The Western Humanities

FIFTH EDITION

Roy T. Matthews & F. DeWitt Platt

MICHIGAN STATE UNIVERSITY

Boston   Burr Ridge, IL   Dubuque, IA   Madison, WI   New York   San Francisco   St. Louis
Bangkok   Bogotá   Caracas   Kuala Lumpur   Lisbon   London   Madrid   Mexico City
Milan   Montreal   New Delhi   Santiago   Seoul   Singapore   Sydney   Taipei   Toronto

The *McGraw-Hill* Companies

Higher Education

THE WESTERN HUMANITIES

Published by McGraw-Hill, an imprint of The McGraw-Hill Companies, Inc., 1221 Avenue of the Americas, New York, NY 10020. Copyright © 2004, 2001, 1998, 1995, 1992 by McGraw-Hill. All rights reserved. No part of this publication may be reproduced or distributed in any form or by any means, or stored in a database or retrieval system, without the prior written consent of The McGraw-Hill Companies, Inc., including, but not limited to, in any network or other electronic storage or transmission, or broadcast for distance learning.

2 3 4 5 6 7 8 9 0 VNH/VNH 0 9 8 7 6 5 4 3

ISBN 0-07-255632-3 (Fourth Edition)
ISBN 0-07-255630-7 (Fourth Edition, Volume I: Beginnings through the Renaissance)
ISBN 0-07-255631-5 (Fourth Edition, Volume II: The Renaissance to the Present)
ISBN 0-07-293176-0 (Fourth Edition, hardbound)

Publisher: Chris Freitag
Senior sponsoring editor: Joe Hanson
Developmental editors: Kate Engelberg and Cynthia Ward
Editorial assistant: Torrii Yamada
Marketing manager: Lisa Berry
Field publisher: Zina Craft
Senior project manager: Christina Gimlin
Senior production supervisor: Richard DeVitto
Media producer: Shannon Gattens
Lead designer: Jean Mailander
Interior designer: Anna George
Cover designer: Jenny El-Shamy
Manager, photo research: Brian J. Pecko
Senior supplements producer: Louis Swaim
Compositor: GTS Graphics
Printer: Von Hoffman Press

On the cover: Vermeer, *Girl Reading a Letter at an Open Window.* © Staatliche Kunstsammlungen, Dresden. Gemäldegalerie Alte Meister.

Library of Congress Cataloging-in-Publication Data
Matthews, Roy T.
  The Western humanities/Roy T. Matthews & F. DeWitt Platt.—5th ed.
    p. cm.
  Includes bibliographical references and index.
  ISBN 0-07-255632-3
  1. Civilization, Western—History. I. Platt, F. DeWitt. II. Title.

CB245.M375   2003
909'.09821—dc21

                                                    2003044594

www.mhhe.com

PREFACE

We offer this new edition of *The Western Humanities* with a great sense of satisfaction. From the start of this project, we wrote from a particular perspective on the arts and humanities, and we wondered how many others shared our point of view. Today, we are gratified to know that our textbook has helped many students develop an understanding and, we hope, an enthusiasm for the arts and humanities. With this fifth edition, we continue in the same spirit with which we first approached our subject. In the first edition, we placed Western cultural achievements within their historical context. In the second and especially the third editions, we expanded coverage of the contributions of women and other artists outside the traditional canon. In the fourth edition, we added a multicultural dimension, with the expectation that students would gain a greater appreciation of world cultures beyond the Western traditions. In this edition, we are expanding our coverage of Islamic civilization, as a way of helping students to better grasp contemporary political and cultural issues. We are also enhancing the pedagogical features to make the text more accessible to students. It is our hope that the fifth edition of *The Western Humanities* will continue to assist instructors in meeting today's teaching challenges as well as help the next generation of students understand and claim their cultural heritage.

AIMS OF *THE WESTERN HUMANITIES*

When we sat down to write the first edition of *The Western Humanities*, we feared that the world of the late twentieth century was in danger of being engulfed by present-minded thinking. Now, we believe this fear is even more real. As historians, we know that history has always had its naysayers, but it seems to us that an ahistorical view is even more prevalent today. For many people, the past is viewed either as a burden to be overcome or as simply irrelevant—and thus safely ignored. Students merely mirror the wider society when they show little knowledge of or even concern about the great artistic and literary monuments and movements of the Western tradition or about the political, economic, and social milestones of Western history. What intensifies present-minded thinking among today's students is their close involvement in popular culture, with its obsessive faddishness, and the Internet, which provides information and voluminous data but not knowledge.

In *The Western Humanities*, we address the problem of present-mindedness by discussing not only the works that were produced in successive periods but also the prevailing historical and material conditions that so powerfully influenced their form and content. Our intention is to demystify the cultural record by showing that literature and the arts do not spring forth spontaneously and independently of each other but reflect a set of specific historical circumstances. By providing this substantial context, out of which both ideas and artifacts emerge, we hope to give students a deeper understanding of the meaning of cultural works and a broader basis for appreciating the humanities.

At the same time that we point out the linkages between cultural expression and historical conditions, we also emphasize the universal aspects of creativity and expression. People everywhere have the impulse to seek answers to the mysteries of human existence; to discover or invent order in the universe; to respond creatively to nature, both inner and outer; to delight the senses and the mind with beauty and truth; to communicate their thoughts and share their visions with others. Thus, another of our intentions is to demonstrate that the desire to express oneself and to create lasting monuments has been a compelling drive in human beings since before the dawn of civilized life. We believe that this emphasis will help students see that they, along with their ideas, questions, and aspirations, are not isolated from the past but belong to a tradition that began thousands of years ago.

Our third aim is to help students prepare themselves for the uncertainties of the future. When they examine the past and learn how earlier generations confronted and overcame crises—and managed to leave enduring legacies—students will discover that the human spirit is irrepressible. In the humanities—in philosophy, religion, art, music, literature—human beings have found answers to their deepest needs and most perplexing questions. We hope that students will be encouraged by this record as they begin to shape the world of the twenty-first century.

In its origin *The Western Humanities* was an outgrowth of our careers as university teachers. Instructing thousands of undergraduate students throughout the years had left us dissatisfied with available textbooks. In our eyes, the existing books failed in one of two ways: They either ignored material developments and focused exclusively on cultural artifacts without context or perspective, or they stressed political, social, and economic history with too little or too disjointed a discussion of literature and the arts. Our goal in writing this book was to balance and integrate these two elements—that is, to provide an analysis and an appreciation of cultural expression and artifacts within an interpretive historical framework.

ORGANIZATION AND CONTENT

The Western Humanities is organized chronologically, in twenty-one chapters, around successive historical periods, from prehistory to the present. In our introduction for students we distinguish three sweeping historical periods—ancient, medieval, and modern—although we do not formally divide our study into parts. We explain that the first of these periods extends from about 3000 B.C. to A.D. 500 and includes the civilizations of Mesopotamia, Egypt, Greece, and Rome (covered in Chapters 1–6 and part of Chapter 7). We then turn our attention to the world of Islam, examining both its origins in the seventh century and its achievements to 1517 (Chapter 8). We resume our coverage of Western civilization, focusing on the second period, which lasts from about 500 to 1500, when the West became centered in Europe and was largely dominated by the Christian church (part of Chapter 7 and Chapters 9–10). The third period, beginning in about 1400 and extending to the present, witnessed the gradual birth of the modern world (Chapters 11–21). Timelines are provided in the introduction to support these distinctions and to give students a basic framework for the study of the humanities.

In the body of the book, the first part of every chapter covers the material conditions of the era—the historical, political, economic, and social developments. From the mass of available historical information we have distilled what we consider the crucial points, always aiming to capture the essence of complex periods and to fashion a coherent narrative framework for the story of Western culture. In this discussion many of the major themes, issues, and problems of the period come into view.

The remaining part of each chapter is devoted to cultural expression, both in the realm of attitude and idea—philosophy, history, religion, science—and in the realm of cultural artifact—art, music, drama, literature, and film. In this part we describe and analyze the significant cultural achievements of the age, focusing on pervasive themes, choices, and elements of style. We examine how intellectuals, artists, writers, and other creative individuals responded to the challenges presented to them by their society and how they chose values and forms by which to live. Included among these individuals are those whom the Western tradition has often neglected or discounted, namely, women and members of racial and ethnic minorities. Their experiences, roles, and rich contributions are given their rightful place alongside those of the more conventionally favored artists, thinkers, and writers.

The Western Humanities strives to balance the historical background with cultural and artistic achievements. We believe that the clearest and most effective way to present this closely woven web of experience and expression is to untangle the various realms and discuss them separately. Thus, our treatment of cultural achievements is broken down into sections on art, architecture, music, literature, and so on. These sections vary in length, order, and focus from chapter to chapter, just as preferred or more developed forms of expression vary from one period to another. This approach gives students an unobstructed view of each form and reveals the continuities—as well as the strains and disruptions—in that form from one period to the next.

At the same time, we work from a unified perspective and stress the integrated nature of the humanities. We emphasize that the creative works of a particular period represent a coherent response to the unique character and deepest urges of that period. By pointing out linkages and reverberations, we show that the various areas of expression are tied together by shared stylistic elements and by the themes and issues that inform and shape the era. Rather than weave our own synthesis so tightly into this discussion that instructors would have to spend their class time sorting out our point of view from the true subject of the book, we prefer to present the material in as direct a way as possible. We believe this approach gives instructors the flexibility to teach from their own strengths and perspectives, and we invite them to do so. We have paid special attention to sorting out and explaining complex ideas and sequences of events carefully and clearly, to make the study of the humanities accessible to a broad range of students.

Each chapter ends with a brief section describing the cultural legacy of that era. Here we show what achievements proved to be of lasting value and endured into succeeding periods, even to the present day. Students will find that some ideas, movements, or artistic methods with which they are familiar have a very long history indeed. They will also discover that the meaning and ascribed value of cultural objects and texts can change from one time and place to another. Our goal here is not only to help students establish a context for their culture but to show that the humanities have developed as a dynamic series of choices made by individuals in one era and transformed by individuals in other eras. We hope to convey both the richness and the energy of the Western tradition, to which so many have contributed and from which so many have drawn.

SPECIAL FEATURES

In addition to the overall distinctive features of *The Western Humanities*—its interpretive context for the humanities, its balanced treatment of history and culture, its focus on the cultural legacy of each period—the book has some special features that we believe contribute to its usefulness and appeal. Chapter 8 offers an extended discussion and analysis of Islamic history and culture, broadening the horizons of the Western tradition to cover this important area. Chapter 15 presents a concise discussion of the seventeenth-century revolutions in science and political philosophy that laid the foundations for what we consider modern thinking. Chapter 21 extends the narrative of Western history and culture to the present day and includes expanded coverage of the global style known as Post-Modernism. Throughout the book, we consider not just art, literature, and music but also less commonly covered topics such as history, theology, and technology.

A special feature introduced in the fourth edition is "Windows on the World," a series of timelines that outline the most important historical events and cultural achievements in Africa, the Americas, and Asia. Placed between chapters where chronologically appropriate, these two-page illustrated tables are designed to help students see the West in the larger context of the entire world. As we seek to nurture global awareness in today's students, "Windows on the World" offers a glimpse of the arts and humanities as they developed in many great civilizations around the world.

"Personal Perspectives," first introduced in the third edition, offer students the opportunity to hear the voices of those who witnessed or participated in the historical and cultural events described in the text. These excerpts from primary sources and original documents are designed to bring history to life for the reader.

"A Humanities Primer: How to Understand the Arts," included at the beginning of the book, is a brief introduction to understanding and appreciating cultural works. It defines and explains terms and concepts that are used in discussions of the arts and humanities as well as analytical methods used to understand them. It also includes samples of artistic, literary, and musical analysis.

CHANGES TO THE FIFTH EDITION

A major change to this fifth edition of *The Western Humanities* is the "Encounters" feature—accounts of meetings between the West and other cultures. The "Encounters," through text and art, focus on critical interchanges that influenced both cultures. Often these cultural exchanges had far-reaching effects, such as the introduction of the Latin language to the Dacians (modern Romanians) or the adoption of Japanese print techniques by French Impressionist artists. Of the eight "Encounters" we chose to describe, some occurred in Europe, such as the encounter between the pagan Vikings and the Christian Europeans, but most occurred around the globe—in Africa, Japan, India, North America, and the West Indies. This new feature helps students see that cultural encounters and exchanges are an enduring part of history and have had both negative and positive consequences.

Another innovation is "Learning Through Maps," a feature that asks students to answer questions and complete intellectual exercises in association with each of the 27 maps in the text. This pedagogical device is designed to help students read maps and to encourage them to use their geographical knowledge to enhance their understanding of the text's historical and cultural material.

A third major change is the reorganization of Chapters 7 and 8. Chapter 7, which formerly focused only on the later Roman Empire, now also includes Byzantium and the Early Medieval West, both previously discussed in Chapter 8. This rearrangement, in part a response to reviewers' suggestions, allowed us space for more coverage of Islam. Chapter 8, modeled on the other chapters in *The Western Humanities,* presents an expanded treatment of the rise of Islam as both a religion and a civilization, along with additional material on Islamic history, scholarship, literature, art and architecture, and music, from the seventh century to 1517.

Another new feature in this edition is Chapter Highlights, a summary table of the most important literary, philosophical, artistic, and musical achievements described in each chapter. Each Chapter Highlights table includes a timeline and the names of relevant artistic styles to help students contextualize these achievements. The tables also include icons that identify the literary selections included in the accompanying anthology of primary readings (*Readings in the Western Humanities*) and the musical selections on the accompanying CD. They are designed both to help students review the significant cultural achievements described in the chapter and to show how various components of the package work together.

We have also significantly revised the art program for this edition. Almost 30 new artworks are included, either replacing works previously illustrated or adding to the overall art program. Each new artwork is discussed both in the text and in a detailed caption. In the revised art program, we added a new section on the Hudson River School in the United States, and we updated the discussion of Romanesque architecture to show the two-stage evolution of this building style. We made major changes in the chapter on Islam, using images to illustrate both cultural developments and art and architecture. Throughout the text new illustrations come from sculpture, painting, architecture, photography, and other media; they include Exekias's *Achilles Killing the Amazon Queen Penthesilea,* Speyer Cathedral, The Dome of the Rock, Bruegel's *The Painter and the Connoisseur,* Rembrandt's *Susanna and the Elders,* Kensett's *Lake George,* and Cameron's *Beatrice.*

Specific changes in the text have been made in response to reviewers' suggestions. In Chapter 5, we reduced the coverage of Roman history. As previously mentioned, we rearranged Chapters 7 and 8, so that Chapter 7 now includes Late Rome, Byzantium, and the Early Medieval West, the whole being somewhat reduced in scope, and Chapter 8 focuses exclusively on Islam, with the coverage greatly expanded. We introduced three new composers—Guillaume de Machaut, Antonio Lucio Vivaldi, and William Grant Still—and included representative works by each of them on the music CD. In Chapter 21, we added a new map to show Europe after the Cold War, and we expanded coverage of events to the present. Finally, we replaced six "Personal Perspectives" with new eyewitness accounts from such historical and contemporary figures as Alcaeus, Abelard and Heloise, Suzanne Gaudry, and Yo-Yo Ma.

TEACHING AND LEARNING RESOURCES

As instructors, we are keenly aware of the problems encountered in teaching the humanities, especially to large, diverse classes. We have therefore created an Instructor's Manual, as well as a comprehensive package of supplementary resource materials, designed to help solve those problems.

The fifth edition of the Instructor's Manual has been revised and expanded. For each chapter the manual includes teaching strategies and suggestions; test items; learning objectives; key cultural terms; film, reading, and Internet site suggestions; and a detailed outline revised to accompany the fifth edition of *The Western Humanities.* Additionally, there is background on the "Personal Perspective" boxes found throughout the book as well as additional information on the cultures and artworks described in each "Windows on the World" feature. References to the accompanying anthology, *Readings in The Western Humanities,* have been added to each chapter so that primary source material can be easily incorporated into each lesson.

In addition to chapter-by-chapter materials, the following features are included in the Instructor's Manual:

- Five basic teaching strategies
- Seven lecture models
- Timeline of developments in non-Western cultures
- Music listening guides
- Comparative questions covering material from more than one chapter (designed to test students on broader patterns)

The Instructor's Manual is available on the Online Learning Center, on the Instructor's CD-ROM, and, by request, in print form. For more information on the Instructor's Manual in print form, please contact your local McGraw-Hill sales representative.

A new audio CD has been created specifically to accompany the fifth edition of *The Western Humanities.* Selections span the broad spectrum of music discussed in the text and include pieces by such composers as Hildegard of Bingen, J.S. Bach, Igor Stravinsky, and Philip Glass. CD selections are indicated in the text with icons in the Chapter Highlights boxes.

For use in presentations, particularly in large lecture settings, two slide sets are available. The art slides present 100 artworks reflecting the range of art and architecture covered in *The Western Humanities*. The 27 map slides reproduce the maps found in the text.

An updated and expanded Online Learning Center accompanies the fifth edition and can be found at http://www.mhhe.com/mp5. Instructors will have access to the Instructor's Manual online, available in both Windows and Macintosh formats. The Online Learning Center also provides resources for students, including quizzes, essay questions, interactive map and Internet exercises, and links to additional information on the Web. Additional resources, including the computerized test bank and the full Instructor's Manual with test items, are available on the Instructor's CD-ROM. The testing program on the CD-ROM allows instructors to design tests using the questions provided, to edit those questions, and to incorporate their own questions.

Available to accompany *The Western Humanities*, as mentioned above, is an anthology of primary source materials, *Readings in The Western Humanities*. The readings are arranged chronologically to follow the 21 chapters of the text and are divided into two volumes. Volume I covers ancient Mesopotamia through the Renaissance; Volume II, the Renaissance through the 20th century. This anthology gives students access to our literary and philosophical heritage, allowing them to experience first-hand the ideas and voices of the great writers and thinkers of the Western tradition.

We believe that both instructors and students will find these supplementary materials and resources useful as they share the experience of the Western humanities.

ACKNOWLEDGMENTS

We are grateful to many people for their help and support in this revision of *The Western Humanities*. We continue to appreciate the many insightful comments of students and former students at Michigan State University over the years. We are also grateful for the many suggestions and comments provided to us by the following reviewers: Thomas T. Barker, Alvin Community College; Penelope A. Blake, Ph.D., Rock Valley College; David Borgmeyer, University of Wisconsin-Green Bay; Bradford Brown, Bradley University; Fleta J. Buckles, Oral Roberts University; Judith Chambers, Hillsborough Community College; Anne Clennon, Montclair State University; Margaret Dahl, Austin Community College; Matthew M. Daude, Austin Community College; Jason DePolo, North Carolina Agricultural and Technical State University; Glen A. Dolberg, San Joaquin Delta College; Jeffrey R. Donovick, St. Petersburg College; Peter F. Dusenbery, Bradley University; Karen Eisenhauer, Brevard Community College; Dr. Honora Finkelstein, University of Southern Indiana; Daniel Getz, Bradley University; William Tell Gifford, Truckee Meadows Community College; Dr. Michael Given, University of Southern Indiana; Robin Hardee, Santa Fe Community College; Shirley F. Harrod, Carl Albert State College; Michael Hinden, University of Wisconsin–Madison; Bobby Horn, Santa Fe Community College; Jill Kinkade, University of Southern Indiana; Jill Kelly-Moore, Santa Rosa Junior College; Scott Koterbay, East Tennessee State University; Barbara Kramer, Santa Fe Community College; Dr. Sandi Landis, St. Johns River Community College; Karyn Ott, Brevard Community College; Amalia Durán Parra, Alvin Community College; Dr. Michael Pinner, East Tennessee State University; Dr. Erich W. Skwara, San Diego State University; Philip Simpson, Brevard Community College; Lynn Spencer, Brevard Community College; David K. Underwood, St. Petersburg College; Charles T. Vehse, West Virginia University; Camille Weiss, West Virginia University; Marcella Whidbee, North Carolina A & T State University; John K. Wise, Thiel College; and Feryle L. Wright, Santa Fe Community College.

A unique aspect of this revision is that we are now with a new publisher, McGraw-Hill, following the acquisition of Mayfield Publishing Company by McGraw-Hill in early 2001. The transition for us has been smooth and encouraging. The credit for this must go, in great part, to Allison McNamara, Sponsoring Editor for Film, Theater, and the Humanities. We thank you, Allison, for calming our fears as well as steering a steady course through this fifth edition revision. Thanks too to Cynthia Ward, a freelance developmental editor outside the McGraw-Hill family, for her knowledgeable support with the new features and with the reconfiguration of Chapters 7 and 8. We also want to express our gratitude to Kate Engelberg, the nurturing developmental editor of the first edition of this book, who came back on board in the middle of our work on this, the fifth edition. Special thanks to Joe Hanson, Senior Sponsoring Editor for Art and Humanities, for his numerous contributions to this edition. And thanks to developmental editor Nadia Bidwell, who prepared and assembled the comprehensive supplements package for this edition. We also wish to thank the Editorial, Design, and Production team at McGraw-Hill for their attention to the many aspects of the book's production: Christina Gimlin, Project Manager; Richard DeVitto, Production Supervisor; Jean Mailander, Lead Designer; Brian J. Pecko, Manager, Photo Research; Emma Ghiselli, Art Editor; and Louis Swaim, Supplements Producer. To all, we express our deep gratitude.

To Lee Ann and Dixie

There is nothing nobler or more admirable than when two people who see eye to eye keep house as man and wife, confounding their enemies and delighting their friends, as they themselves know better than anyone.

—HOMER, *Odyssey*

CONTENTS

6
JUDAISM AND THE RISE OF CHRISTIANITY 145

7
THE CIVILIZATIONS OF LATE ROME, BYZANTIUM, AND THE EARLY MEDIEVAL WEST 169

8
THE WORLD OF ISLAM, 630-1517 203

9
THE HIGH MIDDLE AGES
The Christian Centuries   227

10
THE LATE MIDDLE AGES
1300–1500   263

11
THE EARLY RENAISSANCE
Return to Classical Roots
1400–1494   297

12
THE HIGH RENAISSANCE
AND EARLY MANNERISM
1494–1564   *323*

13
NORTHERN HUMANISM,
NORTHERN RENAISSANCE,
RELIGIOUS REFORMATIONS,
AND LATE MANNERISM
1500–1603   *353*

14
THE BAROQUE AGE
Glamour and Grandiosity
1600–1715   *383*

15
THE BAROQUE AGE II
Revolutions in Scientific and
Political Thought
1600–1715 *413*

16
THE AGE OF REASON
1700–1789 *435*

17
REVOLUTION, REACTION, AND CULTURAL RESPONSE
1760–1830   465

18
THE TRIUMPH OF THE BOURGEOISIE
1830–1871   495

19
THE AGE OF EARLY MODERNISM
1871–1914   527

INTRODUCTION
Why Study Cultural History?

To be ignorant of what occurred before you were born is to remain always a child.

      —CICERO, FIRST CENTURY B.C.

Anyone who cannot give an account to oneself of the past three thousand years remains in darkness, without experience, living from day to day.

    —GOETHE, NINETEENTH CENTURY A.D.

The underlying premise of this book is that some basic knowledge of the Western cultural heritage is necessary for those who want to become educated human beings in charge of their own destinies. If people are not educated into their place in human history—five thousand years of relatively uninterrupted though sometimes topsy-turvy developments—then they are rendered powerless, subject to passing fads and outlandish beliefs. They become vulnerable to the flattery of demagogues who promise heaven on earth, or they fall prey to the misconception that present-day events are unique, without precedent in history, or superior to everything that has gone before.

Perhaps the worst that can happen is to exist in a limbo of ignorance—in Goethe's words, "living from day to day." Without knowledge of the past and the perspective it brings, people may come to believe that their contemporary world will last forever, when in reality much of it is doomed to be forgotten. In contrast to the instant obsolescence of popular culture, the study of Western culture offers an alternative that has passed the unforgiving test of time. Long after today's heroes and celebrities have fallen into oblivion, the achievements of our artistic and literary ancestors—those who have forged the Western tradition—will remain. Their works echo down the ages and seem fresh in every period. The

ancient Roman writer Seneca put it well when he wrote, in the first century A.D., "Life is short but art is long."

When people realize that the rich legacy of Western culture is their own, their view of themselves and the times they live in can expand beyond the present moment. They find that they need not be confined by the limits of today but can draw on the creative insights of people who lived hundreds and even thousands of years ago. They discover that their own culture has a history and a context that give it meaning and shape. Studying and experiencing their cultural legacy can help them understand their place in today's world.

THE BOUNDARIES OF THE WEST

The subject of this text is Western culture, but what exactly do we mean, first, by "culture" and, second, by the "West"? *Culture* is a term with several meanings, but we use it here to mean the artistic and intellectual expressions of a people, their creative achievements. By the *West* we mean that part of the globe that lies west of Asia and Asia Minor and north of Africa, especially Europe—the geographical framework for much of this study.

The Western tradition is not confined exclusively to Europe as defined today, however. The contributions of peoples who lived beyond the boundaries of present-day Europe are also included in Western culture, either because they were forerunners of the West, such as those who created the first civilizations in Mesopotamia and Egypt, or because they were part of the West for periods of time, such as those who lived in the North African and Near Eastern lands bordering the Mediterranean Sea during the Roman and early

Christian eras. Regardless of geography, Western culture draws deeply from ideals forged in these lands.

When areas that had been part of the Western tradition at one time were absorbed into other cultural traditions, as happened in Mesopotamia, Egypt, and North Africa in the seventh century when the people embraced the Muslim faith, then they are generally no longer included in Western cultural history. Because of the enormous influence of Islamic civilization on Western civilization, however, we do include in this volume both an account of Islamic history and a description and appreciation of Islamic culture. Different in many ways from our own, the rich tradition of Islam has an important place in today's world.

After about 1500, with voyages and explorations reaching the farthest parts of the globe, the European focus of Western culture that had held for centuries began to dissolve. Starting from this time, the almost exclusive European mold was broken and Western values and ideals began to be exported throughout the world, largely through the efforts of missionaries, soldiers, colonists, and merchants. Coinciding with this development and further complicating the pattern of change were the actions of those who imported and enslaved countless numbers of black Africans to work on plantations in North and South America. The interplay of Western culture with many previously isolated cultures, whether desired or not, forever changed all who were touched by the process.

The Westernization of the globe that has been going on ever since 1500 is perhaps the dominant theme of our time. What human greed, missionary zeal, and dreams of empire failed to accomplish before 1900 was achieved during the twentieth century by modern technology, the media, and popular culture. The world today is a global village, much of it dominated by Western values and styles of life. In our time, Westernization has become a two-way interchange. When artists and writers from other cultures adopt Western forms or ideas, they are not only Westernizing their own traditions but also injecting fresh sensibilities and habits of thought into the Western tradition. The globalization of culture means that a South American novel or a Japanese film can be as accessible to Western audiences as a European painting and yet carry with it an intriguingly new vocabulary of cultural symbols and meanings.

HISTORICAL PERIODS AND CULTURAL STYLES

In cultural history the past is often divided into historical periods and cultural styles. A historical period is an interval of time that has a certain unity because it is characterized by the prevalence of a unique culture, ideology, or technology or because it is bounded by defining historical events, such as the death of a military leader like Alexander the Great or a political upheaval like the fall of Rome. A cultural style is a combination of features of artistic or literary expression, execution, or performance that define a particular school or era. A historical period may have the identical time frame as a cultural style, or it may embrace more than one style simultaneously or two styles successively. Each chapter of this survey focuses on a historical period and includes significant aspects of culture—usually the arts, architecture, literature, religion, music, and philosophy—organized around a discussion of the relevant style or styles appropriate to that time.

The survey begins with prehistory, the era before writing was invented, setting forth the emergence of human beings from an obscure past. After the appearance of writing in about 3000 B.C., the Western cultural heritage is divided into three sweeping historical periods: ancient, medieval, and modern.

The ancient period dates from 3000 B.C. to A.D. 500 (Timeline 1). During these thirty-five hundred years the light of Western civilization begins to shine in Mesopotamia and Egypt, shines more brightly still in eighth-century-B.C. Greece and Rome, loses some of its luster when Greece succumbs to Rome in 146 B.C., and finally is snuffed out when the Roman empire collapses in the fifth century A.D. Coinciding with these historical periods are the cultural styles of Mesopotamia; Egypt; Greece, including Archaic, Classical (or Hellenic), and Hellenistic styles; and Rome, including Republican and Imperial styles.

The medieval period, or the Middle Ages, covers events between A.D. 500 and 1500, a one-thousand-year span that is further divided into three subperiods (Timeline 2). The Early Middle Ages (500–1000) is typified by frequent barbarian invasions and political chaos so that civilization itself is threatened and barely survives. No single international style characterizes this turbulent period, though several regional styles flourish. The High Middle Ages (1000–1300) is a period of stability and the zenith of medieval culture. Two successive styles appear, the Romanesque and the Gothic, with the latter dominating culture for the rest of the medieval period. The Late Middle Ages (1300–1500) is a transitional period in which the medieval age is dying and the modern age is struggling to be born.

The modern period begins in about 1400 (there is often overlap between historical periods) and continues today (Timeline 3). With the advent of the modern period a new way of defining historical changes starts to make more sense—the division of history into

Timeline 1   THE ANCIENT WORLD

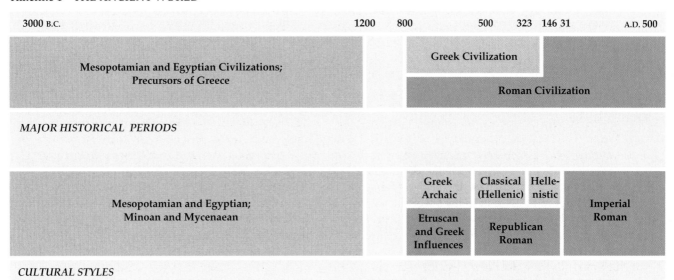

| 3000 B.C. | | | 1200 | 800 | | 500 | 323 | 146 | 31 | A.D. 500 |

MAJOR HISTORICAL PERIODS

Mesopotamian and Egyptian Civilizations; Precursors of Greece

Greek Civilization

Roman Civilization

CULTURAL STYLES

Mesopotamian and Egyptian; Minoan and Mycenaean

Greek Archaic

Classical (Hellenic)

Hellenistic

Etruscan and Greek Influences

Republican Roman

Imperial Roman

movements, the activities of large groups of people united to achieve a common goal. The modern period consists of waves of movements that aim to change the world in some specific way.

The first modern movement is the Renaissance (1400–1600), or "rebirth," which attempts to revive the cultural values of ancient Greece and Rome. It is accompanied by two successive styles, Renaissance style and Mannerism. The next significant movement is the Reformation (1500–1600), which is dedicated to restoring Christianity to the ideals of the early church set forth in the Bible. Although it does not spawn a specific style, this religious upheaval does have a profound impact on the subjects of the arts and literature and the way they are expressed, especially in the Mannerist style.

The Reformation is followed by the Scientific Revolution (1600–1700), a movement that results in the abandonment of ancient science and the birth of modern science. Radical in its conclusions, the Scientific

Revolution is somewhat out of touch with the style of its age, which is known as the Baroque. This magnificent style is devoted to overwhelming the senses through theatrical and sensuous effects and is associated with the attempts of the Roman Catholic Church to reassert its authority in the world.

The Scientific Revolution gives impetus to the Enlightenment (1700–1800), a movement that pledges to reform politics and society according to the principles of the new science. In stylistic terms the eighteenth century is schizophrenic, dominated first by the Rococo, an extravagant and fanciful style that represents the last phase of the Baroque, and then by the Neoclassical, a style inspired by the works of ancient Greece and Rome and reflective of the principles of the Scientific Revolution. Before the eighteenth century is over, the Enlightenment calls forth its antithesis, Romanticism (1770–1870), a movement centered on feeling, fantasy, and everything that cannot be proven scientifically. The Romantic style, marked by a

Timeline 2   THE MEDIEVAL WORLD

| 500 | | | 1000 | 1150 | 1300 | 1500 |

Early Middle Ages   High Middle Ages   Late Middle Ages

MAJOR HISTORICAL PERIODS

Regional Styles   Romanesque   Gothic

CULTURAL STYLES

Timeline 3   THE MODERN WORLD

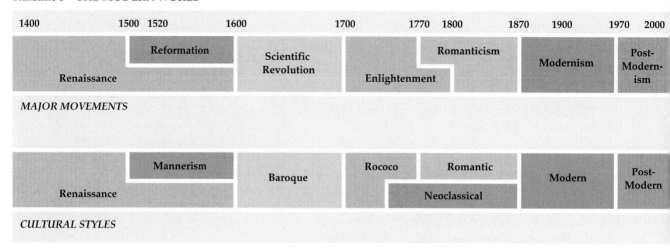

revived taste for the Gothic and a love of nature, is the perfect accompaniment to this movement.

Toward the end of the nineteenth century Modernism (1870–1970) arises, bent on destroying every vestige of both the Greco-Roman tradition and the Christian faith and on fashioning new ways of understanding that are independent of the past. Since 1970 Post-Modernism has emerged, a movement that tries to make peace with the past by embracing old forms of expression while at the same time adopting a global and multivoiced perspective.

Although every cultural period is marked by innovation and creativity, our treatment of them in this book varies somewhat, with more space and greater weight given to the achievements of certain times. We make these adjustments because some periods or styles are more significant than others, especially in the defining influence that their achievements have had on our own era. For example, some styles seem to tower over the rest, such as Classicism in fifth-century-B.C. Greece, the High Renaissance of sixteenth-century Italy, and Modernism in the mid–twentieth century, as compared with other styles, such as that of the Early Middle Ages or the seventeenth-century Baroque.

AN INTEGRATED APPROACH TO CULTURAL HISTORY

Our approach to the Western heritage in this book is to root cultural achievements in their historical settings, showing how the material conditions—the political, social, and economic events of each period—influenced their creation. About one-third of each chapter is devoted to an interpretive discussion of material history, and the remaining two-thirds are devoted to the arts, architecture, philosophy, religion, literature, and music

of the period. These two aspects of history do not occur separately, of course, and one of our aims is to show how they are intertwined.

As just one example of this integrated approach, consider the Gothic cathedral, that lofty, light-filled house of worship marked by pointed arches, towering spires, and radiant stained-glass windows. Gothic cathedrals were erected during the High Middle Ages, following a bleak period when urban life had virtually ceased. Although religion was still the dominant force in European life, trade was starting to flourish once again, town life was reviving, and urban dwellers were beginning to prosper. In part as testimonials to their new wealth, cities and towns commissioned architects and hired workers to erect these soaring churches, which dominated the landscape for miles around and proclaimed the economic well-being of their makers.

We adopt an integrated approach to Western culture not just in considering how the arts are related to material conditions but also in looking for the common themes, aspirations, and ideas that permeate the artistic and literary expressions of every individual era. The creative accomplishments of an age tend to reflect a shared perspective, even when that perspective is not explicitly recognized at the time. Thus, each period possesses a unique outlook that can be analyzed in the cultural record. A good example of this phenomenon is Classical Greece in the fifth century B.C., when the ideal of moderation, or balance in all things, played a major role in sculpture, architecture, philosophy, religion, and tragic drama. The cultural record in other periods is not always as clear as that in ancient Greece, but shared qualities can often be uncovered that distinguish the varied aspects of culture in an era to form a unifying thread.

A corollary of this idea is that creative individuals and their works are very much influenced by the times in which they live. This is not to say that incomparable geniuses—such as Shakespeare in Renaissance England—do not appear and rise above their own ages, speaking directly to the human mind and heart in every age that follows. Yet even Shakespeare reflected the political attitudes and social patterns of his time. Though a man for the ages, he still regarded monarchy as the correct form of government and women as the inferiors of men.

THE SELECTION OF CULTURAL WORKS

The Western cultural heritage is vast, and any selection of works for a survey text reflects choices made by the authors. All the works we chose to include have had a significant impact on Western culture, but for different reasons. We chose some because they blazed a new trail, such as Picasso's *Demoiselles d'Avignon* (see Figure 19.21), which marked the advent of Cubism in painting, or Fielding's *Tom Jones,* one of the earliest novels. Other works were included because they seemed to embody a style to perfection, such as the regal statue called *Poseidon* (or *Zeus*) (see Figure 3.21), executed in the Classical style of fifth-century-B.C. Athens, or Dante's *Divine Comedy,* which epitomized the ideals of the High Middle Ages. On occasion, we chose works on a particular topic, such as the biblical story of David and Goliath, and demonstrated how different sculptors interpreted it, as in sculptures by Donatello (see Figure 11.11), Verrocchio (see Figure 11.12), and Michelangelo (see Figure 12.19). Still other works caught our attention because they served as links between successive styles, as is the case with Giotto's frescoes (see Figure 10.19), or because they represented the end of an age or an artistic style, as in the haunting sculpture called *The Last Pagan* (see Figure 7.12). Finally, we included some works, especially paintings, simply because of their great beauty, such as Ingres's *Madame Jacques Louis Leblanc* (see Figure 17.6).

Through all the ages of Western cultural history, through all the shifting styles and tastes embodied in painting, sculpture, architecture, poetry, and song, there glows a creative spark that can be found in human beings in every period. This diversity is a hallmark of the Western experience, and we celebrate it in this book.

A CHALLENGE TO THE READER

The purpose of all education is and should be self-knowledge. This goal was first established by the ancient Greeks in their injunction to "Know thyself," the inscription carved above the entrance to Apollo's temple at Delphi. Self-knowledge means awareness of oneself and one's place in society and the world. Reaching this goal is not easy, because becoming an educated human being is a lifelong process, requiring time, energy, and commitment. But all journeys begin with a single step, and we intend this volume as a first step toward understanding and defining oneself in terms of one's historical and cultural heritage. Our challenge to the reader is to use this book to begin the long journey to self-knowledge.

A HUMANITIES PRIMER
How to Understand the Arts

INTRODUCTION

We can all appreciate the arts. We can find pleasure or interest in paintings, music, poems, novels, films, and many other art forms, both contemporary and historical. We don't need to know very much about art to know what we like, because we bring ourselves to the work: What we like has as much to do with who we are as with the art itself.

Many of us, for example, will respond positively to a painting like Leonardo da Vinci's *The Virgin of the Rocks.* The faces of the Madonna and angel are lovely; we may have seen images like these on Christmas cards or in other commercial reproductions. We respond with what English poet William Wordsworth calls the "first careless rapture," which activates our imaginations and establishes a connection between us and the work of art. However, if this is all we see, if we never move from a subjective reaction, we can only appreciate the surface, the immediate form, and then, perhaps subconsciously, accept without question the values it implies. We appreciate, but we do not understand.

Sometimes we cannot appreciate because we do not understand. We may reject Picasso's *Les Demoiselles d'Avignon,* for it presents us with images of women that we may not be able to recognize. These women may make us uncomfortable, and the values they imply may frighten us rather than please or reassure us. Rather than rapture, we may experience disgust; but when we realize that this painting is considered a groundbreaking work, we may wonder what we're missing and be willing to look deeper. (*The Virgin of the Rocks* and *Les Demoiselles d'Avignon* are discussed in the text on pages 318–319 and pages 551–552, respectively.)

LEONARDO DA VINCI. *The Virgin of the Rocks.*

To understand a work of art (a building, a poem, a song, a symphony), we need to keep our "rapture" (our emotional response and connection) but make it less "careless," less superficial and subjective, less restricted to that which we recognize. We need to enrich our appreciation by searching for a meaning that goes beyond ourselves. This involves understanding the intent or goal of the artist, the elements of form present in the work, the ways in which those elements contribute to the artist's goal, the context within which the artwork evolved, and the connections of the work to other works. Understanding an artwork requires intellectual involvement as well as an emotional connection. The purpose of this primer is to provide you with some of the tools you will need to understand—as well as appreciate—literature, art, and music.

APPROACHES TO THE ANALYSIS OF LITERATURE, ART, AND MUSIC

When we analyze a work of art, we ask two questions: What is the artist trying to do, and how well is it done? We want to identify the intent of the work, and we want to evaluate its execution. To answer these questions, we can examine the formal elements of the work—an approach known as formalism—and we can explore its context—known as contextualism.

Formalism

A formal analysis is concerned with the aesthetic (artistic) elements of a work separate from context. This type of analysis focuses on medium and technique. The context of the work—where, when, and by whom a work was created—may be interesting but is considered unnecessary to formalist interpretation and understanding. A formal analysis of a painting, sculpture, or architectural structure examines its line, shape, color, texture, and composition, as well as the artist's technical ability within the medium used; it is not concerned with anything extraneous to the work itself. A formal analysis of a literary work, such as a short story or novel, would explore the relationships among theme, plot, characters, and setting, as well as how well the resources of language—word choice, tone, imagery, symbol, and so on—are used to support the other elements. A formal analysis of a film would also explore theme, plot, characters (as developed both verbally and nonverbally), and setting, as well as how the resources of cinematography—camera techniques, lighting, sound, editing, and so on—support the other elements.

A formal analysis of *The Virgin of the Rocks* would examine the artist's use of perspective, the arrangement

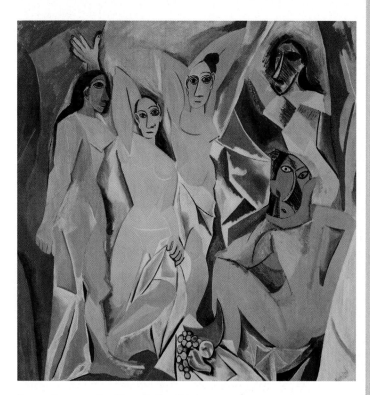

PABLO PICASSO. *Les Desmoiselles d'Avignon.*

of figures as they relate to each other and to the grotto that surrounds them, the technical use of color and line, the dramatic interplay of light and shadow (known as *chiaroscuro*). The same technical considerations would be explored in a formal analysis of *Les Demoiselles d'Avignon*. The fact that the two paintings were completed in 1483 and 1907, respectively, would be important only in terms of the technology and mediums available to the artists. In a formal analysis, time and place exist only within the work.

Contextualism

In contrast, a contextual analysis focuses on factors outside the work: why it was created, in response to what artistic, social, cultural, historical, and political forces, events, and trends; who the artist is, and what his or her intent and motives were in creating the work; how the work fits in with other works of the same genre of the same or different eras; and how the work fits in with the rest of the artist's body of work. Time and place are very important.

A contextual analysis of the da Vinci and Picasso paintings would include information about where and when each painting was completed; the conditions from which it arose; the prevailing artistic styles of the times; the life circumstances of the artists; and so on. The paintings alone do not provide enough information for contextual inquiry. Similarly, contextual analysis of a novel by Dostoevsky would consider both his personal circumstances and the conditions in Russia and Europe when he wrote. A contextual analysis of a chorale and fugue by Bach would include information on Bach's life, his religious beliefs, and the political climate of Germany in the eighteenth century.

An Integrated Approach

In a strictly contextual analysis of an artwork, the work itself can sometimes be lost in the exploration of context. In a strictly formal analysis, important knowledge that can contribute to understanding may remain unknown. The most effective analyses, therefore, combine and integrate the two approaches, examining the formal elements of the work and exploring the context within which it was created. Such an approach is more effective and, in a sense, more honest than either the formal or the contextual approach alone. A work of art, whether a poem or a painting, a cathedral or a cantata, is a complex entity, as are the relationships it fosters between the artist and the art and between the art and its audience. The integrative approach recognizes these relationships and their complexity. This is the approach to artistic and cultural analysis most frequently used in *The Western Humanities*.

A Variety of Perspectives

Many students and critics of culture, while taking an integrative approach, are also especially interested in looking at things from a particular perspective, a set of interests or a way of thinking that informs and influences their investigations and interpretations. Common perspectives are the psychological, the feminist, the religious, the economic, and the historical.

People working from a psychological perspective look for meaning in the psychological features of the work, such as sexual and symbolic associations; they do a kind of retroactive psychological analysis of the artist. They might look for meaning in the facial expressions, gestures, and body positions of Mary and the angel in *The Virgin of the Rocks*. They might be interested in da Vinci's attitudes toward women and his relationships with them, and they might compare this painting with the *Mona Lisa* in a search for clues about who he was.

Someone working from a feminist perspective would examine the art itself and the context in which it arose from a woman's point of view. To take a feminist perspective is to ask how the work depicts women, what it says about women and their relationships in general, and how it may or may not reflect a patriarchal society. Many people have discussed the apparent hatred of women that seems to come through in Picasso's

Les Demoiselles d'Avignon. At the same time, the work, in its size (8 feet by 7 feet 8 inches) and in the unblinking attitude of its subjects, suggests that these women have a kind of raw power. Feminist critics focus on such considerations.

Analysis from a religious perspective is often appropriate when a work of art originated in a religious context. The soaring spires and cruciform floor plans of medieval cathedrals reveal religious meaning, for example, as do Renaissance paintings depicting biblical characters. Many contemporary works of art and literature also have religious content. Religious analyses look to the use of symbolism, the representation of theological doctrines and beliefs, and intercultural connections and influences for meaning.

Someone approaching a work of art from an economic perspective focuses on its economic content—the roles and relationships associated with wealth. Often drawing upon Marx's contention that class is the defining consideration in all human relationships and endeavors, an economic analysis would examine both purpose and content: Was the work created as a display of power by the rich? How does it depict people of different classes? What is the artist saying about the distribution of wealth?

The historical perspective is perhaps the most encompassing of all perspectives, because it can include explorations of psychological, religious, and economic issues, as well as questions about class and gender in various times and places. Historical analysis requires an understanding of the significant events of the time and how they affect the individual and shape the culture. *The Western Humanities* most often takes a historical perspective in its views of art and culture.

The Vocabulary of Analysis

Certain terms and concepts are fundamental to the analysis of any artwork. We review several such general concepts and terms here, before moving on to a consideration of more specific art forms.

Any artwork requires a relationship between itself and its audience. **Audience** is the group for whom a work of art, architecture, literature, drama, film, or music is intended. The audience may be a single person, such as the Medici ruler to whom Machiavelli dedicated his political treatise *The Prince*. The audience can be a small group of people with access to the work, such as the monks who dined in the room where Leonardo da Vinci painted *The Last Supper* on the wall. The audience can also be a special group of people with common interests or education; for example, films like *There's Something About Mary* and *Scream* are intended for a youthful audience. Sometimes the audience is limited by its own understanding of the art; we often feel excluded from what we don't understand. Consequently, some art requires an educated audience.

Composition is the arrangement of constituent elements in an individual work. In music, composition also refers to the process of creating the work.

Content is the subject matter of the work; content can be based on mythology, religion, history, current events, personal history, or almost any idea or feeling deemed appropriate by the artist.

Context is the setting in which the art arose, its own time and place. Context includes the political, economic, social, and cultural conditions of the time; it can also include the personal conditions and circumstances that shape the artist's vision.

A **convention** is an agreed-upon practice, device, technique, or form. A sonnet, for example, is a fourteen-line poem with certain specified rhyme schemes. A poem is not a sonnet unless it follows this formal convention. A convention of the theater is the "willing suspension of disbelief": We know that the events taking place before our eyes are not real, but we agree to believe in them for the duration of the play. Often, conventions in the arts are established as much by political powerbrokers as by artists. The Medicis and the Renaissance popes, for example, wanted portraits and paintings that glorified their reigns, and conventions in Renaissance art reflect these demands. Today, museum directors, wealthy individuals, and government funding agencies play a role in influencing the direction of contemporary art by supporting and showing the work of artists whose conventions they agree with or think are important.

Genre is the type or class to which a work of art, literature, drama, or music belongs, depending on its style, form, or content. In literature, for example, the novel is a genre in itself; the short story is another genre. In music, symphonies, operas, and tone poems are all different genres. Beginning in the Renaissance, genres were carefully distinguished from one another, and a definite set of conventions was expected whenever a new work in a particular genre was created.

The **medium** is the material from which an art object is made—marble or bronze, for example, in sculpture, or water colors or oils in painting. (The plural of *medium* in this sense is often *mediums;* when *medium* is used to refer to a means of mass communication, such as radio or television, the plural is *media.*)

Style is the combination of distinctive elements of creative execution and expression, in terms of both form and content. Artists, artistic schools, movements, and periods can be characterized by their style. Styles often evolve out of existing styles, as when High Renaissance style evolved into Mannerism in the sixteenth century, or in reaction to styles that are perceived as worn out or excessive, as when Impressionism arose to challenge Realism in the nineteenth century.

When we talk about **technique,** we are referring to the systematic procedure whereby a particular creative task is performed. If we were discussing a dancer's technique, we might be referring to the way he executes leaps and turns; a painter's technique might be the way she applies paint to a canvas with broad, swirling brushstrokes.

The dominant idea of a work, the message or emotion the artist intends to convey, is known as the **theme.** The theme, then, is the embodiment of the artist's intent. In a novel, for example, the theme is the abstract concept that is made concrete by character, plot, setting, and other linguistic and structural elements of the work. We often evaluate the theme of a work in terms of how well it speaks to the human condition, how accurate its truth is, how valuable its message or observation is. We usually make these judgments by exploring the extent to which the theme confirms or denies our own experience.

In addition to these general concepts and terms, each art form has its own vocabulary. These more specific terms will be introduced in the sections that follow on literary, artistic, and musical analysis, along with brief illustrative analyses in each area. These informal illustrations are meant not as definitive analyses but as examples of the kinds of productive questions you can ask as you approach a creative work. The analyses differ in their depth and level of detail.

❧ LITERARY ANALYSIS

Literary analysis begins with a consideration of various literary genres and forms. A work of literature is written either in **prose,** the ordinary language used in speaking and writing, or in **poetry,** a more imaginative and concentrated form of expression usually marked by meter, rhythm, or rhyme. Part of poetry's effect comes from the sound of words; it can often best be appreciated when spoken or read aloud. Prose is often divided into nonfiction (essays, biography, autobiography) and fiction (short stories, novels).

In literature, *genre* refers both to form—essay, short story, novel, poem, play, film script, television script—and to specific type within a form—tragedy, comedy, epic, lyric, and so on. According to Aristotle, a **tragedy** must have a tragic hero—a person of high stature who is brought down by his own excessive pride *(hubris);* he doesn't necessarily die at the end, but whatever his greatness was based upon is lost. A **comedy** is a story with a complicated and amusing plot; it usually ends with a happy and peaceful resolution of any conflicts. An **epic** poem, novel, or film is a relatively long recounting of the life of a hero or the glorious history of a people. A **lyric** poem is a short, subjective poem usually expressing an intense personal emotion. In a general sense, an epic tells a story and a lyric expresses an idea or feeling. Lyric poetry includes ballads (dramatic verse meant to be sung or recited, often by more than one singer or speaker), elegies (short, serious meditations, usually on death or other significant themes), odes (short lyric poems dealing with a single theme), and sonnets (formal fourteen-line poems identified by the arrangement of lines as either Italian [Petrarchan] or English [Shakespearean]).

In literature, the author's intent—the message or emotion the author wishes to convey—is usually discussed as the theme of the work. In an essay, the theme is articulated as the thesis: the idea or conclusion that the essay will prove or support. In a novel, story, or play, we infer the theme from the content and the development of ideas and imagery.

In fiction, the action of the story, what Aristotle calls "the arrangement of incidents," is the **plot.** There may be a primary plot that becomes the vehicle by which the theme is expressed, with subplots related to secondary (or even tertiary) themes. Plot can be evaluated by how well it supports the theme. Plot can also be evaluated according to criteria established by Aristotle in his *Poetics.* According to these criteria, the action expressed should be whole, with a beginning that does not follow or depend on anything else, a middle that logically follows what went before, and an end, or logical culmination of all prior action. The plot should be unified, so that every action is necessary and interrelated with all other actions. Few works of fiction adhere to these criteria completely; nevertheless, the criteria do provide a way of beginning to think about how a plot works.

Characters are also important both for themselves and for their effect on the plot and support of the theme. **Characters** provide the human focus, the embodiment, of the theme; they act out and are affected by the plot. The protagonist, or primary character, of the work is changed by the dramatic action of the plot and thus is a dynamic character; static characters remain unchanged throughout the story. An antagonist is a character in direct opposition to the protagonist. Some characters are stock characters, representing a type rather than an individual human being: the romantic fool, the nosy neighbor, the wise old woman, the vain beauty, the plain girl or dumb boy with a heart of gold.

Readers need to believe that characters' actions are authentic reactions to various events. The believability of a work of fiction—the writer's ability to express the truth—is called verisimilitude. Even in works of science fiction or fantasy, where events occur that could not occur in reality, readers must believe that what characters say and do makes sense under the conditions described.

The background against which the action takes place is the **setting.** It can include the geographical location, the environment (political, social, economic) in which the characters live, the historical time in which the action takes place, and the culture and customs of the time, place, and people.

The story or poem is told from the point of view of the **narrator.** The narrator is not necessarily identical with the author of the work. The narrator (or **narrative voice**) can be examined and analyzed like any other element of the work. When a narrator seems to know everything and is not limited by time or place, the work has an omniscient point of view. Such a narrator tells us what everyone is thinking, feeling, and doing. When the story is told from the perspective of a single character who can relate only what he or she knows or witnesses, the work has a first-person point of view. Such a narrator is limited in his or her understanding. Thus, we need to consider the narrator in order to judge how accurate or complete the narrative is.

Sometimes a narrator proves to be unreliable, and we have to piece together an account of the story ourselves. Other times an author uses multiple narrators to tell a story from multiple points of view. William Faulkner uses this device in his novel *The Sound and the Fury* to show that a story can be fully told only when several different characters have a chance to speak. Japanese film director Akira Kurosawa uses a similar device in *Rashomon* to show that there are many equally valid—or invalid—versions of the truth.

A literary analysis of a drama, whether a play for the stage or a film script, will consider not only the elements already mentioned—theme, plot, character, setting, language, and so on—but also the technical considerations specific to the form. In theater, these would include the work of the director, who interprets the play and directs the actors, as well as stage design, light and sound design, costumes, makeup, and so on. In film, technical considerations would include direction, editing, cinematography, musical score, special effects, and so on.

Let's turn now to a poem by Shakespeare and see how to approach it to enrich our understanding. Identifying a poem's intent and evaluating its execution is called an *explication,* from the French *explication de texte.* An explication is a detailed analysis of a poem's meaning, focusing on narrative voice, setting, rhyme, meter, words, and images. An explication begins with what is immediately evident about the poem as a whole, followed by a more careful examination of its parts.

William Shakespeare (1564–1616) was not just a great playwright; he was also a great poet. His works portray human emotions, motives, and relationships that we recognize today as well as the conditions and concerns of his time. In this sense, they are an example of aesthetic universality, the enduring connection between a work of art and its audience.

Shakespeare's sonnets are his most personal work. Scholars disagree about whether they are generic love poems or are addressed to a specific person and, if the latter, who that person might be. Formally, an English (or Shakespearean) sonnet is a 14-line poem consisting of three 4-line stanzas, or quatrains, each with its own rhyme scheme, and a concluding 2-line stanza, or couplet, that provides commentary on the preceding stanzas. The rhyme scheme in a Shakespearean sonnet is abab cdcd efef gg; that is, the first and third lines of each quatrain rhyme with each other, as do the second and fourth lines, though the rhymes are different in each quatrain. The last two lines rhyme with each other.

The meter of most Shakespearean sonnets is iambic pentameter; that is, each line has five feet, or units ("pentameter"), and each foot consists of an iamb, an unaccented syllable followed by an accented syllable (as in *alone*). An example of iambic pentameter is, "My mistress' eyes are nothing like the sun"; each foot consists of an unaccented and an accented syllable, and there are five feet. Unrhymed iambic pentameter—the verse of most of Shakespeare's plays—is known as **blank verse.**

Sonnet 130 ("My mistress' eyes are nothing like the sun") is a poem that not only illustrates sonnet form but also showcases Shakespeare's wit and his attitude toward certain conventions of his time. The poem was originally written in Elizabethan English, which looks and sounds quite different from modern English. We reproduce it in modern English, as is customary today for Shakespeare's works.

Sonnet 130

My mistress' eyes are nothing like the sun;
Coral is far more red than her lips' red;
If snow be white, why then her breasts are dun;
If hairs be wires, black wires grow on her head.

I have seen roses damask'd, red and white,
But no such roses see I in her cheeks,
And in some perfumes is there more delight
Than in the breath that from my mistress reeks.

I love to hear her speak, yet well I know
That music hath a far more pleasing sound;
I grant I never saw a goddess go,
My mistress when she walks treads on the ground.

And yet, by heaven, I think my love as rare
As any she belied with false compare.

Because the poet's intent may not be immediately evident, paraphrasing each line or stanza can point the

reader to the theme or meaning intended by the poet. Let's begin, then, by paraphrasing the lines:

My mistress' eyes are nothing like the sun;
The speaker's lover's eyes are not bright.
Coral is far more red than her lips' red;
Her lips are not very red, certainly not as red as coral.
If snow be white, why then her breasts are dun;
Her breasts are mottled in color, not as white as snow.
If hairs be wires, black wires grow on her head.
Her hair is black (not blond, as was the conventional beauty standard then, when poets referred to women's hair as "golden wires").

I have seen roses damask'd, red and white,
But no such roses see I in her cheeks,
Her cheeks are not rosy.
And in some perfumes is there more delight
Than in the breath that from my mistress reeks.
Her breath doesn't smell as sweet as perfume.

I love to hear her speak, yet well I know
That music hath a far more pleasing sound;
Her voice doesn't sound as melodious as music.
I grant I never saw a goddess go,
My mistress when she walks treads on the ground.
Although the speaker has never seen a goddess walk, he knows his lover does not float above ground, as goddesses are supposed to do, but walks on the ground, a mortal woman.

And yet, by heaven, I think my love as rare
As any she belied with false compare.
His lover is as rare and valuable as any idealized woman glorified by false poetic comparisons.

Remember that to analyze a poem, we ask questions like, What is the theme of the poem, the poet's intent? How does Shakespeare support his point with specific images? From the paraphrased lines it is clear that the narrator is stating that his love is a real woman who walks upon the ground, not an unattainable ideal to be worshiped from afar. Idealized qualities are irrelevant to how he feels about her; the qualities he loves are the ones that make her human.

Closely examining each line of a poem helps to reveal the rhyme scheme (abab cdcd efef gg), the meter (iambic pentameter), and thus the form of the poem (sonnet). Explication of the formal elements of the poem would also include examining the use of language (such as word choice, imagery, comparisons, metaphors), the tone of the narrative voice, and so on.

To understand the context of the poem, we would consider the cultural climate of the time (was "courtly love" a prevalent cultural theme?); common contemporary poetic conventions (were many other poets proclaiming their eternal love for idealized women?); and the political, social, and economic conditions (what roles were open to women in Elizabethan England, and how were they changing? What influence might Queen Elizabeth have had on the poet's point of view? What comments about his society is Shakespeare making?)

Finally, we might consider how honest and accurate we find the emotional content of the poem to be, how relevant its truth. Are Shakespeare's observations germane to today, a time when the mass media present us with a nearly unattainable ideal as the epitome of female beauty?

❧ FINE ARTS ANALYSIS

As with literature, knowledge of a particular vocabulary helps us "speak the language" of art critics. The terms introduced here are in addition to those discussed earlier, such as *medium* and *technique*. They apply to all the visual arts, including drawing and painting, sculpture—the art of shaping material (such as wood, stone, or marble) into three-dimensional works of art—and architecture—the art and science of designing, planning, and building structures, usually for human habitation. In architecture, the critic would also pay attention to the blending of artistry and functionality (how well the structure fulfills its purpose).

Generally, art is more or less representational or more or less abstract. **Representational art** is true to human perception and presents a likeness of the world much as it appears to the naked eye. An important convention of representational art is **perspective,** the appearance of depth and distance on a two-dimensional surface. **Abstract art** presents a subjective view of the world, the artist's emotions or ideas; some abstract art simply presents color, line, or shape for its own sake.

The formal elements of visual art include line, shape, texture, color, composition, and so on. **Line** is the mark made by the artist, whether with pencil, pen, or paintbrush. Lines can be straight or curved, thick or thin, light or dark, spare or plentiful. **Color** is the use in the artwork of hues found in nature; color can enhance the sense of reality presented in a visual image, or it can distort it, depending on how it is used. The primary colors are red, blue, and yellow, and the secondary colors are orange (a combination of red and yellow), green (a combination of yellow and blue), and purple (a combination of blue and red). Blue, green, and purple hues are "cool" colors that appear to recede from the eye; red, yellow, and orange are "warm" colors that appear to move forward. Color has symbolic associations within specific historical and cultural settings. For example, in Western culture, white is a symbol of purity and is worn by brides. In Eastern cultures, white is a symbol of death; Chinese brides wear red to symbolize good luck.

How the artist arranges the work is referred to as the composition. Often the artist controls how the eye

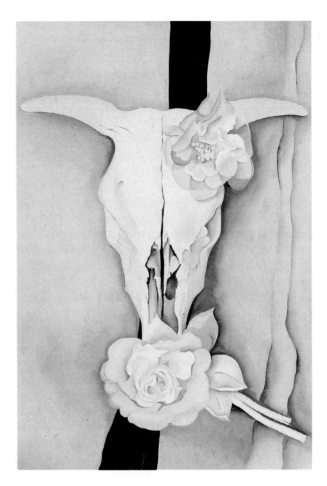

GEORGIA O'KEEFFE. *Cow's Skull with Calico Roses.*

moves from one part to another by means of the composition. Through the composition the artist leads us to see the artwork in a particular way. The setting of an artwork is the time and place depicted in a representational work, as defined by visual cues—the people, how they are dressed, what they are doing, and so on.

With these terms in hand, let's consider *Cow's Skull with Calico Roses* by Georgia O'Keeffe (1887–1986), painted in 1931. What is the artist's intent? How well is that intent executed? Front and center we see the cow's skull, placed so the strong vertical line of the skull, accentuated by the skull's vertical midline crack, aligns with the center of the canvas. A broad band of black extending from the top of the canvas to the bottom behind the skull further reinforces the vertical axis, as do the wavy lines on the right. The skull's horns form a shorter, secondary horizontal line, creating a cross shape. At the bottom of the canvas, the black band seems to open; its expansion to the left is balanced by the rose stem in the lower right and the right-of-center rose at the top. The image overall is balanced and symmetrical, conveying a sense of stillness and repose rather than dynamic action.

The artist has not used broad or bold lines in her painting; rather, the lines of the skull and flowers are drawn delicately against the background; shading suggests contours and subtleties of lighting, and shadows blend softly. The surface is shallow and flat, conveying little sense of depth. The background material is ambiguous; is it cloth, paper, parchment, or some other material? The skull appears to float in front of this background. At the same time, the black band behind the skull seems to open into a mysterious space that recedes from the viewer.

The colors of the painting are muted, subtle, neutral—shades of black, gray, cream, and white. A slightly different color tone comes from the inside of the broken skull, where shades of tan and ochre are revealed. Within this world of muted tones, the white skull stands out rather starkly against the off-white background, and the flowers show up silvery gray against the white, beige, and black. The colors are quiet, almost somber, with a balance between the heavy black band and the other lighter-colored surfaces.

What are we to make of the image itself—a skull dressed up with cloth flowers? The animal almost appears to be eating or nuzzling one flower, and the other adorns its forehead. Many artists have used human skulls to remind us of our mortality, and in this painting suggestions of death and spirituality are reinforced, perhaps to the subconscious mind, by the cross shape that underlies the composition. In this context, the cow skull strikes an odd and discordant note. Cow skulls are often used to suggest the unforgiving nature of the desert, where animals and humans alike perish in a waterless, forbidding landscape. Here, the skull is transformed, first by its placement in an abstract setting and second by its adornment with artificial flowers. Is the image morbid, macabre? Is it humorous, playful, ironic? Or are we meant simply to see the skull in a new way, as a unique and interesting object, apart from the living animal it once was? Aged in the desert, bleached by the sun, the skull, though evocative of death, has its own stark beauty. The flowers too have their beauty; at the same time, the artist makes it clear that they are calico, not real. They are artificial, created by human hands to resemble living flowers

Although the skull and flowers are painted realistically, the ambiguous background suggests that the artist is moving toward abstraction, toward an expression of feeling and mood rather than pure representation. The overall feeling evoked by the painting is one of contemplation, meditation. Faced with the juxtaposition of these incongruous objects, we are reminded of the intimate relationships between life and death, beauty and ugliness, art and nature.

How can we augment our appreciation and understanding of this painting with contextual knowledge?

Georgia O'Keeffe grew up on a farm in Wisconsin, where she reveled in every detail of nature, bringing to it an attention and appreciation that would later be reflected in her paintings. She knew from an early age that she wanted to be an artist, and she studied art in Chicago and New York, developing a highly refined technique that quickly became recognized as uniquely her own. Among important early influences were the paintings and theories of Russian abstract artist Wassily Kandinsky, who believed that art and especially color had powerful spiritual effects. In 1929 O'Keeffe visited Taos, New Mexico, for the first time, where she became enraptured by the desert, the light, the colors of the landscape, the expanse of the sky. She was especially intrigued by bones—their form, shape, color, texture—and she shipped boxes of them back to her studio in New York to paint. Eventually she spent more and more time in the Southwest, developing a style that blends realism and abstraction. Her trademark was the selection and abstraction of an object or a view in nature, which she then transformed in accordance with her inner vision. She became known for her particular way of seeing and for her ability to enable others to see the same way.

When she painted *Cow's Skull with Calico Roses,* O'Keeffe was at a difficult time in her personal life. Perhaps depression led her to paint in subdued colors (rather than the brilliant colors of earlier and later paintings) and to focus on bones and other images of death (rather than the images of flowers for which she was already famous). Some have suggested that the seemingly suspended nature of the skull in this painting was suggestive of her own unsettled frame of mind. Whether or not personal details like these help us appreciate and understand the work, what is clear is that when we contemplate *Cow's Skull with Calico Roses,* we see not just the beauty of natural forms but also the power of nature to transform objects and the power of the artist to transform them once again.

MUSICAL ANALYSIS

Like literature and art, music has its own vocabulary, and we need to be familiar with it in order to analyze a composition. A basic distinction we can apply to music is the one between religious music, or **sacred music**—such as Gregorian chants, Masses, requiems, and hymns—and **secular music**—such as symphonies, songs, and dances. Another distinction we can make is between vocal or choral music, which is sung and generally has lyrics (words), and instrumental music, which is written for and performed on instruments.

In music, composers choose among many different **forms,** or particular structures or arrangements of elements. Symphonies, songs, concertos, string quartets, sonatas, Masses, and operas are some of the many different forms in which composers may write their music. As in literature and the visual arts, various musical forms have been more or less popular according to the styles and fashions of the time. The madrigal, for example, was a popular vocal form of the Renaissance period; the church cantata was a common form in the Baroque period; and the symphony became the most important orchestral form beginning in the eighteenth century.

Music itself is a combination of tone, tempo, and texture. **Tone** is a musical sound of definite pitch (pitch is determined by the frequency of the air waves producing the sound). A set pattern of tones (or notes) arranged from low to high (or high to low) is known as a **scale.** The modern Western scale is the familiar do, re, mi, fa, sol, la, ti, do, with half-steps in between the tones. In other cultures, more or fewer tones may be distinguished in a scale. The term *tone* can also refer to the quality of a sound. **Tempo** is the rate of speed of a musical passage, usually set or suggested by the composer. **Texture** describes the number and the nature of the voices or instruments employed and how the parts are combined. In music a theme is a characteristic musical idea upon which a composition is built or developed.

Melody is a succession of musical tones, usually having a distinctive musical shape, or line, and a definite rhythm (the recurrent alternation of accented and unaccented beats). **Harmony** is the simultaneous combination of two or more tones, producing a chord. More generally, harmony refers to the chordal characteristics of a work and the way in which chords interact with one another.

Music differs from literature and the visual arts in some important ways. First, unlike visual art, which does not change after the artist finishes it, music begins when the composition is complete. Like drama, music is lifeless until it is interpreted and performed. The written music represents the composer's intent, but the actual execution of the work is up to conductors and musicians.

A second difference is the fleeting, temporal nature of music. When we listen to live music, we hear it once and it's gone. We cannot study it like a painting or reread a passage as we can in a novel. Of course, recording devices and musical notation enable us to revisit music again and again, but by its very nature, music exists in time in a way that literature and the visual arts do not. For this reason, it is often particularly difficult to appreciate or understand a piece of music on first hearing; instead, we have to listen to it repeatedly.

Music is also more difficult to describe in words than literature or the visual arts. At best, words can only approximate, suggest, and refer to sounds. Sometimes it's helpful to use imagery from other sense modalities to describe a piece of music. What visual images does the work evoke? What colors? What textures? If you were to choreograph the work, how would the dancers move?

Finally, when we analyze a painting, we can reproduce it for our audience, and when we analyze a poem, we can reprint it. When we analyze music, we often have to hope that members of our audience know the work and can "hear" it in their heads. Alternatively, we can hope to generate enough interest in the work that they will want to make a point of hearing it themselves.

With these few basics in mind, let's consider a well-known musical work, *Rhapsody in Blue,* by George Gershwin (1898–1937). Even if you don't know this piece by name, it's very likely that you've heard it. It's been used in ads and in the sound tracks of numerous movies, including *Fantasia 2000;* it is also a standard accompaniment to images of New York City.

Imagine that you're seated in a concert hall and hearing this piece performed by a symphony orchestra (probably a "pops" orchestra, one that performs more popular classical music). When listening to a new piece of music or one you're not terribly familiar with, it's a good idea to simply try to get a sense of its general mood and character—again, focusing on the creator's intent. What emotions or ideas is the composer trying to convey? What musical elements does the composer use to execute that intent?

You'll notice, first of all, that the work is written for a small orchestra and a solo piano, the same instrumental configuration you would expect for a classical piano concerto (a concerto is a work for one or a few instruments and an orchestra, with much of its interest coming from the contrasts between the solo voice and the ensemble voice). But the opening notes of *Rhapsody in Blue* reveal something other than classical intentions: a solo clarinet begins low and sweeps up the scale in a seemingly endless "smear" of sound, finally reaching a high note, briefly holding it, and then plunging into the playful, zigzag melody that becomes one of the major themes of the work. Within moments, the orchestra enters and repeats the theme in the strings and brass, to be followed by the entry of the solo piano. Throughout the work, piano and orchestra alternate and combine to sing out beautiful melodies and create a varied and colorful texture. Variety also comes from different instrumentation of the themes and tunes, played first by a slinky muted trumpet, then by a sweet solo violin, later by a whole lush string section or a brash horn section.

You'll notice too the constant changes in tempo, now slower, now faster, almost as if the work is being improvised. Complex, syncopated, off-the-beat rhythms give the piece a jazzy feeling, and the combination of tones evokes the blues, a style of music in which certain notes are "bent," or lowered slightly in pitch, creating a particular sound and mood. The general feeling of the piece is upbeat, exciting, energetic, suggestive of a bustling city busy with people on the go. It may also make you think of Fred Astaire and Ginger Rogers movies you've seen on late-night TV—sophisticated, playful, casually elegant—and in fact, Gershwin wrote the music for some of their films.

What can we learn about this work from its title? Musical works often reveal their form in their title ("Fifth Symphony," "Violin Concerto in D," and so on). A rhapsody is a composition of irregular form with an improvisatory character. Although you may have heard themes, repetitions, and echoes in *Rhapsody in Blue,* you probably were not able to discern a regular form such as might be apparent in a classical sonata or symphony. The word *rhapsody* also suggests rapture, elation, bliss, ecstasy—perhaps the feelings conveyed by that soaring first phrase on the clarinet. *Blue,* on the other hand, suggests the melancholy of the blues. The dissonance created by the combination of the two terms—like the combinations and contrasts in the music—creates an energetic tension that arouses our curiosity and heightens our interest.

In making these observations about *Rhapsody in Blue,* we've been noticing many of the formal elements of a musical work and answering questions that can be asked about any composition: What is the form of the work? What kind of instrumentation has the composer chosen? What is the primary melodic theme of the work? What tempos are used? How do the instruments or voices work together to create the texture? What is the overall mood of the piece—joyful, sad, calm, wild, a combination?

Now, at your imaginary concert, there may be notes in the program that will provide you with some context for the work. You'll find that George Gershwin was a gifted and classically trained pianist who quit school at 15 and went to work in Tin Pan Alley, a district in New York City where popular songs were written and published. His goal in writing *Rhapsody in Blue* (1924) was to blend classical and popular music, to put the energy and style of jazz into a symphonic format. Many listeners "see" and "hear" New York City in this piece. Gershwin created his own unique idiom, a fast-paced blend of rhythm, melody, and harmony that followed certain rules of composition but gave the impression of

improvisation. He went on to write musicals, more serious compositions like the opera *Porgy and Bess,* and music for Hollywood films, all in his distinctive style. Information like this can help you begin to compare *Rhapsody in Blue* both with other works of the time and with other works by Gershwin. As in any analysis, integrating the formal and the contextual rounds out your interpretation and understanding of the work.

CONCLUSION

These three brief analyses should give you some ideas about how literature, art, and music can be approached in productive ways. By taking the time to look more closely, we gain access to the great works of our culture. This statement leads us to another issue: What makes a work "great"? Why do some works of art have relevance long beyond their time, while others are forgotten soon after their designated "fifteen minutes of fame"? These questions have been debated throughout history. One answer is that great art reflects some truth of human experience that speaks to us across the centuries. The voice of Shakespeare, the paintings of Georgia O'Keeffe, the music of George Gershwin have a universal quality that doesn't depend on the styles of the time. Great art also enriches us and makes us feel that we share a little more of the human experience than we did before.

As both a student of the humanities and an audience member, you have the opportunity to appreciate and understand the arts. Despite the formal nature of academic inquiry, an aesthetic analysis is a personal endeavor. In looking closely at a creative work, seeking the creator's intent and evaluating its execution, you enrich your appreciation of the work with understanding; you bring the emotional reaction you first experienced to its intellectual completion. As twentieth-century composer Arnold Schoenberg once wrote, "You get from a work about as much as you are able to give to it yourself." This primer has been intended to help you learn how to bring more of yourself to works of art, to couple your subjective appreciation with intellectual understanding. With these tools in hand, you won't have to say you don't know much about art but you know what you like; you'll be able to say you know *about* what you like.

1 PREHISTORY AND NEAR EASTERN CIVILIZATIONS

A Western man or woman born early in the last century has seen more change in a lifetime than previous generations experienced over hundreds of years. Despite this rapid change in modern times, Western civilization stands firmly on a foundation that is almost five thousand years old, and people in the West often return to that foundation to discover their heritage and to reexamine their values. As further changes occur, the past becomes increasingly important as a guide to the future.

Before we begin to explore this heritage and what it means today, we need to discuss two important terms—*culture* and *civilization*. **Culture** usually refers to the sum of human endeavors: methods and practices for survival; political, economic, and social institutions; and values, beliefs, and the arts. **Civilization,** on the other hand, refers to the way people live in a complex political, economic, and social structure, usually in an urban setting; usually after making certain technological and artistic advances and sharing a refinement of thought, manners, and taste. Culture is passed from one generation to another by human behavior, speech, and artifacts; civilization is transmitted primarily by writing (Figure 1.1). The term *culture* can also be used to refer to the creative, artistic, and intellectual expressions of a civilization. We will use the term in both these senses. In the words of Matthew Arnold, the nineteenth-century English poet and critic, culture is "the best that has been thought and said." To this we would add, "and done."

◀ **Detail**   *Selket*. Ca. 1325 B.C. Wood, overlaid with gesso and gilded, ht. 53⅝". Cairo Museum, Egypt.

Figure 1.1   Rosetta Stone. Ca. 197–196 B.C. British Museum. *Although scholars knew that Egypt had a writing system, they were unable to solve the mystery of hieroglyphics until the nineteenth century. The key was provided by the Rosetta Stone, discovered by members of Napoleon's expedition when he invaded Egypt in 1799. On the stone the same event is described in hieroglyphics, in Egyptian cursive script, and in Greek. By comparing the Greek text with the other two, scholars were able to decipher both Egyptian scripts. This discovery marks the origin of modern Egyptology.*

PREHISTORY AND EARLY CULTURES

Where and when does the story of human culture begin? The latest evidence from paleoanthropology, the study of early human life, indicates that human beings originated in the distant past in lands far from western Europe. Human development thus begins during prehistory, long before our predecessors compiled—or could compile—written records of their cultures. The first ancestors of human beings probably appeared four to five million years ago. In comparison, life-forms appeared on earth an estimated two to three billion years ago, and the planet itself is believed to have formed some four to six billion years ago.

The periods of time involved in these processes are so vast that only metaphors can make them comprehensible. If we take the seven-day week, made familiar

by the biblical account of creation, and combine it with recent scientific estimates about when the earth and life began, then the following analogy may be made. The earth was created just after midnight on the first day, the first life appeared at about noon on the fourth day, and the early ancestors of human beings didn't show up until about 11 P.M. on the seventh day. To complete the analogy, the birth of civilization occurred almost an hour later, in the last tenth of a second before midnight on the last day of the week.

Although the record of human evolution is obscure, sufficient evidence exists to show that hominids, the earliest primate ancestors of modern humans, probably originated in eastern Africa. From among them, about two million years ago, in the Pliocene epoch, the genus *Homo* evolved, a form marked by a larger brain and the ability to adapt somewhat to the environment. Hominids of the *Homo* genus made and used tools and developed rudimentary cultures. Anthropologists designate this earliest cultural period as the **Paleolithic,** or Old Stone Age. It corresponds to the geological period known as the Pleistocene epoch, or Ice Age, the time of extensive climate changes caused by the advance and retreat of massive glaciers (Timeline 1.1).

Stone Age culture spread widely over a vast area, but remains of hominid life are scarce. Evidence indicates that hominids lived in packs, followed herds of wandering animals, and ate wild seasonal fruits and vegetables. Anthropologists believe that duties and work divided along sex lines as all-male teams hunted game for meat and fur while females and children gathered plant foods, prepared meals, and tended the young. During the night, all sought shelter together in caves for safety and refuge against the elements. This way of life hinged on cooperation and food sharing among small social groups.

In the early Old Stone Age, or Lower Paleolithic, hominids invented crude stone tools, used fire, and probably developed speech—a major breakthrough that allowed them to communicate in ways denied other animals. Their first tools were simple choppers and, somewhat later, hand axes. In the Middle Paleolithic, more advanced hominids developed pointed tools and scrapers, which they chiseled with precision and care. In the Upper Paleolithic, double-faced blades became common.

By about 200,000 B.C., the species *Homo sapiens* had evolved from earlier hominids. More fully developed physically and mentally, they slowly spread throughout the Eastern Hemisphere and eventually migrated into the Western Hemisphere over the land bridge between Siberia and Alaska. Their more sophisticated tools included bows and arrows, fishhooks, and needles. They lived together cooperatively, buried their dead with rituals, and began to paint and sculpt. Especially through

Timeline 1.1 GEOLOGICAL TIME AND PREHISTORIC CULTURAL PERIODS   **All dates approximate and** B.C.

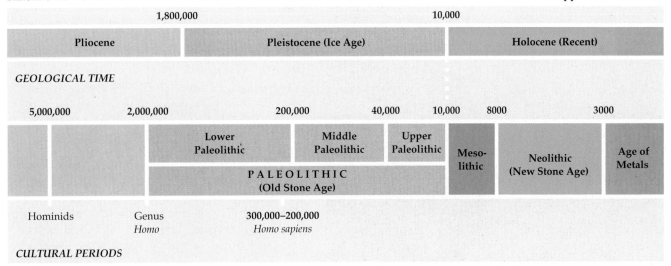

their cave paintings and carved figurines, our ancestors made a breakthrough to symbolic thought.

Ice Age cave paintings of reindeer, bison, rhinoceroses, lions, and horses in Altamira, Spain, and in Lascaux and the Ardèche region of France date from the Upper Paleolithic and are the earliest examples of human art (Figure 1.2). The purposes of the paintings in the recently discovered Chauvet caves in the Ardèche region remain a mystery, but those at Altamira and Lascaux were probably used as part of ceremonies and rituals before hunting. By painting numerous wild animals pierced with arrows, the artists were attempting to ensure a successful hunt.

Another type of Upper Paleolithic art is seen in the carved female figurine found at Willendorf, Austria (Figure 1.3). Made of limestone, the statue is faceless and rotund. The distended stomach and full breasts suggest that the figure may have been used as a fertility symbol and an image of a mother goddess, representing the creative power of nature. As a mythological figure, the mother goddess appeared in many ancient cultures, beginning in Paleolithic times; about thirty thousand miniature sculptures in clay, marble, bone, copper, and gold have been uncovered at about three thousand sites in southeastern Europe alone. The supremacy of the mother goddess was expressed in the earliest myths of creation, which told of the life-giving and nurturing powers of the female. This figurine from Willendorf, with its emphasized breasts, navel, and vulva, symbolic of creativity, may have been used in religious ceremonies to ensure the propagation of the tribe or to guarantee a bountiful supply of food. The statue also reveals the aesthetic interests of the sculptor, who took care to depict the goddess's hands resting on her breasts and her hair in tightly knit rows.

As the last glaciers retreated from Europe, during the Holocene (Recent) epoch of geological time, human beings were forced to adapt to new living conditions. Their stone tools became more advanced and included knives and hammers. Following the Mesolithic transitional period (about 10,000–8000 B.C.), a transformation occurred that has been called the most important event in human history: Hunters and gatherers became farmers and herders. Thus began the **Neolithic** period, or New Stone Age (about 8000 B.C.). In Southeast Asia, Central America, parts of South America, and the Near East, human beings ceased their nomadic existence and learned to domesticate wild animals. They learned to plow the earth and sow seeds, providing themselves with a much more reliable food supply, which in turn encouraged the development of permanent settlements and eventually the rise of urban centers. This agrarian pattern of life dominated the West until about two hundred years ago.

Precisely why and how the agrarian revolution came at this time is a hotly debated topic among anthropologists. Nonetheless, most agree that with the retreat of the last glaciers from Europe, methods of food gathering changed dramatically, causing either surpluses or shortages. In some areas, grain surpluses allowed populations to grow, which led to forced migrations as the number of humans outstripped the available food. In less productive lands, the people began to experiment with domesticating animals and planting grains. These innovations in marginal lands caused food production to rise, soon matching that found in more fertile areas, so that eventually a uniform agricultural economy spread to many parts of the globe. Thus, economic causes accounted for the transformation from food-gathering to food-producing cultures.

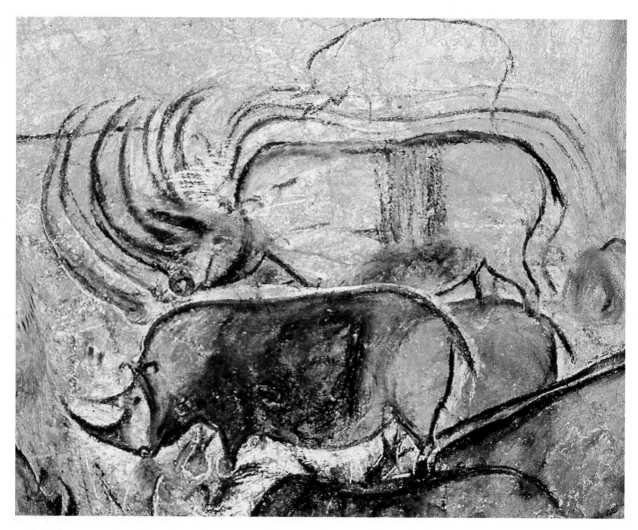

Figure 1.2   Herd of Rhinoceroses. Ca. 32,000–30,000 B.C. Chauvet Cave, Ardèche region, France. *This naturalistic detail of a panel painting includes lions, bison, and a young mammoth (not visible here) moving across a vast expanse of the cave wall. The repeated black lines of the rhinoceroses' horns and backs create a sense of depth and give energy to the work.*

The agricultural revolution expanded across the Near East and probably into Europe and Africa. Between 6000 and 3000 B.C., human beings also learned to mine and use copper, signifying the end of the Neolithic period and ushering in the Age of Metals. In about 3000 B.C., artisans combined copper and tin to produce bronze, a strong alloy, which they used in their tools, weapons, and jewelry.

The Bronze Age, which extended from about 3000 to about 1200 B.C., gave rise to two major civilizations in the Near East. The earlier developed in Mesopotamia, the land between the Tigris and Euphrates Rivers (in present-day Iraq), and the other, probably emerging just slightly later, originated along the Nile River in Egypt. Mesopotamian and Egyptian civilizations shared certain characteristics: Both were ruled by kings who were in turn supported by a priestly caste;

the rulers' power was shared by a few educated elites; their economies were slave-based; their societies were stratified, with class privileges at the upper end; and palaces and religious edifices were built for ceremonial and governmental purposes. These early civilizations made deep and lasting impressions on their neighbors and successors that helped shape life in the Western world.

THE CIVILIZATIONS OF THE TIGRIS AND EUPHRATES RIVER VALLEY: MESOPOTAMIA

The Tigris-Euphrates river valley forms part of what is known as the Fertile Crescent, which starts at the Persian Gulf, runs slightly northwestward through the

Figure 1.3 Figurine from Willendorf. Ca. 25,000 B.C. Ht. 4⅜". Museum Naturhistorisches, Vienna. *Discovered in about A.D. 1908, this female statuette measures just under 5 inches high. Carved from limestone, it still shows evidence of having been painted red. Many other statues like it have been discovered, but this one remains the most famous because of the unusual balance it strikes between symbolism and realism.*

The Sumerian, Akkadian, and Babylonian Kingdoms

Three successive civilizations—Sumerian, Akkadian, and Babylonian—flourished in Mesopotamia for nearly fifteen hundred years (Timeline 1.2). Indeed, as historian Samuel Kramer asserts, "history began at Sumer."

The rulers of Sumer created an exalted image of a just and stable society with a rich cultural life. Sumer's most inspirational king, Gilgamesh [GILL-guh-mesh], ruled during the first dynasty (about 2700 B.C.) of Ur, a state centered between the rivers. His heroic adventures and exploits were later immortalized in the poem *The Epic of Gilgamesh.* A later ruler, Urukagina, is known for reforming law codes and revitalizing the economy near the end of the Sumerian period (2350 B.C.). But Urukagina's successors were unable to maintain Sumer's power, and the cities became easy prey for the Akkadians of northern Mesopotamia.

The Akkadian dynasties, lasting from about 2350 to about 2000 B.C., incorporated Sumerian culture into their own society and carried this hybrid civilization far beyond the Tigris-Euphrates valley. According to legends—which are similar to the later story of the Hebrew leader Moses—Sargon, the first and greatest Akkadian ruler, was born of lowly origins and abandoned at birth in the reed marshes; yet Sargon survived and rose to prominence at the Sumerian court. Excavated inscriptions reveal that Sargon conquered the Sumerians and founded a far-flung empire to the east and northeast. At its height, Sargon's power was felt from Egypt to India, but his successors, lacking his intelligence and skill, could not maintain the Akkadian empire. The incursions of the Guti tribes from the Zagros Mountains brought about the final collapse of the weakened Akkadian empire and the division of southern Mesopotamia into petty kingdoms.

Babylonia was the third civilization in Mesopotamia. From northern Mesopotamia, their power base, the Babylonians governed the entire valley from about 2000 to 1600 B.C. Under their most successful military leader and renowned lawgiver, Hammurabi [ham-uh-RAHB-e] (r. 1792–1750 B.C.), the Babylonians reached their political and cultural ascendancy. However, the Hittites, centered in Asia Minor, invaded Babylon in about 1600 B.C. and toppled the dynasty of Hammurabi.

Agriculture dominated the economy of Mesopotamia. Harsh living conditions and unpredictable floods forced the inhabitants to learn to control the rivers through irrigation systems and cooperative tilling of the soil. Farmers eventually dug a complex canal system to irrigate their cultivated plots, which might have been some distance from the river. As production increased, prosperity allowed larger populations to

Tigris-Euphrates valley, and then turns westerly to the Mediterranean Sea and curves south along the shoreline toward Egypt (Map 1.1). This arc of land contained some of the most arable soil in the Near East, many of the heavily traveled trade routes, and most of the early centers of civilization.

Mesopotamia is a Greek word meaning "land between the two rivers." The hill country and Zagros Mountains rise to the east of the Tigris-Euphrates valley, and the vast Arabian desert stretches to the west. The twin rivers course down to the Persian Gulf, draining an area approximately 600 miles long and 250 miles wide. Near the mouth of the gulf, on the river delta, human wanderers settled in about 6000 B.C., founding villages and tilling the land. Despite heat, marshes, unpredictable and violent floods, and invaders who came from both the mountains and the desert, some of these communities prospered and grew.

Map 1.1   MESOPOTAMIA AND ANCIENT EGYPT
This map shows the two earliest civilizations of the Near East: Mesopotamia and Egypt. **Notice** that much of Mesopotamia is contained within the area known as the Fertile Crescent and that Egypt is settled mainly along the Nile River. **Locate** the cities in Mesopotamia and Egypt. **Compare and contrast** the role and importance of rivers in these civilizations. **Why** was Egypt less exposed to external influences than was Mesopotamia?

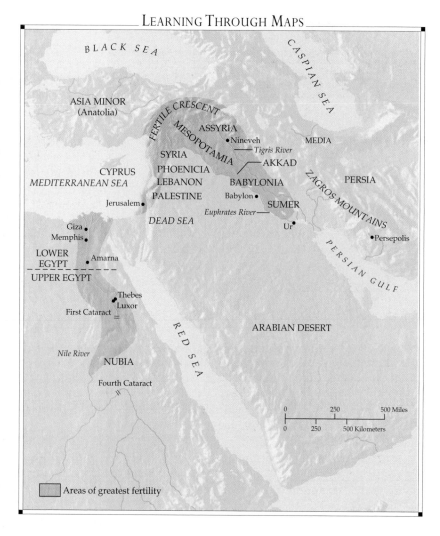

LEARNING THROUGH MAPS

thrive. Villages soon grew into small cities—with populations ranging from 10,000 to 50,000—surrounded by hamlets and tilled fields. Trade developed with nearby areas, and wheeled vehicles—perfected by the Sumerians—and sailboats carried goods up and down Mesopotamia and eventually throughout the Fertile Crescent.

By the beginning of the Bronze Age, the family had replaced the tribe or clan as the basic unit in society. Families now owned their lands outright, and, under the general direction of the religious and secular authorities, they worked their fields and maintained the irrigation ditches. Marriages were arranged by parents, with economics an essential consideration. According to the law codes, women possessed some rights, such as holding property; however, a wife was clearly under her husband's power. Divorce was easier for men than for women, and women were punished more severely than men for breaking moral and marital laws. Recent scholarship has suggested that women's status and

roles became more limited as Mesopotamian society became more complex. In sum, Mesopotamian women were originally able to participate actively in economic, religious, and political life as long as their dependence on and obligation to male kin and husbands were observed, but they progressively lost their relative independence because rulers extended the concept of patriarchy (rule by the fathers) from family practice into public law.

The political structure reflected the order and functions of the social system. At the top stood the ruler, who was supported by an army, a bureaucracy, a judicial system, and a priesthood. The ruler usually obtained advice from prominent leaders, meeting in council, who constituted the next layer of the social order: rich landowners, wealthy merchants, priests, and military chiefs. The next group consisted of artisans, craftspeople, and petty businesspeople and traders. Below them were small landowners and tenant farmers. At the bottom of the social scale were

Timeline 1.2   MESOPOTAMIAN CIVILIZATIONS   All dates approximate and B.C.

3000	2350	2000	1600
Sumerian	Akkadian	Babylonian	

serfs and slaves, who either had been captured in war or had fallen into debt.

The Cradle of Civilization

The three Mesopotamian civilizations responded to the same geography, climate, and natural resources, and their cultures reflected that shared background. The Sumerians were probably the most influential: From Sumer came writing, the lunar calendar, a mathematical computation system, medical and scientific discoveries, and architectural innovations. However, each civilization, through its religion, literature, law, and art, deeply affected other Near Eastern people.

Writing   Thousands of clay tablets inscribed with the wedge-shaped symbols of Sumerian script have been uncovered in Mesopotamia, indicating that the Sumerians had developed a form of writing by 3000 B.C. With the invention of writing, people no longer had to rely on memory, speech, and person-to-person interactions to communicate and transmit information. Instead, they could accumulate a permanent body of knowledge and pass it on from one generation to the next. With writing came the possibility of civilization.

At first, the Sumerians needed a simple way to record agricultural and business information and the deeds and sayings of their rulers. Their earliest symbols were **pictograms,** or pictures, carefully drawn to represent particular objects. To these they added **ideograms,** pictures drawn to represent ideas or concepts. A simple drawing of a bowl, for example, could be used to mean "food." As these pictures became more stylized, meaning began to be transferred from the represented object to the sign itself; that is, the sign began to stand for a word rather than an object.

Later, Sumerian scribes and writers identified the syllabic sounds of spoken words and created **phonograms,** symbols for separate speech sounds, borrowing from and building on the earlier pictograms and ideograms. These simplified and standardized symbols eventually resulted in a phonetic writing system of syllable-based sounds that, when combined, produced words (Figure 1.4). (It was left to later civilizations to separate vowel sounds from syllables and thus create a true alphabet, based on individual speech sounds.)

The Sumerians could now express complex, abstract concepts, and their system could extend to other languages. The Akkadians and the Babylonians adopted and modified the Sumerian script to keep records and preserve their literature, including *The Epic of Gilgamesh* and the Code of Hammurabi. By the end of the Bronze Age (about 1200 B.C.), other written languages existed, but Akkadian-Sumerian was the language of diplomacy and trade in the Near East.

The Sumerian writing system has been labeled **cuneiform,** a term derived from the Latin word *cuneus,* which means "wedge." Using wedge-shaped reeds or styluses, scribes pressed the symbols into wet clay tablets, and artists and craftspeople, wielding metal tools, incised the script into stone monuments or cylindrical pillars. Preserved for thousands of years in hardened clay and stone, cuneiform writing has provided invaluable insight into ancient Mesopotamian culture.

Religion   Sumerian, Akkadian, and Babylonian religions, despite individual differences, shared many basic attitudes and concepts that became the foundation for other Near Eastern belief systems. The underlying beliefs of Mesopotamian religion were that the gods had created human beings to serve them, that the gods were in complete control, and that powerless mortals had no choice but to obey and worship these deities. The hostile climate and unpredictable rivers made life precarious, and the gods appeared capricious. The Mesopotamians held a vague notion of a shadowy netherworld where the dead rested, but they did not believe in an afterlife as such or any rewards or punishments upon death. Happiness seldom was an earthly goal; pessimism ran as a constant theme throughout their religion and literature.

Mesopotamian religion had three important characteristics. It was **polytheistic**—many gods and goddesses existed and often competed with one another; it was **anthropomorphic**—the deities possessed human form and had their own personalities and unique traits; and it was **pantheistic**—hundreds of divinities were found everywhere, in nature and the universe. Since Mesopotamians thought of their gods in human form with all the strengths and weaknesses of mortals, they believed their deities lived in the same way as people, and they were pragmatic in approaching the supernatural powers. For example, they believed that their deities held council, made decisions, and ordered

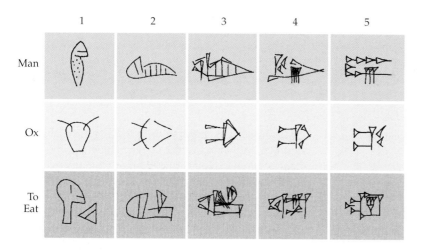

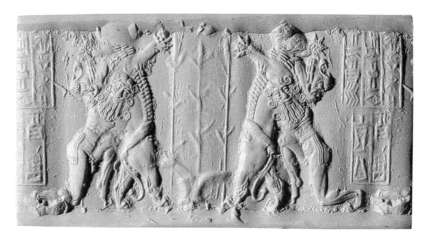

Figure 1.4 Sumerian Cuneiform Writing. Ca. 3000–1000 B.C. *The columns illustrate the evolution of Sumerian writing from pictograms to script. Column 1 shows the pictogram: a man, an ox, and the verb "to eat" (represented by the mouth and a bowl). In column 2, the pictographic symbols have been turned 90 degrees, as the Sumerians did in their first writing. Columns 3 and 4 show how the script changed between 2500 and 1800 B.C. Column 5 is an Assyrian adaptation of the Sumerian cuneiform script.*

Figure 1.5 Gilgamesh Fighting a Lion. Ca. 2500–2000 B.C. Cylinder seal (left) and modern impression of a cylinder seal (right). British Museum. *The separate scenes, rolled out on this impression from the seal, which is about 1 inch high, depict the Sumerian hero in one of his many battles against beasts. The artist heightens the intensity of the physical struggle by placing Gilgamesh, with his legs bent and arms locked around the lion, at a sharp angle under the animal to muster his brute strength against his foe.*

the forces of nature to wreak havoc or to bestow plenty on mortals.

Mesopotamians divided the deities into the sky gods and the earth gods. In these two categories were the four major deities: Anu, the heaven god; Enlil, the air god; Enki, the water god; and Ninhursag, the mother goddess. Enlil emerged as the most powerful god for the Sumerians. He gave mortals the plough and the pickax, and he brought forth for humanity all the productive forces of the universe, such as trees, grains, and "whatever was needful."

Rituals, ceremonies, and the priesthood were absolutely essential to Mesopotamian religion. Although the average Mesopotamian might participate in worship services, the priests played the central role in all religious functions. They also controlled and administered large parcels of land, which enhanced their

power in economic and political matters. Priests carefully formulated and consciously followed the procedures for rites and rituals, which were written down and stored in their temples. This cultic literature not only told the Mesopotamians how to worship but also informed them about their deities' origins, characteristics, and deeds. Religious myths and instructions constituted a major part of Mesopotamian literature and made writing an essential part of the culture.

Literature Of the surviving epics, tales, and legends that offer glimpses into the Mesopotamian mind, the most famous is *The Epic of Gilgamesh*. King Gilgamesh, whose reign in about 2700 B.C. is well documented, became a larger-than-life hero in Sumerian folk tales (Figure 1.5). In all probability, the Gilgamesh epic began as an oral poem and was not written on clay

PERSONAL PERSPECTIVE

A Sumerian Father Lectures His Son

In this Sumerian text, a father rebukes his son for leading a wayward life and admonishes him to reform. The essay was inscribed on clay tablets dating from about 1700 B.C.

"Where did you go?"

"I did not go anywhere."

"If you did not go anywhere, why do you idle about? Go to school, stand before your 'school-father,' recite your assignment, open your schoolbag, write your tablet, let your 'big brother' write your new tablet for you. After you have finished your assignment and reported to your monitor, come to me, and do not wander about in the street. . . .

"You who wander about in the public square, would you achieve success? Then seek out the first generations. Go to school, it will be of benefit to you. My son, seek out the first generations, inquire of them.

"Perverse one over whom I stand watch—I would not be a man did I not stand watch over my son—I spoke to my kin, compared its men, but found none like you among them. . . .

"I, never in all my life did I make you carry reeds to the canebrake. The reed rushes which the young and the little carry, you, never in your life did you carry them. I never said to you 'Follow my caravans.' I never sent you to work, to plow my field. I never sent you to work to dig up my field. I never sent you to work as a laborer. 'Go, work and support me,' I never in my life said to you.

"Others like you support their parents by working. . . .

"I, night and day am I tortured because of you. Night and day you waste in pleasures. You have accumulated much wealth, have expanded far and wide, have become fat, big, broad, powerful, and puffed. But your kin waits expectantly for your misfortune, and will rejoice at it because you looked not to your humanity."

---

tablets for hundreds of years. The most complete surviving version, from 600 B.C., was based on a Babylonian copy written in Akkadian and dating from about 1600 B.C. Although this poem influenced other Near Eastern writings with its characters, plot, and themes, *The Epic of Gilgamesh* stands on its own as a poetic utterance worthy of being favorably compared with later Greek and Roman epics.

Through its royal hero, *The Epic of Gilgamesh* focuses on fundamental themes that concern warriors in an aristocratic society: the need to be brave in the face of danger, the choice of death before dishonor, the conflict between companionship and sexual pleasure, the power of the gods over weak mortals, and the finality of death. Above all, it deals with human beings' vain quest for immortality. As the tale begins, the extravagant and despotic policies of Gilgamesh have led his subjects to pray for relief. In response, a goddess creates from clay a "wild man" of tremendous physical strength and sends him to kill Gilgamesh. But Enkidu, as he is called, is instead tamed by a woman's love, loses his innocence, wrestles Gilgamesh to a draw, and becomes his boon companion.

As the epic unfolds, Gilgamesh chooses friendship with Enkidu rather than the love offered by the goddess Ishtar. Gilgamesh is punished for this choice by being made to watch helplessly as Enkidu dies from an illness sent by the gods. Forced to confront the fate awaiting all mortals, a grieving Gilgamesh begins a search for immortality.

The next section of the epic, which details Gilgamesh's search, includes the Sumerian tale of the great flood, which parallels the later Hebrew story of Noah and the ark. Although the Sumerian account of the flood was probably a later addition to the original story of Gilgamesh, the episode does fit into the narrative and reinforces one of the epic's major themes: the inescapable mortality of human beings. Gilgamesh hears the story of the flood from its sole survivor, Utnapishtim. Utnapishtim tells Gilgamesh how he built an ark and loaded it with animals and his family, how the waters rose, and how he released birds from the ark to discover if the waters were receding. The old man then explains how the gods, feeling sorry for the last remaining human, granted him immortality. Utnapishtim refuses to divulge the secret of eternal life to Gilgamesh, but the old man's wife blurts out where a plant may be found that will renew youth but not give immortality. Although Gilgamesh locates the plant, he loses it on his journey home. Gilgamesh, seeing the city of Uruk that he had built, realizes that the deeds humans do on earth are the measure of their immortality and that death is inevitable.

The Epic of Gilgamesh is essentially a secular morality tale. Gilgamesh's triumphs and failures mirror the lives of all mortals, and the Sumerians saw themselves in Gilgamesh's change from an overly confident and powerful hero to a doubting and fearful human being. Those who, like Gilgamesh, ignore the power of the deities have to pay a heavy price for their pride.

Mesopotamia also gave the world the first known literary figure, Enheduanna (fl. 2330 B.C.), an Akkadian poet who wrote in the Sumerian language. Made priestess of temples in the Sumerian cities of Ur (see Figure 1.9) and Uruk by her father, King Sargon, she used her priestly offices and literary gifts to further his political goal of uniting the Sumerians and the Akkadians. In these posts, she composed hymns to both Sumerian and Akkadian deities, and these hymns— some of which have been identified—became models for later poets. Enheduanna was especially devoted to Inanna, the Sumerian goddess of love, and she made this deity the subject of her best-known literary work, *The Exaltation of Inanna*. In this work, Enheduanna exalted, or raised, Inanna to supremacy in the Sumerian pantheon, her tribute for what she believed was Inanna's role in Sargon's triumph over a general uprising at the end of his reign.

Law   The Mesopotamians produced the fairest law codes before that of the Hebrews. The central theme of Sumerian law, whose first existing records date from about 2050 B.C., was justice. From the earliest times, the Sumerian kings understood justice to mean "the straight thing"—that is, dealing fairly with all their subjects and prohibiting the exploitation of the weak by the strong. This concept of equity applied especially to economic matters, such as debts, contracts, and titles to land.

The most important set of laws from Mesopotamian civilization is that of the Babylonian king Hammurabi. Dating from about 1700 B.C., the Code of Hammurabi was found preserved on a seven-foot-high black stone **stele,** or pillar. At the top, Hammurabi is depicted standing in front of Shamash, the Babylonian and Sumerian god of justice. Like other ancient lawgivers (Moses, for example), Hammurabi received the legal code from a deity. Below the two figures are carved the prologue, the collection of laws, and an epilogue (Figure 1.6). The prologue lists Hammurabi's accomplishments and sings his praises while making it clear that the gods are the source of his power to establish "law and justice." The epilogue warns future rulers to carry out these laws or else be subject to defeat and ruin.

The laws concerning punishment for crimes are based on the judicial principle of *lex talionis,* or retaliation, which demands an "eye for an eye," although Hammurabi's code often substitutes payments in kind for damages done. Every major area of civil and criminal law was covered in the code, including property

Figure 1.6   Code of Hammurabi. Ca. 1700 B.C. Basalt, ht. approx. 3'. Louvre. *Hammurabi stands on the left, his hand raised before his mouth in the traditional Mesopotamian gesture of devotion, and Shamash, the sun god and protector of truth and justice, sits on the right. The cult of Shamash (in Sumeria, Utu) emerged from the earliest times, and this god's representation— flames shooting from the shoulders and hands holding symbols of power—was established in the Sumerian period. The relief, with its incised folds of cloth and ceremonial chair, is carved deep enough into the hard stone stele (7'4") to suggest a three-dimensional sculpture.*

rights, sales, contracts, inheritance, adoption, prices and wages, sexual relations (much more severely restricted for women than for men), and personal rights for women, children, and slaves. Hammurabi's code, like other Mesopotamian laws, was only one part of a complex judicial system that encompassed judges, courts, trials, legal proceedings, and contracts.

Art and Architecture   The art of Mesopotamia, like the rest of its culture, evolved from Sumerian styles to the Akkadian and Babylonian schools. Artisans worked in many forms—small seals, pottery, jewelry, vases, reliefs, and statues—and in many media—clay, stone, precious gems, gold, silver, leather, and ivory. Artifacts and crafted works from all three civilizations recorded the changing techniques of the producers as well as the shifting tastes of the consumers, whether they were rich individuals decorating their homes or officials issuing commissions for statues to adorn their temples. The temples, usually the center of the city and set on high mounds above the other structures, were often splendidly ornamented and housed exquisitely carved statues of gods and goddesses.

A fine example of Sumerian artistry is a bull's head carved on the sound box of a lyre (Figure 1.7). Working in gold leaf and semiprecious gems, the unknown artist has captured the vigor and power of the animal in a bold and simple style. Such elegant musical instruments were played in homes and in palaces to accompany the poets and storytellers as they sang of the heroes' adventures and the deities' powers.

Mesopotamian artists carved thousands of figures, many on the walls of temples and palaces and others as freestanding statues. A notable early type of freestanding statue that became standard in Akkadian temples depicts a figure in a contemplative, worshiping pose, his hands folded and clasped in front of him. Many of these are likenesses of Gudea, a ruler who flourished about 2150 B.C. (Figure 1.8).

In contrast to the finely crafted sculpture, Mesopotamian architecture often seems uninspired, particularly the domestic architecture. Most Mesopotamian houses were square or rectangular. Even though the Mesopotamians knew about the arch, the vault, and the column, they did not employ them widely; they used primarily the basic **post-and-lintel construction** of two vertical posts capped by a horizontal lintel, or beam, for entranceways. The clay bricks used in construction limited the builders in styles and decorations, notably on the exterior. If private homes of clay bricks looked drab from the street, however, they were often attractive inside, built around an open courtyard with decorated rooms. The exteriors of temples and palaces were sometimes adorned with colored glazed bricks, mosaics, and painted cones arranged in patterns or, more rarely, with imported stone and marble.

Archeologists have not yet determined exactly how Mesopotamian cities were laid out. Urban centers were protected by walls, whose imposing and elaborately decorated gates proclaimed the city's wealth and power. The most prominent structure in each Sumerian city was the **ziggurat,** a terraced brick and mudbrick pyramid that served as the center of worship. The ziggurat resembled a hill or a stairway to the sky from which the deities could descend; or perhaps the structure was

Figure 1.7 Restored Sumerian Lyre, from Ur. Ca. 2600 B.C. Wood with gold leaf and inlays, ht. of bull's head, approx. 12". British Museum. *The lyre's sound box, on which the bull's head is carved, is a hollow chamber that increases the resonance of the sound. Music played an important role in Mesopotamian life, and patrons often commissioned the construction of elegant instruments. Thus, even at this early stage of civilization, those with wealth influenced the arts.*

Figure 1.8 *Gudea.* Ca. 2150 B.C. Diorite, ht. 17¾". Louvre. *Little is known of Gudea, but more than thirty small statues of this Guti ruler have been found. The body and the head of this statuette were discovered separately and later joined together.*

conceived as the gods' cosmic mountain. A temple of welcome for the gods stood on the top of the ziggurat, approached by sets of steps. Shrines, storehouses, and administrative offices were constructed around the base or on the several levels of the massive hill. In the low plain of the Tigris-Euphrates valley, the ziggurat literally and figuratively dominated the landscape. The Tower of Babel, described in the Jewish scriptures as reaching to the sky, may have been suggested by the Sumerian ziggurats, some of which had towers.

Of the numerous ziggurats and temples that have survived, the best preserved is at Ur, in southern Mesopotamia, dedicated to the moon god, Nanna (Figure 1.9). Built in about 2100 B.C., this ziggurat was

laid out to the four points of the compass. A central stairway led up to the highest platform, on which the major temple rested. Other cities constructed similar massive podiums in the hopes that they would please the gods and goddesses, that the rivers would be kind to them, and that life would continue. Thus, the central themes of Mesopotamian civilization manifested themselves in the ziggurats.

THE CIVILIZATION OF THE NILE RIVER VALLEY: EGYPT

Another great river, the Nile, provided the setting for Egyptian civilization. Unlike the culture of the Mesopotamian valley, however, Nilotic culture evolved continuously, responding mainly to internal changes rather than to external influences. It thus achieved a unified character that lasted for about three thousand years. Isolated by deserts on either side, Egypt developed an introspective attitude that was little influenced by neighboring cultures (such as Nubia, also called Kush, which flourished between the first and fourth cataracts, or waterfalls, of the Nile River) and that led to a sense of cultural superiority. Subjected to the annual floodings of the Nile and aware of the revolutions of the sun, Egypt saw itself as part of a cyclical pattern in a timeless world.

The periodic overflowings of the Nile made civilized life possible in Egypt. Red sandy deserts stretched east and west of the waterway. Beside the Nile's banks, however, the black alluvial soil of the narrow floodplain offered rich land for planting, although the river's gifts of water and arable land were limited. Irrigation canals and ditches plus patient, backbreaking labor were required to bring the life-giving liquid into the desert.

Because the survival and prosperity of the people depended on the Nile, the river dominated and shaped the Egyptian experience. About 95 percent of the people lived on the less than 5 percent of Egyptian land that was arable and that was located along the Nile. The resulting concentration of people led to the emergence of the agricultural village, the fundamental unit of Egyptian civilization. The reward for farm labor tended to be subsistence living, yet the perennial hope that next year's flood would bring a more bountiful harvest created an optimistic outlook that contrasted with the darker Mesopotamian view.

The Nile linked the "Two Lands," Upper and Lower Egypt, two regions whose differing geography made for two distinct ways of life. Since the Nile flows northward, Lower Egypt referred to the northern lands fed by the river's spreading delta, a region made wealthy by its fertile soil. In contrast, the harsh topography and poor farming conditions of the southern lands made

Figure 1.9   Ziggurat of Ur. Ca. 2100 B.C. Ur (Muqaiyir, Iraq). *A temple to Nanna, the moon god, stood on the top of the ziggurat, which was terraced on three levels. On the first level was an entranceway approached by two sets of steps on each side and one in the front. The base, or lowest stage, which is all that remains of this "Hill of Heaven," measures 200 by 150 feet and stands 70 feet high. In comparison, Chartres cathedral in France is 157 feet wide, with each tower over 240 feet high.*

Upper Egypt an area of near subsistence living. In addition, Lower Egypt, because of its proximity to both Mediterranean and Near Eastern cultures, tended to be more cosmopolitan than the provincial, isolated lands of Upper Egypt.

The earliest Neolithic settlers in the Nile valley probably arrived in about 6000 B.C. These earliest Egyptians took up an agricultural life, wresting control of the surrounding lands, taming the river, and domesticating animals. In the rich alluvial soil, they cultivated barley, wheat, and vegetables for themselves and fodder for their animals. They hunted with bows and arrows and fished with nets, thereby supplementing their simple fare. They also planted flax, from which thread was woven into linen on primitive looms. Most tools and weapons were made of stone or flint, but copper, which had to be imported, became more important after 3500 B.C. The early Egyptians lived in simply furnished, flat-topped houses built of sun-dried bricks. These basic patterns characterized peasant life throughout much of Egypt's history.

Continuity and Change over Three Thousand Years

Egypt stepped from the shadows of its illiterate past in about 3100 B.C., when Menes [MEE-neez] proclaimed himself king and united the upper and lower lands. His power reached from the Mediterranean to the first cataract of the Nile, making Egypt a state to be reckoned with in the Near East. Egypt's lengthy, complex history is conventionally divided into twenty-six dynasties, which are in turn classified into groups. The three major groups of dynasties are known as the Old Kingdom, the Middle Kingdom, and the New Kingdom. They are preceded and followed, respectively, by two dynastic groups known as the Early Dynastic Period and the Late Dynastic Period. In addition, two intermediate dynastic groupings (the First and the Second) precede and follow the Middle Kingdom (Timeline 1.3).

In the Early Dynastic Period (about 3100–2700 B.C.), the kings brought prosperity through their control of the economy and fostered political harmony through diplomacy and dynastic marriages. These rulers, claiming to be gods on earth, adopted the trappings of divinity and built royal tombs to ensure their immortality.

With the Old Kingdom (about 2700–2185 B.C.), Egypt entered a five-hundred-year period of peace and prosperity, as its political institutions matured and its language was adapted to literary uses. The most enduring accomplishment of the Old Kingdom became the pyramid—the royal tomb devised by the Fourth Dynasty kings (Figure 1.10). As the visible symbol of the kings' power, the massive pyramids served to link the rulers with the gods and the cosmos. Yet, although the kings could impress their people with divine claims, they could neither subdue the forces of nature nor make their power last forever. For reasons not fully understood, these rulers loosened their control over the state and thus ushered in an age of political fragmentation called the First Intermediate Period.

Timeline 1.3 EGYPTIAN CIVILIZATION   All dates approximate and B.C.

6000	3100	2700	2185	2050	1800	1552	1079	525
Neolithic and Predynastic Periods	Early Dynastic Period	Old Kingdom	First Intermediate Period	Middle Kingdom	Second Intermediate Period	New Kingdom	Late Dynastic Period	Persian Conquest

Figure 1.10   The Pyramids at Giza. Ground view from the south. Pyramid of Menkure (foreground), ca. 2525 B.C.; Pyramid of Khafre (center), ca. 2590 B.C.; Pyramid of Khufu (rear), ca. 2560 B.C. *The Fourth Dynasty was the Age of Pyramids, when this characteristic shape was standardized and became a symbol of Egyptian civilization. The Great Pyramid, in the center, was the first structure at Giza; it originally stood 480 feet high but today is only 450 feet high.*

In the First Intermediate Period (about 2185–2050 B.C.), civil war raged sporadically and starvation wiped out much of the populace. Eventually, a family from Thebes, in Upper Egypt, reunited the state and initiated the Middle Kingdom (about 2050–1800 B.C.). The new dynasty, the twelfth, fortified the southern frontier with Nubia and helped bring about a cultural renaissance, especially in literature, but unity was short-lived.

The Second Intermediate Period (about 1800–1552 B.C.) was an age of chaos provoked both by repeated failures of the Nile to flood and by a resurgence of local warlords. A weakened Lower Egypt succumbed to the Hyksos, Semitic-speaking invaders from Palestine. Backed by warriors in horse-drawn chariots, the Hyksos with their bronze weapons easily defeated the copper-armed Egyptians. The Hyksos era was crucial in Egypt's history because it ended the isolation that had fed a sense of cultural superiority. Egyptian nobility now joined aristocracies everywhere in employing the horse for war and sport, and Egyptian artisans fully entered the Bronze Age.

Ahmose I [AH-mos], a Theban king, drove out the Hyksos and inaugurated the New Kingdom (1552–1079 B.C.), the most cosmopolitan era in Egyptian history.

Pursuing the Hyksos into Palestine, Ahmose conquered the foreign peoples along the way, creating the first Egyptian empire. To the northeast, Egypt's kings, now called pharaohs, pursued imperial ambitions against the cities in Palestine, Phoenicia, and Syria, a move that provoked deadly warfare with the Hittites of Anatolia. Egypt finally secured its possessions by peacefully dividing up the Near East with the Hittites and the Assyrians. To the south, the pharaohs pushed Egypt's frontiers to the Nile's fourth cataract, conquering the Nubians long in residence there. As the empire grew, Egypt's society underwent the greatest changes of its entire history, including religious innovation by a ruling family, widespread material affluence, extravagant temple building, and artistic and literary experimentation.

But imperial success declined after 1200 B.C., signaled by the pharaoh's growing dependence on unreliable foreign troops. Bands of nomads, called Sea Peoples by the Egyptians, began to disrupt trade and normal social life. Over the course of a century, the invaders forced Egypt to withdraw behind its historic borders and thus ended the empire. The success of the Sea People's challenge, despite their small numbers,

lay in their new weapons, for these destructive migrants were the leading edge of the Age of Iron. Egypt's lack of iron ore probably contributed fatally to its military decline.

Egypt maintained continuity of tradition into the Late Dynastic Period (about 1079–525 B.C.). However, its independence came to an end with its successive incorporations into Nubian, Assyrian, and Persian empires.

Just as the pharaoh dominated the state, so the rulers controlled the predominantly agrarian economy, although departments of government or the priesthood of a temple often exploited the land and the king's serfs. Upper Egypt provided the bulk of farm produce that Lower Egypt exported to Mediterranean neighbors. In prosperous years, the pharaohs claimed up to half of the farm crops to support their building programs, especially funerary monuments. But in years of famine, dynasties fell and the state splintered into separate units.

Foreign trade was also a royal monopoly. The government obtained cedar from Lebanon, olive oil from Palestine, and myrrh from Punt, probably on the Somali coast. Since Egypt never developed a coinage, the pharaohs bartered for these imports with papyrus rolls (for writing), linen, weapons, and furniture. The pharaohs also exported gold from the eastern desert and copper from the Sinai peninsula. In addition, Egypt served as the carrier of tropical African goods—ebony, ivory, and animal skins—to the eastern Mediterranean.

Egyptian society was hierarchical, and at the top stood the pharaoh—the king and god incarnate. Because divine blood coursed through the ruler's veins, he could marry only within his own family. Tradition decreed that the Chief Queen, who was identified with the goddess Hathor, would produce the royal heir. If she failed to produce offspring, the successor pharaoh was selected from sons of the ruler's other wives or royal cousins. On rare occasions, when there was no suitable heir, the Chief Queen became the pharaoh, as did Hatshepsut [hat-SHEP-soot] in the New Kingdom.

Because there was no provision for a female king in Egyptian culture, the appearance of a female ruler is thought by scholars to signal a political crisis. Only four times in Egypt's three-thousand-year history was the king female; in contrast, there were more than two hundred male kings. Of the four female rulers, three appeared at the end of dynasties: Nitiqret in the Sixth Dynasty, Nefrusobk in the Twelfth, and Tausret in the Nineteenth. Hatshepsut's assumption of power was unique in that it occurred in the midst of a flourishing dynasty, though during the infancy of Thutmose III [thoot-MOH-suh], the heir apparent. Acting at first as regent to the young heir, she soon claimed the kingship in her own right and reigned for about ten years. After her death, Thutmose III obliterated her name and image from her monuments, though the reason for their removal is unclear. He may have been expressing hatred of her, or he may have wanted to erase the memory of a woman who had seized power contrary to *maat*, the natural order of things.

Ranked below the ruling family were the royal officials, nobles, large landowners, and priests, all generally hereditary offices. The pharaoh's word was law, but these groups were delegated powers for executing his will. On a lower level, artists and artisans worked for the pharaonic court and the nobility. Peasants and a small number of slaves formed the bulk of Egypt's population. Personal liberty took second place to the general welfare, and peasants were pressed into forced labor during natural disasters, such as floods, and at harvest time.

A Quest for Eternal Cultural Values

Until the invasion of the Hyksos, Egypt, in its splendid isolation, forged a civilization whose serene values and timeless forms deeply mirrored the religious beliefs of the rulers and the stability of the state. But as contact with other cultures and civilizations grew, Egyptian culture changed to reflect new influences. Writers borrowed words from other languages, for example, and sculptors displayed the human figure in more natural settings and poses. Still, Egyptian culture retained its distinctive qualities, and innovations continued to express traditional ideals.

Religion   Egypt was a **theocracy,** or a state ruled by a god. Believing that the deities had planned their country's future from the beginning, the Egyptians thought of their society as sacred. From the time that Menes first united Egypt, religious dogma taught that the king, as god on earth, embodied the state. Egyptian rulers also identified themselves with the deities. For example, Menes claimed to be the "two ladies," the goddesses who stood for Upper and Lower Egypt. Other rulers identified themselves with Ra, the sun god, and with Ra's son, Horus, the sky god, who was always depicted as having the head of a falcon. Because of the king's divinity, the resources of the state were concentrated on giving the ruler proper homage, as in the Old Kingdom's massive tombs, designed on a superhuman scale to ensure his safe passage to the next life.

Egyptian subjects worshiped the pharaoh, but the pharaoh could venerate any deity he pleased. Hence, the shifting fortunes of Egypt's many cults depended

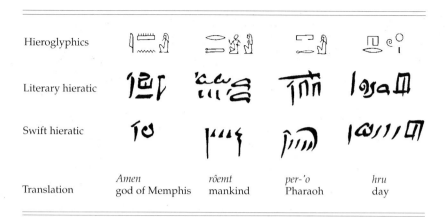

Hieroglyphics				
Literary hieratic				
Swift hieratic				
Translation	*Amen* god of Memphis	*rôemt* mankind	*per-'o* Pharaoh	*hru* day

Figure 1.11   Egyptian Writing. *From the Old Kingdom onward, the hieroglyphs (in the top line) constituted the style of formal writing that appeared on tomb walls and in monuments. Religious and governmental scribes soon devised two distinct types of cursive script, a careful manuscript hand (in the middle line) and a more rapid hand (in the bottom line) for administrative documents and letters.*

on the ruler's preference. For example, Ptah (who, like the Hebrew God in Genesis, created through speech) became the god of Memphis, which was the capital of the Old Kingdom. The kings of the Fifth Dynasty, on the other hand, called themselves sons of Ra, the sun god, and they honored this celestial deity by building him temples more impressive than their own royal tombs. Later, the Twelfth Dynasty replaced Ptah with Amen (a word meaning "hidden one"), and a series of rulers adopted his name, as in Amenemhat [AH-men-EM-het]. Royal favor to a god generally increased the wealth and influence of the god's cult and priests. Consequently, by the time of the New Kingdom, society had become top-heavy with priests and their privileged religious properties.

Egypt came close to having a national deity during the New Kingdom when Akhenaten [ahk-NAHT-uhn] (r. about 1369–1353 B.C.) reshaped the royal religion at his capital, Amarna. Elevating Aten, the god of the sun's disk, to supremacy above the other gods, Akhenaten systematically disavowed the older divinities—a heretical view in tolerant, polytheistic Egypt. This innovation aroused the opposition of conservative nobles who supported the powerful priests of the Theban god, Amen. Akhenaten ultimately failed, and later pharaohs tried to erase his name and memory from history. The Amarna revolution, however, like the religious choices of the pharaohs generally, had little effect on the ordinary Egyptian, who continued to believe that the pharaoh could intervene with the other gods for the benefit of all.

The foremost distinguishing mark of Egyptian religion was its promise of immortality—a belief that generated a more optimistic attitude toward human existence than that found in Mesopotamia. At first, in the Old Kingdom, only the kings were accorded this reward. Eventually, nobles and royal officials were buried in the vicinity of the rulers' tombs, thereby ensuring their immortality as assistants to the risen god in the afterlife. By the First Intermediate Period, the

nobles had claimed their own right to immortality by erecting tombs on which the royal funerary texts were copied. Later, immortality apparently was opened to all Egyptians, although only the wealthy minority could afford the cost of a proper burial.

Writing and Literature   Late predynastic Egypt learned the idea of writing, but not foreign words, from Mesopotamia. The Egyptians initially drew pictographs, called **hieroglyphs,** for such words as *hoe, arrowhead,* and *plow.* This early hieroglyphic script could also depict abstract words for which no adequate picture was available, but because such picture writing was time-consuming and clumsy to execute, the scribes soon made the pictographs function as signs, or clusters of consonants, for other words (Figure 1.11).

Egyptian literature produced no single great work that rivals *Gilgamesh,* but the Egyptian experience was rich in its variety of literary **genres,** or types of literature. For example, pyramid texts, the writings inscribed in burial chambers, formed the chief literary genre in the Old Kingdom. As this era gave way to the First Intermediate Period, new prose genres, such as prophecies and pessimistic writings, arose that addressed the prevalent political disintegration and social upheaval. Such was the tenor of the times that writers expressed views contradicting Egypt's otherwise optimistic attitudes to death and life. *The Dispute of a Man with His Soul* describes a desperate mortal finally choosing the emptiness of death rather than life in a materialistic and violent world.

The prophecies, **hymns** (songs of praise to the gods), and prose narratives of the Middle Kingdom constitute the classical period of Egyptian letters. The most famous work of the Middle Kingdom, as well as of all Egyptian literature, is the *Story of Sinuhe,* a prose tale that celebrates the ruler Senusert I and his subject, the hero named in the title. Fleeing Egypt, Sinuhe earns fame and fortune in Lebanon yet yearns for his beloved homeland. Sinuhe's exploits smack of

Figure 1.12 IMHOTEP. Step Pyramid of King Djoser. Ca. 2680 B.C. Sakkareh, Egypt.
Though isolated from its neighbors until about 1730 B.C., Egypt was influenced by surrounding cultures, as the design for the step pyramid at Sakkareh shows. Resting on a rectangular base and rising in six progressively smaller stages, this pyramid was modeled on Mesopotamia's ziggurat. But unlike the ziggurats, which were made of dried clay bricks, it was built of cut stone, the first building to be so constructed in the world. The step pyramid has six levels on a 411- by 358-foot base and stands 204 feet high.

the folk tale, for in one episode he subdues a taunting giant of a man, much as David defeats Goliath in the Old Testament story. Eventually, a gracious Senusert writes Sinuhe, forgiving his wandering subject's unnamed crime and inviting him to return home. The travel yarn concludes with a homecoming scene in which a joyful Sinuhe is reintegrated into Egyptian court society.

The richest period in Egyptian letters occurred during the New Kingdom. In addition to songs praising the pharaoh, poets now composed lyrics telling of the pain of parted lovers, and new genres included model letters, wisdom literature, and fairy tales. Akhenaten's revolution led to unique forms of literary expression, as in the *Hymn to Aten*, which praised this universal god. Although the hymn has similarities to Psalm 104 of the Old Testament, Akhenaten's text, unlike the Jewish scriptures, was not a declaration of **monotheism,** the belief that there is only one god. Instead, the *Hymn to Aten* recognized a special link between Akhenaten and his family and the god of the solar disk while still acknowledging the worship of other deities.

Architecture The classic Egyptian building was the pyramid, whose shape seemed to embody a constant and eternal order. During the Old Kingdom, the pyramid became the only building deemed suitable for

a ruler-god's resting place preparatory to the afterlife. A modified version of the pyramid appeared first in about 2680 B.C. in the step pyramid of King Djoser [ZHO-ser] at Sakkareh, opposite Memphis (Figure 1.12). Later Egyptian rulers preferred the true pyramid form, and this design did not develop further.

The true pyramid appeared in the Old Kingdom when the Fourth Dynasty ruler Khufu [KOO-foo] erected the Great Pyramid at Giza, across the Nile from Cairo (see Figure 1.10). The anonymous architect executed this largest stone building in the world— 6.25 million tons—with mathematical precision. Many of the tomb's two million stones were quarried on the site, although most were obtained farther upstream and ferried to Giza during the flooding of the Nile. The infinitesimally small deviation between the two sets of opposing base sides of the pyramid showed the scientific spirit already at work in this early stage of Egypt's history. Later, two of Khufu's successors, Khafre [KAF-ray] and Menkure [men-KOO-ray], added their pyramids to make the complex at Giza the symbol of the Old Kingdom and one of the wonders of the ancient world.

The pyramids eventually gave way to funerary temples when the New Kingdom pharaohs began to construct splendid monuments for themselves that reflected Egypt's new imperial status. The temple of

Figure 1.13 SENMUT. Hatshepsut's Temple. Ca. 1490 B.C. Deir el Bahri, across from Luxor, Egypt. *Hatshepsut's temple was planned for the same purpose as the pyramids—to serve as a shrine for the royal remains. In actuality an ascending series of three colonnaded courtyards, this temple provided a spectacular approach to a hidden sanctuary carved in the steep cliffs.*

Queen Hatshepsut is perhaps the most beautiful example of this architectural development (Figure 1.13). Designed by the royal architect Senmut, the temple of Hatshepsut was carved into the face of the mountain at Deir el Bahri, across the Nile from Luxor. Senmut, adopting the post-and-lintel style of construction, gave the queen's temple two levels of pillared colonnades, each accessible by long sloping ramps. The most arresting feature of Hatshepsut's temple is its round columns, which are used alongside rectangular pillars in the **porticoes,** or covered entrances. These columns—with their plain tops and grooved surfaces—suggest the graceful columns of later Greek architecture, although some scholars dismiss this similarity as coincidental. Be that as it may, this Egyptian monument, like the later Greek temples, shows a harmonious sense of proportion throughout its impressive colonnades.

Rulers in both Egypt and Mesopotamia created zoos and botanical gardens, the first in the world, though the earliest evidence of these developments comes from Egypt. Built for pleasure and prestige and to satisfy scientific curiosity, the menageries and gardens originated before 2000 B.C.

Sculpture, Painting, and Minor Arts The Egyptians did not understand art as it is defined today. Indeed, they had no word for art. Rather than being art for art's sake, Egyptian painting and sculpture served as a means to a religious end, specifically to house the *ka*, or spirit of a person or deity. Art was more than mere representation; images embodied all of the subjects' qualities.

In the royal graveyard at Giza, artisans of the Old Kingdom carved from the living rock a mythical creature that stirred the imagination of most peoples in the ancient world—a sphinx, half-lion and half-man (Figure 1.14). Although this creature often inspired feelings of dread, in actuality there was little mystery to the sphinx, since its original purpose was to guard the royal tombs, perhaps to frighten away grave robbers. Indeed, this first sphinx's face was that of Khafre, the Fourth Dynasty king whose pyramid stood nearby. Today, this crumbling relic stands as a reminder of the claims to immortality of the Old Kingdom rulers.

The sheer size and mythical character of the Great Sphinx set it apart from Old Kingdom sculptures in the round, which favored human-scaled figures and realistic images. The life-size statue of King Menkure and his Chief Queen, found beneath the ruler's pyramid at

PERSONAL PERSPECTIVE

The Instruction of Amenemope

Egypt's wisdom literature—aphorisms about the best way to live—culminated in The Instruction of Amenemope, *written in the late New Kingdom. In this work, the author stresses the ethical life rather than the amassing of personal wealth.*

Beginning of the teaching for life,
The instructions for well-being.

. . . .

If you make your life with these [words] in your
    heart,
You will find it a success;
You will find my words a storehouse for life,
Your being will prosper upon earth.

. . . .

Do not move the markers on the borders of fields,
Nor shift the position of the measuring-cord.
Do not be greedy for a cubit of land,
Nor encroach on the boundaries of a widow.

. . . .

Do not set your heart on wealth,
There is no ignoring Fate and Destiny;

. . . .

Do not strain to seek increase,
What you have, let it suffice you.

. . . .

Do not cheat a man (through) pen on scroll,
The god abhors it;
Do not bear witness with false words,
So as to brush aside a man by your tongue.

. . . .

Do not laugh at a blind man,
Nor tease a dwarf,
Nor cause hardship for the lame.

. . . .

Do not sit down in the beer-house
In order to join one greater than you,
Be he a youth great through his office,
Or be he an elder through birth.
Befriend a man of your own measure.

. . . .

Do not revile one older than you,
He has seen Re [the Sun God] before you;
Let (him) not report you to the Aten [the god of the
    sun's disk] at his rising,
Saying: "A youth has reviled an old man."

Figure 1.14 The Great Sphinx. Ca. 2560 B.C. Sandstone, 65' high × 240' long. Giza, Egypt. *Sphinxes, creatures part lion and part human, were often depicted in Egyptian art. The most famous sphinx is the one at Giza, carved from the rock on the site. The sphinx's colossal size prevented the anonymous sculptor from rendering it with any subtle facial expressions. More significant as a monument than as a great work of art, the Great Sphinx had a practical purpose—to guard the nearby pyramid tombs.*

Giza, show this art's brilliant realism (Figure 1.15). The sculpture embodies the characteristics of what became the standard, or classical, Egyptian style: their left legs forward, the king's clenched fists, their headdresses (sacred regalia for him and wig for her), their rigid poses, their serene countenances, and the figures' angularity. Designed to be attached to a wall, the couple was intended to be viewed from the front, so the work has a two-dimensional quality.

In contrast to practices in the Old Kingdom, the wives of rulers in the New Kingdom acquired claims to divinity in their own right. A statue of Hatshepsut represents her in the clothing and with the sacred pose of pharaoh (Figure 1.16). Having first been Chief Queen to

Figure 1.15 *King Menkure and His Chief Queen.* Ca. 2525 B.C. Ht. 54½". Museum expedition. Courtesy Museum of Fine Arts, Boston. *This life-size slate sculpture of Menkure, a Fourth Dynasty ruler, and his Chief Queen was removed from its resting place beneath the king's pyramid at Giza (see Figure 1.10). In this sculpture, the figures are represented as being of comparable size, unlike the usual depiction of husbands as much larger than their wives, indicating their greater importance. The sizes here probably reflect the royal status of the Chief Queen. The queen's subordination to the king is subtly shown in her position on his left side, thought to be inferior to the right, and her arm around his waist, an indication that her role was to encourage and support.*

Figure 1.16 *Hatshepsut.* Ca. 1460 B.C. Marble, ht. 6'5". Courtesy Metropolitan Museum of Art. Rogers Fund and contribution from Edward S. Harkness, 1929. (29.3.2). *This sculpture is one of more than two hundred statues of Hatshepsut intended to adorn her massive and elegant funeral temple at Deir el Bahri in the western hills of Thebes. The authoritative pose and regalia convey her pharaonic status, and she is only subtly represented as a woman.*

Figure 1.17 *Family Scene: Pharaoh Akhenaten, Queen Nefertiti, and Their Three Daughters.* Ca. 1350 B.C. Limestone, 13″ high × 15⅚₂″ wide. Ägyptisches Museum, Berlin. *The religious ideas associated with Akhenaten's reforms are expressed in the lines streaming from the sun's disk above the royal couple. Each ray of the sun ends in a tiny hand that offers a blessing to the royal family.*

Thutmose II in the New Kingdom, after his death she seized leadership, probably with the cooperation of the powerful Theban priesthood of Amen. Although more than a thousand years separated this sculpture from that of Menkure (see Figure 1.15), in its expression of dignity and authority the statue of Hatshepsut bears a strong resemblance to the earlier work, thus demonstrating the continuity of the Egyptian style.

A major challenge to Egypt's traditional, austere forms occurred in Akhenaten's revolutionary reign. A low-relief sculpture of the royal family exemplifies the naturalism and fluid lines that this artistic rebellion favored (Figure 1.17). Akhenaten nuzzles one of his daughters in an intimate pose while his wife dandles another daughter on her knees and allows a third to stand on her left arm. The domesticity of this scene is quite unlike the sacred gestures of traditional Egyptian sculpture, but the religious subject of this relief remains true to that tradition, as the rays streaming from the disk of Aten onto the royal family indicate.

The most extraordinary artistic achievement of the Amarna period is the carved portrait head of Queen Nefertiti (Figure 1.18), a life-size sculpture discovered in 1912 by a team of German archeologists in the desert sands near the long-lost city founded by Akhenaten for the god Aten. This statue-head with its unfinished left eye, deliberate or accidental, is one of the most arresting images of world art. Painted in flesh tones and natural colors and imbued with the naturalism of the Amarna style, the queen has a vitality that is unsurpassed. A modern critic has called her the eternal female, ceaselessly watching.

Nefertiti's unusual headdress signifies her status as a potent force in this culture. Rising straight up from

Figure 1.18 *Nefertiti.* Ca. 1350 B.C. Limestone, ht. 20″. Ägyptisches Museum, Berlin. *This portrait head of Nefertiti is characterized by sleekness and charm, a look achieved through the sculptor's fusing of the fluid Amarna style with the formality of Egypt's traditional art. To create the image of sleekness, the sculptor has pushed Nefertiti's face forward like the prow of a ship cutting through the wind. The figure's charm emerges from the tension between the queen's dreamy, deeply hooded eyes and her lively, arched eyebrows. The artist has succeeded in representing Nefertiti as both a woman and a goddess.*

Figure 1.19 Opening of the Mouth Scene, Funerary Papyrus of Hunefer. Ca. 1305–1195 B.C. British Museum. *Egyptian painters and sculptors always depicted human subjects from the side, with the feet in profile, as in this painting on a papyrus manuscript deposited in a New Kingdom tomb. This painting's treatment of flesh tones of the human figures also typifies the Egyptian style. Egyptian men, represented here by the officiating priests, were consistently shown with red-brown, tanned skins at least partially reflective of their outdoor lives. Egyptian women, such as the mourners directly before the mummy, were usually painted with lighter complexions of yellow or pink or white skin. The Opening of the Mouth was a burial ritual, preparing the deceased to speak in the afterlife.*

her forehead, this crown is decorated with the *uraeus*, the image of a cobra ready to strike. By custom, this powerful and protective symbol was part of the kingly **regalia** (tokens of royal authority) and could be worn only by rulers and their Great (principal) Queens. Modern scholars have proved that Nefertiti was the only Great, or Chief, Queen in Egypt's long history to actually share power with her husband. (Queen Hatshepsut actually ruled alone as pharaoh.) The prevalence of images of Nefertiti in so much of the art that remains from Amarna confirms this queen's importance on the political level and thus underscores her central role in the Amarna revolution.

Just as Egypt's sculpture in the round developed a rigid **canon,** or set of rules, so did two-dimensional representations acquire a fixed formula, whether in relief sculptures or in wall paintings. The Egyptians never discovered the principles of perspective. On a flat surface, the human figures were depicted in profile, with both feet pointing sideways, as in a painting from a New Kingdom funerary papyrus (Figure 1.19). However, the artistic canon required that the eye and the shoulders be shown frontally, and both arms had to be visible along with all the fingers. The artist determined the human proportions exactly, by the use of a grid. Throughout most Egyptian art history, the human figure was conceived as being 18 squares high standing and 14 squares high seated, with each unit equivalent to the width of one "fist"; anatomical parts were made accordingly proportional. The canon of

Figure 1.20   Banqueting Scene. Ca. 1567–1320 B.C. Fresco, 23 × 27¼". British Museum.
*In a small space, the Egyptian painter has created a delightful banqueting scene, a favorite subject
in tomb decoration in the New Kingdom. No one eats at this ritual meal, for the purpose is to set
the stage for the tomb owner's rebirth. The female figures, especially the young seminaked girls
dancing (below) and serving (above), represent the female generative principle. The naked-girl
motif in tomb paintings, which appeared at this time, was probably meant to ensure the tomb
owner's fertility while living and the continuity of the family while the deceased was in the tomb
awaiting rebirth. The lotus flowers on the heads of the female guests and musicians reflect the
rebirth theme, since the lotus was used to symbolize the promise of immortality for the dead. The
frontal pose of two of the lower figures is an artistic innovation. Faces were almost always shown
in profile in Egyptian art (see Figures 1.17 and 1.19).*

proportions was established by the time of the Old
Kingdom, and its continued use, with slight variations,
helped Egyptian art retain its unmistakable style. Wall
paintings, in contrast to relief sculptures, permitted a
greater sense of space to be created, but the rules regarding the human figure still had to be observed
(Figure 1.20). Given those stringent conventions, the
Egyptian artists who worked in two dimensions were
amazingly successful in creating the image of a carefree society bubbling with life.

Royal tombs have yielded incomparable examples
of Egyptian sculpture, as in the burial chamber of the
New Kingdom pharaoh Tutankhamen [too-tahn-
KAHM-en]. Of the thirty-four excavated royal tombs,
only that of King Tut—as he is popularly known—

escaped relatively free from violation by thieves in
ancient times. A freestanding, life-size sculpture of
the funerary goddess Selket was one of four goddess
figures placed outside the gilded shrine that contained the king's internal organs (Figure 1.21). Her arms
are outstretched in a protective fashion around her
royal charge's shrine. A unique feature is the turn of
Selket's head, a violation of the cardinal rule of three-
dimensional Egyptian art that figures face frontward
(see Figures 1.15 and 1.16). Selket's pose suggests that
she was looking for intruders. The sculpture's style,
with its naturalism and fluid lines, reflects the art of
Amarna, the revolutionary style that flourished briefly
in the fourteenth century B.C. before being abandoned
and replaced by Egypt's traditional formal style.

Figure 1.21 *Selket.* Ca. 1325 B.C. Wood, overlaid with gesso and gilded, ht. 53⁵/₈″. Cairo Museum, Egypt. *This statue of the goddess Selket was discovered in King Tutankhamen's tomb in 1923, one of the great archeological finds of the twentieth century. Discovered by Egyptologist Howard Carter, the tomb held thousands of royal artifacts and art objects, including the pharaoh's gold funerary mask, a solid gold coffin, a gold throne, chairs, couches, chariots, jewelry, figurines, drinking cups, clothing, weapons, and games. The fascinating story of the discovery is told in Carter's book,* The Tomb of Tutankhamen.

HEIRS TO THE MESOPOTAMIAN AND EGYPTIAN EMPIRES

With the decline of Mesopotamian and Egyptian empires after 1000 B.C., successor kingdoms arose in the east-ern Mediterranean, notably those of the Hittites, the Assyrians (Figure 1.22), the Medes, and the Persians. If the length of their rule and the richness of their achievements failed to measure up to those of Mesopotamian and Egyptian civilizations, they nevertheless brought law and order to numerous peoples over vast territories and offered a convincing model of civilized life.

The Hittites and the Assyrians were rival empires whose fortunes ebbed and flowed (Timeline 1.4). In 612 B.C., Nineveh, the Assyrian capital city, was sacked by the Medes, an Indo-European people from the southwest Iranian plateau, and the Assyrian empire passed under their control. Medean rule, however, was shortly supplanted when their empire fell to the Persians, another nomadic Indo-European tribe, in about 550 B.C. With masterful skill, successive Persian rulers forged the strongest and largest empire that the eastern Mediterranean had seen until this time. At its height, Persian rule extended from Egypt in the south to central Russia in the north, and from Cyprus in the west to the Indus River in the east. Only Greece eluded Persia's grasp. In 327 B.C., Alexander the Great defeated the last Persian king, thus allowing the Greeks to assimilate the Persian lands.

Persian culture followed in the footsteps of Assyrian culture, but Persian art lacked the savagery associated with the Assyrian style. Instead, Persian art emphasized contemplative themes with less action (Figure 1.23). Persian culture's most original and enduring contribution was the religion of Zoroaster [ZOHR-uh-was-ter], or Zarathustra [zah-ra-THUSH-trah], a prophet who lived

Figure 1.22 Fugitives Swimming with Water-Skins. Ninth century B.C. Limestone, ht. 39″. British Museum. *Assyrian artists were masters of relief sculpture, as in this detail of a battle scene, created for the palace of King Ashurasirpal II at Nimrud. Archers pursue swimming fugitives, two of whom keep afloat with inflated animal skins (lower foreground). Despite the lack flush bottom and unconcern for relative dimensions, the relief vividly evokes Assyria's warrior culture.*

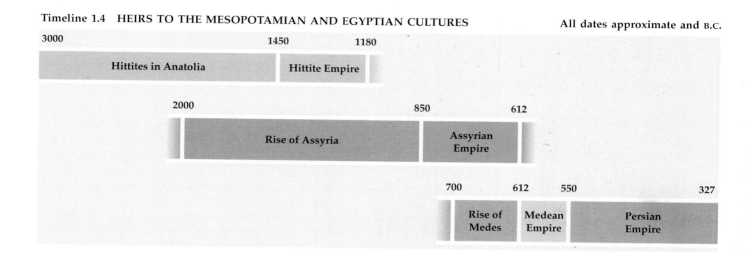

Timeline 1.4   **HEIRS TO THE MESOPOTAMIAN AND EGYPTIAN CULTURES**   All dates approximate and B.C.

Figure 1.23   Darius Giving Audience Before Two Fire Altars. Found in the Treasury, Persepolis. Ca. 512–494 B.C. Limestone, length 20′. Archeological Museum, Teheran. *This relief sculpture, carved on the walls of the Treasury at Persepolis, shows King Darius seated before two fire altars. In front of him is the master of ceremonies, with his hand raised to his lips in a gesture of devotion. Two bodyguards, holding spears, stand to the right. The Persian sculptural style is shown by the stylized hair and beards, precise folds in the clothing, and the formal poses of the figures.*

in about 600 B.C. Rejecting polytheism, Zoroaster taught a dualistic religion in which the god of light, Ahura-mazda, engaged in a universal struggle with the god of darkness, Ahriman. According to Zoroaster, those who lead puritanical lives not only gain favorable treatment in the afterlife but also ensure the triumph of the forces of good. Key ideas of Zoroastrianism influenced other religions: Zoroaster's martyrdom, the prophet's life filled with miracles, the evil spirit as the Prince of Darkness, and the notion of a Last Judgment.

The Legacy of Early Near Eastern Civilizations

Mesopotamia and Egypt provide the earliest models of civilization in the West. In both, large numbers of people were organized into societies characterized by class stratification; a division of labor; complex political, economic, and religious forms; technological advances (pottery and glass-making, the extraction and working of metals, textiles, woodworking, and building techniques); and cultural achievements. They weren't the only ancient civilizations—others developed in China, India, South America, and elsewhere—but they are the ones to which Westerners most directly trace their cultural roots.

Mesopotamia's gifts to Western civilization are impressive. In addition to writing, these societies established urbanism as a way of life in contrast to agrarian or village existence. In more practical matters, they created a mathematical system based on 60 that gave the world the 60-minute hour and the 360-degree circle. They also divided the seasons and devised a lunar calendar to mark off periods of days to aid them in their planting. Trade and commerce forced them to develop methods of counting, measuring, and weighing that became the standard procedures for other Near Eastern peoples for centuries. Mesopotamian myths, legends, and epics found their way into the folk tales and literature of other cultures.

Egypt made equally impressive contributions to the West. Egyptian bureaucrats, who wanted to predict the correct date for the rising of the Nile's waters, originated a solar calendar that is the basis of the Western calendar. The Egyptian model, which divided the year into twelve months of thirty days, each with five days of holiday at the end, was conveyed to Western culture by the Romans. In architecture, Egyptian builders devised the column with a decorated capital, which later Greek architects probably adopted. The Greek builders also borrowed the Egyptian tradition of sound engineering principles rooted in mathematics. Similarly, Greek sculptors owed a debt to Egyptian forms and poses. Indeed, the Egyptian idea of an aesthetic canon influenced both sculptors and artists in Greece.

In literature, the Egyptians explored a variety of genres—such as wisdom writing—and folk tales that influenced the Hebrews and the Greeks. In science, Egyptian physicians became renowned throughout the Near East for their medical learning and knowledge of drugs. Finally, with its priceless treasures, its mysterious pyramids, and its cult of the dead, Egypt inspired curiosity and excitement in foreigners from ancient times onward. One of the first Western tourists to visit Egypt was the Greek historian Herodotus, whose writings in the fifth century B.C. helped to create the Egyptian mystique. The world's fascination with the culture of ancient Egypt has not abated today.

KEY CULTURAL TERMS

culture	post-and-lintel
civilization	construction
Paleolithic	ziggurat
Neolithic	theocracy
pictogram	hieroglyphs
ideogram	genre
phonogram	hymn
cuneiform	monotheism
polytheism	portico
anthropomorphism	regalia
pantheism	canon
stele	

SUGGESTIONS FOR FURTHER READING

Primary Sources

KASTER, J., ed. and trans. *The Literature and Mythology of Ancient Egypt.* London: Allen Lane, 1970. An anthology that includes creation myths, rituals, stories, songs, proverbs, and prayers.

KRAMER, S. N. *History Begins at Sumer.* Philadelphia: University of Pennsylvania Press, 1981. A standard collection of original Sumerian sources by one of the most renowned modern Sumerian scholars.

PRITCHARD, J. B. *Ancient Near Eastern Texts Relating to the Old Testament.* Princeton: Princeton University Press, 1969. For the serious student, a collection of the most important nonbiblical texts, including myths, histories, prayers, and other types of writing.

SANDARS, N. K., ed. *The Epic of Gilgamesh.* New York: Penguin, 1972. The editor's informative introduction sets the tone for this famous ancient epic.

CHAPTER *1* HIGHLIGHTS
Prehistory and Near Eastern Civilizations

B.C.

1.3 Herd of Rhinoceroses (ca. 32,000–30,000 B.C.)

1.4 Figurine from Willendorf (ca. 25,000 B.C.)

B.C.

B.C.

The Exaltation of Inanna (ca. 2330 B.C.)

Code of Hammurabi (ca. 1790–1750 B.C.)

The Epic of Gilgamesh (ca. 1600 B.C.)

1.7 Sumerian Lyre (ca. 2600 B.C.)

1.8 *Gudea* (ca. 2150 B.C.)

1.9 Ziggurat of Ur (ca. 2100 B.C.)

B.C.

B.C.

Story of Sinuhe (ca. 1900 B.C.)

The Dispute of a Man with His Soul (ca. 1850 B.C.)

Great Hymn to the Aten (ca. 1369–1353 B.C.)

1.12 Step Pyramid of King Djoser (ca. 2680 B.C.)

1.10 Pyramids at Giza (ca. 2590–2525 B.C.)

1.14 Great Sphinx (ca. 2560 B.C.)

1.15 King Menkure and His Chief Queen (ca. 2525 B.C.)

1.20 Banqueting Scene (ca. 1567–1320 B.C.)

1.13 SENMUT, Hatshepsut's Temple (ca. 1490 B.C.)

1.16 *Hatshepsut* (ca. 1460 B.C.)

1.17 *Pharaoh Akhenaten, Queen Nefertiti, and Their Three Daughters* (ca. 1350 B.C.)

1.18 *Nefertiti* (ca. 1350 B.C.)

1.21 *Selket* (ca. 1325 B.C.)

1.19 Opening of the Mouth Scene (ca. 1305–1195 B.C.)

1.1 Rosetta Stone (ca. 197–196 B.C.)

B.C.

1.22 Fugitives Swimming with Water-Skins (ninth century B.C.)

1.23 Darius Giving Audience Before Two Fire Altars (ca. 512–494 B.C.)

B.C.

■ *Literature & Philosophy*   ■ *Art & Architecture*   ■ *Music & Dance*

 Readings in the Western Humanities

AFRICA

HISTORY

Neolithic period, ca. 3000–1000 B.C. Pastoral culture (which had begun ca. 8000 B.C.) in the Sahara disappeared as savannas dried up. Hunters and gatherers prevailed elsewhere, though farming slowly spread southward. Three racial groups: Caucasoid peoples in the north and northeast, Khoisan peoples in the open areas from the Sahara south to the Cape, and Negroid peoples in the central forests and the west. *Nubian, or Kushan, culture.* Rule by strong chieftains (ca. 3100–2600 B.C. in Lower Nubia; ca. 2050–1550 B.C. in Upper Nubia) alternated with conquest and occupation by the Egyptians. First Nubian kingdom, Kush, established 1100 B.C.: the first known African kingdom outside Egypt. Noted for art, learning, and trade. One of the first African centers of iron making, ca. 1000 B.C. Kush's kings conquered and ruled Egypt (ca. 750–666 B.C.). Capital shifted from Napata to Meroë (592 B.C.).

ART

Neolithic period. Rock carvings and paintings of animals and people in various regions, with the majority (over 30,000) in the Sahara.

Giraffes. Ca. 5000 B.C. Rock engraving, ht. 6–7". Libya.

ARCHITECTURE

Nubian culture. Kerma, capital of Upper Nubia, was the first settlement in Africa south of Egypt that can be called a city. Kerma in its classical period (ca. 1750–1580 B.C.) reflected Nubian traditions in wood and mudbrick palaces, temples, governmental buildings, and city walls and gates. In the Kushan kingdom, Nubian culture was fully Egyptianized, especially in building styles and city planning.

RELIGION, PHILOSOPHY, LITERATURE

Nubian culture. Kings, especially in the Kushan period, adopted the Egyptian practice of divine rulers supported by hierarchical administrations.

AMERICAS

HISTORY

Ca. 25,000 B.C. Humans may have first entered Western Hemisphere from Asia over Bering Strait land bridge. Had migrated throughout hemisphere by ca. 12,000 B.C.
Mesoamerica Maize introduced ca. 5000 B.C. *Olmec culture,* began 1500 B.C. South coast of Gulf of Mexico. "Mother culture" of Mesoamerican civilizations invented ballcourt, pyramid, pantheon of gods, and perhaps ritual calendar and glyph writing.
Andes *Pre-Ceramic period, 3000–1800 B.C.* Tribes and clans in villages. *Initial period, 1800–800 B.C.* Farming intensified. *Chavín culture, began 1000 B.C.* Center at Chavín de Huantar (Peru); importer of luxury goods.
Native North America *Clovis culture, from ca. 9500 B.C.* Southwest U.S., earliest well-documented archeological remains in North America. *Mississippian culture.* Earthworks at Poverty Point, Louisiana (after 1300 B.C.).

ART

Mesoamerica *Olmec culture.* Altars and massive sculptures of heads, probably of rulers, in religious centers.
Andes Fine textiles from ca. 10,000 B.C. *Pre-Ceramic period.* Animal-figured textiles, mosaics, mirrors, earrings, featherwork, female figurines. *Initial period.* Fired clay pottery for cooking, ca. 1800 B.C. Giant stone sculptures, painted reliefs, and wall murals in public plazas. *Chavín culture.* First unifying Andean artistic style; images of jaguars, snakes, and composites of animals and humans.

ARCHITECTURE

Mesoamerica *Olmec culture.* Elaborate religious and ceremonial centers at San Lorenzo, La Venta, and Trés Zapotes, inhabited by the elite, with temple mounds, huge sculptures and altars, and a complex system of drains and lagoons.
Andes *Pre-Ceramic period.* Monumental public architecture, the oldest in the Americas, with traditional features, such as artificial mounds, plazas, and courtyards.

RELIGION, PHILOSOPHY, LITERATURE

Mesoamerica *Olmec culture.* A pantheon of gods identified with tropical rain-forest fauna, especially the jaguar. The key religious belief was that a shaman, or spiritual leader, could undergo a mystical transformation into a sacred creature or plant.
Andes *Chavín culture.* The capital, Chavín, was a pilgrimage center for Andean people.

Colossal Head 1. Ca. 1200 B.C. Basalt, ht. 112½". San Lorenzo, Veracruz.

ASIA

China

Neolithic period, ca. 5000–1766 B.C. Tribes and clans living in villages in the Yellow River valley in the north, along the Chang (Yangtze) River to the south, and at remote sites in far northeastern China. Hunting, fishing, and farming; diet based on millet. *Shang Dynasty, 1766–1122 B.C.* Rise of Bronze Age culture. Kings controlled much of China with support of warrior landlords. Capital cities Ao and Anyang founded. Rulers buried in pits with equipment and regalia for afterlife. *Chou Dynasty, 1122–481 B.C.* Loose grouping of feudal vassal states; divided into Eastern and Western Chou (771).

India

Indus, or Harappan, culture, ca. 2600–1900 B.C. Urban civilization dominated by the cities of Harappa and Mohenjo-daro in Indus River valley and extending over modern Pakistan and western India. Trading society; no centralized ruler or military elite. Mixed technology of stone and bronze. First literate state east of Mesopotamia. *Aryan culture, 1500–500 B.C.* Aryan peoples from Persia infiltrated and eventually conquered northern India and its resident peoples, setting up an agrarian society arranged into the Vedic caste system, with cattle as the major form of wealth. Iron introduced ca. 1000 B.C.

Japan

Jōmon culture. Beginning (ca. 2500 B.C.) of last phase of village culture, born ca. 11,000 B.C. Hunting, gathering, and fishing. By end of period, cultivation of yams and taro, imported from Asian mainland.

Neolithic period. Much traditional Chinese culture dates from this period, such as the use of jade, wood, silk, ceremonial clay vessels, and perhaps chopsticks. *Shang Dynasty.* Unique type of gray bronze used for ritual objects for royal court. *Chou Dynasty.* Bronzes, with inscriptions and animal motifs. Exaggerated details.

Four-Legged Vessel. Ca. 1523–1028 B.C. Bronze, ht. 15¼". People's Republic of China.

Harappan culture. Seals carved with animal and human forms, pottery, toys, and figurines of important personages.

Bust of a Priest-King or Deity from Mohenjo-daro. Ca. 2000–1750 B.C. Steatite, ht. 6⅞". National Museum of Pakistan, Karachi.

Jōmon culture. Jōmon, or "rope pattern," hand-thrown pottery. Also bracelets and earrings in ivory and bone.

Shang Dynasty. Timber houses with rammed earth floors, wattle and daub walls, and thatched roofs; rammed earth walls to encircle cities and to separate urban nobility from craftspeople and merchants.

Harappan culture. Brick-walled cities, laid out in grids and served by wells, bathhouses, and a system of wastewater drains. *Aryan culture.* No ruins survive.

Jōmon culture. Basic house was either a circular or a rectangular hut with a pit floor.

Shang Dynasty. Writing in characters appeared soon after 1700 B.C. on inscribed bones consulted as oracles about great decisions of state. This pictographic language is the basis of Chinese writing today.

Harappan culture. The writing has not been deciphered. *Aryan culture.* Brought Indo-European languages and Vedism, the Vedic religion centered on sacrifices to deities and presided over by priests, or brahmans, who (between the 15th and 5th centuries B.C.) composed a body of religious texts, known as the Vedic corpus or simply the Vedas. These texts were written in Sanskrit, a language derived from the ancient Indo-European, ancestor of many of today's European languages. Vedism was the starting point for the later Hindu religion.

Jōmon culture. Simple burial rites in small pits dug near dwellings. Aspects of the burial (knees drawn up or stone clasped to chest) suggest either magical or religious practices. Perhaps a belief in fertility goddesses, as indicated by large numbers of female figurines made of clay.

2 AEGEAN CIVILIZATIONS
The Minoans, the Mycenaeans, and the Greeks of the Archaic Age

Although Mesopotamia and Egypt offer successful models of civilization, the tradition of Greece is often the first in which Westerners feel they can recognize themselves. What ties most moderns to ancient Greece is the Greeks' vision of humanity, for they were the first to place human beings at the center of the universe. The Near Eastern cultures focused on deities and godlike rulers, paying little heed to the strivings of humanity. The Greeks, on the other hand, no longer saw mortals as the inconsequential objects of divine whim. Men and women assumed some importance in the scheme of things; they were seen as having some control over their destinies and some moral responsibility for their actions. By the fifth century B.C., the Greek philosopher Protagoras could proclaim, "Man is the measure of all things."

With their new way of thinking, the Greeks surged forward in all areas of creativity, ultimately reaching heights that some think have never been equaled. Because of their grandeur and noble appeal, Greek poetry, sculpture, and architecture became the standard against which later works were frequently judged. From the Greeks the Western tradition has inherited many of its political forms and practices, its views on human behavior, its insistence on philosophical rigor, and its approach to scientific inquiry. In essence, through their human-centered consciousness and their cultural achievements, the Greeks laid the foundation of Western civilization.

Greek culture developed in the basin of the Aegean Sea (Map 2.1). On rocky coasts and rugged islands and peninsulas, the people coaxed a subsistence living from the thin, stony soil and turned to the sea for trade, conquest, and

◀ Acropolis, Athens. *View from the west.*

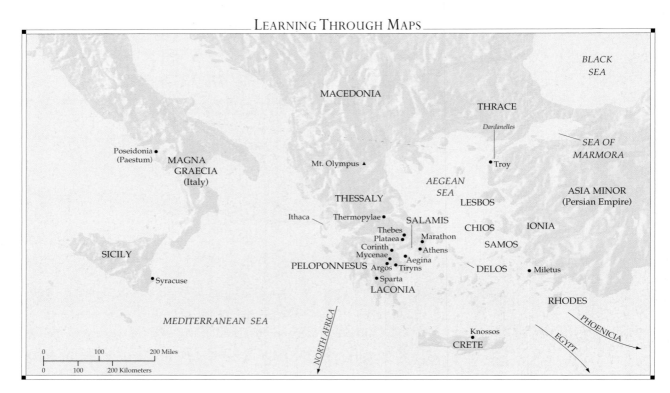

Map 2.1   THE AEGEAN WORLD
This map shows the location of the Minoan, Mycenaean, and Greek Archaic Age
civilizations. **Consider** the role of the Aegean and Mediterranean seas in shaping these
three civilizations. **What** were the centers of Minoan and Mycenaean civilizations?
Why do you think the location of Troy helped to make it a wealthy and strategic city?
Locate the major city-states of the Greek Archaic Age. **How** did geography influence
the origins and strategies of the Persian War?

expansion. During the Bronze Age, the inhabitants of
the island of Crete and the Greek peninsula traded
with the Egyptians and the Hittites of Anatolia. The
early Greeks borrowed and adapted a writing system
from the Phoenicians. They were indebted to the
Egyptians for sculptural techniques and to other Near
Eastern civilizations for techniques in working with
metal and clay, for music and mathematics, and for
elements of their religious system.

The people we refer to as the Greeks were not the
first to thrive in the Aegean basin. Two other distinctive civilizations—the Minoan and the Mycenaean—
established centers of culture in the area and left their
mark on the Greeks of the Archaic Age (which dates
from about 800 B.C.) who followed (Timeline 2.1).

PRELUDE: MINOAN CIVILIZATION, 3000–1100 B.C.

While civilizations were flourishing in Egypt and
Mesopotamia, another culture was developing among
the Neolithic settlements on the island of Crete. By

about 2000 B.C., a prosperous and stable mercantile
civilization had emerged, and between 1700 and
1100 B.C., it reached its high point in wealth, power,
and sophistication. This society, labeled Minoan after
King Minos, a legendary Cretan ruler, apparently was
organized into a complex class system that included
nobles, merchants, artisans, bureaucrats, and laborers.
Noble life was based in palaces, and twentieth-
century archeological excavations of several palace
sites indicate that communities were linked in a loose
political federation, with the major center at Knossos
on the north coast. Remarkably, no fortified walls protected the Minoan palaces, suggesting that the cities
remained at peace with one another and that the
island itself afforded adequate protection against invading sea raiders. Crete's tranquil image is further
supported by the absence of weapons in excavated
remains.

The palace at Knossos has revealed more about
Cretan life than has any other cultural artifact. The
ruins, though no longer paved or walled, still provide
a sense of the grandeur and expanse of this once-
magnificent site (Figure 2.1). It included an impressive

Timeline 2.1   MINOAN AND MYCENAEAN CIVILIZATIONS   All dates approximate and B.C.

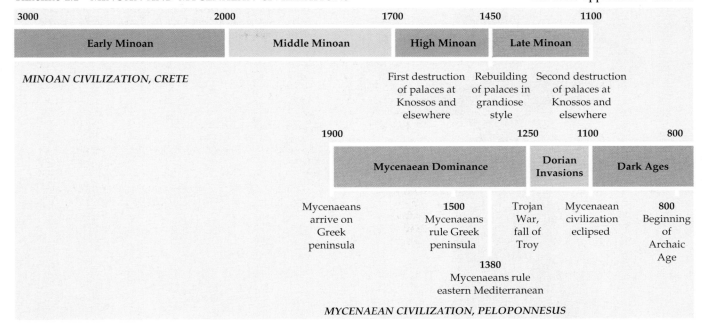

3000	2000	1700	1450	1100

Early Minoan	Middle Minoan	High Minoan	Late Minoan

MINOAN CIVILIZATION, CRETE

First destruction of palaces at Knossos and elsewhere	Rebuilding of palaces in grandiose style	Second destruction of palaces at Knossos and elsewhere

1900	1250	1100	800

Mycenaean Dominance	Dorian Invasions	Dark Ages

Mycenaeans arrive on Greek peninsula	**1500** Mycenaeans rule Greek peninsula	Trojan War, fall of Troy	Mycenaean civilization eclipsed	**800** Beginning of Archaic Age

1380 Mycenaeans rule eastern Mediterranean

MYCENAEAN CIVILIZATION, PELOPONNESUS

Figure 2.1 Palace at Knossos. Aerial view from the east. Ca. 1750–1650 B.C. *The palace complex, with courtyards, staircases, and living areas, now partially restored, indicates that the royal family lived in comfort and security, surrounded by works of art. When British archeologist Sir Arthur Evans uncovered these ruins in 1902, he became convinced that he had discovered the palace of the legendary King Minos and labeled the civilization Minoan—a descriptive term used interchangeably with* Cretan.

plumbing and drainage system and a complex layout of rooms and passageways on several levels. Below-ground, a storage area contained huge earthenware pots that held grains, oils, and wines, probably collected as taxes from the populace and serving as the basis of trade and wealth. Beautiful **friezes** (bands of designs and figures) decorated the walls of rooms and hallways. **Frescoes**—paint applied directly on wet plaster—of dolphins, octopuses, and other ocean creatures enlivened the palace walls.

The early Minoans developed a pictorial form of writing on clay tablets that was replaced in about 1800 B.C. by a still undeciphered script known as Linear A. **Linear B,** which superseded Linear A, flourished from about 1400 to the decline of Minoan civilization in around 1300, though it remained in use in a few scattered places on the Greek mainland for about two hundred years. When Linear B was deciphered, it proved to be an early form of Greek. The Linear B writings revealed nothing of Minoan political, social, or philosophical systems but were used to record commercial transactions.

Minoan religion appears to have been matriarchal, centering on the worship of a mother goddess, or great goddess, creator of the universe and source of all life. Statues of a bare-breasted earth goddess with snakes in

Figure 2.2 Earth Goddess with Snakes. Ca. 1600–1580 B.C. Faience, ht. 13½″. Archaeological Museum, Heraklion, Crete. *This cult figure was discovered in the Treasury of the Knossos Palace. Her triangular dress, with its apron and flounced skirt, is similar to those of Cretan youths in surviving frescoes.*

Figure 2.3 *Bull-Leaping.* Ca. 1500 B.C. Archaeological Museum, Heraklion, Crete. *This fresco (approximately 32 inches high) from the east wing of the palace at Knossos is one of the largest paintings recovered from Crete. The association of young men and women with bulls in this scene brings to mind the legend of the Minotaur, in which seven youths and seven maidens were periodically sacrificed to a monster, half man and half bull, who lived in an underground labyrinth, supposedly on Crete.*

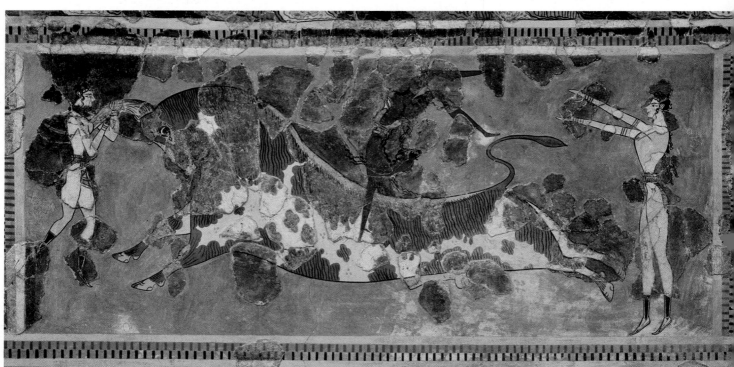

her hands show how the deity was portrayed by the Minoans, but the precise purpose of these statues is unknown (Figure 2.2). Minoans also honored numerous minor household goddesses and venerated trees and stone pillars, to which they probably attributed supernatural powers. Near the end of their era, the Minoans began to bury their dead in underground tombs and chambers, but neither the reason for the new burial practice nor its ritualistic meaning has been discovered.

What has been uncovered on the palace walls is a fresco depicting bull-leaping—a sport or ritual activity that perhaps was associated with a bull cult (Figure 2.3) and that apparently had deep religious significance. Regardless of its meaning, this daring act is probably more fiction than fact: The maidens (painted white) stand at either end of the bull while a male athlete (painted red) somersaults over the beast's back, a feat that is virtually impossible to accomplish.

Minoan trade dominated the eastern Mediterranean until about 1380 B.C., when the island was devastated by a natural catastrophe—perhaps a volcanic eruption on a nearby island, the second natural disaster to assult Crete in about 250 years. Weakened by Mycenaean incursions over the preceding centuries, Minoan civilization quickly fell to these raiders from the Greek mainland or to other invading seafarers. Late Minoan Crete (about 1400–1100 B.C.) was a blend of Cretan and Mycenaean elements, marked by decline in economic activity and artistic quality. Whatever the whole story, the Minoans disappeared suddenly and mysteriously, leaving few remnants of their peaceful civilization.

The Greeks of the later Archaic Age had no direct knowledge of Minoan civilization, but the Greek attitude toward the Minoans was shaped by mythology. Myths are usually considered fiction, but buried within them are often actual folk memories or deep psychological truths.

For example, Crete is traditionally the birthplace of the god Zeus. The Minoans worshiped a Zeus who was born in a cave, grew to manhood, and died. They venerated the site of his birth and honored him as a child. The later Greeks, however, believed Zeus to be the immortal father and ruler of the Olympian deities, and they were incensed by the Minoan belief that the god died. The grain of truth in this story may be that although the Greeks eventually dominated Crete in physical terms, elements of Minoan religion found their way into later Greek beliefs; thus, in a sense, the Olympian gods *were* born in Crete. Cretan influences on Greece may also be detected in language, social organization, and economic pursuits, although the Archaic Greeks did not regard the Minoan past as part of their heritage.

BEGINNINGS: MYCENAEAN CIVILIZATION, 1900–1100 B.C.

Unlike the Minoans, the Mycenaeans continued to live for the Greeks of the Archaic Age through the *Iliad* and the *Odyssey*. The events related in these two epic poems occur during the Mycenaean Age, and the stories furnished the Greeks with many of their heroes—Achilles, the doomed warrior, for example, and Odysseus, the tough and wily wandering sailor. Eventually, the Greeks traced their tradition to Mycenae, honoring its warriors as their ancestors and as models of ideal noble behavior and values.

Mycenaean civilization, named by archeologists for Mycenae, one of its most prominent fortress cities, developed on the rugged lower Greek peninsula known as the Peloponnesus. An aggressive warrior people, perhaps from the plains of southern Russia or from the Tigris-Euphrates valley, the Mycenaeans arrived on the peninsula in about 1900 B.C., and by about 1500 B.C., they ruled the entire Peloponnesus.

A feudal order similar to that found later in medieval Europe characterized the Mycenaean political system. Family ties and marriages, tentative alliances, and uneasy truces bound the local rulers in a confederation of petty kingdoms. The kings of these fortress states and their warriors controlled the surrounding countryside. A staunch loyalty developed between the kings and their noble allies, generating a rigid class structure that exploited those who were not warriors.

A royal tax system created a need for a large bureaucracy of collectors and civil employees. At the low end of the social scale stood the merchants, traders, artisans, small landowners, peasants, and slaves—the last, like the royal servants, probably captured in wars or raids.

The ruins of the Mycenaean fortress-palaces, with their massive double walls, narrow escape passages, and wide gateways, stand as mute testimony to the harshness of the militaristic life and the power of the local king. The best-known palace ruin, at Mycenae, contains the famous Lion Gate, constructed from four massive hewn stones, or **ashlars** (Figure 2.4). On one of these stones, two carved lions, separated by a column, face each other and stretch out their long, muscular bodies. Their heads, now missing, were made of metal, perhaps bronze or gold. Placed there to guard the fortress and to remind the populace of the ruler's power, the beasts must have intimidated all visitors who entered or left the citadel.

Within the fortresses and across the eastern Mediterranean, archeologists have found jars, containers, vessels, and terra-cotta figurines, revealing the high level of the Mycenaeans' artistic skill with clay and

Figure 2.4 The Lion Gate at Mycenae. Ca. 1300 B.C. *The Lion Gate is a massive structure of four gigantic blocks—two posts and a beam forming the entrance and a triangular block on which are carved the two 9-foot-high lions and the central column. So impressive were the megalithic fortresses of the Mycenaeans to the later Greeks that they called them cyclopean, convinced that only a race of giants, the Cyclopes, could have built them.*

their wide-ranging trade and travel. The weapons and personal items crafted for the warriors show especially impressive artistic skills. A decorated sword blade of a lion hunt, inlaid in gold and silver, exemplifies the artisan's attention to delicate detail (Figure 2.5).

Mycenaean religion appears to have been a fusion of Minoan and local deities. Like the Minoans, the Mycenaeans venerated numerous household goddesses and worshiped aspects of nature in caves and natural shrines. Local deities seem to have been of two kinds: Some were predecessors of the Olympian gods and goddesses worshiped by the later Greeks and had the same names; others were nature divinities and spirits. Six **shaft graves** have been excavated at Mycenae (Figure 2.6). These graves have yielded fabulous gold treasures, such as the two carved panels from a sixteenth-century B.C. casket shown in Figure 2.7. The graves have also indicated that the Mycenaeans buried their dead with honor. Perhaps influenced by the Egyptians, they wrapped the bodies and surrounded them with precious objects and pottery. From such practices and attitudes evolved the worship of heroes, a central aspect of Greek culture.

The Mycenaean feudal system flourished for several centuries, and after 1380 B.C., when Crete fell, the Mycenaeans extended their raiding and trading activities throughout the eastern Mediterranean. In about 1250 B.C., they attacked the wealthy and strategic city of Troy, on the western coast of present-day Turkey, near the Dardanelles (see Map 2.1). Although similar expeditions had brought booty to the Mycenaeans on earlier occasions, this long, exhausting foray weakened them, leaving them open to conquest by more vigorous tribes. Ironically, this siege of the Trojan citadel probably inspired the *Iliad* and the *Odyssey*, Homer's enduring epics. Overwhelmed by the Dorians from the north, Mycenaean civilization faded, and by about 1100 B.C., the Age of the Mycenaeans had closed. A three-century hiatus in Greek history—called the Dark Ages—followed, when writing disappeared and cultural activities virtually ceased.

The Mycenaeans, as presented by Homer, gave the Greeks many of their ideals. Heir to three centuries of oral traditions about the Mycenaeans, Homer invented the Age of Heroes. He sang to the Greeks of a glittering past that both inspired and sobered them. In the *Iliad* and the *Odyssey*, the Greeks found a universe with a basic moral order and a people with a distinct ethos, or ethical code. The pursuit of excellence that Homer attributed to his Mycenaean heroes became an ideal of historical Greece. Many aristocrats even traced their ancestry back to Homer's

Figure 2.6   Mycenae. Aerial view of the Acropolis. Ca. 1600–1200 B.C. *Set on top of a hill, this citadel occupied a commanding position over the surrounding countryside, and the fortified wall protected its inhabitants. Hilltop citadels such as this were typical for most cities in Mycenaean culture.*

Figure 2.7   Lion Pursuing a Stag (top); Lion Pursuing a Gazelle (bottom). Ca. 1500 B.C. Two plaques from gold-plated wooden chest. Length, 3¾″ each. National Museum, Athens. *The Mycenaeans, isolated in their fortresses on the Greek mainland, learned to appreciate the beauties of Minoan art through contacts with neighbors on Crete. Mycenaean artisans adapted Cretan subjects and themes, but they ignored their fanciful and lively nature in order to cultivate static effects, as in these gold plaques with their stylized animals and lilies. These plaques, decorating a small wooden chest, were found in a grave at Mycenae, deposited there as part of the burial equipment of a dead king.*

Figure 2.5   Lion Hunt. Ca. sixteenth century B.C. Bronze inlaid with gold and electrum. National Museum, Athens. *An anonymous artisan has decorated every part of this 9-inch dagger. Whether the weapon was ever used in battle is not clear, but its fine details and realistic figures must have made it a prized possession of a Mycenaean warrior. This dagger survived because it was buried alongside its owner in a funeral mound.*

warriors and, through them, to the gods and goddesses. So rich was Homer's world that art and literature drew on it for subjects and incentive throughout Greek history. Through him the Mycenaeans gave the Greeks their myths, their religion, their ethics, their perception of the universe, and their insight into human character.

INTERLUDE: THE DARK AGES, 1100–800 B.C.

With the fall of the Mycenaeans, a period known as the Dark Ages began, and life reverted to simpler patterns. People lived in isolated farming communities and produced only essential tools and domestic objects. Commercial and social interchange among communities, already made hazardous by the mountainous terrain, became even more dangerous, and communication with the eastern Mediterranean kingdoms nearly ceased.

Yet some fundamental changes were slowly occurring. Political power was gradually shifting from kings to the heads of powerful families, laying the foundation for a new form of government, and iron gradually replaced bronze in tools, weapons, and other crafted objects—thus ending the Bronze Age and beginning the Iron Age in Greece. Many Mycenaeans fled to the coast of Asia Minor, which later came to be called Ionia, thus paving the way for the formation of an extended Greek community around the Aegean and Mediterranean Seas.

THE ARCHAIC AGE, 800–479 B.C.

In about 800 B.C., the Greeks emerged from their long years of stagnation and moved into an era of political innovation and cultural experimentation. Although scattered and isolated, they shared a sense of identity based on their common language, their heroic stories and folk tales, their myths and religious practices, and their commercial and trading interests. They claimed a common mythical parent, Hellen, who fathered three sons—the ancestors of the three major Greek tribes, the Ionians, the Aeolians, and the Dorians—and thus they called themselves Hellenes and their land Hellas. In the next three centuries, the Greeks would reconstruct their political and social systems, develop new styles of art and architecture, invent new literary genres, and make the first formal philosophical inquiries into the nature of human behavior and the universe. By the end of this period, they would have laid the foundations for a new world.

Political, Economic, and Social Structures

By the beginning of the Archaic Age (*Archaic* is from the Greek and means "ancient" or "beginning"), the isolated farming community had evolved into the *polis* (plural, *poleis*), a small, well-defined city-state. Several hundred poleis lay scattered over the Greek mainland and abroad. Although each polis had its own separate history and unique traits, each shared certain features with all the others. An *acropolis,* or fortified hilltop, served as a citadel where the rulers usually resided (Figure 2.8). Temples and holy shrines stood on the acropolis or below in an *agora.* The agora, an open area where political leaders held forth, citizens assembled, and the populace congregated to conduct business and socialize, was the center of a polis. The pursuit of both public and private matters in an agora served to connect the citizens of a polis and to foster civic pride and loyalty. In effect, a polis, through its control of the religious, cultural, and psychological components of its relatively closed community, molded the citizenry into an organic body with a collective identity.

Simultaneously with the emergence of the polis, in about 800 B.C., the political system underwent a basic change. The kings had been deposed by the leaders of noble families who owned most of the land and possessed the weapons and horses. These wealthy warriors established **oligarchies,** or government by the few. Although the oligarchies benefited the aristocrats, they were also characterized by exemplary leadership, civic idealism, and cultural and artistic patronage. However, most oligarchies eventually failed because of unforeseen and far-reaching military and economic changes.

New military tactics now made obsolete the aristocratic warriors in their horse-drawn chariots. Foot soldiers—armed with long spears, protected by shields and personal armor, and grouped in closed ranks called phalanxes—were proving more effective in battles. These foot soldiers, or hoplites, were recruited from among independent farmers, merchants, traders, and artisans, who were also profiting from an expanding economy. As their military value became evident, these commoners soon demanded a voice in political decisions.

At the same time, a growing population, beginning to strain the limited agricultural resources, led to an era of overseas expansion and colonization. The Hellenes sent citizens to join their earlier Ionian settlements and to establish new colonies along the coasts of Spain, North Africa, southern Russia (or the Black Sea), and Sicily and southern Italy, which became known as *Magna Graecia,* or Greater Greece.

Foreign ventures and expanded trade increased the wealth of the new middle class and reinforced their desires for more economic opportunities and political

Figure 2.8 Acropolis, Athens. View from the west. *The Acropolis dominates Athens in the twenty-first century just as it did in ancient times when it was the center of Athenian ceremonial and religious life. Today it is the towering symbol of Athens's cultural heritage as well as the center of the local tourist industry. A landmark in the history of town planning, the Acropolis is the ancestor of all carefully laid-out urban environments from ancient Rome to Renaissance Florence to modern Brasilia.*

influence, but the entrenched aristocracy blocked their way to power. Frustrated by the inability of reform efforts to solve deep-seated problems, in the sixth century B.C. many poleis turned to rulers whom they entrusted with extraordinary powers to make sweeping economic and political changes. Many of these tyrants, as the Greeks called them, restructured their societies to allow more citizens to benefit from the growing economy, to move up the social scale, and to participate in the political process. However, some tyrants perpetuated their rule through heirs or political alliances and governed harshly for years, thus giving the word *tyrant* its modern meaning.

Regardless of the different results of the tyrants' reigns, by about 500 B.C. life was similar in many ways in all poleis. Citizens—freeborn males who could claim the right to enter into politics by virtue of family and wealth—voiced their opinions in a widening democratic process. They sat on juries, debated in the assemblies, and defended their polis in time of war. Civic responsibility, recognized as a central element in everyday life, was now passed on by the aristocrats to this new band of citizens.

Although horizons were expanding for the male citizens, other members of this predominantly middle-class society were severely restricted in political and economic matters. Women—except for priestesses such as Lysimache, who was priestess of Athena for sixty-four years in the later fifth and early fourth centuries, and a rare literary figure such as Sappho—were subservient to men. In Athens, for example, women possessed no legal or economic status, for they were by law under the control of the males in the household. Families often married off their daughters for economic gain, and, once married, the daughters were expected to be hardworking, loyal, and obedient.

Foreigners, with a few exceptions, were placed in special categories that restricted their personal rights and limited their economic opportunities. Some poleis, such as Sparta, simply barred most foreigners, whereas Athens was more tolerant. Slaves, on the other hand, had no rights and were treated as property, with little hope of future improvement.

The Greek Polis: Sparta and Athens

Of the hundreds of poleis that evolved during the Archaic Age, Sparta and Athens stand out for their vividly contrasting styles of life and their roles in subsequent Greek history. Sparta, the principal symbol of Dorian civilization, chose to guarantee its integrity

ca. 800		600	590		508	490	479
Dark Ages	Expansion and Colonization	Solon in Athens	Political, Social, Economic Reforms		Cleisthenes in Athens	Persian Wars	Hellenic Age
	Political and cultural activity revives						

and future through stringent and uncompromising policies. The earliest Spartans forcibly enslaved the *Helots*—the original inhabitants of the lower Peloponnesus. To prevent rebellions and to control the Helots, who outnumbered the Spartans ten to one, a vigilant Sparta was forced to keep its military always on the alert. Thus, Sparta created a rigid hierarchical society of well-trained, tough, and athletic men, women, and children. The Spartans also established a genuine oligarchy: a constitutional government operated by five officials elected annually by a small body of citizens. The ruling class, obsessed with keeping social order, passed laws forbidding immigration, limiting material possessions, and restricting creativity. Sparta was admired for its loyal, brave soldiers and its stable social order. But Sparta contributed little to the artistic enrichment of Greece.

By contrast, Athens, the symbol of Ionian civilization, reached greater artistic, intellectual, and literary heights than did any other polis. Athens, both the city and its surrounding countryside of Attica, was a more open society than Sparta. The Attican clans shared a sense of community with the Athenians and supported them in wartime.

The history of Athens echoes the general pattern of change in the poleis during the Archaic Age (Timeline 2.2). Aristocrats initially ruled Athens through councils and assemblies. As long as farming and trading sustained an expanding population, the nobles ruled without challenge. But at the beginning of the sixth century B.C., many peasant farmers were burdened with debts and were threatened with prison or slavery. Having no voice in the government, the farmers began to protest what they perceived as unfair laws.

In about 590 B.C., the Athenians granted an aristocrat named Solon special powers to reform the economy. He abolished debts and guaranteed a free peasantry, overhauled the judicial system, and recorded the laws. Solon also restructured the Athenian constitution by giving the lower ranks of free men—those without great name or noble family but with some property or wealth—the right to participate in government.

Solon's principal successor was Cleisthenes [KLICE-thu-neez], who established democracy in Athens beginning in 508 B.C. He broadened the governmental base by opening it to all free male citizens (called the *demos*) regardless of their property or bloodlines. Cleisthenes' democratic reforms, which lasted for almost

two centuries, created an atmosphere in which civic pride and artistic energy were unleashed, inaugurating the Hellenic Age (sometimes called the Golden Age), which made Athens both the pride and the envy of the other Greek city-states.

For moderns, one of the most surprising contrasts between Sparta and Athens is the difference in the roles and status of women. In general, Spartan women spent their time outside and spoke freely to men; Athenian women were kept in seclusion and rarely talked with their husbands. What made Spartan women so independent was that, above all else, they were to be strong mothers of the vigorous males needed to maintain this warrior society. To that end, Spartan women, alone among Greek women, were given public education, including choral singing and dancing, and athletics, in which they stripped just as Greek men did. Spartan women were also unique in being able to own land and to manage their own property.

In contrast, the women of Athens pursued respectability as an ideal, which meant that they were supposed to marry and stay indoors, overseeing their households and performing domestic chores. It is not clear how strictly this ideal was imposed on them in daily life. Athenian drama contains many instances of female characters complaining about their powerlessness, as when a wife is abandoned (Euripides' *Medea*) or a woman is left during wartime (Aeschylus's *Agamemnon*). These examples probably reflected reality. Athenian women, lacking public education and excluded by law from government and the military, played a subordinate role to Athenian men.

The Persian Wars

Cleisthenes' domestic reforms were one of the two major events that heralded the end of the Archaic Age and the coming of Greece's Hellenic Age. The other event, the Persian Wars, was pivotal not only for Greece but also for Western civilization. If the autocratic and imperialistic Persians had won these wars, then the democratic institutions, the humanistic values, and the cultural landmarks that the Greeks were establishing would have been lost.

By the mid–sixth century B.C., the Persians ruled a huge empire in the Near East encompassing most of the ancient world and including the Greek poleis in Ionia. When Darius [duh-RYE-us], king of the Persians in the late sixth century, demanded taxes from the Ionian Greeks, they revolted and looked to their homeland for support. A few poleis, including Athens, sent an expedition, which Darius defeated. To prevent future uprisings, Darius invaded the Greek peninsula and landed near Athens at Marathon in 490 B.C. The outnumbered Athenian army fought brilliantly, destroying many of the invader's ships and turning back the powerful Persian Empire.

However, the Persians soon found a new and determined ruler in Xerxes [ZIRK-seez], son of Darius, who overran much of northern Greece. Under Spartan leadership, the Greeks planned to trap the Persians at Thermopylae, a northern mountain pass, but they were annihilated by Xerxes' troops. Xerxes moved southward and sacked Athens, whose inhabitants escaped across the Saronic Gulf to the island of Salamis. The Athenians drew the Persian navy into the narrows of the gulf, where the swifter Greek ships outmaneuvered the cumbersome Persian craft. After witnessing the destruction of his fleet, Xerxes returned to Persia. The remainder of the Persian army was routed at Plataea in 479 B.C., thus ending this major threat to Greece. The Greeks' final victory over the mighty Persians created a euphoric mood in Athens and set the stage for the ensuing Hellenic Age.

THE EMERGENCE OF GREEK GENIUS: THE MASTERY OF FORM

During the Archaic Age, the Greeks developed a variety of literary, philosophical, and artistic forms that they used to probe the meaning of the universe and of human existence as well as to celebrate their joyous sense of life. These cultural accomplishments, like those of the older Near Eastern civilizations, were associated with the religious beliefs and practices that played a central role in Greek life and history. In fact, the Greeks believed that creativity itself was a divine gift from the **muses,** the nine goddesses of artistic inspiration (Table 2.1). Guided by their muses, they created enduring works of art, literature, and theater, each with a universal appeal.

Religion

The Greeks made religion an ongoing part of their private and public affairs. Indeed, the polis and religion could not be separated, for in the eyes of the Greeks the fate of each community depended on the civic deity. Public rituals and festivals drew together the citizens,

Table 2.1 THE NINE MUSES AND THEIR AREAS OF CREATIVITY

NAME	ART OR SCIENCE
Calliope	Epic poetry
Clio	History
Erato	Erotic poetry and mime
Euterpe	Lyric poetry and music
Melpomene	Tragedy
Polyhymnia	Sacred hymn
Terpsichore	Dance and song
Thalia	Comedy
Urania	Astronomy

infused them with civic pride, and reminded them of their common heritage. During the Archaic Age, Greek religion—an amalgam of deities derived from the original settlers as well as invaders and foreigners—evolved into two major categories: the Olympian and the chthonian. The **Olympian deities** dwelled in the sky or on mountaintops and were associated with the Homeric heroes and the aristocracy. The **chthonian deities** (from the Greek *chthon,* meaning "the earth") lived underground and were associated with peasant life, the seasons and cycles of nature, and fertility.

The Olympian religion shared some traits with the polytheistic cults of the ancient Near East, including the notion that the deities intervene in daily affairs, the belief that they are like humans in many respects, and the idea of a pantheon of gods and goddesses. The Greeks endowed their deities with physical bodies and individual personalities, creating a fascinating blend of charm and cruelty, beauty and childishness, love of justice and caprice. This family of unruly and willful deities quarreled with one another and played favorites with their mortal worshipers as they pleased. Faced with such favoritism among the deities, the Greeks themselves developed a strong moral sense. They came to believe that as long as they recognized the divinities' power and did not challenge them—and thus become victims of **hubris,** or pride—they would survive and often prosper.

Homer's poems lay out the complex relations and kinships in the Olympic pantheon and explain the functions and roles of the twelve principal deities, but Homer by no means invented these supernatural beings; they had been around long before his time. Indeed, their confusing traits and characters are probably the result of a fusion of numerous gods and goddesses whose origins predate the Greeks. Notwithstanding the deities' erratic characteristics, however, the Greeks never forgot that the Olympian system reflected a moral order and a sense of justice.

Zeus, a sky god and first among the immortals, reigned as king on Mount Olympus, hurling thunderbolts and presiding over the divine councils. He sired both immortals and mortals, for his sexual appetite knew no bounds. Hera, probably the great goddess of earlier cultures, was the sister and wife of Zeus. She watched over the women who appealed to her for help and kept a close eye on her wandering husband. Zeus's two brothers controlled the rest of the universe, Poseidon ruling the seas, all waters, and earthquakes, and Hades guarding the underworld. Zeus's sister Hestia protected the hearth and its sacred flame. Zeus's twin offspring, Apollo and Artemis, symbolized the sun and the moon, respectively. Apollo, Zeus's favorite son, personified the voice of reason. Artemis watched over childbirth and guarded wild creatures. Zeus's lying son Ares delighted in fierce battles, and, as the war god, he possessed a quick temper and few morals. He and Aphrodite—Zeus's daughter and the goddess of love and beauty—were adulterous lovers. Ironically, Homer has Aphrodite married to Hephaestus, the ugly and lame son of Zeus who was a master smith and the patron of craftspeople.

Two other children of Zeus rounded out the Olympic roster. Athena, the goddess of wisdom and patron goddess of Athens, was associated with warfare, the arts, and handicrafts. She was worshiped as a virgin goddess. Hermes, the god of trade and good fortune, was also the patron of thieves, although he was best known as a messenger for his fellow deities (Table 2.2).

The chthonian gods and goddesses were probably derived from ancient earth and harvest deities. At first they were worshiped only by the lower orders, but as the demos grew in influence, chthonian rituals spread and were soon integrated into the civic calendar. Nevertheless, these cults were open only to initiates, who were sworn to silence; hence, they were called mystery cults, from the Greek word *mystos,* "keeping silent."

The chthonian practices originally invoked the powers of the earth to ensure a successful planting and a bountiful harvest. The two most important crops in Greece—grains and grapes, the sources of bread and wine, respectively—led to two major cults, those of Demeter and Dionysus. Demeter, a sister of Zeus, was a harvest goddess. She in turn had a daughter, Persephone, whom Hades abducted to his kingdom belowground. According to her cult legend, Demeter finally rescued Persephone, but not before Hades had tricked Persephone into eating a fruit that made her return to the underworld for part of each year. Thus, during the winter months, the earth is bare, but when Persephone and Demeter are together, the earth is fecund and the grains grow. At Eleusis, a small village in Attica, Demeter was

GOD OR GODDESS	DUTIES AND RESPONSIBILITIES
Zeus	Chief deity and keeper of order on Olympus
Hera	Mother goddess, protector of women
Poseidon	Ruler of waters
Hades	Keeper of the underworld
Hestia	Protector of the hearth
Apollo	God of wisdom and moderation
Artemis	Virgin goddess who aided women
Ares	Amoral god of violence and warfare
Aphrodite	Goddess of passion, love, and beauty
Hephaestus	Patron of craftspeople
Athena	Goddess of wisdom and warfare
Hermes	God of merchants and thieves; messenger for the deities

Table 2.2 THE OLYMPIAN DEITIES AND THE AREAS THEY RULED

the focus of a mystery cult. Prospective initiates from all over Greece traveled there, apparently to receive her promise of immortal life.

Whereas Demeter's followers honored her in a dignified manner, Dionysus's worshipers, through wild dancing and wine drinking, hoped to be reinvigorated by their god and born again. Dionysus came to represent the irrational, emotional, and uncontrolled aspects of human nature to the Greeks. In contrast, the rational, conscious, controlled aspects were associated with Apollo. The two aspects—Dionysian and Apollonian—were considered opposing but complementary. Eventually, a Dionysus cult arose in Athens, where his followers annually held ceremonies honoring his power as god of the vine (Figure 2.9). Over the years these rituals became civic festivals, which in turn spawned the competitive performances of tragic drama in Athens in the sixth century B.C.

Epic Poetry

The originator of the major conventions of **epic poetry** is traditionally believed to be Homer (about 800 B.C.), a **bard,** or poet who sang his verses while accompanying himself on a stringed instrument. In the *Iliad* and the *Odyssey,* Homer sang of the events before, during, and after the Trojan War, stories that had circulated among the Greeks since the fall of Mycenae. Homer entertained an aristocratic audience eager to claim kinship with the Mycenaean past. For many years, his poems were transmitted orally by

Figure 2.9 EXEKIAS. *Dionysus Crossing the Sea.* Ca. 535 B.C. Clay, 12″ diameter. Staatliche Antikensammlungen, Munich. *Painted in the basin of a circular drinking bowl, Dionysus, the god of wine, is depicted sailing alone in a fish-nosed boat. This work by Exekias, one of the most admired artists of the Archaic Age, illustrates the beautiful mastery of space—the making of a convincing pictorial image on a predetermined surface, such as a pot or a tomb—that characterized the best vase painting of the time. Dionysus reclines under a billowing sail, surrounded by gamboling dolphins. Sprouting from the boat is a vine carrying bunches of grapes—the symbol of the god of wine. Exekias's simple design is typical of Archaic painting.*

Figure 2.10 SIGNED BY EXEKIAS. *Achilles Killing the Amazon Queen Penthesilea.* Ca. 530 B.C. Clay, ht. of jar 16″. British Museum, B 210. *Exekias painted this scene on an Athenian amphora, a vase with an oval body, cylindrical neck, and two handles, used for wine or oil. The scene is based on an episode from the Trojan War, which was Exekias's favorite source. Although not recorded by Homer in the* Iliad, *the event is part of the traditions of the siege of Troy. According to some of the stories, Penthesilea, whose warrior women were allies of the Trojans, outfought Achilles on several occasions before he killed her. At the moment he is about to kill Penthesilea, Achilles recognizes her beauty and falls in love. Exekias's skillful composition directs the viewer's eye to Achilles' spear, aimed at Penthesilea's throat. Both figures, simple and dignified, dressed in their armor, which Exekias details, are caught in a tragic scene of war and death, which Achilles' love cannot overcome. Exekias depicted Dionysus, holding an amphora, and his son, Oenopion, with a cup in his hand, on the reverse side. This work and Figure 2.9 are in the black-figure style, characterized by silhouetted figures on a reddish clay background. Greek artists later reversed this technique, creating the red-figure style of reddish figures on a black background (see Figures 3.1, 3.10, and 3.11).*

other bards, and they probably did not exist in written versions until the seventh century B.C. Homer's authorship and, indeed, even his very existence are established solely by tradition; nothing is actually known about him. Nevertheless, by the end of the Archaic Age, the appeal of Homer's poetry had embraced all social levels, and his authority approached that of a modern combination of television, Shakespeare, and the Bible.

The basic appeal of the Homeric epics lies in their well-crafted plots, filled with dramatic episodes and finely drawn characters. Set against the backdrop of the Trojan War, the *Iliad* describes the battle of Ilium, another name for Troy, and the *Odyssey* recounts events after the Greeks defeat the Trojans (Figure 2.10). The earlier of the epics, the *Iliad*, focuses on Achilles, the epitome of heroic Greek manhood. In contrast to the battlefield heroics of the *Iliad*, the *Odyssey* narrates the wanderings of the Greek warrior Odysseus after the fall of Troy. Moreover, the *Odyssey* celebrates marriage, for Odysseus, despite some amorous adventures, remains fixed on thoughts of his wife, Penelope, who waits for him in Ithaca.

In both poems, the deities merrily intrude into the lives of mortals, changing and postponing the fate of friend and enemy alike. So great was Homer's authority that his works made him the theologian of Greek religion. His stories of the gods and goddesses, although not completely replacing other versions of their lives, became the standard that circulated wherever Greek was spoken. Homer presented Zeus, the nominal protector of the moral order, as forever under siege by other gods seeking help for their favorite mortals. Although some later Greeks deplored Homer's

44

SAPPHO
He Seems to Be a God

Sappho's lyrical poems are vehicles for her intensely personal emotions. In this ode, she describes the pangs of jealousy and grief she feels on seeing someone she loves respond to another.

He seems to be a god, that man
Facing you, who leans to be close,
Smiles, and, alert and glad, listens
To your mellow voice

And quickens in love at your laughter
That stings my breasts, jolts my heart
If I dare the shock of a glance.
I cannot speak,

My tongue sticks to my dry mouth,
Thin fire spreads beneath my skin,
My eyes cannot see and my aching ears
Roar in their labyrinths.

Chill sweat slides down my body,
I shake, I turn greener than grass.
I am neither living nor dead and cry
From the narrow between.
But endure, even this grief of love.

ALCAEUS
Longing for Home and Drinking Song

The poet Alcaeus (about 620–about 580 B.C.) was Sappho's contemporary, and he also lived in the polis of Mytilene on the island of Lesbos. Unlike Sappho, Alcaeus wrote about the world of men. His works were collected into ten books in antiquity, but only a few fragments survive today. The first poem describes Alcaeus's anguish in exile, when he was banished for political activities. The second poem describes a drinking party with male friends.

1

Plunged in the wild chaste-woods I live
a rustic life, unhappy me,
longing to hear Assembly called
and Council, Agesilaidas!

From lands my grandfather grew old
possessing, and my father too,
among these citizens who wrong
each other, I've been driven away.

An outland exile: here I dwell
like Onomacles, the Athenian
spear-wolf, out of the fray. To make
peace with . . . is no wise.

So to the precinct of the gods,
treading the dark earth . . .

. . . I live
keeping well out of trouble's reach.

Now Lesbos' long-robed girls are here for the beauty-
     contest. All around,
the women's wondrous annual cry,
the holy alleluia, rings.

When will the gods from all my trials
deliver. . . .

2

Let's drink! Why wait for the lamps? Only an inch of
     day.
Get those bigger cups down, boyo, the fancy ones.
Wine puts cares out of mind, gift of a god to men,
Zeus' and Semele's son. Water it two to one;
pour them full to the brim, cup after cup, without any
     gap.

inattention to moral issues, his roguish portraits of the deities remained indelibly imprinted in the minds of the general populace.

Homer's poetic expression also gave texture to the Greek language. Similes, figures of speech in which two unlike things are compared, help bring the dramatic, exotic events of the stories down to earth. For example, Homer creates a vivid image of Odysseus as a ferocious killer when he compares him to a lion "covered with blood, all his chest and his flanks on either side bloody." In a less violent simile, Homer has Achilles compare his fellow Greeks to "unwinged" baby birds and himself to their nurturing mother. Homer's images also provide a rich repertory of ready phrases and metaphors, known as **Homeric epithets,** such as "the wily Odysseus," "the swift-footed Achilles," and the "rosy-fingered dawn."

Besides shaping the language, Homer served as a guide to behavior for the Archaic Greeks. Because they became part of the Greek educational curriculum, his poems acquired an ethical function. A young man who took Achilles or Odysseus for a model would learn to maintain his well-being, to speak eloquently in company with other men, to give and receive hospitality, to shed tears in public over the death of his closest friend, to admire the beauty of women, to esteem the material wealth of other nobles, to appreciate songs of bravery, and, above all, to protect his reputation as a man and warrior. On the other hand, a young woman who imitated Penelope, the patient and faithful wife of Odysseus, would inhabit a more circumscribed world as she learned to weave at the loom, to manage a household, to cultivate her physical beauty, and to resist the advances of other men. Although much changed, life in the United States today still pays more than lip service to these values—men, esteeming material wealth, admiring women, and protecting their masculine position; women, cultivating beauty, remaining faithful, and keeping the home.

Lyric Poetry

Verses sung to the music of the **lyre** (a stringed instrument), or **lyric poetry,** became the dominant literary expression in the late Archaic Age, and lyric verses have dominated Western poetry ever since. Lyric poetry, which originated later than the epic, expressed an author's personal, private thoughts, though the muse Euterpe was credited with the inspiration. The shift from epic to lyric poetry in the sixth century B.C. coincided with changes in the polis, where the rising democratic spirit encouraged a variety of voices to be heard.

Of the several types of lyric poetry, monody, or the solo lyric, became the most influential in Archaic Greece. Poets of monody achieved relative simplicity by using a single line of verse or by repeating a short stanza pattern. Unlike the Homeric epics, which survive relatively whole, the solo lyrics are extremely fragmented. For example, the bulk of what remains of Sappho's [SAF-oh] verses consists of random lines and references gleaned from later commentators and only one or two entire lyrics. And of the music, the whole has been lost. The ancients, however, regarded Sappho (about 600 B.C.) as the greatest of the writers of solo lyrics. The philosopher Plato hailed her as the tenth muse in a short lyric he dedicated to her. A truly original writer, Sappho apparently owed no debt to Homer or any other poet. Her work is addressed to a small circle of aristocratic women friends on her native island of Lesbos in the Aegean. She was deeply personal in her interests, writing chiefly about herself, her friends, and their feelings for one another. In her elegant but restrained verses,

Table 2.3 **PHILOSOPHERS OF THE ARCHAIC AGE**

PHILOSOPHER	TIME	ACHIEVEMENT
Thales	About 585 B.C.	First philosopher and founder of philosophic materialism
Pythagoras	About 580–about 507 B.C.	Founder of philosophic idealism
Heraclitus	About 545–about 485 B.C.	First dialectical reasoning; belief in continual flux

Sappho sang mostly about moods of romantic passion: of longing, unrequited love, absence, regret, dead feelings, jealousy, and fulfillment. Sappho's willing vulnerability and her love of truth made the solo lyric the perfect vehicle for confessional writing.

Natural Philosophy

The mental attitudes that partly accounted for the democratic challenge to established authority in the Archaic Age also brought forth thinkers who questioned the power and, ultimately, the existence of the gods. Just as the democrats constructed a human-centered state, so did the philosophers conceive of a world where natural causes and effects operated. These Greek thinkers invented what the Romans later called natural philosophy, a term that encompasses what we would call "science" and "philosophy." The close connection between science and philosophy persisted for twenty-two centuries, until the Newtonian revolution of the seventeeth century A.D. From that point on, science simply demonstrated what happened in nature without speculating about its purpose.

The origins of natural philosophy, like those of lyric poetry, are hidden in the incomplete historical record and distorted by the fragmented extant writings, but we can nevertheless say that formal Western philosophy began on the Ionian coast in the sixth century B.C. There, in the polis of Miletus, a set of thinkers known as the Milesian school speculated that beneath the ever-changing natural world was an unchanging matter (Table 2.3).

Thales [THAY-leez] (fl. 585 B.C.), the founder of the Milesian school, reasoned that the fundamental substance was water—an outlook that made him a materialist, because he thought that everything was made of matter. From the standpoint of modern science, Thales

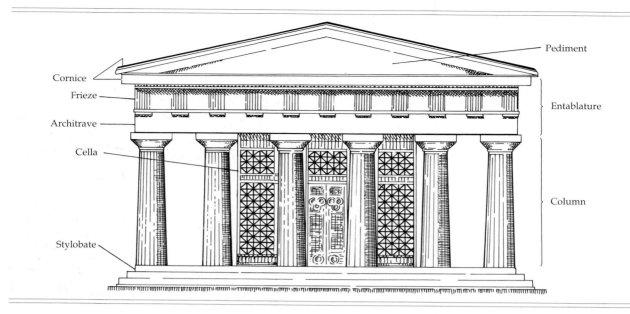

Figure 2.11 Elements of Greek Architecture

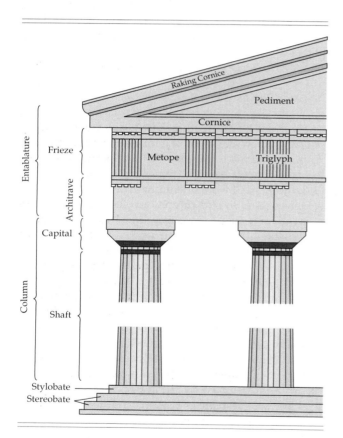

Figure 2.12 Greek Architecture of the Doric Order

in rationality not only determined the direction of speculative thought but also initiated the steps that led to physics, chemistry, botany, and other sciences. Proposing that the universe was governed by natural laws, these first philosophers questioned divine explanations for natural events, a development deplored by those who found the key to life in a divine spirit.

When the Persians conquered Asia Minor near the end of the sixth century B.C., the center of intellectual thought shifted to Athens and to southern Italy and Sicily, where a tradition had emerged that challenged the Milesian school. Pythagoras [puh-THAG-uh-ruhs] (about 580–about 507 B.C.), the leader of the Sicilian school, rejected the concept of an underlying substance. Instead, he proclaimed, "Everything is made of numbers," by which he meant that mathematical relationships explained the basic order in nature—an outlook that made him an idealist, because he thought that an immaterial principle was the root cause of things. His musical studies probably led Pythagoras to this conclusion. He may have observed that a plucked string vibrated, making a certain sound; if the string were cut in half and plucked again, then a new note an octave higher than the first, with twice as many vibrations per second, would be heard. Hence, mathematical ratios determined musical sounds. Pythagoras then concluded that "numbers" explained everything in the "cosmos," his term for the orderly system embracing the earth and the heavens. Later, ancient astronomers building on Pythagorean beliefs claimed that the planets, in moving through their orbits, made music—the "music of the spheres."

A third philosopher, Heraclitus [her-uh-KLITE-uhs] (about 545–about 485 B.C.), appeals more to the modern age than does any other thinker in Archaic Greece. Rejecting the materialism of Thales and the idealism of

was wrong and so were the rest of his circle, who proposed other elements—air and "the infinite"—as the underlying essence. But more important than their conclusions regarding matter were their convictions that there is regularity in the universe and that human reason can ultimately understand the natural order. Their belief

Figure 2.13 Temple of Hera at Paestum. Ca. 560–550 B.C. Limestone. *This temple, with its heavy, squat columns, stands not only as a model of Archaic Greek architecture but also as a reminder of Greek wealth and expansion. Colonists from mainland Greece settled in southern Italy, the land they thought of as "Greater Greece," in the seventh and sixth centuries B.C., bringing with them the Olympian gods and goddesses and ideas of how to build temples in their honor.*

Pythagoras, Heraclitus pioneered a philosophic tradition that found truth in constant change, as in his well-known idea that a person cannot step twice into the same flowing river. In addition, Heraclitus devised the earliest dialectical form of reasoning when he speculated that growth arises out of opposites, a fundamental tenet of dialectic thought. This original idea led him to argue that "strife is justice" and that struggle is necessary for progress. Heraclitus's dialectical reasoning anticipated certain nineteenth-century thinkers, and his notion of continual flux has attracted modern physicists.

Architecture

The supreme architectural achievement of the Greeks, the temple, became the fountainhead of the building components, decorative details, and aesthetic principles that together have largely shaped Western architecture down to Post-Modernism in the early twenty-first century. In its origins during the Archaic Age, the temple was a sacred structure designed to house the cult statues of the civic deities. The early houses of worship were probably made of wood, which explains why no remains of these Greek temples have been discovered. However, as the Archaic Age gathered economic momentum and wealth accumulated, each polis rebuilt its wooden sanctuaries in stone.

A diagram of a typical temple illustrates how much the building has influenced Western architecture (Figure 2.11). Generic Greek architecture is called **post-beam-triangle construction** (also known as post-and-lintel construction). *Post* refers to the columns; *beam* indicates the horizontal members, or **architraves,** resting on the columns; and *triangle* denotes the triangular area, called a **pediment,** at either end of the upper building. Other common features include the **entabla-**

ture, which is the name for all of the building between the columns and the pediment; the **cornice,** the horizontal piece that crowns the entablature; and the **stylobate,** the upper step of the base on which the columns stand. A typical temple had columns on four sides, which in turn enclosed a walled room, called a **cella,** that housed the cult image. Each temple faced east, with the doors to the cella placed so that, when opened, they allowed the sunrise to illuminate the statue of the deity.

The earliest temple style in Greece was called **Doric,** both because it originated in the Dorian poleis and because the style's simplicity of design and scarcity of decorative detail reflected the severe Dorian taste (Figure 2.12). The Doric columns have plain tops, or **capitals,** and the columns rest directly on the stylobate without an intervening footing. On the entablature of each Doric temple is a sculptural band, called a *frieze,* which alternates three-grooved panels, called **triglyphs,** with blank panels, called **metopes,** that could be left plain or filled with **relief** sculptures. The triglyphs are reminders of the temple's origin as a wooden building when logs, faced with bronze, served as overhead beams.

An excellent example of the Doric style in the Archaic Age is the Temple of Hera in Poseidonia, now called Paestum, in southern Italy (Figure 2.13). The Temple of Hera is the oldest (about 550 B.C.) and best preserved of three cult sanctuaries on this site. Constructed from coarse local limestone, this large temple has a somewhat ungainly appearance, due in part to the massive architrave and the small spaces between the columns. The builders attempted to remedy this defect (without total success) by introducing refinements into the temple's design. The columns were made to appear strong and solid enough to support the entablature by enlarging the middles of the shafts, a technique known as **entasis.** The artisans also carved vertical grooves, called **fluting,**

Figure 2.14   Temple of Aphaia, Aegina. 510 B.C. *The Temple of Aphaia in Aegina became the standard for the Doric temple style from its creation until it was superseded by the Athenian Parthenon in the 440s. Built of local limestone and covered in stucco and painted, the Temple of Aphaia gleamed like a jewel in its carefully planned site overlooking the Saronic Gulf. Constructed and decorated with strict attention to artistic refinements, such as the slender columns and the lifelike sculptures, this temple represents the climax of Archaic architecture.*

along the shafts to give the columns a graceful, delicate surface and enhance their visual three-dimensionality.

Eventually, after much experimentation, Greek architects overcame the awkwardness of the early Doric style by deciding that a temple's beauty was a function of mathematical proportions. The Temple of Aphaia—erected in 510 B.C. by the citizens of Aegina, Athens's neighbor and perennial enemy—seemed to embody this principle (Figure 2.14). The architect of this temple achieved its pleasing dimensions by using the ratio 1:2, placing six columns on the ends and twelve columns on the sides. The Temple of Aphaia, with its harmonious proportions and graceful columns, became the widely imitated standard for the Doric style over the next half century.

Sculpture

Like the art of Mesopotamia and Egypt, Greek sculpture was rooted in religious practices and beliefs. The Greek sculptors fashioned images of the gods and goddesses to be used in temples either as objects of worship or as decorations for the pediments and friezes. Of greater importance for the development of Greek sculpture were the **kouros** (plural, *kourai*) and the **kore** (plural, *korai*), freestanding statues of youths and maidens, respectively. Before 600 B.C., these sculptures had evolved from images of gods, into statues of dead heroes, and finally into memorials that might not even relate directly to the dead person to whom they were dedicated.

What made the **Archaic** statues of youths and maidens so different from Egyptian and Mesopotamian art was the Greek delight in the splendor of the human body. In their representations of the human form, the Greeks rejected the sacred approach of the Egyptians and the Mesopotamians, which stressed conventional poses and formal gestures. Instead, Greek sculptors created athletic, muscular males and lively, robust maidens. For the Greeks, the health and beauty of the subjects was as important as the statues' religious purpose.

The first Archaic statues of youths owed much to the Egyptian tradition, but gradually Greek sculpture broke free of its origins. An early example of the kourai type of sculpture is the New York Kouros (Figure 2.15), named for its present location in New York City's Metropolitan Museum of Art. Artistically, this marble statue of a youth with the left foot forward, the clenched fists, the arms held rigidly at the sides, the stylized hair, and the frontality—that is, the quality of being designed for viewing from the front—shows the Egyptian influence (see Figure 1.15). The Greek sculptor has moved beyond Egyptian techniques, however, by incorporating changes that make the figure more lifelike, such as by attempting to show the correct shape of the knees and suggesting an actual person's mouth. That the result is not a realistic or an idealized human figure is less important than that the sculptor has studied the human body with fresh eyes and endeavored to represent it accurately. With such groundbreaking works as the New York Kouros, the Greeks launched a dynamic tradition that later artists continually reshaped.

A generation after the New York Kouros, new sculptors expressed their changed notion of a beautiful living male body in such works as the Ptoon Kouros (Figure 2.16). This sculpture, which was probably a

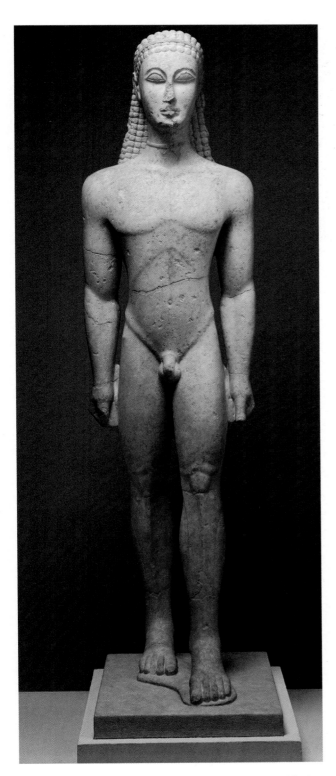

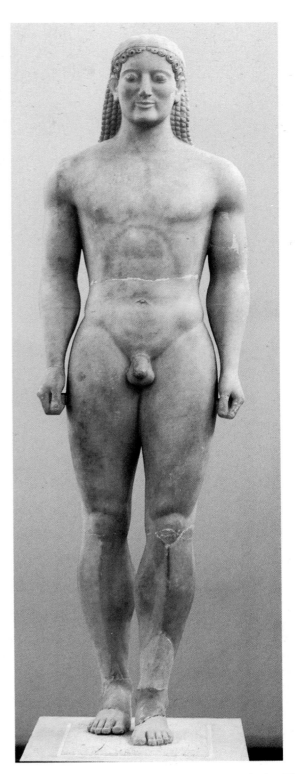

Figure 2.15   New York Kouros. Ca. 615–590 B.C. Marble, ht. 73½". Courtesy Metropolitan Museum of Art. Fletcher Fund, 1932. (32.11.1) *The New York Kouros is one of many similar statues dating from about the beginning of the sixth century B.C. During that century, the male and female statues evolved from stiff and stereotyped models to natural and anatomically correct forms.*

Figure 2.16   Ptoon Kouros. Ca. 540–520 B.C. Marble, ht. 76". National Museum, Athens. *The Ptoon Kouros possesses the distinguishing characteristics of all kourai: frontality, attention to bodily details, and a general formality. However, the Ptoon Kouros's subtle innovations—more precise musculature and more liveliness, as contrasted with Figure 2.15—foreshadow the Hellenic sculpture style.*

Figure 2.17   Auxerre Kore. Ca. 675–600 B.C. Limestone. Louvre. *The Auxerre Kore represents a fairly early stage in the development of this female form. The small size of the sculpture (about 29½″ high) suggests that it may have been part of a burial rite. Traces of red pigment on the bust indicate that this kore was once painted to make it appear more lifelike.*

Figure 2.18   Peplos Kore. Ca. 535–530 B.C. Marble, ht. 48″. Acropolis Museum, Athens. *The kore, a statue of a young draped female, was highly popular during the first phase of Greek art, the Archaic style, which set the standard for later Greek art. The Peplos Kore depicted here—with her beautiful face, elegant dress, and expectant countenance—represents the highest expression of this early style.*

dedicatory offering to a god or a goddess, still shows a powerful Egyptian influence, but it takes a giant step forward to a greater sense of life. The taut body and massive torso convincingly reproduce the athletic qualities of an Olympic competitor, and the curious facial expression, known as the "archaic smile," gives an enigmatic quality to the marble figure.

The korai sculptures, like the statues of youths, evolved from a frozen, lifeless style toward a greater realism, although women were never depicted in the nude at this stage in Greek sculpture. The earliest draped korai sculptures mixed Mesopotamian and Egyptian traditions with Greek ideas, sometimes producing an interesting but awkward effect. Such an early work is the Auxerre Kore (Figure 2.17)—named for the museum in Auxerre, France—whose cylindrical shape is copied from Mesopotamian models and whose stiff pose, wiglike hair, and thin waist are borrowed from Egypt. The Greek sculptor added the broad mouth and the Greek peplos (a loose-fitting outer robe) decorated with a meander pattern, but the Auxerre Kore, despite its charming details, is rigid and inert.

The Peplos Kore (Figure 2.18), dating from about a century later, expresses beautifully the exciting changes that were taking place in late Archaic sculpture. The statue wears a chiton, or tunic, over her upper torso, and a belted peplos. The sculptor has replaced the rigidity of the Egyptian pose with a more graceful one, as shown, for example, by the way the figure holds her right arm. Traces of a painted necklace may be seen, for the Peplos Kore, like all Greek sculpture, was painted to make the figure as true to life as possible. The often awkward archaic smile is here rendered to perfection, giving this lovely maiden an aristocratic demeanor.

The Greek tradition of representing males nude and females clothed persisted throughout the Archaic Age and well into the succeeding Hellenic Age. The Greeks readily accepted male nudity, witnessing it in the army on campaigns, in the gymnasium during exercises, and in the games at Olympia and elsewhere, and this acceptance is reflected in their art. But they were much less comfortable with female nudity (except in Sparta, where women exercised in the nude), so women were usually depicted draped or robed.

The political turmoil brought on by the Persian Wars occurred simultaneously with the revolutionary changes in sculpture that were leading to a new style of art. The Temple of Aphaia at Aegina provides a laboratory setting for the transition from the Archaic to the Hellenic style (480–323 B.C.) because of the different ages of the building's statues: The sculptures for the west pediment (about 500 B.C.) were made some fifteen years earlier than those for the east pediment (about 490–485 B.C.). Their stylistic differences demonstrate the changes that were under way.

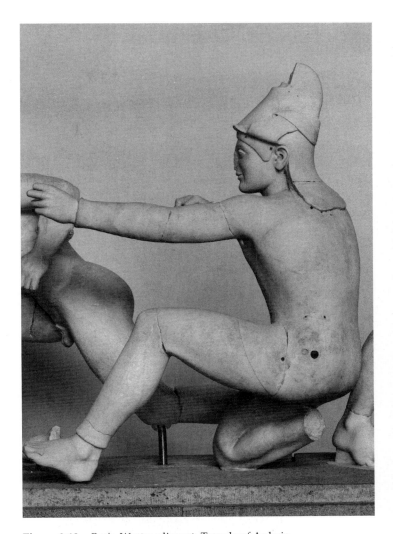

Figure 2.19 *Paris.* West pediment, Temple of Aphaia, Aegina. Ca. 500 B.C. Marble, ht. 41". Staatliche Antikensammlungen, Munich. *The pedimental sculptures on the Temple of Aphaia illustrate the rapid changes that were occurring in artistic ideals and techniques in the period just preceding the Hellenic Age of Athens. The sculpture of Paris from the earlier west pediment is formal and stylized in comparison with its counterpart on the east pediment.*

An earlier statue (from the west pediment) depicts the Trojan hero Paris as a nude, somewhat sensual bowman, poised, ready to release an arrow (Figure 2.19). Paris, his body and face revealing very little tension, might have been posing, rather than preparing for action. A later sculpture (from the east pediment) portrays the legendary hero Herakles as a clothed archer, in a stance copied from the *Paris* figure (Figure 2.20). But what a contrast! Herakles' more muscular body is tensed and ready for action. Although neither face registers emotion, Herakles' gaze and set jawline convey a more lifelike image of a warrior. The *Herakles* figure is a transitional work to the next style—the Hellenic.

Figure 2.20 *Herakles.* East pediment, Temple of Aphaia, Aegina. Ca. 490–485 B.C. Marble, ht. 31″. Staatliche Antiken-sammlungen, Munich. *The statue of Herakles from the east pediment of the Temple of Aphaia shows the advances made in sculpture in the ten to fifteen years after the figure of Paris was crafted for the west pediment. More realistic, detailed, and lifelike than Paris, Herakles is emotionally charged and tense, yet composed and restrained—a state admired and often depicted by Hellenic artists.*

The Legacy of Archaic Greek Civilization

The Archaic Age in Greece was a precious moment in the story of the arts and humanities. Inheriting survival techniques from Neolithic cultures, continuing the urban ways of Mesopotamia and Egypt, and, more important, drawing spiritual and psychological sustenance from the Minoans and the Mycenaeans, the Archaic Greeks developed a unique consciousness that expressed, through original artistic and literary forms, their views about the deities and themselves and how they interacted. A mark of the creative power of the Archaic Greeks is that at the same time that they were inventing epic poetry, lyric poetry, the post-beam-triangle temple, the kore and kouros sculptures, and natural philosophy, they were involved in founding a new and better way to live in the polis.

The new way of life devised by the Archaic Greeks gave rise to what we call, in retrospect, the **humanities**—those original artistic and literary forms that made Greek civilization unique. But the cultural explosion of this brilliant age is inseparable from the Greeks' restless drive to experience life to the fullest and their deep regard for human powers. Having devised their cultural forms, the Archaic Greeks believed passionately that by simply employing these models, either through studying them or by creating new works, the individual became a better human being. In this way, the Archaic Greeks' arts and humanities were imbued with an ethical content, thus suggesting for some—notably philosophers—an alternative way of life to that offered by religion.

Wherever we look in this age, we see creative energy, a trait that has characterized Western civilization through the ages. Even though the different cultural forms did not develop at the same pace during the Archaic Age—sculpture, for example, was not as expressive as lyric poetry—these early aesthetic efforts were fundamentally different from those of the earlier Near Eastern civilizations. The touchstone of the humanistic style developed by the Archaic Greeks was their belief in human powers, both intellectual and physical. Indeed, the most powerful literary voice of this age, Homer, was quoted over and over for his claim that mortals and divinities are part of the same family. Less confident people, hearing this assertion, might have reasoned that human beings are limited in their earthly hopes. But, for the Greeks of this period, Homer meant that humans are capable of godlike actions. The reverence that the Archaic Greeks expressed for all noteworthy deeds, whether in poetry, in warfare, or in the Olympic games, attested to their belief in the basic value of human achievement.

KEY CULTURAL TERMS

frieze
fresco
Linear A
Linear B
ashlar
shaft graves
oligarchy
muse
Olympian deities
chthonian deities
hubris
epic poetry
bard
Homeric epithet
lyre
lyric poetry
post-beam-triangle
    construction

architrave
pediment
entablature
cornice
stylobate
cella
Doric
capital
triglyph
metope
relief
entasis
fluting
kouros
kore
Archaic
humanities

SUGGESTIONS FOR FURTHER READING

Primary Sources

BARNSTONE, W., ed. and trans. *Greek Lyric Poetry*. New York: Bantam Books, 1962. Selections from literary fragments dating from the seventh century B.C. to the sixth century A.D.; includes helpful biographical notes.

HOMER. *Iliad*. R. Fagles. New York: Viking Penguin, 1998. The most recent modern translation of the story of the Trojan War.

———. *Odyssey*. R. Fagles. New York: Viking Penguin, 1996. The epic of Odysseus's adventures after the fall of Troy, again in Fagles's well-received translation.

Sappho, a Garland: The Poems and Fragments of Sappho. Translated by J. Powell. New York: Farrar, Straus & Giroux, 1993. This slim volume contains all of Sappho's existing verses, both whole and fragments, rendered into contemporary language.

WHEELWRIGHT, P., ed. *The Presocratics*. New York: Bobbs-Merrill, 1966. A collection of quotations from early philosophers that captures the flavor of sixth-century Greek thought.

Of all the many translations of Greek literature, the Loeb Classical Library (Harvard University Press) is probably the best.

CHAPTER *2* HIGHLIGHTS

Aegean Civilizations: The Minoans, the Mycenaeans, and the Greeks of the Archaic Age

MINOAN

2.1 Palace at Knossos (ca. 1750–1650 B.C.)

2.2 Earth Goddess with Snakes (ca. 1600–1580 B.C.)

2.3 *Bull-Leaping* (ca. 1500 B.C.)

MYCENAEAN

2.5 Lion Hunt (ca. sixteenth century B.C.)

2.7 Lion Pursuing a Stag; Lion Pursuing a Gazelle (ca. 1500 B.C.)

2.4 Lion Gate at Mycenae (ca. 1300 B.C.)

ARCHAIC GREECE

 HOMER, *Iliad* (ca. 800 B.C.)

 HOMER, *Odyssey* (ca. 800 B.C.)

 SAPPHO, Poems (ca. 600 B.C.)

2.17 Auxerre Kore (ca. 675–600 B.C.)

2.15 New York Kouros (ca. 615–590 B.C.)

2.13 Temple of Hera at Paestum (ca. 560–550 B.C.)

2.16 Ptoon Kouros (ca. 540–520 B.C.)

2.18 Peplos Kore (ca. 535–530 B.C.)

2.9 EXEKIAS, *Dionysus Crossing the Sea* (ca. 535 B.C.)

2.10 EXEKIAS, *Achilles Killing the Amazon Queen Penthesilea* (ca. 530 B.C.)

2.14 Temple of Aphaia, Aegina (510 B.C.)

2.19 *Paris* (ca. 500 B.C.)

2.20 *Herakles* (ca. 490–485 B.C.)

■ *Literature & Philosophy*   ■ *Art & Architecture*   ■ *Music & Dance*

 Readings in the Western Humanities

3 CLASSICAL GREEK CIVILIZATION
The Hellenic Age

With the defeat of the Persians at Plataea in 479 B.C., the Greeks entered the **Hellenic** Age, a period that lasted until the death of Alexander the Great of Macedon in 323 B.C. During the more than 150 years of the Hellenic Age, the Greeks defeated the Persians for a second time and survived a century of destructive civil war, only to succumb ultimately to the Macedonians. But throughout those turbulent times, the Greeks never wavered in their supreme confidence in the superiority of their way of life.

The Greek world consisted of several hundred poleis (city-states), located on the mainland, on the Aegean Islands and the coast of Asia Minor, and in the lands bordering the Mediterranean and Black Seas (Map 3.1). Athens was the cultural center, but many poleis contributed both materially and intellectually to Hellenic civilization. The Hellenic Age was the first stage of Classical civilization, the highest achievement of the ancient Greeks. Chapter 4 describes the second stage of Classical civilization, the Hellenistic Age.

GENERAL CHARACTERISTICS OF HELLENIC CIVILIZATION

Despite diversity among the poleis, the Greeks of the Hellenic Age shared certain characteristics. Competitiveness and rivalry were certainly dominant features, as was an increasingly urban lifestyle (Figure 3.1). Most Greeks still lived in the countryside, but the city now dominated politics, society, and the economy.

Popular attitudes toward the Olympian deities were also changing, and public worship began to be assimilated into civic festivals. The great art of the

◄ **Detail** Poseidon, Apollo, and Artemis. Parthenon frieze. Ca. 448–442 B.C. Marble, ht. 43". Acropolis Museum, Athens.

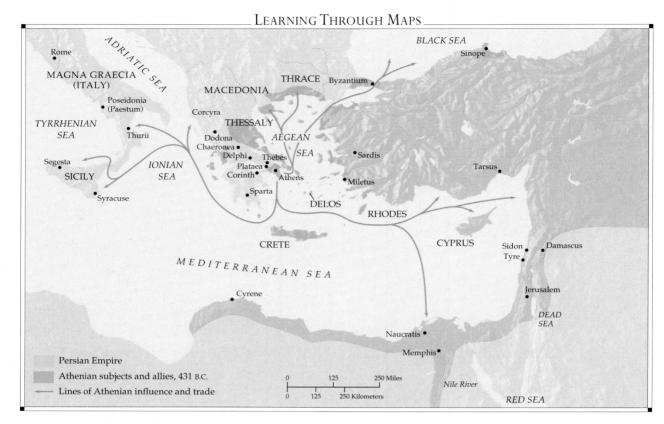

Map 3.1   THE ATHENIAN EMPIRE, 431 B.C.
This map shows the Athenian and Persian empires on the eve of the Peloponnesian War. **Compare** the Athenian and Persian empires, with respect to size and sea and land configuration. **Notice** the difference between Athenian and Spartan influence in the eastern Mediterranean. **How** did the locations of Athens and Sparta influence their respective naval and military policies? **In what way** did the distance between Sicily and Athens affect the course of the Peloponnesian War? **Observe** that Macedonia's proximity to Greece helped in its conquest of the late fourth century B.C.

Figure 3.1   *Torch Race.* Ca. 430–420 B.C. Clay, ht. 14³⁄₁₆″. Arthur M. Sackler Museum, Harvard University Art Museums, Cambridge, Mass. (Bequest of David M. Robinson.) *From the dawn of the Archaic period, about 800 B.C., sports, especially competitive sports, were integral to Greek life. In Hellenic times, artists used sports contests as subjects, as in this painting depicting a torch race, perhaps during the Panathenaea festival. This vase painting is executed in the red-figure style, a reversal of the black-figure style, which is illustrated in Figures 2.9 and 2.10. The relatively uncluttered design, three figures with sparse details, perfectly fits into the small panel on the krater, a mixing vessel.*

age reflected the fusion of civic and sacred in such works as the Parthenon, the temple of the goddess Athena, protector of Athens (Figure 3.2). With gods and goddesses playing increasingly ceremonial roles, religion became demystified and lost some of its personal value in people's lives. Religious dissatisfaction was also triggered by expanded civil rights: The more democratic poleis raised the collective hopes of their citizens but were unable to satisfy all their spiritual longings.

Another characteristic of Hellenic civilization was a high regard for the balanced life and for moderation in achieving it. In Athenian tragedy, a recurrent theme is the danger of great wealth and high position. According to the playwrights, riches and status bred pride and led to envy by other citizens or, worse, envy by the gods. A modest life was the safest way to avoid personal calamity.

The Greeks also sought a balance between the opposite extremes in human nature, symbolized by Apollo, god of moderation, and Dionysus, god of excess. As the god of light, Apollo embodied rational thought, ethical ideals, and aesthetic balance. Apollo's temple with its oracle at Delphi was one of the holiest shrines in Greece, second only to the island of Delos, his birthplace (Figure 3.3).

Dionysus, on the other hand, was the god of wine, drunken revelry, sexual excess, and madness. Women known as **maenads** followed and worshiped him, sometimes tearing apart beasts in their blind frenzy. By the Hellenic Age, these excesses were confined to rural areas, for the Dionysiac impulse was constantly being tamed by the Apollonian spirit and urban life. In Athens, the drunken worship of Dionysus was transformed into a civic festival, the **Dionysia,** from which tragedy, perhaps the highest expression of the Greek ethical genius, was born (Figure 3.4).

Greek citizens of Hellenic times, then, were proud of their own polis, where they participated in civic functions and religious rites. However, despite the many commonalities among the Greek poleis—language, ancestry, history, and Homer—they never shared a politically united Greek world.

Figure 3.2 *Athena Parthenos.* Marble replica based on fifth-century B.C. statue by Phidias. Ht. 3′5⅜″. National Museum, Athens. *Phidias's larger-than-life sculpture, which dominated the inner sanctum of the Parthenon, disappeared in ancient times, but numerous copies, such as this small figurine, have survived. Athena wears a peplos, gathered at her waist, and a helmet, ornamented with a sphinx flanked by two winged horses, and her left hand steadies a shield depicting Greek battle scenes. The statue was composed of gold and ivory sections joined together. A close examination of Athena's head demonstrates the shift from the Archaic to the Hellenic style of sculpture, since it no longer has the Archaic smile and its features are idealized.*

58

Figure 3.3 *Apollo. West pediment, Temple at Olympia. Ca. 460 B.C. Marble, ht. 10'2". Olympia Museum. Apollo's serene countenance in this splendidly crafted head reflects his image as the god of moderation. As the deity who counseled "Nothing in excess," Apollo was a potent force in combating the destructive urges that assailed the Greeks. This sculpture is executed in the Severe style, or the first stage of the Hellenic Classical style, which is evident by the turn of the head to the right. However, its wiglike hair indicates the lingering influence of the Archaic style.*

Figure 3.4 *Dionysus and His Followers. Ca. 430 B.C. Staatliche Museen, Berlin. Scrolling around a perfume vase, this painting depicts a bearded Dionysus seated on the right with his followers. Of his twelve devotees, eleven are maenads, young female revelers; the last is the bearded Silenus, the foster father and former schoolmaster of Dionysus. Silenus is depicted on the lower left in his usual drunken, disorderly state.*

DOMESTIC AND FOREIGN AFFAIRS: WAR, PEACE, AND THE TRIUMPH OF MACEDONIA

On the eve of the Hellenic Age, the Greeks, having defeated the Persians, were united only in their continuing opposition to Persia and in their hostility to any polis that tried to control the others. Although they cooperated on short-term goals that served their common interests, goodwill among the poleis usually evaporated once specific ends were met.

Despite rivalries, the Greek economy expanded. A rising middle class took advantage of the economic opportunities created by the fluctuations of war and politics, causing manufacturing and commerce to flourish. Although the economic base remained agricultural, people increasingly flocked to the polis to make their fortunes, to participate in government, and to find stimulation.

The Hellenic Age can be divided into four distinct phases: (1) the Delian League; (2) wars in Greece and with Persia and the ensuing Thirty Years' Peace; (3) the Peloponnesian War; and (4) Spartan and Theban hegemony and the triumph of Macedonia (Timeline 3.1). While these conflicts raged, life within the polis went on, and in some poleis, notably Athens, extraordinary political, cultural, and intellectual changes were occurring.

After defeating the Persians, the Greeks realized that a mutual defense organization was the key to preventing further Persian attack. In 478 B.C., a number of poleis formed the Delian League, a defensive alliance, with Athens at its head. But Athens soon began to transform the league into an instrument of imperialism. As the oppressive nature of Athenian policies emerged, Athens's independent neighbors became alarmed.

Athenian power, however, was restricted by strained relations with Sparta, by the continuing menace of Persia, and by the highly unstable Delian alliance.

Timeline 3.1 PHASES OF HELLENIC HISTORY   **All dates** B.C.

478	460		431	404		323
Delian League	Wars in Greece and with Persia	Thirty Years' Peace	Peloponnesian War	Spartan and Theban Hegemony		Triumph of Macedonia

When a negotiated settlement finally resolved Persian claims, the Delian League fell apart, leaving Athens vulnerable to its enemies on the Greek mainland. First Thebes and then Sparta led attacks on Athens. The war dragged on, but in 445 B.C., when Sparta unexpectedly withdrew, Athens won a quick victory that forced its enemies to negotiate.

The ensuing Thirty Years' Peace (which lasted only fourteen years) brought the Hellenic Age of Athens to its zenith. Athenian democracy expanded so that even the poorest citizens were empowered with full rights (though women continued to be excluded). Artists and sculptors beautified the Acropolis, and the three great Athenian tragedians—Aeschylus, Sophocles, and Euripides—were active in the drama festivals. Drawing on the Delian treasury, Pericles [PER-uh-kleez], the popular leader and general, launched a glorious building program that was essentially a huge public works project (Figure 3.5). In a speech over Athens's war dead, Pericles offered an eloquent summation of Athenian democracy, praising its use of public debate in reaching decisions, its tolerance of diverse beliefs, its ability to love beauty without sacrificing military strength. His conclusion boasted that Athens was the model for Greece.

However, those poleis that were not enamored of Athenian aggression became convinced that war was the only way to protect themselves. Athens's foreign policy and its expansionism had given rise to an alliance system so delicately balanced that neither side could allow the other to gain the slightest advantage. When Athens's neighbor Corinth went to war with Corcyra (present-day Corfu) in western Greece, Corcyra appealed to Athens for aid. Athens's initial victories frightened Corinth, whose leaders persuaded the Spartans to join together in the Peloponnesian League. The Peloponnesian War (431–404 B.C.) had begun.

Pericles knew the league was superior on land but thought the Athenians could hold out indefinitely within their own walls and win a war of attrition. However, a plague broke out in Athens in 430 B.C., killing many citizens, including Pericles. The first phase of the war ended in 421 B.C., when a demoralized and defeated Athens sued for peace.

Figure 3.5 *Pericles. Ca. 440 B.C. Marble, ht. 19¾". Vatican Museum. Pericles possessed a vision of Athens as the political, economic, and cultural center of the Greek world. Even though this portrait bust is a Roman copy of the Greek original, it conveys Pericles' strong sense of leadership and determination.*

The second half of the Peloponnesian War shifted from the Greek peninsula to distant Sicily and the west—a move that sealed Athens's fate. In 416 B.C., Segesta, a Sicilian polis, begged Athens for military assistance. The Athenians eventually sent help, but in trying to conduct a war so far from home, they were soundly defeated and never recovered their military and economic power.

In the early decades of the fourth century B.C., first Sparta and then Thebes emerged as the preeminent city-state, but these power struggles only further weakened the poleis and made them easy prey for an invader. At the northern edge of the civilized Greek world, that invader was gathering its forces.

Figure 3.6   *Alexander the Great.* Ca. 200 B.C. Marble, ht. 16⅛".
Istanbul Museum. *Alexander's youth and fine features, idealized
perhaps in this portrait bust, add to the legends that have accumulated around one of the most famous conquerors in history. Later
rulers measured themselves against Alexander, whose dream of a
united world was cut short by his early death.*

Macedonia was a primitive Greek state, governed by
kings and populated with a people speaking a rough
dialect of the Greek language. Their king, Philip, having been a hostage in Thebes when young, had become
a *philhellene*—a lover of Greek civilization. A brilliant
soldier, Philip expanded Macedonia to the east as far
as the Black Sea. He then moved southward, conquering the poleis of central Greece. The poleis hastily
raised an army, but Philip's well-disciplined troops
crushed them at Chaeronea in 338 B.C. After establishing a league between Macedonia and the poleis, he
granted the Greeks autonomy in everything except
military affairs. Philip then announced an all-out war
against Persia but was assassinated before he could
launch his first campaign.

Philip's nineteen-year-old son, Alexander, succeeded to the throne. Tutored in philosophy by the
renowned thinker Aristotle, Alexander nevertheless
had the heart of a warrior. When Thebes and other
poleis attempted to take control at Philip's death,
Alexander burned Thebes to the ground, sparing only
the house of the poet Pindar. Placing a general in
command of Greece, Alexander turned his sights to the
east (Figure 3.6).

Alexander dreamed of a world united under his
name and of a culture fused from Hellenic and Persian
roots. His armies marched into Asia Minor, Egypt, and
Mesopotamia, absorbing the great Persian Empire;
then they swept east through Asia to the Indus River in
India. As he conquered, Alexander destroyed and
looted the great centers of Eastern civilization, but he
also founded new cities and spread Greek culture.

Alexander's dream ended abruptly with his death
in 323 B.C. at the age of thirty-two. Seizing the opportunity presented by his sudden death, the Greeks
revolted against the Macedonian oppressors, but
they were quickly overwhelmed. The Macedonians
then occupied Athens and installed an aristocratic
government. Thus ended democracy and Hellenic
civilization—in Greece.

THE PERFECTION OF THE TRADITION: THE GLORY OF HELLENIC GREECE

Throughout this era of shifting political fortunes, artistic and intellectual life flourished. Athens—bursting
with creative energy—was the jewel of the Greek
world. Atop its Acropolis, perfectly proportioned
marble temples gleamed in the brilliant Aegean sun.
Below, in the agora, philosophers debated the most
profound questions of human nature. Hundreds of
citizens congregated outdoors to serve in the assembly,
where they passed laws or sat on juries that made legal
rulings. Other citizens who were at leisure cheered
on the athletes exercising in the open-air gymnasium
(Figure 3.7). During drama festivals, the whole city
turned out to share a gripping tragedy or to laugh up-
roariously at the latest comedy.

The culture that flourished in Greece at this time is
known as **Classic,** or **Classical,** a term with varied
meanings. *Classic* means, first of all, "best" or "preeminent," and the judgment of the Western tradition is
that Greek culture was in fact the highest moment in
the entire history of the humanities. *Classic* also means
having permanent and recognized significance; a classic work establishes a standard against which other
efforts are measured. In this second sense, the aesthetic
values and forms of Greek culture have been studied
and imitated in all later stages of Western history. By
extension, "the classics" are the works that have survived from Greece and Rome.

Classic also refers to the body of specific aesthetic
principles expressed through the art and literature of

Figure 3.7   *Athletes in the Palaestra.* Second quarter of the fifth century B.C. Marble, ht. 12½". National Museum, Athens. *This low-relief sculpture depicts athletes warming up in the open-air exercise area where spectators would congregate to urge on their favorites. The youth on the left is preparing for a foot race, and the one on the right tests his javelin. The pair in the center has just begun to wrestle. This relief was originally part of a sculptured base built into a wall that the Athenians constructed after the Persian Wars.*

Greece and Rome, a system known as **Classicism.** The first stage of Classicism, which originated in the Hellenic Age, emphasized simplicity over complexity; balance, or symmetry, over asymmetry; and restraint over excess. At the heart of Classicism was the search for perfection, for the ideal form—whether expressed in the proportions of a temple constructed in marble or in the canon of the human anatomy molded in bronze or in a philosophical conclusion reached through logic. Hellenic Classicism found expression in many areas: theater, music, history, natural philosophy, architecture, and sculpture.

Theater: Tragedy

One of the most prominent institutions of Greek civilization was the theater, in which the dramatic form known as **tragedy** reached a state of perfection. Greek theater originally arose in connection with the worship of Dionysus. The word *tragedy* in Greek means "goat song," and this word may refer to a prehistoric religious ceremony in which competing male **choruses**—groups of singers—sang and danced, while intoxicated, in homage to the god of wine; the victory prize may have been a sacrificial goat. Whatever its precise origins, during the Archaic Age theater in Athens had taken the form of a series of competitive performances presented annually during the Great Dionysia, celebrated in March.

Features of the Tragic Theater   At first, the chorus served as both the collective actor and the commentator on the events of the drama. Then, in the late sixth century B.C., according to tradition, the poet Thespis—from whose name comes the word *thespian,* or "actor"—introduced an actor with whom the chorus could interact. The theater was born. Initially, the main function of the actor was simply to ask questions of the chorus. During the Hellenic Age, the number of actors was increased to three, and, occasionally, late in the fifth century B.C., a fourth was added. Any number of actors who did not speak might be on the stage, but only the three leading actors engaged in dialogue. In the fifth century B.C., the chorus achieved its classic function as mediator between actors and audience. As time went on, however, the role of the chorus declined and the importance of the actors increased. By the fourth century B.C., the actor had become the focus of the drama.

Because the focus of tragedy was originally the chorus, the need for a space to accommodate their dancing and singing determined the theater's shape. The chorus performed in a circular area called an **orchestra,** or "dancing place," in the center of which was a functioning altar, serving as a reminder that tragedy was a religious rite. The audience sat around two-thirds of the orchestra on wooden bleachers or stone seats under the open sky. The other third of the orchestra was backed by a wooden or stone building

ENCOUNTER

The Representation of Blacks in Greek Art

The Greeks, over the course of their history, encountered other peoples, but their contact with black Africans left the greatest visual legacy. Starting in the Archaic Age, Greek artists created a black type, which became a persistent theme in their tradition. Features that came to characterize the black type in art included black skin, tightly curled hair, broad nose, full lips, and projecting jaw. Once introduced, the black figure flourished for the rest of Greek history (see Figure 4.1) and became part of Roman art. Few life-size statues and heads of the black type have been found, but hundreds of small works, dating from all periods, reflect the enduring popularity of the type, including images on statuettes, vases, engraved gems, coins, lamps, weights, finger rings, earrings, necklaces, and masks.

The Greek word for a black person was *Ethiopian*, a term originally meaning "one with a sun-burned face." As Greeks encountered blacks at home and abroad, the word came to be applied to any dark-skinned person and had no special connection to the land below Egypt.

The black type probably originated in Naucratis, the city founded in Egypt's Nile delta by Greek settlers, in the seventh century B.C. There, artists, impressed by their contacts with black people, may have been the first to portray black figures in Greek art.

A critical date in the evolution of the black type was the arrival in Athens of black troops in the army of Persian king Xerxes in the Persian Wars (479 B.C.). The black type had previously emerged in mainland art, but the large number of blacks in Xerxes' defeated army deeply impressed the Greeks who saw them. Some may eventually have been enslaved and thus became a continuing presence in Greek life. Other blacks also made their way to Greece. Most came as prisoners of war, some as soldiers, diplomats, or members of trade delegations, and a few to study. Many black immigrants held menial positions, but others were soldiers, actors, and athletes.

The portrayal of blacks in Greek art arose from artistic and scientific interest and not from racial prejudice. The Greek world, just as the Roman, was free of color bias, unlike the modern world. The numerous images they created provide striking evidence of contacts between Greeks and black Africans throughout most of Greek history.

Encounter figure 3.1   Attic Head-Vase. 6th–5th centuries B.C. Berlin, Staatliche Museen, F4049. Courtesy Staatliche Museen, Berlin. *The head that forms this vase exhibits the typical features of the black type in Greek art. The vase was fashioned in Athens, sometime between the sixth and fifth centuries B.C.*

Figure 3.8 Theater at Epidauros. Ca. 300 B.C. *The best-preserved theater in Greece is the one at Epidauros. Although tragedy was created only in Athens, the popularity of the art form led to the construction of theaters all over Greece—a telling index of Athens's cultural imperialism. The acoustics in this ancient auditorium were remarkable. Performers' voices could be heard clearly throughout the theater even though it is in the open with fifty-four rows of seats accommodating 14,000 spectators.*

called the *skene,* which could be painted to suggest a scene and through which entrances and exits could be made (Figure 3.8).

Such simple set decorations may have provided a slight bit of realism, but Greek theater was not concerned with either realism or the expressiveness of individual actors. Ideas and language were crucial. The actors—all men, even in the female roles—wore elaborate masks designed to project their voices, platform shoes, and long robes, which helped give the dramas a timeless, otherworldly quality.

Plays were performed in tetralogies (sets of four) on successive days of the Great Dionysia. Each competing playwright offered three tragedies, not necessarily related in theme or subject, that were performed during the day, and a satyr-play that was performed later. A **satyr-play** usually featured the indecent behavior and ribald speech of the satyrs—sexually insatiable half-men, half-goats—who followed Dionysus. That the Greeks liked to watch three deeply serious dramas followed by a play full of obscene high jinks demonstrates the breadth of their sensibility.

Tragic Drama The essence of Greek tragedy is the deeply felt belief that mortals cannot escape pain and sorrow. The dramatists shared with Homer the insight that "we men are wretched things, and the gods . . . have woven sorrow into the very pattern of our lives." Although terrible things happened in the tragedies—murder, incest, suicide, rape, mutilation— the attitude of the play toward these events was deeply moral. Violence for its own sake was not the concern of the playwright, and violence was never depicted onstage.

The tragedies were primarily based on the legends of royal families—usually the dynasties of Thebes, Sparta, and Argos—dating from the Age of Heroes of which Homer sang in his epics (Figure 3.9). Since the audience already knew these stories, their interest focused on the playwright's treatment of a familiar tale, his ideas about its moral significance, and how his language shaped those ideas.

The plots dealt with fundamental human issues with no easy solutions, such as the decrees of the state versus the conscience of the individual or divine law versus human law. Humans were forced to make hard choices without being able to foresee the consequences of their decisions. Nonetheless, the dramatists affirmed that a basic moral order existed underneath the shifting tide of human affairs. The political leaders of Athens recognized and accepted tragedy's ethical significance and educative function and thus made the plays into civic spectacles. For example, the audience was composed of citizens seated according to voting precincts, and Athenian warriors' orphans, who were wards of the polis, were honored at the performances.

According to the Greek philosopher Aristotle, whose immensely influential theory of tragedy, the *Poetics,* was

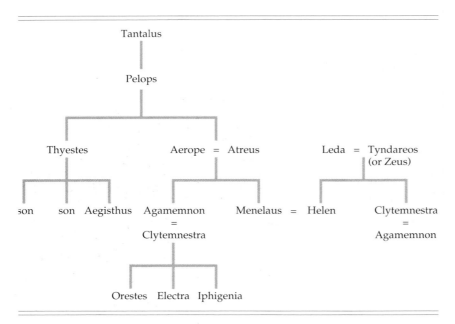

Figure 3.9 Genealogy of the House of Argos. *The tragic fate of the House of Argos (or the family of Atreus) was well under way before the opening scene of Aeschylus's tragedy* Agamemnon. *Thyestes seduced Aerope, the wife of his brother Atreus; in retaliation, Atreus killed Thyestes' two sons and served them to him in a stew. Thyestes then cursed the line of Atreus, and dire consequences followed. Most important, Agamemnon, the son of Atreus, sacrificed his own daughter to gain favorable weather for his planned invasion of Troy. Besides the* Oresteia, *three more tragedies survive that have plots based on the House of Argos—*Iphigenia in Taurus, Iphigenia in Aulis, *and* Electra, *all by Euripides— although they have no inner connection, as does Aeschylus's trilogy.*

based on his study of the dramas of the Hellenic Age, the purpose of tragedy was to work a cathartic, or purging, effect on the audience, to "arouse pity and terror" so that these negative emotions could be drained from the soul. The tragic heroes were warnings, not models; the spectators were instructed to seek modest lives and not aim too high. Many tragedians pursued these themes and competed in the Dionysia, but the works of only three still survive—Aeschylus, Sophocles, and Euripides.

Aeschylus Aeschylus [ES-kuh-luhs] (about 525– about 456 B.C.), the earliest of the three dramatists, won first prize in the Great Dionysia thirteen times. He composed about ninety plays, but only seven are extant. His masterpiece, the *Oresteia,* is the only trilogy that has survived, and even here the satyr-play is missing. The framing plot is the homecoming from Troy of the Greek king Agamemnon, who had sinned by sacrificing his daughter to gain military success; his murder by his vengeful and adulterous wife, Clytemnestra; and the dire consequences of this killing.

Aeschylus's treatment of these terrible events in the *Oresteia* embodies some of the principles of Classicism. In the first place, Aeschylus shows great simplicity by avoiding distracting subplots: The first play, *Agamemnon,* tells the story of the king's death and Clytemnestra's triumph; the second, the *Libation Bearers,* relates the vengeance murder of Clytemnestra by her son, Orestes; and the third, *Eumenides,* halts—with the help of the Olympians Athena and Apollo—the cycle of

revenge by instituting an Athenian court to try such cases. The trilogy is symmetrical in that Agamemnon's murder in the first play serves as punishment for the sacrifice of his daughter, Clytemnestra's death in the second avenges her slaying of Agamemnon, and the courtroom drama of the third absolves Orestes of the crime of matricide.

Finally, Aeschylus shows great restraint inasmuch as all deaths occur offstage, and the chorus or messengers only describe them. However, for the Athenian audience, the *Oresteia* had moral significance as well as stylistic power. By transforming the Furies, the blind champions of vengeance killing, into the "Kindly Ones" (*Eumenides*), Aeschylus, in effect, affirmed the ethical superiority of the rational Olympians over the earthbound chthonian divinities (see Chapter 2). In the *Oresteia,* Aeschylus confronts and resolves the opposition between several seemingly irreconcilable polarities—Olympian and chthonian gods, divine and human justice, religious cult and civic ritual, and fate and free will (Figure 3.10).

Sophocles Sophocles [SOF-uh-kleez] (about 496–406 B.C.), the most prolific of the great tragedians, wrote about 125 plays, but only seven survive. He was popular among the Athenians, who awarded him first prize twenty-four times. Sophocles' *Antigone* (442 B.C.) expresses beautifully the principles of Classical tragedy. The simple plot treats the conflicts between King Creon and his niece Antigone. The principal, although not the sole, philosophical issue explored by the play is whether human or divine law should take precedence.

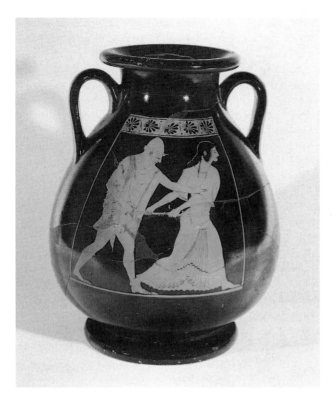 

Figure 3.10 *Orestes Slaying Aegisthus.* Ca. late sixth century B.C. Kunsthistorisches Museum, Vienna. *This red-figure vase painting presents a different version of events in Argos from those given by Aeschylus in the* Libation Bearers, *the second play of the* Oresteia. *The vase painter portrays Clytemnestra bearing an ax (left), a detail Aeschylus omitted, and the sister between Orestes and his mother is not named Electra as she is in the* Oresteia. *However, painter and playwright agree that Orestes killed Aegisthus, his mother's lover.*

Antigone's two brothers have killed each other in a dispute over the Theban crown. Creon decrees that Eteocles, who died defending the city, be buried with honor but that the body of the rebel Polyneices be left as carrion for wild beasts. Antigone, whose name in Greek means "born to oppose," defies his order and buries her brother in compliance with religious teachings. Arrested and imprisoned, Antigone hangs herself, and Creon's son and wife kill themselves. Too late, King Creon sees the light; he gives up his throne saying, "There is no man can bear this guilt but I."

Several tensions are at issue here. Creon represents the typical tyrant, concerned only with "law and order." His son, Haemon, is the voice of democracy, opposing the tyrannical will of his father. Creon believes in the superiority of public power over domestic life, in the necessity of the state to seek power for its own sake, in the priority of war over the commands of love, and in the right of men to control women. When the king tries to persuade his son to renounce his love for the disobedient Antigone, they argue about all four of these issues. Whether the Athenian citizens sided with Creon or Haemon is unknown, but *Antigone* has become the classic example of a tragic dilemma where two rights confront each other. In his desire for balance, Sophocles gives equally powerful arguments to the play's opposing characters.

Sophocles returned to the history of the Theban dynasty in later plays about Antigone's ill-fated father, Oedipus. In *Oedipus the King,* he tells how the Theban ruler unwittingly kills his father and marries his mother and later blinds himself to atone for his guilt. Though fate has a pivotal role in Oedipus's story, the playwright also emphasizes the part the hero's weakness plays in his downfall. Aristotle's *Poetics* held up this work as a model of Greek tragedy. In *Oedipus at Colonus,* his last play, Sophocles portrays the former king at peace with himself and his destiny.

Euripides By the time Euripides [yu-RIP-uh-deez] (about 480–406 B.C.) was writing for the stage, Athens was fighting for its existence in the Peloponnesian War, and with him, the creative phase of Classical theater came to an end. Euripides was in tune with the skeptical mood of the later years of this struggle, and by presenting unorthodox versions of myths and legends, he exposed the foolishness of some popular beliefs and, sometimes, the emptiness of contemporary values. When he staged *The Trojan Women* in 415 B.C., the Athenians could not have missed the parallel between the cruel enslavement of the women of Troy after the Greeks destroyed their city and the fate of the women of Melos, which Athens had just subjugated.

For his ninety or more tragedies (of which eighteen survive), the Athenians awarded the first prize to Euripides only five times, perhaps because his unorthodox plays angered the audience. But later ages, far removed from the stresses of Hellenic times, found his dramas more to their liking. Among the extant works, *The Bacchae* is his masterpiece, a gruesome tale about the introduction of the worship of Dionysus into Thebes. In this play, the bacchae, or bacchantes (another name for the followers of Dionysus), blinded by religious frenzy, kill the king of Thebes under the delusion that he is a wild animal. Euripides' dark tragedy may have been a warning to the citizens of Athens about the dangers of both excess and repression in religion and politics.

Euripides followed Classical principles in *The Bacchae,* using a single plot, offstage violence, and well-defined conflict, but he also extended the range of Classical drama with his unorthodox, even romantic, language and his skeptical treatment of familiar themes. Moreover, Euripides pointed the way toward a different sort of theater by having the severed head of the hero brought onstage at the end of the tragedy.

With Euripides, the creative phase of Classical theater came to an end. The playwrights who followed him seem to have read their works aloud rather than staging them with actors and choruses. The plays of all the Greek dramatists were presented frequently throughout Greece, however, as well as later in the Macedonian and Roman Empires.

Theater: Comedy

Comedies were performed in the Great Dionysia just as the tragedies were, and they were also entered in contests in another festival known as the Lesser Dionysia, celebrated in later winter. The comedies refused to take anyone or anything seriously. They featured burlesque actions, buffoonery, slapstick, obscenity, and horseplay, and actors wore grotesque costumes with padded bellies or rumps to give a ridiculous effect. Comic playwrights invented their own plots and focused on contemporary matters: politics, philosophies, the new

social classes, and well-known personalities. Even the deities were ridiculed and portrayed in embarrassing situations.

The freedom of the comic playwrights could exist only in a democracy. And yet the freedom was limited to a highly ritualized setting—the drama festivals—which allowed, even encouraged, the overturning of rules and the burlesquing of traditions. This controlled expression of the unspeakable provided a catharsis that strengthened communal bonds in the polis. At the same time, the authors demonstrated their faith in the basic good sense of the average citizen.

The comedies of Aristophanes [air-uh-STOF-uh-neez] (about 445–about 388 B.C.) are the primary source for what is known as **Old Comedy,** comic Greek plays with a strong element of political criticism. Aristophanes composed forty-four works in all, of which eleven are extant. Like Euripides, he wrote his plays for war-torn Athens, and he satirized famous contemporaries such as the thinker Socrates, depicting him as a hopeless dreamer. Aristophanes must have stepped on many toes, for the Athenians awarded him first prize only four times.

In *Lysistrata*, Aristophanes transcended the limitations of the comedic form and approached the timeless quality of the tragedies. A sexually explicit and hilarious comedy, *Lysistrata* points out the absurdity of the prolonged Peloponnesian War and, by implication, all war. In the play, Lysistrata, an Athenian matron, persuades the women of Athens and Sparta to withhold sex from their husbands until they sign a peace treaty. Filled with sexual innuendos, obscenities, and ridiculous allusions to tragic dramas, the play ends with stirring reminders to the Greeks of their common ancestry, their joint victory over the Persians earlier in the century, and their reverence for the same gods. First staged in 411 B.C., seven years before Sparta won the Peloponnesian War, this play commented on but failed to derail Athens's headlong rush to disaster (Figure 3.11).

After the Peloponnesian War and the restoration of a harsher democracy in 403 B.C., free speech was severely repressed in Athens. Comedies still relied on burlesque and slapstick, but their political edge was blunted. For all practical purposes, the great creative age of Greek theater was now over.

Music

Like other peoples of the ancient Near East, the Greeks used music both in civic and religious events and in private entertainment. But the Greeks also gave music a new importance, making it one of the humanities along with art, literature, theater, and philosophy. Music became a form of expression subject to rules, styles, and rational analysis. One reason for this was that the Greeks believed music fulfilled an ethical function in the training of young citizens. They also believed that music had divine origins and was inspired by Euterpe, one of the nine muses (thus the word *music*).

Nevertheless, the vast library of Greek music has vanished. What knowledge there is of that lost heritage, which can be only partially reconstructed from surviving treatises on musical theory and references in other writings, shows a tradition that, despite some differences, became the foundation of Western music. Greek music apparently followed the diatonic system, which had been invented by Pythagoras, using a scale of eight notes, each of which was determined by its numerical ratio to the lowest tone. The Greek composers also devised a series of scales, called **modes,** which functioned roughly like major and minor keys in later Western music. The modes, however, were not interchangeable the way keys are, because the Greeks believed that each mode produced a different emotional and ethical effect on the listener. Thus, the Dorian mode, martial and grave in its emotional impact, was thought by the Greeks to make hearers brave and dignified; the tender and sorrowing Lydian mode, to make them sentimental and weak; and the passionate and wild Phrygian mode, to make them excited and headstrong. Believing that such emotional manipulation made free citizens difficult to govern, Plato banished virtually all music from his ideal republic. Modern research has been able to reproduce all the Greek modes, but otherwise this music remains a mystery.

Despite music's high ethical status in Greece, it had no independent role in Hellenic culture. Instead, music was integrated with verse, notably in epic and lyric poetry and in tragedy and comedy, with either the lyre (a stringed instrument) or the aulos (a wind instrument) providing accompaniment.

History

The study of history began in the fifth century B.C., when inquisitive and articulate Greeks started to analyze the meaning of their immediate past and to write down in prose the results of their research, or *historia*—the Greek word for inquiry. The Greeks before the Classical period had only a dim sense of their past; what they knew came from Homer, random artifacts, and the ruins of Mycenaean grandeur. Herodotus [he-ROD-uh-tuhs] (about 484 B.C.–about 430 B.C.) was the first to approach history as a separate study and the first to practice historical writing in anything like the modern sense. He was motivated by the belief that the present had its causes in the past and could be a guide for the future. His *Histories*

Figure 3.11   Detail, Scene from a Comedy. Mid–fourth century B.C. Ht. of vase 15⅔". British Museum. *This scene, painted on a mixing bowl, portrays a situation from a Greek comedy. The actors on the right and left are outfitted in the grotesque costume of comedy with padded rumps and genitals. That these characters are onstage is indicated by the decorations at the bottom of the frame.*

recorded and analyzed the Persian Wars, which Herodotus interpreted as Europe versus Asia, or West versus East. In his desire to be fair to both sides, he traveled to Persia and recorded what he learned there.

The *Histories* have been criticized for implausible and inaccurate information, but Herodotus's clear prose style, his concern for research, his efforts to be impartial, his belief in historical cause and effect, and his desire to leave a record of the past as a legacy to future generations have justly earned him the title "Father of History."

Yet, for all his excellence, Herodotus pales in comparison with Thucydides [thew-SID-uh-deez] (died about 401 B.C.). His subject was the Peloponnesian War, of which he was an eyewitness at times. Thucydides was much more skeptical and inquiring than Herodotus, and although he was an avid democrat and an admirer of Pericles, he strove to be completely fair in his account of Periclean Athens. He saw the weaknesses of his beloved polis and realized the baleful effects of imperialism. In his *History of the Peloponnesian War,* he even wrote objectively of his own role as the losing admiral in a naval battle.

Thucydides also used ordinary events to illuminate human motives and fundamental causes and effects in history. Like the Greek dramatists, he showed that human weaknesses and flaws created the real-life tragedies he observed around him. His insight into human nature was penetrating as he chronicled how individuals shift loyalties and redefine their values to justify their actions.

This masterful writer rose above his narrative to give lessons to future generations, arguing that events that happened in the past would, at some time and in similar ways, recur. Yet he denied that history repeats itself simplistically, and he warned that his book must be read closely and thoughtfully if it was to be understood wisely.

Natural Philosophy

When the Hellenic Age opened, natural philosophy remained divided into two major camps: the materialists and the idealists (see Chapter 2). The materialists, who perpetuated the inquiries of Thales and the Milesian school, believed that the world was made of some basic physical thing. The idealists, in contrast, who stemmed from Pythagoras and the Sicilian school, were nonmaterialists, reasoning that the physical world was illusory and that behind it was a spiritual force or a metaphysical power.

By the mid–fifth century B.C., this simple pattern was being challenged by new philosophies, and by 400 B.C., a revolution in thought had occurred that overshadowed everything that had gone before. The first assault came from Elea, in Sicily, where a new school of thinkers proposed to reconcile materialism and idealism. Then, in Athens, the Sophists questioned philosophical inquiry itself and the notion of absolute truth. These corrosive figures provoked Socrates, the most revolutionary thinker of the entire ancient world, to respond to their claims. Socrates' life is regarded as a watershed in Greek thought. All Greek thinkers before him are now known as Pre-Socratics, and those who came after him—chiefly Plato and Aristotle in Hellenic Greece—followed his lead in studying the human experience (Table 3.1).

The Pre-Socratics   The major pre-Socratic thinkers were concerned with determining the nature of the physical world. For Parmenides [par-MEN-uh-deez] (about 515–? B.C.) and his followers in Elea, for example, the world was a single, unchanging, unmoving object whose order could be known through human reason. This attempt to reconcile materialism and idealism was modified by Parmenides' student Empedocles [em-PED-uh-kleez] (about 484–about 424 B.C.),

Table 3.1 PHILOSOPHY IN THE HELLENIC AGE	
PHILOSOPHY	*EMPHASIS*
Pre-Socratic	The physical world; nature; debate over materialism and idealism
Sophist	Humanistic values; practical skills, such as public speaking and logic
Socratic	Enduring moral and intellectual order of the universe; the psyche (mind/soul); "Virtue is Knowledge"
Platonist	Ideas (Forms) are basis of everything; dualism, the split between the world of Ideas and the everyday world; rationalism; severe moderation in ethics
Aristotelian	Natural world is the only world; empiricism, using observation, classification, and comparison; "golden mean" in ethics

who claimed that everything, animate or inanimate, originated in the four elements of earth, water, fire, and air. These elements were unchanging, but the opposing forces of Love and Strife could combine them in different ways, to the detriment or benefit of humans. This essentially metaphysical explanation of change later influenced Aristotle.

The Atomists, another school of pre-Socratic thinkers, believed that everything was composed of atoms—eternal, invisible bodies of varying size that, by definition, could not be divided into smaller units—and the void, the empty space between the atoms. Atomic theory was developed most fully by Democritus [de-MOK-ruht-us] of Thrace (about 460–? B.C.). The movement and shape of the atoms were sufficient to explain not only physical objects but also feelings, tastes, sight, ideas—in short, every aspect of the physical world.

Anaxagoras [an-ak-SAG-uh-ruhs] (about 500–428 B.C.), although not an Atomist, also explained the world in terms of small particles. His unique contribution was the idea that the combinations and divisions of these particles were controlled by a nonphysical agency he called *nous* (reason or mind). Socrates praised him for the originality of this conception and then faulted him for seeing *nous* only as a mechanical force without religious significance.

The Sophists   The Sophists—from the Greek word *sophia,* or "wisdom"—scorned pre-Socratic speculation about atoms and elements as irrelevant and useless. These traveling teachers claimed to offer their students (for a fee) knowledge that guaranteed success in life. Their emphasis on the development of practical skills, such as effective public speaking, led their critics to accuse them of cynicism and a lack of interest in higher ethical values, but the Sophists were deeply serious and committed to humanistic values. Protagoras [pro-TAG-uh-ruhs] (481–411 B.C.), the most renowned of the Sophists, proclaimed in a dictum that "man is the measure of all things." This summed up the Sophists' argument that human beings, as the center of the universe, have the power to make judgments about themselves and their world. The Sophists helped free the human spirit to be critical and creative. If there was a danger in their teaching, it was a tendency toward unrestrained skepticism. By stressing that human beings had the power to shape the world, the Sophists opened themselves to charges of impiety and undermining traditional values, because the traditional Greek view was that the gods controlled everything.

The Socratic Revolution Socrates [SAH-kruh-teez] (about 470–399 B.C.), the thinker who launched a new era in philosophy, did not hesitate to condemn the Sophists. He claimed to oppose everything they stood for, especially what he thought was the Sophist tendency to overvalue skepticism and thus undermine values without offering new ones in their place. But Socrates shared certain traits with the Sophists, such as his rejection of philosophizing about nature, his focus on human problems, and his desire to empower individuals to make their own moral choices. What basically separated Socrates from the Sophists was his passionate conviction that an enduring moral and intellectual order existed in the universe.

Socrates' method for arriving at true moral and intellectual values was deceptively simple yet maddeningly elusive. At the heart of his thinking was the *psyche* (mind, or soul); being immortal, the psyche was deemed more important than the mortal and doomed body. Those who want wisdom must protect, nourish, and expand their psyches by giving their minds the maximum amount of knowledge, but not just any knowledge. The knowledge the psyche acquired had to be won through stimulating conversations and debates as well as by contemplation of abstract virtues and moral values. Only then could the psyche approach its highest potential.

"Virtue is Knowledge," claimed Socrates; he meant that a person who knows the truth, acquired through personal struggle to self-enlightenment, will not commit evil deeds. And this moral dictum may be reversed: Those who do wrong do so out of ignorance. If people used their psyches to think more deeply and

clearly, they would lead virtuous lives. His belief in the essential goodness of human nature and the necessity of well-defined knowledge became a central tenet of Western thought.

After having pointed out the proper path to wisdom, Socrates left the rest up to his students. Bombarding inquiring youths with questions on such topics as the meaning of justice, he used rigorous logic to refute all the squirming students' attempts at precise definition. Then—as shown by Plato's dialogues, the principal source for what we know about Socrates—the students, collapsing into confusion, admitted the serious gaps in their knowledge. Socrates' step-by-step questions, interspersed with gentle humor and ironic jabs, honed his students' logical skills and compelled them to begin a quest for knowledge in light of their self-confessed ignorance. The Socratic method was adopted by many teachers in Greece and Rome and remains an honored pedagogical device.

The Athenians of this era began to perceive Socrates as a threat to their way of life. This short, homely, and rather insignificant looking man—as surviving statues reveal—aroused suspicion in the polis by his public arguments (Figure 3.12). When Athens fell to the Spartans in 404 B.C., opposition to Socrates began to swell. Many citizens now found subversion or even blasphemy in his words and in the behavior of his followers. Five years after the end of the Peloponnesian War, Socrates was accused of impiety and of corrupting the Athenian youth, and a jury declared him guilty and sentenced him to die. Plato, a former student, was so moved by Socrates' eloquent, though ineffective, defense and by the injustice of his death that the younger man dedicated the remainder of his life to righting the wrong and explaining the Socratic philosophy.

Plato also made Socrates' last days the subject of four works: the *Euthyphro* (a discussion of piety on the eve of his trial), the *Apology* (his defense before the court), the *Crito* (explanation of his willingness to die for his beliefs), and the *Phaedo* (deathbed scene with his argument in support of immortality).

Plato The spirit of Socrates hovers over the rest of Greek philosophy, especially in the accomplishments of his most famous student, Plato (about 427–347 B.C.). Plato's philosophy is the fountainhead of Western **idealism,** a thought system that emphasizes spiritual values and makes ideas, rather than matter, the basis of everything that exists. **Platonism** arose out of certain premises that were Socratic in origin—the concept of the psyche and the theory of remembrance. Like Socrates, Plato emphasized the immortal and immutable psyche over the mortal and changeful body. But Plato advanced a new polarity, favoring the

Figure 3.12 · *Socrates*. Ca. 200 B.C.–A.D. 100. Ht. 10½″. British Museum. *This Roman marble copy of the original Greek statue supports the unflattering descriptions of Socrates by his contemporaries. By portraying the philosopher with a receding hairline and a dumpy body, the anonymous sculptor has made one of the world's most extraordinary human beings look very ordinary.*

invisible world of the Forms, or Ideas, in opposition to the physical world. The psyche's true home was the world of the Forms, which it inhabited before birth and after death—the time when the psyche was lost in wonder among the eternal Ideas. In contrast, the body lived exclusively in the material world, completely absorbed by the life of the senses. Once trapped inside the body, the psyche could glimpse the higher reality, or Forms, only through remembrance.

Nonetheless, Plato thought that through a set of mental exercises the psyche would be able to recall the Ideas to which it had once been exposed. The best training for the psyche was the study of mathematics, since mathematics required signs and symbols to represent other things. After the mastery of mathematics, the student proceeded, with the help of logic, to higher stages of abstract learning, such as defining the Forms of Justice, Beauty, and Love. By showing that wisdom came only after an intellectual progression that culminated in an understanding of the absolute Ideas, Plato silenced the Sophists, who claimed that knowledge was relative.

A major implication of Plato's idealism is that the psyche and the body were constantly at war. The psyche's attempts to remember the lost Ideas meet resistance from the body's pursuit of power, fame, and physical comforts. This dualism especially plagued the philosopher, the lover of wisdom; but the true philosopher took comfort in recognizing that at death the psyche would return freely to the world of the Forms.

Plato identified the Form of the Good, the ultimate Idea, with God, yet the Platonic deity was neither the creator of the world nor the absolute and final power. Instead, Plato's deity was necessary for his idealism to function; in his thought, God was the source from which descended the imperfect objects of the natural world. In a related theological notion, he, like Socrates, attributed the presence of evil to ignorance; but Plato added the psyche's misdirected judgment and insatiable bodily appetites as other causes of evil.

Socrates' death provoked Plato to envision a perfect state where justice flourished. The book that resulted from Plato's speculations—the *Republic*—sets forth his model state and, incidentally, launched the study of political philosophy in the West. Plato thought that a just state could be realized only when all social classes worked together for the good of the whole, each class performing its assigned tasks. Because of the importance of the psyche, social status was determined by the ability to reason and not by wealth or inheritance. A tiny elite of philosopher-kings and -queens, who were the best qualified to run the state, reigned. Possessing wisdom as a result of their education in the Platonic system, they lived simply, shunning the creature comforts that corrupted weaker rulers.

THE PERFECTION OF THE TRADITION

The two lower ranks were similarly equipped for their roles in society by their intellects and their training: A middle group provided police and military protection, and the third and largest segment operated the economy. In Plato's dream world, both the individual and the society aimed for virtue, and the laws and the institutions ensured that the ideal would be achieved.

Aristotle Socrates may have been revolutionary; Plato was certainly poetic; but Aristotle [AIR-uh-stot-uhl] (384–322 B.C.) had the most comprehensive mind of the ancient world. His curiosity and vast intellect led him into every major field of inquiry of his time except mathematics and music. Born in Macedonia, he was connected to some of the most glittering personalities of his day. He first studied philosophy under Plato in Athens and then tutored the future Alexander the Great back at Philip's court. After Philip's conquest of Greece, Aristotle settled in Athens and opened a school, the Lyceum, that quickly rivaled the Academy, the school Plato had established.

Although his philosophy owed much to Platonism, Aristotle emphasized the role of the human senses. To Aristotle, the natural world was the only world; no separate, invisible realm of Ideas existed. Nature could be studied and understood by observation, classification, and comparison of data from the physical world—that is, through the empirical method.

Aristotle rejected the world of the Forms because he believed that Form and Matter were inseparable, both rooted in nature. Each material object contained a predetermined Form that, with proper training or nourishment, would evolve into its final Form and ultimate purpose. This growth process, in his view, was potentiality evolving into actuality, as when an embryo becomes a human or a seed matures into a plant. Thus, the philosopher could conclude that everything had a purpose, or end.

Aristotle's thought rested on the concept of God, which he equated with the First Cause. Aristotle's God was a philosopher's deity, purely rational, self-absorbed, and uncaring about the world or its inhabitants. Had this deity been anything else, Aristotle's God would not have been the supreme power or First Cause.

Rejecting Platonic dualism and its exclusive regard for the psyche, Aristotle devised a down-to-earth ethical goal—a sound mind in a healthy body—that he called happiness. To achieve happiness, he advised, in his *Nicomachean Ethics,* striking a mean, or a balance, between extremes of behavior. For example, courage is the mean between the excess of foolhardiness and the deficiency of cowardice. Noting that actions like murder and adultery are vicious by their very nature, he

condemned them as being unable to be moderated. Although Aristotle disavowed many of Plato's ideas, he agreed with his former mentor that the cultivation of the higher intellect was more important than that of the body.

Aristotle's ethics are related to his politics, for he taught that happiness finally depended on the type of government under which an individual lived. Unlike Plato, who based his politics on speculative thinking, Aristotle reached his political views after careful research. After collecting over 150 state constitutions, Aristotle, in his *Politics,* classified and compared them, concluding that the best form of government was a constitutional regime ruled by the middle class. His preference for the middle class stemmed from his belief that they, exciting neither envy from the poor nor contempt from the wealthy, would honor and work for the good of all.

Aristotle's influence on Western civilization is immeasurable. His writings formed the core of knowledge that Christian scholars later studied as they struggled to keep the light of civilization burning after the collapse of the Roman Empire. Likewise, Jewish and Moslem thinkers ranked his books just below their own religious scriptures. Today, Aristotelianism is embedded in the official theology of the Roman Catholic Church, and Aristotle's logic continues to be taught in college philosophy courses.

Architecture

Of all the Greek art forms, architecture most powerfully embodied the Classical ideals of the Hellenic Age. The stone temple, the supreme expression of the Hellenic building genius, now received its definitive shape. Ironically, the Doric temple, which had originated in the Archaic Age, reached perfection in Ionian Athens. The versatile Athenians also perfected a new architectural order, the **Ionic,** which reflected more clearly their cultural tradition.

Sanctuaries Before there were temples, however, Greece had sanctuaries, places considered sacred to a god or goddess. Of these sacred places, Apollo's shrine at Delphi was the oldest and the most famous (Figure 3.13). Delphi, thought to be the center of the earth, was hallowed ground to the entire Greek world, and the major poleis supported the god's priesthood there. Apollo's temple was the most splendid building on the site. Inside was Apollo's oracle—the only woman permitted at Delphi—to whom people journeyed from all over Greece with their questions.

With the rise of the poleis, the concept of a holy place set aside from the business of everyday life was

Figure 3.13   The Delphic Sanctuary. Aerial view. Late sixth century–late fourth century B.C. *The ruins of Apollo's temple—this is an active earthquake zone—are marked by a rectangular foundation and a few standing columns. A Sacred Way, or road, zigzagged up the mountain to the temple's entrance. During the fourth century* B.C., *a gymnasium for boys and a theater were established in the sanctuary, and a stadium was constructed for athletic contests.*

adapted to the religious needs of each community. By the Hellenic Age, each polis had its own sacred area, usually built on a hill or protected by walls, which contained buildings and altars. Although each polis worshiped the entire pantheon of deities, one god or goddess was gradually singled out as a patron, and a temple was erected to house the statue of that particular divinity.

The Temple: The Perfection of the Form   By Hellenic times, the Greek world was polarized between eastern (the mainland and the Aegean Islands) and western (Magna Graecia) styles of temple design, although in both styles the temples were rectilinear and of post-beam-triangle construction. Influenced by the Pythagorean quest for harmony through mathematical rules, the eastern builders had standardized six as the perfect number of columns for the ends of temples and thirteen, or twice the number of end columns plus one, as the perfect number of columns for the sides. These balanced proportions, along with simple designs and restrained decorative schemes, made the eastern temples majestically expressive of Classical ideals.

Architects in western Greece, somewhat removed from the centers of Classical culture, were more experimental. Their buildings deviated from the eastern ideals, as can be seen in the Second Temple of Hera at Poseidonia, built of limestone in about 450 B.C. (Figure 3.14). The best preserved of all Greek temples, this Doric structure does not have the harmonious proportions of the eastern version of this style. Although the Second Temple of Hera owed much to eastern influences, including the six columns at the ends and the porches, it had too many (fourteen) columns on the sides, its columns were too thick, and the low-pitched roof made the building seem squat.

Between 447 and 438 B.C., the architects Ictinus [ik-TIE-nuhs] and Callicrates [kuh-LICK-ruh-teez] perfected the eastern-style Doric temple in the Parthenon, a temple on Athens's Acropolis dedicated to Athena (Figure 3.15). When completed, this temple established a new standard of Classicism, with eight columns on the ends and seventeen on the sides and with the numerical ratio of 9:4 used throughout, expressed, for example, in the relation of a column's height to its diameter. Inside, the builders designed two chambers, an east room for a 40-foot-high statue of Athena and a smaller room housing the Delian League treasury. The rest of the Acropolis project, finally finished in 405 B.C., included the Propylaea, the gate leading to the sanctuary; the temple of Athena Nike, a gift to Athens's patron goddess thanking her for a military victory (Figure 3.16); and the Erechtheum, a temple dedicated to three deities.

Figure 3.14 Second Temple of Hera at Poseidonia. Ca. 450 B.C. Limestone. *This temple of Hera is among the best-preserved structures from the ancient world. Since Hera may have been a chthonian goddess before becoming consort to Olympian Zeus, it is appropriate that this Doric temple, with its ground-hugging appearance, be her monument.*

Figure 3.15 ICTINUS AND CALLICRATES. The Parthenon. Third quarter of the fifth century B.C. Pentelic marble. Athens. *A great humanistic icon, the Parthenon has had a long history since its days as a Greek temple. It served successively as a Christian church, a mosque, and an ammunitions depot, until it was accidentally blown up at the end of the seventeenth century A.D. Today, concerned nations are cooperating with the Greek government through UNESCO to preserve this noble ruin.*

PERSONAL PERSPECTIVE

XENOPHON
Secrets of a Successful Marriage

Xenophon (ca. 445–355 B.C.) was a Greek military commander, historian, essayist, and student of Socrates. In this selection from Oeconomicus, *he expounds on the secrets of a successful marriage through the characters of Socrates and Ischomachus, a rich landowner.*

I [Socrates] said, "I should very much like you to tell me, Ischomachus, whether you yourself trained your wife to become the sort of woman that she ought to be, or whether she already knew how to carry out her duties when you took her as your wife from her father and mother."

[Ischomachus replied,] "What could she have known when I took her as my wife, Socrates? She was not yet fifteen when she came to me, and had spent her previous years under careful supervision so that she might see and hear and speak as little as possible. . . .

"[A]s soon as she was sufficiently tamed and domesticated so as to be able to carry on a conversation, I questioned her more or less as follows: 'Tell me, wife, have you ever thought about why I married you and why your parents gave you to me? It must be quite obvious to you, I am sure, that there was no shortage of partners with whom we might sleep. I, on my part, and your parents, on your behalf, considered who was the best partner we could choose for managing an estate and for children. And I chose you, and your parents, apparently, chose me, out of those who were eligible. Now if some day the god grants us children, then we shall consider how to train them in the best way possible. For this will be a blessing to us both, to obtain the best allies and support in old age. But at present we two share this estate. I go on paying everything I have into the common fund; and you deposited into it everything you brought with you. There is no need to calculate precisely which of us has contributed more, but to be well aware of this: that the better partner is the one who makes the more valuable contribution. . . .

"'Because both the indoor and the outdoor tasks require work and concern, I think the god, from the very beginning, designed the nature of woman for the indoor work and concerns and the nature of man for the outdoor work. For he prepared man's body and mind to be more capable of enduring cold and heat and travelling and military campaigns, and so he assigned the outdoor work to him. Because the woman was physically less capable of endurance, I think the god has evidently assigned the indoor work to her. . . .

"'Because it is necessary for both of them to give and to take, he gave both of them equal powers of memory and concern. So you would not be able to distinguish whether the female or male sex has the larger share of these. And he gave them both equally the ability to practise self-control too, when it is needed. . . . [B]ecause they are not equally well endowed with all the same natural aptitudes, they are consequently more in need of each other, and the bond is more beneficial to the couple, since one is capable where the other is deficient.'"

Ictinus and Callicrates introduced many subtle variations, called refinements, into their designs, so that no line is exactly straight, horizontal, or perpendicular. For example, the stepped base of the temple forms a gentle arc so that the ends are lower than the middle; the floor slopes slightly to the edges; and the columns tilt inward away from the ends. These and other refinements were no accidents but were intended to be corrections for real and imaginary optical illusions. The Parthenon's fame exerted such authority in later times that these refinements, along with harmonious proportions, became standardized as the essence of Greek architecture.

The second order of Greek architecture, the Ionic, originated in the late Archaic Age and, like the Doric, came to flower in Hellenic times. The Ionic style, freer than the Doric and more graceful, reflected its origins in the Ionian world; traditionally, the Ionians contrasted their opulence with the simplicity of the Dorians. In place of the alternating metopes and triglyphs of Doric buildings, the Ionic temple had a running frieze to which sculptured figures might be added. More decorated than the plain Doric, the Ionic columns had elegant bases, and their tops were crowned with capitals that suggested either a scroll's ends or a ram's horns. What solidified the Ionic temple's impression of elegance were its slender and delicate columns.

The Athenians chose the Ionic style for the exquisite, though eccentric, Erechtheum, the last of the great buildings erected on the Acropolis (Figure 3.17). The artistic freedom associated with the Ionic style may have led the architect, Mnesicles [NES-uh-kleez], to make the floor plan asymmetrical and to introduce so many design variations, but a more likely explanation

Figure 3.16 CALLICRATES. Temple of Athena Nike. Late fifth century B.C. Marble. Athens. *Designed by Callicrates, one of the Parthenon's architects, this miniature temple was begun after 427 B.C. and probably completed before 420 B.C. Like the Parthenon, it was dedicated to the city's patron goddess, Athena, though here she was honored as Nike, goddess of victory. This temple's simple plan includes a square cella with four Ionic columns at the front and back and a sculptural frieze, devoted to scenes of mythic and contemporary battles, encircling the upper exterior walls.*

was Mnesicles' need to integrate three existing shrines into a single building—those of the Olympians Athena and Poseidon and King Erechtheus, who introduced the horse to Athens. Mnesicles took the unusual step of stressing the site's unbalanced nature by adding two Ionic porches and the temple's crowning feature, the Porch of the Maidens. By his bold design, Mnesicles created a marvelous illusion of harmony that was in keeping with the age's Classical ideals.

Sculpture

Equally impressive is the Greek achievement in sculpture. Believing that the task of sculpture was to imitate nature, the Greeks created images of gods and goddesses as well as of men and women that have haunted the Western imagination ever since. They not only forged a canon of idealized human proportions that later sculptors followed but also developed a repertoire of postures, gestures, and subjects that have become embedded in Western art.

During the Hellenic Age, Classical sculpture moved through three separate phases: the **Severe style,** which ushered in the period and lasted until 450 B.C.; the **High Classical style,** which coincided with the zenith of Athenian imperial greatness; and the **Fourth Century style,** which concluded with the death of Alexander the Great in 323 B.C.

Sculpture in the Severe style, inspired perhaps by its association with funeral customs, was characterized by a feeling of dignified nobility. The *Kritios Boy*—showing a figure fully at rest—is an elegant expression of this

Figure 3.17 MNESICLES. The Erechtheum. View from the west. Ca. 410 B.C. Marble. Athens. *The Erechtheum was probably built to quiet conservatives who rejected Athena's new temple, the Parthenon, as a symbol of Athenian imperialism. Reflecting its ties with the past, the Erechtheum housed the ancient wooden cult statue of Athena, which pious Athenians believed had fallen from the sky. Its Ionic porches set the standard for the graceful Ionic order. The Porch of the Maidens (right), which was inaccessible from the outside, fronted the southern wall.*

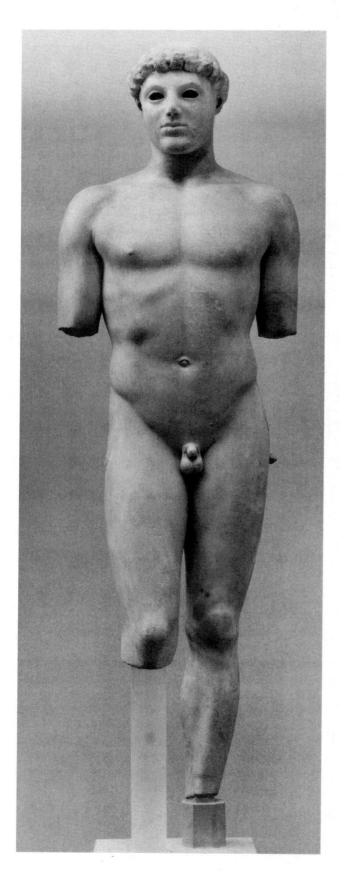

Figure 3.18 *Kritios Boy.* Ca. 480 B.C. Ht. 33". Acropolis Museum, Athens. *This statue is carved from marble probably mined at Mt. Pentelicus in Attica. Two features—the treatment of the eyes, which were originally set with semiprecious stones, and the roll of hair—show that the Kritios sculptor was accustomed to working in bronze. The figure's beautifully rendered muscles and sense of inner life announce the arrival of the Hellenic style; the contrapposto, used sparingly here, foreshadows later developments in Greek sculpture.*

first phase of Classicism (Figure 3.18). Kritios [KRIT-ee-uhs], the supposed sculptor, fixed the mouth severely and altered the frontality, a feature of the Archaic style, by tilting the head subtly to the right and slightly twisting the upper torso. The flat-footed stance of the Archaic *kourai* has given way to a posture that places the body's weight on one leg and uses the other leg as a support. This stance is called **contrapposto** (counterpoise), and its invention, along with the mastery of the representation of musculature, helped to make the Classical revolution (Figure 3.19). Thereafter, sculptors were able to render the human figure in freer and more relaxed poses.

The central panel of the so-called Ludovisi Throne, another sculpture from the same period, conveys an air of quiet gravity (Figure 3.20). The subject is probably the birth of Aphrodite as she rises from the sea, indicated by pebbles under the feet of her attendants, the stooping figures on either side. This relief reflects a perfect blending of late Archaic grace (Aphrodite's stylized hair and the hint of Archaic smile) with the dignity of the Severe style (the delicate transparent draperies and the convincing realism produced by foreshortening the arms of the three figures).

In contrast to the Severe style, which accepted repose as normal, the High Classical style was fascinated with the aesthetic problem of showing motion in a static medium. The sculptors' solution, which became central to High Classicism, was to freeze the action, resisting the impulse to depict agitated movement, in much the same way that the tragic playwrights banished violence from the stage. In effect, the High Classical sculptors stopped time, allowing an ideal world to emerge in which serene gods and mortals showed grace under pressure. A striking representation of this aspect of High Classicism is the bronze statue of Poseidon or Zeus, found in the Aegean Sea off Cape Artemision. It captures to perfection High Classicism's ideal of virile grace (Figure 3.21). The mature god, signified by the beard and fully developed body, is shown poised, ready to hurl some object. In such sculptures as this, the Greeks found visual metaphors for their notion that deities and mortals are kin.

Figure 3.19 *Torso of Miletus. Ca. 480–470 B.C. Marble, ht. 4'4". Louvre. The torso is all that survives from a formerly life-size statue. Scars and plaster residue indicate that it was damaged and restored in antiquity. Although little is known of its origins and first use, the statue eventually was installed in a Roman theater in Miletus, Asia Minor. The torso shows the transition from the Archaic style, marked by frontality and nudity, to Classicism, characterized by well-defined musculature and the hint of contrapposto in the lightly flexed hips.*

Figure 3.20 *The Birth of Aphrodite (?). Ca. 460 B.C. Ht. 2'9". Terme Museum, Rome. The Ludovisi Throne, with its three relief panels, is a controversial work, because scholars disagree about its original function, the interpretation of its panels, and even its date. Discovered in Rome in the late nineteenth century, it probably was carved in Magna Graecia, perhaps for an altar, and brought to Rome in antiquity. The figure of Aphrodite was one of the first naked women depicted in large-scale Greek sculpture. The goddess is rendered in softly curving lines—a marked deviation from the Severe style and a forecast of the sensuous tendency of later Greek art.*

Figure 3.21 *Poseidon* (or *Zeus*). Ca. 460–450 B.C. Bronze, ht. 6'10". National Museum, Athens. *The nobility of the Greek conception of their gods is nowhere better revealed than in this magnificent bronze sculpture of Poseidon (or Zeus). Grace, strength, and intellect are united in this majestic image of a mature deity. Poseidon's eyes originally would have been semiprecious stones, and the statue would have been painted to create a more realistic effect.*

High Classical sculptors wanted to do more than portray figures in motion; some, most especially Polykleitos [pol-e-KLITE-uhs] of Argos, continued to be obsessed with presenting the ideal human form at rest. In his search for perfection, Polykleitos executed a bronze male figure of such strength and beauty—the *Doryphoros*, or *Spearbearer*—that its proportions came to be regarded as a canon, or set of rules, to be imitated by other artists (Figure 3.22). In the *Doryphoros* canon, each of the limbs bears a numerical relation to the body's overall measurements; for example, the length of the foot is one-tenth of the figure's height. Other principles of High Classicism embodied in the *Doryphoros* include the slightly brutal facial features, which were typical of this style's masculine ideal; the relaxed contrapposto; and the controlled muscles.

Greek architecture reached its zenith in the Parthenon, and, similarly, Classical Greek sculpture attained its height in the reliefs and sculptures of this celebrated temple. Under the disciplined eye of the sculptor Phidias [FIHD-e-uhs], craftspeople carved patriotic and mythological subjects destined for various parts of the building. Taken as a whole, the sculptures revealed the Parthenon to be a tribute to Athenian imperialism as much as to the goddess Athena (Figure 3.23).

On the Parthenon's metopes—the rectangular spaces on the Doric frieze—sculptors portrayed scenes in the prevailing High Classical style. In panel after panel, the metope sculptors depicted perfect human forms showing restraint in the midst of struggle, such as Amazons against men, Greeks against Trojans, and gods against giants. The south metopes portrayed the battle between the legendary Lapiths and the half-men, half-horse Centaurs (Figure 3.24). For the Greeks, the struggle between the human Lapiths and the bestial Centaurs symbolized the contest between civilization and barbarism or, possibly, between the Greeks and the Persians.

Inside the columns, running around the perimeter of the upper cella walls in a continuous band, was a low-relief frieze. Borrowed from the Ionic order, this running frieze introduced greater liveliness into High

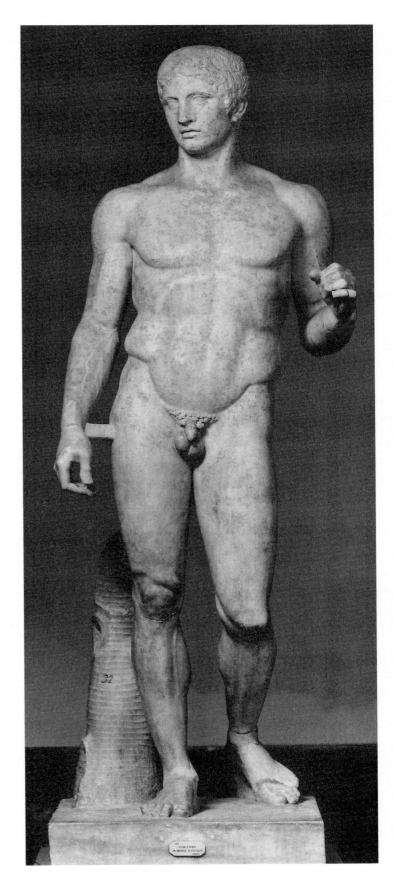

Figure 3.22 *Doryphoros*. Ca. 440 B.C. Marble copy of a bronze original by Polykleitos, ht. 6'6". Museo Nazionale Archeologico, Naples. *The* Doryphoros *expresses the classical ideal of balanced repose. The nude figure rests his weight upon the right leg. The left arm, extended to hold the now missing spear, balances with the right leg. The left foot, barely touching the ground, balances with the relaxed right arm. Besides representing idealized repose, the* Doryphoros *was also recognized as the embodiment of human beauty with its ordered proportions, well-toned musculature, and rugged features.*

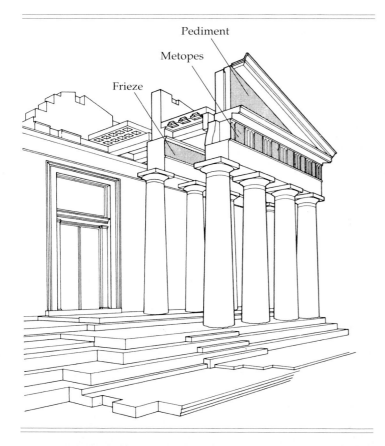

Pediment

Metopes

Frieze

Figure 3.23   The Location of the Sculptures on the Parthenon. *This cutaway view shows the metopes, Ionic frieze, and pediments of the Parthenon, which were covered with sculptures celebrating the glory of Athens.*

Classicism. The 525-foot-long band is filled with hundreds of men and women, walking and riding horses, along with sacrificial animals for Athena and the rest of the Olympians. The subject of this vivid scene is the procession of the Great Panathenaea festival, Athens's most important civic and religious ritual, which was held every four years. This panoramic view of the thrilling procession concluded with a stunning group portrait of the twelve gods and goddesses, seated in casual majesty, awaiting their human worshipers. In one scene, a bearded Poseidon taps the shoulder of Apollo, which causes him to turn, while Artemis, at the right, absentmindedly adjusts her robe (Figure 3.25). Their tranquil faces, their sense of inner life, and the prevailing calm are the marks of mature Classicism. The entire Parthenon frieze was the most ambitious work of sculpture in the Greek tradition.

The transition to Fourth Century style coincided with the end of the creative phase of tragedy and the

Figure 3.24   *Centaur Versus Lapith.* Metope XXX, south face of the Parthenon. Ca. 448–442 B.C. Marble, ht. 56". British Museum. *This struggling pair was designed to fit comfortably into the metope frame, and thus the proportions of the figures in relation to each other and to the small space were worked out with precision. The intertwined limbs of the warrior and the Centaur visibly demonstrate the new freedom of High Classicism. The anguished countenance of the Lapith, however, is almost unique in High Classicism and is a portent of the more emotional faces of the Hellenistic style, the next major artistic development.*

Figure 3.25 *Poseidon, Apollo, and Artemis*. Parthenon frieze. Ca. 448–442 B.C. Marble, ht. 43". Acropolis Museum, Athens. *The Hellenic style always stressed the human dimension of the Greek gods and goddesses, embodying Homer's claim that gods and humans are of the same race. In this section of the Parthenon frieze, the Homeric deities are resplendent in their beautiful bodies and are calmly serene.*

disintegration of the Greek world as it passed into the Macedonian political orbit. Sculpture remained innovative, since each generation seemed to produce a master who challenged the prevailing aesthetic rules, and free expression continued as a leading principle of Fourth Century style. But sculptors now expressed such new ideas as beauty for its own sake and a delight in sensuality. Earlier Classicism had stressed the notion that humans could become godlike, but the last phase concluded that gods and mortals alike reveled in human joys.

This new focus is apparent in Praxiteles' [prax-SIT-uhl-eez] *Hermes with the Infant Dionysus*. This sculpture, perhaps the only original work by a known sculptor that survives from Hellenic Greece, portrays two gods blissfully at play (Figure 3.26). Hermes, lounging in a casual yet dignified pose, probably dangled grapes before the attentive baby god. The contrapposto posture, beautifully defined in Hermes' stance, became widely imitated as the **Praxitelean curve.** Hermes' sensuous body, his intent gaze, and his delicate features are hallmarks of Fourth Century Classicism; by the next generation Praxiteles' treatment of the male figure had superseded the more rugged *Doryphoros* canon.

Figure 3.26 PRAXITELES. *Hermes with the Infant Dionysus*. Ca. 350–340 B.C. Marble, ht. 85". Olympia Museum. *In this statue of Hermes, Praxiteles changed the look of Classical art with his rendering of the god's body. For example, Hermes' small head and long legs contributed to the Praxitelean canon for the male figure. The sculptor has also created a dramatic contrast between Hermes' well-muscled body and his soft face. As a direct result of Praxiteles' new vision, sculptors in the Hellenistic Age became interested in more frankly sensual portrayals of the human figure, both male and female.*

The Legacy of Hellenic Civilization

Although Athens failed in its dream of political mastery of Greece, the Athenian miracle so impressed its contemporaries that Athenian culture dominated the Hellenic Age. Tragic poets, comic playwrights, and natural philosophers made the Athenian dialect the medium of expression for poetry and prose. The buildings on the Acropolis expressed visually the purity and restraint of the Athenian style. And Athenian democracy, which served as the exciting teacher of its citizens, was the envy of most of the other Greek poleis. After the fall of Greece to Macedonia, however, the idea of democracy fell into disrepute. Almost two thousand years passed before some in Europe were ready to give democracy a second chance.

But **humanism,** the other great creation of Athens, survived as a guide to refined living for the cultivated classes in the West. Athenian culture became the heart of the educational curriculum that was followed in Hellenistic civilization; that model was adopted by Rome and transmitted in the humanistic tradition to Europe. In time, the study and the practice of humanistic learning—literature, philosophy, theater, music, and the arts and architecture—became the crowning glory of Western civilization, affecting private individuals and entire societies.

Moreover, Classicism—the style of humanistic achievements in the Hellenic Age—had three great effects on the Western tradition. First, the principles of Greek Classicism—balance, simplicity, and restraint—set the standard by which the styles of other times are often measured. Second, the actual works of Classicism became basic building blocks of Western culture. In the realm of thought, the works of Plato and Aristotle quickly acquired a luster of authority and retained it until the seventeenth century A.D. Aristotle's literary criticism created a new writing genre, and his analysis of tragedy made this type of play the ultimate challenge to ambitious writers. The Greek tragedies themselves—of Aeschylus, Sophocles, and Euripides—are thought by many to be unsurpassed.

The comic plays of Aristophanes are less well known today, but their spirit still lives in period comedies and contemporary political satire. The histories of Herodotus and Thucydides retain their vitality as important sources for their respective eras, although modern research has cast doubt on some of their conclusions. Among Greece's accomplishments, architecture has had the most potent effect; the ruins on the Athenian Acropolis and elsewhere are eternal reminders of this Greek heritage. Finally, the idealized statues of men and women, such as the *Doryphoros*, have inspired Western artists with their vision of noble beings alert to the rich possibilities of human life.

The third and perhaps most important contribution of Classicism to the Western tradition was a skeptical spirit that was rooted in democracy. By asserting that the purpose of human life can best be realized in cities that are shaped by the citizens' needs, as Athenian humanism claimed, the humanists declared war on all tyrants, hierarchical societies, and divinely ordered states—in other words, the prevailing order of the ancient world. Because of this critical aspect of humanism, the Greek heritage has sometimes been called into question and, during repressive periods, been subjected to attack. However, the passion for questioning, for inquiry, which characterizes the skeptical spirit, is at the core of Western consciousness.

KEY CULTURAL TERMS

Hellenic

maenad

Dionysia

Classic (Classical)

Classicism

tragedy

chorus

orchestra

skene

satyr-play

Old Comedy

modes

idealism

Platonism

Ionic

Severe style

High Classical style

Fourth Century style

contrapposto

Praxitelean curve

humanism

SUGGESTIONS FOR FURTHER READING

Primary Sources

AESCHYLUS. *Oresteia.* Translated by R. Fagles. New York: Penguin, 1986. A good modern version of the only dramatic trilogy that survives from ancient Greece.

ARISTOPHANES. *Lysistrata.* Translated by J. Henderson. New York: Oxford University Press, 1987. This modern version captures the antiwar spirit and bawdy humor of the original comedy.

EURIPIDES. *The Bacchae and Other Plays.* Translated by P. Vellacott. New York: Penguin, 1972. An excellent collection of Euripides' dramas, in each of which strong-minded women play major roles.

HERODOTUS. *The Histories*. Translated by A. de Sélincourt. New York: Penguin, 1972. Prefaced with an informative introduction, this translation captures both the language and the narrative of the first history book in Western literature.

KAPLAN, J., ed. *The Pocket Aristotle*. New York: Washington Square Press, 1966. Edited selections from the *Physics*, the *Nicomachean Ethics, Politics,* and *Poetics* give a sense of Aristotle's method of inquiry.

ROUSE, W. H. D., trans. *Great Dialogues of Plato*. New York: New American Library, 1963. Includes the full text of the *Republic*, the *Apology, Phaedo,* and the *Symposium.*

SOPHOCLES. *The Theban Plays*. Translated by E. F. Watling. New York: Penguin, 1974. The three plays about the misfortunes of King Oedipus and his family; includes *Oedipus Rex* and *Antigone.* Unlike Aeschylus's Oresteian trilogy, Sophocles' Theban plays do not constitute a unified work; each was originally performed with other plays (now lost).

THUCYDIDES. *The Peloponnesian War*. Translated by R. Warner. New York: Penguin, 1970. A translation that captures the sweep and drama of the original.

CHAPTER 3 HIGHLIGHTS
Classical Greek Civilization: The Hellenic Age

9 B.C.

HELLENIC GREECE

AESCHYLUS, *Oresteia* (458 B.C.)

SOPHOCLES, *Antigone* (442 B.C.)

HERODOTUS, *Histories* (after 430 B.C.)

SOPHOCLES, *Oedipus Rex* (ca. 429 B.C.)

EURIPIDES, *The Trojan Women* (415 B.C.)

ARISTOPHANES, *Lysistrata* (411 B.C.)

THUCYDIDES, *History of the Peloponnesian War* (ca. 410 B.C.)

SOPHOCLES, *Oedipus at Colonus* (401 B.C.)

PLATO, *Republic* (first half of fourth century B.C.)

PLATO, *Phaedo* (first half of fourth century B.C.)

ARISTOTLE, *Nicomachean Ethics* (last half of fourth century B.C.)

ARISTOTLE, *Poetics* (last half of fourth century B.C.)

ARISTOTLE, *Politics* (last half of fourth century B.C.)

3.2 *Athena Parthenos* (fifth century B.C.)

3.18 *Kritios Boy* (ca. 480 B.C.)

3.19 *Torso of Miletus* (ca. 480–470 B.C.)

3.3 *Apollo* (ca. 460 B.C.)

3.20 *Birth of Aphrodite (?)* (ca. 460 B.C.)

3.21 *Poseidon* or *Zeus* (ca. 460–450 B.C.)

3.14 Second Temple of Hera at Poseidonia (ca. 450 B.C.)

3.24 *Centaur Versus Lapith* (ca. 448–442 B.C.)

3.25 *Poseidon, Apollo, and Artemis* (ca. 448–442 B.C.)

3.15 ICTINUS and CALLICRATES, the Parthenon (third quarter of fifth century B.C.)

3.22 *Doryphoros* (ca. 440 B.C.)

3.1 *Torch Race* (ca. 430–420 B.C.)

3.16 CALLICRATES, Temple of Athena Nike (late fifth century B.C.)

3.17 MNESICLES, Erechtheum (ca. 410 B.C.)

3.26 PRAXITELES, *Hermes with the Infant Dionysus* (ca. 350–340 B.C.)

3.8 Theater at Epidauros (ca. 300 B.C.)

3.6 *Alexander the Great* (ca. 200 B.C.)

3.12 *Socrates* (ca. 200 B.C.–A.D. 100)

3 B.C.

Literature & Philosophy   Art & Architecture   Music & Dance

 Readings in the Western Humanities

AFRICA

AMERICAS

HISTORY

Northeast Africa *Nubian culture, ca. 2000 B.C.–A.D. 350.* Capital Meroë (in modern Sudan); important trade and iron-working center.

West Africa *Nok culture, began 500 B.C.* Well-organized economy and administrative system in northern and central Nigeria; first people in sub-Saharan Africa to make iron tools and weapons. Influenced neighbors in the region.

Mesoamerica *Olmec culture.* Last phase: decline followed by collapse (400 B.C.), for reasons unknown.

Andes *Chavín culture.* Final phase: noted for improved maize and the back-strap loom; spread along coastal Peru.

Native North America *Adena culture, ca. 600 B.C.–A.D. 200.* Ohio Valley; hunter-gatherers with trade network from Canada to Florida.

ART

West Africa *Nok culture.* Terra-cotta heads characterized black Africa's first known sculptural tradition, from ca. 500 B.C.

Jemaa Head. Ca. fifth century B.C. Tsauni Camp, Jemaa. Terra-cotta, ht. 9¹³⁄₁₆". Lagos National Museum.

Mesoamerica *Olmec culture.* Carved stone figures depicting rain god with jaguar or "howling baby" features.

Andes *Chavín culture.* Gold work (in use since ca. 1900 B.C.) for cult objects and as prestige body art for the elite.

Native North America *Adena culture.* Simple pottery, carved pipes, ornaments of copper, mica, and seashells.

Olmec Statue of Priest with Supernatural "Infant." Ca. 600 B.C. Greenstone. Museo de Antropologia de la Universidad Veracruzana, Xalapa, Mexico.

ARCHITECTURE

Northeast Africa *Nubian culture.* About 300 pyramid tombs survive near ancient Meroë, a Kushan city of mud-brick palaces, temples, houses, and baths.

Andes *Chavín culture.* Deliberately disorienting architectural style, as in Chavín's Old Temple complex: a central U-shaped platform embracing a sunken plaza, which could be reached only by a circuitous series of plazas and stairways.

Native North America *Adena culture.* Earthen pyramids and effigy mounds in the shape of sacred animals, such as Great Serpent Mound (Ohio; ca. 2nd century B.C.).

RELIGION, PHILOSOPHY, LITERATURE

Northeast Africa *Nubian culture.* Egyptian hieroglyphs abandoned in favor of an indigenous Meroitic script.

Andes *Chavín culture.* The most common religious image was a figure (possibly a god) with jaguar fangs.

Mesoamerica *Olmec culture.* Glyphs carved on stone sculptures hint at a written language.

Gold Alloy Pectoral (with jaguar face). Found at Chavín de Huantar. Ca. 500 B.C. Former Bliss Collection, Dumbarton Oaks Research Library and Collections, Washington, D.C.

ASIA

China

Warring States period, ended 221 B.C. Endemic warfare among rival states. Spread of culture across China continued. Historic pattern of society: impoverished peasants living in villages and landowning nobility preoccupied with family, ancestor worship, and religious ritual. Iron working began. Crossbow introduced.

India

Aryan culture, ended 323 B.C. Warfare among petty kingdoms.

Japan

Jōmon culture, ended 300 B.C. Hunting, fishing, and gathering continued.

Warring States period. Decorative arts: lacquered wood, inlaid fittings, and bronze vessels. Exotic features show influence of Ch'u people assimilated into Chinese society in this period.

Monster Mask and Ring Handles. 771–221 B.C. Bronze, mask 3⁷/₁₀" diameter, ring 3½" diameter. People's Republic of China.

Jōmon culture. Clay figurines with huge insectlike or shell-shaped eyes.

Warring States period. Ruins of rammed earth walls at Wang Ch'eng, measuring nearly 2 miles in perimeter.

Jōmon culture. Tomb burial in square pits topped by stone "sundials."

Nonakado Stone Group Above Burial Pit. Late Jōmon period. Oyu, Akita.

In philosophy, the "Hundred Schools" period (6th–3rd centuries B.C.), zenith of China's ethical tradition. Confucius (551–479 B.C.) and Confucianism: encouraged reverence for good form and the established order—the family, hierarchy, seniority. Lao-tzu (6th century B.C.) and Taoism: stressed harmony with nature and a positive acceptance of life's variety. Han Fei-tzu (?–233 B.C.) and the Legalists: taught authority of the rulers, duty of the people, and military power.

Aryan culture. India's great epic poems (about 400 B.C.): the *Rāmāyana* and the *Mahābhārata,* including the *Bhagavadgitā.* Vedism evolved into Early Hinduism, changing from a religion grounded in ritual sacrifice to one focused on asceticism and the practice of yoga. Two new religions, Buddhism and Jainism, emerged, led respectively by Siddhārtha Gautama, called Buddha ("Enlightened One"; ca. 563–ca. 483 B.C.), and Vardhamāna, called Mahāvīra ("Great Hero"; ca. 599–527 B.C.).

4 CLASSICAL GREEK CIVILIZATION
The Hellenistic Age

The Hellenistic Age covers the relatively brief period from the death of Alexander the Great in 323 B.C. to the triumph of Rome over Macedonian Greece in 146 B.C. During this time, a new urban civilization developed in the eastern Mediterranean basin. In contrast to Hellenic Greece, this new civilization was dominated by large metropolitan centers linked by trade and commerce. More racially mixed and ethnically varied than Hellenic Greece, this civilization has come to be called **Hellenistic** because of the preeminent role Greece played in its development. Greece, for example, furnished the Hellenistic world with its diplomatic and commercial language, its bureaucrats, and most of its cultural forms. And yet Hellenistic culture was eclectic, for the subjects of the various states made their presence known (Figure 4.1). Several key motifs grew from oriental roots: the concept of a ruler who is also divine, the aesthetic ideal that identifies grandiosity with earthly majesty, and new religious cults that promised immortality.

Although the Hellenistic Age is sometimes overlooked, Alexander's dream of a world community united by a common leader has had an impact reaching into modern times. The multiracial and multicultural kingdoms of the Hellenistic period are the first examples of a type whose modern versions include the United States and the former Soviet Union. And, not least, Hellenistic achievements in philosophy, art, and architecture are considerable.

This creation of a worldly Mediterranean community destroyed the Hellenic political order in which poleis were guided by their citizens. The poleis were replaced mainly by large Hellenistic kingdoms, ruled by men who declared themselves deities. The Hellenistic economic order rested on

◀ **Detail** *Aphrodite of Melos (Venus de Milo).* Ca. 160–150 B.C. Marble, ht. 6′10″. Louvre.

Figure 4.1 Black Youth Singing. Second century B.C. Ht. 7½". Bibliothèque Nationale, Paris. *Since the Archaic Age, Greek artists had occasionally depicted black Africans in their works. During the Hellenistic Age, with the migration of peoples and the increased use of slaves, sculptors frequently chose black figures as subjects. This small bronze statue of a young African is an illustration of the racial diversity of the Hellenistic Age. Originally, the figure held a small musical instrument—now lost—which accounts for its exaggerated pose.*

specialized luxury crafts and professional occupations, international trade and banking, and an abundant and cheap supply of slaves. The large ports exported and imported basic agricultural commodities such as grain, olive oil, wine, and timber, exchanging them for expensive goods like pottery, silks, jewelry, and spices.

Class divisions in Hellenistic society were pronounced. For the rich, urban life was often luxurious and cosmopolitan, but most of society remained provincial. Those in the middle social ranks, primarily tradespeople and skilled artisans, struggled to keep ahead and hoped to prosper. However, for the poorest free classes—laborers, unskilled workers, and small landowners—life offered little. Slaves, whose numbers grew during the wars of this period, were expected to bear the brunt of all backbreaking labor.

Hellenistic women were affected by the period's growing cosmopolitanism. Women, along with men, moved to the newly conquered lands and created new lives for themselves in frontier towns. In Alexandria and other large cities, some restrictions of Hellenic Greece were maintained, but others were relaxed or discarded. For example, royal and non-Greek women were able to conduct their own legal and economic affairs, though nonroyal Greek women were still forced to use a male guardian in such cases. Dowries remained the custom among Greek families, but unmarried respectable women now had the option of working in the liberal arts, as poets and philosophers, and in the professions, as artists and physicians. Hellenistic literature reflects changed mores, portraying women in carefree situations apart from the gaze of their husbands or fathers. In economic matters, some women became prosperous in their own right, and, just as men did, they made charitable bequests and erected impressive gravestones. Despite these changes, Hellenistic society was dominated by masculine thinking. The surest sign of women's subordinate role was that the Greek practice of infanticide continued as a way for families to rid themselves of unwanted females.

THE STAGES OF HELLENISTIC HISTORY

The shadow of Rome hung over the Hellenistic world, although the states—mired in their quarrels and jockeying for power—were unaware that their fate depended on the rising western Mediterranean power. The events of this age fall into two stages: (1) the disintegration of Alexander's empire and the rise of the successor states; and (2) the arrival and triumph of Rome (Timeline 4.1).

Timeline 4.1 THE HELLENISTIC AGE   All dates B.C.

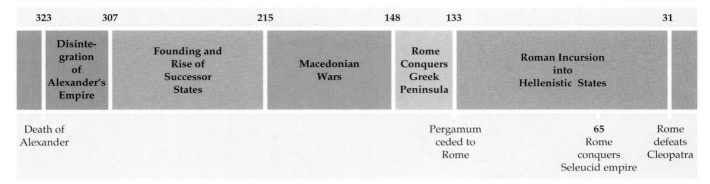

323	307	215	148	133	31
Disinte-gration of Alexander's Empire	Founding and Rise of Successor States	Macedonian Wars	Rome Conquers Greek Peninsula	Roman Incursion into Hellenistic States	

Death of Alexander		Pergamum ceded to Rome	65 Rome conquers Seleucid empire	Rome defeats Cleopatra

The End of the Empire and the Rise of the States

The years from 323 to 307 B.C. saw the shattering of Alexander's dream of a united Greek and Persian civilization. Alexander left no designated successor. After his death, his chief generals (Antigonus, Seleucus, and Ptolemy) divided his empire into three dynastic kingdoms (called the "successor states") that, along with a few minor states and leagues of Greek city-states, survived until Rome moved into the area. The era of the successor states (307 to 215 B.C.) was the zenith of Hellenistic culture. Politically the states were hardly ever at peace, but culturally they were united. Greeks and barbarians mingled freely, and an urban civilization began to emerge. A form of colloquial Greek, called *koine*, spread throughout the Hellenistic world and was spoken from Gaul to Syria.

The three successor states were based in Macedonia, in the former Persian Empire, and in Egypt (Map 4.1). The kingdom of Macedonia, that of Antigonus, controlled Greece until two leagues of poleis challenged Macedonian hegemony. The ensuing warfare with the Greek leagues ultimately weakened this state.

The Seleucid kingdom, that of Seleucus, was built on the ruins of the old Persian Empire. At its height, Seleucid power extended east to present-day Iraq. During the mid–third century B.C., however, the eastern region of the Seleucid kingdom broke away and formed the two smaller states of Parthia and Bactria, which would later prove to be prickly adversaries of Rome. In time, the Seleucid rulers, distracted by the invading Gauls, a wandering tribe of Celtic peoples from central and eastern Europe, lost control of their kingdom and had to relinquish land in Asia Minor to a new kingdom known as Pergamum, named after an old Greek city.

The Ptolemaic kingdom, that of Ptolemy, included Egypt, the oldest civilization surviving in the ancient world. Although the Ptolemaic dynasty was marked by weak and corrupt rulers, Egypt enjoyed a resurgence as a unified and independent state. The capital, Alexandria, became the greatest urban center of the Hellenistic Age, enriched by the grains harvested in the Nile River valley and the goods and traffic that passed through its port.

The Arrival and Triumph of Rome

The second phase of Hellenistic civilization began in the late third century B.C. when Macedonia joined Carthage, a Phoenician state in North Africa, in its struggle against Rome. Thereafter, the unforgiving Romans used every opportunity to humiliate their Greek enemies. Between 215 and 148 B.C., Rome fought four wars with Macedonia, thus becoming entangled in Greek political and military squabbles. Finally, in 146 B.C., Rome brought the entire Greek peninsula under its control. The other Hellenistic kingdoms soon submitted. In 133 B.C., the ruler of Pergamum willed his state to Rome. The Seleucid kingdom was conquered by the Romans in 65 B.C. after three wars. Egypt maintained its freedom until 31 B.C., when Cleopatra and her forces were defeated by Octavian and the Roman navy.

THE CITIES OF HELLENISTIC CIVILIZATION

Alexander's most enduring legacy to the Hellenistic world was his new image of the city. The city is as old as civilization, since urban life is by definition a component of civilized existence. For Alexander, cities were keystones holding together his diverse and vast empire—serving as centers of government, trade, and culture and radiating Greco-Oriental civilization into the hinterland. Alexander is reputed to have founded

LEARNING THROUGH MAPS

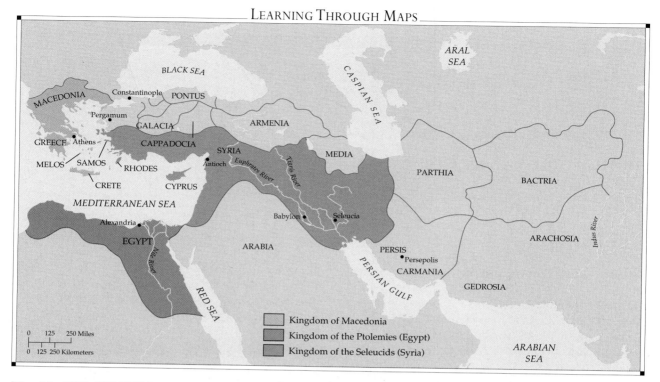

Map 4.1   THE SUCCESSOR STATES AND THE HELLENISTIC WORLD
This map shows the Hellenistic world and the successor states, which emerged after
the breakup of Alexander the Great's Empire. **Notice** the differing size of the successor
states and the respective region controlled by each. **Consider** the impact of geography
and regional cultural traditions on the three kingdoms. **Locate** the major cities of these
kingdoms. **How** did Alexandria's location in Egypt help to make it the dominant city
of the Hellenistic world?

more than seventy cities during his conquests, many of
which were named for him.

Pergamum

During the Hellenistic period, Alexander's successors
emulated him, establishing urban centers such as Antioch, on the Orontes River in southern Asia Minor, and
Seleucia, the new capital of the Seleucid kingdom, near
Babylon. The new city of Pergamum in western Asia
Minor emerged as a brilliant center of art and thought,
bringing together Greek and Persian civilizations. The
Attalids, the ruling dynasty of Pergamum, decorated
their city's acropolis with a splendid palace, a library
second only to the one in Alexandria, and a marble
temple to Athena. Scattered on the hillside beneath the
acropolis were shrines, markets, and private dwellings
of the more prosperous citizens. At the base of the hill,
the tradespeople, artisans, and slaves lived crowded
together (Figure 4.2).

Alexandria in Egypt

For all its claims to grandeur, however, Pergamum
could not surpass the size, wealth, beauty, or culture of the premier Hellenistic city, Alexandria in
Egypt, founded by Alexander (Figure 4.3). Under the
Ptolemies, Alexandria grew to be a world city that
attracted both the ambitious who sought opportunities
and the apathetic who wanted to be left alone. Every
desired attraction is said to have existed here, just as in
the teeming cities of the twenty-first century. By the end
of the first century B.C., Alexandria's population was
about one million, and the city was divided into five
sections, including one reserved for royalty and separate residential quarters for the Egyptians and the Jews,
who were attracted by the city's opportunities and tolerant atmosphere. Whereas the polis of the Hellenic
Age was self-contained, with a relatively homogeneous
population, Alexandria's racially and ethnically diverse groups were held together by economic interests.
With busy harbors, bustling markets, and international

Figure 4.2 Acropolis at Pergamum. Second century B.C. Reconstruction by H. Schlief. Staatliche Museen, Berlin. *Pergamum architecture was in the Hellenic style, but the city's mixed population and economy made it the commercial and political hub of a Hellenistic kingdom. Under Eumenes II, the capital and the country reached its height of power around 160 B.C.*

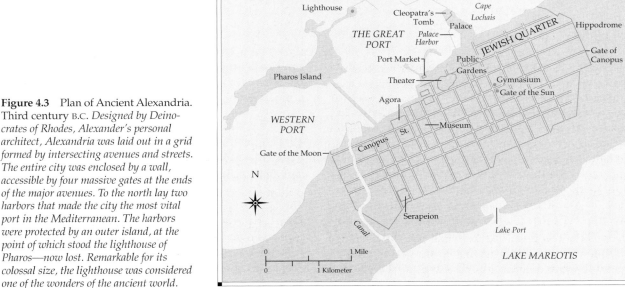

Figure 4.3 Plan of Ancient Alexandria. Third century B.C. *Designed by Deinocrates of Rhodes, Alexander's personal architect, Alexandria was laid out in a grid formed by intersecting avenues and streets. The entire city was enclosed by a wall, accessible by four massive gates at the ends of the major avenues. To the north lay two harbors that made the city the most vital port in the Mediterranean. The harbors were protected by an outer island, at the point of which stood the lighthouse of Pharos—now lost. Remarkable for its colossal size, the lighthouse was considered one of the wonders of the ancient world.*

PERSONAL PERSPECTIVE

THEOCRITUS
Getting to the Concert on Time

Two ladies, Gorgo and Praxinoa, each with her maid (Eutychis and Eunoa, respectively), make their way through the crowded streets of Alexandria, Egypt, on their way to the palace of Ptolemy II to hear a singer perform at the festival of Adonis. The passage is from Theocritus's Idylls, *dating from the third century* B.C.

[GORGO:] [C]ome, get your dress and cloak on,
    and let's go to King Ptolemy's palace
    and take a look at this Adonis.
    The Queen, I hear, is doing things in style.
PRAXINOA: Oh, nothing but the best. Well, they can
        keep it.
GORGO: But when you've seen it, just think,
    you can tell those who haven't all about it.
    Come on, it's time we were off.
PRAXINOA: Every day's a holiday for the idle.

• • •

[Out in the street.]
    Ye Gods, what a crowd! The crush!
    How on earth are we going to get through it?
    They're like ants! Swarms of them, beyond
        counting!
    Well, you've done us many favours, Ptolemy,
    since your father went to heaven.
    We don't get those no-goods now, sliding up to us
    in the street and playing their Egyptian tricks.
    What they used to get up to, those rogues!
    A bunch of villains, each as bad
    as the next, and all utterly cursed!
    Gorgo dear, what will become of us?

Here are the king's horses! Take care,
    my good man, don't tread on me.
    That brown one's reared right up!
    Look how wild he is! He'll kill his groom!
    Eunoa, you fool, get back!
    Thank God I left that child at home.
GORGO: Don't worry, Praxinoa.
    We've got behind them now.
    They're back in their places.
PRAXINOA: I'm all right now.
    Ever since I was a girl, two things
    have always terrified me—horses,
    and long, cold snakes. Let's hurry.
    This great crowd will drown us.

• • •

GORGO: Look, Praxinoa! What a crowd at the door!
PRAXINOA: Fantastic! Gorgo, give me your hand.
    And you, Eunoa, hold on to Eutychis.
    Take care you don't lose each other.
    We must all go in together. Stay close by us.
    Oh no! Gorgo! My coat! It's been ripped
    clean in two! My God, sir, as you hope
    for heaven, mind my coat!
STRANGER: It wasn't my fault. But I'll be careful.
PRAXINOA: What a herd! They push like pigs.
STRANGER: Don't worry, madam, we'll be all right.
PRAXINOA: And may you, sir, be all right
    forever and beyond, for looking after us.
    What a charming man! Where's Eunoa?
    She's getting squashed! Come on, girl, push!
    That's it. "All safely in."

banks, the city became a hub of commercial and financial enterprises, similar to modern port cities.

Alexandria's economic vitality was matched by the splendor of its cultural achievements. The world's first university—a museum dedicated to the muses—was built here as a place for scholars to study and to exchange ideas. Nearby was the famed library, whose staff collected the classics of Greek civilization, including the works of Plato and Aristotle; the tragedies of Aeschylus, Sophocles, and Euripides; the comedies of Aristophanes; and the scientific treatises of Hellenistic philosophers. At the time of the Roman conquest in the late first century B.C., the library contained nearly 700,000 volumes, the largest collection in the ancient world. By then, Alexandria had be-

come a beacon for great minds, who were attracted by the city's rich intellectual life and cosmopolitan atmosphere.

THE ELABORATION OF THE GREEK TRADITION: THE SPREAD OF CLASSICISM TO THE HELLENISTIC WORLD

The Hellenistic world to some extent rejected the simplicity, balance, and restraint that had characterized Hellenism and embraced a more emotional, theatrical view of culture (Figure 4.4). The expansiveness of Alexander's territorial conquests was echoed in the expansion of emotional and expressive content in the

Figure 4.4 *Nike of Samothrace.* Front and side views. Ca. 190 B.C. Marble, ht. 8′. Louvre. *The* Nike of Samothrace—*commonly called the "Winged Victory" because Nike was the Greek goddess of victory—is a perfect symbol of the war-dominated Hellenistic Age. Carved to appear to be striding into the wind, with wildly agitated draperies and soaring wings, this sculpture embodies exuberant action, a defining feature of this turbulent age. Nike's costume also illustrates this age's superb virtuosity; note the transparent band of "fabric" around the navel and the draperies swathing the thighs and legs. Originally part of a sculptural group on the island of Samothrace, which included a war galley, a fountain, and a reflecting pool (now lost), the Nike gives the impression of standing on the prow of a swiftly moving ship.*

arts. As new energies, languages, and traditions were poured into old artistic and literary forms, the seriousness of Hellenism began to give way to a Hellenistic love of playfulness along with an interest in ordinary, everyday subjects.

Hellenistic culture also reflected the tastes and needs of the period's diverse states. Greek tragedy lost its vitality when separated from its roots in the independent polis, but comedy appealed to sophisticated urban audiences who were seeking diversion.

Nondramatic literature became rather artificial as authors concentrated on perfecting their style or pursuing exotic scholarship. New philosophies and religions arose in response to the urban isolation and loneliness that many people experienced. And, finally, grandiose architecture addressed the propaganda needs of autocratic rulers, and realistic sculpture reflected the tastes of an increasingly urban, secular culture.

Nevertheless, the values of Hellenistic culture did not so much replace the standards of Hellenic Classicism as they enriched and elaborated the older ideals. Like Hellenism, the Hellenistic style depicted the realities of the physical world rather than finding truth in fantasy or abstraction. And Hellenistic artists and authors agreed with their Hellenic forebears that art must serve moral purposes, revealed through content and formal order.

Drama and Literature

In the Hellenistic Age, Greek comedy began to resemble modern productions. The grotesque padding worn by the actors gave way to realistic costumes; masks were redesigned to be representative of the portrayed characters; and the actors assumed a dominant status over the chorus. Comedies became a form of popular amusement, and Hellenistic playwrights developed a genre known as **New Comedy** to appeal to the pleasure-seeking audiences who were flocking to the theaters. Avoiding political criticism and casual obscenity, New Comedy presented gently satirical scenes from middle-class life.

The plays were generally comic romances on such themes as frustrated first love or marital misunderstandings, and although the endings were inevitably happy and there was much formula writing—somewhat like today's situation comedies on television—the plays reflected the comprehensive range of the Hellenistic style. The characters, for example, were familiar types drawn from the rich diversity of Hellenistic society—the courtesan, the slave, the fawning parasite. New Comedy remained steadfastly middle-class, however, for the traditional social order always prevailed in the end. For example, a favorite plot device of New Comedy hinged on discovering that a seemingly lowborn character was actually from a respected—and often wealthy—family.

Both ancient and modern critics tend to regard Menander [muh-NAN-duhr] (about 343–about 291 B.C.) as the leading author of New Comedy. He wrote more than one hundred plays for the Dionysia festival in Athens, winning first prize for comedy eight times, and is credited with perfecting the **comedy of manners,** a humorous play that focuses on the way people interact in society.

The Woman from Samos is a robust example of his work. Dating from about 321 B.C., this comedy concerns the identity of an orphaned baby and features stock characters: a courtesan, a young lover, an old lover, a humorous neighbor, and two comic slaves. Menander first presents a household in which the father believes that he and his son are wooing the same woman, when, in actuality, the son is involved with the girl next door. Then, when a foundling appears,

absurd misunderstandings arise and false accusations are made. The play ends happily with all characters reconciled, the son wed to his true love, and the father and mistress married in a joyous ceremony—a typical New Comedy resolution. Western comedy would be inconceivable without Menander. His style was assimilated into Roman comedy, which passed the spirit of his work into the dramas of the Italian Renaissance and from there into the comedies of Shakespeare and Molière.

In nondramatic literature, the Hellenistic Age produced a style known as **Alexandrianism.** The Ptolemaic rulers who built the library and the museum in Alexandria used state subsidies to lure scholars and poets to the city to study the works that found their way, by purchase or plunder, into the library's vast collections. The writers produced works of many types—poetry, history, biography, literary criticism, and essays on geography and mathematics—but their work is generally of historical interest only. Alexandrian literature is often obscure and ornate, derivative, and scholarly.

A writer who stands apart in the Alexandrian school is the poet Theocritus [the-OCK-ruht-us] (about 310–250 B.C.), who worked within the confines of the style but achieved genuine literary distinction. He created a new poetic form, the **pastoral,** which would influence later Classical and modern European literature. These poems describe the lives of shepherds and farmers in a somewhat artificial, idealized way. Theocritus drew his images from his memory of his earlier years in rural Sicily, and his charming, nostalgic verses appealed to many who had also left the quiet rustic life for the excitement of the Hellenistic cities.

Theocritus also wrote what he called **idylls** (from the Greek meaning "little picture"), which offered small portraits, or vignettes, of Hellenistic life. Some of these poems reveal much about everyday affairs, noting the common concerns and aspirations of all generations—love, family, religion, and wealth.

Philosophy and Religion

For many people, everyday life changed drastically during the Hellenistic Age. As urban life became more multicultural, the sense of belonging that had characterized life in the Hellenic poleis was replaced by a feeling of isolation, of loneliness, even of helplessness, particularly in the urban centers. As a consequence, two seemingly contradictory points of view grew up: individualism and internationalism. Those who held these attitudes were searching for continuity in a rapidly changing world; were seeking identity for the individual through common interests, values, and hopes; and were striving to understand events that seemed unpredictable and beyond human control.

Philosophies and religions offered answers that seemed as contradictory as the problems themselves. One philosophy urged a universal brotherhood of all human beings, united regardless of race, status, or birth; another, despairing of the world, excluded most people and appealed to a chosen few. Religions, similarly, provided varying answers. One faith preached salvation in a life after death, and another turned to magic to escape Fate—that blind force that controlled human life.

In the long run, such diversity of choice tended to foster tolerance, since no single set of beliefs prevailed or satisfied everyone (Figure 4.5). Having many alternatives spared society the anguish and bigotry that would have arisen had there been only two or three competing points of view. Because of the ease of communication and travel in the Hellenistic period, these new philosophies and religions quickly gained converts everywhere, regardless of class or geographic location.

The most enduring of this period's philosophies, Cynicism, Skepticism, Epicureanism, and Stoicism, attracted the better-educated and more influential groups in Hellenistic society. Of these four theories, Cynicism and Skepticism appealed to only a few, whereas Epicureanism and Stoicism had a much larger following (Table 4.1).

Cynicism   Of the four schools, **Cynicism** had the least impact on Hellenistic civilization. The Cynics, believing that society diverted the individual from the more important goals of personal independence and freedom, denounced all religions and governments, shunned physical comfort, and advocated the avoidance of personal pleasure. In the Cynics' logic, true freedom came with the realization that if one wanted nothing, one could not lack anything. By isolating themselves from society, they gained a type of self-sufficiency the Greeks called *autarky.*

The most prominent Cynic, Diogenes [die-AHJ-uh-neez] (about 412–about 323 B.C.), openly scorned the ordinary values and crass materialism of his society. His contrary personality so fascinated Alexander the Great that the ruler, upon being insulted by the Cynic, is reported to have said that if he were not Alexander, he would prefer to be Diogenes (Figure 4.6)! A few Cynics earned the respect of some thinkers, but the principles of Cynicism offended the educated, and its pessimism offered no hope to the masses.

Skepticism   The proponents of **Skepticism** argued that nothing could be known for certain, an extreme conclusion they were led to by their belief that the senses were unreliable sources of knowledge. Thinking

Figure 4.5   A Religious Ceremony. A.D. 159. Yale University Art Gallery, New Haven. *Although this relief is dated from the second century A.D., it is characteristic of Hellenistic religious practices that continued into Roman times. In the center is depicted Zeus Olympius–Baalshamin, a combination of Greek and Semitic deities. On the left is a priest burning an offering on an altar and dressed in Near Eastern garb; on the right is a priest wearing Greek clothing.*

Table 4.1   PHILOSOPHY IN THE HELLENISTIC AGE

PHILOSOPHY	EMPHASIS
Cynicism	True freedom arises from realizing that if one wants nothing, then one will never lack anything; *autarky* (self-sufficiency) is goal
Skepticism	Nothing can be known for certain; question all ideas; *autarky* is goal
Epicureanism	Only the atoms and void exist; pleasure is the highest good; death is final in its extinction of consciousness; the gods play no active role in human affairs
Stoicism	The world is governed by the divine *logos*, or reason, or nature; wisdom and freedom consist of living in harmony with the *logos*; all humans share in the divine *logos*; *autarky* is goal

that everything was relative, the Skeptics maintained that all ideas must be questioned and that no single philosophy was true. When their critics pointed out that such unrelenting questioning was clearly not a practical answer to life's uncertainties, the Skeptics replied that certainty could be achieved only by admitting that truth was unknowable—a circular response. The Skeptics

Figure 4.6 *Diogenes and Alexander the Great.* First century A.D. Villa Albani, Rome. *This Roman relief shows that Diogenes and Alexander the Great, two figures of the Hellenistic Age, were living presences for the Romans. The philosopher Diogenes is carved sitting in his famous tub, a symbol of his contempt for creature comforts. The world-conqueror Alexander is on the right, pointing his finger at the Greek thinker. The dog portrayed on top of the tub is a reference to Cynicism (the word* cynic *is from the Greek word for "dog"). Diogenes asserted that humans should live simply—like dogs.*

thought that if they recognized that intellectual inquiry was fruitless, then they could avoid frustration and achieve *autarky,* or self-sufficiency—the same goal as that of the Cynics and the Stoics.

The Skeptics, even though they attracted a smaller audience than the Cynics, had a greater impact on Western reasoning. Pyrrho [PEER-oh] of Elis founded Skepticism and pursued the native strain of Greek thinking to its logical conclusion, but he never recorded his ideas. Skepticism had some appeal for the early Romans, who brought the Greek philosopher and teacher Carneades [kar-NEE-uh-deez] (about 214–129 B.C.) to Rome in 155 B.C. Carneades shocked his pious Roman audience, who took his universal doubt as a denial of the stability and permanence of their state and its values. Although Skepticism faded after Carneades' death, the movement was revived during the Roman Empire and eventually passed into the mainstream of Western thought.

Epicureanism The strict and quiet way of life advocated by **Epicureanism** appealed to aristocrats who were more interested in learning than in politics. It began as the philosophy of the Greek thinker Epicurus

[ep-uh-KYUR-uhs] (about 342–270 B.C.), who founded a school in Athens where pupils, including slaves and women, gathered to discuss ideas (Figure 4.7). For Epicurus, the best way to keep one's wants simple, and thus to achieve happiness, was to abstain from sex and focus instead on friendship. Friendship was a mystic communion, based on shared need, in which men and men, men and women, rich and poor, old and young, of all nationalities and any class supported each other in trusting relationships. This vision guided Epicurus's school, where life became a daily exercise in friendship. It was an ideal that appealed to women since, in making them men's equals, it showed that they had more to give than bearing children and raising families.

Epicurus based his ethical philosophy on the Atomic theory of those Greek thinkers who saw the universe as completely determined by the behavior of atoms moving in empty space (see Chapter 3). Epicurus accepted this picture, but with one significant modification: He argued that because atoms on occasion swerved from their set paths and made unpredictable deviations, it was possible, even in a deterministic universe, for humans to make free choices. Like the Atomists, Epicurus also believed that the senses pre-

Figure 4.7 *Epicurus.* Ca. 290–280 B.C. Courtesy The Metropolitan Museum of Art. Rogers Fund, 1911. (11.90) *This marble bust of Epicurus, discovered in southern Italy and inscribed with his name, is a copy of the original bronze sculpture. Many busts and likenesses of Epicurus have been found, indicating the popularity of his philosophy in Hellenistic times and especially during the Roman era.*

sented an accurate view of the physical world. Thus, by using the mind as a storehouse for sense impressions and by exercising free will in their choices, individuals could reach moral judgments and ultimately form an ethical code.

For Epicurus, the correct ethical code led to happiness, which was realized in a life of quiet—separated and withdrawn from the trying cares of the world. Furthermore, those who would be happy should keep their wants simple, not indulge excessive desires, and resist fame, power, and wealth, which only brought misery and disappointment.

Another characteristic of Epicurean happiness was freedom from fear—fear of the gods, of death, and of the hereafter. Although Epicurus believed that the gods existed, he also believed that they cared nothing about human beings, and therefore no one needed to be afraid of what the gods might or might not do. As for death, there was, again, nothing to agonize over because when it did occur, the atoms that made up the soul simply separated from the body's atoms and united with other particles to create new forms. With death came the end of the human capacity to feel

pleasure or pain and thus the end of suffering. Consequently, death, rather than being feared, should be welcomed as a release from misfortune and trouble. Pleasure, in the Epicurean view, is the absence of pain. The happy Epicurean, standing above the cares of the world, had reached *ataraxia,* the desireless state that the Hellenistic Age deemed so precious.

Stoicism   Both Epicureanism and **Stoicism** claimed that happiness was a final goal of the individual, and both were essentially materialistic, stressing the importance of sense impressions and the natural world. The Stoics, however, identified the supreme deity with nature, thus making the natural world divine and inseparable from the deity. The supreme being was also another name for reason, or *logos,* and hence nature was also rational. Since the Stoics' God was law and the author of law, this led to the notion that the workings of nature were expressed in divine laws.

The Stoics likewise discovered God in humanity. The Stoics' God, being identical with reason, gave a spark to each mortal's soul, conferring the twin gifts of rationality and kinship with divinity. The Stoics thus believed that reason and the senses could be used jointly to uncover the underlying moral law as well as God's design in the world, proving God's wisdom and power over human life and nature.

There was in Stoicism a tendency to leave everything up to God. Stoics came to accept their roles in life, whether rich or poor, master or slave, healthy or afflicted, and such a resigned and deterministic outlook could (and did) lead to apathy or unconcern. However, the ideal Stoic, the Wise Man, never became apathetic. He overcame Stoicism's fatalistic tendency by stressing his own sense of and dedication to duty. Doing one's duty was part of following the deity's plan, and the Stoic willingly performed his tasks, no matter how onerous or laborious. The reward for living a life of duty was virtue. Having achieved virtue, the Stoics were freed from their emotions, which they thought only corrupted them. The Stoics had thus achieved *autarky,* the state of existence sought by many Hellenistic philosophers.

Stoicism was unique among the Hellenistic philosophies in holding out the promise of membership in a worldwide brotherhood. Perhaps inspired by Alexander the Great's dream, the Stoics advocated an ideal state, guided by God and law, that encompassed all of humanity of whatever race, sex, social status, or nationality in a common bond of reason. As humans carried out their duties in this larger community, they would rise above local and national limitations and create a better world.

Because of their practical optimism, the Stoics drew the largest number of followers among political leaders and intellectuals, who found the Cynics, the Skeptics, and the Epicureans too pessimistic. In the end, however, all four philosophies satisfied only a small portion of the vast Hellenistic population. They failed to appeal to persons who were confused by the intellectual theories or who derived no personal satisfaction from the teachings. Instead, the bulk of the people, spurred on by a growing sense of helplessness, began to believe that Fate ruled their lives.

Fate and the Mystery Cults   The belief in Fate, a concept borrowed from Babylonia, gripped the lives of many in the Hellenistic world. To them, Fate ruled the universe, controlled the heavens, and determined the course of life. Although no one could change the path of this nonmoral, predestined force, individuals could try to avoid the cruel consequences of Fate by various methods. The pseudoscience of astrology, also from Babylonia, offered one alternative. Magic was now revived, and many people used sacred objects to conjure up good spirits or to ward off evil ones. Nevertheless, it was the mystery cults—springing from the primitive chthonian religions of Greece (see Chapters 2 and 3) and elsewhere—that eventually emerged as the most popular and effective response to Fate.

During the Hellenistic Age, numerous chthonian cults spread from the Seleucid kingdom and Egypt to the Greek mainland, where they were combined with local beliefs and rituals to create religions that fused different beliefs and practices. By the second century B.C., converts were being attracted from all over the Hellenistic world to the well-established mystery cults of Orpheus and Dionysus in Greece and to the new religions from Egypt and the old Persian lands. The growth of these cults in turn sparked an increase in religious zeal after about 100 B.C., resulting in more ceremonies and public festivals and the revival of older faiths.

The Egyptian mystery cults grew, becoming quite popular across the Hellenistic world. Ptolemy I, the Macedonian founder of the Ptolemaic dynasty in 323 B.C., invented a new god, Serapis, in an effort to unite the Egyptians and the Greeks. Serapis became a favorite deity of the masses outside Egypt, and followers built shrines everywhere.

But the goddess Isis, already well known to the Egyptians, overshadowed the newly minted Serapis. According to her cult legend, Isis rescued her husband-brother, Osiris, from his enemies and brought him back to life with her unwavering love. This resurrection symbolized to the faithful the new life awaiting them at death. In time, Isis became associated with many foreign goddesses, fusing with them to become the most honored goddess of the ancient world (Figure 4.8).

From the Seleucid kingdom, the remnants of Babylonian and Persian cultures offered two radically

Figure 4.8   Isis with Her Son Harpocrates (left) and God Anubis (right). First century A.D. Terra-cotta, ht. approx. 7". British Museum. *This small terra-cotta figurine—probably used as a votive—blends Greek sculptural style with Egyptian symbolism. The goddess is portrayed wearing an Egyptian headdress and is flanked by her son and the jackal-headed Anubis, the god of the dead. Greek features include the goddess's tightly curled hair, her slightly contrapposto pose, and the graceful drapery of her dress. The statue, fired on the Italian peninsula in the first century A.D., testifies to her popularity throughout ancient times and across the Mediterranean world.*

different cults to the Hellenistic Age, the brutal religion of Cybele and the philosophical religion founded by Zoroaster (see Chapter 1). Cybele, the Great Mother goddess, appealed to many women and even a few men, despite the self-mutilation that male believers had to undergo to gain the promise of a new life. Under different names, the Great Mother goddess was worshiped throughout the Hellenistic world and in Rome. Later, Mithraism, an offshoot of Zoroastrianism, with its emphasis on duty and loyalty, caught the attention of Rome's soldiers, thereby ensuring the spread of this belief wherever Roman legions were stationed.

The secret rites of the mystery cults, which communicated the thrill of initiation and the satisfaction of belonging, answered deep psychological needs in their Hellenistic converts. This universal appeal cut across class and racial lines and attracted an ever-widening segment of the populace. With their promise of immortality, these rituals contributed to the atmosphere of the Roman world in which Christianity would later be born.

Architecture

As in Hellenic times, architecture in the Hellenistic Age reflected the central role that religion played in the life of the people. Public buildings served religious, ceremonial, and governmental purposes, and the temple continued as the leading type of structure. The altar, which had originated in Archaic Greece as a simple structure where holy sacrifices or offerings were made, now became a major structural form, second in importance only to the temple, because of its use in state rituals.

Hellenistic architecture modified the basic temple and altar forms inherited from Hellenic models to express the grandeur demanded by the age's rulers. These monarchs were mesmerized by Alexander the Great's claim to divinity, which had opened up a new vision of statecraft. As a result, Alexander's successors built temples and altars whose massive size and elaborate decoration manifested both their own earthly majesty and the divine authority of whatever deity with whom they claimed kinship.

The Corinthian Temple   The **Corinthian** temple came to embody Hellenistic splendor. The Corinthian column had first appeared in the Hellenic period, when it was probably used as a decorative feature. Because it was taller, more slender, and more ornamented than either the Doric or the Ionic column, the Corinthian column was now used on the exterior of temples erected by Hellenistic builders for their kings. In time, Hellenistic taste decreed that the Corinthian column was appropriate for massive buildings. The Corinthian order later became the favorite of the Roman emperors, and it was revived in the Renaissance and diffused throughout the Western world, where it survives today as the most visible sign of Hellenistic influence.

The most outstanding Corinthian temples combined grandeur with grace, as in the Olympieum in Athens, now a ruin (Figure 4.9). Commissioned by the

Figure 4.9   The Olympieum. Various dates: late sixth century B.C.; second quarter of second century B.C.; completed, second quarter of second century A.D. Athens. *The thirteen standing Corinthian columns were part of the original plan of the Olympieum's architect. After the temporary cessation of building in 164 B.C., some of this temple's unfinished columns were transported to Rome and reused in a building there. Their use in Rome helped to popularize the Corinthian style among political leaders and wealthy tastemakers.*

Figure 4.10   Altar of Zeus at Pergamum. (Reconstruction.) 170s B.C. Pergamum Museum, Berlin. *This masterpiece of Hellenistic architecture was erected in the 170s B.C. by Eumenes II, the king of Pergamum, to commemorate his victories over various barbarian states in Asia Minor. Eumenes believed himself to be the savior and disseminator of Greek culture, and this altar with its giant frieze was meant to suggest Hellenic monuments, such as the Athenian Parthenon.*

Seleucid king Antiochus IV [an-TIE-uh-kuhs], the Olympieum expressed his notion of a diverse, international culture united under Zeus, his divine counterpart and the lord of Mount Olympus. The temple, the first to use Corinthian columns, was constructed during three different and distinct historical eras. The stylobate, or base, was laid in the late Archaic Age but then abandoned; the Corinthian columns were raised by Antiochus IV in about 175 B.C., after which work was suspended indefinitely; it was finally completed in A.D. 130 under the Roman emperor Hadrian, a great admirer of Greek culture. The temple is stylistically unified, however, because it was finished according to the surviving plans of its second-century B.C. architect. Despite its massive size and its lack of mathematical refinements, the Olympieum presented an extremely graceful appearance with its forest of delicate Corinthian columns, consisting of double rows of twenty columns each on the sides and triple rows of eight on the ends.

The Altar   Before there were temples, there were altars, the oldest religious structure in the Greek world. The earliest altars were simple slabs, made wide enough to allow sacrificial animals to be slaughtered. During the Hellenistic Age, the altars were substantially enlarged. The biggest appears to have been the 650-foot-long altar, permitting the sacrifice of more than one hundred cattle at one time, funded by the tyrant of Syracuse in the third century B.C.

Although the Syracusan altar has disappeared, the dismantled altar of Zeus at Pergamum has recently been discovered and reassembled. It is easy to see why ancient travelers called it one of the wonders of the world (Figure 4.10). The actual altar, not visible in the photograph, stands lengthwise in a magnificent Ionic colonnaded courtyard. The courtyard itself is raised on a **podium,** or platform; below the courtyard, the sides of the structure are decorated with a sculptured frieze depicting the deities at war. The overall design—with the frieze below the columns—appears to be an inversion of the usual temple plan. Constructed by Eumenes II [YOU-muh-neez] of the Attalid dynasty, this altar was but one part of a concerted effort to transform Pergamum into another Athens. Thus, the idea of a "new" Athens—a recurrent motif in the humanistic tradition—had already been formulated by the Hellenistic Age.

Sculpture

Like Hellenistic architects, Hellenistic sculptors adapted many of the basic forms and ideas of the Hellenic style to meet the tastes of their day. The Hellenistic sculptors perpetuated such Hellenic principles as contrapposto and proportion as well as the Hellenic emphasis on religious and moral themes. But Hellenistic art increasingly expressed a secular, urban viewpoint, and Hellenic restraint often gave way to realism, eroticism, and violence, expressed and enjoyed for their own sake. Some of these Hellenistic qualities are apparent in the refreshingly naturalistic sculpture *Boy Struggling with a Goose* (Figure 4.11). At the same time, this work of art relates ironically to the age's values because it can be understood on two levels: Its subject is both an everyday scene and a mock-heroic battle; its playful nature masks a sense of violence; and its twisting forms and shifting planes seem overdone on such a small scale.

Between 230 and 220 B.C., King Attalos I [AT-uh-luhs] of Pergamum dedicated in Athens a group of bronze sculptures that celebrated his recent victory over the barbaric Gauls. By donating these bronzes to Athens, which was outside of Pergamum's political orbit, the Attalid ruler hoped to establish his cultural credentials as a defender of Greek culture and thus further his claims to rule over the entire Hellenistic world.

One of these pieces, *Dying Gaul* (which survives only in a Roman marble copy), shows a mortally wounded barbarian warrior (Figure 4.12). The torque, or twisted necklace, he wears identifies him as a Gaul. Lying close by are his sword and trumpet. The sculptor

Figure 4.11 *Boy Struggling with a Goose.* Roman copy of a Greek original, dating from second half of second century B.C. Marble, ht. 33½". Capitoline Museum, Rome. *When Hellenistic sculptors freed themselves from the ideals of Hellenic art, one of the results was the production of works on unhackneyed themes, as in* Boy Struggling with a Goose. *So popular was this genre scene that several versions of it are known from antiquity. Its popularity reflects the age's delight in childhood and its joys—perhaps an outgrowth of the rising status of women in Hellenistic times.*

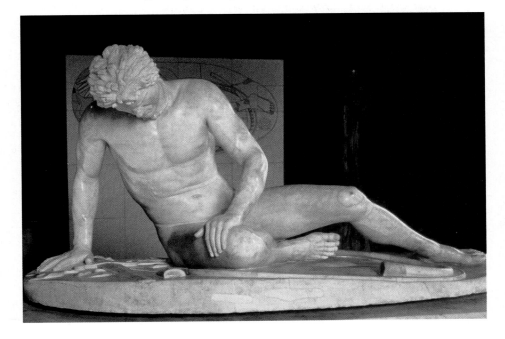

Figure 4.12 *Dying Gaul.* Ca. 230–220 B.C. Roman marble copy of a bronze original, ht. 3'. Capitoline Museum, Rome. *The rulers of the Hellenistic kingdom of Pergamum preferred art that was showy and overwrought, a taste that perhaps stemmed from their insecurity at being a new dynasty. A Pergamene style of sculpture developed under these kings, in which gestures were theatrical and anatomical features were portrayed in exaggerated depth. The* Dying Gaul *is a superb example of this style.*

Figure 4.13 *Old Market Woman.* Third or second century B.C. Roman marble copy of a Hellenistic bronze, ht. 49″. Metropolitan Museum of Art. *Many Hellenistic sculptors depicted old women in pathetic situations, tired, drunk, or begging. Scholars are divided in opinion about whether these statues were meant to be admired for their truthfulness or whether they represented disdain for what Hellenistic aristocrats considered an ugly social phenomenon.*

Figure 4.14 *Athena Battling with Alkyoneus.* From the Great Frieze of the Pergamum altar, east section. 170s B.C. Marble, 7′6″. Pergamum Museum, Berlin. *An unusual aspect of this relief is the diversity of their bodily forms. For example, Alkyoneus's outspread wings identify him as a Giant and an offspring of Gaea, the goddess of the Earth, who is shown on the bottom right.*

demonstrates his keen eye for realistic details in the open wound oozing blood from the warrior's rib cage and by the blank stare as he faces death. The Hellenistic style's appreciation of the melodramatic is evident in the tension between the warrior's sagging body and his efforts to prop himself up. But by treating a foreign enemy with such nobility, the anonymous sculptor perpetuates the deep moral sense that was central to Hellenic art.

A radically different subject is treated in the *Old Market Woman*, which, like a stock character from New Comedy, depicted a well-known social type (Figure 4.13). The old woman, who might have strolled out of the marketplace of any Hellenistic city, represented a **genre subject,** or a scene taken from everyday life. The original third-century B.C. bronze portrayed a stooped figure, straining under the combined weight of her groceries and her advancing years. In this Roman marble copy, the left arm is missing, but she carries a fowl and a brimming bucket. Her deeply lined and wrinkled face and her sagging breasts express the realism of Hellenistic style.

Among the masterpieces of Hellenistic art are the sculptures of the Pergamum altar frieze, which can be seen in Figure 4.10. The subject is a battle between the Olympian deities and the Giants, the monstrous race of pre-Greek gods and goddesses who were the offspring of Gaea (Earth) and Uranus (Sky, or the Heavens)—the first rulers of the universe. The Giants, having overthrown their parents, are then defeated by *their* own children, the Olympian deities. To the Greeks, the final triumph of the Olympian gods and goddesses symbolized the coming of a just and moral order both in the universe and in their own society. Hence, when the Attalid rulers chose this subject for the altar frieze, they affirmed that they were continuing the values of Greek civilization. With the exception of the frieze on the Parthenon, the figures on this altar represent the most ambitious sculptural project in the ancient world.

Filled with high-powered energy, the Pergamum frieze displays figures that threaten to explode from the space in which they are barely contained. In one celebrated panel, Athena grasps the dying Giant Alkyoneus while her sacred snake bites him on the chest (Figure 4.14). Her agitated draperies appear to be billowing in a strong wind, so that the folds hang expressively rather than simply disclosing her body, as in the Hellenic style. The expression of pain on Alkyoneus's face—deeply furrowed brow and bulging eyeballs— and the straining muscles with prominent veins reflect the Pergamum school's taste for exaggeration.

The sculpture of the Hellenistic Age is also characterized by a frank appreciation of female beauty, a famous example of which is the *Aphrodite of Melos*, perhaps better known as the Venus de Milo (Figure 4.15). This original sculpture, carved from Parian marble,

Figure 4.15 *Aphrodite of Melos (Venus de Milo).* Ca. 160–150 B.C. Marble, ht. 6'10". Louvre. *This celebrated statue represents the classicizing tendency, derived from Greek tradition, in Hellenistic art. The head is executed in the pure Hellenic style, as seen in the serene countenance, the exquisitely detailed hair, and the finely chiseled features. However, the body, with its frank sensuality and its rumpled draperies, is clearly in the Hellenistic style.*

Figure 4.16 AGASIAS OF EPHESUS. *Borghese Gladiator.* Ca. 100 B.C. Marble, ht. 5′6½″ Louvre. *The subject here is not a gladiator, for the Greeks were ignorant of the circus games. Instead, based on the upturned gaze and the upraised left arm, the statue depicts a warrior on foot fighting for his life against an unseen opponent on horseback. The outmatched warrior is thus a figure of pathos, a beloved theme during the Hellenistic period. Yet Agasias has injected into this theme the rugged athleticism of the fourth century B.C. Lost in antiquity, the statue was acquired by a Borghese prince on its rediscovery in the seventeenth century A.D. Today, the* Borghese Gladiator, *newly restored in 1997, stands in a place of honor in the Louvre.*

shows many borrowings from the tradition of Praxiteles, as shown in his *Hermes with the Infant Dionysus* (see Figure 3.26). Both Aphrodite and Hermes exhibit exaggerated contrapposto; a sensuous, even erotic, modeling of the body; and a serene countenance with an unmistakable gaze. However, the Hellenistic sculptor, demonstrating a playful flair with the rolled-down draperies, calls attention to Aphrodite's exposed lower torso.

The *Aphrodite of Melos* was part of the growing influence of **Neoclassicism,** which swept the disintegrating Hellenistic world in the wake of Rome's rise to greatness. Neoclassicism, developing first in Athens in the late third century B.C. and later in Pergamum and other cities, was a kind of nostalgia for the glory days of the fifth and fourth centuries B.C. Another famous work in this style was the *Borghese Gladiator,* which combines the well-defined musculature perfected during the Hellenic period with a dramatic lunging pose so favored by Hellenistic taste (Figure 4.16). Probably commissioned by a Roman patron, this sculpture of a warrior standing on a plinth is thought to be either a copy of or inspired by a third- or second-century B.C. original. Its status as a copy is indicated by the tree trunk support—the place where the sculptor, Agasias of Ephesus (in modern Turkey), carved his name.

The *Horse and Jockey,* original bronzes that were retrieved in this century from a sunken ship in the Aegean Sea off Artemision, show Hellenistic fluidity rather than the frozen style of Hellenic art (Figure 4.17). Whether the two figures are a true ensemble is a subject of scholarly debate. Arguing against their unity is the size disparity between the small jockey and the enormous horse, but the balance seems in favor of treating them as a group, especially when the jockey is seated on the horse. In this juxtaposition, the horse's forward motion seems to cause the jockey's cloak to blow behind him. The boy, contorting his face with the strain of the race, stretches out his left hand, as if to urge his mount on to victory. This sculptured pair shows other innovations in Hellenistic art. The boy athlete, who looks rather like a ragged street urchin, represents the new interest in children that arose in Hellenistic art, and the straining horse contrasts dramatically with the serene, well-proportioned horses on the Parthenon frieze.

Figure 4.17 *Horse and Jockey of Artemision.* Mid–second century B.C. Bronze, ht. of jockey 33½″. National Museum, Athens. *The jockey and horse may have been intended by an athlete as a votive offering to a deity for victory in a competition. Such statues had been erected in Greece from the Archaic Age onward.*

Figure 4.18 *Muse (Melpomene or Polyhymnia (?)).* Roman copy, probably of a mid-second-century B.C. original by Philiskos of Rhodes. Ht. 4′11″ without plinth. Capitoline Museum, Rome. *The sculptor has portrayed the muse in a simple but dignified pose—leaning forward on a support, left foot up-turned, chin resting on curved right hand—and swathed her in a thin mantle of fabric that falls into rhythmic folds. The contrast between the serenely meditative face and the dynamic drapery pattern is a typical effect of Hellenistic art (see Figure 4.14).*

Figure 4.19 HAGESANDROS, POLYDOROS, AND ATHANA-DOROS. *The Laocoön Group.* Ca. A.D. 50. Marble, ht. 8′. Vatican Museum. *Parallels are frequently made between the distorted features of the dying Laocoön and those of the mortally wounded Alkyoneus from the Pergamum altar (see Figure 4.14). This similarity points to some connection between the Rhodian and Pergamene schools of sculpture, though the exact relationship is a matter of controversy.*

Rhodes: Late Hellenistic Style

Although much of the Hellenistic world, including Greece, fell into Roman hands in 146 B.C., the Aegean island of Rhodes remained free for over sixty more years (see Map 4.1). During this period, independent Rhodes became a cultural center that rivaled the older cities of Pergamum, Alexandria, and Athens in concentration of scientists, artists, and humanists. The Rhodian style, which alternated between lighthearted and gay on the one hand and colossal and theatrical on the other, was influenced by the Pergamene school and was the final stage of Hellenistic art.

A graceful example of this statuary type is a Roman copy of one figure from a Rhodian sculptural group dating from the mid–second century B.C. (Figure 4.18). The muse is probably either Melpomene, muse of tragedy, or Polyhymnia, muse of the choral hymn. She is portrayed as a young woman leaning against a support, lost in thought. Except for her left foot and left hand, she is swathed in draperies, a typically Hellenistic way of portraying women. The large number of statues of draped women surviving from the Hellenistic era reflects the rising social status of respectable women during this time.

The school of sculpture on Rhodes, even after the island's absorption into Rome, was still able to produce the sublime masterpiece of Rhodian and Hellenistic art, *The Laocoön Group* (Figure 4.19). The sculptors of this famous group, probably Hagesandros [haj-uh-SAN-drohs], Polydoros [pol-e-DOOR-uhs], and Athanadoros [ah-thay-nuh-DOOR-uhs], were all members of a local dynasty of sculptors. Their sculpture depicts the priest Laocoön and his sons. According to Vergil's *Aeneid,* the Roman epic, Laocoön, a priest of Neptune, warned the Trojans not to bring the wooden horse—which, unknown to him, concealed a party of Greek warriors—into their city. (Laocoön's admonition to beware Greeks bearing gifts has become proverbial.) As Laocoön finished his speech, sea serpents, sent by the gods, raced out of the sea and crushed him and his two sons to death. The Trojans interpreted Laocoön's speech as an impious act against the gods, and they hauled the horse into Troy.

In the *Laocoön* sculptural group, the snakes, which grasp and bite the priest and his sons, serve to integrate the three figures into an image of unrelieved horror: Laocoön's face is contorted in anguish as the serpent bites him; on the left, one of his sons is already dead; and the other son seems to be disentangling himself from the serpentine coils. This celebrated work, with its technical virtuosity and its rhetorical violence, is a fitting climax to almost four hundred years of Hellenistic art. The *Laocoön* sculptural group vanished after the fall of Rome, only to be rediscovered in the early sixteenth century A.D., when it influenced the sculptor Michelangelo and the subsequent rise of Baroque art.

The Legacy of the Hellenistic World

In the Hellenistic Age, Athens and its culture achieved the status of an inspiring model to be honored and emulated. But the Hellenistic rulers had no interest in democracy; indeed, their larger political interests often conflicted with the needs of local subjects. Nor did these kings want to further humanism, which they regarded as either irrelevant to imperial goals or subversive of them. What appealed to the Hellenistic kings was a narrow, lifeless humanism, as exemplified by the dynasties of the Attalids in Pergamum and the Ptolemies in Egypt. The Hellenistic monarchs wanted to do no more than create new cultural centers that rivaled the fame of the old Athens. The great Hellenistic centers of Pergamum and Alexandria—with their libraries, poets, scientists, artists, schools of philosophy, marble buildings, and monuments—were perceived as politically useful to these ambitious rulers. In other words, they wanted to harness art to politics for propaganda purposes.

The Hellenistic world bequeathed the idea of a "new Athens" to Rome, which was, in part, inspired by its many cities, urban life, and civic culture. Rome in turn diffused the Greek heritage to the major cities of the entire Mediterranean area. After the fall of Rome, the medieval rulers adopted this tradition, making their governments responsive to the religious and, to a lesser extent, the cultural needs of their citizens. With the rise of the secular state in the eighteenth century A.D., governments began to dissociate themselves from the religious lives of their people. But state support of the arts and humanities increased and remains today a legacy of the Hellenistic Age to the modern world.

Hellenistic sculpture and architecture left their mark on later civilizations. Artists brought to their genre sculpture an invigorating realism that expressed emotions and individualism. They introduced the portrayal of female nudity, a practice that has persisted in Western art to the present day, with the exception of the Christian Middle Ages. Their emphasis on individualism influenced Roman sculptors, who, in carving many lifelike busts during the republic, preserved this tradition in Western art. The Corinthian temple, perfected in the Hellenistic era, set the standard in decoration and proportion for Roman temples and, along with the Doric and Ionic styles, was adopted and modified for many public structures.

A final legacy of the Hellenistic Age was its schools of philosophy—Stoicism, Epicureanism, Skepticism, and Cynicism. Although contradictory of each other, these schools of thought had a common appeal: the promise of a stable belief system and inner peace in the face of a hostile and chaotic environment. From Roman times to the present, these philosophies have attracted followers, but Stoicism has had the most enduring impact (on republican Rome, early Christianity, and the Enlightenment), with Epicureanism the next most influential (on the Scientific Revolution and the twentieth century). With their advice to disengage oneself from either the world or one's own passions, these four schools have provided solace in every age marked by overwhelming events and social disorder.

KEY CULTURAL TERMS

Hellenistic
koine
New Comedy
comedy of manners
Alexandrianism
pastoral
idyll
Cynicism
autarky

Skepticism
Epicureanism
ataraxia
Stoicism
logos
Corinthian
podium
genre subject
Neoclassicism

SUGGESTIONS FOR FURTHER READING

Primary Sources

AUSTIN, M. M., ed. *The Hellenistic World from Alexander to the Roman Conquest: A Selection of Ancient Sources in Translation.* Cambridge: Cambridge University Press, 1981. Letters, decrees, and official pronouncements from the Hellenistic period; provides a real sense of the time.

SHAPIRO, H., AND CURLEY, E., eds. *Hellenistic Philosophy: Selected Readings.* New York: Modern Library, 1965. Selections from writings on Epicureanism, Stoicism, Skepticism, and Neo-Platonism, with short introductions.

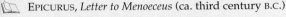

CHAPTER *4* HIGHLIGHTS
Classical Greek Civilization: The Hellenistic Age

MENANDER, *The Woman from Samos* (ca. 321 B.C.)

 THEOCRITUS, *Idylls* (ca. early third century B.C.)

EPICURUS, *Letter to Menoeceus* (ca. third century B.C.)

4.9 Olympieum, various dates: late sixth century B.C.; second quarter of second century B.C.; completed second quarter of second century A.D.

4.7 *Epicurus* (ca. 290–280 B.C.)

4.12 *Dying Gaul* (ca. 230–220 B.C.)

4.13 *Old Market Woman* (third or second century B.C.)

4.4 *Nike of Samothrace* (ca. 190 B.C.)

4.10 Altar of Zeus at Pergamum (170s B.C.)

4.14 *Athena Battling with Alkyoneus* (170s B.C.)

4.15 *Aphrodite of Melos* (ca. 160–150 B.C.)

4.1 Black Youth Singing (second century B.C.)

4.17 *Horse and Jockey of Artemision* (mid–second century B.C.)

4.18 *Muse (Melpomene* or *Polyhymnia (?))* (mid–second century B.C.)

4.11 *Boy Struggling with a Goose* (second half of second century B.C.)

4.16 AGASIAS OF EPHESUS, *Borghese Gladiator* (ca. 100 B.C.)

4.19 HAGESANDROS, POLYDOROS, and ATHANADOROS, *The Laocoön Group* (ca. A.D. 50)

■ *Literature & Philosophy*   ■ *Art & Architecture*   ■ *Music & Dance*

 Readings in the Western Humanities

5 ROMAN CIVILIZATION
The Pre-Christian Centuries

Roman civilization is as ancient as Greek civilization, but it reached its peak later. From its legendary founding in 753 B.C., Rome grew steadily from a tiny city-state ruled by kings to a powerful republic, constantly adjusting to internal and external forces, and ultimately to a vast empire that controlled the known Western world. This chapter surveys Rome from its founding to its near collapse in A.D. 284. Chapter 7 follows the story of Rome through its rejuvenated and Christian period to the last days of the empire. Before that, Chapter 6 examines the Judeo-Christian tradition that wove itself inextricably into the Western heritage during the first centuries of imperial Rome.

THE COLOSSUS OF THE MEDITERRANEAN WORLD

In A.D. 248 the Romans celebrated the one-thousandth anniversary of the founding of their city. By that date, the Roman way of life had not only engulfed the peoples and cultures of the ancient Near East and the eastern Mediterranean but also brought the light of civilized existence to the tribes living in North Africa, in western Europe to the Rhine River, in central Europe to the Danube River, and in England (Map 5.1). So vast was Rome's dominion and so powerful its influence that until the eighteenth century, Rome was the exemplar of power and wealth, one that the nations of Europe could only dream of equaling. Roman civilization had a profound and lasting impact on life in the West.

◀ **Detail** *Augustus*, from Prima Porta. Ca. A.D. 14. Marble, ht. 6′7¹/₂″. Vatican Collection.

LEARNING THROUGH MAPS

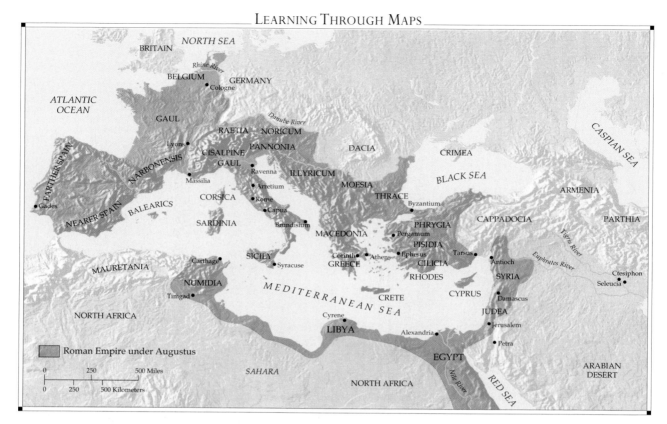

Map 5.1 THE ROMAN EMPIRE UNDER AUGUSTUS, A.D. 14
This map shows the Roman Empire at the death of its founder, Augustus. **Notice** the
wide-ranging lands incorporated into the Roman world. **Compare** this map with Map
1.1, Mesopotamia and Ancient Egypt, and Map 4.1, The Successor States and the
Hellenistic World, and see which ancient civilizations were now included in the
Roman Empire. **What** impact did these ancient civilizations have on Roman cultural
life? **What** role did the Mediterranean Sea play in the Roman Empire? **How** did
Rome's location make it a convenient site for the imperial government?

General Characteristics of Roman Civilization

Who were the Romans, and how did they create such a
successful civilization? The Romans were, above all, a
practical people, interested chiefly in what was useful.
Possessed of a virile moral sense, they were inclined to
view intellectual brilliance with suspicion. Furthermore, Roman authority figures cultivated the virtue
known in Latin as *gravitas,* or gravity, meaning a deep-
seated seriousness (Figure 5.1). By Greek standards,
the Romans were a dull lot, too self-controlled and
afraid of the imagination. But the Romans were ingenious at adapting borrowed cultural forms and had a
gift for governing.

Early Rome was a minor city-state founded by
herdsmen and farmers on seven low hills beside the
Tiber River in central Italy. Over their long rise to
world leadership, the Romans changed radically, but
they never ceased to honor their agrarian roots. Roman
morality and Roman law both echoed a rural ethic by

stressing the importance of nature and of living within
one's means. Roman literary culture was also deeply
imbued with a reverence for a rustic past. When Rome
became prosperous, many writers bemoaned the corrupting power of luxury and appealed to the homespun values of Rome's founders.

Another important Roman value was the sanctity of
the family. Divorce was unheard of until the late republican era, and even then family values continued to be eu-
logized by moralists and honored by leaders. Roles were
strictly defined within the Roman family, which was
guided by the father, the *paterfamilias,* who exercised legal power of life and death over his entire household, including his spouse, children, relatives, servants, and
slaves (Figure 5.2). The paterfamilias wielded greater authority than his Greek counterpart, but, in contrast, the
Roman matron was freer and had more practical influence than did the secluded wives of Greece. In general,
the Roman matron was conspicuously present in society,
attending and presiding at gatherings along with her

Figure 5.1 *Statue of a Republican General.* 75–50 B.C. Marble, ht. 78″. Museo Nazionale, Rome. *This statue portrays an unknown military leader from the Late Republic. The deeply serious though realistic face is typical of the Roman style. By this time, Roman generals were imitating the custom of Hellenistic leaders of having themselves depicted as nude or seminude figures. This fashion ended abruptly with the reign of Augustus, when rulers began to be represented wearing a cuirass, or breastplate (see Figure 5.22).*

mate and supervising the education of both her female and her male offspring (Figure 5.3).

Religion permeated family life, and each Roman household kept an undying fire burning on its hearth, symbolic of the goddess Vesta, to ensure the family's continuity. The family revered the deceased male ancestors, whose funeral masks adorned the walls and were regularly used in domestic rituals.

In sum, the Roman citizen was secure in the knowledge of both Rome's and his place in the world and in the cosmos. And the Roman matron, though lacking the voting rights citizenship gave to her spouse, played many roles that society and tradition demanded of her.

The Etruscan and Greek Connections

Although the Romans took great pride in their native tradition, they were receptive to change and able to assimilate the contributions of superior cultures, as their

Figure 5.2 *Patrician with Busts of Ancestors* (*Barberini Togatus*). Early first century A.D. Marble, ht. 5′5″. Palazzo dei Conservatori, Rome. *The stern and wrinkled faces of the anonymous patrician and his ancestors convey the quiet dignity and authority of the typical paterfamilias. Some scholars think that these portrait busts, with their unflattering realism, were modeled on death masks.*

Figure 5.3 *Eumachia. Mid–first century A.D. Marble. Museo Nazionale, Naples. This statue of Eumachia, which was found at Pompeii, shows that Roman matrons were involved in public life. The inscription on the statue's base praises her for having donated a building in the town's forum for the use of the fullers—workers involved in the making of woolen cloth. Her statue was paid for by the fullers' association in gratitude for her gift. Her idealized face reflects the Hellenic ideal preferred during the reign of Augustus in the first century A.D.*

Etruscan domination, Rome prospered and became a hub of commerce and transportation. Romans also began to put their spoken language into writing, using the Etruscan alphabet. Even what are called Roman numerals were invented by the Etruscans.

Whereas the Etruscans had conquered the Romans, it was the Romans who made the opening move in conquering the Greeks, beginning in 275 B.C. with the Greek colonies in southern Italy, or Magna Graecia. More conquests followed as Rome, between 146 and 31 B.C., assimilated the separate Hellenistic kingdoms into its overseas empire. Styling themselves after the defeated Hellenistic rulers, the Roman emperors eventually claimed to be immortal gods, turning the state into a divine monarchy. The emperors also adopted the civilizing mission of the Hellenistic kingdoms, thus giving Rome's domestic and foreign policies a new moral dimension.

The conquest of the Hellenistic kingdoms propelled Rome to the height of ancient civilization. However, in the end, Greek civilization conquered the conquerors, for when the Greek cultural forms (lyric and epic poetry, the arts, and architecture, among others) were imported into Rome, the Romans were forced out of their exclusively practical ways. The Romans coined the term *humanities* to refer to the artistic, literary, and philosophical activities the Greeks considered basic to civilized life. But the humanities themselves were Greek inventions, as was the belief that the study and practice of the humanities is stimulating to the soul (mind). Thus, the humanities, which originated among the artists and intellectuals of Archaic and Hellenic Greece, were preserved and transmitted by the Romans, an achievement that some historians regard as Rome's finest.

The Roman Empire was centuries in the making, and pre-Christian Roman history can be divided into three periods reflecting the prevailing type of government: monarchy (753–509 B.C.), republic (509–31 B.C.), and empire (31 B.C.–A.D. 284) (Timeline 5.1). In each period, earlier traits and values endured.

Rome in the Age of Kings, 753–509 B.C.

During the Age of Kings, some basic components of Roman political, social, and economic structures were established. The city-state, although ruled by kings, had a balanced system of government in which a council of landowners helped select the ruler and the entire people ratified its choice. This system ended in about 600 B.C. when the Etruscans imposed their rulers on Rome, but it became a model for government under the republic.

Also taking root at this time was another persistent feature of Roman political and economic life—class conflict. As Rome expanded, some urban dwellers,

experience with the Etruscans and the Greeks demonstrates. In the late seventh century B.C., Rome, still a small city-state, was subjugated by the Etruscans, a sophisticated urban people of obscure origins in northern Italy. The Etruscans excelled at commerce and conducted a brisk maritime trade with the advanced cultures of the eastern Mediterranean (Figure 5.4). Under

Figure 5.4 *Apollo of Veii.* Early fifth century B.C. Painted terra-cotta, ht. 70". Museo Nazionale di Villa Guilia, Rome. *This magnificent striding statue of Apollo shows strong influences from the art of Archaic Greece, such as the proportion of the torso to the limbs and the enigmatic smile. But the superb mastery of movement achieved by the Etruscan artist is well in advance of the Greek style.*

Timeline 5.1   THE ROMAN MILLENNIUM, 753 B.C.–A.D. 248

753 B.C	509 B.C		31 B.C.	A.D. 248
	Monarchy	Republic	Empire	
Founding of Rome	ca. 600 Etruscan rulers	Founding of the republic	Founding of the empire	1,000th birthday of Rome

debarred from the aristocracy by poverty and birth, took advantage of commercial opportunities and began to engage in trade. The plebeians, as this class was called, accumulated wealth and began to challenge the social power of the landed aristocrats. When the aristocrats abolished the monarchy and established the republic, they safeguarded their power by denying citizenship to the plebeians. This policy of exclusion laid the groundwork for centuries of class conflict.

The Roman Republic, 509–31 B.C.

In 509 B.C., the Roman aristocrats threw off their Etruscan overlords and founded a republic. Unlike the Greeks, whose political order consisted of short-lived leagues of city-states, the Romans established a republic whose provinces eventually reached the eastern Mediterranean and that lasted almost five hundred years. This republic, in contrast to Athens's direct democracy, was based on a system of representatives and a separation of powers. Rome's achievement is unsurpassed in Western history.

Rome's republic is divided into three principal periods: early, middle, and late. During these tumultuous periods, Rome became a world power (Timeline 5.2).

The Early Republic, 509–264 B.C.   Two major crises, one domestic and one foreign, faced the Early Republic and threatened to overwhelm the fledgling state. The domestic issue stemmed from the division of society into two classes—the landed, aristocratic patricians and the unorganized, disenfranchised plebeians. As the patricians dismantled the monarchy and set up a republic, they continued to exclude the plebeians from political life. They placed executive power with two consuls, each with veto power over the other. They gave legal and fiscal power to magistracies—public offices—and legislative and judicial powers to an assembly. But real power resided with the Senate, the successor to the old council of landowners that had existed under the kings. The plebeians were given no part in these reforms, but, over the years, they steadily won concessions. By 287 B.C., they had gained

all the rights of citizenship enjoyed by the ruling patricians.

The foreign crisis faced by Rome was the military conquest of the various peoples inhabiting the Italian peninsula. During these first foreign wars, the Romans originated the strategy that became the key to their military success. They permitted defeated peoples to remain self-governing, to keep their own religions, and, most especially, to satisfy obligations to Rome by providing troops for her armies instead of paying taxes. This strategy allowed the former foes some freedom and yet subtly tied them to Rome.

The Middle Republic, 264–133 B.C.   Roman armies had conquered Italy, but up and down the peninsula restless tribes were not securely attached to Rome. The challenge was to convert them to the Roman way of life. By founding new towns and enticing settlers with offers of free land and full Roman citizenship, Rome eventually united the entire population. Roman law and the Latin language triumphed on the Italian peninsula.

Beyond the peninsula, Rome faced the challenge of Carthage, a Phoenician state in North Africa that dominated the western Mediterranean and blocked Rome's expansion into that area. In the Punic Wars (from the Latin *poeni,* "Phoenician") (264–146 B.C.), a series of three separate but related conflicts, Rome overwhelmed and finally destroyed Carthage; later, in 29 B.C., the Romans refounded Carthage as the capital of the province of Africa. At the end of the Third Punic War in 146 B.C., Rome added Sicily, Corsica, Sardinia, and North Africa to its realm.

The wars transformed both the Roman state and the Roman character. The republic's imperialistic ambitions were emboldened by its acquisition of new territories to the west. And during the Second Punic War, the Carthaginian general Hannibal had invaded Italy and ravaged the countryside for fourteen years. His scorched-earth policy devastated Italy's farm country, and small farms began to be replaced by huge ranches worked by slaves. Italy's social fabric was permanently changed.

Having made themselves masters in the west, the Romans moved quickly to conquer the Hellenistic kingdoms to the east. The Romans granted greater freedom

Timeline 5.2   THE ROMAN REPUBLIC, 509–31 B.C.

509			264		133	31
Early Republic			Middle Republic		Late Republic	
Rome establishes republican form of government, subdues Italian peninsula			**264–241** First Punic War **219–202** Second Punic War	**149–146** Third Punic War	**133–31** Rome acquires Hellenistic kingdoms; social, political unrest	**44** Julius Caesar assassinated **44–31** civil war

to these older Hellenistic cultures, but they forcefully organized and civilized the western provinces. At the end of the Middle Republic, Romans could justly call the Mediterranean Mare Nostrum—"Our Sea."

The Late Republic, 133–31 B.C.   Rome in the Late Republic was ruled by an oligarchy of patrician families who dominated the Senate and clung stubbornly to their rights and privileges. Although Roman power continued to spread throughout the Mediterranean basin, economic and social problems multiplied.

One problem was generated by the rise of the equestrian order (*equites* in Latin), a social class who had gained wealth during the Punic Wars but who lacked the political power of the patricians. By the mid–first century B.C., open warfare had broken out between the equites and the senators, contributing to the anarchy of the period.

At the same time, the nature of the masses was changing. Increasing numbers of independent farmers were pushed off the land by large estate owners, and many of them went to Rome, where they lived in perpetual poverty and sold their votes to the highest bidders. In an effort to pacify them, the government instituted free bread and public amusements, scornfully referred to by critics as "bread and circuses." The farmer-soldier ideal of early Rome now gave way to a new mentality, one more concerned with bloody sporting events such as gladiatorial contests than with political rights and duties.

The republic's last hope for substantive reform was Julius Caesar, a major figure in Roman politics from 60 to 44 B.C. Caesar had emerged as a great public hero by pacifying Gaul (France). The commander of a loyal and formidable army, he had defeated rival generals to become Rome's sole ruler in 48 B.C. He took his authority from the many titles and powers he held, including dictator for life, consul, and head of the armies. Future Roman emperors recognized him as their predecessor by calling themselves Caesar, or ruler. With the possible exception of Alexander the Great, no other Western ruler has generated such praise or blame from philosophers, poets, and artists.

Caesar, though acting in the name of equestrian interests, held a lofty vision for Rome's future. He initiated building projects that gave work to the urban poor, allowed the Italians outside Rome more self-rule, and founded Rome's first public library. But Caesar's enemies in the Senate believed that the dictator wanted to be king—the dreaded fear dating back to Etruscan Rome. On the Ides of March (March 15) in 44 B.C., a band of senatorial assassins murdered Caesar, and Rome plunged into chaos.

A new leader emerged from the years of unrest that followed: Octavian, Caesar's great-nephew and adopted son. His accession to power in 31 B.C. marked the beginning of the Pax Romana (Roman peace), a two-hundred-year period of unprecedented tranquility and economic growth. But it also marked the gradual dismantling of the republic and the establishment of an autocratic empire.

Growing Autocracy: Imperial Rome, 31 B.C.–A.D. 284

When Octavian returned peace and order to Rome, he pledged to restore the republic. He maintained the government offices, the Senate, and the political machinery, but beneath the surface of the Roman state, power was being transferred to one man, the emperor. With no legal safeguards against the emperor's will, the citizens became subject to his personal whim, and political liberty was gradually strangled. Subsequent Roman emperors enhanced their power by stifling dissent and glorifying themselves, eventually adopting the Hellenistic practice of emperor worship.

The political structure forged by Octavian remained intact from 31 B.C. to A.D. 284. This span of almost three centuries may be broken into two parts: the two-hundred-year Pax Romana and nearly a century of civil wars.

Figure 5.5   Timgad, Algeria. Ca. A.D. 100. *Timgad, strategically located at the intersection of six Roman roads in North Africa, was typical of the towns built from scratch by the Romans during the Pax Romana and populated by ex-soldiers and their families. The town was planned as a square with two main avenues crossing in the middle where the forum stood and all other streets intersecting at right angles. The so-called Arch of Trajan in the foreground marked one of the main thoroughfares, which was lined with columns. Temples, baths, fountains, markets, a theater, and private homes gave the city the reputation of being a pleasant place to live.*

Pax Romana, 31 B.C.–A.D. 193   Octavian, who became known as Augustus Caesar, or "revered ruler," established his power by converting Egypt—Rome's wealthiest province—into his personal property and by making the military the loyal mainstay of his rule. His armies pushed back Rome's frontiers, stopping at what he considered its natural borders, the Rhine and Danube Rivers. Augustus then extended the celebrated Pax Romana to the people whom he conquered. Governors were dispatched to rule and collect taxes, army camps were created to keep law and order, and colonies and municipalities were founded to provide more land for Romans. The amenities of urban life were also expanded: Temples, altars, schools, arenas, libraries, marketplaces, aqueducts, fountains, and baths were built, and paved roads linked each far outpost with Rome (Figure 5.5).

Under Augustus (r. 31 B.C.–A.D. 14), economic life also became centralized. Agriculture, industry, and trade flourished, and most social classes prospered. At the same time, Rome became a true melting pot. Except for the inhabitants of the Greek-speaking East, most people spoke Latin and followed Roman customs. Divisive social and ethnic issues had faded from memory as patrician power waned and equestrian power grew. Senators and emperors now came from the equestrian order as well as from the provinces of Greece and Spain.

Civil Wars, A.D. 193–284   Despite its economic success, however, the empire was profoundly hampered by a major problem: how to select a new emperor. Adoption and inheritance were both tried, often with disastrous results. The murder of the emperor Commodus in A.D. 193 ushered in decades of civil wars, military rule, violence, and chaos. Of the twenty-seven so-called Barrack emperors (rulers drawn from the ranks of the Roman legions) in the third century, only four died natural deaths.

The empire was beset by problems both inside and outside its boundaries. Searching for loot, implacable Germanic tribes began crossing the northern frontiers. Runaway inflation and a debased coinage wiped out fortunes and caused a return to barter exchange. The Roman army forcibly requisitioned food and supplies from civilians. In addition, a plague ravaged the empire, killing perhaps hundreds of thousands. In A.D. 284, Diocletian, a general from Illyricum (modern Croatia) seized power. In time, his reforms would snatch Rome from the brink of destruction, as described in Chapter 7.

THE STYLE OF PRE-CHRISTIAN ROME: FROM GREEK IMITATION TO ROMAN GRANDEUR

Hellenistic culture became the foundation of Roman civilization. Often, Rome simply expanded on Hellenistic ideas, but in areas for which the Romans had a special gift, as in lyric poetry and comedy, they created works that rivaled the Greek originals. And in architecture, the Romans made their greatest mark, because this art form naturally blends the utilitarian with the aesthetic.

As in any civilization, Roman cultural achievements were shaped by their political and social contexts. Especially notable in the long evolution of Roman culture is the shift in style that occurred as the republic gave way to the empire, a shift that can be seen in every area of cultural expression.

Under the republic, artistic achievements were inspired by the Greek model and appealed to the privileged few. Under the empire, a distinctive Roman style began to emerge in response to the tastes of the masses, and spectacle became important in Roman culture. In this atmosphere, philosophy survived mainly as an antidote to the restrictions of the imperial regime. Literature flourished among an educated elite, but flattery and propaganda crept into the works of even the greatest writers. And architecture and sculpture became increasingly monumental and theatrical.

Roman Religion

The native Roman religion was deeply affected by the cults of neighboring and conquered peoples. The **syncretism,** blending of religion, began in earliest times.

Table 5.1	THE CHIEF ROMAN GODS AND GODDESSES AND THEIR GREEK COUNTERPARTS
ROMAN	*GREEK*
Jupiter	Zeus
Juno	Hera
Neptune	Poseidon
Pluto	Hades
Vesta	Hestia
Apollo	Apollo
Diana	Artemis
Mars	Ares
Venus	Aphrodite
Vulcan	Hephaestus
Minerva	Athena
Mercury	Hermes

After their initial contacts with the Greeks in southern Italy, the Romans started to intermingle their divinities with those of the Greek religious system, who seemed to be always either making mischief or making love (Table 5.1). Thereafter, the Greek deities enlivened Rome's religion and inspired her writers, musicians, and artists with thrilling stories. And even after the fall of Rome, the Greco-Roman gods and goddesses continued to live in the art, music, and literature of Europe.

From the Punic Wars onward, innovative cults sprang up in Rome. From Egypt came the worship of Isis (Figure 5.6), a religion that promised immortality, and from Asia Minor the cult of Cybele, a mother goddess. Army veterans returning from Persia brought back Mithra, the mortal son of the sun god, whose cult excluded women (Figure 5.7). Mithra's followers observed each seventh day as Sun Day and December 25 as the god's birthday; the faithful also underwent a baptism in the blood of a sacred bull.

Religious innovation was perpetuated in imperial Rome until Greek and oriental cults finally submerged the old Roman beliefs. Most of all, the emperor cult—the state policy of encouraging public worship of the ruler as a god—succeeded admirably, except among two groups of Roman subjects who refused to recognize the ruler's divinity—the Jews and the Christians, whose story of resistance and rebellion is told in Chapter 6.

Language, Literature, and Drama

Latin, the Roman language, was at first an unimaginative, functional language, suited only to legal

Figure 5.6 *Preparations for a Banquet.* Ca. A.D. 180–190. Detail. Mosaic, total size 7'4⁵/₈" × 6'10⁵/₈". Formerly in Carthage (Sidi-bou-Said), North Africa. Louvre. *This mosaic, depicting a slave-attendant at a banquet, probably decorated a room used by the Isis cult for ritualistic dinners, though no records have been found identifying the building in which it was discovered. The work's style, with its nearly life-size figure set against a plain white ground and the careful rendering of the human body, is typical of the mosaics of this period.*

documents, financial records, and military commands. But with the growth of law and oratory in the Early Republic, grammar was standardized, vocabulary was increased, and word meanings were clarified. As the Romans conquered, they made Latin the language of state, except in the Greek-speaking East. By the late empire, Latin had spread throughout the civilized world and was the common tongue for the vast majority of Roman citizens. Latin literature began to flourish in the Middle Republic (264–133 B.C.) with lyric and epic poetry, comedy, and tragedy, all in the Greek style, although writers were beginning to develop a distinctive Roman style. Roman literature changed with the changing times, evolving through several quite distinct periods.

The First Literary Period, 250–31 B.C. The writing of the first literary period was noteworthy for its strongly

Greek flavor and, in some writers, its grave moral tone. This period also saw the rise of a Roman theatrical tradition influenced both by roots in boisterous Etruscan religious celebrations and by contact with the Greek theater. Many educated Romans in this period could speak Greek, and many had seen performances of tragedies and comedies during their travels.

Plautus [PLAW-tuhs] (about 254–184 B.C.), a plebeian from Italy, launched Rome's great age of comic theater with his almost 130 plays. His genius lay in breathing fresh life into the stale plots and stock characters borrowed from Menander and other Hellenistic, New Comedy playwrights. In his hands, the mistaken identities, verbal misunderstandings, and bungled schemes seemed brand new. Rome's other significant comic playwright was Terence [TAIR-ents] (about 195–159 B.C.), a Carthaginian slave who was brought

Figure 5.7 *Mithra Slaying the Bull.* Third century A.D. Marble, ht. 2′10¼″. Antiquario Comunale, Rome. *This relief depicts the defining moment of the Mithra cult, a standard representation found across the Roman Empire in statues and in paintings. Mithra, dressed in Phrygian cap, tunic, trousers, and flowing cloak, presses his right knee on the bull as he slays it. The various animals and humans surrounding this dramatic scene symbolize the themes of good and evil, light and dark, life and death, which are central to the religion.*

to Rome, educated, and set free. Although he wrote only six plays, he won the acclaim of Rome's educated elite, perhaps because of the pure Greek tone and themes of his works. Terence's highly polished style later inspired the magisterial Cicero.

As Roman comedy began to decline, superseded by the vast spectacles that the masses demanded, two major poets with distinctively different personalities and talents appeared: Lucretius and Catullus. Both were heavily influenced by Greece. Lucretius [lew-KRE-shuhs] (about 94–about 55 B.C.) stands in the long line of instructive literary figures dating from Homer. A gifted poet, with his well-turned Latin phrases and imaginative and vivid language, Lucretius wrote *De Rerum Natura (On the Nature of Things)* to persuade the reader of the truth of Epicureanism, the philosophy based on scientific atomism that denied divine intervention in human affairs (see Chapter 4).

In contrast to Lucretius's lengthy poem, the verses of Catullus [kuh-TUHL-uhs] (about 84–about 54 B.C.) are characterized by brevity, one of the hallmarks of the Alexandrian school of the Hellenistic Age. Catullus's "small" epics, epigrams, and love poems also closely imitate the scholarly and romantic qualities of Alexandrianism. Catullus is best remembered for his love poems, which draw on the lives of his highborn, free-spirited circle in Rome, and which express his innermost feelings of desire, disappointment, and jealousy.

The efforts of Lucretius and Catullus pale, however, when placed beside those of their contemporary Cicero (106–43 B.C.). An equestrian from Italy, he dominated Roman letters in his own day so much that his era is often labeled the Age of Cicero. By translating Greek treatises into Latin, he created a philosophical vocabulary for the Latin language where none had existed before. For centuries, Cicero's collected speeches served as models both of public oratory and of written argument. Similarly, his philosophical tracts set the agenda for generations of thinkers and reformers. Today's readers rank Cicero's collection of letters, most by him, some addressed to him (a few written by his son), as his masterpiece. These nearly nine hundred letters, frank in style and language, offer a unique self-portrait of a major public figure in ancient times (Figure 5.8).

The Second Literary Period: The Golden Age, 31 B.C.– A.D. 14 The second period of Roman literature coincided with the personal reign of Augustus and is considered the Golden Age of Roman letters. This period's three greatest writers, Vergil, Horace, and Ovid, captured the age's euphoric mood as peace and stability once more returned to Rome. Of the three writers, Vergil best represented the times through his vision of Rome and his stirring verses.

The works of Vergil [VUR-jill] (70–19 B.C.), an Italian plebeian, were inspired by Greek literary forms—idylls

PERSONAL PERSPECTIVE

MARCUS, SON OF CICERO
Changing My Ways

Marcus, having been accused of overspending his allowance, writes to Tiro, Cicero's secretary. In the letter, from Athens, 44 B.C., Marcus, knowing that Tiro will inform his father, gives assurances that he has reformed his ways.

I had been looking for a letter when one finally came, forty-six days out. Its arrival brought me the keenest joy; for in addition to the pleasure I got from the kind words of my father your most delightful letter filled my cup of joy to overflowing. Accordingly, I was not sorry that there had been a break in our correspondence, but rather was I glad; for I profit greatly by your writing after my long silence. Therefore I rejoice exceedingly that you have accepted my excuses.

I don't doubt, my dearest Tiro, that you are deeply gratified over the rumors that are reaching your ears, and I will guarantee and strive that with the passing days this nascent good report may be increased twofold. You may, therefore, keep your promise of being a trumpeter of my good repute, for the errors of my youth have brought me such pain and sorrow that not only does my soul recoil at the acts themselves but my ear shrinks from the very mention of them. I know full well that you shared in the anxiety and worry of this experience.

Since I then brought you sorrow, I'll warrant that now I will bring you joy in double measure. Let me tell you that I am associated with Cratippus not as a disciple but as a son, for not only do I listen to his lectures with pleasure but also I am greatly privileged to enjoy him in person. I am with him all day and very often a part of the night since by much pleading I often succeed in getting him to dine with me. Now that he has got used to this habit, he often drops in on me at dinner time and, laying aside the severe demeanor of a college professor, he jokes with me like a human. See to it, therefore, that you embrace the earliest opportunity of meeting the eminent gentleman, of finding out what he is like, and of becoming acquainted with his merry disposition.

What now shall I say of Professor Bruttius? I keep him with me all the time. He is a regular stoic in his habits of life but a jolly good fellow withal, for he is very much of a wit both in his lectures and in his discussions. I have hired lodgings for him next door, and, as best I may, out of my slender purse I relieve him in his slender circumstances.

Besides, I am studying public speaking in Greek with Cassius. I am planning to do the same with Bruttius in Latin. On Cratippus' recommendation I am on very intimate terms with certain learned gentlemen whom he brought with him from Mytilene. I also spend a good deal of time with Epicrates, the chief Athenian, Dean Leonidas, and other men of that sort. So much for what I am doing. . . .

I am deeply grateful to you for looking out for my commissions; please send me as soon as possible a secretary, by all means one who knows Greek; he will save me much labor in copying out my notes. Of all things, be sure to take care of yourself that we may be able to pursue our studies together. I commend you to Anterus (the postman).

(or vignettes), didactic (instructive) poems, and epics— yet his use of native themes and his focus on the best traits in the Roman people give an authentic Roman voice to his work. Deeply moved by Augustus's reforms, he put his art in the service of the state. Vergil's pastoral poetry, the *Eclogues* and *Georgics,* celebrated rural life and urged readers to seek harmony with nature in order to find peace—advice that became a significant moral theme of the Western heritage. But Vergil is best known for the *Aeneid,* an epic poem in twelve books that he wrote in imitation of the Homeric epics. In this work, infused with Roman values and ideals, Vergil gave full voice to his love of country, his respect for Augustus, and his faith in Rome's destiny.

The *Aeneid* tells of Aeneas, the legendary Trojan hero who wandered the Mediterranean before founding Rome. In the first six books, Vergil models his tale on the *Odyssey,* writing of travel and love. The second half is modeled on the *Iliad,* stressing fighting and intrigue. The *Aeneid* became Rome's bible and its literary masterpiece. Children were often required to memorize passages from the poem to instill in them the values that had made Rome great. Aeneas served as the prototype of the faithful leader who would not be diverted from his destined path. The work's rich language led later poets to mine the *Aeneid* for expressions and images. As Homer inspired Vergil, so Vergil became the model for Western poets when imaginative literature was revived in late medieval Europe.

The second major poet of the Golden Age was Horace (65–8 B.C.), another Italian plebeian who also welcomed Augustus as Rome's savior and offered patriotic sentiments in his verses. His poems, which were written to be read aloud, use Alexandrian forms such

Figure 5.8 *Cicero.* First century B.C. Capitoline Museum, Rome. *The anonymous sculptor of this bust of Cicero has caught the character of the man as recalled in literary sources. Honored as one of Rome's finest intellectuals and a patriot devoted to rescuing the state from chaos, he is depicted deep in thought with stern and resolute features. This idealized portrait contributed to the mystique of Cicero as a hero of the Roman republic.*

as odes and letters in verse. He helped to create a new poetic genre, the **satire,** which rebuked the manners of the age. Horace was at his best in addressing the heartbreaking brevity of life: "what has been, has been, and I have had my hour."

Ovid [AHV-uhd] (43 B.C.–about A.D. 17), the third voice of the Golden Age, was a wealthy Italian equestrian who did not devote his verses to patriotic themes or pay lip service to conventional morality. Ovid's love poems speak of the purely sensual and fleeting quality of sex and ignore the enduring value of committed love. His *Art of Love* offers advice, in a manner bordering on the scientific, on how to seduce women, whether willing or not. Such advice contrasted with Vergil's and Horace's attempts to raise the moral level of the Romans.

Ovid's masterpiece was the *Metamorphoses,* or *Transformations.* Somewhat irreverently, he breathed new life

into more than two hundred Greek and Roman myths and legends that centered on the transformation of people into other forms. This work is the source of our knowledge of many Classical myths, and medieval and Renaissance poets turned to it continually for inspiration.

The Third Literary Period: The Silver Age, A.D. *14–200*
In the third literary period, the patriotic style of the previous era was replaced by the critical views of writers who often satirized Roman society and the state. Lacking the originality of the Golden Age, the writers of this era looked to their predecessors for models while they polished their phrases and reworked earlier themes. This shift in literary taste reflected a new educational ideal, which stressed skills in debate and oratory. As a result, moral considerations became secondary to aesthetic effects, with writers using rhetorical flourishes and exaggerated literary conceits.

One of Rome's outstanding Silver Age talents was Seneca [SEN-e-kuh] (4 B.C.–A.D. 65). Born into a wealthy equestrian family in Spain, Seneca became a powerful senator and one of the age's chief thinkers. He is best remembered as a dramatist, though his works failed to measure up to the Greek heritage. His ten extant plays relied on emotionalism, rhetorical excess, and stage violence—the perennial traits of Roman tragedy. After his day, the staging of tragedies ceased, not to be revived for more than fifteen hundred years.

The Silver Age produced Rome's last great Latin poet, Juvenal [JOO-vuh-nuhl] (about A.D. 60–about 140), who trained his censorious gaze on the follies of the empire. Juvenal expressed his outraged observations in sixteen satires, the literary form originated by Horace and others. The voice that speaks in Juvenal's satires is embittered, perhaps a reflection of his obscure social origins. But the carefully crafted language—obscene, bilious, and evocative but always just right—made him the master of this genre in Rome, if not in world letters.

The leading historian of the Silver Age was Tacitus [TASS-i-tus] (A.D. 55?–117), famed also as an orator and politician. He honored the Greek tradition of historical writing, which dictated that history must be written according to literary rules, that the proper study of history is contemporary events, and that effects in history have human, not supernatural, causes.

Tacitus acquired his knowledge of statecraft as the governor of the province of Asia (modern southwest Turkey). Among his works are two that have earned him the front rank among Roman historians. The *Annals* focus on the rulers after the death of Augustus in A.D. 14 until the murder of Nero in 68. The *Histories* then pick up the story of Rome and carry it through 96, when the tyrannical Domitian was assassinated.

Tacitus was a master of the Latin language and had a flair for dramatic narrative. Like other Roman historians, he wrote history with a moral purpose, but his critical spirit set him apart from those who had nothing but glowing praise for Rome. Instead, Tacitus's perspective is that of a proud senator who cannot conceal his distaste for Rome's loss of political freedom. In his works, he sought to uncover the origins of the misrule that had almost destroyed Rome in his day, and he ended by concluding that tyranny was an innate flaw in the imperial office.

Philosophy

The Romans adopted the ethical aspects of Greek thought, but they rejected philosophy itself as dangerous, fearing that its study would draw their young men away from the military to lives of dreamy speculation. As a result, Roman thought stressed rules of behavior with little regard for metaphysics.

In time, Roman versions of Epicureanism and Stoicism reached a wide audience, notably among influential aristocrats. Although Epicureanism had little impact, mainly because its focus on withdrawal from worldly cares contradicted the Roman sense of duty, Stoicism's effect was potent and lasting. Stoic values seemed to confirm the farmer-soldier ideal, suggesting that the early Romans were unintentional Stoics. In addition, Stoicism under the empire caused a few aristocrats to resist, if passively, the growing menace of autocracy; these hardy Stoics, some of whom, like Seneca, willingly sacrificed their lives for their ideas, believed that the natural law was superior to the earthbound justice of the rulers.

Stoicism   Although Stoicism was introduced to Rome by Greek philosophers in the Late Republic, its greatest influence was achieved later, through the writings and teaching of Seneca, Epictetus, and the emperor Marcus Aurelius.

Seneca's fame as a philosopher rests on his *Letters on Morality.* These letters, which were usually written in response to pressing ethical problems, are filled with good advice, even though they break no new philosophical ground. Thus, for example, Seneca counseled a grieving acquaintance to maintain dignity and inner strength in the face of a loved one's death.

Seneca's *Letters* survived the fall of Rome in A.D. 476, but the works of most other thinkers temporarily disappeared. Consequently, he became one of the great guides for Western thought when philosophy was revived in the Middle Ages. In the modern world, however, his reputation has suffered because of his closeness to Nero, an emperor of legendary cruelty. Despite Seneca's noble philosophy, doubt has been cast on his personal morality.

No such cloud hovers over Epictetus [ep-ik-TEET-uhs] (about A.D. 55–115), who not only preached but also lived his Stoic creed. According to tradition, Epictetus, though a slave in Rome, won his freedom because of his teachings. He subsequently founded a school in Asia Minor and attracted enthusiastic converts. He did not write anything, but Arrian, a pupil, composed the *Discourses* and the *Handbook,* both in Greek, which together preserved the essence of his master's ideas.

Epictetus's philosophy reflected his own victory over personal misfortune. He advised patience in the face of trouble, indifference to material things, and acceptance of one's destiny. Although these ideas represented a rehash of basic Stoic beliefs, his moral wholeness gave them a special appeal.

Stoicism's finest hour arrived in A.D. 161 when Marcus Aurelius became emperor (Figure 5.9). Converted to Stoicism in his youth, the emperor wrote an account (in Greek) of his daily musings—called *Meditations*—while he was engaged in almost continuous warfare against Germanic invaders. His journal came to light after his death and was soon recognized as a masterpiece of Stoicism.

Like all Stoics, the emperor admonished himself to play with dignity the role that providence had assigned. If a divine plan guides the universe, then he must accept it; if, however, the world is ruled by chance, then a well-regulated mind is the best defense. Such reasoning enabled Marcus Aurelius to avoid moral confusion. The emperor's death in A.D. 180 signaled the end of Stoicism. The next century witnessed the swamping of all philosophies in the military anarchy and oriental cults of the times.

Neo-Platonism   Some Roman thinkers adopted Greek Stoicism; others were interested in blending the various Greek schools—Platonic, Aristotelian, and Stoic, among others—into a philosophic synthesis. The outstanding example of this latter trend was **Neo-Platonism,** a school of thought founded primarily by Plotinus [plo-TIE-nuhs] (A.D. 205–270) in the third century A.D. Neo-Platonism was the last major school of philosophy in the ancient world. The movement began as an attempt to correct the problem at the heart of Plato's system—the seemingly irreconcilable split between the absolute world of Ideas and the perishable material world. This Platonic dualism could and did lead to the notion that the everyday world has little purpose in the overall scheme of things. Plotinus now succeeded in bridging the two worlds with his theories, and his writings later influenced Christian

Law

The most original contribution of the Roman mind was law. Rome's law created a notion of justice founded on such ideals as fairness for both citizens and subjects, as well as the presumption of innocence in criminal cases. These principles later became central to the Western legal tradition. But the most important facet of Roman law was born in Stoicism: the idea of **natural law,** or a higher justice than that made by human forces. This doctrine of natural law is the basis of the American Declaration of Independence.

Rome's law evolved over many centuries, starting in 450 B.C. with the first written code, the Twelve Tables. These tables, which represented a plebeian victory over the patricians, treated basic aspects of civil life such as personal and property rights, religious practices, and moral behavior. But this milestone did not rid Rome of class distinctions; it merely recognized conflicting rights and the necessity of a judge above both parties. Through the years, class divisions continued to affect the way the law was applied, since the dispensing of justice always favored the rich.

The branch of Roman law dealing with property rights was called civil law and developed through the office of the *praetor.* Each praetor, at the beginning of his term, issued an edict describing the legal procedures and precedents he would follow. The body of decisions handed down by the praetors eventually came to constitute Rome's civil law.

By the Late Republic, the development of law was enhanced by the advice of legal experts, called *jurisconsults* or *jurisprudentes.* They tended to broaden Roman justice with their Stoic views. The most creative phase of Roman law occurred in the second and third centuries A.D., when eminent jurisconsults helped to codify the law and extend its principles to cover all the citizens of the empire.

The Visual Arts

Architecture and sculpture dominated Rome's visual arts, but they were pressed into the service of practical needs. The Romans commissioned buildings and statues to serve the state, religion, or society, but they recognized that the practical did not have to forgo beauty, and many of Rome's engineering feats were beautiful in their functional elegance.

The early Romans learned lessons in architecture from the Etruscans, but after encountering the Greeks of Magna Graecia, they rebuilt Rome along Greek lines. By the second century B.C., wealthy Romans were collecting Greek statues in all styles—Archaic, Hellenic, and Hellenistic. Under Augustus, Hellenic style in sculpture

Figure 5.9 *Marcus Aurelius. Ca. A.D. 173. Bronze, ht. 16'8".*
Piazza del Campidoglio, Rome. *The unknown artist has represented Marcus Aurelius as a warrior-emperor, but the militaristic image is offset somewhat by the Stoic ruler's face. Here we see revealed a human being lost in thought and far removed from pomp and power. This magnificent equestrian statue marked the climax of sculpture in the Roman Empire.*

thinkers in the Middle Ages and the Italian humanists of the Renaissance.

Plotinus resolved Platonic dualism not with logical analysis but with mystical insight, claiming that the union of the physical and spiritual worlds could be grasped only through an ecstatic vision. His retreat from philosophy into mysticism occurred during the turbulent era of the Barrack emperors, when many people fled from urban violence to the relative peace of their villas and estates in the countryside.

and architecture became supreme, inching across the empire over the next two centuries. By the third century A.D., a new architectural style had arisen, blending Greek and Roman styles. This Greco-Roman style carried over into medieval civilization after the collapse of the Roman Empire in the West (see Chapter 7).

Architecture   Over the years, the Romans used many types of materials in their public and private buildings. The architects of the Early Republic built with sundried bricks and used terra cotta, a fired clay, for roofs and decorations. As Rome's wealth grew and new materials were imported, the bricks retained an important though less visible role in buildings, chiefly in foundations and walls. By the Late Republic, two new products were adapted from the Greeks, mortar and ashlars (massive hewn stones), which, in time, revolutionized the face of Rome.

Much of the impetus for the building revolution sprang from the Romans' improvement of mortar. They produced a moldable concrete by mixing lime, sand, small rocks, and rubble, but because the concrete was visually unappealing, the builders began to cover it with slabs of expensive and highly polished marble and granite imported from Greece or quarried in Italy.

The temple became one of Rome's chief architectural forms. The basic source for the Roman temple was the Greek model with its post-beam-triangle

construction, although Etruscan influence was also significant. The Romans adapted the Greek column as either support or decoration, preferring the ornamented Corinthian order to the plainer Doric and Ionic.

The Romans' most significant innovations in architecture were made with the rounded arch, which already had a long history by the time they began to experiment with it. The Mesopotamians probably invented this arch, the Greeks knew about it, and the Etruscans used it in their drainage systems. The arch's basic round form is created with wedge-shaped stones called **voussoirs.** A **keystone** at the center of the semicircle locks the arch in place. The installed arch is amazingly strong, diverting the weight of the upper walls both outward and downward onto columns or other supports (Figure 5.10).

The Romans demonstrated their inventive genius by creating ceilings, or **vaults,** from arches—by transforming the simple rounded arch into barrel vaults, groined vaults, and domes. They created the **barrel vault**—named because it looks like a barrel divided lengthwise—by building a series of contiguous arches. They intersected two barrel vaults at right angles to produce a **groined,** or **cross, vault.** Finally, the dome, the crown jewel of Rome's architectural vocabulary, was constructed essentially by rotating an arch in a full circle (see Figure 5.10). The Romans were also able to build arches more safely after they discovered the

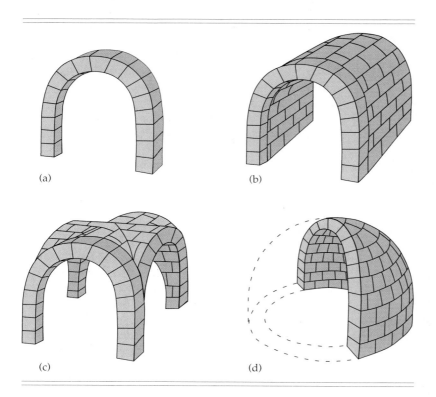

(a)

(b)

(c)

(d)

Figure 5.10 Structures Used in Roman Architecture. *Beginning with the basic arch (a), the Romans created the barrel vault (b) and the cross vault (c). These structural elements, along with the dome (d), which they formed by rotating a series of arches around a central axis, gave the Romans the architectural elements they needed to construct their innovative temples and monuments.*

Figure 5.11 Maison Carrée. Ca. 16 B.C. Base 104'4" × 48'10". Nîmes, France. *This temple was probably modeled on temples in Rome, since buildings with Corinthian columns and similar overall designs were being constructed in the capital at this time. Reproducing architecture in the provincial cities was another way in which the Romans spread civilization throughout their conquered lands.*

correct mathematical ratio (1:2) between the height of an arch and the width of its base.

The prototype of imperial temples is the well-preserved Maison Carrée in Nîmes, France, a major provincial city under Augustus. Built in about 16 B.C., the Maison Carrée incorporated Etruscan and Greek ideas (Figure 5.11). Raised on a platform in the Etruscan manner, this temple shows other Etruscan borrowings in the central stairway, the deep porch, and the engaged columns—that is, the columns built into the walls of the cella, the inner sanctum housing the cult statue. Greek influences are visible in the low gable—the triangular end of the building's roof—and the Corinthian columns. The Greek notion that beauty lies in mathematical harmony is also expressed in the predetermined ratio of the area of the cella to the area of the temple's porch. In the eighteenth century, Thomas Jefferson used it as the model for the statehouse in Richmond, Virginia.

Besides perfecting their version of the rectilinear temple, the Romans also invented the round temple, as seen in the Pantheon, a sanctuary dedicated to all their deities. The Pantheon consists of three different units: the entrance porch, or portico, with its supporting columns; the huge drum, housing the sanctuary proper, which is attached to the porch; and the dome set on top of the drum (Figure 5.12). This design showed the Romans' reliance on a native heritage, because the rounded shape was probably inspired by the circular religious shrines of the pre-Romans, as modern archeology has shown. The Pantheon also combined a religious with a secular image: The dome symbolized both the heaven of the deities and the vastness of the empire.

But the Pantheon did more than reflect the deep longings of the Roman people; its rich interior illustrated the Roman genius for decoration (Figure 5.13). A polychrome marble floor and a dome with recessed panels created a dazzling interior, and statues, decorative columns, triangular pediments, niches, and other architectural details alternated around the circular room. The most unusual effect of all was the round hole, thirty feet in diameter, called the **oculus,** or eye, which opened the dome to the sunlight and the elements. As the oldest standing domed structure in the world, the Pantheon is the direct ancestor of St. Peter's Basilica in Rome and St. Paul's cathedral in London.

Rome's architecture consisted of more than beautiful temples. The city of Rome was the center of government for the Mediterranean world, the nucleus of the state's religious system, and the hub of an international

Figure 5.12 Pantheon Exterior. A.D. 126. Rome. *In modern Rome, the Pantheon is crowded into a piazza where it faces a monument topped by an Egyptian obelisk. However, when built under the emperor Hadrian, the Pantheon was part of a complex of structures that complemented one another, and the temple's facade faced a set of columns in an open forecourt. Its original setting reflected the Roman sense that urban space should be organized harmoniously.*

Figure 5.13 Pantheon Interior. A.D. 126. Rome. *The inner diameter of the dome is 144 feet. The height of the dome is 72 feet, or one-half of the total height (144 feet) of the building. The sunlight sweeps around the interior and plays on the dome's decorations as the earth turns, creating constantly changing patterns of light and design.*

Figure 5.14   Roman Forum. Ca. 100 B.C.–ca. A.D. 400. *The forum was literally the center of the Roman world, for here the Romans erected the Golden Milestone, from which all roads led out across the empire. The temples and public buildings, crowded together in a relatively small area, were rebuilt over several centuries as rulers added to Rome's architectural legacy.*

economy. And at the heart of the city was its **forum,** which functioned like the agora of Greek city-states. In the forum, citizens conducted business, ran the government, and socialized among the complex of public buildings, temples, sacred sites, and monuments (Figure 5.14). The high priest of Roman religion, the Pontifex Maximus, lived in the forum, and nearby stood the curia, or Senate house. Under the empire, the forum became a symbol of Roman power and civilization; the leading cities in each province had forums.

As part of his reforms, Augustus rebuilt and beautified much of the republican forum. Later emperors, such as Trajan (r. A.D. 98–117), constructed their own forums, which not only served as new centers for trade and government but also perpetuated their names. Trajan's forum, which originally included a library, law courts, and plazas for strolling, has vanished except for one of the most significant monuments of

the Roman Empire, a column commemorating Trajan's conquest of Dacia (modern Romania) (Figure 5.15).

Another symbol of empire, the triumphal arch, originated in the republic in the second century B.C. The Romans used both single and triple arches to celebrate military victories and erected them across the empire. The style of these memorials varied until the Arch of Titus, constructed in A.D. 81, became the accepted model. This arch, which commemorated the capture of Jerusalem by the then general Titus in A.D. 70, stood at the entrance to the Via Sacra, the thoroughfare of the Roman Forum (Figure 5.16). Inscribed on the attic, or top story, of the arch is the dedication, and decorating the sides are composite columns, a Roman innovation that intertwined flowers in the capitals of Ionic columns. Inside the arch are reliefs of Titus's victorious march into Rome after subduing the Jews.

In addition to forums, columns, and arches, the emperors commissioned amphitheaters as monuments to

ENCOUNTER

Roman Conquests and Romance Languages

The Romans of the early empire, envisaging Cicero's call for "imperial glory," began to conquer neighboring peoples who threatened the Roman way of life. A superb example of this policy was Trajan's wars (A.D. 101, 105–106) against the Dacians, a people living in a territory roughly equivalent to modern-day Romania. With their strong, loyal tribal system and distinctive advanced material culture based on iron products and weapons, the Dacians refused to succumb to the Romans. Succeeding where other emperors had failed, Trajan conquered the Dacians and colonized the region, bringing in merchants, traders, and government officials.

The Romans, in varying degrees of success, followed their usual patterns of colonization in Dacia, transforming villages into provincial towns, constructing villas or country estates, and settling their veterans in the civic centers and rural areas. The colonizers set examples of the Roman way of life for the local populations, persuaded the tribal leaders to adopt Roman dress and other habits, encouraged them to finance and build amphitheaters, and made Latin the language of state.

Among the Dacians, a new language soon emerged, a language based on Latin but different from that of the invaders. The new tongue was a mingling of the local languages with the Latin spoken by the common Roman citizen—known as the vulgar or ordinary tongue—as opposed to the classical Latin used in official documents and writings. However, when the Western Roman Empire disintegrated, this new language lost its links to Rome and gradually evolved to become what is known as Romanian.

Romanian belongs to the Romance language family, which includes French, Spanish, Italian, Catalan, and Portuguese. These languages, though separate, share some vocabulary and grammar. As Europeans contacted and conquered many parts of the globe, the Romance languages spread, so that today nearly 400 million people speak a Romance language. Romanian, which had it origins under Trajan, is still spoken by about 23 million inhabitants in Romania and by 2.5 million in Russia plus a half million others scattered across the Balkans and southeastern Europe.

Encounter figure 5.1 *Trajan's victory over the Dacians was represented in Trajan's Column, which stands in the ruins of Trajan's forum in Rome. The continuous style narrates Trajan's two campaigns against the Dacians. The bottom scenes depict the Dacians attacking a Roman fort (left), the Dacians crossing the Danube (center), and the Romans ferrying troops over the Danube (right); the top scene shows the Romans attacking Dacian supply wagons.*

Figure 5.15 Trajan's Victory Column. A.D. 106–113. Ht. 125', including base. Rome. *Borrowing the idea of a victory column from Mesopotamia, the pragmatic Trajan used art to enhance his power in the eyes of the citizens. This work commemorated his conquest of Dacia—present-day Romania. The marble column, set on a foundation, enclosed a winding stairway that led to an observation platform and a statue of Trajan. Spiraling around the column's shaft was a stone relief sculpture that told the story of Trajan's victory in lively and painstaking detail.*

Figure 5.16 Arch of Titus. Ca. A.D. 81. Marble, ht. 47'2". Rome. *The Arch of Titus, like so many structures in Rome, was eventually incorporated into other buildings. Only in the early nineteenth century was the arch restored to its original splendor. Inspired by this arch, modern architects have designed similar structures throughout the Western world.*

themselves and as gifts to the citizens. The amphitheaters were the sites of the gladiatorial contests and other blood sports that were the cornerstone of popular culture in the empire. The most famous of these structures was called the Colosseum, although it was actually named the Flavian amphitheater, in honor of the dynasty that built it (Figure 5.17). The name Colosseum, dating from a later time, referred to a large statue of the emperor Nero that stood nearby.

The exterior of the Colosseum was formed by stacking three tiers of rounded arches on top of one another; Greek columns were then inserted between the arches as decorations—Doric columns on the first level, Ionic on the second, and Corinthian on the third. A concrete and marble block foundation supported this immense

Figure 5.18 The Forum at Pompeii. Ca. 150–120 B.C. Pompeii, Italy. *This forum served as the civic center of this provincial town of 15,000 to 20,000 inhabitants. Four streets, from the north, south, east, and west, converged here, but no traffic was allowed in the central area.*

Figure 5.17 Colosseum. Ca. A.D. 72–80. Ht. 166′6″. Rome. *Although the Flavians were a short-lived dynasty, starting with Vespasian in A.D. 69 and ending with Domitian in 96, they left Rome this structure, one of its most enduring landmarks. The Romans created the oval amphitheater (literally "theater on both sides") by joining two semicircular Greek theaters, another example of their ingenuity and practicality.*

amphitheater. The playing area, or arena (Latin for "sand"), was made of wood and usually covered with sand. A honeycomb of rooms, corridors, and cages ran underneath the wooden floor. The Colosseum's vast size and unusual features, such as its retractable overhead awning, made it one of the triumphs of Roman engineering, but the spectacular and brutal contests between men, and sometimes women, and wild beasts, in varied combinations, symbolized the sordid side of Rome.

Up and down the Italian peninsula and across the ancient world, the urban governments built forums, temples, and amphitheaters, laid roads, and engineered aqueducts in emulation of Rome. Sometimes old towns were made to conform to imperial standards. Pompeii, founded by the Greeks in southern Italy, was typical of the older provincial towns that the Romans remodeled to suit their needs. The Romans left Pompeii's earlier temples and public buildings standing, but a new forum gave the old city a modern look, with municipal offices, a business center, temples to the emperors and to Apollo, and a shrine honoring the civic deities (Figure 5.18). On the edge of town were such amenities as a palaestra—an exercise yard with swimming pool—and several markets. But disaster abruptly ended the urban renewal of Pompeii. In A.D. 79 nearby Mount Vesuvius, an active volcano, erupted and buried the city and most of its people—a horrible fate for the city, but one that produced a rich treasure for archeologists, who began excavations in the 1700s.

Like modern urban centers, Roman towns needed a continuous supply of water. In meeting the water demands of the cities, the Romans displayed their talent for organization and their preference for the practical by creating an elaborate network of aqueducts, sluices, and syphons that ran by gravity from a water source in nearby hills and culminated in a town's reservoirs and fountains.

The Romans started building underground aqueducts in about 300 B.C. and constructed the first elevated aqueduct in 144 B.C. Under Augustus, they completed an aqueduct across the Gard River near Nîmes in southern France (Figure 5.19). Known as the Pont du Gard, this aqueduct has a beautiful functional design. Six large arches form the base, and above them are eleven smaller ones supporting a third tier of thirty-five even smaller arches. Atop the third tier is the sluice through which the water flowed, by gravity, to Nîmes. This graceful structure is a reminder of how the Romans transformed an ordinary object into a work of art.

Sculpture Unlike Roman architecture, Roman sculpture was deeply affected by the tastes of artists and

Figure 5.19 Pont du Gard. Ca. late first century A.D. Ht. 161′. Gard River, near Nîmes, France. *This aqueduct spanning the river was only one segment of the 31-mile system that supplied water to Nîmes. Between 8,000 and 12,000 gallons of water were delivered daily, or about 100 gallons per inhabitant.*

Figure 5.20   *Head of Brutus.* Ca. 350–50 B.C. Ht. 20″. Palazzo dei Conservatori, Rome. *The finely detailed hair, beard, and facial lines are the work of a skilled sculptor, perhaps a Greek from southern Italy. The broad range of possible dates for this bronze head (ca. 350–50 B.C.) indicates that scholars still disagree over when it was cast.*

patrons as well as by class interests. For example, certain trends in the republic ran along class lines: The patricians gravitated to the Greek styles and the plebeians favored the local art, called Italo-Roman. Under the empire, the same needs that gave rise to temples and amphitheaters were at work in changing the look of imperial sculpture.

Although Roman portrait sculpture never broke through to a distinct style during this period, it nevertheless passed through three definite phases. The first phase, lasting from the third to the first century B.C., was influenced by the death masks made for the family gallery as part of ancestor worship. This style can be seen in the *Head of Brutus* (Figure 5.20). Brutus, one of the great heroes who helped to turn out the last Etruscan king, is shown as a stern and resolute leader. In contrast, the artist who sculptured the *Republican Portrait of a Man* (Figure 5.21) captured the characteristic

realism of sculpture in the Late Republic. The man's face, clearly troubled and aged, as indicated by the lines in his cheeks and around his eyes, was intended as a warning rather than as an inspiration to the viewer. This type of realistic sculpture, with its sense of unease, represents the second phase of Roman sculpture.

The third phase was shaped by the reign of Augustus. According to his biographer Suetonius, the emperor boasted that he found Rome a city of brick and left it a city of marble, and Augustus certainly did influence the direction of sculpture and architecture. Under his rule, imperial portraiture reverted to the idealism of Hellenic Greece, displacing the realistic art of the Late Republic. But Augustus's pure idealism did not prevail for long, for under his successors sculpture became more propagandistic—that is, more symbolic of imperial power. This move to symbolic idealism reflected the later emperors' need to find a highly visible way in which to overawe, and thus draw together, Rome's increasingly diversified masses.

Two major sculptural works associated with Augustus, the Prima Porta portrait and the Ara Pacis, or the Altar of Peace, helped to popularize the idealistic style. Augustus's statue, commissioned after his death, stood in a garden on his widow's estate, Prima Porta, just outside Rome (Figure 5.22). The pure Hellenic style is evident in Augustus's relaxed stance and idealized face, both of which were modeled on the *Doryphoros* by Polykleitos (see Figure 3.22). However, the accompanying symbols reveal the propagandistic intent of the sculpture and were portents of the path that imperial portraits would take. For example, the cupid represents Venus, the mother of Aeneas, and thus Augustus is symbolically connected to the legendary origins of Rome.

The second idealistic sculpture, the marble Ara Pacis, was funded by the Senate as an offering of thanks to Augustus for his peacekeeping missions. The entire structure was set on a platform and enclosed by three walls. On the fourth side, an entrance with steps led to the altar (Figure 5.23). Relief sculptures decorated the interior and exterior walls, some in an idealized style and others in a realistic style (Figure 5.24). The resulting tension between realism and idealism marked this altar as an early work in the imperial style.

This type of sculpture reached its highest potential as a propaganda tool on triumphal arches and victory columns, such as the Arch of Titus and Trajan's Column. One of the reliefs from the Arch of Titus, the *March of the Legions,* portrayed the army's victory march into Rome after the destruction of the Temple in Jerusalem in A.D. 70 (Figure 5.25).

Figure 5.21 *Republican Portrait of a Man.* Copy of an original from about 30 B.C. Marble, ht. 13". Museum of Art, Rhode Island School of Design, Providence, Rhode Island. *This bust reflects the upheavals of first-century B.C. Rome, as patricians reasserted their power over the crumbling state. Portraits of patrician leaders were characterized by wrinkled skin, clenched jaws, and determined expressions.*

Figure 5.22 *Augustus,* from Prima Porta. Ca. A.D. 14. Marble, ht. 6'7¹/₂". Vatican Collection. *This statue of Caesar Augustus (r. 31 B.C.–A.D. 14), the founder of the Roman Empire, was uncovered at Prima Porta, the villa of his wife, Livia. The statue closely resembled the ruler yet presented him as godlike. Augustus's imperial successors commissioned similar sculptures to convey a sense of their dignity and power.*

Figure 5.23   Ara Pacis. 9 B.C. Marble, width 35'. Rome. *Like the Prima Porta statue, the Ara Pacis became a model for later emperors, who emulated its decorations, symbols, and size. The altar was rediscovered in the sixteenth century, excavated in the nineteenth and early twentieth centuries, and restored in 1938.*

Figure 5.24   *Family of Augustus,* Ara Pacis relief. 9 B.C. Marble, ht. 63". Rome. *The figures in low relief, moving from right to left, are separated yet linked by their placement and clothing. The child to the right of center is given great prominence: He faces right while all the adults in the foreground are looking left and a man places his hand on the child's head. This singling out of the child may be an act of endearment or of recognition that he is to be the emperor.*

Figure 5.25 *March of the Legions,* from the Arch of Titus. Ca. A.D. 80. Marble relief, approx. 6 × 12½'. Rome. *This rectangular marble relief occupies the south side of the Arch of Titus. It commemorates the Roman victory in the Jewish War of A.D. 66–70, when the Romans put down a rebellion by the Jews in Judea and subsequently dispersed them across the Roman world. In the relief, the Roman soldiers hold aloft the Jewish holy relics from the Temple as they seem to press forward and pass under the arch on the right.*

The continuous frieze from Trajan's Victory Column is one of the sculptural marvels of the Roman world (Figure 5.26). This low-relief sculpture winds around the column like a long comic strip, telling the story of Trajan's campaign against Dacia. Scholars still study the carvings of campsites and fortifications on this relief, finding them a rich source for Roman military history.

The last great sculpture from this period is the equestrian statue of Marcus Aurelius (see Figure 5.9). This work reveals a falling away from Augustan idealism to a rugged, individualized style, although one that was still highly propagandistic in its use of symbols. The symbols in this statue stress that Marcus Aurelius was a warrior-emperor, fighting enemies far from his capital in Rome.

Painting and Mosaics **Murals,** or wall paintings, the most popular type of painting in Rome, have been found in private dwellings, public buildings, and temples. Surviving works hint at a highly decorative

and brightly colored art. Originally the Romans applied tempera, or paint set in a binding solution, directly onto a dry wall. However, this quick and easy method produced a painting that soon faded and peeled. Later they adopted fresco painting as the most practical and lasting technique. Paints were mixed and worked into a freshly plastered wall. The colors dried into the wall, resulting in a nearly indestructible painting. The Romans were inspired by many subjects: landscapes, Greek and Roman myths, architectural vistas, religious scenes, and genre scenes, or "slices of life."

Of the many paintings scattered around the Roman world, the murals in the Villa of the Mysteries at Pompeii are the most impressive. These intriguing and controversial scenes, which fill the walls in several rooms, portray twenty-nine nearly life-size figures engaged in some mystery cult rite (Figure 5.27). The grouping of figures—well balanced and separated—create tension among the participants, and the undecipherable

◀ **Figure 5.26**   Detail of Trajan's Victory Column. A.D. 113. Marble, ht. of relief band approx. 36". Rome. *Wrapped around the 100-foot-high column is the 645-foot relief carving with 2,500 figures depicting Trajan's two campaigns against the Dacians. Color was applied to heighten the realistic effect of the work, which, in its original setting, could be viewed from nearby buildings.*

expressions on the faces of the women heighten the sense of theater.

The Romans learned to make **mosaics** from the Hellenistic Greeks in the third century B.C., but by the third century A.D., several local Roman mosaic styles had sprung up across the empire. Although subjects varied, certain ones seemed always to be in vogue, such as still lifes, landscapes, Greek and Roman myths, philosophers and orators, and scenes from the circus and amphitheaters. A mosaic from Tunisia (North Africa) shows the intricacy of design and variety of color that artisans achieved even in the Roman provinces (Figure 5.28).

Music

The absorption of the Greek tradition in music was so complete that later Roman music, in effect, simply perpetuated Greek forms and ideas. And yet the Romans used music only for practical purposes and rejected the Greek notion that music performed an ethical role in educating the soul or mind.

Not until imperial times did music come to play an important role in Roman life. Under the emperors, music became wildly popular, as all classes succumbed to its seductive charms. **Pantomimes**—dramatic productions with instrumental music and dances—became the spectacle favored by the Roman masses. In the long run, the pantomimes became a symbol of music's decadent trend under the empire. The largest of these productions featured three thousand instrumentalists and three thousand dancers, but the more common size was three hundred performers in each category. A more serious sort of music was kept alive by the

Figure 5.27   *Flagellation Scene.* Villa of the Mysteries. Ca. 60–40 B.C. Wall painting, ht. 60". Pompeii, Italy. *The figures in this brilliantly colored wall frieze seem almost to be present in the room, partly because they are just under full life size and partly because the artist has placed them on a narrow painted ledge as if on a stage. The lack of depth in the mysterious scene adds to the illusion.*

Figure 5.29   *The Street Musicians.* Ca. 100 B.C. 16⁷/₈ × 16¹/₈″. Museo Nazionale, Naples. *This mosaic may portray a scene from a comic play. Two masked figures dance and play the tambourine and the finger cymbals while a masked female figure plays the tibia, or double oboe. This mosaic was found in the so-called Villa of Cicero at Pompeii.*

wealthy classes, who maintained household orchestras and choruses for their private amusement. An even more cultivated audience encouraged poets such as Horace to set their verses to music, thus continuing the Greek tradition of lyric poetry.

Although what Roman music actually sounded like remains a subject of conjecture, their musical instruments, borrowed from across the Mediterranean world, can be identified with some certainty. From Greece came the stringed instruments, the lyre and the kithara, along with such woodwinds as the single **aulos,** or oboe, and the double aulos—called by the

Romans the tibia (Figure 5.29). From the Etruscans came the brasses. The Romans delighted in the harsh sounds made by these instruments, incorporating them into their military music just as the Etruscans did. The hydraulic organ, or water organ, was probably perfected in Hellenistic Alexandria, but in imperial Rome it became a crowd pleaser, adding deep, voluminous sounds to the pantomimes. The taste of the imperial Roman audience is evident in the water organ, which was impressive not for its musical qualities but as a feat of engineering expertise.

◄ **Figure 5.28**   Calendar Mosaic. Late second–early third century A.D. From the Maison des Mois at El Djem. Detail of 5 × 4′ mosaic. Sousse Museum, Sousse, Tunisia. *The El Djem Calendar comprises twelve small scenes, each representing a month, the name of which is inscribed in Latin. The Roman year began with March (top middle) and ended with February (top left corner). The months are symbolized by either religious or rural activities, such as in the September panel, which shows two figures standing in a vat crushing grapes.*

The Legacy of Pre-Christian Rome

Western civilization is built on the ruins of Rome. Although no pre-Christian institutions survived to form a basis of European organization, other tangibles persisted in abundance, so that the mark of Rome may still be seen and heard in countless ways. The very languages of Western Europe bear the stamp of Rome, and Roman law forms the basis of the legal codes of many Western countries. Until the beginning of the twentieth century, the European educational ideal was based on the Roman curriculum, in which students studied the *trivium*—the three arts of grammar, logic, and rhetoric—and the *quadrivium*—the four sciences of arithmetic, geometry, music, and astronomy. Even today, this ideal persists at the heart of Western education.

Roman builders and engineers added to the Greek architectural tradition to create the Greco-Roman style, whose principal Roman components included domes, rounded arches, vaulting techniques, domed temples, temples on podiums, triumphal arches, amphitheaters, and victory columns. From the Renaissance, starting in 1400, until the twentieth century, the Greco-Roman style dominated Western architecture. Roman sculptors likewise helped to create the Greco-Roman style; their contributions included realistic portrait sculptures, propagandistic portraits of rulers, and equestrian statues. In literature and drama, Rome gave us the comic plays of Terence and Plautus, which influenced the rebirth of comedy in the Renaissance; the tragedies of Seneca, which inspired the tragedies of Shakespeare and other Renaissance dramatists; the contrasting satire genres invented by Horace and Juvenal, both of which spawned imitators through the ages; and the writings of Vergil, Horace, and Ovid, which became the classical standard for Europeans during the thousand years from the fall of Rome to the Renaissance, when Latin was in the ascendant and Greek had practically disappeared. In philosophy, Cicero taught the Christian West to write and think philosophically, since his works were known to the educated for centuries. And the ideas of Greek thinkers, though in summary or corrupt form, survived through Latin translations.

Rome's greatest legacy to the Western world was its shining image of a healthy civilization: a just and well-regulated society of multiethnic, multiracial citizens. The Idea of Rome, as we may call this achievement, was adapted from the Hellenistic rulers. However, the Hellenistic cities lacked the cohesiveness and longevity—and, most important, the vision—of the Roman creation. When the ancient world was swept away, the Idea of Rome remained a beacon in the darkness that descended over Europe.

KEY CULTURAL TERMS

syncretism
satire
Neo-Platonism
natural law
voussoir
keystone
vault
barrel vault

groined vault
  (cross vault)
oculus
forum
mural
mosaic
pantomime
aulos

SUGGESTIONS FOR FURTHER READING

Primary Sources

APULEIUS. *The Golden Ass*. Translated by R. Graves. New York: Farrar, Straus & Giroux, 1951. A sound translation of one of the most lively and entertaining tales in ancient literature.

HORACE. *The Complete Works of Horace*. Introduction by C. Kraemer. New York: Modern Library, 1936. Masterly translations of the works that made Horace Rome's outstanding lyric poet.

JUVENAL. *The Sixteen Satires*. Translated by P. Green. New York: Penguin, 1970. Superb vernacular versions of Juvenal's bitter works.

VERGIL. *The Aeneid*. Translated by W. F. J. Knight. New York: Penguin, 1964. A sound English prose version of Vergil's poetic epic about Aeneas, the Trojan warrior whose conquests made possible the future supremacy of Rome.

CHAPTER 5 HIGHLIGHTS
Roman Civilization: The Pre-Christian Centuries

Literature & Philosophy   Art & Architecture   Music & Dance

 Readings in the Western Humanities

AFRICA

AMERICAS

HISTORY

North Africa *Sahara.* Camel introduced (1st century A.D.); camel caravans soon linked north Africa with the south.

Northeast Africa *Kush culture, ended A.D. 350.* Amassed great wealth from trade in the Red Sea; conquered by King Ezana of Axum. *Axum culture, began 300 B.C.* Axum (modern Eritrea and parts of Ethiopia and Sudan) dominated trade in the region after A.D. 200; King Ezana minted gold coins and signed a treaty with the Byzantine emperor.

West Africa *Niger River area.* Founding (about 250 B.C.) of Jenne-jero, a farming village and iron-working center. *Nok culture, ended A.D. 200.* Mixed culture of farming, hunting, and gathering.

Mesoamerica *Classic period, began A.D. 150.* Teotihuacán (in modern Mexico), the first true city (125,000 at its height) in the Americas, founded A.D. 250. *Mayan culture.* Zenith: A.D. 250–900 in what is now Yucatán, Guatemala, Honduras. Ritual cities, such as Tikal and Uaxactún. *Veracruz culture.* High culture whose center was El Tajín. *Zapotec culture.* Center was Monte Albán in Oaxaca.

Andes *Chavín culture ended 200 B.C. Paracas culture, ca. 600–175 B.C. Nasca culture, 200 B.C.–A.D. 500. Moche culture, began 200 B.C.* First organized state on North Coast.

Native North America *Plains, from ca. 250 B.C.* Nomadic buffalo hunters began to cultivate maize, established villages. *Hopewell culture, ca. 200 B.C.–A.D. 500.* Ohio and Illinois valleys; mound builders with extensive trade network; maize cultivation ca. A.D. 100. *Southwest, ca. A.D. 100.* Migration from Mesoamerica.

ART

Northeast Africa *Axum culture.* Kings erected granite monuments.

Mesoamerica *Classic period. Teotihuacán culture.* Frescoes, pictographic books, pottery, clay figurines, masks, and stone sculptures. *Veracruz culture.* Stone carvings and hollow clay sculptures. Wheels on toys. *Zapotec culture.* Murals, elaborate inscriptions, pottery, and bowls representing birds, fish, and jaguars.

Andes *Paracas culture.* Ceramics, textiles, embroidery, and gold work. *Nasca culture.* Nasca Lines: carved in geometric and figural shapes, on the Nasca plains. *Moche culture.* Gold ritual objects, including necklaces, scepters, bells, and beads; invented a two-piece press mold for replicating ritual pottery forms.

Animal Figure on Wheels. Ca. A.D. 600–900. Veracruz. Ht. 7¾".
American Museum of Natural History, New York.

ARCHITECTURE

Northeast Africa *Axum culture.* Impressive fortresses and palaces built by kings, though little remains.

West Africa *Nok culture.* The Nok lived in clay huts in the hills and lowlands.

Mesoamerica *Classic period. Teotihuacán culture.* Teotihuacán centered on Pyramids of the Sun and the Moon. *Zapotec culture.* Monte Albán with an astronomical observatory, ritual ballcourt, and necropolis (city of the dead). *Mayan culture.* The corbelled arch, made of overlapping stones. Tikal and Uaxactún: Ceremonial cities with temples, pyramids, platforms, and plazas.

Andes *Nasca culture.* Ruins of about 40 temple mounds, at the capital Cahuachi. *Moche culture.* Forts, palaces, and pyramids, made of molded adobe brick; aqueducts and canals.

Native North America *Plains.* Portable tepees made of poles and buffalo skins for nomadic hunters, and dome-shaped earth lodges for maize-growing tribes.

RELIGION, PHILOSOPHY, LITERATURE

Northeast Africa *Axum culture.* King Ezana converted to Coptic Christianity and made it the official faith of his kingdom (300s). After 451, Coptic Church separated itself from papal control and looked to the Coptic patriarch at Alexandria for new leaders. The Coptic Church is Ethiopia's state religion today.

West Africa *Nok culture.* Polytheism and ancestor worship.

Andes *Paracas culture.* Elaborate burial rituals.

Mesoamerica *Classic period.* Hieroglyphic writing, in both *Mayan* and *Zapotec cultures. Mayan culture.* Daily life and religious ritual based on coordination of the 260-day and the 365-day calendars; astronomical observation (particularly Venus); knowledge of the zero.

Native North America *Hopewell culture.* Developed and spread first North American pan-Indian religion from Minnesota to West Virginia.

Moche Stirrup-Spout Vessel (depicting scene of childbirth). Early Intermediate period. Ceramic. Staatliches Museum für Völkerkunde, Berlin.

ASIA

China

Ch'in Dynasty, 221–206 B.C. Shih Huang-ti, the first emperor, united country for first time; standardized scripts, weights, and measures. The name *China* is derived from *Ch'in*. *Han Dynasty, 210 B.C.–A.D. 220.* Culturally brilliant and militarily expansive period; rule extended to Korea, Mongolia, and southern Manchuria. Trade with Rome via the Silk Road. Paper invented. *Six Dynasties, or Period of Disunity, A.D. 220–581.* Political chaos.

India

Mauryan Empire, ca. 325–185 B.C. First Indian empire to include most of the subcontinent. Buddhist emperor Asoka (r. ca. 265–238 B.C.), efficient and humane ruler. The Lion Capital on Asoka's edict column became the emblem of the Republic of India. *Political disunity, 185 B.C.–A.D. 320.* Rise of regional states; foreign invasions. *Gupta Dynasty, A.D. 320–ca. 550.* A golden age. Zenith under Chandra Gupta II (r. A.D. 375–415).

Edict Column at Sarnath. Ca. 250 B.C. Archaeological Museum, Sarnath.

Japan

Yayoi culture, ca. 300 B.C.–A.D. 300. Migrants (perhaps ancestors of modern Japanese) with new technology: bronze and iron working, wheel-thrown ceramics, and wet-rice farming. *Kofun period, began A.D. 300.* Clan rivalry. The Yamato clan (from whom later emperors claimed descent) became dominant (400s); set up a base in Korea, allowing influence from China.

Ch'in Dynasty. About 6,000 life-size terracotta models of soldiers, in the burial pit of Emperor Shih Huang-ti, at the capital, Ch'ang-an (206 B.C.). *Han Dynasty.* Bronze castings, jade carvings, brush-and-ink paintings on paper, and paintings on silk.

Horse. Bronze, 13⁵/₈ × 17³/₄". Found in a second-century A.D. tomb, Gansu, China.

Mauryan Empire. Stupas (holding Buddhist relics), edict columns, and stone sculptures of divinities. *Political disunity* and *Gupta Dynasty.* Relief stone sculptures, stupas, and two schools of Buddhist art: Mathura in central India, rooted in folk art, and Gandhara (in modern Pakistan), influenced by Greco-Roman styles. The image of the Buddha in the form of a god first introduced.

Yayoi culture. Ceramics, including tableware; ceremonial objects such as bronze bells and swords, mirrors, and semiprecious stones.

Ch'in Dynasty. The Great Wall, extending for more than 1,000 miles along the northern frontier, built to keep out nomadic invaders. *Six Dynasties.* Iconography and temple and tomb building influenced by Buddhism.

Section, Great Wall of China. 215 B.C.

Political disunity. Rock-cut sanctuaries at Bhaja (western India) became models for Jains, Buddhists, and Brahmans. *Gupta Dynasty.* Complex of 29 rock-cut sanctuaries, at Ajanta in central India, including the earliest surviving Indian paintings. *Mauryan Empire.* The capital Pataliputra, a walled city with many gates, stretched for two miles in perimeter.

Kofun period: Yamato clan built *kofun,* or mounded tombs; contained pottery figures *(haniwa).*

Ch'in Dynasty. Shih Huang-ti followed the path of Legalism and rejected the Confucian ideal. *Han Dynasty.* Ssu-ma Ch'ien's *Historical Records,* a history of early China. Hsu Shen's 10,000-character dictionary. Confucianism made an official state cult (A.D. 6) and basis of civil service examinations. Buddhism established at the royal court. Folk songs flourished, as in the *Ballad of Mu Lan* in the militant style of northern Chinese literature. Poets Tao Ch'ien and Hsieh Ling-yun explored the tension between Confucian ideal of public service and Taoist call for withdrawal.

Mauryan culture. A Buddhist convert, Asoka, sent Buddhist missionaries to what is now Myanmar and Sri Lanka. The policies of Asoka were guided by the *Arthashastra,* a political treatise. *Political disunity.* The *Panchatantra,* beast fables. Christianity probably arrived in western port cities. *Gupta Dynasty. Yoga Aphorisms of Patanjali,* classic yoga text; *Eight Anthologies* and *Ten Songs,* classic Tamil poetry; *Kama-sutra,* manual of sexual techniques; Bhartrihari's cynical love poems; Kālidāsa's *Shākuntalā,* first great Indian play. Invention of decimal system. Zenith of Buddhism.

Kofun period. Chinese script arrived by way of Korea, and Chinese characters adapted into Japanese writing by 500.

6 JUDAISM AND THE RISE OF CHRISTIANITY

The great civilizations discussed so far—Mesopotamian, Egyptian, Greek, and Roman—were all wealthy, powerful, and culturally dynamic, and they contributed enormously to the Western heritage. Yet an even greater contribution, one that cannot be measured in buildings or governments, came from a politically insignificant people who lived in a tiny corner of the eastern Mediterranean during ancient times—the Jews. This people created a religion that helped to shape the character of the civilizations of the Western world. Through the Hebrew Bible—the Old Testament to Christians—Judaic beliefs were passed on to both Christianity and Islam and spread around the world. In addition, the fruitful interaction of the Judeo-Christian heritage with the Greco-Roman Classical ideals enriched and transformed the Western humanities.

JUDAISM

Judaism is one of the oldest living religions in the world. It originated in the third millennium B.C. among a tribal Middle Eastern people who placed themselves at the center of world history and created sacred texts for passing on their heritage. Unlike the history and religion of other ancient peoples, the history and religion of the Jews are so inextricably connected that they cannot be separated.

The People and Their Religion

In about 2000 B.C., many displaced tribes were wandering throughout the Middle East because of the political upheavals that accompanied the collapse of the

◄ **Detail** Synagogue. Third century A.D. Dura Europas, Syria.

145

Timeline 6.1   JEWISH CIVILIZATION

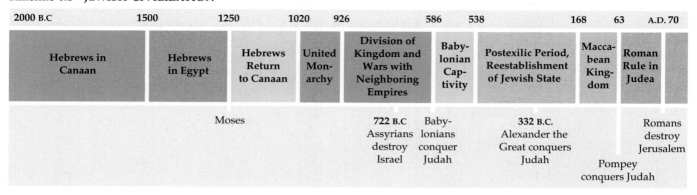

2000 B.C	1500	1250	1020	926		586	538		168	63	A.D. 70
Hebrews in Canaan	Hebrews in Egypt	Hebrews Return to Canaan	United Monarchy	Division of Kingdom and Wars with Neighboring Empires		Babylonian Captivity	Postexilic Period, Reestablishment of Jewish State		Maccabean Kingdom	Roman Rule in Judea	

Moses

722 B.C Assyrians destroy Israel

Babylonians conquer Judah

332 B.C. Alexander the Great conquers Judah

Pompey conquers Judah

Romans destroy Jerusalem

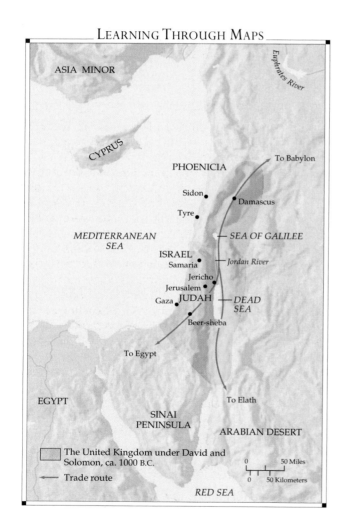

LEARNING THROUGH MAPS

ASIA MINOR

Euphrates River

CYPRUS

PHOENICIA

To Babylon

Sidon

Damascus

Tyre

MEDITERRANEAN SEA

SEA OF GALILEE

ISRAEL

Samaria

Jordan River

Jericho

Jerusalem

Gaza   JUDAH

DEAD SEA

Beer-sheba

To Egypt

EGYPT

To Elath

SINAI PENINSULA

ARABIAN DESERT

☐ The United Kingdom under David and Solomon, ca. 1000 B.C.

→ Trade route

0   50 Miles

0   50 Kilometers

RED SEA

Map 6.1   ANCIENT ISRAEL
This map shows the Hebrews' ancient kingdom, known as the United Monarchy, forged by the rulers David and his son Solomon. The map also shows the kingdoms of Israel and Judah, the two Hebrew states which emerged when the United Monarchy split on the death of Solomon, in 926 B.C. **Locate** the capitals of these two kingdoms. **How** was the cultural life and religious faith of the nation of Israel influenced by foreign neighbors? **What** impact did Israel's size and location have on its history and religious faith? **Notice** the scale of the map and compare it with the scale of Map 5.1, The Roman Empire Under Augustus.

tribes, known as the Hebrews and led by the patriarch Abraham, occupied territory called Canaan, a region identified loosely with ancient Israel (Timeline 6.1). They settled in the hill country, where they tended their flocks and practiced their crafts (Map 6.1).

The Hebrews considered themselves unique, a belief based on the relationship between Abraham and a great supernatural being who spoke to him and whom he obeyed. This deity made a **covenant,** or solemn agreement (the outward sign of which was the circumcision of all male children), with Abraham to protect his family and bring prosperity to his offspring if they agreed to obey his divine commands. Although this Hebrew deity was associated with nature, he differed from other Mesopotamian deities in his commitment to justice and righteousness. He was an ethical god and sought to impose ethical principles on humans.

Egypt, Exodus, and Moses   The Hebrews prospered for decades in Canaan, but around 1500 B.C. a group migrated south into Egypt, which had recently been overrun by the Hyksos, a Semitic people with whom the Hebrews shared language and cultural traits. The Hebrews thrived over the next few centuries, until the Egyptians reconquered their land and enslaved both the Hyksos and the Hebrews. In about 1250 B.C., the extraordinary leader Moses rallied the Hebrews and led them on the Exodus from Egypt—one of the most

Akkadian kingdom and the coming of the Babylonians. Some of these nomads eventually settled along the eastern coast of the Mediterranean Sea that is part of the Fertile Crescent. These patriarchal tribes, under the guidance of the oldest and most respected male members, founded communities united by bloodlines, economic interests, and folk traditions. One of these

Table 6.1 THE TEN COMMANDMENTS

1. You shall have no other gods before me.
2. You shall not make for yourself a graven image, or any likeness of any thing that is in heaven above, or that is on the earth beneath, or that is in the water under the earth. . . .
3. You shall not take the name of the Lord your God in vain. . . .
4. Observe the sabbath day, to keep it holy, as the Lord your God commanded you. . . .
5. Honor your father and your mother. . . .
6. You shall not kill.
7. Neither shall you commit adultery.
8. Neither shall you steal.
9. Neither shall you bear false witness against your neighbor.
10. Neither shall you covet your neighbor's wife . . . or anything that is your neighbor's.

Source: The Bible, Revised Standard Version, Deuteronomy 5:6–21.

Figure 6.1 Stone Menorah. Second century A.D. Ht. 18″. Israel Museum, Jerusalem. *Although this particular menorah dates from the second century A.D., the seven-branched candelabrum had been in use as a religious symbol for centuries. According to Jewish beliefs, God gave Moses explicit instructions on how to craft the menorah, which was made for the tabernacle, or house of prayer. Later the menorah came to symbolize knowledge and understanding as well as the light of God protecting the Jews.*

significant events in Jewish history. Hebrew scriptures describe Moses as a savior sent by God.

As the Hebrews wandered in the desert on the Sinai peninsula, Moses molded his followers into a unified people under a set of ethical and societal laws, which they believed were received from God. The laws of Moses were unique among ancient peoples because they were grounded in the covenant between the Hebrews and God and because no distinction was made between religious and secular offenses. All crimes were seen as sins and all sins as crimes. Those who committed crimes could not simply make reparation to their victims; they also had to seek forgiveness from God. There were some crimes, such as murder, that were so offensive to God that they could not be forgiven by human beings alone. Furthermore, human life was seen as sacred, because it was given by God, who created and owned all things; individual humans were precious because they were made in God's image.

The core of Mosaic law was the Ten Commandments, which set forth the proper behavior of human beings (Table 6.1). The commandments became the basis of a renewed covenant, which was now extended beyond Abraham and his descendants to include the entire people. The Hebrew God tolerated no rivals; he was seen as the sole, omnipotent creator and ruler of the universe. If individuals followed his laws and worshiped him alone, they would be rewarded, and if they strayed, they would be punished. Likewise, if the tribe followed the divine commands, they would prosper, and if they disobeyed, they would meet with adversity. As the mediator of the covenant between God and the Hebrew people, Moses played a crucial role in shaping Judaism into a comprehensive system of ethical monotheism.

As they wandered through the Sinai desert, the Hebrews carried with them a sacred decorated box called the Ark of the Covenant. Within were the stone tablets on which the Ten Commandments were carved. Details of how to craft the Ark and all the other sacred objects used in worship were dictated to Moses by God (Figure 6.1). In the desert, the deity also revealed a new name for himself—YHWH, a name so sacred that pious Jews never speak or write it. In the late Middle Ages, European scholars rendered YHWH as Jehovah, but today this term is generally considered a false reading of the sacred letters. In modern English, YHWH is usually rendered as Yahweh. In biblical times, Jewish priests called the deity Adonai, the Semitic term for Lord.

After forty years of wandering, followed by Moses' death, the Hebrews finally returned to Canaan, the Promised Land pledged by Yahweh to their forefathers. Over the next two centuries, the Hebrews won Canaan and became known as the Israelites.

The Kingdom of Israel In about 1000 b.c., the Israelites established a monarchy, and from the late eleventh century to the end of the tenth century B.C., the nation flourished under a series of kings—Saul, David, and Solomon. The popular king David rallied the scattered Israelite tribes, centralized the government, and shifted the economy away from herding and toward commerce, trade, and farming.

Solomon, David's son, brought the Israelite kingdom to its pinnacle of power and prestige. He signed

Table 6.2 **HISTORICAL STAGES OF THE TEMPLE OF JERUSALEM**

NAME	CONSTRUCTION DETAILS	DATE DESTROYED
Solomon's Temple. Also called First Temple	Completed under King Solomon, 957 B.C.	587/586 B.C., by the Babylonians
Second Temple. Also called Herod's Temple after being rebuilt in A.D. 26	Completed 515 B.C. Rebuilt at order of King Herod (d. 4 B.C.) between 20 B.C. and A.D. 26	A.D. 70, by the Romans. A section of the western wall (also called the Wailing Wall) survived; it was incorporated into the wall around the Muslim Dome of the Rock and al-Aqsa mosque in A.D. 691.

treaties with other states, expanded Israel's trade across the Middle East, and raised the standard of living for many of his subjects. He completed the building of Jerusalem begun by David, which, with its magnificent public structures and great Temple, rivaled the glory of other Middle Eastern cities. The Temple of Solomon, also known as the First Temple, housed Israel's holy relics, including the Ark of the Covenant, and became the focal point of the nation's religion, which required pilgrimages and rituals, based on the religious calendar (Table 6.2; Figure 6.2). The Hebrew religion required ritual offerings (sacrifices of animals on large altars and wine, incense, and grain mixed with oil on small altars) twice daily. These offerings were conducted by priests in the Temple in Jerusalem as a community ritual for the entire Hebrew nation; individuals could also arrange for sacrifices to be made on their own behalf. The early Hebrews sometimes were allowed to make sacrifices outside the Temple, but this practice was later forbidden.

King Solomon considered himself a patron of literature and the arts, and under his rule Hebrew culture expanded, notably in law, writing, music, and dance. As the Hebrews' oral traditions gave way to written records, Hebrew authors wrote down their laws and their earliest histories, which are preserved in the first books of the Bible (Figure 6.3). These Hebrew works predate by five centuries the writings of the great Greek historians Herodotus and Thucydides, but, unlike the Greek writers, the Hebrew historians made God the central force in human history and thus transformed

Figure 6.2 Horned Altar. Tenth century B.C. Carved limestone, ht. 26½". Oriental Institute, University of Chicago. *Middle Eastern peoples made sacrifices to their deities on altars, but the small horned altar, as pictured here, was unique to the Hebrews. Horned altars are described in the Bible, especially as a ritual object in the Temple in Jerusalem, built in the tenth century B.C. However, this horned altar was discovered at Megiddo, one of the cities of the Hebrew kingdom.*

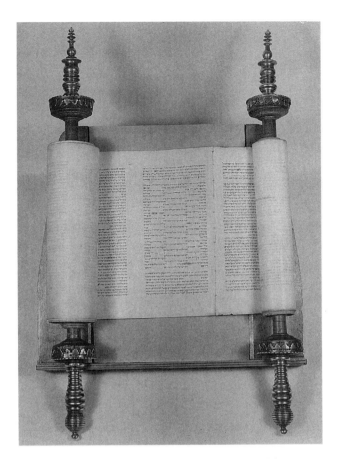

Figure 6.3 Scroll of the Pentateuch. *The ancient Hebrews recorded their scriptures on parchment scrolls. The scroll of the Pentateuch was wound on two staves. The scrolls were not decorated or illuminated with designs, animals, or humans because the Bible forbade any likeness of Yahweh and artistic expressions were not encouraged. However, some sacred books were illustrated and ornamented at various stages of Hebrew history. The carved staves on which the Pentateuch was wound were often embellished. Evidence exists that by the fifth century A.D., the scrolls might have been encased in a container of precious metal, and by the fifteenth century, they were enclosed in containers adorned with reliefs and Hebrew lettering.*

the unfolding of earthly events into a moral drama with cosmic significance.

Solomon's achievements came at a heavy price, however, for they undermined his people's religious foundations, intensified class divisions, and tended to divide the northern and southern tribes. When Solomon died in 926 B.C., the tensions between the regions intensified and the United Monarchy separated into two states: Israel in the north, with its capital at Samaria, and Judah in the south, with its capital at Jerusalem.

During the period of the two Hebrew kingdoms, a new type of religious leader, known as a prophet, appeared. The prophets warned of the fatal consequences of breaking Yahweh's commandments, and in predicting the downfall of surrounding non-Hebrew states, the prophets asserted that God was now using peoples other than the Hebrews to fulfill his divine plan in history. The prophets also demanded social justice for the helpless and the downtrodden. In the face of a widening gulf between rich and poor, the prophets predicted that if the well-off did not aid the less fortunate, Yahweh would bring down the evil rulers and, in the future, punish the selfish and reward the sufferers. But the words of the prophets, such as Hosea and Amos in Israel and Isaiah and Jeremiah in Judah, seemed to go unheeded.

The Babylonian Captivity and the Postexilic Period
Although Israel enjoyed its moments of prosperity and power, the larger empires, especially Egypt and Assyria, wanted to control the military and trade routes crossing this part of the Fertile Crescent. In 722 B.C., the tiny nation of Israel was destroyed by the Assyrians. Judah, to the south, endured for another two hundred years, but in 586 B.C., the Babylonians conquered Judah, destroying Solomon's Temple in Jerusalem and deporting most of the Hebrews to Babylonia. The approximately forty years of exile, known as the Babylonian Captivity, became one of the major turning points in Jewish history.

At the end of the sixth century, the Jews (as the Hebrews are called after the Babylonian Captivity) were freed by the triumphant Persians, who were sweeping across the ancient world under Cyrus (see Chapter 2). Returning to Judah, the Jews rebuilt their Temple, now known as the Second Temple, and their towns. Believing that God had rescued them, they established a theocratic state—a government ruled by those who are recognized as having special divine guidance and approval—and dedicated themselves to the correct formulation and observation of their religious beliefs. The Jews welcomed back many exiles, reestablished their commercial ties, and revived their handicraft industries. But many exiles remained outside the homeland and became known as Jews of the **Diaspora,** or the Dispersion.

After their return from Babylon, the Jews expanded their views of Yahweh. Probably under the indirect impact of the increasingly popular Persian religion, Zoroastrianism—and its description of the twin forces of good and evil or Light and Dark—the Jews began to envision a cosmic dualism in their own beliefs. The Hebrews' earlier perception of themselves as a chosen people under a universal deity was reinforced as they concluded that Yahweh had used the Persians to free them. Furthermore, the Jews started to incorporate two new features into their religion: **eschatology,** or the concern with the end of the world, and an interest in **apocalypse,** prophecies about the coming of God and a

Figure 6.4   Model of the Reconstructed Second Temple (Herod's Temple) in Jerusalem. *This model of the Second Temple shows the strong influence of Hellenistic-style architecture, particularly in the colonnaded arcades, the decorative frieze, and the tall, slender Corinthian columns flanking the main entryway. The Second Temple was destroyed by Roman legions in A.D. 70, but one wall was left standing.*

day of judgment. This future world would be led by a **Messiah,** or Anointed One, who would bring peace and justice to all.

The Hellenistic and Roman Periods   Alexander the Great conquered Judah in 332 B.C., and after his death the area became part of the Seleucid kingdom, centered in Syria. Hellenistic culture and ideas proliferated and deeply affected Jewish life. Growing tensions between the Jews and the Hellenistic leaders erupted in 168 B.C. when the Seleucid king Antiochus IV tried to impose the worship of Greek gods on the Jews, placing a statue of Zeus in the Second Temple in Jerusalem. Antiochus's violation of the sacred place enraged the Maccabean clan, whose inspired leadership and bravery led to a successful revolt and the recapture of the Temple. The

Figure 6.5   Masada, Israel. *This outcropping of rock in the forbidding terrain outside Jerusalem was a natural fortress. King Herod had built one of his palace-fortresses here in the years just before the birth of Christ. For three years the Zealots occupied its ruins, holding out against the Romans after the end of the First Jewish War in A.D. 70.*

Figure 6.6 Synagogue. Third century A.D. Dura Europos, Syria. Reconstructed in the National Museum, Damascus, Syria. *This house-synagogue (a place of worship set up within a private residence) was discovered in the early twentieth century, after having been filled with rubble in A.D. 256, as part of a defense plan for the city of Dura Europos. Only sections of the four painted walls survived. The room featured benches running around the walls and a niche for the Torah scrolls in the western wall. The wall paintings depict various events from the Hebrew Bible, most having to do with national salvation, such as Samuel Anointing David, the Ark Brought to Jerusalem, and the Exodus from Egypt. Painted by anonymous artists, these works were executed in tempera, a medium made of pigments blended with egg yolks and water, applied to dry plaster.*

Maccabean family ruled Judah as an independent commonwealth for approximately one hundred years. Then, in 63 B.C., the Romans conquered most of the Middle East. They subsequently incorporated Judah (in what was now called Palestine) into their empire as Judea and placed the Jewish lands under client kings.

Appointed to these kingships was the Herod dynasty, a family of Jews who had gained favor with the Romans. Herod the Great, who ruled from 37 to 4 B.C., rebuilt Jerusalem, including the Second Temple, and promoted Hellenistic culture (Figure 6.4). But conditions under the Romans became unbearable to the Jews, and in A.D. 66 a rebellion broke out. After four years of fighting, called the First Jewish War, the Romans captured Jerusalem and destroyed the Second Temple (A.D. 70). A revolutionary group known as Zealots held out until 73 at Masada, a sheer-sided mesa on the shores of the Dead Sea (Figure 6.5). When their cause became hopeless, they committed suicide rather than surrender to the Romans.

One wall of the Second Temple in Jerusalem remained standing. Known as the Wailing Wall, it came to symbolize the plight of the Jewish people. As described in Chapter 5, Titus, the victorious Roman general and later emperor, returned to Rome with the holy Jewish relics (see Figure 5.25). To make sure the Jews would no longer be a problem, the Roman government in the late first century A.D. ordered the dispersal of the Jews throughout the empire. However, this second Diaspora did not end the Jews' cultural, intellectual, and religious existence. On the contrary, the Jewish way of life continued, though it changed. With the fall of the Temple in Jerusalem, Jews worshiped in synagogues, or congregations, which eventually were headed by rabbis, or teachers (Figure 6.6). Over the centuries, the rabbis' teachings evolved into Rabbinic Judaism, based on the Torah and the Talmud (from Hebrew, "learning"), a collection of legal rulings and commentaries. Rabbinic Judaism established a mode of worship and moral code that Jews worldwide have followed down to modern times.

Societal and Family Relationships From earliest times to the founding of the monarchy, Jewish families survived in an agrarian economy and society. Although the patriarchal structure set the pattern of life and ensured the dominance of the tribal chieftains, men and women shared duties and responsibilities because in a rural society a family's continuation and the preservation of its property required the efforts of all its members. Within the family, women exercised some freedom, mothers' and sisters' roles were taken seriously, and the family rights of wives and mothers were protected by law.

However, with the coming of the kingdom of Israel and during and after the Babylonian Captivity, the male leaders, in their efforts to protect the new political system, the integrity of their religion, and the Hebrew way of life, formally and informally limited the rights and powers of women. This trend accelerated in the Hellenistic period as urbanism and commercialism made inroads into the Jewish social order and family. Work was increasingly divided according to gender, with women being assigned domestic duties and subordinated and restricted within the economic, social, legal, and cultural system. The changing, and often conflicting, roles for women were reflected in the Hebrew Bible and other literature, which recorded instances of women serving as priestesses or influencing Hebrew officials, defined the qualities of a good wife, justified women's subservient status in a patriarchal order, and blamed them for human transgressions.

The Bible

The Jews enshrined their cultural developments in the Bible, their collection of sacred writings, or **scriptures.**

Known as the Old Testament to Christians, the Hebrew Bible (from the Greek word for "book") contains history, law, poetry, songs, stories, prayers, and philosophical works. Evolving out of a rich and long oral tradition, the Bible probably began to take its earliest written form during the United Monarchy in the tenth century B.C. By then the Hebrews had an alphabet, which, like that of the Greeks, was probably derived from the Phoenicians. Having acquired a written language and a unified political state, the Hebrews shared a consciousness of their past and desired to preserve it. They assembled and recorded various historical accounts, songs, and stories, plus the sayings of the prophets. Sometime in the fifth century B.C., Jewish scholars and religious leaders canonized (officially accepted) parts of these writings as divinely inspired. They became the first five books of the Bible, known as the Torah or the Pentateuch. The Hebrew Bible's ultimate form was reached in A.D. 90 when a council of Jewish scholars added a last set of writings to the **canon.**

Another important development in the transmission of the Hebrew scriptures was their translation into other languages. In the third century B.C., after many Jews had been influenced by Hellenistic culture, a group of Alexandrian scholars collected all the authenticated Jewish writings and translated them into Greek. This Hebrew Greek Bible was called the Septuagint, from the Latin word for "seventy," so named because of the legend that it was translated by seventy scholars. Although traditionalist Jews initially rejected the Septuagint,

Table 6.3 BOOKS OF THE HEBREW BIBLE AND THE CHRISTIAN BIBLE OLD TESTAMENT

HEBREW BIBLE		*CHRISTIAN BIBLE OLD TESTAMENT*	
The Law (Torah)		***The Pentateuch***	
Genesis	Numbers	Genesis	Numbers
Exodus	Deuteronomy	Exodus	Deuteronomy
Leviticus		Leviticus	
The Prophets		***The Historical Books***	
(Early Prophets)		Joshua	2 Chronicles
Joshua	2 Samuel	Judges	Ezra
Judges	1 Kings	Ruth	Nehemiah
1 Samuel	2 Kings	1 Samuel	Tobit*
(Later Prophets)		2 Samuel	Judith*
Isaiah	Micah	1 Kings	Esther
Jeremiah	Nahum	2 Kings	1 Maccabees*
Ezekiel	Habakkuk	1 Chronicles	2 Maccabees*
Hosea	Zephaniah	***The Poetical or Wisdom Books***	
Joel	Haggai	Job	
Amos	Zechariah	Psalms	
Obadiah	Malachi	Proverbs	
Jonah		Ecclesiastes	
The Writings		Song of Solomon (Songs)	
Psalms	Esther	Wisdom*	
Proverbs	Daniel	Sirach*	
Job	Ezra	***The Prophetical Books***	
Song of Songs	Nehemiah	Isaiah	Obadiah
Ruth	1 Chronicles	Jeremiah	Jonah
Lamentations	2 Chronicles	Lamentations	Micah
Ecclesiastes		Baruch*	Nahum
		Ezekiel	Habakkuk
		Daniel	Zephaniah
		Hosea	Haggai
		Joel	Zechariah
		Amos	Malachi

*Roman Catholics include these books in the canon and refer to them as deuterocanonical ("second canon"); Protestants sometimes place them in an appendix with other Apocrypha.

it gradually was accepted as authoritative by Jewish intellectuals and early Christian scholars.

The final version of the Hebrew Bible is divided into three parts: the Law, the Prophets, and the Writings (Table 6.3). (Christians divide the Old Testament into four parts.) The Law, also called the Torah (from Hebrew, "instruction"), recounts the story of God's creation of the world and the early history of the Hebrews. More important, it details the establishment of the covenant and the foundation of the moral and ritualistic codes of personal and societal behavior that underlie Judaism.

The Prophets, canonized in the first century B.C., provide records about Israel and Judah and expand the Hebrews' ideas about God's nature and their relationship to him. They recount the conquest of Canaan, the

Figure 6.7   The Dead Sea Isaiah Scroll (detail). First century B.C.–first century A.D. *The Dead Sea Scrolls are believed to be the work of a Jewish sect known as the Essenes. Living in a monastic community called Qumran, this radical group rejected the leadership of the Jews in Jerusalem and practiced a militant, separatist form of Judaism. The scrolls represent their copies of the Hebrew Bible as well as previously unknown works. The Dead Sea Isaiah Scroll preserves all sixty-six chapters of the Bible's longest book.*

events of the era of the Judges and the period of the United Monarchy, and the fate of Judah after the Babylonian Captivity.

The Writings reflect diverse viewpoints and contain many types of literature, including poetry, wise sayings, stories, and apocalyptic visions of the end of time. Some of these books, such as Job, Ecclesiastes, and Proverbs, reflect the influence of other cultures on Jewish beliefs. The Writings were not deemed canonical until A.D. 90, with the exception of Psalms, a collection of poems, which was given sacred status by 100 B.C.

There is also a body of Jewish literature outside the canon. The Apocrypha are books written between 200 B.C. and A.D. 100 that include wisdom literature, stories, and history, including the history of the Maccabees. Though not part of the Jewish canon, these books were included in the Septuagint, the Greek translation of the Hebrew Bible, and accepted by the Roman Catholic Church as part of the Christian Old Testament.

Copies of many Jewish works, both canonical and noncanonical, were found in a cave near the Dead Sea in 1947. These documents, dating from about 200 B.C. to A.D. 100 and known as the Dead Sea Scrolls, were almost a thousand years older than any other existing manuscripts of the Bible and confirmed that the books had been transmitted faithfully for centuries (Figure 6.7). The scrolls also provided scholars with material about nonmainstream Jewish religious practices in the period before and during the earliest Christian period.

The Hebrew Bible provided Judaism with many of its beliefs and values and much of its worldview. It contrasted a changing view of God with a consistently negative opinion of human nature. Examples abound of humans who, like Adam and Eve or David, failed to uphold their side of the covenant by disobeying

Yahweh, worshiping other gods, exploiting the unfortunate, or breaking moral and social codes. The Bible implied that given the weakness of human nature and Yahweh's strict demands, most mortals were unlikely to attain happiness. Perhaps happiness would be reached when Yahweh's kingdom was established on earth, but no one knew when that would happen or in what form. The individual's life was made more perplexing because no mortal could comprehend the awesome power of Yahweh. Human beings could only try to follow Yahweh's commandments—knowing that they would sin—and hope for happiness through his forgiveness.

In biblical Judaism, the hope for happiness depended on another aspect of the covenant: Jews believed that they would be forgiven for their sins. Redemption by God had occurred over and over in history, and the Bible sustained human hope while revealing Yahweh's love and mercy. Yet such qualities often seemed inconsistent with the Lord's vengeful manner. Consequently, the hearts of worshipers were torn between hope and fear. Their hope was strengthened through the covenant's promise that Yahweh would protect humanity as long as they lived just lives.

Early Jewish Art and Architecture

Jewish culture was profoundly shaped by the Second Commandment, which forbids the making of images or likenesses of God. In art, this meant that Yahweh could not, by definition, be depicted in any recognizable form. Furthermore, creation and creativity are considered the exclusive domain of God and reserved for him alone. Thus, there is no official Jewish sculpture or painting.

The scattered surviving artifacts of the Hebrews from the period before the United Monarchy can seldom be distinguished from the works of their neighbors. Because of the early Hebrews' nomadic existence, what sacred objects they had were transportable and kept in tents. These early works were not for public display because of the very holiness of Yahweh and the Hebrews' sense of their deity's power. Only a few persons were even permitted to see or be in the vicinity of these sacred objects. Once the tribes were united, however, Solomon enshrined the Ark of the Covenant and other ritualistic items in the splendid Temple that he built in Jerusalem. Solomon meant the Temple to be the central national shrine of the Hebrews and a symbol of his dynasty.

Solomon's Temple was destroyed by the Babylonians when they carried off the Jews in the early sixth century B.C. The description of the Temple in 1 Kings makes it sound similar to the "long-house" temples found in other civilizations of that time and probably indicated the influence of foreign neighbors. According to the Bible, Solomon's Temple was a rectangular building comprising three sections: a porch, a sanctuary, or main hall, and an inner sanctum that housed the Ark of the Covenant. Artists and craftspeople decorated the interior with carvings of floral designs and cherubs, highlighting these with gold. The building was made of ashlars, and two large freestanding columns were placed at the entranceway. The Temple may have been raised on a platform. A court surrounded the Temple, and a large altar stood inside the court.

When the Jews were released from the Babylonian Captivity by the Persians, they returned to their homeland and reconstructed the capital city of Jerusalem and its Temple. The Second Temple, completed in the late sixth century B.C., exhibited a simpler design and decoration scheme than did Solomon's Temple. Meanwhile, the Jews of the Diaspora gathered in Hellenistic cities to read the Torah and to pray in buildings that became synagogues, or houses of worship. No record survives of how these synagogues looked or how they might have been decorated until the third century A.D.

Greek influences became apparent in Jewish architecture during Hellenistic times. One Maccabean ruler, John Hyrcanus [hear-KAY-nuhs] (135–106 B.C.), constructed a fortress-palace at present-day Araq el Emir in Jordan that shows this influence clearly. The facade of the palace blended Greek columns and oriental carvings, typical of the Alexandrian architectural and decorative style (Figure 6.8). The edifice and its carvings were probably similar to the Second Temple in Jerusalem. One of the few decorations remaining from this palace is a lion fountain (Figure 6.9). Carved in high relief, the lion is well proportioned and conveys a sense of power with its raised front paw and open mouth.

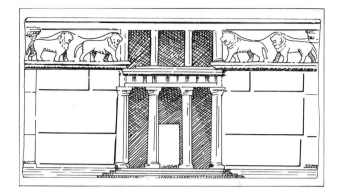

Figure 6.8 Palace of John Hyrcanus. Second century B.C. Araq el Emir, Jordan. *This rendering of the palace of John Hyrcanus is based on ancient literary descriptions and recent archeological excavations. The Corinthian columns and the carved lions show Greek and Persian influences, but the lions appear more lifelike than the typically stylized Persian models.*

Figure 6.9 Lion at the Palace of John Hyrcanus. Second century B.C. Araq el Emir, Jordan. *This lion, Greco-Oriental in style, was carved deeply into the stone's surface to create a high-relief work. The lion's tail, wrapped around his right rear leg, is balanced by the raised left front leg, creating a feeling of strength and agility.*

The lingering influence of late Greek architecture on Jewish structures is also seen in a set of tombs dug out of the soft limestone rocks east of Jerusalem in the Kidron Valley. According to the inscription, these tombs contained the remains of priests from the Hezir family (Figure 6.10). The tomb on the left displays Doric columns, and the one in the center fuses Greek Ionic columns and an Egyptian pyramidal roof. Several other tombs in the vicinity reveal a similar melding of styles.

During the reign of King Herod the Great (r. 37–4 B.C.), architecture in Judea exhibited a further mix of Greek styles with Jewish motifs. King Herod's magnificent

Figure 6.10 Tomb of Bene Hezir. Early first century B.C. Kidron Valley, Israel. *The Tomb of Bene Hezir (on the left) shows the influence of Greek architecture in its post-and-lintel construction and its Doric columns. Even though the area was subject to Roman impact at this time, Roman influence is not apparent in the architecture. The members of the priestly Hezir family, as recorded in 1 Chronicles 24, were buried in what has been determined to be the oldest tomb in Israel's Kidron Valley. Scholars disagree over whether the structure in the center with the pyramidal roof belonged to the Bene Hezir tomb.*

Figure 6.11 Hall of Herod's North Palace. Late first century B.C. Masada, Israel. *These Corinthian columns were originally plastered over and painted. Carved directly out of the hill's rock, they formed a natural corridor around the banqueting hall. Herod built this and other splendid palaces to impress the Jews and win their political sympathy, but he failed to do either.*

Figure 6.12   Mosaic from Herod's Palace. Late first century B.C. Masada, Israel. *The Greek practice of mosaic making was adopted by both the Romans and the Jews. The patterned designs around the borders of this mosaic from Herod's Palace are typically Greek, and the more organic image in the center is typically Jewish.*

fortress-palace at Masada may have been a conscious blending of the two cultures in an effort to bridge the gap between the Roman and Jewish worlds (see Figure 6.5). The various buildings in Herod's complex contained many representative Greco-Roman features, including fluted Corinthian columns and marble facings (Figure 6.11). In Herod's palace, Classical patterned mosaics were combined with traditional Jewish decorations of flowers, fruits, and intertwined vines and branches (Figure 6.12).

Herod also built palaces at Jericho and in Jerusalem, but they were destroyed, and their remains have not been uncovered. The king also supervised the rebuilding of the Second Temple in Jerusalem, whose large dimensions and impressive features were recorded in the writings of the Jewish historian Josephus in his works *The Jewish War* and *Jewish Antiquities* (see Figure 6.4). Like the First Temple, this one contained many rooms, including the Holy of Holies with the menorah and the table where the priests placed the consecrated, unleavened bread eaten during Passover, the festival that commemorates the exodus from Egypt. Whatever may have been Herod's motives in constructing this new Temple, the results were short-lived. When the Romans finally crushed the Jewish revolt in A.D. 70, the Temple, except for the Wailing Wall, was destroyed, and its sacred objects were transported to Rome.

CHRISTIANITY

Like Judaism, Christianity rose from obscurity and gained much of its power from the tremendous moral force of its central beliefs and values. But Christianity went on to become the dominant religion of Western culture. From its origins among the Jews of Judea, Christianity slowly spread until, by the end of the fourth century A.D., it had become the official faith of Rome. When Rome lost control of the western provinces at the end of the fifth century A.D., Christianity's ideas and institutions survived as rays of hope in the surrounding darkness. In the following century, Christians gradually gained the upper hand. Their triumph was powerfully symbolized in the Early Middle Ages when church authorities revised the old Roman calendar to make the birth of Christ the pivotal event in history. Thus, the period before Jesus' birth is known as B.C., or before Christ, and the era after his birth is termed A.D., or ANNO DOMINI, Latin words meaning "in the year of the Lord," the title of respect given to Jesus by Christians. Although Christianity and the church have declined from their zenith in the Middle Ages, the Christian calendar remains in effect throughout the West as well as in many other parts of the world—a symbol of the continuing power of this creed.

Timeline 6.2   **CHRISTIANITY TO** A.D. **284**

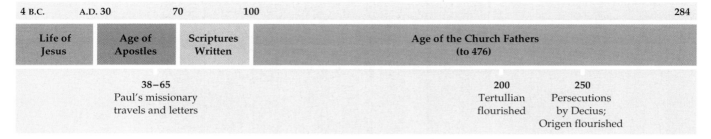

The Life of Jesus Christ and the New Testament

The surviving primary sources for the origin of Christianity are writings in Greek by early believers who were openly partisan. According to them, Christianity began within the Jewish faith among the followers of Jesus, a deeply pious and charismatic Jew who failed to purify his own faith but succeeded in founding a dynamic new religion.

Jesus was born to Mary and Joseph in Judea in about 4 B.C. (a date that reflects changes in the Christian calendar made since its inauguration). After narrating the events surrounding his birth, the accounts of Jesus' life are almost silent until he reaches the age of about thirty, when he commenced a teaching mission that placed him squarely in conflict with prevailing Jewish beliefs and authorities. The poor and outcast in Jewish society heard Jesus' message, and he soon had a small group of followers who believed that he was the Messiah, the Anointed One who would deliver the Jews, promised by God to the prophets. He was also termed the Christ, taken from the Greek for "the anointed one." Performing miracles and healing the sick, he preached that the apocalypse, or the end of the world, was near. In anticipation of what he called the coming of the kingdom of God, he urged his followers to practice a demanding and loving ethic.

Growing discord between the Jewish establishment and this messianic band caused Roman leaders to classify Jesus as a political rebel. In about A.D. 30, Jesus was crucified by the Romans (Timeline 6.2). Three days later, some of his followers reported that Jesus had risen from the dead and reappeared among them. His resurrection became the ultimate miracle associated with his teachings, the sign that immortal life awaited those who believed in him as the son of God and as the Messiah. In after a few days on earth, Jesus ascended into heaven, though not before pledging to return when the world ended.

The outline of Jesus' life is set forth in the first three books, called **Gospels,** of the Christian scriptures. The early Christian community believed that the writers, known as Matthew, Mark, and Luke, were witnesses to Jesus' message; hence they were called **evangelists** after the Greek work *evangelion*—for those who preached the gospel, or the good news. The Gospels, although providing evidence for the historical Jesus, were not intended as histories in the Greco-Roman sense because they were addressed to Christian converts. Mark's Gospel was the earliest, dating from about 70; Matthew's account was written between 80 and 90; and an early version of Luke's narrative probably appeared at about the same time. These three works are known as the synoptic Gospels (from the Greek *syn* for "together" and *opsis* for "view") because they take essentially the same point of view toward their subject. Between 90 and 100, a fourth, and somewhat different, Gospel appeared—that of John—which treats Jesus as a wisdom teacher, a revealer of cosmic truths. The author of the Fourth Gospel has Jesus teach the possibility of being born again to eternal life.

Despite their similarities, the synoptic Gospels reflect a schism, or split, in the early Christian church. Peter, one of Jesus' original disciples, headed a Judaizing group that stressed the necessity of first becoming a Jew before becoming a Christian. Paul, a Jew who converted to Christianity after the death of Jesus, led a group that welcomed gentile, or non-Jewish, members. Mark's Gospel was written in part to support Paul's gentile faction and therefore takes a negative tone toward Jews. Matthew was written in part as a corrective to Mark and made Peter, according to Roman Catholic doctrine, the "rock" on which the church was founded—the biblical source for the belief that Peter was the first pope. Luke's Gospel was an effort by the early Roman church to deny, after the fact, that a schism had ever existed.

Luke also wrote the Acts of the Apostles, the earliest account of the fledgling Christian community. This work records the activities of Jesus' followers immediately after his resurrection and defines some of the church's first rituals and beliefs, including a rejection of Jewish dietary laws and the practice of circumcision. Acts also affirmed the opening of Christianity to gentiles, a policy that in the future would aid in the spread of Christianity. At the time Acts was written,

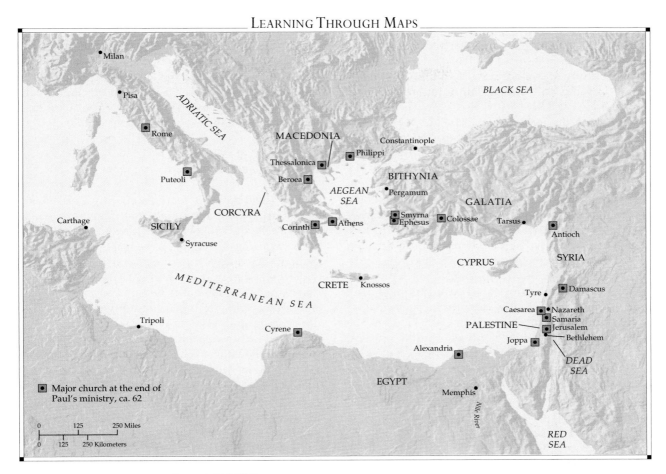

Map 6.2 THE EARLY CHRISTIAN WORLD
This map shows the spread of Christianity after the death of Jesus. **Identify** the major churches in existence by the end of Paul's ministry. **Which** of these churches did St. Paul found? **Which** church was best positioned to become the mother church of Christianity? **Why? Consider** the impact of geography on the location of these churches. **Is** there a connection between the major cities on Map 5.1, The Roman Empire, and the location of the Christian churches in this map?

however, Paul and other missionaries were preaching mainly to Greek-speaking Jews and Jewish converts scattered across the Roman Empire. Paul's Roman citizenship enabled him to move about freely.

The meaning of Jesus' life and teachings was further clarified by Paul, who had persecuted the Christians of Judea before joining the new faith. Between 50 and 62, Paul, who was familiar with Greek philosophy, addressed both local issues and broader theological concerns in epistles, or letters, the earliest writings among the Christian scriptures, although only seven of the fourteen so-called Pauline epistles are generally recognized as having been written by him. These epistles constitute Christianity's first **theology,** or the study of the nature of religious truth. Paul directed his letters to churches he either founded or visited across the Roman Empire: Ephesus and Colossae (Galatia), Philippi and Thessalonica (Macedonia), Corinth (Greece), and Rome (Map 6.2).

Paul's interpretation of the life of Jesus was based on the "Suffering Servant" section of the book of Isaiah in the Old Testament. The Suffering Servant was described as noble and guiltless but misunderstood and suffering on behalf of others. Paul set forth the doctrine of the Atonement, whereby a blameless Christ suffered on the cross to pay for the sins of humankind. Christ's life and death initiated a new moral order by offering salvation to depraved human beings who otherwise were doomed to eternal death and punishment by Adam's first sin. But, according to Paul, human redemption was not automatically given, for a sinner must have faith in Jesus Christ and his sacrifice.

Paul's teachings also stressed that Christ's resurrection, which guaranteed everlasting life for others, was the heart of Christian beliefs, an argument that echoed the synoptic Gospels. Pauline Christianity made a radical break with Judaism by nullifying the old law's authority and claiming that the true heirs of Abraham were not the Jews but the followers of Christ. Paul also affirmed that obedience to Christ led to righteousness. Such righteousness demanded ascetic living, with particular stress on sexual chastity. From Paul's writing came the Roman Catholic Church's teaching that sexuality, except for reproductive purposes, was inherently sinful.

The final section of the Christian scriptures was the Book of Revelation, dating from about 95. This apocalyptic scripture projected the end of the world and the institution of a new moral order on the occasion of Jesus' return and final judgment. Revelation's picture of Rome as a corrupt Babylon destined for destruction reflected the early church's hatred of the existing political and social order. But the book, filled with enigmatic sayings and symbols, proved controversial, and not all ancient church communities accepted its authority.

By the mid–second century, the four Gospels, the Acts of the Apostles, the fourteen Pauline epistles, the seven non-Pauline epistles, and Revelation were accepted as the canon of Christian scriptures, or the New Testament (Table 6.4). Believing themselves to be the new Israel, the early Christians also retained the Hebrew scriptures, called the Old Testament. Although the spoken language of the Jews in Palestine was Aramaic, a Semitic tongue, the Christian canon was composed in Greek, like the Hebrew Septuagint. The use of Greek reflected the triumph of Paul and the gentile party as the church turned away from Jerusalem and toward the Greco-Roman world.

Christians and Jews

Despite the distinctive features of early Christianity, many Jewish ideas and rituals contributed to the new religion. The Christian vision of Yahweh was rooted in Judaism: a single, creating, universal God who spoke through sacred texts (the canon) and who demanded moral behavior from all humans. Both Jewish and Christian ethical standards required social justice for individuals and for the community. Likewise, the Christian image of Jesus as Messiah was framed within the context of Jewish prophetic literature. Christian apocalyptic writing, such as Revelation, also shared a common literary form with Jewish models such as the book of Daniel.

Even when Christians rejected specific Jewish ideas, such as the sanctity of the Mosaic law, the early church continued discussions on human righteousness and sin in terms familiar to Jews. The Christians probably adapted their rite of baptism from a ceremony similar to that of the Jews of the Dispersion. Christians also kept the idea of the Sabbath but changed it from Saturday to Sunday, and they transformed the festival of Passover (a celebration of the Hebrews' escape from Egypt) to Easter (a festival celebrating Jesus' resurrection). The church sanctuary as a focal point for prayer and learning evolved out of the Jewish synagogue, as did Christian priests from the Jewish elders. And the Christian **liturgy,** or the service of public worship, borrowed heavily from the Jewish service with its hymns, prayers, and Bible reading.

Judaism also influenced Christian thought by transmitting certain ideas from Zoroastrianism, including such dualistic concepts as Satan as the personification of evil, heaven and hell as the twin destinies of humankind, and a divine savior who would appear at the end of time. Jesus and the dominant Jewish sect, the Pharisees, though enemies, both integrated these Persian ideas into their religious outlooks.

Despite their common heritage, relations between Christians and Jews were stormy. After the Council at Jamnia in Judea in 90, when the Jews established the final version of their sacred canon, there was no place in Judaism for the Christian message. As revealed in Paul's letters, the Jews viewed the followers of Jesus Christ as apostates, people who had abandoned or

---

Table 6.4 BOOKS OF THE NEW TESTAMENT

Gospels

Matthew	Luke
Mark	John

Acts of the Apostles

Acts

Epistles

Romans	Titus
1 Corinthians	Philemon
2 Corinthians	Hebrews
Galatians	James
Ephesians	1 Peter
Philippians	2 Peter
Colossians	1 John
1 Thessalonians	2 John
2 Thessalonians	3 John
1 Timothy	Jude
2 Timothy	

Apocalypse

Revelation

renounced their true religion. Accordingly, the Jews tried to deny the Christians the protection that Jewish leaders had negotiated with Roman authorities regarding emperor worship and their own unique beliefs and rituals. In some cases, Jews resorted to reporting individual Christians to the Roman authorities. Until the end of the second century, Jews and Christians occasionally engaged in violent clashes. Possibly the strong anti-Jewish bias found in a few of the Christian books like the Gospel of Mark reflected these tensions.

Christianity and Greco-Roman Religions and Philosophies

Christianity also benefited from its contacts with Greco-Roman mystery cults and philosophies. Whether or not the rituals of the cults of Cybele, Isis, or Mithra directly influenced Christianity, they did share religious ideas—for example, salvation through the sacrifice of a savior, sacred meals, and hymns. Christianity, as a monotheistic religion, paralleled movements within the cults of the second and third centuries that were blending all deities into the worship of a single divinity. Among the Greco-Roman philosophies, both Stoicism and Neo-Platonism influenced Christianity as the church shifted from its Jewish roots and became hellenized; the Stoics taught the kinship of humanity, and the Neo-Platonists praised the spiritual realm at the expense of the physical world.

Christians in the Roman Empire

Eventually, the Romans viewed and treated Jews and Christians differently. The Romans initially regarded the Christians as a Jewish sect, but during the First Jewish War, the Christians evidently held aloof. The Christian attitude seemed to be that the Jews had brought calamity upon themselves through their rejection of Christ. Similarly, Christians remained untouched during later persecutions of Jews by Romans in 115–117 and in 132–135.

As their faith expanded during the first century, individual Christians began to experience trouble from the Romans, though no state policy of seizing Christians was introduced. However, if suspected Christians came to the notice of secular officials, they were punished if they did not renounce their beliefs. The same pattern of localized, random persecution continued until the mid–third century, reminding the Christians of their vulnerability. The church, having by that time increased dramatically in membership and accumulated property in buildings and cemeteries, profited from the indifference of imperial and local authorities.

As long as economic prosperity and political stability lasted, the Christians seemed safe.

However, as the chaos of the third century descended on Rome, the Christians were blamed for all the empire's troubles. The emperor Decius [DEE-she-uhs] (r. 249–251) mounted a wide-ranging political test that required all citizens (men, women, and children) to make a token sacrifice to the emperor. When the Christians refused to honor the emperor in this manner, hundreds of them died, including several of their local leaders, or bishops. Decius's sudden death ended this assault, but in 257 Valerian (r. 253–260) renewed the struggle, which resulted in the martyrdom of the bishop of Rome and the age's leading intellectual, Cyprian. Christians were beheaded, buried alive, or burned alive during this persecution. The killings eventually ceased, but for the rest of the century the survival of the Christian church was uncertain and depended on a muted existence.

Despite persecutions from the authorities, the Christian church drew much sustenance from Roman culture. The language of the church in the western provinces became Latin, and in the eastern provinces the religious leaders adopted Greek. The canon law that governed the church was based on the Roman civil law. Most important, the church modeled itself on the Roman state: The bishops had jurisdiction over territories called dioceses just as the secular governors controlled administrative dioceses.

In addition, the church was moving toward a monarchical form of government. Because the authority of the officeholders was believed to descend from Jesus' faithful supporters, those bishoprics established by apostles—such as the one in Rome that tradition claimed was founded by both Peter and Paul—emerged as the most powerful.

From an insignificant number of followers at the end of the first century, the church had attained a membership of perhaps five million, or about a tenth of the population of the empire, by the end of the third century. The smallest communities were scattered along the frontiers, and the largest congregations were in Rome and the older eastern cities. Social composition of the church evolved from primarily lower-class foreign women and slaves, particularly those recruited from among the Jewish communities of the Diaspora, to progressively higher classes. By the late second century, the middle classes, especially merchants and traders, were joining the church. Aristocratic women sought membership, but men of the highest classes tended to remain unconverted, although a few aristocratic converts prepared the way for future adherents.

Christianity's appeal to women was complex, though all seemed to respond to its promise of salvation and the Apostle Paul's egalitarian vision

PERSONAL PERSPECTIVE

VIBIA PERPETUA
Account of Her Last Days Before Martyrdom

Vibia Perpetua, an educated young woman from a wealthy Carthaginian family and a convert to Christianity, defied an edict against proselytizing issued by the emperor in A.D. 202. She was jailed and died in the arena of Carthage in 203.

A few days later we were moved to a prison [in Carthage]. I was frightened, because I had never been in such a dark place. A sad day! The large number of prisoners made the place stifling. The soldiers tried to extort money from us. I was also tormented by worry for my child. Finally, Tertius and Pomponius, the blessed deacons responsible for taking care of us, bribed the guards to allow us a few hours in a better part of the prison to regain our strength. All the prisoners were released from the dungeon and allowed to do as they wished. I gave suck to my starving child. . . . I was permitted to keep my child with me in prison. His strength came back quickly, which alleviated my pain and anguish. The prison was suddenly like a palace; I felt more comfortable there than anywhere else.

(Galatians 3:28): "There is neither Jew nor Greek, there is neither bond nor free, there is neither male nor female: for ye are all one in Christ Jesus." Female converts also found the Christian community to be a refuge from the anonymity and cruelty of Roman society; the church formed a secret underworld of close relationships among people drawn together by an ascetic but loving way of life. That underworld promised to free women from the constraints of marriage and family life; it offered power by allowing them to influence others by their faith; it widened their horizons through intimate contacts with spiritual leaders; it gave them new identities through foreign travel and involvement in a cause that was life-sustaining; and, for those who chose lives of chastity, it could serve as a means of birth control.

Early Christian Literature

By the late second century, the status of the church had attracted the attention of leading Roman intellectuals, such as the philosopher Celsus and the physician Galen. Celsus (second century) ridiculed the Christian notion of the resurrection of the body and the new religion's appeal to women and slaves. On the other hand, Galen (about 130–about 201) found merit in Christianity because of its philosophical approach to life and its emphasis on strict self-discipline.

Christian literature was excluded from secular public discourse from its birth in Paul's letters until 284. But the work of Christian writers, which addressed the evolving needs of this underground religion, began to circulate among the faithful. Of the many Christian writers active during this time, Tertullian [tehr-TULL-yuhn] (about 160–about 230) and Origen [AHR-uh-juhn] (about 185–about 254) were important because they helped to define Christianity's relation to humanistic learning.

Tertullian's life and writings showed the uncompromising nature of Christianity. Trained in Stoic philosophy in Roman Carthage, he later converted to the new faith after he witnessed the serenity of Christians dying for their religion. The strength of his beliefs made him a spokesperson for North Africa, where a cult of martyrs made the area the "Bible belt" of the Roman world. Writing in Latin, he helped to shape the Western church's voice in that language. His diatribes against the pleasures of the theaters and arenas and his intense denunciation of women as sexual temptresses became legendary. In the severest terms he rejected the Greco-Roman humanistic heritage, preferring the culture of Christianity. Such fundamentalist thinking eventually drove this restless intellect into heretical, or false, beliefs. His vehement detestation of the secular world and the institutional church proved to be an uncomfortable legacy for Christianity.

Origen of Alexandria shared Tertullian's puritanical zeal and his defiance of spiritual authority, but he did not repudiate humanistic learning. In his mature writings, composed in Greek, Origen brought Christian thought into harmony with Platonism and Stoicism. Origen's Jesus was not the redeemer of the Gospels but the *logos* of Stoicism (see Chapter 4). The *logos*, or reason, liberated the human soul so that it might move through different levels of reality to reach God. Origen's Platonism led him to reject the notion of the resurrection of the body as described in the Gospels and Paul's letters and to assert instead that the soul is eternal. Not surprisingly, Origen's ideas were condemned as heretical

Figure 6.13 The Roman Catacombs: A Narrow Corridor with Niches for Burials. *Because of their belief in a bodily resurrection, proper burial loomed large in the minds of early Christians. Roman Christians joined with other citizens in burying their dead along subterranean passages underneath the city. In 400, when Christianity triumphed in Rome, the custom of catacomb burial ceased. Knowledge of the catacombs passed into oblivion until 1578, when they were rediscovered and became subjects of study and veneration.*

Figure 6.14 The Good Shepherd. Mid–third century A.D. Fresco. Crypts of Lucina, Catacomb of Callixtus, Rome. *This third-century fresco shows one of the popular religious symbols used by early Christians to disguise evidence of their faith from prying and perhaps hostile eyes. The "Good Shepherd" as an image of Jesus persisted in Christian art until the end of the fifth century.*

by later popes. Nevertheless, his philosophic writings, which were read secretly, helped free Christianity from its Jewish framework and appealed to intellectuals.

Christian women writers in this earliest period were very rare, because intellectual discourse was totally dominated by men. Women did play important roles in the new faith—such as Mary Magdalene, who waited at Jesus' empty tomb, and Lydia and Priscilla, whom Paul met on his travels—but their voices are almost always heard indirectly. In their theoretical writings, men often addressed women's issues, such as Tertullian's "The Apparel of Women." Nevertheless, the voice of one Christian woman from this period has come down to us: that of Vibia Perpetua (about A.D. 181–203) of Carthage in North Africa, one of the first female saints. An anonymous account of the Christian martyrs' struggles includes a verbatim reproduction of Perpetua's writings in prison. Filled with heartbreaking detail, the account describes her prison ordeal as she awaited death while nursing her child. The sentence

was imposed because she refused to obey an edict of the non-Christian emperor Septimius Severus.

Early Christian Art

Had Christians obeyed the Second Commandment, no Christian figurative art would have been produced. Indeed, the earliest Christian writers, including Tertullian and Origen, condemned the depiction of religious subjects as blasphemous. But pious Christians, attracted by the pull of humanism, commissioned frescoes for underground burial chambers and sculptures for their **sarcophagi,** or marble tombs. Christian painters and sculptors slowly fused their religious vision with the Greco-Roman tradition, a style that would dominate the art of the late empire. After the fall of Rome, religious values were central to Western art for almost a thousand years, until the Italian Renaissance.

In imperial Rome, citizens had the legal right to bury their dead in underground rooms beside the Appian Way, the city's chief thoroughfare (Figure 6.13). By the late second century some of the tombs displayed Christian symbols and subjects, suggesting the increased confidence of the new religion in an otherwise hostile Roman environment. In the so-called Catacomb of Callixtus, a third-century fresco depicts a shepherd as a symbol of Jesus (Figure 6.14). This depiction, which is the most popular surviving image in the Christian art of this period, is based on the

Figure 6.15 *Calf Bearer.* Ca. 570 B.C. Marble, ht. 65".
Acropolis Museum, Athens. *This sixth-century B.C. Greek
statue shows a young man carrying a calf probably intended for a
ritual sacrifice. The statue is executed in the kouros style, popular
in the Archaic Age, as indicated by the frontality, stiffness, and
stylized beard. The shepherd image later became associated with
Jesus in the early Christian period.*

idea of Jesus as the kindly shepherd of his flock of
followers, an image derived from many biblical
sources, including the Twenty-third Psalm: "The Lord
is my shepherd." Holding a sheep across his shoulders
with his right hand, the shepherd stands in the center
of a circle, flanked by two sheep. This circle in turn is
surrounded by eight panels with alternating depictions of orants (praying figures) and scenes from the
life of Jonah.

Figure 6.16 *Christian Good Shepherd.* Second century A.D.
Marble, ht. 39". Vatican Museum. *This graceful statue blends
Greek influences with a Christian subject. The casual pose of the
shepherd with his easy contrapposto and dreamy gaze shows that
the influence of Praxiteles, the fourth-century B.C. Greek sculptor,
was still active after more than five centuries. The short cloak
worn by the figure was a typical costume of shepherds in the art of
the times.*

Even though the shepherd and sheep convey a Christian message, the image adapts a familiar Greco-Roman theme—known in both art and literature—that identified such diverse figures as the philosopher Pythagoras and the Orphic cult leader Orpheus with shepherds. The pose of the youth carrying an animal on his shoulders appeared in Archaic Greek sculpture as early as the sixth century B.C. (Figure 6.15). The painter of the Good Shepherd ceiling fresco portrays the shepherd as a beardless youth without distinctive, godlike traits. A statue of a shepherd from the second century attests to the widespread use of this image (Figure 6.16). By such representations as these, the artists in effect declared the limits of their art in penetrating the mystery of Jesus as both God and man.

Catacomb paintings were rich in images, however disguised, of Christian resurrection, salvation, and life after death. The Jewish Bible was a source of subjects for Christian artists, as can be seen in Figure 6.17, *Three Hebrews in the Fiery Furnace*. The youths, Shadrach, Meschach, and Abednego, were rescued from certain death by divine intervention and thus symbolize redemption (Daniel 3). In the painting, they are depicted impressionistically, floating in abstract space. Their feet are hidden in swirls of red paint, representing the fiery torment of the furnace. Their arms are upraised as if praying and constitute an additional symbol: the invocation of God's blessing.

A relief panel sculpted on the marble sarcophagus, dating from about A.D. 270, in the church of Saint Maria Antiqua, Rome, reinforces the message that the Old and New Testaments are not in conflict but exist in religious harmony (Figure 6.18). Reading from left to

Figure 6.17 *Three Hebrews in the Fiery Furnace.* Chamber of the Velatio. Mid–third century A.D. 19½ × 34". Cemetery of Priscilla, Rome. *This catacomb painting of* Three Hebrews in the Fiery Furnace *illustrates the practice of early Christian artists drawing on Jewish stories to symbolize their beliefs. The rescue of the Hebrew youths, who refused to bow down to the golden image set up by the Babylonian king, becomes a symbol of Christian refusal to engage in worship of Rome's emperor. However, the Christian artist has changed the story, so that instead of being rescued by an angel, as recorded in Daniel 3:28, the Hebrews are promised salvation by means of a bird bearing leaves in its beak (above). This symbol probably derives from the Jewish story of Noah and the Flood, in which a dove with an olive leaf was a sign that the dry land had reappeared (Genesis 8:11).*

Figure 6.18 Early Christian Frieze Sarcophagus. Ca. A.D. 270. Marble. Saint Maria Antiqua, Rome. *Most sarcophagi were products of workshops; thus the artistic quality varied greatly. However, this sarcophagus, carved by anonymous artists, exhibits a fairly sophisticated artistic level in the treatment of human figures, such as the variety of poses and gestures, and the attention to detail, such as the draperies and the varied objects used to identify each person. The figures, despite their small size, possess limbs proportional to their bodies, except for the one being baptized.*

right on the panel is the Old Testament story of Jonah: the Prayer in the Ship, Jonah and the Whale, and Jonah Under the Gourd Vine. The three days he spent in the belly of the whale are understood as prefiguring the time Christ spent in the tomb. The rest of the panel shows Christian symbols—a praying figure (with upraised arms), a philosopher (holding a scroll), the Good Shepherd, a baptism (a standing man places his hand on a smaller figure), and a fisherman (with a net). These images, found so often in Christian funerary art, attest to the saving power of their God.

The Legacy of Biblical Judaism and Early Christianity

The entire Jewish tradition has evolved from the early history of the Hebrews—their wandering without a homeland, their role as outsiders in other cultures, their brief period in control of the promised land of Canaan, and, above all, their deep and abiding sense of being the chosen people of the almighty God, Yahweh. Under the Romans, the Jews were punished for their religious views, a portent of the anti-Semitism and violent attacks that have dogged their existence down to the twenty-first century. Despite adversity, the Jews have survived and today have the longest continuous history of any group of people in Western civilization.

Unlike the Greco-Roman deities, who were seen as encouraging and supporting human achievement and excellence in many areas of life, the God of the Hebrews was primarily concerned with the ethical conduct of human beings and their obedience to his laws. Yahweh's jealousy extended to all forms of human expression insofar as they detracted from his worship. As a consequence, the arts and humanities, when allowed in Judaism, tended to be subordinated to religious concerns. Ultimately, Jewish culture found its voice in the ideals of the Bible, among the highest moral standards of any ancient people. The Jewish ethical vision, which even today drives Western reformers and revolutionaries, demanded social justice for every person, no matter how poor or powerless, within the human community.

Inheriting this conception of God and culture, the Christians reinterpreted it and gave it their distinctive stamp. After the fall of Rome, when Christianity emerged as the religion of the West, the Judeo-Christian tradition merged with the Greco-Roman heritage to form the basis of Western civilization. Following the teaching of Jesus, the early Christians perpetuated the Jewish emphasis on God's unity and omnipotence as well as the demands for stringently ethical behavior. Accordingly, Jesus' golden rule—to treat others as one would like to be treated—became the goal of devout Christians. The first Christians also laid great emphasis on taking care of the sick, the impoverished, and the homeless—a tradition that has given rise in Western civilization to a wide variety of private and public social relief programs.

The early Christians, rejecting the relatively closed nature of Judaism, turned their religion into a missionary faith; in the first generation of missionaries, Paul and other church leaders took Jesus' message to all people, addressing them as individuals regardless of their racial and ethnic backgrounds. Today, after two thousand years, nearly one-third of the world's population subscribes—at least nominally—to Christian beliefs.

Under the early Roman Empire, Christian thought also became a transnational, or international, belief system that expressed uncompromising hostility to Greco-Roman culture and to the Roman state. Those Christian writers who, like the author of the Book of Revelation, described Rome as "the great whore" and forecast that city's destruction simply expressed the collective yearnings of the faithful in the early church. Under the onslaught of the Roman persecutions, the Christians anticipated a new order ruled by God's values. Thus, early Christians adopted Greco-Roman ideas not for their own sake but for their usefulness to the Christian religion.

The hostility of the early church to humanism and secular thought was but the opening assault in a running battle between two ways of looking at the world. For the moment, in imperial Rome humanism was triumphant among the people who counted—the aristocrats, the intellectuals, and the ruling class. But by the end of the fourth century, the balance had swung over in favor of Christianity, and the non-Christian intellectuals were rapidly disappearing. This state of affairs prevailed until the Italian Renaissance; then, artists, writers, and intellectuals challenged the reigning Christian worldview by reviving humanistic learning and the Greco-Roman past. As the modern world has taken shape, Christianity has found itself assaulted from many sides and has never regained the preeminence that it held from the time of the fall of Rome to the coming of the Renaissance.

KEY CULTURAL TERMS

covenant	canon
Diaspora	Gospels
eschatology	evangelists
apocalypse	theology
Messiah	liturgy
scripture	sarcophagus

SUGGESTIONS FOR FURTHER READING

Primary Sources

EUSEBIUS. *The History of the Church from Christ to Constantine.* Translated by G. A. Williamson. New York: Penguin, 1965. Though a partisan account written by a credulous observer, this work is the major source of early Christian history.

Holy Bible, New Testament, Old Testament. There are many translations of these sacred books, ranging from the King James version of the early seventeenth century to various twentieth-century translations based on recent scholarship. The Douay edition is the official Bible of the Roman Catholic Church.

JOSEPHUS. *The Jewish War.* Translated by G. A. Williamson. New York: Penguin, 1974. Josephus, a Jew who served Rome, wrote one of the few surviving accounts of this period.

CHAPTER 6 HIGHLIGHTS
Judaism and the Rise of Christianity

B.C.

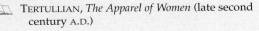 Hebrew Bible: the Law (Torah) (ca. fifth century B.C.); the Prophets (ca. first century B.C.); and the Writings (ca. A.D. 90)

6.10 Tomb of Bene Hezir, Israel (early first century B.C.)

6.11 Hall of Herod's North Palace, Israel (late first century B.C.)

. 90

.C.

 Christian Bible: the Epistles (7) of Paul (ca. A.D. 50–62); the non-Pauline Epistles (7) (late first century A.D.); Gospels (ca. A.D. 70–100); Acts of the Apostles (ca. A.D. 90); and the Book of Revelation (ca. A.D. 95)

TERTULLIAN, *The Apparel of Women* (late second century A.D.)

284

6.9 Lion at the Palace of John Hyrcanus, Araq el Emir, Jordan (second century B.C.)

6.6 Dura Europos Synagogue, Syria (third century A.D.)

6.15 *Calf Bearer* (ca. 570 B.C.)

6.16 *Christian Good Shepherd* (second century A.D.)

6.14 The Good Shepherd, catacombs, Rome (mid–third century A.D.)

6.17 *Three Hebrews in the Fiery Furnace* (mid–third century A.D.)

6.18 Early Christian Frieze Sarcophagus (ca. A.D. 270)

■ *Literature & Philosophy*   ■ *Art & Architecture*   *Music & Dance*

 Readings in the Western Humanities

7

THE CIVILIZATIONS OF LATE ROME, BYZANTIUM, AND THE EARLY MEDIEVAL WEST

After 284, the Roman Empire underwent a radical transformation, sparked by political, social, and economic crises that increasingly seemed beyond human control. At the same time, Christianity was made the official state religion, the church became a prominent feature at all levels of life, and a new cultural ideal emerged that blended Christian beliefs with Classical humanism (Figure 7.1). When the empire fell in 476, Roman civilization as a unifying force around the Mediterranean basin came to an end, and within the power vacuum thus created, three new civilizations gradually emerged: Byzantium, the West, and Islam. All three civilizations borrowed features from Late Rome, and, most especially, Byzantium and the West adopted the cultural ideal of interweaving Christianity and Classical humanism.

Rome's fall meant only the end of the Western Roman Empire. The Eastern Roman Empire, known from this time onward as the Byzantine Empire, endured for nearly one thousand years longer, until 1453. (The Eastern Empire is called "Byzantine" because its capital, Constantinople, was founded on the site of the ancient Greek city of Byzantium.) Of Rome's successors, the Byzantine Empire, with its autocratic government, stable farm economy, Greek intellectual heritage, and what came to be called Orthodox Christianity, seemed to have the greatest prospects for dominance and longevity.

In contrast, the civilization of the West—the name given the surviving lands and peoples of the Western Roman Empire—was all but eclipsed in its first phase, the Early Medieval period. Its political and economic systems, inherited from late Roman practices, were in disarray, and its people huddled in wooden huts beside armed fortresses. In the midst of this chaos, however,

◀ **Detail** *Amor and Psyche* (replacement copy of statuary). Fourth century. Ostia, Italy.

Timeline 7.1   LATE ROME, 284–476

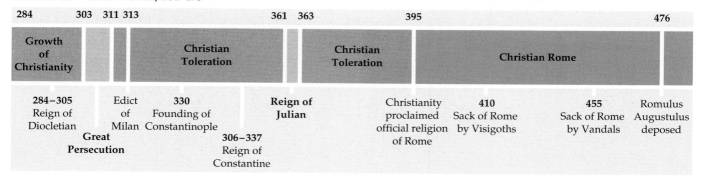

284	303	311	313	361	363	395	476

Growth of Christianity		Christian Toleration	Christian Toleration	Christian Rome		

| 284–305 Reign of Diocletian | Edict of Milan | 330 Founding of Constantinople | Reign of Julian | Christianity proclaimed official religion of Rome | 410 Sack of Rome by Visigoths | 455 Sack of Rome by Vandals | Romulus Augustulus deposed |

Great Persecution

306–337 Reign of Constantine

Figure 7.1   *Young Christ.* Third century. Marble, ht. 27$\frac{1}{2}$". Terme Museum, Rome. *Third-century church leaders, lacking a clear-cut tradition for portraying Jesus, simply borrowed from Classical art, making its tradition their own, as in this portrait of a young Christ. Like the gods on the Parthenon's frieze (see Figure 3.25), Christ is portrayed as a beardless youth, dressed in a Greek garment and seated in repose, his left foot resting against a chair leg. The image of Christ as a beardless youth persisted in the church until the fall of Rome, when it was supplanted by the image of an older, bearded man.*

a new world was being born, built on Classical ruins, spurred by Germanic energies, and animated by the new Christian ethos. This chapter surveys the civilizations of Late Rome, the Byzantine Empire, and the Early Medieval West (Map 7.1). Rome's third successor, Islam, will be covered in Chapter 8.

THE LAST DAYS OF THE ROMAN EMPIRE

When the Roman general Diocletian [die-uh-KLEE-shun] seized power as emperor in 284, the empire faced many problems, chief of which was an out-of-control army whose pressing needs intensified other threats to the state. For more than a century, the office of emperor depended on the army's approval, and increasing numbers of soldiers were recruited to defend the empire's borders. The army payroll drained the state treasury, which was already weakened by inflation and a declining economy. Urban population fell as thousands fled into the countryside to avoid military duty and heavy taxes. Many who stayed in urban areas still clamored for the amenities of Roman life, including bread and circuses, and that further drained precious state resources.

Christian converts presented another problem, for many valued their church membership more than Roman citizenship. They often refused to serve in the army on the grounds that killing was murder, an act forbidden by their faith. With the pool of potential troops reduced, the government recruited soldiers from the barbarians living within Rome's borders—a practice that weakened the loyalty of the military.

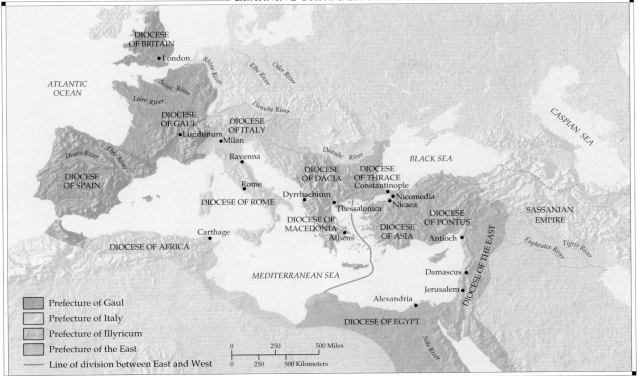

Map 7.1   THE ROMAN EMPIRE IN THE FOURTH CENTURY
This map shows the Roman Empire after the reforms of Diocletian and Constantine.
Notice the role of rivers and bodies of water in determining the empire's frontiers.
What was the impact of geography on establishing the pattern of governmental
dioceses? **Notice** also the dividing line between the Eastern and Western halves of the
empire. **Compare** the location of the Hellenistic kingdoms in Map 4.1, The Hellenistic
World, with the location of the same regions in this map.

Faced with these problems, Diocletian began a series of reforms that virtually refounded the Roman
state. Late Roman civilization may be divided into two
phases: Diocletian's reforms and the triumph of Christianity, 284–395, and Christian Rome and the end of
the Western Empire, 395–476 (Timeline 7.1).

Diocletian's Reforms and the Triumph of Christianity, 284–395

Diocletian (r. 284–305) stands as the creator of late
Rome just as Augustus does of the early empire. Unlike Augustus, however, Diocletian claimed to be
divine, building on the sun-god cult and inflating the
image of the emperor to enhance the power of the office. But whereas Diocletian may have ruled as a god,
he had the soul of a bureaucrat when he turned to the
problems facing Rome. He inaugurated reforms that
reined in the rebellious army, contained barbarian incursions from beyond the borders, and restored modest economic prosperity for most of the fourth century.

Diocletian's efforts to restructure the government met
with mixed success. His greatest reform was the division

of the empire into two separate areas. In the West, Rome
remained the ceremonial capital, although Ravenna became the imperial residence, and thus the actual capital,
for several decades. The Eastern Empire was ultimately
centered in Constantinople (now Istanbul, Turkey) by
Diocletian's successor, Constantine (r. 306–337) (see
Map 7.1). Diocletian's plan for administering the empire
under a tetrarchy, or a rule by four, proved unworkable,
however. Each half of the empire was to be governed by
two tetrarchs, an Augustus supported by a Caesar, but
civil war among rival tetrarchs only made an already
confused situation worse (Figure 7.2). A third reform—
dividing the empire into prefectures and subdividing
these into dioceses—made the vast state more centralized. But the consequences were reduced efficiency and
increased bureaucracy as officials multiplied at all levels.

Diocletian's social and economic reforms changed
the nature of everyday Roman life. He froze wages and
prices in a futile effort to control inflation. When the
old tax system failed to produce adequate funds to
support the enlarged army and the expanded state
bureaucracy, he forced citizens to retain their occupations and sons to inherit their fathers' careers as well
as their tax burdens—even if enslavement for debt

Figure 7.2 *Diocletian's Tetrarchy. Ca. 300. Porphyry, approx. 51". St. Mark's cathedral, Venice. In this group portrait of the tetrarchs, the four rulers—two Augusti, or leaders, joined by their two Caesars, or successors—stand clasping shoulders to signify their unity and loyalty. By this time, the political leaders were no longer wearing imperial togas, as can be seen in the figures' cloaks, tunics, and hats; but the eagle-headed swords and decorated scabbards show that fine workmanship in armor was still practiced in late Rome. Despite the solidarity suggested by the sculpture, the tetrarchy was not a successful reform of the imperial administration.*

resulted. Rural laborers coped with this new tax code by attaching themselves to landed estates, and thus the small independent farmer disappeared—the class that had made early Rome great. Money virtually passed out of circulation, and the economy moved toward a barter system. Citizens now paid taxes in goods or labor or supplied recruits for the army.

One of Diocletian's reforms offers insight into the position of Roman women. Before Diocletian's reign, women, except for wealthy heiresses, were not counted in the state census, presumably because of male prejudice and because women were thought to contribute little to the overall economy. Diocletian now reversed that policy and included women and their wealth in census data. Still, women were not always counted as the equivalent of men; in rural Thrace, for example, two women counted as one man.

The Great Persecution and Christian Toleration At first, Diocletian's religious policy was to tolerate all faiths, but in 303 he began the Great Persecution, whose aim was to stamp out Christianity. Although Diocletian retired in 305, for eight years his successors forbade Christian worship, destroyed churches and books, rebuilt pagan temples, arrested bishops, and imposed a religious test on all citizens. The number of Christians who died in this persecution is unclear, but the imperial policy ultimately failed, for the killings strengthened the church and the courage of Christian martyrs won many converts.

The Great Persecution suddenly ceased in 311, and in 313 toleration was restored to Christians by the Edict of Milan, also known as the Peace of the Church, at the order of the emperor Constantine, a convert to Christianity (Figure 7.3). Priests now joined army units, and

Figure 7.3 Colossal Statue of Constantine. Ca. 313. Marble. Palazzo dei Conservatori, Rome. *Like Diocletian, Constantine consciously nurtured the image of the emperor as a larger-than-life figure. To enhance this image, he commissioned a huge statue of himself, perhaps ten times life size, to stand in the gigantic basilica (which he had also built) in the Roman Forum. All that remains of the statue today are the head, which measures over 8 feet tall, a hand, and some pieces of the limbs. The monument signaled the climax of the emperor cult and the beginning of its decline. With the spread of Christianity, rulers were no longer viewed as gods.*

bishops attended the imperial court. Across the empire, Constantine's policies expanded the restored faith, returned confiscated property to the church, built new churches, and gave tax exemptions to bishops.

Constantine, who after 324 ruled in both the East and the West, built his eastern capital, Constantinople, as a fully Christian city. Dedicated in 330, it was endowed with churches, a Senate building, and mansions for the senators. Standing on a peninsula between Europe and Asia and surrounded by thick walls and water, Constantinople was almost impregnable. It soon became one of Rome's most prosperous cities, thus attesting to the superior vitality and wealth of the East when compared with the Western Empire.

Christianity grew under Constantine's successors, and by 395 most Romans were nominally Christian. Conversions occurred for various motives. Many joined because the church adapted its message to Roman values, promising victory to Roman armies and a bountiful life for believers. Others, especially among the lower classes, found comfort in the Christian ideal of charity and its belief in the spiritual power of the poor.

Early Christian Developments   Christianity, unlike other Roman cults, developed a creed, or set of authorized doctrines, which church leaders imposed on believers. Those who differed were excommunicated as heretics. After the rulers became Christian, the state became entangled in the new religion's problems. Distressed by church squabbles, Constantine tried to end a major controversy over the relationship of Jesus to God. The followers of the priest Arius [uh-RYE-uhs] maintained that Jesus' nature was similar to the divine, a belief that came to be known as Arianism. Those who supported deacon, later bishop, Athanasius [ath-uh-NAY-zhus] believed that the natures of Jesus and God were identical. For Christians, fundamental issues were at stake, such as whether Jesus was eternal and whether God had made the ultimate sacrifice for humanity. To resolve the dispute, Constantine, in 325, called a church council at Nicaea in Asia Minor. Under his guidance, the council issued the Nicene Creed, which supported Athanasius.

Arianism, though condemned, divided the faith for decades and remained strong among church leaders. In addition, most of the Germanic tribes moving into the empire became Arian Christians through the efforts of Ulfilas [UHL-fuh-las], a fellow German and an Arian bishop. Ulfilas's converts were treated as enemies of the true faith, for orthodox Christians recognized no difference between pagans and Christian heretics.

Despite these difficulties, Christianity remained vital. In the fourth century, an ascetic Christian movement began in Egypt and spread across the empire, taking two forms. Both forms taught that the world was evil and must be shunned, but they differed over the best way to earn salvation. Pachomius [puh-KOH-me-uhs] founded an isolated community where followers sought perfection through a life of self-denial and moral rigor. His contemporary Antony chose the solitary life of a hermit, seeking union with God through his individual efforts. Ultimately the dominant form of Christian asceticism became the community style—commonly known as monasticism.

Paganism ceased to be tolerated under Theodosius [the-uh-DOH-she-uhs], called the Great (r. 379–395). The ruler and the law courts ignored the rights of non-Christians, destroyed non-Christian images and temples, and made Christianity the state religion. Paganism disappeared in urban areas, but it survived in the countryside, kept alive by oral traditions, protected by ingrained conservatism, and hidden behind a Christian veneer.

Christian Rome and the End of the Western Empire, 395–476

Despite Diocletian's reforms, Rome ultimately faced insoluble problems: an increasingly non-Roman army, a growing state bureaucracy, and a shrinking tax base. When new waves of Germans began to sweep through the Western Empire in the fifth century, the government was overwhelmed. The Visigoths sacked Rome in 410, and a humbled Senate was forced to pay them a hefty ransom. About 450, the Saxons, Angles, and Jutes invaded Britain, ending its ties to Rome. The Vandals raged through France and Spain, creating a North African kingdom in 442 and sacking Rome in 455. Burgundians settled in central France after 430. Elsewhere, minor tribes exploited Roman weakness.

Western society changed radically. Town life virtually disappeared, leaving only noisy metropolises and the silent countryside. Landowners took over many state functions, and their isolated and relatively secure rural estates attracted desperate city people seeking refuge. Thus began the economic and social world of the Middle Ages.

The Roman Senate and the church responded to the disintegrating conditions quite differently. When Ravenna became the working capital of the Western Empire in the fourth century, the Senate was reduced to the status of a ceremonial body. Yet the senators still collected rents on their estates, doubling the fees when they could. In contrast, some church leaders used the crisis to stamp out troublesome heresies; but, more positively, others offered food and shelter to the homeless and comfort to the poor.

The end of the Western Empire came swiftly when Odoacer [oh-doh-AH-suhr], the leader of a troop of Germans, defeated a Roman army in 476, deposed the young ruler, Romulus Augustulus (r. 475–476), and

PERSONAL PERSPECTIVE

PAULINA
Epitaph for Agorius Praetextatus

Paulina, a Roman matron, composed this inscription for the tomb of her husband of forty years, Agorius Praetextatus (d. 384), an illustrious figure in religion, philosophy, letters, and public life. Although Christianity was rapidly replacing paganism at this time, Paulina praises her husband not only for his teachings but also for his spiritual guidance in pagan worship.

My parents' bright fame gave me nothing greater
   than this—
that, at the time we married, I was thought worthy
   of you.
Yet my whole light and glory is my husband's name,
yours, Agorius, who, born of proud ancestry,
make radiant your land, the senate, and your wife,
by your mind's integrity, your actions and aspirations—
you who have reached the highest peak of excellence.

. . . .

[Y]ou, loyal initiate in the holy
mysteries, bury their insights deep within your mind;
instructed, you worship a manifold divinity
and generously make your wife your comrade

in rites of gods and men: faithful to you, she shares
   your thought.

. . . .

Husband, by your good teaching you liberate me,
innocent and modest, from the bond of death,
you lead me into temples, dedicate me to gods;
with you as my witness, I am steeped in all the mysteries,

. . . .

you teach me the triple secret of Hecate, whom I serve,
and make me worthy of Demeter's liturgy.
Because of you, everyone lauds me as blessed
and holy: it is you who show me to be good, and so
I who was unknown am known throughout the
   world—
how could I fail to please, since you are my husband?

. . . .

How happy I'd have been had the gods let my
   husband live on—yet in the end I *am* happy:
I am and have been yours, and soon, after my death,
   I shall be yours.

sent the symbols of office to the Eastern emperor in Constantinople, thereby signaling that centralized rule had ended in the West. Odoacer prepared to rule not as a Roman emperor but as a Germanic king in northern Italy. The Western Empire was in ruins, fractured into numerous independent Germanic kingdoms.

THE TRANSITION FROM CLASSICAL HUMANISM TO CHRISTIAN CIVILIZATION

Between 284 and 476, Roman civilization moved through two stages, both of which bristled with bitter pagan and Christian tensions. The first phase, which coincided with Diocletian's reforms, was paganism's last flowering; and the second phase, which began when the empire started to break apart after Constantine's reign, was a dynamic Christian age.

Literature, Theology, and History

During Rome's last two centuries, secular writers and Christian writers competed for the hearts and minds of educated Romans through poems, treatises, letters, and essays. The secular authors, who felt threatened by Christian activity and thought, preserved Classical forms and values in their writings. They turned to the humanistic tradition for inspiration and guidance because they believed that their morals and culture were undergirded by Rome's old religion and the farmer-soldier values. Nonetheless, these writers' romantic views of the past were distorted by nostalgia and veneration for a Rome that either was no more or had never been (Figure 7.4).

Secular literature declined in the late empire, and writers did not experiment with new styles or attempt to modify established forms. No one wrote plays, novels, or epics. As a group, the secular Roman authors reflected a growing sense of a lost age. With the exception of a few poets, they seemed unable to define or to analyze the profound changes occurring in their own lifetime.

In contrast, Christian writers looked to the future and a new world to come. They were convinced that Rome was not only dying but also not worth saving. After Constantine decreed toleration for Christians in 313, these authors moved into the mainstream and slowly began to overshadow their pagan rivals. The

Figure 7.4 The House of Amor and Psyche (replacement copy of statuary). Fourth century. Ostia, Italy. *The non-Christian elite of late Rome still revered their Classical past, as shown by this sculpture of Amor and Psyche, the famed lovers from Greek legend, found in the private residence of a wealthy Roman. The erotic pair stood in one of four elegantly decorated, intimate bedrooms, which were dimly lit by small windows and lined in white marble. The tale still caught the fancy of sophisticated Romans living in isolated splendor, perhaps reminding them of the glories of a former age.*

bitter differences of opinion between them and the pagans, which characterized the late fourth century, faded in the early fifth century. By then Christian literature had triumphed, though it remained deeply indebted to Greco-Roman thought and letters.

The Fathers of the Church By about 300, Christian writers began to find a large audience as their religion continued to win converts among the educated. Although they extolled the virtues and benefits of the new faith, they did not necessarily abandon Classical philosophy and literature; they believed that some of these writings conveyed God's veiled truth prior to the coming of Christ, and thus they combined Classical with biblical learning. No longer persecuted, these Christian writers lived either as interpreters of God's word or as bishops. Revered by later ages as the Fathers of the church, they set examples in their personal lives and public deeds. The three most renowned were Ambrose, Jerome, and Augustine. Because of their superior talents, resolute convictions, and commanding personalities, the Fathers not only were powerful figures within the church but also often intervened in secular matters, instructing the local authorities and even

the emperors. Moreover, their writings laid the foundation of medieval Christian doctrine and philosophy.

The first of these men, Ambrose (about 340–397), devoted his life to affairs of the church (Figure 7.5). Born into a well-established Christian family (his sister was a nun), he was trained in the Greco-Roman classics, from which he drew material for sermons, tracts, and letters. Ambrose vigorously opposed the Arian heresy, and as bishop of Milan he aided the urban poor and the victims of barbarian assaults. In scholarly sermons, he condemned the emperors for the social injustices of their reigns. His letters shed light on problems of church government, and his treatises analyzed controversies dividing the church. Ambrose's hymns, perhaps his most memorable contribution, introduced to the Western church another way for Christians to praise their God and enrich their ceremonies.

The second major church Father, Jerome (about 340–420), wrote extensively on religious issues, but his most enduring work was his translation of the Bible into Latin from Greek and Hebrew sources. The Vulgate (from *vulgus*, "common people"), as his version is called, was composed in the common speech of his day; the mark of his Bible's success is that, with some revisions, it remains the standard of the Roman Catholic Church today. Like Ambrose, Jerome received a Classical education. Later, after settling in Bethlehem, he founded a monastery, where he devoted most of his days to his translations of the scriptures. His reclusive habits and his harshly critical opinions of Roman society made him an unattractive figure to his enemies. Yet, as with the other Fathers, Jerome's ascetic life inspired both his own generation and later Christians to emulate his strict denial of personal pleasure.

Of all the Fathers, Augustine (354–430) exercised the greatest influence on Christianity. In his youth in North Africa, he studied Classical literature and thought, including Neo-Platonism (see Chapters 5 and 6). Augustine then journeyed, via Rome, to Milan, where he met Ambrose, whose persuasive sermons assisted in his conversion. Augustine, convinced of Christianity's intellectual integrity and spiritual vitality, retired to North Africa and dedicated himself to the spread of his new faith. However, his winning personality and administrative skills soon propelled him into church politics.

Augustine joined in the debates raging in the church. During his lifetime, his writing came to represent the voice of orthodox beliefs. He opposed the Donatists, who claimed that a priest's sin would make the sacraments useless. Augustine's position—that each sacrament worked in and of itself—became the church's official stance. But his greatest fury was against Pelagianism, which asserted that good works could earn salvation for a sinner. Augustine's argument—that salvation can be achieved only by God's grace—rested on

Figure 7.5 *Ambrose*. Ca. 470. Church of Sant'Ambrogio, Chapel of San Vittore in Ciel d'Oro, Milan. *This portrait of Ambrose conveys some of the spiritual intensity of the powerful fourth-century bishop of Milan. The work is one of few mosaics that survived the destruction brought by Germanic assaults in northern Italy. Although the artist shows some feeling for the shape and movement of the body, the mosaic strongly reflects the artistic ideals developing in the eastern provinces: frontality, flatness, enlarged eyes, and stylized pose.*

his rejection of free will and his insistence on original sin. Once again, he spoke for orthodoxy.

During a long, active life, Augustine wrote many kinds of religious works, but looming over them all are his two major achievements: *The Confessions* and *The City of God*. The *Confessions,* written at the end of the fourth century, trace his search for intellectual and spiritual solace and detail his dramatic conversion. In this spiritual autobiography, he castigates himself for living a sinful, sensual life. Although he was remorseful and laden with guilt for not having found God sooner, he came to believe that his efforts to understand the world by studying Greco-Roman philosophy, literature, and religion affirmed his desire to search for life's ultimate truths.

His conversion occurred in a garden in Milan, where a child's voice commanded him to read the scripture. Opening the Bible at random, he read from Paul, who directed him to arm himself with Jesus Christ as a way of combating the sins of the flesh. Upon reading this passage Augustine wrote: "The light of confidence flooded into my heart and all the darkness of doubt was dispelled." Now certain of his faith, he dedicated himself to his new mission, adopted an ascetic style of life, and, ultimately, accepted church leadership as the bishop of Hippo, in North Africa. Augustine's convictions, so forcefully expressed, helped to raise the standards of Christian literature in the final years of the Roman Empire.

In contrast to the autobiographical *Confessions, The City of God* offered a theological interpretation of history. In this work, written soon after the Visigoths sacked Rome in 410, Augustine addresses the central question confronting the Romans of that generation: Why was their empire subjected to so many catastrophes? To those who blamed the Christians, he replied that the decline of Rome was part of God's plan to prepare the world for the coming of a divine kingdom on earth. If the city fell, it was best for the human race. Augustine expounded and reinforced this argument in the first ten books of *The City of God* as he attacked Greco-Roman philosophies and religions.

In the concluding twelve books of the work, he elaborated his view of world history, which relied on the Hebrew experience and Christian sources. At the heart of his argument lay what he called the two cities in history, the City of God and the City of Man. The inhabitants of

PERSONAL PERSPECTIVE

ST. JEROME
Secular Education; The Fall of Rome

In this passage, St. Jerome defends his use of examples from non-Christian literature in his writings and describes the slide of Rome into chaos. He believed that knowledge of the classics would be necessary in the new world that was emerging.

You ask me at the close of your letter why it is that sometimes in my writings I quote examples from secular literature and thus defile the whiteness of the church with the foulness of heathenism. I will now briefly answer your question. . . . Who is there who does not know that both in Moses and in the prophets there are passages cited from Gentile books and that Solomon proposed questions to the philosophers of Tyre and answered others put to him by them. . . . That leader of the Christian army, that unvanquished pleader for the cause of Christ skillfully turns a chance inscription into a proof of the faith. For he had learned from the true David to wrench the sword of the enemy out of his hand and with his own blade to cut off the head of the arrogant Goliath. . . .

I shudder when I think of the catastrophes of our time. For twenty years and more the blood of Romans has been shed daily between Constantinople and the Julian Alps. . . . How many of God's matrons and virgins, virtuous and noble ladies, have been made the sport of these brutes! Bishops have been made captive, priests and those in minor orders have been put to death. Churches have been overthrown, horses have been stalled by the altars of Christ, the relics of martyrs have been dug up. . . .

The Roman world is falling: yet we hold up our heads instead of bowing them.

---

the City of God were predestined to be saved, but the citizens of the City of Man were condemned to hell. Augustine predicted that the future would eventually expose the nature of the two cities: The City of Man would be destroyed, but the City of God—composed of Christians on their way to heaven—would last forever. In the City of God, the saved would enjoy an eternal happiness that paganism had promised but could not deliver.

Augustine completed *The City of God* shortly before his death and as the Vandals were approaching his city of Hippo. When Augustine's view of history seemed to be validated by the fall of Rome, his fame began to mount. For many centuries, he was venerated by Christians as the supreme authority on nearly every major theological issue.

Church History   In addition to theology, early Christian writing included a new literary genre—church history. Eusebius [you-SEE-be-uhs] (about 260–about 340), bishop of Caesarea in Palestine from 314 until his death, made no claims to impartiality in his *History of the Christian Church*. It makes the bishops the heroes, for Eusebius believed that they ensured the truth of Christianity. He also charted the church's spiritual, intellectual, and institutional life in its martyrs, thinkers, and leaders from its earliest days until 324. Although he is generally reliable in his discussions, modern scholars fault him for siding with the faction that was working to make the bishop of Rome the head of the church in the West.

Written in Greek, Eusebius's history was inspired by the secular Greco-Roman historians, and he followed them in quoting from written sources. He consulted both the Old and the New Testaments, Christian scholars, and the Greek classics, including Homer and Plato. Eusebius's historical account of the early church gained authority from his background. Having been jailed twice and having survived the Great Persecution, he appeared to prove God's power in the world. He also baptized Constantine and delivered the opening oration at the Council of Nicaea.

The Visual Arts

In late Rome, secular and Christian art underwent major transformations. In terms of patronage, tastes shifted as the emperors' dictates were first challenged by the early Christian communities and then forced to bow to the triumphant church. In aesthetic terms, Classical forms and values yielded to a **symbolic realism** in imperial secular art and, later, to abstract spiritual values in Christian works. In geographic terms, church art and architecture in the Eastern Empire moved further away from Greco-Roman ideals, even though the artists and builders continued to modify Classical forms and subjects to fit their faith's themes and needs. A striking example of this trend is the art and architecture of Ravenna, the working capital of the Western Empire. Ravenna naturally had strong political ties with the East, and Ravenna's artistic monuments borrowed heavily from Eastern styles and schools.

Figure 7.6 Diocletian's Palace. Ca. 300. Split, Croatia. *The peristyle, or colonnaded courtyard, screened off the buildings on the left and right, enhanced the enclosed atmosphere, and focused attention on the vestibule. Behind the peristyle, on the left, stood Diocletian's tomb (now a church) and, on the right, the Temple to Jupiter (now the Baptistery of St. John).*

Architecture In the late third century, Diocletian revitalized architecture, following an unproductive period during the previous fifty years of political turmoil. As a part of his efforts to restore centralized rule, Diocletian used art, specifically architecture, as a sign of his new power. Constantine followed Diocletian's lead until the Edict of Milan in 313, after which he promoted Christian architecture and art. He then launched a building campaign of churches and shrines across the empire. Except for the brief reign of Julian (360–363), who renounced Christianity and tried to restore paganism, the later emperors patronized Christian forms and styles, and pagan tastes and schools disappeared.

During the fifth century, the bishops began to vie with the emperors in erecting Christian centers of worship. The invisible forms of the underground church—rooms in private homes, isolated buildings, and converted pagan temples—were abandoned in favor of new standardized structures such as baptisteries and basilicas. Architects, craftspeople, and artists traveled throughout the empire, directing their energies into glorifying the new official religion.

As part of his imperial reforms, Diocletian built a palace on the Dalmatian coast (modern Croatia), where he spent the last twelve years of his life. Strategically located halfway between the Western and Eastern centers of power, his residence resembled a Roman camp in its symmetrical layout. The palace serves as a fitting monument for this soldier who restored law and order to a world racked by civil war and incompetent rulers.

Visitors entered the palace by the main gate on the north side and walked along a path lined with columns across the central intersection and into the **peristyle,** or colonnaded courtyard (Figure 7.6). Those who traveled this far would be reminded of the emperor's presence by such architectural features as the long entranceway, the domed vestibule, and the grandiose courtyard. Beyond the vestibule, on the south side bordering the sea, were the imperial apartments, the guards' barracks, rooms for private audiences, and banquet halls. This residence incorporated nearly all the major designs and techniques, including the arch and mortar mixtures, known to Roman builders. More important, its impressive splendor symbolized divine authority combined with secular political power.

Just as Diocletian's palace was one of the last pagan edifices, the Arch of Constantine was literally the last pagan triumphal arch (Figure 7.7). The arch was erected to celebrate the emperor's victory in 312, which led to the issuing of the Edict of Milan. This well-proportioned monument with its triple arches evolved from the Arch of Titus with its single opening (see Figure 5.16). The circular **medallions** set between the detached columns on the side arches help to balance these smaller arches with the central arch. The decorated **attic,** or crown of the arch, with its statues of Germanic peoples, blends well with the lower sections. The Senate and the Roman people, according to the inscription, gratefully dedicated this arch to Constantine for his deeds as their liberator from civil war and as their new emperor.

Much of the decoration was borrowed from other monuments; for example, some of the reliefs and carvings came from works honoring the victories of Trajan, Hadrian, and Marcus Aurelius; and where a likeness of the emperor is intended, the original has been remodeled to resemble Constantine. Despite Constantine's celebrated conversion to Christianity, however, the arch clearly reflects a strong pagan influence. The symbols and figures stress human action, and only one small frieze hints at divine intervention.

The shift from pagan to Christian architecture began after 313 under Constantine's inspiration and patronage. He ordered the building of churches as places of worship for congregations and as memorials at holy spots in Rome, Palestine, and other parts of the empire. Financed and supported by the state, this ambitious enterprise resulted not only in the spread of Christianity but also in the founding of new artistic values and architectural forms. The basic design of the churches that Constantine had constructed was derived from the **basilica,** a large enclosed rectangular structure that dated back to the second century B.C. and by the early empire was often built to house marketplaces or public assembly halls.

Although basilicas varied in detail, the basic form used for churches was simple: an oblong hall with an **apse,** or curved wall, at the eastern end. Two rows of parallel columns usually divided the hall into a central area, or **nave,** and two side **aisles.** The roof was taller over the nave section, and **clerestory windows** were set high in the outside nave walls to let in light. The apse, where

Figure 7.7 Arch of Constantine. 312–315. Ht. 68'10". Rome. *The frieze that winds around the monument narrates the emperor's preparations for war, his victory, and his triumphant entry into Rome. The scenes depicted on the Arch of Constantine, like those on Trajan's Column, memorialized the Roman ruler's presence at every stage of a military campaign.*

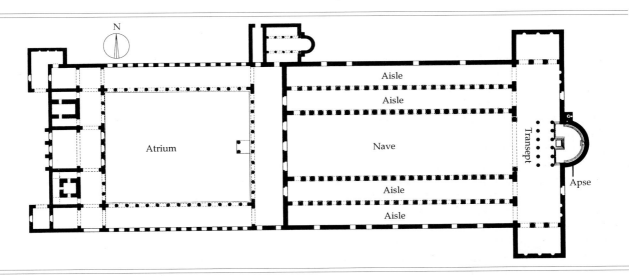

Figure 7.8 Floor Plan of Old St. Peter's Basilica. Ca. 330. Rome. *Old St. Peter's Basilica was the most important structure in Christian Europe until it was demolished in the early sixteenth century to make way for the present St. Peter's. Constantine dedicated Old St. Peter's on the spot believed to be the burial site of Peter, whom the church considered the successor to Jesus. Of the original basilica nothing remains, but sixteenth-century drawings show that it was cruciform (cross-shaped), had a wide central nave with two aisles on either side, and was fronted by an atrium, where worshipers washed their hands and faces before entering the sanctuary.*

ceremonies were performed or where the holy relics were placed, was often screened off from the worshipers, who stood in the nave. In some structures, there was an **atrium,** or open courtyard, in front of the main hall.

No fourth-century Roman basilica churches remain, but drawings, such as that of the floor plan of the basilica of Old St. Peter's, suggest their appearance (Figure 7.8). St. Peter's Basilica, built to mark the grave of the apostle who, by tradition, founded the church in Rome, included a **transept,** or crossing section, that intersected the nave at the apse end of the building, making it **cruciform** (cross-shaped). This first St. Peter's Basilica served

as a shrine for thousands of pilgrims and, in its early years, as a burial ground for Christians.

Constantine ordered the construction of many similar buildings around the empire. In the provincial outpost of Trier, an important administrative and commercial center on the Moselle River (in modern Germany), Constantine erected a complex of government buildings, including an imperial residence and a large basilica that was used as an assembly hall (Figure 7.9). Originally, an atrium fronted the basilica, and the hall connected to other buildings. Its heavily emphasized vertical supports, two tiers of rounded windows, and

Figure 7.9 Constantine's Basilica in Trier. 310. Trier, Germany. *This basilica served first as an audience hall for Roman officials and then as a medieval castle; today it serves as a Lutheran church. Although it is an impressive 220 feet long, 91 feet wide, and 100 feet high, its plan is simple: a narrow hall without aisles, and an apse at the eastern end. Around the exterior of the apse, two stories of round arched windows give a graceful appearance by creating the impression of an arcade. That such a monumental basilica was erected so far from the Roman capital showed the impact of imperial art in the distant provinces.*

Figure 7.11 Baptistery at Frèjus. Fifth century. Frèjus, France. *The Baptistery at Frèjus is one of the earliest surviving examples of the octagonal building. The eight-sided structure has a central dome resting on a solidly constructed drum pierced with windows. At one time it was believed that this style was imported from the East, but now evidence indicates it originated in the West, probably in France.*

Figure 7.10 Sta. Maria Maggiore. Interior, nave. 432–440. Rome. *As Germanic invaders were ending centralized rule in the West, Pope Sixtus III (432–440) and his successors to 470 launched a Classical revival, drawing on the designs of late Classical Roman buildings of the second, third, and fourth centuries. The basilica of Sta. Maria Maggiore is the best surviving example of this revival, as evidenced in the nave's fusion of Classical features—Ionic columns, coffered ceiling, marble floor, clerestory windows topped with rounded pediments, and Classical entablature—into a majestic, symmetrical design.*

large apse established certain basic features that were incorporated into later churches, such as Sta. Maria Maggiore in Rome, built by a fifth-century pope (Figure 7.10). By this date not only had Christians taken over

Classical learning as a tool for studying God's word, but they had also Christianized the pagan basilica. Sta. Maria Maggiore is typical of early churches in its Ionic columns and mosaics from the Greek tradition. By using existing models, Christians not only satisfied their own religious needs but also kept alive the Greco-Roman architectural tradition.

A second important design in Christian architecture was the round or polygonal structure topped by a dome. As these polygonal structures evolved, they came to serve primarily as **baptisteries**—that is, places set aside for baptism. The baptistery was usually separated from the basilica because Christians believed that the unbaptized were unworthy to enter the sanctuary and mingle with the members. This design, which originated in the domed rooms of public baths and funerary architecture and whose most impressive realization was the Pantheon (see Figure 5.12), became standardized as an octagon with a domed roof (Figure 7.11).

Sculpture During Diocletian's reign and before Christianity's conquest of the Roman arts, the late empire produced some unique and monumental works, such as the group portrait of Diocletian's tetrarchy, carved in red porphyry (see Figure 7.2) and the colossal statue of Constantine, a composite of marble and metal (see Figure 7.3). The generalized features of these figures show the trend to symbolic representation characteristic of the art of the late empire and the movement away from the idealized or realistic faces of Classical sculpture. These public works are clearly forms of propaganda art. But Roman artists also continued to execute

Figure 7.13 The Plotinus Sarcophagus. Late third century. Marble, ht. 4'11". Lateran Museum, Rome. *This relief may depict Plotinus, a founder of Neo-Platonism, and his admirers. If so, then the scene is ironic, for Neo-Platonist philosophy rejected realistic art, claiming that art should be viewed with the inner eye. This Neo-Platonist belief influenced Christian mysticism, which in turn helped to create the symbolic art of the Middle Ages, an art that used traditional images to express religious faith.*

Figure 7.12 *The Last Pagan.* Ca. 380–400. Marble, ht. 66". Museo Ostiense, Ostia, Italy. *Evidently this Roman, clad in the toga of an earlier era, has academic interests, since a set of bound books rests beside his right foot. The drapery is cut at severe angles, which increases the overall effect of this care-laden man. The statue is of Greek marble and stands just under 6 feet tall.*

statues for private citizens, whose changing tastes were typified in a statue of a bedraggled scholar (Figure 7.12). Here the artist has fashioned a realistic work that delves into the psychology of his subject. The man's lined features, worried look, and weary slouch convey resignation and defeat. Symmachus, one of the last learned non-Christians, often visited Ostia, where this statue was found; the sculptor may have been depicting this Roman intellectual.

Christian sculpture was undergoing aesthetic changes similar to those taking place in secular art. By the end of the third century, Christian art was symbolic in content and **impressionistic** in style (see Chapter 6). Simple representations of Jesus and the apostles had become common in the underground church. In 313, when the Peace of the Church brought Christian art literally aboveground, artists began to receive the support of the Roman state.

Christian Rome's reshaping of the humanistic tradition can be seen in the carvings on sarcophagi. The

Roman anxiety about life after death and the pursuit of intellectual matters easily evolved into Christian images and themes. The growing acceptance of burial rather than cremation and the resultant increased demand for sarcophagi afforded many artists new opportunities to express themselves. After about the second century, rich Roman families commissioned artists to decorate the sides of these marble boxes with images of Classical heroes and heroines, gods and goddesses, military and political leaders, and scenes of famous events and battles. The Christians borrowed many of these subjects and transformed them into religious symbols pertaining to salvation and life after death. Thus, although the content of sarcophagus art became Christian after the Peace of the Church, the style remained Classical for some time.

Roman sarcophagi also depicted abstract concepts. For example, a carving of a seated philosopher, surrounded by attentive men and women, represents the life of the mind, its attention directed toward more important matters than earthly delights (Figure 7.13). The carvings, finely executed and well balanced, capture this philosophical idea through superbly realized human characters. On either side of the philosopher is a female follower. Neo-Platonism appealed to women because it welcomed them equally with men as students of philosophy. Women also responded favorably to its harsh moral code (sparse vegetarian diet, limited sleep, chastity) because it suited their intellectual striving and made them independent of men's sexual control.

Painting and Mosaics Unlike architecture and sculpture, painting exhibited no changes directly caused by the Peace of the Church. In the fourth century,

Figure 7.14 Illumination from Vergil's *Aeneid*. Fifth century. 6 × 6". Vatican Library. *This page from an illustrated manuscript of Vergil's Aeneid shows an episode from Book IV. Dido, the Queen of Carthage, and Aeneas seek shelter in a cave from a thunderstorm caused by the goddess Juno, who is plotting to bring them together. Outside the cave wait two guards and their horses. A delightful touch is that one of the guards has turned his shield over his head, using it as an umbrella. Although a charming image, this illumination shows a decline in Classical artistic standards, in the lack of balance and perspective in the design, the absence of structure and proportion in the figures, the masklike faces, and the awkwardly placed arms and hands.*

Figure 7.15 *Female Athletes*. Detail from mosaic. 350–400. Villa at Piazza Armerina, Sicily. *This scene may show a female version of games that continued to be conducted in the Christian empire. The mosaic conveys a grace and lightheartedness somewhat at odds with this troubled age and with the changing artistic ideals of Christian art.*

Christian frescoes flourished in the Roman catacombs and continued the symbolic, impressionist style of the previous era (see Chapter 6). Non-Christian paintings are extremely scarce from the fifth century, except for a few works such as a collection of illustrations for Vergil's

Figure 7.16 Putti *Harvesting Grapes*. Mosaic. Fourth century. Church of Sta. Costanza, Rome. *Besides alluding to communion, this scene illustrates the Christian scripture John 15:1, in which Jesus says, "I am the true vine, and my Father is the vinedresser." Putti are depicted trampling grapes and loading grapes into carts pulled by oxen; the rest of the scene is a labyrinth of vines, making up an arbor, amid which other putti are gathering grapes. This scene harkens back to representations of the cult of Dionysus; we know it is Christian only because it is in a Christian church.*

Aeneid, probably painted for a wealthy patron. This extensive picture cycle (Figure 7.14), numbering over 225 scenes, recalls the style of earlier paintings, but it is also an early example of a new medium, the illustrated book. Books were now written on vellum, a parchment made from animal skins, and bound in pages rather than written on scrolls. In the Middle Ages, this type of decorated, or illuminated, book became a major art form. In the late empire, however, the form was in its infancy.

A more vital art form was the mosaic, which, as in other art forms, Christians ultimately turned to their own ends. Pagans continued to place mosaics on both floors and walls, but Christians more often put them on the walls. Christian artists also replaced the stone chips with bits of glass that reflected light, thus adding a glittering, ethereal quality to the basilicas and other buildings.

In the late Roman mosaics, pagan and Christian subjects stand in sharp contrast. Among the many pagan mosaics that survive, one depicting young female athletes from a country villa in Sicily indicates the continued interest of the Romans in the body as the temple of the mind and as an object of admiration (Figure 7.15). The artist has captured the energy and playfulness of these (probably professional) performers in a variety of feats: dancing, running, and exercising. Their movements are realistic, graceful, and strikingly modern. The pagans also liked pictures of young children, or **putti,** in the role of adults at work or play or even in religious scenes. In the very first Christian art, some artists adopted this playful genre for scenes of grape harvesting, as in a mosaic from the Church of Sta. Costanza, Rome (Figure 7.16). In Christian art, however, the scene was a disguised representation of

Figure 7.17 *The Good Shepherd.* Ca. 450. Mausoleum of Galla Placidia, Ravenna, Italy. *The young, beardless Christ, which was still the accepted image of the Christian savior in the fifth century, supports himself with the cross and feeds the sheep, the symbol of the church, with his right hand. Foliage and plants in the background tie in with similar decorations on the mausoleum's ceilings and walls. Upon entering the small tomb, worshipers would immediately be confronted with this large figure of Christ.*

the Christian communion, in which wine made from grapes became the blood of Christ.

The *putti* genre proved not to be popular with Christians. More acceptable was art emphasizing the spiritual and otherworldly qualities of saintly figures, such as the mosaic of the church father Ambrose (see Figure 7.5). Where the *putti*'s movements are fluid, his pose is static, and where their bodies are celebrated, the shape of his body is completely concealed under his clothing, in accordance with the church teaching that the body is sinful and should be hidden from view.

Mosaics became one of the dominant art forms in the Eastern Empire and areas influenced by the Eastern rulers, beginning late in the fifth century. In Ravenna, the small cruciform tomb of Galla Placidia [GALL-uh pluh-SID-e-uh], daughter of Theodosius the Great, contains some splendid mosaics that prefigured the Byzantine style, which in succeeding centuries would dominate Christian art in the Eastern Empire. In the mosaics in the tomb of Galla Placidia, scrolls of vines and leaves wind around the ceiling; large flowers, or rosettes, decorate other sections; and animals and saints adorn parts of the curved walls. Over the entranceway stands the youthful shepherd watching over his flock (Figure 7.17). By the fifth century, the rich and the powerful, such as the relatives of Galla Placidia, were honoring the Good Shepherd in their sanctuaries as the giver of eternal life. The mosaics in the tomb of Galla Placidia

clearly show the adaptation of Classical models to Christian purposes.

Music

The music of late Rome was in decline, but Christian music was just beginning to take shape. The Christians took the principles of Greco-Roman music and integrated them with the Jewish tradition of singing the psalms and the liturgy to make music a dynamic part of their church rituals. In later times, this Christian practice gave birth to a rich body of sacred music that included both singers and instrumentalists.

In late Rome, however, sacred music was limited to chanting and unaccompanied singing. The Antioch church, inspired by the congregational singing in Jewish synagogues, developed a new musical genre, the hymn, a song of praise to God. From Antioch the practice of hymn singing spread to Constantinople and Milan and eventually was integrated into the Christian liturgy everywhere. A few hymns survive from the period before Constantine, but only a fragment of musical notation has come to light. As with other ancient music, how it actually sounded can only be a matter of speculation.

Ambrose, bishop of Milan and a powerful influence at the imperial court, stands out among the earliest hymn writers as one of the founders of the Western sacred song. His hymns, which were written in Latin,

LEARNING THROUGH MAPS

Map 7.2 THE BYZANTINE AND CAROLINGIAN EMPIRES IN 814, THE YEAR OF CHARLEMAGNE'S DEATH

This map shows Charlemagne's Empire during the Early Medieval period in the West, along with the Byzantine Empire. **Consider** the impact of geography and regional cultural traditions on the two empires. **Compare** the size of the Byzantine and Carolingian empires on this map with the size of the Roman Empire in Map 5.1. **Notice** the four rivers in the Carolingian Empire. **What** influence would these rivers have? **What** is the significance of the location of Charlemagne's capital in Aachen, rather than in Rome?

coincided with a new era in the church; up until the fourth century, the liturgy of the early church was in Greek. Ambrose's Latin hymns were probably meant to be sung antiphonally—that is, with lines sung alternately between a leader and a chorus.

THE EASTERN ROMAN EMPIRE AND BYZANTINE CIVILIZATION, 476–1453

The end of centralized rule in Rome's western lands in 476 had little effect on the Eastern Roman Empire. During its one-thousand-year existence, the empire took its Roman heritage and became an autocratic, static entity in a world of great upheaval and movement of populations. The changing boundaries of the Byzantine world tell the story of an empire under continual siege. Byzantium's borders reached their farthest western limits in the sixth century and then contracted over the next eight hundred years. The empire lost territory to

the Arabs in the east and to the Bulgars and other groups in the west. Finally, no longer able to defend even the city of Constantinople itself, the empire fell to the Ottoman Turks in 1453 (Map 7.2).

Although Byzantium was buffeted by rapid and sometimes catastrophic upheavals, great wealth and economic resources allowed the state to survive. The rulers tightly controlled their subjects' economic affairs, a policy that placed state interests above individual gains. A stimulating urban life developed, centered especially in Constantinople, the empire's capital and preeminent city (Figure 7.18). Beyond Constantinople, the countryside was dotted with walled towns and vast farming estates owned by aristocrats and tilled by *coloni,* or serfs. Agriculture remained Byzantium's basic source of wealth.

Even though the frontiers of the empire expanded and contracted over the centuries, its heartland in Greece and Asia Minor remained basically stable. Here, a relatively uniform culture evolved that differed

Timeline 7.2 THE BYZANTINE EMPIRE

476	641	867	1081	1261	1453
	Revival of Empire	Withdrawal and Renewal	The Golden Age	The Challenge from the West	Palaeologian Emperors
Fall of Rome		726–843 Iconoclastic Controversy	1054 Schism between Orthodox and Roman churches		Fall of Constantinople

Figure 7.18 ISIDORE OF MILETUS AND ANTHEMIUS OF TRALLES. Hagia Sophia, Exterior. 532–537. 270' long × 240' wide, ht. of dome 180'. Istanbul. *The Byzantine emperors transformed their capital into a glittering metropolis that easily outshone ravaged Rome. The most magnificent building in the city was Hagia Sophia ("Holy Wisdom"), originally built by Justinian as a church. The building's 101-foot diameter makes it the largest domical structure in the world. Two half-domes at either end double the interior length to more than 200 feet. The beauty of Hagia Sophia made the domed church the ideal of Byzantine architecture.*

markedly from late Rome and the Medieval West. The Byzantine world gave up its pagan and Latin roots to become a Christian, Greek civilization. The Orthodox Church, led by the patriarch of Constantinople, emerged as a powerful force, but without the independence from secular rulers enjoyed by the Western church and the pope. Greek became the language of church, state, and scholarship, just as Latin served those functions in the West. But, like late Rome and unlike the Medieval West, Byzantium remained characterized by ethnic and racial diversity; new peoples, such as the Serbs and the Bulgarians, helped to ensure this diversity as they were slowly assimilated into the Byzantine way of life.

History of the Byzantine Empire

Throughout its history, the Byzantine Empire's fortunes fluctuated depending on its relations with its hostile neighbors. From 476 to 641, the emperors made a valiant but ultimately futile effort to recover the lost western provinces and revive the empire (Timeline 7.2). The memorable emperor Justinian (r. 527–565) conquered several of the Germanic kingdoms that had arisen in the former Western Empire and extended the empire's borders to encompass Italy, southern Spain, and North Africa (Figure 7.19). Justinian's wars exhausted the state treasury, however, leaving his successors unable to maintain the empire.

Between 641 and 867, the second period of Byzantine history, a series of weak rulers lost all the western lands that Justinian had recovered. The emperors were

Figure 7.19 *Justinian and His Courtiers.* Sixth century. Ravenna, Italy. *This mosaic represents a contemporary portrait of Justinian with his courtiers, including the patriarch of Constantinople, who is holding the bejeweled cross. The luxurious trappings of office—purple robes, jeweled crown, and golden scepter—were calculated to enhance the emperor's earthly dignity. The Byzantine Empire's union of church and state is symbolized by the juxtaposition of the soldiers on the emperor's right with the ecclesiastical officials on his left.*

also forced to yield much of Asia Minor to their Arab foes, and in 687 a Bulgarian kingdom was carved out of Byzantine territory in the Balkans. To repel these enemy assaults, Byzantium became more militarized. In the provinces, generals were given vast military and civil powers, and they began to replace the aristocrats as landowners. A style of feudalism—vast estates protected by private armies—slowly arose. Despite the changes in the social structure, important cultural developments occurred, including a major revision of the law code and the establishment of a second university in Constantinople.

With the reign of Basil I (r. 867–886), a new dynasty of capable Macedonian rulers led Byzantium into the Golden Age (867–1081). These rulers again expanded the borders of the empire and restored the state to economic health. Orthodox missionaries eventually tied the peoples of eastern Europe to the religion and civilization of Byzantium, and in the late tenth century they introduced Christianity to Russia. As a result, after the fall of Constantinople in 1453, the Russian state claimed to be the spiritual and cultural heir to Byzantine civilization.

In 1081 an exceptional feudal general, Alexius Comnenus [kahm-NEE-nuhs] (r. 1081–1118), seized the throne, and thus began a new period, characterized by increasing pressure from the West (1081–1261). Despite the energy of Comnenus and his successors, they were unable to solve the empire's social problems. Under the Comneni dynasty, Byzantium became fully militarized and feudalized. The free peasantry disappeared, having been transformed into a vast population of serfs forced to labor on the landlords' estates.

The Comneni rulers tried vainly to win allies, but they were surrounded by enemies—Normans, Seljuk Turks, Hungarians, Serbs, Bulgars, and, after 1095, even the European Crusaders on their way to the Holy Land. In 1204 the soldiers of the Fourth Crusade conquered Constantinople and took over the remaining lands. The empire appeared to be finished except for some scattered holdings in Asia Minor. But in 1261 Michael Palaeologus [pay-lee-AHL-uh-guhs] (r. 1261–1282) regained Constantinople and breathed some new life into the feeble empire.

The Palaeologian dynasty ruled over the Byzantine world during the fifth and last phase of its history (1261–1453), but eventually it was forced to recognize that the empire was only a diminished Greek state. From 1302 onward, the Ottoman Turks built an empire on the ruins of the Byzantine Empire. By 1330 this new state had absorbed Asia Minor, and by 1390 Serbia and Bulgaria were Turkish provinces. In 1453 the Turks took Constantinople, ravaging the city for three days, searching for booty and destroying priceless art treasures. Thus ended the last living vestige of ancient Rome.

Byzantine Culture: Christianity and Classicism

From Rome, Byzantium inherited a legacy of unresolved conflict between Christian and Classical ideals. In the wider Byzantine culture, this conflict was revealed in the division between secular forms of expression, which showed a playful or humorous side of Byzantine life, and religious forms, which were always deeply serious. However, Byzantine culture, whether secular or religious, tended to stress Classical values of serenity, dignity, and restraint. This timeless and even majestic quality was cultivated, perhaps, in compensation for the beleaguered nature of the Byzantine state.

The Orthodox Religion While the bishop of Rome (the pope) was the head of the Christian church in the West, the bishop (or patriarch) of Constantinople was the spiritual and doctrinal head of the Eastern (Orthodox) Church in Byzantium. Many differences existed between the two Christian churches. They disagreed over the issue of whether the pope or a patriarch should lead the church; they also differed in language (Latin in the West, Greek in the East), religious practices (Roman Catholic priests were celibate, Orthodox priests could marry), and fine points of religious doctrine. In 1054 the patriarch of Constantinople refused to yield to the Roman church's demand for submission, and a permanent schism, or split, ended all ties between the two faiths.

The patriarch of Constantinople had to deal with challenges from the pope, rival patriarchs in other Eastern cities, and the Byzantine emperors, who viewed the church as an extension of the government (the patriarchs never had the kind of power enjoyed by the popes). The Eastern Church was also plagued by internal dissension and a variety of heresies.

The most serious issue to confront the Orthodox Church was the Iconoclastic Controversy (726–843), which erupted when the emperor Leo III commanded the removal and destruction of all religious images. The iconoclasts, or image-breakers, claimed that the devotion paid to sacred pictures was blasphemous and idolatrous, a belief perhaps inspired by Judaism or Islam, which both strongly condemned the use of religious images. Siding with the iconoclastic emperors were the bishops, the army, and the civil service; opposed were the monks, many of whom lost their lives in the civil unrest that seized the empire. In the West, the papacy refused to join the iconoclastic frenzy. The controversy lasted for over one hundred years, and by the time the Byzantine rulers restored the veneration of icons, nearly all religious pictures had been destroyed by zealous reformers.

Monasticism, which furnished the chief foes of the iconoclastic emperors, was a basic expression of Orthodox piety. Like Western asceticism, Byzantine monasticism took two forms, hermitic (or isolated) and communal. The monastic communities were basically places where people retreated from the world to lead strictly disciplined lives. For centuries, the monasteries received immense gifts of land and wealth from rulers, merchants, and peasants alike, and eventually they achieved a powerful economic position in Byzantine society.

The most important monastic complex in Byzantium was at Mount Athos, founded in 963. This mountain retreat in northern Greece, which housed about eight thousand monks in the thirteenth century, achieved relative independence from the secular authorities. The style of Mount Athos—self-governing, self-contained, and committed to study and prayer—influenced monastic development in the Orthodox world.

Law and History From the viewpoint of Western culture, Byzantium's greatest accomplishment was the codification of the Roman law made under the emperor Justinian in the sixth century. The Justinian Code, which summarized a thousand years of Roman legal developments, not only laid the foundation of Byzantine law but also later furnished the starting point for the revival of Roman law in the West. This law code preserved such legal principles as requiring court proceedings to settle disputes, protecting the individual against unreasonable demands of society, and setting limits to the legitimate power of the sovereign. Through the Justinian Code, these Roman ideals permeated Byzantine society and served as a restraint on the autocratic emperors. When the West revived the study of the Roman law in the Middle Ages, these principles were adopted by the infant European states. Today, in virtually all the Western states, these principles continue to be honored.

From the viewpoint of world culture, Byzantium was noteworthy for contributing one of the first known works of history by a woman: the *Alexiad,* by Anna Comnena [kawm-NEE-nuh] (1083–about 1153), daughter of Emperor Alexius I Comnenus. Joining Christian and Classical knowledge and following the rigorous method pioneered by the Greek historian Thucydides (see Chapter 3), the *Alexiad* is a scholarly study of the reign of Anna's father, Alexius. Despite the author's obvious bias toward her father and confused chronology, the work is the best source for this period in Byzantine history. Especially valuable for Western readers is its portrait of the soldiers, saints, and hangers-on of the First Crusade (1096) passing through Constantinople on the way to Jerusalem. To Anna Comnena's non-Western eyes, the European Crusaders were a crude, violent bunch, more greedy for loot than concerned about salvation.

Architecture and Mosaics Besides law and history, architecture was the great achievement of the Byzantine world. Byzantine architecture was committed to

Figure 7.20 Isidore of Miletus and Anthemius of Tralles. Hagia Sophia, Interior. 532–537. Istanbul. *Hagia Sophia was the mother church of the Orthodox faith. After the Ottoman conquest, the church became an Islamic mosque, and some of the trappings, such as the calligraphic writings, still survive from this stage of the building's life. Today, Hagia Sophia is a museum, and its striking mixture of Byzantine and Islamic elements makes it a vivid symbol of the meeting of West and East.*

glorifying the state and the emperors and to spreading the Christian message. Most of the Byzantine palaces and state buildings either were destroyed in the fifteenth century or have since fallen into ruins, but many churches still survive and attest to the lost grandeur of this civilization.

By the seventh century, the **Byzantine style** had been born, a style that drew from Greek, Roman, and oriental sources. The Greco-Roman tradition supplied the basic elements of Byzantine architecture: columns, arches, vaults, and domes. Oriental taste contributed a love of rich ornamentation and riotous color. Christianity fused these ingredients, provided wealthy patrons, and suggested subjects for the interior decorations. The **Greek cross,** which has arms of equal length, came to be the preferred floor plan for most later Byzantine churches.

Despite their borrowings, the Byzantines made one significant innovation that became fundamental in their architecture: They invented **pendentives**—supports in the shape of inverted concave triangles—that allowed a dome to be suspended over a square base (Figure 7.20).

Figure 7.21 San Vitale, Exterior. 526–547. Ravenna, Italy. *Ravenna's church of San Vitale, with its octagonal plan and domed central core, is the prototype of the domed church that became standard in Byzantine civilization. From the outside, San Vitale's dome is not visible because it is covered by a timber and tile roof. This church inspired Charlemagne's Royal Chapel in Aachen (see Figure 7.27).*

As a result of this invention, the domed building soon became synonymous with the Byzantine style, notably in churches.

The Byzantine obsession with the dome probably stemmed from its central role in the magnificent church Hagia Sophia, or Holy Wisdom, in Constantinople (see Figures 7.18 and 7.20). The dome had been employed in early Christian architecture (see Figure 7.11) and in important Roman temples such as the Pantheon (see Figure 5.12). Erected by Justinian, Hagia Sophia was intended to awe the worshiper with the twin majesties of God and the emperor. The central dome measures more than 101 feet in diameter and rests on four pendentives that channel the weight to four huge pillars. Half-domes cover the east and west ends of the aisles.

In the vast interior, the architects showed that they were divided about the Classical legacy. On the one hand, they used such Classical features as vaulted aisles, well-proportioned columns, and rounded arches. But they ignored the basic rules of Classical symmetry; for example, they failed to harmonize the floor columns with the columns in the second-story gallery. Their goal was not to produce a unified effect but rather to create an illusion of celestial light. Glittering walls covered with polychrome marbles and brilliant mosaics, which have since disappeared or been covered with whitewash, suggested shimmering cloth to early viewers and contributed to the breathtaking effect of this magnificent church.

Although many later Byzantine architects adopted Hagia Sophia as their model—a floor plan that unites the early Christian longitudinal basilica with a central square surmounted by a dome or domes set upon drums—they also built churches without a dome, particularly in Ravenna on Italy's northeast Adriatic coast. Protected by marshes on the land side and with an escape route to the sea, Ravenna enjoyed the best of both Roman worlds. The Western emperors began to rule from there in 404 and to turn their new capital into an artistic jewel. In the late fifth century, Ravenna fell into the hands of Germanic invaders, who continued to add to the city's splendor. When the city became a Byzantine outpost under Justinian, new churches were built, including San Vitale. San Vitale was domed (Figure 7.21).

Mosaic making had experienced a lively flowering in late Rome, and in Byzantium it became a major form of artistic expression. Unlike the Roman mosaics, which were of stone and laid in the floor, the Byzantine mosaics were usually of glass and set into the walls. Of the Byzantine mosaics, the most beautiful and the most perfectly preserved are those in the churches of Ravenna.

The church of San Vitale is home to a pair of impressive mosaics, one depicting Justinian and his courtiers (see Figure 7.19), the other depicting Justinian's empress, Theodora, and her retinue (Figure 7.22). In these mosaics, debts to late Roman art may be seen in the full frontal presentation of each figure, their large and staring eyes, and their long gowns. But the two-dimensional rendering of the figures reveals the new Byzantine aesthetic; the rulers and their

Figure 7.22 *Theodora and Her Attendants.* Ca. 547. San Vitale, Ravenna. *This mosaic featuring the empress Theodora faces the panel of her husband, Justinian, with his courtiers (see Figure 7.19). Together, these mosaics communicate the pageantry and the luxury of this age. The man on Theodora's right draws back a curtain, inviting the imperial party into some unseen interior. His gesture may mean that this scene was part of a religious procession.*

companions seem to float in space, their feet pointing downward and not touching any surface. In various ways, the mosaics compare Justinian and Theodora to Christ and the Virgin Mary. For example, Justinian is surrounded by twelve companions, and the lower edge of Theodora's robe shows the three Wise Men bearing gifts to the Christ child.

During the Iconoclastic Controversy, the emperors destroyed virtually all figurative religious art that was under their control. After the conclusion of the controversy, a formalized repertory of church decoration evolved that characterized Byzantine art for the rest of its history. The aim of this religious art was strictly theological. For instance, Christ Pantocrator (Ruler of All) dominated each church's dome (Figure 7.23). In these portraits, Christ was presented as the emperor of the universe and the judge of the world. Accordingly, Byzantine art came to picture him with a stern and forceful countenance, in contrast to Western portrayals, which increasingly focused on his suffering.

THE EARLY MEDIEVAL WEST

Since the Italian Renaissance, scholars have described the fall of Rome as the end of the ancient world and the beginning of the thousand-year era known as the medieval period, or the Middle Ages. Although Renaissance intellectuals used the word *medieval* as a negative term, today's scholars believe the civilization of the Middle Ages to be as worthy of study as the ancient and modern worlds. This section is devoted to the first phase of this era, the Early Medieval period, dating from about 500 to about 1000.

The Early Middle Ages: A Romano-Germanic Christianized World

After the fall of Rome, life in the West was precarious for most people. There was a return to an essentially agrarian existence, accompanied by a decline in

Timeline 7.3 THE KINGDOM OF THE FRANKS

476	481		680	700		800	843
	Frankish Self-Rule	**Merovingian Line**		**Carolingian Line**			
End of Western Roman empire	**481–511** Clovis		**680–714** Pepin II	**714–741** Charles Martel	**741–768** Pepin the Short	**768–814** Charlemagne	Division of Charlemagne's empire

Figure 7.23 *Christ Pantocrator.* Central dome, Church of Dafni. 1100. Dafni, near Athens. *In early Christian art, Christ had been portrayed as a beardless youth, often in the guise of the Good Shepherd (see Figure 7.17) or Orpheus. In Byzantine art, starting in the seventh century, Christ began to be depicted as a mature man with a full beard, as in this mosaic. Part of the change was a result of a fashion for full beards at this time, but, more important, the bearded figure reflected Orthodox theology's focus on Christ as the stern judge of the world.*

By about 500, Western life had stabilized to some degree. Three Germanic tribes occupied and ruled vast parts of the old Western Roman Empire: the Visigoths in Spain, the Ostrogoths in Italy and southern Germany, and the Franks in France and western Germany. The Angles and Saxons were dominant in England, the Vandals in North Africa, and the Burgundians in southern France; other Germanic tribes claimed land in central Europe, on the Scandinavian peninsula, and along the Baltic Sea. In Gaul (modern-day France), especially, life was being redefined in ways that would have a profound impact on Western civilization.

While a Germanic tribe known as the Lombards was gaining control of the Italian peninsula, the Franks were centralizing rule in Roman Gaul under Clovis, the first important ruler of the Merovingian dynasty (Timeline 7.3). An early convert to Latin Christianity, through the persuasion of his wife, Clotilda, Clovis supported missionaries in newly conquered territories, strengthening political ties between Gaul and the pope.

During these years of political expansion in the Frankish kingdom, some security and order gradually developed, especially around the rulers' fortress-palaces. As the barbarian invasions subsided in the late sixth century, manorialism developed as a new economic system. Most of the Germanic invaders settled on the manors, or landed estates, of the Frankish warrior class. There they became serfs, indentured servants who were bound to the land. Their value as workers earned them the protection of the lord of the manor in time of war.

Frankish society was composed of three well-defined ranks: those who fought, those who prayed, and those who worked. Each social rank had a rigidly defined hierarchy of subgroups. The warrior class, headed by the king, consisted of the lords of the great manors and their families and, under them, their courtiers, the less wealthy knights, and the lords of small manors. The upper clergy, who shared the high social status of warriors, consisted of the archbishops, bishops, and abbots; the lower clergy comprised priests, monks, nuns, and clerical scribes and secretaries. The

commerce and in the standard of living. Village life was simple and barter the primary medium of exchange. The little security that people had was provided by the Christian church, with its bishops and priests, its increasingly powerful pope in Rome, and its spreading network of monasteries and convents.

working ranks consisted of free farmers, artisans, and a few merchants; the vast population of peasants, serfs, and a few slaves were at the bottom.

In Frankish society, the status of women declined sharply from what it had been in the Roman world. On the manors, noblewomen enjoyed few personal or property rights, since, under Frankish law, land was passed through the male line. The noblewoman's primary function was the bearing of sons, and the peasant woman was simply another laborer. The only leadership role for women was in the nunneries, for women traditionally ruled themselves in these religious institutions.

After 700 the Merovingians gradually lost control of the Frankish kingdom to the Carolingian dynasty. Under Charles Martel ("Charles the Hammer") (r. 714–741), Carolingian troops halted the advance of the Muslims at the Battle of Tours in southern France in 732, thereby ensuring the future of Europe as a Christian land. In 751, Pepin the Short (r. 751–768), the son of Charles Martel, was declared king of the Franks, with the approval of the pope and the votes of the Frankish nobles. Three years later, a new pope crowned Pepin and anointed him as defender of the church. This ceremony, cementing an alliance between the popes and the Franks, set the course for church-state relationships in the West.

In exchange for papal recognition of his royal title, Pepin conquered the Lombards, who ruled most of Italy, and gave their lands in central Italy to the pope. These lands, which later became known as the Papal States, were conveyed in one of the most important documents of the Early Middle Ages, the Donation of Pepin. The alliance symbolized by the Donation of Pepin benefited both parties: The pope's authority and the church's economic foundation were enhanced, and the Frankish kings gained legitimacy and a claim to be the hereditary protectors of Rome. This alliance also redirected the church's interests away from the Eastern Empire and linked Rome's destiny with western Europe.

Charlemagne ("Charles the Great") (r. 768–814), the son of Pepin the Short, established the first real empire in medieval Europe and challenged the Byzantine rulers' claims to the western Roman lands. Because Charlemagne was the most powerful ruler in the Early Middle Ages, historians have named a dynasty and an age for him—Carolingian, from *Carolus*, Latin for Charles. Charlemagne fought the Lombards in Italy, the Saxons in Germany, and the Muslims in Spain, colonizing most of these areas and converting the populace to Christianity. To reward Charlemagne's military and religious triumphs, Pope Leo III crowned him "Charles Augustus, Emperor of the Romans" on Christmas Day, 800. With this act, Leo may have hoped to assert the authority of the church over the state, but Charlemagne continued to believe in the supremacy of the state. The coronation enhanced Charlemagne's

reputation, but it also widened the rift between Byzantium and the West (see Map 7.2).

Charlemagne created an efficient bureaucracy, instituted a fair judicial system, and brought learned people to his court as part of a revival of the arts and humanities. He granted large tracts of land to local warriors and then held them responsible for maintaining law and order in their domains. This administrative system fused the Roman approach to governing an empire with the Germanic warrior tradition, and it worked efficiently as long as Charlemagne lived.

The end of the Carolingian era began in 843 when Charlemagne's grandsons divided the empire into three parts, hastening the splintering of western Europe into smaller kingdoms. In the ninth and tenth centuries, a final wave of invaders entered western Europe—the Vikings from Scandinavia and the Magyars from the Hungarian plains. By the late tenth century, however, two new kingdoms—later to become modern France and Germany—were emerging from the political chaos.

France developed from the ambitions of Hugh Capet (r. 987–996), a noble landowner who was crowned king of the western Franks. From their power base in Paris, the Capetian kings consolidated their grip over the other feudal lords and their lands. The other emerging kingdom was that of Otto the Great (r. 936–973), who was elected king of the Germans and Saxons. A superb military leader and dedicated church reformer, Otto extended his kingdom into Italy. There he released the papacy from the control of corrupt Roman families and forced the pope, in return, to recognize him as emperor. Otto was clearly following the dream of Charlemagne—to restore the lost Roman world (Figure 7.24).

Religion and Culture in the Early Middle Ages

During the Early Middle Ages, literature, art, and architecture degenerated from the already low standards of late Rome. There was a brief, bright moment in the early ninth century under Charlemagne and his successor when literature, learning, and the arts flourished, but by the middle of the ninth century this renaissance had faded in the wake of political disintegration and foreign invasions. Later, Otto the Great encouraged the cultivation of letters within his empire. Notwithstanding their sporadic nature, these intellectual and artistic developments helped to blend the Germanic and Greco-Roman worlds into an emerging Christian Europe.

Christianity: Leadership and Organization   Regardless of internal dissension and external foes in the period between 500 and 1000, Christianity strengthened itself and its hold on society. The early popes faced heresy, disorganization, and a vast world of unbaptized men and women. The energetic and dedicated

PERSONAL PERSPECTIVE

Anna Comnena
The Arrival of the First Crusade in Constantinople

Mutual suspicion, prejudice, and hostility characterized relations between Byzantium and the Early Medieval West. This first selection is from Byzantine historian Anna Comnena's Alexiad *and recounts the arrival of the First Crusade (1096) in Constantinople; the Frankish Crusaders, led by Peter the Hermit, were on their way to Jerusalem to recover Christian holy places from the Muslims.*

Before he [Emperor Alexius I] had enjoyed even a short rest, he heard a report of the approach of innumerable Frankish armies. Now he dreaded their arrival for he knew their irresistible manner of attack, their unstable and mobile character and all the peculiar natural and concomitant characteristics which the Frank retains throughout. . . .

. . . [Peter the Hermit had] contrived to assemble the Franks from all sides, one after the other, with arms, horses and all the other paraphernalia of war. And they were all so zealous and eager that every highroad was full of them. And those Frankish soldiers were accompanied by an unarmed host more numerous than the sand or the stars, carrying palms and crosses on their shoulders, women and children, too, came away from their countries. And the sight of them was like many rivers streaming from all sides, and they were advancing towards us through Dacia generally with all their hosts. Now the coming of these many peoples was preceded by a locust which did not touch the wheat, but made a terrible attack on the vines. This was really a presage as the diviners of the time interpreted it, and meant that this enormous Frankish army would, when it came, refrain from interference in Christian affairs, but fall very heavily upon the barbarian Ishmaelites [Muslims] who were slaves to drunkenness, wine, and Dionysus.

Liudprand of Cremona
A Mission to the Byzantine Court

Bishop Liudprand of Cremona, emissary of the German ruler Otto I (the Great), traveled (968) to Constantinople to arrange a marriage between Otto's son and a Byzantine princess. Here he describes his reception to Otto.

On the fourth of June we arrived at Constantinople, and after a miserable reception, meant as an insult to yourselves, we were given the most miserable and disgusting quarters. . . .

On the sixth of June, which was the Saturday before Pentecost, I was brought before the emperor's brother Leo, marshal of the court and chancellor; and there we tired ourselves with a fierce argument over your imperial title. He called you not emperor, which is Basileus in his tongue, but insultingly Rex, which is king in yours. I told him that the thing meant was the same though the word was different, and he then said that I had come not to make peace but to stir up strife. Finally he got up in a rage, and really wishing to insult us received your letter not in his own hand but through an interpreter. . . .

On the seventh of June, the sacred day of Pentecost, I was brought before Nicephorus himself in the palace called Stephana, that is, the Crown Palace. He is a monstrosity of a man. . . . He began his speech as follows:—

> It was our duty and our desire to give you a courteous and magnificent reception. That, however, has been rendered impossible by the impiety of your master, who in the guise of an hostile invader has laid claim to Rome; . . . has tried to subdue to himself by massacre and conflagration cities belonging to our empire. . . .

To him I made this reply: "My master did not invade the city of Rome by force nor as a tyrant; he freed her from a tyrant's yoke, or rather from the yoke of many tyrants. . . . Your power, methinks, was fast asleep then; and the power of your predecessors, who in name alone are called emperors of the Romans, while the reality is far different. . . .

Pope Gregory the Great (pope 590–604) was the most successful of the early medieval pontiffs. He reformed the clergy, whose poor training and lax habits, in particular their sexual behavior, worked against the church's efforts to set high moral standards. Tradition claims he standardized the use of music in the service of worship, so that the Gregorian chants became synonymous with the medieval church. He encouraged the founding of new monasteries among the Germanic peoples. Abroad, he sent missionaries to England, thus ensuring the triumph of Christianity among the Anglo-Saxons. Despite their successes and reforms, however, Gregory and the later popes could not break the grip of secular power over church affairs.

The church found a new source of strength in monasticism. Western monks followed the guidelines

Figure 7.24 Church of St. Pantaleon. 966–980, restored 1890–1892. Cologne, Germany. *Otto the Great founded this church for a Benedictine monastery in Cologne where his brother was archbishop. As a builder of churches, Otto was following in Charlemagne's footsteps, identifying himself as God's chosen instrument intent on expanding both the Christian faith and his own empire. Of the original fortresslike church, only the west-works with three towers survive. Like many tenth-century churches, St. Pantaleon was flanked by two tall towers and an enclosed entrance. The rest of the church was restored in the late nineteenth century.*

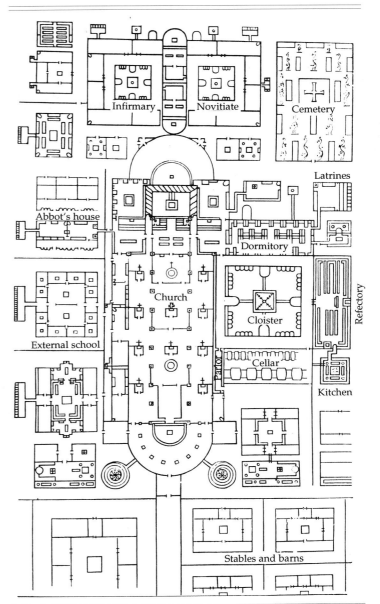

Figure 7.25 Plan of St. Gall Monastery. Ca. 820. *One of the most prominent ninth-century monasteries was the Benedictine House at St. Gall in Switzerland. Although the monastery no longer exists, its original plan, perhaps by Linhard, has been preserved. The plan reveals the self-sufficient system of the monastery, with its school, hospital, dormitories, poorhouse, and various buildings and plots of land.*

that were laid down by St. Benedict (480–543) and observed in the Benedictine order's first monastery at Monte Cassino, south of Rome. Benedictines, after a period of rigorous intellectual training and self-denial, vowed to lead lives of chastity, obedience, and poverty. They divided their days into alternating periods of work, prayer, and study. The monks were known as the regular clergy, because they followed a *regula*, or rule. After the seventh century, women became part of the monastic system, using the Benedictine rules and sharing with monks the same facilities, then known as double monasteries. By the tenth century, separate facilities for women—nunneries—were being established by noblemen and noblewomen. Supervised by an abbess, some of these convents became important centers for women's concerns, and nearly all served as refuges for the devoted or for those forced by their families to take the veil as brides of Christ.

The monasteries and nunneries that spread across Europe served many purposes. They were havens for the populace during invasions. They were centers for copying ancient literary and philosophical texts, which were then studied in their libraries. The monks often established schools for the local young men, and the nuns for young women. These self-sufficient monasteries and nunneries were models of agricultural productivity and economic resourcefulness (Figure 7.25).

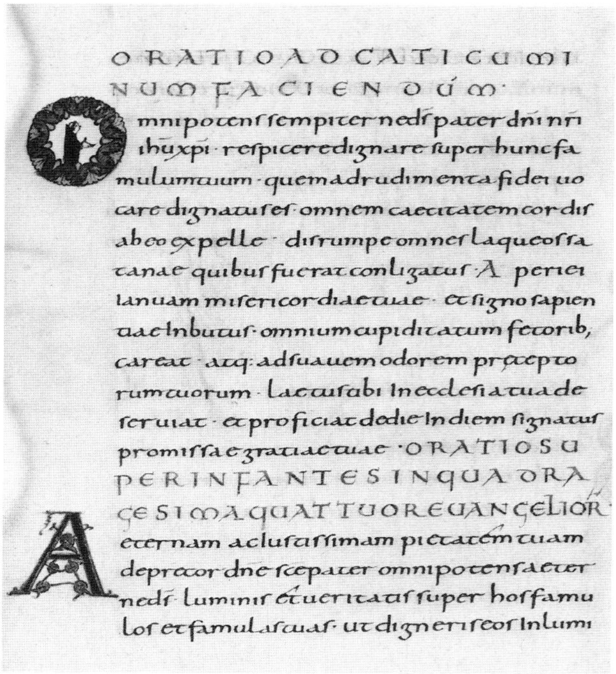

Figure 7.26 Carolingian Minuscule. Ninth century. Bibliothèque Nationale, Paris. *Because Christianity relied heavily on written works, legible texts were important; but the prevailing style of writing, which used separately formed lowercase letters, was almost impossible to read. To overcome this difficulty, scribes during Charlemagne's reign perfected a new style of writing—the Carolingian minuscule—characterized by clearly formed letters linked into words, spaces between words, and capital letters at the beginning of sentences, as shown here. All subsequent Western handwriting styles follow from this tradition.*

Literature, History, and Learning   Writers during this period were more interested in conserving the past than in composing original works. Consequently, literature—all of it written in Latin—was eclectic, blending Christian ideas with Classical thought and often mixing genres, such as history, biography, science, philosophy, and theology.

The most highly educated scholar of the Early Middle Ages was Boethius [bo-E-the-uhs] (about 480–524), a Roman aristocrat and a courtier of Theodoric, the Ostrogoth king in Italy. A rarity in his age, an intellectual who knew Greek, Boethius translated much of Aristotle's vast writings into Latin. In the later Middle Ages, all that Latin scholars knew of Aristotle was through Boethius's translations.

Boethius fell from favor in Theodoric's court and was eventually executed. While in prison, he wrote the *Consolation of Philosophy*, a work widely read throughout the Middle Ages and beyond. In it he described his mental struggle with despair at life's cruel turn of events. He personified Philosophy as a learned woman with whom he argued many issues in search of the meaning of happiness. In the face of imminent death, Boethius finally concluded that true contentment was

reserved for those who combined intellectual inquiry with Christian beliefs.

Although several scholars wrote historical chronicles, only Gregory of Tours and Bede can be classified as historians. Both consulted written documents and other sources and in general strove for (but did not always achieve) objectivity and historical accuracy. Gregory of Tours (about 538–593) left the single surviving record of the sixth-century Merovingian kingdom in his *History of the Franks*. Gregory's account lacks historical cohesion and shows stylistic confusion, but he manages to capture the flavor of his times in his lively and humane character sketches of the Frankish rulers. In Anglo-Saxon England, Bede [BEED] (673–735), an English monk and scholar, composed *A History of the English Church and People*, which described the missionary activities that led to the founding of the English church. Written in a pure Latin style, his *History* is a major source for the chronology of this troubled age.

When Charlemagne came to power, cultural life enjoyed its greatest flowering in the Early Middle Ages. The Carolingian Renaissance, which represented Europe's first genuine rebirth of Classical studies within the context of Christian beliefs, had its roots in educational reform. Recognizing that ignorance posed a threat to his regime, Charlemagne founded a palace school at his residence at Aachen, in present-day western Germany. He invited the most learned men of the day to train his own staff and to teach the sons of the nobility. Leading scholars from England, Ireland, and Italy settled in Aachen, where they pursued their scholarship. Foremost among them was Alcuin [AL-kwin] of York (735–804), who led the palace school, giving instruction in Latin, composing his own textbooks, and overseeing the copying of manuscripts.

Another important scholar and adviser at Aachen was Einhard [INE-hart] (about 770–840), who came from Gaul. His lasting contribution was his brief and simple biography of Charlemagne, the *Vita Caroli* (the *Life of Charles*, usually translated as *The Life of Charlemagne*). Modeled on the lives of the Caesars by the Roman historian Suetonius, this work is a major literary achievement of the Early Middle Ages and still gives today's readers a vivid portrait of Charlemagne and his times.

One of the important achievements of the palace school was a significant innovation in handwriting. Trained scribes developed a flowing style consisting primarily of rounded lowercase letters that became the standard form for all later handwriting styles in the West. With the development of this legible and uniform Latin script, known as Carolingian minuscule, educated men and women gained access to written material and monks, in transcribing books, were liable to fewer errors (Figure 7.26).

During the turbulent ninth and tenth centuries, the light of civilization seemed to grow dimmer, except in monasteries in Ireland and Germany, where many monks and nuns kept the humanities alive. Especially noteworthy among the monastic scholars who balanced Christian faith with the Classics was Hrosvitha [rawts-VEE-tar] (about 935–about 1000), a canoness (a nunlike vocation that did not require vows for life) at Gandersheim convent in Saxony. The first German playwright, Hrosvitha wrote six plays, in Latin, modeled on those of Terence, the Roman dramatist (see Chapter 5), but infused with erudite religious ideas. Rejecting the themes of Roman comedy as spiritually unhealthy, these Christian dramas focused on fall and conversion themes, as in *Abraham,* which tells of a prostitute rescued by a saintly monk. Literary exercises, these plays were probably never performed, except perhaps as recitations with mimed action. Hrosvitha's writings, forgotten until the Renaissance, were rediscovered about 1500 by German humanists who recognized them as major monuments of medieval drama.

Outside the walls of monasteries, storytellers captured the imagination of audiences at royal and aristocratic courts. Written in the first half of the eighth century, *Beowulf* recounts the adventures of a Danish fictionalized warrior hero. Spurred by his loyalty and daring, Beowulf not only kills monsters but also brings peace to his inherited kingdom. The poem, considered to be the finest achievement of Old English literature and the most famous surviving epic poem in a European vernacular language, blends a surface of Christian values with a deep pagan fear of the forces of darkness.

Music   Music became integral to the church liturgy during the Early Middle Ages and kept alive the Greek heritage of music as an art form. From this religious foundation ultimately arose all of the sacred and secular music of the modern West. The name of Pope Gregory the Great is preserved in the early medieval musical form, the **Gregorian chant,** which became the official liturgical music of the early church—used in the Mass (the celebration of the Eucharist) and other services of the yearly cycle of public worship. The chants consisted of a single melodic line sung in unison, without instrumental accompaniment, by male voices. They had an impersonal, nonemotional quality and served religious rather than aesthetic or emotional purposes. Notwithstanding this aim, the chants cast a spell over their listeners, evoking in them feelings of otherworldliness, peace, and purity.

In the ninth century, one of the most important advancements in music history occurred, the rise of polyphony—two lines of melody sounded at the same

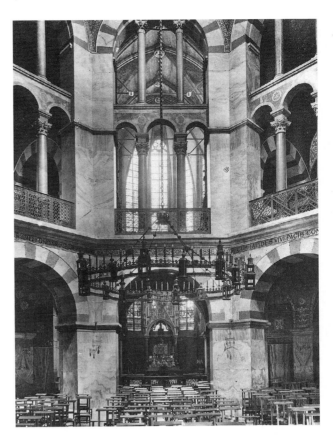

Figure 7.27   Charlemagne's Palace Chapel. Ca. 792–805. Diameter over 50'. Aachen, Germany. *Odo of Metz designed the Royal Chapel for Charlemagne, and Pope Leo III probably dedicated it in 805. Although the chapel is inspired by Byzantine architecture, the decorative scheme and the roof design make it principally a Roman building. From the tenth to the sixteenth century, the Germans crowned their kings in this chapel.*

time. Polyphony, unlike the monophonic Gregorian chants, gave music a vertical as well as a horizontal quality. But further musical developments would have to await more settled social and political conditions.

Architecture   The overall decline of living conditions in western Europe took its toll in architecture and art as patronage evaporated, skills fell into disuse, and artistic talents were necessarily directed to more pragmatic ends. The few artisans and builders who were still in business traveled across western Europe constructing churches and chapels in protected places.

Charlemagne gave full support to the construction of impressive churches and palaces, especially his own royal residence. Today, most of the original apartments and offices of his palace are restored rather than original, but the Palace Chapel remains largely as it was first built (Figure 7.27). Inspired by the design of San Vitale in Ravenna, this magnificent room reflects the architect's reinterpretation of the graceful Byzantine style to incorporate the massive solidity of Roman monuments and the vigor of Germanic taste. The octagonal chapel stands two stories high, and heavy

Figure 7.28 *Adam and Eve.* Genesis, from the St. Paul Bible. Ca. 870. San Paolo Fuori le Mura, Rome. *This miniature painting of Adam and Eve was intended to introduce the Book of Genesis. Divided into three bands, the painting presents, from left to right, the story of the first man and woman, beginning with the creation of Adam and ending with the exile of both from Eden. The decoration is brilliantly colored and extremely inventive, as in the final episode, where Adam is shown digging while Eve stands by suckling her firstborn, Cain. The treatment of the human figures, with carefully modeled limbs and appropriate expressions, shows a full mastery of the human form. The only sour note in the painting is the way the artist has rendered Eve's breasts as pendulous—perhaps a reflection of the artist's lack of access to live models or a conventional depiction of Eve copied by the artist.*

square pillars support the second level, where galleries are framed by graceful arches and columns from Italy. The bronze gratings and mosaic floor were also brought to Aachen from Italy. An **ambulatory,** or passageway for walking, extends around the circumference of the central space behind the pillars. Spiral steps lead to the upper floor, where the tribune, or emperor's throne, was located. From here, Charlemagne observed and participated in church services and ceremonies and was in turn observed by his subjects, enthroned as Christ's representative on earth.

Painting: Illuminated Manuscripts Although nearly all the murals, frescoes, and mosaics from this period have vanished, the surviving **illuminated manuscripts** offer an excellent view of the Early Medieval painting ideal. The art of manuscript illumination was influenced by the Germanic practice of decorating small objects and the Classical tradition of fine metalwork that had been maintained in Italy. During the Early Middle Ages, gifted artists and dedicated monks joined these disparate artistic elements to produce richly illustrated books and bejeweled book covers. Most of these decorated books were used in the liturgy of the Mass, such as the psalters, the collections of the psalms, and the gospel books, which were the texts of

the first four books of the New Testament. For three centuries, in monasteries and abbeys from Ireland to Germany, scribes copied the Bible and their fellow artists adorned the pages with geometric and foliage designs, mythical animals, Christian symbols, and portraits of biblical characters and saints.

Manuscript illumination became both more symbolic and more realistic in the Carolingian Renaissance, partly because Italian artists were now influencing Frankish tastes. For example, the Gospel Book of St. Medard of Soissons follows Italian practice in being filled with Christian symbols and religious icons as well as making visual references to Classical architecture. Perhaps the most impressive of the Carolingian illuminated manuscripts was the St. Paul Bible, one of the presents Charles the Bald (r. 840–877), the grandson of Charlemagne, gave to win the pope's approval for his coronation as emperor in 875. Produced in an unidentified scriptorium in the city of Reims by a team of scribes and illuminators, the St. Paul Bible originally contained twenty-four (today, twenty-three) decorated full-page miniature paintings to introduce some of the books in the Old and New Testaments (Figure 7.28). It also included a dedicatory miniature of Charles the Bald and his wife; a miniature based on the life of St. Jerome, translator of the Vulgate Bible; and a treasure trove of decorated title pages and initial letters. The luxurious style of the St. Paul Bible was typical of the works commissioned by Charles the Bald, who is recognized today as the most important patron of the Carolingian Renaissance.

At the end of the Early Middle Ages, the style of manuscript illumination became even more elaborate and richer in tone, as in the Gospel Book of Otto III, a product of the German Reichnau school. This manuscript represents the enthroned figure of St. Luke in a state of religious ecstasy. The saint supports a host of Jewish prophets and heavenly messengers; books from the Old Testament are stacked in his lap. Hovering above St. Luke's head is his symbol, the ox (Figure 7.29).

Figure 7.29 *St. Luke,* from the Gospel Book of Otto III. Ca. 1000. About 13 × 9³⁄₈″. Bayerische Staatsbibliothek, Munich. *In this illumination from a gospel book, the biblical symbols and images above St. Luke dominate the earthly and human forms. The unnatural colors and placement of the figures suggest a mystical meaning.*

The Legacy of Late Rome, Byzantium, and the Early Medieval West

Late Rome Late Roman civilization created a synthesis of Christian and Greco-Roman values, which became its legacy to the Early Medieval West. Christian intellectuals valued Greco-Roman thought for the support it lent to the spiritual values that were now considered primary. Late Roman art and architecture also blended the two traditions.

This late Roman synthesis of Christian and Greco-Roman values was supremely embodied in the Christian church. From the fall of Rome until the 1800s, the church's culture was nearly synonymous with the wider culture; to be Western was to be Christian. Church leaders were now the patrons of culture. They commanded artists to create only religious works, using a symbolic, impressionistic style; they commissioned architects to build churches in the form of Roman basilicas adapted to religious needs and baptisteries based on round, or polygonal, designs; they asked composers to write music for the church liturgy; they authorized scholars to harmonize faith with Greco-Roman thought; and they ordered sacred books to be decorated—manuscript illumination—by gifted artist-clergy. Most notably, church leaders known as the Fathers left an impressive array of writings, including Jerome's Vulgate Bible, Augustine's vast theological works, and Ambrose's hymns, which soon became authoritative. And Eusebius, a church leader, created the literary form of church history, a popular genre in the Middle Ages.

From late Rome came the structure of everyday life in the medieval world: the sharp division of society into aristocratic landowners and dependent agricultural workers, the church functioning as a state within the state, a barter economy, military power wielded by owners of large estates, and the ideal of a multiethnic but Christian society. In effect, the late Classical world was the womb from which would emerge the next incarnation of Western institutions as well as Western humanities.

Byzantium When Constantinople fell, Byzantine civilization left a profound legacy to the West, some of which is alive today. In Eastern Europe, the Orthodox church continues to influence the Slavic population. Western law owes a great debt to the Code of Justinian, which became the standard legal text studied in medieval universities. Elements of Byzantine art appeared in Renaissance art in Italy, and the Italian cities of Venice, Genoa, and Pisa became major cultural centers in the fifteenth century because of the wealth they had accumulated from Byzantine trade.

Byzantium also served conserving functions for the West. The Byzantine Empire acted as a buffer against the Arabs in the seventh century and against the Seljuk Turks in the twelfth century. Byzantine scholars preserved ancient Greek texts, many of which were carried to Italy, England, and elsewhere in the mid–fifteenth century. When these works were reintroduced into the West, they intensified the cultural revival already under way.

Early Medieval West The Early Medieval West preserved the legacy of the ancient world, notably the Christian church, the papacy, the Latin language, the educational ideal of the arts and the sciences, building and artistic methods, Greek thought, and Greco-Roman literary and artistic forms. The legacy was usually reshaped in some way, such as the reform of monasticism along Benedictine lines and the spread of female monasticism. Most important, this first medieval period added Germanic elements to the Classical and Christian legacy to forge a new civilization centered in Europe rather than in the Mediterranean basin. This new version of Western culture was born in the reign of Charlemagne, and its memory lingered in the monasteries and other isolated outposts. When the barbarian invasions ended, a more enduring Western culture was born.

KEY CULTURAL TERMS

symbolic realism
peristyle
medallion
attic
basilica
apse
nave
aisles

clerestory windows
atrium
transept
cruciform
baptistery
impressionistic
putti
Byzantine style

Greek cross
pendentive
Gregorian chant

ambulatory
illuminated manuscript

SUGGESTIONS FOR FURTHER READING

Primary Sources

AUGUSTINE, SAINT. *Confessions.* Translated by R. S. Pine-Coffin. New York: Penguin, 1966. One of the enduring books of

Western literature; reveals the anguish and the achievements of this influential thinker.

————. *The City of God.* Edited by D. Knowles. New York: Penguin, 1972. A monumental work that illustrates Augustine's blending of Classical and Christian thought.

BEDE. *A History of the English Church and People.* Translated by L. Sherley-Price. New York: Penguin, 1955. Written in 731, this account of the church in Saxon England is an important source for understanding early Christian society and attitudes in England.

BOETHIUS. *The Consolation of Philosophy.* Translated by V. E. Watts. New York: Penguin, 1969. An account, combining verse and prose and written in the early sixth century, that shows how Christian faith and pagan philosophy enabled the author to accept both his fall from power and death.

COMNENA, ANNA. *The Alexiad of Anna Comnena.* Translated and with a brief introduction by E. R. A. Sewter. New York: Penguin, 1979. A fresh, modern translation of this Byzantine classic work of history, with notes, a map, appendixes, and genealogical tables; some of the author's digressions are consigned to footnotes.

EINHARD and NOTKER THE STAMMERER. *Two Lives of Charlemagne.* Translated by L. Thorpe. New York: Penguin, 1969. A useful introduction and many footnotes enlighten the student about these two brief but important contemporary biographies by, respectively, the head of Charlemagne's palace school and a monk.

GREGORY, BISHOP OF TOURS. *History of the Franks.* Translated by L. Thorpe. New York: Penguin, 1974. An engrossing account of this chaotic time by an eyewitness.

HROSVITHA. *The Plays of Hrotsvit [Hrosvitha] of Gandersheim.* Translated and with an introduction by K. Wilson. New York: Garland, 1989. A lively and authoritative translation of these early medieval plays, with scholarly notes.

STANIFORTH, M., trans. *Early Christian Writings: The Apostolic Fathers.* New York: Penguin, 1968. Useful introduction to the issues and personalities of the early Christian church.

CHAPTER *7* HIGHLIGHTS
The Civilizations of Late Rome, Byzantium, and the Early Medieval West

AUGUSTINE, *Confessions* (ca. 390s)
AUGUSTINE, *City of God* (ca. 420s)
EUSEBIUS, *History of the Christian Church* (325)
7.1 *Young Christ* (third century)
7.6 Diocletian's Palace (ca. 300)
7.9 Constantine's Basilica, Trier (310)
7.7 Arch of Constantine (312–315)

7.3 Colossal Statue of Constantine (ca. 313)
7.15 *Female Athletes* (350–400)
7.12 *The Last Pagan* (ca. 380–400)
7.11 Baptistery at Frèjus, France (fifth century)
7.14 Illumination from Vergil's *Aeneid* (fifth century)
7.10 Sta. Maria Maggiore, Rome (432–440)
7.17 *The Good Shepherd* (ca. 450)

COMNENA, *Alexiad* (first half of twelfth century)
7.21 San Vitale, Ravenna (526–547)
7.18 ISIDORE OF MILETUS AND ANTHEMIUS OF TRALLES, Hagia Sophia (532–537)

7.19 *Justinian and His Courtiers* (sixth century)
7.22 *Theodora and Her Attendants* (ca. 547)
7.23 *Christ Pantocrator* (1100)

BOETHIUS, *Consolation of Philosophy* (ca. 520s)
GREGORY OF TOURS, *History of the Franks* (sixth century)
BEDE, *A History of the English Church and People* (ca. 730s)
EINHARD, *The Life of Charlemagne* (829–836)
HROSVITHA, *Abraham* (last half of tenth century)
Beowulf (ca. 1000)

7.27 Charlemagne's Palace Chapel, Aachen, Germany (ca. 798–805)
7.28 *Adam and Eve*, from the St. Paul Bible (ca. 870)
7.24 Church of St. Pantaleon, Cologne, Germany (966–980)
7.29 *St. Luke*, from the Gospel Book of Otto III (ca. 1000)

■ Literature & Philosophy   ■ Art & Architecture   ■ Music & Dance

 Readings in the Western Humanities

AFRICA

AMERICAS

HISTORY

East Africa   *Madagascar.* Settlement by Southeast Asians; introduced new crops (bananas, plantains, and papayas).
North Africa   Egypt and the Maghreb (modern Libya, Tunisia, Algeria, and Morocco) conquered by Arab Muslims (late 7th century).
West Africa   *Ghana* (West Sahara). Rise of kingdom of Ghana; controlled gold and salt caravan trade. Black and Berber population. *Niger Delta.* Jenne-jero, a mudbrick town of about 10,000, flourished; wealth based on gold and salt trade.
Northeast Africa   *Axum culture.* Controlled western Arabia for short time (6th century). Ended 1000.

Andes   *Moche culture.* Collapse ca. 600. *Sicán culture (North Coast),* began 700. Wide-ranging trade network. *Tiwanaku (Lake Titicaca)* and *Wari cultures, 500–800.* Warrior theocracies; long-distance trade; raised-field farming.
Mesoamerica   *Classic period, ended 900. Mayan culture (zenith: 600–900).* Modern Chiapas, Belize, and southern lowlands. *Teotihuacán culture.* Collapse ca. 650. *Zapotec culture.* Strong trading economy. *Early Postclassic period, began 900. Mayan culture.* General decline; Toltecs seized Chichén Itzá in Yucatán ca. 900. *Toltec culture.* Tula (north of Mexico City) and Chichén Itzá. Iron introduced. *Zapotec culture.* Loss of population and abandonment.
Native North America   *Hohokam (ca. 200–1450; Arizona).* Canal irrigation systems and ritual ballcourts. *Anasazi (ca. 400-1300; Arizona, Colorado).* Pueblos connected by road system; dominated turquoise trade.

ART & MUSIC

South Africa   Rock art in Cedar Mountains (Republic of South Africa), painted by hunter-gatherers.
West Africa   *Nigeria, at Igbo-Ukwu.* Terra-cotta and bronze sculptures entombed with dignitaries.

Andes   *Sicán culture.* Silver, gold, and bronze funerary objects; textiles with abstract patterns of deities. *Tiwanaku culture.* Stylized monolithic stone figures, ceramics, metalwork, and pottery. *Wari culture.* Textiles, ceramics, goldwork, and monumental sculpture.
Mesoamerica   *Classic period. Mayan culture.* Various styles of art. Sculptural friezes. *Zapotec culture.* Tomb paintings and ritual clay urns.
Native North America   *Southwest. Mogollon (ca. 200–1250; New Mexico, Arizona).* Mimbres pottery (stylized figurative designs in black on white). *Hohokam.* Etched shells, fine pottery, turquoise mosaics.

The Friar. Carved monolith. Red sandstone, ht. 8'. Tiwanaku, Bolivia.

ARCHITECTURE

Northeast Africa   *Nubia.* Christian cathedral in Faras with frescoes of rulers and saints, rebuilt on earlier church site (begun 707).
South Africa   *Bantu culture.* Egalitarian society with people grouped into villages of conical thatched huts (6th century). By 10th century, chiefs lived separately, behind high-walled enclosures.

Andes   *Tiwanaku culture.* Ceremonial centers with palaces, pyramids, plazas, and sunken courtyards; elaborate post-and-lintel portals. Use of the grid in city design.
Mesoamerica   *Mayan culture.* Palenque Palace; Temple of the Inscriptions, tomb of King Pacal. *Zapotec culture.* Mile-long stone wall around center of Monte Albán; underground tombs.
Native North America   *Anasazi.* Chaco Canyon multi-story "apartment" complexes around plazas with ceremonial subterranean kivas. Cliff-house villages.

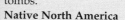

Temple of the Inscriptions, Ca. 750. Palenque, Mexico.

RELIGION, PHILOSOPHY, LITERATURE

North Africa   Islam spreads across the region.
Northeast Africa   *Nubia (Kush).* Converted to Christianity (about 540).
West Africa   *Nigeria.* Elaborate burial rituals.

Altar Stand. Found in Igbo-Ukwu tomb. Ninth century. Bronze, ht. 11¾".
Nigerian Museum, Lagos.

Andes   *Sicán culture.* Sicán Precinct, a religious and funeral site. *Tiwanaku culture.* Religious images suggestive of sun worship. *Wari culture.* Agrarian motifs (especially maize) in religion.
Mesoamerica   *Classic period. Mayan culture.* Inscriptions on stone slabs. *Zapotec culture.* Glyph writing on tombs and in paintings. *Early Postclassic period. Toltec culture.* Ritual sacrifice of defeated enemies; practice also adopted by the Mayas.
Native North America   *Southwest. Anasazi.* Petroglyphs on cliffs depicting historical events, migration routes, astronomical patterns.

ASIA

China

Sui Dynasty, 581–618. China reunited; strong centralized state. *T'ang Dynasty, 618–906.* A culturally vibrant and militarily expansionist period. World's largest empire. *Five Dynasties, 907–960.* End of centralized rule. *Sung Dynasty, began 960.* China reunited; capital Kaifeng, in the north.

Tomb Model of Camel. Eighth century. Glazed pottery. British Museum.

T'ang Dynasty. Relief carvings in Buddhist cave shrines; marble figures of Buddha and bodhisattvas; landscape painting; ceramics, often placed in tombs. A rich period in music.

Sui Dynasty. Great Wall rebuilt and realigned. *T'ang Dynasty.* Cave temples.

Sui Dynasty. Hsieh Ho's *Old Record of the Classifications of Painters*, a classic of art criticism. Spread of Mahayana Buddhism and the cult of bodhisattvas ("enlightened" disciples). *T'ang Dynasty.* Golden Age of poetry. Woodblock printing invented; mass production of Buddhist and Taoist texts.

India

Northern. Gupta Dynasty fell to the Huns (about 550). *Post-Gupta period.* Rival dynasties; most successful was the Buddhist Pala Dynasty (8th–10th centuries). Feudal society. *Southern.* Region controlled by the Hindu Pallava Dynasty (4th–9th centuries); growth of Aryan culture. Built navy and dockyards; rich sea trade. Pallavas defeated (ca. 900) by Cholas and Pandyas (Tamil Dynasties).

Northern. Pala Dynasty. Complex stone sculptures, in response to a new form (Vajrayana) of Buddhism. *Southern. Pallava Dynasty.* Larger-than-life stone sculptures of animals, humans, and gods. Kings were music patrons.

Northern. Pala Dynasty. Buddhist stupas. *Southern. Pallava Dynasty.* Free-standing stone temples at Mamallapuram, a coastal city.

Shore Temple, Mamallapuram. Early eighth century.

Northern. Pala Dynasty. University of Nalanda in Bihar flourished; Buddhism spread to Tibet. *Sind (modern Pakistan).* Conquered by Arab Muslims (712).

Japan

Asuka to Nara periods, 552–794. Height of Chinese influence. The first fixed capital Nara (710–794) modeled after the T'ang capital Ch'ang-an (now Xi'an). A more centralized regime emerged. *Heian period, began 794.* Chinese-style government failed, and capital moved to Heian (modern Kyoto). The apogee of aristocratic Japan. Emperor's power in decline (950) and warrior class (samurai) ascending.

Asuka to Nara periods. Narrative painting, lacquered wood, and embroidery; zenith of Buddhist sculpture. *Heian period.* Huge stone and wood religious sculptures; scroll and screen paintings, in both Chinese and Japanese style. *Gagaku*, court music, based on Chinese models.

Asuka to Nara periods. The Hōryūji, a walled compound at Nara, enclosing several wooden buildings; except for a pagoda derived from Buddhist architecture, the buildings were based on the T'ang Chinese temple. *Heian period.* The Shingon temple of Murōji (near Nara), a five-story pagoda with broad overhanging shingle roof. Buddhist monastery complex (more than 300 buildings) on a mountain near Heian.

Asuka to Nara periods. The history *Kojiki* (*Records of Ancient Matters*, 712), the earliest work of Japanese literature. Chinese Buddhism arrived (552) by way of Korea. Chinese calendar adopted. Japanese National University founded. *Heian period.* *Kokinshū*, a collection of 1,111 poems (905). New school of Buddhism (Tendai), imported from China; offered hope to ordinary men and women.

8 THE WORLD OF ISLAM
630–1517

The Byzantine Empire and the Early Medieval West were two of the three new civilizations that emerged in the power vacuum left by the fall of Rome in 476. Islamic civilization was the third. The word *islam* is Arabic for "submission" (to God); a *muslim* is "one who has submitted" or accepted the beliefs and practices of Islam. At its largest, the Islamic empire extended over an enormous area that included southern Spain, Sicily, North Africa, Syria, Palestine, Mesopotamia, Persia, and the Arabian peninsula (Map 8.1). Building on Arabic roots and the teachings of the Prophet Muhammad while absorbing aspects of Greco-Roman and Persian cultures, Islamic civilization flourished from the mid–eighth to the thirteenth century. It was the source of numerous scholarly advances as well as a wealth of artistic achievements.

The date 630 marks the year when Muhammad's call for a new religion was accepted by the Arab leaders of Mecca and surrounding areas. The date 1517 marks the triumph of the Ottoman Turks, who had converted to Islam, and the beginning of a new era in Islamic history. Modern Islam is no longer identified with a particular country or region or with any one ethnic or racial group. The world's fastest-growing religion, with over one billion adherents across the globe, it is second in size only to Christianity (Figure 8.1.)

The pre-Islamic Arabs inhabited the Arabian peninsula, a dry land wedged between the Red Sea and the Persian Gulf. In the north, nomadic Bedouin tribes herded sheep and goats across the higher plateaus and deserts. In the south, Arabs lived in farming communities and cities. Merchants prospered from trade on the southern caravan route, which began in India, crossed

◄ **Detail** Pyxis. Cordoba. 968.

LEARNING THROUGH MAPS

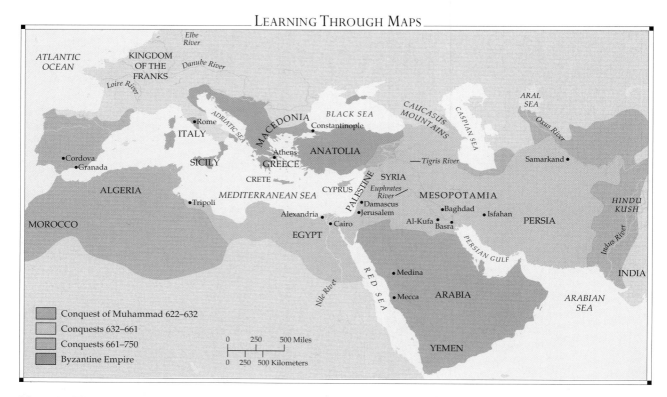

Map 8.1   THE WORLD OF ISLAM, 622–750
This map shows the successive expansion of the Islamic world, between 622 and 750.
Notice the three phases of expansion. **Consider** how the expansion of Islam threatened
the Byzantine Empire and the Kingdom of the Franks. **Identify** the three successive
capitals of the Islamic Empire. **What** problems would the Muslims face in conquering
so much land so quickly and ruling such diverse peoples? **Compare** the size of the
Islamic holdings in 750 with those of the Roman Empire under Augustus in Map 5.1.
Source: Gloria Fiero, *The Humanistic Tradition*, 4e. New York: McGraw-Hill, 2002. Vol. I, p. 219.

southern Arabia, and then followed the west coast
plateau along the Red Sea into the Roman Empire.

By the early seventh century, the Arabic language
had spread throughout the peninsula, binding the
inhabitants with a common tongue and oral literary
tradition. Jews and Christians, lured by the prospects
of wealth and trade, migrated into southern Arabia.
From them the Arabs acquired additional knowledge
of weaponry, textiles, food and wine, and writing. In
Mecca, the leading commercial city on the southern
trade route, Jews, Christians, and Arabs not only
exchanged products and wares but also shared ideas
and values.

MUHAMMAD, THE PROPHET

Muhammad, the founder of Islam and one of the most
commanding figures in history, was born in the city of
Mecca in 570. His father was from a minor but
respected clan within the city's most powerful tribe,
the Quraish or Quraysh. Apparently Muhammad was
orphaned when quite young and was reared by

grandparents and other kinspeople. He is said to
have been a shepherd until he went to work for a caravan company owned by a wealthy widow, Khadija
(kah-DE-jah), his first wife. Their only surviving child,
Fatima (FAT-uh-mah), was to become a revered religious figure (Figure 8.2).

In 610, at the age of forty, Muhammad experienced
a spiritual transformation that convinced him that
Allah had called him to be his prophet to the Arab
people. Other revelations soon followed. Inspired by
these encounters, Muhammad slowly gathered a small
band of converts. As his fame grew, he became known
simply as "the Prophet"—always with an initial capital letter as a sign of deep respect.

At first, the city leaders of Mecca paid scant attention to Muhammad. However, he became a controversial figure when, in the name of Allah, he declared that
there was only one God, attacked the polytheistic
beliefs of his fellow Arabs, and condemned as idolatrous the *Kaaba* (cube), a local pagan shrine that housed
a sacred black rock. Since the *Kaaba* was not only a holy
place but also a source of revenue generated by the
thousands of pilgrims who visited it each year, the

Figure 8.1   The Pilgrimage to Mecca and the Circling of the *Kaaba*. J. Allan Cash photograph. *All Muslims are required to make a pilgrimage to Mecca at least once in their lives. There they circle the* Kaaba, *a sacred shrine, seven times in a counterclockwise direction, trying to touch or kiss its walls. On the ninth day of their pilgrimage, worshipers assemble on the plain of Arafat outside Mecca to make their stand before God. This ten-day journey and its ceremonies often mark the climax of a devout Muslim's life.*

Figure 8.2 *Fatima*. Chester Beatty Library, Dublin. *Fatima, veiled and dressed in white, kneels beside two of Muhammad's wives. Although Fatima is not mentioned in the* Qur'an, *her reputation grew over the years among the Shi'ite Muslims. She became the ideal woman, possessing extraordinary powers similar to those of the Virgin Mary for Roman Catholics. Devout Shi'ite women appeal to her for guidance and protection, and worship at her shrines.*

Quraish tribal leaders feared that they were in danger of losing one of their most profitable attractions. They also considered Muhammad to be socially inferior and uneducated. Soon Quraish hostility turned to persecution. Fearing for his life, Muhammad and a few followers fled, in 622, to Yathrib, a neighboring city. This historic flight, or Hegira *(hijra)*, transformed Muhammad's message of reform into a call for a new religion. And the date, 622 in the Christian Western calendar, marks the year 1 for Muslims.

According to tradition, Muhammad was welcomed into Yathrib and quickly made a name for himself by settling several disputes that had divided its citizens. He emerged as a judge and lawgiver as well as a military leader. In Yathrib, Muhammad was able to found his ideal community, where religion and the state were one. Yathrib became known as Medina, or "the City," a name that denoted its position as Islam's model city.

Before the Hegira, Muhammad had formulated the basic doctrines of Islam. In Medina, he put them into practice to solve social and legal problems and to offer guidelines for everyday life and social interactions. Muhammad, it is believed, also drew up a charter defining relations among the Medinese people, his own followers, and the Jews, who were influential in the city. Most important, this charter established several fundamental principles. Faith, not blood or tribe, unified the believers; Muhammad, as the voice of Allah, was a ruler and not a consensus builder; and Islam was the only source of spiritual and secular authority. In essence, a theocracy was in the making in Medina, as political and religious objectives blurred into one, and a unified, faith-based state government was envisioned. Eventually, tensions between the Jews and the followers of Muhammad reached the point where he exiled the Jews. At the same time, he expunged any rituals that might have had Jewish associations. Specifically, he changed the direction for praying from Jerusalem to Mecca, he called for pilgrimages to the *Kaaba*, and he moved the day of collective prayer from Saturday to Friday.

While Muhammad held sway in his newly adopted home, conflicts between Medina and Mecca grew as Medinese raiders attacked the caravans traveling over the trade routes from Mecca. Desert warfare soon erupted. From 624 to 628, the two cities fought three major battles. The last one resulted in a victory for Muhammad's forces. Now, in full control of Medina and having repelled the Meccan army, he was ready to return to Mecca.

Muhammad and about one thousand of his followers set out as pilgrims to the *Kaaba* shrine. The Quraish leaders faced a dilemma. If they attacked or tried to prevent the pilgrims from worshiping, they would be violating their role as protectors of the shrine. But, if they did nothing, they risked turning their city over to Muhammad and his supporters. As a way out of this impasse, a Quraish delegation negotiated a treaty that allowed Muhammad to visit Mecca the next year as a pilgrim in exchange for his returning to Medina. This peaceful solution convinced many Arab tribes that Muhammad's new faith and tactics were legitimate, and they soon converted to Islam.

In 629, Muhammad made his pilgrimage, winning new converts during a three-day visit. The next year, when the Quraish attacked one of Muhammad's allied tribes, he raised an army of ten thousand to march on Mecca. Faced with these odds, the Quraish opened the city, their leaders accepted the new faith, and the Prophet entered triumphantly. He destroyed the pagan idols at the *Kaaba*, and he forgave his enemies if they became Muslims. Nearby tribes sent delegations to Mecca, from which contacts Muhammad constructed a network of personal and political alliances across the Arabian peninsula based on their recognizing Mecca's power and agreeing not to attack Muslims and their allies. On the eve of his death in 632, he had achieved what no Arab leader before him had done. He had brought peace to Arabia and united its inhabitants; and, at the same time, he had given the Arabs a new faith based on revelation, an ethical code of conduct, and a monotheistic deity. Muhammad's personality, dedication, and resolve had ignited a unification movement that now was energized and directed by a vigorous and resourceful religion.

IMPERIAL ISLAM

Islam evolved through a series of dynasties in the first nine hundred years of its history. They can be divided into five major periods, which sometimes overlapped (Timeline 8.1).

The Post-Muhammad Years

After Muhammad's death, leadership was transferred to a series of caliphs. (*Caliph* means "representative" or "successor.") Those who personally knew the Prophet are identified as *rashidun*, or "rightly guided," to distinguish them from the more secular caliphs in later dynasties.

Abu Bakr (a-bu BAK-er) (573–643), the first of the four *rashidun* caliphs, had been Muhammad's close adviser, friend, and father-in-law. Rather than being elected, which was the custom among Arab tribes, he was picked by a small group of Muslims. Another faction supported Ali, Muhammad's cousin and son-in-law, who, in their view, was the true heir, since he was a blood relative. From this group would emerge the Shi'a party, or Shi'ites, who later challenged the

Timeline 8.1   THE WORLD OF ISLAM, 630–1517

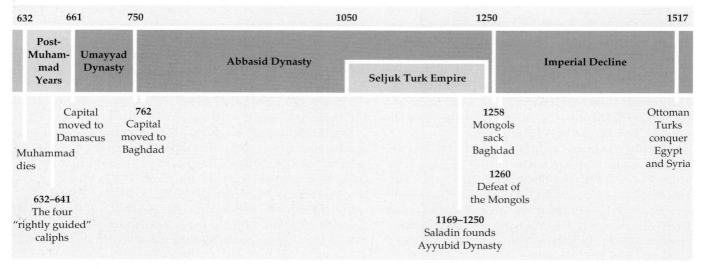

The Abbasid Dynasty

During the 740s, a series of uprisings undermined the weakened Umayyad regime. In 750, an Arab Muslim army, led by a member of the Abbasid clan, defeated the last Umayyad ruler. The Abbasids, who claimed to be descendents of Abbas, the uncle of Muhammad, moved the capital from Damascus to Baghdad in modern Iraq—an old trading city that now became Islam's cultural center and the home of the caliphs. During the Abbasid period, Islamic peoples from other traditions began to play prominent roles in government, society, and culture. The Persians, a people with a centuries-old civilization, now exerted a strong influence in the arts and learning and set the tone and atmosphere at the Abbasid court. Persians also staffed the state bureaucracy and ran the government. Persian prime ministers, who ruled in the name of the caliph, made day-to-day decisions. Turks, Kurds, and other hired mercenaries replaced Arabs in the imperial armies.

The Seljuk Turk Empire

Internal weaknesses and breakaway kingdoms made the Abbasid Empire easy prey for the Seljuk Turks, a nomadic tribe who arrived from Central Asia after converting to Islam in the 990s. By about 1050, they ruled Baghdad in the name of the Abbasid caliphs and soon were in command of much of the Muslim world (Figure 8.3). Watching these events from Constantinople, the alarmed Byzantine rulers realized that the Seljuk

Sunni, or mainstream, Muslims over succession, power, and legal matters. Today, most Shi'ites are found in Iran and southern Iraq.

During his brief rule, Abu Bakr suppressed a revolt of Arab tribes and launched numerous raiding parties beyond the Arab peninsula—a step that inaugurated Islam's imperial period. His successor, Umar (u-mar) (about 586–644), continued the invasions. Although the Arabs took their share of loot, they neither destroyed towns or villages nor tried to convert their new subjects to Islam. Instead, they controlled the conquered peoples through existing governance and administrative systems—a wise policy that helped stabilize the Arab Empire that was emerging. Umar's assassination in 644 opened a period of factionalism that ended with a leader from the Umayyad clan being chosen as caliph.

The Umayyad Dynasty

Muawiyah (mu-A-we-ya) (about 602–680) founded the Umayyad Dynasty in 661, which lasted for about a century. Muawiyah moved the capital of his new empire from Medina to Damascus—a cosmopolitan trade center located more centrally in the Middle East—signifying an important shift in Arab politics and worldviews. During this dynasty, territorial expansion continued. Islam found converts more by example than by coercion, and those who did not convert were usually left to their own faiths. Nonetheless, they had to pay a special tax, were required to recognize the sovereignty of Islamic law, and accept Arab political and military control.

Figure 8.3   Courtyard and mosque. Sultan Han Caravanserai. Aksaray, Turkey. 1229, heavily restored. *This caravanserai, or way station for merchants, pilgrims, and other travelers, was built by the Seljuk Sultan 'Ala ad-Din Kayqubad.* Han *is Turkish for "caravanserai." Located along well-traveled caravan routes, at distances about a day's travel apart (about forty kilometers), caravanserais were usually heavily fortified and offered amenities, such as food and lodging for travelers, fodder and stables for the animals, and protection to all. The courtyard of the Sultan Han caravanserai is surrounded by an arcade that opens to a series of rooms on one side and covered places on the other. A small mosque stands in the center of the courtyard.*

Turks might destroy what remained of their empire. Consequently, they called upon the Christians in Western Europe to rescue them, thus launching the first of nine Crusades, which lasted from 1095 to 1272. Although the Crusades disrupted life in parts of the Muslim world, they proved to be more a nuisance than a danger.

The most famous of the Seljuk Sultans was Saladin (SAL-ed-n) (about 1137–1193), who established the Ayyubid Dynasty, which ruled in what are now modern Syria, northern Iraq, Palestine, and Egypt from 1169 to 1250. He made Cairo a new center for Islam and launched a golden age of learning in the city. Saladin then defeated the Crusaders in Palestine and restored Jerusalem to the Muslims.

Imperial Decline

Soon, however, Islam faced a powerful enemy from the east. The Mongols, a tribe of nomadic warriors out of the Mongolian Plateau in Asia, invaded and ravaged the Muslim lands, starting in the 1220s. In 1258, they sacked Baghdad and dethroned the last Abbasid caliph. The Turkish Mamelukes, who took control of Egypt and Syria after Saladin's death, defeated the Mongols in 1260. Islam had survived, but instead of a unified state there were smaller kingdoms and principalities. Islam's thriving commercial economy gave way to an agrarian system. In 1517, the largest of these kingdoms, located in Egypt and Syria, fell to the Ottoman Turks.

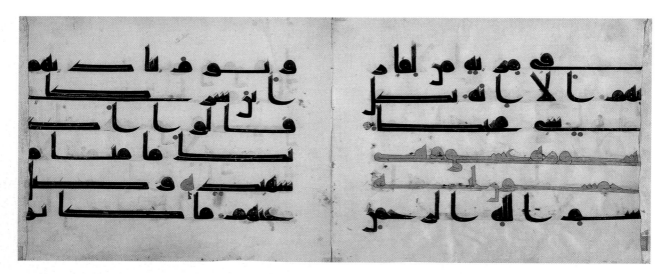

Figure 8.4   Kufic Calligraphy from the *Qur'an*. Ninth–tenth centuries. Ink and gold leaf on vellum, 8½ × 21". Nelson-Atkins Museum of Art, Kansas City, Missouri. Purchase: Nelson Trust. *Kufic calligraphy, which originated in the city of Al-Kufa in Iraq, was used in mosque decoration and the writing of early copies of the* Qur'an. *Because Islam opposed the representation of figures in most art, calligraphy was one of the major forms available to Muslim artists.*

ISLAM AS RELIGION

Islam's fundamental characteristics—monotheism and revelation—are founded on its two central beliefs: There is but one God and Muhammad is his Prophet. Muslims worship the same God as Jews and Christians, but Muslims alone recognize Muhammad as the final Prophet of a tradition that dates from Abraham and Moses in Judaism, and that recognizes Jesus Christ, not as the son of God, but as the giver of the Christian prophecy. However, for devout Muslims, it is Muhammad's voice, above all others, that is the culminating revelation and perfects God's earlier message to Jews and Christians.

Muhammad's prophecies make up the text of the *Qur'an*, a word that literally means "recitation" (Figure 8.4). These prophecies were given final form in the generation after the Prophet's death. Nevertheless, for pious Muslims, the *Qur'an* is the uncreated or eternal word of God revealed through the angel Gabriel, or *Gibril*, to the Prophet. In the historical context, however, the *Qur'an* was created by a committee of Muslims between 640 and 650. They gathered the fragments of texts and sayings of Muhammad and compiled them into an official version of the word of God as had been revealed to the Prophet. They then destroyed all other sources or collections of sayings that might constitute rival texts. The *Qur'an* was now the only text, and it could not be questioned. Over time, Muslims came to be-

lieve that the *Qur'an* should be read only in Arabic. (Most Muslims today cannot read classical Arabic, the language of the *Qur'an*, so translations may be used for instructional purposes. For devotion, only the Arabic is allowed.)

The text of the *Qur'an* is arranged into 114 chapters, each called a *sura*, with the chapters printed according to length, ranging from the longest to the shortest. Each chapter is divided into *ayas*, or verses. The style resembles a type of rhymed prose. Muhammad's utterances reveal him to be a master of literary expression and rhetoric. Many converts came to Islam because they were swayed as much by the *Qur'an*'s evocative language as by its message. Its elevated tone and poetic qualities appeal to the faithful's soul or inner being.

Within a century of Muhammad's death, another source of the Prophet's sayings, proclamations, instructions, and activities, along with those of his companions, appeared with the issuance of the *Hadith*, or the Tradition. Muslims use the *Hadith* as a supplement to the *Qur'an* and regard it as a source to explain their laws, rituals, and dogma. Today, the *Hadith*, the *Qur'an*, commentaries on the *Qur'an*, and the Arabic language make up the core curriculum taught in Islamic religious schools, or **madrasas.**

The *Qur'an* and the *Hadith* offer truth and guidance to the faithful. However, the core of Muslim religious life rests on the Five Pillars, or Supports, of the Faith— which include one verbal affirmation and four required devotional practices. The affirmation of faith

Figure 8.5 Kutubiyya Minbar. Ca. 1137–1145. Bone and colored woods, ht. 12′10″, width, 2′10¼″, depth 11′4¼″. Kutubiyya Mosque, Marrakesh, Morocco. Islamic. Three-quarter view from the right. Photography by Bruce White. Photograph © 1998, The Metropolitan Museum of Art. *Richly decorated* minbars, *or portable pulpits, were used by local prayer leaders to address worshipers during Friday services. A minbar is basically a wooden staircase on wheels, with a seat at the top of the stairs for the prayer leader. This intricately detailed example was assembled from perhaps a million pieces of bone and fine African woods.*

states: There is but one God, Allah, and Muhammad is his Prophet. The four acts of devotion are to pray five times a day facing Mecca (Figure 8.5), to fast during the month of Ramadan, to give alms to the poor, and to make a pilgrimage to Mecca at least once in one's life (see Figure 8.1).

Not one of the five pillars but central to the faith is the idea of **jihad.** *Jihad* basically means "to strive," or "to struggle," or "to make the utmost effort." Muslims "struggle" against sinning, or doing evil, and strive to follow the demands of the *Qur'an* and the five Pillars of the Faith. Thus *jihad* is a moral or spiritual striving or fight within the individual to do the right thing. However, *jihad* has other meanings, such as Holy War, a definition often found in the Western media. Many modern Muslims reject the linkage between *jihad* and Holy War, but certain groups within Islam consider *jihad* to be a Sixth Pillar of the Faith. The belief that *jihad* means Holy War can lead, and has led, to military action on the part of individuals, of groups, or of states to protect the community, to defend the faith, or to promote Islam.

In the eighth century, Muslim orthodoxy, also known as Sunni Islam, was challenged by the rise of Sufism, a mystical movement. Sufism emerged as both a reaction to the worldliness of the Umayyad Dynasty rulers and a desire, on the part of some especially dedicated Muslims, to return to what they perceived to be the simpler faith that Muhammad had taught and practiced. They rejected the legalism and formalism that had crept into Islam, and they challenged the power and influence of the *ulama,* or those men who interpreted the *Qur'an* and guarded the tradition of the faith. A majority rejected the Sunni position that all revelations from Allah were now complete, for they felt that religious truths were to be found in many places, even in other faiths. The word *Sufi* comes from the Arabic word *su,* which means "wool," in reference to the coarse woolen garment worn by the Sufis as a symbol of their ascetic life and in memory of the simple garb worn by Muhammad. In some ways, Sufism resembled monasticism, which became so important in shaping Christianity's early growth and development (see Chapter 9).

Like most societies where codes of law are rooted in religious practice and tradition, the Muslim world established the holy law of Islam—the *Sharia*—on their faith. For Muslims, this body of sacred laws was

Figure 8.6   A Husband and Wife Before a Judge. Bibliothèque Nationale, Paris. *A judge, sitting above an estranged
couple, hears arguments from the husband (on the right) and the
wife (second from the left). A scribe, in the center, records their
complaints. The figure on the far left may be presenting the couple
to the judge. Under Islamic law, a man could divorce his wife
without giving any particular reason. A wife's rights were much
more limited and restricted. Judges became an institution in
Islamic society during the Umayyad Dynasty.*

derived, in its earliest forms, from the *Qur'an*, the *sun-
nah* or habits and personal religious practices of
Muhammad, and the *Hadith*. Although Muslim jurists,
intellectuals, and scholars have added to the Islamic
law over the centuries, the basic purpose remains the
same—to tell the faithful what to believe and how to
live their daily lives (Figure 8.6).

MEDIEVAL ISLAMIC CULTURE

Scholarship

From the ninth to the twelfth century, Islamic scholars
and intellectuals made significant advances in the sciences and in medicine, mathematics, law, philosophy,
and history. At the time of the Arabic expansion, they
became the saviors and successors of the Greek learning tradition by translating Greek philosophy, mathematics, and science into Arabic, which they then
passed on to other cultures (see Chapters 7 and 9). In
addition, they used the Classical heritage as a foundation for numerous advances. (See Encounter box.)

ENCOUNTER

An International Community of Scholars

Islamic scholars during the Abbasid Dynasty (750–1258), which is known as the Golden Age of Islam, preserved the works of Greek mathematicians, adopted and transmitted the contributions of the Hindus, and made original discoveries in mathematics and the sciences. They and Western European scholars, often working together, passed this accumulated knowledge to Western Europe during the twelfth and thirteenth centuries.

These learned men gathered at Islamic centers of study scattered throughout the western reaches of the Muslim Empire. In Spain the university at Córdoba, famed for its tolerance and diversity, attracted monks and scholars from Western Europe who studied the Arabic writings, made copies, and brought them back to their monasteries and schools. There, they were translated into Latin and studied by others.

Islam's Golden Age was the work of an international community of scholars. Al-Khwarizmi (Al-KWAHR-iz-me) (780–850) advanced the field of algebra; he also introduced Hindu numerals, which became known as Arabic numerals, and used them to make calculations. His near contemporary Al-Battani (al-ba-TAN-e) (about 858–929) corrected errors in the Ptolemaic planetary system and constructed an elaborate astronomical table. His writings on equinoxes and eclipses, in which he showed the possibility of solar eclipses, were translated by European scholars into Latin, making him the best known Arab astronomer in medieval Europe. Both Al-Khwarizmi and Al-Battani were associated with the "House of Wisdom" in Baghdad, the capital of the Abbasid Dynasty. Another scholar, who spent his life in Cairo, Ibn al-Haytham (ib-n-al-hi-THAM) (965–1039), studied the Ptolemaic system, expanded on the mathematical work of Euclid, and developed new ideas about optics and light rays. His works, available in Latin in the thirteenth century, later influenced the German astronomer Johannes Kepler and the French mathematician and philosopher René Descartes.

Western scientists and mathematicians during the Renaissance of the fifteenth and sixteenth centuries studied the Islamic works in translation and built upon their discoveries. By 1700, the West had assimilated the knowledge generated by Islamic civilization and applied it to their study of nature, especially the exploration, navigation, and mapping of the earth. Then Europeans, for the first time since the fall of Rome, took the lead in mathematics and science.

Encounter figure 8.1 In the 1570s, Arab astronomers, under the guidance of Taqi al-Din, the head astronomer of the Ottoman Empire, studied the heavens with various instruments at an observatory in Istanbul. To make their observations and calculations, they used astrolabes, hourglasses, globes, and a mechanical clock built by Taqi al-Din. Many of their instruments were similar to those later used by Western astronomers in the explorations of the universe.

Figure 8.7 A Doctor Performing an Operation. Edinburgh University Library. *Muslim physicians normally did not operate on patients, preferring to use medicines and noninvasive procedures. Sometimes operations were necessary, as in this illustration of a woman having a cesarean section. The surgeon is helped by several attendants; on the right, one is holding the patient's head, while the one on the left is handing instruments to the doctor.*

Muslim doctors, whose skills were far superior to those of their Western contemporaries, obtained their knowledge from Greek texts that were translated into Arabic about the middle of the ninth century. In addition, Islamic medicine had a practical approach to the curing of disease, namely through the use of observation and experimentation. Islamic medicine also made advances in ophthalmology, added new drugs to the pharmacopoeia, stressed the role of diet in the treatment of various maladies, and was the first to make the clinical distinction between measles and smallpox. Surgeries, such as amputations, trepanning or opening the skull, and cesarean sections were occasionally performed (Figure 8.7).

Muhammad Al Razi (al RAY-zee) (about 865– between 923–935) set the standard for medicine, both as a practicing doctor and as a scholar. A prolific writer, he compiled a twenty-volume medical encyclopedia in which he noted his own findings and took issue with the ancient Greeks and their medical tradition. Al Razi also treated childhood diseases and wrote a treatise on them, earning him the title "Father of Pediatrics." Most of his writings were translated into Latin and became part of the curriculum in Western medical schools until the nineteenth century.

Ibn Rushd (ib-uhn RUSHT) (1126–1198), Islam's foremost thinker and one of the world's greatest minds, is known in the West as Averroës (uh-VER-uh-weez). Among his vast works, which he wrote while performing judicial duties, were comprehensive commentaries on Aristotle's writings, effectively reconciling the Greek thinker's ideas with Islamic thought. Western scholars used his Arabic versions of Aristotle, translated into Latin, to help reconcile Aristotelian and Christian thought. Ibn Rushd's writings remained basic texts in Western schools and universities until modern times.

The study of history first played a role in Islamic thought because of the supreme significance of Muhammad's life to Islam. Biographies of the Prophet

and histories of his time appeared soon after his death. Later generations developed a taste for diverse historical genres, including accounts of territorial conquests, family genealogies, and town histories. However, Islamic history—and, indeed, the study of history— took a giant step forward in the works of Ibn Khaldun (ib-uhn kal-DOON) (1332–1406).

Ibn Khaldun's fame rests on a multivolume history of the world, and, most especially, the *Muqaddima* or *Prolegomena,* which serves as the introduction to his lengthy study. Khaldun examined ancient societies with an eye to identifying their characteristics and the stages of their evolution. He was one of the first thinkers anywhere to deal with supply and demand, the role and value of currency, and stages of economic development as a society evolves from an agricultural to an urban economy. In Ibn Khaldun's view, which echoes that of the Greek writer Thucydides, the best historical studies downplay the role of religion or divine forces and focus on the role of human activity. Historians, by probing beneath the surface explanations of human behavior, would discover that humans are governed not by religion or idealism but by status concerns and the desires to identify with certain groups. He also offered a theory explaining the rise and fall of civilizations: As a civilization decays, its social bonds weaken, and it falls victim to a more vigorous people from outside its frontiers. The outsiders overthrow the weakened civilization, become powerful, and then cycle into a state of decay, to be invaded by more powerful intruders—an outlook that reflected his knowledge of the dramatic impact of Seljuk Turk, Mongol, and other nomadic forces on Muslim life.

Literature

In pre-Islamic Arabia, Arabic was basically a spoken language, developed by desert Bedouins and spread into urban areas by traders, who adapted it to their needs. Within this tribal culture, poets played a critical role, because they were thought to be wizards inspired by a *jinn*, or spirit. They eventually created a body of works that were transmitted orally by *rawis*, professional reciters of poetry. The preferred poetic form was the *qasida* (ode), composed in varied meters with a single rhyme. These poems, celebrating tribal life, personal glory, and love and wine, helped create a community identity and became the preferred model for poetic expression. Between 800 and 1300, Arabic became standardized as a written language. Called literary Arabic, or classical Arabic, it took the basic form of the language of the *Qur'an*, though modified to suit changing needs.

Critical to understanding Islam's literary culture is the concept of *adab*, an Arabic word initially meaning "rules of conduct," "manners," or "good habits." *Adab* first appeared in the eighth century as a literary genre, with the translation into Arabic of a Persian work on statesmanship. For several hundred years following, many works about *adab* were written, applying the term to all social classes. Among the elite, *adab* came to mean "refinement," which included having certain skills, such as the ability to swim and to ride horses, and, most especially, having deep knowledge of Islamic poetry, prose, and history, and of the Arabic language. In modern Arabic, *adab* simply refers to the whole of "literature."

Poetry Pre-Islamic poetry did not disappear with the advent of Islam. This poetry, consisting of several long and short odes, was now written down and survived to become the model for Islamic poets. The most famous surviving works are *al-Mu'allaqat* ("The Hanged Poems," or "The Seven Odes"), which, according to tradition, were suspended on the walls of the *Kaaba* while it was still a pagan shrine. The Prophet, though rejecting the pagan themes, recognized the poetry's power and called for poets to adapt the ode for religious ends.

Another genre that survived from pre-Islamic times was the elegy, or lament, especially for the dead. Usually composed by a woman, most often the dead hero's sister, the elegy became a favorite of Islamic poets. The best of these pieces were those by the female poet al-Khansa (al-kan-SAH) (d. after 630), who lived into the early Islamic period. Filled with the fatalistic outlook of the pre-Islamic world, these laments for her father and two brothers vividly capture her grief at the inescapable reality of death.

A new literary genre, the *ghazal*, or *ghazel*, a short lyric usually dealing with love, emerged in early Islamic Arabia. Composed in single rhyme, the *ghazal* often drew on the poet's personal life. Of these early poems, those of Jamil (d. 701) set the standard for later writers. His usual theme was impossible love: star-crossed lovers devoted to each other unto death. Persian,

Turkish, and Urdu poets, adapting the *ghazal* into their languages, made it a popular genre in the Islamic world.

Two centuries later in Islamic Spain, Ibn Hazm (ib-n KAZ-um) (994–1064) produced the highly influential *The Ring of the Dove*, which blends poetry with prose and focuses on the art of love. In this work, he argues that the "true" lover finds happiness in pursuit of rather than in union with the beloved—a central idea of Arabic poetry that may have influenced the Provençal poetry of Europe.

The Persian-speaking region of the Islamic world produced the gifted poet Rumi (1207–1273), active in Afghanistan, Persia, and Anatolia (modern Turkey). A Sufi mystic, Rumi greatly influenced Muslim ascetic thought and writing and, most important, Turkish religious life. As part of prayer ritual, Turkish followers created a whirling dance called Whirling Dervishes in the West. Rumi's literary legacy is two-fold: the *Diwan-e Shams*, a collection of poems addressed to a Sufi holy man and the poet's master; and the *Masnavi-ye Ma'navi* ("Spiritual Couplets"), a complex work, part Sufi handbook, part anthology of proverbs and folktales. The theme of the *Diwan-e Shams* is the poet's deep love for his master, a metaphor for the Sufi idea of an all-consuming love for God. The *Masnavi*, written in rhyming couplets, a Persian genre, presents the Sufi "way" through pointed stories and anecdotes.

Prose Literary prose in Arabic originated at the Abbasid court in Baghdad, mainly as the creation of clerks and translators. A vast literature gradually emerged, but the genres were limited because of Islam's moral objection to drama and pure fiction—drama because it "represented" reality and was thus not real and fiction because it made no claim to truth. Early writings from the Abbasid court were collections of proverbs; tales of tribal warfare known as *ayyam al-'Arab*, or "The Days of the Arabs"; and, most especially, "night conversations," or *musamarah*, which evoked lively communal evenings around desert campfires. Organized loosely about a well-worn theme, filled with puns, literary allusions, and colorful vignettes of tribal life, and, above all, animated by love of the Arabic language, the "night conversations" reminded urban Arabs of their past and inspired the *maqamah* genre, a major prose achievement.

The *maqamah* ("assembly") genre was created by al-Hamadhani (al-HAM-uh-tha-NE) (969–1008). Blurring the line between fact and fiction, his *maqamahs* are entertaining works, focusing on rogues, dreamers, and lowlifes, written in rhymed prose to display his learning and literary art.

The foremost writer in the *maqamah* genre was al-Hariri (al-ka-RE-re) (1054–1122), a government official in Basra and a scholar of Arabic language and literature.

Figure 8.8   The "Ardebil" Carpet. Formerly in the Mosque of Ardebil, Iran. 1539–1540. Woolen knotted carpet, 37'9½" × 17'6". Victoria and Albert Museum, London. *Arabesque leaves fill the yellow medallion at the center of this exquisite carpet. The medallion is surrounded by sixteen ogees (pointed ovals), which also contain arabesques. A section of this design is repeated in the corners of the interior rectangle. Praised as "the greatest example of carpet weaving in the world," this carpet of silk and wool was woven for a Persian mosque. At least thirty-two million knots were needed to complete it.*

who devises a storytelling plan to keep the vengeful King Shahryar from his mad scheme of murdering a wife a day because an earlier wife had betrayed him. The tales come from many lands, including India, Iran, Iraq, Egypt, Turkey, and possibly Greece, and represent various genres—fairytales, romances, legends, fables, parables, anecdotes, and realistic adventures. Originally, fewer than a thousand tales existed, but as the stories grew in popularity, new ones were added to make the number exact. This collection has supplied the West with many legendary figures, such as Aladdin, Ali Baba, and Sinbad the Sailor. In the Arab world, however, Islamic scholars have not accepted *The Thousand and One Nights* as classical literature, criticizing it for colloquial language and grammar errors.

A significant prose form, popular from 1000 to 1400, was the "Mirror of Princes," a Persian genre, based on the idea of *adab*. A guide for enlightened rulers, this genre focused on real and legendary statesmen, presenting them as models of refinement and "good habits." This literature influenced a genre of the same name that flourished contemporaneously in the West.

Art and Architecture

Islamic art and architecture developed within a cultural setting dominated by the *Qur'anic* ideal that religion should govern all aspects of living. In an effort to sanctify human life, this ideal made no distinction between the artistic and the practical, the private and the public, the secular and the divine. Thus, art and architecture, like the rest of Islamic culture, had no purpose beyond serving religious faith. Reality, of course, never fully realized this ideal, but it helped to define what Islamic artists and architects could and, of equal importance, could not do.

The *Qur'an* forbade the worship of idols. In time, this ban was extended to mean that artists were prohibited from representing all living things. Accordingly, large-scale paintings and sculptures were not produced, and lifelike figures, whether of humans or of animals, largely disappeared from art. Artists became abundantly inventive in the use of nonrepresentational forms. The **arabesque**—a complex figure made of intertwined flo-

Al-Hariri's poems are noted for verbal fireworks, humor, and exquisite usage of Arabic language and grammar. In the *Maqamat*, or *The Assemblies of al-Hariri*, he focuses on the adventures of the learned rogue and vagabond Abu Zayd, as reported by a narrator, al-Harith. Abu Zayd, who resembles the author in his poetic powers and lively intelligence, repeatedly uses his skills as a storyteller to charm presents from wealthy victims.

During this time, the collection of stories known as *The Thousand and One Nights*, first translated into Arabic from Persian, was circulating in the Muslim world. It is perhaps the most famous example of the "tale within a framing tale" literary genre in all of literature. The framing tale, probably from an Indian source, tells of the woman Shahrazad (Scheherazade),

Figure 8.9 The Dome of the Rock. Ca. 687–ca. 691. Diameter of dome approx. 60′; each outer wall: 60′ wide × 36′ high. Jerusalem. *This Islamic shrine is filled with theological symbolism. The dome itself is a symbol of the heavens, and the dome's thrusting shape represents the correct path for the faithful to follow. The eight-sided figure on which the interior drum rests is an image of the earth, and the rock enclosed within this sacred space is the center of the world—a traditional Islamic belief. This belief arises, in part, because the Dome of the Rock stands on the Temple Mount—the location of Solomon's Temple and its successors. Thus, this building symbolizes Islam's claim to be the successor to and fulfillment of the Judaic and Christian faiths.*

ral, foliate, or geometrical forms—emerged as a highly visible sign of Islamic culture (Figure 8.8). Geometric shapes, floral forms, and **calligraphy,** or writing, decorated walls, books, and mosaics (see Figure 8.4).

Islamic tenets allowed borrowing from other cultures, so long as what was borrowed was adapted to the teachings of the *Qur'an.* From Greco-Roman architecture came the column and the capital, the rib and the vault, and the arcade. From Byzantine architecture came the dome, the most prominent feature of the Islamic style, and the pendentive, the support feature that made the dome possible. From Persian art and architecture came miniature painting, the vaulted hall, the teaching mosque, the pointed arch, and floral and geometric ornamentation. And from Turkish art and architecture came a grand artistic synthesis, which raised Persian influence to a dominant role in Islamic art and architecture, in the zone stretching from Egypt eastward, after 1200.

Architecture The oldest extant Islamic monument is the Dome of the Rock in Jerusalem, a shrine for pilgrims dating from between 687 and about 691 (Figure 8.9). Located in a city already sacred to Jews and Christians, and built over a rock considered holy by Muslims and Jews, the shrine proclaimed by its presence that Islam was now a world religion. For Muslims, the shrine's rock marked the spot from which the founder of their faith, Muhammad, made his Night Journey to heaven. For Jews, it was identified with Abraham's planned sacrifice of his son Isaac. Because Muslims also claim Abraham as their ancestor, the site was thus given added meaning. Today, the Dome of the Rock remains one of Islam's holiest places, after Medina and Mecca.

The architecture of the Dome of the Rock draws mainly on Roman and Byzantine sources, but the aesthetic spirit reflects the new Islamic style. Its basic plan—an octagon covered by a dome—was rooted in

Figure 8.10   The Great Mosque of Kairouan, Tunisia. Ninth century. Stone, approx. 395 × 230′; ht. of minaret without finial 103′. *As in the other civilizations of this period, the dominant building type in Islam was the house of worship. This mosque, with its plain walls and square tower for calling the faithful to prayer, reflects the simple style of early Islam. Inside the walls, a large unadorned courtyard serves as a praying area.*

Roman and Byzantine tradition, and the dome's support system—a tall **drum** or wall, resting on an **arcade,** or a series of arches supported by columns—was derived from Byzantine models. But, unlike the stone domes of Byzantine churches, this dome is made of wood covered with gold. The dome's splendor reflected the opulent aesthetic emerging in the Muslim world, as well as the ambitions of the Umayyad caliph who commissioned it.

The architectural aesthetic of the Dome of the Rock is echoed in its art program. Unlike Byzantine churches, whose plain exteriors contrasted with brilliant interiors, the Dome of the Rock is a feast for the eyes throughout. Everywhere there are mosaics, tiles, and marble, much of which was added later. In obedience to the *Qur'anic* ban, there is no figurative art. Arabesques, foliated shapes, scrolls, and mosaics of purple and gold, inspired by Byzantine and Persian designs, animate the surfaces,

and more than seven hundred feet of Arabic script—repeating passages from the *Qur'an*—are written on both interior and exterior surfaces. Sixteen stained-glass windows allow muted daylight to play across the interior surfaces. This shrine soon became fabled for its beauty, inspiring similar domed sanctuaries and saints' tombs across the Islamic world.

The Dome of the Rock, however, did not set the standard for Islam's dominant building type, the **mosque,** or in Arabic *masjid,* "place for bowing down." The Prophet himself established the basic mosque plan with the house of worship he constructed in Medina. This first mosque, now lost, reflected the simple values of early Islam. It consisted of a rectangular courtyard, covered by a roof that rested on palm trunks and enclosed by walls made of raw bricks. The wall facing Mecca, the direction for prayer, was designated the *qiblah* wall, and a pulpit was erected from which Muhammad led prayers, preached, decreed new laws, and settled disputes. The courtyard also functioned much as the Greek *agora* and the Roman forum, providing a public meeting space. In Muhammad's mosque, it became a gathering place for the Islamic community to discuss religion and any other vital concern. In huts opening onto the courtyard lived the Prophet and his wives. With its varied activities—judicial, political, social, and religious—this first mosque expressed the Islamic ideal of the unity of life.

Later mosque builders followed the example set by the Prophet. Plain in exterior ornament and rectangular in shape, mosques were distinguished from secular buildings by their interior features and spaces—basins and fountains for ritual hand washing, porticoes for instruction, a screened enclosure to shield the prayer leader, and an open area for the group prayers (Figure 8.10). Sometimes the mosque was crowned with a dome, as in the Byzantine churches, but the Islamic dome's high melon shape distinguished it from the more spherical Byzantine form. A thin pointed tower, or **minaret,** from whose top a Muslim official, the *muezzin,* called the faithful to prayer five times a day, also identified the mosque. Inside the mosque, from the earliest times, rich decorations reminded worshipers of the beauty of paradise. Brilliant mosaics and oriental carpets emblazoned the floors, facings and calligraphic friezes beautified the walls, metal or ceramic lamps cast a twilight glow onto the faithful at night, and richly decorated *minbars* or pulpits (see Figure 8.5) elevated the prayer leader above the worshipers.

The mosque type inspired by Muhammad's example is called the **congregational mosque,** or **Friday mosque,** a horizontal structure that houses the Friday worshipers in a central courtyard with a domed fountain for ablutions. With the Arab conquests, mosques of this type were built across the Islamic world, from Morocco to

China. The ninth-century Ibn Tulun mosque at Cairo is an imposing example of the congregational mosque (Figure 8.11). Four rows of arcades stand between the faithful and the east wall (the direction of Mecca), and portals of pointed arches open into the arcaded area. A minaret with a winding stair rises just beyond the mosque, which is built of brick faced with stucco. In later Islamic mosques, the pointed arches and decorated stucco work became basic features of this style. During the Christian Middle Ages, Western architects borrowed the pointed arch and adapted it to their own needs, using it to perfect the Gothic style of architecture.

In the twelfth century in the eastern Islamic lands ruled by the Seljuk Turks, a new type of mosque, inspired by Persian architecture but retaining the basic rectangular plan of the Friday mosque, emerged. The new mosque type was called a teaching mosque, because it provided distinctive areas for *madrasas*, or religious schools for advanced study. The *madrasas* were the ancestors of universities in the Islamic world. The teaching mosque proved to be a popular innovation, and between the twelfth and eighteenth centuries, architects built similar structures in Egypt, Central Asia, and India.

The most famous example of a teaching mosque is the Masjid-i Jami, or Great Mosque, in Isfahan (in modern Iran), the capital of the Seljuk Dynasty in the eleventh and twelfth centuries (Figure 8.12). Four huge vaulted halls, or *iwans*, open into a central courtyard. Prayers are said in the *iwan* that opens toward Mecca, and the other three serve as areas for study, school, and rest. Viewed from the courtyard, the opening in each *iwan* constitutes a huge arch set into a rectangular façade, faced with blue tiles—a specialty of Persian artisans and the signature color of the Seljuk rulers.

Islamic builders also excelled in palace architecture, as exemplified by the Alhambra in Granada, the residence of the last Muslim rulers of Spain. Its exterior of plain red brick contrasts dramatically with its fantastic interior. The presence and sound of water everywhere—fountains, pools, and sluices—enhance the serenity and pleasure of the gardens and buildings. The Court of the Lions illustrates vividly the meaning of the term *arabesque*, with its calligraphic carvings, slender columns, geometric and floral shapes, and lacy decoration (Figure 8.13). The fountain surrounded by stone lions is a rare example of Islamic representational sculpture.

Painting   Notwithstanding the *Qur'anic* prohibition, one branch of Islamic art—book painting, or the art of the book—usually depicted realistic scenes. A few surviving examples show that the art of the book was practiced in the early days of Islam. However, after 1100, in rapid succession, two brilliant schools of book painting emerged, each devoted to representational

Figure 8.11   Ibn Tulun Mosque, Cairo. 876–879. Red brick covered with white stucco, exterior 531 × 532½'. *The finest surviving example of the congregational style, the Ibn Tulun mosque was imitated throughout the Islamic world. This view, from inside the courtyard, shows a domed fountain used for ritual washing. Outside the walls rises the spire of a four-story minaret, set on a square base with a cylindrical second story and an exterior staircase.*

Figure 8.12.   Masjid-i Jami (Great Mosque). Eleventh and twelfth centuries. Isfahan. *The view of the central courtyard and iwan (vaulted hall) of this teaching mosque is framed by the arched opening of the facing iwan. Various mosque facilities, including living quarters for teachers and students, are located in the areas around the iwans.*

PERSONAL PERSPECTIVE

Abu'l-Faraj al-Isfahānī
Marketing a Product

Abu'l-Faraj al-Isfahānī (a-bul-far-AJ al-is-fa-HA-ne) (879–967), an Arab scholar whose home was Baghdad, wrote The Book of Songs, *a collection of stories on Arab composers and poets who lived from pre-Islamic times to the Abbasid Dynasty. In one humorous tale, he recounts how al-Dārimī (al-da-RU-mi), a famous poet and jurist, helped a merchant sell his wares. This tale, underscoring the universality of human behavior, has been called by a famous Islamic scholar one of the first "singing commercials" in history.*

A merchant from Kufa came to Medina with veils. He sold all but the black ones, which were left in his hands. He was a friend of al-Dārimī and complained to him about this. At that time al-Dārimī had become an ascetic and had given up music and poetry. He said to the merchant, "Don't worry. I shall get rid of them for you; you will sell the whole lot." Then he composed these verses:

Go ask the lovely one in the black veil
What have you done to a devout monk?
He had already girded up his garments of prayer
Until you appeared to him by the door of the mosque.

He set it to music, and Sinan the scribe also set it to music, and it became popular. People said, "Al-Dārimī is at it again and has given up his asceticism," and there was not a lady of refinement in Medina who did not buy a black veil, and the Iraqi merchant sold all he had. When al-Dārimī heard this, he returned to his asceticism and again spent his time in the mosque.

Figure 8.13 Court of the Lions. The Alhambra. Thirteenth and fourteenth centuries. Granada, Spain. *The Alhambra is the only Islamic palace surviving from the medieval period. A popular destination for European and American tourists, the ornate Alhambra has played a pivotal role in developing a taste for the arabesque among many Westerners.*

Figure 8.14   YAHYA IBN MAHMUD AL-WASITI. *Abu Zayd Preaching.* Book painting. 1237. *Abu Zayd, here disguised as a religious official, preaches to a group of pilgrims, including their camels. Islamic touches include the beards of male pilgrims and head coverings for both men and women. The artist creates a lively scene, much in the manner of street theater, in the way he shows the pilgrims' varied eye and facial movements, including an exchange of glances, stares into the distance, heads lifted upward, and a head looking down. No earlier pictorial source has been established for this lively and realistic art.*

scenes. Little known in the West, the first school flowered in Syria and Iraq, and its artists were probably Arab, strongly influenced by Persian tradition. The second was the world-famous school of **Persian miniatures,** which flourished in Persia from the thirteenth to the seventeenth century.

Of the Arab painters whose works survive, Yahya ibn Mahmud al-Wasiti (YAK-yah ib-n mak-MOOD al-WAH-see-TEE) (fl. 1230s) is generally recognized as the best. Working in Baghdad, he illustrated al-Hariri's *Maqamat,* a twelfth-century work. Each picture depicts a colorful episode in the life of the con artist Abu Zayd, rendered with an eye to detail (Figure 8.14). The typical format on the page includes arranging the scene's focus into the frontal plane, keeping the background neutral in color, and creating a setting with the barest of details, such as a small hill or a single tree. Near Eastern tradition is apparent in the very large eyes, the dark outline of the figures, and the bunched drapery folds.

The Persian miniatures were produced under the patronage of the Mongol sultans, who had replaced the caliphs as rulers. Although the Mongols brought Chinese influences to the Persian miniatures, the Muslim artists rejected the openness of Chinese space and created their own ordered reality, as shown in a superb example from the fifteenth century (Figure 8.15). The painter records each object with painstaking naturalistic detail. The painting's high horizon and its rectangular format put the two figures in a precise setting. Like all Persian miniatures, this exquisite work is characterized by fine detail, naturalistic figures and landscape, and subtle colors.

Figure 8.15 Scene from the *Khamsah (Five Poems)* of Amir Khosrow. 1485. 6¾ × 4½". Chester Beatty Library, Dublin. *The art of Persian miniatures achieved its classic expression during the fifteenth century, the age of the Mongol rulers in Persia. These small works are immediately recognizable by their rectangular designs, their representation of the human figure as about one-fifth the height of the painting, and their use of extremely refined detail.*

Figure 8.16 Pyxis. Córdoba. 968. *The image on this pyxis—a vessel to hold cosmetics or perfumes—testifies to the high status held by instrumental musicians at the Umayyad court in Córdoba. At the center stands a musician, holding an ud, or lute, as he performs for the two young men flanking him. The listening youths, seated Muslim style, are royalty, as symbolized by the two lions below. The youth on the left holds a vessel and a flower, and the one on the right holds a fan. Executed in the all-over style of Islamic art, the surrounding space is enlivened with human, animal, and vegetal figures and abstract, meandering scrolls. An inscription identifies the pyxis as a gift to al-Mughira, the younger son of Abd al-Rahman III (r. 912–961), the first caliph of the West.*

Music

Music has historically been a controversial topic in Muslim culture. Only a few musical genres have gained universal approval, such as the call to prayer (*adhan*), the chanting of the *Qur'an*, and the chanting of poems and prayers during certain religious events, including the Prophet's birthday, pilgrimages, and Ramadan. Clerics often question other musical forms, especially instrumental music, claiming such music undermines faith. And yet, music traditionally has thrived in the Muslim world.

Early Islamic music employs a microtonal system, in which the intervals, or distances between sounds (pitches) on a scale, are **microtones,** or intervals smaller than a semitone—the smallest interval in mainstream Western music before jazz.

Vocal music initially was dominant in Muslim culture, with instrumental music used only to support singing. Instrumental music later won its freedom under Spain's Umayyad rulers, who were great patrons of musicians and, most notably, of secular music (Figure 8.16). Meanwhile, religious music was given a new direction by the Sufi sect, who, in their pursuit of religious emotion, encouraged singing, chanting, and **recitative,** or vocal passages delivered in a speechlike manner. A major change arose in Turkey, where the Sufi order of Whirling Dervishes introduced music into their mosques.

Musicians across the Muslim world played many instruments, representing three groups of instruments and drawn from varied traditions. These included from the string group, the *ud* (lute), the pandore (a bass lute), the psaltery (a trapezoidal-shaped zither), the harp, the *qithara* (guitar), and the *rabab* (rebec, a lute-shaped fiddle); from the wind group, the flute, the reed pipe, and the horn; and from the percussion group, tambourines (square and round), castanets, and various drums, such as *naqqara* (nakers, or small kettle-drums) and *tabla* (a pair of wooden drums). Most of these instruments were adopted into Western music, especially as a result of cultural encounters during the Crusades.

These illustrated books were made from paper beginning around 800, when a Chinese prisoner of war revealed the secrets of papermaking to his Arab captors. Thereafter, a prodigious paper industry flourished, spreading from Samarkand to Baghdad, Damascus, Tripoli in Syria, Yemen, Maghrib, Egypt, and Spain. Christian Europeans eventually learned how to make paper from the Islamic industry in Spain.

The Legacy of Medieval Islam

The legacy of medieval Islam remains potent in the modern Muslim world. That medieval presence is apparent in distinctive architecture, which uses domes, vaulted halls, arcades, and pointed arches; in decorative patterns made with nonrepresentational designs, such as arabesques, calligraphy, and geometric, floral, and abstract forms; in a music tradition based on a microtonal system; in classical Arabic as a literary and scholarly language; in traditional clothing styles, along with beards for men and headscarves, and sometimes veils, for women; and in daily readings from the *Qur'an* on radio and television.

Medieval Islam also transmitted a legacy of suspicion toward the Christian West as a result of the Crusades; indeed, in parts of Islamic society today, the word *crusader* is a hate-charged term for a Westerner on Muslim soil. When the Greek heritage fell into disrepute in the Muslim world, medieval Islam changed the intellectual climate for scholars. As a result, the Muslim world, which after the fall of Rome had been the leader in scientific knowledge, began to lag behind the West, so that by 1800, Muslim science and universities had become irrelevant. Medieval Islam also transmitted a vision of a unified Islamic empire, stretching from Spain to China, inhabited by millions of Muslims, all worshiping Allah and obeying the *Qur'anic* laws—a vision that appeals to those dissatisfied with their place in today's Western-dominated world. Probably the major legacy of medieval Islam, and the feature of Islamic life that so differs from Western life, is the intermingling of religion and state. In the Muslim world, except for the secular state of Turkey, religion's dominant role is expressed in varied ways from law codes based on the *Qur'an*, mandating severe punishments for crimes such as adultery and theft, to separation of the sexes in public and private life.

Though perhaps not as strong as its impact on modern Islam, the influence of medieval Islam on the civilization of the modern West has been significant. Islam's direct legacy to Western civilization includes the pointed arch, which made the Gothic style possible; musical instruments from the string, the wind, and the percussion groups; poetic forms and themes that may have been imitated by the Provençal poets; love poetry, which inspired modern imitators; the poetry of the Sufi mystic Rumi, much admired by contemporary artists including the writer Doris Lessing and the composer Philip Glass; the tradition of reconciling religion with Aristotle's philosophy, which became the goal of Europe's scholastic thinkers; and algebra and other original mathematical concepts, which became part of the Western educational curriculum.

Besides direct influence, medieval Islam also has had an indirect impact on the West by transmitting legacies from other cultures. Of these mediated legacies, the Classical heritage was probably the most important. Islamic scholars produced Arabic versions of most of the Greek and Roman scholarly writings, which Christian scholars then translated into Latin and used as the textbooks in medieval Europe's schools and universities. From the study of those textbooks, the West's modern scientific tradition was born. Other notable transmitted legacies include, from China, papermaking; and, from India, the Hindu-Arabic numeral system along with other mathematical knowledge and probably the basic form of the *Arabian Nights*, though embellished with stories from various cultures.

KEY CULTURAL TERMS

madrasa	mosque
jihad	*qiblah*
qasida	minaret
adab	*minbar*
ghazal	congregational mosque,
maqamah	or Friday mosque
arabesque	*iwan*
calligraphy	Persian miniature
drum	microtone
arcade	recitative

SUGGESTIONS FOR FURTHER READINGS

Primary Sources

Arabian Nights. Translated by J. Zipes. New York: Dutton Signet, 1991. Selections from the *Arabian Nights,* the alternative name for *The Thousand and One Nights,* by a noted authority on world folktales.

Assemblies of Al-Hariri. Translated and with an introduction by A. Shah. London: Octagon Press, 1981. An up-to-date translation of this classic of Arabic literature, telling of the adventures of the charming and learned rogue Abu Zayd. All fifty episodes or "assemblies" are included.

The Essential Rumi. Translated by C. Barks and others. San Francisco: Harper San Francisco, 1997. Excellent American English free-verse renderings of the difficult poetry in the *Masnavi,* the masterpiece of the Sufi mystic Rumi. Includes selections of Rumi's love poems and teaching parables, along with Barks's insightful introductions.

IBN HAZM. *The Ring of the Dove: A Treatise on the Art and Practice of Arab Love*. Translated by A. J. Arberry. London: Luzac & Company, Ltd., 1953. A didactic work that blends a study of the characteristics and meaning of love, including examples, anecdotes, and poems, with a moral discourse on sinning and the virtues of abstinence.

IBN KHALDUN. *The Muqaddimah: An Introduction to History*. Translated by F. Rosenthal. Edited by N. J. Dawood. Princeton: Princeton University Press, 1969. Introduces the student to Ibn Khaldun's study of the origins and characteristics of civilization. An abridged edition of Rosenthal's three-volume translation.

The Koran [Qur'an]. Translated by N. J. Dawood. New York: Penguin, 2000. Seventh ed. Easy to read, authoritative translation of Islam's holy book. Follows the *Qur'anic* tradition of arrangement of suras, or chapters. The most popular version in the United States today.

The Seven Odes: The First Chapter in Arabic Literature. Translated by A. J. Arberry. London: George Allen & Unwin, 1957. An analysis, history, and modern translation of the earliest Arabic literary works—the seven odes, or *"hanged poems,"* which hung on the walls of the *Kaaba* before the time of Muhammad and the rise of Islam.

CHAPTER *8* HIGHLIGHTS
The World of Islam, 630–1517

MEDIEVAL ISLAM

Literature & Philosophy   Art & Architecture   Music & Dance

 Readings in the Western Humanities   *CD, The Western Humanities*

9 THE HIGH MIDDLE AGES
The Christian Centuries

Although Charlemagne's ambitious hopes for Europe were thwarted by the invasions of the ninth and tenth centuries, society had grown more settled by the early eleventh century, and a brighter era began to unfold in the West. Between 1000 and 1300—the period called the High Middle Ages—a new foundation was laid that would support the future development of Western civilized life.

During this time, the Christian church became the dominant institution of the medieval world. At the same time, feudalism was established as the principal military, economic, and political system, and feudal monarchies in France, England, and central Europe were beginning to form what would become European states. Town life also revived in the West, and a new urban class was born. Situated midway between the feudal aristocrats and the peasants, this middle class included merchants, moneylenders, and skilled artisans—virtually all free persons associated with town life.

These momentous political, social, and economic changes were reflected in cultural interests. Theologians, writers, and architects worked to harmonize the two opposing trends of the time, the secular and the spiritual. They achieved a stunning but short-lived synthesis. Moving from rugged warrior values, supreme between 1000 and 1150, Western culture became more refined, more learned, and increasingly secular between 1150 and 1300. The earlier 150-year period is associated with monastic and feudal themes in literature and the Romanesque style in architecture. The later period saw a growing trend toward urban and courtly themes in literature and the rise of Gothic architecture, the most spectacular realization of which was the Gothic cathedral.

◄ **Detail** Speyer Cathedral. View from the east. Speyer, Germany. Begun about 1030, completed before 1150.

FEUDALISM

Out of feudalism—a military and political system based on personal loyalty and kinship—arose a new social order, a code of conduct, and an artistic and literary tradition. In the beginning, feudalism restored law and order to western Europe, even though local lords often exploited those under them. But during the High Middle Ages, the feudal nobility slowly lost power to the feudal kings, who laid the foundations of the early modern national monarchies. By the early 1300s, feudalism no longer served its original function and was being superseded in many areas by different political, social, and economic forms.

The Feudal System and the Feudal Society

Feudalism evolved in the Early Middle Ages under the Franks and expanded under Charlemagne. As a military system, it offered some protection from invaders but at the cost of fragmenting society into rival states. As the feudal chiefs began to pass their lands on to their eldest sons, Europe became dominated by a military aristocracy (see Chapter 7).

Feudal wealth was reckoned in land; the feudal estate included lands, manor houses, and the serfs who worked the land. The feudal lords attracted warriors, called vassals, to their private armies by offering them estates, and thus feudalism depended on the manorial economy. The feudal estate, called a fief, provided the warrior with the means to outfit himself with the proper military equipment and attendants and to live in an aristocratic style.

Over the generations, feudalism became a complex web of agreements, obligations, and rituals. A written agreement spelled out the mutual duties and obligations of the lord and the vassal. Typically, the lord gave military protection to his vassal and settled quarrels among his supporters through his court. The vassal in turn furnished military or financial aid and sat as counsel in the lord's court. Conflicts between a lord and his vassal were sometimes settled by peers in the lord's court, but more often they escalated into civil wars.

The vassal–lord relationship was the heart of feudalism, but the form of the institution varied geographically. Feudalism's prototype was that of northern France, around Paris, but each area modified the French form to suit its local needs. Those who profited from feudalism retained the institution as long as possible, so that well into the twentieth century its vestiges were evident in central Europe and Russia and were eliminated only by revolution.

The hierarchical feudal social order was defined and elaborated in the unwritten rules of conduct known as the **chivalric code.** In the early eleventh century, chivalry (from the French word *cheval,* meaning "horse") was largely a warrior code, although one rooted in Christian values. More an ideal than a reality, it nevertheless inspired the vassal to honor his lord and to respect his peers. He was also expected to protect the weak from danger and to practice his ideals—bravery, strength, and honesty—with all members of society. The French clergy refined the chivalric code by initiating the Peace of God, a call for an end to fighting at specified times, and other clerics encouraged the knights to treat women, clergy, and peasants more humanely.

By the twelfth century, both the Peace of God and the notion of protected classes—notably women—had been incorporated into the heart of a more refined and courtly version of the chivalric code. Especially influential in altering the status of women was the rise of courtly love, a movement that began in the aristocratic courts of southern France. The love of a lord for a lady (usually an unattainable lady, such as another man's wife) was seen as an ennobling emotion, encouraging the man to ever greater deeds. Aristocratic ladies were idealized and venerated with an almost holy respect, resembling that shown for the Virgin Mary (Figure 9.1). (However, a contemporaneous countertrend also identified women with Eve, who, by tempting Adam to eat the forbidden fruit, brought the burden of original sin to humanity.) Courtly love, one of the greatest contributions of medieval civilization, provided inspiration for much of the secular literature, art, and music of the High Middle Ages because it encouraged the intermingling of men and women in social settings, where dancing, music, and conversation were enjoyed in accordance with the rules of courtesy.

Whatever the image of woman in medieval society, however, on a practical level her position was determined by the social status of her husband or her father or by the support of a powerful family. A few women—such as Eleanor of Aquitaine, wife of King Henry II of England, in the twelfth century— sometimes influenced a spouse's decisions or wielded power on behalf of a son. But their rarity as rulers in their own right testifies to how little power women had in the Middle Ages, despite their exalted image.

Peasant Life

Feudalism and chivalry served the interests of the small noble classes. Life was quite different for the peasants, who constituted the vast majority of the population. Some were free, but many were bound in service. The two most common forms of servitude, slavery and serfdom, were legacies from Rome. Slaves were the personal property of the lord, whereas serfs were

Figure 9.1 *Count Eckhart and Uta.* Naumburg cathedral. Ca. 1245. Limestone, life-size. Naumburg, Germany. *In this representation of a feudal lord and lady, the most striking features are the woman's chaste beauty, reflecting her role as the queen of chivalry and linking her to the Virgin Mary, and the man's great heraldic shield and sword, symbolizing his position as an aristocratic warrior and defender of honor. These two figures are among several that stand in Naumburg cathedral, representing noble men and women associated with the founding of the cathedral. The Naumburg statues are considered among the most beautiful sculptures from this period.*

half-free but tied to the land. Serfs worked for the lord in exchange for living on his land. In eleventh-century Europe, slavery was dying out because the church's teachings had largely convinced the feudal lords of its inhumanity, but serfdom was firmly entrenched.

The routine of the serfs and the free peasants was dictated by custom and regulated by daily and seasonal events (Figure 9.2). With men and women occasionally working together in the fields, they eked out a bare subsistence from their tiny plots of land; they lived in wooden huts, raised their children, and found relief in the church's frequent Holy Days and feast days. As farming innovations were introduced (such as three-field crop rotation, which allowed the land to replenish itself), the plight of the serfs improved. Increasing the productivity of the soil brought economic benefits to the lord, who could then, if he wished, pay the peasants in coin and sell them tracts of land.

As serfs gained a few legal rights, they could become economically independent and gain their freedom from the manorial system. These trends, however, were confined to western Europe, notably England and France. In some areas of central and eastern Europe, serfs continued to be exploited for centuries.

The Rise of Towns

A new trend began to counter the dominance of the feudal system: the rise of urban areas where free individuals pursued their own economic goals. Although rural manors provided work and security for 90 percent of the population at the beginning of the High Middle Ages, the population of Europe nearly doubled between 1000 and 1300, from thirty-five million to almost seventy million, and an increasing number of people sought economic opportunities in the new and revitalized urban areas (Figure 9.3). From that point on, the future of the West lay with town dwellers.

As towns grew larger and urban life became more competitive, the residents formed associations, called guilds, to protect their special interests. The artisan and craft guilds, for example, regulated working con-

Figure 9.2 *Labors of the Months.* Amiens cathedral. Ca. 1220–1230. Amiens, France. *The labors of the months—threshing and fruit-picking—are shown beneath their respective zodiacal signs—Cancer (late June to late July) and Leo (late July to late August). These carefully observed scenes of peasant life from the western portals of Amiens cathedral show peasants engaged in their seasonal tasks. The labors of the months and the zodiacal signs are framed in quatrefoils—four-leafed shapes—which are typical decorative devices in medieval art.*

ditions, created apprenticeship programs, and set wages; the merchant and banking guilds approved new businesses and supervised trade contracts. These guilds often quarreled over issues inside the town walls, but they joined hands against the intrusions of the church and the local nobility.

Figure 9.3 AMBROGIO LORENZETTI (active ca. 1319–1347). *Street Scene in Medieval Siena.* Detail from *Allegory of Good Government in the City.* 1338–1339. Fresco in the Sala della Pace, Palazzo Pubblico, Siena. *Although an idealized image, this painting is nevertheless an accurate representation of medieval Siena as a bustling country town built on a hill. Signs of prosperity abound. In the middle right and center, farmers, perhaps from the nearby countryside, lead pack animals loaded with sacks of wool and other goods. Nearby, three weavers are making textiles. On the lower right, a goatherd coaxes his flock, probably to the city market. In the middle left foreground, a shopkeeper arranges his wares. Through the large opening on the left may be glimpsed a classroom, where a seated teacher addresses his students. On the extreme right, two women, perhaps servants, carry objects, one, most noticeably, with a large bundle balanced on her head.*

Because urban economic life conflicted with the interests of the feudal system, urban dwellers, led by the guilds, founded self-governing towns, called communes, often with written charters that specified their rights in relation to the feudal lords. By about 1200, many towns in northern and western Europe had charters, and their political independence spurred economic growth.

Artisans and merchants needed buyers, secure trade routes, and markets for their products if they were to prosper. The earliest trade routes were the rivers and the old Roman roads. As demand increased in the West for luxury items from the East, new trade routes opened. Italian cities led this international commerce, trading the luxurious woolen cloth of Flanders for the silks of China and the spices of the Middle East (Map 9.1). Along the overland routes in Europe, local lords guaranteed traders safe passage through their territory for a fee. Some nobles and towns along the way sponsored fairs to lure this rich international trade.

As on the feudal manor, the position of women in the medieval urban world was still subordinate to that of men, even though urban women often worked closely with their husbands in trade or crafts. Indeed, in this hierarchical society gender roles became increasingly differentiated through custom and legislation. As a consequence, females could neither hold governmental office nor have any public voice in politics. The few women with economic power—such as those directly involved in manufacturing and trade or the occasional rich widow who kept her husband's business afloat—were exceptions to this general exclusionary rule.

The Feudal Monarchy

Politically, feudalism was leading to a new form of rule. By about 1100, some powerful feudal lords had begun to expand their holdings into larger kingdoms. As these ambitious noblemen subdued weaker ones, they often sealed their victories through marriages with the conquered family. Over the ensuing generations, their heirs extended and consolidated their lands, always seeking to win the loyalty of their new subjects. The greatest problem a feudal monarch faced was building a centralized rule to keep the kingdom from disintegrating into a set of separate, warring states. During the High Middle Ages, four feudal monarchies dominated

LEARNING THROUGH MAPS

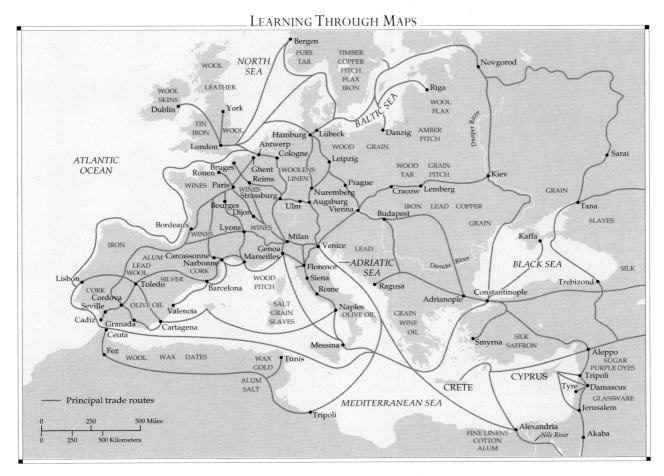

Map 9.1   PRINCIPAL TRADING ROUTES AND TOWNS OF EUROPE, 1300
This map shows the major towns and trading routes in Europe at the end of the
High Middle Ages. **Note** the important role played by sea trade. **Identify** some key
crossroads of trade. **How** did the location of the north Italian cities help to make them
leaders in trade? **Consider** the extensive nature of the long-distance trade between
Europe and its neighbors. **Consider** also the impact of climate on the products made
and produced in various regions.

the West: France, England, the Holy Roman Empire,
and the papacy, which was politically similar to the
three secular monarchies (Timeline 9.1).

The French Monarchy   The origins of modern France
stem from the reign of Hugh Capet (r. 987–996), the
first of the Capetian rulers, who exercised power over
a part of the old Frankish kingdom (see Chapter 7). By
the early eleventh century, the Capetians, having
defeated their rivals, had founded a feudal monarchy
in central France, with Paris as its center.

During the twelfth and thirteenth centuries, a series
of able monarchs managed to consolidate and expand
the Capetian power base and control the great vassals
by forming alliances with the lesser nobles, the middle
class, the clergy, and the popes. The establishment of
central authority in France was a slow process, but by

the beginning of the reign of Philip IV in 1285, France
was the most powerful feudal kingdom in Europe and
the French tradition of royal absolutism was well
established.

The English Monarchy   The English monarchs also
amassed power at the expense of the feudal landowners,
but the English rulers never controlled their kingdom to
the same degree as the Capetians. Moreover, because
some English kings made grievous mistakes, England's
feudal barons won pivotal battles against the monarchy.
In addition, judicial reforms and advisory councils
tended to limit, not to expand, the English kings' power.

Three major events determined English history during the High Middle Ages. The first was the Norman
invasion of England. For five centuries, England had
been ruled by an Anglo-Saxon monarchy, and when

Timeline 9.1   THE FEUDAL MONARCHIES IN THE HIGH MIDDLE AGES

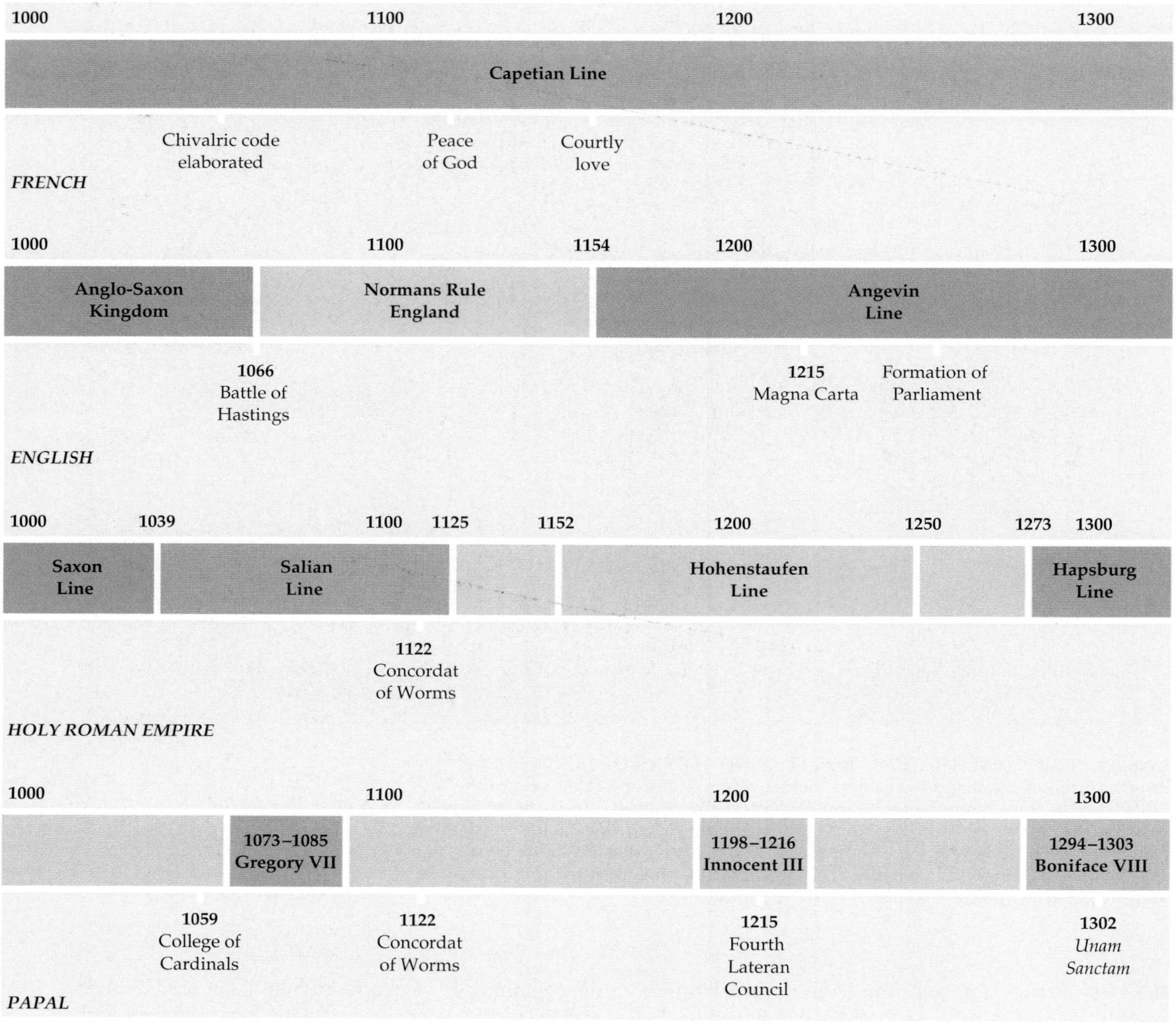

1000	1100	1200	1300

Capetian Line

	Chivalric code elaborated	Peace of God	Courtly love

FRENCH

1000	1100	1154	1200	1300

Anglo-Saxon Kingdom	**Normans Rule England**	**Angevin Line**

1066 Battle of Hastings

1215 Magna Carta   Formation of Parliament

ENGLISH

1000	1039	1100	1125	1152	1200	1250	1273	1300

Saxon Line	**Salian Line**		**Hohenstaufen Line**		**Hapsburg Line**

1122 Concordat of Worms

HOLY ROMAN EMPIRE

1000	1100	1200	1300

	1073–1085 Gregory VII		**1198–1216 Innocent III**		**1294–1303 Boniface VIII**

1059 College of Cardinals

1122 Concordat of Worms

1215 Fourth Lateran Council

1302 *Unam Sanctam*

PAPAL

the king died in 1066 without a clear successor, Duke William, the ruler of the duchy of Normandy in northern France, invaded England to claim the throne. At the Battle of Hastings, in 1066, William conquered the Anglo-Saxon contender, Harold, and became king of England (Figure 9.4). For the rest of the High Middle Ages, England was ruled by Norman kings and their French (Angevin) successors, and conquerors and conquered were blended into one nation and one culture.

The second major event occurred in 1215 when the English feudal barons forced King John (r. 1199–1216) to sign the Magna Carta ("great charter"), a document that limited royal authority and gave the barons

certain financial and governmental controls over the crown. In the long run, the Magna Carta was also a victory for all freemen because it gave them certain judicial rights, such as trial by jury.

The third event was the creation of Parliament, which occurred during the reign of Henry III (r. 1216–1272). Faced with renewed hostility from his English barons, Henry agreed to convene the ancient but little-used Great Council, comprising representatives from every county and town. This body became Parliament (from the French word *parler*, "to talk") and began to advise the king. Initially, Parliament was part of the royal government, but in time it

Figure 9.4 *These Men Wonder at the Star. Harold.* Panel from the Bayeux Tapestry. Third quarter of the eleventh century. Wool embroidery on linen, ht. 20″. Bayeux, France. *Today housed in the cathedral of Bayeux, this famous embroidery provides an important historic record of the events leading up to the Battle of Hastings and presents a justification for the Norman conquest of England. Harold is cast as a villain who breaks his oath of allegiance to William and loses the English crown as a result of this treachery.*

Halley's comet, interpreted as an evil omen, appeared over England in February 1066. The comet is shown in the center of the upper border. On the left, men point to the comet, and on the right Harold also seems upset by the comet. Beneath Harold and his adviser are outlines of boats, implying a possible invasion by the Normans.

represented the people against the crown, as England moved further toward a limited feudal monarchy.

The Holy Roman Empire Whereas France and England grew into unified feudal monarchies, the Holy Roman Empire, which began as the Saxon dynasty of Otto I in the late tenth century, failed to achieve a centralized state. From the early eleventh to the early twelfth century, the empire prospered and trade expanded, but a conflict with the papacy arose that would undermine the empire. It concerned the European-wide practice of lay investiture—the appointment of priests, bishops, and archbishops by local lords and nobles, often for money. Such appointments allowed the secular rulers some control over the wealth and influence of the church within their own territories. The central issue in the long and complicated conflict was whether the bishops and archbishops were the servants of the pope or of the secular rulers.

The issue of lay investiture was settled by the Concordat of Worms in 1122, which allowed the pope to confer spiritual authority on the clergy and the emperor to invest them with land and secular authority. But the rivalry between the Holy Roman rulers and the popes would not die. Under the Hohenstaufen dynasty, Frederick Barbarossa and Frederick II temporarily created an empire in central Europe, which included Italy. Their successors failed to maintain this empire, and the popes resumed their sway over Italian politics. The Holy Roman emperors ceased playing a major role in European affairs until after the coming of the Hapsburg line in 1273.

The Papal Monarchy The papacy during the High Middle Ages closely resembled the feudal monarchies in Europe, except that it was guided by the ideal of Christendom—a universal state ruled by the popes under God's law. The church's most powerful claim to authority was that only through the clergy—those trained and ordained to administer the sacraments—could a Christian hope to gain everlasting life. The church defined society's moral standards at the same time that it participated in the politics of the period.

The key to the church's power was a reform movement that originated in the Benedictine monastery at Cluny, France, and swept through Europe in the 900s. Before this movement, the church had been riddled with scandal and corruption, and many clergy were poorly trained and lived less than exemplary lives. Because of lay investiture, bishops often acted as vassals of feudal lords rather than as agents of the church. The buying and selling of church offices, a practice known as simony, meant that positions often went to the highest bidder. Worst of all, many clergymen expressed blatant disregard for the sacraments.

The monks at Cluny, however, were free of feudal obligations and loyal only to the pope. Little by little, the Cluniacs impressed Europe with their spirituality, and as they established new monasteries and reformed others, the church began to revive, to eliminate corrupt practices, and to reimpose celibacy on the clergy. In 1059 the College of Cardinals was founded to elect the popes, thus freeing the papacy from German and Italian politics. By the late eleventh century, the political power of the reformed popes rivaled that of the feudal monarchs.

Figure 9.5   Arnolfo di Cambio. *Pope Boniface VIII*. Early fourteenth century. Museo dell'Opera del Duomo, Florence, Italy. *Boniface VIII is portrayed in his crown and vestments—the rich trappings of papal monarchical power. The sculptor, Arnolfo di Cambio, who was also the first architect of the Florentine cathedral (see Chapter 10), has depicted Boniface VIII in the elongated Late Gothic style with sagging draperies.*

Of the great medieval popes, the two most powerful were Gregory VII and Innocent III. Gregory VII (pope 1073–1085), brought to the papacy by the Cluniac revival, purified the wayward clergy, demanding full obedience to canon law. Innocent III (pope 1198–1216) was probably the most powerful pontiff in the history of the church. He excommunicated kings; intervened in the secular affairs of England, France, and the Holy Roman Empire; and advocated crusades against the Muslims abroad and the heretics at home. Motivated by the ideal of Christendom, his aim was to unite Europe under the papal banner.

By his extravagant claims, Pope Boniface VIII (pope 1294–1303) unwittingly undid the three centuries' work of his predecessors to build papal power (Figure 9.5). In 1302 he issued the papal bull (from the Latin word *bolla*, "seal") known as *Unam sanctam*, a proclamation of papal superiority over all secular rulers. The French crown swiftly sent an army to arrest the pope, and an unnerved Boniface VIII had to flee and died soon thereafter. This episode precipitated a decline in the prestige of the papacy from which it did not fully recover until the sixteenth century.

MEDIEVAL CHRISTIANITY AND THE CHURCH

In addition to its political significance, the institution of the church had incalculable influence in the High Middle Ages, bringing Christian values to bear on virtually all of medieval life. The church owed its influence not only to the maneuverings of the popes but also to the tireless work of the clergy and the powerful effect of Christian beliefs.

By this time in its history, the church had evolved an elaborate organization to carry out its work. The pope, as the spiritual leader of Christianity, stood at the head of a strict hierarchy. Supporting him was the papal curia—a staff of administrators, financial experts, secretaries, clerics, and legal advisers. A system of ecclesiastical courts handled the church's judicial functions and interpreted canon law, the church's law code based on the Bible. These courts were technically restricted to cases involving clerical personnel, but in actuality their jurisdiction was broader because of the huge number of people enmeshed in the workings of the church. The church's judicial branch rivaled the feudal courts in jurisdiction, and canon law sometimes challenged the authority of feudal law.

Tithes, taxes, and special collections provided funds for the church's daily operations and its charitable obligations. The system was relatively efficient, and as long as the church spent the funds wisely, the populace kept up its generous contributions.

ENCOUNTER

Pagan Vikings versus Christian Europeans

The Vikings, the last Germanic people to be assimilated into European life, began the Early Middle Ages as pagans, linked by trade with Christian Europe but otherwise isolated, living in Norway, Denmark, and Sweden. Starting about 789, that changed, as peaceful coexistence gave way to sometimes violent encounters with European neighbors. For more than three hundred years, the Vikings launched hit-and-run raids, pillaging monasteries, churches, and other unfortified sites along the coasts and rivers of Britain, Ireland, northern France, and occasionally Italy; conquering Normandy, Sicily, and large parts of Russia and Britain; trading with Constantinople and Baghdad; discovering and colonizing Iceland and Greenland; and being the first Europeans to set foot in North America, on the coast of Newfoundland. Any hope for a far-flung Viking culture ended in the tenth and eleventh centuries, mainly because the Vikings converted to Christianity and thus lost their distinctive Scandinavian identity. By 1100, the Viking Age was over; they were now Christian Europeans.

The word *Viking* originally meant only those Scandinavians who went *vikingr*, or plundering, and it probably originated in Britain, where the first raids began about 789. Today, it is applied to all Early Medieval Scandinavians, whether they went "plundering" or not. However, the Viking Age was more than a time for looting. It was a period of migration of peoples, propelled by varied motives, including overpopulation, worsening climate and food supply, infighting among rival chieftains in which the losers were driven overseas, and the search for lucrative trading opportunities.

The Vikings unquestionably altered Western culture. They established the first towns in Ireland, Russia, and Scandinavia, and made Iceland part of Europe by opening it to settlement. In France, they hastened the breakup of the Carolingian Empire and deeply influenced the history of France, England, and Italy by

Encounter figure 9.1   Viking Raid. Tombstone. Lindisfarne (Holy Island). Ninth century. *This tombstone vividly depicts a Viking raid, through simple forms and expressive gestures. The ferocity of the attack is manifest in the massed warriors, each with one leg bent at the knee to suggest movement and one arm brandishing a battle-axe. Found in the monastery of Lindisfarne, on the northeastern coast of England, this image probably depicts the actual sacking of this monastery in 793. The attack on Lindisfarne, a major monastic center, caused some to believe that God was using the Vikings to punish Christians for some terrible sin.*

founding the duchy of Normandy. They set up the first state in Russia; the word *Russia* is derived from *Rus*, the name given Scandinavians by the Slavic majority. The Vikings' greatest impact was probably on Britain, where their small states, though short-lived, destroyed old governing units and thus prepared the way for the founding of the unified kingdoms of England and Scotland.

Christian Beliefs and Practices

A great part of the immense authority of the church sprang from the belief shared by the overwhelming majority of the medieval population that the church held the keys to the kingdom of heaven and provided the only way to salvation. By attempting to adhere to the Christian moral code and by participating in the rituals and ceremonies prescribed by the church and established by tradition, Christians hoped for redemption and eternal life after death.

These rituals and ceremonies were basically inseparable from the doctrines of the religion. They had been derived from the teachings of Jesus and Paul, clarified by the church fathers, particularly Augustine, and further defined by medieval theologians. Finally, the Fourth Lateran Council of 1215, under Pope Innocent III, officially proclaimed the sacraments as the outward signs of God's grace and the only way to heaven.

As established by the council, the sacraments numbered seven: baptism, confirmation, the Eucharist

(Holy Communion), penance, marriage, last rites, and ordination for the priesthood. Baptism, the Eucharist, and penance were deemed of primary importance. In baptism, the parents were assured that the infant had been rescued from original sin. In the Eucharist, the central part of the Mass, the church taught that a miracle occurred whereby the priest turned the bread and wine into the body and blood of Jesus. That the outer appearance of the bread and wine remained the same while their inner nature changed was explained by medieval philosophers in the doctrine of transubstantiation. For the uneducated congregation, however, the Mass and the miracle were simply another sign of the church's spiritual power.

Penance evolved into a rather complicated practice. First, sinners confessed their sins individually to a priest; the priest conveyed God's forgiveness for the mortal penalties of sin so that hell could be avoided; the priest then directed that an earthly punishment—the penance—be carried out in an effort to erase the effects of the sin. Depending on the severity of the sin, penance could range from a few prayers to a pilgrimage or a crusade. This sacrament was made even more complex by its association with purgatory.

With the groundwork laid by Augustine in the fifth century and Pope Gregory the Great in the sixth century, the doctrine of purgatory was given more explicit form by the papacy and scholastic thinkers of the High Middle Ages. Neither hell nor heaven, purgatory was a third place, where those who had died in a state of grace could avoid damnation by being purged, or purified, from all stain of sin. All souls in purgatory were ultimately destined for heaven; penance was a means of reducing time in purgatory. Thus the living could do penance on earth in hope of spending less time in purgatory.

Confession and penance became widespread practices of the eleventh-century church. By 1300, both were integral to Christian rituals and beliefs. In political terms, penance, along with the Mass, was an effective means for controlling the moral behavior of church members.

Religious Orders and Lay Piety

Crucial to the workings of the church were the clergy, who were the most visible signs of the church's presence in everyday life. The "secular" clergy (from *saeculum*, Latin for "world") moved freely in society, and the "regular" clergy lived apart from the world in monasteries under a special rule (*regula* in Latin). The monasteries served as refuges from the world, as schools, and as places of study where manuscripts

could be copied and traditional learning maintained. They also gave rise to the reform movements that periodically cleansed the church of corruption.

As noted earlier, the Cluniac monks originated the reform movement that helped to establish the moral and political authority of the medieval church. Other waves of reform followed, the most important of which was represented by the founding of the Cistercian order in the twelfth century. Bernard of Clairvaux [klair-VOE] (1090–1153), a saint, a mystic, and one of the most forceful personalities of the period, personally founded over 160 Cistercian abbeys. Unlike the moderate Cluniacs, the Cistercians observed a severe rule, living usually in isolated monasteries where the brothers worked with the local peasants. The Cistercians also simplified their worship services, eliminating elaborate ceremonies.

For women, the religious impulse found an outlet in convents and nunneries. Here, women could devote themselves to Christ and follow ascetic lives filled with prayer, contemplation, and service. Convents had existed since the time of Charlemagne, although seldom with the large endowments monasteries enjoyed or with as much influence in local affairs.

Convent life nevertheless did nurture several gifted women who influenced this age, most notably Hildegard of Bingen (1098–1179), founder and abbess of the Benedictine house of Rupertsberg near Bingen (modern Germany). Her writing and preaching attracted scores of supporters in Germany, France, and Switzerland, including most of her male superiors. She was highly influential with major figures of the time, as evidenced by her correspondence with Eleanor of Aquitaine, the Holy Roman emperor Frederick Barbarossa (r. 1152–1190), and various popes. She wrote in the medical arts, theology, and the history of science, but it was mainly through visionary tracts that she had the most impact on her contemporaries. Her first book, entitled *Scivias* (translated variously as *May You Know* or *Know the Ways of the Lord*), included descriptions of her visions, the texts of liturgical songs, and a sung morality play, *Ordo Virtutatum (The Company of the Virtues)*, the first of its kind. She also illuminated manuscripts (Figure 9.6) and composed sacred poetry, which has survived in monophonic musical settings and has found new audiences today. Hildegard was a bold talent and left a superb legacy, especially given the belief of the time that it was dangerous to teach a woman to read and write.

Besides convents and nunneries, another type of religious order appeared in the thirteenth century with the rise of two major mendicant, or begging, orders, the Franciscans and the Dominicans. These new churchmen, called **friars,** were originally dedicated to

Figure 9.6 Hildegard's Awakening: A Self-Portrait from *Scivias*. Ca. 1150. *Hildegard's description of the moment when she received the word of God is effectively captured in this illumination: a "burning light coming from heaven poured into my mind." The Holy Spirit inflames her mind as she etches the word of God on a tablet; Volmar, the priest of the abbey and her loyal secretary, gazes at the event. The simplistic sketch of the towers and building is typical of similar twelfth-century illuminated manuscripts.*

Figure 9.7 ATTRIBUTED TO GIOTTO. *St. Francis of Assisi's Trial by Fire Before the Sultan.* Before 1300. Fresco. Basilica of St. Francis, Assisi, Upper Church, nave. *This painting, from a cycle of twenty-eight frescoes detailing the life and miracles of St. Francis of Assisi, shows the saint (center, with a halo around his head) preaching before the enthroned Sultan al-Malik Kamil (r. 1218–1238), the last of the Ayyubid dynasty (right). The setting is Egypt, the center of the Sultan's holdings, which included Syria and Palestine. Trying to convert the Sultan to Christianity, St. Francis, backed by a second Franciscan friar, challenges the Sultan's Islamic clergy to join in a walk through the blazing fire on the bottom left, as a test of their respective religious faiths. The Sultan gestures toward the fire with his right hand, as four Muslim clergy prepare to leave on the far left. This fresco, completed perhaps seventy years after the saint's death, was painted during a time when Franciscan missionaries were active in Egypt and other Middle Eastern lands.*

working among the urban poor, but by 1250 most of them were also priests and they dominated higher education. For example, Thomas Aquinas, the age's leading scholar, was a Dominican friar. Although both orders made important contributions, the Franciscans had a greater impact on medieval society, largely because of the gentle nature of the order's sainted founder, Francis (1182–1226). Many people still find Francis's piety, selflessness, and legendary humility the personification of a sublime Christian (Figure 9.7).

As monastic reform slowed in the late twelfth century, a wave of lay piety swelled up from the lower ranks of society, triggered by a mixture of religious protest and social and economic causes. Typical of these unorthodox movements were the beguines, independent communities of laywomen dedicated to good works, poverty, chastity, and religious devotion. Unlike nuns, who isolated themselves from the world,

the beguines had regular contact with society—caring for the sick at home and in hospitals, teaching in both girls' and boys' schools, and working in the textile industry. The beguines first established themselves in northern France and then, along with male lay brethren called beghards, spread to Germany and the Netherlands, usually in proximity to Dominican monasteries. These lay communities became centers of freethinking, as some members turned their intellectual gifts to spiritual matters. For example, Mechthild of Magdeburg (about 1207–about 1282) wrote *The Flowing Light of the Godhead,* a mystical account of her religious odyssey. The beguine and beghard communities also provided the audience for medieval Germany's finest devotional writer and a great mystic of the Christian tradition, Meister Eckhart (about 1260–1328), who composed tracts and

238

sermons to guide these laypeople's religious piety into orthodox ways.

Despite a reputation for freethinking, the beguines and the beghards won approval from religious authorities, but other lay groups were condemned as heretics, probably because they failed to amass enough property to found permanent residences and, hence, appeared to the church to be uncontrollable. The most powerful of these heretical sects was the Albigensian, which was centered at Albi in southern France. The Albigensians were also known as the Cathari, from the Greek word for "pure." Their unorthodox beliefs were derived partly from Zoroastrianism, the source of their concept of a universal struggle between a good God and an evil deity, and partly from Manichaeism, the source of their notion that the flesh is evil. The Albigensians stressed that Jesus was divine and not human, that the wealth of the church was a sign of its depravity, and that the goal of Christian living was to achieve the status of Cathari, or perfection.

These unorthodox beliefs spread rapidly across much of southern France, permeating the church and the secular society. In 1214 Pope Innocent III called for the destruction of the hated beliefs. His message appealed to the feudal nobles who were greedy for the heretics' lands. The Albigensians were repressed with incredible ferocity and cruelty. Many Cathari were slaughtered and their property was confiscated; others were tried by the Inquisition and burned at the stake. Such actions reflected the less benign face of the medieval church and its immense power.

THE AGE OF SYNTHESIS: EQUILIBRIUM BETWEEN THE SPIRITUAL AND THE SECULAR

Between 1000 and 1300, Christian values permeated European cultural life. The Christian faith was a unifying agent that reconciled the opposing realms of the spiritual and the secular, the immaterial and the material—as symbolized in many cities and towns by the soaring spires of the local **cathedral** (Figure 9.8). Medieval culture drew from the arts and humanities of the Classical world, the heritage of the various European peoples, and, to a lesser extent, the traditions of Byzantium and Islam. Because of these diverse influences, the culture of the High Middle Ages was by no means uniform. What many writers, thinkers, and artists shared was a set of common concerns and interests, most notably the quest for forms that could transcend the contradictions of the age.

A historical watershed occurred in the mid–twelfth century that was reflected in architecture, sculpture, music, learning, and literature. Before 1150 Western culture tended to express the rugged virtues of the feudal castle and the cloistered monastery; the militant warrior and the ascetic monk were the social ideals; and women were treated as chattel, or property. After 1150 the urban values of the new towns became paramount along with a more courtly attitude toward women. The church indirectly encouraged this trend with the rise of the cult of the Virgin Mary; Mary's status became so great that she was revered almost as much as Christ.

Learning and Theology

From about 1000 onward, scholars revived the school system that had flourished briefly under Charlemagne in the Early Middle Ages. These monastic schools—along with many new cathedral schools—appealed to an age that was hungry for learning and set Europe's intellectual tone until about 1200. During these two centuries, the only serious rival to the schools was a handful of independent scholars who drew crowds of students to their lectures in Paris and elsewhere. By 1200 new educational institutions arose—the universities—that soon surpassed the monastic and cathedral schools and forced the independent masters out of business. Since then, the universities have dominated intellectual life in the West.

Cathedral Schools and the Development of Scholasticism   During the twelfth century, the new cathedral schools reached the height of their power, as Chartres and Paris led the way. Schooling, with rare exceptions, was the exclusive province of men who were preparing for careers in either the church or the dynastic states. For the next three hundred years, the curriculum stayed the same as that codified by Boethius in the sixth century: the trivium (grammar, logic, and rhetoric) and the quadrivium (arithmetic, astronomy, geometry, and music)—the seven liberal arts—which in turn were based on the works of the Classical authors and the early church fathers. Teachers and pupils communicated in Latin, and students read the Christian works in the original Latin. In contrast, Classical writings were known only from misleading Latin summaries until they were replaced in the twelfth century with more accurate Latin versions made from Arabic translations (see Chapter 8).

The introduction of the new versions of the Classical texts, notably those of Aristotle, caused a revolution in education and elevated the Greek thinker to the status of an authority whose word could not be questioned. By 1300 Aristotle's writings virtually monopolized the curriculum at every educational level. The revival of Aristotle contributed to the development of **scholasticism.** In general, the aim of a scholastic thinker was to bring Aristotle's thought into harmony with the Christian faith. Scholasticism was also a system of reasoning that had been perfected in oral debates in the schools. In the scholastic method, a scholar divided each problem into three parts. First, a question was set forth for intellectual analysis; next, a discussion thoroughly summarized the arguments for and against the question, usually citing the Bible, the church fathers, Aristotle, and other ancient authors; finally, a solution was offered, reinforced with support from religious and secular sources.

The scholastic method was not meant to discover new knowledge; rather, it used deductive logic to

Figure 9.8   Auxerre Cathedral. Begun ca. 1225. Auxerre, France. *Looming over the town and dominating the countryside for miles around, the Gothic cathedral symbolized the preeminent role of the Christian church in medieval life. No other building could soar past its spires, either literally or figuratively. People worshiped inside it, built their houses right up to its walls, and conducted their business affairs within the shadows of its towers. Thus, the cathedral also symbolized the integration of the secular and the sacred in medieval life.*

clarify existing issues and to explore the intellectual ramifications of a topic. This method, which tended to uphold rather than to question religious beliefs, was discarded in favor of an inductive, mathematically based style of reasoning in the seventeenth century.

Peter Abelard   The primacy of the cathedral schools of Chartres and Paris in the twelfth century was challenged by a few independent masters who pitted their intellects against the authority of the faculty of these institutions. Of this daring breed of scholars, Peter Abelard [AB-uh-lard] (in French, Pierre Abélard) (1079–1142) was the most brilliant and controversial. More important, he was one of the first medieval thinkers to proclaim a clear distinction between reason and faith. Intellectually curious and reveling in provocative disputes, Abelard attended the lectures of William of Champeaux [shahm-POE] (about 1070–1121), the most revered teacher in the cathedral school of Paris. Dissatisfied with what he was hearing, Abelard began his own lecture series. He quickly became the sensation of Paris and his words found eager listeners. A master logician, Abelard demolished William's arguments and drove his rival into a monastery.

What divided Abelard and William of Champeaux was the problem of universals, the supreme intellectual issue between 1050 and 1150. This controversy revolved around the question of whether or not universals, or general concepts, such as "human being" and "church," truly exist. At stake in this dispute between the two schools of thought, known as **Realism** and **Nominalism,** were basic Christian ideas, such as whether Jesus' sacrifice had removed the stain of original sin from each individual. The Realists, following Plato, reasoned that universals do exist independently of physical objects and the human mind. Hence, "humanity," for example, is constantly present in every individual. In opposition, the Nominalists denied the existence of universals and claimed that only particular objects and events are real. Hence, "church" and "human being" exist only in particular instances.

In these debates, Abelard showed that William of Champeaux's extreme Realism denied human individuality and was thus inconsistent with church teachings. For his part, Abelard taught a moderate Realism that held that the universals existed, but only as mental words, and hence could be used as an intellectual convenience. Later in the century, when new translations of Aristotle became available, thinkers discovered that Abelard and the Greek genius agreed about universals, a discovery that further enhanced Abelard's fame. In the next century, Abelard's moderate Realism was adopted by Thomas Aquinas, the greatest mind of the High Middle Ages.

The Rise of the Universities   After 1100 a period of cultural ferment erupted that brought forth some of the finest achievements of medieval times, including the founding of the universities. By 1200 conditions were ripe for the rise of universities at Bologna, Paris, and Oxford, the first Western schools of higher education since the sixth century. Unlike the ancient universities in Athens and Alexandria, these medieval institutions were organized into self-governing corporations with charters. A century later, similar centers of learning were springing up elsewhere in Italy, France, and England, as well as in Spain, Portugal, and Germany. The University of Paris was the most celebrated institution of advanced learning during the High Middle Ages. Divided into faculties by specialization, it awarded degrees in civil law and canon law, medicine, theology, and the liberal arts. The liberal arts degree was basically devoted to mastering the new translations of Aristotle. Other universities taught a similar curriculum, but their faculties lacked the international renown of the Parisian professors.

Intellectual Controversy and Thomas Aquinas   More and more of Aristotle's works became available in the late twelfth and early thirteenth centuries. Between 1150 and 1200, a few hardy Christian scholars traveled to remote centers of learning, such as Muslim Sicily and Toledo, Spain, to meet Islamic and Jewish scholars and study Aristotle's writings. There they learned Arabic and translated the Greek and Arabic philosophical and scientific works into Latin, the form in which they entered the mainstream of European medieval thought.

At the University of Paris, the introduction of these improved and more complete versions divided the intellectual community. On one side was the theological faculty, who welcomed the Arabic writings but wanted to reconcile them to Christian thinking. Arrayed against them were the members of the arts faculty, who advocated that reason be fully divorced from faith or, in other words, that philosophy be separated from theology. The leaders of the arts faculty were called Latin Averroists because they claimed inspiration from the Arabic philosopher Ibn Rushd [ib-uhn RUSHT], known in the West as Averroës [uh-VER-uh-weez] (see Chapter 8).

Faced with the skeptical Latin Averroists, the Parisian theologians devised two ways to relate the new learning to orthodox beliefs. The more traditional view was set forth by Bonaventure [bahn-uh-VEN-chur] (1221–1274), who was later made a saint. Denying that knowledge was possible apart from God's grace, Bonaventure, following Augustine's mode of reasoning, argued that truth had to begin in the supernatural world and thus could not arise in the senses, as Aristotle had argued. A new and brilliant theological view, and the one that carried the day, was set forth by Thomas Aquinas [uh-KWI-nus] (1226–1274), a Dominican friar who taught at Paris from 1252 to 1259 and again from 1269 to 1272. Within a generation of his death, he was made a saint, and six hundred years later, in 1874, the papacy declared his thought the official basis of Roman Catholic beliefs. Avoiding the pure rationalism of the Latin Averroists and the timidity of Bonaventure, Thomas Aquinas steered a middle path, or *via media,* which gave Aristotle a central role in his theology while honoring traditional Christian beliefs. Known as Thomism, this theological system in its complex design and sheer elegance remains one of the outstanding achievements of the High Middle Ages.

Of Thomas Aquinas's two monumental *Summas*—comprehensive summaries of Christian thought—the *Summa Theologica* is his masterpiece. In this work, he showed that God had given human beings two divine paths to truth: reason and faith. Following Aristotle, he made the senses the only source for human knowledge—a bold step that sharpened the difference between reason and faith. At the same time, Thomism escaped the strict rationalism of the Latin Averroists by denying that philosophy, or reason, could answer all theological questions. Aquinas claimed that reason based on sensory knowledge could prove certain truths, such as the notions that God exists and that the soul exists, but that reason had limits and that faith was necessary for those truths that were beyond sensory proof, such as the beliefs in the soul's immortality and the holy Trinity.

Thomas Aquinas's contributions to medieval thought extended beyond theology into political and economic matters. He saw the secular state as a natural and necessary support to human life. For Aquinas, politics had an ethical root, and this allowed him to write about everyday life in his *Summas*. For example, he reasoned that church law should be used to regulate economic behavior, putting controls on usury (the practice of charging exorbitant interest) and setting a just price for consumer goods.

Aquinas and the other theologians of the High Middle Ages held differing views on a number of subjects, but all shared a confidence in human reason and its ability to comprehend the world. Even though the role of reason was carefully circumscribed and often had to give way to revelation, there was still a genuine rationalist tradition during this period—one that originated in ancient Greece, was transmitted into Renaissance thought, and finally helped to bring about the Scientific Revolution that inaugurated modern times.

Literature

Beyond the rarefied atmosphere of scholastic thought, writing was finding its own way. The literature of the High Middle Ages falls naturally into two chronological parts, with the dividing line at about 1150. The first half, which coincides with Romanesque art, perpetuates the feudal and monastic values of the Early Middle Ages. The second half, which parallels the Gothic style, introduces urban and courtly themes while moving away from the world of the monasteries.

Monastic and Feudal Writing Between 1000 and 1150, most authors were monks, writing in Latin and imitating late Roman literary models such as hymns, sermons, lives of the saints, and historical chronicles. Perhaps most distinctive was the Latin lyric poetry composed during this time, which has been called the best literary work of the Latin-speaking Middle Ages. These poems were rich in metric subtleties, extremely learned in content, and filled with Classical and Christian allusions. Some of the poets have been identified as **goliards,** or roaming scholars, but most were probably clerics. Addressing an audience of church intellectuals, these poets often wrote on religious and moral topics. They also wrote lighthearted love poems, however, which appear to have had a wider audience and whose themes certainly appealed to more secular interests. Even though the love poems sang of carnal

Figure 9.9 Charlemagne Panels. Ca. 1220–1225. Stained-glass window, Chartres cathedral. Chartres, France. *The Song of Roland was so well known and well loved that scenes from the poem were depicted in the stained-glass windows of Chartres cathedral, constructed in the thirteenth century. Even though the Charlemagne panels were inspired by a secular poem, they were situated in the ambulatory behind the main altar, one of the cathedral's most sacred areas. In one scene, Charlemagne is shown arriving too late to save Roland's life. Other panels depict him donating a church and traveling to Constantinople.*

pleasure, these verses were not personal, nor were the poets' erotic yearnings directed toward real women.

While the monks sang of love in Latin, lay poets at the feudal courts of northern France were developing a new literary genre, the **chanson de geste,** or song of brave deeds. Written in the **vernacular,** or popular, spoken language, the *chansons de geste* chiefly honored the heroic adventures of warriors who had lived in France under Charlemagne and his heirs. These medieval epics often memorialized a minor battle or, more rarely, even a defeat. They took Christian values for granted, but supernatural and magical elements were commonly a part of their plots. Of the many *chansons de geste*, the masterpiece is the *Song of Roland*, which became the standard for the genre (Figure 9.9).

Much of the *Song of Roland* was passed down orally for three hundred years, and it did not reach its final written form until about 1100. The narrative claims to be based on a historical event, telling of the destruction of a troop of Frankish warriors led by Count Roland, one of Charlemagne's vassals, and of Charlemagne's revenge for this massacre. Superimposed on this supposedly Carolingian tale are the later values of the High Middle Ages, such as chivalry, militant Christianity, and primitive nationalism. For example, Roland and his men obey the chivalric code, showing devotion to their ruler, to God, and to their personal honor—an ideal unknown in Charlemagne's day. Likewise, the religious zeal of Charlemagne's army against the Spanish Muslims probably derived from the First Crusade in 1095; indeed, modern scholars have shown that Charlemagne's actual enemies in Spain were Christians. Finally, this poem portrayed the Franks as ready to die for "sweet France," a sentiment that would have been incomprehensible to Charlemagne but that was encouraged by the twelfth-century French kings who used the popular *Song of Roland* to further their political ambitions.

Vernacular and Courtly Writing   Between 1150 and 1300, Latin continued to be the dominant language in the universities, but elsewhere lay writers, composing in the vernacular, were beginning to win new audiences and to develop new genres.

For example, inspired by Latin lyric verse, vernacular lyric poetry began to appear in the eleventh century in the Provençal tongue of southern France. This vernacular poetry reached its zenith in the next two centuries. Its supreme expression was the **canzone,** or love poem, the ancestor of all later Western love poetry. At the educated feudal courts of southern France, professional **minstrels,** or entertainers, sang the songs before the assembled court; the poems' composers—called **troubadors**—were often local nobles. Addressed to court ladies whose identities were thinly disguised in the poem, these troubador songs made devotion to a highborn woman the passionate ideal of the chivalrous knight. In the mature Provençal lyrics, adulterous passion was the central theme, and women were idolized and made the masters over men. Where previously adoration had been reserved for God, the troubadour lyrics now celebrated the worship of women.

As the influence of Provençal poetry spread, the status of women in Western literature was revolutionized, a development paralleled in the church, where the cult of the Virgin Mary was beginning to flourish. However, most real-life medieval women were unaffected by these literary and religious changes; their happiness depended on submitting to the limited roles that the masculine society allowed them to fill. After 1400, though, these cultural changes encouraged upperclass women to play a more prominent role in society, as hostesses and as arbiters of social decorum.

After 1150 courtly **romances** quickly replaced the feudal *chansons de geste* in popularity. The romances were long narratives of the chivalric and sentimental adventures of knights and ladies. The name *romance* arose from the mistaken belief that the medieval authors were imitating a Roman literary form. Their subjects derived from stories of ancient Troy and Celtic legends from the British Isles, the most enduring of which proved to be the Celtic stories of King Arthur and his knights of the Round Table.

The first poet to make Arthur and his court his subject was Chrétien de Troyes [KRAY-tyan du-TRWAH], whose versions set the standard for later romances. Chrétien (about 1148–about 1190) wrote his romances for the feudal courts of northern France. His treatment of the adulterous love of the knight Lancelot and Arthur's queen, Guinevere, is characteristic of the way romances combined aristocratic, courtly, and religious themes. In this version, Lancelot rescues Queen Guinevere after experiencing many adventures and personal humiliations for her sake; this humbling of Lancelot is necessary to teach him to love Guinevere with unquestioning obedience.

A curiosity for modern readers is that Chrétien identifies Lancelot with Christ, so that many episodes echo scenes of Jesus' suffering and death. Although the work avoids sacrilege, the net effect is unsettling in its mixing of the sacred with the profane. Chrétien describes Lancelot and Guinevere's passion without judging their behavior. Such moral neutrality was unacceptable to other Christian writers, who believed adultery to be a deadly sin. In an English prose version of this tale—Thomas Malory's *Le Morte d'Arthur,* published in 1485—the lovers are blamed for the collapse of Arthur's court. Perhaps because today's world tends to agree with Malory's more judgmental view, his story of Lancelot is the one better known now.

Another literary genre that flourished simultaneously with the romance was the **lay** (French, *lai*), a short lyric or narrative poem meant to be sung to the accompaniment of an instrument such as a harp. The oldest lays are the twelve surviving by Marie de France (fl. about 1170), a poet from Brittany who lived most of her life in England. Based on Celtic legends, including those of Lancelot, Marie de France's lays were stories of courtly love, often adulterous (for instance, a young wife kept under close watch by a jealous old husband), usually faced with conflict, always with a moral lesson. Writing in Old French, de France addressed the French-speaking nobility of post–Norman Conquest England, an audience that may have included King Henry II and Queen Eleanor of Aquitaine. De France's lays, along with her fables and other works, were part of the outpouring of writing in the twelfth century that made Old French the most influential literature in Europe until the rise of Italian literature in the age of Dante Alighieri.

Dante   Vernacular writing appeared late in Italy; not until the thirteenth century did Italian poetry begin to emerge. But, despite its later start, Italy had brought forth by 1300 the greatest literary figure of the High Middle Ages, Dante Alighieri [DAHN-tay ahl-egg-YEH-ree] (1265–1321). A native of Florence, in the province of Tuscany, Dante was the first of a proud tradition that soon made the Tuscan dialect the standard literary speech of Italy.

Born into a minor aristocratic family, Dante was given an excellent education with a thorough grounding in both Greco-Roman and Christian classics. Attracted to the values of ancient Rome, he combined a career in public office with the life of an intellectual—a tradition of civic duty inherited from the ancient Roman republic. When Dante's political allies fell from office in 1301, he was exiled from Florence for the rest of his life. During these years, poor and wandering about Italy, he composed the *Commedia,* or *Comedy,* which stands as the culmination of the literature of the Middle Ages. The *Comedy's* sublime qualities were immediately recognized, and soon its admirers attached the epithet "divine" to Dante's masterpiece.

Divided into three book-length parts, the *Divine Comedy* narrates Dante's fictional travels through three realms of the Christian afterlife. Led first by the ghost of Vergil, the ancient Roman poet, Dante descends into hell, where he hears from the damned the nature of their various crimes against God and the moral law. Vergil next leads Dante into purgatory, where the lesser sinners expiate their guilt while awaiting the joys of heaven. At a fixed spot in purgatory, Vergil is forced to relinquish his role to Beatrice, a young Florentine woman and Dante's symbol of the eternal female. With Beatrice's guidance, Dante enters paradise and even has a vision of the almighty God.

The majestic complexity of Dante's monumental poem, however, can scarcely be conveyed by this simple synopsis. Written as an allegory, the *Divine Comedy* was meant to be understood on several levels. Read literally, the poem bears witness to the author's personal fears as a moral sinner yet affirms his hope for eternal salvation. Read allegorically, the poem represents a comprehensive synthesis of the opposing tendencies that characterized medieval culture, such as balancing the Classical with the Christian, Aristotle with Aquinas, the ancient with the new, the proud with the humble, and the secular with the spiritual.

Of the great cultural symbols that abound in the *Divine Comedy,* the richest in meaning are the central figures of Vergil and Beatrice, who represent human reason and divine revelation, respectively. In the poem, Vergil is made inferior to Beatrice, thus revealing Dante's acceptance of a basic idea of Thomas Aquinas—reason can lead only to awareness of sin; revelation is necessary to reach God's ultimate truth. Besides this fundamental Christian belief, the two figures convey other meanings. Vergil stands for Classical civilization and the secular literary life; Beatrice (Italian for "blessing") symbolizes spiritualized love and Christianized culture. By turning Beatrice into an image of God's grace, Dante revealed that the High Middle Ages were open to new symbols of Christian truth. (By the time of the Catholic Counter-Reformation in the sixteenth century, however, Dante's image was considered blasphemous and was censured by religious critics.)

Dante's spiritual odyssey is set during the season of Easter. The poet's journey through hell coincided with Jesus' descent into hell on Good Friday, and Dante's ascent up the Mount of Purgatory happens at Easter dawn—the time of Jesus' resurrection; the visit to heaven occupies the rest of Easter week. Thus Dante's allegory has the religious aim of forcing his readers to meditate on the fate of their own immortal souls.

Dante's vision of the afterlife underscored his belief that humans have free will. Predestination had no place in his system, as his picture of hell shows. With one exception, all of the damned earned their fate by their deeds on earth. Excepted were the people consigned to Limbo—the pious pagans who lived before Jesus and thus were denied his message of hope. Moreover, those in Limbo, such as Aristotle and Plato, were not subjected to any punishment other than being removed from God's presence.

The intricate structure of Dante's massive poem owes much to numerology, a pseudoscience of numbers that absorbed the medieval mind. The numbers three and nine, for example, occur prominently in the *Divine Comedy.* Three is a common symbol of the Christian Trinity (the union of the Father, the Son, and the Holy Ghost in one God), and the poem is written in a three-line verse form called **terza rima** (an interlocking rhyme scheme in three-line stanzas, as *aba, bcb, cdc, ded,* and so on, ending in a rhyming couplet), which was Dante's invention. The other number, nine, symbolizes the Trinity squared. More important, Dante identified the number nine with the dead Beatrice, whose soul lived on in the ninth heaven, the one nearest to God. He also divides hell, purgatory, and paradise into nine sections each.

Despite its allegorical and theological features, the *Divine Comedy* is a deeply personal poem. Dante rewards and punishes his Florentine friends and foes by the location that he assigns each in the afterlife. He also reveals his private feelings as he enters into discussions with various saints and sinners along the way. Beyond his desire for salvation, his most cherished idea is to bring about a harmony between the church and the secular state on earth.

Figure 9.10 Scenes from the Life of Christ. Detail. Ca. 1150–1170. Stained-glass windows, each panel: 40⅛" wide × 41⅓" high. West facade. Chartres cathedral. *The stained-glass windows of Chartres cathedral are renowned as the most beautiful examples of this craft to survive from the Gothic period. Of Chartres's windows, those in the west facade have been much praised for the brilliant effects created by their jewel tones of red, blue, and gold, as well as white, with small areas of green and lemon yellow. Taken from the central window of the west facade, this detail shows eighteen of its twenty-four panels, treating the life of Christ. Visible in the detail are panels depicting the annunciation (bottom left row), the visit of the three wise men (left and right, third row from bottom), and the flight into Egypt (left and right, sixth row from bottom). In the design, square panels alternate with roundel forms to frame each scene; red is the ground color for the squares and blue for the roundels. The windows can be awe-inspiring, as in the reaction of the scholar Henry Adams, who described the cathedral's interior as a "delirium of coloured light."*

Architecture and Art

Just as scholars and writers devoted their efforts to exploring religious concerns and Christian values, artists, artisans, and architects channeled their talents into glorifying the Christian house of worship. Because the dominating physical presence of the church made it a ubiquitous symbol in both the countryside and the towns, architecture ranked higher than the other

arts in medieval life. Indeed, the arts lacked an independent status, for they were regarded as mere auxiliary sources of church decoration—wall paintings, statues, and **stained-glass** windows, most of which portrayed saints and biblical heroes (Figure 9.10). In this respect, these art forms conformed to the church's teaching that the purpose of art was to represent Christian truth.

Even though the church dominated art and architecture, it did not prevent architects and artists from experimenting. In about 1000 an international style called the **Romanesque** emerged. The first in a succession of uniform styles to sweep over Europe, the Romanesque was carried along by the monastic revival until about 1200. But by 1150 the **Gothic** style was developing in Paris; it was to become the reigning style of the towns for the remainder of the Middle Ages, succumbing finally to Renaissance fashion in about 1500.

Romanesque Churches and Related Arts The Romanesque style, though based on the architectural language of ancient Rome, was not a pure Roman style but embraced elements inspired by Christianity, along with innovations made by builders, between 1000 and 1200. From Roman architecture, Romanesque builders adapted the basilica plan, rounded arches, vaulted ceilings, and columns for both support and decoration (see Figure 7.8). Inspired by Christian beliefs, they pointed the basilicas toward Jerusalem in the east and curved each building's eastern end into an apse to house the altar. A transept, or crossing arm, was added at the church's eastern end to convert the floor plan into a cruciform shape to symbolize the cross (Figure 9.11). Other Christian beliefs dictated such practices as having three doorways in the western façade—to symbolize the Trinity—and building the baptistery apart from the church to keep the unbaptized out of sacred space. To Roman and Christian elements, Romanesque builders added innovative design features, vaulting techniques, and a wealth of ornamental detail, to create the most expressive and disciplined architectural style since the fall of Rome.

A representative Romanesque church is difficult to identify today for various reasons. Most original structures have been altered significantly over the years, and, of those that were not updated, many have been destroyed or fallen into ruins. The style itself, in its origin, allowed for great diversity and experiment, which reflected the taste of different regions, communities, and patrons; the types of stone available for building; and the knowledge and historical awareness of the master builders and their workshops. The style was also felt at all levels of society, underscoring the

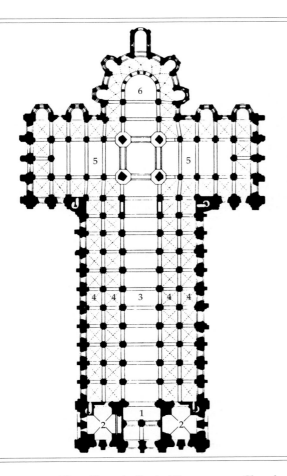

Figure 9.11 Floor Plan of a Typical Romanesque Church. *This floor plan identifies the characteristic features of a Romanesque church with its cruciform floor plan: (1) narthex, (2) towers, (3) nave, (4) side aisles, (5) transept, and (6) apse.*

Figure 9.12 Santa Cruz de la Seros (Aragon), church of San Caprasio, Spain. View from the north. Last quarter of the eleventh century. *This church, though simple in the extreme, embodies the basic elements of the First Romanesque style. These elements include stone rubble walls, which have not been faced; a small number of windows; a flat, wooden roof; and both Lombard bands and Lombard arcades.*

long reach of the church's arms into people's lives, ranging from simple parish churches and sumptuous urban cathedrals to both large and small monastic churches and vast pilgrimage churches.

Within this diversity, two stages of development can be identified: the First Romanesque, about 1000–1080, and the Second Romanesque, 1080–1200.

The **First Romanesque** style originated along the Mediterranean, in the zone ranging from Dalmatia (modern Croatia), across Northern Italy and Provence (Southern France), to Catalonia (Northeast Spain). Simple in design, the First Romanesque churches were built of stone rubble, a Roman technique, and covered with flat, wooden roofs. With high walls and few windows, they resembled fortresses, a trait that came to characterize both Romanesque styles. The defining exterior features of the First Romanesque churches were a web of vertical bands or buttresses along the sides and a sequence of small arcades below the eaves (Figure 9.12). Because these features may have been born in Lombardy (North Central Italy), they are usually called *Lombard bands* and *Lombard arcades*. Later builders experimented with the Lombard bands and arcades, cre-

ating spectacular churches, such as the Speyer Cathedral in Germany (Figure 9.13). At Speyer, Lombard bands establish a rhythmic, vertical sequence on the walls of the apse. And variations on the Lombard arcade form include, on the lower part of the apse, the elongated, relatively windowless arcade attached to the wall; on the top part of the apse, the open, or "dwarf," arcaded gallery; and, on the wall above the apse, the arched niches arranged in stairstep fashion and the line of Lombard arches below the roofline.

The **Second Romanesque** style is associated with the Cluniac monastic order because the order's mother church at Cluny—Cluny III, founded 1088, the third church built on this site—in eastern France was constructed in this style. Cluny III, though destroyed in the 1800s, was greatly admired in its day for its vast scale, including double transepts and crossing towers, towers at the ends of the transepts, a double-aisled nave covered with a barrel vault, and a rich decorative program of religious art, both inside and out. The spectacular success of the Cluniac movement in the eleventh and twelfth centuries led to the spread of the Second Romanesque style over the map of Europe (Figure 9.14). In appearance, this style reflected both the needs of the monastic communities and the physical

Figure 9.13 Speyer Cathedral. View from the east. Speyer, Germany. Begun about 1030, completed before 1150. *Speyer Cathedral, whose massive size rivals that of the great mother church at Cluny, the home of the Cluniac order of monks, represents the climax of the First Romanesque, the first phase of Romanesque style.*

Figure 9.14 Basilica of Sacre-Coeur, Formerly Abbey Church of the Virgin and St. John the Baptist, Paray-le-Monial, France, View of nave, looking east. Begun 1110s–1120s, completed mid–twelfth century. Nave height approx. 147' 7½"; length approx. 72' 2⅛". *The monastery at Paray-le-Monial became part of the Cluniac system in 999. Tradition links St. Hugh, Abbot of Cluny (1049–1109), with the building of the Paray-le-Monial basilica. As head of the Cluniac order, Hugh commissioned Paray to be a scaled-down version of the great mother church, Cluny III. It replicates Cluny III's vaulting techniques, using barrel vaults in the nave and groin vaults in the aisles, combined with pointed arches—derived from Muslim architecture. (The pointed arches used at Cluny III and Paray-le-Monial were not related to the development of Gothic-style architecture.) As in Cluny III, the east end culminates in a semicircular arcade resting on slender columns. The nave, consisting of only three vaulted sections, is markedly shorter than Cluny III's nave, reflecting the lack of pageantry associated with the small monastic community at Paray-le-Monial.*

demands created by the unsettled conditions of the times. These churches were richly decorated and earth hugging, with massive walls and few windows, though more and larger windows than in the First Romanesque. They looked like the spiritual fortresses that they indeed were.

Many Second Romanesque churches were pilgrimage churches—destinations for pilgrims traveling vast distances to see and venerate holy relics, very often the supposed bones of saints. The foremost pilgrimage churches included ambulatories, or semicircular or polygonal aisles behind the apse, to accommodate the expected hordes of religious tourists.

A celebrated pilgrimage church in the Second Romanesque style is Sainte-Marie-Madeleine in Vézelay, France. Attached to a Cluniac convent, this church attracted penitents eager to view the bones of Mary Magdalene. Vézelay's builders followed a basilica design with a cruciform floor plan. Inside, the most striking feature is the nearly 200-foot-long nave, which could hold a large number of pilgrims as well as allow religious processions (Figure 9.15). Typical of Romanesque architecture, the nave is divided into sections called **bays.** Each bay is framed by a pair of rounded arches constructed

from blocks of local pink and grey stones. These colors alternate in the overhead arches and create a dazzling effect for which this church is famous. The ceiling of each bay is a groin vault—a Roman building technique. The support system for the tall nave walls—an arcade, or series of arches resting on clusters of columns—was also taken from Roman architecture. Vézelay's builders used

Figure 9.15 View of nave, looking east. Church of Sainte-Marie-Madeleine, Vézelay, France. Ca. 1089–1206. *Vézelay's nave was made unusually long so that religious pilgrims might make solemn processions along its length. A reliquary, or an area for displaying holy relics, was later set aside in the choir. Within the choir, the design of the ambulatory provided ample space for masses of pilgrims to view all the relics at one time.*

Figure 9.16 *Jacob Wrestling with the Angel.* Decorated column capital. Church of Sainte-Marie-Madeleine, Vézelay, France. Ca. 1089–1206. *The Vézelay capitals survive in near-immaculate condition. Late medieval moralists considered their vivacity and gaiety inappropriate in God's house, and the offending sculptures were plastered over. When they were uncovered during a nineteenth-century restoration of the church's interior, the capitals were revealed in their charming originality.*

sculpture to provide "sermons in stone" for illiterate visitors. Symbolic rather than idealistic, the Romanesque figures were designed to convey religious meanings. For example, instead of copying the ancient Greco-Roman columns, the artisans created their own style of decorated column. The capitals, or tops, of the interior columns are sculptured with religious scenes and motifs, such as one that shows Jacob, one of the Hebrew patriarchs (on the left), wrestling with the angel (Figure 9.16). The angel, clutching his robe in his left hand, raises his right hand to bless Jacob. The simple figures with their dramatic gestures and expressive faces accurately convey the message in Genesis (32:24–30) that Jacob has been chosen by God to lead the Hebrew people. The art is typically Romanesque: The feet point downward, the limbs are placed in angular positions, and the drapery folds are depicted in a stylized manner.

A more mature Romanesque style appears in the carvings on the **tympanum** over the south portal of the tower porch at Moissac, one of the two remaining elements of the twelfth-century abbey church that once stood here. The other surviving element is a cloister, a covered arcade surrounding a quadrangle, which originally connected the church to the monastic community. Although a subject of controversy, the tympanum carvings probably depict a vision of the Christian apocalypse, much of which is based on the Book of Revelation (Figure 9.17). Jesus is portrayed in glory, indicated by the cross-shaped nimbus behind his head and the oval in which he sits enthroned, and wearing a crown. Surrounding him are the four evangelist symbols, namely, Man (Matthew), winged lion (Mark), winged bull (Luke), and eagle (John), and the twenty-four Elders listed in Revelation 4. The Elders hold cups and musical instruments as described in Revelation 5. This tympanum sculpture served as a warning about life's ultimate end to those who passed through the south portal.

Besides church building and church decoration, the Romanesque style was used in manuscript illumination. Originated in late Rome and developed in the

Figure 9.17 *Christ in Glory with Four Evangelist Symbols and the Twenty-Four Elders.* Tympanum over south portal. Church of St. Pierre, Moissac, France. Ca. 1125. *The jam-packed imagery in this tympanum and surrounding space is typical of the allover patterns used in the Romanesque style. Nevertheless, there is artistic order here. Stylized floral forms are aligned rhythmically along the lintel and around the tympanum frame, and human and animal shapes encircle the seated Jesus, who is rendered four times larger than the Elders. The tympanum itself is divided into three zones by the horizontal lines of clouds below Jesus' feet and above the second row of Elders.*

Early Middle Ages, this art remained a cloistered activity in this age of monasticism (see Chapter 7). Perhaps only cloistered painters had the leisure to pursue this painstaking skill. During the High Middle Ages, new local styles arose, inspired by regional tastes and by a knowledge of Byzantine painting brought from the East by Crusaders. The English monks probably developed the finest of these local styles.

The Bury Bible, painted at Bury St. Edmunds monastery, reflects an English taste that is calmer and less exuberant than Continental styles. Two panels from the Bury manuscript, set off by a border of highly colored foliage, show an episode in Moses' life (Figure 9.18). Borrowings from Byzantine art may be detected in the elongated figures, the large eyes, the flowing hair, and the hanging draperies. The naturalness of these scenes presented a vivid contrast with the spirited agitation of French Romanesque art.

Gothic Churches and Related Arts The word *Gothic* was invented by later Renaissance scholars who preferred Greco-Roman styles. They despised medieval architecture, labeling it *Goth-ic*—meaning a barbaric creation of the Goths, or the Germanic peoples. Modern research, however, has shown that this Renaissance view is false. In fact, the Gothic grew out of the Romanesque and was not a German art. Nevertheless, the term *Gothic* is still used today, although its negative connotation has long since been discarded.

Gothic architecture sprang from the religious revival of the twelfth century, when the clergy wanted to bring God's presence more tangibly to their urban congregations. As a result, clerics began to demand taller churches with more windows than were available in the relatively dark Romanesque churches. To the medieval mind, height and light were symbols of the divine. Another impetus behind the Gothic was the rise of the middle class, who wanted churches that reflected their growing economic power. Thus spiritual and economic forces were united in pushing architects to seek a new kind of architecture.

Two problems with the Romanesque stood in the way: The groin vaults were so heavy that the nearly windowless walls had to be extremely thick to support their great weight, and the rounded arches limited the building's height to less than 100 feet. During the early twelfth century, builders constantly sought solutions to these problems.

Eventually, between 1137 and 1144, the Gothic style was created by Suger [sue-ZHAY] (about 1081–1151), the abbot of the royal Abbey Church of St. Denis, near Paris, and an adviser to the French kings. Suger's approach to architecture grew out of his religious faith, as in his words, "Through the beauty of material things we come to understand God." The brilliant innovation employed by Suger and the architects and artisans he

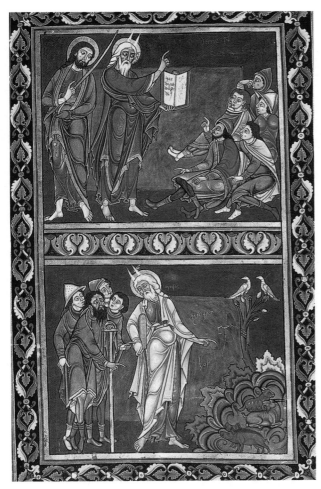

Figure 9.18 *Moses Expounding the Law of the Unclean Beasts.* The Bury Bible. 1130–1140. Approx. 20 × 14″. Bury St. Edmunds, England. Master and Fellows of Corpus Christi College, Cambridge. *These panels depict Moses delivering the dietary laws to the ancient Hebrews. The responses of his audience reveal the sure hand of the artist, known only as Master Hugo. For example, in the upper panel one figure pulls at his nose, while a nearby companion looks skeptical. Moses' head is depicted with horns, which reflected a biblical mistranslation of the term for the radiance that surrounded him after receiving God's law.*

Figure 9.19 Principal Features of a Typical Gothic Church. *In this schematic drawing, the features are numbered from the nave outward: (1) nave arcade, (2) pointed arch, (3) vault, (4) clerestory, (5) flying buttress, (6) buttress, and (7) gargoyle.*

hired was to change the vaulting problem from one of weight to one of stress. First, they replaced the groin vault with a **ribbed vault;** this step allowed lighter materials to be placed between the stone ribs, thus reducing the weight. Next, they abandoned the rounded arch in favor of the Muslim pointed arch. The combination of pointed arch and ribbed vault permitted an increase in the building's height as well as a rechanneling of the ceiling's stresses downward and outward to huge **piers** internally and, in later buildings, to **flying buttresses** externally, which formed a bridge between the upper nave walls and the nearby tall pillars (Figure 9.19). With the support skeleton transferred to the building's exterior, the builders could easily insert stained-glass windows into the non-weight-bearing walls.

The glory of the Gothic church—the **choir**—was all that remained to be built. The plan and inspiration for the choir (the part of the church where the service was sung) were the pilgrimage churches, such as Vézelay, that had enlarged their apses to accommodate religious tourists. In Suger's skillful hands, the east end of St. Denis was now elaborated into an oval-shaped area—the choir—ringed with several small chapels (Figure 9.20). At the heart of the choir was the apse, now arcaded; a spacious ambulatory area divided the apse from the chapels (Figure 9.21).

St. Denis gave only a foretaste of the triumphant art that was called Gothic. Between 1145 and 1500, the Gothic style presented an overwhelming image of God's majesty and the power of the church. A Gothic exterior carried the eye heavenward by impressive vertical spires. A Gothic interior surrounded the daytime

Figure 9.20   Ambulatory. Church of St. Denis, Paris. Ca. 1145. *This view of the choir of St. Denis shows a portion of the ambulatory that allowed pilgrims to view the chapels in the apse. The evenly spaced support columns and the pointed arches create this flowing, curved space. The ribbed arches in the ceiling are also central to the Gothic skeletal construction.*

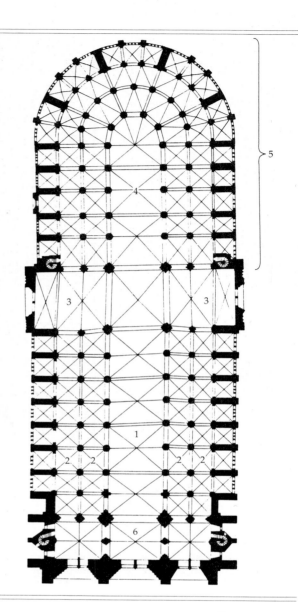

Figure 9.22   Floor Plan of Notre Dame. Paris. 1163–ca. 1250. *This drawing shows the principal features of Notre Dame cathedral: (1) nave, (2) aisle, (3) transept, (4) apse, (5) choir, and (6) narthex, or vestibule.*

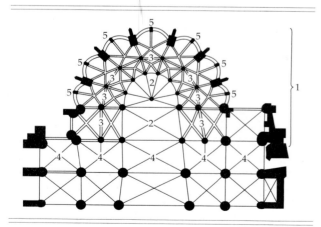

Figure 9.21   Floor Plan, Ambulatory. Church of St. Denis, Paris. Ca. 1145. *This floor plan, based on a similar design used in the pilgrimage churches, became the basis for the reordering of interior space in the Gothic choirs. The features include (1) choir, (2) apse, (3) ambulatory, (4) transept, and (5) chapel.*

worshiper with colored, celestial light; the soaring nave ceiling, sometimes rising to more than 150 feet, was calculated to stir the soul. In its total physicality the Gothic church stood as a towering symbol of the medieval obsession with the divine.

During the High Middle Ages, the Gothic style went through two stages, the Early and the High. The Early Gothic style lasted until 1194 and was best represented by Notre Dame cathedral in Paris. The High Gothic style flourished until 1300 and reached perfection in the cathedral at Amiens, France.

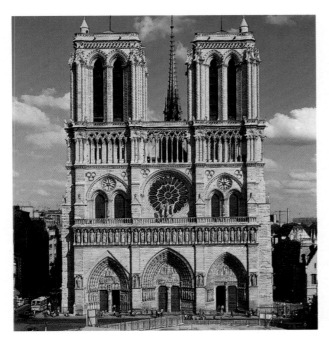

Figure 9.23 Western Facade. Notre Dame. Paris. 1220–1250. *In the gallery above the western portals are twenty-eight images of the kings of Judah, including David and Solomon. These sculptures, which are typical of Gothic churches, are more than decorations: They are reminders that Mary and Jesus were descended from royalty. In the medieval mind, this religious idea was meant to buttress the monarchical style of government.*

EARLY GOTHIC STYLE, 1145–1194 The cathedral of Notre Dame ("Our Lady," the Virgin Mary) in Paris made popular the Early Gothic style, making it a fashion for other cities and towns. Begun in 1163, the cathedral was the most monumental work erected in the West to that time. Its floor plan was cruciform, but the length of the transept barely exceeded the width of the aisle walls (Figure 9.22).

Part of Notre Dame's beauty stems from the rational principles applied by the builders, notably the ideal of harmony, best expressed in the integration of sculpture and decorative details with building units. For instance, the west facade is divided into three equal horizontal bands: the three doorways, the **rose window** and **blind arcades,** and the two towers (Figure 9.23). Within each subdivision of this facade, figurative sculpture or architectural details play a harmonizing role, from the rows of saints flanking each of the portals to the **gargoyles,** or grotesque demons, peering down from the towers.

Inside Notre Dame, the spectacular nave reveals the awe-inspiring effects of Early Gothic art at its best (Figure 9.24). The strong vertical lines and the airy atmosphere represent the essence of this taste. With its ribbed vaults and pointed arches, the nave rises to a height of 115 feet from the pavement to the roof. Like the harmonious west facade, the nave is divided into three equal tiers: the nave and double aisles, the open spectator **gallery** above the aisles,

Figure 9.24 Nave. Notre Dame. Paris. View from the height of the western rose window. 1180–1250. Ht. floor to summit of roof 115′. *The nave is clearly not aligned properly. The choir bends perceptibly to the north, which probably reflected the different building times for various parts of the cathedral. The transept and the choir were finished first, after which the nave and the double aisles were added. The western facade was completed last.*

and, at the top, the clerestory, as the window area is called.

Notre Dame reveals that the choir was coming to dominate the entire Early Gothic church. Notre Dame's choir is almost as long as the nave, so that the transept virtually divides the church into two halves. At first, the choir's walls had no special external supports, but as cracks began to appear in the choir's walls during the thirteenth century, flying buttresses were added to ensure greater stability—a feature that would later characterize High Gothic churches (Figure 9.25).

The Gothic sculptures that decorate Notre Dame differ from the exuberant Romanesque style. The Romanesque's animated images of Jesus have given way to the Gothic's more sober figures. In addition, the

Figure 9.25 Notre Dame. Paris. View from the east. 1163–1182. *Notre Dame's choir, shown on the right, was originally built without chapels and flying buttresses—a sign of its Early Gothic origins. Paris's greatest church caught up with the High Gothic style in the fourteenth century, when these architectural features were added.*

Gothic figures are modeled in three dimensions, and their draperies fall in natural folds (Figure 9.26). At the same time, the rise of the cult of the Virgin meant an increased number of images of Mary as well as of female saints. The name "Notre Dame" itself testifies to the appeal of the Virgin cult. Despite these visual differences, however, the Gothic remained true to the symbolic purposes of Romanesque art.

Before Notre Dame was finished, its architects began to move in new directions, refining the traditional features into a new style, called **Rayonnant,** or Radiant. In the Rayonnant style, the solid walls gave way to sheets of stained glass framed by elegant **traceries,** or rich ornamentation, of stone. This radiant effect was especially evident in the north transept facade, which was rebuilt in this new style. With the addition of this transept's imposing rose window, designed to suggest the rays of the sun, the cathedral's interior was bathed in constantly shifting colors, giving it a mystical atmosphere (Figure 9.27).

Figure 9.26 *The Last Judgment.* Central portal, west facade. Notre Dame, Paris. Ca. 1210. *This tympanum represents Jesus enthroned and presiding over the Last Judgment. Surrounding him are the apostles, the prophets, the church fathers, and the saints—arranged in descending order of their importance in relation to Jesus. Like all the sculptures of Notre Dame's first story, the entire scene was gilded with gold paint until the mid–fifteenth century.*

Figure 9.27 North Rose Window of Notre Dame. Paris. Ca. 1255. *This masterwork by Jehan de Chelles is the only original of Notre Dame's three rose windows. The nineteenth-century restoration genius Viollet-le-Duc re-created the other two. Measuring 43 feet in diameter, the window was installed after workers first removed sections of the existing wall. The bits of predominantly blue glass, encased in iron settings, were then placed inside the stone frame.*

HIGH GOTHIC STYLE, 1194–1300 The High Gothic style is a tribute to the growing confidence of the builders of the thirteenth century. These builders took the Gothic ingredients and refined them, creating grander churches than had been erected earlier. In comparison with Early Gothic architecture, High Gothic churches were taller and had greater volume; artistic values now stressed wholeness rather than the division of space into harmonious units. Rejecting the restrained decorative ideal used in the Early Gothic style, the High Gothic architects covered the entire surface of their churches' western facades with sculptural and architectural designs.

The cathedral in Amiens is a perfect embodiment of the High Gothic style. Amiens was planned so that flying buttresses would surround its choir and march along its nave walls (Figure 9.28). Instead of trying to

Figure 9.28 Amiens Cathedral. Amiens, France. Ca. 1220–1270. *This photograph shows the brilliantly articulated exterior skeleton of Amiens cathedral. The Gothic churches openly displayed the exterior support system that made their interior beauty possible. In the Renaissance, this aspect of Gothicism was decried for its clumsiness. Renaissance architects preferred Classical structures that hid their stresses and strains.*

Figure 9.29   Nave. Amiens cathedral. View from the west. Amiens, France. Ca. 1220–1236. Ht. floor to summit of vault, 139'. *Gothic architecture was built to appeal to the emotions. The overwhelming height and the celestial light were intended to create a spiritual environment. This spiritual feeling may be sensed even in a photograph. The dramatic contrast between the human elements—the chairs—and the voluminous space is a reminder of the frailty of mortals.*

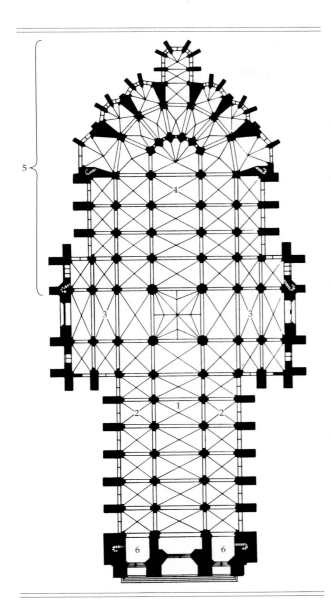

Figure 9.30 Floor Plan of Amiens Cathedral. Amiens, France. Ca. 1220–1236. *This drawing shows the principal features of Amiens cathedral: (1) nave, (2) aisle, (3) transept, (4) apse, (5) choir, and (6) narthex.*

Figure 9.31 Western Facade. Amiens cathedral. Amiens, France. Ca. 1220–1236. *Comparison of Amiens's facade with that of Notre Dame in Paris (see Figure 9.23) shows how the High Gothic differs from the Early Gothic. The basic form remains the same, but Amiens's surface is richer in detail and more splendid overall. The pointed features, such as the arches over the portals and over the openings in the towers, are the most characteristic visual element in the High Gothic style.*

disguise these supports, the architect made the exterior skeleton central to his overall plan. As a result, more spacious window openings could be made in the nave and the choir walls than had been the case in Notre Dame. Furthermore, the design of Amiens's nave was also changed so that the entire space was perceived as a homogeneous volume. The division of the nave walls into three equal horizontal bands was eliminated, and the system of arches and bays overhead became less emphatic (Figure 9.29). Amiens's overall floor plan was conservative, however, for it resembled that of Notre Dame; for example, its transept bisected a choir and a nave of equal length (Figure 9.30).

The western facade of Amiens shows how decoration changed in the High Gothic style (Figure 9.31). Amiens's western wall and towers are pierced with rich and intricate openings. The elegant tracery has the effect of dissolving the wall's apparent solidity. What surface remains intact is covered with an elaborate tapestry of architectural devices and sculptural figures (Figure 9.32).

The finest stained glass from the High Gothic era is from the cathedral in Chartres, a bishopric in Hugh Capet's old lands. Indeed, Chartres's windows are often recognized as the most exquisite of all Gothic stained glass. Chartres has 176 windows, and most are the thirteenth-century originals. Outstanding

Figure 9.32 *Golden Virgin.* Amiens cathedral. Ca. 1260. Amiens, France. *The* Golden Virgin *of* Amiens, *so called because it was originally covered with a thin layer of gold, is one of the most admired works of Gothic art. The artist has depicted Mary as a loving earthly mother with fine features, a high forehead, and a shy smile. This sculpture shows the new tenderness that was creeping into art during the High Middle Ages as part of the rise of the cult of the Virgin.*

examples of this art are the Charlemagne panels depicting scenes from the *Song of Roland,* illustrated earlier in this chapter (see Figure 9.9). Each figure is precisely rendered, though many are cropped off at the edge of the pictorial space. The glass itself is brilliant, notably in the dominant blue tones.

High Gothic painting survives best in the manuscript illuminations of the late thirteenth century. By that time, these small paintings were being influenced by developments elsewhere in Gothic art. The Gothic illuminators abandoned the lively draperies of the Romanesque and instead showed gowns hanging in a natural manner. More important, they sometimes allowed the architectural frame to dominate the painting, as in the Psalter of St. Louis IX of France. Commissioned by the sainted French king (r. 1226–1270), this volume contains seventy-eight full-page paintings of scenes from the Old Testament. Of these paintings, "Balaam and His Ass" is a typical representation of the anonymous painter's style (Figure 9.33). The scene unfolds before a High Gothic church; two gables with rose windows are symmetrically balanced on the page. Although this painting owes much to changes in Gothic sculpture, the animated figures of the men, the angel, and the ass are reminiscent of the exuberant Romanesque style.

Music

As with the other arts, the purpose of music during the High Middle Ages was the glorification of God. At first, the monophonic (single-line) Gregorian chants were still the main form of musical expression, but two innovations—the introduction of tropes and

Figure 9.33 *Balaam and His Ass.* Psalter of St. Louis IX. 1252–1270. Bibliothèque Nationale, Paris. *The architectural details in this miniature painting show a correspondence with the Rayonnant architectural style: the two gabled roofs, the two rose windows with exterior traceries, the pointed arches, and the pinnacles. Just as Gothic architects emphasized the decorative aspects of their buildings, so did this anonymous miniature painter. The story of Balaam and his ass (Numbers 22:22–35 in the Old Testament) was a beast fable—a popular literary genre in the Middle Ages. In the biblical story, the ass could speak and see things of which his master, Balaam, was ignorant. In the painting, the ass turns his head and opens his mouth as if to speak.*

the development of polyphony—led the way to a different sound in the future.

Among the compositions of sacred music written during this period, the works of Hildegard of Bingen, the learned and gifted abbess of the Rupertsberg monastery on the Rhine River (modern Germany), have a lasting appeal. Hildegard composed within the tradition of Gregorian chant (see Chapter 7), though she, a devout mystic, claimed ecstatic visions as the inspiration for her musical ideas. The words for her texts were drawn from the Bible, her theological writings, and the church's liturgy. Hildegard's works were unusual not only because they were written by a woman but also because they were performed by women singers before audiences of women—Hildegard's fellow nuns. Besides the previously mentioned sung morality play *Ordo Virtutatum (The Company of Virtues)* (see this chapter, Religious Orders and Lay Piety), she composed 77 songs, chants, and hymns for the church's liturgy, including such works as *O Pastor Animarum (O Shepherd of Souls), Spiritui Sancto (Holy Spirit),* and *O Jerusalem.* She also wrote a Kyrie (a chant sung during the Mass asking God for mercy); and an Alleluia (a chant sung during the Mass offering praise), as well as two longer works composed specifically for women, one dedicated to virgins and the other to widows.

The **tropes,** or turns, were new texts and melodies inserted into the existing Gregorian chants. Added for both poetic and doctrinal reasons, these musical embellishments slowly changed the plainchants into more elaborate songs. Culminating in about 1150, this musical development coincided with the appearance of the richly articulated Gothic churches.

The tropes also gave a powerful impetus to Western drama. From the practice of troping grew a new musical genre, the **liturgical drama,** which at first was sung and performed in the church but gradually moved outdoors. From the twelfth century onward, these works were staged in the area in front of the church as sacred dramas or mystery plays (*mystery* is derived from the Latin *ministerium,* "handicraft" or "occupation"). As their popularity increased, they began to be sung in the vernacular instead of Latin. Ultimately, the liturgical drama supplied one of the threads that led to the revival of the secular theater.

Gregorian chants were also being modified by the development of **polyphony,** in which two or more lines of melody are sung or played at the same time. In the early eleventh century, polyphony was extremely simple and was known as **organum.** It consisted of a main melody, called the *cantus firmus,* accompanied by an identical melody sung four or five tones higher or lower. By about 1150, the second line began to have its own independent melody rather than duplicating the

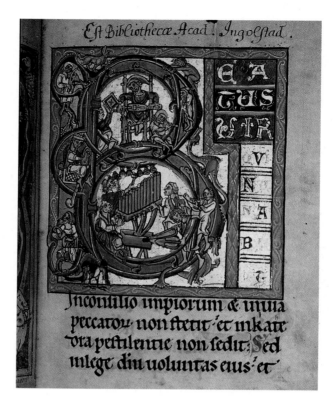

Figure 9.34   Embellished Letter *B*. Psalter from Würzburg-Ebrach. Early thirteenth century. Universitäts Bibliothek, Munich. *In illuminated manuscripts, the initial letter of a sentence was often embellished with intricate details, drawn from the artist's imagination and experience. In this example from a thirteenth-century German psalter, the letter* B *is interwoven with a band of musicians playing instruments typical of the era: organ (with bellows), bells, ivory horn, flute, stringed instruments, and an instrument for bows. The artist who painted this miniature scene has captured the liveliness of a musical performance, depicting several players singing.*

first. During the thirteenth century, two-voiced organum gave way to multivoiced songs called **motets,** which employed more complex melodies. In the motets, the main singer used the liturgy as a text while up to five other voices sang either commentaries or vernacular translations of the text. The result was a complex web of separate voices woven into a harmonious tapestry. By about 1250, the motet composers had laid the foundations of modern musical composition.

Notwithstanding these developments in sacred music, the church could not stop the rise of secular music any more than it could prevent the spread of courtly love. Indeed, the first secular music was associated with the same feudal courts where the *chansons de geste* and the troubador songs flourished in the twelfth century. At first, France was the center of this musical movement, but in the early thirteenth century, German poets took the lead. At the same time, music began to be practiced not just by aristocratic poets but also by

middle-class minstrels, and new musical instruments—some, such as the **lute** (a multistringed instrument with neck and soundbox) and the bagpipe, banned by the church—started to find their way into secular music (Figure 9.34).

The High Middle Ages also gave rise to some innovations that made modern music possible. Guido of Arezzo [GWEE-doe/uh-RET-so] (about 995–about 1050), an Italian monk, modernized musical notation by his invention of the music staff, the set of five horizontal lines and four intermediate spaces on which notes may be drawn. Guido also began the practice of naming the musical tones by the syllables *ut* (or *do*), *re, mi, fa, sol,* and *la,* a step that greatly simplified the teaching of music. The music composed according to Guido's system can be reproduced by today's music historians; thus, Western music may be said to descend in an unbroken line from the music of this period.

The Legacy of the Christian Centuries

The grandeur of this age of synthesis declined after 1300, when the secular and the spiritual began to go their separate ways. But the legacy of the Christian centuries survives, particularly in the writings of Dante, the theology of Thomas Aquinas, and the Gothic cathedrals. Of Dante's works, the *Divine Comedy* is his most enduring gift to world literature; his poetic style and literary forms influenced Italian writers for centuries. Furthermore, Dante's love for Beatrice has deeply influenced Western literature by encouraging poets to seek inspiration from a living woman.

The Roman Catholic world is the most significant beneficiary of the philosophy of Thomas Aquinas. Since the late nineteenth century, Thomism has been regarded as the basis of orthodox beliefs. As for the Gothic style, it ceased to be practiced after about 1500, although it was revived in the nineteenth century as part of the Romantic movement, and even today universities often adopt Gothic elements in their official architecture.

Besides these great gifts, the Christian centuries have left the modern world other significant cultural legacies. First and foremost was the birth of the courtly love movement that glorified individual romantic affection—the idea that *this* man loves *this* woman. Vernacular literature finally found its voice during this time in the first European poetry. Of special note, the vernacular writers created one of the richest literary traditions in the West through the stories of King Arthur and the knights of the Round Table. The basic theoretical system for composing music was developed during this period under the auspices of the church. Outside the church, the ancestor of all Western love songs was invented by the Provençal poets. In Gothic sculpture, artists began to move away from symbolic representation to a more realistic art.

Notwithstanding these innovations, the Christian centuries transmitted many of the legacies that had been received from ancient and other sources. The liberal arts, the Christian religion, the rationalist tradition, Muslim science, and the entire Greco-Roman heritage are only the major ingredients of this invaluable legacy to later ages.

KEY CULTURAL TERMS

chivalric code
friars
cathedral
scholasticism
Realism
Nominalism
via media
goliard
chanson de geste
vernacular language
canzone
minstrel
troubador
romance

First Romanesque
Second Romanesque
bay
tympanum
ribbed vault
pier
flying buttress
choir
rose window
blind arcade
gargoyle
gallery
Rayonnant
tracery

lay
Lombard arcades
Lombard bands
terza rima
stained glass
Romanesque style
Gothic style

trope
liturgical drama
polyphony
organum
motet
lute

SUGGESTIONS FOR FURTHER READING

Primary Sources

CHRÉTIEN DE TROYES. *Arthurian Romances.* Translated by W. W. Comfort. New York: Everyman's Library, 1955. A good prose version of Chrétien's romances, including *Lancelot.*

DANTE. *The Divine Comedy. The Inferno. The Purgatorio. The Paradiso.* Translated by J. Ciardi. New York: New American Library, 1982. The best contemporary English translation.

HILDEGARD OF BINGEN. *Scivias.* Translated by C. Hart and J. Bishop. New York: Paulist Press, 1990. A modern, readable translation of Hildegard's writings.

The Lais of Marie de France. Translated and with an introduction by R. Hanning and J. Ferrante. Durham: Labyrinth Press, 1982. A modern, free-verse translation of these Old French poems; with notes and an extremely useful introductory essay.

The Song of Roland. Translated by F. Golden. New York: Norton, 1978. A readable and modern translation that still captures the language and drama of the original.

ST. THOMAS AQUINAS. *Summa Theologica.* 3 vols. Translated by Fathers of the English Dominican Province. New York: Benziger, 1947. A good English version of St. Thomas's monumental work, which underlies Roman Catholic theology.

TIERNEY, B. *The Crisis of Church and State, 1050–1300.* Englewood Cliffs, N.J.: Prentice-Hall, 1964. Primary documents linked together by sound interpretations and explanations.

CHAPTER *9* HIGHLIGHTS
The High Middle Ages: The Christian Centuries

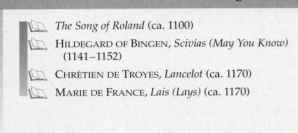

The Song of Roland (ca. 1100)

HILDEGARD OF BINGEN, *Scivias (May You Know)* (1141–1152)

CHRÈTIEN DE TROYES, *Lancelot* (ca. 1170)

MARIE DE FRANCE, *Lais (Lays)* (ca. 1170)

MECHTHILD OF MAGDEBURG, *The Flowing Light of the Godhead* (mid–thirteenth century)

AQUINAS, *Summa Theologica* (ca. 1265–1273)

DANTE, *The Divine Comedy* (ca. 1314)

9.6 HILDEGARD OF BINGEN, *Scivias* (mid–twelfth century)

HILDEGARD OF BINGEN, *O Pastor Animarum* (mid–twelfth century)

9.13 Speyer Cathedral, Germany (1030–about 1150)

9.4 Bayeux Tapestry (third quarter of eleventh century)

9.7 *St. Francis of Assisi's Trial by Fire Before the Sultan* (1290s)

9.12 Santa Cruz de la Seros (Aragon) Church of San Caprasio, Spain (last quarter of eleventh century)

9.14 Basilica of Sacre Coeur, Formerly Abbey Church of the Virgin and St. John the Baptist, France (ca. 1110–ca. 1150)

9.15 Church of Sainte-Marie-Madeleine, France (ca. 1089–1206)

9.17 Tympanum, Church of St. Pierre, France (ca. 1125)

9.18 Illumination from the Bury Bible (1130–1140)

9.20 Church of St. Denis, France (ca. 1145)

9.23 Notre Dame, Paris (ca. 1220–1250)

9.26 Tympanum, Central Portal, Notre Dame, Paris (ca. 1210)

9.27 North Rose Window, Notre Dame, Paris (ca. 1255)

9.28 Amiens Cathedral, France (ca. 1220–1270)

9.32 *Golden Virgin,* Amiens Cathedral, France (ca. 1260)

9.33 Illumination from Psalter St. Louis IX (1252–1270)

 Literature & Philosophy   Art & Architecture   Music & Dance

 Readings in the Western Humanities   CD, *The Western Humanities*

AFRICA

AMERICAS

HISTORY

East Africa Swahili-speaking coastal city-states, with black African and Arab Muslim traders; trading links with Far East and Middle East.

North Africa *Maghreb.* Islamized Berber dynasties, from about 1050. Settled farming society became tribal and nomadic. *Egypt.* Arab Muslim dynasties.

Northeast Africa *Axum culture.* Collapse, ca. 1000. *Ethiopia. Zagwe Dynasty, 1137–1270.* Evolved from Axum empire. Kings extended the Christian faith inland. *Solomonic Dynasty, began 1270.*

West Africa *Ghana Empire.* Traded slaves for salt and cloth. Muslim invaders sacked capital (1076). Fell to Mali Empire, led by Sundiata (1235). *Mali Empire.* Covered 1,000 miles from Atlantic to Middle Niger River. *Yoruba culture.* Ife, the political and religious center.

Andes *Late Intermediate period, 900–1400.* Chimú, north and central coasts; Ica, south coast. Sicán fell under the sway of Chimú about 1100.

Mesoamerica *Early Postclassic period, 900–1200.* Toltec culture. The capital, Tula, abandoned about 1200, though its art, architecture, and myths influenced the Aztecs. *Zapotec culture.* Ritual city of Mitla. *Late Postclassic period, began 1200. Toltec culture.* Sack and abandonment of Chichén Itzá (early 1300s). *Mayan culture.* Loose confederation of cities on Yucatán peninsula, centered on Mayapán.

Native North America *Mississippian culture, ca. 700–1500.* Theocratic village-states, mainly along Mississippi River and tributaries; trade network throughout continent. Cahokia (Illinois) was major urban and ceremonial center (ca. 900–1200).

ART & MUSIC

North Africa *Morocco* and *Tunisia.* Under the Almohad Dynasty (about 1121–1269), Berber power and culture at its zenith. Urban life and the arts flourished.

West Africa *Yoruba culture.* Ife sculptural arts in bronze and terra cotta (1100s); two distinct styles: idealized naturalism and extreme stylization.

An Oni (Local Priest-King) of Ife. Twelfth century or earlier. Brass, ht. 18⅜". Ife Museum, Nigeria.

Andes *Chimú culture.* Mass-produced art objects for the elite, displayed in residences and buried in tombs; long-distance trade to import emeralds and amber. *Sicán culture.* Gold and silver metalwork, ceramics, textiles.

Mesoamerica *Early Postclassic period. Toltec culture.* Plumbate pottery, made to look like metal.

Native North America *Mississippian culture.* Elaborate headdresses, wooden masks, effigy pottery; motifs included feathered serpent, human figures, geometric shapes.

Ceremonial Tumi Knife. About 1250. Gold, silver, and turquoise. Sicán. Royal Ontario Museum, Toronto.

ARCHITECTURE

Northeast Africa *Ethiopian culture.* Eleven churches carved from native rock at Roha.

West Africa *Ghana culture.* The capital Koumbi Saleh (in modern Mauritania) laid out in two towns: round mud huts where the ruler lived in a palace encircled by a wall; stone houses for the Muslim merchants.

Andes At the Chimú capital Chan Chan (pop. about 30,000), a complex of adobe buildings, consisting of royal compounds, palaces, and home workshops.

Mesoamerica *Early Postclassic period. Zapotec culture.* Mitla: palaces, open plazas, and buildings faced with geometric mosaics and stonework. *Toltec culture.* Tula: pyramids linked by spacious courtyards and colonnades. Chichén Itzá: pyramids, temples, courtyards, an observatory, and the largest ballcourt in Mesoamerica.

Native North America *Mississippian culture.* Ceremonial plazas bordered by pyramidal or oval earth mounds with temple or palace on top. Monks Mound (ca. 1100), the largest in Cahokia.

RELIGION, PHILOSOPHY, LITERATURE

North Africa *Egypt.* Saladin, a mythic hero to Muslims and Christians, founded the Ayyubid Dynasty. *Morocco and Tunisia.* Ibn Rushd (Averroës, 1126–1198), Islamic philosopher and court physician. The Almohads swept to power based on Sufism, a mystical form of Islam.

Northeast Africa *Ethiopian culture.* Geez language used by clerical elite; Amharic language spoken by ordinary people. The Solomonic Dynasty claimed descent from the marriage of biblical King Solomon and the Queen of Sheba.

Western Africa Islam spread into Ghana about 1050. Elsewhere, various African religions prevailed. Among the Yoruba, oracles were used to forecast the future through poems that became sacred texts.

Mesoamerica *Early Postclassic period. Toltec culture.* Rise of the cult of Quetzalcoatl; the legend forecasting his return helped Cortés's conquest of the Aztecs in 1519. *Late Postclassic period. Mayan culture.* Four books (codices) survive, covering mathematics and astronomy, prophecies, ritual observances, and a table of movements of the planet Venus.

Native North America *Mississippian culture.* Religion centered on sun worship; high chief's title was the Great Sun. Ceremonies included ritual ballgames.

The Caracol (Astronomical Observatory). After 1000. Chichén Itzá.

ASIA

China

Sung Dynasty, ended 1279. Turkic invaders (the Chin) conquered north China (1127); made Beijing the capital. Southern Sung state founded (1128), with Hangzhou as capital. Advances in medicine and technology. *Yüan Dynasty, 1260–1368.* China united under its first foreign dynasty (Mongol), founded by Kublai Khan; capital, Beijing; peace established, trade expanded, and links renewed with the West.

India

Chola Dynasty, 907–1279. Dominated south India, including Sri Lanka and Malay Archipelago; defeated by two rival dynasties, the Pāndyas and the Hoysalas. *Medieval period, began 550.* In north India, Hindu dynasties fought for control, as Muslim power moved into the region. *Delhi Sultanate, began 1192.* Delhi, the capital of six successive Muslim dynasties.

JŌCHŌ. Amida, Buddha of the Western Paradise. *1053. Gold leaf and lacquer on wood, ht. 116". Phoenix Hall. Byōdōin, Kyōto.*

Japan

Heian period, ended 1185. Imperial family weakened; power shifted to Fujiwara clan (after 897). Onset of feudalism. *Kamakura period, 1185–1333.* Clan warfare (1156–85) over the office of shōgun (military dictator); shōgun's headquarters moved to Kamakura; emperor remained in Kyōto (pop. [1185]: 500,000). Samurai increased power.

Sung Dynasty. A golden age of calligraphy and ink painting. Three ink-painting styles: Northern Sung (mountain landscape), Southern Sung (romantic landscape), and the Ch'an (Zen) Buddhist style of sophisticated "simplicity." Woven and embroidered silks, tapestry, lacquer, carved jades, and ivory. Music: the tz'u genre blended poetry and song.

Chola Dynasty. Bronze sculptures of deities, such as Shiva Nataraja, the Lord of the Dance, both creator and destroyer of the universe.

Kamakura period. Revitalization of art: portrait sculpture, portrait painting, and sword making. Buddhist-influenced art.

Sung Dynasty. Lin Chieh's *Ying-tsao fa-shih,* the oldest treatise on Chinese architecture. *Yüan Dynasty.* Tibetan-style White Pagoda in Beijing's royal gardens, built (1272) by Kublai Khan.

Chola Dynasty. The Hindu Rajarajeshvara Temple, the supreme expression of the South Indian style, built by King Rājarāja I in his capital, Tanjore (about 1000). *Delhi Sultanate.* Islamic mosques.

View of the Phoenix Hall, Byōdōin. 1053. Uji, Kyōto.

Heian period. The Byōdōin, the private chapel of the regent Fujiwara Yorimichi (994–1074). *Kamakura period.* After civil war, Buddhist monasteries rebuilt in many styles. A secular "warrior style" emerged: buildings and training grounds surrounded by narrow moats or stockades.

Sung Dynasty. Li Ch'ing-chao, composer of tz'u, one of China's greatest female poets. Southern Sung scholars influenced by Ch'an Buddhism. *Yüan Dynasty.* Golden era of the dramatic form *tsa-chü,* such as Wang Shih-fu's *The Pavilion of the West.* Short stories and novels. *Marco Polo's Travels,* an account of the Venetian's years at the Mongol court. Toleration for many faiths, such as Tibetan lamaism, Islam, and Nestorian Christianity.

Shiva Nataraja. *Eleventh–twelfth centuries (Chola Dynasty). Bronze, ht. 32¼". Von der Heydt Collection, Museum Rietberg, Zurich.*

Chola Dynasty. Hinduism, the official faith. *Medieval period.* Buddhism introduced into Tibet under the Pala Dynasty.

Heian period. Perfection of *kana*-style calligraphy. Women writers flourished: Lady Murasaki's classic, *The Tale of Genji,* and *The Pillow-Book of Sei Shōnagon,* the diary of a lady-in-waiting. Chinese-style Buddhism, especially the Amida Pure Land Paradise cult, adopted by the ruling class. *Kamakura period. The Confessions of Lady Nyō,* a novel of a court lady's love affairs; and *An Account of My Hut,* by Kamo Chōmei, a Buddhist poet disenchanted with the world. Samurai warriors sought support either in the native Shinto religion or in Zen Buddhism, imported from China. Zen monks adopted the ritual tea ceremony.

10 THE LATE MIDDLE AGES
1300–1500

Many who lived during what a modern historian has termed the "calamitous" fourteenth century believed that the biblical apocalypse had arrived, attended by plague, famine, and war. Amid this turbulence, the unique culture of the High Middle Ages, which blended the spiritual with the secular, began to unravel. In the Late Middle Ages, the church had to relinquish its dream of a united Christendom when faced with the reality of warring European states. New military tactics and weapons rendered chivalry obsolete, and the chivalric code began to seem a romantic fiction. In the universities, new intellectual currents drove a wedge between philosophy and theology, which had been so carefully integrated by Thomas Aquinas. And the balanced High Gothic style in art and architecture gave way to the florid Late Gothic style.

This chapter examines the third and final period of medieval civilization, between 1300 and 1500 (see Chapters 7 and 9). It also explores the rise of secularism in this contradictory age and the technological and artistic innovations that were guiding the Western world in a new direction (Figure 10.1). The specific developments in the 1400s that ushered in the Renaissance and the modern era will be the focus of the next chapter.

HARD TIMES COME TO EUROPE

Shortly after the opening of the fourteenth century, Europe entered a disastrous period of economic depression, accompanied by soaring prices and widespread famine. Against the backdrop of the Hundred Years' War between England and France (1337–1453), social unrest increased and renegade feudal

◀ **Detail** *Wine-Making*. Fifteenth century. Tapestry. Cluny Museum, Paris.

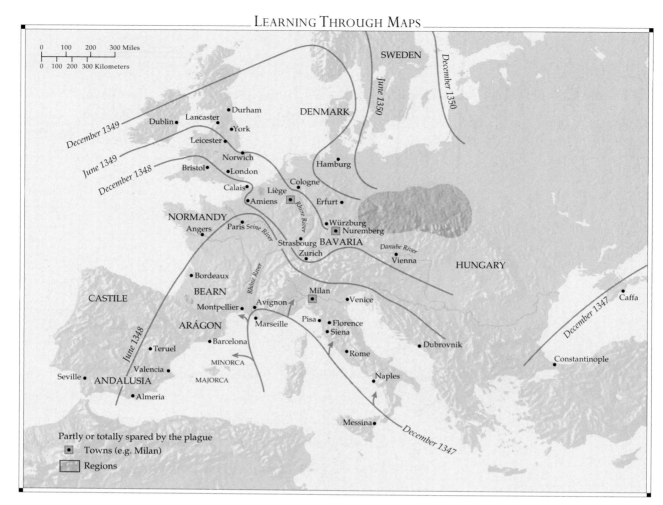

Map 10.1 PROGRESS OF THE BLACK DEATH ACROSS EUROPE IN THE FOURTEENTH CENTURY

This map shows the spread of the plague across Europe in the mid-fourteenth century. **Notice** how the dark lines mark the progress of the plague at a specific time. **Where** and **when** does the Black Death appear in Europe? **Where** and **when** does it end? **What** regions and cities were partly or totally spared of the plague? **Consider** the role of various types of travelers in spreading the Black Death.

Figure 10.1 *Wine-Making*. Fifteenth century. Tapestry. Cluny Museum, Paris. *Wine production became a specialty of certain regions in the Late Middle Ages, as represented in this fifteenth-century tapestry. In the center of the tapestry, two means of wine-making are shown: above, a wine press, and, below, the more traditional stomping of the grapes in a vat. In the left foreground, the lord and lady of the manor, recognizable by their rich gowns, supervise the making of the wine.*

Figure 10.2 *The Dance of Death. Fifteenth century. In the wake of the Black Death, art and literature became filled with themes affirming the biblical message that life is short and death certain. A vivid image of this theme was the* Danse Macabre, *or Dance of Death, which took many artistic and literary forms. In this example, a miniature painting taken from a fifteenth-century Spanish manuscript, the corpses are shown nude, stripped of their human dignity, and dancing with wild abandon.*

armies ravaged much of western Europe. The church, in disgrace and disarray for much of this period, was unable to provide moral or political leadership. As old certainties evaporated, the optimistic mood of the High Middle Ages gave way to a sense of impending doom.

Ordeal by Plague, Famine, and War

Of all the calamities that now befell Europe, the worst was the plague, an animal-to-human illness, which first appeared in northern Italy in 1347 (Map 10.1). Imported from the East along newly opened trade routes, the plague bacillus was carried over sea and land by fleas. Fleas, infected from biting diseased rats, then transmitted the bacillus to other rats and human. From Italy, the disease spread rapidly over most of Europe, halted by the frost line in the north. A few cities and areas—such as Milan and central Germany—were free of plague, but elsewhere it raged from 1348 until 1351, and further onslaughts occurred at random into the next century. So deadly was the disease that more than a third of Europe's seventy million people died in the first epidemic alone.

The mechanism of disease transmission was not fully understood, and the plague created panic. Using medieval accounts of the disease, modern researchers have detected three forms of plague: bubonic (infected lymph nodes), pneumonic (infected lungs), and septicemic (blood poisoning). All three forms were extremely painful, and death could result in a matter of hours or days. People in the Late Middle Ages referred to these disease types collectively as "the plague"; in

the sixteenth century, historians began to label the epidemic the "Black Death," which has become the common term.

The Black Death cast a long shadow over the Late Middle Ages. Many writers and artists reflected the melancholy times, occasionally brightening their dark works with an end-of-the-world gaiety. The age's leading image became the Dance of Death, often portrayed as a skeleton democratically joining hands with kings, queens, popes, merchants, peasants, and prostitutes as they danced their way to destruction. In the direct manner of medieval thinking, this symbol forcefully showed the folly of human ambition and the transitory nature of life (Figure 10.2).

The plague was compounded by growing famine conditions across the European continent. Starting in 1315, agricultural harvests failed with some regularity for more than a century. Besides raising the death rate, these famines weakened the populace and made them more susceptible to diseases.

War also disrupted the pattern of social and economic life. By 1450 the kings of Aragon in eastern Spain had defeated and replaced the French rulers of Naples, Sicily, and Sardinia. The increasingly powerful northern Italian cities waged war among themselves for commercial and political advantage. Farther east, from 1347 on, the Ottoman Turks had been on the move, occupying Greece and the Balkan peninsula, conquering Constantinople in 1453 and menacing Bohemia and Hungary as the century ended. During the same period in the west, England and France fought the seemingly endless Hundred Years' War, while the dukes of Burgundy attempted to carve out a "middle kingdom" between France and the German empire.

One consequence of this almost constant warfare was a growing number of renegade soldiers who wandered the land. The countryside was filled with bands of roving knights—nobles, younger sons or bastards of aristocratic families, and outlaws—who blackmailed both landowners and peasants. Throughout Europe, these dangerous circumstances compelled town dwellers to retreat behind their city walls.

Depopulation, Rebellion, and Industrialization

The chief consequence of the plagues, famines, and wars was depopulation, which affected the commercial centers of Europe. In general, the regions hardest hit economically were those that had benefited most in the earlier boom, particularly France. New centers rose to economic importance, including Bohemia, Poland, Hungary, Scandinavia, and Portugal. The northern Italian cities of Florence, Genoa, and Venice, the largest cities in Europe, rallied from the plague's devastating losses in the fifteenth century to make a remarkable economic recovery.

Population decline also caused dramatic social dislocations. Plague-free regions lost population as healthy people flocked to plague-stricken areas, where laborers were in great demand. The rural population decreased, and thousands of villages simply disappeared as peasants abandoned their farms and settled in the towns. A short-term effect of the population shift was the widening of the gap between rich and poor. As a once relatively homogeneous population began to split into antagonistic classes, the established social order broke down, and society experienced warfare between peasants and landowners, guildsmen and merchants, and town laborers and middle-class elites. These social uprisings often had an anticlerical element, with the rebels attacking church property and denouncing the collection of tithes.

Starting in Flanders in 1296, social unrest mounted across Europe. In 1358 the French Jacquerie, or rural renegades, made common cause with Parisian workers and killed many nobles. In England during the brief Peasants' Revolt in 1381, insurgents seized and occupied London. Among their demands was that the English king abolish the nobility. In the end, these uprisings failed to remedy the inequalities in the social order.

Although the immediate consequence of the demographic crisis was increased social unrest, the long-term effect was a higher standard of living for the survivors (see Figure 10.1). Peasants in western Europe found their labor more in demand and their bargaining positions with the landowners improved. Many broke free from servitude and became rent-paying farmers. Others, less fortunate, moved from the status of serf to that of sharecropper. As a result of all these changes, manorialism was dying out in most of western Europe by 1500. But in central and eastern Europe, where the plague had been less devastating and the landlords could hold firm, estate owners bound the serfs ever more tightly to their farm labors.

As farming changed, so did Europe's fledgling industrial life. Hand-loomed textile manufacturing remained the leading industry, but its production and distribution centers shifted. Cut off by war from their former wool supplies and their retail markets, the Flemish and French weavers were challenged by woolen manufacturers from northern Italy, the Rhineland, and Poland. The greatest change in textile manufacturing, however, was ultimately precipitated by England's shift from the export of raw wool to the export of finished cloth, a change that disrupted the traditional rural way of life.

New industries also developed around the production of rag paper, a Chinese invention perfected by the Arabs and manufactured widely in Spain after 1300; of salt, distributed by Venice and Lisbon and used in tanning leather and preserving food; and of iron, in demand for weapons, armor, and horseshoes. New technology, such as the suction pump and the spinning wheel, increased productivity in other industries, and older inventions, such as eyeglasses, clocks, and gunpowder, were perfected in this age of rapid change. The development of movable type in the mid–fifteenth century was the most significant technological innovation of the Late Middle Ages; it gave rise to the printing and publishing industries and had enormous repercussions on education and literature.

The Secular Monarchies

France and England maintained their leading positions in Europe, but they exhausted their economies with wasteful wars. The Hundred Years' War, as the group of conflicts between the mid–fourteenth and the mid–fifteenth centuries is called, arose over feudal and military rivalries dating from the High Middle Ages (Timeline 10.1). The war was fought entirely on French soil. The Valois dynasty had to contend not only with England but also with the dukes of Burgundy, who threatened to break their ties with the French crown and establish an independent kingdom on the northeast border of France. The Burgundian court at Dijon was the most brilliant in northern Europe, attracting the leading artists and humanists of the age. A heroic figure who emerged from this war was Joan of Arc (1412–1431), who rallied the French to victory, only to be burned at the stake by the English; in modern times,

Timeline 10.1   ROYAL DYNASTIES IN LATE MEDIEVAL FRANCE AND ENGLAND

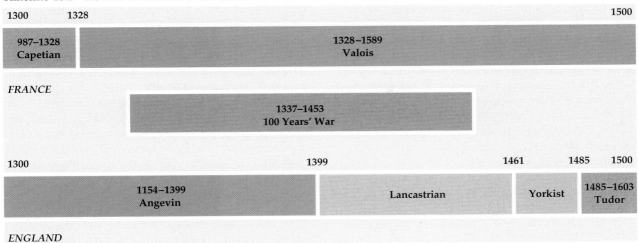

she became one of France's national heroines and a Roman Catholic saint.

Despite the ravages of the Hundred Years' War, the Valois kings ultimately increased their territory. Except for the port of Calais in northern France, England was forced to cede its overseas lands to the French crown. The dukes of Burgundy were brought under French control. And the northwestern region of Brittany, the last major territory that had escaped the French crown, was acquired through marriage. The contour of modern France was now complete.

While the Hundred Years' War raged on the Continent, life in England was disrupted by feudal rebellion, peasant unrest, and urban strife. Like France, England was emerging from the feudal system, but it was moving in a different direction. The English Parliament, which represented the interests of the nobles, the towns, and the rural counties, gained power at the expense of the king. Parliament also reflected popular feeling when it passed laws curbing papal power in England.

When Henry VII (r. 1485–1509) became king, however, it became apparent that a key reason for the dominance of Parliament had been the weakness of the kings. This founder of England's brilliant Tudor dynasty avoided the quarrels his predecessors had had with Parliament by abandoning foreign wars, living off his own estates, and relying on his own advisers. Henry VII's policies deflated parliamentary power and made him as potent as his contemporaries in France.

The success of the French and the English kings in centralizing their states attracted many imitators. Their ruling style—with royal secretaries, efficient treasuries, national judiciaries, and representative assemblies—was adopted in part by other states.

Spain was the most successful in achieving unity. Dynastic politics and civil war kept central Europe and Scandinavia from becoming strong and centralized. The Holy Roman Empire was the least successful of these political entities, and Germany remained divided into combative states.

The Papal Monarchy

From its pinnacle of power and prestige in 1200 under Pope Innocent III, the church entered a period of decline in about 1300, and for the next century it was beset with schism and heresy. For most of the fourteenth century, the seat of the papacy was located in Avignon, a papal fief on the Rhône River, to escape from Rome's factional politics. Opponents of the relocation of the papacy, which had never happened before, claimed these popes were in the pocket of the French king. The chief success of the Avignonese popes was to centralize the papacy, an accomplishment comparable to what was happening in the secular kingdoms. These popes reorganized the church's financial system and changed payments from kind to money. At the same time, unfortunately, they rarely made moral reforms. Their reigns lapsed into worldliness and greed, which made the papacy more vulnerable to criticism.

The Avignonese papacy had barely ended in 1378 when a new calamity, the Great Schism, threw the church into even more confusion. Under Pope Gregory XI, the papacy had returned to Rome in 1377, and the cardinals had elected an Italian pope when Gregory died. The French cardinals did not approve of this pope, and they elected another pontiff to rule from

Avignon. Western Christendom was thus divided into two obediences with two popes, two colleges of cardinals, two curias, and two church tax systems. The rising power of the secular states became evident as rulers cast their support along political lines. France, Sicily, Scotland, Castile, Aragon, and Portugal rallied behind the Avignon pope; England, Flanders, Poland, Hungary, Germany, and the rest of Italy stayed loyal to the Roman pope. The papal office suffered the most; the pope's authority diminished as pious Christians became bewildered and disgusted.

The worst was yet to come. In 1409 both sets of cardinals summoned a church council in Pisa to heal the fissure. The Pisan Council elected a new pope and

called on the other two to resign. They refused, and the church was faced with *three* rulers claiming papal authority. The Great Schism was finally resolved at the Council of Constance (1414–1418), which deposed the Avignon ruler, accepted the resignation of the Roman claimant, ignored the Pisan Council's choice, and elected a new pope, Martin V.

With the success of the Council of Constance, conciliar rule (rule by councils) as a way of curbing the power of the popes seemed to be gaining support in the church. But Martin V (pope 1417–1431) rejected this idea as soon as he was elected to the papal throne. Nevertheless, the conciliar movement remained alive until the mid–fifteenth century, when strong popes reasserted the monarchical power of their office. Although powerful, these popes failed to address pressing moral and spiritual concerns, for they were deeply involved in Italian politics and other worldly interests, ruling almost as secular princes in papal states.

THE CULTURAL FLOWERING OF THE LATE MIDDLE AGES

The calamitous political, social, and economic events of the Late Middle Ages were echoed in the cultural sphere by the breakdown of the medieval synthesis in religion, in theology, in literature, and in art. New secular voices began to be heard, challenging traditional views, and the interests of the bourgeoisie started to have an impact on art and architecture. Although the church remained the principal financial supporter of the arts, rich town dwellers, notably bankers and merchants, were emerging as the new patrons of art (Figure 10.3). Conspicuous art patronage made them the equals of the most powerful figures in society, but they still had few political rights.

Religion

Monastic reform had been a major force within the church in the High Middle Ages, but such collective acts of piety were largely unknown in the Late Middle Ages. Dedicated and virtuous monks and nuns were increasingly rare, and their influence was waning. Innovative forms of religious expression did not come from members of religious orders but from laypeople, inspired perhaps to protest and react against what they perceived as the increasing worldliness of the church and the declining commitment of many clergy.

Lay piety was thus one of the most significant developments in the religious landscape. By 1400 the Brethren and Sisters of the Common Life and the Friends of God were rising in the Rhineland, the Low

Figure 10.3 Jacques Coeur's House. 1443–1451. Bourges, France. *Coeur was an immensely successful entrepreneur who at one point bankrolled the French kings. His magnificent mansion at Bourges spawned many imitations among wealthy businessmen across Europe. The building's spiky turrets, fanciful balconies, and highly decorated windows are all secular adaptations of the Late Gothic style more commonly seen in church architecture. Coeur conducted his Europe-wide financial and commercial dealings from this house, sending messages by carrier pigeons released through holes on the roof.*

Countries, and Flanders. This lay movement constituted the *devotio moderna,* or the "new devotion," with its ideal of a pious lay society. Disappointed with traditionally trained priests, members of these groups often rejected higher education and practiced the strict discipline of the earlier monastic orders, but without withdrawing into a monastery. Among the most important expressions of this new devotion was *The Imitation of Christ,* by Thomas à Kempis (1380–1471). His manual, with its stern asceticism, reflected the harsh ideals of the Brethren of the Common Life, the group of which Kempis was a member.

Within the pietistic movement, extreme ascetic practices that verged on heresy increased in these turbulent years. The bizarre behavior of the flagellants, for example, was triggered by the plague. They regarded this disease as God's way to judge and punish an evil society. The flagellants staged public processions in which they engaged in ritual whippings in an attempt to divert divine wrath from others (Figure 10.4).

The flagellants managed to escape official censure, but those more openly critical of the church did not. The leaders who attempted to reform the church in England and Bohemia met stout resistance from the popes. The English reform movement sprang from the teachings of John Wycliffe (about 1320–1384), an Oxford teacher whose message attracted both nobility and common folk. Wishing to purify the church of worldliness, Wycliffe urged the abolition of ecclesiastical property, the subservience of the church to the state, and the denial of papal authority. The most lasting achievement of Wycliffe's movement was the introduction of the first complete English-language Bible, produced by scholars inspired by his teaching. After his followers (known as Lollards) were condemned as heretical, the secular officials launched savage persecutions that resulted in the murder of those supporters who did not recant.

The Bohemian reformers in the Holy Roman Empire were indebted to Wycliffe, whom some had met at Oxford; but, more important, their strength was rooted in the popular piety and evangelical preachers of mid-fourteenth-century Prague. The heresy became identified with Jan Hus (about 1369–1415), a Czech theologian who accepted Wycliffe's political views but rejected some of his religious teachings. Hus was invited to the Council of Constance in 1415, where his ideas were condemned, and he was burned at the stake by state authorities. His death outraged his fellow Czechs, many of whom, including the powerful and wealthy, now adopted his views. Hussite beliefs became a vehicle for Czech nationalism, as his ethnic comrades fought against German overlords and attacked church property. Because of the backing of

Figure 10.4   *Flagellation Scene. Annales of Gilles Le Muisit.* Bibliothèque Royale Albert Ier, Brussels. *This miniature painting represents a familiar scene across Europe during the plague years. The penitents, depicted with bare backs and feet, marched through towns scourging themselves with whips. By this self-punishment, they hoped to atone for their own and society's sins and thus end the plague.*

powerful lay leaders, the Hussites survived into the next century. They gained more followers during the Protestant Reformation and exist today as the Moravian Brethren.

Although the secular authorities, instigated by the church, could usually be counted on to put down the heresies, the church had a more powerful internal weapon at its disposal: the Inquisition (from the Latin *inquisitio,* meaning "inquiry"). Born in the aftermath of the Albigensian heresy in the twelfth century (see Chapter 9), the Inquisition was a religious court for identifying and condemning heretics. The Inquisition reached its cruel height during the Late Middle Ages, particularly in Italy and Spain.

Because of its procedures, the Inquisition became the most notorious instrument ever created by the Christian church. Ignoring the basic ideals of Roman law, this church court allowed suspects to be condemned without ever facing their accusers. Confessions made under torture were also allowed to serve as evidence against other persons. Forbidden by the Bible to shed blood, the leaders of the Inquisition turned convicted heretics over to the state authorities, who then executed them by burning. By modern estimates, thousands of men and women perished in this way.

The Inquisition was also used to rid society of women—and to a lesser extent of men—who were suspected of being in league with the devil. The belief in witchcraft, an occult legacy of the ancient world, was next to universal during the Middle Ages. Many educated people sincerely believed that certain women were witches and that magical devices could protect the

PERSONAL PERSPECTIVE

Henry Knighton
Political and Religious Rebels

An excellent source for the Late Middle Ages in England is the Chronicle *of the cleric Henry Knighton (?–1396). An attentive observer of public affairs, he recorded the political and religious unrest of his age. He lived mainly in Leicestershire, far from London, but he had well-placed contacts and reliable sources. In the first excerpt, Knighton details events of the 1381 rebellion of Wat Tyler. The second excerpt records an instance of religious unrest, which may be related to the Lollards, who believed that women could be priests.*

1

The next day, which was Saturday [15 June 1381], they all came together again in Smithfield, where the king [Richard II] came early to meet them, and showed that although he was young in years he was possessed of a shrewd mind. He was approached by their leader, Wat Tyler, who had now changed his name to Jack Straw. He stood close to the king, speaking for the others, and carrying an unsheathed knife, of the kind people call a dagger, which he tossed from hand to hand as a child might play with it, and looked as though he might suddenly seize the opportunity to stab the king if he should refuse their requests, and those accompanying the king therefore greatly feared what might come to pass. The commons asked of the king that all game, whether in waters or in parks and woods should become common to all, so that everywhere in the realm, in rivers and fishponds, and woods and forests, they might take the wild beasts, and hunt the hare in the fields, and do many other such things without restraint.

And when the king wanted time to consider such a concession, Jack Straw drew closer to him, with menacing words, and though I know not how he dared, took the reins of the king's horse in his hand. Seeing that, [William] Walworth, a citizen of London, fearing that he was about to kill the king, drew his basilard and ran Jack Straw through the neck. Thereupon another esquire, called Ralph Standish, stabbed him in the side with his basilard. And he fell to the ground on his back, and after rising to his hands and knees, he died.

2

A woman in London celebrates mass. At that time there was a woman in the city of London who had an only daughter whom she taught to celebrate the mass; and she privily set up and furnished an altar in her own bedroom, and there she caused her daughter on many occasions to dress as a priest and in her fashion to celebrate mass, though when she came to the sacramental words she prostrated herself before the altar and did not complete the sacrament. But then she would rise for the rest of the mass and recite it to the end, her mother assisting her and showing her devotion.

That nonsense went on for some time, until it was revealed by a neighbour who had been admitted to the secret, when it came to the ears of the bishop of London. He summoned them to his presence and showed them the error of their ways, and compelled them to display the child's priestly tonsure in public, for her head was found to be quite bald. The bishop greatly deplored and bewailed such misconduct in the church in his time, uttering many lamentations, and put an end to it by enjoining penance upon them.

---

faithful from their spells. Consequently, hundreds of suspected individuals were killed by the Inquisition or by unruly mobs. Fear of witchcraft persisted as a dangerous part of popular lore into the eighteenth century.

Theology, Philosophy, and Science

Although the popes betrayed their spiritual mission in these years, the church was not without dedicated followers who cared deeply about theological issues. Many of these clerical thinkers were affiliated with the universities, principally in Paris and at Oxford. Their major disputes were over Thomism, the theological system of Thomas Aquinas, which in the Late Middle Ages was losing supporters and coming increasingly under attack. At the same time, the ongoing philosophical struggle between Realism and Nominalism finally ended with a Nominalist victory. In the long run, those who questioned Thomism and those who accepted Nominalism set philosophy and theology on separate paths and thus paved the way to the Renaissance and the Scientific Revolution.

The Via Antiqua *Versus the* Via Moderna   The opening round in the theological war against Thomism

began soon after the death of Thomas Aquinas in 1274 and before the High Middle Ages was over. In 1277 church officials in Paris condemned the Latin Averroists at the local university for their rationalist ideas. As part of their attack on extreme rationalism, the church authorities rejected some of Aquinas's arguments. The censure of Thomism led to a heated controversy that raged for much of the Late Middle Ages among university scholars. In particular, Thomas's fellow Dominican friars waged an acrimonious battle with the Franciscan masters, their great rivals in theological studies.

During these theological debates, new labels were invented and assumed by the opposing sides. Aquinas's *via media* came to be termed by his opponents the *via antiqua,* or the old-fashioned way. Broadly speaking, the *via antiqua* followed Thomism in urging that faith and reason be combined as the correct approach to divine truth. In contrast, the *via moderna,* or the modern way, made a complete separation of biblical beliefs and rationalism. In time the *via moderna* prevailed, driving the *via antiqua* underground until it was rescued from oblivion in the modern period.

Duns Scotus and William of Ockham

The conflict between the *via antiqua* and the *via moderna* was best exemplified in the writings of John Duns Scotus and William of Ockham, respectively. The first of these commentators was sympathetic to the theology of Thomas Aquinas, but the second scholar was unmistakably hostile and tried to discredit Thomism.

Duns Scotus [duhnz SKOAT-us] (about 1265–1308), the most persuasive voice of the *via antiqua,* was a Scottish thinker who was trained as a Franciscan and lectured at the universities in Oxford, Paris, and Cologne. Even though he was a supporter of Thomism, Duns Scotus unwittingly undermined Aquinas's synthesis by stressing that faith was superior to reason, a shift in focus that arose from his belief in God's absolute and limitless power. Pointing out that God's existence could not be proven either through the senses or by reason, he asserted that only faith could explain the divine mystery. Furthermore, Duns Scotus concluded that because the theologian and the philosopher have different intellectual tasks, theology and science (that is, the study of nature) should be independent fields of inquiry.

What Duns Scotus unintentionally began, William of Ockham (about 1300–about 1349) purposely completed. Under the assaults of Ockham's keen intellect, the Thomist theological edifice collapsed. An Oxford-trained theologian, he recognized the importance of both reason and faith; but, like Scotus, he did not see how reason could prove God's existence. Both thinkers believed that only personal feelings and mystical experiences could reveal God and the divine moral order. Yet Ockham went further than Scotus by asserting that reason, the senses, and empirical evidence could enable human beings to discover and hence understand the natural world. To Ockham, faith and reason were both valid approaches to truth, but they should be kept apart so that each could achieve its respective end.

In the seemingly endless medieval debate between the Realists and the Nominalists, Ockham's reasoning swept Nominalism to its final victory. Like the Nominalists of the twelfth century, Ockham denied the existence of universals and claimed that only individual objects existed. He concluded that human beings can have clear and distinct knowledge only of specific things in the physical world; no useful knowledge can be gained through reason or the senses about the spiritual realm. Ockham's conclusion did not mean that human beings were cast adrift without access to the world of God. A corollary of his approach was that understanding of the spiritual realm rested solely on the truths of faith and theology.

In his reasoning, William of Ockham asserted a principle of economy that stripped away all that was irrelevant: Arguments should be drawn from a minimum of data and founded on closely constructed logic. "It is vain to do with more what can be done with fewer," he says in one of his works. Ockham's "razor" of logic eliminated superfluous information that could not be verified, thus enabling a student to cut to the core of a philosophical problem. The Ockhamites, following their mentor's logic and empiricism, challenged the Realists and dominated the intellectual life of the universities for the next two hundred years.

Developments in Science

Ockham's ideas broadened the path to modern science that had been opened by two thirteenth-century thinkers. In that earlier time, Robert Grosseteste [GROAS-test] (about 1175–1253), a Franciscan at Oxford University, had devised a scientific method for investigating natural phenomena; using step-by-step procedures, he employed mathematics and tested hypotheses until he reached satisfactory conclusions. Roger Bacon (about 1220–1292), another Franciscan and a follower of Grosseteste, advocated the use of the experimental method, which he demonstrated in his studies of optics, solar eclipses, and rainbows and in his treatises on mathematics, physics, and philosophy. From the modern standpoint, Bacon was perhaps the most original mind of this generally barren period in the history of science.

In the fourteenth century, other thinkers, with Grosseteste and Bacon as guides and Ockham's logic as a weapon, made further contributions to the advance of science. Outstanding among these men was one bold Parisian scholar who took advantage of the growing interest in the experimental method, Nicholas Oresme [O-REM] (about 1330–1382). Oresme answered all of Aristotle's objections to the idea that the earth moved. Using pure reason and applying theoretical arguments, he concluded that it was as plausible that the earth moved around the sun as that it was fixed. Having used reason to show that the earth may move, however, Oresme then chose to accept church doctrine, denying what he had demonstrated. Nevertheless, Oresme's arguments, along with Ockham's separation of natural philosophy from theology and Bacon's formulation of the experimental method, foreshadowed the end of the medieval concept of the physical and celestial worlds.

Literature

The powerful forces that were reshaping the wider culture—the rising new monarchies, the growing national consciousness among diverse peoples, the emerging secularism, and the developing urban environment—were also transforming literature in the Late Middle Ages. The rise of literacy produced a growing educated class who learned to read and write the local languages rather than Latin, and a shift to vernacular literature began to occur. Two new groups—the monarchs and their courts and the urban middle class—started to supplant the nobility and the church as patrons and audiences. And, ultimately most important of all, in the mid–fifteenth century Johann Gutenberg developed a practicable method of using movable type to print books. This invention helped to seal the doom of medieval civilization and signaled the commencement of the modern world.

Northern Italian Literature: Petrarch and Boccaccio

New literary forms emerged in the areas where the chivalric and feudal modes were weakest—northern Italy and England. Petrarch and Boccaccio, both Florentines, like Dante, grew up in a Christian world that was rapidly being secularized. These two writers captured the mood of this transition era as Florence and the other Italian city-states shed their medieval outlook. Both authors looked back to the Classical world for inspiration, and yet both found in the bustling world of the nearby towns the materials and characters for their stories. Of the two, Petrarch was the more dedicated Classicist and often used ancient themes in his writings.

Francesco Petrarch [PEE-trark] ("Petrarca" in Italian) (1304–1374), though Florentine by birth and in spirit, flourished in Avignon amid the splendor and learning of the papal court. As a diplomat for popes and Italian princes, he won fame and wealth, but his reputation arose from his career as a professional man of letters. Rejecting the age's trend toward the vernacular, he dedicated his life to Latin writing and to the recovery of ancient manuscripts, although the work for which he is most renowned, a collection of love lyrics and sonnets called *Canzoniere,* or *Songbook,* is written in Italian. His devotion struck a responsive chord among his fellow Italians, who in 1341 proclaimed him poet laureate for his lyrics, sonnets, treatises, and epics. In many ways, Petrarch, despite a clerical training, shows the typical secular interests of his times. A conventional Christian, he only occasionally addressed religious issues in his works.

A religious theme is touched on in *Secretum,* or *My Secret,* in which Petrarch deals with the state of his soul. In this dialogue, "Augustinus," or St. Augustine, hounds "Franciscus," or Petrarch, about his innermost thoughts and desires, charging him with all the deadly sins. Freely admitting his moral lapses, Franciscus pleads that he is the same as any other man—driven by a love of learning, a weakness for fleshly attractions, and an appetite for personal comforts. Despite this confession, with its modern overtones, the dialogue shows that Petrarch could not liberate himself fully from medieval values.

Even more than his lifelong friend Petrarch, Giovanni Boccaccio [bo-KACH-e-o] (1313–1375) was a man of the world. The son of a banker, Boccaccio began his literary career by penning prose romances along with poetic pastorals and sonnets, many of which were dedicated to Fiammetta, a young woman who was both his consuming passion and his literary muse. His early efforts, however, were overshadowed by his Italian prose masterpiece, *The Decameron.* Written in about 1351, this work reflects the grim conditions of the Black Death, which had just swept through Florence (Figure 10.5). In *The Decameron* (from the Greek for "ten days"), Boccaccio describes how ten young men and women, in their efforts to escape the plague, flee the city to a country villa, where they pass the time, each telling a story a day for ten days. Most of their one hundred tales were based on folk stories and popular legends. Although some tales deal lightly with social mores and a few contain moral messages, the majority simply entertain the listener. Boccaccio, speaking through a cross section of urban voices and relying on well-known stories, helped develop a form of literature that eventually led to the modern short story.

English Literature: Geoffrey Chaucer

Like its Italian counterpart, English literature rapidly matured into its

Figure 10.5 Francesco Traini. *Triumph of Death*. Detail. Ca. 1350. Entire fresco 18′6″ ×
49′2″. Pisa, Italy. *Like the storytellers in* The Decameron, *these well-dressed travelers have left
their plague-stricken city, perhaps in search of safety or hoping for a day's pleasant diversion in
the countryside. Instead, they come on three corpses rotting in coffins—even the dogs are afraid—
and a hermit who points out the lesson: Death triumphs over all. This detail is from a huge fresco
painted on the wall of the cemetery next to the Pisa cathedral.*

own forms during the Late Middle Ages. The development of an English literary style was aided immensely
by the evolution of a common language. Until this
time, most educated English people read and spoke
French, but a rising sense of national consciousness,
triggered by the Hundred Years' War and by an emerging educated urban class, hastened the spread of
English as the native tongue. England's kings came to
see themselves as different from their French ancestors
and purposely began to speak English instead of
French; they also made English the official language of
government.

By 1300 important works in English were beginning
to appear, such as *The Vision of Piers Plowman,* a moral
allegory, probably written by William Langland (about
1332–1400), that graphically exposes the plight of the
poor and calls for a return to Christian virtues. This
work provides insight into England's social and eco-

nomic system and, through the author's anguish, reveals the social tension around the time of the Peasants' Revolt in 1381.

English literature was still establishing its own
identity and a common language was slowly emerging
when Geoffrey Chaucer (about 1340–1400) appeared
on the scene. He wrote in an East Midland dialect
of English that became the standard form for his generation as well as the foundation of modern English.
The son of a wealthy London merchant, Chaucer spent
his professional life as a courtier, a diplomat, and a
public servant for the English crown. The profession of
"writer" or "poet" was unknown in Chaucer's day. But
his poetry brought him renown, and when he died he
was the first commoner to be buried in Westminster
Abbey, a favored burial spot for English royalty.

Chaucer began composing his most famous work,
The Canterbury Tales, in 1385. He set the tales in the

context of a pilgrimage to the tomb of Thomas à Becket, the twelfth-century martyr. Even though the journey has a religious purpose, Chaucer makes it plain that the travelers intend to have a good time along the way. To make the journey from London to Canterbury more interesting, the thirty-one pilgrims (including Chaucer himself) agree to tell tales—two each going and returning—and to award a prize for the best story told.

Chaucer completed only twenty-three tales and the general Prologue, in which he introduces the pilgrims. Each person on the pilgrimage not only represents an English social type but also is a unique and believable human being. In this poetic narrative about a group of ordinary people, the spiritual is mixed with the temporal and the serious with the comic.

Chaucer drew his pilgrims from nearly all walks of medieval society. The Knight, in this late stage of feudalism, personified much that was noble and honorable in the chivalric code; his bravery could not be questioned, but he was also a mercenary and cruel to his enemies. Certain representatives of the church are also somewhat skeptically treated. The Prioress, the head of a convent and from the upper class, is more concerned about her refined manners and polished language than the state of her soul. Similarly, the Monk lives a life of the flesh and enjoys good food, fine wines, and expensive clothing. The Friar seems the very opposite of his sworn ideals; he is eager to hear a confession for a fee, and he never goes among the poor or aids the sick. However, in the country Parson, Chaucer portrays a true servant of God who preaches to his parish, looks after the infirm and dying, and never takes more than his share from his religious flock.

Among the secular travelers, the most vivid is the Wife of Bath. A widow five times over, this jolly woman is full of life and loves to talk. She has been on many pilgrimages and not only knows about foreign places but also has a keen insight into people (Figure 10.6).

As for the tales they tell, the pilgrims' choices often reflect their own moral values. The worthy Knight tells a chivalric love story, but the Miller, a coarse, rough man well versed in lying and cheating, relates how a young wife took on a lover and deceived her husband—an example of the popular medieval tale known as a *fabliau*. Thus the pilgrims' stories, based on folk and fairy tales, romances, classical stories, and beast fables, reveal as much about the narrators as they do about late medieval culture.

French Literature: Christine de Pizan France was also touched by the winds of change blowing through Europe during the Late Middle Ages. Christine de Pizan, the leading French writer of the day, began to

Figure 10.6 *The Wife of Bath.* Ellesmere Manuscript. Early fifteenth century. Bancroft Library, University of California at Berkeley. *In the Ellesmere Manuscript, an early edition of* The Canterbury Tales *issued soon after Chaucer's death, each story was accompanied by a sketch of the pilgrim who was narrating it. This portrait of the Wife of Bath shows her riding an ambler, a horse that walks with an easy gait, and wearing a wimple, the typical headdress of nuns as well as laywomen of the period.*

explore in her works the status and role of women, giving voice in the process to one of the most prominent issues in the Post-Modern world (see Chapter 21). She also contributed to the triumph of vernacular over Latin language by writing in a graceful French with the learnedness of Latin.

Christine de Pizan (sometimes written as "de Pisan," or "of Pisa") (1364–about 1430) was by birth an Italian whose literary gifts blossomed under the patronage of the French kings and dukes of Burgundy. She began a life of study and learning after the death of her husband, a royal official, in 1389, left her with a family to support. The first known Western woman to earn a living through her writings, de Pizan was a pioneer who blazed the trail for women authors.

De Pizan wrote on diverse topics, working within the well-established literary genres of her day, including love poems, lays, biography, letters, political tracts, and moral proverbs. Two themes dominate her writing: calls for peace and appeals for the recognition of women's contributions to culture and social life. Both themes reflect the era in which she lived—an age beset by civil strife because of the Hundred Years' War and a time in which women were scarcely allowed to express an opinion in public.

The work of de Pizan's that has excited the most interest among modern readers is *The Book of the City of Ladies* (1405), a book that forcefully tries to raise the status of women and to give them dignity. Offering one of the first histories of women and arguing that women have the right to be educated, based on her premise that women are moral and intellectual equals of men, this book seems almost feminist in a modern sense; however, a close reading shows that de Pizan is writing within a medieval framework. Nowhere in this book or in any other writings does she advocate that women abandon their traditional roles and strike out on a new path. It is proper nevertheless to claim that de Pizan is the first Western writer to raise the issue of women's rights in society and culture.

Art and Architecture

The Gothic style continued to dominate architecture throughout this period (see Chapter 9), but the balanced and unified High Gothic of the thirteenth century was now replaced with the ornate effects of the **Late Gothic style.** Virtuosity became the chief aesthetic goal, as the architects took basic forms and pushed them to the stylistic limits.

Late Gothic sculpture and painting also became more virtuosic. Statues and sculptured figures were given willowy, swaying bodies, rendered in exquisite detail, and illuminated manuscripts and painted wooden panels became ever more refined. At the same time, Giotto, an early-fourteenth-century Florentine painter, was revolutionizing art with a new approach to painting. The trend toward naturalism embodied in his works was the most significant new artistic development of this period and was destined to be the wave of the future.

Late Gothic Architecture France—the home of the Gothic style—remained a potent source of architectural innovation. French architects now abandoned the balanced ideal of the High Gothic and made extravagance their guiding principle, creating a Late Gothic style typified by ever greater heights and elaborate decoration. In the fifteenth century, this tendency culminated in the **Flamboyant style,** so named for its flamelike effects. French churches built in this style had sky-piercing spires, and their facades were embroidered with lacy or wavy decorations

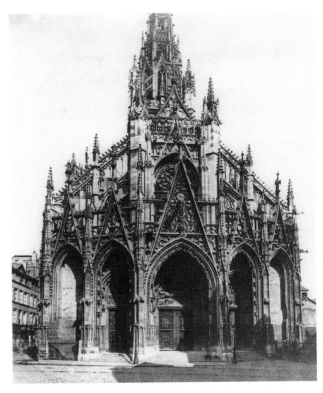

Figure 10.7   The Church of St. Maclou. 1435–ca. 1514. Rouen, France. *St. Maclou's exterior illustrates the ornate Late Gothic style. Its west facade, unlike a square High Gothic front, fans out to form a semicircular entrance. There are five portals (rather than the usual three), two of which are blind, and set above them are steeply pitched stone arches of intricate design.*

that obscured the buildings' structural components (Figure 10.7).

During the fourteenth century, the Late Gothic spread, becoming an international style. All across Europe, the focus shifted to fanciful designs: The churches were smaller, the roofs and towers taller, the naves wider, and the decorations more luxuriant. Regional tastes, however, made for local variations in the general style.

In England, the Late Gothic was called **Perpendicular** because of its dramatic emphasis on verticality. This Perpendicular style was characterized by an increased use of paneled decorations on the walls and overhead vaults, resulting in a variation of rib vaulting, called **fan vaulting,** in which stone ribs arch out from a single point in the ceiling to form a delicate pattern. This style also increased the number of window openings, which necessitated additional flying buttresses. The best example of the English Perpendicular is the cathedral in Gloucester.

In the choir, the vertical lines, extending from the floor to the ceiling, where the tracery is interwoven,

Figure 10.8 Choir of Gloucester Cathedral. Ca. 1330–1357. Gloucester, England. *The choir and apse of Gloucester cathedral were rebuilt in the Perpendicular Gothic style in about 1330, when King Edward III chose the church as the burial shrine for his murdered father, Edward II. The architects made the earlier Norman apse into a square and filled the east end with glass panels. Inside, the builders redesigned the support system, using thin vertical piers; these piers were attached to the walls and laced together on the ceiling, creating elaborate patterns that complemented the glass decorations.*

unite the building's interior into an upward-moving volume (Figure 10.8). Just as impressive as the interior is the nearby cloister with its fan tracery vaulting that weaves a pattern overhead while tying the walls and ceiling into a complex unit (Figure 10.9).

In Italy, the Gothic had put down only shallow roots because the Italians felt that the French builders had little to teach them about architecture. Italian Gothic has strong affinities with the Romanesque style—the large hall with its basilica floor plan and massive walls. In addition, most of the key Gothic features are missing from the Italian Gothic, such as the flying buttresses, the twin towers, and the vast numbers of stained-glass windows.

A key example of the Late Italian Gothic is the cathedral in Siena. Filled with civic pride, Siena's citizens urged their leaders to build a cathedral more splendid than those of their neighbors. Begun in the mid–thirteenth century, the cathedral was constructed over the next hundred and fifty years, and, as a result, the building complex shows a mixture of styles: The **campanile,** or bell tower, is executed in the Italian Romanesque, but the overall cathedral complex is Italian Gothic (Figure 10.10). The facade, for the first time in Italy, incorporated nearly life-size figures into the total design, thus heightening its resemblance to the French Gothic. However, many features distinguish the style of Siena from the French style. For example, the decorative statues on Siena's facade were placed above the gables and not set in niches. Furthermore, the Sienese builders put mosaics into the spaces in the gables and above the central rose window.

Florence, Siena's greatest military and trade rival, refused to be outdone by its nearby competitor. The Florentine city fathers asked Giotto [JAWT-toe] (about 1276–1337), the city's most renowned painter, to design a campanile for their own cathedral. Today, the first story of the bell tower—with its carvings, interlaced patterns of pink and white marble, and hexagonal inlays—still stands as conceived by Giotto (Figure 10.11). Giotto's plan, as left in a drawing, called for an open tower with a spire on top, as in a French Gothic tower. But later architects constructed a rectangular top instead and decorated it with marble—making it distinctively Italian rather than reminiscent of the French.

Figure 10.9 South Cloister of Gloucester Cathedral. Ca. 1370. Gloucester, England. *Fan vaulting, an intricate pattern in which ribs arch out from a single point in the ceiling, first appeared at Gloucester cathedral and inspired many imitations. Although the ribs may appear to be structurally necessary, they are really a richly decorative device carved from stone. In Gloucester's south cloister, the tracery fans out from the top of each column and then merges in the center of the ceiling, giving the impression of a delicate screen.*

Figure 10.10 Siena Cathedral. 1250–1400. Siena, Italy. *Extant records and floor plans show that the Sienese changed their minds several times before deciding on the cathedral's final shape. At one time, in about 1322, a commission of architects advised that the existing cathedral be demolished because the foundations and walls were not strong enough to support new additions. Nonetheless, construction went forward, and the cathedral is still standing after more than six hundred years.*

Late Gothic Sculpture During the Late Middle Ages, sculpture, like architecture, continued to undergo stylistic changes, among which two general trends may be identified. One trend centered in Italy, notably in Siena, where the Pisano [pee-SAHN-o] family began to experiment with sculptural forms that foreshadowed Renaissance art, with its return to Classical themes and values (see Chapter 11). Outstanding among the members of the gifted Pisano family was Giovanni Pisano

(1245–1314), who designed the intricate Late Gothic facade of the Siena cathedral (see Figure 10.10). Giovanni's great artistic reputation is largely based on the massive marble pulpit that he carved for the cathedral at Pisa. Using Classical themes derived from Roman art (as Renaissance artists were to do), he designed the pulpit to rest on acanthus leaves at the top of eight Corinthian columns (Figure 10.12). The lions that support two of the columns were modeled on those on

Figure 10.11 GIOTTO. Campanile of the Florentine Cathedral. Ca. 1334–1350. Ht. approx. 200′. Florence, Italy. *Giotto's Tower, as this campanile is known in Florence, is one of the city's most cherished landmarks. Today, its bells still toll the time. The two sets of windows in the central section and the taller openings at the top give the campanile a strong sense of balanced proportion. Thus, despite being built in the fourteenth century, the tower anticipates the Classical ideal that was revived in the Renaissance.*

Figure 10.12 GIOVANNI PISANO. Pulpit in the Pisa Cathedral. Ca. 1302–1310. Pisa, Italy.
Pisano built and carved this massive (17-foot-high) pulpit at the height of his reputation. A superb artist but a quarrelsome man, Pisano recorded his frustrations in the lengthy inscription around the pulpit's base. In it he claimed that he had achieved much, had been condemned by many, and took full responsibility for this work of art. Pisano's advance from anonymity to a position of great artistic repute was typical of a new breed of artist appearing in fourteenth-century Italy.

Figure 10.13 GIOVANNI PISANO. Nativity Scene. Pulpit in the Pisa cathedral. Ca. 1302–1310. 33½ × 44½″. Pisa, Italy. *In this Late Gothic sculpture, Pisano cut deeply into the marble's surface to give a nearly three-dimensional effect. His many figures seem involved in their own tasks but are nevertheless linked with one another around the Madonna and child. For example, the two shepherds (the head of one has been lost) in the upper right corner appear to be listening to the angels approaching from the left, while at the far right, sheep rest and graze. Such balanced placements are evidence of Pisano's classicizing tendencies. Pisano's relief retains a prominent Gothic feature, however, by presenting the Virgin and child twice—in the central scene and in the lower left corner, where a seated Mary, balancing the baby Jesus on her right leg, stretches her left hand to test the temperature of the water in an elaborate basin.*

an ancient Roman sarcophagus. Just as late Roman art blended Christian and Classical symbols, so Giovanni's treatment of the pulpit's base mixed images of the cardinal virtues, such as Justice and Temperance, with the figure of the Greek hero Herakles.

Pisano's octagonal pulpit includes eight panels in high relief that depict scenes from the lives of either John the Baptist or Christ. Of these panels, the scene depicting the Nativity ranks as his finest work. In this scene, he portrays a natural vitality through the careful balance and orderly spacing of the animals and people (Figure 10.13). The placement and the calm actions of

the surrounding figures frame the Virgin and child so that the viewer's attention is focused on these two central figures. Giovanni's swaying figures with their smooth draperies were rooted in Late Gothic art, but their quiet serenity attested to his classicizing manner.

The other trend in sculpture during this time centered in Burgundy, where Philip the Bold (r. 1364–1404) supported scholars and artists at his ducal court in Dijon. Preeminent among these was Claus Sluter [SLUE-tuhr] (about 1350–1406), a sculptor of Netherlandish origin who helped to define this last phase of Gothic art. Sluter's masterly sculptures are still housed in a monastery near Dijon, and his most famous work, *The Well of Moses*, was commissioned for the cloister of this monastic retreat.

The Well of Moses, which was designed as a decorative cover for an actual well in a courtyard, is surrounded at its base with Old Testament prophets symbolizing the sacraments of communion and baptism. The most beautifully rendered of the surviving life-size statues is Moses, encased in a flowing robe and standing erect with a finely chiseled head (Figure 10.14). Sluter's sense of the dramatic moment, of the prophet's personal emotions, and of the individual features makes the statue nearly an individual portrait. Sluter rendered Moses' beard and the unfurled scroll in precise detail and carved the figure with the head turned to the side, eyes looking into the future.

Late Gothic Painting and the Rise of New Trends

Of all the arts, painting underwent the most radical changes in the Late Middle Ages. Illuminated manuscripts maintained their popularity, but their themes became more secular under the patronage of titled aristocrats and wealthy merchants. At the same time, painters of frescoes and wooden panels introduced new techniques for applying paint and mixing colors. Stylistically, painters preferred to work in the extravagant Late Gothic manner with its elegant refinement and its undulating lines. Nevertheless, as mentioned earlier, Giotto and other Italian painters discovered fresh ways of depicting human figures that started to revolutionize art.

ILLUMINATED MANUSCRIPTS   The Burgundian court played a pivotal role in the production of one of the outstanding illuminated manuscripts of the medieval period, the *Très Riches Heures du Duc de Berry*. This famous collection of miniatures was painted by the three Limbourg brothers for the duke of Berry, brother of Philip the Bold of Burgundy. These illustrations stand above the others of their time for their exquisite detail, general liveliness, and intricately designed crowd scenes—some of the marks of the Late Gothic style.

The *Très Riches Heures*, or the *Very Rich Hours*, represents a type of small prayer book that was a favorite of nobles and businessmen. These personal books of worship, with their litanies and prayers, were often handsomely hand-illustrated to enhance their value. The duke of Berry's prayer book contained some 130 miniature paintings, including scenes from the life of Christ and the calendar cycle. In the calendar series, each tiny painting, finely detailed and colored in jewel-like tones, notes a seasonal activity appropriate for the month. Some represent the brilliant court life of the duke, and others depict the drudgery of peasant life, sharply differentiated from the court scenes by

Figure 10.14   CLAUS SLUTER. *Moses*, from *The Well of Moses*. Ca. 1395–1406. Ht. of full figure approx. 6'. Chartreuse de Champmol, Dijon, France. *Sluter followed the allegorical tradition of medieval art in this portrait of the Hebrew prophet Moses. The book in Moses' right hand and the scroll over his left shoulder symbolize the Word of God. Sluter also depicted Moses with "horns" growing out of his forehead, as was characteristic in medieval representations.*

their action and color. The illustration for January shows the duke of Berry surrounded by his well-dressed courtiers and enjoying a sumptuous feast (Figure 10.15).

THE PRINT   The print, a new artistic medium, developed in the Late Middle Ages in the Austrian-Bavarian regions, eastern France, and the Netherlands. Sparked by the growth of lay piety, the earliest prints were devotional woodcuts to be used as aids to personal meditation. The prints initially featured scenes from the lives of the Virgin and Christ. For the **woodcut print,** the artist drew an image on a woodblock, which was

Figure 10.15 LIMBOURG BROTHERS. Month of January, from the *Très Riches Heures du Duc de Berry.* 1413–1416. Approx. 8½ × 5½". Musée Condé, Chantilly, France. *This miniature painting provides insightful social history in its exquisite details. The duke, seated in the right center, is dressed in a blue patterned cloak and is greeting his guests for what was probably a New Year's celebration. Behind the duke stands a servant, over whose head are written the words "aproche, aproche," a welcome that is the equivalent of "Come in, come in." Above this festive scene, the zodiac signs of Capricorn and Aquarius identify the month as January.*

then cut by a woodcutter and printed by the artist; some were then hand-tinted by a colorist. By 1500 the new techniques of **engraving** (using a sharp tool to draw an image onto a metal plate overlaid with wax, dipping the plate in acid, and then printing it) and **drypoint** (marking an image onto a copper plate with a metal stylus and then printing it) were becoming increasingly popular.

Probably the outstanding set of prints dating from this period was that in the Medieval Housebook, a late-fifteenth-century German manuscript. The so-called Medieval Housebook was a gathering of 192 prints, of which only 126 remain. Most of the prints are in black and white, though a few are partially colored. The printing techniques vary from drypoint and engraving to simple drawings on vellum. Stylistic differences indicate that at least three artists contributed to the work, thus suggesting that the Housebook may have been produced in a workshop. For convenience, however, the artist is called simply the Housebook Master.

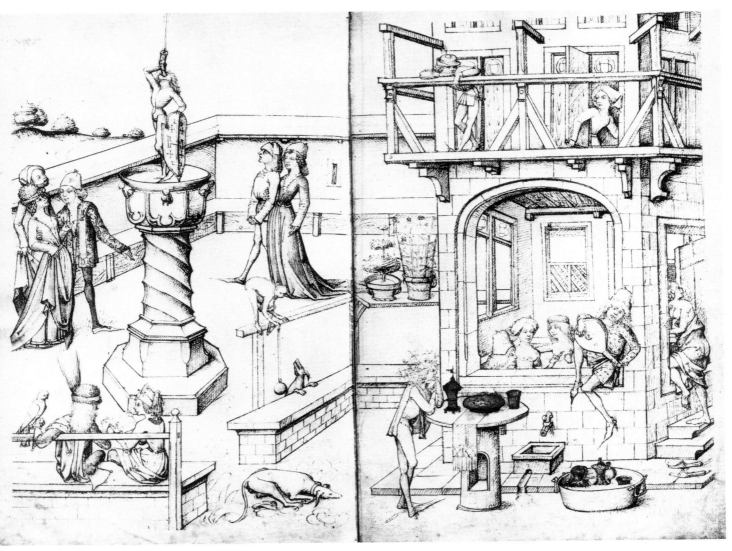

Figure 10.16 Housebook Master. *Leisure Time at the Bath.* Ca. 1475–1490. Ink on vellum drawing, partially colored. Private collection. *This print reveals the upper classes at play as well as the strict social order. On the left, young couples converse or flirt around a fountain in a courtyard; the pets (a falcon, two dogs, and a monkey) are indicators of the high status of their owners; a lady-in-waiting holds the skirt of her mistress. On the right, young aristocrats (a man and two women) enjoy bathing, while a third woman is entering the bathhouse. A servant serenades the bathers on a stringed instrument, as another waits in attendance. On the balcony, two servants enjoy a flirtatious moment. This Chaucerian-like scene, with its frank sensuality, indicates that within the increasingly secular world of the Late Middle Ages the pleasures of the flesh could be a fit subject for an artist.*

Of the surviving 126 prints, the subjects range over late medieval life, from the workaday world to jousting scenes to court life. Some offer realistic views of medieval buildings, including barnyards, private dwellings, and palaces; most are highly detailed, showing hair and clothing styles. Others are lively and playful, depicting relations between the sexes and the classes (Figure 10.16).

NEW TRENDS IN ITALY: GIOTTO While the illuminated manuscript and the print were popular in northern Europe, a revolution in painting was under way in Italy. The paintings of Giotto are generally recognized as having established a new direction in Western art, one that led into the Renaissance. In Giotto's own day, Dante praised him and the citizens of Florence honored him. Later, Vasari, the famous sixteenth-century painter and biographer, declared that Giotto had "rescued and restored" painting.

Giotto's revolution in painting was directed against the prevailing **Italo-Byzantine style,** which blended Late Gothic with Byzantine influences. He turned this painting style, with its two-dimensional, lifeless quality, into a three-dimensional art characterized by naturalism and the full expression of human emotions. Partly through the innovative use of light and shade and the placement of figures so as to create nonmathematical **perspective,** or depth, Giotto was able to paint realistic-looking figures, rather than the flat, ornamental depictions found in most illuminated manuscripts or the Italian altar paintings.

A painting by one of Giotto's contemporaries, Cimabue [chee-muh-BU-a] (about 1240–1302), the *Madonna Enthroned,* reveals the state of Italian painting at this time (Figure 10.17). The angels on the side are rendered stiffly, aligned vertically without any sense of space between them, and placed flat on the wood panel without any precise relationship with the four

Figure 10.17 CIMABUE. *Madonna Enthroned.* Ca. 1280. Tempera on panel, 12'7½" × 7'4". Uffizi Gallery, Florence. *Although Cimabue was experiencing the same desire for freedom in art as the sculptor Giovanni Pisano, this painting of the Madonna shows that he still was strongly under the spell of the Italo-Byzantine tradition. Rather than showing the intense feeling of Giotto's portraits, Cimabue's Virgin and child remain medieval and mystical.*

Figure 10.18 GIOTTO. *Madonna Enthroned*. Ca. 1310. Tempera on panel, 10'8" × 6'8". Uffizi Gallery, Florence. *Giotto's* Madonna Enthroned, *so revolutionary in its composition and spatial dimensions, has been called the most influential painting of the fourteenth century. Especially innovative in this altarpiece is the realistic treatment of the Virgin's eyes. They are shaped like ordinary eyes and peer out at the viewer rather than gazing into the distance, as in the Italo-Byzantine style.*

prophets below them. Although Cimabue's angels were balanced in their placement and the depiction of the figures of the Madonna and Christ child offered some sense of rounded form, the overall effect of the work confirms its debt to the two-dimensional tradition of Italo-Byzantine art.

In contrast, Giotto's *Madonna Enthroned*, painted about twenty years after Cimabue's, shows how Giotto was transforming Florentine art (Figure 10.18). His Madonna seems to be actually sitting on her throne, and the four angels on either side of her chair are placed to give a sense of spatial depth, or perspective.

The angels' distinctive gazes are highly expressive, suggesting feelings of wonder and respect. The Virgin resembles an individual woman and Christ a believable child, not a shrunken adult. Although Giotto uses Gothic touches—the pointed arch, the haloes, and the applied gold leaf—the natural rendering of the figures foreshadows great changes in art.

Giotto was a prolific artist whose paintings adorned churches in Florence and cities all over Italy. At the Arena Chapel in Padua, Giotto painted his masterpiece, two sets of frescoes, one of the life of the Virgin and the other of the life of Christ. These thirty-eight scenes show

Figure 10.19 GIOTTO. *Lamentation.* Ca. 1305–1310. Fresco, 7′7″ × 7′9″. Arena Chapel, Padua, Italy. *Such works gained Giotto his reputation as the modern reviver of realistic art— a tradition that had been lost with the fall of ancient Rome. In this fresco, he created three-dimensional space in ways that even the Greeks and the Romans had not used. Giotto's illusion of depth was conveyed by surrounding the dead Christ with numerous figures and, in particular, by placing two mourners in the foreground with their backs to the viewer. Giotto's use of perspective was convincing to his generation even though it lacked mathematical precision.*

Giotto at the height of his powers, rendering space with a sense of depth and organizing figures so as to create dramatic tension. An outstanding scene from the Padua frescoes is the *Pietà,* or *Lamentation* (Figure 10.19). This scene, which portrays the grief for the dead Christ, expresses total despair through the mourners' faces and gestures, from Mary, who cradles the body of Jesus, to John, who stands with arms outstretched, to the hovering angels. In the fresco's stark and rugged landscape, even nature seems to mourn, notably in the barren tree that symbolizes the wood of the cross on which Jesus was crucified. After Giotto died in 1337, no painter for the rest of the century was able to match his remarkable treatment of nature and human emotions.

FLEMISH PAINTING: JAN VAN EYCK AND HANS MEMLING
When Philip the Good (r. 1419–1467) became duke of Burgundy, he expanded his territories to include the wealthy counties of Holland, Zeeland, and Luxembourg. Philip was the greatest secular patron of the arts of his day. Of the artists encouraged by his patronage, the brothers Jan and Hubert van Eyck are the most famous, and their religious works and portraits established the Flemish style of art. Little is known of Hubert, but Jan van Eyck [YAHN van IKE] (about 1370–1441) is considered the founder of the Flemish school.

As a general principle, Flemish art sought reality through an accumulation of precise and often symbolic details, in contrast to Italian art, which tended to be more concerned with psychological truth, as in Giotto's frescoes in the Arena Chapel. This national style, expressed primarily through painting with oils on wood panels, turned each artwork into a brilliant and precise reproduction of the original scene. The finest detail in a patterned carpet, the reflected light on a copper vase, or the wrinkled features of an elderly patron were laboriously and meticulously recorded. The Flemish style, with its close attention to detail, was widely appreciated and quickly spread to Italy and England.

Jan van Eyck, probably with his brother's help, painted an altarpiece for the cathedral at Ghent, Belgium (Figure 10.20). This large work—originally

Figure 10.20 HUBERT AND JAN VAN EYCK. *Ghent Altarpiece.* Ca. 1432. Oil on panel, 11'3" × 14'5". St. Bavo cathedral, Ghent, Belgium. *This large altarpiece may seem to be a collection of separate paintings, but the work is united in themes and symbolism. What links the panels is their portrayal of Christ's redemption of humanity. From "The Sin of Adam and Eve" to the mystic "Adoration of the Lamb," all the paintings touch in some manner on Christ's sacrifice.*

commissioned to beautify the high altar—still remains in its original place. The twenty panels are hinged together so that when opened twelve are visible. These twelve panels are divided into two levels—heavenly figures and symbols on the upper level and earthly figures on the lower level. On the ends of the upper level are nude portraits of Adam and Eve, next to angels singing and playing musical instruments. Mary on the left and John the Baptist on the right flank a portrayal of God the Father, resplendent in a jewel-encrusted robe and triple crown. Below, on the lower level, are human figures who are depicted as moving toward the center panel. On the left, knights and judges ride on horseback, while, on the right, pilgrims and hermits approach on foot.

The focus of the *Ghent Altarpiece,* when opened, is the lower center panel, the *Adoration of the Lamb.* In this work, the sacrificial death of Jesus is symbolized by the cross, the baptismal font in the foreground, and the blood issuing from the lamb into the communion chalice. The surrounding worshipers include holy virgins,

Figure 10.22   Jan van Eyck. *Arnolfini Wedding Portrait.* 1434. Oil on wood, 33 × 22½". Reproduced by courtesy of the Trustees, National Gallery, London. *This work is a perfect expression of the symbolic realism that dominated northern European painting in the Late Middle Ages. The wedding is celebrated in a room filled with religious symbols of the marriage rite. For example, the bride and groom stand shoeless, indicating that they are in holy space, and above them is a chandelier with a single lighted candle, a sign of God's presence.*

martyrs, and prophets, plus the four evangelists and the Twelve Apostles, who stand and kneel in groups amid plants and trees (Figure 10.21).

In contrast to this mystical work, Jan van Eyck painted a decidedly secular but still symbolic work in his *Arnolfini Wedding Portrait* (Figure 10.22). In this painting, nearly every object—the lighted candle, the shoes, the fruit, the dog—refers to a wedding custom or belief. Yet, the details—for example, the mirror on the rear wall reflecting the couple's backs, the artist, and a fourth person—create a worldly setting. Van Eyck's painting is not an imaginary scene but a recording of an

Figure 10.21   Hubert and Jan van Eyck. *Adoration of the Lamb.* Detail of the *Ghent Altarpiece.* Ca. 1432. St. Bavo cathedral, Ghent, Belgium. *This lower center section of the opened altarpiece dramatically shows how the Flemish school could use religious symbolism to evoke a mystical effect. The refined details, which derived from the tradition of manuscript painting, make this scene both credible and otherworldly.*

Figure 10.23 HANS MEMLING. *Madonna and Child with Angels.* After 1479. Oil on panel, 23⅛ × 18⅞". Andrew W. Mellon Collection. National Gallery of Art, Washington, D.C. (1937.1.41) Photograph © Board of Trustees. *Memling, though part of the Flemish tradition, appeared to be aware of developments in Renaissance Italy. He introduced some Italian elements into this painting, such as the putti, or small angels (used as decorations on the columns and arch), and the stringed musical instruments held by the angels.*

actual event, for Arnolfini was an Italian businessman who lived in Bruges. Thus, the commerce and wealth of Burgundy and the Italian cities are symbolically united by van Eyck in this wedding portrait.

A second outstanding artist working in Flanders during the Late Middle Ages was Hans Memling (about 1430–1494), the most popular painter of his day in Bruges. Long a northern commercial center, Bruges was now entering a period of decline, hastened by the displacement of the Burgundian ruling house by that of the Hapsburgs. Before settling in Bruges, the German-born Memling studied painting in Cologne and the Netherlands, where he fully absorbed the northern tradition. Memling's painting style, which borrowed heavily from that of Jan van Eyck and his generation, was characterized by serenity and graceful elegance, traits that stand in marked contrast to this turbulent era. After starting his workshop in Bruges, Memling grew wealthy from commissions, mainly for altarpieces and portraits, paid for by church leaders, local businesspeople, and resident foreign merchants. More than eighty of his works have survived.

Memling was particularly celebrated for the piety of his Madonna paintings, such as the *Madonna and Child with Angels* (Figure 10.23). Following the Flemish tradition, this painting is filled with religious symbolism, which reinforces the message that Christ died to atone for the sins of humankind. The baby Christ reaches for an apple held by an angel, the fruit symbolizing original sin. The second angel, dressed in a vestment associated with the High Mass, plays a harp, possibly a reference to heavenly music. A carved vine of grapes, depicted on the arch, is an emblem of Holy Communion. On the left column stands David, an ancestor of Christ, and on the right column stands Isaiah, a prophet who foretold the birth of the Messiah.

The format and the details of Memling's enthroned Madonna harken back to Jan van Eyck, but without the intensity or sense of reality. Memling's style is static and somewhat artificial. The painting space is clearly arranged, but the landscape and architectural background function as a stage set; the figures are so composed that they constitute a veritable *tableau vivant*, a staged scene in which costumed actors remain silent as if in a picture. Each of the three figures is treated in similar fashion—thin bodies; oval faces; blank, emotionless stares. Adding to the air of artificiality is the absence of shadows, for the painting is bathed in unmodulated light.

Music

The forces of change transforming Europe in the 1300s also had an impact on the field of music. Sacred music began to be overshadowed by secular music, with the rise of new secular forms—such as the ballade and rondeau—based on the **chanson,** a song set to a French text and scored for one or more voices, often with instrumental accompaniment. Polyphony remained the dominant composing style, but composers now wrote secular polyphonic pieces that were not based on Gregorian chants. These changes were made possible by innovations that coalesced into what came to be called the *new art* (**ars nova** in Latin), particularly in Paris, the capital of polyphonic music. The innovations included a new system of music notation, along with new rhythmic patterns such as **isorhythm**—the use of a single rhythmic pattern from the beginning to the end of a work, despite changes in the melodic structure. The chief exponent of *ars nova* was the French composer and poet Guillaume de Machaut [gee-yom duh mah-show] (ca. 1300–1377).

Machaut, who trained as a priest and musician, first made his mark as a court official to the King of Bohemia. For his services, he was rewarded with an appointment to the cathedral in Reims (1337), where he worked for much of the rest of his life. His music circulated widely in his day, largely because he made gifts of his music manuscripts to wealthy patrons. Thus, he became one of the first composers whose works have survived. Reflecting the decline in church music, his output consists mainly of secular love themes. In England, his verses influenced the great poet Geoffrey Chaucer.

Although famous for secular music, Machaut's reputation rests on his *Notre Dame* Mass, the first polyphonic version of the Mass Ordinary by a known composer. "Ordinary" refers to the five parts of the Mass that remain unchanged throughout the liturgical year, namely the Kyrie ("Lord, have mercy"), Gloria ("Glory"), Credo ("the Nicene Creed"), Sanctus and Benedictus ("Holy" and "Blessed"), and Agnus Dei ("Lamb of God"). Written for four voices, some of which may have been performed by instrumentalists, Machaut's Mass made liberal use of isorhythm in most of its parts. Following his lead, composers for more than six hundred years made the Mass Ordinary the central point of choral music.

The Legacy of the Late Middle Ages

All historical eras are periods of transition, but the changes of the Late Middle Ages were especially momentous. The medieval world was dying, and the modern era was struggling to be born. Dating from this turbulent period were many of the cultural tensions that defined the history of Europe for the next four hundred years.

The most revolutionary happening in the Late Middle Ages was the release of a powerful secular spirit that began to make its presence felt everywhere. The upsurge of vernacular literature, the rise of literary themes questioning the low status of women, the increasing popularity of secular music, and the divergence of philosophy and theology are four examples of this new development. But the greatest impact of the rise of secularism on cultural life was that painting and sculpture began to be liberated from the service of architecture. The first stirrings of this change were expressed in the works of Giotto and other Italian and Flemish artists. By the next century, painting in Italy

had freed itself from the tutelage of architecture and become the most important artistic genre in the West.

This period also saw the emergence of a new breed of secular ruler who was prepared to mount a sustained drive against the church's combined political and spiritual powers. The victories of the English and the French kings over the papacy—each ruler was able to secure control over his national church—were signs of the breakup of Christendom.

Another important legacy of these years is that the towns, led by their bourgeois citizens, began to exercise their influence over the countryside. From today's perspective, the growth of the middle class as a dominant force in society was perhaps the most critical development of this age. Finally, this period witnessed the unusual spectacle of the common people revolting against the aristocratic control of the culture and society. Their sporadic efforts failed, but the seeds of future revolution were planted.

KEY CULTURAL TERMS

devotio moderna	woodcut
via antiqua	engraving
via moderna	drypoint
Late Gothic style	Italo-Byzantine style
Flamboyant style	perspective
Perpendicular style	*chanson*
fan vault	*ars nova*
campanile	isorhythm

SUGGESTIONS FOR FURTHER READING

Primary Sources

BOCCACCIO, G. *The Decameron.* Translated by M. Musa and P. E. Bondanella. New York: Norton, 1977. An updated translation of the hundred stories—some learned, some coarse, but all humorous—that make up this work; first published about 1351.

CHAUCER, G. *The Canterbury Tales.* Edited by N. Coghill. New York: Penguin, 1978. Of many versions of these bawdy and lighthearted tales, Coghill's is one of the most readable and enjoyable; the original work dates from 1385.

CHRISTINE DE PIZAN. *The Book of the City of Ladies.* Translated by E. J. Richards. New York: Persea Books, 1982. An accessible, modern translation of this Late Medieval work, which argues that the political and cultural dignity of women depends on their being educated properly, just as men are; first published in 1405.

LANGLAND, W. *The Vision of Piers Plowman.* Translated by H. W. Wells. New York: Sheed and Ward, 1959. A good modern version of Langland's work criticizing the religious establishment of his day and calling for a new order; written between 1362 and 1394.

SUGGESTION FOR LISTENING

GUILLAUME DE MACHAUT (ca. 1300–1377). Machaut's innovations in rhythm helped inaugurate the **ars nova** style. His *Notre Dame* Mass, which employed isorhythms, is the first setting of the Mass Ordinary by a known composer.

CHAPTER *10* HIGHLIGHTS
The Late Middle Ages, 1300–1500

 PETRARCH, *Canzoniere (Songbook)* (mid–fourteenth century)

PETRARCH, *Secretum* or *My Secret* (1342–1343)

 BOCCACCIO, *The Decameron* (ca. 1351)

LANGLAND, *The Vision of Piers Plowman* (ca. 1380s)

CHAUCER, *The Canterbury Tales* (1385–1400)

CHRISTINE DE PIZAN, *The Book of the City of Ladies* (1405)

10.10 Siena Cathedral, Italy (1250–1400)

10.17 CIMABUE, *Madonna Enthroned* (ca. 1280)

10.12 PISANO, Pulpit in the Pisa Cathedral, Italy (ca. 1302–1310)

10.19 GIOTTO, *Lamentation* (ca. 1305–1310)

10.18 GIOTTO, *Madonna Enthroned* (ca. 1310)

10.8 Choir of Gloucester Cathedral, England (ca. 1330–1357)

10.11 GIOTTO, Campanile of the Florentine Cathedral (ca. 1334–1350)

10.15 LIMBOURG BROTHERS, Illustration from *Très Riches Heures du Duc de Berry* (1413–1416)

10.20 HUBERT AND JAN VAN EYCK, *Ghent Altarpiece* (ca. 1432)

10.22 JAN VAN EYCK, *Arnolfini Wedding Portrait* (1434)

10.7 Church of St. Maclou, Rouen, France, (1435–ca. 1514)

10.16 HOUSEBOOK MASTER, Illustration from Medieval Housebook (ca. 1475–1490)

10.23 MEMLING, *Madonna and Child with Angels* (after 1479)

 MACHAUT, *Notre Dame* Mass (mid–fourteenth century)

 *Literature & Philosophy*    *Art & Architecture*    *Music & Dance*

 *Readings in the Western Humanities*    *CD, The Western Humanities*

AFRICA

AMERICAS

HISTORY

East Africa *Coastal trading states.* Arab-Swahili society; trade with inland peoples and Ming China. *Zimbabwe.* Bantu state; based on gold; height of Great Zimbabwean civilization. *Zambezi Valley.* Rival states fought to control trade.
North Africa *Egypt.* Mameluke Dynasty, ended 1517. *Morocco.* Merinid Dynasty lost Atlantic port to Portuguese.
West Africa *Songhai Empire.* Successor to Ghana and Mali; controlled salt and gold through Timbuktu, Jenne-jero, and Gao. *Kongo Kingdom.* Bantu trading state; under Portuguese influence (1482). *Yoruba culture.* Ife, a religious center; Benin and Oyo, trading states; Benin dominant (after 1440) and free of European control.
South Africa Portuguese made contact with Bushmen, Hottentots, and Bantu-speaking peoples.

Andes *Sicán culture.* Ended 1400. *Inca culture.* Conquered Chimú and Ica (ca. 1460). Empire ranged from Peru to Chile.
Mesoamerica *Late Postclassic period, ended 1519. Mayan culture.* Faded away after peasant revolt in Mayapán (about 1460). *Aztec culture.* Began 1426. Capital Tenochtitlán (Mexico City); ruled much of modern Mexico, Guatemala, and El Salvador. Warrior culture devoted to conquest and ritual sacrifice of captured enemies.
Native North America *Southwest.* Descendants of Anasazi (including Hopi, Zuni, Acoma tribes) migrated to river areas (1300–1700). *Eastern woodlands.* Five Lake Ontario tribes formed Iroquois League (ca. 1390).
Caribbean Arawaks greeted Columbus when he landed on Hispaniola (1492); decimated by epidemics in wake of contact with Europeans (1508–11).

ART & MUSIC

West Africa *Yoruba culture.* Ife bronzes: naturalistic life-size heads of kings and queens. Benin bronzes: life-size and miniature statues of people and animals; portrait heads; influenced by Nok and Ife art. *Oriki,* or praise song, flourished, encompassing daily chores and life's passages.

Bronze Head. Benin. Fifteenth century. British Museum.

Andes *Chancay culture.* Textiles (ponchos and clothing) and ceramics (figurines and whistling pots). *Inca culture.* Tapestries and ceramics. *Colombia.* Jewelry and pectorals, made from alloys of copper, silver, and gold.
Mesoamerica *Late Postclassic period. Mayan culture.* At Mayapán: stone stelae depicting gods; at Tulum: polychrome, ceramic figures, especially images of the deity Chac. *Aztec culture.* Clay figurines of deities. Monumental stone sculptures.
Native North America *Koniag culture.* Alaska. Wooden masks representing real people. *Mississippian culture. Calusa culture.* Florida. Wooden feline figurines. *Southwest.* Pueblo. Elaborate kachina masks representing supernatural beings in ritual ceremonies.

ARCHITECTURE

East Africa *Coastal trading states.* Mosques and palaces. *Zimbabwe.* Mortarless stone buildings, built for Bantu kings, priests, and ruling class. Round mud huts with pole-and-thatch roofs for ordinary Bantu.

Andes *Inca culture.* The mountaintop fortress city of Machu Picchu, built of massive interlocked stones fitted together without mortar.
Mesoamerica *Late Postclassic period. Mayan culture.* Walled city of Mayapán. *Aztec culture.* Tenochtitlán, modeled on Teotihuacán, laid out on a grid dominated by two pyramids; Tlatelolco, largest trading center in the Americas.
Native North America *Iroquois culture, northeastern U.S.* Communal longhouses, made of poles covered with sheets of bark.

General View. Machu Picchu, Peru. Fifteenth century.

RELIGION, PHILOSOPHY, LITERATURE

West Africa *Songhai Empire.* Islamized merchant class; progressive Islamization of society (after 1493). *Kongo Kingdom.* Portuguese Christian missionaries arrived (1482).

Andes *Inca culture.* Daily and periodic offerings (a llama, a fine textile, a child) to the gods. Royal mummies ritually fed, dressed, consulted, and carried in processions.
Mesoamerica *Late Postclassic period. Aztec culture.* Tenochtitlán's twin pyramids dedicated to the chief gods. At Tepeyacac: worship of mother goddess Tonantzín; site later identified with Virgin of Guadalupe.

Aztec Calendar Stone. Fifteenth century. Basalt, diam. 360".
Tenochtitlán. National Museum of Anthropology, Mexico City.

ASIA

China

Ming Dynasty. At first, expanded influence, forcing tribute from Mongolia, Japan, and Korea and sending maritime expeditions to Southeast Asia and East Africa. Later, turned inward to support farming, commerce, and social change. Zenith: Yung-lo (r. 1402–24).

India

Medieval period. Hindu and Muslim states at war: Vijayanagar Empire (1336–1565), the most successful Hindu state; Bahmani Kingdom (about 1347–1518), the strongest Islamic state. *Delhi Sultanate, ended 1526.* Political instability: three dynasties between 1413 and 1451, when the Lodis brought stability and territorial expansion.

The Forbidden City, Beijing. General view of one of the inner courtyards of the palace. Fifteenth century.

Japan

Muromachi period, began 1333. Weak shōguns; continual warfare among the *daimyō* (feudal lords) and their samurai retainers.

Ming Dynasty. Height of blue and white porcelain; silk brocades. Two schools of landscape painting: the court artists, or Zhe School, centered in province of Zhejiang; the Wu School, based in Suzhou, the cultural capital. A Wu School legacy: poem painting (including a complementary poem in a painting).

Medieval period. In Vijayanagar Empire: carved stone figures of deities on Hindu temples.

Muromachi period. Chinese (Yüan, Ming, and Zen Buddhist) influences; silk paintings, fine arts, decorations, and ink paintings (landscape, poem, and portrait). Chinese art collected by shōguns and the ruling class.

Ming Dynasty. Splendid imperial tombs with many above-ground rooms. Emperor Yung-lo made Beijing the capital (1403); built the Forbidden City, a 250-acre compound containing the administrative center of the country and palaces, temples, and tombs for the royal family; style characterized by wooden beams and pillars and wide tile roofs.

Vijayanagar Empire. Lotus Mahal, a two-story pavilion. *Delhi Sultanate.* Persian-style buildings (low domes and thick walls).

Muromachi period. Chinese-style pavilions built by shōguns, often as retreats; teahouses; and rock and dry landscape gardens.

Golden Pavilion, Kyōto. General view. 1398; rebuilt, 1964.

Yüan Dynasty. First color printing in the world. *Ming Dynasty.* Definitive Confucian texts, arranged by Emperor Yung-lo. Encyclopedia (about 11,000 volumes) began to be issued (1403).

Delhi Sultanate. Lodi rulers cultivated a transplanted Persian culture. One of India's greatest Persian writers, the poet and historian Amir Khosrow (see Figure 8.15).

Muromachi period. Nō drama created: Nobumitsu's classic play *Ataka* and 240 plays by Motokiyo Zeami. *Tsurezuregusa* (casual jottings), the period's chief prose genre.

11 THE EARLY RENAISSANCE

Return to Classical Roots

1400–1494

Believing they had broken radically with the past, Italian artists and intellectuals in the fifteenth century began to speak of a rebirth of civilization. Since the nineteenth century, the term *Renaissance* (meaning "rebirth") has described the cultural and artistic activities of the fifteenth and sixteenth centuries that began in Italy and spread northward. The Renaissance profoundly altered the course of Western culture, although scholars have differing interpretations of the significance of this first modern period.

THE RENAISSANCE: SCHOOLS OF INTERPRETATION

In the 1860s, Swiss historian Jacob Burckhardt, agreeing with the fifteenth-century Italians, asserted that the Renaissance was a rebirth of ideas after centuries of cultural stagnation. He maintained that a new way of understanding the world had emerged, as the Italians looked back to ancient Greece and Rome for inspiration and declared themselves part of a revitalized civilization that was distinctive and superior to the immediate past.

By the mid–twentieth century, Burckhardt's interpretation began to be viewed as too simplistic. According to some scholars, the Italians, after the fall of Rome, never lost sight of their Classical roots. These historians considered the revival of learning in the fifteenth century to be more of a shift in educational and cultural emphasis than a rediscovery of antiquity. They also noted that the Renaissance had at least two phases, the Early and the High, each with different contributions.

◀ **Detail** GIOVANNI BELLINI. *St. Francis in Ecstasy.* 1470s. Oil in tempera on panel, 49 × 55⁷/₈". Frick Collection, New York.

Figure 11.1 DOMENICO GHIRLANDAIO. *Old Man with a Child.* Ca. 1480. Panel 24½ × 18″. Louvre. *This double portrait summarizes many of the new secular values of the Early Renaissance, such as its human-centeredness and its preference for simple scenes. The work's subject, a man possibly with his grandchild, indicates the important role that the family played during the times. The age's commitment to direct observation of the physical world is evident in the treatment of the man's diseased nose (rosacea) and the landscape glimpsed through the open window.*

Since the 1960s, a third interpretation has dominated Renaissance studies. In this view, the Renaissance label should be used cautiously and only to describe what was happening in learning and the arts, not in politics and society. The authors of this book tend to agree with this third interpretation. In politics, economics, and society, Italy in the 1400s differed little from Italy in the 1300s; however, the Italians of the 1400s did start down a new *cultural* path (Figure 11.1).

This chapter examines the first phase of this new cultural style, the Early Renaissance (1400–1494); Chapter 12 is devoted to the brief High Renaissance (1494–1520) and to Early Mannerism (1520–1564), an anti-Classical phase of the Renaissance. Chapter 13 considers Northern Humanism, the Northern Renaissance, the early-sixteenth-century religious reformations, and Late Mannerism (1564–1603), when Renaissance style was slowly undermined by new trends (Timeline 11.1).

EARLY RENAISSANCE HISTORY AND INSTITUTIONS

For most of the fifteenth century, the city-states of northern Italy were prosperous and peaceful enough to sustain upper-class artists and writers. This supportive climate encouraged the innovations of Renaissance culture. By the end of the century, however, disputes among Italy's city-states and a shift in maritime trade from the Mediterranean to the Atlantic, coupled with the French invasion of Florence in 1494, had dimmed northern Italy's cultural preeminence.

Italian City-States During the Early Renaissance

The erratic fortunes of Italy's economy were a major factor in the region's politics in this period. The northern Italian city-states had emerged from the High Middle Ages in 1300 as Europe's leading commercial center and manufacturer of finished woolens (see Chapter 9), but by 1500 they had been eclipsed by various European nations to the north. In the 1300s, Italian population, productivity, and prosperity declined because of the Black Death and the birth of the English woolen industry. Although the Italians made a limited economic recovery in the 1400s, history was moving against them. Even their domination of international banking was challenged by German businessmen.

During the Early Renaissance, five Italian states competed for dominance: the Republic of Venice, the Duchy of Milan, the Republic of Florence, the Papal States, and the Kingdom of Naples. Other small states, such as the artistic and intellectual centers of Ferrara and Modena, played minor but crucial roles (Map 11.1). In the first half of the fifteenth century, the Italian states waged incessant wars among themselves, shifting sides when it was to their advantage.

The continuous warfare and the uncertain economy provided the conditions for the emergence of autocratic rulers called *signori,* who were from ruling families or elitist factions. Taking advantage of economic and class tensions, these autocrats pledged to solve local problems, and in so doing they proceeded to accumulate power in their own hands. What influence the guilds, the business leaders, and the middle class had wielded in the fourteenth century gave way to these despots, ending the great medieval legacy of republicanism in Venice, Milan, and Florence.

Under the *signori,* the conduct of warfare also changed. Technological developments changed weaponry, and battles were fought with mercenary troops led by *condottieri,* soldiers of fortune who sold their military expertise to the highest bidder. But the most

Timeline 11.1 STAGES OF THE ITALIAN RENAISSANCE

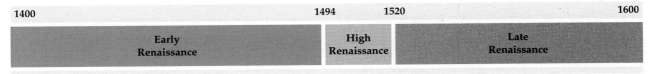

1400	1494	1520	1600
Early Renaissance	High Renaissance	Late Renaissance	

LEARNING THROUGH MAPS

Map 11.1   THE STATES OF ITALY DURING THE RENAISSANCE, CA. 1494
This map shows the many states and principalities of Italy in the Early Renaissance. **Consider** the size of each state with its role in competing for dominance of the Italian peninsula. **Notice** the large number of states in the north as compared with the small number in the south. **Notice** also the four forms of government—duchy, republic, kingdom, and papal states. **Identify** the major ports of the Italian state system. **What** geographic advantage made the Papal States such a force in Italian politics?

significant change in Renaissance warfare was the emergence of diplomacy as a peaceful alternative to arms, a practice that gradually spread throughout the Continent. The Italian regimes began sending representatives to other states, and it soon became customary for these diplomats to negotiate peace settlements. In turbulent fifteenth-century Italy, these agreements seldom lasted long—with the notable exception of the Peace of Lodi. This defensive pact, signed in 1454 by Milan, Florence, and Venice, established a delicate balance of power and ensured peace in Italy for forty years.

The Peace of Lodi came apart in 1494, when a French army led by Charles VIII entered Italy in the hope of promoting French monarchic ambitions. Outside Italy, three events further weakened the region's prospects for regaining its position as a major

Figure 11.2 PEDRO BERRUGUETE (?). *Federico da Montefeltro and His Son Guidobaldo. Ca. 1476–1477. Oil on panel, 4′5⅛″ × 2′5⅞″. Galleria Nazionale della Marche, Urbino. Urbino, under the Montefeltro dynasty, was transformed from a sleepy hill town with no cultural history into a major center of Renaissance life. Federico, the founder of the dynasty and one of the greatest* condottieri *of his day, was created duke of Urbino and captain of the papal forces by Pope Sixtus IV in 1474. Federico then devoted his energies to making Urbino a model for Italian Renaissance courts. In this portrait, the seated Federico wears the armor of a papal officer while reading a book—symbols that established him as both a soldier and a scholar, later the ideal of Castiglione's Courtier. At the duke's right knee stands his son and heir, Guidobaldo, wearing an elaborate robe and holding a scepter, a symbol of power. Federico's dream ended with his son, the last of the Montefeltro line.*

At the Urbino court, artists combined Flemish and Italian styles, as in this double portrait. The internal lighting, emanating from some unseen source on the left, is adopted from the tradition pioneered by Jan van Eyck; the profile portrait of the duke follows the Italian practice, based on portrait heads rendered on medals. This double portrait was probably painted by Pedro Berruguete, Spain's first great Renaissance artist, who studied painting in Naples and worked briefly in Urbino before returning to his homeland.

economic power: the fall of Constantinople in 1453, Portugal's opening of the sea route around Africa to India at the end of the century, and Columbus's Spanish-sponsored voyage to the New World.

These three events shifted the focus of international trade from the Mediterranean to the Atlantic. The fall of Constantinople to the Ottoman Turks in 1453 temporarily closed the eastern Mediterranean markets to the Italian city-states. At the same time, by virtue of the wide-ranging global explorations they sponsored, some European powers—most notably Portugal and Spain—were extending their political and economic interests beyond the geographical limits of continental Europe.

Before the Italian city-states were eclipsed by other European powers, however, upper-class families enjoyed unprecedented wealth, which they used to cultivate their tastes in literature and art and thus substantially determine the culture of the Early Renaissance (Figure 11.2). One reason for the importance these families gave to cultural matters is that they put high value on family prestige and on educating their sons for their predestined roles as heads of family businesses and their daughters as loyal wives and successful household managers (Figure 11.3). The courts of the local rulers, or *grandi*, became places where educated men—and, on occasion, women—could exchange ideas and discuss philosophical issues.

Although the status of women did not improve appreciably, more were educated than ever before. Many ended up behind the walls of a convent, however, if their parents could not afford the costly dowry expected of an upper-class bride. The few upper-class women with an independent role in society were those who had been widowed young. The women at the ducal courts who exercised any political influence did so because of their family alliances. One of the most powerful of these women was Lucrezia Borgia [loo-KRET-syah BOR-juh] (1480–1519), the illegitimate daughter of Pope Alexander VI. Married three times before the age of twenty-one, she held court in Ferrara and was the patron of many writers and artists. Most women who tried to exercise real power, however, found it unattainable.

Florence, the Center of the Renaissance

Amid the artistic and intellectual activity occurring throughout Italy, Florence, the capital of the Tuscan region, was the most prominent of the city-states. After 1300 Florence's political system went through three phases, evolving from republic to oligarchy to family rule. During these turbulent political times, however, Florentine artists and writers made their city-state the center of the Early Renaissance (Timeline 11.2).

Timeline 11.2 THE EARLY RENAISSANCE IN FLORENCE, 1400–1494

1400							1494
			Early Renaissance				

1403–1424 Ghiberti's north doors, Florentine Baptistery	1425 Invention of linear perspective (Brunelleschi)	1429–1437 Ghiberti's east doors, Florentine Baptistery	1438–1445 Fra Angelico's *Annunciation*	1461 Completion of Pazzi Chapel by Brunelleschi	1473–1475 Verrocchio's *David*	1480s Botticelli's *Primavera* and *The Birth of Venus*	1483 Leonardo da Vinci's *The Virgin of the Rocks*
	1425–1428 Masaccio's frescoes for Santa Maria Novella	1430–1432 Donatello's *David*		1462 Founding of Platonic Academy, Florence			
		1435 Alberti's *On Painting*					

The republic, which began in the fourteenth century with hopes for political equality, fell into the hands of a wealthy oligarchy. This oligarchy, composed of rich bankers, merchants, and successful guildsmen and craftsmen, ruled until the early fifteenth century, when the Medici family gained control. The Medicis dominated Florentine politics and cultural life from 1434 to 1494, sometimes functioning as despots.

The Medicis rose from modest circumstances. Giovanni di Bicci de' Medici [jo-VAHN-nee dee BEET-chee day MED-uh-chee] (1360–1429) amassed the family's first large fortune through banking and close financial ties with the papacy. His son Cosimo (1389–1464) added to the Medicis' wealth and outmaneuvered his political enemies, becoming the unacknowledged ruler of Florence. He spent his money on books, paintings, sculptures, and palaces, and, claiming to be the common man's friend, he was eventually awarded the title

Figure 11.3 DOMENICO GHIRLANDAIO. *Giovanna degli Albizzi Tornabuoni.* Ca. 1489–1490. Tempera and (?) oil on panel, 29½ × 19¼". Madrid, Thyssen-Bornemisza Collection (cat. no. 46). *This likeness of Giovanna degli Albizzi Tornabuoni (1468–1486) embodies the Florentine ethos of family, city, and church. Her husband, Lorenzo Tornabuoni, a member of a prominent Florentine family, commissioned it as a memorial. Probably painted after his wife's death, it was much admired by Lorenzo, who, according to household records, kept it hanging in his bedroom, even after his remarriage. The subject's gold bodice is decorated with emblems—interlaced Ls and diamonds—which are symbolic of Lorenzo and his family. The brooch, the coral necklace, and the prayer book allude to Giovanna's high social status and piety. In the background, the Latin epigram "O Art, if thou were able to depict conduct and the soul, no lovelier painting would exist on earth" evokes the Renaissance ideal that equates physical beauty with moral perfection. The epitaph is based on a line from an ancient Roman poet.*

Pater patriae, Father of His Country—a Roman title revived during the Renaissance.

Cosimo's son, Piero, ruled for only a short time and was succeeded by his son Lorenzo (1449–1492), called the Magnificent because of his grand style of living. Lorenzo and his brother Giuliano controlled Florence until Giuliano was assassinated in 1478 by the Pazzi family, rivals of the Medicis. Lorenzo brutally executed the conspirators and then governed autocratically for the next fourteen years.

Within two years of Lorenzo's death, the great power and prestige of Florence began to weaken. Two events are symptomatic of this decline in Florentine authority. The first was the invasion by Charles VIII's French army in 1494. The invasion initiated a political and cultural decline that would eventually overtake Italy, whose small city-states could not withstand the incursions of the European monarchies. The French army drove the Medici family from Florence; they remained in exile until 1512.

The second event was the iconoclastic crusade against the city led by the Dominican monk Fra Savonarola [sav-uh-nuh-ROH-luh] (1452–1498). He opposed the Medicis' rule and wanted to restore a republican form of government. In his fire-and-brimstone sermons, he denounced Florence's leaders and the city's infatuation with the arts. He eventually ran afoul of the papacy and was excommunicated and publicly executed, but not before he had had an enormous effect on the citizens—including the painter Botticelli, who is said to have burned some of his paintings while under the sway of Savonarola's reforming zeal.

The Resurgent Papacy, 1450–1500

The Great Schism was ended by the Council of Constance in 1418, and a tattered Christendom reunited under a Roman pope (see Chapter 10). By 1447 the so-called Renaissance popes were in command and had turned their attention to consolidating the Papal States and pursuing power. Like the secular despots, these popes engaged in war and, when that failed, diplomacy. They brought artistic riches to the church but also lowered its moral tone by accepting bribes for church offices and filling positions with kinsmen. But above all, these popes patronized Renaissance culture.

Three of the most aggressive and successful of these church rulers were Nicholas V (pope 1447–1455), Pius II (pope 1458–1464), and Sixtus IV (pope 1471–1484). Nicholas V, who had been librarian for Cosimo de' Medici, founded the Vatican Library, an institution virtually unrivaled today for its holdings of manuscripts and books. He also continued the rebuilding of Rome begun by his predecessors. Pius II, often considered the most representative of the Renaissance popes because of his interest in the Greek and Roman classics and in writing poetry himself, rose rapidly through the ecclesiastical ranks. This clever politician practiced both war and diplomacy with astounding success. As a student of the new learning and as a brilliant writer in Latin, Pius II attracted intellectuals and artists to Rome. His personal recollections, or *Commentaries,* reveal much about him and his turbulent times.

Sixtus IV came from the powerful and scheming della Rovere family, and he increased his personal power through nepotism, the practice of giving offices to relatives. He continued the papal tradition of making Rome the most beautiful city in the world. The construction of the Sistine Chapel, later adorned with paintings by Botticelli and Michelangelo, was his greatest achievement (see Chapter 12).

THE SPIRIT AND STYLE OF THE EARLY RENAISSANCE

Drawing inspiration from ancient Greek and Roman models, the thinkers and the artists of the Early Renaissance explored such perennial questions as, What is human nature? How are human beings related to God? and What is the best way to achieve human happiness? Although they did not reject Christian explanations outright, they were intrigued by the secular and humanistic values of the Greco-Roman tradition and the answers they might provide to these questions. They also rightfully claimed kinship with certain fourteenth-century predecessors such as the writer Petrarch and the artist Giotto (see Chapter 10).

Those artists, scholars, and writers who are identified with the Early Renaissance and who embodied its spirit were linked, through shared tastes and patronage, with the entrepreneurial nobility, the progressive middle class, and the secular clergy. Until about 1450, most artistic works were commissioned by wealthy patrons for family chapels in churches and for public buildings; later, patrons commissioned paintings and sculptures for their private dwellings.

Even though artists, scholars, and writers stamped this age with their fresh perspectives, some of the old cultural traits remained. Unsettling secular values emerged in the midst of long-accepted religious beliefs, creating contradictions and tensions within society. In other ways, however, the past held firm, and certain values seemed immune to change. For example, Early Renaissance thought made little headway in science, and church patronage still strongly affected the evolution of the arts and architecture, despite the growing impact of the urban class on artistic tastes.

The artists, scholars, and writers who flourished in the Early Renaissance were almost exclusively men, in contrast with the Middle Ages, when women occasionally played cultural roles. Recent scholarship has pointed out that women living in the Italian Renaissance were subjected to new constraints, especially in well-to-do families. For example, the learned Laura Cereta [che-RAY-tah], daughter of a physician in Brescia, was silenced at eighteen years of age for her outspokenness, though not before she had published a defense of herself, asserting the right of women to be educated the same as men.

Humanism, Scholarship, and Schooling

Toward the end of the 1300s, Italy's educated circles became fascinated by ancient Roman civilization. Inspired by Petrarch's interest in Latin literature and language, scholars began to collect and translate Roman manuscripts uncovered in monastic libraries and other out-of-the-way depositories. There was a shift in emphasis from the church Latin of the Middle Ages to the pure Latin style of Cicero, the first-century B.C. Roman writer whose eloquent essays established a high moral and literary standard (see Chapter 5).

In the 1400s, these scholars spoke of their literary interests and new learning as *studia humanitatis.* They defined this term, which may be translated as humanistic studies, as a set of intellectual pursuits that included moral philosophy, history, grammar, rhetoric, and poetry. At first, the men who studied these disciplines read the appropriate works in Latin, but after the Greek originals began to appear about 1400 and the study of ancient languages spread, they learned from the Greek texts as well.

In response to the demand for humanistic learning, new schools sprang up in most Italian city-states. In these schools was born the Renaissance ideal of an education intended to free or to liberate the mind—a liberal education. To that end, study was based on the recently recovered Latin and Greek works rather than on the more narrowly defined curriculum of scholasticism and Aristotelianism that had been favored in the Middle Ages.

The first Renaissance scholars, who were primarily searching for original Latin manuscripts, were philologists—that is, experts in the study of languages and linguistics. In time, they came to call themselves humanists because of their training in the *studia humanitatis.* These early humanists created a branch of learning, now called textual criticism, that compares various versions of a text to determine which one is most correct or authentic. They recognized that knowledge of the evolution of language was necessary to make a critical judgment on the authenticity of a text. As a result of their studies, they revealed writing errors committed by medieval monks when they copied ancient manuscripts—revelations that, in the case of religious documents, raised grave problems for the church.

The most spectacular application of textual criticism was made by Lorenzo Valla (1406–1457), who exposed the Donation of Constantine as a forgery. Throughout the Middle Ages, this famous document had been cited by the popes as proof of their political authority over Christendom. By the terms of the document, the Roman emperor Constantine gave the popes his western lands and recognized their power to rule in them. But by comparing the Latin of the fourth century, when Constantine reigned, with the Latin of the eighth century, when the document first came to light, Valla concluded that the Donation must have been produced then and not in the fourth century.

Other humanists played an active role in the life of their states, modeling themselves on the heroes of the Roman republic. Outstanding among them is Leonardo Bruni (1374–1444), who typifies the practical, civic humanist. A one-time chancellor, or chief secretary, of Florence's governing body, or *signoria,* Bruni also worked for both the Medicis and the papacy and wrote the *History of the Florentine People.* This work reflected his humanistic values, combining as it did his political experience with his knowledge of ancient history. To Bruni, the study of history illuminated contemporary events. Bruni and the other civic humanists, through their writings and their governmental service, set an example for later generations of Florentines and helped infuse them with love of their city. Moreover, by expanding the concept of humanistic studies, they contributed new insights into the ongoing debate about the role of the individual in history and in the social order.

An important consequence of humanistic studies was the rise of educational reforms. Vittorino da Feltre [veet-toe-REE-no dah FEL-tray] (1378–1446) made the most significant contributions. Vittorino favored a curriculum that exercised the body and the mind—the ideal of the ancient Greek schools. His educational theories were put into practice at the school he founded in Mantua at the ruler's request. At this school, called the Happy House, Vittorino included humanistic studies along with the medieval curriculum. A major innovation was the stress on physical exercise, which arose from his emphasis on moral training. At first, only the sons and daughters of Mantuan nobility attended his school, but gradually the student body became more democratic as young people from all classes were enrolled. Vittorino's reforms were slowly introduced into the new urban schools in northern Europe, and their

PERSONAL PERSPECTIVE

LAURA CERETA
Battle of the Sexes, Fifteenth-Century Style

In this letter, dated January 13, 1488, the young Laura Cereta responds fiercely to a critic who admired her writing by wondering how it could possibly be the work of a woman.

My ears are wearied by your carping. You brashly and publicly not merely wonder but indeed lament that I am said to possess as fine a mind as nature ever bestowed upon the most learned man. You seem to think that so learned a woman has scarcely before been seen in the world. You are wrong on both counts. . . .

I would have been silent, believe me, if that savage old enmity of yours had attacked me alone. . . . But I cannot tolerate your having attacked my entire sex. For this reason my thirsty soul seeks revenge, my sleeping pen is aroused to literary struggle, raging anger stirs mental passions long chained by silence. With just cause I am moved to demonstrate how great a reputation for learning and virtue women have won by their inborn excellence, manifested in every age as knowledge. . . .

Only the question of the rarity of outstanding women remains to be addressed. The explanation is clear: women have been able by nature to be exceptional, but have chosen lesser goals. For some women are concerned with parting their hair correctly, adorning themselves with lovely dresses, or decorating their fingers with pearls and other gems. Others delight in mouthing carefully composed phrases, indulging in dancing, or managing spoiled puppies. Still others wish to gaze at lavish banquet tables, to rest in sleep, or, standing at mirrors, to smear their lovely faces. But those in whom a deeper integrity yearns for virtue, restrain from the start their youthful souls, reflect on higher things, harden the body with sobriety and trials, and curb their tongues, open their ears, compose their thoughts in wakeful hours, their minds in contemplation, to letters bonded to righteousness. For knowledge is not given as a gift, but [is gained] with diligence. The free mind, not shirking effort, always soars zealously toward the good, and the desire to know grows ever more wide and deep. It is because of no special holiness, therefore, that we [women] are rewarded by God the Giver with the gift of exceptional talent. Nature has generously lavished its gifts upon all people, opening to all the doors of choice through which reason sends envoys to the will, from which they learn and convey its desires. The will must choose to exercise the gift of reason. . . .

I have been praised too much; showing your contempt for women, you pretend that I alone am admirable because of the good fortune of my intellect. . . . Do you suppose, O most contemptible man on earth, that I think myself sprung [like Athena] from the head of Jove? I am a school girl, possessed of the sleeping embers of an ordinary mind. Indeed I am too hurt, and my mind, offended, too swayed by passions, sighs, tormenting itself, conscious of the obligation to defend my sex. For absolutely everything—that which is within us and that which is without—is made weak by association with my sex.

model—the well-rounded student of sound body, solid learning, and high morals—helped to lay the foundation for future European schools and education.

Thought and Philosophy

The Italian humanists were not satisfied with medieval answers to the perennial inquiries of philosophy because those answers did not go beyond Aristotelian philosophy and Christian dogma. Casting their nets wider, the Renaissance thinkers concluded that the ancients had given worthwhile responses to many of the same issues as Christians and that they should not be dismissed simply because they were non-Christian.

Renaissance scholars came to advocate more tolerance toward unorthodox beliefs and began to focus on the important role played by the individual in society. Individual fulfillment became a leading Renaissance idea and remains a central notion in Western thought today. During the Renaissance, the growing emphasis on the individual resulted in a more optimistic assessment of human nature—a development that in time led to a rejection of Christianity's stress on original sin.

After the fall of Constantinople in 1453 and the flight of Byzantine scholars bearing precious manuscripts, the humanists began to focus increasingly on Greek literature, language, and, in particular, philosophy. The philosophy of Plato found a home in Italy in 1462 when Cosimo de' Medici established the Platonic Academy at one of his villas near Florence. Here, scholars gathered to examine and to discuss the writings of Plato as well as the Neo-Platonists, whose reinterpreted Platonism had influenced early Christian

Figure 11.4 SANDRO BOTTICELLI. *The Birth of Venus.* 1480s. Tempera on canvas, 5′8″ × 9′1″. Uffizi Gallery, Florence. *With the paintings of Botticelli, the nude female form reappeared in Western art for the first time since the Greco-Roman period. Botticelli's* Venus *contains many Classical echoes, such as the goddess's lovely features and her modest pose. But the artist used these pre-Christian images to convey a Christian message and to embody the principles of Ficino's Neo-Platonist philosophy.*

theology. The academy was under the direction of the brilliant humanist Marsilio Ficino [mar-SILL-e-o fe-CHEE-no] (1433–1499), whom Cosimo commissioned to translate Plato's works into Latin.

In two major treatises, Ficino made himself the leading voice of Florentine Neo-Platonism by harmonizing Platonic ideas with Christian teachings. Believing that Platonism came from God, Ficino began with the principle that both thought systems rested on divine authority. Like Plato, Ficino believed that the soul was immortal and that complete enjoyment of God would be possible only in the afterlife, when the soul was in the divine realm. Ficino also revived the Platonic notion of free will. In Ficino's hands, free will became the source of human dignity because human beings were able to choose to love God.

Ficino had the most powerful impact on the Early Renaissance when he made Plato's teaching on love central to Neo-Platonism. Following Platonism, he taught that love is a divine gift that binds all human beings together. Love expresses itself in human experience by the desire for and the appreciation of beauty in

its myriad forms. Platonic love, like erotic love, is aroused first by the physical appearance of the beloved. But Platonic love, dissatisfied by mere physical enjoyment, cannot rest until it moves upward to the highest spiritual level, where it finally meets its goal of union with the Divine. Under the promptings of Platonism, the human form became a metaphor of the soul's desire for God. Many Renaissance writers and artists came under the influence of Ficino's Neo-Platonism, embracing its principles and embodying them in their works. Sandro Botticelli, for example, created several allegorical paintings in which divine love and beauty were represented by an image from pre-Christian Rome—Venus, goddess of love (Figure 11.4).

Ficino's most prized student, Pico della Mirandola [PEE-koh DAYL-lah me-RAHN-do-lah] (1463–1494), surpassed his master's accomplishments by the breadth of his learning and the virtuosity of his mind. Pico—a wealthy and charming aristocrat—impressed everyone with his command of languages, his range of knowledge, and his spirited arguments. His goal was the synthesis of Platonism and Aristotelianism within

Figure 11.5 LEONE BATTISTA ALBERTI. Tempio Malatestiano (Malatesta Temple) (Church of San Francesco). Ca. 1450. Rimini, Italy. *Although unfinished, this church strikingly demonstrates the revolution in architecture represented by Early Renaissance ideals. Nothing could be further from the spires of Late Gothic cathedrals than this simple, symmetrical structure with its plain facade, post-and-lintel entrance, rounded arches, and Classical columns. Designed by the leading theoretician of the new style, the Malatesta Temple served as a model for artists and architects of the later Renaissance.*

a Christian framework that also encompassed Hebraic, Arabic, and Persian ideas. Church authorities and traditional scholars attacked Pico's efforts once they grasped the implication of his ambitious project—that all knowledge shared basic common truths and that Christians could benefit from studying non-Western, non-Christian writings.

Pico's second important contribution—the concept of individual worth—had been foreshadowed by Ficino. Pico's *Oration on the Dignity of Man* gives the highest expression to this idea, which is inherent in the humanist tradition. According to Pico, human beings, endowed with reason and speech, are created as a microcosm of the universe. Set at the midpoint in the scale of God's creatures, they are blessed with free will—the power to make of themselves what they wish—which enables them either to raise themselves to God or to sink lower than the beasts. This liberty to determine private fate makes human beings the masters of their individual destinies and, at the same time, focuses attention on each human being as the measure of all things—a Classical belief now reborn.

Architecture, Sculpture, and Painting

It was in architecture, sculpture, and painting that the Renaissance made its most dramatic break with the medieval past. The **Early Renaissance style** was launched in Florence by artists who wanted to make a complete break with the Late Gothic style (Figure 11.5). Led by the architect Filippo Brunelleschi [bru-nayl-LAYS-kee] (1377–1446), this group studied the ruins of Classical buildings and ancient works of sculpture to unlock the secrets of their harmonious style. They believed that once the Classical ideals were rescued from obscurity, new works could be fashioned that captured the spirit of ancient art and architecture without slavishly copying it.

Artistic Ideals and Innovations Guided by Brunelleschi's findings, architects, sculptors, and painters made the Classical principles of balance, simplicity, and restraint the central ideals of the Early Renaissance style. The heaviest debt to the past was owed by the architects, for they revived the Classical orders—the Doric, the Ionic, and the Corinthian. The new buildings, though constructed to accommodate modern needs, were symmetrical in plan and relied on simple decorative designs. The theoretician of Early Renaissance style and its other guiding light was Leone Battista Alberti [ahl-BAIR-tee] (1404–1472), who wrote at length on Brunelleschi's innovations and published a highly influential book on the new painting. Alberti believed that architecture should embody the humanistic qualities of dignity, balance, control, and harmony and that a building's ultimate beauty rested on the mathematical harmony of its separate parts.

Sculpture and painting, freed from their subordination to architecture, regained their ancient status as independent art forms and in time became the most cherished of the visual arts. Renaissance sculptors and painters aspired to greater realism than had been achieved in the Gothic style, seeking to depict human musculature and anatomy with a greater degree of credibility. Sculptors, led by this period's genius Donatello [dah-nah-TEL-lo] (about 1386–1466), revived Classical practices that had not been seen in the West for more than a thousand years: the free-standing figure; the technique of contrapposto, or a figure balanced with most of the weight resting on one leg (see Figure 3.22); the life-size nude statue; and the equestrian statue.

Whereas architecture and sculpture looked back to ancient Greek and Roman traditions, developments in painting grew from late medieval sources. In the early fourteenth century, Giotto had founded a new realistic and expressive style (see Chapter 10), on which Florentine painters began to build at the opening of the fifteenth century. Much of Giotto's genius lay in his ability to show perspective, or the appearance of spatial depth, in his frescoes, an illusion he achieved largely through the placement of the figures (see Figure 10.19). Approximately one hundred years after Giotto, painters learned to enhance the realism of their pictures by the use of linear perspective, the most significant artistic innovation of the age.

The invention of linear perspective was another of Brunelleschi's accomplishments. Using principles of architecture and optics, he conducted experiments in 1425 that provided the mathematical basis for achieving the illusion of depth on a two-dimensional surface (and, coincidentally, contributed to the enhancement of the status of the arts by grounding them in scholarly learning). Brunelleschi's solution to the problem of linear perspective was to organize the picture space around the center point, or **vanishing point.** After determining the painting's vanishing point, he devised a structural grid for placing objects in precise relation to each other within the picture space. He also computed the ratios by which objects diminish in size as they recede from view, so that pictorial reality seems to correspond visually with physical accuracy. He then subjected the design to a mirror test—checking its truthfulness in its reflected image.

When the camera appeared in the nineteenth century, it was discovered that the photographic lens "saw" nature according to Brunelleschi's mathematical rules. After the 1420s, Brunelleschi's studies led to the concept of Renaissance space, the notion that a composition should be viewed from one single position. For four hundred years, or until first challenged by Manet in the nineteenth century, linear perspective and Renaissance space played a leading role in Western painting (see Chapter 18).

A second type of perspective, atmospheric or aerial, was perfected by painters north of the Alps in the first half of the fifteenth century, although the Italian painter Masaccio was the first to revive atmospheric perspective in the 1420s, based on the Roman tradition. Through the use of colors, these artists created an illusion of depth by subtly diminishing the tones as the distance between the eye and the object increased; at the horizon line, the colors become grayish and the objects blurry in appearance. When atmospheric perspective was joined to linear perspective, as happened later in the century, a greater illusion of reality was achieved than was possible with either type used independently.

Again commenting on the innovations of Brunelleschi was Alberti, who published a treatise in 1435 that elaborated on the mathematical aspects of painting and set forth brilliantly the humanistic and secular values of the Early Renaissance. Alberti was an aristocratic humanist with both a deep knowledge of Classicism and a commitment to its ideals. In his treatise, he praised master painters in rousing terms, comparing their creativity to God's—a notion that would have been considered blasphemous by medieval thinkers. He asserted that paintings, in addition to pleasing the eye, should appeal to the mind with optical and mathematical accuracy. But paintings, he went on, should also present a noble subject, such as a Classical hero, and should be characterized by a small number of figures, by carefully observed and varied details, by graceful poses, by harmonious relationships among all elements, and by a judicious use of colors. These Classical ideals were quickly adopted by Florentine artists eager to establish a new aesthetic code.

Architecture   In the High Middle Ages, most architects were stonemasons and were regarded as artisans, like shoemakers or potters. But by the fifteenth century, the status of architects had changed. Because of the newly discovered scientific aspects of their craft, the leading architects were now grouped with those practicing the learned professions of medicine and law. By 1450 Italian architects had freed architecture from Late Gothicism, as well as from the other arts. Unlike Gothic cathedrals adorned with sculptures and paintings, these new buildings drew on the Classical tradition for whatever simple decorative details were needed. This transformation became the most visible symbol of Early Renaissance architecture.

Although Brunelleschi established the new standards in architecture, most of his buildings have been either destroyed or altered considerably by later hands. However, the earliest work to bring him fame still survives in Florence largely as he had planned it— the dome of the city's cathedral (Figure 11.6). Although the rest of the cathedral—nave, transept, and choir— was finished before 1400, no one had been able to devise a method for erecting the projected dome until Brunelleschi received the commission in 1420. Using the learning he had gained from his researches in Rome as well as his knowledge of Gothic building styles, he developed an ingenious plan for raising the dome, which was virtually completed in 1436.

Faced with a domical base of 140 feet, Brunelleschi realized that a hemispheric dome in the Roman manner, like the dome of the Pantheon, would not work (see Figure 5.13). Traditional building techniques could not span the Florentine cathedral's vast domical base, nor could the cathedral's walls be buttressed to support a massive dome. So he turned to Gothic methods, using diagonal ribs based on the pointed arch. This innovative dome had a double shell of two relatively thin walls held together by twenty-four stone ribs, of which only eight are visible. His crowning touch was to add a lantern that sits atop the dome and locks the ribs into place (Figure 11.7). The dome's rounded windows echo the openings in the upper nave walls, thereby ensuring that his addition would harmonize with the existing elements. But the octagonal-shaped dome was Brunelleschi's own creation and expresses a logical, even inevitable, structure. Today,

Figure 11.6 FILIPPO BRUNELLESCHI. Cathedral Dome, Florence. 1420–1436. Ht. of dome from floor 367'. *After the dome of the Florence cathedral was erected according to Brunelleschi's plan, another architect was employed to add small galleries in the area above the circular windows. But the Florentine authorities halted his work before the galleries were fully installed, leaving the structure in its present state.*

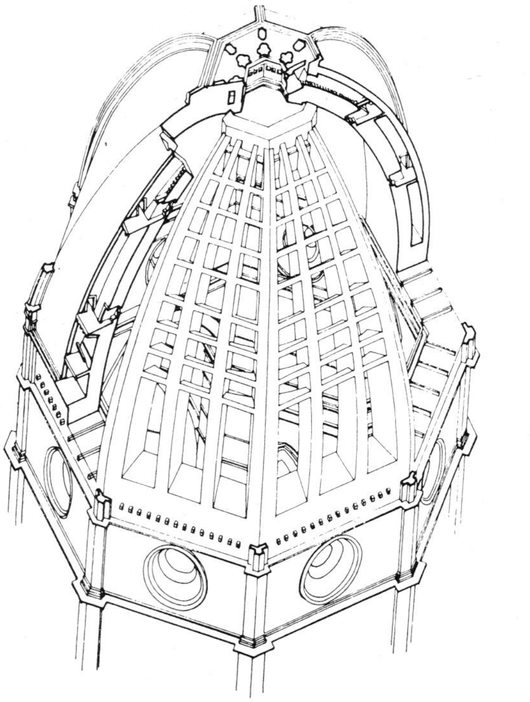

Figure 11.7 FILIPPO BRUNELLESCHI. Design for Construction of Dome of Florence Cathedral. *Brunelleschi designed the dome of the Florence cathedral with an inner and an outer shell, both of which are attached to the eight ribs of the octagonal-shaped structure. Sixteen smaller ribs, invisible from the outside, were placed between the shells to give added support. What held these elements together and gave them stability was the lantern, based on his design, that was anchored to the dome's top sometime after 1446.*

the cathedral still dominates the skyline of Florence, a lasting symbol of Brunelleschi's creative genius.

Brunelleschi's most representative building is the Pazzi Chapel, as the chapter house, or meeting room, of the monks of Santa Croce is called. This small church embodies the harmonious proportions and Classical features that are the hallmark of the Early Renaissance style. In his architectural plan, Brunelleschi centered a dome over an oblong area whose width equals the dome's diameter and whose length is twice its width and then covered each of the chapel's elongated ends with a barrel vault. Double doors opened into the center wall on one long side, and two rounded arch windows flanked this doorway. A loggia, or porch, which Brunelleschi may not have designed, preceded the entrance (Figure 11.8). Inside the chapel, following the Classical rules of measure and proportion, Brunelleschi employed medallions, rosettes, **pilasters** (or applied columns), and square panels. In addition to these Classical details, the rounded arches and the barrel vaults further exemplify the new Renaissance style (Figure 11.9). His Classical theories were shared by Florence's humanist elite, who found religious

significance in mathematical harmony. Both they and Brunelleschi believed that a well-ordered building such as the Pazzi Chapel mirrored God's plan of the universe.

The other towering figure in Early Renaissance architecture was Alberti. Despite the influence of his ideas, which dominated architecture until 1600, no completed building based on his design remains. A splendid unfinished effort is the Tempio Malatestiano in Rimini (see Figure 11.5), a structure that replaced the existing church of San Francesco. Rimini's despot, Sigismondo Malatesta, planned to have himself, his mistress, and his court buried in the refurbished

Figure 11.8 (Inset), FILIPPO BRUNELLESCHI AND OTHERS. Exterior, Pazzi Chapel, Santa Croce Church. 1433–1461. Florence. *The Pazzi Chapel's harmonious facade reflects the Classical principles of the Early Renaissance style: symmetry and simplicity. By breaking the rhythm of the facade with the rounded arch, the architect emphasizes its surface symmetry so that the left side is a mirror image of the right side. Simplicity is achieved in the architectural decorations, which are either Greco-Roman devices or mathematically inspired divisions.*

Figure 11.9 FILIPPO BRUNELLESCHI. Interior. Pazzi Chapel, Santa Croce Church. Ca. 1433–1461. 59′9″ long × 35′8″ wide. Florence. *Decorations on the white walls of the Pazzi Chapel's interior break up its plain surface and draw the viewer's eye to the architectural structure: pilasters, window and panel frames, medallions, capitals, and dome ribs. The only nonarchitecturally related decorations are the terra-cotta sculptures by Luca della Robbia of the four evangelists and the Pazzi family coat of arms, mounted inside the medallions.*

Figure 11.10 DONATELLO. *The Feast of Herod.* Ca. 1425. Gilt bronze, 23½″ square. Baptismal font, San Giovanni, Siena. *The first low-relief sculpture executed in the Early Renaissance style,* The Feast of Herod *is a stunning example of the power of this new approach to art. Its theatrical force arises from the successful use of linear perspective and the orderly placement of the figures throughout the three rooms.*

structure, and he appointed Alberti to supervise the church's reconstruction.

Alberti's monument represents the first modern attempt to give a Classical exterior to a church. Abandoning the Gothic pointed arch, he designed this church's unfinished facade with its three rounded arches after a nearby triumphal arch. He framed the arches with Corinthian columns, one of his favorite decorative devices. Although the architect apparently planned to cover the church's interior with a dome comparable to Brunelleschi's on the Florentine cathedral, Malatesta's fortunes failed, and the projected temple had to be abandoned. Nevertheless, Alberti's unfinished church was admired by later builders and helped to point the way to the new Renaissance architecture.

Figure 11.11 DONATELLO. *David.* Ca. 1430–1432. Bronze, ht. 62¼″. Bargello, Florence. *The David and Goliath story was often allegorized into a prophecy of Christ's triumph over Satan. But Donatello's sculpture undermines such an interpretation, for his* David *is less a heroic figure than a provocative image of refined sensuality, as suggested by the undeveloped but elegant body, the dandified pose, and the incongruous boots and hat. Donatello's* David *is a splendid modern portrayal of youthful male power, self-aware and poised on the brink of manhood.*

Sculpture Like architecture, sculpture blossomed in Florence in the early 1400s. Donatello, the leader of the sculptural revival, was imbued with Classical ideals but obsessed with realism. He used a variety of techniques—expressive gestures, direct observation, and mathematical precision—to reproduce what his eyes saw. Donatello accompanied Brunelleschi to Rome to study ancient art, and he adapted linear perspective as early as 1425 into a small **relief** called *The Feast of Herod* (Figure 11.10).

The subject is the tragic end of John the Baptist, Florence's patron saint, as recounted in Mark 6:20–29. In Donatello's square bronze panel, the saint's severed head is being displayed on a dish to King Herod at the left, while the scorned Salome stands near the right end of the table. A puzzled guest leans toward the ruler, who recoils with upraised hands; two children at the left back away from the bloody head; and a diner leans back from the center of the table—all depicted under the rounded arches of the new Brunelleschian architecture. The sculpture's rich details and use of linear perspective point up the horror of the scene and thus achieve the heightened realism that was among the artistic goals of this era. The scene's vanishing point runs through the middle set of arches, so that the leaning motions of the two figures in the foreground not only express their inner turmoil but also cause them to fall away from the viewer's line of sight.

Donatello also revived the free-standing male nude, one of the supreme expressions of ancient art. Donatello's bronze *David*, probably executed for Cosimo de' Medici, portrays David standing with his left foot on the severed head of the Philistine warrior Goliath—a pose based on the biblical story (Figure 11.11). This sculpture had a profound influence on later sculptors, who admired Donatello's creation but produced rival interpretations of David (Figure 11.12). Donatello and his successors used the image of David to pay homage to male power—a major preoccupation of Renaissance artists and intellectuals.

Like other Renaissance masters, Donatello owed debts to Classical artists, but he also challenged them by adapting their principles to his own times. For example, the Roman statue of Marcus Aurelius (see Figure 5.9) inspired Donatello's bronze called the *Gattamelata*, the first successful equestrian sculpture in over twelve hundred years (Figure 11.13). As Donatello's *David* portrays the subtleties of adolescent male beauty, his *Gattamelata* pays homage to mature masculine power. This work honored the memory of Erasmo da Narni, a Venetian *condottiere* nicknamed Gattamelata, or "Honey Cat." The warrior's pose resembles the Roman imperial style, but in almost every other way, the sculptor violates the harmonious ideas of ancient art.

Figure 11.12 ANDREA DEL VERROCCHIO. *David.* 1473–1475. Bronze, ht. 4'2". Bargello, Florence. *Verrocchio's David inaugurated the tradition in Renaissance Florence of identifying the Jewish giant-killer with the city's freedom-loving spirit. A masterpiece of bravado, Verrocchio's boyish hero stands challengingly over the severed head of Goliath. In its virility, this work surpasses the sculpture that inspired it, Donatello's David (see Figure 11.11). Florence's ruling council liked Verrocchio's statue so much that they placed it in the Palazzo Vecchio, the seat of government, where it remained until Michelangelo's David (see Figure 12.19) displaced it.*

Most significant, the rider's face owes its sharp realism—firm jawline, bushy eyebrows, widely set eyes, and close-cropped hair—to fifteenth-century sources, especially to the cult of the ugly, an aesthetic attitude that claimed to find moral strength in coarse features that did not conform to the Classical ideals (Figure 11.14). Since this work was commissioned after the hero's death and since Donatello had no way of knowing how the soldier looked, he sculptured the face to conform to his notion of a strong-minded general. The massive horse, with flaring nostrils, open mouth, and lifted foreleg, seems to be an extension of the soldier's forceful personality.

The only serious rival to Donatello in the Early Renaissance was another Florentine, Lorenzo Ghiberti [gee-BAIR-tee] (about 1381–1455), who slowly adapted to the new style of art. In 1401 he defeated Brunelleschi

Figure 11.13 DONATELLO. *Equestrian Monument of Erasmo da Narni, Called "Gattamelata."* 1447–1453. Bronze, approx. 11 × 13'. Piazza del Santo, Padua. *This equestrian statue of the* condottiere *was funded by his family but authorized by a grateful Venetian senate in honor of his military exploits. Conceiving of the dead military leader as a "triumphant Caesar," Donatello dressed him in Classical costume and decorated his saddle and armor with many allusions to antique art, such as flying cupids and victory depicted as a goddess.*

in a competition to select a sculptor for the north doors of Florence's Baptistery. The north doors consist of twenty-eight panels, arranged in four columns of seven panels, each depicting a New Testament scene. These doors, completed between 1403 and 1424, show Ghiberti still under the influence of the International Gothic style that prevailed in about 1400. Illustrative of this tendency is the panel of *The Annunciation* (Luke 1:26–38), which depicts the moment when Mary learns from an angelic messenger that she will become the mother of Christ (Figure 11.15). The Gothic quatrefoil, or four-leafed frame, was standard for these panels, and many of Ghiberti's techniques are typical of the Gothic style—the niche in which the Virgin stands, her

Figure 11.14 DONATELLO. Detail of *"Gattamelata."* 1447–1453. Piazza del Santo, Padua. *Donatello deliberately designed the monument's stern, deeply lined, and serious face to conform to the Renaissance ideal of a strong military commander.*

Figure 11.15 LORENZO GHIBERTI. *The Annunciation.* Panel from the north doors of the Baptistery. 1403–1424. Gilt bronze, 20½ × 17¾". Florence. *Ghiberti's rendition of the Annunciation was typical of his panels on the north doors. Mary and the angel are placed in the shallow foreground and are modeled almost completely in the round. The background details, including a sharply foreshortened representation of God on the left, are scarcely raised from the metal. The contrast between these design elements enhances the illusion of depth.*

Figure 11.16 LORENZO GHIBERTI. *The Story of Cain and Abel.* Detail from the east doors of the Baptistery (the "Gates of Paradise"). 1425–1452. Gilt bronze, 31¼ × 31¼". Florence. *This exquisite panel from the Florence Baptistery's east doors is a testament to Ghiberti's absorption of Early Renaissance taste. He followed Brunelleschi's new rules for linear perspective by placing the vanishing point in the middle of the tree trunks in the center of the panel, and he adhered to Alberti's principle of varied details by adding the oxen, sheep, and altar.*

swaying body, and the angel depicted in flight. Nevertheless, Ghiberti always exhibited a strong feeling for Classical forms and harmony, as in the angel's well-rounded body and Mary's serene face.

The artistic world of Florence was a rapidly changing one, however, and Ghiberti adapted his art to conform to the emerging Early Renaissance style of Donatello. Between 1425 and 1452, Ghiberti brought his mature art to its fullest expression in the east doors, the last of the Baptistery's three sculptured portals. These panels, larger than those on the north doors, depict scenes from the Old Testament, such as the story of Cain and Abel from Genesis (Figure 11.16). Most of the Gothic touches are eliminated, including the framing quatrefoils, which are now replaced with rectangular panels. In many other ways, the Cain and Abel panel on the east doors shows Ghiberti's growing dedication to Classical ideals: the graceful contrapposto of the standing figures and their proportional relationships, for example. This work translates Albertian aesthetics into bronze by creating an illusion of depth. But according to Ghiberti's *Commentaries*, the sculptor's purpose was not illusion for its own sake but, rather, a clear presentation of the biblical story. Five incidents from the story of Cain and Abel are illustrated: (1) Cain and Abel as children with their parents, Adam and Eve, at the top left; (2) Cain and Abel making sacrifices before an altar, at the top right; (3) Cain plowing with oxen and Abel watching his sheep, in the middle and foreground, respectively, on the left; (4) Cain slaying Abel with a club, in the right middle; and (5) Cain being questioned by God, in the right foreground. So sublime was Ghiberti's accomplishment that Michelangelo, in the next century, is said to have referred to these doors as "the Gates of Paradise."

Painting The radical changes taking place in architecture and sculpture were minor compared with the changes in painting. Inspired by Classicism though lacking significant examples from ancient times, painters were relatively free to experiment and to define their own path. As in the other arts of the 1400s, Florentine painters led the way and established the standards for the new style—realism, linear perspective, and psychological truth. This movement climaxed at the end of the century with the early work of Leonardo da Vinci.

After 1450 Florence's dominance was challenged by Venetian painters, who were forging their own artistic tradition. Venice, having won its freedom from the Byzantine Empire only in the High Middle Ages, was still in the thrall of Byzantine culture (see Chapter 7). As a result, Venetian painters and their patrons showed a pronounced taste for the stylized effects and sensual surfaces typical of Byzantine art. However, a distinct school of Venetian painters emerged, which

Figure 11.17 MASACCIO. *The Holy Trinity*. 1427 or 1428. Fresco, 21′10½″ × 10′5″. Santa Maria Novella, Florence. *Masaccio achieved a remarkable illusion of depth in this fresco by using linear and atmospheric perspective. Below the simulated chapel he painted a skeleton in a wall sarcophagus (not visible in this photograph) with a melancholy inscription reading, "I was once that which you are, and what I am you also will be." This memento mori, or reminder of death, was probably ordered by the donor, a member of the Lenzi family. His tomb is built into the floor and lies directly in front of the fresco.*

eventually was to have a major impact on the course of painting in the West.

North of the Alps, a third Early Renaissance development was taking place in Burgundy and the Low Countries. There, the painters pursued an art more religious than that of Italy and closer in spirit to the Late Gothic. The northern artists concentrated on minute details and landscapes rather than on the problems of depth and composition that concerned Italy's painters. This survey confines itself to the major figures

in the Florentine school, which is divided into two generations, and to the founder of the Venetian school.

The guiding genius of the revolution in painting in the earlier Florentine school was the youthful Masaccio [mah-ZAHT-cho] (1401–1428), whose career was probably cut short by the plague. He adopted mathematical perspective in his works almost simultaneously with its invention by Brunelleschi. In the history of Western painting, Masaccio's *Holy Trinity* fresco, painted in 1425, is the first successful depiction in painting of the new concept of Renaissance space.

Masaccio's design for this fresco in the church of Santa Maria Novella, Florence, shows that he was well aware of the new currents flowing in the art of his day. The painting offers an architectural setting in the style of Brunelleschi, and the solidity and vitality of the figures indicate that Masaccio had also absorbed the values of Donatello's new sculpture. Masaccio's fresco portrays the Holy Trinity—the three divine beings who make up the Christian idea of God—within a simulated chapel (Figure 11.17). Jesus' crucified body appears to be held up by God the Father, who stands on a platform behind the cross; between the heads of God and Jesus is a dove, symbolizing the Holy Spirit and completing the Trinitarian image. Mary and Saint John, both clothed in contemporary dress, flank the holy trio. Mary points dramatically to the Savior. Just outside the chapel's frame, the donors kneel in prayer—the typical way of presenting patrons in Renaissance art.

In the Trinity fresco, Masaccio uses a variety of innovations. He is the first painter to show light falling from a single source, in this instance, from the left, bathing the body of Christ and coinciding with the actual lighting in Santa Maria Novella. This realistic feature adds to the three-dimensional effect of the well-modeled figures. The use of linear perspective further heightens the scene's realism. Finally, the perspective, converging to the midpoint between the kneeling donors, reinforces the hierarchy of beings within the fresco: from God the Father at the top to the human figures at the sides. In effect, mathematical tidiness is used to reveal the divine order—an ideal congenial to Florence's intellectual elite.

A second fresco by Masaccio, *The Tribute Money*, painted in the Brancacci Chapel of the church of Santa Maria del Carmine, Florence, is recognized as Masaccio's masterpiece (Figure 11.18). This fresco illustrates the Gospel account (Matthew 17:24–27) in which Jesus advises Peter, his chief disciple, to pay the Roman taxes. Because this painting depicts a biblical subject virtually unrepresented in Christian art, it was probably commissioned by a donor to justify a new and heavy Florentine tax. Whether the fresco had any effect on tax collection is debatable, but other artists were captivated by Masaccio's stunning technical effects:

Figure 11.18 MASACCIO. *The Tribute Money.* Ca. 1425. Fresco, 8′2⅜″ × 19′8¼″. Santa Maria del Carmine, Florence. *This fresco represents the highest expression of the art of Masaccio, particularly in his realistic portrayal of the tax collector. This official, who appears twice, first confronting Christ in the center and then receiving money from Peter on the right, is depicted with coarse features—a typical man of the Florentine streets. Even his posture, though rendered with Classical contrapposto, suggests a swagger—a man at home in his body and content with his difficult occupation.*

the use of perspective and **chiaroscuro,** or the modeling with light and shade.

The Tribute Money fresco follows the continuous narrative form of medieval art. Three separate episodes are depicted at the same time—in the center, Jesus is confronted by the tax collector; on the left, Peter, as foretold by Jesus, finds a coin in the mouth of a fish; and, on the right, Peter pays the coin to the Roman official. Despite this Gothic effect, the fresco's central section is able to stand alone because of its spatial integrity and unified composition. Jesus is partially encircled by his apostles, and the tax gatherer, viewed from the back, stands to the right. In this central group, the heads are all at the same height, for Masaccio aligned them according to Brunelleschi's principles. Fully modeled in the round, each human form occupies a precise, mathematical space.

Painters such as the Dominican friar Fra Angelico (about 1400–1455) extended Masaccio's innovations. Fra Angelico's later works, painted for the renovated monastery of San Marco in Florence and partially funded by Cosimo de' Medici, show his mature blending of biblical motifs in Renaissance space. *The Annunciation* portrays a reflective Virgin receiving the angel Gabriel (Figure 11.19). Mary and Gabriel are framed in niches in the Gothic manner, but the other elements—the mastery of depth, the simplicity of gestures, the purity of colors, and the integrated scene—are rendered in the new, simple Renaissance style. The painting's vanishing point is placed to the right of center in

the small barred window looking out from the Virgin's bedroom. The loggia, or open porch, in which the scene takes place was based on a new architectural fashion popular among Florence's wealthy elite. Religious images abound in this painting; the enclosed garden symbolizes Mary's virginity, and the barred window attests to the purity of her life. Because of his gracious mastery of form and space, Fra Angelico's influence on later artists was pronounced.

One of those he influenced was Piero della Francesca [PYER-o DAYL-lah frahn-CHAY-skah] (about 1420–1492), a great painter of the second Florentine generation, who grew up in a Tuscan country town near Florence. His panel painting *The Flagellation* shows the powerful though mysterious aesthetic effects of his controversial style (Figure 11.20). The sunlight flooding the scene unites the figures, but the composition places them in two distinct areas. At the extreme left sits Pilate, the judge, on a dais. The painting's subject—the scourging of Christ before his crucifixion—is placed to the left rear. Reinforcing this odd displacement are the figures on the right, who are apparently lost in their own conversation. Aesthetically this strange juxtaposition arises because della Francesca has placed the horizon line around the hips of the figures beating Christ, causing the three men on the right to loom in such high perspective; thus the men in the foreground appear to be indifferent to Christ and unaware of his importance. The effect is distinctly unsettling in a religious scene. The modern

Figure 11.19 FRA ANGELICO. *Annunciation.* 1438–1445. Fresco, 7'6" × 10'5". Monastery of San Marco, Florence. *Fra Angelico's portrayal of the Virgin at the moment when she receives the news that she will bear the baby Jesus is a wonderful illustration of the painter's use of religious symbols. Mary's questioning expression and her arms crossed in a maternal gesture help to establish the painting's subject. Moreover, the physical setting of the scene, bare except for the rough bench on which she sits, suggests an ascetic existence—an appropriate detail for the painting's original setting, a monastery.*

world, which loves conundrums, has developed a strong passion for the private vision of della Francesca as represented in his art.

Sandro Botticelli [baht-tuh-CHEL-lee] (1445–1510) is the best representative of a lyrical aspect of this second generation and one of the most admired painters in the Western tradition. One of the first Florentine artists to master both linear and atmospheric perspective, he was less interested in the technical aspects of painting than he was in depicting languid beauty and poetical truth.

Until the 1480s, Botticelli's art was shaped by the Neo-Platonic philosophy of the Florentine Academy, and thus he often allegorized pagan myths, giving them a Christian slant. Especially prominent in Neo-Platonic thought was the identification of Venus, the Roman goddess of love, with the Christian belief that "God is love." Botticelli, with the support of his patrons, notably the Medici family, made the Roman goddess the subject of two splendid paintings, the *Primavera* and *The Birth of Venus.* In this way, female nudes once again became a proper subject for art, though male nudes had appeared earlier, in Donatello's generation (see Figure 11.11).

Botticelli's *Primavera,* or *Allegory of Spring,* presents Venus as a Christianized deity, dressed in a revealingly

Figure 11.20 Piero della Francesca. *The Flagellation.* 1460s. Oil on panel, 23 × 32″. Galleria Nazionale della Marche, Palazzo Ducale, Urbino. *A secondary religious message may be found in this work. In 1439 the Orthodox Church discussed union with Rome at the Council of Florence but later repudiated the merger when the Byzantine populace rioted in favor of Turkish rule. The hats on Pilate (seated at the left) and the third man from the right are copies of Greek headdresses that were worn at the council. In effect, these figures suggest that the Greek Church is a persecutor of true Christianity, for the papacy regarded the Greek Orthodox faith as schismatic.*

transparent gown (Figure 11.21). At first glance, the goddess, standing just slightly to the right of center, appears lost amid the general agitation, but on closer view she is seen to be presiding over the revels. Venus tilts her head coyly and holds up her right hand, establishing by these commanding gestures that this orange grove is her garden and the other figures are her familiars, or associates, all of them symbolically linked with divine love.

Even though the *Primavera* is one of the most beloved works of Western art, in technical terms the painting shows that Botticelli was out of step with the Early Renaissance. He has placed the scene in the near foreground, stressing this area's extreme shallowness by the entangled backdrop of trees and shrubs. The figures are flattened, and the background appears more decorative than real.

An even more famous work by Botticelli, and one of the great landmarks of Western art, is *The Birth of Venus* (see Figure 11.4). Painted in an even more flattened style than the *Primavera*, this masterpiece was probably intended as a visual complement to it. In Neo-Platonic terms, Venus is an image of beauty and love as it is born and grows in the human mind; the birth of Venus corresponds to the baptism of Jesus, because baptism is a symbol of rebirth.

In the 1480s, Florentine art was moving toward its culmination in the early works of Leonardo da Vinci (1452–1519). Leonardo is the quintessential representative of a new breed of artist: the Renaissance man, who takes the universe of learning as his province. Not only did he defy the authority of the church by secretly studying human cadavers, but he also rejected the Classical values that had guided the first generation of

Figure 11.21 SANDRO BOTTICELLI. *Primavera*. Ca. 1482. Tempera on panel, 6′8″ × 10′4″. Uffizi Gallery, Florence. *Botticelli's lyricism is evident in his refined images of human beauty. His figures' elegant features and gestures, such as the sloping shoulders and the tilted heads, were copied by later artists. The women's blond, ropelike hair and transparent gowns are typical of Botticelli's style.*

the Early Renaissance. He relied solely on empirical truth and what the human eye could discover. His notebooks, encoded so as to be legible only when read in a mirror, recorded and detailed his lifelong curiosity about both the human and the natural worlds. In his habits of mind, Leonardo joined intellectual curiosity with the skills of sculptor, architect, engineer, scientist, and painter.

Among his few surviving paintings from this period, the first version of *The Virgin of the Rocks* reveals both his scientific eye and his desire to create a haunting image uniquely his own (Figure 11.22). In this scene, set in a grotto or cave, Mary is portrayed with the infant Jesus, as a half-kneeling infant John the Baptist prays and an angel watches. The plants underfoot and the rocks in the background are a treasure of precise documentation. Nevertheless, the setting is Leonardo's own invention—without a scriptural or a traditional basis—and is a testimony to his creative genius.

Leonardo's plan of *The Virgin of the Rocks* shows the rich workings of his mind. Ignoring Brunelleschian perspective, he placed the figures his own way. He also developed a pyramid design for arranging the figures in relation to one another; Mary's head is the pyramid's apex, and her seat and the other three figures anchor its corners. Within this pyramid, Leonardo creates a dynamic tension by using gestures to suggest a circular motion: The angel points to John the Baptist, who in turn directs his praying hands toward Jesus. A second, vertical, line of stress is seen in the gesturing hands of Mary, the angel, and Christ. Later artists so admired this painting that its pyramidal composition became the standard in the High Renaissance.

No prior artist had used chiaroscuro to such advantage as Leonardo does in this work, causing the figures to stand out miraculously from the surrounding gloom. And unlike earlier artists, he colors the atmosphere, softening the edges of surfaces with a fine haze called *sfumato*. As a result, the painting looks more like a vision than a realistic scene. Leonardo's later works are part of the High Renaissance (see Chapter 12), but his early works represent the fullest expression of the scientific spirit of the second generation of Early Renaissance painting.

While the Florentine painters were establishing themselves as the driving force in the Early Renaissance, a rival school was beginning to emerge in Venice. The Venetian school, dedicated to exploring the effects of light and air and re-creating the sensuous effects of textured surfaces, was eventually to play a major role in the history of painting in Italy and the West. Founded by Giovanni Bellini, a member of a dynasty of painters, the Venetian school began its rise to greatness.

Giovanni Bellini (about 1430–1516), who trained in the workshop of his father, the Late Gothic painter Jacopo Bellini (about 1400–about 1470), made Venice a center of Renaissance art comparable to Florence and Rome. Ever experimenting, always striving to keep up with the latest trends, he frequently reinvented himself. Nevertheless, there were constants in his approach to painting. He combined the traditions of the Florentine school (the use of linear perspective and the direct observation of nature) and the Flemish school (the technique of oil painting, the use of landscape as background, and the practice of religious symbolism). Made aware of the importance of atmosphere by the Venetian setting, Bellini also experimented with a range of colors, variations in color intensity, and changes in light. In particular, Bellini perfected the landscape format as a backdrop for foreground figures. A great teacher, Bellini founded a workshop where his methods were taught to young painters, including Giorgione and Titian (see Chapter 12).

An excellent example of Bellini's use of landscape may be seen in *St. Francis in Ecstasy* (Figure 11.23). This work, which depicts an ecstatic St. Francis displaying the stigmata, shows Bellini's typical treatment of landscape. He divides the painting surface into zones, beginning with the area around the saint in the foreground, continuing through a second zone occupied by a donkey and a crane, to a third zone featuring Italian castles nestled into a hillside, and concluding with a fourth zone marked by a fortress and the sky. To heighten the realism, Bellini uses both a rich palette of colors and numerous objects to lead the viewer's eye into the vast distance. He adds to the realism by suffusing the scene with natural light. The landscape, with its vivid rendering of flora and fauna, expresses the Franciscan belief that humankind should live in harmony with the natural world (see Chapter 9).

Music

The changes affecting the cultural life of fifteenth-century Europe naturally also affected the music of the time. The impetus for a new musical direction, however, did not spring from Classical sources, because ancient musical texts had virtually perished. Instead, the new

Figure 11.22 LEONARDO DA VINCI. *The Virgin of the Rocks.* 1483. Oil on panel, approx. 6'3" × 3'7". Louvre. *Two slightly different versions of this work exist, this one dating from 1483 and a later one done in 1506 and on view in the National Gallery in London. The Louvre painting, with its carefully observed botanical specimens, is the culmination of the scientific side of the Early Renaissance. The painting's arbitrary features—the grotto setting and the unusual perspective—point ahead to the High Renaissance; the dramatic use of chiaroscuro foreshadows the "night pictures" of the Baroque period (see Figure 14.8).*

music owed its existence to meetings between English and Continental composers at the church councils that were called to settle the Great Schism (see Chapter 10) and the Continental composers' deep regard for the seductive sound of English music. The English composer John Dunstable [DUHN-stuh-bull] (about 1380–1453) was a central figure in the new musical era that began with the opening of the fifteenth century. Working in England and in France, he wrote mainly religious works—motets for multiple voices and settings for the Mass—that showed his increasingly harmonic approach to polyphony. The special quality of his music is its freedom from the use of mathematical proportion—the source of medieval music's dissonance.

Dunstable's music influenced composers in France, in Burgundy, and in Flanders, known collectively as the Franco-Netherlandish school. This school, which

Figure 11.23 GIOVANNI BELLINI. *St. Francis in Ecstasy.* 1470s. Oil in tempera on panel, 49 × 55⅞". Frick Collection, New York. *In the foreground, Bellini renders his vision of the grotto at Alvernia, a mountain retreat near Assisi, where St. Francis went to pray and fast for forty days, in imitation of Christ's forty days in the wilderness. The artist reinforces the scene's religious significance through various symbols, such as the grapevine and the stigmata, alluding to the sacrifice of Christ, and the donkey (in the middle distance), emblematic of Jesus' entry into Jerusalem before to the Crucifixion.*

became the dominant force in fifteenth-century music, blended Dunstable's harmonics with northern European and Italian traditions. The principal works of this group were Latin **Masses,** or musical settings of the most sacred Christian rite; motets, or multivoiced songs set to Latin texts; and secular *chansons*, or songs, with French texts, including such types as the French ballade and the Italian madrigal, poems set to music for two and six voices, respectively. Together, these polyphonic compositions established the musical ideal of the Early Renaissance: multiple voices of equal importance singing *a cappella* (without instrumental accompaniment) and stressing the words so they could be understood by listeners.

Between 1430 and 1500, the Continent's musical life was guided by composers from the Franco-Netherlandish school, the most important of whom was the Burgundian Josquin des Prez [zho-SKAN day PRAY] (about 1440–1521). Josquin was influential in his day and is now recognized as one of the greatest composers of all time. He was the first important composer to use music expressively so that the sounds matched the words of the text, thereby moving away from the abstract church style of the Middle Ages. One of his motets was described at the time as evoking Christ's suffering in a manner superior to painting. Josquin also began to organize music in the modern way, using major and minor scales with their related harmonies. All in all, he is probably the first Western composer whose music on first hearing appeals to modern ears.

The Legacy of the Early Renaissance

Today, modern times are considered to begin with the Early Renaissance in Italy. This period saw the rebirth of the study and practice of the arts and the humanities and the rise of the idea of the "Renaissance man," the supreme genius who makes all of human knowledge his province. Under the powerful stimulus of humanism, the liberal arts were restored to primacy over religion in the educational curriculum, a place they had not held for a thousand years, since the triumph of Christianity in the fourth century. With humanism also came a skeptical outlook that expressed itself in a new regard for the direct role of human causality in history and the rise of textual criticism. A new ingredient in Renaissance humanism was the drive to individual fulfillment, perhaps the defining trait of Western civilization from this point onward.

The greatest cultural changes took place in the arts and in architecture, largely under the spell of humanistic learning. Now freed from subordination to architecture, sculpture and painting became independent art forms. Fifteenth-century architects, inspired by the Greco-Roman tradition, adapted Classical forms and ideals to their own needs. For the next four hundred years, until the Gothic revival in the nineteenth century, Classicism was the ruling force in a succession of architectural styles. Sculpture also used its Classical roots to redefine its direction, reviving ancient forms and the practice of depicting male and female nudes. Of all the visual arts, painting was least influenced by the Classical tradition, except for its ideals of simplicity and realism. Perhaps as a consequence of its artistic freedom, painting became the dominant art form of this era and continues to hold first rank today.

KEY CULTURAL TERMS

Renaissance	relief
studia humanitatis	chiaroscuro
Early Renaissance style	*sfumato*
vanishing point	Mass
pilaster	*a cappella*

SUGGESTIONS FOR FURTHER READING

Primary Sources

CASSIRER, E., KRISTELLER, P. O., AND RANDALL, J., eds. *The Renaissance Philosophy of Man*. Chicago: University of Chicago Press, 1948. Selections from Pico, Valla, and other Renaissance scholars accompanied by a useful text.

PICO DELLA MIRANDOLA. *On the Dignity of Man*. Indianapolis: Bobbs-Merrill, 1956. A succinct statement on Renaissance thought by one of its leading scholars.

SUGGESTIONS FOR LISTENING

DUNSTABLE (or DUNSTAPLE), JOHN (about 1380–1453). Dunstable's sweet-sounding harmonies helped inaugurate Early Renaissance music. Predominantly a composer of sacred music, he is best represented by motets, including *Veni Sancte Spiritus—Veni Creator Spiritus* and *Sancta Maria, non est similis*. He also wrote a few secular songs, of which the two most familiar are *O Rosa bella* and *Puisque m'amour*.

JOSQUIN DES PREZ (1440–1521). Josquin's Masses, motets, and *chansons* all illustrate his skill at combining popular melodies with intricate counterpoint and his use of harmonies commonly heard today. The motet *Ave Maria*, the *chanson Faulte d'argent*, and the Mass *Malheur me bat* are good examples of his style.

CHAPTER *11* HIGHLIGHTS

The Early Renaissance: Return to Classical Roots, 1400–1494

 ALBERTI, *On Painting* (1435)

BRUNI, *History of the Florentine People* (mid–fifteenth century)

PIUS II, *The Commentaries* (mid–fifteenth century)

 PICO DELLA MIRANDOLA, *Oration on the Dignity of Man* (1487)

11.15 GHIBERTI, *The Annunciation*, panel from North Doors of the Florentine Baptistery (1403–1424)

11.6 BRUNELLESCHI, Cathedral Dome, Florence (1420–1436)

11.10 DONATELLO, *The Feast of Herod* (ca. 1425)

11.18 MASACCIO, *The Tribute Money* (ca. 1425)

11.16 GHIBERTI, *The Story of Cain and Abel*, from the East Doors of the Florentine Baptistery (1425–1452)

11.17 MASACCIO, *The Holy Trinity* (1427 or 1428)

11.11 DONATELLO, *David* (ca. 1430–1432)

11.8 BRUNELLESCHI AND OTHERS, Pazzi Chapel, Florence (1433–1461)

11.19 FRA ANGELICO, *Annunciation* (1438–1445)

11.13 DONATELLO, "*Gattamelata*" (1447–1453)

11.5 ALBERTI, Malatesta Temple (ca. 1450)

11.20 PIERO DELLA FRANCESCA, *The Flagellation* (1460s)

11.23 BELLINI, *St. Francis in Ecstasy* (1470s)

11.12 VERROCCHIO, *David* (1473–1475)

11.4 BOTTICELLI, *The Birth of Venus* (1480s)

11.21 BOTTICELLI, *Primavera* (ca. 1482)

11.22 DA VINCI, *The Virgin of the Rocks* (1483)

 JOSQUIN DES PREZ, *Ave Maria . . . virgo serena* (ca. 1475)

■ *Literature & Philosophy*   ■ *Art & Architecture*   ■ *Music & Dance*

 Readings in the Western Humanities   *CD, The Western Humanities*

12 THE HIGH RENAISSANCE AND EARLY MANNERISM

1494–1564

Between 1494 and 1564, one of the most brilliantly creative periods in Western history unfolded in Italy. During this span of seventy years, there flourished three artists—Leonardo da Vinci, Raphael, and Michelangelo—and a writer—Machiavelli—whose achievements became legendary. The works of these geniuses, and of other talented but less well known artists and intellectuals, affected the basic Western concept of art and fundamentally influenced how we understand ourselves and the world (Figure 12.1).

The **High Renaissance,** lasting from 1494 to 1520, was the first phase of this creative period and was a time when the Classical principles of beauty, balance, order, serenity, harmony, and rational design reached a state of near perfection. The center of culture shifted from Florence, the heart of the Early Renaissance, to Rome, where the popes became the leading patrons of the new style in their desire to make Rome the world's most beautiful city. Florence even had to yield the services of Michelangelo, its favorite son, to the wealthy and powerful Roman pontiffs (Figure 12.1).

After 1520, however, the Renaissance veered away from the humanistic values of Classicism toward an antihumanistic vision of the world, labeled **Mannerism** because of the self-conscious, or "mannered," style adopted by its artists and intellectuals. Mannerist art and culture endured from 1520 until the end of the century, when the style was affected by religious controversy. This chapter covers the High Renaissance style and the Mannerist style through the end of its first phase in 1564, with the death of Michelangelo.

◄ **Detail** RAPHAEL. *Baldassare Castiglione.* 1514. Oil on canvas, 32¼ × 26½".

THE RISE OF THE MODERN SOVEREIGN STATE

The most important political development in the first half of the sixteenth century was the emergence of powerful sovereign states in the newly unified and stabilized nations of France, England, and Spain. This process was already under way in the late fifteenth century (see Chapter 10), but it now began to influence foreign affairs. The ongoing rivalries of these aggressive national kingdoms led to the concept of balance of power—a principle that still dominates politics today.

From 1494 to 1569, Europe's international political life was controlled, either directly or indirectly, by France and Spain. France's central role resulted from the policies of its strong Valois kings, who had governed France since the early fourteenth century. Spain's fortunes soared during this period, first under the joint rule of Ferdinand V and Isabella and then under Charles I. In 1519 Charles I was also elected Holy Roman Emperor as Charles V (he was of the royal house of Hapsburg), thus joining the interests of Spain and the Holy Roman Empire until his abdication in 1556. England kept aloof from Continental affairs during this time.

After 1591 the French and the Spanish rulers increasingly dispatched their armies and allies into the weaker states, where they fought and claimed new lands. As the sovereign monarchs gained power, the medieval dream of a united Christendom—pursued by Charlemagne, the popes, and the Holy Roman emperors—slowly faded away. These new states were strong because they were united around rulers who exercised increasing central control. Although most kings claimed to rule by divine right, their practical policies were more important in increasing their power. They surrounded themselves with ministers and consultative councils, both dependent on the crown. The ministers were often chosen from the bourgeois class, and they advised the rulers on such weighty matters as religion and war and also ran the developing bureaucracies. The bureaucracies in turn strengthened centralized rule by extending royal

Figure 12.1 MICHELANGELO. *Dying Slave*. 1513–1516. Marble, approx. 7′5″. Louvre. *Michelangelo's so-called* Dying Slave *embodies the conflicting artistic tendencies at work between 1494 and 1564. The statue's idealized traits—the perfectly proportioned figure, the restrained facial expression, and the body's gentle S-curve shape—are hallmarks of the High Renaissance style. But the figure's overall sleekness and exaggerated arm movements—probably based on one of the figures in the first-century A.D.* Laocoön Group *(see Figure 4.19), which had recently been rediscovered—were portents of Early Mannerism.*

jurisdiction into matters formerly administered by the feudal nobility, such as the justice system.

The crown further eroded the status of the feudal nobles by relying on mercenary armies rather than on the warrior class, a shift that began in the Late Middle Ages. To pay these armies, the kings had to consult with representative bodies, such as Parliament in England, and make them a part of their regular administration.

The Struggle for Italy, 1494–1529

Italy's relative tranquility, established by the Peace of Lodi in 1454, was shattered by the French invasion in 1494. For the next thirty-five years, Italy was a battleground where France, Spain, and the Holy Roman Empire fought among themselves, as well as with the papacy and most of the Italian states.

The struggle began when France, eager to reassert a hereditary claim to Naples, agreed to help Milan in a controversy involving Naples, Florence, and the pope. The French king, Charles VIII (r. 1483–1498), took Florence in 1494 and then advanced to Rome and Naples. But the Italians did not relinquish ground easily. Joined by Venice and the pope and supported by the Holy Roman emperor and the Spanish monarch, they drove out the French. In 1499 the French returned to Italy to activate their claim to Milan, and the Spanish and the Germans joined with the Italians to defeat the French. Over the next several decades, however, France continued to invade Italy intermittently. In the course of their campaigns, the French rulers, who were enamored of the Italian Renaissance, brought its artistic and intellectual ideals to northern Europe (Figure 12.2).

In 1522 full-scale hostilities broke out between France and the Holy Roman Empire over Italy's future, a struggle that pitted the old Europe against the new. The Holy Roman Empire, ruled by Charles V, was a decentralized relic from the feudal age. France, under the bold and intellectual leadership of Francis I (r. 1515–1547) of the royal house of Valois, was the epitome of the new sovereign state.

The first Hapsburg-Valois war was the only one fought in Italy. In 1527 the troops of Charles V ran riot in Rome, raping, looting, and killing. This notorious sack of Rome had two major consequences. First, it cast doubt on Rome's ability to control Italy—long a goal of the popes—for it showed that the secular leaders no longer respected the temporal power of the papacy. Second, it ended papal patronage of the arts for almost a decade, thus weakening Rome's role as a cultural leader. It also had a chilling effect on artistic ideals and contributed to the rise of Mannerism.

Figure 12.2 JEAN CLOUET. *Francis I.* Ca. 1525. Oil on panel, 37¾ × 29⅛". Louvre. *During his thirty-two-year-long reign, Francis I was a major force in sixteenth-century European affairs. He also embarked on an extensive artistic program, inspired by the Italian Renaissance, to make his court the most splendid in Europe. Under his personal direction, Italian artworks and artists, including Leonardo da Vinci, were imported into France. Ironically, this rather stylized portrait by Jean Clouet, Francis's chief court artist, owes more to the conventionalized portraits of the Gothic style than it does to the realistic works of the Italian Renaissance.*

In 1529 the Treaty of Cambrai ended this first phase of the Hapsburg-Valois rivalry. Years of invasions and wars had left most of Italy divided and exhausted. Some cities had suffered nearly irreparable harm. Florence, because it had so much to lose, fared the worst. In the 1530s, the Medici rulers resumed ducal power, but they were little more than puppets of the foreigners who controlled much of the peninsula. The only Italian state to keep its political independence was Venice, which became the last haven for artists and intellectuals in Italy for the rest of the sixteenth century.

Charles V and the Hapsburg Empire

By 1530 the struggle between the Valois and the Hapsburgs had shifted to central Europe. The French felt hemmed in by the Spanish in the south, the Germans to the east, and the Dutch to the north—peoples all

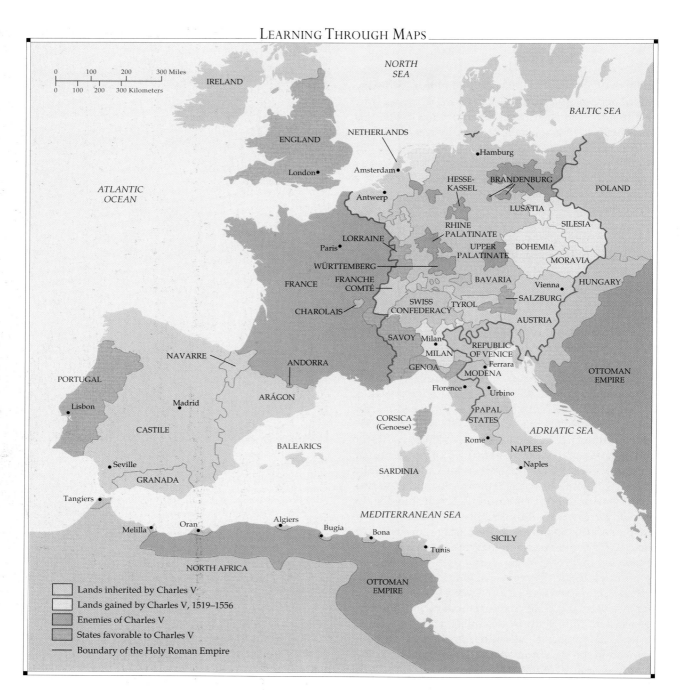

Map 12.1   EUROPEAN EMPIRE OF CHARLES V, CA. 1556
This map shows the extensive holdings of the Holy Roman emperor Charles V, also known as King Charles I of Spain. **Notice** the lands inherited and the lands gained by Charles V. **Identify** the boundary of the Holy Roman Empire. **Who** were Charles V's enemies within the Holy Roman Empire and elsewhere? **Consider** the challenges Charles V faced in governing his widely scattered and culturally diverse empire. **What** impact did geography have on France's attitude toward Charles V's empire?

ruled by the Hapsburg emperor Charles V. In French eyes, Charles had an insatiable appetite for power and for control of the Continent. In turn, the Hapsburg ruler considered the French king a land-hungry upstart who stood in the way of a Europe united under a Christian prince—in other words, the dream of Christendom. In 1559, after a number of exhausting wars and a series of French victories, the belligerents signed the Treaty of Cateau-Cambrésis, which ushered in a brief period of peace (Map 12.1).

Charles V, the man at the center of most of these events, lived a life filled with paradoxes (Figure 12.3).

Because of the size of his empire, he was in theory one of the most powerful rulers ever to live; but in actuality, again because of the vastness of his lands, he never quite succeeded in gaining complete control of his empire. In some ways, he was the last of medieval kings; in other ways, he foreshadowed a new age driven by sovereign kings, standing armies, diplomatic agreements, and strong religious differences.

Charles V's unique position at the center of Europe's political storm was the result of a series of timely deaths and births and politically astute arranged marriages. These circumstances had permitted the Hapsburg rulers to accumulate vast power, wealth, and land. Charles was born in 1500 to a German father and a Spanish mother, and he was the grandson of both the Holy Roman emperor Maximilian I and the Spanish king Ferdinand V. He held lands in present-day Spain, France, Italy, Germany, and Austria—along with the unimaginable riches of the recently acquired lands in the New World. By 1519 Charles V—simultaneously Charles I of Spain—ruled the largest empire the world has ever known.

For most of his life, Charles traveled from one of his possessions to another, fighting battles, arranging peace treaties, and attempting to unify his empire by personal control and compromise. His attention was often divided, and he found himself caught between two powerful foes—especially the French to the west and the Ottoman Turks in the east—who drained both his personal energies and his imperial resources.

Within the Holy Roman Empire, the princes of the German principalities often took advantage of his prolonged absences and his preoccupation with the French and the Turks. Their ability to gain political power at the emperor's expense increased after Martin Luther's revolt and the beginning of the Protestant Reformation (see Chapter 13). Charles also weakened his own position by his contradictory policies. At times he angered the disaffected German princes by meddling in their affairs and condemning Lutheran doctrines, and at other times he angered the popes by making concessions to the Protestants.

Exhausted and disillusioned by his inability to prevail in Europe, Charles abdicated in 1556 and retired to a monastery. His brother Ferdinand took control of the German-Austrian inheritance and was soon elected Holy Roman emperor. His son Philip assumed control of the Spanish Hapsburg holdings, including Spain, the New World territories, and the Netherlands. Thus ended Charles's vision of a united Europe and Christendom, which had turned into a nightmare of endless meetings, gory battles, and false hopes of peace and unity.

Figure 12.3   Titian. *Charles V with a Dog.* Ca. 1533. Oil on canvas, 6′3″ × 3′8″. Prado, Madrid. *Titian's full-length, standing portrait of Charles V was painted when the Hapsburg emperor was at the height of his power. By rendering the "ruler of the world" in contrapposto, his fingers casually holding the collar of his dog, Titian endows the emperor with a natural grace. The lighting that illuminates Charles from the dark background and the breathless hush that seems to envelop the man and dog are trademarks of Titian's style.*

ECONOMIC EXPANSION AND SOCIAL DEVELOPMENTS

By the end of the fifteenth century, Europe had nearly recovered from the impact of the plague; the sixteenth century continued to be a time of growing population and increasing prosperity. The center of commerce shifted from the Mediterranean to the Atlantic coast, making cities like London and Antwerp financial and merchandising centers. Skilled craftspeople turned out quality products, and enterprising merchants distributed these finished goods across much of northwestern Europe. The daring sailing expeditions and discoveries of the late fifteenth and early sixteenth centuries provided new raw materials from America. Innovative manufacturing methods spurred economic growth and expanded worldwide markets.

Although the data are scattered and often unreliable, evidence indicates that the population of Europe increased from about 45 million in 1400 to 69 million in 1500 and to about 89 million by 1600. There was a major population shift from rural to urban areas, and the number of cities with populations over 100,000 grew from five to eight between 1500 and 1600. Rome, for example, grew from about 50,000 in 1526—the year before the sack—to 100,000 by the end of the century.

Prosperity brought a higher standard of living to most of the urban middle class, but throughout much of the century prices rose faster than wages. Those who were not profiting from increased economic growth, such as poor peasants or impoverished nobility living on unproductive farms, suffered the most. In areas of Europe hardest hit by inflation or agricultural and commercial stagnation, economic crises often became intertwined with social and religious matters that intensified long-standing regional and local differences.

Yet the boom offered economic opportunities to some. Many merchants made fortunes and provided employment for others. These merchants and the bankers who offered loans were also accumulating capital, which they then invested in other types of commercial activity. The campaigns of Charles V were financed by wealthy bankers operating in a well-organized money market. The amassing of surplus capital and its reinvestment ushered in the opening phase of commercial capitalism that laid the foundation for Europe's future economic expansion.

During the first half of the sixteenth century, the abundance of raw materials and the vast market potential of the New World had just begun to affect Europe's economy. South American gold and silver played an important role in the upward price spiral. After 1650 New World agricultural products, such as tobacco, cotton, and cocoa, were used in new manufactured goods and profoundly altered consumer habits.

In the late 1500s, a major economic change had occurred that would make it possible to bring the natural resources of the New World to Europe. Some Europeans, taking advantage of the institution of slavery and the existing slave trade in western Africa, mercilessly exploited the local Africans by buying them and shipping them to European colonies in the New World. The Africans were forced to work in the gold and silver mines of Central and South America and on the cotton and sugarcane plantations in the West Indies, where they became a major factor in the production of these new forms of wealth.

FROM HIGH RENAISSANCE TO EARLY MANNERISM

The characteristics of High Renaissance style were largely derived from the visual arts. Led by painters, sculptors, and architects who worshiped ancient Classical ideals, notably those of late-fifth-century B.C. Greece, the High Renaissance was filled with images of repose, harmony, and heroism. Under the spell of Classicism and the values of simplicity and restraint, artists sought to conquer unruly physical reality by subjecting it to the principle of a seemingly effortless order.

Although the visual arts dominated the High Renaissance, literary figures also contributed to this era. From Classicism, the High Renaissance authors appropriated two of their chief aesthetic aims, secularism and idealism. Like their ancient predecessors, historians showed that contemporary events arose from human causes rather than from divine action—unmistakable evidence of a mounting secular spirit. Actually, secularism more deeply affected the writing of history than it did the arts and architecture, where church patronage and religious subjects still held sway. A rising secular consciousness can also be seen in the popular handbooks on manners that offered advice on how to become a perfect gentleman or lady. Although they have no counterpart in ancient literature, these books nevertheless have the Classical quality of treating their subject in idealized terms.

What distinguished the High Renaissance preoccupation with the Classical past from the Early Renaissance's renewed interest in ancient matters was largely a shift in creative sensibility. The Early Renaissance artists, in the course of growing away from the Late Gothic style, had invented new ways of recapturing the harmonious spirit of ancient art and architecture. The geniuses of the next generation, benefiting from the experiments of the Early Renaissance, succeeded in creating masterpieces of disciplined form and idealized beauty. The High Renaissance masters' superb confidence allowed them to produce works that were in harmony with themselves and the physical world—a hallmark of Classical art.

In spite of its brilliance, the High Renaissance existed for only a fleeting moment in the history of Western culture—from the French invasion of Italy in 1494 until the death of Raphael in 1520 (preceded by the death of Leonardo in 1519) (Timeline 12.1). In this era, the Renaissance popes spared no expense in their patronage of the arts and letters. After the disasters of the fourteenth century, the papacy seemed to have

Timeline 12.1 ITALIAN CULTURAL STYLES BETWEEN 1494 AND 1564

1494	1520	1564
	High Renaissance	Early Mannerism	

| French invasion of Italy | 1508–1512 Michelangelo's Sistine Chapel ceiling frescoes | 1519 Death of Leonardo da Vinci 1520 Death of Raphael | 1532 Publication of Machiavelli's *The Prince* | 1536–1541 Michelangelo's *Last Judgment* fresco | 1550 Palladio's Villa Rotonda | 1564 Death of Michel-angelo |

Figure 12.4 *Pope Clement VII Besieged in Castel Sant' Angelo.* 1554. Engraving, 6⅛ × 9". Kunsthalle, Hamburg. *This engraving shows the imperial army of Charles V besieging Castel Sant' Angelo, one of the pope's palaces, during the sack of Rome in 1527. The engraver's sympathies with the pope are revealed by the huge statues of St. Peter (with keys, on the right) and St. Paul (with sword, on the left), who look on disapprovingly. Pope Clement VII, imprisoned in his own fortress, peers down on the scene from a balcony at the center top.*

restored the church to the vitality that it had enjoyed in the High Middle Ages. In reality, however, the popes of the early sixteenth century presided over a shaky ecclesiastical foundation. To the north, in Germany, a theological storm was brewing that would eventually split Christendom and destroy the papacy's claim to rule over the Christian world. This religious crisis, coupled with increasing tendencies to exaggeration in High Renaissance art and with the sack of Rome in 1527, contributed to the development of Mannerism and its spread through Italy and later across western Europe (Figure 12.4).

Mannerist painters, sculptors, and architects moved away from two of the guiding principles of the High Renaissance: the imitation of nature and the devotion to Classical ideals. In contrast to the High Renaissance masters, Mannerist painters deliberately chose odd perspectives that called attention to the artists' technical effects and their individual points of view. Mannerist sculptors, rejecting idealism, turned and twisted the human figure into unusual and bizarre poses to express their own notions of beauty. Likewise, Mannerist

architects toyed with the emotions and expectations of their audience by designing buildings that were intended to surprise. Behind the Mannerist aesthetic lay a questioning or even a denial of the inherent worth of human beings and a negative image of human nature, along with a sense of the growing instability of the world.

Literature

The leading writers of the High Renaissance in Italy drew their themes and values from the Greco-Roman classics. Their artistic vision sprang from the Classical virtue of *humanitas*—a term coined by Cicero in antiquity (see Chapter 5) that can be translated as "humanity," meaning the wisdom, humor, tolerance, and passion of the person of good sense. With some reservations, they also believed in Classicism's basic tenet that human nature is inherently rational and good. One of the finest expressions of Classicism in Renaissance literature was the poetry of the Venetian

Gaspara Stampa, whose lyric verses, though devoted to obsessive sexual love, asserted the moral worth of the lover.

But even as High Renaissance literature was enjoying its brief reign, the Mannerist works of the Florentine author Niccolò Machiavelli began to appear, and at the heart of his thought is an anti-Classical spirit. Despite his education in Classicism and his strict rationalism, Machiavelli concluded that the human race was irremediably flawed. The contrast between the idealizing spirit of the High Renaissance and the anti-traditionalist views of Mannerism can be clearly seen by placing the work of the diplomat and courtier Baldassare Castiglione beside that of Machiavelli. Each wrote a book that can fairly be described as a manual of behavior—but there the resemblance ends.

Gaspara Stampa Gaspara Stampa (about 1524–1554) embraced the classical tradition renewed by Petrarch in the 1300s; her work is thus typical of High Renaissance poetry. She adopted the Petrarchan sonnet as the preferred vehicle for her thoughts, and, like the earlier poet, she used her poetic gifts to investigate the byways of love. Rather than glorifying the distant beloved, however, she asserted the moral worth of the suffering lover, thus transforming the essentially male Petrarchan ideal into a female point of view. Stampa poured out her heart in her verses, confessing vulnerability and lamenting abandonment. She portrayed the abandoned one as superior to the unresponsive loved one—the same lesson taught by Socrates in one of Plato's dialogues (see Chapter 3).

That Gaspara Stampa became a poet at all is testimony to the changing mores of Renaissance Venice, a city fabled for its love of luxury and pleasure. Her autobiographical poetry grew out of her situation in Venice's marginal world of writers, musicians, and artists, including aristocrats and high officials of church and state, who were notably indifferent to Christian values. As a courtesan, or kept woman, she was a welcome member of this twilight world where sexuality was fused with art. Although she seems to have had several liaisons in her brief life, it was Count Collaltino di Collalto, a soldier, who won her heart. In time, Collaltino wearied of her, but Stampa transformed her hopeless love into some of the West's most touching poetry.

Castiglione The reputation of Castiglione [kahs-teel-YOH-nay] (1478–1529) rests on *The Book of Courtier* or simply, *The Courtier,* one of the most influential and famous books of the High Renaissance. Intended for Italian court society, *The Courtier* was published in 1528 and translated into most Western languages by the end of the century. It quickly became the bible of courteous behavior for Europe's upper classes and remained so over the next two hundred years. Even today, at the beginning of the twenty-first century, Castiglione's rules for civilized behavior are still not completely outmoded.

A Mantuan by birth, Castiglione (Figure 12.5) based his guide to manners on life at the north Italian court of Urbino, where, between 1504 and 1517, he was the beneficiary of the patronage of its resident duke, Guidobaldo da Montefeltro (see Figure 11.2). Impressed by the graceful conversations of his fellow courtiers and most especially taken with the charms of Urbino's duchess, Elisabetta, Castiglione was moved to memorialize his experiences in writing. *The Courtier* is composed as a dialogue, a literary form originated by Plato and favored by Cicero. Castiglione's dialogue is set in Urbino over a period of four evenings and peopled with actual individuals for whom he invents urbane and witty conversations that suit their known characters. Despite this realistic touch, his book's overall tone is definitely idealistic and hence expressive of High Renaissance style.

Castiglione's idealism shines forth most clearly in the sections in which the invited company try to define the perfect courtier, or gentleman. Under Duchess Elisabetta's eye, the guests cannot agree on which aspect of the ideal gentleman's training should take precedence: education in the arts and humanities or skill in horsemanship and swordplay. Some claim that a gentleman should be first a man of letters as well as proficient in music, drawing, and dance. In contrast, others believe that a courtier's profession is first to be ready for war, and hence athletics should play the central role. At any rate, both sides agree that the ideal courtier should be proficient in each of these areas. A sign that the Renaissance had raised the status of painting and sculpture was the group's expectation that a gentleman should be knowledgeable about both of these art forms.

The Courtier also describes the perfect court lady. In the minds of the dialogue participants, the ideal lady is a civilizing influence on men, who would otherwise be crude. To that end, the perfect lady should be a consummate hostess, charming, witty, graceful, physically attractive, and utterly feminine. She ought to be well versed in the same areas as a man, except for athletics and the mastery of arms. With these social attributes, the cultivated lady can then bring out the best in a courtier. But she must not seem his inferior, for she contributes to society in her own way.

Castiglione's book turned away from medieval values and led his followers into the modern world. First, he argued that social relations between the sexes ought to be governed by Platonic love—a spiritual passion that surpassed physical conquest—and thus he rejected medieval courtly love and its adulterous focus. Second, he reasoned that women in society should be the educated equals of men, thereby sweeping away the barrier that had been erected when women were excluded from the medieval universities. In the short run, the impact of Castiglione's social rules was to keep women on a pedestal, as courtly love had done. But for the future, his advice allowed women to participate actively in every aspect of society and encouraged their education in much the same way as men's.

Machiavelli In contrast to Castiglione's optimism, the Florentine Machiavelli [mak-ee-uh-VEL-ee] (1469–1527) had a negative view of human nature and made human weakness the central message of his writings. If *The Courtier* seems to be taking place in a highly refined never-never land where decorum and gentility are the primary interests, Machiavelli returns the reader to the solid ground of political reality. His Mannerist cynicism about his fellow human beings sprang from a wounded idealism, for life had taught him that his early optimism was wrong. His varied works, by means of their frank assessments of the human condition, were meant to restore sanity to a world that he thought had gone mad.

Except for Martin Luther, Machiavelli left a stronger imprint on Western culture than any other figure who lived between 1494 and 1564. His most enduring contribution was *The Prince,* which inaugurated a revolution in political thought. Rejecting the medieval tradition of framing political discussions in Christian terms, Machiavelli treated the state as a human invention that ought not necessarily conform to religious or moral rules. He began the modern search for a science of politics that has absorbed political thinkers and policymakers ever since.

Machiavelli's career in sixteenth-century Italy, like that of many writers in antiquity, was split between a life of action and a life of the mind. Between 1498 and 1512, he served the newly reborn Florentine republic as a senior official and diplomat, learning statecraft first-hand. During these turbulent years, he was particularly impressed by the daring and unscrupulous Cesare Borgia, Pope Alexander VI's son. In 1512, after the fall of the Florentine republic to the resurgent Medici party, Machiavelli was imprisoned, tortured, and finally exiled to his family estate outside the city. There, as he recounts in one of his famous letters, he divided his time between idle games with the local farmers at a nearby inn and nightly communion with the best minds of antiquity in his study. From this background emerged in 1513 the small work known as *The Prince,* which circulated in manuscript until after his death. In 1532 it was finally published.

Machiavelli had several motives in writing this masterpiece. Despairing over Italy's dismemberment

Figure 12.5 RAPHAEL. *Baldassare Castiglione.* 1514. Oil on canvas, 32¼ × 26½". *Castiglione, author of a famous book on manners, was memorialized in this handsome portrait by Raphael, one of the great portrait painters of the High Renaissance. Elegantly groomed and completely at ease, Castiglione appears here as the age's ideal courtier—an ideal that he helped to establish.*

by the French and the Spanish kings, he hoped the book would inspire an indigenous leader to unify the peninsula and drive out the foreigners. Enlightened by his personal experience in Florence's affairs, he wanted to capture in writing the truth of the politics to which he had been a witness. And, of equal importance, by dedicating *The Prince* to the restored Medici ruler, he hoped to regain employment in the Florentine state. Like other writers in this age, Machiavelli could not live by his wits but had to rely on secular or religious patronage.

Machiavelli's work failed to gain its immediate objectives: The Medici despot brushed it aside, and Italy remained fragmented until 1870. But as a work that exposed the ruthlessness needed to succeed in practical politics, *The Prince* was an instant, though controversial, success. The book was denounced by religious leaders for its amoral treatment of political power and read secretly by secular rulers for its sage advice. In the prevailing climate of opinion in the sixteenth century, which was still under the sway of

Figure 12.6 LEONARDO DA VINCI. *The Last Supper.* (Restored.) 1495–1498. Oil-tempera on wall, 13′10″ × 29′7½″. Refectory, Santa Maria delle Grazie, Milan. *Classical restraint is one of the defining characteristics of this High Renaissance masterpiece. Instead of overwhelming the viewer with distracting details, Leonardo reduces the objects to a minimum, from the austere room in which the meal is being celebrated to the simple articles on the dining table. The viewer's gaze is thereby held on the unfolding human drama rather than on secondary aspects of the scene.*

Christian ideals, the name "Machiavelli" became synonymous with dishonesty and treachery, and the word **Machiavellianism** was coined to describe the amoral notion that "the end justifies any means."

From the modern perspective, this negative valuation of Machiavelli is both too simplistic and too harsh. Above all else he was a clear-eyed patriot who was anguished by the tragedy unfolding in Italy. *The Prince* describes the power politics that the new sovereign states of France and Spain were pursuing in Italian affairs. Machiavelli realized that the only way to rid Italy of foreigners was to adopt the methods of its successful foes. Seeing his countrymen as cowardly and greedy, he had no illusions that a popular uprising would spring up and drive out Italy's oppressors. Only a strong-willed monarch, not bound by a finicky moral code, could bring Italy back from political chaos.

The controversial heart of Machiavelli's political treatise was the section that advised the ruler on the best way to govern. He counseled the prince to practice conscious duplicity, since that was the only way to maintain power and to ensure peace—the two basic goals of any state. By appearing virtuous and upright while at the same time acting as the situation demanded, the prince could achieve these fundamental ends. Machiavelli's startling advice reflected both his involvement in Italian affairs and his own view of human nature.

Painting

In the arts, the period between 1494 and 1564 was preeminently an age of painting, though several sculptors and architects created major works in their respective fields. The Classical values of idealism, balance, and restraint were translated by High Renaissance painters into harmonious colors, naturally posed figures with serene faces, realistic space and perspectives, and perfectly proportioned human bodies. After 1520 Mannerist tendencies became more and more evident, reflected in abnormal subjects, contorted figures with emotionally expressive faces, and garish colors.

Leonardo da Vinci The inauguration of the High Renaissance in painting is usually dated from Leonardo's *The Last Supper,* which was completed between 1495 and 1498 (Figure 12.6). Painted for the Dominican friars of the church of Santa Maria delle Grazie in Milan, *The Last Supper* heralded the lucidity and harmony that were the essence of High Renaissance style. In executing the fresco, Leonardo unfortunately made use of a flawed technique, and the painting began to flake during his lifetime. Over the centuries, the work has been touched up frequently and restored seven times, with the most recent restoration completed in 1999. Nevertheless, enough of his noble intention is evident to ensure the reputation of *The Last Supper* as one of the best-known and most beloved paintings of Western art.

Leonardo's design for *The Last Supper* is highly idealized—a guiding principle of the High Renaissance. The fresco depicts the moment when Jesus says that one of the twelve disciples at the table will betray him. Ignoring the tradition that integrated this symbolic meal into an actual refectory, Leonardo separated the scene from its surroundings so that the figures would seem to hover over the heads of the clergy as they ate in their dining room. Idealism is also evident in Leonardo's straightforward perspective. The artist makes Jesus the focal center by framing him in the middle window and locating the vanishing point behind his head. In addition, the arrangement of the banqueting party—Jesus is flanked by six followers on either side—gives the painting a balanced effect. This harmonious composition breaks with the medieval custom of putting the traitor Judas on the opposite side of the table from the others.

A final idealistic touch may be seen in the way that Leonardo hides the face of Judas, the third figure on Jesus' right, in shadow while illuminating the other figures in bright light. Judas, though no longer seated apart from the rest, can still be readily identified, sitting cloaked in shadows, reaching for the bread with his left hand and clutching a bag of silver—symbolic of his treason—in the other hand. For generations, admirers have found Leonardo's fresco so natural and inevitable that it has become the standard version of this Christian subject.

Leonardo's setting and placement of the figures in *The Last Supper* are idealized, but his depiction of the individual figures is meant to convey the psychological truth about each of them. Jesus is portrayed with eyes cast down and arms outstretched in a gesture of resignation, while on either side a tumultuous scene erupts. As the disciples react to Jesus' charge of treason, Leonardo reveals the inner truth about each one through bodily gestures and facial expressions: Beneath the visual tumult, however, the artistic rules of the High Renaissance are firmly in place. Since neither biblical sources nor sacred tradition offered an ordering principle, Leonardo used mathematics to guide his arrangement of the disciples. He divides them into four groups of three figures; each set in turn is composed of two older men and a younger one. In his conception, not only does each figure respond individually, but also each interacts with other group members.

Besides mastering a narrative subject like *The Last Supper*, Leonardo also created a new type of portrait when he painted a half-length view of the seated *Mona Lisa* (Figure 12.7). As the fame of this work spread, other painters (and later, photographers) adopted Leonardo's half-length model as a basic artistic format for portraits. This painting, perhaps the most famous portrait in Western art, was commissioned by a

Figure 12.7   LEONARDO DA VINCI. *Mona Lisa*. 1503. Oil on panel, 30¼ × 21″. Musée du Louvre, Paris. *Leonardo's* Mona Lisa, *a likeness of the wife of the merchant Giocondo, illustrates the new status of Italy's urban middle class. This class was beginning to take its social cues from the fashionable world of the courts, the milieu described by Castiglione. Leonardo treats his middle-class subject as a model court lady, imbuing her presence with calm seriousness and quiet dignity.*

wealthy Florentine merchant. Avoiding the directness of *The Last Supper*, Leonardo hints at the sitter's demure nature through her shy smile and the charmingly awkward gesture of having the fingers of her right hand caress her left arm. In her face, celebrated in song and legend, he blends the likeness of a real person with an everlasting ideal to create a miraculous image. Further heightening the painting's eternal quality, the craggy background isolates the figure in space and time, in much the same way that the grotto functioned in Leonardo's *Virgin of the Rocks* (see Figure 11.22). Finally, he enhances the *Mona Lisa*'s mystery by enveloping the subject in the smoky atmosphere called *sfumato*—made possible by the oil medium—that softens her delicate features and the landscape in the background.

Figure 12.8 MICHELANGELO. Sistine Chapel Ceiling. (Restored.) 1508–1512. Full ceiling 45 × 128'. The Vatican. *Michelangelo's knowledge of architecture prompted him to paint illusionistic niches for the Hebrew prophets and the pagan sibyls on either side of the nine central panels. Neo-Platonism inspired his use of triangles, circles, and squares, for these geometric shapes were believed to hold the key to the mystery of the universe. These various framing devices enabled him to give visual order to the more than three hundred figures in his monumental scheme.*

During the High Renaissance, Leonardo's great works contributed to the cult of genius—the high regard, even reverence, that the age accorded to a few select artists, poets, and intellectuals. *The Last Supper* earned him great fame while he was alive. The history of the *Mona Lisa* was more complicated, since it was unseen while he lived and found among his effects when he died in 1519. After his death, as the *Mona Lisa* became widely known, first as a possession of the king of France and later as a jewel in the Louvre collection, Leonardo was elevated to membership among the immortals of Western art.

Michelangelo While Leonardo was working in Milan during most of the 1490s, Michelangelo Buonarroti [my-kuh-LAN-juh-lo bwo-nahr-ROH-tee] (1475–1564) was beginning a career that would propel him to the forefront of first the Florentine and later the Roman Renaissance, making him the most formidable artist of the sixteenth century.

Michelangelo's initial fame rested on his sculptural genius, which manifested itself at the age of thirteen when he was apprenticed to the Early Renaissance master Ghirlandaio and then, one year later, taken into the household of Lorenzo the Magnificent, the Medici ruler of Florence. In time, Michelangelo achieved greatness in painting and architecture as well as in sculpture, but he always remained a sculptor at heart.

Michelangelo's artistic credo was formed early, and he remained faithful to it over his long life. Sculpture, he believed, was the art form whereby human figures were liberated from the lifeless prison of their surrounding material. In this sense, he compared the sculptor's creativity with the activity of God—a notion that would have been judged blasphemous in prior Christian ages. Michelangelo himself, unlike the skeptical Leonardo, was a deeply pious man given to bouts of spiritual anxiety. His art constituted a form of divine worship.

Central to Michelangelo's artistic vision was his most celebrated image, the heroic nude male. Like the ancient Greek and Roman sculptors whose works he studied and admired, Michelangelo viewed the nude male form as a symbol of human dignity. In the High Renaissance, Michelangelo's nudes were based on Classical models, with robust bodies and serene faces. But in the 1530s, with the onset of Mannerism, the growing spiritual crisis in the church, and his own failing health, Michelangelo's depiction of the human figure changed. His later nudes had distorted body proportions and unusually expressive faces.

In 1508 Michelangelo was asked by Pope Julius II to decorate the Sistine Chapel ceiling. Michelangelo tried to avoid this commission, claiming that he was a sculptor and without expertise in frescoes, but the pope was unyielding in his insistence. The chapel had been built by Julius II's uncle, Pope Sixtus IV, in the late 1400s, and most of the walls had already been covered with frescoes. Michelangelo's frescoes were intended to bring the chapel's decorative plan closer to completion.

The challenge of painting the Sistine Chapel ceiling was enormous, for it was almost 70 feet from the floor, its sides were curved downward, necessitating numerous perspective changes, and its area covered some 5,800 square feet. Michelangelo overcame all these difficulties, teaching himself fresco technique and working for four years on scaffolding, to create one of the glories of the High Renaissance and unquestionably the greatest cycle of paintings in Western art (Figure 12.8).

Michelangelo, probably with the support of a papal adviser, designed a complex layout (Figure 12.9) for the ceiling frescoes that combined biblical narrative, theology, Neo-Platonist philosophy, and Classical allusions. In the ceiling's center, running from the altar to the rear of the chapel, he painted nine panels that illustrate the early history of the world, encompassing the creation of the universe, the fall of Adam and Eve,

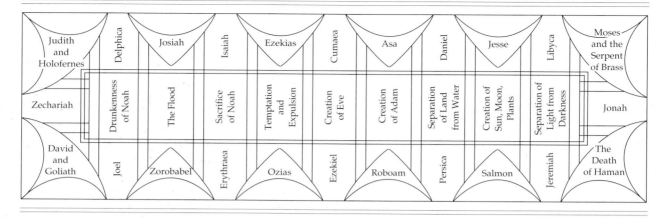

Judith and Holofernes	Delphica	Josiah	Isaiah	Ezekias	Cumaea	Asa	Daniel	Jesse	Libyca	Moses and the Serpent of Brass
Zechariah	Drunkenness of Noah	The Flood	Sacrifice of Noah	Temptation and Expulsion	Creation of Eve	Creation of Adam	Separation of Land from Water	Creation of Sun, Moon, Plants	Separation of Light from Darkness	Jonah
David and Goliath	Joel	Zorobabel	Erythraea	Ozias	Ezekiel	Roboam	Persica	Salmon	Jeremiah	The Death of Haman

Figure 12.9 Plan of Ceiling Frescoes, Sistine Chapel. 1508–1512. *The paintings on the Sistine Chapel ceiling may be grouped as follows: (1) the central section, which presents the history of the world from the creation (called "The Separation of Light from the Darkness") through the "Drunkenness of Noah"; (2) the gallery of portraits on both sides and at either end, which depict biblical prophets and pagan oracles; and (3) the four corner panels depicting Jewish heroes and heroines who overcame difficulties to help their people survive.*

Figure 12.10 MICHELANGELO. *The Delphic Oracle* (Delphica). Detail of the Sistine Chapel ceiling. 1508–1512. The Vatican. *Michelangelo, despite his manifold gifts as painter, sculptor, architect, and poet, always thought of himself as a sculptor, and this is nowhere more evident than in his portrait of the Delphic Oracle from the Sistine Chapel ceiling frescoes. The oracle, or Delphica (her Latin name), is painted to resemble a sculpture, seated on an illusory throne and holding an open scroll, from whose reading she appears interrupted. Delphica's muscular body is a deviation from Classical sculptural ideals of feminine beauty and reflects, instead, Michelangelo's practice of using male models for female subjects. He was also fascinated by the anatomy of position, as in the effect on Delphica's body of her head turned to the left and of one arm upraised and the other at rest. In symbolic terms, Delphica, according to the ceiling's Neo-Platonic plan, represented the pagan Greek prophetess foretelling the coming of Jesus Christ.*

and episodes in the life of Noah. Framing each of these biblical scenes were nude youths, whose presence shows Michelangelo's belief that the male form is an expression of divine power.

On either side of the center panels, he depicted Hebrew prophets and pagan sibyls, or oracles—all foretelling the coming of Christ (Figure 12.10). The pagan sibyls represent the Neo-Platonist idea that God's word was revealed in the prophecies of pre-Christian seers. At the corners of the ceiling, he placed four Old

Testament scenes of violence and death that had been allegorized as foreshadowing the coming of Christ. Michelangelo unified this complex of human and divine figures with an illusionistic architectural frame, and he used a plain background to make the figures stand out.

The most famous image from this vast work is a panel from the central section, *The Creation of Adam* (Figure 12.11). In the treatment of this episode from the book of Genesis, Michelangelo reduces the scene to a

Figure 12.11   MICHELANGELO. *The Creation of Adam.* Detail (restored) of the Sistine Chapel ceiling. 1511. 9′5″ × 18′8″. The Vatican. *One of the most celebrated details of this fresco is the outstretched fingers of God and Adam that approach but do not touch. By means of this vivid symbol, Michelangelo suggests that a divine spark is about to pass from God into the body of Adam, electrifying it into the fullness of life. The image demonstrates the restraint characteristic of the High Renaissance style. The Vatican's ongoing restoration of the Sistine Chapel frescoes has revealed the brilliant colors of the original, apparent in this detail.*

few details, in accordance with the High Renaissance love of simplicity. Adam, stretched out on a barely sketched bit of ground, seems to exist in some timeless space. Michelangelo depicts Adam as a pulsing, breathing human being. Such wondrous vitality in human flesh had not been seen in Western art since the vigorous nudes of ancient Greek art. In a bold move, Michelangelo ignored the Genesis story that told of God's molding Adam from dust. Instead, the artist paints Adam as half-awakened and reaching to God, who will implant a soul with his divine touch—an illustration of the Neo-Platonic idea of flesh yearning toward the spiritual.

By the 1530s, Michelangelo was painting in the Mannerist style, reflecting his disappointment with Florence's loss of freedom and his own spiritual torment. In this new style, he replaced his heroic vision with a fearful view of the world. A compelling example of this transformation is *The Last Judgment*, painted on the wall behind the Sistine Chapel's altar. This fresco conveys his own sense of sinfulness as well as humanity's future doom (Figure 12.12). Executed twenty-five years after the ceiling frescoes, *The Last Judgment*, with its images of justice and punishment, also reflects the crisis atmosphere of a Europe divided

into militant Protestant and Catholic camps. In the center of the fresco, Michelangelo depicts Jesus as the divine and final judge, with right arm raised in a commanding gesture. At the bottom of the fresco, the open graves yield up the dead, and the saved and the damned (on Jesus' right and left, respectively) rise to meet their fate.

In this painting, Michelangelo abandons the architectural framework that had given order to the ceiling frescoes. Instead, the viewer is confronted with a chaotic surface on which a circle of bodies seems to swirl around the central image of Jesus. Michelangelo elongates the bodies and changes their proportions by reducing the size of the heads. There is no classical serenity here; each figure's countenance shows the anguish provoked by this dreaded moment. Faced with judgment, some gesture wildly while others look beseechingly to their Savior. In this Mannerist masterpiece, simplicity has been replaced by exuberant abundance, and order has given way to rich diversity.

Raphael   The youngest of the trio of great High Renaissance painters is Raphael [RAFF-ee-uhl] Santi (1483–1520). Lacking Leonardo's scientific spirit and Michelangelo's brooding genius, Raphael nevertheless

Figure 12.12 MICHELANGELO. *The Last Judgment.* 1536–1541. 48 × 44′. Sistine Chapel, the Vatican. *This* Last Judgment *summarizes the anti-Classicism that was sweeping through the visual arts. Other painters studied this fresco for inspiration, borrowing its seemingly chaotic composition, its focus on large numbers of male nudes, and its use of bizarre perspective and odd postures as expressions of the Mannerist sensibility. This fresco was recently restored, its colors returned to the vivid primary colors of Michelangelo's original design and the draperies removed (they had been added during the Catholic Reformation).*

Figure 12.13 RAPHAEL. *The School of Athens.* 1510–1511. Fresco, 18 × 26'. Stanza della Segnatura, the Vatican. *Much of Raphael's success stemmed from the ease with which he assimilated the prevailing ideas of his age. For instance, the posture of the statue of Apollo in the wall niche on the left is probably derived from Michelangelo's* Dying Slave *(see Figure 12.1). For all his artistic borrowings, however, Raphael could be very generous, as indicated by the conspicuous way he highlights Michelangelo's presence in this fresco: The brooding genius sits alone in the foreground, lost in his thoughts and oblivious to the hubbub swirling about him.*

had such artistry that his graceful works expressed the ideals of this style better than did those of any other painter. Trained in Urbino, Raphael spent four years (from 1504 to 1508) in Florence, where he absorbed the local painting tradition, learning from the public works of both Leonardo and Michelangelo. Inspired by what he saw, Raphael developed his artistic ideal of well-ordered space in which human beauty and spatial harmony were given equal treatment.

Moving to Rome, Raphael had an abundance of patrons, especially the popes. At the heart of Raphael's success was his talent for blending the sacred and the secular, and in an age when a pope led troops into battle or went on hunting parties, this gift was appreciated and rewarded. Perhaps Raphael's most outstanding work in Rome was the cycle of paintings for the *stanze,* or rooms, of the Vatican apartment—one of the finest patronage plums of the High Renaissance. Commissioned by Julius II, the *stanze* frescoes show the same harmonization of Christianity and Classicism that Michelangelo brought to the Sistine Chapel ceiling.

Raphael's plan for the four walls of the Stanza della Segnatura in the papal chambers had as its subjects philosophy, poetry, theology, and law. Of these, the most famous is the fresco devoted to philosophy called *The School of Athens* (Figure 12.13). In this work, Raphael depicts a sober discussion among a group of ancient philosophers drawn from all periods. Following Leonardo's treatment of the disciples in *The Last Supper,* Raphael arranges the philosophers in groups, giving each scholar a characteristic gesture that reveals the essence of his thought. For example, Diogenes sprawls on the steps apart from the rest—a vivid symbol of the arch Cynic's contempt for his fellow man. In the right foreground, Euclid, the author of a standard text on geometry, illustrates the proof of one of his theorems. In his careful arrangement of this crowd scene, Raphael demonstrates that he is a master of ordered space.

The School of Athens has a majestic aura because of Raphael's adherence to Classical forms and ideas. The architectural setting, with its round arches, medallions, and coffered ceilings, is inspired by Classical architectural ruins and also perhaps by

Figure 12.14 RAPHAEL. *Sistine Madonna*. 1513. Oil on canvas, 8'8½" × 6'5". Gemäldegalerie, Dresden. *Raphael's adherence to the rules of Classical art in the* Sistine Madonna *is nowhere more evident than in the painting's balanced composition. Bracketing the central image of the Virgin and child are a variety of pairings: At the top, two curtains are drawn open; toward the middle, two human figures kneel in prayer; and the open space between the draperies above is echoed by the two angels below. These artful pairings not only give visual variety to the simple scene but also outline and define the sacred space surrounding the Virgin and child.*

Figure 12.15 GIORGIONE. *The Tempest*. 1505. Oil on canvas, 31¼ × 28¾". Galleria dell' Accademia, Venice. *Giorgione's mysterious painting evokes the period—called an "anxious hush"—that sometimes attends the prelude to a violent thunderstorm. He creates this tense mood through atmospheric effects that suggest a gathering storm: billowing clouds; a flash of lightning and its watery reflection; and, in particular, the stark color contrasts between the harshly lighted buildings and the somber hues of earth, sky, and river. The mood is also heightened by the presence of two vulnerable figures, especially the nursing mother who gazes quizzically at the viewer, about to be engulfed by the storm. The painting has a typical Venetian feature in its carefully rendered textures—flesh, cloth, wood, stone, and foliage. Giorgione's painting blazed the path for later artists, chiefly in northern Europe, who took the landscape as a subject.*

contemporary structures. Perfectly balanced, the scene is focused on Plato and Aristotle, who stand under the series of arches at the painting's center. Raphael reinforces their central position by placing the vanishing point just above and between their heads. The two thinkers' contrasting gestures symbolize the difference between their philosophies: Plato, on the left, points his finger skyward, suggesting the world of the Forms, or abstract thought, and Aristotle, on the right, motions toward the earth, indicating his more practical and empirical method. Raphael also uses these two thinkers as part of his ordering scheme to represent the division of philosophy into the arts and sciences. On Plato's side, the poetic thinkers are gathered under the statue of Apollo, the Greek god of music and lyric verse; Aristotle's half includes the scientists under the statue of Athena, the Greek goddess of wisdom.

Of even greater fame than Raphael's narrative paintings are his portraits of the Virgin Mary. They set the standard for this form of portraiture with their exquisite sweetness and harmonious composition. The *Sistine Madonna* is probably the best known of this group (Figure 12.14). This painting shows Raphael at his best, borrowing from several sources yet creating his own convincing style. It is composed in the pyramid shape first popularized by Leonardo da Vinci (see Figure 11.22). The Virgin's head forms the apex of the pyramid, Pope Julius II (whose death the painting commemorates) stands bareheaded on her right, and St. Barbara, the patron saint of the arrival of death, on her left; the drape of the curtains underscores the pyramidal design. Raphael relieves the scene's somber mood by painting below the hovering figures two mischievous *putti*, or angels, who look upward, unimpressed with the scene-stealing baby Jesus. Raphael's assurance in handling these complex effects makes the *Sistine Madonna* a glowing masterpiece of the High Renaissance.

Figure 12.16   TITIAN. *Presentation of the Virgin in the Temple.* 1534–1538. 11′4″ × 25′5″.
Originally in the Scuola Grande di Santa Maria della Carità, now part of the Accademia
di Belle Arte, Venice. *Titian's painting is filled with symbols conveying Christian ideas. The
Virgin is bathed in an oval of light of which she is the source; light is a traditional symbol of God's
presence. On the left, the tall, thin pyramid alludes to Mary's divine status; it is a Renaissance
symbol of Holy Wisdom, an attribute of the Virgin. The large cumulus cloud in the distance refers
to the Holy Spirit, and the begging woman at the rear of the procession symbolizes Charity, or
Almsgiving. Most complex of all are the two images in front of the stairway: the old egg seller who
appears oblivious to the momentous event taking place above her head, and, to the right of the
door, an ancient bust. Scholars identify these two images, respectively, with Judaism and
paganism, both of which were to be superseded by the coming of Christ.*

The Venetian School: Giorgione and Titian   Venice
maintained its autonomy during the High Renaissance both politically and culturally. Despite the artistic pull of the Roman and Florentine schools, the Venetian artists stayed true to their Byzantine-influenced
tradition of sensual surfaces, rich colors, and theatrical lighting. The two greatest painters of the Venetian High Renaissance were Giorgione [jor-JO-na]
(about 1477–1510), who was acknowledged to be
Venice's premier artist at the end of his life, and Titian
[TISH-uhn] (about 1488–1576), who in his later years
was revered as Europe's supreme painter.

Little is known of Giorgione's life until the last years
of his brief career. A student of Bellini, he won early
fame, indicated by the rich private and public commissions he was awarded. Although only a few of his
works survive, Giorgione's influence on the course of
European art was substantial. His two major innovations, the female nude and the landscape, contributed
to the growing secularization of European painting.
These developments helped to make Venetian art distinctive from that of Rome and Florence.

The Tempest (Figure 12.15) is probably his best-known
work. Breaking free of Bellini's influence, Giorgione created a dramatic landscape, framed on the left by a
soldier and on the right by a partly clothed mother nursing a child, that did not allude to mythology, the Bible,
or allegorical stories. Whereas Bellini's *St. Francis in
Ecstasy* (see Figure 11.23) made the saint the focus of the

painting, in *The Tempest* the framing figures are overshadowed by the menacing storm. Thus, Giorgione's
landscape, freed of storytelling elements, becomes the
subject and should be appreciated on its own terms.

Titian's paintings were prized not only for their easy
grace and natural lighting—characteristics of the Venetian High Renaissance—but also for the masterful use
of rich color to create dramatic effects (see Figure 12.3).
Titian's adherence to the principles of High Renaissance
style is evident in such narrative paintings as his *Presentation of the Virgin in the Temple,* a subject based on a
legendary account of the life of Mary (Figure 12.16).
Titian's careful arrangement of this complicated
scene—with its landscape, classicizing architecture, and
gathering of accessory figures—reflects his commitment to the principles of simplicity and naturalism. He
conceived of the scene as a sweeping pageant, starting
on the left with the pious procession and culminating
with the young Mary, standing on the temple stairs in
the middle right. Waiting to greet her at the head of the
stairs are the high priest and other officials.

One deviation from Classical principles in this painting is the asymmetry of the closed architectural forms
on the right set against the open landscape on the left.
Instead of symmetry, Titian uses color as a unifying element. Cool colors, primarily blue, are prominent in the
sky and the mountains on the left; warm colors, mainly
brown and pink, are the primary hues of the buildings
and the vestments of the temple leaders on the right.

Figure 12.17 PARMIGIANINO. *Madonna with the Long Neck.* 1534–1540. Oil on panel, 7'1" × 4'4". Uffizi Gallery, Florence. *This Madonna by Parmigianino is one of the landmark works in the rise of the Mannerist style. Ignoring Classical ideals, Parmigianino exaggerates the Virgin's body proportions, especially the slender hands and long neck, and elongates the body of the sleeping Jesus. This anti-Classical portrait was greatly at odds with the prevailing High Renaissance image of the Madonna established by Raphael.*

Because he used subtle modulations of color to create harmony in his works, Titian became the leading "colorist"—as opposed to those more concerned with form—to future generations of painters.

The School of Parma: Parmigianino   Parma, in northern Italy, was another center of High Renaissance art, but the city's best-known artist is a founder of Mannerism, Parmigianino [pahr-mee-jah-NEE-noh] (1503–1540). The *Madonna with the Long Neck* shows Parmigianino's delight in ambiguity, distortion, and dissonance and his love of eccentric composition (Figure 12.17). Mary is portrayed with sloping shoulders and long arms in the manner of Botticelli, and her sensuous figure is not quite hidden under diaphanous draperies—a disturbing mix of sacred and profane love. A similar confusion exists in the depiction of the infant Christ: The bald baby Jesus appears more dead than alive, so that the subject invokes the Pietà image of the dead Christ stretched on his mother's lap along with the image of the Virgin and child. On the left, five figures stare in various directions. In the background, unfinished columns and an old man reading a scroll, perhaps an allusion to biblical prophecies of Jesus' birth, add to the feeling of multiple focuses and contradictory scales. Unlike the art of the High Renaissance, which offered readily understood subjects, this Mannerist painting, with its uneasy blend of religious piety and disguised sexuality, is enigmatic.

Sculpture

Michelangelo's art is as central to the High Renaissance style in sculpture as it is in painting. An early sculpture that helped to inaugurate this style was the *Pietà*, executed when he was twenty-one (Figure 12.18). The

Figure 12.18 MICHELANGELO. *Pietà.* 1498–1499. Marble, ht. 5'8½". St. Peter's, the Vatican. *This* Pietà *is the only one of Michelangelo's sculptures to be signed. Initially, it was exhibited without a signature, but, according to a legend, when Michelangelo overheard spectators attributing the statue to a rival sculptor, he carved his signature into the marble strap that crosses Mary's chest.*

GIORGIO VASARI
Michelangelo Has the Last Word

Vasari (1511–1574) actually studied painting under Michelangelo, but he is known today for his accounts of the lives of Renaissance artists, sculptors, and architects. In this excerpt, he describes how Michelangelo executed his most famous work, the David.

Some of his [Michelangelo's] friends wrote to him from Florence urging him to return there as it seemed very probable that he would be able to obtain the block of marble that was standing in the Office of Works. Piero Soderini, who about that time was elected Gonfalonier for life [head of the Florentine republic], had often talked of handing it over to Leonardo da Vinci, but he was then arranging to give it to Andrea Contucci of Monte Sansovino, an accomplished sculptor who was very keen to have it. Now, although it seemed impossible to carve from the block a complete figure (and only Michelangelo was bold enough to try this without adding fresh pieces) Buonarroti had felt the desire to work on it many years before; and he tried to obtain it when he came back to Florence. The marble was eighteen feet high, but unfortunately an artist called Simone da Fiesole had started to carve a giant figure, and had bungled the work so badly that he had hacked a hole between the legs and left the block completely botched and misshapen. So the wardens of Santa Maria del Fiore (who were in charge of the undertaking) threw the block aside and it stayed abandoned for many years and seemed likely to remain so indefinitely. However, Michelangelo measured it again and calculated whether he could carve a satisfactory figure from the block by accommodating its attitude to the shape of the stone. Then he made up his mind to ask for it. Soderini and the wardens decided that they would let him have it, as being something of little value, and telling themselves that since the stone was of no use to their building, either botched as it was or broken up, whatever Michelangelo made would be worthwhile. So Michelangelo made a wax model of the young David with a sling in his hand; this was intended as a symbol of liberty for the Palace, signifying that just as David had protected his people and governed them justly, so whoever ruled Florence should vigorously defend the city and govern it with justice. He began work on the statue in the Office of Works of Santa Maria del Fiore, erecting a partition of planks and trestles around the marble; and working on it continuously he brought it to perfect completion, without letting anyone see it. . . .

When he saw the David in place Piero Soderini was delighted; but while Michelangelo was retouching it he remarked that he thought the nose was too thick. Michelangelo, noticing that the Gonfalonier was standing beneath the Giant and that from where he was he could not see the figure properly, to satisfy him climbed on the scaffolding by the shoulders, seized hold of a chisel in his left hand, together with some of the marble dust lying on the planks, and as he tapped lightly with the chisel let the dust fall little by little, without altering anything. Then he looked down at the Gonfalonier, who had stopped to watch, and said:

"Now look at it."

"Ah, that's much better," replied Soderini. "Now you've really brought it to life."

And then Michelangelo climbed down, feeling sorry for those critics who talk nonsense in the hope of appearing well informed.

touching subject of the **Pietà**—Mary holding the body of the dead Christ—struck a responsive chord in Michelangelo, for he created several sculptural variations on the Pietà theme during his lifetime.

The first *Pietà*, executed in 1498–1499, about the same time as Leonardo's *Last Supper,* shows Michelangelo already at the height of his creative powers. He has captured completely a bewildering sense of loss in his quiet rendering of Mary's suffering. Everything about the sculpture reinforces the somber subject: the superb modeling of Jesus' dead body, with its heavy head and dangling legs; Mary's outstretched gown, which serves as a shroud; and Mary's body, burdened by the weight of her son. Like some ancient funeral monument, which the *Pietà* brings to mind, this sculpture of Mary and Jesus overwhelms the viewer with its sorrowful but serene mood.

In 1501, two years after finishing the *Pietà*, Michelangelo was given the commission by the city of Florence for the sculpture that is generally recognized as his supreme masterpiece, the *David* (Figure 12.19). Michelangelo was eager for this commission because it allowed him to test himself against other great sculptors who had tackled this subject, such as Donatello in the Early Renaissance (see Figure 11.11). Moreover, Michelangelo, a great Florentine patriot, identified David with the aggressive spirit of his native city. Michelangelo's *David* was instantly successful, and the

Figure 12.19 MICHELANGELO. *David.* 1501–1504. Marble, ht. 14'3". Accademia, Florence. *Michelangelo's colossal David—standing more than 14 feet tall—captures the balanced ideal of High Renaissance art. The "closed" right side with its tensed hanging arm echoes the right leg, which supports the figure's weight; in the same way, the "open" left side with its bent arm is the precise counterpart of the flexed left leg. Further tension arises from the contrast between David's steady stare and the readiness of the right fist, which holds the stone. Through these means, Michelangelo reinforces the image of a young man wavering between thought and action.*

Figure 12.20 MICHELANGELO. *Pietà.* Before 1555. Marble, ht. 7′8″. Santa Maria del Fiore, Florence. *The rage that seemed to infuse Michelangelo's Mannerist vision in* The Last Judgment *appears purged in this* Pietà—*the work he was finishing when he died at the age of eighty-eight. Mannerist distortions are still present, particularly in the twisted body of the dead Christ and the implied downward motion of the entire ensemble. But the gentle faces suggest that serenity has been restored to Michelangelo's art.*

republic of Florence adopted the statue as its civic symbol, placing the work in the open square before the Palazzo Vecchio, the town hall. Damage to the statue through weathering and local unrest caused the civic leaders eventually to house Michelangelo's most famous sculpture indoors, where it remains today.

Michelangelo's *David,* rather than imitating Donatello's partly clothed and somewhat effete version, portrays the young Jewish warrior as a nude, Classical hero. Taking a damaged and abandoned block of marble, Michelangelo carved the colossal *David* as a muscular adolescent with his weight gracefully balanced on the right leg, in Classical contrapposto. The *David* perfectly represents Michelangelo's conception

of sculpture; imaging a human figure imprisoned inside marble, he simply used his chisel to set it free.

Michelangelo also made minor deviations from Classical principles in his rendition of David in the name of higher ideals, just as ancient artists had done. David's large hands, for example, are outside Classical proportions and suggest a youth who has yet to grow to his potential. And his furrowed brow violates the Classical ideal of serene faces but reflects his intense concentration.

Michelangelo's later sculpture is Mannerist in style, as are his later paintings. A second *Pietà* group—with Christ, Mary, Mary Magdalene, and Joseph of Arimathea—shows the change in his depiction of the human form (Figure 12.20). In this somber group,

Figure 12.21 BRAMANTE. Tempietto. After 1502. Marble, ht. 46'; diameter of colonnade 29'. San Pietro in Montorio, Rome. *Bramante's Tempietto is the earliest surviving High Renaissance building and an exquisite example of this style. Fashioned from pure Classical forms, the building is almost devoid of decoration except for architectural features, and the separate parts—dome, cylindrical drum, and base—are brought into a harmonious whole. The only significant missing feature (since High Renaissance buildings were always planned in relation to their enveloping space) is the never-finished courtyard.*

Michelangelo's anti-Classical spirit is paramount. Jesus' body is elongated and unnaturally twisted in death; the other figures, with great difficulty, struggle to support his dead weight. But rather than detracting from the sculpture's impact, the awkward body adds to the scene's emotional interest—an aim of Mannerist art, which did not trust the viewer to respond to more orderly images. Joseph, the rich man who, according to the Gospel, donated his own tomb to Jesus, has Michelangelo's face—a face that is more a death mask than a human countenance.

Architecture

The architectural heir to Alberti in the early sixteenth century was Donato Bramante [brah-MAHN-tay] (1444–1514), who became the moving force behind the High Renaissance in architecture. Trained as a painter, Bramante rejected the reigning building style, called **scenographic,** in which buildings are composed of discrete, individual units. Instead, by concentrating on space and volume, Bramante created an architecture that was unified in all its components and that followed the rules of the Classical orders.

The clearest surviving expression of Bramante's architectural genius is the Tempietto, or little temple, in Rome (Figure 12.21). This small structure was designed both as a church, seating ten worshipers, and as a building marking the site of the martyrdom of

St. Peter. Copied from the circular temples of ancient Rome, this small domed building became the prototype of the central plan church popularized in the High Renaissance and later.

Bramante's design for the Tempietto sprang from ancient Classical principles. Foremost was his belief that architecture should appeal to human reason and that a building should present a severe appearance and not seek to please through specially planned effects. Further, he thought that a building should be unified like a piece of sculpture and that ornamentation should be restricted to a few architectural details.

In accordance with this artistic credo, the Tempietto functions like a work of sculpture; it is raised on a pedestal with steps leading up to its colonnaded porch. In the absence of sculptural decorations, the temple's exterior is accented with architectural details: the columns; the **balustrade,** or rail with supporting posts; and the dome with barely visible ribs. The proportions of its various features, such as the ratio of column widths to column heights, were based on ancient mathematical formulas. Unfortunately for Bramante's final conception, the plan to integrate the small temple into a circular courtyard of a nearby church was never completed. Despite the absence of this crowning touch, the Tempietto is one of the jewels of the High Renaissance.

Bramante had been commissioned by Pope Julius II to rebuild St. Peter's Basilica, the world's most famous church, but he died before his plans could be carried

Figure 12.22 MICHELANGELO. Dome of St. Peter's. View from the southwest. 1546–1564. (Completed by Giacomo della Porta, 1590.) Ht. of dome 452'. Rome. *Its harmonious design and its reliance on Classical forms made Michelangelo's dome an object of universal admiration when it was completed in 1590, after his death. From then to the present day, other architects have used his dome as a model, hoping to reproduce its Classical spirit.*

out. The supervision of the rebuilding of St. Peter's fell to other architects; eventually Michelangelo, at the age of seventy-one, was given this vital task. From 1546 until his death in 1564, Michelangelo, among his other artistic tasks, was occupied with St. Peter's, especially with the construction of the dome. Over the years, other building projects had come his way, but nothing could compare with the significance of this one. Although the dome was completed after his death and slightly modified, it remains Michelangelo's outstanding architectural monument and a splendid climax to his career.

Michelangelo's sculptural approach to architecture was similar to that of Bramante. In an attempt to integrate the dome of St. Peter's with the rest of the existing structure, Michelangelo used double Corinthian columns as a unifying agent. Because the facade of St. Peter's was altered in the 1600s, Michelangelo's dome is best observed from the southwest (Figure 12.22). Beginning at ground level, the Corinthian order provides the artistic cement that pulls the entire building together. Sometimes as columns, sometimes as pilasters, and sometimes as ribs, the double Corinthian units move up the walls, eventually up the dome's drum, and up the dome itself.

This plan for St. Peter's shows that Michelangelo the architect differed from Michelangelo the painter and sculptor. In painting and sculpture, he had by the 1530s become a Mannerist in his use of exaggeration and expressive effects. But in architecture, he stayed faithful to the High Renaissance and its ideal of harmonious design.

The preeminent architect of the Mannerist style was Andrea di Pietro (1508–1580), known as Palladio [pah-LAHD-yo], whose base of operations was Vicenza, in northern Italy. The name Palladio derives from Pallas, a name for Athena, the goddess of wisdom. Palladio's artistic creed was rooted in Classicism, but his forte was the richly inventive way in which he could arrange the Classical elements of a building to guarantee surprise. He played with the effects of light and shadow, adding feature on top of feature, to create buildings that possess infinite variety in the midst of a certain decorative solemnity.

Palladio's most influential domestic design was the Villa Capra, more commonly called the Villa Rotonda because of its central circular area and covering dome (Figure 12.23). Inspired by ancient Roman farmhouses, the Villa Rotonda is a sixteenth-century country house built of brick and faced with stucco and located on a rise overlooking Vicenza. A dome provides a central axis from which four symmetrical wings radiate. Each of the four wings in turn opens to the outdoors through an Ionic-style porch raised on a pedestal. The porticoes, or covered porches supported by columns, then lead to the ground level through deeply recessed stairways. Statues stand on the corners and peak of each of the four pediments, and others flank the four stairways.

Palladio's Mannerist spirit can be seen at work in the design of this building. Although the coldly formal

Figure 12.23 PALLADIO. Villa Rotonda (Villa Capra). Begun 1550. (Completed by Vincenzo Scamozzi.) Ht. of dome 70', villa 80' square. Vicenza. *Despite its harmonious proportions and Classical features, the Villa Rotonda belongs to the Mannerist style. Unlike High Renaissance buildings, which were designed to be integrated with their settings, this boxlike country house stands in an antagonistic relationship to its surrounding garden space. Furthermore, the Mannerist principle of elongation is apparent in its four long stairways. But the Villa Rotonda's most striking Mannerist feature is the surprise inherent in a plan that includes four identical porches.*

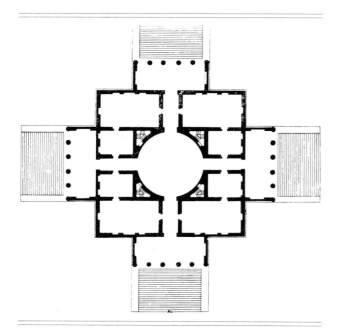

porches are Classical in appearance, no Greek or Roman temple would have had four such identical porches, one on each side of the building (Figure 12.24). Palladio's design incorporates the unexpected and the contradictory within an apparently Classical structure.

Besides designing buildings, Palladio also wrote about architecture in his treatise *Quattro libri dell' architettura,* or *The Four Books of Architecture.* Through its English translation, this work gained wide currency and led to the vogue of Palladianism in the English-speaking world. English aristocrats in the eighteenth century commissioned country houses built on Palladian principles, as did plantation owners in America's antebellum South.

Figure 12.24 PALLADIO. Floor Plan of the Villa Rotonda. *Palladio designed the Villa Rotonda to further the social ambitions of its wealthy Venetian owner, so he made its most prominent interior feature a central circular area, or rotunda. Surmounted by a dome, this area was ideal for concerts, parties, and other entertainments. Palladio surrounded the rotunda with four identically shaped sets of rooms on two levels, where the family lived and guests were housed. Passageways led to the four porches, where villa residents could obtain relief from the summer's heat and enjoy diverting views of the surrounding countryside.*

Music

No radical break separates the music of the High Renaissance from that of the Early Renaissance. Josquin des Prez, the leading composer of the dominant Franco-Netherlandish school, had brought to a climax the Early Renaissance style of music while he was employed in Italy by the popes and the local aristocrats (see Chapter 11). Josquin's sixteenth-century pieces, which consist chiefly of religious Masses and motets along with secular *chansons,* or songs, simply heightened the ideal already present in his earlier works: a sweet sound produced by multiple voices, usually two to six, singing *a cappella* and expressing the feelings described in the text. Despite his interest in music's emotional power, Josquin continued to subordinate the song to the words—thus reflecting the needs of the church, the foremost patron of the age. This balancing act between the music and the words, resulting in a clearly sung text, was also evidence of the Classical restraint of his High Renaissance style. A striking feature of this style was the rich multichoral effect produced when the singing group was subdivided into different combinations of voices.

Experimentation with choral effects was carried into the next generation by Adrian Willaert [VIL-art] (about 1490–1562), a member of the Netherlandish school and a disciple of Josquin's. After the death of his mentor, Willaert was probably Europe's most influential composer. He made his mark on musical history from his post as chapel master of the cathedral of St. Mark's in Venice, and he is considered the founder of the Venetian school of music. Taking advantage of St. Mark's two organs and the Venetian practice of blending instruments with voices, he wrote music for two choirs as well. By a variety of musical mechanisms, such as alternating and combining voices, contrasting soft and loud, and arranging echo effects, Willaert created beautiful and expressive sounds that were the ancestor of the splendid church concertos of the Baroque era. A benefit of Willaert's innovations was that the organ was released from its dependence on vocal music.

Except for the stylistic perfection achieved by Josquin and Willaert, the musical scene during this period witnessed only minor changes from that of the Early Renaissance. Instrumental music still played a secondary role to the human voice, though Josquin and Willaert composed a few pieces for specific instruments, either transposing melodies that originally had been intended for singers or adapting music forms from dance tunes.

One development was the appearance of the violin, which evolved from the Arabic *rebec* and the medieval fiddle and its Italian cousin (Figure 12.25). A bowed, stringed musical instrument, the violin is probably the most popular musical instrument in the world today.

Figure 12.25   GIOVANNI DI LUTERO, KNOWN AS DOSSO DOSSI. *Apollo and Daphne.* Ca. 1538. Oil on canvas, 6'2" × 3'9". Galleria Borghese, Rome. *Dosso Dossi (ca. 1490–1542), who lived in Ferrara and was influenced by Giorgione, Titian, and probably Raphael, painted many allegorical and mythological scenes. His sense of color and understanding of light added to the magic and fantasy of his works. Apollo, the patron of poetry and music and leader of the Muses, is placed in the foreground, while Daphne, whom he constantly chased, is in the middle ground, fleeing from her pursuer. An Italian city, perhaps Bologna (identified by its Twin Towers), fills in the background. Apollo, rather than playing the lyre, an ancient Greek string instrument, is holding a violin. This painting may be one of the first to feature the violin, since it had only appeared about 1510. By the 1570s, Andrea Amati, who is recognized as the designer of the first violin was making the instrument at his workshop in Cremona, a city within eighty miles of Ferrara. Antonio Stradivari and Andrea Guarneri, two of the most famous violin makers in history, were pupils of Niccolo Amati, Andrea's grandson. Antonio Stradivari brought violin making to its highest level of perfection. He produced 540 violins along with many other string instruments. Today, a Stradivari violin is considered one of the most precious musical instruments in the world.*

By the end of the sixteenth century Italian violin makers had determined the instrument's basic size and shape, though the number of strings continued to vary for several decades.

The development that had the most promise for the future was the invention of families of instruments, ranging from the low bass to the high treble, which blended to make a pleasant sound. In most cases, these families, called **consorts,** consisted of either recorders or viols. The consorts represented the principle of the mixed instrumental ensemble, and from this beginning would emerge the orchestra. Recorders and viols could also be blended to make an agreeable sound; when human voices were added to the mixture, the conditions were ripe for opera.

The Legacy of the High Renaissance and Early Mannerism

From a contemporary perspective, the seventy-year period during which the High Renaissance and Early Mannerism flourished is the Golden Age of the West in certain artistic and humanistic areas. In the visual arts—painting, sculpture, and architecture—standards were set and indelible images created that have not been surpassed. In political theory, this age produced the Mannerist thinker Machiavelli, who is the founder of modern political thought.

Beyond those achievements, two other important steps were being taken on the road to the modern world. On a political level, the beginnings of the modern secular state may be seen in the changes taking place in France, Spain, and England. What was innovative, even revolutionary, for these countries in the early sixteenth century has become second nature to the states of the twenty-first century, both in the Western world and beyond. On a social level, a new code of behavior appeared in the Italian courts and was in time adopted throughout Europe. Not only did the rules of courtesy finally penetrate into the European aristocracy and alter their behavior, but also they eventually trickled down to the middle classes. By our day, the behavior of Castiglione's courtier and lady, though in diluted form, has become the model for all Western people with any shred of social ambition.

Another new idea was beginning to develop now as well. The Classical and the medieval worlds had praised what was corporate and public, in conformity with traditional, universal values. But in the 1500s a few artists and humanists, along with their patrons, began to revere what was individual and private. The supreme example of free expression and of the "cult of genius" in the High Renaissance was Leonardo da Vinci, whose encoded notebooks were meant for his personal use and not for general publication. Early Mannerism carried individual expression to extremes by finding merit in personal eccentricities and unrestrained behavior. That patrons supported the new works of these artists and humanists demonstrates the rise of the belief that free expression is both a social and a private good. Both the High Renaissance and Early Mannerism encouraged the daring idea of individualism and thereby introduced what has become a defining theme of Western culture.

KEY CULTURAL TERMS

High Renaissance
Mannerism
Machiavellianism
Pietà

scenographic
balustrade
consort

SUGGESTIONS FOR FURTHER READING

Primary Sources

CASTIGLIONE, B. *The Book of the Courtier.* Translated by G. Bull. New York: Penguin, 1967. A flowing translation; includes a helpful introduction and descriptions of characters who participate in the conversations recorded by Castiglione; first published in 1528.

MACHIAVELLI, N. *The Prince.* Translated by G. Bull. New York: Penguin, 1971. The introduction covers Machiavelli's life and other writings to set the stage for this important political work; written in 1513.

SUGGESTIONS FOR LISTENING

WILLAERT, ADRIAN (about 1490–1562). Willaert is particularly noted for his motets, such as *Sub tuum praesidium,* which reflect the Renaissance humanist ideal of setting the words precisely to the music. His *Musica nova,* published in 1559 and including motets, madrigals, and instrumental music, illustrates the complex polyphony and sensuous sounds that made him a widely imitated composer in the second half of the sixteenth century.

CHAPTER *12* HIGHLIGHTS
The High Renaissance and Early Mannerism, 1494–1564

 CASTIGLIONE, *The Book of the Courtier* (1528)

STAMPA, Poems (mid–sixteenth century)

12.6 DA VINCI, *The Last Supper* (1495–1498)

12.18 MICHELANGELO, *Pietà* (1498–1499)

12.19 MICHELANGELO, *David* (1501–1504)

12.21 BRAMANTE, Tempietto (after 1502)

12.7 DA VINCI, *Mona Lisa* (1503)

12.15 GIORGIONE, *The Tempest* (1505)

12.8 MICHELANGELO, *Sistine Chapel Ceiling* (1508–1512)

12.13 RAPHAEL, *The School of Athens* (1510–1511)

12.14 RAPHAEL, *Sistine Madonna* (1513)

12.1 MICHELANGELO, *Dying Slave* (1513–1516)

12.5 RAPHAEL, *Baldassare Castiglione* (1514)

12.16 TITIAN, *Presentation of the Virgin in the Temple* (1534–1538)

12.22 MICHELANGELO, Dome of St. Peter's (1546–1564)

WILLAERT, *Agnus Dei* (sixteenth century)

 MACHIAVELLI, *The Prince* (1513)

PALLADIO, *The Four Books of Architecture* (1570)

12.17 PARMIGIANINO, *Madonna with the Long Neck* (1534–1540)

12.12 MICHELANGELO, *The Last Judgment* (1536–1541)

12.23 PALLADIO, Villa Rotonda (begun 1550)

12.20 MICHELANGELO, *Pietà* (before 1555)

■ *Literature & Philosophy*   ■ *Art & Architecture*   ■ *Music & Dance*

Readings in the Western Humanities   ⊚ *CD, The Western Humanities*

1500

AD

 Albertus Durerus Nor
ipsum me proprijs sic ef
gebam coloribus atatis
anno XXVIII.

13 NORTHERN HUMANISM, NORTHERN RENAISSANCE, RELIGIOUS REFORMATIONS, AND LATE MANNERISM

1500–1603

As the High Renaissance and Early Mannerism were unfolding in Italy (see Chapter 12), the rest of Europe was being transformed by three developments: a literary movement, two new artistic styles, and a religious crisis. The literary movement and the new artistic styles were partially inspired by the cultural changes under way in Italy. However, the religious crisis, in its early years, was unique to northern Europe; by midcentury, it had become intertwined with local and international politics. Northern (or Christian) humanism, as the literary movement was called, was inspired by both the Italian Renaissance, with its emphasis on Classical studies, and Late Medieval lay piety, with its focus on a simpler Christianity. Two distinct artistic styles now appeared in Europe: the Northern Renaissance, lasting from 1500 until about 1560, and Late Mannerism, enduring for the rest of the century. The course of these literary and artistic developments was, in turn, affected by the religious crisis that soon engulfed all of Europe (Timeline 13.1).

Germany became the epicenter of the spiritual earthquake called the **Reformation,** a movement that forever shattered the religious unity of the West. The Reformation, like the Renaissance, looked to the past for inspiration and ideas, but rather than focusing on the Classical world of Greece and Rome, the religious leaders of the Reformation looked to the early Christian church before it became hierarchical and bureaucratic. Almost immediately, these reformers met with unbending resistance from the contemporary church and its officials. From the confrontations between these hostile groups emerged the labels the two sides still wear today: the Protestants, who wanted a

◄ **Detail** ALBRECHT DÜRER. *Self-Portrait*. 1500. Oil on panel, 26¼ × 19¼". Alte Pinakothek, Munich.

Timeline 13.1   THE SIXTEENTH CENTURY

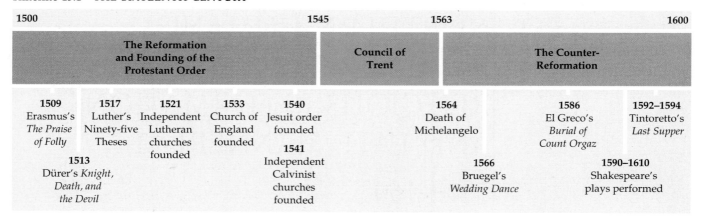

complete renovation of the church, and the Roman Catholics, who were largely satisfied with the church as it was.

The Catholics did not oppose all change, however. In the second half of the sixteenth century, they conducted the **Counter-Reformation,** purifying the church and setting it on the path that it followed until the 1960s. In contrast, the Protestants disagreed over basic Christian doctrines and soon split into separate sects.

In the 1560s, the Counter-Reformation began to have a strong impact on culture, especially in Spain and Italy. Late Mannerism in the arts, architecture, and music flourished in these areas, until the Baroque style rose at the end of the century. One outstanding exception to this late Mannerist trend was found in Spanish literature. Spanish writing, which had entered its Golden Age in about 1500, reached its zenith with the works of Cervantes.

NORTHERN HUMANISM

Northern humanism, also known as **Christian humanism,** shared some of the aesthetic values of the High Renaissance, such as idealism, rationalism, and a deep love for Classical literature. Unlike the humanist movement in Italy, however, the northern humanists were preoccupied with the condition of the church and the wider Christian world. For these northern thinkers, the study of Christian writings went hand in hand with research on the Greco-Roman classics, and their scholarship was meant to further the cause of ecclesiastical reform.

Like the lay pietists of the Late Middle Ages (see Chapter 10), from whom they drew inspiration, the northern humanists approached their faith in simple terms. They taught that any Christian who had a pure and humble heart could pray directly to God. These scholars further strengthened the appeal of this simple creed by claiming that it was identical with Christ's scriptural message, which they were discovering in their vernacular translations of the New Testament.

The thinking of the Christian humanists, notably in Germany, was tinged with national feeling and hostility toward Italian interference in their local religious affairs. Their Christian humanism with its simple faith led them to believe that by imitating the early church—freed of corrupt Italian leaders—they could revitalize Christianity and restore it to its original purpose.

A notable French humanist was François Rabelais [RAB-uh-lay] (about 1494–1553), who wrote a five-part satire collectively titled *The Histories of Gargantua and Pantagruel.* In these works, Rabelais vigorously attacked the church's abuses and ridiculed the clergy and theologians. Beneath the satire, he affirmed the goodness of human nature and the ability of men and women to lead useful lives based on reason and common sense. However, his skepticism and secularism, as well as the ribald humor, obscene references, and grotesque escapades of his heroes, put Rabelais in a unique category, well outside the mainstream of northern humanism.

Another northern humanist outside the mainstream was Marguerite of Angoulême, queen of Navarre (1492–1549), sister of King Francis I. She was an important protector of Rabelais, Protestant reformers, and other free spirits. Most famously in literary history, Marguerite of Navarre—her more usual name—was associated with the *Heptameron* (from the Greek for "seven"), a collection of seventy frankly sexual tales in the style of Boccaccio's *Decameron* (see Chapter 10). Whether or not Marguerite actually wrote these tales is an unresolved topic of scholarly debate, although it is generally agreed that the stories were written for the

Figure 13.1   HANS HOLBEIN THE YOUNGER. *Erasmus of Rotterdam.* Ca. 1523–1524. Oil on panel, 16½ × 12½". Louvre. *This sensitive likeness of the great humanist was painted by one of the most successful Northern Renaissance portraitists, Hans Holbein. The artist conveys his subject's humanity and intellectual authority by depicting him engaged in writing one of his many treatises. The realistic detail, warm colors, and dramatic lighting are typical of Holbein's work.*

completed his education at the University of Paris. This training was supposed to lead to a church career, but Erasmus never wore clerical garb or lived as a priest, although he was ordained. On the contrary, with the aid of patrons he patiently pursued a writing career, enjoying the comforts of a scholarly life. He also traveled widely throughout western Europe, eventually finding a second home in England among the intellectual circle gathered around Thomas More, England's lord chancellor and another well-known humanist.

As a humanist, Erasmus believed in education in the *humanitas* sense advocated by Cicero, emphasizing study of the Classics and honoring the dignity of the individual. As a Christian, he promoted the "philosophy of Christ" as expressed in the Sermon on the Mount and in Jesus' example of a humble and virtuous life. Erasmus earnestly felt that the church could reform itself and avoid division by adopting the moderate approach that he advanced.

Despite a prodigious output of books that include treatises, commentaries, collections of proverbs, a manual for rulers, and a definitive edition of the Greek New Testament, Erasmus's fame rests on his most popular work, *The Praise of Folly*, written in 1509. This lively book, filled with learned humor, captures the gentle grace and good sense of the Christian humanists. Even this work's Latin title, *Encomium Moriae*, reflects a lighthearted spirit, for it is a punning reference to the name of More—the English friend to whom the book is dedicated.

In this work, Erasmus pokes fun at the human race by making his mouthpiece a personified Folly—an imaginary creation who symbolizes human foolishness. In a series of sermons, Folly ridicules every social group, from scholars and lawyers to priests and cardinals. Erasmus's jolly satire, especially in its exposure of clerical hypocrisy, struck a responsive chord among educated people. But with the rapid growth of Protestantism, such cultivated criticism only got Erasmus into trouble. Roman Catholics felt betrayed by his mild barbs, and Protestants accused him of not going far enough. In the end, this mild reformer and gentle scholar sadly witnessed the breakup of his beloved church while being denounced by both sides.

For a time, Luther had hoped for the support of Erasmus in his reforming crusade. But that changed in 1524 when Erasmus asserted, contrary to Luther, that the human will was free; otherwise, according to Erasmus, the Bible would not have urged sinners to repent. Erasmus's argument so enraged Luther that he countered with a tract in which he declared that the human will was irrevocably flawed; in Luther's view, only God's free grace could save any man or woman from the fires of hell. So intemperate was Luther's reply that the two scholars never communicated again. Erasmus's

French court. Based on the evidence of the stories, the French nobility welcomed outspokenness in sexual matters (the themes of the tales are rape, seductions bordering on rape, incest, and trespasses of the sexual and marital codes of aristocratic life) and condoned Protestant-like religious views (the tale's villains are often members of monastic orders and are consistently portrayed as gluttons, parasites, and rapists). The social matrix that spawned the *Heptameron* was northern humanism, a world hostile to the dying ethos of medieval monasticism.

The outstanding figure among the northern humanists—and possibly among all humanists—is the Dutch scholar Desiderius Erasmus (Figure 13.1). Erasmus (about 1466–1536) was fully prepared for the great role that he played in the Christian humanist movement. He studied in the pietistic atmosphere of a school run by the Brethren of the Common Life, where he was introduced to the Greek and Roman classics. He later calm voice went unheeded amid the wild rhetoric and religious mayhem that characterized this age.

THE NORTHERN RENAISSANCE

While Italy was experiencing the High Renaissance and Early Mannerism, northern Europe was also bursting with cultural vitality. The cultural scene was affected by the contemporaneous religious upheavals; late medieval trends, such as Gothic forms and mysticism; northern humanism; and Italy's High Renaissance and Mannerism. The result of these dissimilar tendencies was that the **Northern Renaissance,** the term used to describe the culture of sixteenth-century northern Europe, was a period marked by competing styles. By midcentury, however, the principles of Mannerism were encroaching on the ideals of Renaissance painting and literature.

Northern Renaissance Literature

The sixteenth century was truly an amazing period in literature, for the vernacular tongues now definitively showed that they were the equal of Latin as vehicles for literary expression. In the High Middle Ages, Dante led the way with his *Divine Comedy;* now, other authors writing in the vernacular found their voices. Montaigne, writing in French, and Shakespeare, writing in English, left such a rich legacy that, by common consent, each is revered as the outstanding writer of his respective tradition.

Michel de Montaigne   Like an ancient Roman senator, Michel de Montaigne [mee-SHEL duh mahn-TAYN] (1533–1592) balanced a public career with a life devoted to letters. While serving as a judge and a mayor, he worked on his lifelong project, which he called *Essays.* This collection of discursive meditations is essentially the autobiography of his mind and is thus representative of the individualistic spirit of the Renaissance. What emerges is a self-portrait of a man who is both intellectually curious and fascinated by his own mental processes and personality. He describes his contradictions, accidental as well as deliberate, though he writes that his loyalty is always to truth. What keeps the *Essays* from falling into sterile self-absorption is Montaigne's firm sense that in revealing himself he is speaking for others.

But the *Essays* are more than an early example of confessional literature. They also constitute, in the French tradition, the earliest work of *moralisme,* or moralism, and the beginning of modern skepticism. In terms of morality, Montaigne attached little importance to Christian ethics, since cruelty and barbarism in the name of religion were justified equally by Protestant and Catholic. His musings reflected France's chaotic condition during the religious wars, causing him to question the Renaissance's natural optimism. Montaigne searched for, without ever discovering, a moral code that was centered on a human world and that no one could deny. In his skeptical outlook, Montaigne rejected the Renaissance view of humanity as a microcosm of the universe. Indeed, he claimed that he saw nothing except vanity and insignificance in human beings and their reasoning. Montaigne, however, avoided total skepticism, for although he denied that humans could ever achieve perfect knowledge, he held that practical understanding was possible.

William Shakespeare   Montaigne wrote during a period when religious wars were disrupting France, but England at the same time was enjoying a relatively calm period of cultural exuberance, the Age of Elizabeth. Under Queen Elizabeth I, who reigned from 1558 to 1603, London rose to an eminence that rivaled that of Florence of the Early Renaissance. English playwrights rescued tragedy and comedy from the oblivion into which they had fallen with the collapse of Rome. As in ancient Greece, tragedy and comedy again became part of popular culture. A purely secular and commercial theater now emerged, with professional playwrights and actors, playhouses, and a ticket-buying public (Figures 13.2 and 13.3).

The revived popularity of the theater represented a dramatic reversal of a cultural outlook that had prevailed in the West since the time of Augustine in the fifth century (see Chapter 7). Christian scholars had condemned the stage for its wicked displays and seductive delights. On occasion, medieval culture had spawned morality plays and dramas with biblical themes, but those edifying works remained primitive in form with little care given to language, character, or plot. A play like the fifteenth-century *Everyman,* for example, was intended mainly to reinforce Christian values and only incidentally to entertain or to provoke thought. Under Elizabeth, many able dramatists began to appear, such as Thomas Kyd (about 1557–1595) and Christopher Marlowe (1564–1593). These playwrights revolutionized drama in a single generation. However, first honors must be given to William Shakespeare, the greatest dramatist in the English language.

Shakespeare (1564–1616) was born in Stratford-upon-Avon, a market-town, and educated in its grammar school. By 1590 his plays were being performed on the London stage, and his active public career continued until 1610, when he returned home to Stratford to enjoy country life. His early retirement reflected the

The Globe Playhouse 1599–1613

KEY

A Main entrance
B The Yard, where the 'groundlings' stood (for one penny admission)
CC Entrances to lowest gallery (on payment of another penny)
D Entrances to staircase and upper galleries
E Corridor serving the different sections of the middle gallery
F Middle gallery (The 'Twopenny' Rooms')
G 'Gentlemen's Rooms' or 'Lords' Rooms'
H The stage
J The hanging being put up round the stage (N.B. In some theatres this was boarded in)
K The 'Hell' under the stage
L The stage trap, leading down to the Hell
M Stage doors, leading into the tiring-house
N Curtained 'place behind the stage', sometimes opened for special scenes
O Gallery above the stage, used as required sometimes by musicians, sometimes by spectators, and often as part of the play (e.g. *Romeo and Juliet*)
P Back-stage area (the tiring-house)
Q Tiring-house door
R Dressing rooms
S Wardrobe and storage
T The hut housing the machine for lowering enthroned gods, etc., to the stage
U The 'Heavens'
W Hoisting the playhouse flag

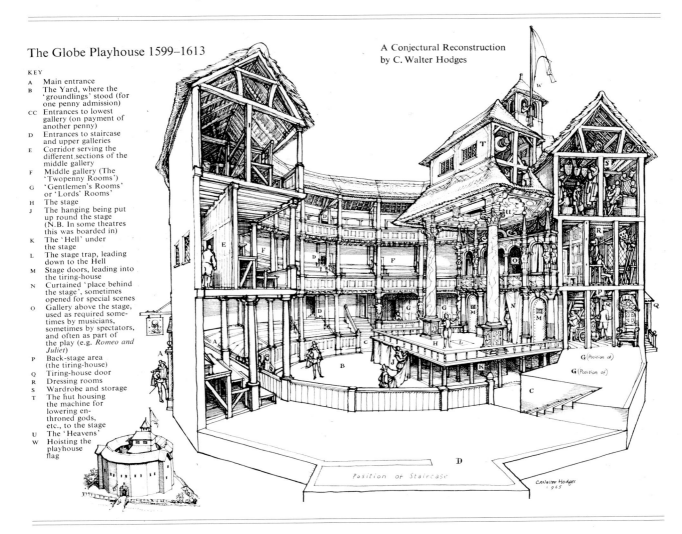

Figure 13.2 Reconstruction of the Globe Playhouse, 1599–1613. *When the Globe Playhouse of London was razed in 1644 to make way for new buildings, one of the most significant monuments of Renaissance England disappeared: the theater where most of Shakespeare's plays were first performed. This cutaway drawing, made by C. W. Hodges, a leading expert on the theaters of the period, attempts to depict the Globe Playhouse as it appeared in Shakespeare's day. As shown in the drawing, the Globe was a sixteen-sided structure with the stage erected in an open courtyard bounded on three sides by three tiers of seats.*

Figure 13.3 The Reconstructed Globe Playhouse. 1996. London, England. *Spurred by the vision of the American actor Sam Wanamaker, an international effort resulted in the construction of a modern Globe Playhouse, near the site of the original theater of Shakespeare's time. This theater, which staged its first performances in August 1996, is true to Elizabethan design and construction methods, including wooden nails and thatched roof. Performances are staged in the daytime, when weather permits—just as they were four centuries ago.*

success that he had achieved as an actor, a theater owner, and a playwright. But it was as the age's leading dramatist that he earned undying fame, mastering the three different genres of history, comedy, and tragedy. His thirty-seven dramas constitute his legacy to the world. Just as tragedies ranked higher than comedies in ancient Greece, so have Shakespeare's tragedies enjoyed a reputation superior to that of his other writings. Of the eleven tragedies, many are regarded as masterpieces; *King Lear, Othello, Julius Caesar, Macbeth,* and *Romeo and Juliet* are constantly performed on the stage and often presented in films, in English as well as other languages. Perhaps the Shakespearean tragedy that stands above the rest, however, and that is reckoned by many as his supreme achievement, is *Hamlet*.

Hamlet is a **revenge tragedy,** among the most popular dramatic forms in the Elizabethan theater. The revenge play had its own special rules, consisting chiefly of a murder that requires a relative of the victim, usually with the prompting of a ghost, to avenge the crime by the drama's end. The origin of this type of play, with its characteristic violence and suspense, has been obscured by time, although Seneca's Roman tragedies, which were known and studied in England, are almost certainly a source.

The basic plot, characters, and setting of *Hamlet* are drawn from a medieval chronicle of evil doings at the Danish court. Elizabethan theatergoers had seen an earlier dramatized version (now lost) before Shakespeare's play was performed in 1600–1601. Shakespeare thus took a well-known story but stamped it with his own genius and feeling for character. In its basic conception, *Hamlet* is a consummate expression of Mannerist principles. Shakespeare presents Hamlet from shifting perspectives, preferring ambiguity, rather than portraying him from a single vantage point in accordance with the Classical ideal. By turns, Hamlet veers from madman to scholar to prince to swordsman, so that a unified, coherent personality is never exposed to the audience. Because of Hamlet's elusive character, he has become the most frequently analyzed and performed of all Shakespeare's heroes.

Another aspect of this play reminiscent of the Mannerist aesthetic is the self-disgust that seems to rule Hamlet's character when he is alone with his thoughts. Whereas the High Renaissance reserved its finest praise for the basic dignity of the human being, Hamlet finds little to value in himself, in others, or in life. Instead, he offers a contradictory vision:

It goes so heavily with my disposition that this goodly frame, the earth, seems to me a sterile promontory; this most excellent canopy, the air . . . this majestical roof fretted with golden fire, why, it appears no other thing to me but a foul and pestilent congregation of vapours.

What a piece of work is a man, how noble in reason, how infinite in faculty; in form and moving how express and admirable, in action how like an angel, in apprehension how like a god! the beauty of the world, the paragon of animals! And yet to me what is this quintessence of dust? Man delights not me. . . .

(Act 2, Scene 2)

In its construction, the tragedy of *Hamlet* is typical of Shakespeare's plays. All his dramas were written for commercial theater troupes and were not intended especially for a reading public. Only after Shakespeare's death were his plays published and circulated to a general audience and thus regarded as "literature."

Northern Renaissance Painting

The Northern Renaissance emerged during an era of cultural crisis. In about 1500 the Late Gothic style of the Flemish school was starting to lose its appeal, except for one extraordinary artist, Hieronymus Bosch. At the same time, growing numbers of artists were attracted to the new Italian art, especially to Mannerism. In the 1520s, the influence of the Protestant Reformation also began to become apparent in the arts. Individual tastes and styles became important, and secular subjects were acceptable, in part because some of the more fervent Protestants looked on enjoyment of the visual arts as a form of idol worship. They even destroyed some paintings, statues, and stained glass that portrayed religious subjects. The combined influences of Mannerism and Protestantism produced three artists of unique stature who reflected the turbulent world of post-Lutheran Europe in quite different ways: Dürer, Grünewald, and Bruegel.

Albrecht Dürer Albrecht Dürer [AHL-brekt DYOU-ruhr] (1471–1528), the son of a goldsmith, pursued a career as an engraver and painter. After studying in Germany, he traveled widely in Italy, where he absorbed the lessons of Renaissance art. Between 1510 and 1519, he earned great fame for the works that he executed for the Holy Roman emperor, but he also discovered that his true artistic bent was for engraving, either on wood or on metal. His engravings, which were issued in multiple editions, enhanced his reputation, and as a result he received many commissions throughout Germany and the Netherlands. Near the end of his life, Dürer became a Lutheran, and some of his last paintings indicate his new faith.

Fully aware of himself and his place in the world, Dürer showed a Renaissance sensibility in introspective self-portraits, especially in the famous work in which he depicts himself as a Christ figure (Figure 13.4). In this stunning image—the intense stare suggests that it was

Figure 13.4 ALBRECHT DÜRER. *Self-Portrait.* 1500. Oil on panel, 26¼ × 19¼″. Alte Pinakothek, Munich. *The Northern Renaissance shared with the Italian Renaissance an emphasis on the individual, as shown in this self-portrait by the German artist Albrecht Dürer—one of the first artists to make himself the subject of some of his paintings. In a series of self-portraits, starting at the age of thirteen, he examined his face and upper torso and rendered them in precise detail, recording his passing age and moods. An unusual aspect of Dürer's self-portrait is that it suggests that he has taken on the role of artist in much the manner that Jesus had taken on the role of Savior.*

painted while the artist was looking in the mirror—Dürer blends a dandified likeness of himself with a standard Flemish representation of Christ. Such an identification of his artistic self with Jesus' divine power would have been unthinkable before the Renaissance. Nevertheless, Dürer remained true to the spirit of the Middle Ages, for he was also following the tradition of mysticism in which he saw himself as striving to imitate the example of Christ.

Although Dürer's paintings brought him recognition and wealth in his day, his engravings constitute his greatest artistic legacy. At the time of Luther's revolt, Dürer engraved the scene called *Knight, Death, and the Devil* (Figure 13.5). This magnificent engraving shows a knight riding through a forest, ignoring both the taunts of Death, who holds up an hourglass to remind him of his mortality, and the fiendish Devil, who watches nearby. The knight is probably meant as a symbol of the Christian who has to live in the practical world.

Dürer's *Knight, Death, and the Devil* combines Late Gothic and Renaissance elements to make a disquieting scene. From the northern tradition are derived the exquisite details, the grotesque demon, and the varied landscape in the background. From Renaissance sources comes the horse, which Dürer copied from models seen during his Italian tour.

Matthias Grünewald A second major German artist in this period is Matthias Grünewald [muh-THI-uhs GREW-nuh-vahlt] (about 1460–1528), who was less influenced by Italian art and more northern in his

Figure 13.5 ALBRECHT DÜRER. *Knight, Death, and the Devil.* 1513. Engraving, approx. 9⅝ × 7⁷⁄₁₂″. The Fogg Art Museum, Harvard University. Gift of William Gray from the Collection of Francis Calley Gray. *Dürer's plan for this work probably derived from a manual by Erasmus that advised a Christian prince on the best way to rule. In his version, Dürer portrays the Christian layman who has put on the armor of faith and rides steadfastly, oblivious to the various pitfalls that lie in his path. The knight is sometimes identified with Erasmus, whom Dürer venerated.*

Figure 13.6 MATTHIAS GRÜNEWALD. *The Crucifixion,* from the *Isenheim Altarpiece.* 1515. Oil on panel, 9'9½" × 10'9". Musée d'Unterlinden, Colmar, France. *Jesus' suffering and death were a central theme in north European piety, particularly after the plague of the fourteenth century. Northern artists typically rendered Christ's death in vivid and gory detail. Grünewald's* Crucifixion *comes out of this tradition; Christ's broken body symbolizes both his sacrificial death and the mortality of all human beings.*

techniques than Dürer. His paintings represent a continuation of the Late Gothic style rather than a northern development of Renaissance tendencies.

Grünewald's supreme achievement is the *Isenheim Altarpiece,* painted for the church of St. Anthony in Isenheim, Germany. The altarpiece includes nine painted panels that can be displayed in three different positions, depending on the church calendar. When the *Isenheim Altarpiece* is closed, the large central panel depicts the Crucifixion (Figure 13.6). By crowding the five figures and the symbolic lamb into the foreground and making Christ's body larger than the rest, Grünewald followed the Late Gothic style. This style is similarly apparent in every detail of Christ's tortured,

twisted body: the gaping mouth, the exposed teeth, the slumped head, and the torso raked by thorns. And Grünewald's Late Gothic emotionalism is evident in his treatment of the secondary figures in this crucifixion panel. On the right, John the Baptist points toward Jesus, stressing the meaning of his sacrificial death. John the Baptist's calmness contrasts with the grief of the figures on the left, including Mary Magdalene, who kneels at Jesus' feet, and the apostle John, who supports a swooning Mary. The swaying bodies of these three figures reinforce the anguish on their faces. One Renaissance feature in this otherwise Gothic painting is the low horizon line, which shows Grünewald's knowledge of Italian perspective.

Figure 13.7 HIERONYMUS BOSCH. *Garden of Earthly Delights.* Ca. 1510–1515. Oil on wood, center panel 86⅝ × 76¾"; each side panel 86⅝ × 38¼". Prado, Madrid. *Careful study of the minute details of this triptych has uncovered the major sources of Bosch's artistic inspiration—namely, medieval folklore, common proverbs, exotic learning, and sacred beliefs. For example, folklore inspired the ravens and owl (left panel), traditional emblems of nonbelievers and witchcraft, respectively; the Flemish proverb "Good fortune, like glass, is easily broken" is illustrated by the lovemaking couple under the glass globe; allusions to exotic learning may be seen in the egg shapes (all three panels), symbolic of the world and sex in the pseudoscience of alchemy; and Christian belief is evident throughout the triptych, but especially in the right panel, showing the punishment of sinners.*

Hieronymus Bosch Hieronymus Bosch [BOSH] (about 1450–1516), whose personal life is a mystery, painted works that still puzzle modern experts. Treating common religious subjects in bizarre and fantastic ways, he earned a reputation even among his contemporaries for being enigmatic.

Much of Bosch's distinctive art may be explained by the changes under way in northern Europe during his day. In the late fifteenth century, political upheavals in Burgundy caused aristocratic patronage to decline, and, at the same time, a feeling of dread, born perhaps of the periodic ravages of the plague, stalked the land. In the early sixteenth century, serious religious trouble that would end with the revolt of Martin Luther was brewing. Influenced by the foregoing forces and also perhaps subjected to his own private demons, Bosch created a body of art that defies strict classification in the stylistic sense.

In his paintings, Bosch seems torn between the declining Late Gothic style and the soon-to-be-born Mannerist style. His addiction to precise detail and his frequent use of sweeping landscapes are clear signs of the debt he owed Flemish art and, in particular, the age's illuminated manuscripts; but his tendency to endow his works with ambiguous, or even cynical, moral messages points to the works of later Dutch artists, such as Pieter Bruegel the Elder. Perhaps the best way to look at Bosch is as an artist whose originality was so pronounced that he stands outside any historical period.

Of Bosch's thirty or more paintings, the most well known and controversial is *The Garden of Earthly Delights,* a work in oil on three wood panels, called a **triptych** (Figure 13.7). When open, the triptych displays three separate but interrelated scenes, organized around the theme of the creation, fall, and damnation of the human race. Most confusingly, the center and right panels are crowded with tiny figures—mostly human, though some are grotesquely monstrous—performing a variety of peculiar actions. Although no scholarly consensus exists as to the ultimate meaning of this work, certain features can be identified that may help the viewer understand it.

The left panel of *The Garden of Earthly Delights* shows the Garden of Eden, with Adam and Eve in the foreground and the first plants and animals (including "natural" animals but also weird monsters) scattered around. Contrary to the story in the Bible, Jesus holds the newly created Eve's hand and introduces her to Adam. Many scholars interpret this panel as making Eve the source of original sin.

The center panel—the dramatic focus of the triptych—depicts the sins of the flesh in lurid and metaphorical detail. In the top horizontal band, the waters of the earth converge to make a fountain, an image that has been identified as a false symbol of human happiness. In the middle band, naked young women cavort in a pool while a parade of naked youths riding animals—partly realistic, partly fantastic—encircles them. In the lower band, more naked men and women engage in various sex acts or are involved with huge birds, fruits, flowers, or fish. The diverse images in this central panel symbolize Bosch's perspective on the human condition: perpetual enslavement to the sexual appetite unleashed by Adam and Eve's first sin. Also worthy of note is that this crowded scene includes many black males and females, an early instance of nonwhites in Western art.

Figure 13.8 PIETER BRUEGEL THE ELDER. *Wedding Dance.* 1566. Oil on panel, 47 × 62". Detroit Institute of Arts. *Bruegel has made a sensuous arrangement out of the dancers and bystanders at this country wedding. The line of dancers winds from the foreground back through the trees, where it reverses itself and returns to its original starting point. The sense of lively movement is reinforced by the vivid red colors in the hats and vests and by the stomping feet and flailing arms.*

The triptych's right panel is a repulsive portrait of Hell and the pains human beings must suffer for their sins. A horrific scene of fiery ruins and grisly instruments of torture, this panel proclaims Bosch's hopeless vision of the futility of life on earth. For the artist, human beings cause their own destruction through wicked desires. Nowhere in the entire work is there a hint of salvation.

A few scholars reject this gloomy view of Bosch's message by trying to link the triptych to the beliefs of the Adamites, an underground, heretical sect. If their interpretation is correct, then the central panel may be understood as the Adamites' unusual vision of Paradise. Most scholars reject this view, however, and hold instead that Bosch was a stern moralist, mocking the corrupt society of his day.

Pieter Bruegel the Elder   The life and work of Pieter Bruegel [BREW-gul or BROY-gul] the Elder (about 1525–1569) indicate the changes in northern European art in the mid–sixteenth century. The great German artists Dürer and Grünewald were now dead, and German art, which had dominated northern Europe in the early sixteenth century, was in decline. Protestant iconoclasm had taken its toll, and the demand for religious art had markedly diminished. Within this milieu, Bruegel chose a novel set of artistic subjects—landscapes, country life scenes, and folk narratives—and in the process became the first truly modern painter in northern Europe. Bruegel's subjects, rooted in the Flemish tradition, were often devoid of overt religious content and presented simply as secular art, although he also painted a number of pictures on standard religious themes such as the adoration of the Magi.

Bruegel's most memorable paintings are his scenes of peasant life. The peasants are always depicted in natural settings, neither romanticized nor patronized. Rather, Bruegel represents the common folk as types, never as individuals, and often as expressions of the blind forces of nature. For some viewers, these scenes also convey a pessimism tinged with grudging admiration about human nature as reflected in the peasants' simple, lusty behavior.

A painting that illustrates Bruegel's attitude toward country folk is his lively *Wedding Dance* (Figure 13.8). The painting records the exuberant revels of the lusty men and the kerchief-wearing women. The bride and groom cannot be distinguished from the other dancers. Typical of Bruegel's style, there is a high horizon and a high point of view, so that we look at the scene from above. This effect, along with the crude faces of the peasants, underscores the impression that these are types and not individuals. The painting's composition reinforces the sense of peasant types in the way that

Figure 13.9   PIETER BRUEGEL THE ELDER. *The Painter and the Connoisseur.* Mid-1560s. Pen and gray-brown ink, with touches of light brown ink, 10 × 8 ½". Graphische Sammlung Albertina, Vienna. *Bruegel's drawing was probably intended as an inside joke about the artistic community and not as an artwork to be engraved or sold. The painter, with his skullcap and bushy hair and beard, is depicted as a dreamer, his mind lost in thought as he stares into the distance. Behind him stands an art expert, who clutches the "money" pouch at his waist and stares in a different direction from that of the painter.*

the swirling figures in the foreground are repeated in the background in ever-diminishing size.

Besides paintings, Bruegel is also known for his sixty-one drawings, which were devoted to either fantastic or naturalistic subjects. About half of the drawings were made as preparations for engravings, and, as such, they establish Bruegel as the heir to the Netherlandish artists who developed the print as a new artistic medium in the Late Middle Ages (see Chapter 10). One of Bruegel's drawings, which was not intended for printmaking, is *The Painter and the Connoisseur* (Figure 13.9). This work pioneered a new subject in art: a satiric view of the relations between an artist and an art expert. Bruegel depicts the painter as an eccentric visionary, and the connoisseur as a self-deluded ignoramus who wears glasses and a ridiculous cap that covers his ears. Other details confirm this negative

LEARNING THROUGH MAPS

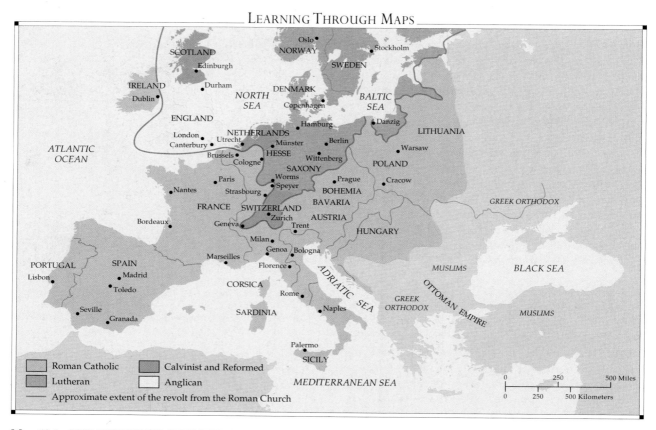

Map 13.1   THE RELIGIOUS SITUATION IN EUROPE IN 1560.
This map shows the religious divisions in Europe in the middle of the sixteenth century. **Notice** the line that separates Protestant Europe from Catholic Europe. **Which** of the two areas is larger? **Identify** the three major Protestant religions and their locations. **Which** Protestant religion covered the largest land area? **What** region was the most likely battleground between Protestants and Catholics? **Which** area of Charles V's Empire (see Map 12.1) was most affected by the Protestant Reformation, as seen in this map?

image of the connoisseur: the hairless face, the nonexistent lips, and the pinched expression.

THE BREAKUP OF CHRISTENDOM: CAUSES OF THE RELIGIOUS REFORMATIONS

Although the reasons for the breakup of Europe's religious unity are complicated, two basic causes are clear: the radical reshaping of Western society and culture that began about 1350 and the timeless spiritual yearnings of human beings. After 1500 these two forces came together in Germany to make conditions ripe for religious revolution. What made change virtually inevitable was the combination of the historical trends occurring during the Late Middle Ages: the corruption and abuses inside the church, the rise of sovereign states, the decay of medieval thought, and the revival of humanism.

The church had been plagued with problems since the Avignon papacy and the Great Schism of the fourteenth century and the challenges to its time-honored practices posed by the growth of heretical groups like the Hussites (see Chapter 10). Without firm guidance from the popes, many clergy led less than exemplary lives, particularly those inside the monasteries. Lay writers, now unafraid of the church, delighted in describing clerical scandals, and the populace gossiped about their priests' latest sins. Everywhere anticlericalism seemed on the rise.

Perhaps the church could have reformed the clergy and stemmed the tide of a rising anticlericalism if the papacy had been morally and politically strong, but such was not the case. By 1500 the popes were deeply distracted by Italian politics and fully committed to worldly interests. The church also lost power to secular rulers, who were determined to bring all their subjects under state control. By 1500 the English and the

Figure 13.10 LUCAS CRANACH THE ELDER. *Martin Luther.* 1520. Copper engraving, 5⁷⁄₁₆ × 3¹³⁄₁₆″. Courtesy of the Metropolitan Museum of Art. Gift of Felix Warburg, 1920. (20.64.21). *This portrait of Martin Luther, with its vivid rendering of his steel jaw and piercing eyes, shows some of the qualities that made him such a force during the Reformation. The admiring likeness was done by the German artist Lucas Cranach, a supporter of the new faith and a close friend of Luther's. At the time of this engraving, the Reformation was barely under way; the thirty-seven-year-old Luther was still in communion with the church in Rome and a member of a monastic order.*

Figure 13.11 ALBRECHT DÜRER. *Elector Frederick the Wise.* 1524. Copper engraving, 7³⁄₈ × 4³⁄₄″. Print collection, Miriam and Ira D. Wallach Division of Art, Prints, and Photographs, The New York Public Library, Astor, Lenox, and Tilden Foundations. *Dürer's portrait captures the princely bearing of Frederick the Wise, the ruler of Electoral Saxony and Luther's great patron. Ironically, Frederick owned one of the largest collections of relics in Christendom. It has been estimated that the 17,443 artifacts in the elector's collection in 1518 could reduce the time in purgatory by 127,799 years and 116 days.*

French kings, to the envy of other European rulers, had made their national churches relatively free of papal control.

In Germany, however, where no unified nation-state had developed, the local secular leaders had no say about clerical appointments and were unable to control the ecclesiastical courts or prevent the Church from collecting taxes—conditions that intensified anticlericalism and hatred of Rome. The German princes, who were already struggling to be free from the control of Charles V, made church reform a rallying cry and turned against Rome as well as the Holy Roman emperor. As events unfolded, the popes were incapable of preventing these princes from converting their lands into independent states outside papal jurisdiction (Map 13.1).

The Protestant Order

Protestantism first appeared in Germany, where Martin Luther led the founding of a new religious sect in the 1520s. In the 1530s a second generation of Protestants acted on the opportunity created by Luther. John Calvin, a French scholar, formed an independent church in Geneva, Switzerland, and King Henry VIII removed the English church from Roman rule (see Timeline 13.1).

Luther's Revolt One of the church's more glaring abuses was the selling of indulgences—pardons that reduced the amount of penance that Christians had to perform to atone for their sins—a practice that dated from the High Middle Ages. In 1517, in response to the archbishop of Mainz's sale of indulgences to raise money, Martin Luther (1483–1546), a monk teaching at nearby Wittenberg University, published his famous Ninety-five Theses (Figure 13.10). These were questions and arguments about the legitimacy of indulgences, and they implicitly challenged the sacraments of confession and penance and the authority of the pope. Luther had simply hoped to arouse a debate in the university, but instead he ignited criticism against the church and placed himself in the vanguard of a reform movement.

The church's response to Luther was initially hesitant, but in 1520 Pope Leo X excommunicated him. When Luther burned the papal document of excommunication in public, the church branded him a heretic and an outlaw. Luther survived because he was under the protection of his patron, Elector Frederick the Wise of Saxony, who had led the German princes opposed to the Holy Roman emperor (Figure 13.11).

Figure 13.12   WORKSHOP OF LUCAS CRANACH. *Katherine von Bora.* Ca 1526. Oil on panel, 7½ × 5″. Wartburg-Stiftung, Germany. *Katherine von Bora was one of a dozen nuns liberated from a convent near Wittenberg in the heady days of 1523. She joined the mixed collection who lived with Luther in the Black Cloisters, his old monastery given him by Frederick the Wise. Despite Luther's protests, she determined to become his wife, and she did. He treated her with great deference, calling her "My lord Kate," though he poked fun at her supposed greed for property. This small portrait was executed in the workshop of Lucas Cranach the Elder, who was also a witness to the marriage of Luther and Katherine von Bora.*

cal precedents and reminiscent of the early church. He believed that the sole source of religious authority was the Bible, not the pope or church councils, and that people could lead simple lives of piety and repentance without the need for priests to mediate with God. Luther also repudiated the mystical definition of the sacraments, the notion of purgatory, the adoration of the saints, and Masses for the dead; he retained only baptism and the Lord's Supper, as he called the Eucharist. Preaching in German became the heart of the liturgy, replacing the Latin Mass.

Luther's voluminous writings constitute the largest legacy of any German author. Among his vast output of tracts, essays, and letters, his German translation of the Bible has had the most enduring influence. He introduced a new era in biblical scholarship by basing his translation on the original languages of the scriptures, the technique that had been developed by the northern humanists, particularly Erasmus. He also set the path followed by subsequent Protestant reformers in choosing what books to include in the Bible: Rejecting the Apocrypha of the Jewish Septuagint, Luther relied on the canonical books of the Hebrew Bible, or Old Testament, and the New Testament. Although nineteen German Bibles were in print by 1518, Luther's version was the one that survived and left its stamp on the German language. His pithy style engaged the reader's emotions with realistic images and idiomatic speech.

SOCIAL AND POLITICAL IMPLICATIONS OF LUTHER'S REVOLT   The Ninety-five Theses circulated widely throughout Germany, and in 1521 Lutheran churches sprang up in most German towns. Simultaneously, radical followers of Luther fomented new problems, causing riots, driving priests from their homes, closing monasteries, and destroying religious images. Luther rejected this violence and advocated moderation. He did accept the abolition of monasticism, however, dropping the monk's habit in 1523 and marrying Katherine von Bora, a former nun, in 1525 (Figure 13.12). When he

LUTHER'S BELIEFS   Luther's attack on indulgences arose from the spiritual quest to understand sin and salvation that had led him to become a monk. Through long study of the scriptures, he reached the understanding that salvation comes not from good works but from God's unmerited love, or grace, or, as Luther phrased it, "justification by faith alone." According to Luther, salvation is achieved by faith in Jesus' sacrificial death; thus, buying indulgences is trying to buy salvation—a direct contradiction of the biblical truth Luther had experienced in his theological studies.

In his theology, which became known as **Lutheranism,** he tried to revive a Christianity based on bibli-

PERSONAL PERSPECTIVE

Albrecht Dürer
Fears for Luther's Safety

The German artist Dürer, writing in 1521, feared for Martin Luther's life when he heard rumors that the reformer had been taken prisoner by the Holy Roman emperor's soldiers. The rumors later proved false; Luther had been kidnapped for his own safety by his protector, Frederick the Wise.

On Friday before Whitsunday in the year 1521, came tidings to me at Antwerp that Martin Luther had been so treacherously taken prisoner; for he was escorted by Emperor Charles' herald with imperial safe-conduct and to him he was entrusted. But as soon as the herald had conveyed him to an unfriendly place near Eisenach he rode away, saying that he no longer needed him. Straightway there appeared ten horsemen and they treacherously carried off the pious man, betrayed into their hand, a man enlightened by the Holy Ghost, a follower of Christ and the true Christian faith. And whether he yet lives, or whether they have put him to death—which I know not—he has suffered this for the sake of Christian truth and because he rebuked the unchristian Papacy, which strives with its heavy load of human laws against the redemption of Christ; and

because we are so robbed and stripped of our blood and sweat, and that the same is so shamefully and scandalously eaten up by idle-going folk, while the poor and the sick therefore die of hunger. But this is above all the most grievous to me, that, maybe, God will suffer us to remain still longer under their false, blind doctrine, invented and drawn up by the men alone whom they call Fathers, by which also the precious Word of God is in many places wrongly expounded to us or not taught at all. . . .

May every man who reads Martin Luther's books see how clear and transparent is his doctrine, when he sets forth the Holy Gospel. Wherefore his books are to be held in great honor and not to be burnt; unless indeed his adversaries, who ever strive against the truth were cast also into the fire, together with all their opinions which would make gods out of men, provided, however, books of Luther's were printed anew again. Oh God, if Luther be dead, who will henceforth expound to us the Holy Gospel with such clearness? What, of God, might he not still have written for us in ten or twenty years? . . .

---

and Katherine had children, they created a familial tradition for Lutheran clergy, unlike the celibate tradition of Catholic Europe. Lutheran women thus seemed to make gains with the closing of convents and the giving of new respectability to married life, but these steps proved illusory, since Luther affirmed male rule and female submission within the family.

Another area profoundly altered by Luther's beliefs was that of education. His supporters set up their own schools and universities, replacing Catholic foundations. Unlike church-run Catholic schools, the Lutheran schools were financed by taxes, so that teachers became state employees—a reflection of Luther's belief that church and state should work hand in hand. For Lutheran women, the changes in education created a dilemma. On the one hand, women were denied access to these schools, but, on the other hand, they were expected to know their Bibles, as both pious Lutherans and knowledgeable mothers capable of guiding their children's moral education.

Luther distanced himself from the anti-government political and social reforms espoused by some of his

followers. In 1523 a brief Peasants' War erupted under the banner of Luther's faith, but Luther urged suppression of the workers by the nobility, clearly showing his preference for the status quo. His reliance on Saxony's rulers for protection set the model for his religion; in the Lutheran faith, the church acted as an arm of the state, and the clergy's salaries were paid from public funds. Luther's revolt did not embrace individual rights in the political or social arena; indeed, the Protestant princes were more powerful than their predecessors, since their powers were not limited by Rome.

The Reforms of John Calvin   Among the second generation of Protestant reformers, the most influential was John Calvin (1509–1564) (Figure 13.13). After earning a law degree in Paris, he experienced a religious conversion and cast his lot with the Reformation. Coming under the suspicion of the French authorities, he fled to Basel, Switzerland, a Lutheran center, where he began to publish *The Institutes of the Christian Religion,* which, in its final form, became a theological document of immense importance.

Figure 13.13   ANONYMOUS. *John Calvin.* 1550s. Bibliothèque Publique et Universitaire de Geneva. *This anonymous portrait of Calvin shows the way that he probably wanted to be viewed rather than a natural likeness. Still, the angular features, the intense gaze, and the set mouth suggest that the reputation Calvin had for strict discipline was justified. The well-trimmed beard and somewhat extravagant fur collar, although typical of middle-class fashion of the era, create an ironic contradiction in this otherwise austere portrait.*

In his theology, Calvin, like Luther, advocated beliefs and practices having biblical roots. He differed from Luther over the nature of God, church–state relations, and Christian morals. Calvin's religious thought, called **Calvinism,** rested on his concept of an awesome, even angry, God, which led him to make predestination (the belief that God predestines certain souls to salvation and others to damnation) central to his faith. Calvin also espoused a theocratic state in which the government was subordinate to the church. Within this state, he favored strict ethical demands, regulating everything from laughter in church to public shows of affection between the sexes. Because of such rules, which later became associated with the reform movement known as **Puritanism,** Calvinism acquired the reputation for being a joyless creed.

More important than the puritanical streak in Calvin's theology was the impact of his thought on political, social, and economic life. Calvinism encouraged thrift, industry, sobriety, and discipline—precisely the same traits that made for business success. Calvin's teachings spurred on the Christian capitalist in his accumulation of wealth, so that gradually there developed the idea that worldly success was tantamount to God's approval and that poverty was a sign of God's disfavor. In addition, of all the new sects, Calvinism was the most international, and reformed congregations spread across Europe, especially in Scotland and the Netherlands (see Map 13.1). The readiness of Calvin's followers to oppose tyranny with arms also made them dangerous everywhere.

The Reform of the English Church   A second major religious reformer in the 1530s was King Henry VIII (r. 1509–1547), who founded the Church of England (also called the Anglican Church) largely out of political considerations. In 1529 Henry asked the pope to annul his marriage to Catherine of Aragon, who, though she gave birth to a daughter, had failed to produce a male heir. In Henry's eyes, Catherine's supposed failure was a divine punishment for his sin of having married his dead brother's widow—an incestuous union in the eyes of the church. In favorable times, the pope might have given Henry a dispensation, but the troops of Holy Roman Emperor Charles V, Catherine's nephew, had just sacked Rome and virtually imprisoned the pontiff. Charles also opposed any step that would nullify his aunt's marriage and make her daughter a bastard. In 1533 Henry pushed through Parliament the laws setting up the Church of England with himself as the head and granting him a divorce.

Although **Anglicanism** was founded by Henry VIII, the ground had been prepared locally by Christian humanists and English Lutherans. The work of both groups led to the so-called Reformation Parliament (1529–1535), which had begun to reform the English church even before Henry made the decisive break with Rome.

Religious turmoil followed Henry's death in 1547, and the fate of the English Reformation stayed in doubt until his daughter Elizabeth (r. 1558–1603) became queen and the head of the Anglican Church (Figure 13.14). In 1559 Elizabeth resolved the crisis, with the aid of Parliament, by steering a middle course between Catholicism and Calvinism, which had gained many English converts. Anglican beliefs were summarized in the Thirty-nine Articles, and people who wished to sit in Parliament, earn university degrees, or serve as military officers had to swear allegiance to them. Hence, Calvinists and Catholics were excluded by law from English public life and remained so for about 275 years.

Figure 13.14 MARCUS GHEERAERTS THE YOUNGER. *Elizabeth I.* Late sixteenth century. Oil on panel, 7'11" × 5'. National Portrait Gallery, London. *The so-called Ditchley portrait presented Queen Elizabeth in all her Renaissance finery. Following the Spanish fashion, the queen wears a neck ruff and yards of pearls, and she carries a fan. She stands atop a map of England, which she ruled for forty-five years with compassion and firmness, until her death in 1603.*

The Counter-Reformation

Before Martin Luther took his stand in Germany, a Roman Catholic reform movement had begun quietly in isolated parts of Europe. Confronted with the surprising successes of the various Protestant groups, the Roman Catholic Church, as it was now called, struck back with a Counter-Reformation. By 1600 this superbly organized campaign had slowed Protestantism and won back many adherents. The Catholics held on to southern and most of central Europe, halting Protestantism's spread in Poland, France, and Switzerland and limiting the movement to northern Europe. The Counter-Reformation moved forward on three fronts:

a revitalized papacy, new monastic orders, and an effective reforming council. Together, these forces confronted the Protestant threat, purified the church of abuses, and reorganized its structure.

The Reformed Papacy With the reign of Paul III (pope 1534–1549), there appeared a series of reform-minded popes who reinvigorated the church. To counter the inroads made by Protestantism, Paul enlisted the support of the full church by convening a council representing Roman Catholic clergy from all over Europe and launched new monastic orders.

Paul and his successors reclaimed the moral leadership of the church and reorganized the papal bureaucracy so that discipline was now enforced throughout the ecclesiastical hierarchy. Sensing that Protestantism would not go away and recognizing the increasing availability of written material now that the printing press had appeared, these popes tried to isolate the church from deviant ideas. A committee of churchmen drew up an Index of Forbidden Books, which listed writings that were off limits to Roman Catholic readers because they were considered prejudicial to faith or morals. The first Index included the works of Luther, Calvin, and other Protestants. In the long run, this tactic failed to suppress hated ideas, but the Index continued to be updated until the 1960s.

New Monastic Orders The work of new monastic orders also contributed to the Counter-Reformation. Since the High Middle Ages, monastic reform had played only a small role in the life of the church. Suddenly in the sixteenth century, new monastic groups arose to fill a variety of needs, such as preparing men and women to minister directly to the masses and reclaiming lapsed believers to the faith.

Typical of monastic reform for women in Counter-Reformation Europe was the fate of the Company of St. Ursula, or the Ursulines, founded in 1535 in Brescia, Italy, by Angela Merici [ma-REE-chee] (about 1470–1540). The Ursulines were named after a legendary British princess who, with eleven thousand virgin companions, was martyred on the way to her wedding. Reflecting the same ideals as contemporary early Protestantism in stressing individual grace and keeping apart from clerical rule, the Ursulines were originally intended to be exclusively for laywomen, without any intrusion by male church officials. Merici's followers, divided into "daughters" and "matrons," were to live in their own homes, practice chastity without taking formal vows, serve the sick and the poor, and educate the young. In 1540, after Merici's death and under pressure from Protestantism, the Ursulines were reformed by church leaders, who cloistered the order and placed its members under

Figure 13.15   ATTRIBUTED TO JUAN DE ROELAS. *St. Ignatius Loyola.* 1622. Oil on canvas, approx. 7'3" × 5'6". Museo Provincial de Bellas Artes, Seville, Spain. *This portrait, painted the year Loyola was canonized and nearly seventy-five years after his death, evokes the determination and strength of the founder of the Society of Jesus. In his right hand Ignatius holds the graphic symbol of Jesus' name, and under his left arm he carries a Bible. Such posthumous portraits were not intended to be exact likenesses but were designed to confirm the high status of the distinguished subject.*

male control. What happened to the Ursulines became the way of life for women in Catholicism: Laywomen were to be organized into formal structures under male supervision.

The most significant new order was the Society of Jesus, commonly known as the **Jesuits.** Recognized by Pope Paul III in 1540, the Jesuits had emerged by 1600 as the church's leading monastic order, with special blessings from the popes. The dedicated members helped to curb Protestantism in Europe, and their missionary efforts abroad represented the first steps in making Roman Catholicism a global faith. After a shaky beginning, their rise to power was quick, and

their success was largely due to the order's founder, the Spaniard Ignatius Loyola (about 1493–1556) (Figure 13.15).

Loyola's life was imbued with more than a touch of medieval knight errantry. His first calling was as a professional warrior, defending his country from invaders. When in 1521 a battle injury to his leg left Loyola crippled for life, he underwent a religious conversion that led him to become a "soldier" in the army of Christ. Eventually, he founded the Society of Jesus, which resembled a military company in its rigid hierarchy, close discipline, and absolute obedience to the founder.

The Jesuits were initially concerned with working among the unchurched and the poor, focusing especially on teaching their children. But that mission was modified in the 1540s. Guided by the Spaniard Francis Xavier (1506–1552), they established outposts in the Far East and converted thousands to the Christian faith. Other Jesuits had similar success in missions to North and South America.

The Jesuits' special vow of loyalty to the pope set them apart from other monastic orders. Because of this connection and their expertise in education, the Jesuits soon became the church's chief weapon against the Protestants. In their writings, the Jesuits answered the church's critics, setting forth their orthodox beliefs in a clear and straightforward manner.

The Council of Trent   The third force contributing to the Counter-Reformation was the reform established by the council conducted at Trent in northern Italy, meeting in three separate sessions between 1545 and 1563. Dominated by papal supporters, Italian delegates, and the Jesuits, the Council of Trent offered no sympathy to the Protestants and thus accepted the split in Christian Europe as an unfortunate fact of life. The council reaffirmed all the practices condemned by the Protestants, such as monasticism, indulgences, and holy relics, although mechanisms were set in motion to eliminate abuse of these practices. In addition, the council initiated some clerical reforms, notably in the realm of education and training.

The council's unyielding position toward the Protestants was based on its belief that both the Bible and church tradition—not the Bible alone as advocated by the Protestants—were the bases of authority and the word of God. To the council, the Vulgate (including the Apocrypha of the Jewish Septuagint) was the official and only Bible; all other versions were rejected. The council reaffirmed that salvation should be sought by faith *and* by good works, not by faith alone; it also reaffirmed the seven sacraments. The moral, doctrinal, and disciplinary results of the Council of Trent laid the foundations for present-day Roman Catholic policies and thought.

Warfare as a Response to Religious Dissent, 1520–1603

As religious dissent spread, the secular rulers watched with mounting concern. Until 1530 compromise between the Lutheran rebels and the dominant faith seemed possible, but with the constant growth of mutually hostile sects, secular rulers increasingly relied on warfare to deal with the crisis.

War between Charles V's armies and the Lutheran forces erupted on German lands in 1546, the year Luther died, and lasted until 1555, when the Religious Peace of Augsburg brought it to an end. This armistice granted toleration to the Lutheran states, but on strict terms. The ruler's religion became the official faith of each territory; members of religious minorities, whether Roman Catholic or Lutheran, could migrate and join their coreligionists in nearby lands. But because the rights of other minority sects, such as the Calvinists, were ignored, the Peace of Augsburg contained the seeds of future wars.

In 1556 Philip II (r. 1556–1598) inherited the Spanish crown from Charles V and became the head of the Roman Catholic cause. Besides Spain, Roman Catholic regimes now ruled Italy, Portugal, and Austria; Protestants reigned in Scandinavia. Elsewhere the religious rivals vied for supremacy. For the rest of the century, until 1603, Germany was at peace, but western Europe suffered religious violence.

Financed by gold and silver from Mexico and Peru, Philip dominated European politics. His well-prepared armies enabled him to control much of Europe. He expelled suspected Muslims from Spain and defeated the Turks in the Mediterranean; he invaded Portugal and joined that country to Spain. But his fortunes declined when he launched a bloody campaign against the United Provinces in the northern Netherlands. (Eventually, in 1609, the United Provinces became an independent Protestant state.) As the Dutch war was winding down, Philip turned his attention to Protestant England, a supporter of the Dutch revolt. In Philip's eyes, only England stood between him and a reunited Christendom; moreover, Spain and England were rivals for the precious metals of the New World. Philip's solution was to attempt an invasion of England. In 1588 his scheme ended in disaster when the Spanish Armada was defeated by English sea power and a violent storm.

Philip II's dream of a reunited Christendom had been impossible from the beginning. The Protestant world was too dedicated, the growth of national consciousness too powerful, and the rise of a system of sovereign states too far advanced for any one monarch to succeed in unifying Europe under a single banner or cause. When Philip died in 1598, Spain was declining and Europe was divided into independent states and several religions.

LATE MANNERISM

The strongest impact of the Counter-Reformation on the arts, architecture, and music began after the Council of Trent, in 1563. Spain and the Italian states, the areas least attracted to Protestantism, were greatly influenced by the council's decisions. The council decreed that the arts and music should be easily accessible to the uneducated. In sacred music, for example, the intelligibility of the words should take precedence over the melody, and in architecture the building should create a worshipful environment. The church council envisioned paintings and sculptures that were simple and direct as well as unobjectionable and decent in appearance. Guided by this principle, the Counter-Reformation popes declared that some of the male nudes in Michelangelo's *Last Judgment* were obscene and ordered loincloths to be painted over them. General church policy now returned to the medieval ideal of an art and music whose sole aim was to serve and clarify the Christian faith.

Since the Roman Catholic Church after Trent wanted a simplified art that spoke to the masses, its artistic policy tended to clash with Mannerism, which embodied a self-conscious vision that was elitist and deliberately complex. Only with the rise of the Baroque after 1600 was there a style that could conform to the church's need for art with a mass appeal. In the meantime, the general effect of Trent on the last stage of Mannerism was to intensify its spiritual values.

Late Mannerism, which emerged across Europe after 1564, dominated Spanish painting, but it had little influence on Spanish literature. Under the influence of the Renaissance, Spanish literature flourished with the revival of the theater and the birth of new literary genres.

Spanish Painting

No Catholic artist expressed the spirit of the Counter-Reformation better than El Greco (1541–1614) in his Spanish paintings after 1576. These visionary works epitomize the spirit of Late Mannerism. El Greco's real name was Domenikos Theotokopoulos. A native of Crete, he had lived in Venice, where he adopted the colorful style of Venetian painting. Unsuccessful in Venice, he also failed to find rich patrons in Rome, though he learned from the works of Michelangelo and the Mannerists. He arrived in Toledo, Spain, about 1576, and there he found an appreciative public among

Figure 13.16   EL GRECO. *The Burial of Count Orgaz.* 1586. Oil on canvas, 16′ × 11′10″. Church of Santo Tomé, Toledo, Spain. *A Manneristic invention in* The Burial of Count Orgaz *was the rich treatment of the robe of St. Stephen, the first Christian martyr and, in this painting, the beardless figure supporting the body of the dead count. Sewn onto the bottom of this robe is a picture of the stoning of St. Stephen, an episode narrated in the New Testament. By depicting one event inside another, El Greco created an illusionistic device—a typical notion of Mannerist painters, who were skeptical about conventional reality.*

the wealthy nobility. But much to El Greco's despair, he never became a favorite of the Spanish ruler, Philip II, who found the Greek painter's works too bizarre.

For his select audience of aristocrats and Roman Catholic clergy, however, El Greco could do no wrong. They believed that his paintings of saints, martyrs, and other religious figures caught the essence of Spanish emotionalism and religious zeal—the same qualities that had led Loyola to found the Jesuits. In effect, El Greco's extravagant images gave visible form to his patrons' spiritual yearnings. In his paintings, he rejected a naturalistic world with conventional perspective, especially when a divine dimension was present or implied; his spiritualized vision came to be distinguished by elongated bodies, sharp lines in the folds of cloth, and luminous colors.

El Greco's masterpiece is *The Burial of Count Orgaz,* painted to honor the founder of the church of Santo

Tomé in Toledo (Figure 13.16). This painting was designed to fit into a special place beside the church's high altar. Its subject is the miraculous scene that, according to legend, occurred during the count's burial, when two saints, Augustine and Stephen, appeared and assisted with the last rites.

From this legend, El Greco fashioned an arresting painting. The large canvas is divided into two halves, with the lower section devoted to the count's actual burial and the upper section focused on the reception of his soul in heaven. Except for a few men who tilt their faces upward, the town dignitaries seem unaware of what is happening just above their heads. El Greco has devised two distinct styles to deal with these different planes of reality. The dignitaries below are rendered in realistic terms, showing fashions of El Greco's era, such as the neck ruffs, mustaches, and goatees. The heavenly spectacle is depicted in the

Figure 13.17 EL GRECO. *Cardinal Guevara.* 1596–1600. Oil on canvas, 67¼ × 42½". Courtesy of the Metropolitan Museum of Art. The H. O. Havemeyer Collection. Bequest of Mrs. H. O. Havemeyer, 1929. (29.100.5). *El Greco's painting of Cardinal Guevara illustrates his mastery of Mannerist portraiture. Disturbing details are visible everywhere. Guevara's head is almost too small for his large body, made even grander by the red cardinal's robe, and the divided background—half wooden panel, half rich tapestry—sets up a dissonant effect. Even the cardinal's chair contributes to the air of uneasiness, for its one visible leg seems barely to touch the floor.*

Figure 13.18 SOFONISBA ANGUISSOLA. *Bernardino Campi Painting Sofonisba Anguissola.* Ca. 1550. Oil on canvas, 43¹¹⁄₁₆ × 43⁵⁄₁₆". Pinacoteca Nazionale, Siena. *Unusual for her time, the aristocratic Sofonisba Anguissola pursued a painting career, and, even rarer, she studied painting apart from her parents' household, under the artist Bernardino Campi (1522–1591), living in his home as a paying guest. From him, she learned the Mannerist style, as in this double portrait of herself and her mentor, both presented in three-quarter length. Within the painting, she depicts her likeness on a canvas supported by an easel. Campi, standing before her likeness, holds a paintbrush in his right hand, which is steadied by a hand rest (a device used to prevent smudges). The sharp contrasts of light and dark and the characteristic "square-U" shape to the hands are typical of Anguissola's Mannerist style. By depicting Campi at work, she also broke new ground in the portrait genre, which hitherto had focused on subjects seated or standing, but always in static situations (see Figures 12.2 and 12.7).*

ethereal manner that he increasingly used in his later works.

El Greco also painted several portraits of church officials; the best known is *Cardinal Guevara* (Figure 13.17). This painting portrays the Chief Inquisitor, dressed in his splendid red robes. El Greco has captured the personality of this austere and iron-willed churchman who vigorously pursued heretics and sentenced them to die in an *auto-da-fé,* Portuguese for "act of faith"—that is, a public ceremony in which heretics were executed, usually by being burned at the stake.

El Greco's likeness suggests much about the inner man: Cardinal Guevara seems to have an uneasy conscience, as betrayed by the shifty expression of the eyes, the left hand clutching the chair arm, and the general sense that the subject is restraining himself. Through these means El Greco created another model for Mannerist portraiture.

Another Mannerist artist-in-exile working in Spain in the late sixteenth century was Sofonisba Anguissola [an-gwee-SOL-uh] (about 1532–1625), a northern Italian from Cremona who, along with El Greco, is credited with helping to introduce the Italian school of painting into Spanish culture (Figure 13.18). Praised

Figure 13.19   SOFONISBA ANGUISSOLA. (Formerly attributed to Alonzo Sánchez Coello.) *Portrait of Don Carlos.* Ca. 1560. Oil on canvas, 42¹⁵⁄₁₆ × 34³⁄₁₆". Prado, Madrid. *This painting of Prince Don Carlos shows typical features of the artist's personal style. Like most women of the period, Anguissola was skilled in the needle arts, and she reveals this knowledge in the painstaking detail she has lavished on the prince's court costume—her trademark, according to one scholar. She also had a signature way of rendering hands—in a "square-U" pattern, so that the index and little fingers are parallel and act as the raised portions of a "U" connected by an imaginary line—which may be seen in both of Don Carlos's hands.*

and encouraged by the aging Michelangelo, Anguissola began her rise to international fame when King Philip II of Spain chose her to be his court painter from 1559 to 1579. She painted mainly portraits, as, for example, the *Portrait of Don Carlos* (Figure 13.19). In this three-quarter-length likeness of Spain's crown prince, Anguissola shows her mastery of the Mannerist style, including the challenging gaze of the young subject and the painting's highly polished surface and dark olive background. Portraits such as that of *Don Carlos* made Anguissola a celebrity, the first internationally acclaimed Italian woman artist. Her painting career at the Spanish court ended in 1580, when she married a Sicilian nobleman and settled with him in Palermo, Sicily, where she lived and worked for much of the rest of her life. Most of her works are lost, but the surviving court portraits stand as vivid testaments to her brilliant gifts as an artist.

Anguissola's international acclaim was due, in part, to her aristocratic breeding and her education in

Renaissance learning, rare for women of the times. This background, coupled with rich artistic gifts, enabled her to overcome the prejudices and guild restrictions that had previously kept women from pursuing careers in the arts. Sofonisba Anguissola was the ablest of the women artists who began to emerge in sixteenth-century Europe.

Spanish Literature

Known in Spanish as *Siglo de Oro,* or Golden Century, the sixteenth century is the high point in Spain's literary history. The writings were characterized by direct observation of life, satiric treatment of earlier epics and ballads, religious zeal, and Spanish themes, values, and subject matter; they also reflected minor influence from Renaissance humanism. Plays and novels were the most popular forms of literary expression.

As in England, theater was now revived in Spain for the first time in centuries. Spanish playwrights began to write dramas, including tragedies and comedies, and invent new dramatic forms, such as allegorical religious plays. The dramatist Lope de Vega [BAY-gah] (1562–1635), author of 426 secular plays and 42 religious dramas, is generally credited with almost single-handedly founding the Spanish national theater.

The **chivalric novel,** a late medieval literary form that presented romantic stories of knights and their ladies, was now challenged by the more realistic **picaresque novel.** The picaresque novel (Spanish *picaro,* "rogue") recounted the comic misadventures of a roguish hero who lived by his wits, often at the expense of those above him in society. Although having the hero question the social order was a revolutionary step, the novels were immensely popular in Spain and across Europe. The first picaresque novel was the anonymous *Lazarillo de Tormes,* published in 1554, in which the poor hero, Lazaro, encounters several masters, each of whom is a shady character suffering from self-deception. In translation, *Lazarillo de Tormes* found new audiences across Europe and influenced the writing of novels in England, France, and Germany for about two hundred years.

The Spanish novel was raised to new heights by Miguel de Cervantes Saavedra [sir-VAN-tez] (1547–1616) in his masterpiece *Don Quixote* (part I, 1605; part II, 1615). Poet, playwright, and novelist, Cervantes is the greatest figure in Spanish literature and one of the most respected writers in the world. In *Don Quixote* he satirized the chivalric novel, mocking its anachronistic ideals. Although the long, rambling structure was borrowed from the chivalric novel, *Don Quixote* is the prototype of the modern novel, with its

Figure 13.20   TINTORETTO. *The Last Supper.* 1592–1594. Oil on canvas, 12′ × 18′8″. San Giorgio Maggiore, Venice. *Nothing better illustrates the distance between the High Renaissance and Mannerism than a comparison of Leonardo's Last Supper (Figure 12.6) with that of Tintoretto. Everything about Tintoretto's spiritualized scene contradicts the quiet Classicism of Leonardo's work. Leonardo's painting is meant to appeal to the viewer's reason; Tintoretto's shadowy scene is calculated to stir the feelings.*

psychological realism, or probing into the motives of the main characters. These characters, the hero, Don Quixote, and his servant, Sancho Panza, whose lives are intertwined, embody the major themes of the work. The tormented Don Quixote, driven half-mad by his unreachable quest, represents the hopeless visionary, while the plodding Sancho Panza, never taken in by his master's madness, stands for the hardheaded realist. At one level, the characters signify the dual nature of the Spanish soul, the idealistic aristocrat and the down-to-earth peasant. At a higher level, the characters personify a universal theme, that idealism and realism must go hand in hand.

Late Mannerist Painting in Italy: Tintoretto

With the death of Michelangelo in 1564, Venice displaced Rome as the dominant artistic center in Italy. From then until the end of the century, Venetian painters carried the banner of the Italian Renaissance, bringing Mannerism to a brilliant sunset. The leading exponent of Late Mannerism in Italy is Tintoretto [tin-tuh-RAY-toe] (1518–1594). This Venetian artist created a feverish, emotional style that reflected impetuosity in its execution. With his haste, Tintoretto was reacting against his famous Venetian predecessor Titian, who had been noted for extraordinary discipline. But in other respects, he followed Titian, adopting his love of color and his use of theatrical lighting. The special quality of Tintoretto's art, which he achieved in his earliest paintings, was to place his human figures in arrangements that suggest a sculptural frieze.

Tintoretto's rendition of the familiar biblical account of the Last Supper shows his feverish style (Figure 13.20). Unlike the serene, classically balanced scene that Leonardo had painted (see Figure 12.6), Tintoretto portrays an ethereal gathering, illuminated by eerie light and filled with swooping angels. The diagonal table divides the pictorial space into two halves; on the left is the spiritual world of Jesus and his disciples, and on the right is the earthly realm of the servants. Tintoretto's depiction of these different levels of reality is reminiscent of a similar division in El Greco's *The Burial of Count Orgaz* (see Figure 13.16). Especially notable is Jesus' body, including the feet, which glows as if in a spotlight. *The Last Supper,* finished in Tintoretto's final year, is a fitting climax to Mannerist painting.

Music in Late-Sixteenth-Century Italy and England

Unlike painting, Italian music remained under the sway of High Renaissance ideals, keeping to the path pioneered by Josquin des Prez (see Chapter 12). Nevertheless, the Council of Trent, along with other forces, led to the decline of the High Renaissance style and created the conditions for the rise of the Baroque. For one thing, the council ruled that the Gregorian chant was preferable to polyphony for church liturgy and that the traditional chants should be simplified to ensure that the words could be easily understood. Most composers, considering the chants to be barbarous, continued to use polyphony but pruned its extravagant effects. The best of these composers and the chief representative of Counter-Reformation music was Giovanni Pierluigi da Palestrina [pal-uh-STREE-nuh] (about 1525–1594). His controlled style established the Roman Catholic ideal for the next few centuries— polyphonic masses sung by choirs and with clearly enunciated and expressive texts.

Nevertheless, the future of Italian music lay outside the church. Ironically, secular vocal music was also moving toward an ideal in which the words took precedence over the sound, but secular composers, unlike those in the church, rejected polyphony because it did not allow the text to be fully understood. The move to make the words primary in secular music was triggered by Renaissance humanists who were convinced that ancient music's power stemmed from the expressive way that the setting suited the clearly articulated words of the text. The most evident signs of this humanistic belief were in the works of the Florentine Camerata, a group of musical amateurs. Rejecting polyphony, the Florentine musicians composed pieces for a text with a single line of melody accompanied by simple chords and sung in a declamatory style.

The trend to expressive secular music in Italy was reflected most completely in the **madrigal,** a song for four or five voices composed with great care for the words of the poetic text. The novelty of this vocal music was that it vividly illustrated the meanings and emotions in the words, rather than the structure of the music. Madrigals were first written in the 1520s, but their heyday was the second half of the sixteenth century. Late in the century, they were imported to England and quickly became the height of fashion there. The success of madrigals in England had to do with the vogue there for Italianate things, as is evident from the settings and sources of Shakespeare's plays and the translation into English of Castiglione's *The Book of the Courtier* during this period.

England's leading madrigal composer was Thomas Weelkes [WILKS] (about 1575–1623), whose works often made use of the technique called **word paintings,** or word illustrations, a musical illustration of the written text. For example, in the madrigal "As Vesta was from Latmos hill descending," Weelkes uses a descending scale for the word "descending," an ascending scale for the words "a maiden queen ascending," and a hill-shaped melodic phrase for the words "Latmos hill descending." Such clever fusing of music and lyrics appealed to listeners, many of whom, in the spirit of the Renaissance, were amateur musicians themselves.

Madrigals eventually achieved a European-wide popularity, but it ended with the Renaissance. Nevertheless, the technique of word painting continued to be a favorite of composers, down through Bach and Handel in the Baroque age (see Chapter 14).

The Legacy of Northern Humanism, Northern Renaissance, Religious Reformations, and Late Mannerism

The period from 1500 until 1520 in northern Europe witnessed important developments in painting and literature. The German painters Grünewald and Dürer and the Flemish painter Bosch brought the Late Gothic style to its final flower, though Dürer was also influenced by the methods of the Italian Renaissance. In the Netherlands, Erasmus launched Christian humanism, and, in France, Rabelais and Marguerite of Angoulême followed in this tradition. The movement was undermined by Luther's break with the Roman Catholic Church and was finally ended by the wars of religion.

The period from 1520 until 1603 brings to a close the third and final phase of the Renaissance. This eighty-three-year period, framed by the deaths of Raphael and Queen Elizabeth I, saw the foundations of early modern Europe move firmly into place. A world culture and economy, in embryo, begins during this period. This momentous development was foreshadowed in the shift of Europe's commercial axis from the Mediterranean to the Atlantic, as well as in the start of Europe's exportation of peoples, technology, religions, and ideas to colonies in Asia, Africa, and the Americas.

Probably the most important material change during this era was the rise of a system of sovereign and mutually hostile states. No single state was able to assert its authority over the others; the pattern set by their struggles would govern Western affairs until the emergence of global politics in the twentieth century. The European state system also spelled the doom of a united Christendom.

The religious reformations further split Christian Europe, dividing it into Protestant and Catholic armed camps. As a result, religious wars afflicted this century and the next, fading away only by about 1700. On a local level, religious differences led to intolerance and persecution. Although Europe's religious boundaries today remain roughly the same as they were in 1600, it took over three hundred years for Protestants and Catholics to accept that they could live together in harmony.

The reformations also left different cultural legacies to their respective Christian denominations. From Protestantism came a glorification of the work ethic, Puritanism, and a justification for capitalism. At the heart of the Protestant revolution, despite its insistence on the doctrine of original sin, was the notion that human beings can commune directly with God without church mediation. Whereas Protestantism tended to view human beings as adrift in the universe, the Catholic Church tried to control the spiritual and moral lives of its members and to insulate them from the surrounding world. This policy eventually placed the church on a collision course with the forces of modernity, but it nevertheless was followed by most of the popes until after World War II.

In the aftermath of the religious crisis, the legacy of northern humanism—rational morals allied to a simple faith—went unheeded by Protestants and Catholics alike. Not until the eighteenth century and the rationalist program of the Enlightenment did Christian humanist ideas find a willing audience.

In the arts and humanities, however, the legacy was clear: This period left a rich and varied inheritance, including the work of Cervantes and the rest of Spain's Golden Age authors and the work of Shakespeare, the most gifted and influential individual writer in the history of Western civilization.

	AFRICA	AMERICAS
HISTORY	**East Africa** *Coastal trading states.* Portuguese took control of gold trade. *Zimbabwe.* In decline, but a cult center for the Shona. *Zambezi Valley.* Butwa, the most prosperous state. Portuguese (ca. 1575) tried to control trade. **North Africa** Egypt and the Maghreb conquered by Ottoman Empire (after 1517). *Morocco.* Sharifian Dynasty founded (1524); still rules today. Repelled Portuguese invaders (1578). **West Africa** *Songhai Empire.* Greatest expanse under Askia Muhammad I (d. 1528). Fell to Moroccans (1591). *Yoruba culture.* Oyo Empire rose to power. Benin Kingdom grew powerful under Oba Esgi; became involved in the slave trade.	Throughout the Americas epidemics of European diseases, introduced by the explorers, decimated native populations. **South America** *Inca culture.* Francisco Pizarro conquered Incas for Spain (1534). *Early Colonial period, 1534–1600.* Spanish founded Buenos Aires, Bogotá, Caracas. Pedro Álvares Cabral claimed Brazil for Portugal (1500). African slave trade began. **Mesoamerica** *Aztec culture.* Hernán Cortés defeated Montezuma II. Tenochtitlán became Mexico City, capital of New Spain. **Native North America** *Mississippian culture.* Calusas and Timucuas (Florida) resisted Spanish expeditions (1513–28). Hernán de Soto's expedition from Florida to Texas (1539–43). *Eastern woodlands.* Hurons traded furs and fish to French. *Southwest.* Francisco Coronado's expedition through Pueblo lands (1540–41).
ART & MUSIC	**West Africa** *Yoruba culture.* Height of Benin bronzes.	**South America** *Early Colonial period.* A hybrid style that fused Inca and Spanish Christian traditions. **Mesoamerica** *Aztec culture.* Stone chacmools; feathered headdresses; and polychrome ceramics. Temple Stone, a throne for Montezuma II (1507). *Early Postconquest period, from 1519.* Wall painting; painted manuscripts (codices) of native history and religion, at the request of Franciscan friars.  *Drinking Cup (Qero). Sixteenth century. Wood. Peru. University Museum of Archeology and Ethnology, Cambridge.*
ARCHITECTURE	**West Africa** *Songhai Empire.* Gao, the capital, became an Islamic city, with mosques, minarets, and the tomb of Emperor Askia Muhammad I.	**South America** *Early Colonial period.* Inca's main temple in Cuzco—the Qorikancha, or "Golden House"—incorporated into a Christian church. **Mesoamerica** *Aztec culture.* Tenochtitlán reached its final form (1487). *Early Postconquest period.* Spanish recycled stones from indigenous temples into civic buildings, churches, and homes. Monastic complexes for missionary friars and open-air chapels for converts.
RELIGION, PHILOSOPHY, LITERATURE	Islam, paramount in North Africa, made inroads into coastal and inland East and West Africa but failed to penetrate south of inland central Africa. Christianity was the state religion in Ethiopia; Christian missionaries in scattered areas on the tropical east and west coasts. Native religions and practices in rest of Africa.	**South America** *Early Colonial period.* Founding of University of Lima (1551) and Central University of Quito (1594). **Mesoamerica** *Early Postconquest period.* Indigenous scribes, sponsored by Franciscans, wrote histories, almanacs, and religious tracts. Aztec dictionary published (1555). *Florentine Codex: General History of the Things of New Spain* (ca. 1566–77, 1585), compiled by Father Bernardino de Sahagún. *Eagle in a Cactus (Symbol of Mexico), from frontispiece,* Codex Mendoza. *Ca. 1550. Mexico. Bodleian Library, Oxford MS Arch. Selden A1.*

ASIA

China

Ming Dynasty. Weak rulers; peaceful period; Portuguese traders settled in Macao (1517); legal restrictions on foreigners and foreign trade (after 1570); breakdown in relations with Japan (1592).

India

Mogul Empire, began 1526. Delhi Sultanate conquered by Bābur, head of the Moguls, a Muslim dynasty from central Asia. Empire (zenith: Akbar, r. 1556–1605) included all of India, except for extreme south. Strong and effective centralized government. Portuguese made Goa headquarters of their Far Eastern trading empire.

Japan

Muromachi period, ended 1573. Civil war among feudal overlords. Portuguese traders arrived (1543). The samurai Oda Nobunaga overthrew the shōgun (1573). *Azuchi-Momoyama period, 1573–1603.* Period named for castle-towns of the two main warlords. The samurai Hideyoshi brought feudal lords under control (1591); restored internal peace and stability; invaded Korea (1592, 1597); thousands of Koreans massacred.

CH'IU YING. *Saying Farewell at Hsün-yang. Detail of handscroll painting. First half sixteenth century. China. Nelson Gallery–Atkins Museum, Kansas City.*

Ming Dynasty. Increased use of color in landscape scroll painting and five-color porcelains.

Deccan Plateau. Idealized version of the Persian miniature, with native Indian and Western features; practiced at Hindu and Muslim courts. *Mogul Empire.* During Akbar's reign, a realistic approach to the Persian miniature, combining European realism and native Indian tradition, as in the manuscript *Romance of Amir Hamza.* Hindustani music at its zenith.

Gardeners Beating the Giant Zamurrad Trapped in a Well, from Romance of Amir Hamza. *1567–82. Paint on cloth. India. Victoria and Albert Museum, London.*

Azuchi-Momoyama period. Zen landscape painting at its height; screen painting by Kanō Eitoku at Azuchi castle; Kanō school colors-on-gold paintings; ink-wash murals by Hasegawa Tōhaku.

Ming Dynasty. Continued building of Forbidden City; developed small courtyard gardens (such as the Wang Shiyuan garden) and large parklike gardens.

The Wang Shiyuan Garden. Sixteenth century. Suzhou.

Mogul Dynasty. Tomb of Akbar's father, Humāyūn (1565), a blend of Persian and Indian features. New cities with public buildings and tombs. Fatehpur Sikri, a city planned by Emperor Akbar, based on Islamic and Hindu designs, only partially completed.

Panch Mahal (Palace of Five Stories). Begun 1571. Fatehpur Sikri, India.

Azuchi-Momoyama period. Two building styles: fortified stone castles with small windows and timbered roofs and the Shōin style with built-in desks and shelves, and rooms divided by sliding rice-paper screens (used by samurai as private retreats). Rustic teahouses influenced domestic architecture.

Ming Dynasty. Voyage to the West (1570), a classic comic novel; *The Peony Pavilion* (1598), with libretto by T'ang Hsien-tsu, a classic of K'un-ch'u opera; Tung Ch'i-ch'ang's *Talking of Painting,* a highly influential critique. Jesuit missionaries, headed by Matteo Ricci, arrived.

Delhi Sultanate. Under Sultan Sikander (1489–1517) poetry, music, and scholarship flourished. *Mogul Dynasty.* During Akbar's reign, Tul-sī-dās, Hindu author of poetic works on the god Rama; the *ghazal,* a type of Urdu lyric poetry. Akbar introduced religious toleration; the Sikh religion founded by the poet Nānak.

Muromachi period. Kabuki theater originated. Dance added to Nō plays. Jesuits active (after 1549). *Azuchi-Momoyama period.* Christians persecuted (1590s).

14 THE BAROQUE AGE
Glamour and Grandiosity
1600–1715

As the Roman Catholic Church pursued its goal of eradicating Protestantism, and as powerful sovereign secular states became established in Europe, a new age—the **Baroque**—dawned in the early seventeenth century. It was a period characterized by grandeur, opulence, and expanding horizons. Baroque art and architecture provided spectacular and compelling images with which the church could reassert its presence and dazzle and indoctrinate the faithful. The Baroque also offered secular rulers a magnificence and vastness that enhanced their political power. Art became a propagandistic tool in a way that the individualistic Mannerist art of the previous period—with its focus on the distorted and the eccentric—never was.

The term *baroque* was coined by eighteenth-century artists and scholars whose tastes were attuned to Classical ideals. To them, much seventeenth-century culture was imperfect, or "baroque," a term probably derived from the Portuguese word *barroco,* meaning an irregular pearl. Not until the mid–nineteenth century did the word acquire a positive meaning, and now "Baroque" is a label for the prevailing cultural style of the seventeenth century.

The Baroque period was an era of constant turmoil, and until midcentury, Europe was plagued by religious warfare, a legacy of the Reformation. The conflicts of the second half of the century had secular motivations: territorial expansion and the race for overseas empires. The seventeenth century was also a period of great scientific discoveries and intellectual change. Because

◀ **Detail** CHARLES LEBRUN AND JULES HARDOUIN-MANSART. Hall of Mirrors, Versailles Palace. 1678–1684. Versailles, France.

LEARNING THROUGH MAPS

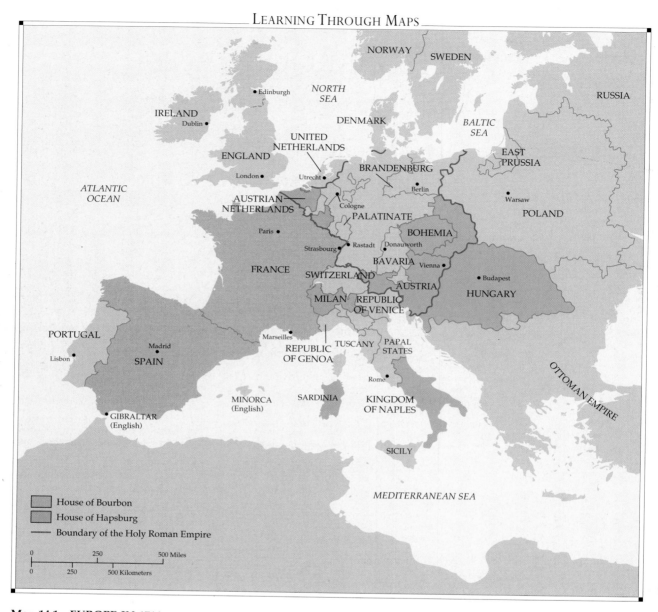

Map 14.1 EUROPE IN 1714
This map shows Europe in the early eighteenth century. **Compare** the lands of the Hapsburg dynasty in this map with the holdings of Hapsburg emperor Charles V in Map 12.1. **Compare** the Holy Roman Empire's size in this map with its size on Map 12.1. **Which** of the two dynasties—Bourbon or Hapsburg—had the larger land holdings in 1714? **How** did the size and location of England and the United Netherlands help make them major maritime powers? **Note** the large number of small states in central Europe and north Italy.

the Scientific Revolution, as this intellectual movement is called, so keenly influenced the making of the modern world, it is covered separately in Chapter 15, along with related philosophical ideas. This chapter focuses on the art, literature, and music of the Baroque age and their historical, political, and social contexts.

ABSOLUTISM, MONARCHY, AND THE BALANCE OF POWER

Although the Baroque style in art originated in Rome and from there spread across the Continent, the Italian city-states and the popes were no longer at the center of European political life. By the time Europe had

Figure 14.1   Attributed to François de Troy. *Louis XIV and His Heirs.* Ca. 1710. Oil on canvas, 4'2¾" × 5'3¾". Wallace Collection, London. *Louis XIV's dynastic ambitions are reflected in this collective portrait of himself surrounded by his heirs. To his right stands his only legitimate son, the "Grand Dauphin," and the king's infant great-grandson, the duc de Bretagne, who is attended by a governess. To the king's left is his grandson, Louis, the duc de Bourgogne. Ironically, none of these heirs became king, because all of them died of illness within two years. In the painting, the Baroque love of grandeur is apparent in the opulent setting, the formal poses, and ornate dress. The king and the dauphin wear rich velvet suits and large, full-bottomed wigs, typical of seventeenth-century style. In contrast, the duc de Bourgogne represents the younger generation with his bright-colored suit and less formal wig. The wall painting within this portrait depicts the Greek sun god Helios, driving his chariot—a reference to Louis's claim to be the Sun King.*

recovered from the first wave of religious wars in 1600, a new system of sovereign states had replaced the old dream of a united Christendom. By 1715 there was a balance of power in Europe among five great military states—England, France, Austria, Prussia, and Russia (Map 14.1). The rise of these states was due to a new breed of rulers fascinated with power. Known as *absolutists,* they wanted complete control over state affairs, unlike the medieval monarchs, who had to share authority with the church and the feudal nobles. Steeped in the works of Machiavelli, the new monarchs buttressed their claims to power with theories of divine right and natural law. France's greatest monarch, Louis XIV, was the most extreme in his claims, glorifying himself as the Sun King—a title derived from the late Roman emperors (Figure 14.1).

In their bid for absolute power, these monarchs founded new institutions and reformed old ones. For example, administrative bureaucracies, which had existed since the High Middle Ages, were reformed to become the exclusive domain of university-trained officials drawn from the middle classes. These career bureaucrats began to displace the great lords who had previously dominated the kings' advisory councils. As a consequence, the authority of the feudal nobility began to diminish.

The absolute monarchs also established permanent diplomatic corps to assist in foreign policy. The great states of Europe set up diplomatic missions in the major capitals, staffed with trusted officials who served as their rulers' eyes and ears in foreign cities. Another new institution was the standing army funded from state revenues, led by noble officers, and manned by lower-class soldiers. New weapons—the flintlock rifle and the bayonet—and an improved breed of horse made these armies more efficient.

France: The Supreme Example of Absolutism

At the opening of the seventeenth century, France was ruled by Henry IV, the first of the Bourbon dynasty, who had converted from Calvinism to Catholicism to restore peace to his largely Roman Catholic state. Like the medieval kings, Henry shared authority with the feudal nobles, though he began to reward middle-class supporters with high office. Henry was a pragmatist; he felt no need to force his adopted faith on the Huguenots, as the French Calvinists were called, and allowed them limited freedom of worship. The atmosphere changed when Henry was assassinated in 1610. Between then and 1715, France became the model absolutist state (Timeline 14.1).

Henry IV was succeeded by Louis XIII, but real authority passed to Cardinal Richelieu, who was the virtual ruler of France from 1624 until his death in 1642. Gifted with political acumen, Richelieu worked tirelessly to wrest power from the nobles. He was also

Timeline 14.1   RULERS OF FRANCE AND ENGLAND DURING THE BAROQUE PERIOD

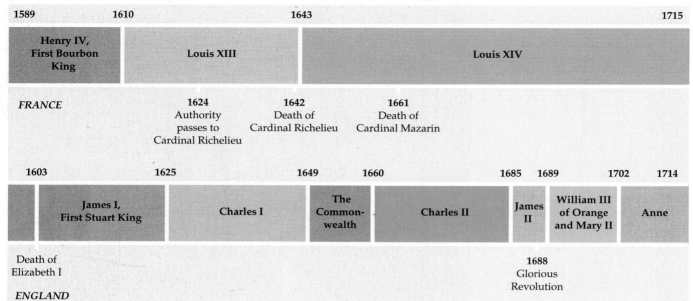

a pragmatic statesman. For example, at home he restricted the freedom of the Protestant Huguenots, but abroad he allied himself with Swedish Protestants. His pragmatic policies were continued by his protégé and iron-fisted successor, Cardinal Mazarin, who served as regent for the young Louis XIV. Mazarin's rule moved France closer to absolutism, but it also coincided with the beginning of a golden age in France; for more than a century, French politics and culture dominated Europe, and French was the language of diplomacy.

When Mazarin died, Louis XIV, aged twenty-three, decided to rule France in his own right. Throughout his fifty-four-year reign, Louis made his private and public life the embodiment of the French state: "L'État c'est moi"—"I am the state"—is what he allegedly said about his concept of government. Determined that nothing should escape his grasp, Louis XIV canceled what freedom remained to the Huguenots, persecuting them until they converted to Roman Catholicism, fled into exile, or were killed. As king, he perfected the policies of his Bourbon predecessors, becoming the chief of a bureaucratic machine that regulated every phase of French life, from economics to culture. His economic policy was called mercantilism, a system that rested on state control. Through his ministers, Louis regulated exports and imports, subsidized local industries, and set tariffs, customs duties, and quotas.

Louis waged a spectacular campaign of self-glorification, and in so doing he made France the center of European arts and letters. His palace at

Versailles became the symbol of his regal style (Figure 14.2). He also encouraged the work of the emerging academies, particularly the French Academy, founded in 1635 by Cardinal Richelieu to purify the French language and honor the state's most distinguished living authors, and the Royal Academy of Painting and Sculpture, founded by Cardinal Mazarin in 1648 to recognize the country's best artists. These seventeenth-century French academies became the models for similar institutions in other Western states.

England: From Monarchy to Republic to Limited Monarchy

Like France, England turned toward absolutism at the beginning of the seventeenth century. Following the death of Elizabeth I, the new Stuart dynasty assumed the throne. King James I considered himself ruler by divine right, but certain aspects of English life held royal power in check. Specifically, the English nobles made common cause with the middle-class members of Parliament; England's Parliament met regularly and considered itself the king's partner rather than his enemy; and England's Calvinist minority, called Puritans, were not despised by the Anglican majority, many of whom shared their zeal. When England became embroiled in a constitutional crisis between Parliament and the headstrong Charles I, Puritan leaders in Parliament led a successful civil war, toppling the monarchy and setting

Figure 14.2 LOUIS LE VAU AND JULES HARDOUIN-MANSART. Palace of Versailles. *1661–1688. Versailles, France. As the seat of government and the center of fashionable society, Versailles was the greatest symbol of this age of kings. Here, nobles competed for Louis XIV's favors and a royal post. He shrewdly rewarded them with menial positions and lofty titles and thus undermined their political influence. At the height of Louis's power, this complex of buildings could house ten thousand people—members of the royal court, hangers-on, and servants.*

up a republic, called the Commonwealth, in 1649. But the Commonwealth soon lost its allure when its leader, the Puritan Oliver Cromwell, turned it into a military dictatorship.

Disappointed by the republic, the English restored monarchy in 1660, recalling Charles I's son from exile in France to become Charles II, an event known as the Restoration. The king's powers were now tempered by vague restrictions, but lack of clarity about the arrangement soon led to renewed conflicts between the crown and Parliament. In 1688 King James II, brother of Charles II, was expelled in a bloodless coup known as the Glorious Revolution, and his daughter and son-in-law, Mary II and William III of the Netherlands, became England's joint sovereigns. With their reign, England's constitutional crisis was finally resolved, for they understood that they could rule only if they recognized citizens' rights and Parliament's power over most financial matters. By 1715 England had become the classic example of limited monarchy under written laws. In the ensuing years, political philosophers cited England's experience as a successful example of the principle that government should rest on the consent of the people.

Warfare in the Baroque Period: Maintaining the Balance of Power

Warfare was crucial in establishing the configuration of the great powers because the most successful states were those in which the king could marshal his country's resources behind his military goals. But when one state began to stand out from the rest, the other states pursued policies designed to hold it in check—that is, to keep a balance of power. This system had several consequences. For one, it prevented any single state from controlling the rest. For another, it was a practical way to discourage the ambition of empires like that of the Ottoman Turks, because the great powers were willing to unite to stop Turkish expansion. Finally, this system relegated many countries, such as Spain and Poland, to secondary power status and spelled the end of a significant international role for city-states like Florence and Venice.

The Thirty Years' War, 1618–1648 The first half of the seventeenth century was mired in the destructive Thirty Years' War (actually a series of four wars), the last great European-wide struggle between the Protestants and the Roman Catholics. Besides the great

PERSONAL PERSPECTIVE

LOUIS XIV
Reflections on Power

During the last fifty years of the seventeenth century, France, under Louis XIV, led Europe in centralizing political power, creating an efficient bureaucracy, fielding a superior army, and setting the cultural and artistic standards. Conscious of his impact on France and Europe, Louis XIV knew how to increase his personal power at home and his country's influence abroad. Louis XIV's private thoughts about wielding power are excerpted here.

Kings are often obliged to do things against their natural inclination and which wound their natural goodness. They ought to love making people happy, and they must often chastise and condemn people whom they naturally wish well. The interest of the state must come first. One must overcome one's inclinations and not put oneself into a position of reproaching oneself, in something important, for not having done better because personal interests prevented one from doing

so and distorted the views which one should have had for the grandeur, the good, and the power of the state. . . .

One must guard against oneself, guard against one's inclinations, and ever be on guard against one's own nature. The king's craft is great, noble, and extremely pleasant when one feels oneself worthy of carrying out everything one sets out to do; but it is not exempt from pain, fatigue, cares. Uncertainty sometimes leads to despair; and when one has passed a reasonable amount of time in examining a matter, one must decide and choose the side believed to be best.

When one keeps the state in mind, one works for oneself. The good of the one makes the *gloire* of the other. When the former is happy, eminent and powerful, he who is the cause as a result is *glorieux* and consequently must savor more than his subjects, if the two are compared, all of the most agreeable things in life.

DUKE OF SAINT-SIMON
Memoirs

The following excerpt, describing Louis XIV's public image, is a striking contrast to the preceding one. The Duke of Saint-Simon (1675–1755) was a soldier and courtier at the French court.

In everything [Louis XIV] loved splendor, magnificence, profusion. He turned this taste to a maxim for political reasons, and stilled it into his court on all matters. One could please him by throwing oneself into fine food, clothes, retinue, buildings, gambling. These were occasions which enabled him to talk to people. The essence of it was that by this he attempted and

succeeded in exhausting everyone by making luxury a virtue, and for certain persons a necessity, and thus he gradually reduced everyone to depending entirely upon his generosity in order to subsist. . . . This is an evil which, once introduced, became the internal cancer which is devouring all individuals—because from the court it promptly spread to Paris and into the provinces and the armies, where persons, whatever their position, are considered important only in proportion to the table they lay and their magnificence ever since this unfortunate innovation.

---

powers of Austria, France, and Brandenburg (soon to be Prussia), states involved at one time or another included Denmark, Sweden, Spain, Venice, the United Provinces of the Netherlands, and Poland. Germany suffered the most because the war was fought largely on its soil, wiping out a generation of Germans and inaugurating more than a century of cultural decline.

The Treaty of Westphalia, which ended the war in 1648, nullified the religious objectives that had caused the war and also created the conditions for the rise of Brandenburg-Prussia to great power status. Germany itself remained divided; Calvinism was now tolerated,

but true religious freedom did not appear, for the principle established at Augsburg in 1555 was retained: The religion of each state was to be dictated by its ruler (see Chapter 13). A divided Germany served the interests of Brandenburg-Prussia and its rulers. Commencing with the Treaty of Westphalia, these Calvinist leaders began to amass additional territories, becoming kings of Prussia in 1701 and finally emperors of a united Germany in 1871.

The Thirty Years' War also had major consequences for the emerging system of great powers. The peace conference was the first in which decisions were arranged through congresses of ambassadors. Both the war and the conference revealed Spain's impotence, showing that it had fallen from its peak in the 1500s. In contrast, Sweden and the Netherlands gained advantages that made them major powers for the rest of the century. The Hapsburg rulers were forced to accept that Protestantism could not be turned back in their German lands; henceforth they concentrated on their Austrian holdings, ignoring the Holy Roman Empire, which now seemed a relic of the feudal age.

France profited the most from the Thirty Years' War. By shifting sides to support first Roman Catholics and then Protestants, the French rulers demonstrated a particularly shrewd understanding of power politics. Even after the religious wars were over, France continued to struggle against Roman Catholic Spain until 1659. Having taken control of France in 1661, Louis XIV launched a series of aggressive wars four years later against various coalitions of European states that lasted until 1713.

The Wars of Louis XIV, 1665–1713   Louis XIV used various means, including marriage and diplomacy, to assert French might on the Continent, but it was chiefly through warfare that he left his enduring mark. In his own mind, he fought for *la gloire* ("glory"), an elusive term that reflected his image as the Sun King but that in practice meant the expansion of France to imperial status.

Louis XIV fought the states of Europe in four separate wars and was finally defeated by a coalition that included virtually all of Europe's major and minor powers. Because of its wide-ranging nature, Louis's last struggle, the War of the Spanish Succession, is generally regarded as the first of the world wars—a new type of war. The Treaty of Utrecht, signed in 1713, not only settled this last war but also showed that the great power system was working.

The peace constructed at Utrecht was a reaffirmation of the balance-of-power principle. The victors set aside Louis's most extravagant acquisitions of land, but they granted those additions that still serve as France's borders today. Brandenburg-Prussia gained territory, and England emerged with the lion's share of the spoils, acquiring Gibraltar and the island of Minorca from Spain and areas of Canada from France. From this augmented base, England became the leader of world trade in the 1700s.

THE BAROQUE: VARIATIONS ON AN INTERNATIONAL STYLE

The Baroque mentality originated in a search for stability and order in a restless age. Encouraged by the Catholic Church, artists and writers sought to reveal the order they believed lay beneath the seeming chaos of life. In this, they shared certain aims with the artists of the High Renaissance. But although both styles were devoted to order, they differed in their concept of how harmony was best achieved. High Renaissance artists valued repose; a single, static perspective; and designs that were complete in themselves. Baroque artists, on the other hand, created dynamic, open-ended works that threaten to explode beyond their formal boundaries. These exuberant works are characterized by grand, sweeping gestures; flowing, expansive movement; and curving lines and oval and elliptical shapes. Reflecting the excitement of overseas explorations and of the new discoveries in astronomy, Baroque artists were fascinated with the concept of infinite space.

Despite religious differences among various regions of Europe, the Baroque style spread readily from its origin in Rome to the entire Continent and to England. Lines of communication—through trade, diplomacy, and marriage—facilitated its spread, as did the persistence of Latin as the common language of scholarly works and diplomatic exchanges. Travel was also a factor in the export of Baroque ideals to the rest of Europe. Many Protestant families in northern and western Europe sent their sons, and sometimes their daughters, on grand tours of the Continent to "complete their education." English travelers to Rome and other Catholic bastions included such faithful Protestants as poet John Milton and architect Christopher Wren.

Although the Baroque was an international style, it was reinterpreted in different regions, so that three distinct manifestations of the style emerged. The Florid Baroque, dominated by Roman Catholic religious ideals and motivations, was a product of the Counter-Reformation. This style developed in Italy and flourished there and in Spain and central Europe. The Classical Baroque, aristocratic and courtly, was a more subdued interpretation of Baroque ideals. This style was associated with French taste, which had been guided by the values of simplicity and harmony since the early 1500s, when Renaissance culture was first introduced into France. The French preference for the Classical fit well with the absolutist policies of Louis XIV, who promoted the adoption of strict rules in all aspects of cultural life as a way to reinforce his own obsession with order and control.

The third manifestation of this style was the Restrained Baroque, which arose in the middle-class United Provinces of the Netherlands and aristocratic England. Repelled equally by Catholicism and French absolutism, the artists and writers of the Restrained Baroque cultivated a style in keeping with their own Protestant values, a style simpler and less ornate than either the Florid or the Classical Baroque.

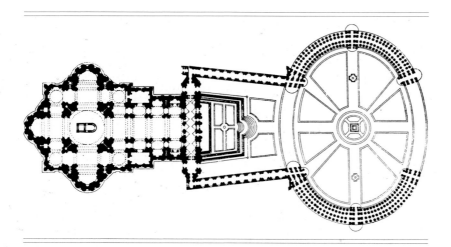

Figure 14.3   CARLO MADERNO AND GIANLORENZO BERNINI. Plan of St. Peter's Basilica with Adjoining Piazza. 1607–1615 and 1665–1667. *This plan of St. Peter's Basilica shows the design of Maderno for the church (left), dating from 1607–1615, and the adjoining piazza and colonnade (right) by Bernini, dating from 1665–1667.*

The Florid Baroque

The most important formative influence on the evolution of the Baroque style in the arts and architecture was the Council of Trent (see Chapter 13). In this series of sessions held between 1545 and 1563, church leaders had reaffirmed all the values and doctrines rejected by the Protestants and called for a new art that was geared to the teaching needs of the church and that set forth correct theological ideas easily understood by the masses. To achieve these goals, the popes of the late sixteenth century began to hold a tighter rein on artists and architects and to discourage the individualistic tendencies of the Mannerist style.

The seventeenth-century popes used their patronage powers to bring to life the **Florid Baroque** style. Once again, as in the Middle Ages, aesthetic values were subordinated to spiritual purposes. The popes enlisted architects, painters, and sculptors to glorify the Catholic message. Architects responded with grand building plans and elaborate decorative schemes that symbolized the power and richness of the church. Painters and sculptors represented dramatic incidents and emotion-charged moments, particularly favoring the ecstatic visions of the saints and the suffering and death of Jesus. They portrayed these subjects with a powerful realism intended to convey the physical presence and immediacy of the church's holiest figures. In everything, vitality and theatrical effects were prized over such Classical elements as restraint and repose.

Architecture   The church of St. Peter's in Rome became the age's preeminent expression of the Florid Baroque building style. First conceived in the early 1500s by Donato Bramante as a High Renaissance temple in the shape of a Greek cross, St. Peter's was now redesigned to conform to the ideals of the Council

Trent. Rejecting the Greek cross as a pagan symbol, Pope Paul V commissioned Carlo Maderno [mah-DAIR-noh] (1556–1629) to add a long nave, thereby giving the floor plan the shape of a Latin cross (Figure 14.3). Not only did the elongated nave satisfy the need to house the large crowds drawn to the mother church of Roman Catholicism, but also the enormous size of the building signified the church's power.

St. Peter's exterior was basically finished after Maderno designed and built the building's facade, but the popes wanted to integrate this huge church into its urban setting—a Classical ideal that was now adapted to Baroque taste. For this task, Pope Alexander VII commissioned Gianlorenzo Bernini [bayr-NEE-nee] (1598–1680). Bernini's solution was a masterstroke of Florid Baroque design in which he followed the principle of abolishing all straight lines. He tore down the buildings around St. Peter's and replaced them with a huge public square where the faithful could gather to see and hear the pope. Bernini then outlined this keyhole-shaped space with a sweeping colonnade topped with statues of saints (Figure 14.4). For worshipers assembled in the square, the curved double colonnade stood as a symbol of the church's welcoming arms.

From its origin in Rome, the Florid Baroque style in architecture spread to Spain, Austria, and southern Germany. By 1650 this lush style had appeared in Spanish and Portuguese colonies in the Americas, and there it flourished until well into the nineteenth century.

Sculpture   During the Baroque period, sculpture once again became a necessary complement to architecture, as it had been in medieval times. This change was hastened by the Council of Trent's advocacy of religious images to communicate the faith as well as the need to decorate the niches, recessed bays, and pedestals that

Figure 14.4 GIANLORENZO BERNINI. Piazza of St. Peter's. 1665–1667. The Vatican. *Bernini's plan for the piazza leading up to St. Peter's was instrumental in making exterior space a major concern of Baroque architects. The ancient Romans had integrated buildings into their urban settings, as had High Renaissance planners, but no architect had ever achieved such a natural blending of a monumental structure with its surroundings as Bernini did in this design.*

were part of building facades in Florid Baroque architecture. The demand for sculpture called forth an army of talented artists, of whom the most outstanding was Bernini, one of the architects of St. Peter's.

Bernini brought the Florid Baroque to a dazzling climax in his sculptural works. His pieces, executed for such diverse projects as churches, fountains, and piazzas, or squares, often combined architecture with sculpture. His sculptural ideal was a dynamic composition that used undulating forms to delight the eye. His sensuous sculptures with their implicit movement were the perfect accompaniments to Florid Baroque structures with their highly decorated walls.

Bernini's most famous sculptures are those he made for the interior of St. Peter's—including altars, tombs, reliefs, statues, and liturgical furniture—during a fifty-year period, commencing in 1629. His masterpiece among these ornate works is the **baldacchino,** the canopy, mainly bronze and partly gilt, that covers the spot where the bones of St. Peter are believed to lie—directly under Michelangelo's dome. Combining architectural and sculptural features, the baldacchino is supported by four huge columns whose convoluted surfaces are covered with climbing vines (Figure 14.5). Bernini crowned this colossal work with a magnificent display of four large angels at the corners, four groups of cherubs in the centers of the sides, and behind the angels four scrolled arches that rise to support a ball and cross at the top.

The baldacchino's twisting columns were modeled on the type that by tradition supported Solomon's Temple in Jerusalem and had been used in the old St. Peter's Basilica. Thus these columns symbolized the church's claim to be the true successor to the Jewish faith. So popular was Bernini's Solomonic canopy that in southern Germany it inspired many imitators and became the standard covering for altars for the next two centuries.

The sculpture that marks the highest expression of Bernini's art is *The Ecstasy of St. Teresa* (Figure 14.6). Using stone, metal, and glass, he portrays the divine moment when the saint receives the vision of the Holy Spirit—symbolized here by the arrow with which the angel pierces her heart. In his conception, Bernini imagines the pair floating on a cloud and bathed by light from a hidden source; the light rays seem to turn into golden rods that cascade onto the angel and the saint. The intensity of the saint's expression, the agitation of the draperies, and the billowing clouds all contribute to the illusion that the pair are sensuously real. By depicting St. Teresa's supernatural experience in physical terms, Bernini intended to force the viewer to suspend disbelief and accept the religious truth of the scene.

Painting   In the Baroque period, painting once again became an essential part of church decoration. In pursuit of church ideals, the painters of this tradition tended to use rich color and unusual lighting effects to depict spectacular or dramatic moments. They represented nature

Figure 14.5 GIANLORENZO BERNINI. The Baldacchino. 1624–1633. Ht., approx. 100'. St. Peter's, Rome. *This magnificent canopy reflects the grandiose ambitions of its patron, Pope Urban VIII, a member of the Barberini family. The Barberini crest was the source for the huge stylized bees displayed on the flaps of the bronze canopy. In his desire for worldly immortality, this pope shared a common outlook with the secular rulers of the Baroque age.*

and the human form realistically to make art intelligible and meaningful to the ordinary viewer.

The earliest great Florid Baroque painter was Michelangelo Merisi (1573–1610), better known as Caravaggio [kahr-ah-VAHD-jo]. Caravaggio rejected the antinaturalism of Mannerism in favor of a dramatic realism. His concern with realism led him to pick his models directly from the streets, and he refused to idealize his subjects. To make his works more dramatic and emotionally stirring, he experimented with light and the placement of figures. His paintings offer startling contrasts of light and dark—the technique known as chiaroscuro—and he banished landscape from his canvases, often focusing on human figures grouped tightly in the foreground.

A superb example of Caravaggio's work is *The Conversion of St. Paul* (Figure 14.7), which is paired with his *Crucifixion of St. Peter* in a Roman church. The two works were part of a commission to paint the founders of the Church of Rome, who, according to the New Testament, preached in the city. Caravaggio's revolutionary use of chiaroscuro emphasizes the dramatic event of Paul's conversion. The light, coming from the upper right, focuses on St. Paul and part of the horse's body. This makes the background nearly indistinct except for the groomsman, on the right, who holds the reins of the horse. St. Paul's head is thrown toward the viewer, and his eyes are shut as he is blinded by the light of Jesus' presence, who, as recorded in the Scripture (Acts 9:3–9), did not appear in human form but only as light.

Caravaggio had an enormous influence on other painters both in Italy and elsewhere, notably France, Spain, and the Netherlands. Perhaps the most original

Figure 14.6 GIANLORENZO BERNINI. *The Ecstasy of St. Teresa.* 1645–1652. Marble, glass, metal, life-size. Cornaro Chapel, Santa Maria della Vittoria, Rome. *Even though this sculpture captures an ecstatic vision, its portrayal reflects the naturalism that was central to the Baroque style. Bernini based this work on the saint's personal account, in which she described how an angel pierced her heart with a golden spear—a mystical moment the tableau faithfully reproduces. The sculpture's subject, St. Teresa of Avila (Spain) (1515–1582), founded the Carmelite order of nuns (1562); she recorded her mystic visions in works such as* Camino de perfección (The Road to Perfection).

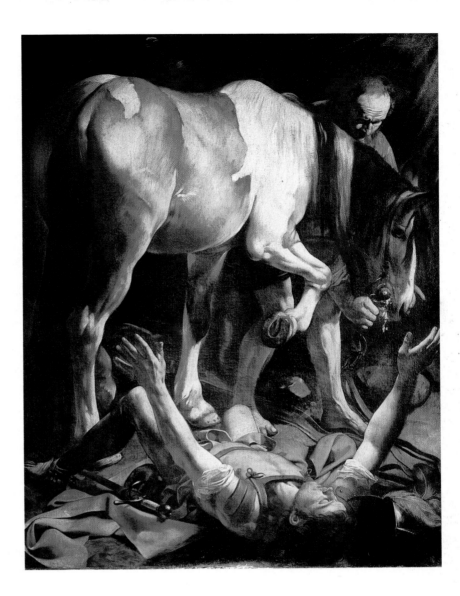

Figure 14.7 CARAVAGGIO. *The Conversion of St. Paul.* 1600–1601. Oil on canvas, approx. 7'5" × 5'8". Cerasi Chapel, Santa Maria del Popolo, Rome. *Caravaggio's paintings made monumentality an important feature of the Florid Baroque. By presenting St. Paul's figure in close-up, and giving full weight and presence to both him and the horse, the artist filled the canvas not only to capture a turning point in St. Paul's life and in the history of Christianity but also to teach the faithful a lesson about forgiveness and the power of God. Saul of Tarsus, the persecutor of Christians, will now become St. Paul, the convert who has been chosen to bring Jesus' message to the Gentiles.*

of Caravaggio's Italian disciples—known as Caravaggisti—was Artemisia Gentileschi [ahrt-uh-MEEZ-e-uh jain-teel-ESS-key] (1593–1653), his only female follower. Unlike most women artists of the early modern period, who limited their art to portraits, such as the late-sixteenth-century painter Sofonisba Anguissola (see Chapter 13), Gentileschi concentrated on biblical and mythical subjects, as many male artists did. Trained by her painter-father Orazio, himself a disciple of Caravaggio, Gentileschi adapted the flamboyant and dramatic style of Caravaggesque realism and made it her own. In almost thirty surviving paintings, she followed this style's preference for "night pictures," dark scenes whose blackness is illuminated by a single internal light source.

What distinguishes Artemisia Gentileschi's art from that of the rest of the Caravaggisti is its female assertiveness, a highly unusual quality in the Baroque period, when women artists were still making their way without guild support or access to nude modeling. Female assertiveness is expressed throughout her

works in an androgynous (having female and male characteristics) ideal, as may be seen in *Judith and Her Maidservant with the Head of Holofernes* (Figure 14.8), which depicts a scene from an apocryphal book of the Old Testament, the Book of Judith. The painting's central figure—Judith—is decidedly female (as shown in the vulnerable throat and fleshy body) and yet exhibits masculine strength (as shown in the commanding gesture accentuated by the firmly grasped sword). Judith, often treated in Italian painting and sculpture in the Renaissance and Baroque eras, is a perfect subject for Gentileschi, since the biblical story describes a woman of destiny. In the story, Judith saves the Jewish people by beheading their enemy Holofernes having first seduced him. In the painting, Holofernes' bloody head, partly visible in the basket, starkly dramatizes the point that Judith is a forthright woman who plans and acts, just as men do. Gentileschi's Judith typifies a heroic female ideal who is endowed with the traits of that fuller humanity that by tradition had been allowed only to male figures. Through such dramatic

Figure 14.8 ARTEMISIA GENTILESCHI. *Judith and Her Maidservant with the Head of Holofernes.* Ca. 1625. Oil on canvas. Detroit Institute of Arts. *Gentileschi's style in this painting is strongly indebted to the style of Caravaggio: The natural background is painted black and thus virtually eliminated, the central figures are shown in tight close-up, and the action is frozen like a single frame in a film sequence. The aesthetic impact of this cinematic method is to draw viewers into the scene and to personalize the figures. The artist's interest in the personal psychology of her characters is part of the trend toward naturalism that characterized Baroque culture in general.*

works as this, Gentileschi helped to spread the Caravaggesque style in Italy.

About the same time that Caravaggio was creating his dramatic works, a new form caught the imagination of painters in the Florid Baroque tradition—the illusionistic ceiling fresco. In these paintings, artists constructed imaginary continuations of the architectural features already present in the room, expanding up through layers of carefully foreshortened, sculptured figures and culminating in patches of sky. Looking up as if at the heavens, the viewer is overawed by the superhuman spectacle that seems to begin just overhead.

The superb example of this **illusionism** is the nave ceiling of the church of Sant' Ignazio (St. Ignatius) in Rome, painted by Andrea Pozzo [POE-tzo] (1642–1709). In this fresco, entitled *Allegory of the Missionary Work of the Jesuits,* Pozzo reveals a firm mastery of the technique of architectural perspective (Figure 14.9). The great nave ceiling is painted to appear as if the viewer were looking up through an immense open colonnade. Figures stand and cling to the encircling architectural supports, and, in the center, an expansive vista opens to reveal Ignatius, the founder of the Jesuit order, being received by an open-armed Christ. The clusters of columns on either side are labeled for the four continents—Europe, Asia, America, and Africa—symbolizing the missionary zeal of the Jesuits around the globe. Pozzo was motivated by spiritual concerns when he painted this supernatural vision. He believed that the illusion of infinite space could evoke feelings of spiritual exaltation and even religious rapture in the viewer. Illusionism, infinite space, and spectacular effects make this a masterpiece of the Florid Baroque. To see the dramatic differences between Baroque and High Renaissance ideals, compare this ceiling fresco with the ceiling of the Sistine Chapel by Michelangelo (see Figure 12.8).

Outside Italy, the principal centers of Florid Baroque painting were the studio of Velázquez in Spain and the workshop of Rubens in Flanders (present-day Belgium). Whereas Velázquez softened the Florid Baroque to his country's taste, Rubens fully

Figure 14.10 VELÁZQUEZ. *Las Meninas (The Maids of Honor).* 1656. Oil on canvas, 10'5" × 9'. Prado, Madrid. *Velázquez uses the mirror on the back wall, reflecting the Spanish king and queen, to enhance the dynamic feeling of the scene. This illusionistic device explodes the pictorial space by calling up presences within and outside the painting.*

◀ **Figure 14.9** ANDREA POZZO. *Allegory of the Missionary Work of the Jesuits.* Ca. 1621–1625. Ceiling fresco. Sant' Ignazio, Rome. *The meaning of Pozzo's fresco is based on* ignus, *Latin for "fire," a pun on the name of St. Ignatius (Loyola), the founder of the Jesuit order. In church tradition, the saint and the Jesuit mission are linked with the power of fire and light. At the fresco's center, Christ, holding the cross, emits rays of light from his wounded side, which pierce the figure of Ignatius (sitting on the cloud bank nearest Christ), who acts as a mirror; from him the light then radiates to the four corners, symbolic of the four continents. Thus, Ignatius and his missionary followers mediate Christ's saving light to the whole earth, as commanded by the scriptures.*

embraced this sensual style to become its most representative painter.

The work of Diego Velázquez [vuh-LAS-kus] (1599–1660) owes much to the tradition of Caravaggio but without the intense drama of the Italian's painting. Velázquez also used chiaroscuro, but he avoided the extreme contrasts that made Caravaggio's paintings controversial. Velázquez's greatest work is *Las Meninas,* or *The Maids of Honor* (Figure 14.10). In his role as official artist to the Spanish court, Velázquez painted this group portrait of the Infanta, or princess, surrounded by her maids of honor (one of whom is a dwarf). What makes this painting so haunting is the artful play of soft light over the various figures. In the background, a man is illuminated by the light streaming through the open door, and even more abundant sunshine falls on the princess from the window on the right.

Velázquez also plays with space and illusion in this painting. On the left side, he depicts himself, standing before a huge canvas with brush and palette in hand. The artist gazes directly at the viewer—or is he greeting the king and queen, who have just entered the room and are reflected in the mirror on the rear wall?

Figure 14.11 PETER PAUL RUBENS. *The Education of Marie de' Medici.* 1621–1625. Oil on canvas, 12'11" × 9'8". Louvre. *The Medici cycle, of which this work is a superb example, not only established the artist's European-wide reputation but also defined historical narrative—the combining of a historical event with mythological motifs—as one of the great themes of Baroque art. By 1715 the French Academy had created a ranked set of painting subjects, of which historical narrative occupied the highest level.*

The princess and two of her maids also look attentively out of the picture, but whether at the artist painting their portrait, at the royal couple, or at the viewer is left unclear. This fascination with illusion and with the effects of light and shade reveals Velázquez's links with Caravaggio and the art of the Florid Baroque.

In contrast to Velázquez's devotion to the ideal of grave beauty, the work of Peter Paul Rubens (1577–1640) is known for its ripe sensuality and for his portrayal of voluptuous female nudes. Rubens had already forged a sensuous style before he sojourned in Italy for eight years, but his encounters with Caravaggio's tradition impressed him deeply, causing him to intensify his use of explosive forms and chiaroscuro. From the Venetian painters, especially Titian, he derived his love and mastery of gorgeous color. In his mature works, he placed human figures in a shallow foreground, bathed them in golden light with dark contours, and painted their clothes and flesh in sensuous tones.

As the most sought-after artist of his day, Rubens was often given commissions by the kings of the great states, and he produced works for royalty, for the church, and for wealthy private patrons. As official painter to the French court before the ascendancy of Louis XIV, who preferred the Classical style, Rubens was commissioned to paint a cycle of works glamorizing the life of Queen Marie de' Medici, widow of Henry IV and powerful regent for her son, Louis XIII. One of the typical works from this series is *The Education of Marie de' Medici* (Figure 14.11). In this huge canvas, Rubens used Roman mythological figures to transform a mundane episode in the life of a queen into a splendid pageant of the French monarchy. All action is centered on the kneeling future queen. Minerva, the goddess of wisdom, offers instruction in reading and writing; Mercury, the god of eloquence, hovers overhead and offers his blessing; Apollo (or Orpheus, or Harmony) plays a stringed instrument, thereby inculcating a love of music; and the three Graces, attendants of the goddess Venus, encourage the perfection of feminine grace. A waterfall cascades in the background, a drapery billows above, and various images of Greco-Roman culture (a mask of tragedy and a musical instrument) are displayed in the foreground. Rubens's mastery of both spiritual and secular subjects and the turbulent drama of his works made him the finest artist of the Florid Baroque.

The Classical Baroque

Although the Baroque originated in Rome, the pronouncements of the church had little effect on the art and architecture of France. Here, the royal court was the guiding force in the artistic life of the nation. The rulers and the royal ministers provided rich commissions that helped to shape the **Classical Baroque,** giving this style a secular focus and identifying it with absolutism. A second powerful influence on the Baroque in France was the pervasiveness of the Classical values of simplicity and grave dignity. Accordingly, after Louis XIV became king, French artists and architects found the Florid Baroque alien and even offensive; their adaptation of the Baroque was more impersonal, controlled, and measured.

Architecture The palace of Versailles was the consummate architectural expression of the Classical Baroque. Versailles, a former hunting lodge, was transformed by Louis XIV into a magnificent royal residence that became the prototype of princely courts in the West. At Versailles, where all power was concentrated in the royal court, were collected the best architects, sculptors, painters, and landscape architects as well as the finest writers, composers, and musicians that France could produce. The duty of this talented assemblage was to use their gifts to

Figure 14.12 ANDRÉ LE NÔTRE, LANDSCAPE ARCHITECT, AND VARIOUS SCULPTORS. Versailles Gardens. The Pool of Latona with adjacent parterres. 1660s. Versailles, France. *This fountain, composed of four concentric marble basins, is named for its crowning statue of Latona, the mother of the sun god Apollo, who was the inspiration for Louis XIV's reign. On either side of the fountain are parterres, or flower gardens with beds and paths arranged into patterns. Beyond the fountain stretches an avenue flanked by wooded areas that culminates in the grand canal, which extends the view into infinity. The rich profusion of this scene is a hallmark of Baroque design.*

surround Louis XIV with the splendor appropriate to the Sun King.

The redesign of Versailles gave Louis XIV the most splendid palace that has ever been seen in Europe. The chief architects of this revamped palace were Louis Le Vau [luh-VO] (1612–1670) and Jules Hardouin-Mansart [ar-DWAN mahn-SAR] (1646–1708), but the guiding spirit was the Sun King himself. When finished, the palace consisted of a huge central structure with two immense wings (see Figure 14.2). The architecture is basically in the style of the Renaissance, with rounded arches, Classical columns, and porticoes inspired by Roman temples, but the overall effect is a Baroque style that is dignified yet regal.

The most striking aspect of Versailles is its monumentality: The palace is part of an elaborate complex that includes a royal chapel and various support structures, all of which are set in an elaborate park over two miles long. The park, designed by André Le Nôtre [luh-NOH-truh] (1613–1700), is studded with a rich display of fountains, reflecting pools, geometric flower beds, manicured woods, exotic trees, statues, urns, and graveled walks—a gorgeous outdoor setting for royal receptions and entertainments (Figure 14.12).

The most famous room in Versailles Palace is the Hall of Mirrors, a central chamber with a tunnel-vaulted ceiling (Figure 14.13). The grandiose design of this hallway reflects its original function as the throne room of Louis XIV. Named for its most prominent feature, this long hall is decorated with Baroque profusion, including, in addition to the mirrors, wood parquetry floors of intricate design, multicolored marbles, ceiling paintings depicting military victories and other deeds of Louis XIV, and gilded statues at the base of the paintings. In modern times, major political events have taken place in the Hall of Mirrors: The Germans proclaimed their empire from here in 1871 after having vanquished the French, and the peace treaty that ended World War I was signed here in 1919.

Painting Classical values dominated Baroque painting in France even more completely than architecture. In pursuit of ancient Roman ideals, Classical Baroque artists painted mythological subjects, stressed idealized human bodies, and cultivated a quietly elegant style. The outstanding Classical Baroque artist was Nicolas Poussin [poo-SAN] (1594–1665). Ironically, except for two disappointing years in Paris, Poussin spent his professional life in Rome, the home of the Florid Baroque. Although he was inspired by Caravaggio's use of light and dark, the style that Poussin forged was uniquely his own, a detached, almost cold approach to his subject matter and a feeling for the unity of human beings with nature.

A beautiful example of Poussin's detached style is *Et in Arcadia Ego*, a painting in which the human figures are integrated into a quiet landscape (Figure 14.14). In ancient mythology, Arcadia was a land of pastures and flocks. In Poussin's painting, four shepherds, modeled on ancient statuary and clothed in Roman dress, are portrayed standing around a tomb, evidently absorbed in a discussion provoked by the Latin words carved into the tomb: *Et in Arcadia Ego*, that is, "I too once dwelled in Arcadia." One shepherd traces the letters with his finger, spelling out the words. The magnificent stillness, the mythological subject, and the gentle melancholy evoked by this reminder of death were central to Poussin's art and evidence of his Classical spirit. Typically Baroque are the use of chiaroscuro, which makes the exposed limbs and the faces of the shepherds stand out vividly from the shadowy middle ground, and the sensual tones and rich colors.

Figure 14.13 CHARLES LEBRUN AND JULES HARDOUIN-MANSART. Hall of Mirrors, Versailles Palace. 1678–1684. Versailles, France. *The French architects Lebrun and Mansart designed this enormous hall to overlook the vast park at Versailles—the court and showplace of the French king, Louis XIV, the most powerful ruler in seventeenth-century Europe. Viewed through the floor-to-ceiling windows, which are placed along the width of the room, the majestic park outside becomes an extension of the interior space. The inside space in turn is enlarged by the tall mirrors that match the windows, echoing the exterior views.*

The Restrained Baroque

The Protestant culture of northern and western Europe created simpler works that humanized Baroque exuberance, appealed to democratic sentiments, and reflected common human experience. This style of art is called the **Restrained Baroque,** and it was founded by the painters and architects of the Netherlands and England.

Painting The Calvinist Netherlands pointed the way in the arts in Protestant Europe until 1675. The Dutch Republic was ruled by a well-to-do middle class whose wealth was based largely on their dominant role in international shipping. Led by these sober-minded burghers, as the townspeople were called, the Netherlands was briefly one of Europe's great powers. During the middle of the century, the Dutch virtually controlled northern Europe, using their military and naval might to fight England, check French ascendancy, and destroy Spanish sea power. Amsterdam became one of Europe's largest cities, and an important school of painting flourished there. In about 1675 a series of military disasters ended the Netherlands' economic expansion, and the state's fortunes declined sharply. By this time, the great days of Dutch art were over.

During the heyday of the Dutch Republic, a school of painters arose whose works defined the Restrained Baroque. Attuned to the sober values of their religion and sympathetic to the civic ideals of the republic, these artists created a secular style that mirrored the

Figure 14.13 NICOLAS POUSSIN. *Et in Arcadia Ego.* Ca. 1640. Oil on canvas, 34 × 48". Louvre. *In sacred art, painters expressed the theme of the inevitability of death in portraits of the sufferings of Jesus and the saints, and in secular art, in depictions of skeletons and death's heads, or images of human skulls. But Poussin, whose art was fired by Classical ideals and who was thus more reflective than others of his age, treated death in a much more detached way, as in this painting. Poussin's puzzled shepherds are a gentle reminder that the reality of death always comes as a surprise in the midst of everyday existence.*

Figure 14.15 REMBRANDT VAN RIJN. *The Night Watch (The Militia Company of Captain Frans Banning Cocq).* 1642. Oil on canvas, 12′2″ × 14′7″. Rijksmuseum, Amsterdam. *Because of its murky appearance, this painting acquired its nickname,* The Night Watch, *in the nineteenth century. But a cleaning of the painting's deteriorated surface showed that it was actually set in daylight. Restored to its original conception, this work now reveals Rembrandt's spectacular use of light and dark.*

pious outlook of the ruling middle class. An important development that helped to shape the course of Dutch painting was the rise of an art market. Venice had shown some tendencies in this direction in the 1500s, but in the Netherlands in the 1600s the first full-fledged art market made its debut. The impact of this market on the Dutch school was instantaneous and dramatic. Driven by a demand for home decoration, especially small works to hang on the wall, the market responded with specific subjects—still lifes, land-scapes, portraits, and genre, or "slice-of-life," scenes. Paintings were sold by dealers as wares, and buyers speculated in art objects. The market dictated success or failure; some painters pursued other careers as a hedge against financial ruin.

The greatest artist of the Dutch school and probably one of the two or three greatest painters of Western art was Rembrandt van Rijn (1606–1669). His early genius lay in his subtle and dramatic use of lighting and his

forceful expressiveness—both qualities that reflected the distant influence of Caravaggio. He also was supremely gifted in his ability to portray the range of moods and emotions he found in humanity, as ex-pressed through the ordinary people he used as models.

The culmination of Rembrandt's early style is a painting entitled *The Militia Company of Captain Frans Banning Cocq* but commonly known as *The Night Watch* (Figure 14.15). The painting was commissioned by one of Amsterdam's municipal guard troops in a typical display of Dutch civic pride. Instead of painting a conventional group portrait, however, Rembrandt cre-ated a theatrical work filled with exuberant and dra-matic gestures and highly charged chiaroscuro effects. He gave the composition added energy by depicting the guardsmen marching toward the viewer. The militia is led by Captain Cocq, the black-suited figure with the red sash and white ruff who marches with arm outstretched in the center foreground. On his left

Figure 14.16 REMBRANDT VAN RIJN. *Susanna and the Elders.* 1647. Oil on mahogany panel, 2'5" × 4'. Gemäldegalerie Staatliche Museen, Berlin. *The scene is the garden of Susanna's wealthy husband, Joacim, whose palace looms in the upper left background. As Susanna steps into the pond, the two Elders appear. The first one lunges after her, trying to disrobe her, while the other stands nearby and leers. Rembrandt's masterful command of chiaroscuro, his placement of the three figures so as to make the scene more threatening, and his deployment of light on Susanna's body heighten the dramatic incident.*

marches his attentive lieutenant, dressed in yellow, with his halberd in his hand. Behind them, the members of the surging crowd, engaged in various soldierly activities and looking in different directions with expressive faces, seem ready to burst forth from the space in which they are enclosed. Of Rembrandt's vast repertory, this painting is one of his most representative.

However, by 1647, five years after *The Night Watch,* Rembrandt's reputation was in decline, and by 1656 he was bankrupt. During these years, his paintings and etchings, which often had a religious theme, began to express his deepest emotions and convictions. He also often illustrated moral lessons, as he did in *Susanna and the Elders* (Figure 14.16).

The story is found in the Apocrypha, the collection of important writings preserved outside the Hebrew canon. Daniel, a young, learned Jew, was deported

from Israel to Babylon. There, through his storytelling ability and predictions, he became an adviser to King Nebuchadnezzar. In the Apocrypha version, he challenges two powerful men to save the life and reputation of an innocent woman, Susanna. The two men, filled with lust, spy upon her while she is bathing. They demand that she yield to them or they will swear that they had seen her with a young man. She refuses to succumb to their advances and yells for her servants. The next day, the Elders repeat their accusation against Susanna. Because of their standing in the community, the crowd believes them until Daniel appears and demands a new trial. He shows, through his cross-examining, that the two Elders had lied. They are condemned to death and Susanna is exonerated. Innocence and honor are vindicated, and false testimony given by the powerful is proven worthless when exposed to the truth and God's sense of right and wrong. Rembrandt, the devout Protestant, understood the meaning of the story and, in his painting, captured the climactic moment when the elders startle the naked Susanna who appears vulnerable and helpless.

In the later work painted in the mid-1640s, Rembrandt's style became more personal and simpler. His paintings now expressed a stronger naturalism and an inner calm, a change that paralleled the rise of the quieter Classical Baroque. This final stage of his art is most beautifully and movingly rendered in his last self-portrait (Figure 14.17). During his career, he had often painted his own likeness, coolly revealing the effects of the aging process on his face. The last self-portrait is most remarkable for the expressive eyes, which, though anguished, seem resigned to whatever happens next. Rembrandt's pursuit of truth—inspired by his own meditations—is revealed here with clarity and acceptance. Looking into this time-ravaged face, the viewer recognizes the universality of growing old and the inevitability of death.

Another great Dutch artist was Jan Vermeer [ver-MEER] (1632–1675), who specialized in domestic genre scenes. His works reveal a calm world where ordinary objects possess a timeless gravity. Color was important for establishing the domesticity and peacefulness of this closed-off world; Vermeer's favorites were yellow and blue. These serene works evoked the fabled cleanliness of Delft, the city where he lived and worked.

One of the most beautiful of his domestic scenes is *The Lacemaker* (Figure 14.18). Like most of his thirty-five extant paintings, *The Lacemaker* depicts an interior room where a single figure is encircled by everyday things. She is lit by a clear light falling on her from the side, another characteristic of Vermeer's paintings. The composition (the woman at the table and the rear wall parallel to the picture frame), the basic colors (yellow and blue), and the subject's absorption in her task typified Vermeer's works. *The Lacemaker* also has a moral message, for a woman engaged in household tasks symbolized the virtue of domesticity for Vermeer.

One of the few Dutch female artists was Judith Leyster (1609–1660), who, like her male colleagues, was a member of an artists' guild (in Haarlem) and painted for the art market. She opened her own studio, where she also instructed aspiring artists. Leyster's specialties were genre scenes, portraits, and still lifes. Her *Self-Portrait* (Figure 14.19), painted when she was about twenty, demonstrates early mastery of artistic technique. Leyster's skill at genre painting enabled her to experience modest success in her profession.

England also contributed to the creation of the Restrained Baroque, but conditions there led to a style markedly different from that of the Dutch school.

Figure 14.17 REMBRANDT VAN RIJN. *Self-Portrait.* 1669. Oil on canvas, 23¼ × 20″. Mauritshuis, The Hague. *In this last self-portrait, Rembrandt's eyes reveal the personal anguish of a man who has outlived wife, beloved mistress, and children. By this means, Rembrandt expresses one of the most popular themes of Baroque art, that of pathos—the quality that arouses feelings of pity and sorrow.*

Unlike the Netherlands, England had no art market, was dominated by an aristocracy, and, most important, had as yet no native-born painters of note. Painting in England was controlled by aristocratic patrons who preferred portraits to all other subjects and whose taste was courtly but restrained. The painter whose style suited these aristocratic demands was a Flemish artist, Anthony van Dyck [vahn DIKE] (1599–1641). A pupil of Rubens, van Dyck eventually settled in England and became court painter to Charles I.

Van Dyck's elegant style captured the courtly qualities prized by his noble patrons. He depicted his subjects' splendid costumes in all their radiant glory, using vibrant colors to reproduce their textures. He invented a repertory of poses for individual and group portraits that showed his subjects to their greatest advantage. But van Dyck did more than cater to the vanity of his titled patrons. With superb sensitivity, he portrayed their characters in their faces, showing such qualities as intelligence, self-doubt, and obstinacy. His psychological insights make his courtly portraits genuine works of art.

Van Dyck's fluent style is clearly shown in his double portrait of Lords John and Bernard Stuart, two of the dandies of the court of Charles I (Figure 14.20). This painting indicates the artist's mastery of the society portrait. The subjects' fashionable dress and haughty expressions establish their high social status. Van Dyck skillfully renders the play of light on the silk fabrics of

Figure 14.18 JAN VERMEER. *The Lacemaker.* Ca. 1664. Oil on canvas, 9⅝ × 8¼". Louvre. *Unlike Rembrandt, Vermeer was not concerned with human personality as such. Rather, his aim was to create scenes that registered his deep pleasure in bourgeois order and comfort. In* The Lacemaker, *he gives his female subject generalized features, turning her into a social type, but renders her sewing in exquisite detail, giving it a monumental presence. The painting thus becomes a visual metaphor of a virtuous household.*

Figure 14.19 JUDITH LEYSTER. *Self-Portrait.* Ca. 1630. Oil on canvas, 29 × 25½". National Gallery of Art, Washington, D.C. Gift of Mr. and Mrs. Robert Wood Bliss. Photo by Lorene Emerson. (1949.6.1). *Leyster's Self-Portrait shows her command of the painting tradition in which she was trained. The casual pose—a model turned in a chair with an arm resting on its back—was pioneered by the Dutch artist Franz Hals (see Figure 15.7), who may have been Leyster's teacher in Haarlem. Her smiling, open mouth represents a "speaking portrait," a frequent pose in this period, in which the subject seems to be wanting to make a statement. The merrymaking fiddler in the easel painting within the portrait was a popular genre subject among the Dutch art-buying public.*

Figure 14.20 ANTHONY VAN DYCK. *Lords John and Bernard Stuart.* Ca. 1639. Oil on canvas, 7'9⅓" × 4'9½". National Gallery, London. *Van Dyck has depicted these dandies in the carefully disheveled style preferred by the era's aristocrats. Their doublets (jackets) are of plain, muted colors and slashed on the chest and sleeves to allow a contrasting color to show. The deliberately casual look is especially prominent in the unbuttoned doublet worn by Lord John (left) and the cloak thrown over the shoulder of Lord Bernard (right). Both men wear the soft leather boots, partly rolled down the legs, that were now replacing the shoes of an earlier time.*

their clothing. He creates an interesting design by placing their bodies opposite one another, but this positioning also offers psychological insight into their characters as the mirrorlike pose suggests that they are vain young men. Van Dyck's deftness at creating elegant likenesses set the standard for English portraiture and influenced French artists well into the eighteenth century.

Architecture The architecture of the Restrained Baroque drew strongly on the Classical tradition. One of the most influential English architects of this period was Sir Christopher Wren (1632–1723), whose Baroque style had two sources. From the Classical Baroque of Versailles came his love of rich ornamentation, and from Bramante's High Renaissance style came his devotion to pure Classical forms, such as the dome and the Classical orders. Following those traditions, Wren created his own unique style, with spacious interiors and elaborately decorated facades.

Although Wren created many brilliant secular works, he is best known for his churches, which he built in the aftermath of the Great Fire of London in 1666. His masterpiece is St. Paul's cathedral in London (Figure 14.21). Intended as a Protestant rival to St. Peter's in Rome, St. Paul's has a longitudinal floor plan similar to St. Peter's but with Gothic features in the interior, including transept and choir and a dome reminiscent of Bramante's Tempietto (see Figure 12.21). The church has many Classical elements, such as the pairs of columns on two levels, the symmetrical towers and

Figure 14.21 CHRISTOPHER WREN. St. Paul's Cathedral. 1675–1710. London. *Wren was a true child of the Baroque age. An astronomy professor at Oxford University, he made discoveries that brought him to the attention of the age's greatest scientist, Isaac Newton. When opportunity called and Wren was given the royal commission to rebuild the churches of London, he approached this task with the same passionate love of geometry that had motivated his scientific researches. St. Paul's design united his sense of beauty with his mathematical bent.*

decorations, and the elaborate pediment. At the same time, its Baroque nature is revealed in the ornate facade punctuated by niches, the robust twin steeples with their shadowy recesses and staggered columns, and the dramatic play of light across the face of the building. The most outstanding feature of St. Paul's is the magnificent dome, inspired by the one designed by Michelangelo for St. Peter's (see Figure 12.22), with its encircling colonnade. This elegant dome still dominates central London's skyline, a splendid reminder of Baroque glory.

Literature

The Council of Trent's decrees, which had such a powerful impact on artists and architects, were hardly felt by seventeenth-century writers. Nevertheless, a style of literary expression arose that is called Baroque and that became international in scope. The most enduring literary legacy of this period is drama. Baroque audiences delighted in works that blended different forms, and drama mixed literature, costume design, set painting, and theatrical spectacle. Tragedy, based on Roman models, was the supreme achievement of the Baroque stage, but comedies of all types, including satires, farces, and sexual comedies, were also important. After centuries of neglect, tragedy and comedy had been brilliantly revived in Elizabethan England, and their appearance in France was evidence of the continuing growth of secular consciousness. Another ancient literary genre that gained wide favor was the epic, a reflection of the love of power typical of the age. Finally, Baroque literature began to acknowledge the world outside Europe, as may be seen in the rise of writings with a non-Western dimension. These non-Western aspects included settings (for example, Mexico in the poetry of the Mexican nun Sor Juana Inés de la Cruz [1648–1695]), characters (for example, the Aztec ruler Montezuma, the hero of the play *The Indian Emperor* [1665], by John Dryden [1631–1700]), and themes (especially the comparison of Western and non-Western customs in travel literature, as in *A New Voyage Round the World* [1697], by William Dampier [1652–1715], and *Travels in Persia* [1686], by Jean Chardin [1643–1713]).

Despite the variety of their works, the Baroque writers had common characteristics, including a love of ornate language and a fascination with characterization, either of individuals or of types. Baroque authors often dealt with emotional extremes, such as gross sensuality versus pangs of conscience. With such emotionally charged themes, Baroque writers could and did employ dramatic rhetoric, slipping occasionally into empty bombast.

Baroque Literature in France Drama was France's greatest contribution to the literature of the Baroque period. Secular drama revived under the patronage of Louis XIII in the 1630s and reached a climax during Louis XIV's reign. Strict control was exercised over the plays staged at the royal court, although comic playwrights were given more freedom, as long as they did not offend common decency or good taste.

The tragic playwrights were expected to obey the rules of literary composition identified by the French Academy and based on the theories of Aristotle (see Chapter 3). The ideal play must observe the unities of time, place, and action—that is, it must take place during a twenty-four-hour time span, have no scene changes, and have a single uncomplicated plot. Furthermore, the plays were supposed to use formal language and to focus on universal problems as reflected in dilemmas experienced by highborn men and women. Because of the playwrights' strict adherence to these rules, it is sometimes claimed that the dramas of this period are expressive of a Classical style. But the French preference for order, gravity, and severity was evidence of a Baroque sensibility—just as was the case in the French style of Baroque painting and architecture.

The two great French tragedians of the Baroque period are Pierre Corneille [kor-NAY] (1606–1684) and Jean Racine [ra-SEEN] (1639–1699). Corneille wrote tragedies in verse based on Spanish legends and Roman themes. Drawing on the Hellenistic philosophy of Stoicism, his dramas stressed the importance of duty, patriotism, and loyalty—ideals that appealed to his courtly audience. His finest work is *Le Cid*, based on a legendary figure of Spanish history and concerned with the hero's choice between personal feelings and honor.

In Racine, drama found a voice whose refined language and penetrating psychological insight have never been equaled in the French theater. Preoccupied with the moral struggle between the will and the emotions, Racine created intensely human characters in classically constructed plays. A subject that intrigued Racine was the doomed woman who was swept to her destruction by obsessive sexual passion. This Baroque theme was most perfectly expressed in his masterpiece, *Phèdre* (*Phaedra*), his version of the Greek tale of incestuous love first dramatized by Euripides in the fifth century B.C. Where Euripides makes fate a central reason for the heroine's, Phèdre's, downfall, Racine portrays the unfortunate woman as a victim of her passion for her stepson. Even though he explored other types of love in his plays, such as mother love and even political passion, it was in his study of sex as a powerful motive for action that Racine was most original.

The Baroque period in French drama also produced one of the comic geniuses of the Western theatre, Jean Baptiste Poquelin, better known as Molière [mole-YAIR] (1622–1673). Molière analyzed the foibles of French life in twelve penetrating satirical comedies that had the lasting impact of tragedy. He peopled his plays with social types—the idler, the miser, the pedant, the seducer, the hypochondriac, the medical quack, the would-be gentleman, the pretentiously cultured lady—exposing the follies of the entire society. To create his comedic effects, Molière used not only topical humor and social satire but all the trappings of farce, including pratfalls, mistaken identities, sight gags, puns, and slapstick.

Molière was appointed official entertainer to Louis XIV in 1658; even so, he made many enemies among those who felt they were the butt of his jokes. When he died, for example, the French clergy refused to give him an official burial because they believed some of his plays to be attacks on the church. The testament to Molière's enduring brilliance is that many of his comedies are still performed today, including *Tartuffe, The Miser, The Would-Be Gentleman,* and *The Misanthrope,* and they are still enormously entertaining.

Baroque Literature in England   The outstanding contribution in English to the literature of the Baroque period was provided by John Milton (1608–1674), a stern Puritan who held high office in Cromwell's Commonwealth. The deeply learned Milton had a grand moral vision that led him to see the universe as locked in a struggle between the forces of darkness and the forces of light. Only an epic was capable of expressing such a monumental conception.

His supreme literary accomplishment was to Christianize the epic in his long poem *Paradise Lost.* Inspired by Homer's and Vergil's ancient works, but also intended as a Protestant response to Dante's *Divine Comedy,* Milton's poem became an immediate classic. His grandiose themes in *Paradise Lost* were the rebellion of the angels led by Lucifer, the fall of Adam and Eve in the Garden of Eden, and Christ's redemption of humanity.

An astonishing aspect of *Paradise Lost* is Milton's portrait of Lucifer, which some readers have seen as a Baroque glamorization of evil. Lucifer is characterized as a creature of titanic ambition and deceitful charm. Despite his powerful presence, however, this epic story has moral balance. At the end, Adam, the author of original sin, is saved instead of being condemned to Hell. Adam's redemption occurs when he accepts Jesus as Lord. Adam's choice reflected Milton's belief in free will and the necessity of taking responsibility for one's actions.

In addition to its grand theme, *Paradise Lost* is Baroque in other ways. The mixing of Christian legend and ancient epic, for example, is typical of Baroque taste. Milton's convoluted style is Baroque with its occasionally odd word order, Latinisms, and complex metaphors. Most of all, Milton's epic is Baroque in its lofty tone and exaggerated rhetoric—literary equivalents, perhaps, of Rubens or Rembrandt.

A secondary achievement of the literary Baroque in England was that literature began to reflect the West's overseas expansion, as in the publishing of travel books, memoirs, and letters describing real and fictional contacts with peoples and lands around the globe. Part of a European-wide trend, the growth of English literature with a non-European dimension expressed the Baroque theme of pushing against the boundaries of life and art. A pioneering work on this Baroque theme was the short prose story *Oroonoko* (1688) by Aphra Behn (1640–1689), an English writer who exploited her firsthand experiences as a resident of Surinam (modern Suriname) to provide a vivid, exotic setting. Situated in South America and told with a blend of realism and romance, *Oroonoko* condemns the culture of slavery through the story of the doomed love affair between a black slave-prince and a slave woman. The author portrays the black hero as untutored in Western ways yet polished and educated on his own terms, and, above all, superior to the natural depravity of the European characters. This is an early version of the myth of the noble savage, the cultural archetype that reached its climax in the Romantic era (see Chapter 17). England's first professional woman writer, Behn also wrote about twenty comedies for the stage and a poem collection, but *Oroonoko* is her chief claim to renown.

Music

Unlike the Renaissance, when a single musical sound prevailed (see Chapter 12), the Baroque had no single musical ideal. Nonetheless, four trends during the Baroque period give its music distinctive qualities. First, the development of major and minor tonality, which had been prefigured in Josquin des Prez's music in the early 1500s, was a central feature of the works of this time, making it the first stage in the rise of modern music. Second, the mixing of genres, which has been noted in literature and the arts, also occurred in Baroque music. Third, the expressiveness that had entered music in the late 1500s now became even more exaggerated, being used to stress meanings and emotions in the musical texts that otherwise might not have been heard. And last, this was an age of **virtuosos,** master musicians, especially singers, who performed with great technical skill and vivid personal style, and of a growing variety of musical instruments

Figure 14.22   JAN BRUEGEL. *Hearing.* Ca. 1620. Oil on canvas, approx. 2′3″ × 3′6″. Prado, Madrid. *One of a series of allegorical paintings representing the five senses, this work by Jan Bruegel depicts the sense of hearing. Set in a Renaissance interior framed by three rounded arches, it shows a variety of sources that make sounds pleasing to the human ear. Most prominent are the musical instruments, which collectively constitute an anthology of the instruments used in Baroque music.*

(Figure 14.22). The musical form that drew these trends together was **opera,** making it the quintessential symbol of the age.

Opera originated in Italy in the late sixteenth century among a group of Florentine musicians and poets with aristocratic ties. The first great composer of opera was Claudio Monteverdi [mon-teh-VAIR-dee] (1567–1643), whose earliest opera, *Orfeo* (1607), was based on the legend of the ancient Greek poet-musician Orpheus. *Orfeo* united drama, dance, elaborate stage mechanisms, and painted scenery with music. Monteverdi wrote melodic arias, or songs, for the individual singers, and he increased the opera's dramatic appeal by concluding each of its five acts with a powerful chorus. His setting truly mirrored the text, using musical phrases to serve as aural symbols and thus to enhance the unfolding of events.

By the 1630s, opera began to shed its aristocratic origins and become a popular entertainment. This change did not affect opera's focus on ancient myths and histories about noble men and women, nor did it halt the trend to brilliant singing called *bel canto*, literally

"beautiful song." However, to appeal to a wider audience, operatic composers added elements from Italy's popular comic theater, such as farcical scenes and stock characters, notably humorous servants. By the end of this age, the operatic form was stylized into a recipe, including improbable plots, inadequate motivations for the characters, and magical transformations—signs of its Baroque nature.

Opera became immensely popular in Europe, especially in Italy, where it remains so today. By 1750 opera houses had been built in many major cities; Venice led the way with more than a dozen establishments. The rise of opera in Italy during the 1600s, like the founding of a commercial theater in London in the 1500s, presaged the downfall of the aristocratic patronage system and the emergence of entertainments with mass appeal.

The winding down of the Thirty Years' War allowed Italian opera to be exported to the rest of Europe. Only in France were composers able to defy the overpowering Italian influence and create an independent type of opera. This development was made possible by the grandeur of Louis XIV's court and by French taste, which was more restrained than the opulent Italian. Nevertheless, French opera was founded by an Italian, Jean-Baptiste Lully [loo-LEE] (1632–1687), who later became a French citizen and Louis's court composer. Under Lully's direction, French opera developed its identifying features: dignified music, the full use of choruses, the inclusion of a ballet, and, most important, a French text. Lully's patron, the Sun King, sometimes performed in the opera's ballet sequences himself, dancing side by side with the composer. Lully's works, which dominated French music until 1750, ensured a powerful role for French music in the Western tradition.

Baroque music reached its climax after 1715. Three composers were responsible for this development: in Protestant northern Europe, the Germans Bach and Handel, and in Roman Catholic Italy, Vivaldi.

The greatest of these late Baroque masters was Johann Sebastian Bach (1685–1750). A devout Lutheran who worked for German courts and municipalities far from the major cities, Bach created a body of sacred music that transcends all religious creeds and nationalities. Employing all the Baroque musical genres, his works are distinguished by their inventiveness and complete mastery of major and minor tonality. His most memorable achievements are the Passions, the musical settings of the liturgy to be performed on Good Friday—the most tragic day in the Christian calendar. Composed in about 1727, the *St. Matthew Passion* expresses the collective grief of the Christian community for the death of Jesus. Bach used a German text with arias and choruses, making the music bring out all the emotional implications of the words. Thus, the *St. Matthew Passion* is more dramatic than most operas and a sublime religious experience in itself.

Although Bach's religious music is his greatest legacy, he also left a body of secular music, including orchestral works and works for various instrumental groups. A musician's musician, Bach composed *The Well-Tempered Clavier* as an ordered set of studies in all the major and minor keys. The forty-eight preludes and fugues in this work set a heroic challenge for keyboard performers and are still an essential part of the piano repertoire today. (A **clavier** is an early keyboard instrument; a **fugue** is a composition in which a theme is introduced by one instrument and then repeated by each successively entering instrument until a complicated interweaving of themes, variations, imitations, and echoes results.) This work contributed to the standardization of the pitches of the notes of the musical scale and of the tuning of keyboard instruments.

Of Bach's secular works, the most popular today are probably the six *Brandenburg Concertos* (written for the duke of Brandenburg), whose tunefulness and rhythmic variety the composer rarely surpassed. The concertos were composed for the type of ensemble found in the German princely courts of the time—a group of string players of average ability along with a few woodwind and brass instruments, perhaps a total of twenty to twenty-five musicians. Bach's dominant idea in these concertos was to demonstrate the interplay between individual soloists and the larger group. As in most of his work, the composer wove different melodic lines and different harmonies together into elaborate, complex structures of tremendous variety, power, and scope.

The other great late Baroque German master, George Frideric Handel (1685–1759), who was renowned for his Italian-style operas. More cosmopolitan than Bach, Handel eventually settled in London, where he composed thirty-six operatic works. His operas succeeded in their day because of the brilliant way in which the music allows the singers to show their virtuosity, but they are generally not to the taste of modern audiences and have not found a place in the standard operatic repertory. In contrast, his mastery of sacred music, particularly the **oratorio**—an opera-like form but without any stage action—which he perfected, has made his name immortal. Of the oratorios, *Messiah*, based on biblical texts and sung in English, holds first place. Its popularity stems from its Baroque qualities: the emotionally stirring choruses and the delightful embellishments the soloists are permitted in their arias. As a result, *Messiah* is probably the best-known work of sacred music in the English-speaking world.

Antonio Lucio Vivaldi (1678–1741), the late Baroque Italian composer and violinist, set a new standard for instrumental music. Unlike Bach and Handel, who worked almost exclusively within secular settings, Vivaldi supported himself through church patronage, serving as both a priest (briefly) and a musician and composer (mainly) at a church orphanage for females in Venice. He also was a freelance composer, producing works for patrons and customers across Europe. Employing diverse musical genres, he wrote nearly fifty operas, of which about sixteen survive complete; about forty cantatas; fifty sacred vocal works; ninety **sonatas** (a sonata is a work for a small group of instruments); and nearly five hundred **concertos** (a concerto is a piece for solo instrument and orchestra), of which nearly half were written for solo violin. Vivaldi's music is little performed today except for the concertos, whose innovations and style raise him to the first rank of composers. His innovations typically include a three-movement form, arranged in a fast-slow-fast pattern, and, most important, the use of a **refrain** (in Italian, *ritornello*), that is, a recurring musical phrase, in combination with brief passages performed by a solo instrument, which together provide a unifying thread to the work. Vivaldi's concerto form influenced the late Baroque works of Bach and helped to set the standard for Classical music in general (see Chapter 16).

The best known of Vivaldi's concertos are those collectively titled *The Four Seasons* (1725), a set of four violin concertos, each named after a season of the year, beginning with spring. Using both major and minor tonality, Vivaldi's music passionately evokes a feeling of each passing season. This work established the tradition of **program music,** or music that represents a nonmusical image, idea, or story without the use of words. Later, Beethoven made program music a central feature of his music (see Chapter 17).

The Legacy of the Baroque Age

The Baroque period left a potent legacy to the modern world in politics, economics, religion, and the arts. The system of great states governed by a balance of power dominated European affairs until 1945. From the Baroque period date the roles of France and England as Europe's trendsetters, both politically and culturally. The concept and practice of "world war" also dates from this period. The economic system known as mercantilism originated during the Baroque period and prevailed in Europe into the nineteenth century. The religious orientation of the European states became well established in the seventeenth century, along with the division of the vast majority of Westerners into Protestant and Catholic camps. In the Netherlands, artists operated in an open market, painting works for wealthy citizens, thus launching the trend toward today's commercial art world. The Baroque idea of spectacle is a thread that runs throughout the culture of this period and helps to explain not only the propagandistic aspects of politics and religion but also the theatrical elements in the arts and entertainment. Culturally, the Baroque is still with us, even though much about this style seems excessive to modern taste. Although Baroque operas are not often performed, the idea of opera originated in this age of spectacle. Other Baroque musical works, notably the majestic oratorios of Handel and the powerful compositions of Bach for church and court, are part of the regular concert repertoire in the West today. Some of the most admired and enduring artworks in Western history were created during this time, including Bernini's *Ecstasy of St. Teresa* and the paintings of Rembrandt. Many cities of Europe are still showcases of Baroque splendor. The church of St. Peter's in Rome, St. Paul's cathedral in London, and the palace and gardens at Versailles are but three of the living monuments of this period, reminding us of the grand religious and political ideals of a very different age.

KEY CULTURAL TERMS

Baroque	*bel canto*
Florid Baroque style	clavier
baldacchino	fugue
illusionism	oratorio
Classical Baroque style	sonata
Restrained Baroque style	concerto
virtuoso	refrain
opera	program music

SUGGESTIONS FOR FURTHER READING

Primary Sources

BEHN, A. *Oroonoko and Other Stories.* Edited and introduced by M. Duffy. London: Methuen, 1985. An edition of Behn's stories, with a useful introduction; these short works prepared the way for the novel genre, born after 1700. *Oroonoko* was first published in 1678.

CORNEILLE, P. *The Cid.* Translated by V. J. Cheng. Newark: University of Delaware Press, 1987. A version of Corneille's drama, recounting the story of a hero torn between honor and love; imitates the poetic form of the original, first staged in 1636.

MILTON, J. *Paradise Lost.* New York: Norton, 1975. Milton's Baroque epic about rebellion—Lucifer's revolt in heaven and Adam and Eve's defiance on earth; Scott Elledge provides a useful introduction and notes to the text, which was first published in 1667.

MOLIÈRE (POQUELIN, J. B.). *The Misanthrope.* Translated by R. Wilbur. London: Methuen, 1967. A good translation by a leading American poet. Useful English versions by various translators of Molière's other frequently performed comedies are also available, including *The Miser* (New York: Applause Theatre Book Publishers, 1987), *Tartuffe* (London: Faber and Faber, 1984), and *The Bourgeois Gentleman (The Would-Be Gentleman)* (New York: Applause Theatre Book Publishers, 1987).

RACINE, J. B. *Phaedra* [*Phèdre*]. Translated by R. Wilbur. New York: Harcourt Brace Jovanovich, 1986. A solid translation of this French tragic drama.

SOR JUANA INÉS DE LA CRUZ. *Poems, Protest, and a Dream.* Translated by M. S. Peden. New York: Penguin, 1997. A selection of Sor Juana's writings, including ironic, courtly poems and the first defense by a New World author of the right of women to be educated, *La Respuesta de la poetisa a la muy ilustre Sor Filotea de la Cruz (Response to the Most Illustrious Poetess Sor Filotea de la Cruz)*, first published in 1691. With a helpful introduction by I. Stavans.

SUGGESTIONS FOR LISTENING

BACH, JOHANN SEBASTIAN (1685–1750). The greatest composer of the Baroque era, Bach is best known for his sacred music, which has tremendous emotional power. His church music for voices includes more than two hundred cantatas, or musical settings of biblical and choral texts, such as *Jesu der du meine Seele (Jesus, Thou Hast My Soul)*, *Wachet Auf (Sleepers Awake)*, and *O Haupt voll Blut und Wunden (O Sacred Head Now Wounded)*; six motets, such as *Jesu meine Freude (Jesus, My Joy)*; two Passions, or musical settings of biblical passages and commentaries on the Easter season (the *St. Matthew Passion* and the *St. John Passion*); and a Mass, the *Mass in B Minor.* He also composed instrumental church music, notably about 170 organ chorales required by the liturgy for the church year. Besides sacred music, Bach wrote secular music, including the "Little" *Fugue in G Minor*, the *Brandenburg Concertos*, and *The Well-Tempered Clavier* (1722; 1740), a collection of works for keyboard that consisted of one prelude and fugue for each of the twelve major and minor keys.

HANDEL, GEORGE FRIDERIC (1685–1759). The German-born Handel, who lived and worked mainly in England, made eighteenth-century England a center of Baroque music. Of the thirty-six Italian-style operas that he composed and produced in London, three of the best known are *Rinaldo* (1711), *Giulio Cesare* (1724), and *Serse* (1738). His oratorios—including *Messiah*—were performed in public theaters rather than churches and especially appealed to the rising middle classes. Handel also produced a body of instrumental music, of which the most significant are the two suites known as the *Fireworks Music* (1749) and the *Water Music* (about 1717) and six concertos for woodwinds and strings.

LULLY, JEAN-BAPTISTE (1632–1687). Lully's eleven operas helped to define the operatic genre in France, giving it an opening overture and a ballet movement. Of his operas, the best known are probably *Theseus* (1675) and *Amadis* (1684). Especially appealing to modern ears are the massed choruses and rhythmic dances of his operas.

MONTEVERDI, CLAUDIO (1567–1643). A prodigious composer of madrigals and sacred music, Monteverdi is best remembered as a pioneer of opera. He composed his operas in a highly expressive style that matched the spirit of the music to the meaning of words in the text, as in *Orfeo* (1607) and *The Coronation of Poppea* (1642).

VIVALDI, ANTONIO LUCIO (1678–1741). Vivaldi's concertos—scored for a solo instrument (including violin, bassoon, cello, oboe, or flute) and orchestra—perfected the form for later composers. Rhythmical and full of feeling, these works often were given picturesque or evocative titles, as in *The Four Seasons* (1725), a cycle of four violin concertos, named for the seasons of the year. One of the most popular works of serious music, *The Four Seasons* was part of a larger suite of twelve, known as *The Trial Between Harmony and Invention.*

CHAPTER *14* HIGHLIGHTS

The Baroque Age: Glamour and Grandiosity, 1600–1715

■ *Literature & Philosophy* ■ *Art & Architecture* ■ *Music & Dance*

 Readings in the Western Humanities   *CD, The Western Humanities*

AFRICA

HISTORY

North Africa Part of Ottoman Empire. *Tunisia.* Ruled by beys (provincial governors) (after 1612).
Northeast Africa *Ethiopia.* Unrest after Catholic missionaries arrived. Europeans expelled (1648). Beset by Muslim states.
East Africa *Zambezi Valley.* Butwa expelled Portuguese (about 1700). Monomotapa collapsed (1666). *Zimbabwe.* Absorbed by Rozvi Empire (1693).
West Africa Small traditional kingdoms (e.g., Mossi and Ashanti) competed for trade routes; repulsed Islamic and European inroads. *Niger Bend.* Timbuktu, Gao, and Jennejero escaped Moroccan control (1618). *Yoruba culture.* Oyo Empire at height (after 1650). Benin prospered. *Dahomey Kingdom.* Founded (about 1645).
South Africa Dutch (Boers) founded coastal colony (1652).

ART & MUSIC

East Africa *Zambezi Valley.* Kingdom of Butwa: royal control of weaving, ivory and stone carvings.
West Africa *Yoruba culture.* Benin bronze plaques and figures, some with Western influences; artistic tradition suddenly ended (1700).

European Soldier with Firearm. Sixteenth or seventeenth century. Bronze, ht. 25". Benin. Nigerian Museum, Lagos.

ARCHITECTURE

East Africa *Zambezi Valley.* Kingdom of Butwa: stone palaces and fortresses.

RELIGION, PHILOSOPHY, LITERATURE

Northeast Africa *Ethiopia.* Coptic Church only unifying element in country (after 1667).
West Africa *Dahomey.* Ritual sacrifice of slaves on the death of a king.

AMERICAS

HISTORY

Latin America *Caribbean.* French, English, and Dutch challenged Spanish rule. *Mexico and Central America.* Ruled by Spanish viceroy from Mexico City; native peoples continued to lose land to Spanish; slave trade grew. *South America.* Ruled by Spanish viceroy from Lima; Europeans settled along the coasts.
Brazil Slave-based economy flourished.
Native North America *Eastern woodlands.* English built Jamestown on Powhatan land (1607). French built Québec on site of old Iroquois village (1608). English built Plymouth on Wampanoag land (1620). Dutch obtained Manhattan Island from Shinnecocks (1626). Iroquois Wars between Dutch-allied tribes and French-allied tribes (1643–1701). *Southwest.* After Spanish introduced sheep, Navajo became sheepherding culture.

ART & MUSIC

Latin America Catholic European styles prevailed, influenced by native and regional tastes. *Mexico.* Native sculptors (until the 1700s) ignored church rulings against Renaissance nudity and other "pagan" practices, so sculpture strongly reflected native points of view.
Native North America *Eastern woodlands.* European floral designs introduced into beadwork by students of Catholic nuns in Canada (ca. 1640).

ARCHITECTURE

Latin America Late Renaissance, Plateresque, and Baroque styles imported from Spain and Portugal; influenced by geography, local materials, and indigenous and (especially in Brazil) African tastes. Churches built over native cult sites. *Mexico.* Church of Santa Clara (1633). Cathedral of Puebla (dedicated 1649). *Peru.* Cuzco cathedral (facade carved 1651–54) and Jesuit church (1651–68) blended European Baroque style with native elements, such as Indian faces, native birds, and ears of corn.

Facade of Jesuit church. Detail. 1698. Arequipa, Peru.

RELIGION, PHILOSOPHY, LITERATURE

Latin America Catholic public ceremonies, such as processions, pilgrimages, and mystery plays introduced. *Mexico.* Sister (Sor) Juana Inés de la Cruz, nun and poet, supported education for women.
Native North America *Eastern woodlands.* Jesuit missionaries from France (1612). *Southwest.* Spanish soldiers raided kivas and burned kachina masks in attempt to eradicate Pueblo religion (1661); rebellion led by Pueblo religious leaders drove Spanish out of New Mexico for 12 years (1680).

ASIA

China

Ming Dynasty, ended 1644. Decadence and decline. Tea trade with Europe began. *Ch'ing Dynasty, began 1644.* Country unified a second time under foreign rulers (Manchus from Manchuria). Kept the Confucian classics central to governmental service. Emperor K'ang-hsi extended empire, adding Taiwan (1683); raised culture to new heights.

India

Mogul Empire. Religious toleration and arts support ended with overthrow (1659) of Shāh Jahān by his son Aurangzeb, who imposed Muslim orthodoxy, ended art patronage, and expanded the empire. Civil war with Sikhs and Maratha Hindus. Sikhs became a military theocracy.

BICHITR. Shāh Jahān. Ca. 1632. Paint on paper. India. Victoria and Albert Museum, London.

Japan

Edo period, began 1603. Tokugawa shōgunate with capital Edo (modern Tokyo); founded by Tokugawa Ieyasu (1603). Centralized rule; rapid urbanization; a merchant aristocracy challenged the feudal order; foreigners expelled and country closed to world; dramatic rise in literacy; 250-year period of peace began.

Ming Dynasty. Colorful porcelains, burial ware, enamel on metalwork *(cloisonné),* and rich silks and rugs. *Ch'ing Dynasty.* Two painting schools: court artists, including the Four Wangs school (imitated historic styles, yet borrowed from Western realism); and "individualists" (commercial artists who freed themselves from traditional art). K'ang-hsi founded imperial ceramic factories; porcelains decorated with polychrome landscapes.

Mogul Empire. Miniature paintings, made in the imperial workshop (to 1659) and at various Hindu courts, such as Rajasthan; often depicted courtiers or the ruler.

Edo period. Rinpa school artists, such as Tawaraya Sōtatsu and Ōgata Kōrin. Calligraphy, lacquered boxes, and silk garments. Hishikawa Moronobu pioneered black-and-white *ukiyo-e* woodblock prints, depicting lively scenes of Edo life.

View of Shōin. Katsura Imperial Villa. 1620–24. Kyōto.

Ch'ing Dynasty. Rebuilding of structures in Forbidden City, Beijing, such as the Pao-ho-tien, a banquet hall built in official Chinese style but painted with bright colors reflecting Manchu taste.

Pao-ho-tien. Ca. 1700. Beijing. Wood with tile roof.

Mogul Empire. The Golden Age of Indian Muslim architecture: the Tāj Mahal, the Jami Masjid mosque, the Red Fort towns, the Peacock Throne, the Great Mosque at Lahore, and the Golden Temple of the Sikhs. The Tāj Mahal, perhaps the most famous building in India, was constructed by Shāh Jahān as a domed tomb for his favorite wife, Mumtāz Mahal ("Chosen One of the Palace").

Tāj Mahal. 1632–1654. White marble. Agra, India.

Edo period. Edo Castle; Nikko Pagoda; urban entertainment districts for merchants. *Sukiya* style, inspired by wooden rustic teahouses; used for lower-class housing. The Shōin style, developed in the Momoyama period for the samurai, influenced the simple style of the Katsura imperial villa complex (residences, gardens, and teahouse), built as a retreat for the royal family.

Ch'ing Dynasty. K'ang-hsi sponsored scholarship (a history of the Ming Dynasty; dictionaries and encyclopedias); welcomed Jesuits at court.

Mogul period. Adi Granth (1604), the Sikhs' sacred scriptures.

Edo period. Saikaku Ihara's *Life of an Amorous Man,* a classic novel; Matsuo Bashō revitalized *haiku* verse with the spirit of Zen Buddhism. Kabuki theater (catering to the merchant class) began; performed solely by male actors (by 1700). Massacre of Christians (about 37,000) (1637).

15 THE BAROQUE AGE II
Revolutions in Scientific and Political Thought
1600–1715

The Baroque age was more than a time of political upheaval and artistic spectacle. It was also the period when the Scientific Revolution took place. As centuries-old beliefs were challenged by discoveries in astronomy and physics, a whole new way of viewing the universe emerged. In England, a revolution in political philosophy was also occurring, leading to the notion that states ought to be governed by the people rather than by paternalistic rulers. These momentous changes added to the pervasive restlessness of the times.

The term *Scientific Revolution* applies chiefly to astronomy and physics, although major advances were also made in medical science, and changes occurred in chemistry, biology, and embryology. In addition, the Scientific Revolution gave rise to a type of literature that considered the impact of the new science on secular and religious thought. A few scholars composed literary works that redefined the place of human beings in the cosmos and the purpose of human life. The chief result was to bring to a climax the separation of philosophy from theology, a gap that had been widening since the 1300s (see Chapter 10). From this point, philosophy begins to address secular concerns, and theology is relegated to a minor cultural role.

The climax of this revolutionary age occurred between 1685 and 1715, a period that witnessed what one twentieth-century historian called "the crisis of the European conscience." For a handful of scholars, the balance tipped from traditional ideas to modern views. These early modern scientists and philosophers countered faith with reason, dogma with skepticism, and divine intervention with natural law. They made mathematics their guiding

◀ Detail MARIA SIBYLLA MER-IAN. *Insect Metamorphoses in Surinam.* 1705. Hand-colored engraving. (Reprinted in F. Schnack, *Das Kleine Buch der Tropenwander.* Leipzig: Insel-Verlag, 1935. Plate 11. 4¾ × 7".)

Timeline 15.1   REVOLUTIONS IN SCIENTIFIC AND POLITICAL THOUGHT

1543	1600	1700	1715

The Scientific Revolution and Early Modern Political Philosophy

1543	1570–1600	1609	1625	1637	1651	1687	1690
Copernicus's *Revolutions of the Heavenly Bodies*	Brahe's observations	Kepler's *On the Motion of Mars*	Grotius's *The Law of War and Peace*	Descartes's *Discourse on Method*	Hobbes's *Leviathan*	Newton's *Mathematical Principles*	Locke's *Two Treatises of Government* and *An Essay Concerning Human Understanding*
		1610 Galileo sights four moons of Jupiter	**1632** Galileo's *Dialogues on the Two Chief Systems of the World*				

star in the search for truth, accepting as true those things that could be proven mathematically and rejecting as untrue those that could not. Their new philosophy eventually concluded that the universe was like a great clock that operated according to universal laws. Although we today tend to discount this clockwork image, we still owe a debt to these thinkers, who set Western culture on its present course and brought modernity into being (Timeline 15.1).

THEORIES OF THE UNIVERSE BEFORE THE SCIENTIFIC REVOLUTION

The Scientific Revolution was both an outgrowth and a rejection of the Aristotelian cosmology that had held Western thinkers in thrall for two thousand years. The Aristotelian system, named for the fourth-century B.C. philosopher, was developed by the ancient Greeks and transmitted to the West through Roman and Islamic culture and the medieval scholastic tradition. The fundamental principle of this cosmology is **geocentrism,** the theory that the universe is earth-centered. Around the earth revolved the five known planets (Mercury, Venus, Mars, Jupiter, and Saturn) and the sun and the moon, each held aloft by a crystalline sphere. The earth, which did not move, was not considered a planet. Nearest the earth was the moon, and there was a complete division between the supralunar world, the region beyond the moon, and the sublunar world, the region beneath the moon (Figure 15.1). In the supralunar world, the planets moved in circular orbits and were made of an incorruptible element, aether; in the sublunar world, change was constant, motion was rectilinear, and matter was composed of the four elements, earth, air, fire, and water. This system had an

Figure 15.1   PETER APIAN. Geocentric Diagram of the Universe, from the *Cosmographia*. 1539. The Bancroft Library, University of California, Berkeley. *This schematic diagram illustrates the geocentric universe in the pre-Copernican era. The unmoving earth is at the center and is surrounded by ten moving spheres, containing, in sequential order, the moon, Mercury, Venus, the sun, Mars, Jupiter, Saturn, the fixed stars, the* aqueous *or* crystalline heaven, *and the* empty *sphere called the* primum mobile. *The ninth sphere, the crystalline heaven, was added by medieval scholars to address a problem raised by the account of creation in Genesis. The tenth sphere, the* primum mobile, *was logically necessary in Aristotle's theory because it moved first and brought the other nine into motion. Beyond the tenth sphere was the Empyrean, home of the Unmoved Mover in philosophy or of God in theology.*

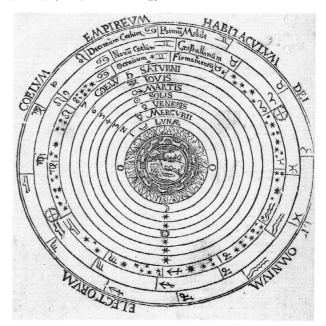

absolute up and down: "Up" referred to the area beyond the spheres inhabited by the Unmoved Mover—Aristotle's philosophical term for the source of all celestial motion—and "down" referred to the center of the earth.

In the second century A.D., the Egyptian scholar Ptolemy updated Aristotle's geocentric theory with new astronomical data and improved mathematical calculations. During the golden age of Muslim culture (800–1000 A.D.), Arab intellectuals preserved this geocentric legacy, improving and refining it to reflect new planetary sightings. In the High Middle Ages (1000–1300), Western scholars recovered the Ptolemaic heritage—with its Muslim additions—and gave it a Christian interpretation: Medieval Christian scientists began to identify the Unmoved Mover as God and the space beyond the spheres as heaven. More important, the church became attached to the geocentric theory because it seemed to validate the doctrine of original sin: The corrupt earth—inhabited by fallen mortals—corresponded to the sublunar world of decay and constant change.

At the University of Paris in the 1300s, a more self-assured and skeptical outlook arose among a few thinkers. Unconvinced by Aristotle's solution to the problem of motion (which was to attribute the forward motion of a projectile to air movement), the Parisian scholars offered an alternative explanation. They asserted that a projectile acquired "impetus," a propulsive quality that gradually diminished as the projectile moved through space. The theory of "impetus" commanded scholars' attention for centuries, leading them to consider a new range of scientific problems.

From the modern perspective, it matters little that the theory of "impetus" was untrue. It was a first step away from the Aristotelian tradition because it made Western scientists aware that the great Greek thinker was not always right. And scholars at Paris and other universities began to advocate applying mathematics to practical problems as well as directly observing nature—in other words, collecting data (**empiricism**) and framing hypotheses from observable facts (**inductive reasoning**).

Aristotle had also used empirical data and inductive logic, but his writings had become so revered that for generations scholars did not examine his methodology and were afraid to tamper with his conclusions. Indeed, his followers relied on **deductive reasoning;** that is, they only explored the ramifications of accepted truths. But with the new critical spirit that appeared in the Late Middle Ages, scholars began to look at the world with new eyes. In time, this spirit led to the greatest achievement of Baroque science, the Scientific Revolution that overturned the geocentric Ptolemaic system and established **heliocentrism,** the theory that the universe is centered on the sun.

Figure 15.2 MARIA SIBYLLA MERIAN. *Insect Metamorphoses in Surinam.* 1705. Hand-colored engraving. (Reprinted in F. Schnack, *Das Kleine Buch der Tropenwander.* Leipzig: Insel-Verlag, 1935. Plate 11. 4¾ × 7".) *A painter and a scientist, the German-born Maria Sibylla Merian (1647–1717) traveled to the South American Dutch colony of Surinam, where, for two years, she collected and raised insects and made notes and illustrations. Her illustration of the metamorphosis of a moth, from caterpillar through pupa (covered by a cocoon) to mature adult, along with a flowering branch of an orange tree, captures the exotic character of the New World, adds to the growing body of scientific knowledge, and reflects the high standards of seventeenth-century Dutch art.*

THE MAGICAL AND THE PRACTICAL IN THE SCIENTIFIC REVOLUTION

The Scientific Revolution is notable for the paradoxes and ironies that the movement gave rise to, some of which will be discussed in a later section of this chapter. A paradox that should be noted at the outset, however, is that this revolution in human thought, which ushered in modern science, was rooted in both magical beliefs and practical technological achievements. With one or two exceptions, the makers of the Scientific Revolution were motivated by two divergent and rather contradictory sets of beliefs. On the one hand, they followed the lead of late medieval science by collecting empirical data, reasoning inductively, and using mathematics to verify results (Figure 15.2). Significantly, the most startling changes occurred in those areas where mathematics was applied to long-existing intellectual problems, namely in astronomy, physics, and biology.

On the other hand, the makers of the Scientific Revolution were entranced by Neo-Platonism, the philosophy that revived the ancient Greek philosophy in the Early Renaissance (see Chapter 11). Like late medieval science, Neo-Platonism stressed the role of mathematics in problem solving, but Neo-Platonism also had a mystical streak—a legacy from Pythagoras—that led its devotees to seek harmony through numbers (see Chapter 2). Thinkers who followed Neo-Platonism believed that simplicity was superior to complexity in mathematical figuring because simplicity was the supreme sign that a solution was correct. This belief has become a guiding ideal of modern science, although other aspects of Neo-Platonism are rejected today, such as the attribution of mysterious powers to the sun. One effect of Neo-Platonism's occult side was to tighten the link between astronomy and astrology, a connection as old as Greek science. Most of those who made the revolution in science supported this linkage, and a few even cast horoscopes for wealthy clients.

As for the role of technology in the Scientific Revolution, many of its achievements would have been impossible without the telescope and the microscope, both of which were invented in about 1600 in the Netherlands. Without them, scholars would have simply remained "thinkers," as they had been since the time of the ancient Greeks. But with the telescope and the microscope, they could penetrate deep into hitherto inaccessible areas—outer space and the inner workings of the human body. Henceforward, scholars with a scientific bent allied themselves with the crafts tradition, becoming experimenters and empiricists.

Astronomy and Physics: From Copernicus to Newton

The intellectual shift from the earth-centered to the sun-centered universe was almost 150 years in the making and involved an international community of scholars. Heliocentrism, the new model of the world, was first broached in modern times by the Polish thinker Copernicus in 1543, and incontrovertible mathematical calculations to prove this view were published by the English scholar Newton in 1687. Between those dates, major steps in the revolution in science were taken by Tycho Brahe of Denmark, Johannes Kepler of Germany, and Galileo Galilei of Italy. Isaac Newton spoke the truth when he claimed that he "stood on the shoulders of giants" (see Timeline 15.1).

Nicolas Copernicus When Nicolas Copernicus (1473–1543) published *Revolutions of the Heavenly*

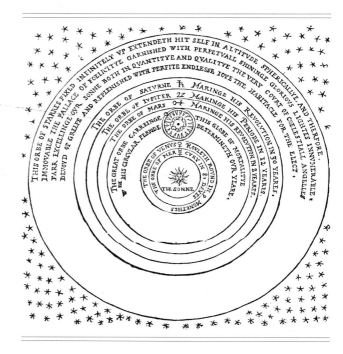

Figure 15.3   Thomas Digges. The Sun-Centered Universe of Copernicus, from *A Perfit Description of the Celestiall Orbes.* 1576. The Huntington Library, San Marino, California. *This diagram drawn by the Englishman Thomas Digges agrees with the Copernican system except in one major way. Copernicus believed the universe was a finite, closed system, but Digges represents it as infinite, expressed in the stars scattered outside the orbit of fixed stars.*

Bodies in 1543, he was reviving the discarded heliocentric theory of the third-century B.C. Greek thinker Aristarchus. In this highly technical work, Copernicus launched a head-on assault against Ptolemaic geocentrism. The main issue between Copernican astronomy and the older worldview was not one of mathematical precision, for both were mathematically solid and thus equally able to predict planetary positions and solar and lunar eclipses. Rather, the basic question between the two systems was which one was simpler. Copernicus reasoned that a more convincing picture of the universe could be achieved by transposing the positions of the sun and the earth. Instead of the Ptolemaic notion of a finite world centered on a fixed earth, Copernicus envisioned a vastly expanded, but not infinite, universe with the planets orbiting the sun (Figure 15.3).

Recognizing the revolutionary nature of his hypothesis, Copernicus delayed printing his ideas until he was dying. In an attempt to mollify clerical critics, he dedicated his book to the pope, Paul III. Later the religious establishment concluded that heliocentrism was dangerous and contrary to scripture; they therefore condemned it as a false system. What disturbed them was that when the earth was removed from the center of the universe, the place of human beings in the divine order was also reduced. In effect, human beings were no longer the leading actors in a cosmic drama staged for them alone.

Catholics and Protestants alike denounced the ideas of Copernicus. Lutheran and Calvinist authorities condemned his views as unbiblical, and in 1610 the pope placed *Revolutions of the Heavenly Bodies* on the Index, the list of forbidden books created during the Counter-Reformation. Eventually, the two religious groups came to a parting of the ways over Copernican ideas. For more than two hundred years, until 1822, the Roman Catholic Church, with all of its considerable power and influence, opposed the sun-centered theory, thus reversing a centuries-old tradition of being open to innovative scientific thought. However, in Protestantism—where authority was not centralized as it was in Roman Catholicism—some sects slowly accepted and adapted their beliefs to the new astronomy.

Johannes Kepler   The reception of Copernican astronomy by the scientific community was neither immediate nor enthusiastic. For example, the great Danish astronomer Tycho Brahe [TEE-ko BRAH-hee] (1546–1601) adopted a modified Copernicanism, believing that the other planets moved around the sun but that the earth did not. Brahe nevertheless contributed to the ultimate triumph of heliocentrism through his copious observations of planetary movement. So accurate were his sightings (without the aid of a telescope) that they set a new standard for astronomical data (Figure 15.4).

Among Brahe's assistants was Johannes Kepler (1571–1630), a brilliant mathematician who dedicated his life to clarifying the theory of heliocentrism. When the Danish astronomer died, Kepler inherited his astronomical data. Inspired by Neo-Platonism to make sense of the regular and continuous sightings of Brahe, Kepler in 1609 published *On the Motion of Mars*, setting forth his solution to the problem of what kept the planets in their orbits. His findings were expressed in two scientific laws that were elegant in their simplicity. In the first planetary law, Kepler substituted the ellipse for the circle as the descriptive shape of planetary orbits. And his second planetary law, which was set forth in a precise mathematical formula, accounted for each planet's variable speed within its respective orbit by showing that nearness to the sun affected its behavior —the closer to the sun, the faster the speed, and the farther from the sun, the slower the speed. Together, these laws validated sun-centered astronomy.

Kepler continued to manipulate Brahe's undigested data, convinced that other mathematical laws could be

Figure 15.4   *Tycho Brahe in his Observatory.* Engraving, from Brahe's *Astronomiae Instauratae Mechanica.* 1598. Joseph Regenstein Library, University of Chicago. *Tycho Brahe, the Danish astronomer who contributed to the Scientific Revolution, is shown in his observatory at Uraniborg, on the island of Ven, in Denmark. With right hand pointing upward, he instructs his assistants in the use of the wall quadrant, the semicircular, calibrated instrument (on his left) he developed for measuring the position of stars. In the background, other assistants work with various astronomical instruments and perform chemical experiments.*

derived from observations of the heavens. In 1619 he arrived at a third planetary law, which relates the movement of one planet to another. He showed that the squares of the length of time for each planet's orbit are in the same ratios as the cubes of their respective mean distances from the sun. Through this formula, he affirmed that the solar system itself was regular and organized by mathematically determined relationships. This was the first expression of the notion that the universe operates with clocklike regularity, an idea that became an article of faith by the end of the Baroque age. Kepler took great pride in this discovery, because it confirmed his Neo-Platonist belief that there is a hidden mathematical harmony in the universe.

Galileo Galilei   While Kepler moved in the rarefied realm of theoretical, even mystical, science, one of his contemporaries was making major breakthroughs with experiments that relied on precise mathematics and careful logic. This patient experimenter was Galileo Galilei (1564–1642), whose most valuable contributions were his accurate celestial observations and his work in terrestrial mechanics, the study of the action of forces on matter. Inspired by news that Dutch lens grinders had made a device for viewing distant objects, in 1609 Galileo made his own telescope, which enabled him to see stars invisible to the naked eye.

With these sightings, Galileo demonstrated that the size of the universe was exponentially greater than that computed on Ptolemaic principles. Further, his observations of the moon's rough surface and the sun's shifting dark spots provided additional proofs against the ancient arguments that the heavenly bodies were perfectly formed and never changed. But his most telling discovery was that the planet Jupiter has moons, a fact that contradicted the Ptolemaic belief that all celestial bodies must move about a common center. Galileo's research affirmed that Jupiter's four satellites rotated around it in much the same way that the six planets orbited the sun. These telescope observations hastened the demise of geocentrism.

Similarly, Galileo's research in terrestrial mechanics proved conclusively that both Aristotle and his fourteenth-century critics in Paris were wrong about one of the central questions of earthly motion—that is, the behavior of projectiles. Aristotle had claimed that projectiles stayed in flight because of the pushing motion of the air, and the Parisian scholars had countered with the theory of "impetus." Through experimentation, Galileo showed that a mass that is moving will go on moving until some force acts to stop it—the earliest expression of the modern law of inertia.

Galileo was probably the first scientist to make a clock a basic means for measuring time in his experiments. Like his contemporary Kepler, he reported his findings in the form of simple mathematical laws. Galileo's work was later validated by Newton, who proved that the laws of mechanics on earth were the same as the laws of mechanics in the sky.

At the same time that Galileo was conducting the experiments that would make him a hero of modern science, he ran afoul of the religious authorities, who brought his career to a humiliating end. The church, as noted previously, had by now abandoned its relative openness to ideas and was moving to stifle dissent. In 1633 Galileo was arrested by the Inquisition, the church court created in the 1200s to find and punish heretics. The great astronomer was charged with false teachings for his published support of the idea that the earth moves, a notion central to Copernicanism but

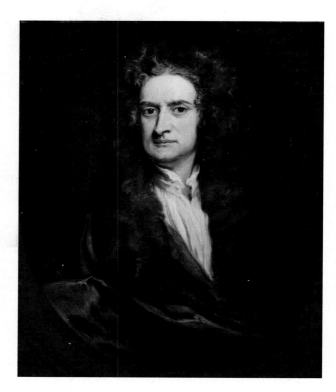

Figure 15.5   GODFREY KNELLER. *Sir Isaac Newton.* 1702. Oil on canvas, 29¾ × 24½". National Portrait Gallery, London. *As the most celebrated intellectual of his generation, the middle-class Newton was given star treatment in this portrait by the reigning society painter in England. Decked out fashionably in an elaborate Baroque wig, Newton peers somewhat uncomfortably at the viewer. The likeness tends to support Newton's reputation for vanity and ostentation.*

untrue according to Aristotle and the church. Threatened with torture, Galileo recanted his views and was released. Despite living on for several years, he died a broken man. This episode abruptly ended Italy's role in the burgeoning revolution in science.

Isaac Newton   Building on the research of the heirs to Copernicus, including Kepler's laws of planetary motion and Galileo's law of inertia, the English mathematician Isaac Newton (1642–1727) conceived a model of the universe that decisively overturned the Ptolemaic scheme and finished the revolution in astronomy begun by Copernicus. In Newton's world picture, there is uniform motion on earth and in the heavens. More significant, Newton presented a satisfactory explanation for what held the planets in their orbits. Newton's solution was the force of gravity, and this topic formed the heart of his theory of the universe (Figure 15.5).

In a precise mathematical formula, Newton computed the law of universal gravitation, the formula whereby every object in the world exerts an attraction to a greater or a lesser degree on all other objects. By this law, the sun held in its grip each of the six planets, and each in turn lightly influenced the sun and the other planets. The earth and its single moon as well as Jupiter and its four satellites similarly interacted. In effect, because of gravity, the heavenly bodies formed a harmonious system in which each attracted the others.

Having described gravity and asserted its universal nature, Newton declined to speculate about what caused it to operate. For him, the universe behaved precisely as a machine, and his law was nothing but a description of its operation. Because Newton refused to speculate beyond what mathematics could prove, he has been called a "mind without metaphysics." Modern scientists have followed Newton's lead, preferring to ignore the *why* of things and to concentrate on the *how* and *what*.

Newton's views were set forth in his authoritative work *Mathematical Principles of Natural Philosophy*. Known more familiarly as the *Principia* (the first word of its Latin title), this book quickly gained an authority that made Newton the modern world's equivalent of Aristotle. By the eighteenth century, the English poet Alexander Pope could justifiably write:

Nature and Nature's Laws lay hid in Night;
God said, *Let Newton be!* and All was *Light*.

Even though Newton's work was the culmination of the revolution that brought modern science into being, he was not fully free of older attitudes. True, he believed that the discovery of scientific truth was simply a matter of using methodical principles. He made mathematics his guiding ideal and used patient and careful observation. But Newton cared little for his own scientific achievement, believing that his lasting monument would be his religious writings. A pious Christian, he devoted his last years to demonstrating that the prophecies in the Bible were coming true.

Newton also invented a form of calculus, a mathematical method of analysis that uses a symbolic notation. This breakthrough had huge potential for solving problems in physics and mechanics by providing a tool for computing quantities that had nonlinear variations. Simultaneously and independently of Newton, Gottfried Wilhelm von Leibniz [LIBE-nits] (1646–1716), a German thinker, invented a more useful version of calculus. By 1800 Leibniz's symbols had become the universally accepted language of calculus.

Medicine and Chemistry

At the same time that Western understanding of the universe at its outer limits was being radically altered, another breakthrough involved anatomical knowledge and the discovery of the true circulation of the human blood. Unlike developments in astronomy, this breakthrough in medical science happened largely without the aid of technology. Only during the last step in the solving of the mystery of the blood's circulation did early modern scientists use the newly invented microscope.

In 1600 anatomical knowledge was extremely limited, primarily because the church forbade the violation of corpses, a position based on the teaching that the body would be resurrected from the dead. Biological research had been limited to the dissection of animals, with generalizations then applied to the human body, leading to a great deal of misinformation and half-truths.

Besides, in biology as in astronomy and physics, the authority of ancient Greek thinkers reigned supreme —Aristotle since the fourth century B.C. and Galen since the second century A.D. Galen's vast researches covering nearly all aspects of ancient medicine were lost in the fall of Rome, but some works were preserved by Arab scholars and were translated from Arabic into Latin by Western scholars from the eleventh century onward (see Chapter 8). Though offering rival theories, Aristotle and Galen shared many false ideas, namely the notions that air ran directly from the lungs into the heart, that blood flowed from the veins to the outer part of the body, and that different types of blood coursed in the arteries and the veins.

The problem of the circulation of the blood was eventually resolved by scientists at the University of Padua in Italy, the most prominent of whom was Andreas Vesalius [vuh-SAY-lee-us] (1514–1564). His painstaking observations led him to deny Galen's theory that blood passed from one side of the heart to the other through the septum, an impermeable membrane (Figure 15.6).

The research of Vesalius and his successors set the stage for William Harvey (1578–1657), an English scientist who studied and taught at the University of Padua. In 1628 Harvey published his groundbreaking work, which produced the correct view of circulation, including the roles of the heart, the lungs, the arteries, and the veins. Mathematical calculation played a decisive role in this scientific triumph, just as it had in Newton's gravitation theory. Using arithmetic, Harvey proved that a constant quantity of blood continuously circulated throughout the body, thereby invalidating Galen's ebb-and-flow theory. However, Harvey lacked knowledge of the capillaries, the connectors between the arteries and the veins. In 1661 the Italian scientist Marcello Malpighi [mahl-PEE-gee] (1628–1694) identified these tiny vessels with the aid of the microscope, and with this critical piece of information an

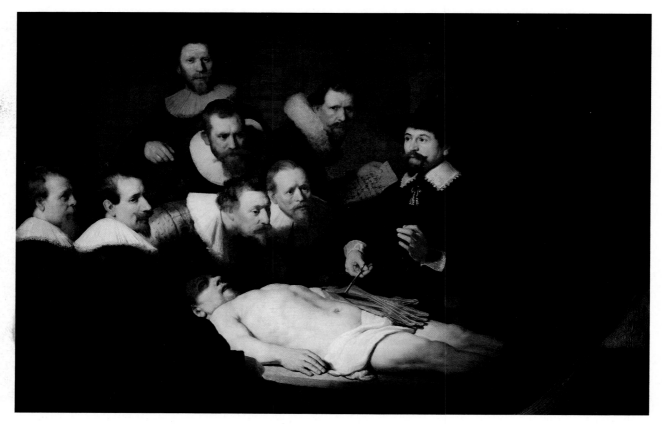

Figure 15.6 REMBRANDT VAN RIJN. *The Anatomy Lesson of Dr. Tulp.* 1632. Oil on canvas, 66¾ × 85¼". Mauritshuis, The Hague. *The pioneering work of Vesalius made the study of anatomy a central concern of medical science in the seventeenth century. In this painting, Rembrandt depicts Dr. Nicholas Tulp of Amsterdam as he demonstrates the dissection of the left arm. Rembrandt's use of Baroque effects, such as the dramatic light on the corpse, the contrast between Dr. Tulp's calm demeanor and the inquisitive faces of his pupils, and the flayed arm of the corpse, make this an arresting image.*

essentially correct, modern description of the blood's circulation was complete.

Chemistry did not become a separate discipline in the Baroque age, but the English physicist Robert Boyle (1627–1691) did establish the groundwork for modern chemistry. A major aspect of Boyle's thought linked him to Newton, for both believed that the universe is a machine. Boyle believed that the workings of nature could be revealed only through experimental study—the inductive method. Boyle's zeal for experimentation led him to study the behavior of gases and to formulate the famous law that bears his name.

Boyle was also one of the first to distinguish chemistry from alchemy, a set of magical practices that had been allied with chemistry since the time of the ancient Greeks. In medieval Europe, alchemy had led scholars to search vainly for the "philosopher's stone" that would miraculously turn a base metal such as lead into gold. Rejecting alchemy's assumptions and

methodology, Boyle sought to understand only those chemical reactions that happened naturally and could be analyzed in mathematical terms.

The Impact of Science on Philosophy

The Scientific Revolution had a profound influence on Western thought and also gave rise to a type of literature that reflected the impact of science on the wider culture. Three prominent contributors to this literature were the English jurist and statesman Francis Bacon and two brilliant French mathematicians, René Descartes and Blaise Pascal, whose speculative writings continued the French rationalist tradition begun by Montaigne in the 1500s (see Chapter 13).

Francis Bacon Francis Bacon (1561–1626) owes his fame to his ability to write lucid prose about science and its methodology. In a field that was dominated by scholars whose writings were accessible only to those learned in mathematics, Bacon's clear prose informed a curious and educated public. In the process of clarifying the techniques and the aims of the new science, he became the spokesman for the "experimenters," those who believed that the future of science lay in discarding Aristotle. Condemning Aristotle for relying on deductive reasoning and unproven axioms, Bacon advocated the inductive method, the procedure that embraced the conducting of experiments, the drawing of conclusions, and the testing of results in other experiments. His claims were not new, but they were forcibly and memorably expressed; few scholars exhibited Bacon's optimism about the usefulness of science. He sincerely believed that the march of science inevitably led to mastery over the natural world, a view summarized in the famous phrase attributed to him, "knowledge is power."

René Descartes   An outstanding critic of the belief that the experimental method was the correct path to knowledge was René Descartes [day-KAHRT] (1596–1650), a philosopher who urged a purely mathematical approach in science (Figure 15.7). Descartes's love of numbers came from a mystical side of his personality, as illustrated by his confession that a dream had inspired his belief that mathematics holds the key to nature. Descartes was the founder of analytic geometry, that branch of mathematics that describes geometric figures by the formulas of algebra, and the author of a widely influential philosophical treatise, *Discourse on Method*, published in 1637.

In the *Discourse on Method*, Descartes outlined four steps in his approach to knowledge: to accept nothing as true unless it is self-evident; to split problems into manageable parts; to solve problems starting with the simplest and moving to the most complex; and to review and reexamine the solutions. He used deductive logic in his method, making inferences only from general statements. But more important than his stress on deductive reasoning was his insistence on mathematical clarity. He refused to accept anything as true unless it had the persuasiveness of a proof in geometry.

Descartes's most influential gifts to Western philosophy were skepticism and a dualistic theory of knowledge. He rejected the authoritarian method of medieval scholasticism and began with universal doubt in order to determine what was absolutely certain in the universe. Step-by-step, he questioned the existence of God, of the world, and of his own body. But he soon established that he could not doubt the existence of his own doubting self. He reached this absolute conclusion in the oft-quoted phrase *"Cogito ergo sum"*—I think, therefore I am. Having first

Figure 15.7   FRANZ HALS. *René Descartes*. After 1649. Oil on canvas, 30¾ × 26¾". Louvre. *In this likeness, Frans Hals, the great Dutch portrait artist and contemporary of Rembrandt, has captured the complex personality of the great French philosopher and mathematician. Descartes's piercing gaze shows his skeptical spirit. His disdainful presence and rough features reveal his early background as a soldier. Hals apparently felt no need to flatter his sitter in this compelling portrait.*

destroyed the age-old certainties, he then, through deduction, reestablished the existence of his own body, the world, and, finally, God.

Descartes's speculations were aimed at identifying clear and distinct ideas that were certain for everyone, but his efforts had a deeply ironic result. In the long run, his thought fostered the growing awareness among the educated elite that absolute truth was not possible. Many who read his *Discourse* were unimpressed by his rational arguments, but they nevertheless accepted his radical doubt, and some even became atheists. That his work contributed to the rise of atheism would have horrified Descartes, since, to his own way of thinking, he had proven the existence of God. He had used skepticism merely as a means of achieving certainty.

Descartes's other great legacy, dualism, made a division between the material world and the human soul or mind. According to him, mathematics permitted natural truths to be revealed to the human understanding. He thought, however, that the mind itself was beyond mathematical knowing and hence was not a fit subject for study. From this dichotomy arise two contrasting traditions, the scientists who reduce the natural world to order through mathematics and the thinkers who focus on human psychology. The second group—the psychologists—represent another ironic legacy, for through the study of such topics as depth psychology and alienation they want to prove that Descartes was wrong and that the human self is knowable in all of its irrationality.

Even though Descartes's speculations were aimed at achieving certainty, his focus on deductive logic has not withstood the test of time. This is because modern scientists think that inductive reasoning—building a model of truth on the facts—is more valid. But Descartes was proven correct in assigning to mathematics its paramount role in establishing precision and certainty in science. Today, those sciences that have the greatest degree of mathematical rigor have better reputations for accuracy and believability than those sciences whose formulations cannot be achieved mathematically.

Descartes made another contribution to the Scientific Revolution when he applied his method to terrestrial mechanics. It was he, rather than Galileo, who gave final expression to the law of inertia. He concluded that a projectile would continue to move in a straight line until it was interrupted by some force. With this language Descartes finally debunked the myth of circular motion, and his definition of the law of inertia became part of the scientific synthesis of Newton.

Blaise Pascal   Descartes's work was barely published before it elicited a strong reaction from Blaise Pascal [BLEHZ pas-KAHL] (1623–1662), an anguished thinker who made radical doubt the cornerstone of his beliefs. Like Descartes, Pascal left his mark in mathematics, notably in geometry and in the study of probability. Pascal was a Jansenist, a member of a Catholic sect that to some observers was Calvinistic because it stressed original sin and denied free will. Pascal's Jansenism permeates his masterpiece, the *Pensées*, or *Thoughts*, a meditative work of intense feeling published in 1670, eight years after his death.

In the *Pensées*, Pascal went beyond Descartes's skepticism, concluding that human beings can know neither the natural world nor themselves. Despite this seemingly universal doubt, Pascal still reasoned that there were different levels of truth. Regarding science, he thought that what he called the geometric spirit—that is, mathematics—could lead scholars to a limited knowledge of nature. Pascal's most controversial opinions, however, concerned human psychology. He felt that the passions enabled human beings to comprehend truths about God and religion directly. He summed up this idea in his often quoted words, "The heart has reasons that reason does not know." In another passage, he justified his continued belief in God, not by intellectual proofs in the manner of Descartes, but by a wager—a notion he derived from his probability studies. Pascal claimed his faith in God rested on a bet: If God exists, then the bettor wins everything, but if God does not exist, then nothing is lost. Pascal's fervent belief in God in the face of debilitating doubt makes him a forerunner of modern Christian existentialism.

Ironies and Contradictions of the Scientific Revolution

Ironies abound in the seventeenth century's most characteristic development, the Scientific Revolution. To begin with, it must be remembered that only a handful of thinkers contributed to the scientific changes, that the vast majority of the populace remained unaware of their findings, and that they could not have understood them even if they had been informed of them. Furthermore, those who made the scientific discoveries were engaged primarily in solving practical problems rather than in trying to build a new model of the universe. They also believed that what they were doing was entirely within an orthodox Christian framework (although some were aware that religious leaders might think otherwise), and few foresaw that their efforts would eventually lead to a conflict between religion and science.

Another irony was that the scientific advancements were not always completely original creations but were rooted in late medieval rationalism and the Renaissance revival of Classical learning. Indeed, the new thinkers were often more concerned with working out minor inconsistencies in the calculations of medieval scholars than in overturning the accepted picture of the universe.

Not only did seventeenth-century science have roots in medieval science, but it was also influenced by superstitions and mystical beliefs. During the Scientific Revolution, even the greatest intellectuals still held firmly to nonrational medieval views. Brahe and Kepler, for example, supported their research by pursuing careers as court astrologers. Harvey imagined that the heart restored a "spiritous" quality to the blood during circulation. Newton and Boyle were both involved in secret experiments with alchemy. A mystical experience lay behind Descartes's mathematical zeal, and Neo-Platonism motivated the thought of Copernicus, Kepler, and Galileo. Many scholars were conventionally devout in their religious convictions,

PERSONAL PERSPECTIVE

Suzanne Gaudry
A Witch's Trial

In 1652, Suzanne Gaudry, an illiterate old woman, was accused of witchcraft—of renouncing "God, Lent, and baptism," worshiping the devil, attending witches' Sabbaths, desecrating the Eucharist wafer, and committing other crimes. Questioned by the local court at Rieux, France, she confessed to some charges but later recanted. Because confession was necessary for conviction, she was subjected to torture, and once again she confessed. She was then condemned and sentenced to be tied to a gallows, strangled to death, and her body burned. This passage is taken from the court record.

On [June 27], . . . this prisoner [Suzanne Gaudry], before being strapped down, was admonished to maintain herself in her first confessions and to renounce her lover [the devil].

—Said that she denies everything she has said, and that she has no lover. Feeling herself being strapped down, says that she is not a witch, while struggling to cry.[1] . . .

—Says . . . she is not a witch. And upon being asked why she confessed to being one, said that she was forced to say it.

Told that she was not forced, that on the contrary she declared herself to be a witch without any threat.

—Says that she confessed it and that she is not a witch, and being a little stretched [on the rack] screams ceaselessly that she is not a witch, invoking the name of

Jesús and Our Lady of Grace, not wanting to say any other thing. . . .

The mark having been probed by the officer, in the presence of Doctor Bouchain, it was adjudged by the aforesaid doctor and officer truly to be the mark of the devil.[2]

Being more tightly stretched upon the torture-rack, urged to maintain her confessions.

—Said that it was true that she is a witch and that she would maintain what she has said.

Asked how long she has been in subjugation to the devil.

—Answers that it was twenty years ago that the devil appeared to her, being in her lodgings in the form of a man dressed in a little cow-hide and black breeches. . . .

Asked if her lover has had carnal copulation with her, and how many times.

—To that she did not answer anything; then, making believe that she was ill, not another word could be drawn from her.

---

[1] Not crying was thought to be a sign of witchcraft.
[2] Perhaps a birthmark or other skin blemish. It was commonly believed that witches were marked by the devil, as a sign of their intimate union, and when the mark was pricked, no pain would occur nor any blood flow out.

---

and Newton tried to correlate biblical prophecy with history. Despite their medieval roots, these scholars did point European thought in a new direction. In the next century, a new generation of intellectuals constructed a set of beliefs based on the achievements of the Scientific Revolution and their implications for the improvement of humanity.

THE REVOLUTION IN POLITICAL THOUGHT

Political philosophy reflected the nature of the shifting political, economic, social, scientific, and religious institutions of the seventeenth century. The Thirty Years' War, the Wars of Louis XIV, and the English Civil War (see Chapter 14) forced political theorists to reconsider such basic themes as the nature of government, the relations between rulers and subjects, the rivalries among sovereign states, and the consequences of war on society and the individual.

Political writers, stimulated by the rise of the nation-state in the 1500s, addressed themselves in the 1600s to the fundamental questions of who holds the final sovereignty in a state and how power should be exercised. Realizing that new states were rapidly extinguishing the rights held by the feudal estates, these theorists tried to define the best form of government. They all supported their arguments with the same sources—the Bible, the concept of natural law, scientific discoveries, and their own views of human nature—but they came to widely differing conclusions.

Natural Law and Divine Right: Grotius and Bossuet

Hugo Grotius [GRO-she-us] (1583–1645) thought that natural law should govern the relations between states. He arrived at this belief chiefly because of his personal sufferings during the Thirty Years' War and the intolerance that he observed in religious disputes.

A Dutch citizen but also an ambassador for Sweden, he saw at first hand the ambiguity of diplomatic relations between the great powers.

Drawing on the idea of natural law as set forth by the ancient Stoic thinkers, Grotius urged that the states follow a law that applied to all nations, was eternal and unchanging, and could be understood by human reason. Like the Stoics, Grotius was convinced that natural law was founded on human reason and was not the gift of a loving God. He rejected original sin, believing instead that human beings were not motivated merely by selfish drives. He thought that because all mortals were rational, they wanted to improve themselves and to create a just and fair society. In his treatise *The Law of War and Peace,* he applied this rational view of human nature to his description of sovereign states. He concluded that nations, like individuals, should treat each other as they would expect to be treated. Today, the writings of Grotius are recognized as the starting point of international law.

Taking a contrary point of view to Grotius was Bishop Bossuet [bo-SWAY] (1627–1704), who defended the theory that kings rule by divine right. This French church leader echoed the opinions of James I of England, who maintained that God bestowed power on certain national monarchs. The French bishop avowed that absolutism, as ordained by God in past societies, was now manifested in the rule of Louis XIV, king of France. Louis, as God's chosen vessel on earth, had the power to intervene in the lives of his subjects, not because of natural law, but by divine right. According to this theory, for corrupt and sinful humans to rebel against the king was to go against God's plan. The bishop believed that the age's conflicts made autocratic rule a political necessity. Bossuet's belief in autocracy was shared by the Englishman Thomas Hobbes, although he explained absolute rule in different terms.

Absolutism and Liberalism: Hobbes and Locke

Thomas Hobbes (1588–1679) grew up in an England increasingly torn by religious, social, and political discord. A trained Classicist and a student of the new science, Hobbes came to believe that everything, including human beings and their social acts, could be explained by using mechanistic, natural laws to describe various states of motion or movement.

Hobbes's efforts to synthesize a universal philosophy founded on a geometric design and activated by some form of energy culminated in his best-known work, *The Leviathan,* published in 1651 (Figure 15.8). *The Leviathan* sets forth a theory of government based on the pessimistic view that individuals are driven by two basic forces, the fear of death and the quest for

power. Hobbes imagined what life would be like if these two natural inclinations were allowed free rein and there were no supreme power to control them. Hobbes described human life under these circumstances as "solitary, poor, nasty, brutish, and short."

Hobbes thought that human beings, recognizing the awfulness of their situation, would decide to give up such an existence and form a civil society under the rule of one man. This first step in the evolution of government was achieved by means of a **social contract** drawn up between the ruler and his subjects. By the terms of this covenant, the subjects surrendered all their claims to sovereignty and bestowed absolute power on the ruler. The sovereign's commands were then to be carried out by all under him, including the religious and civic leaders. Armed with the sword, the sovereign would keep peace at home and protect the land from its enemies abroad.

Hobbes made no distinction between the ruler of a monarchy and the head of a commonwealth, for he was less concerned with the form of government than with the need to hold in check destructive human impulses. In the next generation, Hobbes's pessimistic philosophy provoked a reaction from John Locke, who repudiated absolutism and advocated a theory of government by the people.

Despite their contradictory messages, Hobbes and John Locke (1632–1704) had been subjected to similar influences. Both adapted ideas from the new science, witnessed the English Civil War, and sought safety on the Continent because of their political views. But Locke rejected Hobbes's gloomy view of humanity and his theory of absolutism; he taught instead that human nature was potentially good and that human beings were capable of governing themselves. The two thinkers originated opposing schools of modern political thought: From Hobbes stems the absolutist, authoritarian tradition, and from Locke descends the school of liberalism. Their works represent two of the most significant legacies of the Baroque age to the modern world.

Locke set forth his political theories in his *Two Treatises of Government,* which he published anonymously in 1690. In the *First Treatise* he refuted the divine right of kings, and in the *Second Treatise* he laid out the model for rule by the people. The latter work has become the classic expression of early **liberalism.** In it Locke described the origins, characteristics, and purpose of the ideal political system—a government limited by laws, subject to the will of its citizens, and existing to protect life and property.

Locke's treatise shared some of Hobbes's ideas, such as the view that human life is violent and disorderly in the state of nature, that human beings must form civil governments to protect themselves, and

Figure 15.8 Frontispiece of *The Leviathan.* 1651. The Bancroft Library, University of California, Berkeley. *The original illustration for Hobbes's Leviathan conveys the political message of this controversial work in symbolic terms. Towering over the landscape is the mythical ruler, whose body is a composite of all his subjects and in whose hands are the sword and the scepter, symbols of his absolute power. Below this awesome figure is a well-ordered and peaceful village and countryside—Hobbes's political dream come true.*

that a social contract is the necessary basis of civil society. But Locke believed that basic rights, including life and property, exist in the state of nature. He also believed that human beings possess reason, are fundamentally decent and law abiding, and are slow to want change. From these principles, he concluded that human beings would contract together to create a limited government that had no other purpose than the protection of the basic natural rights of life and property.

Locke rejected the idea that by making a social contract citizens surrender their sovereignty to a ruler. He argued instead that the people choose rulers who protect their rights in a fiduciary trust; that is, they expect their rulers to obey the social contract and govern equitably. If the rulers break the agreement, then the people have the right to revolt, overthrow the government, and reclaim their natural rights. Unlike Hobbes, Locke asserted that rulers possess only limited authority and that their control must be held in

LEARNING THROUGH MAPS

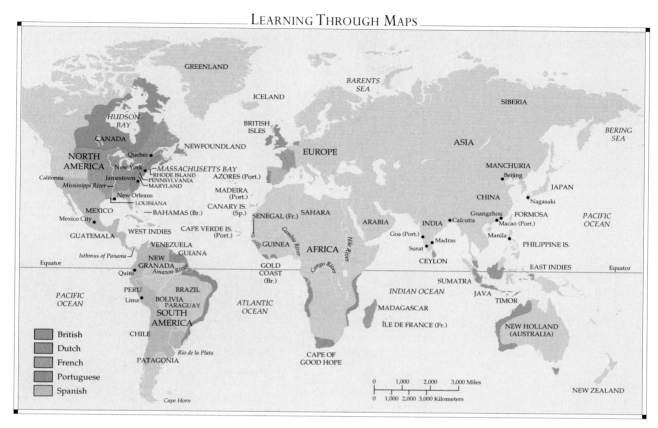

Map 15.1 EXPANSION OF EUROPE, 1715
This map shows the presence of Europeans around the globe in the early eighteenth century. **Notice** the overseas holdings of the five European countries identified on the map. **Observe** the differing encounter patterns—coastal and inland—on the various continents. **Which** country has the largest number of overseas holdings? **On which** continent is there the greatest European presence? **Where** are conflicts among European powers most likely to occur? **Which** areas of the world seem less touched by European expansion?

check by a balanced governmental system and a separation of powers. In later years, Locke's tract influenced American and French political thinkers and patriots who used its ideas to justify the right to revolt against a tyrant and to establish a government of checks and balances.

Locke was not only a political theorist but also the preeminent English philosopher of his day. He grappled with many of the same problems as Descartes, although his conclusions were radically different from the French thinker's. In his important philosophical work *An Essay Concerning Human Understanding,* published in 1690 (the same year he published *Two Treatises of Government*), Locke addressed the question, How is knowledge acquired? Descartes had proposed that the germs of ideas were inborn and that people were born knowing certain truths, such as mathemat-

ical principles and logical relationships; education required nothing more than the strenuous use of the intellect without concern for new information from the senses.

Locke repudiated these views and described the mind at birth as a ***tabula rasa*** (blank tablet) on which all human experiences were recorded. Locke maintained that all that human beings can know must first be received through their senses (a basically Aristotelian viewpoint) and then registered on their minds. The raw sensory data are manipulated by the mental faculties, such as comparing and contrasting, so that abstract concepts and generalizations are formed in the mind. As a result, reason and experience are united in human thought and together determine what is real for each person. Locke's explanation of the origin of ideas is the basis of modern empiricism—the theory

that all knowledge is derived from or originates in human experience. His influence has been so great that many of his ideas seem to the modern reader to be just "common sense."

EUROPEAN EXPLORATION AND EXPANSION

The exploration begun in the late fifteenth century had led to a series of encounters with new peoples that slowly eroded the isolation and self-absorption of Europe. In the sixteenth century, the pace of exploration quickened, and the globe was circumnavigated—events that intensified rivalries among the European states, increased the Continent's economic power, and diffused European culture and customs around the world.

The greatest success of European expansion was achieved through a series of permanent settlements in North and South America and by the opening of new trade routes to the Far East (Map 15.1). Expansion and colonization affected Europe in numerous ways: the introduction of new foodstuffs and other products, the establishment of innovative business methods, the disruption of old economic and social patterns, the introduction of novel ways of looking at the world, and the adoption of new symbols and themes in the arts. Whatever may have been the beneficial or harmful effects of these changes on European life, the negative impact on non-Europeans tended to outweigh the good that came with the introduction of Western culture. In Africa, the Europeans expanded the slave trade; in North, Central, and South America and the Caribbean, they annihilated many native tribes; and everywhere they forced trade agreements favorable to themselves on the local people.

The earliest leaders in the European penetration of the Western Hemisphere were Spain and Portugal. Since the 1500s, these two states had claimed South and Central America and the southern reaches of North America. Where possible, they mined the rich gold and silver veins, flooding Europe with the new wealth and gaining power and influence for themselves. But during the seventeenth century, the mines were nearing exhaustion, and the glory days were a thing of the past.

While Spain's and Portugal's ties with the New World languished during the Baroque age, England, France, and the Netherlands were accelerating theirs, especially with North America (Table 15.1). In 1607 English farmers settled along the Atlantic seaboard in Virginia, ready to exploit the land, and in 1620 English Puritans emigrated to New England in search of

Table 15.1	SETTLEMENTS IN THE NEW WORLD DURING THE BAROQUE AGE		
LOCATION		**DATE OF FOUNDING**	**SETTLERS**
Jamestown (Virginia)		1607	English
Quebec (Canada)		1608	French
Plymouth (Massachusetts)		1620	English
St. Kitts (West Indies)		1623	English
New Amsterdam (New York)		1624	Dutch
Barbados		1627	English
Brazil		1632–1654	Dutch
Curaçao (West Indies)		1634	Dutch
Martinique (West Indies)		1635	French
Saint Lucia (West Indies)		1635	French
Honduras (Belize)		1638	English
Saint Domingue (Haiti)		1644	French
Bahamas (West Indies)		1648	English
Jamaica (West Indies) (Captured from Spain)		1655	English

religious freedom (Figure 15.9). To the north, French explorers, missionaries, and fur traders founded Quebec in 1608 and then spread along the St. Lawrence River valley and southward into the Great Lakes region. At the same time, the French moved into the Caribbean basin, occupying many islands in the West Indies. After 1655 the English worked their way into the southern part of the Atlantic coast and the West Indies. These newly arrived colonists eventually either drove out the Spaniards or drastically reduced their influence. Meanwhile, the Dutch set up their own colonies in North America, on the banks of the Hudson River and in scattered areas of the mid-Atlantic region.

The English, French, and Dutch recognized the economic advantages of sending more explorers and families abroad and encouraged the founding of colonies. Relying chiefly on state or royal charters, they created large overseas settlements that soon led to a brisk trade in which raw products from the New World were exchanged for finished goods from the Old World. William Penn (1644–1718) founded Pennsylvania in 1681 on the basis of such a charter from England.

In the Far East, colonial developments relied less on charters than on joint-stock companies, a private enterprise technique exploited by both England and the

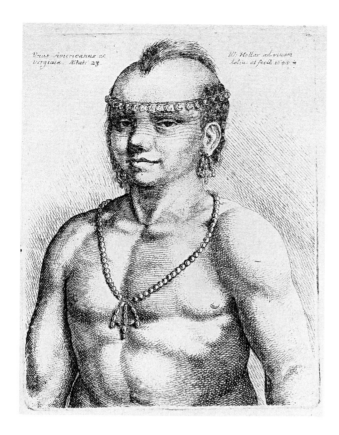

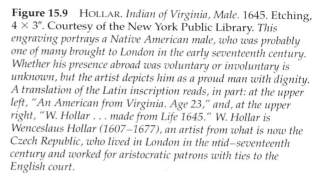

Figure 15.9 HOLLAR. *Indian of Virginia, Male.* 1645. Etching, 4 × 3". Courtesy of the New York Public Library. *This engraving portrays a Native American male, who was probably one of many brought to London in the early seventeenth century. Whether his presence abroad was voluntary or involuntary is unknown, but the artist depicts him as a proud man with dignity. A translation of the Latin inscription reads, in part: at the upper left, "An American from Virginia. Age 23," and, at the upper right, "W. Hollar . . . made from Life 1645." W. Hollar is Wenceslaus Hollar (1607–1677), an artist from what is now the Czech Republic, who lived in London in the mid–seventeenth century and worked for aristocratic patrons with ties to the English court.*

Netherlands. The English East India Company and the Dutch East India Company were the means whereby England and the Netherlands, respectively, opened trade routes and secured markets in the Far East. The two companies made lucrative contracts with Indian princes and Japanese and Chinese state officials (Figure 15.10).

RESPONSES TO THE REVOLUTIONS IN THOUGHT

The scientific discoveries, the growth of skepticism, the new political theories, and the overseas explorations provoked a variety of responses among the artists, intellectuals, and educated public of the 1600s. In the aristocracy, for example, a new social type appeared—the **virtuoso,** a person who dabbled in the latest science and gave it respectability. A new type of literature also appeared, in which scientific concepts and discoveries were popularized for the consumption of an educated elite. Overall, the innovations and changes of the seventeenth century found ample creative expression in the attitudes and images of the period.

Figure 15.10 *A Chinese Interpretation of Dutch Traders.* Porcelain. Ch'ing Dynasty, K'ang-hsi period, seventeenth century. Formerly owned by the Dutch East Indies Company. *As Europeans spread Western culture around the globe in the seventeenth century, they were sometimes confronted with images of themselves created by artists in older cultures, as in these Chinese representations of Dutch traders. These figures express a stereotype of a European man, dressed in the costume of the day (long coat, knee breeches, and hat) and with distinctive features (marked cheekbones, curly hair [wig?], and smiling face). Dating from the reign of China's Emperor K'ang-hsi (1661–1722), these porcelains were made as "curiosities" for the European market. They are enameled glaze porcelains, in which green, yellow, purple, and white enamels were applied to a prefired, or biscuit, body and then given a second firing.*

ENCOUNTER

The Sinews of Trade

In 1616 Sir Thomas Roe, King James I's ambassador, paid homage, with gifts, to Jahangir (je-HAN-ger) (1569–1617), or the Great Mogul, at his court in Agra, India. Roe, through his strong personality, patience, and palace intrigues, managed to gain a trade outlet, or "factory," for the English trading business venture, the East India Company, at Surat on the west coast. This seemingly insignificant encounter linked together one of the richest and most powerful empires in the world and a small island kingdom whose futures would be intertwined until the mid–twentieth century.

The English, as the Portuguese and the Dutch before them, were interested only in turning a profit from Indian goods and products. They held in contempt or viewed with amazement the rich eclectic Mogul civilization of Persian, Indian, and central Asian elements that had emerged in the aftermath of the Mongol invaders and rulers of the thirteenth century. As Christians they were offended by many of the Hindu and Muslim religious practices and beliefs. Although unimpressed with the Mogul's achievements in architecture and technology, in the metal arts, and in much of their fine arts and jewelry, they immediately recognized the economic value of Indian textiles, especially cotton goods. English merchants began to import linen cloth from the Gujarat area of western India to be made into household goods and, later in the seventeenth century, into wearing apparel. Madras cotton cloth, from the town of Madras, and chintz, a type of printed cotton cloth, along with Persian silks also became popular.

During the 1600s, the East India Company forced more concessions from the Mogul rulers, and as the Mogul empire collapsed in the early 1700s, the English meddled in local political affairs. In the mid–eighteenth century they drove out their remaining rival, the French, and gained control of the country through a network of princes and by economic pressures. In the nineteenth century the Industrial Revolution in Europe ruined the Indian textile industry, for the British could now ship their own finished cotton goods to India and sell them at a profit. India still remained vital to British interests for her raw materials and as a market for English manufactured products, becoming the mainstay of Great Britain's worldwide holdings. Her central role in the British Empire became self-evident in 1876 when Queen Victoria was made Empress of India. Yet, within seventy-five years, in 1947, India, led by the Indian nationalist and spiritual leader Mahatma Gandhi (ma-HAT-ma GAN-de) (1869–1948), gained its independence, emerging as the most populous democracy in the world. Her independence also initiated the beginning of the dismantling of the British Empire.

Encounter figure 15.1 *Jahangir, whose name means "World Seizer," sits on a throne supported by an hourglass, which may be a reference to the fleeting of time and the emperor's reign. Jahangir's head is encircled in a halo with the sun and the moon. Before him stands a mullah, or Islamic teacher, to whom the ruler is handing a book. The two figures who are placed below the mullah—a symbolic ranking to show Jahangir's preference of spiritual over worldly matters—have been identified by art historians as the Ottoman sultan and James I of England. At the lower left, the man holding a painting may be Bichitr, the famous court artist who created this miniature.*

Figure 15.11 J. GOYTON after a painting by S. Leclerc. *Louis XIV at the Academy of Science.* 1671. Engraving. Bibliothèque Nationale, Paris. *Science became fashionable during the Baroque age, and rulers provided funds to advance the new discoveries. Louis XIV, king of France, is shown here visiting the Royal Academy of Science, the premier organization of scientists in France. From this period dates the close alliance between science and government, a linkage based on mutual self-interest.*

The Spread of Ideas

In the exciting dawn of the Scientific Revolution, some scientists and intellectuals realized that new scientific findings needed to be given the widest dissemination possible, since the information would be of inestimable value to others who were engaged in their own research. Their enthusiasm for this task led them to share ideas. At first, they exchanged information informally through personal contacts or by chance encounters in the universities. But by midcentury, the scientific society became the usual method for communicating new knowledge. The first one was in England, where King Charles II gave a charter to the Royal Society in 1662. Only a few years later, in 1666, Louis XIV supported the creation of the French Academy of Science (Figure 15.11), and in 1700

German scientists instituted the Berlin Academy of Science.

At the same time, many intellectually curious men and women, who wanted to learn more about the changes taking place in science and mathematics but who lacked specialized training, turned to writers who could demystify the new discoveries and explain them in popular language. One who responded to this interest was the French thinker Bernard de Fontenelle [fon-tuh-NELL] (1657–1757), the long-lived secretary of the Academy of Science. His *Conversations on the Plurality of Worlds* set the early standard for this type of popular literature. With learning and wit, Fontenelle created a dialogue between himself and an inquiring countess in which Newtonian physics and the new astronomy were explained in an informative and entertaining way. Through publicists like Fontenelle, the new theories and ideas became available to a general public and entered the broader culture.

Another French publicist, Pierre Bayle [BEL] (1647–1706), launched the intellectual fashion for arranging ideas in systematic form, as in dictionaries and encyclopedias. Bayle's great popularizing work was called the *Historical and Critical Dictionary,* and it was probably the most controversial book of the Baroque age. For this encyclopedic work, Bayle wrote articles on biblical heroes, Classical and medieval thinkers, and contemporary scholars, many of which challenged Christian beliefs. Each article was a little essay with a text and lengthy footnotes. He approached the work with the aim of setting forth rival and contradictory opinions on each topic; if the result proved to be offensive to the pious, he pointed out that he himself was only following the Bible and the teachings of the Christian faith. Many readers responded to the essays by becoming skeptical about the subjects, as Bayle clearly was. Others questioned Bayle's motives and accused him of atheism. The controversy over his works did not cease with his death. By 1750 his *Dictionary* had been reprinted many times and had spawned many imitations.

Bayle's *Dictionary* marked a new stage in the history of literature for two reasons. First, the work was sold to subscribers, which meant that royal, aristocratic, or ecclesiastical patronage was no longer necessary to publish a book. Second, the extravagant success of his venture showed that a literate public now existed that would buy books if they appealed to its interests. Both of these facts were understood very well by authors in the next generation, who freed writing from the patronage system and inaugurated the world of modern literature with its specialized audiences.

Impact on the Arts

The innovations in science and philosophy coincided with and fostered a changed consciousness not only in the educated public but also in artists and writers.

New attitudes, values, and tastes reflecting these ideas are evident in the creative works of the Baroque period, many of which are discussed and illustrated in Chapter 14. Central among the new ideas was the belief that there is a hidden harmony in nature that may be expressed in mathematical laws. In the arts, this belief was expressed by order and wholeness beneath wild profusion, such as the geometric order that organizes the gardens and grounds of Versailles or the theme of redemption that unifies Milton's sprawling epic, *Paradise Lost.*

A second reflection of the Scientific Revolution, and particularly of the discoveries in astronomy, is the feeling of infinite space that pervades Baroque art. The love of curving lines, elliptical shapes, and flowing contours may be related to the new, expansive views of the planets and the universe. The ultimate expression of these interests and feelings, of course, is the illusionistic ceiling painting (see Figure 14.9).

A final effect of the Scientific Revolution was the elevation of analytic reasoning skills to a position of high esteem in the arts. Just as Newton's genius led him to grasp concepts and laws that had eluded others, so artists and humanists were inspired to use their powers of analysis to look below the surface of human life and search out its hidden truth. Racine's plays, for example, reveal acute insight into human psychology, as do the political philosophies of Hobbes and Locke; and Rembrandt's cycle of self-portraits shows his ability and his desire to reveal his innermost feelings. Baroque art and literature demonstrate that although the Scientific Revolution may have displaced men and women from the center of the universe, an optimistic view of the human predicament was still possible.

The Legacy of the Revolutions in Scientific and Political Thought

One historian of science claims that the Scientific Revolution "outshines everything since the rise of Christianity and reduces the Renaissance and Reformation to the rank of mere episodes . . . within the system of medieval Christendom." Although others hesitate to go that far in praise of this singular event, enough evidence exists to show that the revolution in science caused a dramatic shift in the way people viewed themselves and their world. The Newtonian system became the accepted view of the universe until the twentieth century. Likewise, the new methodology—collecting raw data, reasoning inductively to hypotheses, and verifying results with mathematics—remains the standard in modern science. Out of the gradual spread of this method of reasoning to other areas of thought have emerged the modern social sciences. Even certain disciplines in the humanities—such as linguistics, the study of language—use scientific methods to the extent that is possible.

At the same time that science held out the promise that it could unlock the secrets of nature, it was also contributing to a dramatic upsurge in skepticism. Since the end of the Baroque age, virtually everything in Western culture has been subjected to systematic doubt, including religious beliefs, artistic theories, and social mores. Although many causes besides science lie behind this trend to question all existing standards, the Scientific Revolution created a highly visible model and ready tools for universal doubt. In effect, because Aristotle's and other ancient thinkers' ideas were proven false, modern scholars were inclined to question all other beliefs received from the past. This trend has encouraged the intellectual restlessness that is perhaps the most prominent feature of modern life.

The legacies left by the innovations in Baroque political thought and the expansion of European culture cannot compare with the effects of the rise of modern science. Nevertheless, the changes in political theory and in the relations of Europe with the rest of the world did have strong consequences for modern life. In general, the new political theories gave rise to two rival heritages, the authoritarian tradition, which claims that a strong centralized government is the best way to ensure justice for all citizens, and the liberal tradition, which holds that the citizens are capable of ruling themselves. From this time forward, politics in the West has been organized around the conflicting claims of these two points of view. Until relatively recently, the symbol of this development was the division of the world between the supporters of the authoritarian Soviet Union and the supporters of the democratic United States.

The colonizing efforts in the New World during the 1600s served to extend the geographic limits of the West. As a result, Western ideas and technology may be found today even in the most far-flung reaches of the globe. A negative consequence of the opening of the New World was that slavery, an institution that had virtually died in Europe in the early Middle Ages, was reintroduced, with destructive consequences for the non-Western people who became enslaved. We in the modern age are reaping the bitter harvest of this development.

KEY CULTURAL TERMS

Scientific Revolution
geocentrism
empiricism
inductive reasoning
deductive reasoning

heliocentrism
social contract
liberalism
tabula rasa
virtuoso

SUGGESTIONS FOR FURTHER READING

Primary Sources

BACON, F. *The Essays*. New York: Penguin, 1985. Judiciously edited version of Bacon's highly readable text, dating from 1625, which contributed significantly to the rise of modern scientific thinking.

BAYLE, P. *Historical and Critical Dictionary: Selections*. Translated by R. H. Popkin and C. Brush. Indianapolis: Bobbs-Merrill, 1965. Typical and controversial excerpts from one of the first modern dictionaries; a work originally published in 1697.

DESCARTES, R. *Discourse on Method*. Edited and translated by E. Anscombe and P. T. Geach. Indianapolis: Bobbs-Merrill, 1971. A lucid translation of one of the key tracts of modern philosophy; Descartes's arguments and evidence are relatively easy to understand. First published in 1637.

GALILEI, G. *Dialogue Concerning the Two Chief World Systems—Ptolemaic and Copernican*. Translated by S. Drake, foreword by A. Einstein. Berkeley: University of California Press, 1953. Written in a conversational style, this work—first published in 1632—aligned Galileo with the supporters of the Copernican system and led to his trial by the Roman Catholic authorities.

HOBBES, T. *The Leviathan*. Buffalo, N.Y.: Prometheus Books, 1988. A recent edition of Hobbes's most important work—first issued in 1651—advocating absolutist government without any restraint by the people; this work has inspired many modern forms of authoritarian rule.

LOCKE, J. *An Essay Concerning Human Understanding.* New York: Collier Books, 1965. A good edition, introduced by M. Cranston, of Locke's essay arguing that the mind is shaped by the environment, an assertion that made the progressive theories of the modern world possible; first published in 1690.

———. *Two Treatises of Government.* Cambridge: Cambridge University Press, 1967. An excellent edition with introduction and notes by the distinguished scholar P. Laslett; Locke's *Second Treatise,* making the case for the doctrine of government by consent of the governed, has become the bible of modern liberalism.

CHAPTER *15* HIGHLIGHTS

The Baroque Age II: Revolutions in Scientific and Political Thought, 1600–1715

COPERNICUS, *Revolutions of the Heavenly Bodies* (1543)

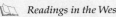 BACON, *Essays* (1597)

KEPLER, *On the Motion of Mars* (1609)

GROTIUS, *The Law of War and Peace* (1625)

 GALILEO, *Dialogue Concerning the Two Chief World Systems—Ptolemaic and Copernican* (1632)

DESCARTES, *Discourse on Method* (1637)

HOBBES, *The Leviathan* (1651)

PASCAL, *Pensées* or *Thoughts* (1670)

FONTENELLE, *Conversations on the Plurality of Worlds* (1686)

NEWTON, *Mathematical Principles of Natural Philosophy* (1687)

LOCKE, *An Essay Concerning Human Understanding* (1690)

LOCKE, *Second Treatise of Civil Government* (1690)

BAYLE, *Historical and Critical Dictionary* (1697)

15.6 REMBRANDT, *The Anatomy Lesson of Dr. Tulp* (1632)

15.9 HOLLAR, *Indian of Virginia, Male* (1645)

15.7 HALS, *René Descartes* (after 1649)

15.5 KNELLER, *Sir Isaac Newton* (1702)

15.2 MERIAN, *Insect Metamorphoses in Surinam* (1705)

Literature & Philosophy   Art & Architecture   Music & Dance

Readings in the Western Humanities   CD, The Western Humanities

16 THE AGE OF REASON
1700–1789

The scientific discoveries and philosophic ideas that made the seventeenth century so intellectually exciting bore fruit in the eighteenth century, a period often referred to as the Age of Reason. The great revelations of the Scientific Revolution led thinkers in the 1700s to believe they were living in a time of illumination and enlightenment. Committed to scientific methodology, mathematical reasoning, and a healthy skepticism, they fervently believed their knowledge could lead to the improvement of both the individual and society.

The Age of Reason was marked by four different trends. The first was the growing concentration of political power in the great states, a process that had begun during the Baroque era. France was the most powerful state, followed by Great Britain (the new name of a unified England and Scotland), Prussia, Austria, Russia, and the Netherlands (Map 16.1). The second trend was the return of the aristocracy to prominence after a century or more of decline. In time, the ostentatious culture spawned by the resurgent aristocrats proved to be their swan song, as the French Revolution, at the end of the century, destroyed their bases of power (see Chapter 17). The third trend was the rise to political and cultural eminence of the middle class who supported those progressive thinkers who advocated social equality, social justice, and a thorough revamping of society. The intellectual and cultural movement spawned by these thinkers is called the **Enlightenment,** which constitutes the fourth and most important trend that helped to reshape Western life in the 1700s.

◄ **Detail** SIR JOSHUA REYNOLDS. *Mrs. Siddons as the Tragic Muse.* 1784. Oil on canvas, 7′9″ × 4′9″. Huntington Art Gallery, San Marino, California.

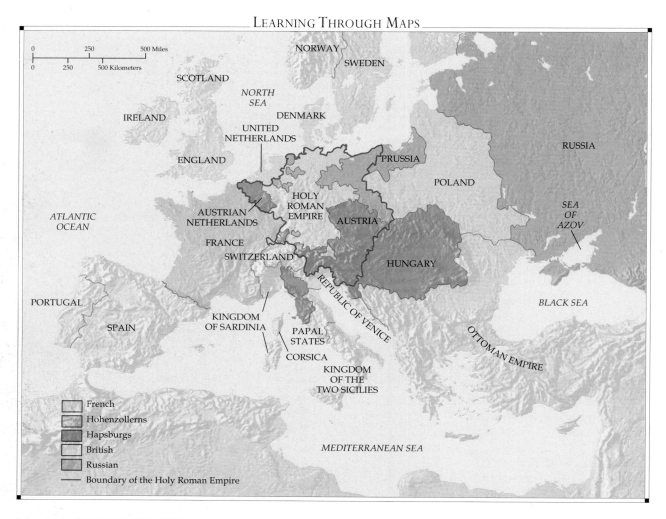

Map 16.1 EUROPE, 1763–1789
This map shows the political divisions of Europe in the mid–eighteenth century.
Locate the territories of France, Great Britain, Russia, the Hohenzollern dynasty, and the Hapsburg dynasty—the five great powers. **Which** great power has the most compact state? **Which** great power has the most widely dispersed lands? **How** would geography and cultural diversity influence a state's ability to maintain great power status? **Notice** the vastness of the Ottoman Empire, a Muslim state, in the southeast corner of Europe.

At the same time that these political and social trends were occurring, a new style in art, architecture, and music was developing in France in reaction to the excesses of the Baroque. This style, known as Rococo, was more informal and graceful, less ponderous and oppressive than the Baroque (Figure 16.1). After about 1750, in reaction to both the Rococo and the Baroque, a very different style—the Neoclassical—developed. Unlike the Rococo, the Neoclassical style in art and architecture spread widely throughout Europe and the United States. In music, a refined and elegant Classical style developed, graced by the incomparable presence of Mozart, arguably the greatest musical genius who ever lived.

THE ENLIGHTENMENT

Eighteenth-century thinkers derived their ideals and goals from a variety of sources. Following the example of ancient Greece and Rome, they rejected superstition, sought truth through the use of reason, and viewed the world from a secular, human-centered perspective. Drawing on the Renaissance, they embraced humanism—the belief that a human being becomes a better person through the study and practice of literature, philosophy, music, and the arts. And from the seventeenth-century revolutions in science and philosophy, particularly the works of Newton, Bacon, Descartes, and Locke, they derived a reliance on rationalism, empiricism, skepticism, and the experimental method, along with a belief in human perfectibility through education and unlimited progress.

Despite the power of these ideas, they reached a relatively small percentage of Europe's population. The Enlightenment had its greatest effect in the cultural capitals of France and Great Britain—Paris, London, and Edinburgh. Many aristocrats read the works of Enlightenment writers, as did many members of the middle class, particularly educators, lawyers, journalists, and clergymen. Ultimately, enough literate and influential people were converted to the goals of the Enlightenment to have an effect on the revolutionary events that occurred later in the eighteenth century (Timeline 16.1).

The *Philosophes* and Their Program

The central figures of the Enlightenment were a small band of writers known as ***philosophes,*** the French word for "philosophers." Not philosophers in a formal sense, the *philosophes* were more likely to be popularizers who wanted to influence public opinion. They avoided the methods of academic scholars, such as engaging in philosophical debates or writing only for colleagues, and tried to reach large audiences through novels, essays, pamphlets, plays, poems, and histories. In this they were following the lead of Fontenelle, who had popularized the new astronomy in his *Conversations on the Plurality of Worlds* (see Chapter 15). When possible, they openly attacked what they deemed to be the evils of society and supported those rulers who favored change, the so-called enlightened despots. When the censors threatened, however, they disguised their radical messages or else published their criticisms in the Netherlands—the most liberal state in Europe at the time.

The Enlightenment was essentially a product of French cultural life, and Paris was its capital. The principal *philosophes* were Voltaire, Diderot, Montesquieu—all French—and by adoption the French-speaking Swiss writer Rousseau. But major *philosophes* appeared elsewhere in Europe, notably in Great Britain, and in Britain's North American colonies. The most influential of these voices were the English historian Edward Gibbon, the American writer Benjamin Franklin, and two Scottish thinkers, the economist Adam Smith and the philosopher David Hume.

The *philosophes,* though never in complete agreement and often diametrically opposed, shared certain assumptions. They had full confidence in reason; they were convinced that nature was orderly and fundamentally good and could be understood through the

Figure 16.1 SIR JOSHUA REYNOLDS. *Mrs. Siddons as the Tragic Muse.* 1784. Oil on canvas, 7′9″ × 4′9″. Huntington Art Gallery, San Marino, California. *The Rococo portrait painter Sir Joshua Reynolds painted many English personalities of his day, including Sarah Siddons. Mrs. Siddons, who came from a theater family, won the applause of England's knowledgeable and discerning audiences to emerge as the most famous actress of tragic drama in the late eighteenth century. Reynolds distances Mrs. Siddons from the viewer and surrounds her with elaborate scenery as if she were on a proscenium stage in a darkened theater. The two figures behind her represent Aristotle's definitions of tragedy—pity and terror.*

empirical method; they believed that change and progress would improve society, since human beings were perfectible. Faith in reason led them to reject religious doctrine, in particular Roman Catholic dogma; to denounce bigotry and intolerance; and to advocate freedom of religious choice. Maintaining

Timeline 16.1   THE AGE OF REASON

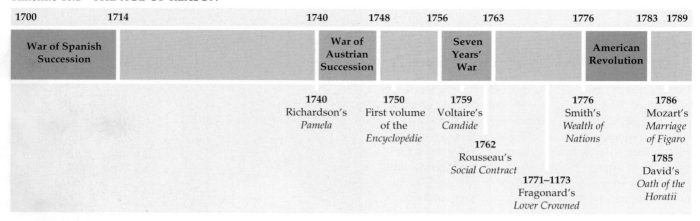

that education liberated humanity from ignorance and superstition, the *philosophes* called for an expanded educational system independent of ecclesiastical control.

The *philosophes* thought that the political, economic, and religious institutions should be reformed to bring "the greatest happiness for the greatest numbers"—a phrase that expresses a key Enlightenment ideal and that, in the nineteenth century, became the battle cry of the English thinker and reformer Jeremy Bentham (see Chapter 18). These theorists anticipated a general overhaul of society, leading to universal peace and a golden age for humanity. In effect, they preached a secular gospel that happiness need not be delayed until after death but could be enjoyed here on earth.

Envisioning a rejuvenated society that guaranteed natural rights to its citizens, the *philosophes* were almost unanimous in thinking exclusively in terms of men and not of women. They still considered women their intellectual and physical inferiors and thus in need of male protection or guidance. Not until the next period were voices raised on behalf of women's rights and only then under the inspiration of the French Revolution.

One of those moved by the revolutionary winds blowing from France was the English writer Mary Wollstonecraft (1759–1797), who, in *A Vindication of the Rights of Woman* (1792), used Enlightenment ideals to urge the liberation of her own sex. Like Rousseau, Wollstonecraft was a democrat and opposed to hierarchy in all forms: in the aristocracy, the military, and the clergy to the extent that promotion was based on obsequiousness. Unlike Rousseau, she was dedicated to the rights of women, whom she repeatedly called "one-half of the human race." Rejecting the "Adam's rib" explanation of woman's inferiority as being simply a male fabrication, she

claimed that women were as rational as men and thus should be treated the same. The heart of this latter-day *philosophe*'s argument was that women should abandon feminine artifice and cunning, especially the all-consuming need to be socially pleasing, and through education become equal partners with educated men. Starting in the nineteenth century, reformers gradually began to take up Wollstonecraft's challenge, particularly her call for female education and women's suffrage.

Deism

Newtonian science implied that God had set the universe in motion and then left it to run by its own natural laws. The *philosophes* accepted this metaphor of God as a clockmaker, and in place of traditional Christianity some thinkers now offered a version of Christianity called **Deism.** Deists focused on the worship of a Supreme Being, a God who created the universe and set the laws of nature in motion but who never again interfered in natural or human matters. Believing in this idea of a clockmaker God, the Deists rejected the efficacy of prayer and reduced the role of Jesus from that of savior to that of a good moral example.

Deism was espoused by only a relatively small percentage of Westerners, however, such as Benjamin Franklin in the British colony of Pennsylvania. Religions that ran counter to the Enlightenment's ideas—including the new sect of Methodists founded by John Wesley (1703–1791) in England—continued to attract most of the populace. Although it did not find wide acceptance, Deism's appeal marked another shift in religious attitudes and was added evidence of the growing secularization of European consciousness in the 1700s.

Figure 16.2 Illustration from the *Encyclopédie: Cotton Plantation in the French West Indies. 1751–1765. As principal editor of the* Encyclopédie, *Diderot adopted Francis Bacon's notion that all knowledge is useful. Thus, the articles and the illustrations for this reference work focused on practical data such as soapmaking, human anatomy, and military drill. In this drawing, for example, the readers could peruse the romanticized plantation scene to discover how raw cotton was prepared for shipment to European mills.*

The *Encyclopédie*

The message of the *philosophes* was communicated by a variety of means: through pamphlets, essays, and books, through private and public discussions and debates, through the new journalistic press, and, especially in France, through the salon—the half-social, half-serious gatherings where the fashionable elite met to discuss ideas. But the principal work of the *philosophes* was the *Encyclopédie*—the monumental project that remains the summation of the Enlightenment. Two earlier works, Chambers's *Cyclopedia* in England (1728) and Bayle's *Dictionary* in France (1697) (see Chapter 15), paved the way for the *Encyclopédie*. Begun in 1750 and completed in 1772, the original work comprised seventeen text volumes and eleven books of plates and illustrations (Figure 16.2). More than 161 writers wrote articles for this educational venture, which was intended as a summary of existing knowledge in the arts, crafts, and sciences.

The editor of the *Encyclopédie* was Denis Diderot [DEED-uh-roh] (1713–1784), one of the giants of the Enlightenment. Diderot was constantly in trouble with the authorities because of the work's controversial essays, which he asserted were meant "to change the general way of thinking." Publication was halted in 1759 by the state censor but resumed secretly with the collusion of other government officials. Unlike most publications of the period, the project was funded by its readers, not by the crown or the church, and private circulating libraries rented the volumes to untold numbers of customers.

The Physiocrats

Under the broad umbrella of Enlightenment ideas, the *philosophes* were joined by a group of French writers concerned with economic matters—the **Physiocrats,** as they called themselves. (The term is a coined word, from Greek, meaning "rule of, or from, the earth.") The Physiocrats examined the general nature of the economy and, in particular, the strengths and weaknesses of mercantilism, the prevailing economic system, in which the state regulated trade and production for its own benefit. In their eyes, this state-run system had hindered the growth of the economies of the various European countries. Contrary to its goals, mercantilism had lowered the productivity of workers, especially farmers, and had led to labor unrest and riots.

Guided by Enlightenment doctrine that "natural laws" governed society, the Physiocrats assumed that similar "laws" applied to economic growth and decline. After a thorough analysis of the French economy, they concluded that certain fundamental economic principles did exist, such as the law of supply and demand, and that these laws operated best when free from governmental interference. Accordingly, they recommended the dismantling of mercantilism and the adoption of *laissez faire*, French for "to let alone"—in other words, an economy where the self-regulating laws of free trade were in effect. In addition, they argued that unrestricted enjoyment of private property was necessary for individual freedom. These French thinkers concluded that both the individual and the entire society automatically benefited when all people

Figure 16.3 JEAN-BAPTISTE-SIMEON CHARDIN. *The Morning Toilette*. 1741. Oil on canvas, 19¼ × 15⅓″. National-museum, Stockholm. *Chardin's* The Morning Toilette *serves as a symbol of the middle class, whose rise to cultural promi-nence in the Age of Reason was a foretaste of their political power in the nineteenth century. The painting depicts a middle-class interior, as identified by the furniture, the toilet articles, and, most especially, the mother engaged in a task that a servant, in an aristocratic house, would have performed. More than a simple genre scene, the painting also conveys a moral message that appealed to moralistic middle-class taste. In effect, Chardin warns of the vanity of women by showing the little girl, whose hair is being combed by her mother, turned so as to look at her reflection in the mirror.*

THE GREAT POWERS DURING THE AGE OF REASON

In comparison with the seventeenth century, the period between 1715 and 1789 was relatively peaceful; national conflicts were few and brief. In addition, Europe experienced a slow but steady economic expansion that was supported by a continuing increase in population. The prosperity fueled the rise of the middle classes, especially in Great Britain and Holland. In France, however, the middle class made only modest gains, and in central and eastern Europe they were a small fraction of the population.

Society: Continuity and Change

A major consequence of the century's modest eco-nomic growth was the growing urbanization of society. Although most Europeans still followed tra-ditional livelihoods on farms and in villages, cities and towns offered increasing opportunities for ambi-tious folk. The rural-to-urban shift originated in Eng-land, the home of the Industrial Revolution, and to a lesser extent in France. Only in the next century did it slowly spread to some parts of central and eastern Europe.

The traditional social hierarchy kept each class in its place. The aristocracy constituted only about 3 percent of the total population, but it possessed tremendous power and wealth. The upper middle class—encompassing rich merchants, bankers, and professionals—normally resided in the rapidly expanding urban areas and influ-enced business and governmental affairs. In the broad middle class were the smaller merchants, shopkeepers, skilled artisans, and bureaucrats (Figure 16.3). Beneath the middle ranks were the lesser artisans and craftspeo-ple, and below them, the metropolitan poor, who per-formed menial labor and were often unemployed.

In the countryside, the nobility and the prosperous farmers owned large sections of the land and con-trolled the rural populace. The small cultivators, tenant farmers, landless workers, and indentured con-tract laborers constituted a complex group whose legal, social, and personal rights varied widely across Europe. Next were the peasants, whose status ranged from freedom in western Europe to serfdom in Russia. (Serfs were bound to the land they worked, but they had customary rights, and strictly speaking they were not slaves.) These impoverished people often bore the brunt of the taxes and the contempt of the other classes.

With few exceptions, such as the upper-middle-class women who played influential roles in the salons, women remained subordinate to men. As mentioned

were allowed to serve their own self-interest instead of working for the good of the state.

At about the same time, the Scottish economist Adam Smith (1723–1790) was developing similar ideas. He reported his conclusions in *An Inquiry into the Nature and Causes of the Wealth of Nations* (1776), a book that became the bible of industrial capitalism and remains so today. In this work, Smith blamed mercan-tilism for the economic woes of his time, identified the central role played by labor in manufacturing, and called for open and competitive trade so that the "in-visible hand" of a free-market economy could operate. Smith's ideas were quickly absorbed by budding en-trepreneurs and had an immediate impact on the changes being generated by the Industrial Revolution (see Chapter 17).

earlier, the *philosophes,* who thoroughly critiqued society, failed to recognize women's contributions or champion their rights. Even Jean-Jacques Rousseau, who was often at odds with his fellow writers, agreed with the *philosophes* that women were inferior to men and should be submissive to them.

Another group who gained little from the Enlightenment were the African slaves in Europe's overseas colonies. During the eighteenth century, ships from England, France, and Holland carried about six million Africans to enslavement in the New World. Efforts to abolish the slave trade or even to improve the conditions of the slaves proved futile despite the moral disapproval of the *philosophes* and the pleas of English Christians.

Absolutism, Limited Monarchy, and Enlightened Despotism

The eighteenth century was the last great age of kings in the West. In most countries, the royal rulers followed traditional policies even in the face of criticism or opposition. Supported by inefficient bureaucracies and costly armies, they controlled the masses through heavy taxes and threats of brutality while holding in check the privileged groups. Although a few rulers attempted reforms, by the end of the century most of the monarchies were weakening as democratic sentiments continued to rise.

In France, the kings struggled to hold on to the power they inherited from Louis XIV. In Great Britain, the kings fought a losing battle against Parliament and the restrictions of constitutional monarchy. In Prussia and Austria, so-called enlightened despots experimented with reforms to strengthen their states, while in Russia the czars found new ways to expand absolutism. By midcentury, the Continent had undergone a series of brief wars that ended the several relatively peaceful decades Europe had enjoyed (see Timeline 16.1). For France and England, the Continental conflicts soon escalated into global commercial, territorial, and colonial rivalries that were resolved only with the outcome of the American Revolutionary War (1775–1783).

France: The Successors to the Sun King   No French ruler was able to recapture the splendor of Louis XIV. Louis XV (r. 1715–1774), who succeeded to full political control at age thirteen and never acquired a strong will to rule, only compounded the problems of the French state. Those he chose as his subordinates were not always talented or loyal, and he permitted his mistresses, who were not trained in government, to influence his decisions about official matters. When

Louis XV, despairing over a military defeat, expressed his misgivings about the future of France to his royal favorite, Madame de Pompadour, she reportedly replied with the prophetic words *"Après nous le déluge"* ("After us, the flood").

Life at Louis XV's court could not be sustained in the grand manner of the late Sun King, and the nobles began to leave Versailles for Paris. Whether at Versailles or elsewhere, educated aristocrats were becoming fascinated by Enlightenment ideas, and they and their wives read the *Encyclopédie* and studied the writings of the *philosophes.* Upper-class women played influential roles in presiding over salons, where the enlightened thinkers and their admirers gathered to dine and converse. Two of the most well known salons were conducted by Madame du Deffand [day-FAHN] (1679–1780) and Julie Lespinasse [les-pee-NAHS] (1732–1776). For a number of years, Madame du Deffand (Marie de Marquise du Deffand) claimed Voltaire as her most prominent literary celebrity, and his presence ensured that other *philosophes* would attend her gatherings. Julie de Lespinasse, serving first as companion to Madame du Deffand, broke away to found her own salon, where Jean d'Alembert, coeditor of Diderot's *Encyclopédie,* was a favored guest.

Even though the French elite debated the merits of reform and the more controversial topics raised by the *philosophes,* Louis XV clearly did not accept the movement's call for change. It is ironic that the country where the Enlightenment began failed to undertake any of its progressive reforms. Indeed, when changes were finally introduced under Louis XVI (r. 1774–1792), they were too little and too late.

Handicapped by the weak Louis XVI, France found its preeminent position in foreign affairs challenged by Great Britain, Austria, and Prussia. As a result of the Seven Years' War, which began in 1756, France suffered defeats in Europe and lost its holdings in North America and India. During the American Revolution, France sided with the colonists against Great Britain, its foe at home and overseas. France's aid to the Americans further diminished the government's financial resources and forced the nation deeper into debt.

France's kings also failed to solve the nation's domestic problems, the consequence of their own failures of leadership and that of the royal officials called *intendants,* who were supposed to coordinate the loose federation of provinces into a functioning French state. Meanwhile, the tax collectors failed to provide adequate revenues for the state because of the corrupt tax system. And, most important, the crown was faced with a resurgent aristocracy determined to recover the feudal privileges it had lost under Louis XIV. Rather than joining the king's efforts to reform the judicial system, the nobility blocked the crown at every step. The middle class combined forces with some sympathetic aristocrats, transforming what had been a feudal issue into a struggle for freedom in the name of the people. In 1789, during the reign of Louis XVI, France started on a revolutionary course that united most of French society against the crown and that culminated in the French Revolution (1789–1799) (see Chapter 17).

Great Britain and the Hanoverian Kings To the *philosophes,* Great Britain was the ideal model of a nation. To them, Britain seemed more stable and prosperous than the states on the Continent, a success they attributed to the limited powers of the English monarchy imposed by Parliament during the Glorious Revolution of 1688. Britain's laws guaranteed to every Englishman certain political and social rights, such as free speech and fair and speedy trials. Britain's economy was strong as well. Prompted by enterprising merchants and progressive landowners, the nation was dominant in an expanding global market; at home, the standard of living was rising for the growing population.

After the death of Queen Anne in 1714, the English crown was inherited by George I, a great-grandson of James I and the Protestant ruler of the German principality of Hanover. The first two Hanoverian kings seemed more interested in events in Germany than in England, leading to a decline in their powers, and eventually the kings reigned in splendid isolation at the royal court. George I (r. 1714–1727) allowed Parliament to run the country. Under George II (r. 1727–1760), Britain was drawn into the Seven Years' War but emerged victorious, the dominant presence in world trade. From this pinnacle of international power, Great Britain occupied center stage until the outbreak of World War I in 1914.

Nevertheless, Great Britain faced serious domestic problems under George III (r. 1760–1820) because he sought to restore royal powers lost to Parliament by his predecessors. This internal struggle affected foreign policy when the king and Parliament offered differing proposals to control the economic development of the American colonies through export and import quotas, duties, and taxes. The differences between the two proposals hastened the onset of the American Revolution and probably contributed to Britain's eventual defeat.

Enlightened Despotism in Central and Eastern Europe
The system of European states underwent some modifications during the Age of Reason. Great Britain and France now dominated western Europe; the less populous countries of Holland and Sweden declined in power; Spain turned increasingly inward and all but

disappeared from Continental affairs; and Italy, under Austrian and papal control, remained an economic backwater. Meanwhile, Prussia, Austria, and Russia jockeyed for control of central and eastern Europe. Under their absolutist rulers, these states pursued aggressive policies, seizing territories from one another and their weaker neighbors. Although these rulers portrayed themselves as enlightened despots, their regimes were generally characterized by oppressive and authoritarian policies.

By 1740 Prussia had a solid economic base, a hardworking bureaucracy, and an efficient army. Capitalizing on these advantages, Frederick II, known as Frederick the Great (r. 1740–1786), turned Prussia into a leading European power. A pragmatic diplomat, a skilled military tactician, and a student of the Enlightenment and French culture, Frederick was an enlightened despot of the type beloved by the *philosophes.* He even attempted (though failed) to reform his state's agrarian economy and social system in accordance with the rational principle that all individuals have the natural right to choose personally the best way to live.

Prussia's chief rival in central Europe was Austria. Throughout the 1700s, Austria's rulers struggled to govern a multiethnic population that included large numbers of Germans, Hungarians, Czechs, and Slovaks along with Poles, Italians, and various Slavic minorities. At the same time, the emperors tried, with mixed success, to assert Austria's role as a great power, both politically and culturally. Schönbrunn Palace in Vienna, for example, was built as a rival to France's Versailles (Figure 16.4). Two rulers stand out—the Hapsburg emperors Maria Theresa and Joseph, her son, whose combined reigns lasted from 1740 to 1790.

Unlike Frederick II of Prussia, Maria Theresa (r. 1740–1780) was not attracted to the ideas of the *philosophes.* More important was her Roman Catholic faith, which led her to portray herself to her subjects as their universal mother. She was perhaps the most beloved monarch in this age of kings. Maria Theresa's reforming zeal sprang not from philosophic principle but from a reaction against Austria's territorial losses during military defeats. She used all her royal prerogatives to overhaul the political and military machinery of the state. Along with universal military conscription, increased revenues, and more equitable distribution of taxes, she wanted a general reorganization of society that gave more uniform treatment to all citizens. Her efforts were not wasted, for her son Joseph II took up her uncompleted task and became the ultimate personification of enlightened despotism.

During his brief reign, from 1780 to 1790, Joseph II launched far-reaching changes to raise farm production

Figure 16.4 JOHANN FERDINAND HETZENDORF VON HOHENBERG. Gloriette, or "The Temple of Fame." Schönbrunn Palace Gardens. 1768. Vienna. *The Gloriette, a triumphal arch flanked by colonnaded screens, is situated on the highest point within the vast gardens of Schönbrunn Palace. Designed by Johann Ferdinand Hetzendorf von Hohenberg (1732–1816), court architect to Empress Maria Theresa, it is the crowning touch of his beautification campaign for the palace grounds. It functioned as a theatrical backdrop for court rituals and receptions. Constructed partly from the ruins of a castle near the site, the Gloriette uses Classical features (colonnades, balustrades, and statuary and urns) though its style is Baroque (profuse decorative details and the reflecting pool).*

and to provide more economic opportunities for the peasants. Convinced that his country's economic and social institutions had to be fully modernized if it was to survive, he abolished serfdom and passed decrees guaranteeing religious toleration and free speech. In the 1790s much of what he had accomplished was undone by his successors, who, fearing the excesses of the French Revolution, restored aristocratic and ecclesiastic control and privileges.

Russia was the newest member of the family of great powers, having achieved this stature during the reign of Peter the Great (r. 1682–1725). Abroad, Peter had made Russia's presence known, and at home he had begun to reform political, economic, and social institutions along Western lines. Most of his eighteenth-century successors were ineffective, if not incompetent, until Catherine the Great (r. 1762–1796) became empress. She pursued the unifying policies of Peter, but unlike him she was able to win the powerful support of the large landowners. A patron of the Enlightenment, Catherine sought the advice of a few *philosophes,* including Diderot. She also attempted to improve the low farm productivity and the nearly enslaved condition of the peasants, but the vastness of Russia's problems and the reactionary autocratic government defeated any genuine reforms.

CULTURAL TRENDS IN THE EIGHTEENTH CENTURY: FROM ROCOCO TO NEOCLASSICAL

Even though the eighteenth century was dominated by the Enlightenment, other cultural trends also held sway. The Rococo style in the arts mirrored the taste of the French nobility; the succeeding Neoclassical style was adopted and supported by the progressive writers, artists, intellectuals, and ambitious members of the middle class. Meanwhile, innovations in literature were pointing the way toward the modern world.

The Rococo Style in the Arts

Conceived on a more intimate scale than the Baroque and committed to frivolous subjects and themes, the **Rococo** style arose in France in the waning years of the Sun King's reign. With his death in 1715 and the succession of his five-year-old heir, Louis XV, the nobility were released both from Versailles and from the ponderous Baroque style. Paris once again became the capital of art, ideas, and fashion in the Western world. There, the Rococo style was created for the French elite almost single-handedly by the Flemish painter and decorator Jean-Antoine Watteau.

Figure 16.5 JEAN-ANTOINE WATTEAU. *Departure from Cythera*. 1717. Oil on canvas, 4′3″ × 6′4½″. Louvre. *Watteau's aristocratic lovers, savoring a last few moments of pleasure, represent the idealized image that the eighteenth-century elite wanted to present to the world. No hint of the age's problems is allowed to disturb this idyllic scene. From the court costumes to the hovering cupids, this painting transforms reality into a stage set—the ideal of Rococo art.*

The Rococo gradually spread to most of Europe, but its acceptance was tied to religion and class. It was embraced by the aristocracy in Germany, Italy, and Austria; Roman Catholic nobles in Austria developed a version of Rococo that was second in importance only to that of France. The English, on the other hand, rejected the Rococo, possibly because its erotic undercurrent and sexual themes offended the Protestant middle-class sensibility. Consequently, Rococo style is a purely Continental phenomenon; there is no English Rococo.

Rococo Painting Jean-Antoine Watteau [wah-TOE] (1684–1721) specialized in paintings that depict *fêtes galantes,* or aristocratic entertainments. In these works, Watteau portrays the intimate world of the aristocracy, dressed in sumptuous clothing, grouped in parks and gardens, and often accompanied by costumed actors, another of Watteau's favorite subjects. He filled these bucolic settings with air and lightness and grace—all of which were a contrast to the occasionally heavy-handed Baroque. Mythological allusions made Watteau's works depictions of Classical themes rather than merely scenes of aristocratic life.

In 1717 Watteau became the first Rococo painter to be elected to membership in the Royal Academy of Painting and Sculpture in Paris. As required by the terms of election, he submitted as his diploma piece *Departure from Cythera* (Figure 16.5). The setting is Cythera, the legendary island of Venus, whose bust on the right is garlanded with her devotees' roses. Forming a wavering line, the lovers express hesitation as they make their farewells: The couple under the statue are lost in reverie as a clothed cupid tugs at the woman's skirt; beside this group a suitor assists his lady to her feet; and next to them a gentleman accompanies his companion to the waiting boat as she longingly gazes backward. This melancholy scene, signified by the setting sun and the departing lovers, represents Watteau's homage to the brevity of human passion.

In *Departure from Cythera,* many of the new values of the Rococo style can be seen. Where the Baroque

Figure 16.6 JEAN-ANTOINE WATTEAU. *The Sign for Gersaint's Shop.* Ca. 1720. Oil on canvas, 5'11⅝" × 10'1⅛". Schloss Charlottenburg, Berlin. *This painting of a shop interior illustrates the social dynamics of the emerging art market in the eighteenth century. The aristocratic customers act as if they own the place, turning it into a genteel lounge. The shop employees, on the other hand, have clearly inferior social roles; one brings forward a heavy painting for inspection, another holds a miniature work up to view, and a third stands downcast at the left. Through such details, Watteau reveals the social gulf between classes that was implicit in the Rococo style.*

favored tumultuous scenes depicting the passions and ecstasies of the saints, the Rococo focused on smaller, gentler moments, usually involving love of one variety or another, whether erotic, romantic, or sentimental. Where the Baroque used intense colors to convey feelings of power and grandeur, the Rococo used soft pastels to evoke nostalgia and melancholy. The monumentality and sweeping movement of Baroque art were brought down to a human scale in the Rococo, making it more suited to interiors, furniture, and architectural details than to architecture itself. *Departure from Cythera* shows the Rococo to be a refined, sensual style, perfect for providing a charming backdrop to the private social life of the eighteenth-century aristocracy.

In one of his last works, *The Sign for Gersaint's Shop,* Watteau removed all mythological and idyllic references (Figure 16.6). His subject, a shop where paintings are sold (François-Edmé Gersaint [1696–1750] was one of the outstanding art dealers of the eighteenth century), indicates the importance of the new commercial art market that was soon to replace the aristocratic patronage system. Within the store's interior, elegantly dressed customers browse, flirt, and study the shopkeeper's wares. The sexual motifs in the pictures on the walls and in the oval canvas on the right reinforce the sensuous atmosphere of this painting. But Watteau also makes this Parisian scene dignified by giving equal focus to the human figures and the role each plays in the overall composition.

Watteau's painting is a telling metaphor of the end of an age and the beginning of another. This meaning can be interpreted in the crating of the portrait of Louis XIV (on the left), a punning metaphor for the demise of the old political order and the style of Louis XIV. Art collecting in the age of Louis XIV had been restricted largely to kings, princes, and nobles, but in the Rococo period, many new collectors came from the world of the upper bourgeoisie and shopped in commercial galleries like Gersaint's shop.

Watteau's paintings convey a dreamy eroticism, but those of François Boucher [boo-SHAY] (1703–1770)

Figure 16.7 FRANÇOIS BOUCHER. *Nude on a Sofa.* 1752. Oil on canvas, 23⅜ × 25⅜″. Alte Pinakothek, Munich. *The trend toward the secularization of consciousness that had been building since the Late Middle Ages reached a high point in this nude by Boucher. Boucher's frank enjoyment of sensual pleasure and his desire to convey that feeling to the viewer represented a new stage in the relationship between artists and the public. By portraying his subject without any justification except eroticism, Boucher embodied a new artistic sensibility.*

Figure 16.8 ELISABETH-LOUISE VIGÉE-LEBRUN. *Marie Antoinette and Her Children.* 1787. Oil on canvas, 9′1¼″ × 7′5⅝″. Musée National du Château de Versailles. *Like the greatest court painters, Vigée-Lebrun is able to provide psychological insight into her highborn subjects while flattering them. Here, Marie Antoinette, though surrounded by adoring children, seems uncomfortable in a maternal role. Instead, with her head held in an imperious manner and her face a beautiful mask, she looks every inch the lady of fashion, which she indeed was. Vigée-Lebrun has muted this psychological insight by providing rich distractions for the viewer's eye, such as the shiny surfaces of the queen's attire (satin gown, pearls, and hat) and the elegant room (carpet, chest, and tasseled cushion).*

are characterized by unabashed sexuality. Boucher was the supreme exponent of the graceful Louis XV style, becoming official painter to the French crown in 1765. His voluptuous nudes, which were made more titillating by their realistic portrayal without Classical trappings, appealed to the king and to the decadent court nobility. Boucher's *Nude on a Sofa* is probably a study of one of Louis XV's mistresses (Figure 16.7). The casually suggestive pose, the rumpled bedclothes, and the delicate pastel shades are all designed to charm and to seduce. Boucher's art, though masterful, epitomizes the lax morals of French noble life that were becoming increasingly offensive even to other Rococo artists.

A different focus is evident in the Rococo portraits of Elisabeth-Louise Vigée-Lebrun [vee-ZHAY-luh-BRUHN] (1755–1842), who became the leading society painter of the later eighteenth century and one of the relatively few women to gain independent fame as an artist. In 1787 she painted a famous family portrait of Louis XVI's queen, Marie Antoinette, whom she served as court painter (Figure 16.8). With this work, Vigée-Lebrun solidified her status as the equal of the best court portraitists of the century. Elements of the Rococo style can be seen in this elegant portrait of the queen and her children in the dainty colors, the graceful gestures, and the feeling of domestic intimacy. The queen's role as mother is the focus as she sits with the baby Duke of Normandy in her lap, the small Madame Royale at her side, and the little Dauphin pointing at the empty cradle. Vigée-Lebrun's depiction of Marie Antoinette dressed as a lady of fashion instead of in the traditional trappings of royalty reflects the queen's well-known fondness for simplicity. Stifled by the formality of court life, the queen promoted a more relaxed social code at Le Hameau, a rustic hideaway she had built for herself at Versailles, where all rules of court etiquette were set aside.

The last great French Rococo painter, Jean-Honoré Fragonard [frag-uh-NAHR] (1732–1806), revived Watteau's graceful, debonair themes, as in *The Lover Crowned* (Figure 16.9). A young woman crowns her kneeling lover with a wreath of flowers, while an artist in the lower right corner sketches the enraptured pair. The man's red suit and the woman's yellow dress cause them to stand out dramatically from the setting in which they are placed. The terrace setting is rich in sensual, if not erotic, details, including rose blossoms, boxed orange trees, two guitars, and sheet music. The statue of a sleeping cupid, mounted on a pedestal, presides over this erotic episode.

What is fresh in Fragonard's art and prefigures Romanticism is his finely detailed treatment of the natural background, which, although resembling the idealized backgrounds of Watteau, has a vivid, luxuriant

Figure 16.9 JEAN-HONORÉ FRAGONARD. *The Lover Crowned.* 1771–1773. Oil on panel, 10′5⅛″ × 7′11¾″. The Frick Collection, New York. *This painting was one of a series of four panels known as* The Progress of Love, *commissioned by Madame du Barry, Louis XV's mistress and rival to Madame de Pompadour. Intended to adorn a pavilion nicknamed the "sanctuary of pleasure" at her palace, the panels were rejected by Madame du Barry, for reasons unknown, before they were installed. Like the other panels in this series,* The Lover Crowned *is a symbolic allegory. In effect, the couple's love has been consummated, as symbolized by the floral wreath and the sleeping cupid. All that remains is for the artist, a reference to Fragonard himself, to transform the lovers' passion into a work of art.*

life of its own. In Fragonard's painting, nature seems almost to threaten the couple's romantic idyll. Despite his interest in landscape, however, Fragonard remained faithful to the Rococo style even after it fell out of fashion. His paintings continued to focus on the playful themes of flirtation and pursuit in a frivolous, timeless world.

Rococo Interiors The decorative refinement and graceful detail of the Rococo style made it well suited to interior design. A major Rococo design element was *rocaille:* fanciful stucco ornaments in the shape of ribbons, leaves, stems, flowers, interlaces, arabesques, and elongated, curving lines applied to walls and ceilings. The effect of *rocaille* was to make solid surfaces look more like fleeting illusions.

Figure 16.10 GERMAIN BOFFRAND. Salon de la Princesse, Hôtel de Soubise. Ca. 1735–1740. Paris. *The Salon de la Princesse was a reception room designed for the apartment of the Princess de Soubise. The graceful undulations of Boffrand's design represent the exquisite style of the Louis XV era. A typical Rococo design element is the blurring of the line between the walls and the ceiling.*

Figure 16.11 BALTHASAR NEUMANN AND OTHERS. Kaisersaal, the Residenz. View toward the south wall. 1719–1744. Würzburg, Germany. *In this magnificent room, the ceiling fresco by Tiepolo is gorgeously framed with multicolored marble curtains pulled back by stucco angels. Other sumptuous details include ornate framed paintings, cartouches, and mirrors; gilded Corinthian capitals and arabesques; and crystal chandeliers suspended low over a polychrome marble floor.*

Mirrors further deceived the senses, and chandeliers provided jewel-like lighting; all elements worked together to create a glittering, luxurious setting for an ultrarefined society.

Germain Boffrand [bo-FRAHN] (1667–1754), France's royal architect, helped to establish Rococo's popularity with his "Salon de la Princesse" in the Hôtel de Soubise in Paris (Figure 16.10). Exploiting the room's oval shape, Boffrand eliminated the shadows and omitted Classical details such as pilasters and columns, which had been elements of decoration since the Renaissance. The floor-to-ceiling windows admit light freely, and the strategically placed mirrors reinforce the airy feeling. Instead of using a large overhead fresco, Boffrand divided the ceiling into many panel pictures. The characteristically nervous Rococo line—

Figure 16.12   WILLIAM HOGARTH.
The Countess' Levée, or *Morning Party,*
from *Marriage à la Mode.* 1743–1745.
Oil on canvas, 27 × 35″. Reproduced
by courtesy of the Trustees, The National Gallery, London. *Hogarth's
painterly techniques—learned in France—
have transformed a potentially banal topic
into a glittering social satire. On the left,
a pig-snouted singer is used to ridicule
the popular* castrati—*men who were
emasculated as youths to preserve their
boyish tenor voices. Hovering over the
castrato is a flutist—his coarse features
demonstrating the artist's loathing for
this social type. Other rich details, such
as the tea-sipping dandy in hair curlers
and the female guest who is gesticulating
wildly, confirm Hogarth's contempt for
the entire gathering.*

seen in the intricate designs of the gold edging—
integrates the interior into a harmonious whole. The
overall effect of airiness, radiance, and grace is worthy
of a Watteau setting of aristocratic revelry.

German decoration followed the French lead. The
Residenz, a palace commissioned by the prince-
bishop of the German city of Würzburg, is an example
of Baroque architecture with Rococo interiors. Designed chiefly by Balthasar Neumann [NOI-mahn]
(1687–1753), the building's glory is the main reception
room, called the Kaisersaal, or Emperor's Room
(Figure 16.11). The ceiling frescoes are by Giovanni
Battista Tiepolo [tee-AY-puh-loh] (1696–1770), an
Italian-born Rococo master. His paintings combine
the theatricality of the Italian Florid Baroque and the
love of light and color characteristic of Rubens and
the Flemish school. But Tiepolo's frescoes are only one
facet of the riotous splendor of this room, which
abounds in crystal chandeliers, gilt ornamentation,
marble statues, Corinthian capitals and arabesques,
gold-edged mirrors, and cartouches, or scroll-like
frames. In rooms such as this, the age's painters and
decorators catered to their patrons' wildest dreams of
grandeur.

The English Response   In Great Britain, where the
Rococo was condemned as tasteless and corrupt, the
painter William Hogarth (1697–1764) won fame as a
social satirist, working in a style quite different from
that of his French contemporaries. Even though his
mocking works appealed to all social groups,
the Protestant middle class most enthusiastically

welcomed his biting satires. In the paintings, which
sometimes ridicule idle aristocrats and always take a
moralistic view of life, his bourgeois admirers discovered the same values that caused them to embrace the
English novel. Taking advantage of his popularity,
Hogarth made engravings of his paintings, printing
multiple copies—the first major artist to take this step
to reach a new clientele.

Among the most popular of Hogarth's moral
works was the series of paintings that depict the
course of a loveless marriage between a profligate
nobleman and the daughter of a wealthy middle-
class businessman. Entitled *Marriage à la Mode,* this
series comprises six scenes that show in exquisite
detail the bitter consequences of an arranged marriage by following the husband and the wife to their
untimely deaths. By the fourth episode, called *The
Countess' Levée,* or *Morning Party,* Hogarth portrays
the wife plotting a rendezvous with a potential lover
(Figure 16.12). In this scene, which was typical of the
age's aristocratic entertainments, the hostess is having her hair curled while the would-be suitor
lounges on a sofa, charming her with conversation.
Nearby, guests, servants, and musicians play their
supporting roles in this sad tale. Hogarth, never willing to let the viewers draw their own conclusions,
provides the moral lesson. In the right foreground,
a black child-servant points to a small horned
creature—a symbol of the cuckold, or the deceived
husband—thus alluding to the wife's planned
infidelity. Even the paintings on the walls echo
Hogarth's theme of sexual abandon.

Figure 16.13 JACQUES-LOUIS DAVID. *The Oath of the Horatii.* 1784. Oil on canvas, 10'10" × 14'. Louvre. *David achieved a Classical effect in his works by arranging the figures so they could be read from left to right as in a sculptural frieze and by giving them the idealized bodies of Classical art. He further enhanced the sense that his central figures had been sculptured instead of painted by omitting distracting details. The resulting stark images contrast sharply with Rococo paintings and their luxuriant backgrounds (see Figures 16.5 and 16.9).*

The Challenge of Neoclassicism

Soon after the middle of the eighteenth century, the Rococo began to be supplanted by a new style, known as **Neoclassical.** With its backward glance to the restrained style of antiquity, the Neoclassical had its origins both in a rejection of the Rococo and in a fascination with the new archeological discoveries made at midcentury. Excavations of Pompeii and Herculaneum—Roman cities buried by Mt. Vesuvius in A.D. 79 and only recently rediscovered—had greatly heightened the curiosity of educated Europeans about the ancient world. At the same time, scholars began to publish books that showed Greek art to be the original source of ancient Classicism. The English authorities James Stuart and Nicholas Revett pointed out the differences between Greek and Roman art in *The Antiquities of Athens,* published in 1762. In 1764 the German Johann Joachim Winckelmann (1717–1768) distinguished Greek sculpture from the Roman in his *History of Art*—a study that led to the founding of the academic discipline of art history. The importance of Neoclassicism is indicated by the decision made in 1775 by the Paris Salon—the biennial exhibition that introduced the latest paintings to the public—to rebuff works with Rococo subjects and to encourage those with Classical themes.

Neoclassical Painting   In 1775, the first year of Louis XVI's reign and the same year the Salon began to promote Neoclassicism, the king appointed Joseph-Marie Vien to head the *Académie de France* in Rome, a leading art school. A strict disciplinarian, Vien returned the study of art to the basics by instructing his students to focus on perspective, anatomy, and life drawing, efforts that resulted in the purified style of Jacques-Louis David [dah-VEED] (1748–1825), the principal exponent of the Neoclassical style.

David's response to a commission from Louis XVI for a historical painting was the *Oath of the Horatii,* a work that electrified the Salon of 1785 (Figure 16.13). Taking a page from the history of the early Roman republic, this painting depicts the brothers Horatii vowing to protect the state, even though their stand means killing a sister who loves one of Rome's enemies. The patriotic subject with its tension between civic duty and family loyalty appealed to the *philosophes,* who preferred Neoclassicism, with its implicitly revolutionary morality, to the Rococo, with its frivolous themes.

David's *Oath of the Horatii* established the techniques and ideals that soon became typical of Neoclassical painting. His inspirational model was the seventeenth-century French artist Poussin, with his Classical themes and assured mastery of linear

Figure 16.14   JACQUES-LOUIS DAVID. *The Death of Socrates.* 1787. Oil on canvas, 4'11"
× 6'6". Metropolitan Museum of Art. Wolfe Fund, 1931. *Neoclassicism usually relied on
ancient literature and traditions for inspiration, as in this painting by David. The scene is based
on Plato's dialogue* Phaedo, *though David has chosen to depict Plato present (at the foot of the
bed), unlike in the literary account. Two of the domestic details, the lamp and the bed, are modeled
on artifacts uncovered at Pompeii. The shackles and cuffs under the bed refer to the fact that
Socrates was in chains just before drinking the hemlock.*

perspective. Rejecting the weightless, floating images
of Rococo painting, David portrayed his figures as
frozen sculptures, painted in strong colors. The Classical ideals of balance, simplicity, and restraint served as
a basis for many of David's artistic choices.

David showed his mastery of these techniques and
ideals in *The Death of Socrates,* which was exhibited in
the Salon of 1787 (Figure 16.14). Like Jesus in scenes
of the Last Supper, Socrates is portrayed shortly before his death, encircled by those men who will later
spread his message. Just as in the *Oath of the Horatii,*
David's arrangement of the figures reflected the
Classical ideal of balance. Surrounded by grieving
followers, the white-haired Socrates reaches for the
cup of poison and gestures toward his heavenly
goal—serene in his willingness to die for intellectual
freedom.

Neoclassical Architecture   No other painter could
compare with David, but the Scotsman Robert Adam
(1728–1792) developed a Neoclassical style in interior
decor that was the reigning favorite from 1760 until
1800. Classicism had dominated British architecture
since the 1600s, and Adam reinvigorated this tradition
with forms and motifs gathered during his archeological investigations. Kenwood House in London shows
his application of Roman design to the exterior of a domestic dwelling, combining Ionic columns, a running
frieze, and a triangular pediment to form a graceful
portico, or porch, in the manner of a Roman temple
(Figure 16.15). In the library, Adam mixed Classical
elements with the pastel colors of the Rococo to produce an eclectic harmony (Figure 16.16). To continue
this theme, he borrowed from Roman buildings with
his barrel-vaulted ceiling and adjoining apse.

Figure 16.15 ROBERT ADAM. Kenwood House. 1764. Exterior, the north front. London. *Adam's restrained style in the late eighteenth century represented a strong reinfusion of Classical principles into the English tradition. His style, with its reliance on the Classical orders and principles of balance and proportion, appealed to all classes but especially to the sober-minded middle class.*

Figure 16.16 ROBERT ADAM. Library, Kenwood House. Begun in 1767. London. *Adam designed the library of Kenwood House with several basic elements of Classical architecture: columns, pilasters, and apses. By and large, he followed the Renaissance dictum of letting the architectural elements determine the chamber's decorative details. Nonetheless, he achieved a dazzling effect by his daring addition of mirrors and color.*

French architects too began to embrace the Neoclassical style in the late 1700s. The leader of this movement was Jacques Germain Soufflot [soo-FLOH] (1713–1780), who designed buildings based on Roman temples. Soufflot's severe Neoclassicism is characterized by its reliance on architectural detail rather than on sculptural decoration. Avoiding Adam's occasional intermingling of Rococo and Classical effects, Soufflot preferred pure Roman forms. The most perfect expression of Soufflot's style is the Pantheon in Paris. Soufflot's Classical ideal is mirrored in the Pantheon's basic plan, with its enormous portico supported by huge Corinthian columns (Figure 16.17). Except for the statues in the pediment, the building's surface is almost devoid of sculptural detail. The only other decoration on the stark exterior is a frieze of stone garlands around the upper walls. For the dome, Soufflot found his inspiration not in Rome but in London—a sign that English architecture had come of age: The Pantheon's spectacular dome, with its surrounding Corinthian colonnade, is based on the dome of St. Paul's cathedral (see Figure 14.21).

Political Philosophy

Modern political theory continued to evolve after its founding in the seventeenth century. Absolutism, the reigning form of government in the eighteenth century, still had many staunch defenders. Voltaire, convinced that the people lacked political wisdom, advocated enlightened despotism. But the other leading *philosophes* of the Age of Reason rejected absolutism and supported alternative forms of government.

The Enlightenment's chief political theorists were Baron de Montesquieu and Jean-Jacques Rousseau, whose contrasting social origins probably to some extent account for their radically different definitions of the ideal state. Montesquieu, a titled Frenchman and a provincial judge, believed that rule by an enlightened aristocracy would ensure justice and tranquility. Rousseau, an impoverished citizen of the Swiss city-state of Geneva, advocated a kind of pure democracy. Rousseau's ideas about who should control the state were more far-reaching and revolutionary than Montesquieu's.

Montesquieu [mahnt-us-KYOO] (1689–1755) most persuasively expressed his political ideas in *The Spirit of the Laws* (1748), a work that compares systems of government in an effort to establish underlying principles. He concludes that climate, geography, religion, and education, among other factors, account for the world's different types of laws as well as governmental systems. Despite his misunderstanding of the roles of climate and geography, Montesquieu's analytical approach identified influences on governments that had not been considered before. One enduring idea in *The Spirit of the Laws* is that a separation of governmental powers provides an effective defense against despotic rule. Montesquieu was an admirer of England's parliamentary democracy and of the work of the English political philosopher John Locke, whose influence is evident here. American patriots adopted this principle of the separation of powers in the 1780s when they framed the Constitution, dividing the federal government's power into executive, legislative, and judicial branches.

In contrast to the conservative Montesquieu, Jean-Jacques Rousseau [roo-SOH] (1712–1778) framed his political theories within a more libertarian tradition. Rousseau set forth his model of the ideal state in *The Social Contract*, published in 1762. He agreed with John Locke that human beings are free and equal in

Figure 16.17 JACQUES GERMAIN SOUFFLOT. The Pantheon. 1755–1792. Paris. *By 1789 advanced thinkers in France had begun to appropriate Classical images for their movement, with David's Neoclassical paintings leading the way. When the revolution began, its leaders determined to build a suitable monument to house the remains of those philosophes whose works had furthered the cause of reform. Hence, it was natural that the revolutionary government turn Soufflot's Classical church—with its portico modeled from Roman styles—into a patriotic shrine.*

nature, but he defined the "state of nature" as a paradoxical condition in which individuals can follow any whim and hence possess no moral purpose. On the other hand, the state, which is founded on a social contract (an agreement among people), gives its citizens basic civil rights (freedom, equality, and property) and a moral purpose—precisely the things that they lack in nature. That morality arises within the civil state is a function of the "General Will," his term for what is best for the entire community. If each citizen is granted the right to vote, and if each citizen votes on the laws in accord with the General Will, then the laws will embody what is best for the whole society. Thus, in Rousseau's thinking, citizens who obey the laws become moral beings. (It should be noted that who defines and implements the General Will and how it affects individual freedom remain ambiguous in *The Social Contract*.)

In contrast to Locke's form of democracy, where a representative group such as a legislature acts in the name of the people, Rousseau's asserted that the people themselves collectively personify the state through the General Will. Rousseau's ideal state, therefore, has to be relatively small, so that all

Figure 16.18   JEAN-ANTOINE HOUDON. *Voltaire.* 1780. Life-size. Bibliothèque Nationale, Paris. *Houdon's Neoclassical portrait in plaster of Voltaire shows the sculptor's determination to portray his subject as an ancient Roman. Houdon seated Voltaire in an armchair copied from ancient models and draped him in an ample robe that suggested Roman dress (but was actually based on the robe worn by the great* philosophe *to keep out the cold). He endowed his sculpture with a vivid sense of life, as may be seen in the fine details and the expressive face.*

citizens can know and recognize one another. His model for the ideal state was based on his experience as a citizen of the tiny Genevan republic. Nevertheless, Rousseau has had an incalculable influence on thinkers and politicians concerned about much larger states. Indeed, his impact in the nineteenth century extended far beyond democratic circles. Nationalistic philosophers such as G. W. F. Hegel borrowed Rousseau's theory of the all-encompassing state, and radical theorists such as Karl Marx adopted his doctrine of the General Will (see Chapters 17 and 18).

Literature

Western literature in the Age of Reason was dominated by French authors and the French language, which now replaced Latin as the international language of scholarship, diplomacy, and commerce. French writers made common cause with the pro-gressive *philosophes,* sharing their faith in a glorious future. They wrote for the growing middle-class audience that was replacing the aristocratic patrons. Since these authors were under the constant threat of state censorship, they were often forced to disguise their more barbed social criticisms or to sugarcoat their beliefs. Those restrictions did not, however, deter them from their mission to liberate the consciousness of their readers and usher in an enlightened society.

French Writers: The Development of New Forms   The two political philosophers discussed earlier—Montesquieu and Rousseau—were also prominent figures in French literature. Early in his career, Montesquieu wrote *Persian Letters,* a cleverly devised, wide-ranging critique of French institutions and customs in the guise of letters purporting to be written by and to Persian travelers during a trip to Paris. Through the eyes of the "Persians," Montesquieu ridiculed the despotism of the French crown, the idleness of the aristocracy, and the intolerance of the Roman Catholic Church. His device of the detached observer of Western life was a safeguard against censorship, as was the decision to print *Persian Letters* in the Netherlands. Montesquieu's publication inspired a new type of literature, a genre in which a "foreign" traveler voices the author's social criticisms.

Rousseau foreshadowed the Romantic sensibility of the next century with his intensely personal autobiography, *The Confessions.* Published after his death, this work was the frankest self-revelation that had yet been seen in print. It narrated Rousseau's lifelong follies and difficulties, including sexual problems, religious vacillation, a mismatched marriage, and his decision to place his five offspring in an orphanage as soon as each was born. Not only did he reveal his personal secrets, but he also tried to justify his failings, pleading with his audience that he not be judged too harshly. The revelations shocked many readers, but others praised him for his emotional truthfulness and were willing to overlook his rather self-serving treatment of a number of the facts of his own life. After Rousseau's candid admissions, the genre of autobiography was never the same again.

The third great French writer of the eighteenth century was François-Marie Arouet, better known by his pen name, Voltaire (1694–1778)—the outspoken leader of the Age of Reason and the *philosophe* who best personifies the Enlightenment (Figure 16.18). A restless genius, Voltaire earned success in many forms, including dramas, essays, poems, histories, treatises, novels, a philosophical dictionary, letters, and the first work of history—the *Essay on Customs*—to survey civilization from a world perspective.

Of Voltaire's voluminous writings, only one work is still widely read today: the novel *Candide,* published in 1759. The most popular novel of the Age of Reason, *Candide* exhibits Voltaire's urbane style, his shrewd mixture of philosophy and wit, and his ability to jolt the reader with an unexpected word or detail. Beneath its frivolous surface, this work has the serious purpose of ridiculing the fashionable optimism of eighteenth-century thinkers who, Voltaire believed, denied the existence of evil and insisted that the world was essentially good.

At one time an optimist himself, Voltaire altered his beliefs about evil after the 1755 Lisbon earthquake, a calamity that figures prominently in *Candide.* This comic adventure tale recounts the coming of age of the aptly named Candide, who is introduced to optimism by Dr. Pangloss, a caricature of a German professor. The naive hero suffers many misfortunes—war, poverty, religious bigotry, trial by the Inquisition, shipwreck—and through them all holds fast to Pangloss's teaching that "this is the best of all possible worlds." But finally, faced with mounting incidents of pain and injustice, Candide renounces optimism. The story ends with the hero's newly acquired wisdom for combating the evils of boredom, vice, and want: "We must cultivate our garden."

Neoclassicism in English Literature In England, the presence of a Protestant middle class, which was growing larger and increasingly literate, created a demand for a literature that was decorous, conservative, and basically moralistic and religious in tone, even if that religion were little more than deference to nature and nature's God. The poetry of Alexander Pope and the monumental historical work of Edward Gibbon are typical of this style of literature, which is referred to as Neoclassical.

Alexander Pope (1688–1744) is the most representative voice of the English Neoclassical style. His poems celebrate the order and decorum that were prized by the middle classes—the social group from which he sprang. He became his age's leading spokesman for humane values such as reason, Classical learning, good sense and good taste, and hatred of hypocrisy and ostentation. His verses, marked by their satirical tone and sophisticated wit, made Pope the supreme inspiration of the Age of Reason until the Romantics, led by William Wordsworth in the 1790s, turned away from the Neoclassical ideal.

Pope wrote many kinds of poetry—pastorals, elegies, and satires, among others—but the work closest to the spirit of the Age of Reason is his *Essay on Man,* a didactic work combining philosophy and verse, published in 1733–1734. Issued in four sections and composed in rhymed couplets, this poem brings together one of the age's central ideas, optimism, with some notions inherited from antiquity. In the first section of this poem, Pope argues that God in his infinite power has created the best possible world—not a perfect universe—and that God's design rests on the concept of the great chain of being: Reaching from God to microscopic creatures, this chain links all living things together. Human beings occupy the chain's midpoint, where the human and animal species meet. Because of this position, two different natures fight in the human breast: "Created half to rise, and half to fall; / Great lord of all things, yet a prey to all."

Since humanity's place is unchanging, human reason is limited, and God does not make mistakes, humans should not question the divine plan. Pope concludes that "whatever is, is right." From this fatalistic principle it follows that what humans perceive as evil is simply misunderstood good. This qualified optimism was satirized by Voltaire in *Candide* through the character of Dr. Pangloss.

Having established a fatalistic outlook in the first section of *Essay on Man,* Pope became more optimistic in the remaining sections. Although God's ways may be unknowable, he reasoned that some truths may still be learned by human beings: "The proper study of mankind is man." From this belief he concluded that a paradise could be created on Earth if human beings would think and act rationally—an attitude dear to the hearts of the *philosophes.*

Edward Gibbon's (1737–1794) *History of the Decline and Fall of the Roman Empire* appeared in six volumes between 1776 and 1788. Gibbon's recognition was instant and universal; he was hailed across Europe both for the breadth of his historical knowledge and for the brilliance of his style. His subject, the history of Rome, appealed to the age's Classical interests, and his skepticism, notably regarding the Christian faith, echoed the sentiments of the *philosophes.* Although Gibbon's authority as a scholar was eclipsed in the next century because of the progress of historical science, his work remains one of the Enlightenment's genuine literary masterpieces.

Gibbon's massive work reflects both the ancient historical tradition and the ideals of the Enlightenment. Following the ancient historians, he wrote with secular detachment and offered reasons for historical change based on human motives and natural causes. From the Enlightenment, he determined that history should be philosophy teaching through example. These influences come together in his history when he attributes Rome's decay to an unpatriotic and subversive Christian faith along with the Germanic invasions. In effect, Gibbon's history praises secular civilization and covertly warns against the perils of religious enthusiasm.

PERSONAL PERSPECTIVE

LADY MARY WORTLEY MONTAGU
Lady Mary Manipulates the System

Lady Montagu (1689–1762) was one of the great letter writers in the Western tradition. A free spirit and a keen observer, she lived apart from her husband, Lord Edward Wortley Montagu, for about twenty years, four of which were spent in Avignon, France. In this letter to her husband, dated 25 March 1744, Lady Mary explains how she was able to save a group of French Protestant Huguenots from being galley slaves.

I take this opportunity of informing you in what manner I came acquainted with the secret I hinted at in my letter of the 5th of Feb. The Society of Freemasons at Nîmes presented the Duke of Richelieu, governor of Languedoc, with a magnificent entertainment. It is but one day's post from hence, and the Duchess of Crillon with some other ladies of this town resolved to be at it, and almost by force carried me with them, which I am tempted to believe an act of Providence, considering my great reluctance and the service it proved to be to unhappy, innocent people.

The greatest part of the town of Nîmes are secret Protestants, which are still severely punished according to the edicts of Louis XIV whenever they are detected in any public worship. A few days before we came they had assembled; their minister and about a dozen of his congregation were seized and imprisoned. I knew nothing of this, but I had not been in the town two hours when I was visited by two of the most considerable of the Huguenots, who came to beg of me with tears to speak in their favour to the Duke of Richelieu, saying none of the Catholics would do it and the Protestants durst not, and that God had sent me for their protection, [that] the Duke of Richelieu was too well bred to refuse to listen to a lady, and I was of a rank and nation to have liberty to say what I pleased. They moved my compassion so much I resolved to use my endeavours to serve them, though I had little hope of succeeding.

I would not therefore dress myself for the supper, but went in a domino to the ball, a mask giving opportunity of talking in a freer manner than I could have done without it. I was at no trouble in engaging his conversation. The ladies having told him I was there, he immediately advanced towards me, and I found from a different motive he had a great desire to be acquainted with me, having heard a great deal of me. After abundance of compliments of that sort, I made my request for the liberty of the poor Protestants. He with great freedom told me that he was so little a bigot, he pitied them as much as I did, but his orders from Court were to send them to the galleys. However, to show how much he desired my good opinion he was returning and would solicit their freedom (which he has since obtained).

The Rise of the Novel Despite the contributions of Pope and Gibbon to Western letters, the most important literary development in England during the Age of Reason was the rise of the modern novel. The hallmark of the early English novel was its realism. In the spirit of the Scientific Revolution, the new authors broke with the past and began to study the world with fresh eyes. Previous writers had based their plots on historical events or fables, but now individual experience became the keystone of the writer's art, and authors turned away from traditional plots in favor of an accurate representation of real-life events.

The English novel was realistic in several ways. It focused on individual persons rather than universal types and on particular circumstances rather than settings determined by literary custom. Furthermore, its plots followed the development of characters over the course of minutely observed time. The sense of realism was complete when the author adopted a narrative voice that contributed to the air of authenticity.

The novel captured the wholehearted attention of the reading public, many of them women. The works of Samuel Richardson and Henry Fielding especially appealed to these new readers. The writings of these two Englishmen helped to define the modern novel and at the same time set the standards for later fiction. For centuries, tragedy, with its plots about aristocratic heroes and heroines, had been regarded as the highest literary form. But since the age of Richardson and Fielding, the novel, with its focus on ordinary people, has been and remains the dominant literary genre.

The novels of Samuel Richardson (1689–1761) focus on love between the sexes. For more than a thousand pages in *Pamela, or Virtue Rewarded* (1740) and almost two thousand pages in *Clarissa Harlowe* (1747–1748), he tells the contrasting stories of two young women whose virtue is sorely tested by repeated seduction attempts. Pamela, a resourceful and somewhat calculating maidservant, eventually finds happiness in marriage to her prosperous would-be seducer. Clarissa, from a higher social class but of weaker mettle, runs off with her seducer and dies of shame.

In contrast to Richardson's sentimental domestic dramas, the novels of Henry Fielding (1707–1754) depict a robust world of comedy and adventure. His best work is *The History of Tom Jones, a Foundling* (1749), a comic masterpiece that has been called the finest English novel. Tom, the hero, is a high-spirited young man who makes little effort to resist the temptations that come his way. His wealthy guardian rejects him for his immoral behavior, but Tom is shown to be good-hearted and honest and thus worthy of the good fortune that befalls him at the novel's end when he has learned the virtues of moderation. The novel contains a great deal of amusing satire, aimed particularly at the upper classes.

Music

The standard in music in the early part of the eighteenth century was set by the French, as it was in art and decoration. Rococo music, like Rococo art, represented a reaction against the Baroque. Instead of the complex, formal structure of Baroque music, eighteenth-century French composers strove for a light and charming sound with graceful melodies over simple harmonies. Known as the *style galant* (gallant style), this music was particularly fashionable during the reign of Louis XV.

The perfect instrument for Rococo music was the harpsichord, a keyboard instrument whose strings are plucked, giving it a delicate, refined sound. At the same time, improved instruments, such as brasses and woodwinds, were joining the musical family, and the violin was perfected by Antonio Stradivari. The earliest piano was invented in the first decade of the eighteenth century by Bartolommeo Cristofori, who installed a mechanism in a harpsichord that would strike the strings with hammers rather than pluck them. With this new instrument, a player could vary the loudness of the sound depending on the force exerted on the keys, something impossible to do on the harpsichord—thus the name **pianoforte,** from the Italian for "soft" and "loud."

The two outstanding composers of Rococo music were the Frenchmen François Couperin and Jean-Philippe Rameau. Couperin [koop-uh-RAN] (1668–1733) set the tone in court society for the early part of the eighteenth century. His finest works were written for the harpsichord; many contain dance pieces and are noted for their rhythmic virtuosity. His highly ornamented compositions are the perfect musical counterpart of Watteau's painting.

Rameau [rah-MOH] (1683–1764) shared Couperin's fascination with the harpsichord and small-scale works, but his major achievement was as a composer of dramatic operas. Following in the footsteps of the French-Italian operatic composer Jean-Baptiste Lully, he made a ballet sequence with a large corps of dancers a central feature of his operatic works. The best of his operas was *Hippolyte and Aricie* (1733), based on the French playwright Racine's tragedy *Phèdre.* Rameau heightened the tension of the gripping plot through his expressive music, underscoring the sexual tension between the doomed heroine and her stepson.

Like Rococo art, Rococo music was supplanted in the second half of the eighteenth century by the new **Classical** style, in which more serious expression seemed possible. An important characteristic of Classical music was its emphasis on form and structure. The most versatile and widely used form to emerge was the **sonata form,** in which a musical piece is written in three main sections, known as the exposition, the development, and the recapitulation. In the first, melodies and themes are stated; in the second, the same material is expanded and changed in various ways; and in the third, the themes are stated again but with richer harmonies and more complex associations for the listener.

The sonata form was also used as the basis for whole compositions, including the **symphony** (a composition for orchestra), the concerto (a piece for a solo instrument and orchestra), and the sonata (a work for a small group of instruments). Such pieces often had three movements varying in **key, tempo,** and **mood.** The first was usually the longest and had a quick tempo. The second was slow and reflective, and the third was as quick as the first if not quicker. If there were four movements, the third was either a minuet, based on a French dance, or a **scherzo,** a lively Italian form. The sonata form provided general principles of composition that governed each movement and yet allowed composers to express their own ideas. Classical music retained the Rococo love of elegant melodic lines and clear, simple harmonies, but by using the sonata form, composers were able to add length and depth to their works.

Franz Joseph Haydn [HIDE-'n] (1732–1809) was the first master of the Classical style. Haydn spent almost thirty years as music director at the palace of a Hungarian noble family, where his status was that of a skilled servant of the reigning prince. At his death, however, he was both comfortably off and famous throughout Europe. He is largely responsible for the development of the sonata form, and his 104 symphonies helped to define the standard, four-movement symphony. Despite their formal regularity, the symphonies show Haydn's inventiveness and sense of

Figure 16.19 Performance of a Haydn Opera. *This print depicts a scene from Haydn's* L'incontro improvviso, *or* The Chance Meeting, *staged around 1775 at Esterháza, the summer castle of the Esterházy family, his patron and employer. Dignitaries and music lovers flocked to Esterháza to hear Haydn's latest works and to walk the grounds. In the print, the proscenium stage, the painted scenery, the costumed singers, and the orchestra below in the pit indicate that the presentations of operas have not changed much over the past 225 years. Some scholars assert that Haydn is playing the harpsichord, at the lower left. Although isolated at Esterháza, Haydn's reputation grew, and his symphonies and concertos were performed across Europe.*

freedom as he experiments with a large and imaginative variety of moods and structures.

Similarly, Haydn's more than seventy string quartets, each composed for first and second violins, viola, and cello, became the accepted norm for this type of chamber music. His supreme innovation was to allow each instrument to show its independence from the rest. Although the first violin has the most prominent role, the musical effect of a Haydn quartet is of four persons conversing. His operas (about twenty), popular in his day, are now seldom performed (Figure 16.19).

However prodigious Haydn's efforts, they are overshadowed by the greatest exponent of the Classical style, Wolfgang Amadeus Mozart (1756–1791). From the age of six, he wrote music, alternating composing with performing. His travels around Europe as a child prodigy exposed him to the musical currents of his day, which he eagerly adapted into his own works. For nine years of his adult life, he was a court musician in the service of the archbishop of Salzburg, a post that caused him great anguish because of its low social position. Unlike Haydn, he would not accept the conventional position of musician as a liveried (uniformed) servant of a wealthy patron. The last decade of his life was spent as a freelance musician in Vienna, where he died in extreme poverty. Despite his brief and tragic life, Mozart left a huge body of music that later generations have pronounced sublime.

Mozart's gift was not for creating new musical forms; Mozart already had at hand the sonata, the opera, the symphony, and the quartet. Rather, his inimitable talent was for composing music with a seemingly effortless line of melody, growing naturally from the opening bars until the finale. His disciplined and harmonious works embody the spirit of the Enlightenment.

The transparency of Mozart's composing technique allowed him to give a unique stamp to every type of music that he touched, and he composed in every genre available to him. In vocal music, he composed religious works (such as Masses, oratorios, and an unfinished Requiem Mass) and dramatic works (for example, operas and a ballet). In instrumental music, he wrote orchestral and ensemble music, including symphonies, serenades, divertimentos, marches, minuets, and German dances; concertos for piano, violin, horn, flute, trumpet, and clarinet; chamber music for strings and winds; violin sonatas; and keyboard sonatas.

The fullest expression of Mozart's genius was reached in his operas, especially his comic operas, where he gave free rein to the playful side of his temperament, blending broad humor with dramatic characterization. His masterpiece in this genre is probably *The Marriage of Figaro,* based on a play by the French *philosophe* Pierre Beaumarchais [boh-mahr-SHAY] (1732–1799). Since its first performance in 1786, *Figaro's* knockabout humor and rich musical texture have made it one of the most popular works in the entire operatic repertory. Beneath the farcical scenes and the enchanting melodies, however, lies a serious theme: By allowing the servant, Figaro, to outwit his arrogant master, Mozart joined the growing ranks of those who criticized the privileged classes and attacked the injustices of their times. In Mozart's other music, his personal presence was always obscured. But in *Figaro,* the disgruntled servant-musician who chafes at his hard lot speaks with Mozart's authentic voice.

The Legacy of the Age of Reason

After the Enlightenment, Western civilization was never the same. By the end of the period, the prevailing form of government—absolutism—was on the defensive, facing condemnation from all sides. Supporters of absolutism argued for enlightened despotism, aristocratic critics advocated a division of centralized rule into rival branches, and democrats wanted to abolish monarchy and give the power to the people. Under these assaults, absolutist governments began to crumble.

Another development in the eighteenth century with long-term consequences was the emergence of the middle classes as a potent force for change. By and large, the Enlightenment reflected their political, social, and economic agenda, though their advocates claimed to speak for all people regardless of background. The rise of the middle classes also opened the door to popular forms of culture, such as the novel. Today, this democratizing tendency continues and is one of the hallmarks of modern civilization.

Many of the ideas and principles of the Enlightenment are now articles of faith in the Western heritage. From it come the beliefs that governments should rest on the consent of the people, that the least amount of state interference in the lives of citizens is best, and that all people are created equal. More fundamentally, from the Enlightenment come the views that human nature is good and that happiness is the proper goal of human life.

Although the Enlightenment pointed the way to the future, we must not be misled by the modern-sounding language of the times. The *philosophes* wrote endlessly in support of free speech and religious toleration, and yet censorship and bigotry remained the normal condition of existence for most Europeans. Despite their brave words, most of these enlightened thinkers did not move from ideas to action, believing that ideas would triumph because of their inner logic and inherent justice. Moreover, they thought that the ruling classes would surrender their privileges once reason had shown them the error of their ways. The Enlightenment was the last era in which such simplistic beliefs held sway. The world in 1789 stood poised on the brink of an era in which ideas became politicized through action, war, and social agitation. In the postrevolutionary world, the radical power of ideas would be understood by all.

KEY CULTURAL TERMS

Enlightenment
philosophes
Deism
Physiocrats

Rococo style
fête galante
rocaille
Neoclassical style

style galant
pianoforte
Classical style (in music)
sonata form
symphony
key

tempo
mood
scherzo

SUGGESTIONS FOR FURTHER READING

Primary Sources

DIDEROT, D. *The Encyclopedia: Selections.* Edited and translated by S. J. Gendzier. New York: Harper & Row, 1967. Well-chosen selections from the most influential work of the Enlightenment; originally published between 1750 and 1772.

FIELDING, H. *The History of Tom Jones, a Foundling.* Middletown, Conn.: Wesleyan University Press, 1975. A recent edition of this rollicking novel about an orphan who through personal charm, good looks, and honesty survives misadventures and is finally restored to his rightful inheritance; first issued in 1749.

GIBBON, E. *The History of the Decline and Fall of the Roman Empire.* Abridged by M. Hadas. New York: Putnam, 1962. One of the landmarks of the Enlightenment, Gibbon's history attributes the fall of Rome to the rise of Christianity; published between 1776 and 1788.

HARDT, U. H. *A Critical Edition of Mary Wollstonecraft's "A Vindication of the Rights of Woman, with Strictures on Political and Moral Subjects."* Troy, N.Y.: Whitston, 1982. An authoritative text of one of the books that helped launch the modern feminist movement.

MONTESQUIEU, BARON DE. *The Persian Letters.* Translated by G. R. Healy. Indianapolis: Bobbs-Merrill, 1964. An excellent English version of this epistolary novel that satirizes European customs through the eyes of imaginary Persian travelers; the original dates from 1721.

———. *The Spirit of the Laws.* Translated and edited by A. M. Cohler, B. C. Miller, and H. S. Stone. New York: Cambridge University Press, 1989. A good recent English version of this groundbreaking work that claims people's choices are influenced by such matters as climate, geography, and religion.

POPE, A. *An Essay on Man.* Edited by M. Mack. London: Methuen, 1964. A poetic statement of the ideals of the Enlightenment by the leading English poet of the age.

RICHARDSON, S. *Pamela.* London: Dent, 1962. A modern edition of one of the earliest novels in the English language, recounting the tale of a servant girl whose fine moral sense enables her to prevail over adversity and rise to the top of aristocratic society.

ROUSSEAU, J.-J. *Basic Political Writings.* Translated and edited by D. A. Cress. Indianapolis: Hackett, 1987. Includes selections from *First Discourse* (1750), *The Social Contract* (1762), *Emile* (1762), and other writings.

———. *Confessions.* Translated by J. M. Cohen. New York: Penguin, 1954. A highly original book, the first in the tradition of confessional autobiographies; bridges the Enlightenment and the Romantic period.

SMITH, A. *The Wealth of Nations: Representative Selections.* Indianapolis: Bobbs-Merrill, 1961. The basic writings that set forth the theory of free-market economics; first published in 1776.

VOLTAIRE. *Candide.* Translated by L. Bair. New York: Bantam Books, 1981. The most popular novel of the eighteenth century; first published in 1759.

SUGGESTIONS FOR LISTENING

COUPERIN, FRANÇOIS (1668–1733). The harpsichord, with its delicate and lively sounds, was the symbol of Rococo music; Couperin's more than two hundred harpsichord works, composed usually in highly stylized and stately dance rhythms, helped to define the Rococo musical style. Typical works are *La visionaire (The Dreamer)* and *La misterieuse (The Mysterious One)*, both from 1730.

HAYDN, FRANZ JOSEPH (1732–1809). Over a long and laborious career, Haydn honed his approach to music, moving from late Baroque forms until he established the sonata form of composition as the basic ingredient of the Classical musical style. Of the string quartets, those in Opuses 17 and 20, composed respectively in 1771 and 1772, show his pure Classical style; the quartets he wrote in the 1790s (Opuses 76 and 77) illustrate his later style, bursting with rhythmic vitality and harmonic innovation. Good examples of his more than one hundred symphonies are Symphony No. 45 (*Farewell*) (1772), Symphony No. 85 (*La reine,* or *The Queen*) (1785), Symphony No. 94 (*Surprise*), and Symphony No. 103 (*Drum Roll*) (1795). Besides instrumental music, Haydn composed religious works, notably the oratorios for orchestra and massed chorus, *The Creation* (1798) and *The Seasons* (1801)—inspired by Handel's *Messiah.*

MOZART, WOLFGANG AMADEUS (1756–1791). The most gifted composer of the period, Mozart helped to define the Classical style in virtually all forms of musical expression, including the symphony, the piano sonata, the concerto for piano and orchestra, the string quartet, and the comic opera. Mozart's religious music includes Masses, motets, and settings of sacred songs, such as *Solemn Vespers of the Confessor* (1780), with its serene "Laudate Dominum" section, as well as the *Epistle Sonatas* for organ and orchestra, composed between 1767 and 1780 as part of the Mass. Among his best-loved compositions are his last two symphonies, Nos. 40 and 41, composed in 1788; the six concertos for piano and orchestra written in 1784; the six string quartets in Opus 10 (1785), dedicated to Haydn; the opera *Don Giovanni* (1787) in Italian, combining comic and dramatic elements; and the comic operas *The Marriage of Figaro* (1786) and *Cosi fan Tutte (They All Do It This Way)* (1790) in Italian and *The Magic Flute* (1791) in German.

RAMEAU, JEAN-PHILIPPE (1683–1764). Rameau's musical fame rests largely on his operas, which combine late Baroque forms with Rococo elegance and grace. His best-known operas include *Hippolyte et Aricie* (1733), *Les Indes galantes (The Gallant Indies)* (1735), and *Castor et Pollux* (1737).

CHAPTER *16* HIGHLIGHTS
The Age of Reason, 1700–1789

MONTESQUIEU, *Persian Letters* (1721)

POPE, *Essay on Man* (1733–1734)

RICHARDSON, *Pamela* (1740)

MONTESQUIEU, *The Spirit of the Laws* (1748)

FIELDING, *The History of Tom Jones* (1749)

Encyclopédie (1750–1772)

VOLTAIRE, *Candide* (1759)

ROUSSEAU, *The Social Contract* (1762)

GIBBON, *History of the Decline and Fall of the Roman Empire* (1776–1788)

ROUSSEAU, *Confessions* (1781)

KANT, "Answer to the Question: What is Enlightenment" (1784)

WOLLSTONECRAFT, *A Vindication of the Rights of Woman* (1792)

16.5 WATTEAU, *Departure from Cythera* (1717)

16.11 NEUMANN AND OTHERS, Kaisersaal, The Residenz, Würzburg (1719–1744)

16.6 WATTEAU, *The Sign for Gersaint's Shop* (ca. 1720)

16.10 BOFFRAND, Salon de la Princesse, Hôtel de Soubise, Paris (ca. 1735–1740)

16.3 CHARDIN, *The Morning Toilette* (1741)

16.12 HOGARTH, *Marriage à la Mode* (1743–1745)

16.7 BOUCHER, *Nude on a Sofa* (1752)

16.4 VON HOHENBERG, Gloriette, Vienna (1768)

16.9 FRAGONARD, *The Lover Crowned* (1771–1773)

16.1 REYNOLDS, *Mrs. Siddons as the Tragic Muse* (1784)

16.8 VIGÉE-LEBRUN, *Marie Antoinette and Her Children* (1787)

RAMEAU, *Hippolyte et Aricie* (1733)

16.17 SOUFFLOT, The Pantheon, Paris (1755–1792)

16.15 ADAM, Kenwood House, London (1764)

16.13 DAVID, *The Oath of the Horatii* (1784)

16.14 DAVID, *The Death of Socrates* (1787)

MOZART, *The Marriage of Figaro* (1786)

MOZART, *Eine kleine Nachtmusik* (1787)

HAYDN, Symphony No. 94 *(Surprise)* (1791)

Literature & Philosophy   Art & Architecture   Music & Dance

 Readings in the Western Humanities   CD, The Western Humanities

AFRICA

AMERICAS

HISTORY

Central Africa *Kongo Kingdom.* Slave trade, civil war, collapse. *Luba Kingdom.* Strong state (modern Democratic Republic of Congo) with satellite kingdoms.
East Africa *Zambezi Valley.* Butwa, the most prosperous kingdom.
North Africa Part of Ottoman Empire; Muslim way of life clashed with Western-style reforms. *Algeria* and *Tunisia.* Piracy flourished. *Egypt.* Napoleon invaded (1798).
South Africa Warfare between Boers and Xhosa.
West Africa *Niger Bend.* Berber tribal confederations raided cities and farms and controlled trade routes. *Dahomey Empire.* Expansive state based on slave trade; subjugated by Oyo Empire (1730). *Ghana.* Asante tribal confederacy founded (1701); trade, including gold and slaves.

Caribbean Spread of sugarcane plantations; African slaves replaced native workers.
Latin America *Mexico.* Roads linked capital with sea. Rapid urbanization. *Viceroyalty of La Plata (modern Argentina, Uruguay, Paraguay, Bolivia).* Potosí, economic hub of South America. *Viceroyalty of Peru.* Inca insurrection, led by Tupac Amarú (1780).
Brazil Economy based on coffee and wild rubber surpassed Portugal's. Diamond and gold mining began. Slave trade grew.
Native North America *Plains.* Sioux began hunting buffalo with Spanish horses from Southwest. *Eastern Woodlands.* French and Indian War; some tribes allied with French, others with British. Revolutionary War (1775–1781); some tribes sided with British, others with colonists. From 1783, forced to cede land to U.S. government. Settlers took over hunting grounds of Shawnee, Delaware, and Cherokee.

ART & MUSIC

Central Africa *Kongo Kingdom. Mintindi* stone figures (of kings?), seated with legs crossed. *Luba Kingdom.* Wooden bow stands and women's heads.
West Africa *Ghana.* Asante Kingdom: golden objects, including royal stools, staffs, chains, and swords; *kente* cloth woven from cotton. *Yoruba culture.* Benin Kingdom: sculpted bronze heads, mounted on tall staffs around graves and altars.

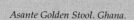

Asante Golden Stool. Ghana.

Latin America Baroque style imported from Europe. *Mexico:* Florid sculptures at the Cathedral of Mexico City; local styles with native influences in small towns. *Viceroyalty of La Plata. Mestizo* (male and female) sculptors and painters at Cuzco and Potosí. *Brazil.* Many African-Portuguese artists, especially the sculptor and architect Antônio Francisco Lisboa, "Aleijadinho." Yoruban influence on music, religion, and the arts.

ANTÔNIO FRANCISCO LISBOA. Daniel. *1757–1777. Soapstone. Courtyard, Church of Bom Jesus de Matozinhos, Congonhas do Campo, Minas Gerais, Brazil.*

ARCHITECTURE

East Africa *Zambezi Valley.* Butwa: ceremonial and high prestige buildings made of stone.
North Africa *Egypt.* Ottoman style dominated, but Egyptian taste expressed in woodcarving and other crafts.

Latin America *Mexico.* Richly decorated churches: polychrome plasterwork, glazed tilework, pilasters based on inverted pyramid, and elaborately carved facades. Indigenous influences in interior towns and cities. *Brazil.* Mulatto influences, especially inland. Neoclassicism introduced (after 1780). *Viceroyalty of Peru.* Fusion of indigenous tradition with European Baroque, especially in the interior.

Church of Santiago. 1700s. Pomata, Peru.

RELIGION, PHILOSOPHY, LITERATURE

West Africa *Niger Bend.* Kunta tribe of Berbers: Sidi Mukhtar, spiritual leader of the Muslim Sufi sect, author, and educator. His schools opened the door to Islam for "outsider" black people.

Caribbean *Cuba, Trinidad, and Haiti.* Yoruban slaves influenced religious beliefs, music, and myth.
Latin America *Viceroyalty of La Plata.* First Argentine university, at Córdoba.
Native North America *California.* 21 Spanish missions founded by Father Junípero Serra (1769–1780); Chumash, Costanoan, and other Indians became laborers on mission lands.

ASIA

China

Ch'ing Dynasty. Height of power under Emperor Ch'ien-lung: greatest territorial extent (Outer Mongolia, Tibet, and Taiwan); farming, trade, and manufacturing grew; population more than doubled in 70 years; exodus of Chinese traders across Far East; foreign merchants restricted (1757).

India

Mogul Dynasty. Disintegration of empire into petty states, including two major Muslim kingdoms (Bengal and Deccan), two major Hindu dynasties (Rajputs and Marathas), and a Sikh kingdom (Punjab). British defeat French for trading rights and territories. Britain's East India Company became leading power (1757).

Japan

Edo period. Peace reigned under a despotic shōgunate; feudal order continued to be undermined by merchant class; extremes of wealth. Isolated from the world, except for Chinese contacts and medical texts imported from West. Shōgun's court became extravagant and inefficient. Edo's population of about 1 million (1800) made it one of the world's largest cities.

Ch'ing Dynasty. Ch'ien-lung supported the arts and patronized Jesuit painters and architects; Jesuit influence (expressed through rich ornamentation or nontraditional forms) in landscapes, portraits, and the applied arts, including embroidery, cloisonné, and jade carving. Commercial art market flourished; colored printmaking introduced; brisk art export trade to Europe.

Mogul Dynasty. Provincial schools, devoted to miniature painting, flourished, especially in northwestern Hindu courts, such as Kangra and Jaipur.

TŌSHŪSAI SHARAKU. Segawa Tomisaburō II as Yadorigi, Ōgishi Kurando's Wife. 1794. Polychrome woodblock print on paper, 5 × 9½". Tokyo National Museum.

Edo period. Traditional and innovative schools of painting, including Literati, Western, and Maruyama (mixing Western realism and traditional style, founded by Ōkyo). *Ukiyo-e* prints matured with the introduction of color by Harunobu (1770s); *ukiyo-e* artists specialized in popular subjects, such as beautiful women (Kitagawa) and Kabuki actors (Sharaku).

Ch'ing Dynasty. Jesuit architects designed Yuan-ming-yuan, a complex of parks, fountains, water works, and pavilions, including the Summer Palace, Peking. Altar of Heaven restored.

Mogul Dynasty. Capital of Sikh Kingdom founded at Lahore.

Edo period. Edo struck by fire (1772); rebuilt.

Rikugi-en, "Garden of the Six Principles of Poetry." Completed 1702. Tokyo.

Ch'ing Dynasty. The classic novel *The Dream of the Red Chamber.* Tai Chen, a scientist, scholar, and philosopher. Renewed interest in textual criticism. Emperor, court, and merchants patronized writers and scholars. Jesuits translated literary and philosophical works, which were transmitted to the West; fostered studies of astronomy, cartography, and mathematics.

Mogul Dynasty. Religious separatism, as Hindus, Muslims, and Sikhs formed their own states.

Edo period. Taniguchi Buson, painter and poet, master of *haiku;* Akinari Ueda's *Tales of the Rainy Moon,* supernatural stories. *Bunraku* (puppet theater) founded; many plays by Chikamatsu Monzaemon; appealed to merchant class. Shōguns encouraged Confucianism as an ethical framework for government.

17 REVOLUTION, REACTION, AND CULTURAL RESPONSE 1760–1830

The Age of Reason was a time of radical talk and little action, but by the end of the eighteenth century, three revolutions had changed the Western world forever—and today the period between 1760 and 1830 is considered a historical watershed. The Industrial Revolution created an industrialism that replaced agriculture as the soundest basis for the economic well-being of a state. The American Revolution demonstrated that government by the people was a workable alternative to monarchy. And the French Revolution forced sweeping changes in the distribution of political power in Europe (Figure 17.1).

These changes were not welcomed by all, and many groups tried to prevent the spread of revolutionary political ideas. However, the middle class, known as the *bourgeoisie*, benefited the most from these revolutions. The emboldened middle class asserted itself as the new standard-bearer of culture, first embracing Neoclassicism and then shifting favor to the powerful new spirit and style of the age—Romanticism.

THE INDUSTRIAL REVOLUTION

Even before the Industrial Revolution, agricultural innovations in England made industrialization possible. The shift toward enclosure, whereby common lands were fenced off by their wealthy owner and consolidated into one large estate, brought hardship to smaller farmers but resulted in increased farm productivity. Improvements in farming techniques increased crop yields and farm income. Better technology also led to improved tools and farm implements, such as the iron plow and the reaper.

◄ **Detail** JACQUES-LOUIS DAVID. *Death of Marat.* 1793. Oil on canvas, 65 × 50½". Musées Royaux des Beaux-Arts, Brussels.

Figure 17.1 Jean-Auguste-Dominique Ingres. *Napoleon I.* 1806. Oil on canvas, 8′6″ × 5′4″. Musée de l'Armée, Paris. *Napoleon, Emperor of France, 1804–1815, is depicted on a throne in the style of an ancient ruler but with references that link him to the French monarchy. He wears a wreath, a Greek symbol of victory, and in his right hand he holds a long rod topped by a gold fleur-de-lis, or French lily—France's national symbol since the Middle Ages. His left hand holds the ivory hand of justice, an image adopted by France's kings in 1314 and revived by Napoleon at his coronation in 1804. Ingres's portrait helped to establish Napoleon's authority and image.*

Three economic changes were necessary before these conditions could combine to produce industrialism: the substitution of machines for manual labor; the replacement of animal and human power with new sources of energy such as water and steam (the steam engine, patented by James Watt in 1769, transformed the generation of power); and the introduction of new and large amounts of raw materials, such as iron ore and coal. By 1800 these changes had taken place (Figure 17.2).

The changes in the cotton cloth industry dramatically illustrate the impact of the Industrial Revolution. Local woolen producers, threatened by competition from cotton, persuaded Parliament to prohibit the importation of inexpensive cotton goods from India; but still the demand grew. The English industry tried to meet the demand for cotton through the putting-out system—a method of hand manufacture in which workers wove the fabric in their homes—but this medieval technique proved hopelessly outdated. As a result, industrialists developed the factory system to speed manufacturing; flying shuttles and power looms were located under one roof, and this building was situated near a swiftly flowing stream that supplied the water for the steam engines that drove the massive equipment.

The laborers had to adjust their entire lives to the demands of the factory system. No longer could most rural workers stay at home and weave at their own pace. Towns near the factories rapidly expanded, and new ones sprang up in the countryside next to the mills. In both cases, employees were crowded into miserable living quarters, with little regard given for the basic amenities of human existence.

With the factories came the "working class." A realigned class system—with the capitalists and the workers at either extreme—transformed the social order, created new indicators of wealth and success, and established different patterns of class behavior. The earlier cooperation between the gentry and small farmers was replaced by increasingly strained relations between the factory owners and the working class.

Industrialization in England

By the mid–eighteenth century, changes at home and abroad had created conditions that steered England toward industrialization. A population increase provided both a labor force and a consumer market. Money to invest was available because of surplus capital generated by sound fiscal practices. Several decades of peace had created an atmosphere conducive to economic growth, and the government's policies promoted further expansion. Free of internal tariffs or duties, goods moved easily throughout Britain, and Britain's acquisition of colonies gave merchants access to raw materials and new overseas markets.

Figure 17.2 MICHAEL ANGELO ROOKER. *The Cast Iron Bridge at Coalbrookdale.* 1782. Approx. 15½ × 24½″. Aberdeen Art Gallery, Aberdeen, Scotland. *The earliest iron bridges, made from the superior grade of iron that was being produced in the new factories, were molded and cast to look like wooden bridges. The first iron bridge, located at Coalbrookdale, became a favorite subject for many artists. Architects did not begin to use iron in building construction until the early 1800s.*

Classical Economics: The Rationale for Industrialization

Although industrialization did not produce a school of philosophy, it did generate serious thinking about the newly emerging economic system. Much of this thought could be interpreted as a rationale for industrialization and a justification for profit-seeking. The French Physiocrats and the Scotsman Adam Smith both advocated the abolition of mercantilism—the economy at the service of the state—and its replacement with a laissez-faire system—the economy at the service of the individual entrepreneur. In England, Smith's ideas attracted a band of thinkers who became known as the Classical economists and included Thomas Malthus and David Ricardo.

Smith's key contribution to Classical economics was his advocacy of a free-market system based on private property that would automatically regulate prices and profits to the benefit of all. He focused his *Wealth of Nations* (1776) on agriculture and commerce, while only glancing at manufacturing. As manufacturing gained power in the English economy, however, businessmen read into his work a rationale for their activities. Smith argued that entrepreneurs acting mutually in enlightened self-interest would not only raise the standard of living for all but also get rich—if the government left them alone. Such an argument was welcome news to businessmen, factory owners, and other capitalists.

Thomas Malthus (1766–1834) and David Ricardo (1772–1823) also lent support to the changes wrought by the Industrial Revolution. In his *Essay on the Principle of Population* (1788), Malthus forecast a world burdened with misery that would worsen if the human population continued to increase. Since the population grew at a geometric rate and the food supply advanced at an arithmetical rate, the number of human beings would soon far exceed the amount of food, leading Malthus to conclude that famines, plagues, and wars were necessary to limit the world's population. His gloomy prediction persuaded most of the middle classes that laborers were victims of their own thoughtless habits, including unrestrained sexuality, and could not be helped.

In *Principles of Political Economy and Taxation* (1821), David Ricardo maintained that wages for laborers would always hover around the subsistence level and that workers would never be able to improve their standard of living beyond that level—his "iron law of wages." Tying Malthus's conclusion to his own, he argued that the working class was inevitably mired in poverty. Thus, the theories of the Classical economists provided the rationales for the business classes as they sought arguments to justify the methods of industrialization and the degradation it brought to workers.

POLITICAL REVOLUTIONS, 1760–1815

During the approximately fifty years between the Treaty of Paris (1763) and the Battle of Waterloo (1815), Europe saw monarchies fall and old societies swept away. By 1830 Europe was divided into a conservative eastern Europe and a progressive western Europe that included the former colonies in the New World. This twofold division persisted well into the twentieth century (Timeline 17.1).

Timeline 17.1   REVOLUTION, REACTION, AND CULTURAL RESPONSE

1760		1775	1783	1789		1799		1815		1830
Industrial Revolution in England		**American Revolution**			**French Revolution**		**Napoleon and the French Empire**		**Restored Bourbon Monarchy in France**	

| | **1769** Watt's steam engine | **1776** Smith's *Wealth of Nations* | | | **1793** David's *Death of Marat* | | **1803** Beethoven's *Third Symphony* | **1808** Goethe's *Faust* (Part 1) | | **1818** Géricault's *Raft of the "Medusa"* | **1830** Berlioz's *Symphonie fantastique* |

| | **1774** Goethe's *The Sorrows of Young Werther* | | | **1798** Wordsworth and Coleridge's *Lyrical Ballads* | | **1813** Austen's *Pride and Prejudice* | **1821** Constable's *Hay Wain* |

The American Revolution

Although Great Britain was leading the way to industrialization, it was also suffering from an outmoded tax structure and from debts contracted in the Seven Years' War. The royal ministers tried numerous schemes and taxes to make the American colonists share in the burden of empire. The colonists, calling the British government's new taxes on sugar, stamps, and tea unconstitutional, claimed immunity from imperial taxation because, they asserted, they were not represented in the British Parliament.

Protests and violence succeeded in nullifying the parliamentary taxes and uniting the colonies in a common cause. In 1774 the colonists convened a Continental Congress in Philadelphia, which spoke for the American people against the "foreign power" of Great Britain. In April 1775 conflict between British troops and colonists in Massachusetts triggered a war. The congress in Philadelphia proclaimed the American goals in the Declaration of Independence, signed on July 4, 1776: government by consent of the governed and the rights to life, liberty, and the pursuit of happiness. The American Revolution lasted until 1783 and resulted in victory and independence for the colonies.

To realize their democratic goals, the Americans developed two new ideas: the constitutional convention and a written constitution. Wary of centralized power, the framers of the United States Constitution met in Philadelphia in 1787 and created three coordinate branches of government—legislative, judiciary, and executive—with specified powers delegated to each. (The idea of a balance of powers is derived from the works of both the English political theorist John Locke and the French *philosophe* Montesquieu.) The central government could assess and collect its own taxes, regulate commerce, and make and enforce laws.

The framers also limited the government's role in everyday life by accepting the superior claims of human rights.

The founders failed to extend rights to slaves, whose existence was barely noted, and women were not given the right to vote. Still, the Constitution made America the most democratic society of its day and the first successful democracy since Athens in the fifth century B.C. As an exemplary democracy, America offered hope to the oppressed, and the successful struggle for independence provided a model for future revolution.

The French Revolution

Despite the importance of the American Revolution, the revolution in France overshadowed it. Because of its dramatic break with the past and its lasting worldwide effects, the French Revolution is a key event of modern times.

When Louis XVI took the throne in 1774, the French crown was confronted with a challenge from two sides: the aristocrats, who were resurgent after the death of Louis XIV, and the emerging bourgeoisie, who were clamoring for power. The affluent bourgeoisie aligned themselves with the nobles in supporting laissez-faire economics, but they joined the king in calling for an end to the feudal privileges of the aristocracy.

The peasant farmers endured burdensome taxes and continued to be subjected to feudal claims. In urban France, the lower middle class, consisting of small shopkeepers, salaried workers, and semiskilled artisans, had little opportunity to escape their bleak existence. Below them existed wage earners, menial workers, and the marginal groups who drifted in and out of the criminal world. Oppressed by high taxes and

Table 17.1 SHIFTS IN THE FRENCH GOVERNMENT, 1789–1830	
July 1789–September 1792	Limited constitutional kingdom; the Assembly
September 1792–August 1795	First Republic; Reign of Terror (1793–1794)
August 1795–November 1799	Directory
November 1799–May 1804	Consulate
May 1804–June 1815	First Empire
June 1815–July 1830	Restored Bourbon Monarchy

harboring ill-disguised hatred for the classes above them, the lower orders schemed to stay one jump ahead of the tax collector.

In the 1780s, France began to develop a huge national debt, fueled by its support of America in its revolution. In 1789 Louis XVI finally agreed to convene the Estates-General, a representative body similar to the English Parliament, which had last met in the early 1600s. When this body gathered, the middle-class representatives shunted aside the nobles and the church leaders and formed themselves into the National Constituent Assembly. The Assembly then proceeded to end royal despotism and to turn France into a limited, constitutional kingdom similar to England (Table 17.1).

This first phase of the revolution lasted from 1789 until September 1792. Dominated by the well-to-do middle classes, the Assembly embraced laissez faire, restricted the vote to property owners, overhauled the legal system, and introduced representative government. Especially impressive was this body's approval of *The Declaration of the Rights of Man and Citizen* (1789), a document that guaranteed both natural and civil rights and that has served as the basis of subsequent French regimes. In framing the constitution of 1791, the Assembly attempted to embody the slogans of the revolution—liberty, equality, and fraternity—but class hatred made fraternity more an ideal than a reality. This stage of the revolution failed, however, because Louis XVI proved to be untrustworthy and forces inside France were pressing its leaders for increasingly radical reforms. In 1792 the constitution of 1791 was suspended along with the monarchy.

The revolution entered its second and most violent phase, which lasted from September 1792 to August 1795. This phase was dominated by leaders from the lower bourgeois and working classes, who executed the king, founded the French Republic, and briefly replaced Christianity with a state religion organized on rational ideals (Figure 17.3). Full voting rights were

Figure 17.3   LOUIS-LEOPOLD BOILLY. *Simon Chenard as a Sans-culotte*. 1792. Oil on canvas, 13⅙ × 8⅝". Musée Carnavalet, Paris. *As French workers came into their own during the second phase of the revolution, their clothing became fashionable. The men dressed in short jackets and baggy trousers, rather than in the aristocratic costume of waistcoats and breeches, or culottes, with silk stockings. Because of the long trousers, these workers were known as sans-culottes ("without breeches"). The artist Boilly, a supporter of the revolution, sought to glorify the sans-culottes in this portrait of a typical worker—actually his friend, the actor Simon Chenard. Clad in worker's attire, including wooden shoes, and holding the tricolor (the red, white and blue banner of the revolution), Chenard strikes a heroic pose, as if ready to defend his newly won rights. Boilly has placed Chenard in the foreground so that he towers over the landscape, just as the newly enfranchised workers dominated the political scene.*

ENCOUNTER

Slavery and the French Revolution

When African slaves were introduced into the West Indies and North America, many whites accepted slavery as embedded in history, sanctioned by the Bible, and necessary to large-scale agricultural production. After 1750, those attitudes were challenged, as thinkers and religious groups, especially the Quakers, began to question slavery's legitimacy. The turning point came later, during the French Revolution, when whites, struggling to overthrow repressive regimes in France, inspired slaves in the French West Indies to fight for their freedom—and the ideals of the French Revolution: liberty, equality, and brotherhood.

By the 1780s, New World slave owners were importing nearly 75,000 slaves a year, many of them destined for the sugar plantations in the French colony of St. Domingue or modern Haiti. St. Domingue, at that time, formed the western half of the island of Hispaniola; the eastern half was Spain's colony of Santo Domingo. The slaves in French St. Domingue, with no rights, were at the bottom of a rigid social and racial system. Above them were the free people of color—those of mixed blood who had some rights but were still subject to discrimination. Next, constituting a group of second-class citizens, were less influential whites, who served as plantation overseers and ran the small but necessary businesses. At the top stood the white plantation owners, prosperous merchants, some French noblemen, the clergy, and government officials. In 1789, when news of the outbreak of the French Revolution reached St. Domingue, the colony's old social and racial order began to crumble.

In the opening phases of the French Revolution, the upper-class whites on St. Domingue set up their own government, sent delegates to the Estates-General in France, and pressed for more economic freedom. From 1790 to 1794, a series of revolts by the free people of color, the poorer whites, and the slaves occurred and spread to the Spanish side of the island. The island's revolutionary government abolished slavery in 1793, and the French government did likewise in 1794. By then, Toussaint L'Ouverture (TOO-san LOO-ver-tchur) (1743–1803), an ex-slave who was literate and familiar with the writings of the French *philosophes*, had emerged as a military and political leader. In 1801, after defeating both British and French forces, he ruled the island as a military dictator—the first black-led government in the New World. A year later Toussaint was arrested and sent to France, where he died in prison.

Out of the mixing of an economic enterprise to supply slave labor for an expanding plantation system for

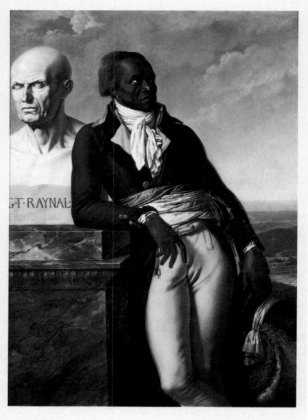

Encounter figure 17.1   Jean-Baptiste Bellay (buh-LAY) joined the slave revolt led by Toussaint L'Ouverture, before being elected as one of three delegates to the constitutional assembly, or Convention, in 1793. He lost his seat in 1797, returned home, and faded into history. Elegantly dressed and wearing the French tricolor in his sash and on his hat, Bellay leans against the bust of Abbé Raynal (re-NAHL), the French *philosophe* whose antislavery writings inspired Toussaint and probably Bellay. Including and relating a dead person to the individual in the portrait was a popular device in eighteenth-century paintings. The background, on the right, represents the Haitian countryside.

Europeans, a debate among European intellectuals over human rights and freedom, and a series of revolutions in France and wars in Europe, an independent republic emerged, in 1803, on the island of Haiti. This government was the first black republic in history and the second republic in the New World. A new society had been born, and its future now rested in the hands of an emancipated and self-governing people.

given to all males, including blacks and Jews, state education was opened to all, conquered people were allowed to vote on their future, and the slave trade was abolished. Women, however, were denied the vote and citizenship, but they acquired certain rights, as in marriage contracts.

Such far-reaching reforms alarmed many, and soon the fledgling Republic faced civil war at home and invasions from abroad, which in turn set off more domestic political and financial crises. These events led to the year-long Reign of Terror (1793–1794), the controversial policy whereby suspected enemies of the revolution were executed. Its excesses overshadowed many of the Republic's accomplishments and discredited the idea of revolution among many of its early supporters. In August 1795 a more moderate republic, known as the Directory, was instituted, in which power was shared between two legislative houses and five directors.

The Directory lasted only four years. Although this government favored the commercial middle classes, it remained revolutionary. Its leaders faced nearly insurmountable problems, such as a growing counterrevolution, the collapse of the currency, and a breakdown in law and order. The directors appealed to the military for aid against their enemies, and in November 1799 General Napoleon Bonaparte staged a coup d'état that abolished the Directory and established the Consulate.

With the rise of Napoleon (1769–1821), events had come full circle, in effect returning France to a monarchy. Napoleon was a dictator and military genius who embodied the enlightened despotism of his century and at the same time anticipated modern totalitarianism. Above all, he was heir to the French Revolution.

Although the cost of Napoleonic rule between 1799 and 1815 was the loss of political liberty for the French, in exchange France received internal peace and a consolidation of most of the revolution's policies. Napoleon kept careers open to talent, suppressed aristocratic privilege, rewarded wealthy property owners, and refashioned public education. He welcomed home revolutionaries who had emigrated— provided they were loyal to his regime. He restored relations with the papacy, though his efforts failed to achieve religious harmony. He also ended the civil war that had raged for more than a decade, and he stabilized the economy.

Napoleon's most enduring legacy was the law code he helped draft. Intended for universal application, the Napoleonic Code introduced rational legal principles and legitimized the idea of the lay state. The code rested on reforms of the revolutionary era, such as the abolition of serfdom, the guilds, and feudal property.

Despite its reactionary ideas of paternal rule and the subservience of women—thus reversing the small gains made by women in the revolutionary era—the code remains the basis of civil law in both France and its former colonies.

Napoleon's military conquests and diplomatic successes soon eclipsed his domestic achievements. A brilliant field general before he seized power, Napoleon launched a series of victorious wars once he became emperor in 1804 (see Figure 17.1). When not winning battles, he managed to make the coalitions allied against him fall apart by exploiting his foes' basic distrust of one another. In particular, he worked to keep Great Britain out of Continental affairs while he crushed Prussia and Austria, who then sued for peace. Simultaneously, he annexed land for France and established satellite kingdoms ruled by members of his family or by his generals. As the self-proclaimed heir of the Age of Reason and the French Revolution, Napoleon reorganized his newly conquered territories along the lines of France. At first, many local reformers welcomed the French, but they soon learned the high costs of occupation and began to resist their "liberators" (Map 17.1).

Napoleon's empire upset the European balance of power at a basic level, so that ultimately the other nations united to defeat him once he was proven vulnerable in battle by the failure of his invasion of Russia in 1812. An alliance of Great Britain and the European states defeated Napoleon in June 1815 at Waterloo (in modern Belgium). Exiled to an island in the South Atlantic, Napoleon died there in 1821, but his spirit hovered over France and Europe for much of the nineteenth century.

REACTION, 1815–1830

After 1815 the victorious nations tried to restore Europe to its prerevolutionary status, but the forces of change had already altered the future of Western— and world—history. As heirs of the Enlightenment notion that they were citizens of the world, the French largely ignored the traditions of the peoples whom they had conquered, believing that the principles of their revolutionary society represented what was best for humanity. Ultimately, however, the French were not as successful as they had hoped in exporting their revolution. The European states and Great Britain shared a conservative agenda that aimed to suppress the advance of liberal ideas. At the Congress of Vienna in 1815, the victors stripped France of most of its conquests, restored the balance of power, halted or reduced reform programs, and inaugurated a period of reaction.

LEARNING THROUGH MAPS

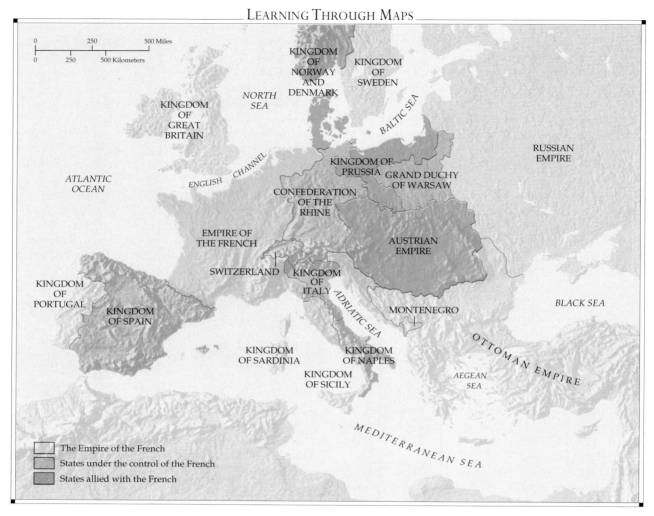

Map 17.1   EUROPE AT THE HEIGHT OF NAPOLEON'S POWER, 1810–1811
This map shows the maximum expansion of Napoleonic power across the map of
Europe. **Compare** the borders of the French Empire in this map with those of France
in Map 16.1, Europe, 1763–1789. **Identify** the states now under the control of France.
Which states were allied with the French? **Notice** the various states that appear in
Map 14.1 but no longer exist or have new names in Map 17.1. **Consider** the influence
of geography in helping make Great Britain and Russia the enemies of Napoleon.

Despite this redesign of the map, many Napoleonic
reforms remained in force until 1830 and beyond. Even
in France, where the allies restored the Bourbons,
Louis XVIII (r. 1815–1824) issued a charter that guaranteed a constitutional regime resembling the limited
monarchy of 1791. Most western European states now
had governments elected by their citizens and civil law
based on the Napoleonic Code. In contrast, Prussia,
Russia, and Austria remained basically untouched by
democracy and representative government.

The fate of reform in Europe between 1815 and 1830
varied from modest changes in England to repression
in Russia. In the immediate postwar period in Great

Britain, the government resisted attempts to reform
Parliament or to institute free trade, but in the 1820s,
Britain began to modernize itself. France regressed
toward absolutism as the restored Bourbon monarchy
chipped away at the revolutionary heritage. By 1830
resistance to the crown was mounting, and in the July
Revolution the people revolted and replaced the Bourbon monarchy with Louis Philippe, the Duke of Or-
léans (r. 1830–1848). Constitutional government now
put the middle class in power.

In central Europe, Austria kept liberal sentiments
under tight control at home and within the region.
Prussia, which had made important liberal reforms in

the Napoleonic era, now seemed more interested in efficiency than in modernizing the state. Russia became increasingly reactionary and repressive. Until the 1860s, Russia's autocratic regime and Austria's domination of central Europe widened the gulf between eastern and western Europe.

REVOLUTIONS IN ART AND IDEAS: FROM NEOCLASSICISM TO ROMANTICISM

The makers of the French Revolution had at hand an artistic style that was perfectly suited to their purposes—the Neoclassical. In contrast to the frivolous Rococo, this style was high-minded, ethical, and serious. Neoclassical artists and architects followed the ancient Greco-Roman ideals of balance, simplicity, and restraint, principles that were thought to embody the underlying order of the universe. Truth was seen as eternal, unchanging, the same for one and all. Art and literature created according to Classical principles were believed to be both morally uplifting and aesthetically satisfying.

In England, Classicism lingered on in the novels of Jane Austen. Untouched by the revolutions that dominated this age, Austen created fictional works that took England's deep countryside for their setting and dealt with the lives of the less wealthy gentry, an essentially middle-class world that appealed to her audience.

Advanced thinkers in France made the Neoclassical paintings of David a symbol of the new rational order they wanted to introduce into the world. The revolution intensified devotion to Classical ideals, and David became its official artist. Later, when the revolution lost its way and France began to see itself as a new Rome, Napoleon made David his court painter. After 1800 David transformed Neoclassicism into an imperial style that lingered on in France and on the Continent long after the French emperor was exiled from Europe in 1815.

Even earlier, starting about 1770, a new movement was emerging across Europe, one that was to have lasting effects on the Western consciousness. **Romanticism** was a whole way of thinking that came to dominate European arts and letters in the nineteenth century. Rejecting Neoclassicism as cold and artificial, the Romantics glorified unruly nature, uncontrolled feeling, and the mysteries of the human soul. They claimed that their ideals were more in tune with human nature than the order, reason, and harmony of Classicism. Certain ideas and elements of Romanticism have permeated our Western way of thinking and become articles of faith in the modern world.

Neoclassicism in Literature After 1789

During her brief life, Jane Austen (1775–1817) wrote six novels that together rank as the finest body of fiction produced in this period. Austen approached novel writing in a Classical spirit, portraying her characters as inhabiting a serene environment reminiscent of the quiet domestic scenes of the seventeenth-century Dutch painter Vermeer (see Chapter 14). Calling herself a miniaturist, she concentrated her author's eye on a vanishing world where the smallest important unit was the family and the most significant problems involved the adjustment of social relationships.

In the hands of a lesser writer, such a literary program might have failed by being too narrow, but Austen transcended her limited framework. She did this through clear writing, ironic understatement, and, above all, beautifully realized descriptions of the manners and little rituals of provincial life: the balls attended, the letters and conversations, the visits to relatives, and the unexpected social breakdowns, such as an elopement, a betrayed confidence, or a broken engagement. She was especially sensitive to the constraints her society imposed on women, depicting with great wit a world in which women were given little access to formal education, confined to the domestic sphere, kept economically dependent on men, and socialized to be weak and sentimental. The best known of Austen's novels is *Pride and Prejudice* (1813), a gently satirical work whose plot revolves around the problems that arise when the Bennets—a shabby genteel family—try to find suitable husbands for five daughters.

Neoclassical Painting and Architecture After 1789

Jacques-Louis David founded Neoclassicism in painting in the 1780s and remained its consummate exponent until his death in 1825. As official artist of the French Revolution, he rendered contemporary events in the ancient manner. David's most successful painting from this period was his study of the revolution's famous martyr Jean Paul Marat [muh-RAH], who was assassinated while seated in his bath (Figure 17.4). Himself an ardent supporter of the revolution, David meticulously planned this work to give universal meaning to a specific moment in French history. The setting is historically accurate because Marat suffered from a skin disorder and often conducted official business while seated in the bathtub. Once having established the scene, David suppresses every detail that does not contribute to the general impression of tragedy. As a result, the few details take on a highly charged quality. The figure of Marat resembles a piece

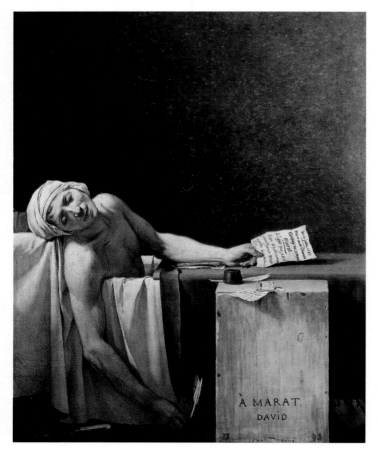

Figure 17.4 JACQUES-LOUIS DAVID. *Death of Marat.* 1793. Oil on canvas, 65 × 50½". Musées Royaux des Beaux-Arts, Brussels. *David's presentation of figures in the nude in his Neoclassical history paintings was often denounced by literal-minded critics as unrealistic, but David defended this choice as consistent with "the customs of antiquity." The critics were silenced by David's depiction of the Marat murder scene, since in this case the nudity was true to life. In this painting, David's Classical principles and the demands of realistic portrayal combined to produce a timeless image.*

of Classical sculpture against the stark background. His torso is twisted so that the bleeding wound and the peaceful face are fully visible. The pen and the inkwell remind the viewer that Marat was killed while serving the revolution. In effect, David has portrayed Marat as a secular saint.

Barely escaping the revolution's most violent phase, David survived to become court painter to Napoleon, and modifications in the cause of political propaganda now appeared in his art. Napoleon, to enhance his image as a new Augustus, encouraged David to make his painting reflect the pomp and grandeur of the Napoleonic court. *The Coronation of Napoleon and Josephine* is typical of David's imperial paintings (Figure 17.5). This pictorial record of the investiture conveys the opulent splendor and theatrical ceremony that Napoleon craved as a way of validating his empire in the eyes of Europe's older monarchs, who regarded him as an upstart. Napoleon's family members, who had been made kings, princes, princesses, and so on, are depicted in elaborate court dress. In addition, David's treatment of the coronation reveals the modern conception of political power. Instead of being crowned by the pope, Napoleon placed the crown on his own head. This painting shows Napoleon preparing to crown his empress, who is kneeling. Virtually ignored in this splendid moment for the Bonaparte family is the pope, who is seated at the right.

The only Neoclassical painter comparable to David is his pupil Jean-Auguste-Dominique Ingres [ANG-gruh] (1780–1867). Ingres inherited the mantle of Neoclassicism from David, but he lacked his teacher's moral enthusiasm. As a result, Ingres's Classicism is

Figure 17.5 JACQUES-LOUIS DAVID. *The Coronation of Napoleon and Josephine.* 1805–1808. Oil on canvas, 20' × 30'6½". Louvre. *Napoleon orchestrated his own coronation and then guided David in painting it. For instance, Napoleon's mother did not attend, probably because of her disapproval of her son's grandiose ambitions, but Napoleon insisted that David depict her seated prominently at the center of the festivities. David also shows the pope's hand raised in benediction, contrary to the report of eye-witnesses who described him sitting with both hands resting on his knees.*

Figure 17.6 Jean-Auguste-Dominique Ingres. *Madame Jacques Louis Leblanc. 1823. Oil on canvas, 47 × 36½".* Metropolitan Museum of Art. Wolfe Fund, 1918. *Ingres was the last great painter of portraits in a field that was to be taken over by the camera after 1840. A keen observer of the human face and form, he was able to render intense, idealized but realistic likenesses, as evidenced in Madame Leblanc's portrait, which he painted in Florence during his years in Italy. Ingres conveys physical presence by placing his subject in the immediate foreground, by highlighting her physical features and the color of her flesh—in Ingres's words, making one side of the portrait light and the other dark—and by depicting the gleaming surfaces of her clothing and jewelry.*

almost cold-blooded and stark in its simple images. The finest expressions of Ingres's art are his portraits. With clean lines drawn with a sure and steady hand, he created almost photographic images of his subjects. Of Ingres's numerous portraits, one of the most exquisite is that of Madame Leblanc [luh-BLAH(N)], a member of the new social order of Napoleonic France (Figure 17.6). Ingres's portrait may not probe deeply into the subject's psychology, but he does convey the sitter's high social position, stressing her poise and alluding to her wealth through the rich details of the marble-topped table and the dangling watch and chain. In his own way, Ingres gives this member of the new bourgeois aristocracy the same glamorous treatment that had been accorded prerevolutionary nobles in Rococo portraits.

After 1789 the Neoclassical style in architecture spread to the European colonies, notably to the former British territories in North America. In the United States, the middle-class founders of the new republic made Neoclassicism synonymous with their own time, which is known as the Federal Period. They graced their capital, Washington, with the Classical architecture that symbolized devotion to republican and democratic sentiments.

The most profound influence on America's Classical heritage was exercised by Thomas Jefferson (1743–1826), the coauthor of the Declaration of Independence and the third president of the United States. Jefferson was also a master architect. Like other architects in this era, he was deeply indebted to the principles of the Italian Andrea Palladio (1508–1580), whose book on architecture he had read. Palladio's Villa Rotonda near Vicenza served as the model for Jefferson's home at Monticello near Charlottesville, Virginia (Figure 17.7). Like the Villa Rotonda (see Figure 12.23), Monticello is a country dwelling arranged around a domed central area, though it features only two symmetrical connecting wings. Executed in brick with wooden trim, Monticello has inspired so many imitations that it has come to symbolize the American dream of gracious living.

Just as Jefferson's plan for his personal residence influenced American domestic architecture, his design for Virginia's state capitol in Richmond has deeply influenced public architecture (Figure 17.8). From his plan for the Virginia statehouse arose the tradition of building public structures in the form of ancient temples. His model for the capitol was the Maison Carrée (see Figure 5.11), a Roman temple dating from the first century A.D. Though small by today's standards for public buildings, Jefferson's statehouse has a strong presence and is a marvel of refined elegance and simple charm. The most pleasing part of his original design is the central building, with its perfectly proportioned features—columns, pediment, and windows. Even though two smaller wings were added later, they enhance rather than detract from Jefferson's symmetrical and harmonious plan.

Romanticism: Its Spirit and Expression

In contrast to Neoclassicism, Romanticism stood for everything that was unbounded and untamed. The Romantics' patron saint was Rousseau, whose emotionalism and love of nature had made him out of step with his own time. Like Rousseau, the Romantics preferred to be guided by emotion and intuition. Following these guides, they conjured up an image of the world that was deeply personal and alive with hidden

Figure 17.7 THOMAS JEFFERSON. Monticello. 1770–1784; remodeled 1796–1806. Charlottesville, Virginia. *The Palladio-inspired architecture of Monticello reflected Jefferson's ethical vision. Its portico in the plain style of a Roman temple mirrored his admiration for the Roman republic and its ideals of simplicity and order. Its overall devotion to mathematical principles and unobtrusive details were expressions of his commitment to disciplined living. Though built for one of America's elite, Monticello was conceived on a modest scale as a visual rebuke to the luxurious palaces of Europe's aristocrats.*

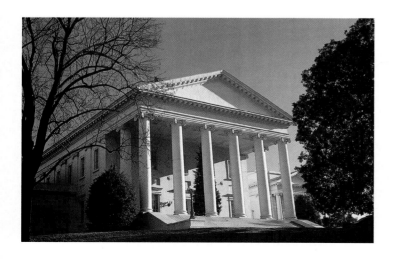

Figure 17.8 THOMAS JEFFERSON. State Capitol of Virginia. 1785–1796. Richmond, Virginia. *Jefferson described the Maison Carrée, the model for this statehouse, as "the most perfect and precious remain of antiquity in existence." Political considerations also influenced Jefferson's choice, for he identified this Roman temple as a symbol of Roman republican values. Like Monticello, Jefferson's statehouse design was an outgrowth of his ethical vision.*

Figure 17.9 Philip Jacques de Loutherbourg. *Coalbrookdale by Night.* 1801. Oil on canvas, 26¾ × 42". Science and Society Picture Library, London. *At first glance, this painting seems to portray the world engulfed in a flaming inferno. Only gradually does the meaning of the scene—a depiction of one of England's new industrialized towns—emerge. As a terrifying symbol of industrialism, the painting helps to explain what Romantic art was rebelling against.*

meanings. Nature itself became God for many Romantics, who spiritualized nature so that divinity was expressed through bucolic scenes as well as terrifying natural forces. To characterize the latter face of nature they invented the term *Sublime* to convey the awesome and majestic power of earthquakes, floods, and storms.

The Romantic reverence for nature stemmed partly from a desire to escape from the effects of the Industrial Revolution, which was altering the countryside for the worse (Figure 17.9). Not surprisingly, England, the first home of industrialization, became the center of a movement that exalted the Middle Ages, creating a world of natural sentiment that existed only in imagination. The Romantics' rejection of the industrial world had many other consequences, including a preoccupation with the exotic East and the domains of the imagination, dreams, drugs, and nonrational mental states.

Another formative force in Romanticism was the French Revolution. Many early Romantics willingly saw in this awesome upheaval Europe's future. The revolutionary watchwords "liberty," "rights of man," "the individual," and "equality" became the basis of a moral and humanitarian viewpoint that could be applied beyond the orbit of the French Revolution. When Greece declared its independence from the feeble Ottoman Empire and fought for its freedom in the 1820s, for example, many Europeans, influenced by revolutionary principles, declared their solidarity with the rebels. Among them was the English Romantic poet Lord Byron, who died in Greece while aiding in the cause of Greek independence.

The French Revolution also sparked a strong negative reaction among some Romantics, who criticized its seemingly random violence. They likewise deplored Napoleonic imperialism, which squeezed the life out of other cultures by conquering them and then imposing French customs. These conservative Romantics renounced the French Revolution's stress on abstract ideas and natural rights and focused their attention on history and the rights and traditions native to each country. They especially disagreed with the revolution's international spirit and advocated instead a nationalistic point of view.

At first, Romantic nationalism was little more than a rejection of foreign influences and a reverence for those unique aspects of culture that are created by the common people—folk dancing, folk sayings, folk tales, folk music, and folk customs. This benign nationalism later developed into an aggressive attitude that insisted on the moral superiority of one people over all others and expressed unrelenting hostility toward outsiders. In its extreme form, militant nationalism encouraged the expulsion of "alien" groups who were not recognized as members of the national heritage. Aggressive nationalism lasted almost a century, from 1848 to 1945, climaxing in Nazi Germany, and still remains a potent force today.

The Romantics also generated a cult of nonconformity and held in great esteem outlaws, gypsies, and those who lived outside middle-class society. This hostility toward middle-class life has an ironic twist because those who professed it generally came from this class and sought its patronage. The unruly presence of Romanticism coincided with the rise to political dominance of the middle class. Out of the love-hate relationship between Romantics and the middle class emerged another familiar emblem of modern life, the anti-bourgeois bourgeois—that is, middle-class people who scorn their own social origins. From the dawn of the Romantic period until the present day, modern culture has been filled with middle-class rebels in revolt against their class.

France played a central role in Romanticism because of its culturally strategic position, and England also produced major figures in Romanticism, particularly in poetry and painting. Notwithstanding these achievements, the heart of Romanticism was German-speaking Europe. The French writer Madame de Staël (1766–1817) helped popularize German culture and writers with her book *On Germany* (1810). So great was the German cultural response that Romanticism is often called a German invention.

The Romantic Movement in Literature

Romanticism in literature was foreshadowed in the German literary movement known as **Sturm und Drang,** or Storm and Stress. This movement flourished briefly in the 1770s and early 1780s, arising as a revolt against Classical restraint and drawing inspiration from Rousseau's emotionalism. On a positive level, this literary movement idealized peasant life and the unconventional, liberated mind. The Sturm und Drang writers attacked organized religion because of its hypocrisy and followed Rousseau in finding God in nature. These middle-class authors objected to the formality and tedium of eighteenth-century life and letters and valued free expression in language, dress, behavior, and love. By the mid-1780s, the movement had settled down, drained of its rebelliousness. The most influential members became fully integrated into the German literary scene.

The Sturm und Drang movement's outstanding writer was Johann Wolfgang von Goethe [GUHR-tuh] (1749–1832), the greatest of German writers. In 1774, while still in his twenties, Goethe acquired a Europe-wide reputation with *The Sorrows of Young Werther,* a novel in which the young hero commits suicide because of disappointment in love. So successful was this novel that it led to Wertherism, the social phenomenon in which young men imitated the hero's emotionalism, sometimes even to the point of killing themselves. Werther is a complex character: passionate and excitable, given to inappropriate outbursts, moved by the innocence of children, attracted to social misfits, and overwhelmed by God's presence in nature. He embodies many characteristics of Romanticism.

With the publication in England in 1798 of *Lyrical Ballads* by William Wordsworth (1770–1850) and Samuel Taylor Coleridge (1772–1834), a turning point in the history of literary style was reached, and Romanticism truly began. Rejecting what they considered to be the artificiality of the Neoclassicists, the two poets turned to more natural types of verse, Coleridge to ballad forms and Wordsworth to simple lyrics of plain

folks, voiced in the common language of the "middle and lower classes of society." Henceforth many Romantic writers, both in poetry and in prose, sought to reproduce the language of customary speech—a literary revolution that was the equivalent of the coming of democracy.

The task Wordsworth assigned himself in *Lyrical Ballads* was to compose verses about the pleasures of everyday existence. He responded to this challenge with poems filled with deep feeling, which were mainly about finding wisdom in simple things. A famous poem from this collection entitled "Lines Composed a Few Miles Above Tintern Abbey" shows Wordsworth's pantheism, or the belief that God lives in nature. In it, speaking to his sister Dorothy, he recalls the strong emotions he felt in his early life when he "bounded o'er the mountains, by the sides / of the deep rivers, and the lonely streams, / wherever nature led." Now he describes himself as subdued but still "a worshipper of Nature." Wordsworth's nature is a world of overgrown hedgerows, meadows, orchards, and peasant cottages. The beauty of the ordinary became Wordsworth's lifelong preoccupation; he is regarded as the English language's most stirring poet of nature.

Soon after the appearance of the *Lyrical Ballads,* Goethe published his verse play *Faust* (Part I, 1808). Goethe's Werther had been a social rebel, the prototype of the anti-bourgeois bourgeois. But his Faust was a universal rebel, unwilling to let any moral scruple stand in the way of his spiritual quest for the meaning of life. Faust's two distinguishing marks are his relentless pursuit of knowledge and his all-consuming restlessness. Having exhausted book learning, Faust hopes that experience will satisfy his spiritual hunger, and thus he turns to the Devil (Mephistopheles), who proposes to give Faust all the exciting experiences that have so far been lacking in his life. If Faust finds any moment satisfying, then his immortal soul is forever condemned to hell. Under such conditions Faust signs the compact, in his blood, with Mephistopheles.

Mephistopheles helps Faust recover his youth and involves him in a series of adventures that include drunkenness, sexual excess, seduction, and murder. His mistress kills their illegitimate child and perishes in despair. *Faust,* Part I, concludes with Faust more dissatisfied than when he began and no nearer to his goal. Goethe later added Part II (1832) to his drama, in which God redeems Faust because of his willingness to sacrifice his life for others, but lacking the emotional intensity of the first part, this second half failed to reach a large audience.

Goethe's *Faust,* Part I, however, proved irresistible. His drama became the most often performed German-language play in the world. It inspired numerous

Figure 17.10   RICHARD WESTALL. *George Gordon, Lord Byron.* 1813. Oil on canvas, 36 × 28″. National Portrait Gallery, London. *Westall's portrait of Lord Byron captures the brooding and dark good looks that made him the exemplar of the Romantic hero. Gazing intently into the distance while resting his chin on his hand, Byron seems lost in thought. His isolation is heightened by the overall darkness except for his face, hand, and shirt collar. It was this image of Byron—a person coiled tight as a spring—that caused one female admirer to describe him as "mad, bad, and dangerous to know."*

paintings and several works of music. The word *Faustian* came into use to characterize one who is willing to sacrifice spiritual values for knowledge, experience, or mastery.

Another powerful voice in Romantic literature was the English poet George Gordon, Lord Byron (1788–1824). Better known on the Continent than his compatriots Wordsworth and Coleridge, Byron was called by Goethe the "herald of world literature." The personality of Byron has fascinated successive generations of Western artists and thinkers. At a time when the middle classes were ruled by a restrictive code of respectability, he created a model for rebellious youth with his flowing hair, open shirt collar, and love of ungovernable forces (Figure 17.10). His greatest Romantic creation was probably himself—the "Byronic hero," who was moody, passionate, absorbed in exploring and expressing his innermost self.

Yet the English treated Byron as a pariah and drove him into exile for his unconventional life. Perhaps in retaliation, Byron, in his most admired poem, *Don Juan* (1819–1824), presented the notorious seducer as a virtuous hero—a literary device intended to expose the hypocrisy of society. Like Goethe's *Faust,* Byron's *Don Juan* was a study in moral duality and reflected the author's fascination with subterranean drives in human nature.

Byron was the best known of the trio of Romantic poets whose enduring lyrical works helped to define the period from 1810 to 1824 as England's great Age of Poetry. The other two poets were Byron's friend Percy Bysshe Shelley (1792–1822), famed for poetry that was often charged with radical politics, and John Keats (1795–1820), who drew on a tragic personal history to create works of quiet beauty and stoic calm. That all three writers led tragically shortened lives—Byron dying at age thirty-six, Shelley at twenty-nine, and Keats at twenty-five—contributed in later years to their Romantic image as doomed poets.

English Romanticism also produced two of the most pervasive figures of Western culture—Frankenstein and his manufactured monster. Made familiar through countless films and cartoons, these two fictional characters first appeared in the novel *Frankenstein* (1818) by Mary Wollstonecraft Shelley (1797–1851). Shelley was well connected to two of the most unconventional literary families of the day; she was the daughter of Mary Wollstonecraft, a founder of modern feminism (see Chapter 16), and she was the wife of the poet Percy Bysshe Shelley. In Shelley's novel, Dr. Frankenstein, having thoughtlessly constructed a humanlike being with no prospect for personal happiness, is eventually hunted down and killed by his own despairing creature. Part of the Romantic reaction against Enlightenment rationalism, which began with Rousseau (see Chapter 16), Shelley's novel presented Frankenstein as a man driven by excessive and obsessive intellectual curiosity and the monster as a tragic symbol of science out of control. Written in the optimistic dawn of the industrialized age, when humanity seemed on the verge of taming the natural world, Shelley's *Frankenstein* is one of the earliest warnings that scientific research divorced from morality is an open invitation to personal and social disaster.

Romantic Painting

Romanticism in painting appeared first in England, manifesting itself as part of a cult of nature with two distinct aspects, the pastoral and the Sublime. Painters of pastoral scenes specialized in landscapes in which peasant life was equated with the divine order of

Figure 17.11   JOHN CONSTABLE. *The Hay Wain.* 1821. Oil on canvas, 51¼ × 73″. Reproduced by courtesy of the Trustees, The National Gallery, London. *Although the pastoral subject was alien to them at the time, French Romantic painters recognized in Constable a kindred spirit when* The Hay Wain *was exhibited at the Paris Salon of 1824. The scene's informality, the strong colors, and the natural lighting converted them, and a later French school of landscape painters was influenced by Constable.*

things, thus forging a moral link between human beings and the natural environment. The painter John Constable was the chief exponent of the pastoral. In contrast, painters of Sublime subjects focused on devastating natural or human-made calamities, reflecting a world order beyond mortal control or understanding. The leading exponent of the Sublime was the painter J. M. W. Turner.

Like the Dutch masters of the 1600s, John Constable (1776–1837) preferred to paint simple country landscapes. But more important than the Dutch influence on his art was the Romantic "cult of nature." Constable's landscapes, like Wordsworth's poetry, reflected the sense of God's universal presence in nature. Wordsworth claimed that nature aroused feelings that "connect the landscape with the quiet of the sky." In his canvases, Constable tried to awaken the viewer to the divinity in nature by focusing on ordinary scenes such as one might see on a country walk.

Constable had an almost holy vision that was true to nature without using what he called tricks or crass emotional appeals.

Constable's landscapes often convey a feeling of having been painted right on the spot. In actuality, he liked to sketch on a site and then transform his impressions into a finished painting that preserved the feeling of immediacy. This two-step method resulted in a style that was both solid and sensitive to the natural world. Constable's innocent and sincere style was meant to convey the feeling that his vision sprang from a mystical communion with nature, rather than being an artificial scene conceived in an artist's studio.

Although Constable's art was not fully appreciated by his contemporaries, a few works won acclaim and helped to redefine the way that the public looked at nature. Of these the most famous is *The Hay Wain* (Figure 17.11). Over the years, this painting has been

Figure 17.12 JOHN CONSTABLE. *Cloud Study.* 1821. Oil on paper on panel, 8⅜ × 11½". Yale Center for British Art, New Haven. Paul Mellon Collection. *As Constable made his cloud paintings, he kept precise records of the weather conditions. For example, in this* Cloud Study, *he recorded the date and time, September 21, 1821, between 2 and 3 P.M. and noted: "strong Wind at west, bright light coming through the Clouds which are laying one on the other." Thus, these paintings combine the scientist's meticulous eye with the artist's sensitive response to nature.*

reproduced so often that it is sometimes dismissed as "calendar art," but when it first appeared, it excited admiration at home and in Paris. The freshness of the simple images attracted viewers to the beauty of the scene. *The Hay Wain* added many features of everyday rural life to the repertoire of Romantic motifs, including a thatch-roofed cottage, a gently flowing stream, a dog running along a river bank, cows grazing in the background, and overhead the ever-changing English sky.

The sky, for Constable, served as the unique source of light. In 1821–1822, he conducted a program that he called "skying," capturing on canvas the cloud-filled English sky as it moved from sunshine to rain and back again (Figure 17.12). Dissatisfied with earlier artists who used artificial means to represent nature, Constable worked as a naturalist to record the truth in nature. Constable's cloud studies echoed Romantic poets, like Goethe and Wordsworth, who identified clouds as a symbol of various themes, such as loneliness and the fleeting quality of life. In his attempt to portray the out-of-doors in its lively colors and ever-changing light, Constable was an important influence on the nineteenth-century Impressionists.

As for the Sublime, Joseph Mallord William Turner (1775–1851) created a new type of subject, "the sublime catastrophe," in which he specialized from 1800 until about 1830. He was the most original artist of his age, prefiguring the Impressionists with his virtuosic use of color and anticipating modern abstract painting in his depictions of wild nature. An example of

Turner's sublime catastrophes is *Snowstorm: Hannibal and His Army Crossing the Alps* (Figure 17.13). Although inspired by an episode from Roman history, this painting is more about the fury of nature than it is about the Carthaginian general Hannibal. The actual subject is the snowstorm, whose sweeping savagery threatens to annihilate everything, including soldiers and horses. No artist before Turner had handled paint in the way that he does here. He turns the sky, which occupies at least three-fourths of the canvas, into an abstract composition, a series of interpenetrating planes of differently colored light.

Turner also dealt with another aspect of the Sublime theme, the notion that all human endeavor is doomed, in *The Bay of Baiae, with Apollo and the Sibyl* (Figure 17.14). Inspired by his first visit to Italy, he portrays Classical motifs in a Romantic landscape. In ancient Rome, the imperial court built splendid villas and baths at the Bay of Baiae (near Naples), which by Turner's time stood in ruins. The painter, using artistic license, rearranged the actual scene to make this vista much more appealing. By placing Apollo and the Sibyl in the foreground, Turner alludes to a Greek myth associated with the nearby port of Cumae, the home of the Cumaean Sibyl.

About the time the Sublime developed in England, it also was launched in Germany by Caspar David Friedrich (1774–1840), a painter who specialized in brooding landscapes, usually with a few human figures to give them a spiritual scale. A lifelong

Figure 17.13   JOSEPH MALLORD WILLIAM TURNER. *Snowstorm: Hannibal and His Army Crossing the Alps*. 1810–1812. Oil on canvas, 4'9½" × 7'9½". Tate Gallery. *Hannibal and his troops, stretching from left to right in the bottom third of the painting, are almost invisible; above them and dominating the scene is a raging snowstorm, through which may be glimpsed a ghostly sun. This painting, based on a Gothic novel of the time, was less about the ancient struggle between the Carthaginian general Hannibal and Rome than about the French general Napoleon and England in the 1800s; thus, this work implicitly reflects the period's political climate—a rare occurrence in Turner's art.*

Figure 17.14   JOSEPH MALLORD WILLIAM TURNER. *The Bay of Baiae, with Apollo and the Sibyl*. 1823. Oil on canvas, 57¼ × 94". Tate Gallery. *Turner has deftly focused the viewer's eye on the painting's center by means of a circular arrangement of objects (boats, ruins, and rocks) and the use of shadows and light. Within this space, Turner places Apollo making overtures to the Sibyl, a tactic whose outcome is symbolized by the rabbit and the snake. The rabbit (center) represents love, referring to Apollo's pursuit of the Sibyl, and the snake (lower right) alludes to lurking evil, perhaps a reference to the Sibyl's fate for spurning Apollo. The god curses her so that she will grow old but never die— just as the ruins at the Bay of Baiae are reminders of Rome's former glory.*

Figure 17.15   CASPAR DAVID FRIEDRICH. *Monk by the Sea.* 1808–1810. Oil on canvas, 43¼ × 67½". Stiftung Preussischer Kulturbesitz, Schloss Charlottenburg, Berlin. *This painting is revolutionary in form and content. In form, it violates Classical perspective by using a low horizon line to create a sky of limitless space; it also rejects traditional design by reducing figures and setting to a minimum level. In content, the meaning is left deliberately ambiguous. These simplifications make the painting a nearly abstract image, and thus it points the way to Modernist art (see Chapter 19).*

resident of Pomerania on northern Europe's Baltic coast, he drew artistic inspiration from his homeland's deserted beaches, dense forests, and chalky cliffs. What sets his landscapes apart from those of earlier artists on the same subject is his desire to turn natural scenes into glimpses of the divine mystery. Avoiding traditional Christian subjects, Friedrich invented his own symbols for conveying God's presence in the world.

In *Monk by the Sea* (Figure 17.15), the setting is the stark Baltic seacoast, where a hooded figure stands on the dunes before a great wall of sky. This figure—the "monk" of the title—forms the only vertical line in an otherwise horizontal painting. Below is the angry sea, but the sky is calm except for a bank of clouds lit by the moon or perhaps the coming dawn. By showing the

monk from the back—he rarely painted faces— Friedrich encourages the viewer to see what the monk sees and to feel what he feels. Perhaps, filled with optimism, he awaits a new day. Or perhaps, despairing, he watches the descent of night. Or perhaps he feels insignificant when confronted with the limitless sky and sea. Infrared photographs have revealed that Friedrich originally included two ships struggling against the waves in the painting. Ships are often present in Friedrich's works, symbolic of a divine messenger to the human realm. By painting them out, Friedrich removed an optimistic note that may have guided the viewer's interpretation. Nevertheless, the finished painting represents twin Romantic themes and favorites of Friedrich's—love of solitude and fascination with the infinite.

Figure 17.16   FRANCISCO GOYA. *The Family of Charles IV.*
1800. Oil on canvas, 9'2" × 11'. Prado, Madrid. *Following a
well-established Spanish tradition, Goya has painted himself into
the canvas on the left, from which vantage point in the shadows he
observes the royal family. Velázquez had followed this tradition
150 years earlier (see Figure 14.10), which this painting echoes.
Goya portrayed the ravaged face of the king's sister on the left as a
reminder of the fleeting nature of human beauty.*

Figure 17.17   FRANCISCO GOYA. *The Sleep of Reason.* 1797.
Etching and aquatint, approx. 8½ × 6". Courtesy, Museum
of Fine Arts, Boston. Bequest of William P. Babcock. *Goya's
artistic technique in the* Caprichos *series is aquatint, a process
that uses acid on a metal plate to create subtle shades of light and
dark. The absence of color in the resulting engravings heightens
the moral message of these works.*

In Spain, Romanticism flourished in the anti-
Classical paintings of Francisco Goya (1746–1828), a
major figure in Spanish culture. Reflecting a nightmarish vision of the world, his art ranges from Rococo fantasies to sensual portraits to grim studies of human
folly to spiritual evil and finally to scenes of utter
hopelessness. Various reasons have been suggested for
Goya's descent into despair, but certainly his dashed
hopes for the regeneration of Spain's political and social order were central to his advancing pessimism, as
was his slow decline into deafness.

In the 1790s, Goya was serving as court painter
to King Charles IV, and signs of the artist's political
disaffection can be detected in his revealing portrait of
the royal family (Figure 17.16). He depicts the queen
(center) as a vain, foolish woman and the king (right,
front) as a royal simpleton. History has judged Goya's
interpretations to be accurate, for this was a corrupt
and stupid court. Perhaps the lace-covered gowns, the
glittering medals, and the general elegance of the ensemble allowed him to get away with such unflattering
portraits and survive within this dangerous environment.

In 1797 Goya published a collection of etchings that
set forth his savage indictment of the age's social evils
and established him as an outstanding humanitarian

artist. The title of this series was *Caprichos*, or *Caprices*,
a Romantic genre that allowed artists to express their
personal feelings on any subject. One of the eighty
caprichos, *The Sleep of Reason* was intended as the series'
frontispiece and is the key to Goya's artistic purpose
(Figure 17.17). The inscription on the desk reads, "The
sleep of reason brings forth monsters," a statement
that conveys the need for eternal vigilance against cruelty and superstition. The nocturnal creatures—bats,
owls, and cats—symbolize the dark forces that continually threaten rationality.

Napoleon's conquest of Spain and the subsequent
Spanish war of liberation form the background to
Goya's masterpiece, *The Execution of the Third of May,
1808* (Figure 17.18). This protest against French imperialism is one of the world's most compelling depictions
of the horrors of war. It shows Spanish captives being

Figure 17.18   Francisco Goya. *The Execution of the Third of May, 1808. 1814–1815.*
Oil on canvas, 8′9″ × 13′4″. Prado, Madrid. *A comparison of this painting by Goya with
David's portrait of the assassinated Marat (see Figure 17.4) shows the difference in tone between
Romantic and Neoclassical art. David makes Marat's death a heroic sacrifice despite its tragic
circumstances. In contrast, Goya's passionate portrayal of the Spanish martyrs shows that there
is nothing heroic about their deaths; their cause may be just, but the manner of their death is
pitiless and squalid.*

executed by a French firing squad. The French troops
are a faceless line of disciplined automatons, and the
Spanish soldiers a band of ill-assorted irregulars. The
Spanish patriots are arranged in three groups: Those
covered with blood and lying on the ground are already dead, those facing the firing squad will be dead
in an instant, and those marching forward with faces
covered are scheduled for the next round. The emotional center of this otherwise somber-hued painting is
the white-shirted man bathed in brilliant light. With
his arms outstretched, he becomes a Christ figure,
symbolizing Goya's compassion for all victims who
die for a "good cause."

Romantic painting arrived in France in 1819 with
the appearance of *The Raft of the "Medusa,"* a work by

Théodore Géricault [zhay-rih-KOH] (1791–1824) that
was based on an actual incident (Figure 17.19). The
Medusa, a sailing ship, had foundered in the South
Atlantic, and it was believed that all aboard were
lost. Then, after almost two months, a handful of survivors were rescued from a makeshift raft. From
their story came shocking details of mutiny, crimes
by officers, murder, cannibalism, and a government
cover-up.

Géricault was attracted to this incident in which
a few men outwitted death against all odds. Focusing
on the precise moment of their rescue, he depicts these
ordinary humans as noble heroes nearly overwhelmed
by the terrible forces of nature. The nude and partially
clad bodies in the foreground convey a powerful sense

Figure 17.19   THÉODORE GÉRICAULT. *The Raft of the "Medusa."* 1818. Oil on canvas,
16'1" × 23'6". Louvre. *Other artists, including Turner and Friedrich, painted shipwrecks and
their victims, but Géricault's enormous canvas is probably the best known. He so vividly caught
his subjects' desperation and hope that his work received instant praise, regardless of the controversies surrounding the subject and its relationships to social and political issues. With his usual
thorough preparation, Géricault made over fifty studies of the incident, rearranging the figures on
the raft until he had created a pyramidal structure, moving from the lower left corner to the center
and upper right.*

of dignity and suffering. From here, the figures surge
upward toward the black youth who is hoisted aloft
and waving a flag at the unseen rescue ship. Géricault wanted his painting to convey a political statement about the government and to be as realistic as
possible—he interviewed survivors and had a replica
of the raft constructed—but at the same time, he imbued it with expression and pathos. The result was a
highly emotional work that embodied the spirit of
Romanticism.

Géricault's *Raft of the "Medusa"* also illustrates Romanticism's connection to liberal political ideas. The
devastated humanity on the raft underscored the
breakdown in civilization that the entire *Medusa* incident came to represent. The painting itself became a
rallying point for the critics of the restored Bourbon
monarchy, who saw in the portrayal of a crew cast
adrift a metaphor for the French nation.

Many of Géricault's ideas were taken up by Eugène
Delacroix [del-uh-KWAH] (1798–1863), who became
the leader of a school of Romantic painting that was in
open rivalry with Ingres and the Neoclassicists. Like
Géricault, Delacroix was a humanitarian who drew
artistic inspiration from his violent times. In the 1820s,
he identified with the Greeks in their war of independence against the Turks, expressing his support in the
allegorical painting *Greece Expiring on the Ruins of
Missolonghi* (Figure 17.20). Lord Byron had died at
Missolonghi while trying to bring warring Greek factions together, an event the painting commemorates.
Delacroix portrays Greece as a grieving woman kneeling on a group of blasted stones from which a dead
hand protrudes. Behind her stands a turbaned Turk,
the symbol of Greece's oppressors.

Delacroix's *Liberty Leading the People* was also inspired by a political incident, the July Revolution of

1830, which resulted in the establishment of a constitutional government (Figure 17.21). The painting combines realism and allegory, depicting revolutionaries on the barricades led by an idealized, barebreasted goddess of Liberty. Surrounding Liberty are three central figures who symbolize the various classes that constitute "the People": The man in the tall hat represents the middle classes, the chief beneficiaries of the revolution; the kneeling figure in the cap stands for the working-class rebels; and the boy brandishing the twin pistols is an image of the street urchin, among the lowest social groups.

The focal point of the painting is the tricolor, the revolutionary flag adopted in the revolution of 1789, outlawed from 1815 until 1830 and now restored as France's unifying symbol. The flag's red, white, and blue determine the harmony of color in the rest of this painting. Completed soon after the 1830 revolution, this work was purchased by the new king as a fitting tribute to the struggle that brought him to power. It was quickly hidden away, however, for the bourgeois establishment found the revolutionary heritage an embarrassment. Only later, with the creation of the Second Republic in 1848, did the French public see the painting.

German Idealism

In philosophy, the Romantic spirit led to idealism, a system of thought that flourished mainly in Germany and that espoused a spiritual view of life. From Kant through Hegel, the Germans constructed idealism as a philosophic alternative to conventional religion. In the 1790s, Immanuel Kant [KAHNT] (1724–1804) began the revolution in thought when he distinguished the world of phenomena ("appearances") from the world of noumena ("things-in-themselves," or spirit). In Kantian terms, the phenomenal world may be understood by science, but the noumenal world may be studied, if at all, only by intuitive means.

Kant's followers, nonetheless, tried the impossible when they began to map out the spiritual realm. Johann Gottlieb Fichte [FICK-tuh] (1762–1814) found reality in the World Spirit, a force having consciousness and seeking self-awareness. Friedrich Wilhelm Joseph von Schelling [SHEL-ing] (1775–1854) equated nature with the Absolute, his name for ultimate reality. He also was the first to espouse the romantic belief in the religion of art by claiming that artists reveal divine truths in inspired works. Schelling's teaching on art influenced the English poet Coleridge and through him English Romanticism in general.

The climax of idealism came with Georg Wilhelm Friedrich Hegel [HAY-guhl] (1770–1831), who ex-

Figure 17.20 EUGÈNE DELACROIX. *Greece Expiring on the Ruins of Missolonghi.* 1826. Oil on canvas, 6'11½" × 4'8¼". Musée des Beaux-Arts, Bordeaux. *Delacroix's representation of Greece as a woman was part of the Romantic convention of using female figures as national symbols. This trend climaxed in the writings of the French historian Jules Michelet, who concluded in 1846 that "France is a woman herself."*

plained human history as the record of the World Spirit seeking to know its true nature. Self-knowledge for the World Spirit arose only through a dialectical struggle. In the first stage, the Spirit developed a thesis that in turn produced an antithesis; in the second stage, a conflict ensued between these two ideas that led to a synthesis, or a new thesis, which in turn gradually provoked new strife—a third stage, and so on ad infinitum. Hegel's theory of history ignored individuals because humans in the mass became tools of the World Spirit in its quest for freedom. In this view, wars, riots, and revolts were merely evidence of

Figure 17.21 Eugène Delacroix. *Liberty Leading the People.* 1831. Oil on canvas, 8'6" × 10'8". Louvre. *Delacroix's canvas bears some meaningful resemblances to Géricault's* Raft of the "Medusa." *Each painting takes a contemporary event as its subject and transforms it into a symbol of France. Moreover, Delacroix's placement of two dead male figures, one partially nude and the other clothed, echoes similar figures in Géricault's work. Delacroix's portrayal of the people triumphant thus seems to be an optimistic response to Géricault's image of France adrift.*

spiritual growth. For this reason, Hegel characterized Napoleon and his wars as embodiments of the World Spirit.

Hegelianism had a tremendous impact on later Western thought. Revolutionaries such as Karl Marx borrowed his dialectical approach to history. Conservatives, especially in Germany, used Hegel's thought as a justification for a strong centralized state, and nationalists everywhere drew inspiration from his thought. Other thinkers rejected his denial of human responsibility and founded existentialist philosophies that glorified the individual.

The Birth of Romantic Music

As the middle class gained political power between 1789 and 1830, they converted the musical scene into a marketplace; that is, laissez-faire economics and music became intertwined. Replacing elite forms of patronage, programs that the bourgeoisie now attended required admission fees and paid performers. Salaries and the demand for performances freed musicians from the patronage system. With their newly won independence, they became eccentric and individualistic—attitudes that were encouraged by the Romantic cult of the artist. Music grew more accessible as democracy progressed, and new industrial techniques and production allowed more people to own inexpensive musical instruments.

The most gifted composer of this period, and one of the greatest musical geniuses of all time, was Ludwig van Beethoven [BAY-toe-vuhn] (1770–1827), a German who spent most of his life in Vienna. He personified the new breed of musician, supporting himself through concerts, lessons, and the sales of his music (Figure 17.22). His works represent both the culmination of Classical music and the introduction of Romantic music. Working

PERSONAL PERSPECTIVE

HECTOR BERLIOZ
This Harmonious Revolution

Berlioz was an eyewitness to the 1830 Revolution in Paris, as well as a participant in the events of the day. In his memoirs, he recorded the frenzy and jubilation of the crowds rebelling against the Bourbon monarchy.

It was in the year 1830. I was just finishing my cantata when the Revolution broke out.

A number of families had taken shelter in the Palais de l'Institut, and it looked strangely transformed— with long-barreled muskets protruding from the barred doors, and its façade riddled with bullets, the air filled with the shrieks of women, and, in the lulls between the discharges of musketry, the shrill twitter of the swallows. I hurriedly dashed off the last pages of my cantata to the tune of the dry thud of the bullets as they struck close to my windows or on the walls of my room; and on the 24th I was free to loaf about Paris with the "*sacred rabble*," and my pistol in my pocket, till the next day.

I shall never forget the aspect of Paris during those memorable days—the wild bravado of the street Arabs, the enthusiasm of the men, the frenzy of the women, the mournful resignation of the Swiss and Royal Guards, the curious pride which the workmen exhibited in not pillaging Paris though they were masters of the situa-

tion, the astounding stories told by young fellows of their exploits, in which the real bravery of the deed was lost in the sense of the ridiculous aroused by the manner in which it was told; as, for instance, when they described the storming of the cavalry barracks of the Rue de Babylone—in which considerable loss had been incurred—with a gaiety worthy of Alexander's veterans, as "the capture of Babylon"—an abbreviation forced on them by the length of the real name. With what pompous prolongation of the "o" the name of "Babylon" was pronounced! . . . Oh Parisians, what buffoons you are! Great, if you will, but still buffoons! . . .

No words can give any idea of the music, the songs and the hoarse voices which rang through the streets!

And yet it was only a few days after this harmonious revolution that I received a most extraordinary musical impression, or shock. I was crossing the Palais Royal when I heard a tune which I seemed to recognize, issuing from among a crowd of people. As I drew nearer I perceived that ten or twelve young fellows were singing a war song of my own, the words of which, translated from one of Moore's *Irish Melodies* (Thomas Moore [1779–1852], Irish poet and satirist), happened exactly to suit the situation.

Figure 17.22 FERDINAND GEORG WALDMÜLLER. *Ludwig van Beethoven*. 1823. Oil on canvas, approx. 28⅓ × 22⅝". Archiv Breitkopf and Härtel, Leipzig, Germany. Original destroyed in World War II. *Beethoven in his later years was the embodiment of the Romantic genius, disheveled, singing to himself as he strolled Vienna's streets, mocked by street urchins; once, he was even arrested by the police as a tramp. In this 1823 portrait, Waldmüller suggests Beethoven's unkempt appearance, but through the strong expression, fixed jaw, and broad forehead he also conveys the great composer's fierce determination and intelligence.*

with the standard Classical forms—the sonata, the symphony, and the string quartet—he created longer works, doubling and even tripling their length. He also wrote music that was increasingly expressive and that showed more warmth and variety of feeling, particularly in his program music—that is, music that portrays a particular setting or tells a story. He made several other significant musical innovations, including the use of choral voices within the symphonic form and the composing of music that expressed the power of the human will.

Beethoven's career may be divided into three phases, but his extreme individualism left his unique stamp on everything that he composed. In the first phase, from the 1790s until 1803, he was under the shadow of Haydn, with whom he studied in Vienna. His First Symphony (1800) may be termed a Classical work, but in it he reveals a new spirit by lengthening the first and third movements and making the middle movement more lively than usual.

In the second phase, from 1803 until 1816, Beethoven's genius gave birth to Romantic music. He began to find his own voice, enriching and deepening the older forms. The Third Symphony (1803), which Beethoven called the *Eroica* ("Heroic"), is the most characteristic work from this second stage. The composer originally dedicated this symphony to Napoleon, whom he admired as a champion of democracy. But when the French ruler declared himself emperor in 1804, Beethoven angrily tore up the page and dedicated it instead "to the memory of a great man." In the Third Symphony, Beethoven substantially expands the musical material beyond the limits characteristic of earlier symphonies, making it longer and more complex. The music is grand, serious, and dignified, a truly heroic work.

In the third phase, from 1816 until 1827, Beethoven's music became freer and more contemplative, reaching its culmination in the Ninth Symphony (1822–1824), the last of his large-scale works. In the last movement of this work, Beethoven included a choral finale in which he set to music the poem "Ode to Joy" by the German Romantic poet Friedrich von Schiller [SHIL-uhr] (1759–1805). Despite a life of personal adversities that included deafness from the age of thirty, Beethoven affirmed in this piece his faith in both humanity and God—"Millions, be you embraced! For the universe, this kiss!" The magnificent music and the idealistic text have led to the virtual canonization of this inspirational work.

Across these three phases, Beethoven was a prolific composer in all musical genres; many of these works are unrivaled in their expressiveness and originality. Besides the nine symphonies, he wrote two Masses, two ballets, one opera *(Fidelio)*, sixteen string quartets, thirty-two piano sonatas (most notably the *Pathétique* and *Moonlight* sonatas), five concertos for piano, one concerto for violin, and numerous chamber and choral compositions.

Vienna contributed another outstanding composer in Franz Schubert [SHOO-bert] (1797–1828), who was famous for the beauty of his melodies and the simple grace of his songs. He lived a rather bohemian life, supporting himself, like Beethoven, by giving lessons and concerts. But unlike Beethoven, Schubert wrote mainly for the living rooms of Vienna rather than for the concert hall and is most famous for perfecting the **art song,** called in German *lied* (plural, *lieder*). The emergence of this musical form in the Romantic period was tied to the revival of lyric poetry. Schubert composed the music for over six hundred *lieder,* with texts by Goethe ("Gretchen at the Spinning Wheel"), Shakespeare ("Who Is Sylvia?"), and other poets. His efforts raised the song to the level of great art.

A final composer of significance in this first period of Romanticism was the Frenchman Hector Berlioz [BAIR-lee-ohz] (1803–1869). His most famous work is the *Symphonie fantastique (Fantastic Symphony)* (1830), a superb example of program music. Subtitled "Episode of an Artist's Life," this symphonic work illustrates musically a story that Berlioz described in accompanying written notes. In the tale, which takes the form of an opium dream, an artist-hero hopelessly adores an unfaithful woman and eventually dies for her. Relatively conventional in form, the symphony is most original in its use of a recurring musical theme, called an *idée fixe,* or "fixed idea," that becomes an image of the hero's beloved. Because every section contains the *idée fixe* in a modified form, it unifies the symphony in an innovative way. The success of Berlioz's symphony helped to strengthen the fashion for program music in the Romantic period.

The Legacy of the Age of Revolution and Reaction

During this period of revolution and reaction, the West turned away from the past, with its monarchical forms of government, its hierarchical society dominated by aristocratic landowners, its glacial rate of change, and its patronage system ruled by social, ecclesiastical, and political elites. Three events in particular—the Industrial Revolution and the American and the French Revolutions—have left an indelible stamp on the modern world. The Industrial Revolution, which continues today, has gradually made humanity master of the earth and its resources, while at the same time accelerating the pace of life and creating the two leading modern social groups, the middle class and the working class. The Industrial Revolution also spawned Classical economics, the school of economists who justified the doctrine of laissez faire that is still held to be the best argument for capitalism and continuous industrial growth. This same doctrine altered the patronage system, subjecting the creative works of modern artists, writers, musicians, and humanists to the law of the marketplace.

The American Revolution produced the first successful modern democracy, one that today stands as a beacon of hope for those oppressed by authoritarian regimes. The French Revolution contributed the idea of an all-encompassing upheaval that would sweep away the past and create a new secular order characterized by social justice and fairness. Although viewed with skepticism by some, for multitudes of others the notion of such a revolution became a sustaining belief. From the French Revolution also arose the idea that race and religion should not be used to exclude people from the right to vote—a reflection of its emphasis on the "brotherhood of man." Another outgrowth of the French Revolution is the Napoleonic Code, the law code that is used in the French-speaking world today.

Both the French and the American Revolutions contributed certain beliefs that have become basic statements of Western political life, such as the idea that constitutions should be written down and that basic human liberties should be identified. Indeed, the progressive expansion of natural and civil rights to embrace all of society is an outgrowth of these two revolutions.

Other enduring legacies of this late-eighteenth- and early-nineteenth-century period are the Neoclassical buildings in Washington, D.C., and in most of the state capitals of the United States, the body of music of the Romantic composers, and the paintings of the Neoclassical and early Romantic schools. An ambiguous legacy of this period has been nationalism, the belief in one's own country and its people. At its best, nationalism is a noble concept, for it encourages people to examine their roots and preserve their collective identity and heritage. At its worst, it has led to cutthroat behavior, dividing the people of a country against one another and leading to the disintegration of nations. Both forms of nationalism remain potent forces in the world today.

On a more personal level, this period saw the development of the Romantic view of life, an attitude that stresses informality, identification with the common people, the importance of feeling and imagination, and enjoyment of simple pleasures. Perhaps more than any other legacy of this period, the Romantic outlook has helped to shape the way that most Western men and women live in today's world.

KEY CULTURAL TERMS

Romanticism
Sublime
Sturm und Drang
Faustian
art song (lied)
idée fixe

SUGGESTIONS FOR FURTHER READING

Primary Sources

AUSTEN, J. *Pride and Prejudice. Sense and Sensibility.* Introduction by D. Daiches. New York: Modern Library, 1950. Both novels deal with English provincial life. *Pride and Prejudice* (1813) focuses on the proud Mr. Darcy, who must be humbled before the "prejudiced" Elizabeth Bennet can take seriously his marriage proposal; *Sense and Sensibility* (1811) uses practical-mindedness ("sense") to expose the self-indulgence of the "picturesque" spirit ("sensibility"), an aspect of genteel taste in the late eighteenth century.

BYRON, G. G., Lord. *Don Juan.* Edited by T. G. Steffan, E. Steffan, and W. W. Pratt. New York: Penguin, 1973. One of Byron's most admired works, full of autobiographical references; dates from 1819–1824.

FICHTE, J. G. *Addresses to the German Nation.* Translated by R. F. Jones and G. H. Turnbull. Chicago: Open Court, 1923. The work that helped to launch German nationalism when first published in the early 1800s.

GOETHE, J. W. v. *Faust.* Part I. Translated by M. Greenberg. New Haven: Yale University Press, 1992. A good recent English version of Goethe's drama of a man prepared to sacrifice his soul for the sake of knowledge based on feeling; originally published in 1808.

————. *The Sorrows of Young Werther.* Translated by E. Mayer and L. Bogan. Foreword by W. H. Auden. New York: Vintage, 1990. The 1774 Romantic novel that brought Goethe his earliest Europe-wide fame, translated by modern poets.

HEGEL, G. W. F. *Reason in History.* Translated and with an introduction by R. S. Hartman. New York: Liberal Arts Press, 1953. The best source for Hegel's theory that history moves through a dialectical process; first published in 1837.

KANT, I. *Critique of Pure Reason.* Introduction and glossary by W. Schwarz. Aalen, Germany: Scientia, 1982. A good version of Kant's difficult work that tried to establish what human reason can know apart from experience; dates from 1781.

MALTHUS, T. *On Population.* Edited and with an introduction by G. Himmelfarb. New York: Random House, 1960. One of the more recent editions of the influential essay, first published in 1788, that identified the modern dilemma of keeping population growth in equilibrium with food production.

RICARDO, D. *On the Principles of Political Economy and Taxation.* New York: Penguin, 1971. Ricardo's "iron law of wages"—that wages tend to hover around the subsistence level—became a central tenet of nineteenth-century laissez-faire theory.

SCHELLING, F. W. J. v. *Ideas for a Philosophy of Nature.* Translated by E. E. Harris. New York: Cambridge University Press, 1988. An excellent translation of Schelling's 1799 work, which helped shape Romantic thinking by claiming to find God both in nature and in the human intellect.

SHELLEY, M. *Frankenstein.* With an introduction by D. Johnson. New York: Bantam Books, 1991. The original source of the Frankenstein legend, published in 1818 when Shelley was twenty-one years old; inspired by an evening of reading and discussing ghost stories.

WORDSWORTH, W. *Lyrical Ballads.* Edited by R. L. Braett and A. R. Jones. London: Routledge and Kegan Paul, 1988. A new edition of the original volume (1798) by Wordsworth and Coleridge that initiated the age of Romantic poetry in England; contains good introductory material.

SUGGESTIONS FOR LISTENING

BEETHOVEN, LUDWIG VAN (1770–1827). Composing mainly in Classical forms, notably the symphony and the string quartet, Beethoven moved from a Classical style in the manner of Haydn and Mozart to a Romantic style that was his own. The First Symphony (1800) shows his Classical approach; the Third Symphony, the *Eroica* (1803), inaugurated his Romantic style with its intense emotionalism and rich thematic variations. Of special note is the Ninth Symphony (1822–1826), a semimystical work whose final section blends full orchestra with a massed chorus. The emotional nature of the Violin Sonata No. 9 (*Kreutzer* Sonata) inspired the Russian writer Leo Tolstoy to use the piece as a catalyst for murder in his story "The Kreutzer Sonata." Beethoven's stylistic development can also be traced in his sixteen string quartets: The first six quartets, dating from 1800, reflect the grace of Haydn and Mozart, and the last five, Nos. 12 through 16 (1823–1826), are technically difficult to play, enormously long, and characterized by mood shifts from light to tragic and unusual harmonic juxtapositions. The familiar piano piece "Für Elise" is a fine example of the rondo form.

BERLIOZ, HECTOR (1803–1869). Berlioz was typically Romantic in going beyond the forms of Classicism and stressing the emotional possibilities of his music. For example, his *Requiem* (1837) is less a religious work than a dramatic symphony for orchestra and voices; its inspiration was the tradition of patriotic festivals originated during the French Revolution. Similarly, his opera *Damnation of Faust* (1846) is not an opera in a conventional sense but a series of episodes based on Goethe's play, a form that allowed the composer to focus on those scenes that seemed full of theatrical potential. Finally, the *Symphonie fantastique* (1830) is more than a symphony; it has been called "a musical drama without words"—the prototype of Romantic program music.

SCHUBERT, FRANZ (1797–1828). Though a prolific composer of symphonies, operas, and piano sonatas, Schubert is most famous for perfecting the art song, or *lied*. Two of his best-known songs, with texts by Goethe, are "Gretchen am Spinnrade" ("Gretchen at the Spinning Wheel," 1814) and "Erlkönig" ("The Erlking," 1815). One of Schubert's most celebrated chamber works, a quintet for piano and strings, is "Die Forelle" ("The Trout," 1821), in which the lively, fluid music suggests the energetic movements of a swimming fish.

CHAPTER *17* HIGHLIGHTS
Revolution, Reaction, and Cultural Response, 1760–1830

50

The Declaration of Independence (1776)

SMITH, *The Wealth of Nations* (1776)

MALTHUS, *Essay on the Principle of Population* (1788)

The Declaration of the Rights of Man and Citizen (1789)

AUSTEN, *Pride and Prejudice* (1813)

RICARDO, *Principles of Political Economy and Taxation* (1821)

30

17.7 JEFFERSON, Monticello, Virginia (1770–1784)

17.8 JEFFERSON, State Capitol of Virginia (1785–1796)

17.4 DAVID, *Death of Marat* (1793)

17.5 DAVID, *The Coronation of Napoleon and Josephine* (1805–1808)

17.1 INGRES, *Napoleon I* (1806)

17.6 INGRES, *Madame Jacques Louis Leblanc* (1823)

70

WORDSWORTH, "Lines Composed a Few Miles Above Tintern Abbey" (1798)

GOETHE, *Faust* (Part I, 1808); (Part II, 1832)

MARY W. SHELLEY, *Frankenstein* (1818)

BYRON, *Don Juan* (1819–1824)

PERCY B. SHELLEY, Poems (first quarter of nineteenth century)

KEATS, Poems (first quarter of nineteenth century)

HEGEL, *Reason in History* (1837)

17.17 GOYA, *The Sleep of Reason* (1797)

17.16 GOYA, *The Family of Charles IV* (1800)

17.15 FRIEDRICH, *Monk by the Sea* (1808–1810)

17.13 TURNER, *Snowstorm: Hannibal and His Army Crossing the Alps* (1810–1812)

30

17.18 GOYA, *The Execution of the Third of May, 1808* (1814–1815)

17.19 GÉRICAULT, *The Raft of the "Medusa"* (1818)

17.11 CONSTABLE, *The Hay Wain* (1821)

17.12 CONSTABLE, *Cloud Study* (1821)

17.14 TURNER, *The Bay of Baiae, with Apollo and the Sibyl* (1823)

17.20 DELACROIX, *Greece Expiring on the Ruins of Missolonghi* (1826)

17.21 DELACROIX, *Liberty Leading the People* (1831)

BEETHOVEN, Symphony No. 5 (1808)

SCHUBERT, "The Erlking" (1815)

BERLIOZ, *Symphonie fantastique* (1830)

■ *Literature & Philosophy*　■ *Art & Architecture*　■ *Music & Dance*

📖 *Readings in the Western Humanities*　💿 *CD, The Western Humanities*

18 THE TRIUMPH OF THE BOURGEOISIE
1830–1871

The French and American Revolutions offered the hope of political power to all disenfranchised groups, and the Industrial Revolution promised material gains to the impoverished. Those expectations remained largely unfulfilled in Europe, however, as the nineteenth century unfolded. Benefits were reaped mainly by one group—the middle class, especially its wealthiest sector.

Left behind was a new group created by industrialization—the proletariat, or working class. These urban workers expressed their frustrations through political uprisings and social movements, and often the lower middle class joined them in demanding universal suffrage and a fairer distribution of power and wealth. Against the liberalism of the bourgeoisie some of the workers set forth the ideals of socialism. But reform was limited at best, and successive waves of revolutionary uprisings failed to win significant improvements (Figure 18.1).

These changes were echoed in the cultural realm. From its brief peak in the 1820s, Romanticism declined and finally faded away. Embraced by the middle class, it gained respectability and lost much of its creative fire. By midcentury, a new, realistic style was emerging that reflected changing political and social conditions. Realism focused on ordinary people and attempted to depict in objective terms "the heroism of everyday life." At the same time, industrialization continued to spread, and people's ideas about themselves and the world were being challenged by everything from the theories of Charles Darwin to the invention of the camera (Timeline 18.1).

◄ **Detail** ÉDOUARD MANET. *A Bar at the Folies-Bergère*. 1882. 3′1½″ × 4′3″. Courtald Institute Galleries, London (Courtald Collection).

Timeline 18.1   THE AGE OF THE BOURGEOISIE

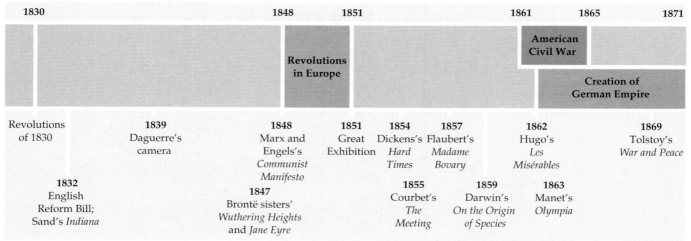

1830			1848	1851				1861	1865		1871
			Revolutions in Europe					**American Civil War**			
									Creation of German Empire		

| Revolutions of 1830 | 1839 Daguerre's camera | | 1848 Marx and Engels's *Communist Manifesto* | 1851 Great Exhibition | 1854 Dickens's *Hard Times* | 1857 Flaubert's *Madame Bovary* | | 1862 Hugo's *Les Misérables* | | | 1869 Tolstoy's *War and Peace* |
| 1832 English Reform Bill; Sand's *Indiana* | | | 1847 Brontë sisters' *Wuthering Heights* and *Jane Eyre* | | 1855 Courbet's *The Meeting* | 1859 Darwin's *On the Origin of Species* | | 1863 Manet's *Olympia* | | | |

Figure 18.1 FRANÇOIS RUDE. *The Departure of the Volunteers.* 1833–1836. Approx. 42 × 26′. Paris. *This group sculpture, depicting a crowd of warriors inspired by the winged Liberty, symbolizes the French people on the march during the revolution of 1830, the first of a series of revolutions in nineteenth-century Europe. Designed for the Arch of Triumph in Paris, the work came to be known affectionately as* La Marseillaise, *the name of the French national anthem.*

THE POLITICAL AND ECONOMIC SCENE: LIBERALISM AND NATIONALISM

The powerful forces of liberalism and nationalism drove many nineteenth-century events. The basic premise of liberalism was that the individual should be free from external control, a notion that resonated with the American and French Revolutions and the need of the bourgeoisie to liberate themselves from aristocratic society. The liberal political agenda included constitutionally guaranteed political and civil rights such as free speech, religious toleration, and voting rights for the propertied classes. Perhaps most important, liberalism embraced the laissez-faire economic ideals that allowed the wealthy middle class to maximize their profits in the business world. Liberalism was most successful in England, France, and Belgium; it failed to take root in Italy and central and eastern Europe, and Russia remained reactionary.

The other driving force of this era, nationalism, emphasized cooperation among all of a country's people who shared a common language and heritage. Overlooking class divisions, nationalists advocated humanitarian values, stressing the concept that all members of a nation are brothers and sisters. As nationalism spread, these concepts were often expanded to include liberal ideals, republican principles, and even democratic beliefs. Nationalism became a force in central, southern, and eastern Europe, where the states of what would become Germany and Italy were still little more than "geographic expressions" (Map 18.1). After 1848 nationalism became increasingly militant.

LEARNING THROUGH MAPS

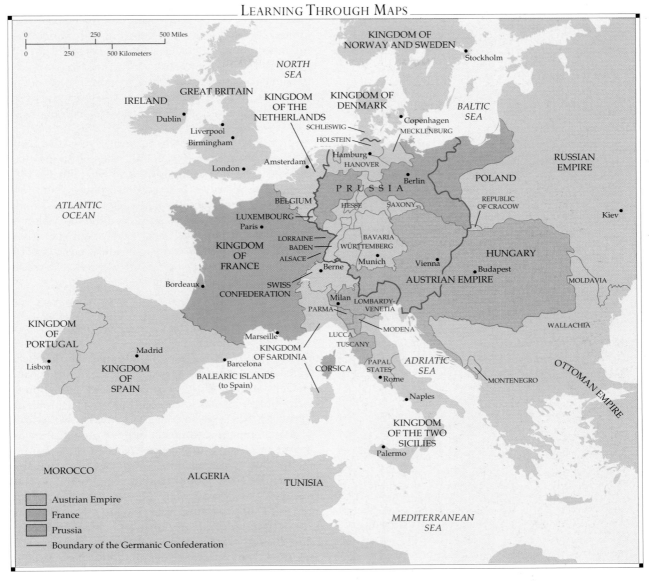

Map 18.1   EUROPE AFTER THE CONGRESS OF VIENNA, 1815
This map shows the political divisions of Europe after the defeat of Napoleon.
Compare this map with Map 17.1, Europe at the Height of Napoleon's Power. **Notice**
the trend toward larger but fewer states. **Which** states improved their territorial
holdings at the Congress of Vienna? **Which** states were the losers at the congress?
Identify the German Confederation and its boundary. **Which** state, Austria or Prussia,
was better positioned to emerge as leader of the German Confederation?

The Revolutions of 1830 and 1848

The repressive policies imposed by the Congress of
Vienna in 1815 were challenged in 1830 by a series of
uprisings, beginning with the July Revolution in
France and the French overthrow of the Bourbon
monarchy and the installation of Louis Philippe
(r. 1830–1848), who pledged to uphold a liberal constitution. This regime increasingly became the tool of
the rich middle class at the expense of the workers,

however. Voting was limited to wealthy male property
owners, and laws favored unregulated economic expansion. Having gained political dominance, the middle class intended to keep the benefits of the liberal
agenda for themselves.

Liberal revolutions followed elsewhere, including
in Belgium and areas of central and southern Europe,
but they were unsuccessful. In central Europe, local
conservatives backed by Austrian troops quickly
crushed the liberal uprisings of 1830 and punished

Table 18.1 MAJOR POLITICAL EVENTS OF THE 1815–1871 PERIOD

EVENT AND DATE	OUTCOME
Congress of Vienna, 1815	Inaugurates an era of repression
July Revolution in France, 1830	Ends the Bourbon dynasty and installs the bourgeois monarchy
First English Reform Bill, 1832	Extends voting rights to wealthy middle-class males
Revolution in France, 1848	Ends the bourgeois monarchy and installs the Second Republic, with Louis-Napoleon as president
Revolutions in Europe, 1848–1851	Their failure leads to an era dominated by realpolitik
Creation of Second French Empire, 1851	Louis-Napoleon becomes Napoleon III and leads empire until 1870
Kingdom of Italy, 1860	Sicily joins Piedmont
Creation of German Empire, 1862–1871	Engineered by Bismarck using a policy of "blood and iron"; unites German states around Prussia
American Civil War, 1861–1865	Preserves national union and abolishes slavery
Second English Reform Bill, 1867	Extends voting rights to working-class males
Franco-Prussian War, 1871	Destroys the Second French Empire, proclaims the German Empire, and leaves a legacy of French bitterness toward Germany

rebels, imposed martial law, reinstituted censorship, and took control of the school systems. Although liberals continued to hope for moderate reforms, conservatives made it difficult for them. Across central and eastern Europe, the one force emerging as a rallying point was nationalism, focusing as it did on ethnic identity and common cultural heritage.

In 1848 accumulated dissatisfactions and frustrations erupted in another series of uprisings across Europe (Table 18.1), starting with demonstrations and riots in February 1848 in Paris. The rebellions were propelled by liberal ideals and nationalistic goals, but their immediate causes were declining production, rising unemployment, and falling agricultural prices. By the spring of 1848, the path of revolution ran from Paris through Berlin to Vienna, and all along this route the bourgeoisie, intellectuals, workers, students, and nationalists toppled kings and ministers. Temporary

governments, led by liberals and reformers, drove out foreign troops and set up constitutional monarchies, republics, or democracies with universal male suffrage. A few governments—influenced by the new movement known as socialism—addressed economic problems by passing laws to stimulate productivity, improve working conditions, and aid the poor with relief or employment programs.

By the fall of 1848, the conservatives—the army, aristocrats, and church—had rallied to defeat the often disorganized revolutionaries, and by January 1849 many of the old rulers had reclaimed power. After 1848 the idealism of the liberals, social reformers, and nationalists gave way to an unsentimental vision of politics and diplomacy backed by pragmatic use of force. This perspective came to be known as *realpolitik*, a German term that means "practical politics," a tactful way of saying "power politics."

European Affairs in the Grip of Realpolitik

From 1850 to 1871, realpolitik guided the European states as conservative regimes turned to strong and efficient armies, short, fierce wars, and ambiguously written agreements to resolve the various problems that had surfaced in the 1848 revolts. Otto von Bismarck, the prime minister of Prussia and future architect of German unification, mocked the failure of the liberals' parliamentary reforms and asserted that his country's fate would be settled not with speeches but with "blood and iron." Nationalists in Austrian-occupied Italy learned that Italian unity could be achieved only by military force and clever diplomacy. The Russian czars, seldom supporters of any type of reform, became even more committed to the belief that if any change did come, it would begin at the top, not the bottom, of society.

Limited Reform in France and Great Britain One of the most astute observers of the 1848 revolutions was Louis-Napoleon Bonaparte, nephew of the former French emperor. He became Emperor Napoleon III (r. 1852–1870) of the Second French Empire by appealing to both the bourgeoisie and the working class. A benign despot, he ruled over a sham representative government supported by a growing middle class made prosperous by the expanding industrial base. He also provided the poor with social services, and with an economic plan and subsidies, he enabled most urban workers and farmers to maintain a high standard of living.

In Great Britain, a liberal coalition of landed and business interests pushed a reform bill through the Parliament in 1832 over the protests of the

Figure 18.2 CHARLES BARRY AND A. W. N. PUGIN. The Houses of Parliament. 1836–1860. Big Ben (right) 320′ high; Victoria Tower (left) 336′ high; riverfront width 800′. London. *In contrast to the revolutionary tradition on the Continent, Great Britain struggled to respond to changing political and social realities through debate and reform. To many observers in England and abroad, Parliament symbolized the success of liberalism and the representative legislative system. The Gothic spires of the Houses of Parliament rose in the mid–nineteenth century after the old buildings burned. Along with the neighboring clock tower known as "Big Ben" (a name applied originally only to the bell), they still stand today as the most recognizable image of modern London.*

conservatives. This new law redrew the political map of England to reflect the tremendous shift in population resulting from industrialization, and it enfranchised thousands of new male voters by lowering the property qualifications for voting, although millions of British citizens were still denied the vote. In 1867 a second reform bill extended voting rights to working-class males. With Queen Victoria (r. 1837–1901) on the throne and political forces balanced evenly between liberals and conservatives, Great Britain reached its apex of economic power and prestige (Figure 18.2).

Wars and Unification in Central Europe Among the German-speaking states, the small principalities tended to discard liberalism and embrace militant nationalism. Their concerns were overshadowed, however, by the power struggle between Prussia and Austria for control of central Europe. William I became king of Prussia in 1861, and Bismarck was appointed his prime minister. Over the next few years, Bismarck built the Prussian army into a fierce fighting machine, at the same time ignoring liberal protests and the Prussian assembly and its laws. Nationalism replaced liberalism as the rallying cry of the Prussians, and Bismarck used this shift to unite the Germans around the Prussian state at the expense of France and of Austria (see Map 18.1).

Bismarck achieved his goal by neutralizing potential enemies through deft diplomacy and, failing that, through force. By 1866 he had united the German states into the North German Confederation, a union that excluded Austria. In 1870 he engineered a diplomatic crisis that forced France to declare war on Prussia. Costly French defeats brought the Franco-Prussian War to an abrupt end later that year, toppled the Second Empire of Napoleon III, and resulted in France's humiliation in the treaty signed at Versailles in 1871, proclaiming the German Empire. The seeds of World War I were sown by this crucial turn of events (Map 18.2).

On the Italian peninsula, most of which was ruled by Austrian princes, liberalism and nationalism were also causes of disruption. In the 1830s, Italian liberals inspired by the revolutionary writings of Giuseppe Mazzini [maht-SEE-nee] (1805–1872) banded together to form Young Italy, a nationalistic movement, and the independent Italian state of Piedmont-Sardinia emerged as the hope of liberals. Piedmont was a constitutional monarchy that honored its subjects' civil and political rights. Its economy was well balanced between farming and trade, and under Prime Minister Count Camillo Benso di Cavour [kuh-VOOR] (1810–1861), the standard of living was raised for many Piedmontese, especially middle-class merchants and manufacturers.

Between 1859 and 1871, Piedmont expelled most of the Austrians. As part of his grand strategy to unite Italy, Cavour, with the encouragement of Napoleon III of France, annexed parts of central and southern Italy. Further assistance came from the fiercely patriotic soldier Giuseppe Garibaldi [gahr-uh-BAHL-dee] (1807–1882), who, with his personal army of a thousand "Red Shirts," invaded and liberated the Kingdom of the Two Sicilies (see Map 18.1) from its Spanish Bourbon ruler. In 1860 Sicilians voted overwhelmingly to join Piedmont in a Kingdom of Italy, and soon thereafter the Italian mosaic fell into place. In 1866 Austria gave up Venetia, and in 1870 Rome fell to nationalist troops and became Italy's capital.

Map 18.2 EUROPE IN 1871

This map shows the political divisions of Europe in the third quarter of the nineteenth century. **Compare** this map with Map 18.1, Europe After the Congress of Vienna. **Notice** the sacrifice of the small states in the Germanic Confederation and on the Italian peninsula to the unified countries of Germany and Italy. **Observe** the changes in the European holdings of the Ottoman Empire. **Consider** how the unification of Germany threatened the dominance of France in Europe. **Which** states divided Poland among themselves?

Figure 18.3 JOSEPH MALLORD WILLIAM TURNER. *The Slave Ship (Slavers Throwing Overboard the Dead and Dying, Typhoon Coming On).* Ca. 1840. Oil on canvas, 35¾ × 48¼". Courtesy, Museum of Fine Arts, Boston. Henry Lillie Pierce Fund. *Growing revulsion against slavery led Parliament to abolish it in the British colonies in the 1830s, but the slaves in the United States were not freed until 1863. Turner's terrifying image of natural calamity and human cruelty reflected the humanitarian values that had surfaced during the parliamentary and national debates about slavery. The ghoulish scene, painted in Turner's unique Romantic style, depicts the castaway bodies of the dead and dying, encircled by hungry fish, as they sink into the stormy sea.*

Figure 18.4 W. P. FRITH. *The Railway Station.* Ca. 1862. Oil on canvas, 3'10" × 8'5". Royal Holloway College and Bedford New College, Surrey, England. *London was the hub of England's economy long before the Industrial Revolution, and with the coming of the railroads its position was enhanced. The massive new railway stations, often constructed of glass and iron, symbolized the changing business and leisure habits of life. In this painting of one of London's new rail stations, Frith's well-dressed middle-class citizens convey the excitement of travel as well as its novelty and uncertainty.*

Civil War in the United States

Paralleling the turbulent unification of the modern states of Italy and Germany, the United States was also undergoing expansion and centralization, processes that carried within themselves the seeds of conflict. The economy was mixed and regionally divided. On one side stood the Northeast, the national leader in commerce, trade, and banking and the site of a growing factory system; on the other side was the South, dominated by huge cotton plantations cultivated by thousands of black slaves. The unsettled western lands formed a third region.

After 1830 the economic issues that divided the northern and southern states became intensified over the question of slavery (Figure 18.3). As settlers moved west, the debate over the spread of slavery into these new territories and states aggravated sectional interests. In 1861 the southern states seceded from the union, provoking a civil war.

Unlike Europe's contemporaneous wars, which were short and resulted in relatively few deaths, the American Civil War lasted four years and resulted in huge losses on both sides. The northern victory in 1865, engineered by President Abraham Lincoln (1861–1865), saved the union and guaranteed freedom for the slaves. But animosity between the North and the South continued to smolder during the war's aftermath, called Reconstruction (1865–1876), and relations remained strained, particularly over racial matters, for more than a century.

The Spread of Industrialism

Underlying all the political upheavals of the nineteenth century was the growing industrialization of the Western world. After its eighteenth-century beginnings in England (see Chapter 17), industrialism started to take root in France in the 1830s, and a short time later Belgium entered the industrial age. For the next forty years, Belgium and France were the chief economic powers on the Continent, with factory and railway systems radiating from Paris and Brussels to Vienna and Milan by 1871. The expansion of rail lines meant that factories no longer needed to be near coal mines or clustered in urban areas. Inventions in communications, such as the telegraph, made it easier for industrialists to take advantage of distant resources and markets, and in 1866 engineers laid a transatlantic telegraph cable, linking Europe and America.

In the meantime, Great Britain passed into the second phase of the Industrial Revolution. It continued to build ships, to construct factories, and to lay rail lines; by 1850 all its major cities were linked (Figure 18.4). In England and on the Continent, the mining of new coal

Figure 18.5 JOSEPH NASH. Detail of *The Crystal Palace.* 1851. Color lithograph with watercolor, approx. 21½ × 29⅝". Victoria and Albert Museum, London. *This detail illustrates the splendor and pageantry surrounding the moment when Queen Victoria opened the Great Exhibition. After the fair closed, the Crystal Palace was disassembled and rebuilt in a suburb in south London, where it stood as an arts and entertainment center until it was destroyed by fire in 1936. Nevertheless, the "pre-fab" construction principles of the Crystal Palace foreshadowed modern building methods.*

Figure 18.6 ANONYMOUS. *Suez Canal Opening.* 1869. Colored engraving. British Library, London. *Just as Great Britain showed the world what it could achieve through industry and agriculture, so France demonstrated its technological and engineering genius in digging the Suez Canal. The Suez Canal Company, headed by the French entrepreneur Ferdinand de Lesseps [duh lay-SEPS] (1805–1894), began its work in 1859 and completed the canal ten years later.*

and iron deposits and the rise of imports in materials for textiles and other goods kept the machines of industry humming. British financiers, joined by Continental bankers, made loans to fledgling companies for new factories, warehouses, ships, and railways, thereby generating more wealth for capitalists who had surplus funds to invest.

As Europe's economy grew, two marvels of the industrial age—the Crystal Palace in London and the Suez Canal in Egypt—captured the world's

imagination. The iron and glass Crystal Palace housed the Great Exhibition of 1851—in effect, the first world's fair. In a structure that used advanced architectural methods and building materials, the newest inventions and machine-made goods were displayed for everyone, rich and poor alike. Although other nations displayed products and inventions, Britain's exhibits were the most impressive and proved that it was the world's leading industrial and agricultural power (Figure 18.5).

The second marvel was the digging of the Suez Canal to link the Gulf of Suez and the Red Sea with the Mediterranean Sea. Funded by a French company and opened in 1869, the canal shortened the distance between Europe and India, thus enabling steamships to ferry passengers and goods around the globe more quickly and comfortably (Figure 18.6).

The Crystal Palace, the Suez Canal, and other wonders of the age were made possible by the labor of millions of workers—men, women, and children. On the Continent, the working and living conditions of this group were no better than the squalid circumstances found in Great Britain in the first stage of the Industrial Revolution. The social costs of industrialism, notably the rapid growth of cities that threw poor and ill-trained people into slums and ghettos, were part of its negative side. The slums became breeding grounds for class hatred and offered ready audiences for revolutionaries and socialists advocating revolt and social changes. The rebellions that flashed across the Continent in 1848 were caused partly by the mounting frustrations in these working-class areas.

Even a large segment of the middle class remained cut off from economic and political power. In the United States, all white males were granted suffrage in the 1820s, and in England voting rights were granted

ENCOUNTER

The Tragedy of the Cherokee Nation

When the first European settlers were establishing colonies on the Atlantic coast, the Cherokees lived farther inland, in farming villages surrounded by hunting and fishing lands, in western Virginia and the Carolinas, eastern Kentucky and Tennessee, and northern Alabama and Georgia. Their villages, composed of five hundred to two thousand people each and ruled by chiefs and priests, were fairly independent, though linked in loose regional federations. Although they had contact with the settlers, the Cherokees kept to the traditions of their ancestors.

However, as whites moved west after 1700, their impact on Cherokee landholdings was devastating. During the Revolutionary War Era, when the Cherokees sided with the British, American forces broke their power and forced them to surrender much of their land. Additional land was lost in the Georgia colony, when the Cherokees were forced to give up two million acres to pay off debts to white traders. By 1800, they were confined to parts of northern Georgia, the western Carolinas, and eastern Tennessee. The Cherokee population, however, remained the same—about 22,000 people—as it had been in 1650.

Recognizing their inability to stem the tide of white settlement, Cherokee leaders devised a strategy for survival: They would forsake the old ways and Westernize their culture. Cherokee leaders and their people adopted white techniques of farming and home construction and began to acquire property. They fought alongside Americans in wars against other Native Americans and the British. Most important, Sequoyah (b. between 1760 and 1770, d. 1843), a Cherokee, invented a writing system, called a syllabary, for his native tongue. The syllabary quickly enabled many Cherokees to read and write. In 1827, tribal leaders established the Cherokee Nation (northern Georgia), with separate legislative, executive, and judicial branches, a bill of rights, and a written constitution—based on the U.S. model. A bilingual newspaper, *The Cherokee Phoenix*, began publishing in 1828.

Despite their efforts to Westernize, the Cherokees soon learned that this was not enough. In 1830, the Cherokees, along with other tribes, were ordered to

Encounter figure 18.1   Chief Vann House. 1804. James Vann, a Cherokee chief, built this three-story brick house in northern Georgia during the period when the Cherokees were emulating white culture. In 1834, Vann's son and heir, Joseph Vann, was dragged from this house by white men who seized the surrounding property. The Vann estate included 800 acres of farmland, peach trees, apple trees, 42 cabins, 6 barns, 5 smokehouses, assorted shops, and a trading post. Houses for rank-and-file Cherokees were more modest in appearance and layout. Courtesy, Historic Preservation Section, Georgia Department of Natural Resources.

move to the Oklahoma Indian Territory. The Cherokee Nation sued to protect their lands, and the U.S. Supreme Court sided with them, but President Andrew Jackson (1828–1836) refused to enforce the court's decision. Jackson's refusal is bitterly ironic, for he said his goal was "to reclaim [Native Americans] from their wandering habits and make them a happy, prosperous people"—the same goal sought by the Cherokees. In 1838–1839, American soldiers evicted the Cherokees from their homes and lands, and more than 4,000 died on the 116-day journey to Oklahoma, a trek that became known as the Trail of Tears. In Oklahoma they joined with other Southeastern tribes—the Creek, the Chickasaw, the Choctaw, and the Seminole, all of whom had been forcibly relocated earlier.

to working-class males in the Reform Act of 1867. The revolutions of 1830 and 1848 widened the franchise for French, Italian, German, and Austrian men, although important government posts were always reserved for aristocrats. Women still could not vote in 1871, nor could wage earners (except for British and American workers) and members of the lower middle class. Universal suffrage was not yet a reality.

NINETEENTH-CENTURY THOUGHT: PHILOSOPHY, RELIGION, AND SCIENCE

At the heart of the debate over liberalism was the question, Which is primary, the individual or the group? Liberalism glorified the value of free expression for each human being, and capitalists used liberal arguments to justify their economic policies. But the corollaries of these policies seemed to be poverty, degradation, and injustice for workers, and new voices began to be raised in support of other approaches that promised antidotes to the injustices of industrial capitalism. Primary among these were a variety of socialisms, a form of political and social organization in which material goods are owned and distributed by the community or the government.

Liberalism Redefined

In the late eighteenth century, English philosopher and social theorist Jeremy Bentham (1748–1832) had developed a variant of liberalism known as **Utilitarianism.** Bentham made "utility" his supreme moral principle, meaning that what gave pleasure to both the individual and society was right and what gave pain was wrong. Utility for society was always identified with "the greatest happiness for the greatest number"—a view that reflected Bentham's commitment to democracy. Accepting liberalism's laissez-faire ideal, yet tempering it with the principle of utility, Bentham pushed for a renovation of the repressive and outmoded governments of his time, including reform of the legal system, prisons, and education.

After 1830 Bentham's ideas were eloquently reinterpreted by bourgeois liberalism's strongest defender, the English philosopher John Stuart Mill (1806–1873). Growing to maturity in the second phase of the industrial age, Mill became increasingly fearful that the masses and a powerful state would ultimately destroy individual rights and human dignity. In his essay *On Liberty* (1859), Mill argued that the continued existence of the "civilized community" required the fullest freedom of speech, discussion, and behavior that was possible among all citizens, as long as no person was physically harmed. Mill's essay represents the high point of English liberalism.

After having advocated laissez-faire economics in his 1848 edition of the *Principles of Political Economy*, in later editions Mill embraced a mild form of socialism. Condemning unbridled economic competition, he reasoned that though production was subject to economic laws, distribution was not, and thus humans should divide the benefits of industrialism along rational lines. Mill also campaigned for religious toleration and minority rights and became a staunch supporter of women's right to vote and own property. In many of his writings, Mill collaborated with Harriet Taylor, his wife.

Socialism

Liberalism provided support for bourgeois values, but **socialism** seemed to many to be the irresistible wave of the future. Socialism began as a reaction to industrialism

and came to be its most severe critic, holding out a vision of what society might become if only certain fundamental reforms were made. Two main groups spoke for socialism in the 1800s: the utopian socialists and the Marxists. The utopians, who reached their peak before 1848, believed that the ills of industrial society could be overcome through cooperation between workers and capitalists. In contrast, the Marxists, who flourished after 1848, held the utopians in contempt as naive idealists and called for revolutions, violence, and the inevitable triumph of scientific socialism.

The principal utopian socialists—Robert Owen (1771–1858) (himself a wealthy industrialist), Comte de Saint-Simon [san-see-MOH(N)] (1760–1825), and Charles Fourier [FOOR-ee-ay] (1772–1837)—shared the belief that a more just society could be introduced using the discoveries about society made in communal associations that served as laboratories for their philosophical ideas. All three thinkers were concerned more about the consumption of the fruits of industrialism than they were about the creation of goods. To them, the workers were simply not receiving a fair share for their efforts and were being victimized by a ruthless, competitive system. To solve these problems, the utopian socialists proposed a number of alternatives, but their often impracticable schemes had little chance of succeeding in an age that was becoming more scientific and realistic.

The utopian socialists and their supporters quickly faded from view once Karl Marx (1818–1883) appeared on the scene. As a student at the University of Berlin, Marx studied Hegel's dialectical explanation of historical change, but as an atheist he rejected Hegel's emphasis on Spirit. Since Marx's radical politics made a teaching post untenable in reactionary Prussia, he became editor of a Cologne newspaper. When the police shut down the paper, Marx sought refuge abroad. From Brussels, he and Friedrich Engels (1820–1895), his lifelong friend and coauthor, were asked to develop a set of principles for a German worker's society. The resulting pamphlet, *The Communist Manifesto* (1848), became the bible of socialism. Both men played minor roles in the 1848 revolts, seeing in them the first steps of a proletarian revolution. Marx spent his last years in London, writing his major work, *Capital* (volume 1, 1867; volumes 2 and 3, completed by Engels, 1885–1894), and founding an international workers' association to implement his ideas.

Marx's approach to historical change differed radically from the utopian view. According to Marx, history moved in a dialectical pattern as the Hegelians had argued, but not in rhythm with abstract ideas or the World Spirit. Instead, Marx thought that material reality conditioned historical development; the various stages of history, which were propelled by class conflicts, unfolded as one economic group replaced another. For example, the middle class, which had emerged out of the collapse of the feudal system, represented only a moment in history, destined dialectically to bring forth its own gravedigger, the proletariat, or the urban working class. Moreover, the institutions and ideas of a society constituted a superstructure erected on the foundation of economic reality; governments, law, the arts, and the humanities merely reflected the values of a particular ruling class.

Marx then forecast a revolt by the proletariat, who would install a classless society. Marx believed that the workers' revolution would be international in scope and that communist intellectuals would assist in bringing an end to bourgeois rule. Elaborating on his political, economic, and social theories, Marx's followers created Marxism and, inspired by his ideal society, organized to abolish the capitalist system, although their impact before 1871 was minimal.

From the first, socialism appealed especially to women, because it condemned existing social relations and called for universal emancipation. The ideal communal world would be free of every inequality, including sexual inequality. Utopian socialists were the most welcoming to supporters of female rights. For example, Fourier claimed that female freedom was the touchstone for measuring human liberation everywhere; Robert Owen espoused a new moral order in which sexual and class differences would be overcome in cooperative, loving communities; and Saint-Simon preached the moral superiority of women, though he preferred sexual complementarity to sexual equality.

Marx and Engels's views on women were ambiguous. They urged the full integration of women into the workforce as a condition of female emancipation, but insisted that freedom for male workers was key to radical social change. So, they encouraged women to curb their aspirations in the name of the greater good—that is, for an ideal Marxian workers' society.

Religion and the Challenge of Science

The growing interest in objective, rational analysis was not confined to investigations of the workings of society. In a development that alarmed some Christians, a group of Protestant scholars in Germany began to study the Bible not as a divinely inspired book incapable of error but simply as a set of human writings susceptible to varied interpretations. In Germany, this movement to treat the Bible like any other book was called **higher criticism.** Scholars began to try to identify the author or authors of each of the biblical books rather than rely on old accounts of their origins, to study each text to determine its sources rather than

treat each book as a divine revelation, and, most important, to assess the accuracy of each account rather than accept it as God's final word. By 1871 orthodox Christians were engaged in intellectual battles with the higher critics, some of whom portrayed Jesus not as God's son but as a mythological figure or a human teacher.

While the higher critics chipped away at Christianity from within, science assaulted it from outside. Geologists first discredited the biblical story of creation, and then biologists questioned the divine origin of human beings. The challenge from geology was led by the Englishman Charles Lyell [LIE-uhl] (1797–1875), whose fossil research showed that the earth was much older than Christians claimed. By treating each of God's six days of creation as symbolic of thousands of years of divine activity, Protestant Christians were able to weather this particular intellectual storm. Not so easily overcome, however, was biology's threat to biblical authority.

Following the Bible, the church was clear in its explanation of humanity's origin: Adam and Eve were the first parents, having been created by God after he had fashioned the rest of the animate world. Paralleling this divine account was a secular argument for evolution. Based on Greek thought, but without solid proofs, it remained a theory and nothing more for centuries. In 1859, however, the theory of **evolution** gained dramatic support when the Englishman Charles Darwin (1809–1882) published *On the Origin of Species*. Marshaling data to prove that evolution was a principle of biological development rather than a mere hypothesis, Darwin showed that over the course of millennia modern plants and animals had evolved from simpler forms through a process of natural selection.

In 1871, in *Descent of Man*, Darwin applied his findings to human beings, portraying them as the outcome of millions of years of evolution. Outraged clergy attacked Darwin for his atheism, and equally zealous Darwinians heaped ridicule on the creationists for their credulity. Today, the theory of evolution is one of the cornerstones of biological science, despite some continuing criticism.

Other advances in science were helping to lay the groundwork for the modern world. In the 1850s, French scientist Louis Pasteur [pass-TUHR] (1822–1895) proposed the germ theory of disease, the notion that many diseases are caused by microorganisms. This seminal idea led him to important discoveries and proposals for change. Claiming that germs were responsible for the spread of disease, he campaigned for improved sanitation and sterilization and thus paved the way for antiseptic surgery. He demonstrated that food spoilage could be prevented by killing microorganisms through heating, a discovery

PERSONAL PERSPECTIVE

CHARLOTTE BRONTË
The First World's Fair, 1851

Charlotte Brontë, while visiting the Great Exhibition, praised the benefits of the Industrial Revolution, including the new machines and tools and wealth from around the world. She was especially pleased by the orderly behavior of the crowds.

Yesterday I went for the second time to the Crystal Palace. We remained in it about three hours, and I must say I was more struck with it on this occasion than at my first visit. It is a wonderful place—vast, strange, new, and impossible to describe. Its grandeur does not consist in *one* thing, but in the unique assemblage of *all* things. Whatever human industry has created you find there, from the great compartments filled with railway engines and boilers, with mill machinery in full work, with splendid carriages of all kinds, with harness of every description, to the glass-covered and velvet-spread stands loaded with the most gorgeous work of the goldsmith and silversmith, and the carefully guarded caskets full of real diamonds and pearls worth hundreds of thousands of pounds. It may be called a bazaar or a fair, but it is such a bazaar or fair as Eastern genii might have created. It seems as if only magic could have gathered this mass of wealth from all the ends of the earth—as if none but supernatural hands could have arranged it thus, with such a blaze and contrast of colours and marvellous power of effect. The multitude filling the great aisles seems ruled and subdued by some invisible influence. Amongst the thirty thousand souls that peopled it the day I was there not one loud noise was to be heard, not one irregular movement seen; the living tide rolls on quietly, with a deep hum like the sea heard from the distance.

HIPPOLYTE TAINE
A Day at the Races, 28 May 1861

Hippolyte Taine (1828–1893), a French philosopher, historian, and critic, was a spectator at the annual Derby Day Horse Races. He described the lively scene, including the landscape, the race course, and the spectators drawn from all levels of society. As a visitor to England, the world's most advanced industrial country, Taine was shocked by the miserable conditions of the lower classes in attendance.

Races at Epsom: it is the Derby Day, a day of jollification; Parliament does not sit; for three days all the talk has been about horses and their trainers. . . .

Epsom course is a large, green plain, slightly undulating; on one side are reared three public stands and several other smaller ones. In front, tents, hundreds of shops, temporary stables under canvas, and an incredible confusion of carriages, of horses, of horsemen, of private omnibuses; there are perhaps 200,000 human heads here. Nothing beautiful or even elegant; the carriages are ordinary vehicles, and toilettes are rare; one does not come here to exhibit them but to witness a spectacle: the spectacle is interesting only on account of its size. From the top of the Stand the enormous antheap swarms, and its din ascends. But beyond, on the right, a row of large trees, behind them the faint bluish undulations of the verdant country, make a magnificent frame to a mediocre

---

that resulted in the "pasteurization" of milk. His studies of rabies and anthrax led him to the first use of vaccines against these diseases. As the founder of bacteriology and an important figure in the development of modern medicine, Pasteur is the embodiment of Francis Bacon's seventeenth-century assertion, "knowledge is power."

In chemistry, a fruitful way of thinking about atoms was finally formulated, moving beyond the simplistic notions that had been in vogue since fifth-century B.C. Greece. In about 1808 the Englishman John Dalton (1766–1844) invented an effective atomic theory, and in 1869 the Russian Dmitri Mendeleev [men-duh-LAY-uhf] (1834–1907) worked out a periodic table of elements, based on atomic weights, a system that, with modifications, is still in use. By 1871 other chemists had moved from regarding molecules as clusters of atoms to conceiving of them as structured into stable patterns. Nevertheless, without means and equipment for studying the actual atoms, atomism remained merely a useful theory until the twentieth century.

Advances in chemistry also led to changes in anesthetics and surgery. In the 1840s, chemists introduced nitrous oxide, chloroform, and other compounds that could block pain in human beings. Use of these new painkillers in obstetrics increased after Queen Victoria was given chloroform to assist her in childbirth in 1853. These desensitizers revolutionized the treatment of many diseases and wounds and made modern surgery possible.

picture. Some clouds as white as swans float in the sky, and their shadow sweeps over the grass; a light mist, charged with sunshine, flits in the distance, and the illuminated air, like a glory, envelops the plain, the heights, the vast area, and all the disorder of the human carnival.

It is a carnival, in fact; they have come to amuse themselves in a noisy fashion. Everywhere are gypsies, comic singers and dancers disguised as negroes, shooting galleries where bows and arrows or guns are used, charlatans who by dint of eloquence palm off watch chains, games of skittles and sticks, musicians of all sorts, and the most astonishing row of cabs, barouches, droskies, four-in-hands, with pies, cold meats, melons, fruits, wines, especially champagne. They unpack; they proceed to drink and eat; that restores the creature and excites him; coarse joy and open laughter are the result of a full stomach. In presence of this ready-made feast the aspect of the poor is pitiable to behold; they endeavour to sell you penny dolls, remembrances of the Derby; to induce you to play at Aunt Sally,[1] to black your boots. Nearly all of them resemble wretched, hungry, beaten, mangy dogs, waiting for a bone, without hope of finding much on it. They arrived on foot during the night, and count upon dining off crumbs from the great feast. Many are lying on the ground, among the feet of the passers-by, and sleep open-mouthed, face upwards. Their countenances have an expression of stupidity and of painful hardness. The majority of them have bare feet, all are terribly dirty, and most absurd-looking; the reason is that they wear gentlemen's old clothes, worn-out fashionable dresses, small bonnets, formerly worn by young ladies. The sight of these cast-off things, which have covered several bodies, becoming more shabby in passing from one to the other, always makes me uncomfortable. To wear these old clothes is degrading; in doing so the human being shows or avows that he is the off-scouring of society. Among us [the French] a peasant, a workman, a labourer, is a different man, not an inferior person; his blouse belongs to him, as my coat belongs to me—it has clothed no one but him. The employment of ragged clothes is more than a peculiarity; the poor resign themselves here to be the footstool of others.

One of these women, with an old shawl that appeared to have been dragged in the gutter, with battered head-gear, which had been a bonnet, made limp by the rain, with a poor, dirty, pale baby in her arms, came and prowled round our omnibus, picked up a castaway bottle, and drained the dregs. Her second girl, who could walk, also picked up and munched a rind of melon. We gave them a shilling and cakes. The humble smile of thankfulness they returned, it is impossible to describe. They had the look of saying, like Sterne's[2] poor donkey, "Do not beat me, I beseech you—yet you may beat me if you wish." Their countenances were burned, tanned by the sun; the mother had a scar on her right cheek, as if she had been struck by a boot; both of them, the child in particular, were grown wild and stunted. The great social mill crushes and grinds here, beneath its steel gearing, the lowest human stratum.

---

[1] A game played at fairs, featuring an effigy of an old woman smoking a pipe, at which fairgoers threw missiles to win prizes
[2] Laurence Sterne (1713–1768), British novelist

CULTURAL TRENDS: FROM ROMANTICISM TO REALISM

In its triumph, the middle class embraced both Neoclassical and Romantic styles in the arts. In Neoclassicism, the bourgeoisie found a devotion to order that appealed to their belief that the seemingly chaotic marketplace was actually regulated by economic laws. In Romanticism, they found escape from the sordid and ugly side of industrialism.

But both styles slowly grew routinized and pretentious under the patronage of the middle class, partly because of the inevitable loss of creative energy that sets in when any style becomes established and partly because of the conversion of the cultural arena into a marketplace. Because they lacked the deep learning that had guided many aristocratic patrons in the past, the new bourgeois audiences demanded art and literature that mirrored their less refined values. Catering to this need, artists and writers produced works that were spectacular, sentimental, and moralistic. Simply put, successful art did not offend respectable public taste.

Adding to this bourgeois influence was the growing ability of state institutions to control what was expressed in art and literature. The most powerful of these was France's Royal Academy of Painting and Sculpture, founded in 1648 for the purpose of honoring the nation's best painters. After 1830 its leaders became obsessed with rigid rules, thus creating what was called "official art." Those artists who could not obtain the academy's approval for exhibiting their works in the annual government-sponsored Salons, or art shows, were virtually condemned to poverty unless they had other means of financial support. Rejected artists soon identified the Royal Academy as a defender of the status quo and an enemy of innovation. No other Western state had a national academy with as

Figure 18.7 ÉDOUARD MANET. *A Bar at the Folies-Bergère.* 1882. 3'1½" × 4'3". Courtauld Institute Galleries, London (Courtauld Collection). *The Folies-Bergère was the grandest of the glorified beer halls, or cafés-concerts, which sprang up in Paris after 1850, offering drinks and raucous stage entertainment. Catering initially to a lower middle class prospering from the booming economy, these cafés-concerts soon became classless settings in which all strata of society could anonymously rub elbows. In this painting, Manet captures the spectacle of the cafés-concerts: the ghastly white light, the crush of customers, the stoic barmaid, the trapeze artist whose green feet are just visible in the top left corner. Most of these details are shown in the mirror behind the barmaid. The painting presents a problem in the impossibly placed mirror; the barmaid appears to be looking at the viewer but is also standing before the top-hatted man reflected in the mirror.*

much power as France's Royal Academy, although in other European countries similar bodies tried to regulate both art and literature.

In reaction to the empty, overblown qualities of official art, a new style began to appear in the 1840s. Known as **Realism,** this style focused on the everyday lives of the middle and lower classes (Figure 18.7). The Realists depicted ordinary people without idealizing or romanticizing them, although a moral point of view was always implied. Condemning Neoclassicism as cold and Romanticism as exaggerated, the Realists sought to convey what they saw around them in a serious, accurate, and unsentimental way. Merchants, housewives, workers, peasants, and even prostitutes replaced kings, aristocrats, goddesses, saints, and heroes as the subjects of paintings and novels.

Many forces contributed to the rise of Realism. In diplomacy, this was the era of Bismarck's realpolitik, the hard-nosed style that replaced more cautious and civilized negotiation. In science, Darwin demystified earthly existence by rejecting the biblical view of creation and concluding that the various species, including human beings, evolved from simpler organisms. The spread of democracy encouraged the Realists to take an interest in ordinary people, and the camera, invented in the 1830s, probably inspired the Realists in their goal of truthful accuracy. All these influences combined to make Realism a style intent on scientific objectivity in its depiction of the world as it is.

Literature

In literature, the Romantic style continued to dominate poetry, essays, and novels until midcentury, when it began to be displaced by Realism. The Romantic authors were concerned with the depth of their characters' emotions and had great faith in the power of the individual to transform his or her own life and the lives of others. The Realists, by contrast, tended to be determinists who preferred to let the facts speak for themselves. They rejected the bourgeois world as flawed by hypocrisy and materialism and denounced the machine age for its mechanization of human relationships. Realism in literature flourished between 1848 and 1871, chiefly in France, England, and Russia. A special contribution to Realistic literature was made by African American writers who found their voices during the slavery controversy preceding the Civil War.

The Height of French Romanticism   In France, the leading exponent of Romanticism was the poet, dramatist, and novelist Victor Hugo (1802–1885). His poetry established his fame, and the performance of his tragedy *Hernani* in February 1830 solidified his position as the leader of the Romantic movement. Enlivened with scenes of rousing action and by characters with limitless ambition, this play seemed with one stroke to sweep away the artificialities of Classicism. Its premiere created a huge scandal. When the bourgeois revolution erupted in July 1830, many French people believed that Hugo's *Hernani* had been a literary prophecy of the political upheaval.

Hugo became something of a national institution, noted as much for his humane values as for his writing. Because of his opposition to the regime of Napoleon III, he was exiled from France for eighteen years, beginning in 1851. While in exile, he published his most celebrated novel, the epic-length *Les Misérables (The Wretched)* (1862), which expresses his revulsion at the morally bankrupt society he believed France had become after Napoleon I.

The hero and moral center of the book is the pauper Jean Valjean, who is imprisoned for seventeen years for stealing a loaf of bread. He escapes and becomes a prosperous, respectable merchant, but the law is unrelenting in its pursuit of him, and he is forced into a life of hiding and subterfuge. Hugo makes Valjean a symbol of the rising masses' will to freedom, and his bourgeois readers were fascinated and horrified at the same time by Valjean's ultimate triumph.

Another popular Romantic literary figure was the French novelist and playwright George Sand (1804–1876), who was forced by need to become a writer. Amandine-Aurore-Lucie Dupin took the name George Sand in part to keep from embarrassing her own and her estranged husband's families and in part to assert herself in the male literary world; she was addressed by her friends as Madame George Sand.

Sand has been called "the first modern, liberated woman." She courted controversy as she engaged in highly public sexual liaisons with leading men of the times, including Romantic composer and pianist Frédéric Chopin. She often dressed as a typical bourgeois gentleman: coat and vest, cravat, trousers, steel-tipped boots, and top hat. Sand was the first Western woman to play an active part in a revolutionary government. In the Paris uprising of 1848, she sat on committees, delivered speeches and debated issues, and wrote in support of the short-lived radical socialist regime.

Because her father was descended from Polish royalty and her mother was the daughter of a Parisian birdseller, Sand found herself in a socially equivocal position in class-conscious France. Thus, she was predisposed to focus her writings on people without power, such as women, artists, and laborers. Her novels and plays, with their strong political undertones, illustrate Victor Hugo's claim that Romanticism was "liberalism in literature." For Sand, idealism simply meant another way to call for social reform.

Sand's first novel, *Indiana* (1832), is usually regarded as her best and is praised for its multifaceted characters and its accurate depiction of the constraints imposed on married women at that time. Indiana, the nineteen-year-old heroine, is unhappily married to an older man; she seeks true love apart from her spouse and in a relationship of equals. Unfortunately, because of her lover's treachery and society's inflexible marital code, she has to flee from France and scandal to Bourbon Island (modern Réunion), then a French colony in the Indian Ocean. There she finds a soul mate with whom she settles down in a Rousseau-like paradise. Critics read the work as an attack on France's Napoleonic Code, which placed wives under their husband's control (see Chapter 17). *Indiana* made Sand's reputation, and she followed it with about eighty more novels and twenty plays, a book of travel writings, and two volumes of children's stories.

Romanticism in the English Novel In England, Romanticism found its most expressive voices in the novels of the Brontë sisters, Charlotte (1816–1855) and Emily (1818–1848). Reared in the Yorkshire countryside far from the mainstream of cultured life, they created two of the most beloved novels in the English language. Their circumscribed lives seemed to uphold the Romantic dictum that true artistic genius springs from the imagination alone.

Emily Brontë's *Wuthering Heights* (1847) creates a Romantic atmosphere through mysterious events, ghostly apparitions, and graveyard scenes, but it rises above the typical Gothic romance. The work is suffused with a mystical radiance that invests the characters and the natural world with spiritual meanings beyond the visible. A tale of love and redemption, the story focuses on a mismatched couple, the genteel Catherine and the outcast Heathcliff, who are nevertheless soul mates. In the uncouth, passionate Heathcliff, Brontë creates a Byronic hero who lives outside conventional morality. Her portrayal of him as a man made vengeful by cruel circumstances has led some to label this the first sociorevolutionary novel.

Charlotte Brontë published *Jane Eyre* in the same year *Wuthering Heights* appeared. A dark and melancholy novel, the work tells the story of a governess's love for her brooding and mysterious employer. Her hopes for happiness are crushed by the discovery that the cause of his despair is his deranged wife, kept hidden in the attic. Narrated in the first person, the novel reveals the heroine's deep longings and passions as well as her ultimate willingness to sacrifice her feelings for moral values. Recognized at the time as a revolutionary work that dispensed with the conventions of sentimental novels, *Jane Eyre* was attacked by critics but welcomed by the reading public, who made it a best-seller.

Romanticism in American Literature Romanticism reached a milestone with the American literary and philosophical movement known as **Transcendentalism.**

Flourishing in New England in the early and middle part of the nineteenth century, this movement was critical of formal religions and drew inspiration from the belief that divinity is accessible without the necessity of mediation. Unlike the God of traditional religion, the divine spirit (Transcendence) manifested itself in many forms, including the physical universe, all constructive practical activity, all great cultural achievements, and all types of spiritual expression. In their goal of seeking union with the world's underlying metaphysical order, the Transcendentalists followed in the steps of the German Idealists (see Chapter 17). Of the Transcendentalists, Henry David Thoreau (1817–1862) was probably the most influential. His most celebrated book, *Walden* (1854), the lyrical journal of the months he spent living in the rough on Walden Pond, is virtually the bible of today's environmental movement. Thoreau's *On the Duty of Civil Disobedience* (1849), an essay on the necessity of disobeying an unjust law, was one of the texts that inspired Martin Luther King, Jr.'s, protests of the 1950s and 1960s against America's segregated social system.

American poetry now became a major presence in Western literature with the writings of Emily Dickinson and Walt Whitman. Both poets worked within the Romantic style, drawing on intimate histories, in the manner of other Romantic poets. They also adopted offbeat techniques, including verse forms and punctuation, that have greatly influenced twentieth-century poets. Today, Dickinson and Whitman are regarded as two of the most innovative poets of nineteenth-century American literature. Dickinson, a virtual recluse in her day, published only seven poems during her lifetime. Since her death, her reputation has increased dramatically, based on the almost 1,800 poems that make up the Dickinson canon. Whitman, vilified at first by the establishment, lived long enough to see himself become an American icon, the model of the good gray-haired poet. During his career, he effected a revolution in American poetry by creating a body of works based on his experience as an American, written in a specifically American language.

Realism in French and English Novels Realism began in France in the 1830s with the novels of Honoré de Balzac [BAHL-zak] (1799–1850). Balzac foreshadowed the major traits of Realism in the nearly one hundred novels that make up the series he called *The Human Comedy*. Set in France in the Napoleonic era and the early industrial age, this voluminous series deals with the lives of over two thousand characters, both in Paris and in the provinces. Balzac condemns the hollowness of middle-class society, pointing out how industrialism has caused many people to value material things more than friendship and family, although there are virtuous and sympathetic characters as well.

France's outstanding Realist was Gustave Flaubert [floh-BAIR] (1821–1880), who advocated a novel free from conventional, accepted moral or philosophical views. His masterpiece is *Madame Bovary* (1857), which caused a scandal with its unvarnished tale of adultery. In contrast to Balzac's broad sweep, Flaubert focused on a single person, the unhappy and misguided Emma Bovary. In careful detail, he sets forth the inner turmoil of a frustrated middle-class woman trapped by her dull marriage and her social standing. By stressing objectivity and withholding judgment, Flaubert believed he was following the precepts of modern science. As a social critic, he portrays everyday life among the smug members of this small-town, bourgeois society. Notwithstanding the scandal it caused, *Madame Bovary* was an instant success and established the new style of Realism. For most readers, Emma Bovary became a poignant symbol of people whose unrealistic dreams and aspirations doom their lives to failure.

English novelists also wrote in the new Realist style. Like their French counterparts, they railed against the vulgarity, selfishness, and hypocrisy of the middle class, but unlike the French, who were interested in creating unique characters, they spoke out for social justice. England's most popular writer of Realist fiction was Charles Dickens (1812–1870), who favored stories dealing with the harsh realities of urban and industrial life. Writing to meet deadlines for serialized magazine stories, Dickens poured out a torrent of words over a long literary career that began when he was in his twenties.

In early works, such as *Oliver Twist* (1837–1839) and *David Copperfield* (1849–1850), Dickens was optimistic, holding out hope for his characters and, by implication, for society in general. But in later novels, such as *Bleak House* and *Hard Times,* both published between 1851 and 1854, he was pessimistic about social reform and the possibility of correcting the excesses of industrialism. Dickens's rich descriptions, convoluted plots with unexpected coincidences, and topical satire were much admired by Victorian readers, and his finely developed and very British characters, such as Mr. Pickwick, Oliver Twist, and Ebenezer Scrooge, have survived as a memorable gift to literature.

Realist fiction in England was also represented by important female writers. The two most successful were Elizabeth Gaskell (1810–1865) and Mary Ann Evans (1819–1880), better known by her pen name, George Eliot. Both wrote novels about the hardships imposed on the less fortunate by England's industrial economy. Gaskell's *North and South* (1855) underscores the widening gap between the rich, particularly in England's urban north, and the poor, concentrated in the rural south, within the context of the rise of the labor unions. Typically, her themes involve contrasts, contradictions, and conflicts, such as the helplessness of the individual in the face of impersonal forces and the simultaneous need to affirm the human spirit against the inequalities of the factory system. Similarly, in *Middlemarch* (1872) and other novels, George Eliot explores the ways human beings are trapped in social systems that shape and mold their lives, for good or ill. Eliot's outlook is less deterministic, however, stressing the possibility of individual fulfillment despite social constraints as well as the freedom to make moral choices.

The Russian Realists   During the Realist period, Russia for the first time produced writers whose works received international acclaim: Leo Tolstoy [TOHL-stoy] (1828–1910) and Feodor Dostoevsky [duhs-tuh-YEF-skee] (1821–1881). Like English and French Realists, these Russians depicted the grim face of early industrialism and dealt with social problems, notably the plight of the newly liberated serfs. Their realism is tempered by a typically Russian concern: Should Russia embrace Western values or follow its own traditions, relying on its Slavic and Oriental past? Significantly, Tolstoy and Dostoevsky transcend Western Realism by stressing religious and spiritual themes.

In his early works, Tolstoy wrote objectively, without moralizing. The novel *Anna Karenina* (1875–1877) describes the unhappy consequences of adultery in a sophisticated but unforgiving society. *War and Peace* (1865–1869), his greatest work, is a monumental survey of Russia during the Napoleonic era, portraying a huge cast of characters caught up in the surging tides of history. Although Tolstoy focuses on the upper class in this Russian epic, he places them in realistic situations without romanticizing them. In these early works, he was a determinist, convinced that human beings were at the mercy of forces beyond them. But in 1876, after he had a religious conversion to a simple form of Christianity that stressed pacifism, plain living, and radical social reform, he repudiated all art that lacked a moral vision, including his own. Tolstoy devoted the rest of his life to this plain faith, following what he believed to be Jesus' teachings and working for a Christian anarchist society.

Feodor Dostoevsky was a powerful innovator who introduced literary devices that have become standard in Western letters. For example, *Crime and Punishment* (1866), written long before Sigmund Freud developed psychoanalysis, analyzes the inner life of a severely disturbed personality. In *Notes from Underground* (1864), the unnamed narrator is the first depiction of a modern literary type, the anti-hero, the character who lacks the virtues conventionally associated with heroism but who is not a villain.

In *The Brothers Karamazov* (1879–1880), Dostoevsky reaches the height of his powers. Like Flaubert in *Madame Bovary*, Dostoevsky sets his story in a small town and builds the narrative around a single family. Each of the Karamazov brothers personifies certain traits of human behavior, though none is a one-dimensional figure. Using the novel to address one of life's most vexing questions—If God exists, why is there suffering and evil in the world?—Dostoevsky offers no easy solution. Indeed, he reaches the radical conclusion that the question is insoluble, that suffering is an essential part of earthly existence and without it human beings can have no moral life.

Realism Among African American Writers   In the 1840s, as public opinion in the United States became polarized over slavery, a new literary genre, the **slave narrative,** emerged. The narratives, whether composed by slaves or told by slaves to secretaries who wrote them down, were filled with gritty, harsh details of the unjust slave system; these stories in turn influenced Realist fiction and also fueled the fires of antislavery rhetoric. Many slave narratives were eventually published, but probably the most compelling was the *Narrative of the Life of Frederick Douglass* (1845), written by Douglass himself, which launched this literary tradition. Douglass's (1817–1895) narrative described a heroic struggle, starting from an early awareness of the burden of being a slave, continuing through successful efforts to educate himself, and concluding with a bolt to freedom and a new life as a spokesman for abolitionism. This eloquent narrative was one of the first great modern books in the West to be written by a person of color. Besides establishing a new genre, Douglass made a splendid addition to the old genre of autobiography and opened the door to a more inclusive world literature free from the racial segregation that had characterized the varied literatures of the world since the fall of Rome.

Another African American who contributed to the Realist tradition was Sojourner Truth (1795–1883). Given the slave name of Isabell ("Bell") Hardenberg at birth, she won her freedom and took a new name, symbolic of her vow to "sojourn" the American landscape and always speak the truth. Truth's voice, captured by her secretary, Olive Gilbert, is both colloquial and eloquent, teasing and sincere, homespun and filled with biblical knowledge. Her actual voice electrified listeners, causing Truth to be remembered as one of the most natural orators in the nineteenth-century United States. Sojourner Truth's "Ain't I a Woman?" speech, delivered in 1851 before the Women's Rights convention in Akron, Ohio, shows the simple eloquence that made her a legend in her own time.

Figure 18.8 Jean-Auguste-Dominique Ingres. *The Turkish Bath.* Ca. 1852–1863. Oil on canvas, diameter 42½". Louvre. *Interest in oriental themes was a continuous thread in France's nineteenth-century bourgeois culture. In his rendering of a Turkish bath, Ingres used a harem setting in which to depict more than twenty nudes in various erotic and nonerotic poses. The nudes nevertheless are portrayed in typical Classical manner, suggesting studio models rather than sensual human beings.*

Art and Architecture

Realism in art grew up alongside an exaggerated version of Romanticism that persisted well beyond midcentury. Even Neoclassicism was represented in the official art of France throughout this period. Both styles found favor with the wealthy bourgeoisie.

Neoclassicism and Romanticism After 1830 Jean-Auguste-Dominique Ingres, who had inherited the position of Neoclassical master painter from Jacques-Louis David, virtually controlled French academic art until his death in 1867. He understood the mentality of the Salon crowds, and his works catered to their tastes. What particularly pleased this audience—composed almost exclusively of the wealthy, educated middle class—were chaste nudes in mythological or exotic settings, as in *The Turkish Bath* (Figure 18.8). The women's tactile flesh and the abandoned poses, though superbly realized, are depicted in a cold, Classical style and lack the immediacy of Ingres's great portraits.

Eugène Delacroix, Ingres's chief rival, remained a significant force in French culture with almost comparable artistic power. Delacroix perfected a Romantic style filled with superb mastery of color and human feeling. One of his finest works from this period is *Hamlet and Horatio in the Graveyard,* based on Act 5, Scene 1, of Shakespeare's drama (Figure 18.9). In the painting, one of the gravediggers holds up a skull to

Hamlet and Horatio. Delacroix, faithful to the Shakespearean text, captures the men's differing reactions: Hamlet, on the right, seems to recoil slightly, while Horatio appears more curious. In this and later paintings, Delacroix tried to work out the laws governing colors—especially the effects that they have on the viewer. The results in *Hamlet and Horatio in the Graveyard* are somber hues that reinforce the melancholy atmosphere. Later, the Impressionists based some of their color theories on Delacroix's experiments.

Romantic painting, especially of landscapes, became popular in the United States as Americans pushed westward. The grandeur, vastness, and beauty of the new country and God's presence in Nature, as explained by the Transcendental poet and essayist Ralph Waldo Emerson (1803–1882), inspired landscape artists to glorify Nature, to portray Nature as Sublime, and to relate the individual to the natural world. One group of artists, known as the Hudson River School (ca. 1825–1870), specialized in images of the mountains and valleys of New England and New York (Figure 18.10). For them, following Emerson's teachings, God and Nature were one, and they attempted to infuse their works with a mystical quality while also showing that the individual had a role to play in understanding and affecting Nature.

Like Romantic painting, nineteenth-century architecture tended to be romantically nostalgic, intrigued by times and places far removed from the industrial present. Particularly appealing were medieval times,

Figure 18.9 EUGÈNE DELACROIX. *Hamlet and Horatio in the Graveyard. 1839. Oil on canvas, 32 × 26".* Louvre. *Shakespeare's Hamlet, a tragedy of doomed love, became a touchstone for Romantic artists and poets. Delacroix, after having seen* Hamlet *performed in Paris, was so taken by the graveyard scene that he created at least three lithographs and two paintings of it. In this painting, he has reduced the scene to its bare essentials: The two gravediggers (foreground) confront Hamlet and Horatio (middle ground), while a cloud-filled sky takes up nearly half of the canvas. He makes the dark skull the focus of the painting by having all four figures gaze at it and placing it against the light sky. Dynamic tension is added by the diagonal line running from the upper right to the lower left side of the painting, a line made up of the descending hill and the gravedigger's upraised arm.*

Figure 18.10 JOHN FREDERICK KENSETT. *Lake George. 1869. Oil on canvas, 44 × 66¼".* The Metropolitan Museum of Art. Bequest of Maria DeWit Jesup. *John Frederick Kensett (1816–1872), one of the fashionable landscape artists of his day, traveled, studied, and painted in Europe and England during the 1840s; and, in 1848, he opened his studio in New York City. Kensett belonged to the **luminists,** as the second generation of the Hudson River School were called. The luminists focused on pristine images of Nature, emphasizing the play of light over the natural scene and downplaying any human presence. In* Lake George, *Kensett positions the mountains in the background and the trees and rocks in the foreground to frame the still lake as if not a single breeze were blowing.*

Figure 18.11 GUSTAVE COURBET. *The Meeting,* or *"Bonjour Monsieur Courbet."* 1854. Oil on canvas, 50¾ × 58⅝". Musée Fabre, Montpellier. *This painting is an allegory of the artistic and financial pact made between Courbet and his wealthy patron, Bruyas. Deeply attracted to Fourier's socialist ideas, both men thought they had found the solution, a Fourierist term, to the problem of uniting genius, capital, and work for the benefit of all. Recently published letters between the two show them involved in a mutual compact: for Bruyas, greater access to art circles and society, and for Courbet, the gaining of spiritual and economic freedom. Despite their partnership, the figural placement in the painting proclaims the preeminence of the artist: With his head tilted haughtily, the painter is privileged, placed nearest the viewer and isolated from the other two figures.*

which were considered exotic and even ethically superior to the present. Patriotism also contributed to the trend among Romantic architects to adapt medieval building styles, notably the Gothic, to nineteenth-century conditions, since the Middle Ages was when the national character of many states was being formed.

In London, when the old Houses of Parliament burned to the ground in 1834, a decision had to be made about the style of their replacement. Since English rights and liberties traditionally dated from the Magna Carta in 1215, during the Middle Ages, a parliamentary commission chose a Gothic style for the new building (see Figure 18.2). Designed by Charles Barry (1795–1860) and A. W. N. Pugin (1812–1852), the Houses of Parliament show a true understanding of the essential features of the Gothic style, using pointed arches and picturesque towers. Despite these features, this building is not genuinely Gothic, for it adheres to Classical principles in the regularity of its decorations and its emphasis on the horizontal.

The Rise of Realism in Art Dissatisfied with the emotional, exotic, and escapist tendencies of Romanticism, a new breed of painters wanted to depict the real-life events they saw around them. In 1848 the jury of the Salon, influenced by the democratic sentiments unleashed by the social revolutions during the year, allowed a new kind of painting to be shown. The artist most identified with this new style was Gustave

Courbet [koor-BAY] (1819–1877), a painter renowned for his refusal to prettify his works in the name of an aesthetic theory. His provocative canvases outraged middle-class audiences and made him the guiding spirit of militant Realism. Until about 1900, most painters in one way or another followed in Courbet's footsteps. A man of the people, a largely self-taught painter, and a combative individual, Courbet began to attract notice in 1849 by painting common people engaged in their day-to-day activities. Above all, he strove for an art that reflected the conditions of ordinary life.

Courbet's art was not readily accepted under France's Second Empire. Salon juries rejected his pioneering works, such as *The Meeting,* or *"Bonjour Monsieur Courbet,"* a visual record of an encounter between the painter and his wealthy patron, Alfred Bruyas (1821–1877) of Montpellier (Figure 18.11). With an expansive gesture, the well-dressed Bruyas (center) greets Courbet (right), as a manservant (left) stands with head bowed. The painter's informal costume— with painting equipment and belongings strapped to his back—helped promote Courbet's image as a carefree artist serving the cause of Realism. With Bruyas's financial backing, Courbet installed this painting at the Realism Pavilion, next door to the official Salon of 1855. Critics ridiculed *The Meeting,* claiming it had no narrative, dramatic, or anecdotal subject, and accused Courbet of self-promotion and narcissism. Relishing the controversy, Courbet remained true to his vision

Figure 18.12 GUSTAVE COURBET. *Interior of My Studio: A Real Allegory Summing Up Seven Years of My Life as an Artist.* 1855. Oil on canvas, 11′9¾″ × 19′6⅝″. Louvre. *Romanticism and Realism are joined in this allegorical work. The subjects—the artist and artistic genius—were major preoccupations of the Romantic era, as was the use of allegory. But undeniably Realist is Courbet's mocking attitude toward academic art and society. This painting's fame rests on its deft three-part composition, its allegorical biography of the artist, and its painterly technique, which captures the sensuosity of different textures, such as the female model's skin, a lace shawl, and a dog's ruffled fur.*

and continued to make art from his own life—an ideal that influenced Manet and the Impressionists.

Another of Courbet's paintings rejected by the 1855 Salon jury and exhibited in the Realism Pavilion was his masterpiece, *Interior of My Studio* (Figure 18.12). An intensely personal painting that visually summarizes his approach to art until this time, this work uses realistic contemporary figures to convey allegorical meaning. Its subtitle suggests Courbet's intent: *A Real Allegory Summing Up Seven Years of My Life as an Artist.* At the center of this canvas is the artist himself, in full light and painting a landscape while he is watched by a naked model and a small boy. The model and the fabric may be ironic references to the Salon's preference for nudes and still lifes. To the left of this central group, in shadow, are depicted those who have to work for a living, the usual subjects of Courbet's paintings, including peasants (the hunter and his dog) and a laborer. To the right, also in shadow, are grouped those for whom he paints, including his friends and mentors, each representing a specific idea. For example, the man reading a book is the poet Charles Baudelaire [bohd-LAIR], a personification of lyricism in art. As a total work, *Interior of My Studio* shows Courbet as the craftsman who mediates between the ordinary people pur-

suing everyday lives and the world of art and culture, bringing both to life in the process.

Although Courbet is considered the principal founder of the Realist style in art, he had a worthy predecessor in Honoré Daumier [DOH-m'yay] (1808–1879), a painter of realistic scenes before Realism emerged as a recognized style. Daumier chronicled the life of Paris with a dispassionate eye. In thousands of satirical lithographs, from which he earned his living, and hundreds of paintings, he depicted its mean streets, corrupt law courts, squalid rented rooms, ignorant art connoisseurs, bored musicians, cowardly bourgeoisie, and countless other urban characters and scenes. His works not only conjure up Paris in the mid-century but also symbolize the city as a living hell where daily existence could be a form of punishment.

No one and nothing were safe from Daumier's gaze. For example, in *The Freedom of the Press,* he depicts a muscular printer, symbolic of free ideas, ready to fight oppressive regimes (Figure 18.13). On the right, Charles X, attended by two ministers, has been knocked down—a reference to the role of the press in the king's fall from power in the 1830 revolution. On the left, top-hatted Louis Philippe threatens the printer with an umbrella, egged on by two attendants. For such satire, Daumier

Figure 18.13 HONORÉ DAUMIER. *The Freedom of the Press.* Caption: "Watch It!!" ["*Ne vous y Frottez Pas!!*"]. 1834. Lithograph, 16½ × 11½". British Museum, Department of Prints and Drawings, London. *Daumier's career as a caricaturist was made possible by technological advances associated with the industrial era. After drawing a cartoon, he reproduced it for the ever-expanding popular market using the lithographic process, the first application of industrial methods to art. In early lithography, the artist rendered an image on a flat stone surface and treated it so the nonimage areas would repel ink. Today's lithography makes use of zinc or aluminum surfaces instead of stone.*

Figure 18.14 HONORÉ DAUMIER. *The Third-Class Carriage.* Ca. 1862. Oil on canvas, 25¾ × 35½". Metropolitan Museum of Art. Bequest of Mrs. H. O. Havemeyer, 1929. *Close study of this oil painting reveals Daumier's genius for social observation: the mother's doting expression, the old woman's stoicism, and the melancholy profile of the top-hatted man in the shadows at the far left. None of the figures is individualized, however, for all represent social types. Despite the cramped quarters, Daumier stresses the isolation of individual travelers.*

was awarded a six-month prison term in 1832, but to his adoring audience he was a hero. Daumier often included printers in his political drawings until tighter censorship laws were passed in 1835.

One of Daumier's well-known paintings is entitled *The Third-Class Carriage* (Figure 18.14). In Paris, third-class coach was the cheapest sort of rail travel, and the resulting accommodations were cramped and plain. In Daumier's scene the foreground is dominated by three figures—a mother with her sleeping child, an old woman, and a sleeping boy. Behind them are crowded other peasants and middle-class businessmen, the latter recognizable by their tall hats. Although caricature is hinted at in this painting, it is a realistic portrayal of the growing democratization of society brought on by the railway.

In contrast to Daumier with his urban scenes, Jean-François Millet [mee-YAY] (1814–1875) painted the countryside near Barbizon, a village south of Paris where an artists' colony was located in the 1840s.

Figure 18.15 JEAN-FRANÇOIS MILLET. *The Sower.* 1850. Oil on canvas, 40 × 32½". Courtesy, Museum of Fine Arts, Boston. Gift of Quincy Adams Shaw through Quincy A. Shaw, Jr., and Mrs. Marian Shaw Haughton. *Like Daumier's peasant travelers, Millet's farmhand is depicted as a social type rather than as an individual. But Millet's Realist vision of peasant life is less forgiving than that of Daumier. He portrays the sower as little more than an animal and places him in a dark, nearly monochromatic landscape. Whereas Daumier's caricatures had provoked laughter or anger, Millet's painting produced fear.*

Figure 18.16 ROSA BONHEUR. *The Horse Fair.* 1853. Oil on canvas, 8′ × 13′4″. Metropolitan Museum of Art. Gift of Cornelius Vanderbilt, 1867. *Artists specializing in animal scenes usually painted their subjects in loving detail but only sketched in the background—perhaps reflecting lack of landscape technique. In contrast, Bonheur fully renders the setting of* The Horse Fair, *including the feathery trees and dusty cobblestones. So precise is her design that the cupola in the distance has been identified as that of La Salpêtrière hospital in Paris—a landmark near a midcentury horse market. Such realism led to the work's favorable reception from Napoleon III, which in turn helped promote Bonheur as one of France's best painters. In 1864 Bonheur became the first woman to receive the Legion of Honor, France's highest award. However, the award was bestowed privately by the empress, for the emperor refused to give the medal to a woman in a public ceremony.*

Millet and the Barbizon school were influenced by the English Romantic Constable, whose painting *The Hay Wain* had been admired in the Paris Salon of 1824 (see Figure 17.11). Unlike Constable, who treated human beings only incidentally in his landscapes, Millet made the rural folk and their labors his primary subject.

One of Millet's early Barbizon paintings was *The Sower,* which he exhibited in the Salon of 1850 (Figure 18.15). This work depicts a youth casting seeds onto a freshly plowed field; dimly visible in the background are a flock of birds and two oxen with a plowman. Ordinarily, such a pastoral scene would have been a romantic idyll symbolizing the dignity of human work, but in Millet's canvas the monotonous toil degrades the laborer. Millet forces attention on the solitary peasant, isolated from the world in a desolate landscape. The resulting image is that of a hulking presence, powerfully muscled and striding boldly across the canvas. Salon critics reacted by calling the picture "savage" and "violent," and its artist a "socialist."

However, Realist painters could focus on rural life and not be accused of socialism, as the career of Rosa Bonheur [boh-NURR] (1822–1899) reveals. Specializing in animal subjects, Bonheur enjoyed success with critics and public alike, starting with the Salon of 1841, when she was nineteen. In 1848 the Salon jury awarded Bonheur a Medal First Class for an animal scene. In

1853 *The Horse Fair* (Figure 18.16)—portraying spirited horses and their handlers at a horse market—made her an international celebrity, after a lithograph copy sold well in France, Britain, and the United States. What makes Bonheur's horses different from those painted by the Romantic Delacroix was her accuracy in depicting anatomy and movement—a reflection of her Realist faith in science. To prepare for this painting, Bonheur, dressed as a man, visited a horse market twice a week for two years to make sketches. Today, the work is considered her masterpiece, both for its impressive scale and for its knowledgeable portrayal of nineteenth-century country life.

If the Parisian art world was gratified by the paintings of Bonheur, it was outraged by the work of Édouard Manet [mah-NAY] (1832–1883), a painter whose style is difficult to classify. He contributed to the events that gradually discredited the Salon and the Academy, encouraging painters to express themselves as they pleased, and thus was a bridge between the Realists of the 1860s and the group that became known in the 1870s as the Impressionists. His notoriety arose in 1863 when Napoleon III authorized a Salon des Refusés (Salon of the Rejects) for the hundreds of artists excluded from the official exhibit. An audacious painting by Manet in this first of the counter-Salons made him the talk of Paris and the recognized leader of new painting.

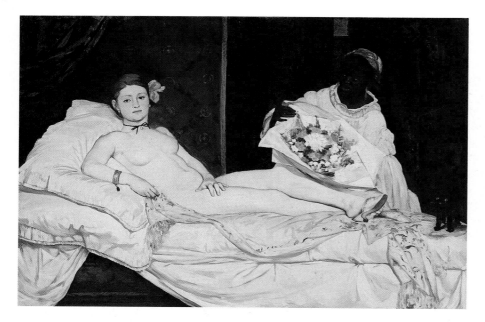

Figure 18.17 ÉDOUARD MANET. *Olympia.* 1863. Oil on canvas, 51¼ × 74¾". Musée d'Orsay, Paris. *Despite its references to traditional art, Olympia created a furor among the prudish and conservative public and critics. Parisian bourgeoisie expected to see nudes in the official Salon, but they were shocked by the appearance of a notorious prostitute, completely nude. The art critics, likewise, found the painting indecent and also condemned Manet's harsh, brilliant light, which tended to eliminate any details of the room's interior. Regardless of its initial negative reception, Olympia today is admired as a work that made a break with traditional art practices and opened the way for a modern art centered on the painter's own theories.*

In the official Salon of 1865, Manet exhibited *Olympia,* painted two years earlier, which also created a scandal (Figure 18.17). The painting presents a nude woman on a bed, a subject established by the painter Titian in the sixteenth century, but which Manet now modernized. Titian presented his nude as the goddess Venus in an idealized setting, but Manet rejected the trappings of mythology and depicted his nude realistically as a Parisian courtesan in her bedroom. The name Olympia was adopted by many Parisian prostitutes at the time, and Manet has portrayed her as being as imperious as a Greek goddess from Mount Olympus. Manet's Olympia is neither demure nor flirtatious; she gazes challengingly at the observer in a mixture of coldness and coyness. Her posture speaks of her boldness, as she sits propped up by pillows and dangles a shoe on her foot. She is attended by a black maid, whose deferential expression is in sharp contrast to Olympia's haughty demeanor. At her feet lies a black cat, an emblem of sexuality and gloom, perhaps inspired by a poem by the artist's friend Baudelaire.

More important than these historical connections, however, are Manet's artistic theories and practices, which strained against the boundaries of Realism. Unlike the other Realists, whose moral or ideological

Figure 18.18 MATHEW BRADY. *Abraham Lincoln.* 1860. Library of Congress. *Urged by his supporters in New York City, Lincoln hastily arranged to have Brady photograph him. Typical of the* carte-de-visite, *Lincoln is shown standing in a three-quarter-length frontal pose, a position influenced by the Western tradition of portrait painting. Dressed in the proper attire of the successful attorney that he was, Lincoln looks steadily at the viewer, while resting his left hand lightly on a stack of books. This photograph enhanced the Honest Abe image, with its dignity, seriousness, and air of calm resolve. On the left is the photographer's logo: Brady N.Y.*

feelings were reflected in the subjects they painted, Manet moved toward a dispassionate art in which the subject and the artist have no necessary connection. Manet's achievement was revolutionary, for he had discarded the intellectual themes of virtually all Western art: reliance on anecdote, the Bible, Christian saints, politics, nostalgia, Greece and Rome, the Middle Ages, and sentimental topics. With his work, he opened the door to an art that had no other purpose than to depict what the artist chose to paint—that is, "art for art's sake." In sum, Manet was the first truly modern painter.

Photography

One of the forces impelling painting toward a more realistic and detached style of expression was the invention of the camera. Two types of camera techniques were perfected in 1839. In France, Louis-Jacques-Mandé Daguerre [duh-GAIR] (1787–1851) discovered a chemical method for implanting images on silvered copper plates to produce photographs called daguerreotypes. In England, William Henry Fox Talbot (1800–1877) was pioneering the negative-positive process of photographic images, which he called "the pencil of nature." Not only did the camera undermine the reality of the painted image, but it also quickly created a new art form, photography. From the beginning, many photographers began to experiment with the camera's artistic potential, though only recently has photography received wide acceptance as serious art.

Among the early photographers were the American Mathew Brady (about 1823–1896) and the English Julia Margaret Cameron (1815–1879). Both made important contributions to photography, but their techniques and results were quite different. Brady attempted, through a sharp focus, to capture his subject in a realistic manner, whereas Cameron, by using a soft focus, delved into the personality and character of the individual in a near-mystical way.

Brady's reputation today is based mainly on his pictorial record of the American Civil War. Before the war, he operated a spacious studio and gallery in New York City, and there, in February 1860, he photographed Abraham Lincoln, who was campaigning to be the Republican nominee for president (Figure 18.18). This portrait introduced Lincoln to the East Coast public, who previously had thought the Midwesterner to be a coarse, backwoods politician. The original photograph achieved wide circulation when it was printed on a *carte-de-visite,* a 2½-inch print that was mounted as a calling card or collected as a personal memento. After Lincoln was elected president, he acknowledged to Brady that the photograph had been instrumental in securing his victory.

Figure 18.19 Julia Margaret Cameron. *Beatrice.* 1866. Victoria and Albert Museum, London. *Cameron photographed many women representing religious, historical, Classical, and literary females. Turning to* The Divine Comedy, *Cameron tries to capture the compelling beauty of Beatrice, who was one of the guiding inspirations of Dante's famous work. The light, coming in from the upper right, accentuates Beatrice's contemplative pose and her allure. In 1864, eight years before Cameron took this picture and when she was beginning her career, she wrote that she wanted to ennoble photography "by combining the real & Ideal and sacrificing nothing of Truth by all possible devotion to Poetry and beauty."*

While Brady and his staff were photographing battlefield scenes as well as portraits, Cameron, in 1863, at age 48, began to photograph her family and friends—many of whom were prominent Victorians (Figure 18.19). Within two years her talent was recognized, and soon she was exhibiting her works and winning awards. Her photographs document her conventional views of a woman's place in society, her deep Christian faith, and the impact of the Romantic movement. In her effort to catch the consciousness of each sitter, Cameron experimented with lighting, used props and costumes, tried different cameras, and often developed her own plates.

Music

Originating shortly after 1800, Romantic music reigned supreme from 1830 until 1871. Romantic works grew longer and more expressive as composers forged styles reflecting their individual feelings. To achieve unique voices, Romantic composers adopted varied techniques such as shifting rhythms, complex musical structures, discordant passages, and minor keys. In addition, with the spread of nationalistic feelings across Europe, especially after 1850, composers began to incorporate folk songs, national anthems, and indigenous dance rhythms into their music. Nonetheless, throughout this era Romantic composers stayed true to the established forms of Classical music composition—the opera, the sonata, and the symphony.

Although a Baroque creation, opera rose to splendid heights under Romanticism. The bourgeois public, bedazzled by opera's spectacle and virtuoso singers, eagerly embraced this art form. Operatic composers sometimes wrote works specifically to show off the vocal talents of particular performers. So prolific were these musicians that they wrote over half of the operas performed today.

Romanticism had an important impact on opera. The orchestras for operas became larger, inspiring composers to write long, elaborate works requiring many performers. Composers also began to integrate the entire musical drama, creating orchestral music that accentuated the actions and thoughts of the characters onstage. Most important, the form of opera itself was transformed. At first, composers imitated the form that they had inherited, writing operas in which a series of independent musical numbers—that is, **arias** (melodious songs)—alternated with recitatives (text either declaimed in the rhythms of natural speech with slight musical variations or sung with fuller musical support). The Italian composer Verdi brought this type of opera to its peak, advancing beyond the mechanical aria-recitative alternation. But even as Verdi was being lionized for his operatic achievements, a new style of opera was arising in Germany in the works of Wagner, which were written not as independent musical sections but as continuous musical scenes.

Giuseppe Verdi [VAYR-dee] (1813–1901), Italy's greatest composer of opera, followed the practice of the time and borrowed many of his plots from the works of Romantic writers filled with passion and full-blooded emotionalism.

One of the operas that brought him international fame was *Rigoletto* (1851), based on a play by Victor Hugo. What makes it such a favorite with audiences are its strong characters, its beautiful melodies, and its dramatic unity—features that typify Verdi's mature works. A study in Romantic opposites, this work tells of a crippled court jester, Rigoletto, deformed physically but emotionally sensitive, coarse in public but a devoted parent in private. The jester's daughter, Gilda, is also a study in contrasts, torn between love for her father and attraction to a corrupt noble.

In *Rigoletto,* Verdi continues to alternate arias with sung recitatives, but overall his music for the orchestra

skillfully underscores the events taking place onstage. In addition, he employs musical passages to illustrate the characters' psychology, using convoluted orchestral backgrounds to accompany Rigoletto's monologues, for example, or shifting from simple to showy musical settings to demonstrate Gilda's conflicted nature. Other operas followed, enhancing Verdi's mounting celebrity: *La Traviata* in 1853, based on a play written by the French Romantic writer Alexandre Dumas [doo-MAH] the younger, and *Aïda* in 1871, commissioned by Egypt's ruler and first performed in the Cairo opera house.

Romantic opera reached its climax in the works of Richard Wagner [VAHG-nuhr] (1813–1883), who sought a union of music and drama. A political revolutionary in his youth and a visionary thinker, Wagner was deeply impressed by the Romantic idea that the supreme expression of artistic genius occurred only when the arts were fused. To that end, he not only composed his own scores but also wrote the **librettos,** or texts, frequently conducted the music, and even planned the opera house in Bayreuth, Germany, where his later works were staged.

Wagner's major musical achievement was the monumental project entitled *The Ring of the Nibelung* (1853–1874), a cycle of four operas—or **music dramas,** as Wagner called them—that fulfilled his ideal of fusing music, verse, and staging. In these works, the distinction between arias and recitatives was nearly erased, giving a continuously flowing melodic line. This unified sound was marked by the appearance of recurring themes associated with particular characters, things, or ideas, known as **leitmotifs.** Based on a popular Romantic source—the medieval Norse myths—the *Ring* also reflected Wagner's belief that opera should be moral. The *Ring* cycle warns against overweening ambition, its plot relating a titanic struggle for world mastery in which both human beings and gods are destroyed because of their lust for power. Wagner may have been addressing this warning to the Faustian spirit that dominated capitalism in the industrial age—a message that went unheeded.

Another German, Johannes Brahms (1833–1897), dominated orchestral and chamber music after 1850 in much the same way that Wagner did opera. Unlike Wagner, Brahms was no musical innovator. A classical Romanticist, he took up the mantle vacated by Beethoven, and he admired the Baroque works of Bach. In Vienna, his adopted home, Brahms became the hero of the traditionalists who opposed the new music of Wagner. Neglecting the characteristic Romantic works of operas and program music, he won fame with his symphonies and chamber music. His characteristic sound is mellow, always harmonic, delighting equally in joy and melancholy.

Despite his conservative musicianship, Brahms's work incorporates many Romantic elements. Continuing the art-song tradition established by Schubert (see Chapter 17), he introduced folk melodies into his pieces. In his instrumental works, he often aimed for the expressiveness of the human voice, the "singing" style preferred in Romanticism. He was also indebted to the Romantic style for the length of his symphonies, the use of rhythmic variations in all his works, and, above all, the rich lyricism and songfulness of his music.

Despite the dominance of Classical musical forms, this period was the zenith of Romantic *lieder,* or art songs. The continuing popularity of *lieder* reflected bourgeois taste and power, since amateur performances of these songs were a staple of home entertainment for the well-to-do, especially in Germany and Austria. In the generation after Schubert, the best composer of *lieder* was the German Robert Schumann (1810–1856), a pianist who shifted to music journalism and composition when his right hand became crippled in 1832. Splendid fusions of words and music, his songs are essentially duets for voice and piano.

Schumann's *lieder* are often parts of song cycles held together with unifying themes. One of his best-known song cycles is *Dichterliebe (A Poet's Love)* (1840), set to verses by Heinrich Heine (1797–1856), Germany's preeminent lyric poet. This song cycle superbly illustrates the Romantic preoccupation with program music. For instance, the song "Im Wunderschönen Monat Mai" ("In the Marvelously Beautiful Month of May") conveys the longing of Heine's text through ascending lines of melody and an unresolved climax. The passion in this song cycle was inspired by Schumann's marriage to Clara Wieck (1819–1896), a piano virtuoso and composer in her own right.

The Legacy of the Bourgeois Age

We in the modern world still live in the shadow of the bourgeois age. The revolutions of 1830 and 1848 demonstrated that uprisings could bring about change but not always the desired results and that more drastic methods might be necessary in the future. These failed revolutions inspired the amoral concept of realpolitik, a guiding principle in much of today's politics. Realpolitik also contributed to the unification of Germany in 1871, which upset the balance of power on the Continent, unleashed German militarism, and led to France's smoldering resentment of Germany. The two world wars of the twentieth century had their seeds in these events.

With liberalism in the ascendant, the middle-class values of hard work, thrift, ambition, and respectability became paramount, as did the notion that the individual should take precedence over the group. However, the utopian socialists and the Marxian socialists, in criticizing liberalism and the industrial system, offered alternative solutions to social and economic problems. Their proposals foreshadowed approaches such as labor unions, mass political parties, and state planning.

The intellectual and artistic developments of this age had far-reaching repercussions. There is still interest in Marx's controversial analysis of history, despite the collapse of global communism; Darwin's theory of evolution, though intensely debated, is central to modern thought; Pasteur's contributions in immunology and microbiology have helped make the world a safer place; and higher criticism, by challenging the Hebrew Bible and the New Testament, has diminished the notion of religious revelation itself.

Romanticism, although under siege from other modes of thought after 1850, has not disappeared from the West, even today. Realism, its immediate successor, became the reigning style until 1900, partly because of the development of the camera and the art of photography. London's Crystal Palace inaugurated the high-tech tradition in art and architecture, and inventions and new techniques in printing and publishing laid the foundation for a mass market in the visual arts. Perhaps the most significant artistic development during this time was Manet's adoption of the credo "art for art's sake," which terminated the debate over the representational nature of art. Most artists in the post-1871 period followed Manet's bold move.

KEY CULTURAL TERMS

Utilitarianism	slave narrative
socialism	luminism
higher criticism	aria
evolution	libretto
Realism	music drama
Transcendentalism	leitmotif

SUGGESTIONS FOR FURTHER READING

Primary Sources

BALZAC, H. DE. *Cousin Bette.* Translated by M. A. Crawford. New York: Penguin, 1972. A representative novel from the *Human Comedy* series, Balzac's monumental commentary on French bourgeois society in the post-Napoleonic era.

———. *Père Goriot.* Translated by J. M. Sedgwick. New York: Dodd, Mead, 1954. Another of the best known of Balzac's almost one hundred novels in the *Human Comedy* series.

BRONTË, C. *Jane Eyre.* Edited and with an introduction by M. Smith. London: Oxford University Press, 1973. A classic of Romanticism, this novel deals with a theme dear to the hearts of nineteenth-century women readers, the life and tribulations of a governess.

BRONTË, E. *Wuthering Heights.* Edited and with an introduction by I. Jack. New York: Oxford University Press, 1983. A classic of Romanticism, this novel recounts the doomed affair of the socially mismatched but passionate soul mates Heathcliff and Catherine.

DICKENS, C. *Hard Times.* London: Methuen, 1987. A depiction of life in the new industrialized cities, this grim tale of forced marriage and its consequences reveals what happens when practical, utilitarian thinking replaces human values.

———. *Oliver Twist.* London: Longman, 1984. Dickens's moving tale of the orphan Oliver and his experiences among London's poor in the sordid conditions of the 1830s.

DICKINSON, E. *Complete Poems of Emily Dickinson.* Edited by T. H. Johnson. Boston: Little Brown & Co., 1976. Excellent gathering of the complete corpus—all 1,775 works—of Dickinson's poetry, arranged in chronological order from awkward juvenilia to the morbid, hell-obsessed verses of her later years. Compiled by a respected Dickinson scholar.

DOSTOEVSKY, F. *The Brothers Karamazov.* Translated by D. Magarshack. New York: Penguin, 1982. In his novel, Dostoevsky deals with broad metaphysical and psychological themes, such as the right of human beings to reject the world made by God because it contains so much evil and suffering. These themes are dramatized through the actions and personalities of the brothers and their father.

———. *Crime and Punishment.* Translated by S. Monas. New York: New American Library, 1980. A masterpiece of psychological insight, this gripping tale of murder explores the themes of suffering, guilt, redemption, and the limits of individual freedom.

DOUGLASS, F. *Narrative of the Life of Frederick Douglass, an American Slave, Written by Himself.* Introduction by Henry Louis Gates. Bedford Books in American History. Bedford Press, 1993. A heartbreaking, but ultimately uplifting, autobiography of perhaps the most influential and celebrated African American of the nineteenth century. Originally published in 1845, this work launched the literary genre known as the slave narrative. A reprint of the 1960 Harvard University Press publication.

ELIOT, G. *Middlemarch.* New York: Penguin, 1965. This classic of Realist fiction explores the psychology and growth in self-understanding of the principal characters, Dorothea Brooke and Dr. Lydgate.

FLAUBERT, G. *Madame Bovary.* Translated by A. Russell. New York: Penguin, 1961. One of the first Realist novels, and possibly the finest, Flaubert's work details Emma Bovary's futile attempts to find happiness in a stifling bourgeois world.

GASKELL, E. C. *North and South.* New York: Dutton, 1975. A portrait of economic and social disparities in mid-nineteenth-century England.

GILBERT, O., AND TRUTH, S. *The Narrative of Sojourner Truth.* Dover Thrift Editions, 1997. This autobiography, as told to a secretary, recounts the amazing life story of the nineteenth-century African American woman who endured thirty years of slavery in upstate New York, after which she became a leading abolitionist and a fighter for various reforms including women's suffrage. Originally published in 1850.

HUGO, V. *Les Misérables.* Translated by L. Wraxall. New York: Heritage Press, 1938. A good English version of Hugo's epic novel of social injustice in early-nineteenth-century France.

MARX, K., AND ENGELS, F. *Basic Writings on Politics and Philosophy.* Edited by L. Feuer. Boston: Peter Smith, 1975. A representative selection of their prodigious writings, which challenged industrial capitalism in the mid–nineteenth century and provided the theoretical basis for socialism and communism.

MILL, J. S. *On Liberty.* New York: Norton, 1975. Mill's examination of the relationship between the individual and society.

———. *Utilitarianism.* Indianapolis: Hackett, 1978. A defense of the belief that the proper goal of government is to provide the greatest happiness for the greatest number.

SAND, G. *Indiana.* Translated by G. B. Ives. Chicago: Academy Chicago, 1977. Sand's first novel, with its Romantic themes and feminist message, established her as a writer of great promise.

TOLSTOY, L. *War and Peace.* Translated by L. and A. Maude. London: Oxford University Press, 1984. Tolstoy's epic novel traces the impact of the Napoleonic wars on the lives of his Russian characters and explores such themes as the role of individual human beings in the flow of history.

WHITMAN, W. *The Complete Poems.* Edited by F. Murphy. New York: Viking Press, 1990. The complete poems of arguably the best poet yet produced in the United States. An authoritative edition compiled by a longtime Whitman scholar.

SUGGESTIONS FOR LISTENING

BRAHMS, JOHANNES (1833–1897). Brahms's four symphonies (1876, 1877, 1883, and 1885) demonstrate the disciplined style and majestic lyricism that made him the leader of the anti-Wagner school. Brahms also excelled in chamber music, a genre usually ignored by Romantic composers. His chamber works show him to be a worthy successor to Beethoven, especially in the Piano Quartet in G minor, Op. 25 (late 1850s), the Clarinet Quintet in B minor, Op. 115 (1891), and three string quartets, composed between 1873 and 1876.

SCHUMANN, ROBERT (1810–1856). Continuing the art-song tradition perfected by Schubert, Schumann composed song cycles such as *Dichterliebe (A Poet's Love)* (1840) and *Frauenliebe undleben (A Woman's Love and Life)* (1840), both filled with heartfelt passion and set to verses by Romantic poets. Schumann also had much success with his works for solo piano, including the delightful *Kinderszenen (Scenes from Childhood)* (1839), which he called "reminiscences of a grown-up for grown-ups." Unlike the *lieder* and piano music, Schumann's other works are often neglected today, such as his four symphonies (1841, 1845–1846, 1850, 1851); two choral offerings, *Das Paradies und die Peri (Paradise and the Peri)* (1843) and *Der Rose Pilgefahrt (The Pilgrimage of the Rose)* (1851); incidental music for the stage (Byron's *Manfred*); and assorted chamber works.

VERDI, GIUSEPPE (1813–1901). Primarily a composer of opera, Verdi worked exclusively in the Romantic tradition, bringing to perfection the style of opera that alternated arias and recitatives. His operatic subjects are based mainly on works by Romantic authors, such as *Il Corsaro (The Corsair)* (1848), adapted from Lord Byron, and *La Traviata (The Lost One)* (1853), adapted from Alexandre Dumas the younger. Shakespeare, whom the Romantics revered as a consummate genius, inspired the librettos for *Otello* (1887) and *Falstaff* (1893). Like the Romantics generally, Verdi had strong nationalistic feelings that he expressed in, for example, *Les Vêpres Siciliennes (The Sicilian Vespers)* (1855) and *La Battaglia di Legnano (The Battle of Legnano)* (1849).

WAGNER, RICHARD (1813–1883). Wagner created a new form, music drama, that fused all the arts—a development that reflected his theory that music should serve the theater. His early style may be heard in *Der Fliegende Holländer (The Flying Dutchman)* (1842), which alternates arias and recitatives in the traditional way. By 1850, in *Lohengrin*, he was moving toward a more comprehensive operatic style, using continuously flowing music and the technique of recurring themes called leitmotifs. He reached his maturity with *Der Ring des Nibelungen (The Ring of the Nibelung)*, written between 1853 and 1874; in this cycle of four operas, he focuses on the orchestral web, with the arias being simply one factor in the constantly shifting sounds. His works composed after 1853 pushed the limits of Classical tonality and became the starting point for modern music.

CHAPTER *18* HIGHLIGHTS
The Triumph of the Bourgeoisie, 1830–1871

■ Literature & Philosophy   ■ Art & Architecture   ■ Music & Dance

 Readings in the Western Humanities   *CD, The Western Humanities*

AFRICA

AMERICAS

HISTORY

Algeria, Tunisia, Madagascar, Mali, Chad, Dahomey, and Senegal under French control. Egypt, Asante Kingdom, and most of Yorubaland under British control.

North Africa Tripoli and Algiers fought U.S.; slave trade and piracy suppressed. Suez Canal opened.

Northeast Africa *Ethiopia.* Defeated Italian invaders.

West Africa *Liberia.* Founded as haven for freed U.S. slaves. *Asante Kingdom.* Decline after end of slave trade (1807).

East Africa Cecil Rhodes's South Africa Company took over Nguni states, Matabeleland and Mashonaland.

South Africa British took Boer coastal lands; displaced Boers founded Transvaal and Orange Free State; gold and diamonds discovered. Boer War (1899–1902) between British and Boers. *Zululand.* Military regime under King Shaka overran Natal. Defeated by Britain (1879).

Latin America Successful wars of independence against Spain (1816–25). *Mexico.* After independence came civil wars, foreign wars (Texas and U.S.), and French occupation. *Argentina.* Large immigration from Spain and Italy. Made wealthy by export trade. *Peru.* Failed Inca uprising (1814). Lost war with Chile (1889). *Brazil.* Portugal's emperor ruled from Brazil (to 1821). Became independent as monarchy and republic. Slavery abolished (1888). *Cuba.* Spain defeated (1898); U.S. troops occupied island (1899).

Native North America *Eastern Woodlands.* Cherokee Trail of Tears, forced march from Georgia to Oklahoma. By 1880s, all eastern Indian nations had been moved west to reservations. *Plains.* Gold discovered on Indian lands. Battle of Little Bighorn. *Southwest.* Navajo forced onto reservation. Apache resistance to relocation, led by Geronimo.

ART & MUSIC

Central Africa *Kwele culture (Gabon).* Ritual masks in antelope and gorilla forms.

West Africa *Benin.* Carved ivory leopards with spots made from copper. *Dahomey. Bocios* (wood carvings or metal sculptures of human figures), meant to ward off evil.

AKATI EKPLEKENDO. Warrior Figure (bocio). 1858–1889. Benin. Iron, ht. 5'5". Musée de l'Homme, Paris.

Latin America Painting and sculpture: academic art in European styles, including Romantic, Neoclassic, Realist, and Impressionist; and popular art drawing on New World themes, ideas, and attitudes. After 1850, artists increasingly worked with local themes. *Brazil.* Antônio Carlos Gomes, opera composer.

Native North America *Southwest.* Navajo renowned for intricately designed blankets; began silversmithing (1853).

JOSÉ MARÍA VELASCO. View of the Valley of Mexico from Hill of Santa Isabel. 1877. Oil on canvas, 63 × 90½". Mexico City, Museum of Modern Art.

ARCHITECTURE

East Africa *Swahili Language Areas.* Doors ornamented with a mixture of Islamic and African styles.

West Africa *Fulani Empire of Sokoto.* Caliph Muhammad Bello built capital city, Sokoto. *Yoruba culture.* Afro-Brazilian building style emerged after freed slaves returned from Brazil.

Latin America In urban and public architecture, Spanish Baroque, which patriots identified with tyranny, was replaced by French Neoclassicism, expressive of Enlightenment ideals and the newly independent states. Local traditions continued to be expressed in countryside.

MANUEL TOLSÁ. Interior Courtyard, School of Mines, Mexico City. 1797–1813.

RELIGION, PHILOSOPHY, LITERATURE

South Africa M. K. Gandhi, the future leader of India, lived here (after 1893), becoming a successful lawyer and perfecting his technique of nonviolent resistance. Feminist Olive Schreiner's novel, *The Story of an African Farm* (1883).

West Africa *Fulani Empire of Sokoto.* Over 260 works on religion, law, politics, history, and poetry by Sheik Usman dan Fodio and his brother and his son. *Yoruba culture.* Samuel Crowther, first black African bishop (1864–90) of the Anglican Church, translated Bible into Yoruba. *History of the Yorubas* (1897), by Samuel Johnson, a Yoruba cleric.

Brazil Joaquim Machado de Assis's *Epitaph for a Small Winner* (1881), a classic novel.

Native North America By 1880s, traditional religious observances, such as Sun Dance and Ghost Dance, outlawed; Indian children forced to attend boarding schools, learn English, become Christian. *Eastern Woodlands.* Sequoyah invented Cherokee alphabet (1828); Cherokee-language newspaper (1828–35).

China

Ch'ing Dynasty. Social conditions and state corruption worsened. Defeated by Britain in Opium War (1839–42); trade and port concessions extracted by Europeans. T'ai-p'ing revolt (1850–64) undermined regime. Officials and students studied in Japan and West. Boxer Rebellion (1900).

India

Mogul Dynasty, ended 1858. Country run by British East India Company. Indian Mutiny led to abolition of East India Company; power passed to the British state. *British Crown (Raj), began 1858.* British legal and bureaucratic systems introduced; industrialization began. Indian National Congress founded; began campaign for Indian self-rule (1885).

Japan

Edo period, ended 1867. Economic slowdown and threats of insurrection. U.S., followed by Europeans, forced opening of ports and trade concessions. Shōgunate abolished and Meiji Dynasty founded. *Meiji Restoration, began 1868.* Institution of Meiji Constitution (1889). Social, economic, and political reforms moved country toward becoming centralized and industrialized. Defeated China and awarded Taiwan (1895).

Ch'ing Dynasty. Scholarly painting, favored by imperial court, became stagnant. Schools of art drawing on Western models or on popular themes flourished in Guangzhou and Shanghai.

REN BONIAN, also known as REN YI. Young Woman at a Window with Plum Blossoms. 1884. Hanging scroll on paper. Liaoning Provincial Museum, Shenyang, China.

Mogul Dynasty. Miniature painting, as practiced in provincial courts, ended. Sikh portrait painting declined. Western influence on the rise. *British Crown.* Rabindranath Tagore's musical settings of Bengali poems.

Edo period. Ukiyo-e prints were produced by Utagawa School and landscape artists Katsushika Hokusai and Andō Hiroshige. *Meiji Restoration.* Traditional, Western style, and hybrid schools of painting. Western textiles and art influenced by Japanese crafts and woodblock prints.

HOKUSAI. Mt. Fuji. 1823–1831. Woodblock print, 10 × 15".

Ch'ing Dynasty. Hybrid style, mixing traditional and Western features. Western-style mercantile buildings, schools, and churches built in port cities. British troops burned Imperial Summer Palace.

Meiji Restoration. Western influence on urban buildings and public parks. Stone replaced wood for building.

TATSUNO KINGO. Bank of Japan (foreground). Completed 1896. Tokyo.

Ch'ing Dynasty. Shanghai's first illustrated magazine, the *Dianshi Studio Pictorial* (1884). Decreased government support of scholarship. Western science and religion made inroads. T'ai-p'ing rebels advocated an egalitarian and communal society, based on Chinese and Christian ideals.

British Crown. The Bengali poet Rabindranath Tagore wrote *Mānasi* (1890) and *Chitra* (1896).

Meiji Restoration. Literature influenced by Western Realism; many Western works translated into Japanese. Tsubouchi Shōyō's critical work *The Essence of the Novel* helped shape the Japanese novel; Futabatei Shimei's *The Drifting Cloud*, first modern Japanese novel; female poet and short story writer, Higuchi Ichiyō; Kawatake Mokuami, a prolific playwright (about 360 plays) for Kabuki theater. Bacteriologist Kiyoshi Shiga identified cause of endemic dysentery (1897).

19 THE AGE OF EARLY MODERNISM

1871–1914

Between 1871 and 1914, the European continent enjoyed an almost unprecedented period of tranquility, free of military conflict and considered by many to be the new age predicted by Enlightenment thinkers. But hindsight exposes this period as one of rampant nationalism, aggressive imperialism, and growing militarism, culminating in the outbreak of World War I in 1914. The prolonged, violent nature of that global struggle ended the optimism of prewar Europe.

At the same time, the phenomenon known as "modern life" was emerging, with people sharing in the benefits of strong nation-states and of the Second Industrial Revolution. In the cultural realm, **Modernism** was born; this movement rejected both the Greco-Roman and the Judeo-Christian legacies and tried to forge a new perspective that was true to modern secular experience (Figure 19.1). Modernism lasted about one hundred years, going through three distinct stages. During its first phase (1871–1914), which is treated in this chapter, artists, writers, and thinkers established the movement's principles through their creative and innovative works. The second phase, the zenith of Modernism (1914–1945), is the subject of Chapter 20; and the exhaustion and decline of the movement, the third phase (1945–1970), is covered in Chapter 21.

EUROPE'S RISE TO WORLD LEADERSHIP

The period between 1871 and 1914 was an age of accelerated and stressful change stimulated by imperialism, nationalism, and militarism. Acting as a catalyst was the middle class of central and western Europe (Figure 19.2).

◀ **Detail** Umberto Boccioni. *Unique Forms of Continuity in Space.* 1913. Bronze (cast 1931), 43⅞ × 34⅞ × 15¾" (111.2 × 88.5 × 40 cm). The Museum of Modern Art, New York.

Figure 19.1 UMBERTO BOCCIONI. *Unique Forms of Continuity in Space.* 1913. Bronze (cast 1931), 43⅞ × 34⅞ × 15¾" (111.2 × 88.5 × 40 cm). The Museum of Modern Art, New York. Acquired through the Lillie P. Bliss Bequest. Photograph © 1997 The Museum of Modern Art, New York. *Umberto Boccioni and his fellow Futurists—an Italian-based literary and artistic movement that typified Early Modernism's rejection of the past—set out to create a new concept of art. The Futurists called for the destruction of museums, libraries, and all existing art forms. In this striding bronze figure, Boccioni distorts form and space to create an airstreamed image of speed, the new modern icon.*

Figure 19.2 PIERRE BONNARD. *Paris, Rue de Parme on Bastille Day.* 1890. Oil on canvas, 31¼ × 15¾". National Gallery, Washington, D.C. *Bonnard's colorful depiction of Bastille Day, France's independence day, is a fitting symbol of nationalism and middle-class life. Middle-class men, women, and children, identified by their dress, leisurely stroll the street or ride in carriages. The tricolor flags lining the streets were patriotic reminders of France's revolutionary heritage.*

Imperialism—the quest for colonies—began as a search for new markets and increased wealth. As Europe became a world power with a network of political and economic interests around the globe, rivalries among European states intensified, transforming most of them into armed camps. Combined with growing feelings of nationalism, imperialistic and militaristic impulses created an atmosphere that eventually led rival states to war.

The Second Industrial Revolution and the Making of Modern Life

The Second Industrial Revolution differed from the first in several significant ways. First, Great Britain, the world's industrial leader since 1760, now faced strong competition from Germany and the United States. Second, science and research provided new and better industrial products and had a stronger influence than in the basically pragmatic first revolution. Finally, steam and water power were replaced by newer forms of industrial energy, such as oil and electricity. The internal combustion engine replaced the steam engine in ships and in the early 1900s gave rise to the automobile and the airplane.

Figure 19.3   MARY CASSATT. *Reading "Le Figaro."* 1878. Oil on canvas, 41 × 33". National Gallery, Washington, D.C. *Cassatt's woman reading a newspaper was a rare subject in the nineteenth century. Artists usually depicted women reading books rather than newspapers, which were identified with the man's world outside the home. The woman is the artist's mother, Katherine Cassatt, who is reading* Le Figaro, *one of Paris's leading newspapers. Rich and well-educated, Mrs. Cassatt was a strong influence in her daughter's life and career. The formidable figure of the mother takes up much of the painting, and the mirror on the left reflects her and her surroundings. The artist has cropped the mirror, much in the style of a photograph, a popular technique among Early Modernist painters.*

Technology, the offspring of science, was also reshaping the world. The wireless superseded the telegraph, the telephone made its debut, and national and international postal services were instituted. Typewriters and tabulators transformed business practices. Rotary presses printed thousands of copies of daily newspapers for an increasingly literate public (Figure 19.3).

The Second Industrial Revolution affected almost every aspect of the economy. In transportation, more efficient engines meant lower transportation costs and cheaper products. Refrigeration permitted perishable foods to be transported great distances without spoiling. Advertising became both a significant source of revenue for publishers and a powerful force in the consumer economy. Increased wealth meant more leisure for more people, and new recreations appeared, such as seaside resorts, music halls, movies, and bicycles—all contributing to the phenomenon known as modern life.

Industrialized cities, with their promises of well-paying jobs, comfortable lives, and noisy entertainments, drew residents of small towns and farms, and by 1900 nearly 30 percent of the people in the West lived in cities (Figure 19.4). As cities grew in industrialized countries, the standard of living improved. Consumers benefited from a general decline in prices and from steady wages and salaries. The period from 1900 to the outbreak of World War I in 1914 was a golden age for the affluent and leisured middle classes.

While the middle and upper classes enjoyed unprecedented prosperity, misery mounted among urban workers despite the creation of state-funded social welfare programs. Urban slums grew more crowded, and living conditions worsened. The presence of squalor in the midst of plenty pricked the conscience of many citizens, who began to work for better housing and less dangerous working conditions for laborers.

Figure 19.4 CAMILLE PISSARRO. *The Great Bridge to Rouen.* 1896. Oil on canvas, 29³⁄₁₆ × 36½". Carnegie Museum of Art, Pittsburgh. Purchase. *Pissarro's painting captures the energy of Rouen and transforms this French river town into a symbol of the new industrial age. Contributing to the sense of vitality are the belching smokestack, the bridge crowded with hurrying people, and the dockworkers busy with their machinery. The fast pace is underscored by the Impressionist technique of "broken color," giving an immediacy to the scene.*

Figure 19.5 EYRE CROWE. *The Dinner Hour at Wigan.* 1874. Oil on canvas, 30 × 42¼". Manchester City Art Gallery, Manchester, England. *Social possibilities for English women expanded to some degree during this era. This painting depicts a factory scene in which the young female workers gain a brief respite from their tasks. A few talk together quietly, while others remain apart or finish a chore. They all seem dwarfed by the huge mill with the smokestacks in the background, a fitting symbol of industrial power.*

When these reform efforts proved inadequate, labor unions arose, along with their best weapon, the strike.

One reform did succeed spectacularly: the founding of secular public education. Reformers claimed that public schools, financed by taxes and supervised by state agencies, would prepare workers for jobs in industrialized society and create an informed and literate citizenry—two basic needs of modern life. An unanticipated result of the establishment of public school systems was that ties between children and their parents were loosened.

The status of women also changed dramatically. New employment opportunities opened for teachers, nurses, office workers, and sales clerks. Because some of these jobs required special skills, colleges and degree programs were developed to teach them to women. Many young women still turned to domestic service, but new household appliances reduced the need for servants. Female labor in factories was now regulated by state laws, but small shopkeepers continued to work long hours in family businesses (Figure 19.5).

Figure 19.6 ANTON VON WERNER. *The Proclamation of the King of Prussia as German Emperor at Versailles. 1877. Oil on canvas. This painting commemorates the moment when the German Empire was proclaimed and King William of Prussia became its first emperor. Von Werner uses reflections from the famed Hall of Mirrors at Versailles to make the stirring scene more theatrical, and added drama comes from the raised swords of the officers. The strong presence of the army was prophetic of the dominant role the military was destined to play in the German Empire.*

Some women reformers, primarily from the middle class, advocated more freedom for women, continuing a tradition that had begun on a limited scale before 1871. These reformers launched successful campaigns to revise property and divorce laws, giving women greater control over their wealth and their lives. In several countries, they founded suffrage movements, using protests and marches to dramatize their situation. The word *feminism* entered the English vocabulary in 1895. Following a vigorous, occasionally violent, campaign, women won the right to vote in Great Britain in 1918 and in the United States in 1920.

Response to Industrialism: Politics and Crisis

At the dawn of Early Modernism, the assumptions of liberalism in industrialized countries were being challenged from many quarters. Except in Britain and the United States, liberals were under siege in national legislatures both by socialists—who wanted more central planning and more state services for the workers—and by conservatives—who feared the masses and supported militant nationalism as a way to unify their societies. After 1900 political parties representing workers and trade unionists, which were strong enough to push successfully for laws to correct some social problems of industrialism, further threatened the liberals' hold on power.

Events also seemed to discredit liberal theory. Theoretically, under free trade the population ought to decline or at least stabilize, and the economy ought to operate harmoniously, but neither happened. Population was surging and industrial capitalism was erratic, leading many to conclude that the so-called laws of liberal economics did not work.

Domestic Policies in the Heavily Industrialized West
Germany, France, Great Britain, and the United States all faced domestic problems during this period. Founded in 1871, the German Reich, or Empire, moved toward unity under the astute leadership of its first chancellor, Otto von Bismarck, and the new kaiser, or emperor, William I (r. 1871–1888), former King of Prussia (Figure 19.6). Despite the illusion of parliamentary rule, the tone of this imperial reich was conservative, militaristic, and nationalistic.

In France, the Third Republic was founded after the humiliating defeat of the Second Empire by Germany in 1871. Even though the government remained hopelessly divided between republicans and monarchists, it agreed on the need to correct the most glaring social injustices in an attempt to counteract the growing appeal of the workers' parties and socialism. The nation's liberal center gradually evaporated, creating bitter deadlocks between socialists and conservatives that no government could resolve.

Great Britain was more successful in solving its domestic problems during this period. Controlled by political parties that represented the upper and middle classes, the British government passed social legislation that improved the working and living conditions of many poor families and created opportunities for social mobility through a state secondary-school system. As in Germany and France, these reform efforts did not prevent workers from forming their own political party, the Labour party. Within a decade after World War I, it had gained enough support to elect a majority of Parliament and the prime minister.

Across the Atlantic, the United States began to challenge British industrial supremacy. America's rapidly expanding economy allowed big business to dominate politics at all levels until the reform movements of the

PERSONAL PERSPECTIVE

Lady Constance Lytton
Paying a Price for the Right to Vote

Lady Constance Lytton was a leader of the women's suffrage movement in Great Britain. Arrested during a protest in Liverpool in 1910, she assumed the name and status of a working-class woman, Jane Warton, because she feared that her high social position would prompt the police to release her. As Jane Warton, she went on a hunger strike and was force-fed by a doctor and wardresses (female guards), a horrifying tactic experienced by many suffragettes.

I was visited again by the Senior Medical Officer, who asked me how long I had been without food. I said I had eaten a buttered scone and a banana sent in by friends to the police station on Friday at about midnight. He said, "Oh, then, this is the fourth day; that is too long, I shall feed you, I must feed you at once," but he went out and nothing happened till about six o'clock in the evening, when he returned with, I think, five wardresses and the feeding apparatus. He urged me to take food voluntarily. I told him that was absolutely out of the question, that when our legislators ceased to resist enfranchising women then I should cease to resist taking food in prison. He did not examine my heart nor feel my pulse; he did not ask to do so, nor did I say anything which could possibly induce him to think I would refuse to be examined. I offered no resistance to being placed in position, but lay down voluntarily on the plank bed. Two of the wardresses took hold of my arms, one held my head and one my feet. One wardress helped to pour the food. The doctor leant on my knees as he stooped over my chest to get at my mouth. I shut my mouth and clenched my teeth. I had looked forward to this moment with so much anxiety lest my identity should be discovered beforehand, that I felt positively glad when the time had come. The sense of being overpowered by more force than I could possibly resist was complete, but I resisted nothing except with my mouth. The doctor offered me the choice of a wooden or steel gag; he explained elaborately, as he did on most subsequent occasions, that the steel gag would hurt and the wooden one not, and he urged me not to force him to use the steel gag. But I did not speak nor open my mouth, so that after playing about for a moment or two with the wooden one he finally had recourse to the steel. He seemed annoyed at my resistance and he broke into a temper as he plied my teeth with the steel implement. He found that on either side at the back I had false teeth mounted on a bridge which did not take out. The superintending wardress asked if I had any false teeth, if so, that they must be taken out; I made no answer and the process went on. He dug his instrument down on to the sham tooth, it pressed fearfully on the gum. He said if I resisted so much with my teeth, he would have to feed me through the nose. The pain of it was intense and at last I must have given way for he got the gag between my teeth, when he proceeded to turn it much more than necessary until my jaws were fastened wide apart, far more than they could go naturally. Then he put down my throat a tube which seemed to me much too wide and was something like four feet in length. The irritation of the tube was excessive. I choked the moment it touched my throat until it had got down. Then the food was poured in quickly; it made me sick a few seconds after it was down and the action of the sickness made my body and legs double up, but the wardresses instantly pressed back my head and the doctor leant on my knees. The horror of it was more than I can describe. I was sick over the doctor and wardresses, and it seemed a long time before they took the tube out. As the doctor left he gave me a slap on the cheek, not violently, but, as it were, to express his contemptuous disapproval, and he seemed to take for granted that my distress was assumed. At first it seemed such an utterly contemptible thing to have done that I could only laugh in my mind. Then suddenly I saw Jane Warton lying before me, and it seemed as if I were outside of her. She was the most despised, ignorant and helpless prisoner that I had seen. When she had served her time and was out of the prison, no one would believe anything she said, and the doctor when he had fed her by force and tortured her body, struck her on the cheek to show how he despised her! That was Jane Warton, and I had come to help her.

---

early 1900s (Figure 19.7). These movements, spurred by America's democratic tradition, temporarily derailed the power of the large business conglomerations called trusts.

In the late nineteenth century, Europeans came to America in the largest migration of human population ever recorded. These immigrants—after painful adjustments, particularly in the crowded slums of the eastern cities—gradually entered the mainstream of American life. Largely from eastern and central Europe, they transformed the United States into a much richer ethnic society and made valuable contributions to the culture.

Figure 19.7 EDGAR DEGAS. *The Cotton Bureau in New Orleans.* 1873. Oil on canvas, 29⅛ × 36¼". Musée des Beaux-Arts, Pau, France. *By the third quarter of the nineteenth century, the United States was challenging English supremacy in world trade. The French painter Degas must have observed this scene—the interior of a cotton exchange in New Orleans—while visiting relatives in Louisiana. Whether consciously or not, Degas accurately depicted the social realities of this bourgeois work space: the capitalist idlers reading a newspaper or lounging against a wall and, in contrast, the paid employees intent on their work.*

Domestic Policies in Central and Eastern Europe

The less industrialized states of central, southern, and eastern Europe faced more difficult problems. As the factory system began to appear in the region, these countries had no well-developed political and economic policies for handling the problems that came with industrialization. Because some regional leaders were stronger than the prime ministers, the Italian government allowed the northern regions to become industrialized while the southern regions, including Sicily, remained in a semifeudal condition. As a result, the north, driven by an expanding middle class, moved far ahead of the agrarian south, where vast estates were worked by peasant labor.

In the Austro-Hungarian Empire, the government's biggest problem was ethnic unrest, a direct outgrowth of the denial of political freedom to Slavic minorities, notably the Czechs and the Slovaks. In 1867 the Austrian Germans had given political parity to the Hungarians, allowing them free rein within their land. But nothing was done to address the simmering discontent among the Slavs. Even while the region seethed with ethnic violence, its capital, Vienna, became a glittering symbol of Modernism. From *fin-de-siècle* ("end-of-the-century") Vienna came the cultural style called Expressionism and the psychology of Sigmund Freud.

Farther east, the Russian Empire slowly entered the industrial age, hampered by its vast size and its sluggish agrarian economy and its inefficient bureaucracy. Adding to Russia's woes were violent underground revolutionaries who despaired of any substantial reform in this autocratic society. In 1881 an anarchist assassinated the liberal Czar Alexander II, and his successors dismantled his reforms. Under them, Russia's economy worsened and the imperial ministers grew more reactionary. In 1905 Japan defeated Russia in the brief Russo-Japanese War (1904–1905), setting off a short-lived revolution led by underpaid factory workers and starving peasants. By promising relief, Czar Nicholas II weathered the storm, but few of his pledges were fulfilled. Instead the state violently repressed dissent, and, as a result, the imperial court grew dangerously isolated.

Imperialism and International Relations

In 1871 most European nations believed that domestic issues were more important than colonial matters and that internal law and order was the first priority. By 1914 those beliefs had been reversed. Domestic politics were no longer primary, and national interests tended to be calculated by each state's role in the global economy and in foreign affairs.

The Scramble for Colonies

Before 1875 the common wisdom was that a colony brought both benefits and problems to a modern state, but after that year Western thinking abruptly changed. Europe's industrialized states began to compete for colonies and for trade rights around the world. To maintain their high standard of

LEARNING THROUGH MAPS

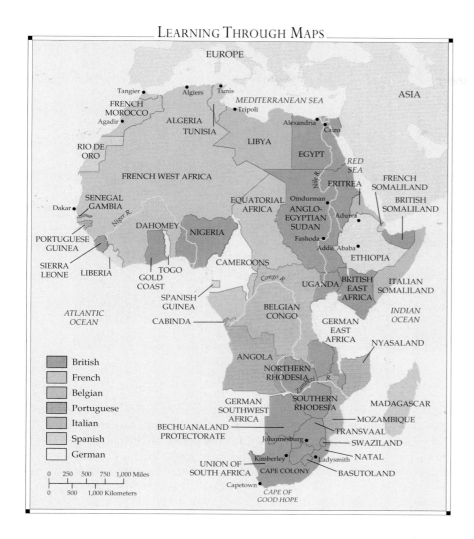

MAP 19.1   IMPERIALISM IN AFRICA: COLONIAL STATES, 1914
This map shows Europe's colonies in Africa on the eve of World War I. **Notice** the movement of Europeans from the coastal lands of Africa in Map 15.1, Expansion of Europe, to the founding of colonies across the continent in this map. **Identify** the holdings of the European powers. **Which** country had the largest number of colonies? **Which** country had the smallest number? **Locate** centers of potential conflict among the colonial powers. **Which** two countries remained independent of European control? Source: Felix Gilbert, *The End of the European Era, 1890 to the Present.* New York: Norton, 1970, p. 23.

living, they had to find new markets, underdeveloped areas in which to invest capital, and cheap sources of raw materials. Given these needs, the continent of Africa was an imperialist's dream. The European states claimed lands and shared the spoils of this product-rich continent. France and Britain got the best lands; Germany and Italy received the more barren, less commercially desirable areas (Map 19.1). In the Far East, imperialists competed for colonies in the South Pacific and China, making the Europeans rivals for land with the United States and Japan (the leading power in the Far East after military victories over China in 1895 and Russia in 1905) (Map 19.2).

Imperialism fomented many crises, particularly in Africa, but no major conflict occurred. In this mostly tranquil climate, people began to believe that peace depended on the secret alliances constructed by the major powers. The diplomatic pacts, reinforced by strong armies and navies, had originated after the Franco-Prussian War in 1871. By 1914 Europe was divided into two armed camps—France, Great Britain, and Russia (called the Triple Entente) against Germany, Austria-Hungary, and Italy (known as the Triple Alliance) (Map 19.3).

The Outbreak of World War I   In June 1914 an incident took place in Sarajevo for which diplomacy had no peaceful remedy: the assassination of the heir to the Austro-Hungarian throne, Archduke Francis Ferdinand. The Austrians were convinced that Serbia, a Balkan state and an ally of Russia, was behind the murder of the crown prince. They demanded a full apology and punishment of the guilty parties. Serbia's reply proved unsatisfactory and Austria declared war.

Austria's action set in motion the mobilization plans required by the alliance system. Frantic efforts to restore peace failed. By August 4, 1914, Russia, France, and Britain were fighting Germany and Austria-Hungary while Italy (a member of the Triple Alliance)

LEARNING THROUGH MAPS

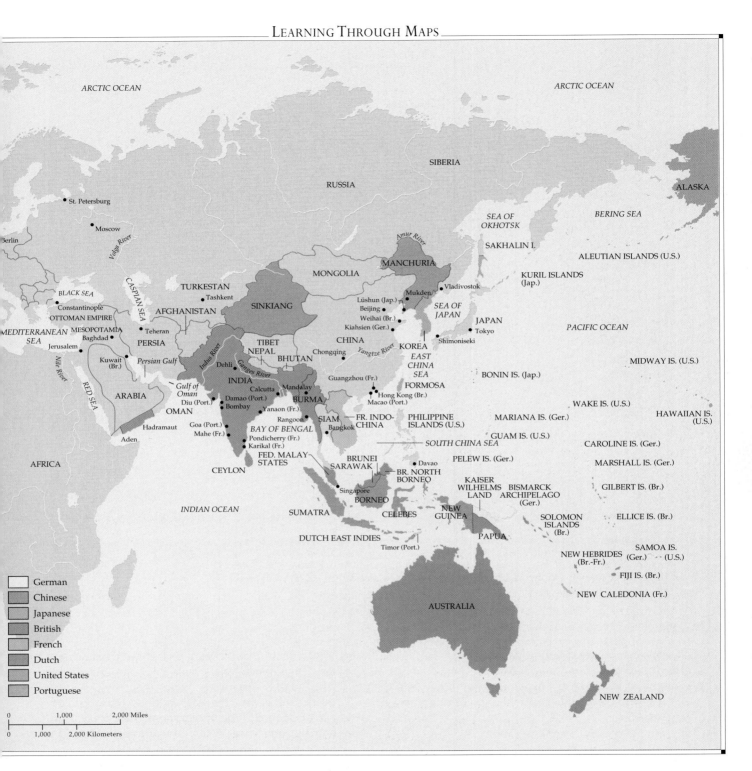

MAP 19.2   IMPERIALISM IN ASIA: COLONIAL STATES, 1914
This map shows Europe's expansion into Asia on the eve of World War I. **Compare**
the small presence of Europeans in Asia in Map 15.1, Expansion of Europe, with their
extensive holdings in this map. **Identify** holdings of the European powers. **Notice** that
China, Japan, and the United States have become colonial powers. **Which** country was
the dominant colonial power? **What** countries occupied islands in the Pacific Ocean?
Which continent, Africa in Map 19.1 or Asia in this map, was more subject to European
occupation? Source: Felix Gilbert, *The End of the European Era, 1890 to the Present.* New York: Norton,
1970, pp. 24–25.

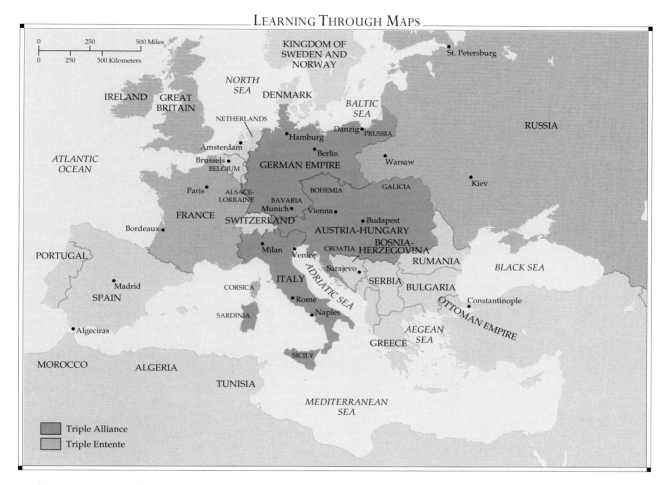

MAP 19.3   EUROPE ON THE EVE OF WORLD WAR I
This map shows the political divisions in Europe in 1914. **Identify** the member states of the Triple Alliance and the Triple Entente. **Which** of the two alliances would have the geographic advantage when defending its member states? **Which** small states might become battlegrounds if war broke out between the two alliances? **Locate** Sarajevo, the city where an incident occurred that set off World War I. **Notice** the lost lands of the Ottoman Empire and the creation of nation-states on this map, compared with the same territories in Map 18.2, Europe in 1871.

watched from the sidelines. Modern life—symbolized by huge armies, military technology, and industrial might—had plunged Europe and, later, much of the world into the bloodiest war that civilization had yet witnessed.

EARLY MODERNISM

As previously noted, at the dawn of the age of Modernism it was widely believed that the human race had turned a corner, that a golden era was about to begin. This sanguine outlook was fueled by the spread of self-government, new technology, and advances in science that held the promise of unlimited moral and material

progress for humanity. As a result, there was everywhere a passion for novelty, a desire to cast off the dead hand of the past.

At the same time, however, a mood of uncertainty began to creep into the Modernist vocabulary and undercut the optimism. A few artists and thinkers, for whom rebellion was a primary response to the world, questioned traditional Western ethics, religion, customs, and other deeply held beliefs. They expressed their doubts in many ways, but chiefly through constant experimentation, through a desire to return to aesthetic fundamentals, and, especially among the painters, through a belief that the art process itself was more valuable than the completed work. As the pace of events accelerated in every area of life, a vigorous

avant-garde, or vanguard, of writers, artists, and intellectuals, pushed Western culture toward an elusive, uncertain future (see Figure 19.1).

Philosophy and Psychology

Toward the end of the nineteenth century, new directions in philosophy and psychology reshaped these intellectual disciplines and fostered the shift to Modernism. These German-inspired ideas undercut cherished Western beliefs that dated from the Enlightenment—ideas about human rationality, universal moral order, and personal freedom. The creators of these seminal innovations were the philosopher Friedrich Nietzsche and the psychologists Sigmund Freud and Carl Jung.

Friedrich Nietzsche [NEE-chuh] (1844–1900) was a prophet of Modernism who was notorious for his corrosive thought. He saw beyond the optimism of his times and correctly predicted the general disasters, both moral and material, that would afflict Western culture in the twentieth century. To him, the philosophies of the past were all false because they were built on nonexistent absolute principles. Denying moral certainty, Nietzsche asserted that he was the philosopher of the "perhaps," deliberately cultivating ambiguity. Nietzsche vehemently rejected middle-class and Judeo-Christian ideals, identifying them with "herd" or "slave" values. For the same reason, he heaped scorn on many of the "isms" of his day—liberalism, socialism, and Marxism—claiming that they appealed to humanity's lowest common denominator and were thus destroying Western civilization.

Nevertheless, there were affirmative, positive aspects to Nietzsche's thought. He believed in a new morality that glorified human life, creativity, and personal heroism. He forecast the appearance of a few *Übermenschen,* or supermen, who had the "will to power," the primeval urge to live beyond the herd and its debased values. He praised these supermen for living "beyond good and evil," for refusing to be bound by society's rules and mores.

Virtually unknown when he died, Nietzsche became one of the giants of twentieth-century thought. His radical thinking—notably in affirming that civilization itself is nothing more than a human invention—has touched nearly every phase of modern thought, including religion, philosophy, literary criticism, and psychology. An extreme individualist, he was contemptuous of the strong German state, though the Nazis in the 1930s used his writings to justify their theory of Aryan supremacy. His glorification of individualism was also a powerful stimulus to many artists, writers, and musicians.

Rather than making a blanket condemnation of much of human morality and behavior, Sigmund Freud [FROID] (1856–1939) offered an approach to human psychology that could be used for further explorations into the study of the self. Part of the highly influential group of intellectuals and artists who flourished in Vienna around 1900, Freud, a neurologist, invented a new way of thinking about human nature that profoundly affected Western society.

Freud's analysis of the human mind challenged the Enlightenment's belief that human beings are fully rational. Freud argued that the human personality is the product of an intense internal struggle between instinctual drives and social reality. According to Freud, each psyche, or self, is composed of an *id,* a *superego,* and an *ego.* The id is the source of primitive, instinctual drives and desires, notably sex and aggression. The superego corresponds to the will of society internalized as the conscience. The ego represents the conscious public face that emerges from the conflict between the inborn instincts and the conscience and acts as the balancing component that establishes inner resolutions. In Freud's view, a true, lasting equilibrium among the three components of the psyche cannot be reached; the internal struggle is constant and inescapable. Those in whom the imbalance is pronounced suffer varying degrees of mental illness, ranging from mild neurosis to extreme psychosis. Even though Freud's theory tends toward determinism, he had hope for human freedom. For those who accepted their inescapable limitations, he believed that the truth about the human condition would liberate them from damaging habits of thought and enable them to function as morally free individuals.

Freud's greatest achievement was the founding of psychoanalysis, a type of therapy dedicated to the principle that once the roots of neurotic behavior are unraveled, a patient can lead a freer, healthier life. As part of treatment, he devised the "free association" method whereby his patients were asked to say, spontaneously and without inhibition, whatever came into their minds—memories, random observations, anything at all—and thus uncover traumas buried in their unconscious. He also studied his patients' dreams, which he thought were forms of wish fulfillment, a theory he set forth in *The Interpretation of Dreams* (1899). Freud's influence is pervasive today in Western culture, but recent research has called into question not only his conclusions but also his ethics.

A challenge was made to Freud's views by a former associate, the Swiss psychologist Carl Jung [YOONG] (1875–1961). Jung developed a theory of a universal, collective unconscious, shared by all humans, that exists in conjunction with each individual's own "personal" unconscious. Jung speculated that the secrets of

Timeline 19.1   EARLY MODERNISM

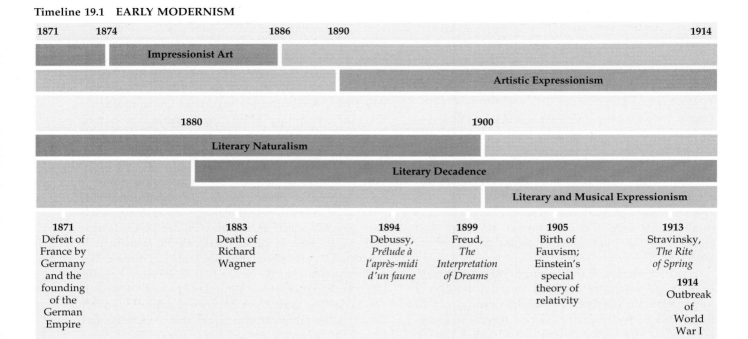

the unconscious could be revealed by studying archetypes, ancient images that recur again and again in human experience and appear in dreams, myths, and folktales. His conception of archetypes opened a rich source of images and subjects for many Modernist artists and writers. Despite their differences, however, Freud and Jung agreed that the conscious mind is only a very small part of individual personality—a belief that is a cornerstone of Modernism.

Literature

Three overlapping and contradictory styles characterize the literature of Early Modernism: Naturalism, Decadence, and Expressionism. The first of these, **Naturalism,** was inspired by the methods of science and the insights of sociology to focus on such issues as working-class unrest and women's rights. Naturalistic writers strove for objectivity and tended to see modern industrial society in a harsh light. **Decadent** writers rejected material values, scorned science, and were in flight from bourgeois society, which they identified with respectability and mediocrity. **Expressionism** was built on the premise that bourgeois culture had robbed the traditional vocabulary of the arts of its capacity to express the truth and therefore new methods and forms of expression must be sought. To a greater or lesser degree, these three styles share a disdain for middle-class life and values (Timeline 19.1).

Naturalistic Literature   The founder and chief exponent of Naturalism was Émile Zola [ZOH-luh] (1840–1902), the French writer whose fame rests on the *Rougon-Macquart* series (1870–1893), twenty novels depicting the history of a single family under France's Second Empire. The novels treat socially provocative themes such as prostitution (*Nana*, 1880) and the horrifying conditions in the coal-mining industry (*Germinal*, 1884). They offer a richly detailed portrait of French society in the mid–nineteenth century and also illustrate Zola's belief in biological determinism. Whether the novels' characters became prostitutes or virtuous housewives, family men or drunken suicides, Zola traces their ultimate fates to inborn dispositions. Nevertheless, Zola was no rigid fatalist. His novels convincingly portray people fervently trying to control their destinies in an uncaring universe.

Another outstanding Naturalist was the Norwegian dramatist Henrik Ibsen (1828–1906). An important playwright, Ibsen helped to establish the **problem play** dealing with social issues such as the public welfare versus private interest. This type of play became the staple of the modern theater and Ibsen its most eloquent practitioner. Ibsen lived mainly in Germany and Italy, writing about the middle-class Norwegian world he had fled, treating with frankness such previously taboo themes as venereal disease, suicide, and the decay of Christian values.

In *A Doll's House* (1879), Ibsen portrays a contemporary marriage and questions the wife's subservient role. Perhaps because of its controversial ending—the wife leaves her husband, asserting that her duties to herself are more sacred than her duties to him—this play created a tremendous first impression. In Ibsen's play, Nora is treated by her husband, Torvald, as a charming child whose sole purpose is to amuse him. When Nora borrows money to save Torvald's life, she deceives him about it because she knows how "painful and humiliating" it would be for him to know he owed her anything. But his reaction when he discovers it—condemning her bitterly and then forgiving her like a father—makes her realize she is living with a stranger. Faced with such lack of understanding, she deserts both husband and family, closing the door on bourgeois "decency." Ibsen's play was an international success, and its liberated heroine became the symbol of the new woman of the late 1800s.

The preeminent Naturalistic writer from eastern Europe was the Russian Anton Chekhov [CHEK-ahf] (1860–1904), a physician turned playwright and short-story writer, who found his subject in the suffocating life of Russia's small towns. He peopled his gently ironic plays with men and women in anguish over their ordinary lives, although his most arresting characters are those who endure disappointment without overt complaint. It is this latter quality that has made Chekhov's comedies, as these bittersweet plays are called, such favorites of both actors and audiences.

The Three Sisters (1901), a play that dramatizes the uneventful lives of a landowning family confined to the drab provinces, is characteristic of Chekhov's work. The characters conceal their depression behind false gaiety and self-deceit. His heroines, the three sisters, are bored, restless, and frustrated, not quite resigned to their mediocre existence. They talk constantly of a trip to Moscow, a journey longed for but never made. Today, Chekhov's plays suggest the dying world of Russia's out-of-touch ruling class, who were about to be swept away by the Marxist revolution of 1917.

An important Naturalistic writer in the United States was Kate Chopin (born Catherine O'Flaherty, 1851–1904), a short-story writer and novelist whose fiction reflected the general trend in nineteenth-century American literature away from Romanticism and toward Realism and Naturalism. A prevalent theme in Chopin's writings was a romantic awakening, usually by a female character. The setting for it was sketched out in **local color,** or regional details, and her method of tracking the action was Naturalistic—that is, she based plot twists on biological and socioeconomic factors. A St. Louis native, Chopin focused her stories and novels on **Creole** and **Cajun** life in Louisiana, a world that caught her imagination during a twelve-year-long marriage to a Creole planter and merchant.

The Awakening (1899) was Kate Chopin's masterpiece and the novel that abruptly ended her literary career, as she was stunned into silence by a hostile public reaction. A tale of adulterous passion, this novel is an American *Madame Bovary* (see Chapter 18). The story of Edna Pontellier, the Kentucky-born wife of a Creole husband, *The Awakening* explores a woman's passionate nature and its relation to self, marriage, and society. Edna rejects conventional morality, social duty, and personal obligations to her husband and children. She establishes her own home, earns money with her painting, accepts one lover, and pursues another. Ultimately, however, Edna's bid for freedom fails. She drowns herself—brought down by tradition, prejudice, and other societal pressures. Chopin's ending has been criticized for its shift to commonplace morality, but the novel nevertheless is an early attempt to deal with the issue of woman's liberation. More than a simple Naturalist, Chopin is hailed today as a precursor of Post-Modernism (see Chapter 21) because of her keen interest in marginal people and feminist themes.

Decadence in Literature   The Decadent movement began in France with Joris-Karl Huysmans [wees-MAHNS] (1848–1907), a follower of Zola's, who in 1884 broke with the social-documentary style of Naturalism and wrote the perverse novel *À rebours (Against Nature)*. Paris was astonished by this partly autobiographical work. In it, Huysmans presents an exotic hero, Des Esseintes, bristling with vivid eccentricity and neurotic feelings and yet filled with inexpressible spiritual yearnings. Des Esseintes, hating modern life for its vulgarity and materialism, creates a completely encapsulated, silent world where he cultivates affected pleasures. He collects plants whose very nature is to appear diseased. He stimulates his senses with unusual sounds, colors, and smells, orchestrating them to music so that he experiences a sensory overload. And, in a violent rejection of Classicism, he embraces the crude Latin works of late Rome.

In Great Britain, Oscar Wilde (1854–1900) was the center of the 1890s Decadent movement, with its generally relaxed view of morals and cynically amused approach to life (Figure 19.8). Like Huysmans, Wilde's own outrageous manner can scarcely be separated from his literary achievements. Dressed in velvet and carrying a lily as he sauntered down London's main streets, Wilde gained notoriety as an **aesthete**—one unusually sensitive to the beautiful in art, music, and literature—even before he achieved fame as a dramatist of witty comedies of manners, such as *The Importance of Being Earnest* (1895). Wilde's only novel, *The Picture of Dorian Gray* (1894), features a hero immersed in exotic pleasures and secret vices, his youth preserved while his portrait ages horribly.

Figure 19.8 AUBREY BEARDSLEY. *The Dancer's Reward* from "Salomé." 1894. Pen Drawing, 9 × 6½". Fogg Art Museum, Harvard University. *The visual counterpart to Wilde's decadent style in literature was Art Nouveau, especially as practiced by Aubrey Beardsley. Typical of his work is this black-and-white illustration for Wilde's play-poem* Salomé, *based on the biblical story of the dancer. In this print, depicting the climactic scene, Salomé grabs a lock of the hair of the beheaded John the Baptist, whose death she has ordered. With her left finger, she touches the blood as if to confirm that it is real. The device in the left corner of three vertical lines and three arrow- or heart-shaped forms is a signature adopted by Beardsley in 1893. The floral motif—the carnations on Salomé's cloak and at her throat—allude to Oscar Wilde's fondness for wearing flowers. Blending organic shapes and flowing lines with perverse themes, Beardsley's artificial style reveals Art Nouveau's affinity with an underworld of depravity.*

Today's most widely admired Decadent writer, the Frenchman Marcel Proust [PROOST] (1871–1922), made his appearance at the end of this period. Starting in 1913 and concluding in 1927, Proust published a series of seven autobiographical novels collectively entitled *À la recherche du temps perdu (Remembrance of Things Past)*. In this massive undertaking, he re-creates the world of upper bourgeois society that he had known as a young man but had deserted in 1903. Withdrawn into a cork-lined retreat reminiscent of Des Esseintes's silent hideaway in *À rebours*, Proust resurrected in the pages of his novels the aristocratic salons, the vulgar

bourgeois world, and the riffraff of mistresses, prostitutes, and rich homosexuals. Today, Proust's novels may be read in contradictory ways, as the supreme expression of a life lived for art or as the exemplification of a life empty of spiritual meaning.

Expressionist Literature Expressionism, the third of these styles, was the only one that did not originate in France. Instead, it arose in Scandinavia in the works of the Swedish playwright August Strindberg and in central Europe in the fiction of Franz Kafka. Strindberg (1849–1912), having first achieved fame through Naturalistic drama, shifted to an Expressionist style in the 1890s. *The Dream Play* (first produced in 1907) is typical of his Expressionist dramas in employing generic figures with symbolic, all-purpose names ("Daughter," "Father," and so on), shadowy plots, and absurd fancies. In *The Dream Play*, time and place become meaningless, as, for instance, when a lovesick soldier suddenly becomes old and shabby and his bouquet of flowers withers before the audience's eyes. Strindberg's innovative techniques were not meant to obscure his meaning but rather to initiate the public into new ways of seeing and understanding life.

The ultimate pioneer of Expressionism was Franz Kafka (1883–1924), whose strange, boldly symbolic stories question traditional concepts of reality. One of Kafka's most striking achievements is the short story *Metamorphosis* (1919), in which the hero awakens to discover that while asleep he has been transformed into a giant insect—a vivid image of an identity crisis and a gripping parable of what happens to a person who is suddenly perceived to be totally different from other people.

The Trial, a novel completed in 1914 and published in 1925, features a doomed main character with the generic name of Joseph K. An obscure minor government official, Joseph K. has his well-ordered world shattered when he is accused of a nameless crime. Unable to identify either his accusers or his misdeed and denied justice by the authorities, Joseph K. is eventually convicted by a mysterious court and executed by two bureaucrats in top hats. Kafka's faceless, powerless hero has become one of the most widely discussed figures of Modernism. In effect, Kafka has transformed his own alienation—as a German-speaking Jew from the Czech-speaking, Protestant section of predominantly Roman Catholic Austria—into a modern Everyman victimized by forces beyond human control (Figure 19.9).

The Advance of Science

Biology and chemistry, in particular, made rapid advances around the turn of the century. In biology, the

Figure 19.9 EDVARD MUNCH. *The Scream.* 1893. Oil on canvas, 36 × 29″. Nasjonalgalleriet, Oslo. *The Expressionists, whether writers, artists, or musicians, responded to the uncertainty of the modern world with images of despair, anxiety, and helplessness. The work of the Norwegian painter Edvard Munch provides a visual counterpart to the bleak and brooding plays of Strindberg and the terrifying stories of Kafka. Munch, whose paintings reflect a nightmarish vision of life as a tormented existence never free from pain, once said, "I hear the scream in nature." The Scream is a visual metaphor of modern alienation. The skullheaded, sexless figure, with mouth opened and hands over ears, seems to be ignored by the couple walking away in the background. Typical of Expressionism, Munch depicts the world as unnatural, as evidenced by the painting's swirling patterns of lines and colors.*

Austrian monk Gregor Johann Mendel (1822–1884) had summarized his groundbreaking research in 1865, but his findings, the basis for the new science of genetics, were ignored until three researchers, working independently, rediscovered his reports in 1900. By applying mathematics to biological theory, Mendel proved the existence of dominant and recessive traits, and using the laws of probability, he worked out the pattern for offspring over the generations. Subsequent research showed that Mendelian laws applied to virtually all animals and plants.

In chemistry, the outstanding development was radiochemistry, the study of radioactive materials. The founder of this new discipline was Marie Sklodowska Curie (1867–1934), a Polish physicist and the first scientist to be awarded two Nobel prizes. Working with her French husband, Pierre Curie (1859–1906), Madame Curie identified two new radioactive elements, polonium and radium. The isolation of radium stimulated research in atomic physics. Another contributor to radiochemistry was the German physicist Wilhelm Conrad Roentgen [RENT-guhn] (1845–1923), whose 1895 discovery of X rays led to their use in diagnostic medicine.

The discoveries in genetics and radiochemistry boosted the optimism and faith in progress that characterized this period, but developments in physics had the opposite effect, adding to the undercurrent of uncertainty and doubt that also existed. Three brilliant scientists—Max Planck, Niels Bohr, and Albert Einstein—launched a revolution that led other scientists to discard the previously accepted belief that Newton's laws of motion were universal.

Max Planck (1858–1947) laid the foundation for modern physics in 1900 with research in quantum theory. His research called into question the wave theory of radiation, which dated from the 1700s. Working with hot objects, Planck observed that the radiative energy that emanated from a heat source did not issue in a smooth wave but in discrete bursts. He measured each burst of radiation and computed a mathematical formula for expressing the released energy, a unit that he called a *quantum*—a word meaning a specified amount, derived from the Latin *quanta*, or "how much." When Planck could not fit his quantum formula into traditional wave-theory physics, he realized the revolutionary nature of his discovery. Planck's quantum theory became a primary building block in the speculation of the second of the trio, Danish physicist Niels Bohr.

Bohr (1885–1962) was the prime mover in solving the mystery of the structure of the atom. When he began his research, the ancient Greek idea of the indivisible atom had already been laid to rest. Scientists in the early 1900s had proved that each atom is a neutral body containing a positive nucleus with negatively charged particles called electrons. And one researcher had speculated that electrons orbit a nucleus in much the same way that the planets move around the sun—suggesting a correspondence with Newtonian theory.

Until Bohr's theory of atomic structure was set forth in 1912, however, no one could explain how these miniature solar systems actually worked. Bohr's solution was based on bold assumptions: that an electron could revolve about a nucleus only in certain privileged orbits and that when it was in these orbits, it did not emit radiation. He concluded that an electron radiated only when it leaped from orbit to orbit. Using

Planck's quantum theory, he called these leaps quantum jumps, referring to the amount of radiative energy released. Bohr's discovery had tremendous consequences, leading eventually to the development of nuclear energy for weaponry and electrical generation.

German-born Albert Einstein (1879–1955) also did important theoretical work in atomic physics, but his most significant research in the early twentieth century involved the relationship between time and space. Newton had maintained that there existed absolute rest and absolute velocity, absolute space and absolute time. Einstein asserted that the only absolute in the universe is the speed of light, which is the same for all observers. He concluded that all motion is relative and that concepts of absolute space and time are meaningless. If two systems move with relatively uniform motion toward each other, there exist two different spaces and two different times. He called this finding the special theory of relativity. This theory replaces Newtonian absolute space with a grid of light beams that in effect determines the meaning of space in each situation. Einstein's special theory was the first step in a reformulation of scientific concepts of space and time.

The Modernist Revolution in Art

After 1871 a revolution began in the arts and architecture whose aim was to replace Renaissance ideals with Modernist principles. Although there were many trends within this revolution, in painting and sculpture it generally meant a shift from an art that reflected the natural world to one rooted in the artist's inner vision, from an art based on representational or naturalistic images to one devoted to nonrepresentational or nonobjective forms, and from an art focused on content to one dedicated to the process of creation itself. By the time the revolution in painting and sculpture was complete, artists had given up realism and made **abstraction** their ideal. In architecture, the Modernist revolution was less radical, though architects slowly turned away from the forms of the Greco-Roman and Gothic styles and created functional buildings devoid of decoration.

Impressionism   The stylistic innovation in painting known as **Impressionism** began in the 1870s. In spite of owing much to Realism and even to Romanticism, this new style marked a genuine break with the realistic tradition that had dominated Western art since the fourteenth century. The Impressionists wanted to depict what they saw in nature, but they were inspired by the increasingly fast pace of modern life to portray transient moments. They concentrated on the play of light over objects, people, and nature, breaking up seemingly solid surfaces, stressing vivid contrasts between colors in sunlight and shade, and depicting reflected light in all its possibilities. Unlike earlier artists, they did not want to observe the world from indoors. They abandoned the studio, painting in the open air and recording spontaneous impressions of their subjects instead of making sketches outside and then moving indoors to complete the work from memory.

Some of the Impressionists' painting methods were influenced by technological advances. For example, the shift from the studio to the open air was made possible by the advent of cheap rail travel, which permitted easy access to the countryside or seashore, and by the discovery of chemical dyes and oils that allowed paint to be kept in tubes that the artists could carry with them.

Although Impressionism was a product of industrial society, it was at the same time indebted to the past. From Realism the Impressionist painters learned to find beauty in the everyday world. From the Barbizon painters (a group of French landscape painters active in the mid–nineteenth century) they took the practice of painting in the open air. From the Romantics they borrowed the techniques of "broken color"— splitting up complex colors into their basic hues—and of using subtle color shadings to create a shimmering surface effect (see Chapter 18).

Impressionism acquired its name not from supporters but from angry art lovers who felt threatened by the new painting. The term *Impressionism* was born in 1874, when a group of artists organized an exhibition of their paintings. Reaction from the public and the press was immediate, and derisive. Among the 165 paintings exhibited was *Impression: Sunrise,* by Claude Monet [moh-NAY] (1840–1926). Viewed through hostile eyes, Monet's painting of a rising sun over a misty, watery scene seemed messy, slapdash, and an affront to good taste (Figure 19.10). Borrowing Monet's title, art critics extended the term *Impressionism* to the entire exhibit. In response, Monet and his twenty-nine fellow artists in the exhibit adopted the name as a badge of their unity, despite individual differences. From then until 1886, Impressionism had all the zeal of a "church," as the painter Renoir put it. The Impressionists gave eight art shows. Monet was faithful to the Impressionist creed until his death, although many of the others moved on to new styles.

Monet wanted to re-create the optical sensations he experienced. Rejecting traditional content, he focused on light and atmosphere, simulating the visual effects of fog, haze, or mist over a landscape and, most especially, over water. That this approach succeeded so well shows the harmony between Monet's scientific

Figure 19.10 CLAUDE MONET. *Impression: Sunrise.* 1872. Oil on canvas, 19½ × 25½". Musée Marmottan, Paris. *Monet's* Impression: Sunrise *illustrates the immediacy of Impressionism. From his window overlooking Le Havre harbor, he painted what he recorded in a letter to a friend: "sun in the mist and a few masts of boats sticking up in the foreground." The artist has transformed the substantial world of nature into fragmented daubs of broken color.*

eye and painterly hand. His studies of changing light and atmosphere, whether depicting haystacks, the Rouen cathedral, or water lilies (Figure 19.11), demonstrate Monet's lifelong devotion to Impressionism.

Unlike Monet, Auguste Renoir [REN-wahr] (1841–1919) did not remain faithful to the Impressionist movement. In the early 1880s, personal and aesthetic motives led him to move away from Impressionism and exhibit in the official Salon (when he could get his work accepted). In his modified style, he shifted from a soft-focus image to a concentration on form, a move that brought quick support from art critics and wealthy patrons.

Painted about the time of his break with Impressionism, *The Luncheon of the Boating Party* demonstrates Renoir's splendid mastery of form (Figure 19.12). Its subject is a carefree summer outing on a restaurant terrace on an island in the Seine, the company being composed of the painter's friends, including fellow artists, a journalist, the cafe owner, and an actress. *The Boating Party* shows that Renoir had not given up—nor would he ever—his Impressionist ties, for his stress in this work on the fleeting, pleasure-filled moment was basic to the style, as was his use of broken color in a natural background. Nevertheless, what remained central to Renoir's creed were the foreground figures, treated clearly and with substance.

In contrast to Monet and Renoir, whose careers bloomed in poverty, Berthe Morisot [mohr-ee-ZOH]

(1841–1895) was a member of the upper middle class. Her wealth and artistic connections—Fragonard was her grandfather and Manet her brother-in-law—allowed her to apply herself to painting and play an important role in the founding of the Impressionist school. In her work, she focused on atmosphere and the play of light on the human form, although she never sacrificed her subjects to the cause of color alone. Her subjects were modern life, though limited to the confined world of domestic interiors and gardens (Figure 19.13).

A few Americans also made significant contributions to Impressionism. The most important of them was Mary Cassatt [kuh-SAT] (1845–1926), a young woman who joined the Impressionist circle while studying painting in Paris. Cassatt was from a prosperous, well-connected Philadelphia family, and it is largely through her social ties that Impressionist painting was introduced to America. She suggested to her wealthy friends that this art was worth collecting, and some of the most notable Impressionist works in American museums are there because of her influence.

Cassatt, however, was not devoted exclusively to Impressionism. Like other artists of this era, she was fascinated by Japanese prints from French collections that were on exhibit in Paris in 1890, and she was the first to imitate all aspects, including color, of the *ukiyo-e* [U-kee-oy] prints—the woodcuts that had developed

Figure 19.11 CLAUDE MONET. *Water Lilies.* Ca. 1920. Oil on canvas, 16′ × 5′ 15/16″. Carnegie Museum of Art, Pittsburgh. Acquired through the generosity of Mrs. Alan M. Scaife. *Knowledgeable about the art market and determined to escape a life of poverty, Monet produced nonthreatening works that appealed to conservative middle-class collectors. For these patrons, he painted natural scenes, such as water lilies, that evoked pleasant memories of simple rural values. Begun in 1899, the water lily series occupied him for the rest of his life. Setting up his easel in his splendid garden at Giverny and working at different times of the day, Monet captured the effect of changing sunlight on this beloved subject.*

◀ **Figure 19.12** AUGUSTE RENOIR. *The Luncheon of the Boating Party.* 1881. Oil on canvas, 51 × 68". The Phillips Collection, Washington, D.C. *Renoir's return to traditional values is reflected in this vivid painting. He uses the restaurant's terrace to establish conventional perspective, the left railing forming a diagonal line that runs into the distance. He balances the composition, weaving the young men and women into a harmonious ensemble, painting some standing and others sitting. He also employs colors effectively, using orange, blue, and black to offset the expanses of white in the tablecloth and the men's shirts and women's blouses.*

Figure 19.13 BERTHE MORISOT. *Laundresses Hanging Out the Wash.* 1875. Oil on canvas, 13 × 16". National Gallery of Art, Washington, D.C. Collection of Mr. and Mrs. Paul Mellon. *Morisot's* Laundresses Hanging Out the Wash, *shown with the Impressionists in 1876, was praised by critics for its clarity of color and handling of light. It depicts, from a high vantage point, a group of commercial washerwomen hanging out laundry in a garden. Morisot was one of the few Impressionists to depict urban workers, because, in rapidly urbanizing France, artists nostalgically focused on farm laborers at their tasks. Typical of her art, she emphasizes the flatness of the picture plane, which is unlike the three-dimensionality of paintings such as Renoir's* The Luncheon of the Boating Party *(see Figure 19.12). Her vigorous brushwork, making the painting difficult to decipher, gives a feeling of immediacy—the aim of Impressionist art.*

ENCOUNTER

The French Impressionists Meet Ukiyo-e *Art*

Europeans, except for the Dutch, lost access to Japan in 1638, when Japan's military ruler, the shōgun, closed the country to foreigners. For the next 225 years, the Dutch colony on Deshima, an island in Nagasaki harbor, operated as Japan's window on the world, conducting from there a highly regulated but lucrative two-way trade. The Dutch also kept Japan up-to-date on selected developments in the West through the import of scientific books and art prints. Japan's isolationist policy began to change in 1853, in response to American gunboats demanding trade relations. At first, five ports were opened; others soon followed.

With trade renewed, Japanese culture flowed into the West. Especially impressive were woodblock prints, or *ukiyo-e* [U-kee-oy] ("pictures of the floating world")—then unknown in the West. Executed at first in black and white, *ukiyo-e* prints entered a golden age with the introduction of color in about 1770. When

these prints reached Europe, their simple design and bold colors fascinated the Impressionist and Post-Impressionist painters.

Numerous artists, including Édouard Manet, Claude Monet, Pierre Renoir, Mary Cassatt (see Figure 19.14), Paul Cézanne, and Paul Gauguin, played with Japanese motifs in their works, but Vincent van Gogh had the greatest affinity with the *ukiyo-e* prints. Van Gogh especially admired and collected the prints of Ando Hiroshige (1797–1858), with their flat areas of pure color and figures drawn with a few wispy lines. Hiroshige's *Rain Shower over Ōhashi Bridge* inspired van Gogh's oil painting *The Bridge in the Rain,* one of three studies he made of Japanese prints. Van Gogh did more than "copy" the print; he transformed it by heightening the color contrasts and adding a decorative border. Learning from his *ukiyo-e* studies, van Gogh forged his own unique style of painting, thus establishing a link between Japanese and Western art.

Encounter figure 19.1   ANDŌ HIROSHIGE. *Rain Shower over Ōhashi Bridge.* Ca. 1857. Woodcut. Hiroshige created a new genre, the travelogue print, based on sketches made on the spot, in all weathers and at different times of day. *Rain Shower over Ōhashi Bridge* is from the series *One Hundred Famous Views of Edo.* He boldly crops the composition, shows the human figures dwarfed by the setting, and uses unusual perspective—typical features of his art.

Encounter figure 19.2   VINCENT VAN GOGH. *The Bridge in the Rain (after Hiroshige).* 1887. Oil on canvas. Van Gogh Museum, Amsterdam (Vincent van Gogh Foundation). This painting shows the lessons van Gogh learned by copying Hiroshige's *ukiyo-e* print: strong, dark color to outline figures, bold color contrasts, cropping of the composition, and dramatic perspective. Van Gogh made these techniques his own in his later works.

in Japan in the 1600s—as in *The Bath,* or *The Tub* (about 1891; Figure 19.14). A mother and child was a typical subject in Cassatt's art.

Post-Impressionism The rebellious, experimental spirit instilled by the Impressionists had freed art from the tyranny of a single style. Artists now moved in many directions, united only by a common desire to extend the boundaries of Impressionism. This ambition signified the triumph of the Modernist notion that art must constantly change in order to reflect new historical conditions—the opposite of the Classical ideal of eternal truths. Impressionism was succeeded by **Post-Impressionism** (1886–1900), whose four most important artists are Georges Seurat, Paul Cézanne, Paul Gauguin, and Vincent van Gogh.

Like the Impressionists, Georges Seurat [suh-RAH] (1859–1891) painted the ordinary pleasures of Parisian life in a sunlit atmosphere, but his way of doing so was formulaic and theoretical, markedly different from the approach of, say, Monet. After studying scientific color theory, Seurat developed a technique known as **Pointillism** (or Divisionism), which meant applying to the canvas thousands of tiny dots of pure color juxtaposed in such a way that, when viewed from the proper distance, they merged to form a natural, harmonious effect of color, light, and shade. His most famous Pointillist work is *A Sunday Afternoon on the Island of La Grande Jatte* (Figure 19.15), an affectionate, good-humored look at Parisians enjoying themselves. The technique may be novel and "scientific," but the composition is Classical and serene, with carefully placed and balanced figures and repeated curved shapes, visible in the umbrellas, hats, and other objects. Seurat's style led to a minor school of painters, but his influence was overshadowed by that of Cézanne.

Paul Cézanne [say-ZAN] (1839–1906), a pivotal figure in Western art, was the prophet of abstraction in Post-Impressionism and a precursor of Cubism. With Édouard Manet, he is one of the founders of modern painting. He had exhibited with the original Impressionist group in 1874 but by 1878 had rejected the movement because its depiction of nature lacked substance and weight. He sought a new way to portray nature so as to reveal its underlying solidity and order. After experimentation, Cézanne concluded that nature was composed of such geometric forms as cylinders, spheres, cubes, and cones. By trying to reveal this idea in his works, he opened up a new way of painting that has influenced art to the present day.

Cézanne's greatest works came after 1886, when he left Paris for his quiet home in Aix-en-Provence in southern France. Among his favorite subjects was the nearby mountain Mont Sainte-Victoire (Figure 19.16). Like many of his later works, *Mont Sainte-Victoire*

Figure 19.14 MARY CASSATT. *The Bath.* Ca. 1891. Soft-ground etching with aquatint and drypoint on paper, 12⅜ × 8⅞″. National Museum of Women in the Arts, Washington, D.C. *This Cassatt print, in Japanese-inspired style, symbolizes the globalization of Western culture that was well under way in Early Modernism. The first of ten prints in a series, it is the only one that could be called a true imitation. It uses simple design, Japanese spatial pattern, flat areas of color, and a hint of Japanese facial features to create a Western version of a* ukiyo-e *print—except that it is made on a metal plate and not a woodblock. In the rest of this series, Cassatt adopted a more Western style, notably adding a complete background, such as wallpaper and windows. Her interest in Japanese prints coincided with Gauguin's experiments (see Figure 19.17) with Tahitian-inspired art; both are forerunners of Post-Modernism.*

points toward abstraction but never quite gives up representation. Amid the dense geometric forms in the picture's lower half, house shapes peek through daubs of green foliage, reminding the viewer that this is a realistic landscape. Later artists, such as Kandinsky and Malevich, took up Cézanne's challenge of telescoping the two-dimensional and the three-dimensional and created the first truly abstract paintings, the most visible signs of twentieth-century art (see Chapter 20).

The Post-Impressionist Paul Gauguin [go-GAN] (1848–1903) began the movement known as **primitivism** —the term used to describe the West's fascination with non-Western culture as well as pre-Renaissance art. Gauguin's eccentric personal life also made him a

Figure 19.15 GEORGES SEURAT. *A Sunday Afternoon on the Island of La Grande Jatte.*
1884–1886. Oil on canvas, 6'9" × 10'1". Art Institute of Chicago. Helen Birch Bartlett
Memorial Collection, 1926. *Unlike most Impressionists, Seurat worked slowly and
methodically. In the case of* La Grande Jatte, *he spent years organizing the canvas and then
painting the thousands of dots required by the Pointillist technique. Such painstaking attention to
detail was necessary to achieve the harmonious effect his finished paintings demonstrate.*

Figure 19.16 PAUL CÉZANNE. *Mont Sainte-Victoire.*
1904–1906. Oil on canvas, 28⅞ × 36¼". Philadelphia
Museum of Art. George W. Elkins Collection. *Although
Cézanne was the founder of the Post-Impressionist movement that
culminated in abstraction, he had a conservative approach to art.
He wanted to create paintings that had the solidity of the art in the
museums, especially the works of the seventeenth-century painter
Nicolas Poussin. Hence, Cézanne continued to rely on line and
geometric arrangement as well as on color and light, simplifying
his paintings into austere images of order and peaceful color. In
this painting of Mont Sainte-Victoire—visible from his studio in
Aix-en-Provence—Cézanne's closeness to abstract art may be
seen. The distant mountain has a solid presence, but the houses,
foliage, fields, and road disappear into a set of ambiguous forms
and color planes. Cézanne's handling of the color planes, with
their jagged edges and abrupt juxtapositions, inspired the Cubists
to search for a new way to represent the world.*

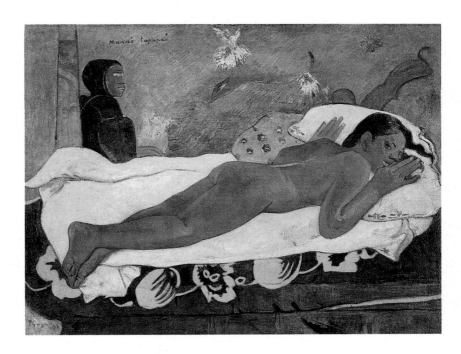

Figure 19.17 PAUL GAUGUIN. *Manao Tupapau: The Spirit of the Dead Watching.* 1892. Oil on burlap mounted on canvas, 28½ × 36⅜″. Albright-Knox Art Gallery, Buffalo. A. Conger Goodyear Collection, 1965. *Gauguin wrote of this painting that he wanted to convey the presence of* tupapau, *or the Spirit of the Dead, as envisioned by the young girl on the bed. He implies her fear through the mixture of the yellow, purple, and blue colors; by the sparks of light, or phosphorescences, which symbolize the spirits of the dead; and by the ghost depicted as an old woman in the left background. He felt it necessary "to make very simple paintings, with primitive, childlike themes" and to use "a minimum of literary means" in order for western Europeans to understand how Tahitians viewed life and death.*

legendary figure of Modernism. Rejecting the comforts of Parisian bourgeois life, he abandoned his career and his family and exiled himself to the French colony of Tahiti, living a decadent, bohemian existence.

Before moving to the South Pacific, Gauguin lived and painted among Breton peasants. He developed a personal style that favored flattened shapes and bright colors and avoided conventional perspective and modeling. He also became interested in non-Western, "primitive" religions, and many of his Tahitian works refer to indigenous beliefs and practices, as in *Manao Tupapau: The Spirit of the Dead Watching* (Figure 19.17). When exhibited in Paris, this painting created an uproar, for Western audiences were not accustomed to seeing dark-skinned nudes in art, and certainly not presented reclining on a bed, a customary pose for female nudes since the Renaissance (see Figure 16.7). Furthermore, the seated ghost at the left was a direct challenge to a secular worldview. Today, Gauguin's role in art has been reevaluated. He is now honored for his introduction of other cultural traditions into Western art, which enriched its vocabulary, and for his expressive use of color.

With the Post-Impressionist Vincent van Gogh [van GO] (1853–1890), the tradition of Expressionism began to emerge in Western art, although he was not part of any of the various Expressionist schools of painters. "Expressionism" in his case meant that the work of art served as a vehicle for his private emotions to an unprecedented degree. Van Gogh sometimes allowed his moods to determine what colors to use and how to apply paint to canvas, a principle that led to a highly idiosyncratic style. Van Gogh's life was filled with

misfortune, and even his painting had little recognition in his lifetime. In his early years, he was rebuffed in his efforts to do missionary work among poverty-stricken Belgian coal miners. All his attempts at friendship ended in failure, including a celebrated episode in the south of France with the painter Gauguin. Throughout his life, overtures to women resulted in utter humiliation. In the end, he became mentally unstable and committed suicide.

From his personal pain he created a memorably expressive style, however. Rejecting the smooth look of traditional painting and stirred by the colorful canvases of the Impressionists, he sometimes applied raw pigments with his palette knife or fingers instead of with a brush. His slashing strokes and brilliant colors often mirrored his mental states, giving the viewer a glimpse into his volatile personality. For instance, his *Self-Portrait with a Gray Hat* is dominated by shades of blue, suggesting his profound melancholy (Figure 19.18). The anguish in his eyes is reinforced by the vortex of color framing the head and the deep facial lines.

The most memorable of van Gogh's paintings is *The Starry Night* (Figure 19.19). Executed in the last year of van Gogh's life, the painting depicts a tranquil village under an agitated sky filled with pulsating stars, an unnatural crescent moon, and whirling rivers of light. Intensifying the strange imagery is the grove of cypress trees (left foreground), rendered in the shape of flames. The ensemble of convoluted shapes and bold colors expresses the artist's inner turmoil. In a sense, van Gogh's works constitute his psychological signature; his style is perhaps the most easily recognizable one in Western art.

Figure 19.18 VINCENT VAN GOGH. *Self-Portrait with a Gray Hat.* 1887. Oil on canvas, 17¼ × 14¾". Vincent van Gogh Foundation/National Museum Vincent van Gogh, Amsterdam. *Van Gogh's self-absorption is reflected in the thirty-six self-portraits he painted during his eleven-year artistic career. Anguished and prone to mental breakdown, he must have found a measure of reassurance in recording the subtle changes in his own countenance. A constant in all his likenesses is the haunted eyes, showing the inner torment from which he could never quite escape. The very execution of this work demonstrates van Gogh's passionate mood, as in the aggressive brushstrokes that congeal into a radiating pattern of energy lines covering the painting's surface.*

Fauvism, Cubism, and Expressionism The preeminence of Paris as the hub of Western culture was enhanced by the arrival of Henri Matisse and Pablo Picasso in about 1900. These innovative and prolific artists emerged as the leaders of the pre–World War I generation, later dominating the art world in the twentieth century in much the same way that Ingres and Delacroix had in the nineteenth century.

Henri Matisse [ma-TEES] (1869–1954) rose to fame in 1905 as a leader of **Fauvism.** The Fauves—French for "wild beasts," a name their detractors gave to them—were a group of loosely aligned painters who exhibited together. Matisse's work, like that of his colleagues, stemmed from the tradition of van Gogh, with color as its overriding concern. In *Open Window,*

Figure 19.19 VINCENT VAN GOGH. *The Starry Night.* 1889. Oil on canvas, 29 × 36¼" (73.7 × 92.1 cm). The Museum of Modern Art, New York. Acquired through the Lillie P. Bliss Bequest. Photograph © 1997 The Museum of Modern Art, New York. *Van Gogh's* The Starry Night *is a stunning symbol of the unstable world of Early Modernism. The whirling, luminous sky, formed with wild patches of color and tormented brushstrokes, reflects the psychic disturbance of the painter— an early example of Expressionist art. But van Gogh was more than an artist beset by personal demons; he wanted to follow Delacroix (see Chapters 17 and 18) and depict nature, using color and drawing, without slavishly copying reality. In van Gogh—as in his contemporary, the philosopher Nietzsche—psychic turmoil and artistic vision were virtually inseparable.*

Figure 19.20 HENRI MATISSE. *Open Window, Collioure*. 1905. Oil on canvas, 21¾ × 18⅛". Courtesy Mrs. John Hay Whitney, New York. *Like van Gogh, Matisse resisted quiet surface effects, preferring the look of paint applied in thick daubs and strips of varying length. His dazzling optical art was created by his use and placement of vibrant colors. In this painting, Matisse interprets the glorious view from his studio overlooking the Mediterranean.*

Collioure, Matisse paints a kaleidoscope of colors—pinks, mauves, bluish greens, bright reds, oranges, and purples—that do not derive from the direct observation of nature but from the artist's belief that color harmonies can control the composition (Figure 19.20). The colors are "arbitrary" in the sense that they bear little resemblance to what one would actually see from the window, but they are far from arbitrary in their relation to one another—which is what interests Matisse.

Pablo Picasso [pih-KAH-so] (1881–1973), a talented young Spanish painter, was attracted to Paris's avant-garde art community in about 1900. In 1907 he proved his genius with *Les Demoiselles d'Avignon (The Young Ladies of Avignon)*, perhaps the most influential painting of the twentieth century (Figure 19.21). This revolutionary work moved painting close to abstraction—the realization of Cézanne's dream. An unfinished work, *Les Demoiselles* reflects the multiple influences operating on Picasso at the time—the primitivism of African masks, the geometric forms of Cézanne, and the ancient sculpture of pre-Roman Spain. Despite its radical methods, this painting still has a conventional composition: five figures with a still life in the foreground. Nevertheless, with this painting Picasso redirected objective art

beyond abstraction and into the development of nonobjective painting—thus overturning a standard founded in the Renaissance.

Les Demoiselles was the prelude to **Cubism,** one of the early-twentieth-century styles leading Western art toward abstraction. With his French colleague Georges Braque [BRAHK] (1882–1963), Picasso developed Cubism. This style of painting, which went through different phases at the hands of different artists, basically fragments three-dimensional objects and reassembles them in a pattern that stresses their geometric structure and the relationships of these basic geometric forms. Braque and Picasso worked so closely together that their paintings could sometimes not be separately identified, even, it is said, by the artists themselves. An example of Picasso's Cubist style is *Man with a Hat* (also known as *Portrait of Braque*) (Figure 19.22). With Cubism, Picasso gave up Renaissance space completely, representing the subject from multiple angles simultaneously and shaping the figures into geometric designs. He also added a new feature to Cubism when he applied bits and pieces of other objects to the canvas, a technique called **collage** (French for "pasting"). Collage nudged Cubism closer to pure abstraction; the flat

Figure 19.21 PABLO PICASSO. *Les Demoiselles d'Avignon. (The Young Ladies of Avignon.)* Paris (June–July 1907). Oil on canvas, 8′ × 7′8″ (243.9 × 233.7 cm). The Museum of Modern Art, New York. Acquired through the Lillie P. Bliss Bequest. Photograph © 1997 The Museum of Modern Art, New York. *This painting's title derives from Picasso's native Barcelona, where Avignon Street ran through the red-light district. First intended as a moral work warning of the dangers of venereal disease (the figures still show provocative poses), the painting evolved over the months, changing as Picasso's horizons expanded. That he left the painting unfinished—like a scientist's record of a failed laboratory experiment—illustrates a leading trait of Modernism, the belief that truth is best expressed in the artistic process itself.*

plane of the painting's surface was now simply a two-dimensional showcase for objects.

Although Paris remained the capital of Western art, other cities were also the scene of aesthetic experiment. Oslo, Munich, Vienna, and Dresden became artistic meccas, especially for Expressionist painters who followed the path opened by van Gogh and the Fauves.

In Munich, for example, Expressionism led to the formation of an international school of artists known as Der Blaue Reiter (The Blue Rider), named after a painting of the same name. Rejecting the importance of artistic content and refusing to paint "safe" objects, this group of painters concentrated on basics such as color and line, which were meant to express inner feelings. Founded by

Figure 19.22 PABLO PICASSO. *Man with a Hat.* (Also known as *Portrait of Braque.*) Paris (after December 3, 1912). Pasted paper, charcoal and ink on paper, 24 × 19⅝″ (62.2 × 47.3 cm). The Museum of Modern Art, New York. Purchase. Photograph © 1997 The Museum of Modern Art, New York. *This image alludes to the close working relationship between Picasso and Braque. Whether the portrait is of Braque is debatable, especially since Picasso denied it. He claimed he worked without a model and added, "Braque and I [later] pretended it was his portrait." This anecdote forcibly stresses the point that Picasso and Braque, the founders of Cubism, were less interested in content than in creating a new visual reality through nontraditional means.*

Figure 19.23 WASSILY KANDINSKY. *Improvisation 33 for "Orient."* 1913. Oil on canvas, 34¾ × 39¼". Stedelijk Museum, Amsterdam. *Kandinsky's radical Expressionism rested on the Romantic idea that serious art can function as a substitute for religion; the artist serves as a sort of "priest" who, through mystical insight, can tap into the divine. In 1912 he published his aesthetic beliefs in the treatise* Concerning the Spiritual in Art, *which became a fundamental text for modern artists. Later abstract artists, such as Robert Rauschenberg (see Chapter 21), ridiculed this theory as pretentious and showed that a nonrepresentational art that has no meaning outside itself is possible.*

the Russian exile Wassily Kandinsky [kan-DIN-skee] (1866–1944) in 1911, this school made the first breakthrough to abstract art—nonrepresentational or nonobjective paintings that defy any sense of reality or connection to nature and are, as the artist himself put it, "largely unconscious, spontaneous expressions of inner character, nonmaterial in nature." Kandinsky's "improvisations," as he labeled them, were free forms, possessing no objective content, consisting only of meandering lines and amorphous blobs of color (Figure 19.23). For all their seeming randomness, however, his paintings were planned to look that way. He consciously worked out the placement of the lines and the choices of color, leaving nothing to chance. He also linked the fluidity of painting with the lyricism of music, a connection suggested in this work by the meandering lines.

New Directions in Sculpture and Architecture Few sculptors of any consequence appeared in the 1871–1914 period and only one genius: Auguste Rodin [roh-DAN] (1840–1917). Rejecting the static Classicism of the mid–nineteenth century, Rodin forged an eclectic style that blended Romantic subject matter, Renaissance simplicity, and Gothic angularity with the radical changes under way in painting. In the sculpture *Eve* (Figure 19.24), he created a rough Gothic effect using modern means, torturing the surface, especially of the stomach and the head. The result was both Impressionistic (the play of light on the scored surfaces) and Expressionistic (the traces of Rodin's fingers on the

bronze medium, which so dramatically suggest the intensity of the artist's involvement).

Having lagged behind the other arts for most of the century, architecture began to catch up in the 1880s. The United States led the way, notably in the works of the Chicago School. The skyscraper, perfected by Chicago-based architects, became synonymous with Modernism and modern life. Unlike Modernist painting and sculpture, the new architecture arose for practical reasons: dense populations and soaring real estate values.

Using the aesthetic dictum that "form follows function," the Chicago School solved design problems without relying on past techniques and traditions. This dictum means that a building ought to be a workable organism where the pressure of daily existence is channeled into a harmonious, functioning whole; in practical terms, the pressure is called function, the resultant building, form. The author of this dictum, Louis Sullivan (1856–1924), produced a masterly example of the Chicago School's style in the Guaranty Building in Buffalo, New York, a structure whose steel frame is covered by a skin of stone and glass (Figure 19.25). Sullivan's imprint can be seen in the way he allows the building to speak for itself: The plan of the exterior skin reflects the internal steel skeleton in the thin, continuous piers between the windows that rise from the base to the rounded arches at the top. The effect of this organization is to turn the building's exterior into a grid, a visual expression of the structural frame underneath. Although Sullivan rejected the rich ornamentation of

Figure 19.24 AUGUSTE RODIN. *Eve.* 1881. Bronze, ht. 67″. Rodin Museum, Philadelphia Museum of Art. *This life-size statue of Eve was originally conceived as half a pair, with Adam, to flank* The Gates of Hell, *Rodin's masterpiece, loosely based on Dante's* Inferno *(see Chapter 9). The figure of Eve owed much to Michelangelo's expressive forms, particularly that of Eve in* The Expulsion from the Garden of Eden *on the Sistine Chapel ceiling. Reflecting her dual roles as first mother and coauthor of original sin, Rodin's Eve is both voluptuous (beautiful face and curvaceous form) and ashamed (face averted and, in gestures of modesty, arms shielding breasts and left leg raised).*

the nineteenth-century Gothic as well as the balanced decorations of Classicism, he nevertheless devised his own decorative scheme, which may be seen in the vertical and horizontal elements, for example, and the spaces (blocks) between the windows.

Sullivan defined the public building for the twentieth century, and his disciple Frank Lloyd Wright (1869–1959) did the same for domestic architecture in about 1910. In the Victorian era, architects had discovered that the middle-class demand for comfortable, spacious housing was an excellent source of income. This same class of patrons continued to demand well-built homes, and for them Wright created a new type of dwelling he called "organic," a term he coined to describe a building that was constructed of local woods and stone and therefore harmonized with the physical environment. Although unconventional in his own life, he was rather a romantic about his bourgeois patrons. To strengthen domestic values, he planned houses that encouraged the inhabitants to identify with the natural surroundings; his structures also broke down the typical reliance on fixed interior walls to encourage fluid family relationships and a free flow of traffic. In time, Wright's style became standard for progressive architects throughout the United States, expressed in the exterior in strong horizontal lines, overhanging eaves, banks of windows, and a minimum of decorative detail (Figure 19.26).

Music: From Impressionism to Jazz

Richard Wagner died in 1883 (see Chapter 18), but in certain respects he is the commanding musical presence in Early Modernism. Most composers were either utilizing in their own way the harmonic advances he had made, working out the implications of those advances, or reacting to his influence by elaborately rejecting it. For example, a musical style influenced by Wagner was Impressionism, which was in part inspired by his shimmering, constantly alternating chords. The Impressionist composers did not stay under his tutelage, however. Where Wagner was philosophical and literary, seeking to fuse all the arts, the Impressionists explored sound for its own sake. Like Impressionist painters, Impressionist composers thought that all moments—no matter how real—were fleeting and fragmentary, and their musical compositions illustrated this principle. Their music, without conventional thematic development or dramatic buildup and release, often sounds veiled or amorphous when compared with the music of, for example, Haydn.

Claude Debussy [duh-byoo-SEE] (1862–1918), a French composer, founded the Impressionist style. He

Figure 19.25 Louis Sullivan. Guaranty Building, Buffalo. 1895. © Wayne Andrews/Esto. *Purity became an identifying characteristic of Modernist style. It was apparent in Matisse's color experiments, in Picasso's abstract Cubist forms, and even in the Expressionist goal of unvarnished truth. In architecture, Louis Sullivan introduced the purity principal with his artistic credo that "form follows function."*

created constantly shifting colors and moods through such musical methods as gliding chords and chromatic scales derived from non-Western sources. Debussy's music represents the climax of the nineteenth-century interest in programmatic titles, large orchestras, rich chords, and relatively free rhythms and forms.

One of Debussy's programmatic works, *Prélude à l'après-midi d'un faune (Prelude to the Afternoon of a Faun)* (1894) is generally recognized as the first Impressionist orchestral masterpiece. This work is a sensuous confection of blurred sounds and elusive rhythms. To achieve its mood of reverie, Debussy used a meandering musical line played by a soulful solo flute, backed by muted strings and delicately voiced brasses and woodwinds.

Impressionist music produced a second major voice in France during this period: Maurice Ravel [ruh-VEL] (1875–1937), a composer loosely indebted to Debussy. Unlike Debussy, Ravel had a taste for the clear structure of Classical musical forms as well as established

dance forms. Perhaps the most Impressionistic of Ravel's compositions is *Jeux d'eau (Fountains)* (1901), a programmatic work for piano marked by sounds evoking sparkling and splashing water. Even before the writing of *Jeux d'eau*, Ravel's Classical inclinations were evident in *Pavane pour une infante defunte (Pavane for a Dead Princess)* (1899), a work for piano with a melancholy quality; here, the music captured the stately rhythm of the Baroque **pavane,** an English court dance of Italian origin. Dance also inspired Ravel's *Valses nobles et sentimentales (Waltzes Noble and Sentimental)* (1911), a work for piano based on the waltzes of Schubert (see Chapter 17) and the Parisian ballrooms of the 1820s, and *La Valse (The Waltz)* (1920), an orchestral work that is a sardonic homage to the waltzes of nineteenth-century Vienna. Ravel's best-known work, *La Valse* is in actuality an embittered metaphor in which the increasingly discordant sounds of the music represent the forces that generated the catastrophe of World War I.

Figure 19.26 FRANK LLOYD WRIGHT. W. W. Willits House. 1902. Highland Park, Illinois. Copyright © Chicago Historical Society. *Between 1900 and 1910, Wright introduced his "prairie houses," named for the* Ladies Home Journal *article (1901) in which their designs first appeared. The Willits house, built in an affluent Chicago suburb, is a fine example of this Midwestern American style that became a model for domestic buildings all over the United States. Laid out in a cruciform shape, this dwelling has a central chimney core. The style's strong focus on horizontal lines, resulting in shifting planes of light across the facade, may be compared to the multiple perspectives of Cubism, the parallel development in painting.*

A trend in opposition to Wagner was Expressionism, which developed simultaneously with Expressionist art in Vienna. Drawing on the insights of Freudian psychology, musical Expressionism offered a distorted view of the world, focusing on anguish and pain. Its most striking feature was its embrace of **atonality,** a type of music without major or minor keys. To the listener, atonal music sounds discordant and even disturbing, because it offers no harmonious frame of reference. It is characterized by wide leaps from one tone to another, melody fragments, interrupted rhythms, and violent contrasts. Rejecting traditional forms, Expressionist composers made experimentation central to their musical vision.

The founder and leader of the Expressionist school was Arnold Schoenberg [SHUHN-burg] (1874–1951), who gave up a Wagnerian style in about 1907 and moved toward atonality. At first, Schoenberg employed traditional musical forms, as in the Second String Quartet (1908), although no string quartet had ever sounded like his dissonant creation. Scored without a designated key and filled with snatches of melody, this work offered the listener no recognizable frame of reference. Violinists were required on occasion to play the most extreme notes of which their instruments were capable.

Besides traditional forms, Schoenberg also established a favorite compositional method of Expressionism: setting a literary text to music and following its changes in character and feeling. An influential example of Expressionist music with text was *Pierrot lunaire (Moonstruck Pierrot)* (1912), based on poems by a Belgian writer and scored for chamber quintet and voice. Though Schoenberg downplayed the source text's importance, the music's violent shifts and prevailing discord clearly complement the alienated psychology and shocking language of the text. Instead of conventionally singing the text, the solo vocalist declaims or chants the text by combining speech and song.

Pierrot lunaire represents the extreme of Schoenberg's Expressionism before World War I. This work made him one of the two most highly respected composers of Early Modernism. Unwilling to rest on his laurels, he continued to experiment with innovative musical techniques (see Chapter 20).

The other outstanding twentieth-century musical genius active during this period was the Russian Igor Stravinsky [struh-VIN-skee] (1882–1971). Untouched by Wagnerism but attuned to the revolutionary events unfolding in the arts and in literature, Stravinsky acquired his reputation at about the same time as Schoenberg. In 1913 Stravinsky wrote the music for *The Rite of Spring,* a ballet produced by Sergei Diaghilev [dee-AHG-uh-lef] (1872–1929) for the Ballets Russes in Paris. Stravinsky's music and the ballet's choreography tapped into the theme of primitivism in art that was currently the rage in the French capital. Stravinsky's pounding rhythms evoke a pagan ritual, using abrupt meter changes, a hypnotic beat, and furious **syncopation,** the musical technique of accenting a weak beat when a strong beat is expected. The "savage" music coupled with the erotic dancing created a scandal that made Stravinsky the leading avant-garde composer in the world. Despite his innovative rhythms, Stravinsky was no relentless experimenter. After World War I, Stravinsky, though touched by Modernism's influences, became the head of a Classical school that was centered in France and opposed the more extreme theories being introduced by Schoenberg through his work in Vienna.

As Western music moved away from ancient and medieval sources, a new tradition, **jazz,** rooted in African American tradition, began to emerge in the United States. The word *jazz,* originally a slang term for sexual intercourse, reflects the music's origins in the New Orleans sexual underworld. Jazz combined West African and African-Caribbean rhythms with Western harmony, along with an improvisatory call-and-response style rooted both in African songs and in gospel songs of the urban Protestant revival in the 1850s. Jazz drew on two other African American musical forms as well—ragtime, which was chiefly instrumental, and the blues, which originated as a vocal art.

Ragtime flourished from 1890 to 1920. The word *ragtime* is derived from the phrase "ragged time," the original name for this type of syncopated music perfected by black pianist and composer Scott Joplin (1868–1917) and based on a blend of African American rhythms and Western harmony. The **blues** grew out of the rural African American tradition of work songs and spirituals and evokes the pain to be found in life, love, poverty, and hard work. Blues and jazz are both powerfully expressive musical forms, considered specifically American contributions to world music.

The Legacy of Early Modernism

From the unsettled period of 1871–1914 come many of the trends that made the twentieth century such an exciting—and dangerous—era. The legacy of militant nationalism gave birth to the two great world wars that devastated the century. Even today, nationalism remains a potent force, threatening to overturn state boundaries and governments. Imperialism, another legacy, had radically contradictory consequences. On the one hand, it exported Western peoples, values, and technology around the globe, bringing a higher standard of living and greater expectations for the future. On the other hand, it disturbed if not destroyed older ways of life and led to a series of wars as colonial peoples struggled to cast off the yoke of Western oppression. And militarism, a third legacy, made rivalry among states a perpetual source of anxiety and destruction.

On the cultural scene, the era of Early Modernism set the stage for the twentieth century. The rise of the masses led to a growing proletarization of culture. As a result, the middle classes were subjected to a cultural assault from urban workers in much the same way that aristocrats had been attacked and displaced by the middle classes. Technology fueled the rise of mass culture. A second legacy of this era was the avant-garde, whose leaders systematically tried to destroy the last vestiges of Judeo-Christian and Classical Greco-Roman traditions. In rejecting the Classical ideal of the search for eternal truths, artists followed the Impressionists' lead and continued to strive for change as a reflection of the new historical conditions that surrounded them. And finally, Early Modernism established the emotional and aesthetic climate of the century—its addiction to experimentalism, its love-hate relationship with uncertainty and restlessness, its obsession with abstraction, its belief in the hidden depths of the human personality, and its willingness to think the unthinkable.

KEY CULTURAL TERMS

Modernism	Post-Impressionism
avant-garde	Pointillism
Naturalism	primitivism
Decadence	Fauvism
Expressionism	Cubism
problem play	collage
local color	pavane
Creole	atonality
Cajun	syncopation
aesthete	jazz
abstraction	ragtime
Impressionism	blues
ukiyo-e	

SUGGESTIONS FOR FURTHER READING

Primary Sources

CHEKHOV, A. P. *Plays.* Translated and edited by E. K. Bristow. New York: Norton, 1977. Excellent versions of Chekhov's most memorable plays: *The Sea Gull, Uncle Vanya, The Three Sisters,* and *The Cherry Orchard.*

CHOPIN, K. *The Awakening.* Edited by M. Culley. New York: Norton, 1976. The story of a sensual woman's coming of age that shocked the American public, whose outrage then silenced its author; with notes, excerpts from contemporary reviews, and essays in criticism. The novel was first published in 1899.

FREUD, S. *Civilization and Its Discontents.* Translated and edited by J. Strachey. New York: Norton, 1962. Freud's ideas about history and civilization, based on his psychological findings and theories; Strachey is the editor of the Standard Edition of Freud's complete works.

————. *The Interpretation of Dreams.* Translated and edited by J. Strachey. New York: Basic Books, 1955. Freud's seminal work about the role of the unconscious in human psychology and his new theory of psychoanalysis; considered by many his most important work.

HUYSMANS, J.-K. *Against Nature.* Translated by R. Baldick. New York: Penguin, 1966. A superb English version of this curious work, first published in 1884.

IBSEN, H. *A Doll's House.* Translated by C. Hampton. New York: S. French, 1972. An excellent English version of Ibsen's most often performed play, the story of a woman's awakening to the facts of her oppressive marriage.

JUNG, C. G. *Basic Writings.* Edited with an introduction by V. S. de Laszlo. New York: Modern Library, 1959. A good selection of the most important works of the Swiss psychiatrist who explored the importance of myths and symbols in human psychology.

————. *Memories, Dreams, Reflections.* Edited by A. Jaffé. New York: Vintage, 1963. Jung's highly readable autobiography, in which he describes the origins of his theories.

KAFKA, F. *The Metamorphosis, The Penal Colony, and Other Stories.* Translated by W. and E. Muir. New York: Schocken Books, 1988. This volume contains the best of Kafka's brilliant short prose works, all concerned with anxiety and alienation in a hostile and incomprehensible world.

————. *The Trial.* Translated by W. and E. Muir. New York: Schocken Books, 1968. A definitive edition of Kafka's nightmare novel in which the lead character is tried and convicted of a crime whose nature he cannot discover.

NIETZSCHE, F. W. *The Portable Nietzsche.* Selected and translated by W. Kaufmann. New York: Penguin, 1976. A collection of the most important writings of the German philosopher, compiled by the American scholar who rescued Nietzsche from the charge of proto-Nazism into which his philosophy had fallen during the Nazi era.

PROUST, M. *Remembrance of Things Past.* Translated by C. K. Scott Moncrieff, T. Kilmartin, and A. Mayor. London: Chatto & Windus, 1981. Contains all seven volumes of Proust's monumental work, which portrays the early twentieth century as a transitional period with the old aristocracy in decline and the middle class on the rise.

WILDE, O. *The Picture of Dorian Gray.* New York: Oxford University Press, 1981. Wilde's only novel recounts the story of a man whose portrait ages and decays while he remains young and handsome despite a dissolute life; the most enduring work of the Decadent school of late-nineteenth-century English literature.

ZOLA, E. *Germinal.* Translated and with an introduction by L. Tancock. New York: Penguin, 1954. A Realist novel that exposes the sordid conditions in the French mining industry.

SUGGESTIONS FOR LISTENING

DEBUSSY, CLAUDE (1862–1918). Debussy's veiled, subtly shifting harmonies helped to found Impressionist music. Excellent examples of his style may be heard in the orchestral works *Prélude à l'après-midi d'un faune (Prelude to the Afternoon of a Faun)* (1894) and *Nocturnes* (1899); in the collections for piano called *Estampes (Prints)* (1913) and *Préludes* (1910–1913); and in the opera *Pelléas et Mélisande* (1902). Not all of his music was Impressionistic, however; for example, in the piano music called *Children's Corner* (1908), he blended Classical values with his typical harmonic structures.

JOPLIN, SCOTT (1868–1917). Typical of Joplin's ragtime compositions with a syncopated beat are *Maple Leaf Rag* (1899), *Sugar Cane Rag* (1908), and *Magnetic Rag* (1914). He also wrote a ragtime opera *Treemonisha* (1911), a failure in his lifetime but a modest success in recent revivals.

RAVEL, MAURICE (1875–1937). Working in the shadow of Debussy, Ravel was an Impressionist with Classical inclinations; where Debussy was rhapsodic, Ravel was restrained. The work for solo piano *Jeux d'eau (Fountains)* (1901) shows Ravel's Impressionist style to perfection. His Classicism is most evident in compositions indebted to dance forms, including two works for solo piano, *Pavane pour une infante defunte (Pavane for a Dead Princess)* (1899) and *Valses nobles et sentimentales (Waltzes Noble and Sentimental)* (1911), and two works for orchestra, *La Valse (The Waltz)* (1920) and *Boléro* (1928).

SCHOENBERG, ARNOLD (1874–1951). By the end of this period, in 1914, Schoenberg was recognized as the leader of Expressionist music, particularly with the atonal work *Pierrot lunaire (Moonstruck Pierrot)* (1912), scored for chamber quintet and voice. In earlier works, he was less radical, as in the Second String Quartet (1908), which fused Classical forms and fragmentary melodies. Only after 1923 did Schoenberg make a breakthrough to serial composition, the type of music with which he is most identified (see Chapter 20).

STRAVINSKY, IGOR (1882–1971). Stravinsky, who along with Schoenberg dominated twentieth-century music, also began writing music during this period, principally as a composer of ballet scores based on Russian folk tales and traditions. These were *The Firebird* (1910), *Petrushka* (1911), and *Le Sacre du printemps (The Rite of Spring)* (1913). With *Le Sacre*, he established his originality as a composer, especially in his innovative rhythms and his handling of folk themes.

CHAPTER *19* HIGHLIGHTS
The Age of Early Modernism, 1871–1914

 NIETZSCHE, *Thus Spake Zarathustra* (1883)

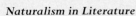 FREUD, *Civilization and Its Discontents* (1929)

Naturalism in Literature

IBSEN, *A Doll's House* (1879)

ZOLA, *Germinal* (1884)

CHOPIN, "The Story of an Hour" (1894)

CHEKHOV, *The Three Sisters* (1901)

Decadence in Literature

HUYSMANS, *Against Nature* (1884)

WILDE, *The Picture of Dorian Gray* (1894)

PROUST, *Remembrance of Things Past* (1913–1927)

19.8 BEARDSLEY, *The Dancer's Reward* from "Salomé" (1894)

Expressionism

STRINDBERG, *The Dream Play* (1907)

KAFKA, *Metamorphosis* (1915)

19.9 MUNCH, *The Scream* (1893)

19.1 BOCCIONI, *Unique Forms of Continuity in Space* (1913)

19.23 KANDINSKY, *Improvisation 33 for "Orient"* (1913)

SCHOENBERG, *Pierrot lunaire (Moonstruck Pierrot)* (1912)

Impressionism

19.10 MONET, *Impression: Sunrise* (1872)

19.13 MORISOT, *Laundresses Hanging Out the Wash* (1875)

19.12 RENOIR, *The Luncheon of the Boating Party* (1881)

19.14 CASSATT, *The Bath* (ca. 1891)

19.11 MONET, *Water Lilies* (ca. 1920)

DEBUSSY, *Prélude à l'après-midi d'un faune (Prelude to the Afternoon of a Faun)* (1894)

RAVEL, *Jeux d'eau (Fountains)* (1901)

Post-Impressionism

19.15 SEURAT, *A Sunday Afternoon on the Island of La Grande Jatte* (1884–1886)

19.18 VAN GOGH, *Self-Portrait with a Gray Hat* (1887)

19.19 VAN GOGH, *The Starry Night* (1889)

19.17 GAUGUIN, *Manao Tupapau: The Spirit of the Dead Watching* (1892)

19.16 CÉZANNE, *Mont Saint-Victoire* (1904–1906)

Fauvism and Cubism

19.20 MATISSE, *Open Window, Collioure* (1905)

19.21 PICASSO, *Les Demoiselles d'Avignon* (1907)

19.22 PICASSO, *Man with a Hat* (also known as *Portrait of Braque*) (1912)

19.24 RODIN, *Eve* (1881)

19.25 SULLIVAN, Guaranty Building, Buffalo (1895)

19.26 WRIGHT, W. W. Willits House, Chicago (1902)

JOPLIN, *Maple Leaf Rag* (1899)

STRAVINSKY, *The Rite of Spring* (1913)

■ Literature & Philosophy   ■ Art & Architecture   ■ Music & Dance

 Readings in the Western Humanities   CD, The Western Humanities

EARLY MODERNISM

Pinté mi retrato en el año de 1940
para el Doctor Leo Eloesser, mi médico y
mi mejor amigo. Con todo mi cariño. Frida Kahlo

20 THE AGE OF THE MASSES AND THE ZENITH OF MODERNISM

1914–1945

The events of the first half of the twentieth century are seen quite differently today from the way they were seen at the time. Historians are beginning to view World War I (1914–1918) and World War II (1939–1945) not as two separate conflicts but as a single struggle divided by a twenty-year peace. They believe that the Great Depression of the 1930s was not a signal that the capitalist system did not work but was simply an episode of economic downturn. And they know that the making of the masses into a historically powerful force was the most significant event of this time. The rise of the masses heralded the onset of a new phase of culture in which ordinary men and women from the lower middle class and the working class challenged bourgeois dominance in much the same way that the bourgeoisie had earlier challenged and eventually overcome the aristocracy.

The needs of this public led to the birth of mass culture, resulting in fresh forms of popular expression. Mass culture triggered negative responses in most serious artists, writers, and musicians, who preferred the difficult and somewhat remote style of Modernism. The leaders of Modernism, partly because of the extreme popularity of mass culture, now fashioned works that grew more and more revolutionary in form, constantly testing the limits of the arts (Figure 20.1). The period between 1914 and 1945 thus saw both the rise of mass culture and the zenith of Modernism.

◀ **Detail** FRIDA KAHLO. *Self-Portrait Dedicated to Dr. Eloesser.* 1940. Oil on masonite, 22¼ × 15¾". Private collection, U.S.A.

Figure 20.1 FRIDA KAHLO. *Self-Portrait Dedicated to Dr. Eloesser.* 1940. Oil on masonite, 22¼ × 15¾". Private collection, U.S.A. *Kahlo reveals a Modernist sensibility in this likeness, which draws on multicultural sources, including Christianity and her indigenous Mexican heritage. The necklace of thorns, which makes her neck bleed, refers both to Christ's crown of thorns worn during the Crucifixion and to the Aztec prophetic ritual that required self-mortification with maguey thorns. The earring in the form of a hand—a gift from Picasso—symbolizes the hand of fate, and the jungle of oversized leaves evokes an image of nature out of control.*

THE COLLAPSE OF OLD CERTAINTIES AND THE SEARCH FOR NEW VALUES

Before World War I, liberal values guided most people's expectations. Between the outbreak of World War I and the ending of World War II, however, the values of liberalism were severely tested and in some cases overthrown. Wars, revolutions, and social upheavals often dominated both domestic and foreign affairs. To those who clung to liberal ideals, the world seemed to have gone mad (Figure 20.2). In Russia, Italy, Germany, and Spain, individual rights became secondary to the

Figure 20.2 PABLO PICASSO. *Guernica.* 1937. Oil on canvas, 11'5½" × 25'5¾". Prado, Madrid. *Picasso's* Guernica *is a vivid symbol of the violent twenty years between World War I and World War II. Depicting the bombing of the unarmed town of Guernica by Nazi planes during the Spanish Civil War, the painting transforms the local struggle into an international battle between totalitarianism and human freedom—the issue that also dominated the age's ideological debates.*

Figure 20.3   PAUL NASH. *"We Are Making a New World."* 1918. Oil on canvas, 28 × 36". Imperial War Museum, London. *Paul Nash, one of Britain's official artists during World War I, made the reality of the war's destructive power evident to civilians at home. In his battle scenes, farmlands were turned into quagmires and forests into "no-man's lands." The artist's choice of the title for this painting mocks the politicians' promises that tomorrow will be better.*

needs of society or simply to the wishes of the ruling totalitarian party. The doctrine of laissez faire also fell into discredit during the Depression of the 1930s, bringing capitalism itself into question and leading to the rise of state-controlled economies.

World War I and Its Aftermath

In 1914 came the war that nobody expected and that took an estimated ten million lives. On one side were the Central Powers—Germany, Austria-Hungary (members of the Triple Alliance), Turkey, and Bulgaria. The principal war aim of these countries was to assert the power of the central European region, which had been eclipsed by western Europe for almost two hundred years. Central Europe's new sense of importance was due to the unification of Germany in 1871, which had made the German Empire the most powerful industrial and military state on the Continent.

Opposed to the Central Powers were the Allied Powers: France, Russia, and Great Britain (members of the Triple Entente), joined in 1915 by Italy (a former member of the Triple Alliance). The Allies refused to allow the Central Powers to revise the balance of power and, in particular, were determined to keep Germany from gaining new lands. The two sides found themselves bogged down in siege warfare that led to huge losses on the battlefield and appalling hardships at home (Figure 20.3).

In the spring of 1917, the stalemate between the two sides was upset by two key events. First, the United States entered the war on the Allied side, promising fresh troops and supplies. Second, revolution broke out in Russia, interrupting its war effort

and eventually causing the newly formed Communist regime to make peace with the Central Powers in 1918. The Germans launched a massive attack on the western front, but the Allies, supported by American troops, foiled the Germans and forced them to surrender in November 1918.

The peace that ended the war—the 1919 Treaty of Versailles—was based partly on a plan of the U.S. president, Woodrow Wilson (1913–1921). The goal of Wilson's plan was to keep Europe safe from war, and it called for the self-determination of nations, democratic governments, and the establishment of the League of Nations, an international agency to maintain the peace. Despite the optimism surrounding its signing, the Versailles Treaty sowed the seeds of discord in Germany that contributed to World War II (Map 20.1). Defeated German officials and officers would later rally nationalistic feelings by denouncing the treaty as a humiliation for their country.

Peace brought boom times to the economies of the victorious Allied Powers, however. Britain and France returned to business as usual. The United States reverted to its prewar isolationism, and between 1924 and 1929 it exhibited the best and the worst of free enterprise—unprecedented prosperity and rampant greed.

The Central Powers also rebuilt their economies in the 1920s. After a shaky start, Germany survived near bankruptcy to regain its status as the leading industrial state on the Continent. Under the Weimar Republic, Germany's first democratic parliamentary government, the country once again became a center for European culture, providing key leaders in avant-garde painting and literature. Conversely, Austria-Hungary was divided into separate nations, and its

LEARNING THROUGH MAPS

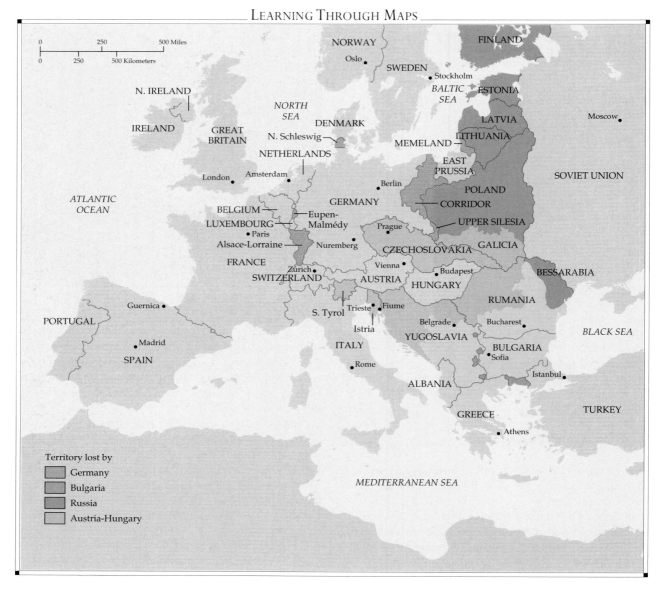

Map 20.1 EUROPE AFTER WORLD WAR I
This map shows Europe's political divisions in the early 1920s. **Notice** the territories lost by Germany, Bulgaria, Russia, and Austria-Hungary. **What** name was now given to Russia? **Which** countries lost the most territory? **How** did these lost lands affect European politics? **Observe** the increase in the size of countries in southeast Europe in this map, as compared with their smaller size in Map 19.3, Europe on the Eve of World War I. **Notice** that the Ottoman Empire in Map 19.3 has become Turkey in this map.

Slavic population dispersed among several states. Lacking a sound economic base, the one-time empire never fully recovered from its defeat.

As the 1920s drew to a close, a warning signal sounded: the crash of the New York stock market in October 1929. After the crash, the buoyant atmosphere of the twenties lingered for only a few months. Then economic depression in the United States, a key player in the world's economy, pulled down Europe's financial house.

The Great Depression of the 1930s

The Depression wiped out prosperity and brought mass unemployment, street demonstrations, and near starvation for many people. In Europe and the United States, governments were forced to take extreme measures to restore their economies. Great Britain and France had to discard free trade and move toward government-controlled economies. Under President Franklin Delano Roosevelt (1933–1945) and

Figure 20.4 DOROTHEA LANGE. *Migrant Mother, Nipomo, California.* 1936. Library of Congress. *Migrant workers were increasingly attracted to the vegetable fields of California during the Great Depression. Seasonal laborers, they harvested crops for very low wages under miserable working conditions and usually lived in crowded, unsanitary camps. This photograph shows a migrant mother, surrounded by three children, whose bleak future has been made worse by the failure of the pea crop. Dorothea Lange's poignant photographs, collected in* An American Exodus: A Record of Human Erosion *(1939), reflected her strong sense of social justice, her sympathy for the downtrodden, and her own life as the child of a broken home.*

his New Deal program, the United States followed a policy of state intervention to revitalize the economy (Figure 20.4). Roosevelt started public works projects, sponsored programs such as social security and unemployment insurance to benefit working people, and moved to regulate Wall Street and the banks. Depressed conditions hung on until World War II, however.

Germany suffered the most in Europe. Domestic problems, brought on in part by bank failures and rising unemployment, led to political crises that doomed the Weimar experiment in democracy and set the stage for the coming to power of the National Socialists, or Nazis, under Adolf Hitler.

While Europe suffered, Japan prospered. Since 1926 Japan had been ruled by Emperor Hirohito (r. 1926–1989), who was worshiped as a god, although actual power was wielded by military leaders and businessmen. In the 1930s, these groups pursued expansionist and militaristic policies, first taking over Manchuria and then making war on China. As the situation worsened in Europe in the late 1930s, Japan was able to take a free hand in Southeast Asia.

The Rise of Totalitarianism

With the peace treaty of 1919, democracy seemed triumphant. By 1939, a mere twenty years later, most of the new democracies—including Germany, Austria, Hungary, Italy, Spain, Bulgaria, and Rumania—had become totalitarian. Totalitarianism on such a huge scale is a twentieth-century phenomenon, but its roots reach back to the policies of Robespierre during the French Revolution. Totalitarian governments control every aspect of the lives and thoughts of their citizens. Art, literature, and the press exist only in the service of the state. "Truth" itself becomes a matter of what the state says it is. Between the wars, totalitarianism emerged in two forms: Russian communism and European fascism.

Russian Communism Russian communism was based on the writings of Karl Marx, whose theory was reinterpreted by the revolutionary leader V. I. Lenin (1917–1924). Lenin accepted Marx's basic premise that economic conditions determine the course of history and his conclusion that history leads inevitably to a communist society run by and for the workers. Unlike Marx, Lenin believed that radical reform could occur only when a small, elite group—rather than a mass movement—seized power in the name of the people.

In 1917 Russia was plagued by an incompetent ruler, an inefficient military staff, a weak economy, and rising social and political discord. Revolution broke out in February, and a small band of Marxist communists—the Bolsheviks—seized control of the government in October. Led by Lenin, the Bolsheviks began to restructure the economy and the political system. Under their plan, the state would control production and distribution, and soviets—or councils of workers, military personnel, and peasants—would restructure the social and economic order at the local level, as directed by the Communist party under Lenin.

After Lenin's death, Joseph Stalin (1928–1953) eventually emerged as the sole ruler of the Union of Soviet Socialist Republics, as the Russian Empire was now called, and he proceeded to impose his will over the state with a vengeance. Production was increased and modernization accomplished through state-owned farms, factories, and heavy industry. No political party other than the Communist party was permitted, however, and Stalin was ruthless in dealing with his opponents and critics. He had them either murdered or imprisoned in a vast network of forced-labor camps, known as the Gulag, in the wilderness of Siberia. The number of Stalin's victims is beyond imagining: More than ten million men, women, and children met unnatural deaths in the period of forced collectivization of agriculture, 1929–1936, and millions more were murdered during purges and in the Gulag.

European Fascism   European fascism was based on the idea that the masses should participate directly in the state—not through a legislative or deliberative body such as a parliament, but through a fusion of the population into one "spirit." Fascism sought to bind the masses by appealing to nonrational sentiments about national destiny. Like communists, fascists believed that the individual was insignificant and the nation-state was the supreme embodiment of the destiny of its people.

In practice, fascism led to loss of personal freedom, as did communism, because its ideals of economic stability and social peace could be achieved only through dictatorship and tight control over the press, education, police, and the judicial system. Because of its idealistic nationalism, fascism was also hostile both to foreigners and to internal groups that did not share the majority's history, race, or politics. The movement's innate aggressiveness led to strong military establishments, which were used to conquer new lands in Europe and to win colonial empires. Fascism first appeared in Italy in the 1920s and then in Germany and Spain in the 1930s.

In Italy, a floundering economy and mounting national frustration led more and more people to follow the Fascists. Led by Benito Mussolini [moo-suh-LEE-nee] (1922–1945), the Fascists dreamed of a revitalized Italy restored to its ancient glory. After seizing power in 1922, Mussolini achieved some success with his programs, and as the rest of Europe suffered through the Depression, his pragmatic policies gained admirers elsewhere.

Germany in the early 1930s was wracked by the Depression, unemployment, and political extremism, and in 1933 the German voters turned to the National Socialist (Nazi) party. Within three years, the Nazis had restored industrial productivity, eliminated unemployment, and gained the support of many business leaders and farmers. The success of the National Socialists depended ultimately on their *Führer*, or "leader," Adolf Hitler (1933–1945), a middle-class Austrian and veteran who had hammered together a strong mass movement built on anti-Semitism and anticommunism. He used his magnetic personality to attract devoted followers with promises to restore Germany to prewar glory. From the beginning, the Nazis' ruthless treatment of political enemies, of the Jews, and of any dissidents aroused fears, but most Europeans ignored these barbaric acts, preferring to focus on the regime's successes (Figure 20.5).

Spain's agrarian economy and traditional institutions began to be strained by industrial growth in the 1920s, and in the early 1930s a coalition of reformers overthrew the king and created a secular republic with a constitution guaranteeing civil rights. Conservative forces plotted to restore monarchical rule and the church's influence. In 1936 civil war broke out. General Francisco Franco (1939–1975) led the conservatives to victory in 1939, defeating an alliance of reformers. During hostilities, Hitler and Mussolini supplied Franco's fascist army with troops and equipment, and Stalin backed the losing faction. For the Germans and the Italians, Spain's civil war was a practice run for World War II. For example, the bombing of unarmed towns such as Guernica (see Figure 20.2) foreshadowed the indiscriminate bombing and killing of civilians that characterized the later war.

World War II: Origins and Outcome

The origins of World War II lay in the Treaty of Versailles (which many Germans denounced as a "dictated peace" that brought the loss of territory in France and Poland), the Great Depression, and nationalism.

Figure 20.5   Nuremberg Nazi
Party Rally. 1933. *Under the skillful
orchestration of their propaganda chief,
Joseph Goebbels, the National Socialists
staged massive demonstrations whose
goal was to overpower the emotions of
participants and observers alike. In this
anonymous photograph, Nazi party
members and private army units pass in
review. In the 1930s, such demonstrations
succeeded in uniting the German masses
with the Nazi leader.*

Figure 20.6   MARGARET BOURKE-WHITE. Russian Tank
Driver. 1941. *Photojournalism, a popular form in which the
photograph rather than the text dominates the story, reached new
heights during World War II, particularly in illustrated magazines
such as* Life. *Margaret Bourke-White, one of the first women war
journalists, was the only foreign correspondent–photographer
present in the Soviet Union when the Germans invaded in June
1941. In this photograph, a Russian tank driver peers through his
window with the cannon jutting out over his head—a vivid image
of the integration of human beings into mechanized warfare.*

After less than a year in office, Hitler launched a campaign to revise the Versailles Treaty and engaged in a
propaganda crusade that focused on Germany's glorious past. His regime, he boasted, was the Third Reich,
or empire, which would last for a thousand years—
like the centuries-long Holy Roman Empire (1000–
1806) rather than the short-lived German Empire
(1871–1918). In 1936 he marched troops into the
Rhineland, the industrial heartland of Germany, which
had been demilitarized by the Versailles Treaty. When
the world failed to respond to this challenge, Hitler
concluded that Germany's former enemies were weak,
and he initiated a plan to conquer Europe. In the next
two years, Europe watched as Hitler took Austria and
Czechoslovakia. World War II began on September 1,
1939, when Germany invaded Poland; France and
Britain responded with declarations of war.

Within nine months, the Nazis occupied most of
western Europe. By the fall of 1940, the British, under
their wartime leader Winston Churchill, were bravely
holding on, taking the brunt of the German air raids.

Unable to defeat England by air, Hitler turned eastward
and invaded the Soviet Union in 1941 (Figure 20.6).
Shortly thereafter, the Soviet Union and Great Britain
became allies against Nazi Germany. Then, on December 7, 1941, Japan attacked Pearl Harbor, an
American military base in the Pacific, and a few days

PERSONAL PERSPECTIVE

ELIE WIESEL
Surviving in a Nazi Death Camp

In this excerpt from his autobiographical novel Night, *Wiesel describes the arrival of his family at Auschwitz, a Nazi death camp.*

The cherished objects we had brought with us thus far were left behind in the train, and with them, at last, our illusions.

Every two yards or so an SS man held his tommy gun trained on us. Hand in hand we followed the crowd.

An SS noncommissioned officer came to meet us, a truncheon in his hand. He gave the order:

"Men to the left! Women to the right!"

Eight words spoken quietly, indifferently, without emotion. Eight short, simple words. Yet that was the moment when I parted from my mother. I had not had time to think, but already I felt the pressure of my father's hand: we were alone. For a part of a second I glimpsed my mother and my sisters moving away to the right. Tzipora held Mother's hand. I saw them disappear into the distance; my mother was stroking my sister's fair hair, as though to protect her, while I walked on with my father and the other men. And I did not know that in that place, at that moment, I was parting from my mother and Tzipora forever. I went on walking. My father held onto my hand.

Behind me, an old man fell to the ground. Near him was an SS man, putting his revolver back in its holster.

My hand shifted on my father's arm. I had one thought—not to lose him. Not to be left alone.

The SS officers gave the order:

"Form fives!"

Commotion. At all costs we must keep together.

"Here, kid, how old are you?"

It was one of the prisoners who asked me this. I could not see his face, but his voice was tense and weary.

"I'm not quite fifteen yet."

"No. Eighteen."

"But I'm not," I said. "Fifteen."

"Fool. Listen to what *I* say."

Then he questioned my father, who replied:

"Fifty."

The other grew more furious than ever.

"No, not fifty. Forty. Do you understand? Eighteen and forty."

He disappeared into the night shadows.

---

later Germany and Italy followed Japan in declaring war on the United States.

The war in Europe lasted until May 1945, when the combined armies of the Allied Powers—Britain, the Soviet Union, and the United States—forced Germany to surrender. Italy had already negotiated an armistice with the Allies in September 1943 after anti-Fascists overthrew Mussolini and set up a republic. In the Pacific, where the Allies had captured key Japanese island strongholds, the war against Japan was brought to an abrupt end in August 1945, when the United States dropped atomic bombs on the Japanese cities of Hiroshima and Nagasaki. The more than 200,000 Japanese killed in these two raids climaxed the bloody six years of World War II, adding to its estimated thirty to fifty million deaths.

By 1945 the world had witnessed some of the most brutal examples of human behavior in history, but few were prepared for the shock of the Nazi death camps. Gradually it became known to the world that the Nazis had rounded up the Jews of Germany and eastern Europe and transported them in cattle cars to extermination camps, where they were killed in gas chambers.

The Nazis referred to their plan to eliminate the Jewish people as the Final Solution, but the rest of the world called it the Holocaust. This genocidal policy involved the murder of six million Jews out of a population of nine million, along with millions of other people the Nazis deemed undesirable, such as Gypsies and homosexuals (Figure 20.7).

In 1945, after six years of war, Germany and Japan lay in ruins. Italy escaped with less damage. France, partly occupied by the Germans for most of the war, was readmitted to the councils of the Allies. England, though victorious, emerged exhausted and in the shadow of her former allies, the United States and the Soviet Union. The old European order had passed away. The Soviet Union and the United States were now the two most powerful states in the world.

THE ZENITH OF MODERNISM

Modernism had originated in the latter part of the nineteenth century as a reflection of the fast-paced modern world whose foundations and boundaries

Figure 20.7 Nazi Death Camp in Belsen, Germany. 1945. *When the Nazis came to power in Germany in 1933, they secretly began to imprison their political enemies in concentration camps, where they were tortured or executed. By 1942 the Nazis had extended this secret policy across Europe to include minority civilians, particularly Jews. Photographs such as this one revealed to the world the atrocities committed by the Nazi regime.*

seemed to be constantly shifting. The Modernist sensibility, with its underlying spirit of skepticism and experimentation, continued to guide artistic and literary expression in the twentieth century. But this style was limited in its appeal, and an ever-growing general public was isolated from avant-garde developments in art, music, and literature. When this wider audience was exposed to Modernist works, they often responded negatively to them, considering them incomprehensible, obscene, or decidedly provocative in some way. They turned instead to the increasingly available and affordable pleasures offered by **mass culture.**

Like Modernism, mass culture was a direct outgrowth of industrialized society. Its roots reached back to the late nineteenth century, when skilled workers began to enjoy a better standard of living than had previously been possible for members of the lower classes. This new generation of consumers demanded products and amusements that appealed to their tastes: inexpensive, energetic, and easily accessible.

In response to their desires, entrepreneurs using new technologies flooded the market with consumer goods and developed new entertainments. Unlike the folk culture or popular culture of earlier times, modern mass culture was also mass-produced culture. The untapped consumers' market led to the creation or expansion of new industries, in particular automobiles, household products, and domestic appliances. Most forms of mass culture—the radio, newspaper comic strips and cartoons, professional sports, picture magazines, recordings, movies, and musical comedies—had originated before World War I, but now, between the wars, they came into their own. The 1920s was the golden age of Broadway's musical comedies, and radio reached its peak in the years after 1935.

The spread of mass culture heightened the prestige of the United States as it became known as the source of the most vigorous and imaginative popular works. The outstanding symbol of America's dominance of popular culture is Walt Disney (1901–1966), the creator of the cartoon figures of Mickey Mouse (1928) and other characters. By 1945, mass culture was playing an ever-growing role in the public and the private lives of most citizens in the more advanced societies. A handful of creative people began to incorporate elements of mass culture into their works, using jazz in "serious" music or film in theatrical performances, for example, but in the main most artists, writers, and musicians stood apart from mass culture. Their isolation reflected an almost sacred commitment to the Modernist ideals of experimentation, newness, and deliberate difficulty. And some Modernists, especially among the visual artists, imbued these ideals with spiritual meaning.

Experimentation in Literature

Modernist writers between 1914 and 1945 maintained Early Modernism's dedication to experimentation, a stance that reflected their despair over the instability of their era. By challenging the traditional norms and methods of literature through their carefully composed experimental works, the Modernists were convinced that they could impose an order on the seeming randomness and meaninglessness of human existence.

The Novel Depiction of the narrator's subjective consciousness was a principal concern of the Modernist novelists, who otherwise differed markedly from one another. The most distinctive method that arose from this concern was **stream-of-consciousness** writing, a method in which the narrative consists of the unedited thoughts of one of the characters, through whose mind readers experience the story. Stream-of-consciousness fiction differs from a story told in the first person—the grammatical "I"—by one of the characters (for example, Dickens's *David Copperfield*) in that it is an attempt to emulate the actual experience of thinking and feeling, even to the point of sounding fragmented, random, and arbitrary.

The Irish author James Joyce and the English writer Virginia Woolf were important innovators with the stream-of-consciousness technique. In his novel *Ulysses,* James Joyce (1882–1941) uses this device as a way of making the novel's characters speak directly to readers. For instance, no narrator's voice intrudes in the novel's final forty-five pages, which are the scattered thoughts of the character Molly Bloom as she sinks into sleep. This long monologue is a single run-on sentence without any punctuation except for a final period.

Despite the experimental style of *Ulysses,* Joyce aspired to more than technical virtuosity in this monumental work. He planned it as a modern version of the *Odyssey,* contrasting Homer's twenty-four books of heroic exploits with an ordinary day in the lives of three Dubliners. Joyce's sexual language, although natural to his characters, offended bourgeois morals. *Ulysses,* first published in France in 1922, became the era's test case for artistic freedom, not appearing in America or England until the 1930s.

Rejecting traditional narrative techniques, Virginia Woolf (1882–1941) experimented with innovative ways of exploring time, space, and reality. In her early novel *Jacob's Room* (1922), for example, she develops the title character through fragments of other people's comments about him. In *Mrs. Dalloway* (1925), she uses interior monologues to trace a woman's experiences over the course of a day in London. Like her contemporaries Joyce and Freud, Woolf was interested in examining the realities that lie below surface consciousness. Many consider *To the Lighthouse* (1927) Woolf's finest novel. In it she uses stream-of-consciousness to strip the story of a fixed point of view and capture the differing senses of reality experienced by the characters—in much the same way that the Cubist painters aimed at representing multiple views. To that end, she focuses on the characters' inner selves, creating diverse effects through interior monologues. For instance, one character's narrow, matter-of-fact mentality differs from his wife's emotional, free-ranging consciousness. A distinguished literary critic and the author of well-known feminist works such as *A Room of One's Own* (1929), Woolf gathered around her the avant-garde writers, artists, and intellectuals known as the Bloomsbury Group and founded, with her husband, Leonard, the Hogarth Press.

American writers also contributed experimental fiction to the Modernist revolution. By and large, these Americans made their first contacts with Europe during World War I and stayed on until the Great Depression drove them home (Figure 20.8). Ernest Hemingway (1899–1961) was the first of the Americans living abroad to emerge as a major literary star. His severely disciplined prose style relied heavily on dialogue, and he often omitted details of setting and background. His writing owed a debt to popular culture: From the era's hardboiled detective fiction he borrowed a terse, world-weary voice to narrate his works, as in his 1926 novel, *The Sun Also Rises.* In this novel, he portrays his fellow American exiles as a "lost generation" whose future was blighted by World War I—a Modernist message. In Hemingway's cynical vision, politics is of little importance; what matter most are drinking bouts with male friends and casual sex with beautiful women.

William Faulkner (1897–1962) was another American who became one of the giants of twentieth-century literature. The stream-of-consciousness technique is central to his 1929 masterpiece, *The Sound and the Fury.* With a story line repeated several times but from different perspectives, this novel is especially audacious in its opening section, which narrates events through the eyes of a mentally defective character. More important than his use of such Modernist devices was his lifelong identification with his home state of Mississippi, where, after a brief sojourn in Europe, he began to explore themes about extended families bound together by sexual secrets. Faulkner's universe became the fictional county of Yoknapatawpha, which he peopled with decaying gentry, ambitious poor whites, and exploited blacks. His artistic power lay in his ability not only to relate these characters to their region but also to turn them into universal symbols.

Although experimentalism was a highly visible aspect of Modernist fiction, not all Modernist writers were preoccupied with innovative methods. Other writers were identified with the Modernists because of their pessimistic viewpoints or their explosive themes. The Modernism of the British writer D. H. Lawrence (1885–1930), for example, was expressed in novels of sexual liberation. Frustrated by the coldness of sexual relations in bourgeois culture, Lawrence, the son of a miner, concluded that the machine age emasculated men. As an antidote, he preached a religion of erotic passion. He set forth his doctrine of sexual freedom most clearly in the 1928 novel *Lady Chatterley's Lover,* issued privately and quickly banned for its explicit language and scenes. Not until the 1960s, and only after bitter court battles, was this novel allowed to circulate freely. In the novel, the love-making episodes between Lady Chatterley, wed to an impotent aristocrat, and the lower-class gamekeeper Mellors were presented as models of sexual fulfillment with their mix of erotic candor and moral fervor.

Falling outside the Modernist classification is the English novelist and essayist George Orwell (1903–1950), who nevertheless was one of the major figures of the interwar period. Born Eric Blair to an established middle-class family, Orwell changed his name, rejected his background, lived and worked among the poor and downtrodden, and became a writer. He also became the conscience of his generation because he remained skeptical of all the political ideologies of his day. In the allegorical novel *Animal Farm* (1945), he satirized Stalinist Russia. In the anti-utopian novel *1984* (1948), he made totalitarianism the enemy, especially as practiced in the Soviet Union, but he also warned of the dangers of repression in capitalist society. What made Orwell remarkable in this age torn by ideological excess was his claim to be merely an ordinary, decent man. It is perhaps for this reason that today Orwell is claimed by socialists, liberals, and conservatives alike.

Poetry Modern poetry found its first great master in William Butler Yeats (1865–1939). His early poems are filled with Romantic mysticism, drawing on the myths of his native Ireland. By 1910 he had stripped his verses of Romantic allusions, and yet in his later works, he never gave up entirely his belief in the occult or the importance of myth. As Irish patriots grew more hostile to their country's continued submersion in the

Figure 20.8 Pablo Picasso. *Gertrude Stein.* 1906. Oil on canvas, 39¼ × 32". Metropolitan Museum of Art. Bequest of Gertrude Stein, 1946. *Talented Americans were introduced to Paris by American writer and expatriate Gertrude Stein, who made her studio a gathering place for the Parisian avant-garde. There she entertained Matisse and Picasso, composer Igor Stravinsky, writers Ernest Hemingway and F. Scott Fitzgerald, and many other brilliant exponents of Modernism. Stein was shocked at first by the starkness and brooding presence of Picasso's portrait of her, but she came to regard it as an accurate likeness, saying, "For me it is I, and it is the only reproduction of me which is always I."*

United Kingdom, climaxing in the Easter Rebellion of 1916, Yeats's poems took on a political cast. His best verses came in the 1920s, when his primary sources were Irish history and Greco-Roman myth. Perhaps his finest lyric is "Sailing to Byzantium," a poem that conjures up the Classical past to reaffirm ancient wisdom and redeem the tawdry industrialized world.

T. S. Eliot (1888–1965) was another founder of Modern poetry. Reared in St. Louis and educated at Harvard, Eliot moved to London in 1915, becoming an English citizen in 1927. He and Ezra Pound (1885–1972), another American exile, established a school of poetry that reflected the crisis of confidence that seized Europe's intellectuals after World War I. Like those of

Figure 20.9 JACOB LAWRENCE. *Migration Series, No. 58.* The original caption reads, "In the North the Negro had better educational facilities." 1940–1941. Tempera on gesso on composition board, 12 × 18". The Museum of Modern Art, New York. Gift of Mrs. David M. Levy. *Jacob Lawrence's* The Migration Series, *a cycle of paintings commissioned by* Fortune *magazine, depicted the mass flight of African Americans from the American South to the North in their quest for a better life. Lawrence (1917–2000) was a Harlem resident and the son of black migrants. These works are simplistic in format (standard small size and common color scheme); nevertheless, they reveal Lawrence's knowledge of High Modernism, especially in the flatness and angularity of the figures and the unusual perspective. The painting titled* No. 58 *evokes a sense of rhythm by having the number sequence repeated by the young girls' arm and leg movements and their swaying dresses. This series established Lawrence as a serious artist, and in 1941 he became the first African American included in the permanent collection of New York's Museum of Modern Art.*

the late Roman poets, Eliot's verses relied heavily on literary references and quotations.

"The Waste Land," published in 1922, showed Eliot's difficult, eclectic style; in 403 irregular lines, he quotes from or imitates thirty-five authors, including Shakespeare and Dante, adapts snatches from popular songs, and uses phrases in six foreign languages. Form matches content because the "waste land" itself represents a sterile, godless region without a future, a symbol drawn from medieval legend but changed by Eliot into a symbol of the hollowness of modern life. In 1927 he moved beyond such atheistic pessimism, finding solace by being received into the Church of England— a step he celebrated in the poem "Ash Wednesday," published in 1930.

The black American poet Langston Hughes (1902–1967) also belongs with the outstanding Modernists. Hughes drew inspiration from many sources, including Africa, Europe, and Mexico, but the ultimate

power of his poetry came from the American experience: jazz, spirituals, and his anguish as a black man in a white world. Hughes's emergence, like that of many African American writers, occurred during a population shift that began in 1914 when thousands of blacks from the American South settled in northern cities such as New York, Chicago, and Detroit in hopes of a better life (Figure 20.9).

At the same time that America's ethnographic map was being redrawn, a craze for Negro culture sprang up that was fueled by jazz and the avant-garde cult of primitivism. This craze sparked the Harlem Renaissance, a 1920s cultural revival in the predominantly black area of New York City called Harlem. Hughes was a major figure in this black literary movement. His earliest book of verses, *The Weary Blues* (1926), contains his most famous poem, "The Negro Speaks of Rivers." Dedicated to W. E. B. DuBois (1868–1963), the founder of the National Association for the Advancement of

Figure 20.10 GEORGE GROSZ. *Nude.* Ca. 1919. Watercolor, India ink, and collage, approx. 16½ × 11½″. Thyssen-Bornemisza Foundation Collection, Madrid, Spain. © 1997 Estate of George Grosz/Licensed by VAGA, New York, NY. *The works of German artist George Grosz provide a visual counterpart to the dramas of Brecht. Grosz portrays bourgeois society as morally bankrupt, as in this painting of a brothel scene that shows a prosttute as a willing victim—note the prostitute's complicitous glance. Brecht makes the same point in the drama* Mother Courage *by presenting a businesswoman heroine interested only in making money even though it means sacrificing her sons in war. Grosz's* Life Model *reflected the influence of Dada art, which was imported into Berlin from Zurich in late 1918, at the end of World War I. Typical of Berlin Dadaists, Grosz added a political message to this subversive art, and he underscored his corrosive vision with a brutal, unsentimental collage technique, using photographic and painted images and overlapping planes of color.*

Colored People, Hughes's verse memorializes the deathless spirit of his race by linking black history to the rivers of the world.

Another outstanding figure of the Harlem Renaissance was Zora Neale Hurston (about 1901–1960), the most prolific African American woman writer of her generation. Poet, novelist, folklorist, essayist, Hurston made her literary task the exploration of what it means to be black and female in a white- and male-dominated society. An excellent example of her handling of this theme is the essay "How It Feels to Be Colored Me," published in 1928. In this short work, filled with self-mocking irony, she presents herself as torn between black and white culture and sometimes forced to choose between two then current stereotypes: the "happy Negro" who performs for white folks for money and sheer joy and the "exotic primitive," the educated black who, despite a veneer of learning, remains "uncivilized." Nevertheless, she rejects both stereotypes as caused by being born black in a white culture. In certain moments,

she claims to transcend race though not gender: "I belong to no race nor time. I am the eternal feminine with its string of beads." Her ideal is of a future, free of racism, in which African Americans no longer have to struggle with culturally imposed identities.

Drama During the interwar years, drama moved in new directions in both Europe and America. An Expressionist in aesthetics and a Marxist in politics, the German Bertolt Brecht [BREKT] (1898–1956) blended a discordant style learned from the Berlin streets with his hatred of bourgeois society into what he called **"epic theater."** Rebelling against traditional theater, which he thought merely reinforced class prejudices, he devised a radical theater centered on a technique called the "alienation effect," whose purpose was to make the bourgeois audience uncomfortable (Figure 20.10). Alienation effects could take any form, such as outlandish props, inappropriate accents, or ludicrous dialogue. By breaking the magic spell of the stage,

Brecht's epic theater challenged the viewers' expectations and prepared them for his moral and political message. A victim of Nazi oppression, Brecht fled first to Scandinavia and then to America, where he lived for fifteen years before moving to East Berlin in 1952 to found a highly influential theater company.

A year before he officially embraced Marxism, Brecht teamed with the German-born composer Kurt Weill [WILE or VILE] (1900–1950) to create one of the best-known musicals in modern theater, *The Three-penny Opera* (1928). Loosely based on an eighteenth-century English opera, Brecht and Weill's Expressionist version was raucous, discordant, violent, and hostile to bourgeois values. The playwright, believing that bourgeois audiences wanted goodness to triumph over evil, made the hero a small-time hoodlum ("Mack the Knife") and then saved him at the last moment from a hanging that he richly deserved.

Besides such pathfinders as Brecht, this period also produced two major Modernist playwrights. The first of these was Jean Cocteau [kahk-TOE] (1889–1963), a French dramatist who helped to launch the French trend for modernizing the Greek classics. For example, Cocteau's *The Infernal Machine* (1934) updates Sophocles' *Oedipus*. In this modern retelling, the story is filled with Freudian overtones—Oedipus is portrayed as a "mother's boy"—and film clips are introduced for flashbacks. A second major Modernist was Eugene O'Neill (1888–1953), America's first dramatist to earn worldwide fame. Like Cocteau, O'Neill sometimes wrote new versions of Greek tragedies, as in *Mourning Becomes Electra* (1931), which was modeled on Aeschylus's *Oresteia*. O'Neill's best plays are his tense family dramas in which generations battle one another, as in *Long Day's Journey into Night*, staged posthumously in 1956.

Philosophy and Science: The End of Certainty

During this period, the Idealist philosophy that had dominated Continental speculation since the early 1800s was replaced by two new schools of thought. First, in Austria and England Ludwig Wittgenstein developed ideas that helped establish the logical positivist school, which became known after World War II as the analytical school. Second, in Germany Martin Heidegger founded the existentialist school. Both schools tried to create new philosophies that were in harmony with Modernist developments.

The Austrian Ludwig Wittgenstein [VIT-guhn-stine] (1889–1951) believed that the West was in a moral and intellectual decline that he attributed to faulty language, for which, he surmised, current philosophical methods were to blame. Wittgenstein asserted that traditional philosophical speculation was senseless because, of necessity, it relied on language that could not rise above simple truisms.

Wittgenstein's solution to this intellectual impasse was to dethrone philosophy and make it simply the servant of science. He set forth his conclusion in his *Tractatus Logico-Philosophicus* in 1922. In this treatise, he reasoned that, although language might be faulty, there were mathematical and scientific tools for comprehending the world. He proposed that thinkers give up the study of values and morals and assist scientists in a quest for truth. This conclusion led to **logical positivism,** a school of philosophy dedicated to defining terms and clarifying statements.

Wittgenstein later rejected the idea that language is a flawed instrument and substituted a theory of language as games, in the manner of children's play. Nevertheless, it was the point of view set forth in the *Tractatus* that made Wittgenstein so influential in the universities in England between 1930 and 1960 and in America after World War II.

While Wittgenstein was challenging philosophy's ancient role, Martin Heidegger [HI-deg-uhr] (1889–1976) was assaulting traditional philosophy from another angle by founding modern **existentialism.** The result of Heidegger's extensive criticism, however, was to restore philosophy to its central position as the definer of values for culture. Heidegger's major work, *Being and Time,* was published in 1927. The focal point of his thinking was the peculiar nature of human existence (the source of the term *existentialism*) as compared with other objects in the world. In his view, human existence leads to anxiety, a condition that arises because of the consciousness that there is a future that includes choices and death. He noted that most people try to avoid facing their inevitable fate by immersing themselves in trivial activities. For a few, however, Heidegger thought that the existential moment offered an opportunity in which they could seize the initiative and make themselves into authentic human beings. "Authenticity" became the ultimate human goal: to confront death and to strive for genuine creativity—a typical German philosophical attitude shared with Goethe and Nietzsche.

Heidegger is among the twentieth century's foremost philosophers, but his political activities have made him a controversial figure. He used his post as a German university professor to support the rise of Nazism in the 1930s. To hostile eyes, Heidegger's existential views—which acknowledged that individuals, powerless to reshape the world, could only accept it—seemed to support his political position. Indeed, some commentators have condemned existentialism for that reason.

Heidegger's best-known disciple, though one who rejected Nazism, was the French thinker Jean-Paul Sartre [SAHR-truh] (1905–1980). Sartre's major

Figure 20.11   ALBERTO GIACOMETTI. *Hands Holding the Void.*
1934. Plaster sculpture, original cast, ht. 61½″. Yale University
Art Gallery, New Haven, Connecticut. Anonymous gift. *The
uncertainty of the modern world—as demonstrated by both physics
and the economic and social realities of daily life—is poignantly
symbolized in Giacometti's sculpture. His melancholy figure,
clutching an invisible object, evokes the anguish humans suffered
in no longer being able to expect answers from traditional sources,
such as science and philosophy. Giacometti personally shared
these fears as he created, in this Surrealistic work (inspired by his
admiration for Egyptian sculpture), a semiseated female whose face
is a mask. She seems to be, in the opinion of one critic, searching
for what is truly human in a state of painful ignorance—the
predicament of those in the modern world.*

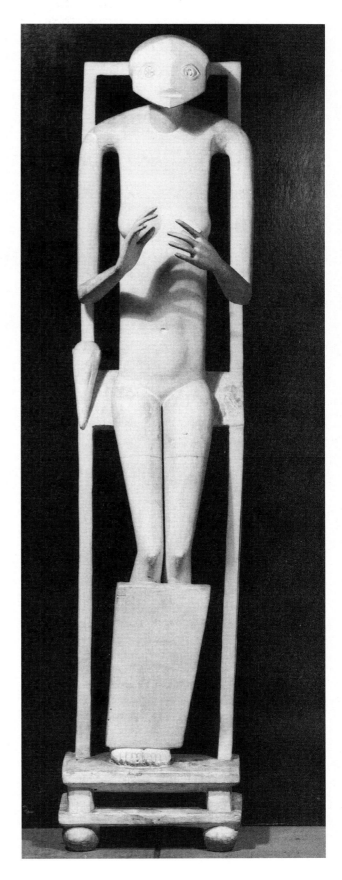

philosophical work, *Being and Nothingness* (1943), was
heavily indebted to his mentor's concepts. From Heidegger came his definition of existentialism as an attitude characterized by concern for human freedom,
personal responsibility, and individual choices. Sartre
used these ideas to frame his guiding rule: Because human beings are condemned to freedom—that is, not free
not to choose—they must take responsibility for their
actions and live "without excuses." After 1945 Sartre rejected existentialism as overly individualistic and thereafter tended to support Marxist collectivist action.

In the sciences, physics remained the field of dynamic activity. The breakthroughs made before World
War I were now corroborated by new research that
compelled scientists to discard the Newtonian model
of the universe as a simple machine. They replaced it
with a complex, sense-defying structure based on the
discoveries of Albert Einstein and Werner Heisenberg
(Figure 20.11).

Einstein was the leading scientist in the West, comparable to Newton in the eighteenth century. His special relativity theory, dating from 1905, overturned the
Newtonian concept of fixed dimensions of time and
space (see Chapter 19). In Einstein's view, absolute
space and time are meaningless categories, since they
vary with the situation. In 1915 he expanded this
earlier finding into a general theory of relativity, a universal law based on complex equations that apply
throughout the cosmos.

The heart of the general theory is that space is
curved as a result of the acceleration of objects (planets, stars, moons, meteors, and so on) as they move
through undulating trajectories. The earth's orbit
about the sun is caused not by a gravitational "force"
but by the curvature of space-time around the sun. In
1919 a team of scientists observed the curvature of
space in the vicinity of the sun and confirmed that
space curves to the degree that Einstein's theory had
forecast. Since then, his general theory has survived
many tests of its validity and has opened new paths of
theoretical speculation.

Timeline 20.1   HIGH MODERNISM, 1914–1945

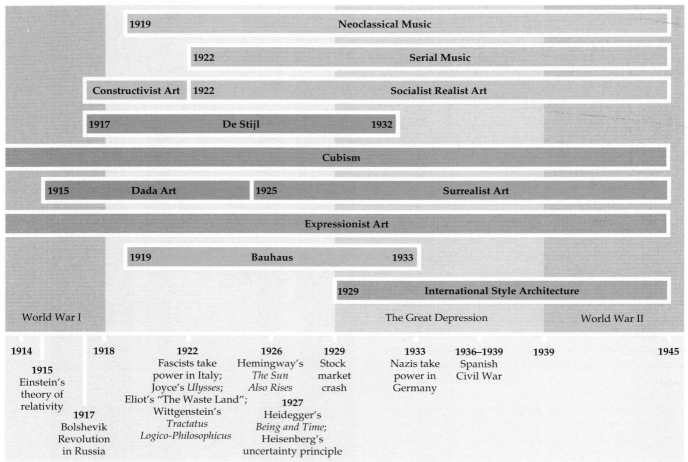

The other great breakthrough of modern physics was the establishment of quantum physics. Before 1914 the German physicist Max Planck had discovered the quantum nature of radiation in the subatomic realm (see Chapter 19). Ignoring the classical theory that energy is radiated continuously, he proved that energy is emitted in separate units that he called *quanta,* after the Latin for "how much" (as in *quantity*), and he symbolized these units by the letter *h.*

Working with Planck's *h* in 1927, which by now was accepted as a fundamental constant of nature, the German physicist Werner Heisenberg [HIZE-uhn-berg] (1901–1976) arrived at the uncertainty principle, a step that constituted a decisive break with classical physics. Heisenberg showed that a scientist could identify either an electronic particle's exact location or its path, but not both. This dilemma led to the conclusion that absolute certitude in subatomic science is impossible because scientists with their instruments inevitably interfere with the accuracy of their own work—the uncertainty principle. The incertitude involved in quantum theory caused Einstein to remark, "God does not play dice with the

world." Nevertheless, quantum theory joined relativity theory as a founding principle of modern physics.

A practical result of the revolution in physics was the opening of the nuclear age in August 1945. The American physicist J. Robert Oppenheimer [AHP-uhn-hi-muhr] (1904–1967), having made basic contributions to quantum theory, was the logical choice to head the team that built the first atomic bomb. Oppenheimer's other role as a member of the panel that advised that the atomic bombs be dropped on Japan raised ethical questions that divided the scientific community then and continue to do so.

Art, Architecture, and Film

The art, architecture, and film of the interwar period were driven by the same forces that were transforming literature and philosophy. Modernism reached its zenith in painting and architecture, and the movies became established as the world's most popular form of mass culture (Timeline 20.1).

Painting Painting dominated the visual arts in the interwar period. Painters launched new art movements every two or three years, although certain prevailing themes and interests could be discerned underneath the shifting styles: abstraction, primitivism and fantasy, and Expressionism. This era's most explosive art was produced within these stylistic categories. Picasso and Matisse, the two giants of twentieth-century art, continued to exercise their influence, yet they too worked within these three categories, all of which had arisen in the Post-Impressionist period.

ABSTRACTION The history of modern painting has been rewritten in the past forty years to accommodate the contributions of Soviet painters to abstract art. No one questions the primary role played by Picasso and Braque in Cubist paintings before World War I, but Soviet painters, beginning in 1917, moved beyond Cubism and toward full abstraction, thus staking out claims as early founders of modern abstract art. The most influential of these Soviet artists was Kasimir Malevich [mahl-YAY-vich] (1878–1935).

Influenced by the Cubists and the Futurists—an Italian school of artists who depicted forms in surging, violent motion—Malevich was already working in an abstract style when World War I began in 1914. Four years later, he was painting completely nonobjective canvases. Believing that art should convey ethical and philosophical values, he created a style of painting devoted to purity, in which he made line, color, and shape the only purposes in his art. He called this style **Suprematism,** named for his belief that the feelings are "supreme" over every other element of life— "feelings," that is, expressed in a purely rational way.

Searching for a way to visualize emotions on canvas, Malevich adopted geometric shapes as nonobjective symbols, as in *Suprematist Painting* (Figure 20.12). In this painting, design has triumphed over representation. There are only geometric shapes of different sizes and varying lengths. The choice of the geometric shapes reflects their role as basic elements of composition with no relation to nature. The qualities shown in Malevich's painting—flatness, coolness, and severe rationality—remain central to one branch of abstract art today.

Malevich's Suprematism helped to shape **Constructivism,** the first art style launched by Lenin's regime in 1917 and the last modern-art movement in Russia. Malevich's philosophical views, which were rooted in Christian mysticism, ran counter to the materialism of the Marxist government, however, and the flowering of abstraction in the Soviet Union was abruptly snuffed out in 1922. In that year, Lenin pronounced it a decadent form of bourgeois expression, and its leaders were imprisoned or exiled. In place of Constructivism,

Figure 20.12 KASIMIR MALEVICH. *Suprematist Composition.* 1916–1917. Oil on canvas, 29 × 36¼″ (73.7 × 92.1 cm). The Museum of Modern Art, New York. Photograph © 1997 The Museum of Modern Art. *Malevich's geometric style reflected his belief that abstract images had a spiritual quality comparable to that of religious icons. Thus, if approached in the proper spirit, an abstract form could become a meditation device that could lead the viewer's thoughts beyond the physical realm. For Malevich, the physical realm was no longer of use, and painting was a search for visual metaphors (mainly geometric elements) that could evoke awareness of unconscious and conscious experiences in the individual. His belief was typical of thinking among the German and Russian avant-garde in the early 1900s.*

the Soviet leaders proclaimed the doctrine of **Socialist Realism,** which demanded the use of traditional techniques and styles and the glorification of the communist ideal. This type of realistic art also had greater appeal to the Soviet masses, who had been alienated by the abstract style of Constructivism.

A movement similar to Suprematism and Constructivism, called **de Stijl** (The Style), originated in the

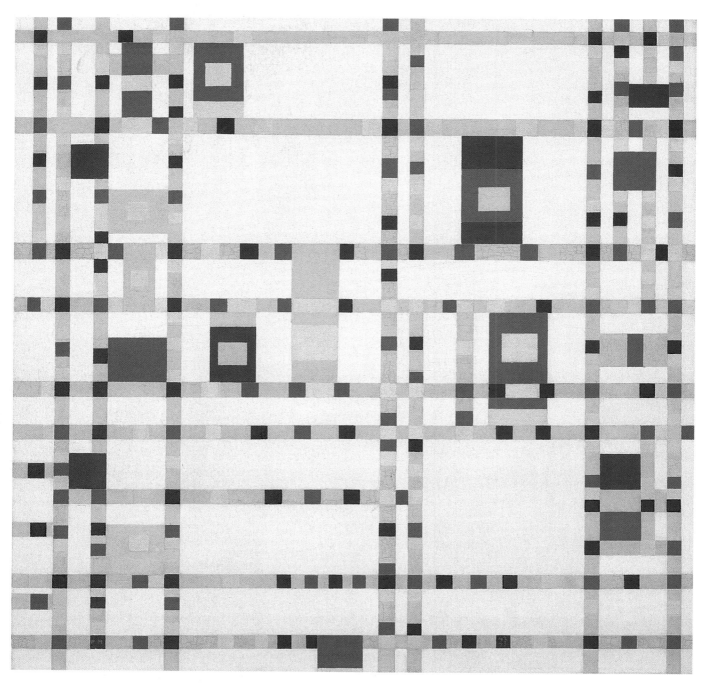

Figure 20.13 PIET MONDRIAN. *Broadway Boogie Woogie.* 1942–1943. Oil on canvas, 50 × 50". The Museum of Modern Art, New York. *Allied with those artists who identified abstract forms with spiritual values, Mondrian originated "the grid" as the ideal way to approach the canvas, allowing the verticals and horizontals to establish the painting area. In this painting, he pays homage to his new home and a dance craze of the era: The interaction of the colored lines evokes both the street map of Manhattan and the syncopated pattern of the Boogie Woogie. Mondrian's devotion to "the grid," along with his sparse use of color, gave rise to many of the dominant trends in art after World War II: two-dimensional images, geometric shapes, and "all over" paintings without a specific up or down.*

Figure 20.14 PABLO PICASSO. *The Three Musicians.* 1921. Oil on canvas, 6'8" × 6'2". Philadelphia Museum of Art. The A. E. Gallatin Collection. *This Cubist painting captures the energy of a musical performance. Here and there among the flattened shapes can be seen hints of musical instruments being fingered by disembodied hands. Only a little imagination is needed to bring this masked trio to life. The brilliant colors coupled with the broken and resynthesized forms evoke the jagged rhythms the musicians must have been playing.*

Netherlands during this period and lasted from 1917 to 1932. De Stijl artists shared the belief that art should have spiritual values and that if artists were to revamp society along rational lines, from town planning to eating utensils, a more harmonious vision of life would result.

The de Stijl movement was led by the painter Piet Mondrian [MAHN-dree-ahn] (1872–1944), who after 1919 worked successively in Paris, London, and New York. He developed an elaborate theory to give a metaphysical meaning to his abstract paintings. A member of the Theosophists—a mystical cult that flourished in about 1900—he adapted some of their beliefs to arrive at a grid format for his later paintings, notably using the Theosophists' stress on cosmic duality, in which the vertical represented the male and the horizontal the female. His paintings took the form of a rectangle divided by heavy black lines against a white background. Into this highly charged field he introduced rectangles of the primary colors—blue, yellow,

and red—which in his mystic vision stood as symbols of the sky, the sun, and dynamic union, respectively. After 1932, Mondrian began to tire of black but it was only with the coming of World War II, when he emigrated to New York City, that he was able to eliminate black. However, he remained faithful to the grid and the primary colors (Figure 20.13).

Despite the pioneering work of Suprematism and the de Stijl school, Cubism remained the leading art movement of this period, and Pablo Picasso was still the reigning Cubist. Picasso's protean genius revealed itself in multiple styles after 1920, but he continually reverted to his Cubist roots, as in *The Three Musicians* (Figure 20.14). Like the rest of his works, this painting is based on a realistic source, in this case a group of masked musicians playing their instruments. The forms appear flattened, as if they were shapes that had been cut out and then pasted to the pictorial surface—the ideal of flatness so prized by Modern painters.

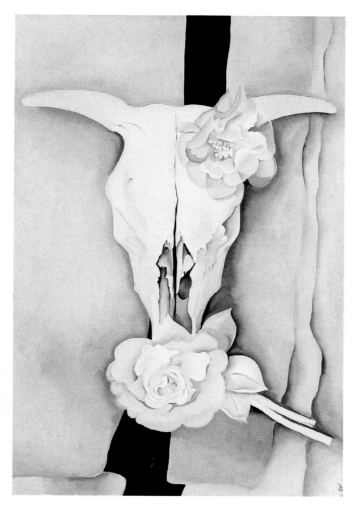

Figure 20.15   GEORGIA O'KEEFFE. *Cow's Skull with Calico Roses.* 1932. Oil on canvas, 36⁵⁄₁₆ × 24⅛". Art Institute of Chicago. Gift of Georgia O'Keeffe. *The simplified forms—the skull and the rose—link this painting to the period's trend to abstraction, but their placement so as to suggest the image of a "face" devouring a rose implies a connection with another development of this period, Surrealism, a style that delighted in realistic images with double meanings (see Figure 20.17). Whether intentional or not, O'Keeffe's overlapping of stylistic boundaries was typical of the fluid artistic scene in the years between the two world wars.*

The most famous work of Picasso's long career also dates from this period: the protest canvas *Guernica,* painted in a modified Cubist style. Picasso named this painting for an unarmed town that had been bombed by the Nazi air force (in the service of Franco) during the Spanish Civil War. Picasso used every element in the work to register his rage against this senseless destruction of human life (see Figure 20.2). The black, white, and gray tones conjure up newspaper

images, suggesting the casual way that newspapers report daily disasters. An all-seeing eye looks down on a scene of horror made visible to the world through the modern media—as symbolized by the electric bulb that acts as a retina in the cosmic eye. Images of death and destruction—the mother cradling a child's body, the stabbed horse, the enraged bull, the fallen man, and the screaming woman—are made even more terrifying by their angular forms. In retrospect, *Guernica* was a watershed painting both topically and stylistically. The blending of Cubism with social protest was new—as was Franco's type of unbridled warfare. *Guernica* forecast even more horrifying events to come.

The American painter Georgia O'Keeffe (1887–1986) refused to follow European painters down the path to pure abstraction. Instead, she pursued a distinctively American type of abstraction, using American subjects drawn from nature, which she pared to their pure form and color; at the same time, she kept representation of the natural world as a primary goal of her art. A native of Wisconsin, she found a spiritual home in the American Southwest—Texas and especially New Mexico—whose sun-drenched, stark landscapes inspired some of her most famous images. Sensitive to light, color, texture, and atmosphere, she registered in her paintings the previously hidden beauties of this desert world, as in *Cow's Skull with Calico Roses* (Figure 20.15). As early as the Renaissance, painters had occasionally used death's heads as memento mori (reminders of death), but no artist before O'Keeffe had thought of presenting a cow's skull as an art subject. The already abstract form of the cow's skull, stripped bare of flesh, became even more abstract as she simplified it and presented it close up with two roses nearby. The result is an image of shocking beauty.

PRIMITIVISM AND FANTASY   The Modernists' admiration for primitivism led to **Dada,** the most unusual art movement of the twentieth century. Named for a nonsense word chosen for its ridiculous sound, Dada flourished in Zurich and Paris between 1915 and 1925, chiefly as unruly pranks by disaffected artists who wanted to "hurl gobs of spit in the faces of the bourgeoisie." They staged exhibits in public lavatories, planned meetings in cemeteries, and arranged lectures where the speaker was drowned out by a bell. Slowly it became evident that these outrageous acts conveyed the message that World War I had made all values meaningless. These artists could no longer support the spiritual claims and traditional beliefs of Western humanism. The Dada group embraced anti-art as the only ethical position possible for an artist in the modern era.

Figure 20.16 MARCEL DUCHAMP. *The Bride Stripped Bare by Her Bachelors, Even* (or, *The Large Glass*). 1915–1923. Oil and lead wire on glass, 9'1¼" × 5'9⅛". Philadelphia Museum of Art. Bequest of Katherine M. Dreier. *Shortly after this legendary assemblage was built, the glass shattered. Duchamp repaired the work, replacing the glass with heavier panes and installing a reinforced frame. But effects of the accident are still apparent. Duchamp claimed to be delighted by these chance additions to his original design. In making this claim, he was the forerunner of the Modernist idea that chance should play a guiding role in art. After World War II, many artists began to incorporate random effects into their works.*

The most influential exponent of Dada was the French artist Marcel Duchamp [doo-SHAHN] (1887–1968), who abandoned Cubism in about 1915. His best-known Dada piece is the "definitely incomplete" work called *The Bride Stripped Bare by Her Bachelors, Even,* a mixture of oil, wire, and lead foil on two glass panels made between 1915 and 1923, sometimes called *The Large Glass* (Figure 20.16). Although it is certainly enigmatic, and in the eyes of many viewers it looked like a giant swindle, much is clear about *The Large Glass.* It has an erotic theme, typical of Dada art. Duchamp makes this theme manifest in the sculpture by devoting the upper half to the bride (the amorphous shape floating on the left) and her "apartment" (the stretch of gauze with three holes) and populating the lower "chamber" with the bachelors (the nine objects to the left) and their sex organ (the contraption made of a water mill, grinder, and

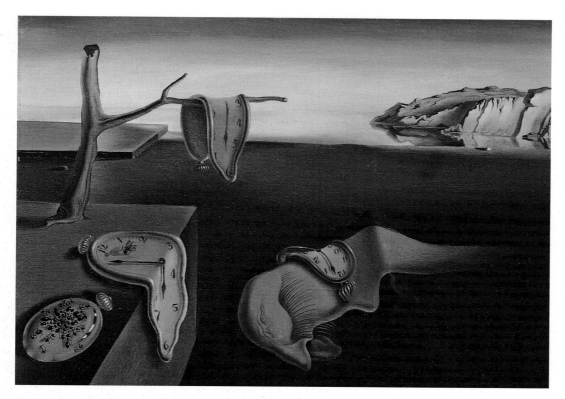

Figure 20.17   SALVADOR DALI. *The Persistence of Memory (Persistance de la mémoire).* 1931. Oil on canvas, 9½ × 13" (24.1 × 33 cm). The Museum of Modern Art, New York. Given anonymously. Photograph © 1997 The Museum of Modern Art. *Dali liked to paint images that were actually optical illusions. In this painting, the watch depicted on the right is draped over an amorphous shape that, on inspection, appears to be that of a man. Dali's use of such optical effects reflected his often-stated belief that life is irrational.*

other bits of metal). Linking the bride with the bachelors are tiny capillaries, or thin tubes, filled with oil—symbolic of fertilization with sperm. Duchamp's point seems to be similar to that of the novelist D. H. Lawrence: Sex in the machine age has become boring and mechanized.

Dada led to **Surrealism,** an art movement that began in the 1920s. Unlike Dada, Surrealism was basically a pictorial art. Inspired by Freud's teaching that the human mind conceals hidden depths, the Surrealists wanted to create a vision of reality that also included the truths harbored in the unconscious. They portrayed dream imagery, fantasies, and hallucinations in a direct fashion that made their paintings more startling than Dada. Among the leading Surrealists were Salvador Dali and Paul Klee.

The Spanish painter Salvador Dali [DAH-lee] (1904–1989) concentrated on subjects that surfaced from his lively imagination and often contained thinly disguised sexual symbols. Probably his most famous work is the poetically named painting *The Persistence of Memory,* which depicts soft, melting watches in a

desertlike setting (Figure 20.17). Sexual themes may be read in the limp images of watches—perhaps a reference to sexual impotence. Regardless of its meaning, the painting gives a strange twist to ordinary things, evoking the sense of a half-remembered dream—the goal of Surrealist art. Despite obvious painterly skills, Dali cultivated a controversial, even scandalous, personal image. His escapades earned him the public's ridicule, and the Surrealists even disowned him. From today's vantage point, however, Dali is admired for two reasons: for having created some of Modernism's most fantastic images and for being a link with the Pop artists of the 1960s.

The Swiss painter Paul Klee [KLAY] (1879–1940) may be grouped with the Surrealists, but he was too changeable to be restricted to a single style. He is best known for an innocent approach to art, which was triggered by his fondness for children's uninhibited scrawls. The childlike wonder portrayed in his whimsical works has made him a favorite with collectors and viewers. A professor from 1920 until 1930 at the Bauhaus, Germany's leading art institute between the

wars, Klee created poetic images, rich in color and gentle wit, as in *Revolution of the Viaduct* (Figure 20.18). This painting depicts the breakup of a viaduct—a series of arches built to carry a road across a wide valley—when each arch, marching on thin "legs" and footlike bases, goes its own way. More than a cartoon, this whimsical work is Klee's allegorical response to Europe's growing fascist culture—an atypical gesture by this usually apolitical artist. Klee equates the viaduct with the neo-Roman buildings favored by the Nazis as an expression of a homogeneous community ideal. The viaduct's breakup into individualized arches forecasts the downfall of Nazism. Klee thus espouses a quiet faith that fascist mass conformity may be undermined by the subversive acts of cultural revolutionaries—such as himself.

The Mexican painter Frida Kahlo [KAH-low] (1907–1954), famed for her unsettling self-portraits, might be classified with the Surrealists, though she is usually linked with the Mexican Muralists, the politically motivated artists who flourished between the two world wars and who painted mural (wall) cycles in public buildings to dramatize their socialist vision and solidarity with Mexico's native peoples. For most of her life, she was involved in a tempestuous marriage to Diego Rivera (1886–1957), a leading Mexican Muralist, but she was much more than the wife of a famous painter. Kahlo was an important artist in her own right, creating works that reflected her physical and spiritual suffering (she had polio at age six and was in a serious accident at eighteen). Today, she is known as an artist who turned private anguish into art with universal resonance.

Kahlo's self-portrait (see Figure 20.1) dates from a dark period in her life. Beset by marital and health problems and distraught over the assassination of her friend the Russian Marxist Leon Trotsky, who had been living in exile in Mexico, Kahlo was restored to health by the strict regimen of Dr. Eloesser of San Francisco. In gratitude, she dedicated this work to him, as indicated by the flying banner, which reads, in part, "to my doctor and my best friend, with all my love." Despite this upbeat motif, the portrait reflects Kahlo's obsession with death and suffering.

EXPRESSIONISM   The chief Expressionist painters in this era were Henri Matisse, a founder of Fauvism before World War I (see Chapter 19), and Max Beckmann, the heir to German Expressionism. In the 1930s Matisse's art was distinguished by its decorative quality, a tendency since his Fauvist days. *Large Reclining Nude* shows his new style, which is characterized by a fresh approach to the human figure: enlarged, simplified, though clearly recognizable (Figure 20.19). The nude figure is depicted completely flat, without modeling or

Figure 20.18   PAUL KLEE. *Revolution of the Viaduct.* 1937. Oil on canvas, 25⅝ × 19⅝". Kunsthalle, Hamburg. *Klee painted this work in the aftermath of the* Degenerate Art *exhibition, which opened in Munich in July 1937. Mounted by the Nazis to showcase what they called subversive art—art that encouraged "political anarchy and cultural anarchy"—the show was a frontal assault on Modernism. Klee, living in Switzerland after having been fired from his German teaching post in 1933, was represented by seventeen works in this show, displayed under the topics "confusion" and "insanity." Klee's* Revolution of the Viaduct *was part of the response of the international Modernist art world to the Nazi challenge.*

shading, so that it looks as if it has been cut out and glued to the gridded surface. Matisse has also abandoned the highly saturated colors of Fauvism and replaced them with cooler tones—in this case a cotton-candy pink. Nevertheless, he stayed true to the leading Expressionist principle of distortion, as demonstrated by the nude figure's elongated body and dangling limbs.

Matisse was rebuked for concentrating on pretty subjects while the world slipped into anarchy. No such charge can be made against the German painter Max Beckmann (1884–1950), whose Expressionist paintings register horror at the era's turbulent events. *The Departure* is typical of his works, being concerned with

Figure 20.19 HENRI MATISSE. *Large Reclining Nude.* 1935. Oil on canvas, approx. 26 × 36⅕″. Baltimore Museum of Art. The Cone Collection. *Matisse's* Large Reclining Nude *established the archetypal images—a still life and a model in an interior—that Matisse painted for the rest of his life. It was also the first expression of his later style, which was characterized by the human figure's being simply another element in an overall design.*

both personal and spiritual issues (Figure 20.20). The structure of the painting—divided into three panels (a triptych) like a medieval altarpiece—suggests that it has religious meaning. It was the first of nine completed triptychs. Influenced by the mystical teachings of the German thinker Arthur Schopenhauer, East Asian philosophy, and the Jewish cabala (medieval writings), *The Departure* represents a yearning to be free of the horrors of earthly existence. In the side panels, Beckmann depicts images of cruelty, including bound human figures, one of whom is gagged, being subjected to torture—perhaps reflecting his fears of the rise of Nazism. In contrast, the central panel, in which a man, woman, and child are ferried across a lake by a

hooded boatman, evokes the theme of deliverance. When the Nazis came to power in 1933, they declared Beckmann a degenerate artist, confiscated his works, and fired him from his academic post. In 1937, he sought refuge in Amsterdam, where he managed to survive World War II.

Architecture In the 1920s and 1930s, architects continued their search for a pure style, free of decoration and totally functional. Their research resembled a mystical quest, stemming from the belief that new architecture could solve social problems by creating a new physical environment—a recurrent theme in European Modernism.

Figure 20.20 MAX BECKMANN. *The Departure.* 1932–1935. Oil on canvas, center panel 7' × 3'9", side panels 7' × 3'3". The Museum of Modern Art, New York. *In* The Departure, *Beckmann's Expressionism is revealed through the treatment of form and color. The flat, angular figures, arranged into awkward positions, and the unusual perspective reinforce the painting's disturbing theme. The dark hues of the side panel, appropriate for the violent images, contrast with the bright colors of the central panel and its message of salvation.*

This visionary conception of architecture was best expressed in Germany's Bauhaus, an educational institution whose aim was to bring about social reform through a new visual environment, especially in the design of everyday objects. To that end, the school brought together artists, craftspeople, and architects. During its brief lifetime, which lasted from its founding in 1919 until 1933 when it was closed by the Nazis, the Bauhaus, under Walter Gropius [GROH-pee-uhs] (1883–1969), was the center of abstract art in Germany. The Bauhaus affected later culture in two ways. First, it developed a spartan type of interior decoration characterized by all-white rooms and wooden floors, streamlined furniture, and lighting supplied by banks of windows by day and recessed lamps at night. Second, it introduced the **Interna-**

tional style in architecture, which is sleek, geometrical, and devoid of ornament.

The International style's most distinguished representative in the period between the wars was the Swiss architect Charles-Edouard Jeanneret, better known as Le Corbusier [luh kor-boo-ZYAY] (1887–1965). Le Corbusier's artistic credo was expressed in the dictum "a house is a machine for living." In pursuit of this ideal, he pioneered building methods such as prefabricated housing and reinforced concrete as ways to eliminate ordinary walls. His Savoye House became the prototype of private houses for the wealthy after World War II (Figure 20.21). The Savoye House was painted stark white and raised on columns; its ground floor had a curved wall; and its windows were slits. A painter before becoming an architect, Le Corbusier designed

Figure 20.21   LE CORBUSIER. Savoye House. 1929–1931. Poissy, near Paris. *Le Corbusier wanted to make a break with previous styles of architecture and create a new style in tune with the machine age. His design for the Savoye House realizes this ambition completely through its severe geometrical form, its absence of decoration except for architectural details, and its sparkling white walls. When finished, the Savoye House had the streamlined look associated with industrial machinery, an achievement much admired in the 1930s.*

architecture that combined Cubism's abstractness (the raised box) with Constructivism's purity (whiteness).

Film   Motion pictures—the movies—were immediately popular when they were introduced early in the twentieth century, and by the mid-1920s they had become the most popular mass entertainment, drawing larger audiences than the theater, vaudeville, and the music halls. The American film director D. W. Griffith (1875–1948) showed in such pioneering works as *The Birth of a Nation* (1915) and *Intolerance* (1916) that it was possible to make movies that were serious, sustained works of art. His technical innovations, such as cross-cutting and the close-up, made more complex film narratives possible, but such attempts to develop the medium were rare. Although other directors quickly appropriated Griffith's techniques, few went beyond them, and the movies remained resolutely lowbrow. The present-day distinction between "movies" (the

widest possible audience) and "film" (appealing to more educated, intellectual audiences) had not yet arisen.

One of the era's most inventive directors was the Russian Sergei Eisenstein [IZE-uhn-stine] (1898–1948), who introduced directorial techniques that had an enormous influence on the rise of art films. In *The Battleship Potemkin* (1925), he pioneered the montage technique, which consisted of highly elaborate editing patterns and rhythms. He developed the montage because he believed that the key element in films was the way the scenes were arranged, how they faded out and faded in, and how they looked in juxtaposition to one another. By focusing on the material of the film itself instead of highlighting the plot or the characters' psychology, Eisenstein showed his allegiance to the artistic aspect of moviemaking.

The United States (which eventually meant Hollywood, California) had dominated the motion picture industry since World War I, and the industry underwent important changes during the interwar years. Sound movies became technically feasible in the late 1920s, and in the early 1930s three-color cinematography processes were developed. Both these technical developments became basic to the movies throughout the world, but other experiments, such as wide-screen and three-dimensional photography, were less successful. Another important development in this period was the descent on Hollywood of many German filmmakers in flight from the Nazis. In the Hollywood of the 1930s, these exiles helped to create some of the outstanding achievements in world cinema.

A sign of the excellence of Hollywood movies in these years is Orson Welles's *Citizen Kane* (1941), often called America's best film. An American, Welles (1915–1985) had learned from the German exiles and borrowed their Expressionist methods, such as theatrical lighting and multiple narrative voices. Welles's own commanding presence in the lead role also contributed to making this an unforgettable movie. But one of the hallmarks of the movie—its dark look, which underscores the brooding theme of unbridled lust for power—was in actuality a money-saving device to disguise the absence of studio sets. Is *Citizen Kane* a "film" or a "movie"? It is a measure of Welles's success that it is triumphantly both: Its frequent showing both on television and in theaters attests to its popularity, yet its discussion and analysis in film journals and books points to its high prominence as a film.

Music: Atonality, Neoclassicism, and an American Idiom

During the 1920s and 1930s, Western music was fragmented into two rival camps as a result of developments that had begun in the period before World War I (see Chapter 19). On one side was the Austro-German school headed by Arnold Schoenberg, who had introduced atonality before 1914 and in the 1920s pioneered serial music. On the other side was the French school led by Igor Stravinsky, who had experimented with primitive rhythms and harsh dissonances in the early 1900s but after World War I adopted a stern Neoclassical style.

Having abandoned tonality in 1909, Schoenberg in the 1920s introduced **serial music,** a method of composing with a **twelve-tone scale**—twelve tones that are related not to a tonal center in a major or minor key but only to each other. Lacking harmonious structure, serial music sounded dissonant and random and tended to create anxiety in listeners. As a result, serial music appealed to cult rather than mass audiences. Lack of a huge responsive public did not halt Schoenberg's

Figure 20.22 PABLO PICASSO. *Stravinsky.* 1920. Pencil on gray paper, 24⅜ × 19⅛". Musée Picasso, Paris. *Picasso's pencil sketch of Stravinsky is a perceptive character study. Long before Stravinsky became almost unapproachable, Picasso portrayed him as an aloof, self-absorbed young man. Stravinsky's cold demeanor is obvious in the tense posture, the harsh stare, and the clasped hands and crossed legs. Picasso's sketch also hints at Stravinsky's genius by exaggerating the size of his hands, perhaps to emphasize their role in the composer's creative life.*

pursuit of atonality. His serial system culminated in *Variations for Orchestra* (1928), a composition that uses the Classical form of theme with variations. In 1933 he emigrated to America, where his devotion to atonality mellowed. Some of Schoenberg's later works mix twelve-tone writing with tonality.

Stravinsky, in exile from the Soviet Union after 1917, went to live in Paris, where he became the dominant figure of **Neoclassicism** in music, borrowing features from seventeenth- and eighteenth-century music (Figure 20.22). In his Neoclassical works, he abandoned many of the techniques that had become common to music since the Baroque period, such as Romantic emotionalism and programmatic composition as well as Impressionism's use of dense orchestral sounds. Austere and cool, his Neoclassical compositions used simple instrumental combinations and sounded harmonious. Stravinsky's works from this period made him the outstanding composer of the twentieth century.

Stravinsky originated Neoclassicism in 1919 with the ballet *Pulcinella* and brought the style to a close in 1951 with the opera *The Rake's Progress*. Between these two major works is one of his most admired compositions, the *Symphony of Psalms,* dating from 1930. *Pulcinella* and *The Rake's Progress* owe much to the music and comic operas of the Classical composers Pergolesi and Mozart, respectively, and the *Symphony of Psalms* follows a Baroque model in its small orchestra and musical structure. Despite borrowing forms and ideas, Stravinsky made them his own, introducing occasional dissonances and continuing to experiment with complex rhythmic patterns.

American music, meanwhile, was discovering its own idiom. Charles Ives (1874–1954) focused on American melodies, including folk songs, hymns, marches, patriotic songs, ragtime tunes, and music of his beloved New England. Working without models, Ives experimented with tonality and rhythm in ways similar to those of the European avant-garde. Typical of his work is the *Concord Sonata* for piano (1909–1915). Another American composer, Aaron Copland (1900–1990), had achieved some success by imitating European styles, but in the 1930s he began to develop a distinctive American style. His ballet scores *Billy the Kid* (1938), *Rodeo* (1942), and *Appalachian Spring* (1944), commissioned by choreographers Agnes de Mille and Martha Graham, drew on hymns, ballads, folk tunes, and popular songs of the period. His delightful melodies, brilliant sound, jazzy experimentation, and upbeat rhythms ensured the popularity of these pieces.

A major American composer who cared less about developing a purely American idiom and more about exploring music's frontiers was George Antheil [an-TILE] (1900–1959). Living in Europe from 1922 to 1933, Antheil became part of the intellectual avant-garde who were intrigued by the machine-oriented culture of the Age of the Masses. In worshiping the machine, these artists and musicians followed in the steps of the Futurists, the Italian group who had raised "speed" to an artistic principle before World War I (see Figure 19.1). As part of the 1920s European scene, Antheil was led to incorporate industrial sounds—the music of the masses—into his compositions. Hence, his *Ballet méchanique (Mechanical Ballet)* (1924; revised 1952) included scoring for unusual "instruments" (electric bells, small wood propeller, large wood propeller, metal propeller, siren, and sixteen player pianos) as well as more traditional instruments (piano and three xylophones). Antheil claimed this as his goal in composing this iconoclastic work: "It is the rhythm of machinery, presented as beautifully as an artist knows how. . . . It is the life, the manufacturing, the industry of today."

The African American composer William Grant Still (1895–1978), who was born in the heart of the Old South, in Mississippi, also left his defining mark on this period. Still was uniquely positioned to make a major contribution to serious music. He was educated in both black and white institutions of higher learning, a student first of medicine and then of music composition and steeped in Western musical styles, both traditional and radically avant-garde, along with jazz idioms created by both white and black performers. His eclectic musical style used traditional Western musical forms infused with elements of jazz and various other forms of black musical expression, as well as popular music and orchestration. He wrote ballets, five symphonies, orchestral suites, symphonic poems, chamber works, songs, arrangements of spirituals, and operas, including *The Troubled Island* (1938), with a libretto by Langston Hughes, the first opera by an African American to be staged by a professional opera company (the New York City Opera). His most popular work today is the *Afro-American Symphony* (1931), the first symphony by a black American to be performed by a major symphony orchestra.

During this period, jazz began to reach larger audiences, in part because of the development of the radio and the phonograph. Many jazz greats created their reputations in these years. The fame of the finest jazz composer, Duke Ellington (born Edward Kennedy Ellington, 1899–1974), dated from 1927 at Harlem's Cotton Club. Ellington's songs balanced superb orchestration with improvisation and ranged from popular melodies, such as "Sophisticated Lady" (1932), to major suites, such as *Such Sweet Thunder* (1957), based on Shakespeare. Jazz's premiere female vocalist, Billie Holiday (1915–1959), whose bittersweet style was marked by innovative phrasing, also appeared then.

Two jazz performers whose careers extended well beyond this period are Louis Armstrong (1901–1971) and Ella Fitzgerald (1918–1996). Armstrong, better known as "Satchmo," became a goodwill ambassador for the United States with his loud and relaxed New Orleans–style trumpet playing. Ella Fitzgerald, a vocalist noted for her bell-like voice and elegant phrasing, became the peerless interpreter of jazz standards as well as pop tunes. In the next period, jazz fragmented into a host of styles and was a vital ingredient in the explosive birth of rock and roll, the popular music form originating in the 1950s that has since dominated popular music.

The Legacy of the Age of the Masses and High Modernism

The Age of the Masses has transformed material civilization in the West in both good and bad ways. It has given us the most destructive wars of history, the greatest economic depression since the fourteenth century, the most absolute forms of government since the late Roman Empire, the first modern attempt to eliminate an entire people, and a weapon capable of destroying the planet. At the same time, it has brought a better standard of living to most people in the West and given millions of Westerners their first taste of democracy.

This age has also had a contradictory impact on cultural developments. On the one hand, it saw the growth of a worldwide mass culture, led by American ingenuity, which began to dominate public and private life for most people. On the other hand, it inspired a revolt by Modernist artists, writers, and musicians to create works free of mass culture's influence. Their creations were experimental, perplexing, and often committed to what they defined as spiritual values. A few Modernists refused to become mass culture's adversaries, and these moderating voices pointed toward a healthier relationship between mass culture and the elitist tradition after World War II.

Besides the polarization of mass and high culture, this period left other cultural legacies. Films became accepted as a serious art form, and they remain the greatest legacy of mass culture to the twentieth century. It was also during this period that America emerged as a significant cultural force in the West, partly because of the tide of intellectuals flowing from Europe, partly because of America's growing political, economic, and military power, and partly because of excellent native schools of writers, musicians, and artists. And finally, a questioning mood became the normative way of looking at the world, replacing the certainty of previous centuries.

The Modernists had pioneered a questioning spirit in about 1900, and in this period the revolution in physics seemed to reinforce it. Einstein's conclusion that space and time are interchangeable was echoed by artists, writers, and musicians who focused on form to define content in their work. And Heisenberg's uncertainty principle seemed to reverberate everywhere—from Wittgenstein's toying with language to the highly personal narrative voices that dominated the novel to the constantly shrinking set of basic beliefs that characterized the period's religious thought and, ultimately, to the widespread belief that Western civilization had lost its course.

KEY CULTURAL TERMS

mass culture
stream-of-consciousness
epic theater
logical positivism
existentialism
Suprematism
Constructivism
Socialist Realism

de Stijl
Dada
Surrealism
International style
serial music
twelve-tone scale
Neoclassicism

SUGGESTIONS FOR FURTHER READING

Primary Sources

BRECHT, B. *The Threepenny Opera.* English version by D. Vesey and English lyrics by E. Bentley. New York: Limited Editions Club, 1982. An excellent adaptation of Brecht's biting drama about the underworld in Victorian England; Bentley's lyrics capture the slangy flavor of the German play first staged in 1928.

COCTEAU, J. *The Infernal Machine and Other Plays.* Norfolk, Conn.: New Directions, 1964. Cocteau fuses Classicism with experimental methods in his Modernist plays; he updates the Oedipus legend, for example, by introducing Freudian ideas and using film clips to present flashbacks.

ELIOT, T. S. *Collected Poems, 1909–1962.* New York: Harcourt, Brace & World, 1963. Eliot, a pillar of Modernism, portrayed his times as exhausted and abandoned by God.

FAULKNER, W. *The Sound and the Fury.* New York: Modern Library, 1946. The most admired novel from the Yoknapatawpha series, Faulkner's monumental study of post–Civil War Mississippi society.

HEIDEGGER, M. *Being and Time.* Translated by J. Macquarrie and E. Robinson. New York: Harper, 1962. First published in 1927, this work helped launch the existentialist movement by portraying the universe as a meaningless place and human existence as a never-ending quest for authenticity.

HEMINGWAY, E. *The Sun Also Rises.* New York: Scribner's, 1970. Hemingway's semiautobiographical first novel, set in France and Spain in 1925.

HUGHES, L. *Selected Poems of Langston Hughes.* London: Pluto, 1986. Poetry by one of the twentieth century's outstanding writers.

JOYCE, J. *Ulysses.* New York: Penguin, 1986. This classic of Modernism uses a tapestry of narrative styles to portray a day in the lives of three middle-class citizens of Dublin.

LAWRENCE, D. H. *Lady Chatterley's Lover.* New York: Modern Library, 1983. A controversial work that poses sex as a panacea for the ills of contemporary industrialized life.

O'NEILL, E. *Three Plays: Desire Under the Elms, Strange Interlude, Mourning Becomes Electra*. New York: Vintage, 1961. O'Neill's trilogy of plays based on Aeschylus's *Oresteia* and involving a contemporary New England family.

ORWELL, G. *Animal Farm; Burmese Days; A Clergyman's Daughter; Coming Up for Air; Keep the Aspidistra Flying; Nineteen Eighty-four*. New York: Octopus/Heinemann, 1980. This volume contains Orwell's most significant writings, most of which convey the author's hatred of tyranny and his skepticism about the future of humanity.

SARTRE, J.-P. *Being and Nothingness: An Essay in Phenomenological Ontology*. Translated and with an introduction by H. E. Barnes. Abridged. New York: Citadel Press, 1956. Sartre sets forth his existentialist philosophy, focusing on such key ideas as individual freedom and personal responsibility.

WALKER, A., ed. *I Love Myself When I Am Laughing . . . And Then Again When I Am Looking Mean and Impressive: A Zora Neale Hurston Reader*. Introduction by M. H. Washington. Old Westbury, N.Y.: The Feminist Press, 1979. A judicious collection of Hurston's writings, including excerpts from novels (*Their Eyes Were Watching God*, 1936) and autobiography (*Dust Tracks on a Road*, 1942); essays ("How It Feels to Be Colored Me," 1928, "Crazy for Democracy," 1945); and short stories ("The Gilded Six-bits," 1933); with an admiring "afterword" by the celebrated writer Alice Walker.

WITTGENSTEIN, L. *Tractatus Logico-Philosophicus*. Translated by D. F. Pears and B. F. McGuiness, with an introduction by B. Russell. London: Routledge and Kegan Paul, 1974. An excellent English-language version of the treatise that led to logical positivism in philosophy.

WOOLF, V. *To the Lighthouse*. London: Hogarth Press, 1974. A typical Woolf novel in its stream-of-consciousness technique and its exquisitely detailed observations of contemporary thinking.

YEATS, W. B. *The Collected Poems of W. B. Yeats*. Edited by R. J. Finneran. New York: Collier Books, 1989. One of Modernism's leading voices, Yeats wrote poetry devoted to such themes as Celtic myth, the tragic violence of Irish history, and the mystical nature of human existence.

SUGGESTIONS FOR LISTENING

ANTHEIL, GEORGE (1900–1959). An American composer who worked in both experimental and traditional forms, Antheil lived in Europe in the 1920s and 1930s. His best-known experimental work is *Ballet mécanique (Mechanical Ballet)* (1924; revised 1952), scored for airplane propellers and other industrial noises. Recognizing that his mechanical aesthetic was at a dead end with this work, Antheil spent the rest of his career searching for a personal style: from Neoclassicism (1925–1927), as in the lyrical *Piano Concerto* (1926); to Americana experiments (1927–1942), as in the opera *Transatlantic* (1927–1928), a political farce about an American presidential election; to neoromanticism, as in Symphony No. 4 (1942) and Symphony No. 5 (1947–1948), which blend melodic and rhythmic experiments with Classical forms.

COPLAND, AARON (1900–1990). Copland's most popular works incorporate folk melodies and pay homage to the American way of life. Copland used cowboy songs in the ballet scores *Billy the Kid* (1938) and *Rodeo* (1942); he incorporated variations on the Shaker hymn "Simple Gifts" in *Appalachian Spring* (1944), originally a ballet score that was later re-arranged as a suite for symphony orchestra. His faith in the future of democracy is expressed most fully in the short, often-performed work *Fanfare for the Common Man*.

ELLINGTON, EDWARD KENNEDY ("DUKE") (1899–1974). Ellington's jazz style blended careful orchestration with ample opportunity for improvisation. Many of his songs have become standards in the popular music repertory, such as "Creole Love Call" (1928), "Mood Indigo" (1934), "Don't Get Around Much Anymore" (1940), and "Sophisticated Lady" (1932). Less well known are his serious compositions, such as *Such Sweet Thunder* (1957) and *In the Beginning God* (1965), a religious work.

IVES, CHARLES (1874–1954). America's first great composer, Ives experimented with atonality, clashing rhythms, and dissonant harmony long before they became a standard part of twentieth-century music. He frequently drew on American themes, as in the *Concord Sonata* for piano (1909–1915) and the orchestral *Three Places in New England* (1903–1914, first performed in 1931), works that evoked the landscape of his native region. A good example of one of his atonal works is *The Unanswered Question* (1908), a small work for trumpet, four flutes, and strings.

SCHOENBERG, ARNOLD (1874–1951). During this period, Schoenberg, the leader of the school of atonality, originated serialism as a method of composing, as may be heard in *Variations for Orchestra* (1928), the unfinished opera *Moses and Aaron* (1932), and *Violin Concerto* (1936).

STILL, WILLIAM GRANT (1895–1978). Still's eclectic style usually relied on traditional Western musical forms while drawing on diverse elements of his African American background and hybrid educational experience, including jazz, popular music and orchestration, Negro spirituals, and Western avant-garde music. Notable achievements include the ballet *Lenox Avenue* (1937), the opera *The Troubled Island* (1938), with a libretto by Langston Hughes, and the *Afro-American Symphony* (1931).

STRAVINSKY, IGOR (1882–1971). Schoenberg's rival Stravinsky became the leader of Neoclassicism in music with the ballet *Pulcinella* (1919) and continued this musical style in such works as the *Symphony of Psalms* (1930), the opera-oratorio *Oedipus Rex (Oedipus the King)* (1927), the *Symphony in C* (1940), and the opera *The Rake's Progress* (1951).

CHAPTER *20* HIGHLIGHTS
The Age of the Masses and the Zenith of Modernism, 1914—1945

ELIOT, *The Love Song of J. Alfred Prufrock* (1915)

YEATS, Poems (1919–1927)

HUGHES, Poems (1921–1951)

JOYCE, *Ulysses* (1922)

WITTGENSTEIN, *Tractatus Logico-Philosophicus* (1922)

HEMINGWAY, *The Sun Also Rises* (1926)

HEIDEGGER, *Being and Time* (1927)

LAWRENCE, *Lady Chatterley's Lover* (1928)

HURSTON, "How It Feels to Be Colored Me" (1928)

FAULKNER, *The Sound and the Fury* (1929)

WOOLF, *A Room of One's Own* (1929)

O'NEILL, *Mourning Becomes Electra* (1931)

STEIN, *The Autobiography of Alice B. Toklas* (1933)

COCTEAU, *The Infernal Machine* (1934)

SARTRE, *Being and Nothingness* (1943)

ORWELL, *Animal Farm* (1945)

WIESEL, *Night* (1960)

20.16 DUCHAMP, *The Bride Stripped Bare by Her Bachelors, Even (or, The Large Glass)* (1915–1923)

20.12 MALEVICH, *Suprematist Composition* (1916–1917)

20.14 PICASSO, *The Three Musicians* (1921)

20.21 LE CORBUSIER, Savoye House, France (1929–1931)

20.17 DALI, *The Persistence of Memory* (1931)

20.15 O'KEEFFE, *Cow's Skull with Calico Roses* (1932)

20.20 BECKMANN, *The Departure* (1932–1935)

20.11 GIACOMETTI, *Hands Holding the Void* (1934)

20.19 MATISSE, *Large Reclining Nude* (1935)

20.2 PICASSO, *Guernica* (1937)

20.18 KLEE, *Revolution of the Viaduct* (1937)

20.1 KAHLO, *Self-Portrait Dedicated to Dr. Eloesser* (1940)

20.9 LAWRENCE, *Migration Series, No. 58* (1940–1941)

20.13 MONDRIAN, *Broadway Boogie Woogie* (1942–1943)

IVES, *Concord Sonata* (1909–1915)

ANTHEIL, *Ballet méchanique* (1924)

BRECHT AND WEILL, *The Threepenny Opera* (1928)

SCHOENBERG, *Variations for Orchestra* (1928)

STRAVINSKY, *Symphony of Psalms* (1930)

STILL, *Afro-American Symphony* (1931)

ELLINGTON, "Mood Indigo" (1934)

COPLAND, *Appalachian Spring* (1944)

 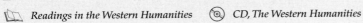

Literature & Philosophy   *Art & Architecture*   *Music & Dance*

Readings in the Western Humanities   *CD, The Western Humanities*

AFRICA

HISTORY

North Africa   Site of major WWII campaign. *Egypt*. British protectorate, then independent. *Libya*. Italian colony. *Morocco*. French, Spanish, and Moroccan zones.

Northeast Africa   *Ethiopia*. Haile Selassie's reign began (1928). Conquered by Italy; liberated by Britain.

West Africa   *French Equatorial Africa*. Modern Chad made French. *French West Africa*. French colony (modern Benin, Burkina Faso, Ivory Coast, Guinea, Senegal, Mauritania, Mali, and Niger). *Liberia*. Prosperity from rubber exports. *Nigeria*. Fulani Empire of Sokoto fell to British.

Central Africa   *Congo Free State*. Annexed to Belgium.

East Africa   *Tanganyika* (with Zanzibar, modern Tanzania). German, then British rule.

South Africa   *Union of South Africa*. British and Dutch colonies united in self-governing state under British (1910).

ART & MUSIC

East Africa   *Tanganyika*. Carved wooden canes and swagger sticks; figure heads on musical instruments and lids or stoppers on medicinal containers; ritual masks; and tomb figures.

South Africa   *Union of South Africa*. Ndebele: beadwork (cloaks and long trains); mural art. Zulu: carved wooden ear plugs.

West Africa   *Nigeria*. Carved wooden verandah and interior posts; palace doors; ritual vessels; shrine figures; headdresses and masks. Iron staffs with decorated ends. Decorated leather bags.

Olowe of Ise. Decorated column from the Palace of Ikere, Nigeria. 1910–1914. Wood and pigment. Art Institute of Chicago.

ARCHITECTURE

RELIGION, PHILOSOPHY, LITERATURE

South Africa   Poet Nicolaas Petrus van Wyk Louw, perhaps the greatest figure in Afrikaans literature.

West Africa   *Nigeria*. Daniel O. Fagunwa, Yoruba chief, first original writer in Yoruba, and popular novelist. *Senegal*. Poet and president of Senegal (1960–80) Léopold Senghor helped develop concept of Négritude, or blackness.

AMERICAS

HISTORY

Caribbean   *Cuba*. Became independent with end of U.S. occupation (1902). Corrupt, brutal regimes followed; frequent U.S. intervention. *Jamaica*. Racial tension; weak economy.

Latin America   *Mexico*. Revolution (1910–21). Natural resources, including oil, nationalized; church property appropriated by state; great estates broken up; education made secular. *Argentina*. Economic depression; military dominated politics. *Brazil*. Fascist under Getúlio Vargas. *Colombia*. Lost Panama after civil war. *Peru*. Prosperity under dictator Augusto Leguía (to 1930). Campaign for Indian rights (from 1920s).

Native North America   Most Indians lived in poverty on 200 federal reservations. By end of WWII, uranium, oil, and other mineral resources found under many reservations in West.

ART & MUSIC

Caribbean   *Cuba*. Wilfredo Lam, inspired by Picasso, Surrealism, and Afro-Cuban culture. *Haiti*. Primitivist school of art begun.

Latin America   *Mexico*. Nationalist art and Symbolist-style painting (to 1920). Muralists including Diego Rivera, David Alfaro Siqueiros, and José Clemente Orozco produced public murals with political messages (1920–50). *Argentina*. Tango dance and music born in brothels and dance halls. *Brazil*. Cubist and Expressionist art with Brazilian themes (1920s). Nationalist art (1930s). *Peru*. Christ of the Andes sculpture, on Chile-Argentine border, commemorating peaceful settlement of border dispute.

Native North America   Edward Curtis published 20 volumes of photographs of Native American peoples (1899–1924).

ARCHITECTURE

Latin America   *Mexico*. Retail stores in major cities built in Art Nouveau style. Introduction of new materials (cast iron and reinforced concrete). *Brazil*. International style (to 1930s). Functional Modernism, marked by the sensuous curve (after 1936). *Peru*. Lima's Gran Hotel Bolívar (1924), the country's central meeting place.

DIEGO RIVERA. The Arsenal, or Distribution of Arms. 1928. Mural, south wall, Courtyard of the Fiestas, Ministry of Public Education, Mexico City.

RELIGION, PHILOSOPHY, LITERATURE

Caribbean   *Jamaica*. Rise of Rastafarianism, a religious movement with political goals, especially returning black people to Africa (1904). *Martinique*. Poet Aimé Césaire helped develop concept of Négritude, or blackness.

Latin America   *Mexico*. *Revista Moderna*, a journal read by artists and intellectuals. José Clemente Orozco's *Autobiography* (1945). *Nicaragua*. Poet Rubén Darío founded Spanish American Modernist literary movement. *Argentina*. Author Jorge Luis Borges, a founder of magic realism. *Chile*. Avantgarde poet and novelist Vicente Huidobro. Gabriela Mistral, first Latin American and first woman poet to be awarded Nobel Prize for literature (1945). *Peru*. César Vallejo, author of *Human Poems* (1939).

Native North America   *Black Elk Speaks*, biography of Oglala Sioux holy man by John Neihardt (1932).

ASIA

China

Ch'ing Dynasty, ended 1911. Last emperor abdicates (1911). *Republic of China, 1912–49.* Fragmented into regions controlled by rival warlords. Sun Yat-sen, the father of modern China, led the Kuomintang, or Nationalist Party, based on nationalism, democracy, and socialism. China mistreated at Versailles Conference; anti-Western feelings grew. Chiang Kai-shek set up Nationalist Government at Nanjing (1928). Japan invaded Manchuria (1931). Communists, led by Mao Zedong, made "Long March" into north China. War with Japan (1937–45).

India

British Crown (Raj), ended 1947. Amritsar riots against Britain. Indians allowed to sit in legislative councils (1919); Gandhi's nonviolent campaign for independence begun (1920). Britain separated India from Burma and Aden, and ruled India through 11 provinces, each with a governor. Vital to Allies in World War II.

Japan

Meiji Restoration, ended 1912. Emerged as a major Far East power, after defeating Russia (1905) and annexing Korea (1910). *Taishō period, 1912–26.* Forced trade concessions from China (1915). Less militant (1924–31). *Shōwa period, began 1926.* Turbulent reign of Emperor Hirohito. Resurgence of militarism and expansionism (1930s). Invasion of Manchuria (1931); war with China (1937–45); pact with Axis powers Germany and Italy (1940); war with U.S. and its allies (1941–45).

Republic of China. Kuomintang party pushed for official style blending traditional and Western art, but traditional painting, free of Western influence, was most popular.

Gao Jianfu. Flying in the Rain. *Ca. 1920–1930. Art Museum of the Chinese Museum, Hong Kong (73.831).7*

Fragmented art world; Western styles challenged traditional styles.

YOSHIDA HIROSHAI. Sailboat, Morning. 1926. Polychrome woodblock print on paper, 20⅛ × 14⅛". Museum of Art, Atami, Shizuoka prefecture, Japan.

Meiji and Taishō periods. Quest for authentic Japanese painting (to 1921). Sculptors inspired by Western artists, mainly Rodin. Demise of *ukiyo-e* prints; new woodblock styles emerged. Hostile climate for innovation (after 1921). *Shōwa period.* Rival factions (1930s). Arts regulated during WWII.

Republic of China. Chung Shan Hospital, Shanghai, built in Chinese Revival style (1937).

British Crown. Sir Edwin L. Luytens, British architect, laid out the capital New Delhi and designed Viceroy House, which blended traditional Indian with European Classical forms.

Taishō and Shōwa periods. Strong direct and indirect influence from the West, including Frank Lloyd Wright's Imperial Hotel (1923), Tokyo, and the Diet Building (1936), based on Western forms, designed by a committee of Japanese architects.

EDWIN L. LUYTENS. Viceroy House, East Front. 1931. Buff and rhubarb-red sandstone. New Delhi.

Ch'ing Dynasty. Lui E's novel, *The Travels of Lao Ts'an,* about the Boxer Rebellion. *Republic of China.* Writers and thinkers influenced by Western literature and thought, especially Marxism. Lu Hsün, a short story writer and translator of Western works. The author and philologist Lin Yu-t'ang wrote works of nonfiction (for example, *My Country and My People* [1936]) and novels and founded first satirical journal in China. Peking University established.

British Crown. British and Western styles of writing and learning flourished. Two trends in Hindi fiction: social realism and psychological profiles. Rabindranath Tagore awarded the Nobel Prize for literature (1913).

Meiji Restoration. Writing reflected Western and native themes. Mori Ōgai, a founder of modern Japanese literature. Shimazaki Tōson's *Broken Commandment,* a work of social realism (1906). *Taishō period.* Sōseki Natsume's novel *Kokoro* (1914), dealing with the crisis of Modernism. Akutagawa Ryūnosuke's "Rashōmon" short story (1915). *Shirakaba (White Birch),* a journal that introduced Western styles. *Shōwa period.* Jun'ichirō Tanizaki's *Some Prefer Nettles* (1929), a novel of erotic despair.

21 THE AGE OF ANXIETY AND BEYOND

1945–

Fear of nuclear war had a pervasive effect on attitudes and events after 1945 and led to an enormous buildup of weapons by the United States and the Soviet Union. This arms buildup in turn contributed to uncontrolled military spending at the expense of domestic programs. For some, anxiety about nuclear war produced a sense of absurdity and a mood of despair. Against the backdrop of these realities, the cultural style known as Late Modernism captured the anguish experienced by many artists, writers, and intellectuals.

FROM A EUROPEAN TO A WORLD CIVILIZATION

The end of World War II brought the cold war, an era of international tensions and conflicting ideologies. World relations were governed by a bipolar balance of power between the United States and the Union of Soviet Socialist Republics (USSR) (Figure 21.1). The American bloc included Western Europe, the British Commonwealth, and their former enemies, Japan, West Germany, and Italy. The Soviet bloc embraced virtually all of Eastern Europe and, after 1949, when the Communists took power, China.

The cold war escalated for two main reasons. First, the superpowers extended their confrontations to the Third World, rushing in to influence events as the West's colonial empires fell and were replaced by struggling independent states. Second, the development of ballistic missiles capable of hurtling nuclear weapons across intercontinental distances raised the possibility of sudden strikes and mass destruction without warning.

Detail JOHN BENNETT,
◀ GUSTAVO BONEVARDI,
RICHARD NASH GOULD,
JULIAN LAVERDIERE, PAUL
MARANTZ, AND PAUL MYODA.
"Tribute in Light." Photo: Vincent Laforet. The New York Times.

Figure 21.1   WALLACE K. HARRISON INTERNATIONAL COMMITTEE OF ARCHITECTS. United Nations Headquarters. 1949–1951. New York. *The decision to locate the United Nations Headquarters in New York made that city the unofficial capital of the free world—a term that was applied to the United States and its allies during the cold war. And the choice of a "glass box" skyscraper for the United Nations Secretariat building helped to ensure that the International style would be the reigning style of architecture in the postwar period, until about 1970.*

The last thirty years of the twentieth century brought more uncertainty but, at the same time, an emerging sense of optimism—and an increasingly globalized culture. International population explosions raised the specter of food shortages and famines, new technological breakthroughs seemed to entail economic and employment crises, and environmental calamities threatened the earth's ecosystem. These issues were recognized as world problems and not simply Western dilemmas. On the other hand, the easing of the tensions of the cold war, culminating with the fall of communism in 1989, the economic booms of the eighties and nineties, and the advances in the biological sciences counterbalanced some of the negative trends. In the 1990s, especially, the growth of globalization was hastened by the continued economic prosperity in

the West, the revolutions in the computer and telecommunication industries, and the unprecedented migration of peoples from undeveloped countries to the industrialized world.

However, the renewed sense of hope, which marked the beginning of the twenty-first century, quickly dissipated. The economic euphoria of the nineties disappeared, conflicts over the Middle East intensified, and terrorism spread around the world, including attacks on the United States.

The Era of the Superpowers, 1945–1970

Between 1945 and 1970, the West followed two patterns. For the American bloc, democracy was the rule, social welfare was slowly expanded, and the economies were booming. For the Soviet bloc, collectivist regimes prevailed, social welfare was comprehensive, and the economies either stagnated or grew slowly. The two systems emerged as seemingly inevitable consequences of World War II.

Postwar Recovery and the New World Order   The chief Allied powers—the United States, Great Britain, and the Soviet Union—began to plan for the postwar era before World War II ended. They agreed to occupy Germany and Japan, giving those nations representative forms of government and drastically curbing their military systems. They joined with forty-eight other countries in 1945 to found the United Nations, a peacekeeping and human rights organization dealing with international disputes (see Figure 21.1). They also prepared for worldwide economic recovery by establishing a transnational monetary fund to help nations devastated by the war; however, the Soviet Union refused to participate in these economic arrangements.

When peace came in 1945, the Allies split Germany into four occupied zones. In 1949 Britain, France, and the United States united their zones into the Federal Republic of Germany (West Germany), and the USSR set up its zone as the German Democratic Republic (East Germany). By 1969 West Germany, led by moderates devoted to capitalism, had become Europe's chief industrial power, and East Germany, under a collectivist regime, lagged far behind.

In Japan, the American victors imposed a democratic constitution that kept the emperor as a figurehead; introduced a parliamentary system; gave the vote to women, workers, and farmers; and virtually eliminated the military. Between 1950 and 1973, under this renovated system, Japan's domestic product grew more than 10 percent a year on average, surpassing that of any other industrialized nation.

By the early 1950s, both Great Britain and France were enjoying moderate economic growth, although each was beset by continuing labor unrest. Left-wing governments in both countries nationalized major industries and founded national health-care systems, although conservatives periodically returned some businesses to private hands.

France and West Germany recognized that in the age of the superpowers the era of the small state was over and that it was necessary to join economic forces to gain economic stability. In 1957 they initiated a free-trade zone that also included Belgium, the Netherlands, Luxembourg, and Italy. Called the European Economic Community, or the Common Market, this organization became the driving force in Europe's prosperity over the next decade.

A large reason for the formation of the Common Market was that the USSR threatened to dominate Europe. After World War II, Soviet troops occupied neighboring countries in Eastern Europe, ostensibly to provide a military shield for the USSR. By 1948 the Soviets had converted these countries into Communist satellites, their industrial and agricultural systems tied to the Soviet economy. Thus, the USSR loomed more as a menace to than an ally of Western Europe.

The architect of the Soviet Union's rise to superpower status was Joseph Stalin, who was determined to keep the collectivist system free of the taint of capitalism and the Western idea of freedom. He demanded extreme sacrifices from Soviet citizenry to bring their war-shattered economy up to the level of the advanced industrialized countries. After Stalin's death in 1953, his successors were more moderate, but they continued the policies of censorship and repression.

The United States took up the torch of free-world leadership in 1945, claiming to have earned this status because of crucial contributions to Allied victory. It further believed that the war had been a moral crusade for human freedom, and thus it should protect the rights of people everywhere. On the basis of these beliefs, the United States justified an activist foreign policy, and between 1945 and 1970 it was probably the wealthiest and most powerful country that ever existed.

American domestic life was marked by a radical shift in mood from the 1950s to the 1960s. The 1950s was a decade of complacency and blandness. The 1960s, in contrast, was a turbulent decade around the world, of which the American experience was only a part. In the 1960s, millions of people protested against the Vietnam War, racism, and old ways of thinking. Hippies cultivated a bohemian lifestyle and contributed to the emergence of a counterculture that rejected mainstream values and traditions.

Racial prejudice was the most pressing domestic problem in the United States because it was so embedded in the nation's history. In 1954 the Supreme Court declared segregation in public schools unconstitutional. The next year, Rosa Parks, a black Alabaman, refused to move to the back of a bus as required by state law and was jailed. The social protest that was sparked by the jailing of Parks marked a watershed in American race relations. Rejecting a historically passive role, black citizens began to use the tactics of civil disobedience in their crusade to win equal rights. Nevertheless, the civil rights movement did not begin on a national scale until the 1960s. After some stalling, the federal government instigated changes in education, living conditions, and voting rights. In 1968 the civil rights struggle temporarily lost direction and momentum when its leader, Martin Luther King, Jr., was assassinated, but new leaders arose in America's black community who have continued the struggle against racism.

The Cold War   Hope for peace and cooperation among the victorious powers disappeared after 1945 as the USSR and the United States defined their respective spheres of influence. By 1949 an "iron curtain" had descended in Europe, dividing the West from the East (Map 21.1). In 1949 fear of a Soviet invasion led the Western democracies to form a military alliance called the North Atlantic Treaty Organization (NATO) with the United States as its leader. The Eastern bloc countered with the Warsaw Pact (1955), an alliance led by the Soviet Union. A race to stockpile weapons ensued, dividing the industrial world into armed camps. By 1955 a balance of terror seemed to have been reached because both the United States and the USSR possessed the atomic and hydrogen bombs. Nevertheless, the race for more weapons continued.

The East-West contest for power spread to other regions of the world. In 1949 Chinese Communists defeated the ruling Kuomintang party and commenced to build a socialist system under the leadership of Mao Zedong [MAU (D)ZE-DUHNG] (1949–1976) (Figure 21.2). The struggle between the superpowers shifted to the Far East, where a limited war emerged between North and South Korea, which had been divided after World War II into two independent states. In 1950 Soviet-dominated North Korea invaded South Korea to reunite the two states. Alarmed at this expansion of communism, the United States, under the auspices of the United Nations, sent troops in support of the South Koreans. Later in the year, China dispatched its soldiers to aid the North Koreans. After months of fighting, a stalemate resulted along the old borders, which were finally guaranteed in 1953 by an armistice. The Korean War ended in a draw, but it established one of the guiding principles of the nuclear age—that wars would not necessarily escalate into

LEARNING THROUGH MAPS

Map 21.1   EUROPE IN 1955
This map shows Europe at the height of the cold war. **Notice** the division of Europe between NATO and the Communist bloc. **Which** countries were not members of either alliance? **Which** countries would most likely be battlegrounds if war occurred between the two power blocs? **Notice** also the division between East Germany and West Germany. **Observe** the westward expansion of the Soviet Union in this map, as compared with the smaller Soviet Union on Map 20.1, Europe After World War I.

nuclear confrontations; they could be fought with conventional weapons rather than with nuclear arms.

Cold war tensions were heightened—and symbolized—by the Berlin Wall, which was built in 1961 by East Germany to prevent its citizens from going to West Berlin. Conceived as a way to save communism, this armed border only intensified divisions between Western and Eastern Europe. But the severest strain on the superpower system was the Vietnam War, which erupted in the early 1960s. Originating as a civil war, it became a cold war contest when the United States joined South Vietnam to repel the Communist troops invading from the north. For American soldiers, the war was doubly difficult to wage because it was fought in unfamiliar jungle terrain against a guerrilla army and because it became so violently unpopular at home. Protests culminated in confrontations at universities in Ohio and Mississippi, leaving six students killed in clashes with public authorities (Figure 21.3).

The Vietnam War was a turning point in world affairs. The United States withdrew from South Vietnam in 1973, thereby allowing its conquest by North Vietnam in 1975. Certain conclusions were quickly drawn from this setback to American might. First, the country's superpower status was cast into doubt, and its leaders became reluctant to exercise military power. Second, the war illustrated a new principle of foreign relations—namely, that even superpowers could not defeat small states by means of conventional warfare. Taken together, these post–Vietnam era principles suggested that the international influence of the United States was in decline and opened the door to new forms of global cooperation in the 1970s.

Emergence of the Third World   After 1945 Europe's overseas territories began to struggle for freedom and self-government, and by 1964 most of the empires had been replaced by independent countries. In 1946 the

United States let go of a former colony, the Philippines. In 1947 Great Britain agreed to divide India into a Hindu-dominated state—India—and a separate Muslim state—Pakistan. The Dutch gave up the East Indies, which in 1950 became Indonesia. France tried to retain Indochina but in 1954 was driven out, and the former colony was divided into North and South Vietnam.

In the Middle East, Arab states were freed by France and Britain, who had dominated them since 1919. After 1945 the region was in continual turmoil because its oil was needed by the industrialized states, its geopolitical position in the eastern Mediterranean attracted the superpowers, and Islamic fundamentalism led to militant Arab nationalism. But the founding of Israel as a Jewish state in 1948, following World War II and the Holocaust, contributed the most to an unstable Middle East. Israel's founding resulted in the expulsion of more than a half million Arabs from Palestine, and the fate of these refugees has contributed to constant conflict in the region. Further instability has been caused by the decline of Iran and the rise of Iraq as an independent state.

In Africa, nearly all colonies became free, although through often painful and costly transitions. In the 1960s, France concluded a bloody war in Algeria, relinquishing it and most of its other colonies in West Africa. The British withdrew gradually from East Africa, leaving behind bureaucracies that could serve the new states. In southern Africa, Rhodesia became Zimbabwe in 1980, achieving independence from Great Britain and gaining black majority rule.

Figure 21.2 ANDY WARHOL. *Mao.* 1973. Acrylic and silk-screen on canvas, 14′6⅞″ × 11′4½″. Art Institute of Chicago. Mr. and Mrs. Frank G. Logan Purchase Prize and Wilson L. Mead Funds. *A feature of totalitarian societies in the twentieth century was the personality cult, the practice of giving a political leader heroic dimensions. In Communist China, the cult of Mao Zedong established Mao as a secular god. American Pop artist Andy Warhol turned Mao's official photograph into a pop culture icon, suggesting that there was no difference between propaganda in a totalitarian state and media stardom in a free society.*

Figure 21.3 The National Guard at Kent State, Ohio. 1970. *This photograph bears a striking resemblance to Goya's* Execution of the Third of May, 1808 *(see Figure 17.18), a painting that protested the killing of Spanish civilians by French soldiers. In the tense days after the Kent State deaths, this photograph served a similar function in American society as many people began to think of the dead students as martyrs to the anti–Vietnam War cause.*

LEARNING THROUGH MAPS

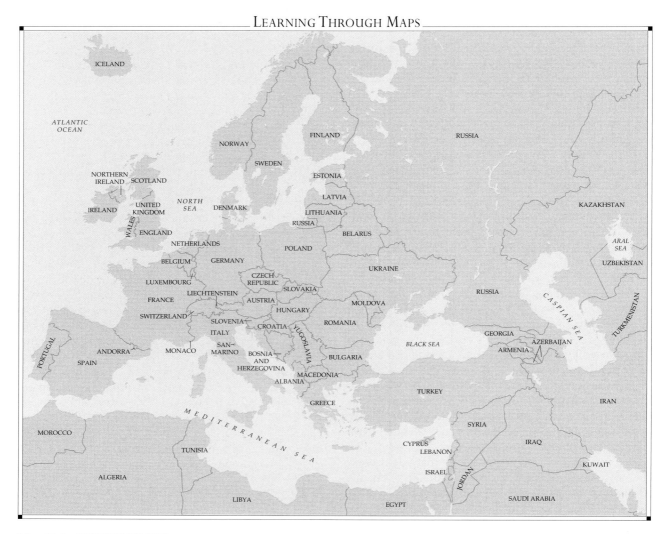

Map 21.2   EUROPE IN 1996
This map shows Europe after the end of the cold war. Use this map and Map 21.1, Europe in 1955, as references for the following. **Notice** the breakup of the Soviet Union and its replacement by Russia and numerous independent states. **Consider** the impact on Russia of its loss of control of the former republics in the Soviet Union as well as the member states of the Communist bloc. **Notice** the changes in southeastern Europe. **What** has happened to Germany? **Consider** the stability of borders in western Europe in relation to those in eastern and central Europe.

Toward a New Global Order, 1970 and Beyond

The year 1970 marked a turning point in history, not only for Western civilization but also for the world. The balance of political power began to shift from the bipolar, superpower model to a multipolar system that included Japan, China, and Western Europe. This global shift began when the superpowers moved toward détente, a French term meaning a waning of hostility. By the early 1970s, détente had produced several arms-limitation treaties between the USSR and the United States, creating a favorable climate for a reappraisal of cold war attitudes and a reduction of other global ideological battles. China, a previously closed country, began to open slowly to interaction with the United States and other Western countries. In addition, the industrialized nations began to experience energy shortages that revealed their dependence on the oil-producing countries, which had formerly exerted little influence on world events.

National Issues and International Realignment In the early 1970s, the standard of living declined for most citizens in Western Europe and the United States when the Organization of Petroleum Exporting Countries (OPEC), a cartel of the oil-rich states of the Middle East, raised prices. As a result, most Western nations went into a recession that resulted in rising unemployment and inflation. In the Soviet Union, it was becoming clear that the regimented system could no longer produce both arms and consumer goods.

The 1970s were a time of political drift in the United States in the wake of the Watergate scandal and President Nixon's resignation; in contrast, the 1980s brought dramatic changes both nationally and internationally. The government adopted laissez-faire economic policies and experienced an economic turnaround. The nation paid for this prosperity, however, with increased spending, a huge national debt, and a shift in foreign trade from creditor to debtor status. The gap between rich and poor also widened, leading to increasing polarization in American society.

Two events, both setbacks for détente, clouded the international scene: a Soviet invasion of Afghanistan in 1979 in support of local Communist leaders and the founding in 1980 of Solidarity in Poland, a labor movement that pushed for economic reform. The Polish government, supported by the USSR, ruthlessly suppressed the movement. Cold war sentiments revived, ongoing disarmament talks between the superpowers broke down, and an intensified arms race seemed imminent.

The international tension dissipated in 1985 with the appearance of Mikhail Gorbachev [GOR-bah-chof] (1985–1991) as the new moderate leader of the Soviet Union, whose economy was now in shambles. He introduced a new era of détente and helped guide the cold war to a peaceful close. His overtures to the United States resulted in limited arms reductions and opened communication between the two superpowers.

At home, Gorbachev made changes in the state bureaucracy and the Communist party that were designed to raise the standard of living. His plans dramatically altered the course of history in the USSR, Eastern Europe, and the world. Gorbachev's domestic reforms contributed to the breakup of the centralized structure of the USSR, as some member states declared their independence and others gained more local control. From the old Soviet system, following more than seventy years of communism, a desperately weakened Russia reemerged, shorn of its vast empire yet still managing to retain some ethnic republics through a commonwealth arrangement (Map 21.2).

After 1989 Gorbachev's policies toward the satellite states led to the dissolution of the Communist bloc in Eastern Europe, symbolized by the actual destruction of the Berlin Wall (Figure 21.4). Newly independent, these former Communist states, including Russia itself, are struggling to maintain their social welfare programs and worker protection legislation and at the same time to move toward democratic government and a market economy. Within Russia, which is increasingly subject to ethnic and regional crises, Boris Yeltsin (1991–1999) tried to steer a course in uncharted political waters between the nationalists and Communists who wanted to restore their country's former imperial and economic systems and the reformers who wanted to expand the marketplace economy and ensure political freedom. With Vladimir Putin (1999–) as president, Russia seems poised to, once again, become one of the family of nations.

Starting in about 1970, however, the threat of nuclear war began to subside and international tensions relaxed. In the arts, a more upbeat style, referred to as Post-Modernism, began to emerge. Characterized by a cautious optimism and an interest in reinterpreting past styles, Post-Modernism reflects a search for more positive responses to the world. Events in the late 1980s further altered and influenced the shape of the modern world. Political and economic changes in the former Soviet Union and Eastern Europe, a broadening of international influence beyond the traditional Western powers, and pressing worldwide environmental and economic issues have all contributed to the emergence of a global perspective. The growth of a global culture is reflected in Post-Modernism, which is democratic and embraces diversity. The trend for the future seems to be toward a world civilization that recognizes common human concerns and honors the creative impulse in all people (Timeline 21.1), but, after 1990, the revival of militant nationalism and ethnic violence and the intensification of terrorism threaten the realization of this goal.

The Post–Cold War World   In the 1990s, the multipolar system of international politics, which had been expected since the 1970s, did not emerge, leaving the United States as the world's lone superpower. The other countries who were to have been part of a multipolar arrangement have serious problems to deal with. Russia, beset by lawlessness and corruption, is too weakened to remain a superpower. Japan has yet to recover from the downturn its financial markets experienced in the early 1990s. The European Union successfully launched the Euro as an alternative currency to the American dollar, and with the help of the United States and NATO, finally brought peace to the Balkans. China, though undergoing rapid economic growth in the private sector, has its hands full with democratic groups calling for a more open society.

As other nations have fallen by the wayside, the United States basks in its role as the lone superpower. It has achieved this position because its military arsenal and system of international alliances, dating from the cold war period, are still in place and, in part,

Figure 21.4   Fall of the Berlin Wall. 1989. *Given the Soviet Union's previous use of force in Eastern Europe, no one had predicted that the collapse of the Communist states would be so quick and bloodless. The most symbolic event of this extraordinary period was the dismantling of the wall that separated East Berlin from West Berlin.*

because its tireless consumers have driven the global economic boom since the early 1980s. Contributing further to America's role as global leader is its unwillingness to work in full harmony with the United Nations. Believing the U.N. to be dominated by Third World interests, the United States often prefers to act alone or through coalitions of its own choosing or to work with established regional alliances.

An ironic consequence of the end of the cold war is the resurgence of late-nineteenth-century trends, especially nationalism and ethnic violence, which had been suppressed during the era of the superpowers. Nationalistic and ethnic interests today are often intertwined and occasionally involve religious issues.

Throughout the 1990s, economic globalization further developed because of the spread of free-market systems, but volatility in financial markets led to social and political unrest and brought into question some of the assumptions of laissez-faire capitalism. In the decade's early years, the Pacific Rim countries, except for Japan, continued to enjoy an economic boom, but by 1998, the euphoria had disappeared. Paralleling globalization has been the rise of regional economic alliances, such as the formation of the European Union into a free-trade zone and the creation of the North Atlantic Free Trade Asso-

ciation (NAFTA) among Canada, the United States, and Mexico. Other countries are exploring similar regional economic organizations. Fueling these trends are fast-paced technological innovations, such as the Internet and electronic commerce, which are revolutionizing the way the world conducts its business.

The emergence of the United States as the only superpower has enhanced its presence in Post-Modernism, which had a strong American component to begin with. Thus, the progress of Post-Modernism around the world leads to a paradoxical situation: American culture, especially popular culture, values, and technology, is eagerly adopted abroad, but with this adoption come voices denouncing America's cultural imperialism as well as its military strength and economic power.

The symbolic meaning of the far-reaching military and economic might of the United States—often manifested in its buildings—came to be a target of anti-Americanism on September 11, 2001. Previous terrorist attacks on America, both abroad and at home, paled in comparison with the devastating assault on two of America's structural icons—the Twin Towers of the World Trade Center in New York City (Figure 21.5) and the Pentagon in Washington, D.C. Organized by radical

Timeline 21.1   CULTURAL STYLES, 1945–PRESENT

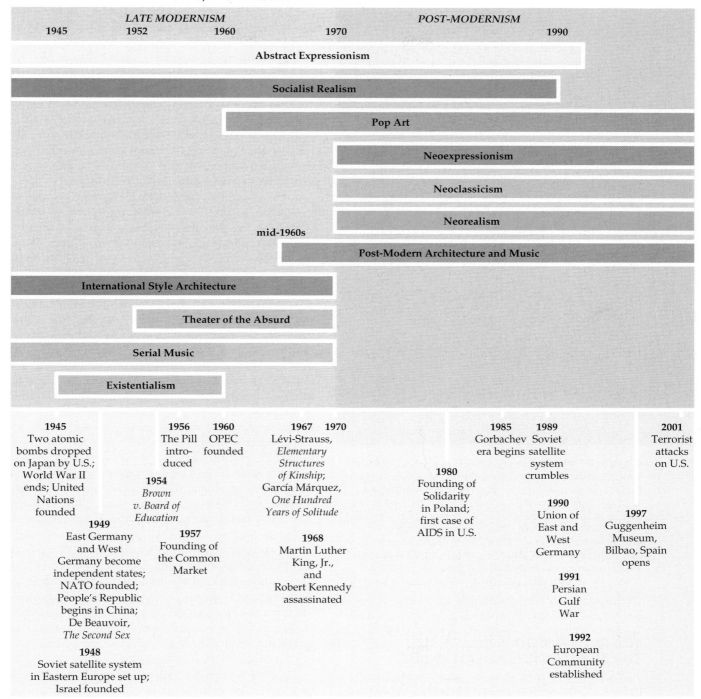

Muslims from the Middle East, who used America's open-door policy and technological know-how to launch their destructive scheme, the 9/11 attacks, as they are commonly called, affected nearly every phase of life in the United States and had an impact in many countries. Only now are the United States and other nations beginning to understand and to react to the changes triggered by these acts of terrorism: fighting an elusive band of revolutionaries, with no particular state identity and no visible government, and, thus, having no way to determine when, and if, the war is won. A small radical Islamic sect, Al Qaeda, widely believed to be behind the attacks, has probably altered the course of history for much of the first half of the twenty-first century.

Figure 21.5 JOHN BENNETT, GUSTAVO BONEVARDI, RICHARD NASH GOULD, JULIAN LAVERDIERE, PAUL MARANTZ, AND PAUL MYODA. "Tribute in Light." Photo: Vincent Laforet. The New York Times. *The "Tribute in Light," designed by New York–based artists and architects and mounted on the site of the former World Trade Center, served as a brief memorial to those killed in the terrorist attack. The columns of light, powered by eighty-eight searchlights, functioned as two votive candles and could be seen for miles around, during its month-long display. What eventually will be constructed on this site is the subject of a great debate.*

THE END OF MODERNISM AND THE BIRTH OF POST-MODERNISM

In 1947 the British-American author W. H. Auden published a poem entitled "The Age of Anxiety," which expressed the melancholy spirit of his times. He described a period caught between a frantic quest for certainty and a recognition of the futility of that search. Responding to the unparalleled violence of World War II, Auden's anxious age was haunted by death and destruction, fueled by memories of the Holocaust in Europe and the two atomic bombs dropped on Japan. While relations between the Soviet Union and the

United States deteriorated and World War III seemed inevitable, melancholy could and often did turn into despair. In this gloomy setting, Modernism entered its final phase.

Late Modernism, flourishing from 1945 until 1970, expressed the vision of a group of artists, writers, and thinkers who seemed almost overwhelmed by this despairing age. Existentialism—with its advice to forget the past and the future and to live passionately for the present—appeared to be the only philosophy that made sense. Paradoxically, diminished faith in humanity kept the Modernists at their creative tasks and prevented them from falling into hopeless silence.

Like earlier Modernists, Late Modernists thought of themselves as an elite. They were committed to saving what they considered worth saving in Western culture while destroying all in the past that was irrelevant, ignoring mass culture, and borrowing insights from depth psychology and non-Western sources. Armed with a sense of mission, they stripped their works down to the most basic components, abandoning strict rationality and making randomness the rule. They threw subject matter out the window and pressed experimentation to the extreme, reducing painting to lines and colors, sculpture to textures and shapes, and music to random collections of sound. Like earlier Modernists, they then invested these works with spiritual or metaphysical meaning by claiming that abstract paintings and sculptures were meditation devices and that music that mixed noise and harmony echoed the natural world.

In the early 1970s, Late Modernism was challenged by a new movement that became known as **Post-Modernism.** Having grown to maturity after World War II and feeling that Late Modernism's anxiety was outdated, the Post-Modernists turned from existentialism to **structuralism,** a type of thinking that affirmed the universality of the human mind in all places and times. Unlike the Late Modernists, this new generation embraced mass culture and preferred a more playful approach to creativity (Figure 21.6). Because the United States is a microcosm of global society, its artists and scholars have played a key role in establishing the culture of Post-Modernism.

The Post-Modernists' cultural vision causes them to look in two directions at the same time—forward to an emerging global civilization that is many-voiced and democratic, and backward to the roots of the Western tradition. This vision embraces the works of women, minority group members, and representatives of the Third World at the same time that it reexamines both Classical and pre-Classical civilizations. Only time will tell if Post-Modernism is merely a period of fragmentation before regrouping or the beginning of a cultural revolution.

Philosophical, Political, and Social Thought

Existentialism, born between the two world wars, dominated Western thought from 1945 until the 1960s, when it was eclipsed by structuralism and other intellectual movements, notably feminism and black consciousness. Unlike existentialism, with its focus on freedom and choice, structuralism asserts that human freedom is limited. Structuralists maintain that innate mental patterns cause human beings to interact with nature and one another in consistent and recurring ways, regardless of the historical period or the social setting. It follows that civilization (as represented in governments, social relations, and language, for example) and ideas (such as freedom, health, and beauty) arise from deep-seated modes of thought instead of from the environment or progressive enlightenment. Structuralists reason that not only is all knowledge conditioned by the mind but also civilization itself reflects the mind's inborn nature. By defining and analyzing the substrata of culture, they attempt to garner some understanding of the elemental nature of the human mind.

The two leading structuralists are Noam Chomsky [CHAHM-skee] (b. 1928), an American linguist, and Claude Lévi-Strauss [lay-vee-STRAUS] (b. 1908), a French anthropologist. Chomsky's *Syntactic Structures* (1957) prompted a revolution in linguistics, the scientific study of languages. He argues that below the surface form of sentences (that is, the grammar) lies a deeper linguistic structure that is intuitively grasped by the mind and is common to all languages. Similarly, Lévi-Strauss made war on empirical thinking with his 1967 study, *The Elementary Structures of Kinship*. He claimed that beneath the varied relations among clans in different societies exist certain kinship archetypes with such common themes as the incest taboo and marriage patterns. Chomsky and Lévi-Strauss imply the existence of common universal structures running through all minds and all societies that can be expressed as a general code. This conclusion gives a strong psychoanalytic cast to structuralist thought, because it leads researchers to focus on the subconscious mind.

Following Chomsky and Lévi-Strauss, other scholars have studied subsurface patterns in such disciplines as history, child development, and literature. No thinker has yet unified the various structuralisms into a coherent theory of mind. It is an intriguing coincidence, however, that the trend of thought that points to a universally shared mind-set parallels the rise of a global culture under Post-Modernism.

The revival of feminist thought has been another significant development in philosophy since World War II. The French thinker and novelist Simone de Beauvoir [duh boh-VWAHR] (1908–1986) sparked this revival,

Figure 21.6 NAM JUNE PAIK. *My Faust-Channel 5-Nationalism.* 1989–1991. Twenty-five Quasar 10-inch televisions, three Sony laser disc players, neogothic wood frame with base, 104 × 50 × 32". Private Collection, Seoul. *Designed by the Korean American artist Nam June Paik, this artwork is a playful commentary on war as a form of national religion. Housed in a neogothic frame, inspired by medieval altarpieces, the art is filled with military objects, such as bombs, jackboots, and helmets, as well as television screens and laser disc players. By covering the top and sides of the frame with flags from many of the world's nations, he suggests that all countries make sacred cults of their military establishments.*

following the dry spell that set in after many Western women won the right to vote in the 1920s. In her 1949 treatise *The Second Sex*, de Beauvoir argued that women are treated as "the Other," an anthropological term meaning that men accord women a different and lower existence than themselves. Drawing on personal anecdote and existentialist thought, she advised women

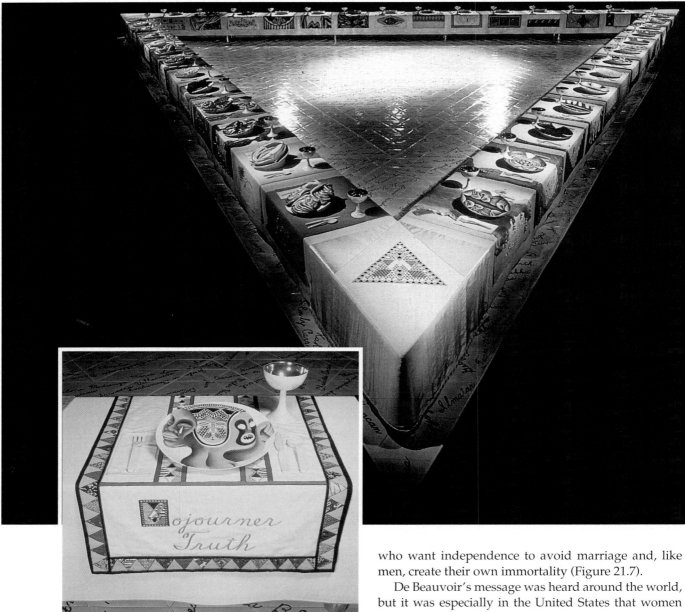

Figure 21.7 JUDY CHICAGO. *The Dinner Party.* 1979. Installation view. Multimedia, china painting on porcelain, needlework, 48 × 48 × 48' installed. © Judy Chicago. *The rebirth of feminism led some women artists to adopt explicit feminist themes in their art, as in the works of Judy Chicago (born Gerowitz, 1939). Chicago abandoned Abstract Expressionism in the late 1960s, at about the same time she changed her name, thereafter devoting her art to the feminist cause.* The Dinner Party, *her most ambitious project to date, is dedicated to leading historical and mythological women of Western civilization. In this work, she arranges a triangular-shaped dining table with thirty-nine places decorated in individual styles, honoring such famous women as Sappho and Sojourner Truth (inset; see also Chapter 18).*

who want independence to avoid marriage and, like men, create their own immortality (Figure 21.7).

De Beauvoir's message was heard around the world, but it was especially in the United States that women heeded her. America's best-known feminist in the 1960s was Betty Friedan (b. 1921). She awakened the dormant women's movement with *The Feminine Mystique* (1963), arguing that society conspired to idealize women and thus discourage them from competing with men. In 1966 she founded the National Organization for Women (NOW), a pressure group that has attracted millions of members. According to its founding manifesto, NOW supports "equal partnership with men" and is committed to "integrating women into the power, privileges, and responsibilities of the public arena." Friedan did not always agree with the more radical feminists of the 1970s, and in 1982 she showed that she was still a moderate in *The Second Stage*, a book that advocated men's liberation as a condition for women's equality.

Figure 21.8 ROMARE BEARDEN. *The Prevalence of Ritual: Baptism.* 1964. Collage on board, 9 × 12″. The Hirshhorn Museum and Sculpture Garden, Smithsonian Institution, Washington, D.C. © Romare Bearden Foundation/Licensed by VAGA, New York, NY. *Romare Bearden (1914–1988), the United States' most honored post–World War II black painter, blended Modernism with elements from his cultural heritage. In the 1960s, he developed a style reminiscent of Cubism that used collage and flattened, angular figures and that drew on his personal experiences, as in this collage of a baptismal scene—an allusion to the important role of churches in the black American tradition. Bearden places the person to be baptized in the center of the composition, a large hand over his head. The references to African masks suggest that this ritual unites an ancient way of life with the present.*

Like feminism, the black consciousness movement has grown and flourished since 1945 (Figure 21.8). The earliest significant theorist of black identity was Frantz Fanon [fah-NOHN] (1925–1961), a psychiatrist from French Martinique who practiced medicine among the Arabs of Algeria. An eyewitness to French colonialism and oppression, Fanon became convinced that the West had doomed itself by abandoning its own moral ideals. By the late 1950s, Fanon had begun to justify black revolution against white society on the basis of existential choice and Marxism. In 1961 in *The Wretched of the Earth*, he issued an angry call to arms, urging nonwhites to build a separate culture. Some black leaders in America welcomed Fanon's message in the 1960s, as did Third World thinkers who turned their backs on Western ideologies in the 1970s.

America in the 1960s produced a radical black voice in Malcolm X (1925–1965), the pseudonym of Malcolm Little. A fiery personality, he made sharp ideological shifts, moving from advocacy of black separatism to a call for an interracial civil war and, after his conversion to orthodox Islam, to support of racial harmony. Assassinated allegedly by former colleagues, he remains today a prophetic voice for many African Americans who want a clearer sense of their history, culture, and accomplishments in a predominantly white society.

In the turbulent 1960s, Malcolm X's voice was overpowered by that of Martin Luther King, Jr. (1929–1968), a visionary who dreamed of a world free from racial discord. Probably the most famous black figure in Western history, King was an advocate of civil disobedience—based on Christian teachings,

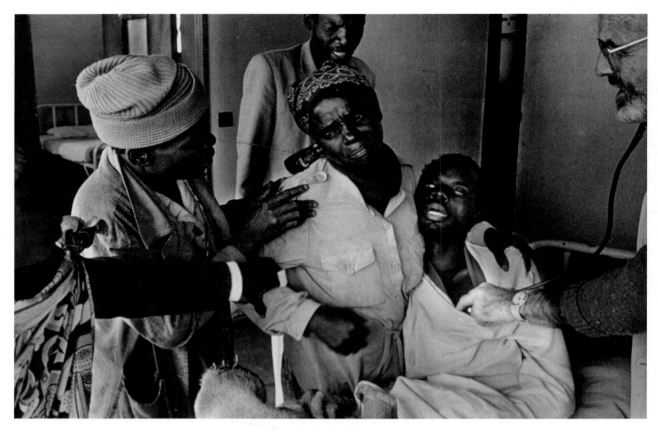

Figure 21.9 AIDS Patient Dies from Kidney Failure While Surrounded by Family Members. Mission Hospital, Southern Africa. 2002. Gideon Mendel/Network—Saba. *The dying man in the photograph is a victim of the AIDS epidemic. According to a recent estimate, AIDS will soon have killed more people than all the wars of the twentieth century. As a global threat, it not only kills in the present but also affects the future by leaving many children orphaned or with a single parent. The United Nations and some of its members have taken steps to combat AIDS, but other U.N. countries have been less supportive, and even indifferent, which lessens the hopes of conquering the disease.*

the writings of the New England philosopher and abolitionist Henry David Thoreau, and the example of India's liberator, Gandhi. An inspirational leader and a superb orator, King galvanized blacks, along with many whites, into the Southern Christian Leadership Conference, organized by ministers to end segregation in American life, notably in schools and universities. Though King was assassinated before his dream was fully realized, his vision of an integrated society lives on, but the movement has taken many directions.

Science and Technology

Although important theories were developed in biology and physics during the postwar period, the spectacular advances in applied science affected people more immediately. Ordinary life and manners have been irretrievably altered by an unending stream of inventions and discoveries, notably the birth control pill, communication satellites, and the computer. The invention of a safe birth control pill in 1956 triggered a

sexual revolution that slowed down only in the 1980s with the advent of AIDS (acquired immune deficiency syndrome) and a dramatic rise in the incidence of other sexually transmissible diseases (Figure 21.9). The introduction of communication satellites, a by-product of the United States space program of the 1960s, has made a global culture possible. Multinational corporations are linked by these satellites, and individuals all over the world watch televised events at the same time thanks to satellite communication.

Perhaps most important, the computer and the Internet have revolutionized life on every level, making previously unimaginable quantities of data immediately accessible, simplifying complex tasks, and transforming the traditional habits of personal and public life across the globe. Consumers, through e-commerce, purchase goods and services directly and, through e-trade, buy and sell stocks and bonds without brokers. Scholars, through IT (information technology), access journals, books, libraries, and databases to keep up with areas of expertise. From websites, businesses place orders, restock inventories, and sell to customers.

Individuals can e-mail friends and family, keep up with current events, and pursue interests and hobbies. These developments have contributed to "cocooning," a mode of living in which people center their lives in their homes, surrounded by electronic devices, and venture out into the public domain for amusement and social contact less and less. Political and militant groups, whether mainstream or not, have also used electronic technology to spread their message and rally support.

Breakthroughs in medicine also changed the nature of human life for millions. In the 1950s, polio was eradicated through vaccines developed by the American physicians Jonas Salk (1914–1995) and Albert Sabin (1906–1993). Innovative surgical methods, radiation treatment, and chemotherapy drastically reduced cancer mortality. Organ transplants and the use of artificial organs have prolonged life for many otherwise without hope. However, these practices have embroiled the medical profession in ethical controversy, including charges that only a few can afford these procedures and that they drain the health-care system. Likewise, new methods in human reproduction, such as test-tube fertilization and surrogate parenting, although helping a few, have raised moral dilemmas and led to court cases.

Advances in the biological sciences are revealing basic information about the origin of life. Since 1953, when Francis Crick (b. 1916) and James Watson (b. 1928) reported their discovery of the structure of deoxyribonucleic acid (DNA), the chemical substance ultimately responsible for determining individual hereditary characteristics, new findings have been made with regularity. In genetics, researchers have decoded the human genome, composed of perhaps three billion units of DNA, arranged into twenty-three pairs of chromosomes. In biogenetics, scientists have cloned animal and plant products and organs, as well as their most spectacular achievement, whole sheep and mice. As in medicine, these breakthroughs are raising serious ethical questions, such as: What use will be made of the genome map? Should attempts be made to clone humans? Are genetically modified fruits and vegetables safe for human consumption? Despite attempts to resolve these questions within the scientific community, their final resolution will probably be determined within the legal system.

The Literature of Late Modernism: Fiction, Poetry, and Drama

France's leading postwar thinkers, Jean-Paul Sartre and Albert Camus, were among Late Modernism's outstanding voices. In a trio of novels called *Roads to Freedom*, published between 1945 and 1950, Sartre interwove Marxist collectivist beliefs with existentialism's focus on the individual. Although accepting the existentialist view that life is cruel and must be confronted, he portrayed his characters as cooperating for a new and better world, presumably one in which they would be able to live in harmony. Sartre also wrote a series of plays on current issues that are infrequently performed today. His most successful drama, and perhaps his most enduring literary work, was *No Exit* (1944), which shows how three characters turn their lives into living hells because of their unfortunate choices in desperate situations.

Like Sartre, the Algerian-born writer and thinker Albert Camus [kah-MOO] (1913–1960) wrote novels, plays, and philosophical works that mirrored his political thinking and personal values. His finest literary work was *The Fall* (1956), a novel published at the height of his reputation as one of the West's main moral voices. In 1957 he was awarded the Nobel Prize in literature, an honor that Sartre declined in 1964. Written as a single rambling monologue, *The Fall* portrays an anguished, self-doubting central character who accuses himself of moral fraud. When admirers recognized Camus himself in the narrator's voice, they were shocked because they were unwilling to accept this harsh self-judgment. Whether this self-mocking confession heralded Camus's move toward God—as some critics have maintained—can never be known, for an auto accident prematurely ended his life.

Existentialism's rejection of bourgeois values and its affirmation of identity through action appealed to black writers in the United States. As outsiders in a white-dominated society, these writers identified with the French thinkers' call to rebellion. The first black author to adopt an existential perspective was Richard Wright (1908–1960), whose outlook was shaped by his birth on a Mississippi plantation. His works, such as his novel *Native Son* (1940) and his autobiography, *Black Boy* (1945), were filled with too much rage at racism to be accepted by white literary critics in the 1940s. His later years were spent in Paris, where he further developed his interest in existentialism.

The most successful black American author of this time was James Baldwin (1924–1987), who began to write during a self-imposed exile in France (1948–1957), where he had fled from racial discrimination. In a series of novels and essays, he explored the consequences of growing up black in a predominantly white world. In his first novel, *Go Tell It on the Mountain* (1953), he drew on his Christian beliefs to mute his anger against the injustices that he believed blacks daily endured. This novel, which held out hope for an integrated society, established the literary theme that he pursued until Martin Luther King, Jr.'s, assassination caused his vision to darken. In later novels, such as *No Name in the Street* (1972), he regretfully accepted violence as the only path to racial justice for black Americans.

In postwar fiction, existentialism sometimes took second place to a realistic literary style that concentrated on exposing society's failings. Three major writers who blended existential despair with Realism's moral outrage were Norman Mailer (b. 1923), Doris Lessing (b. 1919), and Alexander Solzhenitsyn [sol-zhuh-NEET-suhn] (b. 1918). Their goal was to uncover the hypocrisy of their age.

Mailer, an American, drew on his experience as a soldier in World War II to capture the horror of modern war in his first and finest novel, *The Naked and the Dead* (1948). This work portrays a handful of enlisted men, a microcosm of America, as victims of their leaders' bad choices. He describes their officers as pursuing fantasies of glory, inspired by a notion that the world is godless and without lasting values. In the late 1960s, Mailer began to write journalism, eventually achieving so much fame that today his essays overshadow his novels. His best journalism is the booklength essay *The Armies of the Night* (1968), an account of the October 1967 peace march on Washington, D.C., in which he participated. This book won Mailer a Pulitzer Prize.

Doris Lessing, a white eastern African writer, used Realism to show the contradictions at work in her homeland, Rhodesia (modern Zimbabwe), between blacks and whites, British and Dutch, British and colonials, capitalists and Marxists, and, always, women and men. In the *Children of Violence* series (1950–1969), consisting of five novels, she presents the story of the rise of black freedom fighters and the diminishing of white control in what was then a British colony. This disintegrating world serves as a backdrop to the existential struggle for self-knowledge and independence by the main character, Martha Quest. In her best-known novel, *The Golden Notebook* (1962), Lessing addresses, among other issues, the socialization process that stifles women's creativity. Her concerns, however, are not just female identity but also the moral and intellectual fragmentation and confusion she sees in the modern world. In recent years, she has turned to science fiction to address these issues.

The Russian Solzhenitsyn writes realistic novels that praise the Russian people while damning Marxism, which he regards as a "Western heresy," opposed to Orthodox Christianity. His short novel *One Day in the Life of Ivan Denisovich* (1962) reflects his own rage at being unjustly imprisoned under Stalin. This novel, published during Nikita Khrushchev's (1958–1964) de-Stalinization drive, offers an indelible image of the tedium, harassment, and cruelty of life in a forced labor camp. And yet Ivan Denisovich remains a Soviet John Doe, dedicated to Marxism, his work, and his comrades (Figure 21.10).

When Solzhenitsyn's later books, which were banned in the Soviet Union until its fading years, revealed his hatred for communism, he was deported, in 1974. Choosing exile in the United States, he settled in a Vermont hideaway from which he expressed moral disgust with the West for its atheistic materialism and softness toward the Soviet system. His values—Christian fundamentalism and Slavophilism, or advocacy of Russia's cultural supremacy—resemble those of Russia's great nineteenth-century preexistentialist novelist Dostoevsky. Believing that communism was finally dead, Solzhenitsyn returned to his homeland in 1994, but he has not become a moral force in post-Soviet Russia.

Many Late Modernist poets used a private language to such a degree that their verses were often unintelligible to ordinary people and thus did not have a wide audience. A few who used more conventional verse styles, however, earned a large readership. Of this latter group, the Welsh poet Dylan Thomas (1914–1953) was the most famous and remains so today. Thomas's poems mirror the obscurity favored by the Modernist critics, but what makes his works so memorable is their glorious sound. With their strong emotional content, jaunty rhythms, and melodious words, they are perfect to read aloud.

Better known than Thomas's poems, though, is his verse play *Under Milk Wood* (1954), arguably the best-loved poetic work of Late Modernism. Unlike the poems, this verse play is direct and imbued with simple emotions. Originally a play for radio, it presents a typical day in a Welsh village, a world he knew well, having grown up in such a place. His portrait of the colorful speech and intertwined lives of the eccentric villagers has moved millions of listeners, evoking for them bittersweet memories of their own youth.

A Late Modernist poet who was able to be experimental and yet win a large audience was the American writer Allen Ginsberg (1926–1997), the most significant poet produced by the Beat Generation of the 1950s. Like Dylan Thomas, he had an ear for colloquial speech, and his ability to construct new forms to convey iconoclastic views was unequaled by any other poet of his time. His most famous poem is "Howl" (1956), a work of homage to rebel youth and illicit drugs and sex. Overcoming censorship, this poem of Ginsberg's opposed capitalist, heterosexual, bourgeois society and became the anthem of the Beat Generation.

During Late Modernism, the most radical changes in literature took place in drama. Sharing existentialism's bleak vision and determined to find new ways to express that outlook, a group of dramatists called the **"theater of the absurd"** emerged. The absurdists shifted the focus of their plays away from the study of the characters' psychology to stress poetic language and abandoned realistic plots to concentrate on outrageous situations. A typical absurdist play mixed tragedy with comedy, as if the playwright thought that the pain of existence could be tolerated only if blended with humor.

Figure 21.10 VITALY KOMAR AND ALEKSANDER MELAMID. *Stroke (About March 3, 1953).* 1982–1983. Oil on canvas, 6' × 3'11". Collection of Evander D. Schley. Courtesy Ronald Feldman Fine Arts, New York. Photo credit: D. James Dee. *The two Russian émigré painters Komar and Melamid—who work as a team—painted this work,* Stroke, *soon after arriving in the United States. In it, they depict the lonely death of Stalin and the discovery of his body by a member of his inner circle. The artists subtly criticize both Stalin and the Soviet system in the way the official stares unmoved at the dead tyrant. Komar and Melamid show their Post-Modernist tendencies in their use of elements from earlier styles of art, such as the theatrical lighting and unusual perspective typical of Caravaggio.*

Samuel Beckett (1906–1989), an Irish writer who lived in Paris, was the best-known dramatist of absurdist theater. His *Waiting for Godot* (1952) is a play in which almost nothing "happens" in the conventional sense of that word. Combining elements of tragedy and farce, *Waiting for Godot* broke new ground with its repetitive structure (the second act is almost a replica of the first); its lack of scenery (the stage is bare except for a single tree); and its meager action (the characters engage in futile exchanges based on British music hall routines). What plot there is also reinforces the idea of futility, as the characters wait for the mysterious Godot, who never appears.

In later years, Beckett's works explored the dramatic possibilities of silence, as in the one-act drama *Not I* (1973). In this play, a voice—seen only as a mouth illuminated in a spotlight—tries to, but cannot, stop talking. Beckett's plays portrayed human consciousness as a curse; yet, at the same time, his works affirmed the human spirit's survival in the face of despair.

The Literature of Post-Modernism

Post-Modernist literature is notable for the inclusion of new literary voices in Latin America and in central and eastern Europe, marking a shift away from the dominance of the Paris–New York cultural axis and the rise of a more global culture. For the first time, Latin

American authors attracted international acclaim. Most of these writers were distinguished by left-wing political opinions and devotion to a literary style called **"magic realism,"** which mixed realistic and supernatural elements. The ground had been prepared for the magic realists by the Argentinian author Jorge Luis Borges [BOR-hays] (1899–1986), whose brief, enigmatic stories stressed fantasy and linguistic experimentation.

The outstanding representative of the magic realist school is Gabriel García Márquez [gahr-SEE-uh MAHR-kays] (b. 1928) of Colombia, who received the 1982 Nobel Prize for literature—the first Latin American novelist to be so honored. His *One Hundred Years of Solitude* (1967) is among the most highly acclaimed novels of the postwar era. Inspired by William Faulkner's fictional county of Yoknapatawpha, Mississippi, García Márquez invented the town of Macondo as a symbol of his Colombian birthplace. Through the eyes of an omniscient narrator—probably an unnamed peasant—who sees Macondo as moving toward a predestined doom, he produced a hallucinatory novel that blends details from Latin American history with magical events, such as a character's ascent into heaven.

While Latin America's authors were enjoying international renown for the first time, the writers of central and eastern Europe—the other new center of Post-Modernism—were simply renewing an old tradition. From the early 1800s until Communist regimes were installed in this century, the finest writers of central and eastern Europe had often been honored in the West. The revival of the literature of this region was heralded by the 1950s cultural thaw initiated by Soviet leader Khrushchev, but this thaw proved premature, since controversial writers were either silenced or forced to seek refuge in the West.

Exile was the choice of the novelist Milan Kundera [KOON-deh-rah] (b. 1929) of Czechoslovakia, who moved to France after his first novel, *The Joke* (1969), put him in disfavor with Czech authorities. Kundera's style has affinities with magic realism, notably the blending of fantasy with national history, but unlike the Latin American authors, he uses fantasy to emphasize moral themes, never for its own sake. He is also more optimistic than the magic realists, hinting that the power of love can lead to a different and better life. Indeed, Kundera tends to identify sexual freedom with political freedom.

The equation of sexual and political freedom is certainly the message of Kundera's finest novel to date, *The Unbearable Lightness of Being* (1984). He made the center of this work two historic events—the coming of communism to Czechoslovakia in 1948 and its reimposition after the 1968 uprising. He describes the obsessive and ultimately destructive behavior of his main characters as they try to define their sexual natures in the repressive Czech state. Although his novel shows how insignificant human existence is in the face of political repression, he refuses to despair. That his characters struggle for sexual fulfillment, even when faced with overpowering odds, is his way of affirming the strength of human nature. Ultimately, Kundera endorsed the belief of humanism that the human spirit can be diminished but never broken.

A similar belief is apparent in the work of the American writer Alice Walker (b. 1944). In her poetry, essays, and fiction, she brings a positive tone to her exploration of the African American experience. Her novel *The Color Purple* (1982) is the story of a black woman abused by black men and victimized by white society. The literary device she uses to express this woman's anguish is an old one, a story told through an exchange of letters. What is unique is that in some letters the suffering woman simply pours out her heart to God—an unexpected but moving twist in the skeptical atmosphere of the postwar world. *The Color Purple* also drew on Walker's feminist consciousness, showing that the heroine's survival depended on her solidarity with other black women.

Toni Morrison, another American writer, is the first African American to win the Nobel Prize for literature. Awarded in 1993, the prize recognized her for a group of novels that explored the plight of black people in American society. Except for *The Song of Solomon* (1977), which has a male narrator, her novels focus on female characters who are victims of a racist society. For example, in her first novel, *The Bluest Eye* (1970), a young black girl, attracted by the standard of white beauty, yearns to have blue eyes. Morrison also shows how violence is a central part of the black experience, as, for instance, in *Sula* (1973), when a grandmother, wanting to support her family, deliberately injures herself in order to collect insurance money. Inspired by her sense of an African heritage, she draws on folklore, mythology, and sometimes the supernatural, as in *Beloved* (1987), where a ghost is the central character. Along with the racism and the violence, Morrison imbues her novels with spiritual longing, thus offering hope for a more just society in the future.

Maxine Hong Kingston (b. 1940) has enriched Post-Modernism by putting Chinese Americans into American literature through her autobiographical books, a novel, short stories, and articles. Her avowed aim as a writer has been to "claim America," meaning to show that the Chinese have the right to belong through their labor in building the country and supporting themselves. In staking out this claim, she was influenced by the poet William Carlos Williams (1883–1963), a Modernist who envisioned an American culture distinct from Europe and fashioned from indigenous

Figure 21.11 JACKSON POLLOCK. *Blue Poles*. 1952. Oil, enamel, and aluminum paint, 6'11" × 16'. Collection, Australian National Gallery, Canberra. *This painting is virtually unique among Pollock's drip canvases by having a recognizable image, the eight long, vertical, dark blue "poles." He achieved this effect by first swirling paint onto the canvas and then applying a stick covered in blue pigment onto its surface. His refusal to use traditional methods reflects his belief that rational approaches to art are flawed and his faith that subconscious feelings, when released, reveal hidden truths—an attitude typical of the Abstract Expressionists.*

materials and forms. Kingston's writing not only celebrates Chinese strength and achievement but also serves to avenge wrongs—by calling exploitation, racism, and ignorance by their true names.

The daughter of Chinese immigrants whose language was Say Yup, a dialect of Cantonese, Kingston has used her own life as a paradigm of the Chinese American experience. Drawing on childhood stories told in the immigrant community, she wrote two works that summarize her Chinese heritage: *The Woman Warrior: Memoirs of a Girlhood Among Ghosts* (1976), dealing with matriarchal influence, and *China Men* (1980), telling of the patriarchal side.

Late Modernism and the Arts

In the postwar art world, leadership shifted from Paris to New York. The end of Parisian dominance had been predicted since the swift fall of France to the Nazis in 1940, and the economic and military superiority of the United States at the war's end ensured that America's largest city would be the new hub of Western culture. New York's cultural leaders were divided in 1945, however. On one side stood those who wanted to build on the native school of American art, which was realistic and provincial. On the other side was a group ready to take up the mantle of leadership of the West's avant-garde. The chief institutional ally of this latter group, which soon dominated the field, was the Museum of

Modern Art (MOMA) in New York City, founded principally by the Rockefeller family in 1929.

In determining the direction of Modern art, the New York artists had to contend with the domination of painting by Picasso, whose restless experimentation seemed to define art's leading edge; the prevalence of psychological theories that encouraged artists to experiment with spontaneous gestures and to seek insights from primitive peoples and from religious experience; and the cardinal need for constant newness. These had all been forces in Modernism since 1900, but as a result of World War II, the Holocaust, and the postwar arms race, the need to dispel illusions was greater and the level of despair higher.

Painting Shortly after 1945, an energetic style of painting came to dominate Late Modernism and still plays a major role: **Abstract Expressionism,** sometimes called Action Painting. Like earlier Modernists, the Abstract Expressionists made spiritual claims for their work, saying their spontaneous methods liberated the human spirit. One of the founders of Abstract Expressionism was the American Jackson Pollock (1912–1956), who launched this style with his "drip paintings," created between 1947 and 1950. Influenced by Jungian therapy to experiment with spontaneous gestures, Pollock nailed his canvases to the floor of his studio and dripped loops of house paint onto them from buckets with holes punched in their bottoms (Figure 21.11). The drip canvases led to a new

Figure 21.12 MARK ROTHKO. *Ochre and Red on Red*. 1954. Oil on canvas, 7′8⅝″ × 5′3¾″. The Phillips Collection, Washington, D.C. *In his paintings, Rothko aims to create secular icons for a nonreligious age, a spiritual theory inherited from the Russian Constructivist tradition. Accordingly, he banishes all references to nature from his art and focuses on fields of color floating in space—timeless, universal images.*

ing huge paintings that focused on no more than two or three fields of color (Figure 21.12).

By the mid-1950s, a new generation of Abstract Expressionists had emerged, the most important of whom were Helen Frankenthaler [FRANK-un-thahl-uhr] (b. 1928), Jasper Johns (b. 1930), and Robert Rauschenberg [RAU-shun-buhrg] (b. 1925). Following in Pollock's footsteps, Frankenthaler adopted a method of spilling pigment onto canvas from coffee cans. By guiding the paint's flowing trajectory, she stained the canvas into exquisite, amorphous shapes that, though completely flat, seem to suggest a third dimension (Figure 21.13).

Johns and Rauschenberg found Abstract Expressionism too confining and overly serious, however. Although he did not abandon Expressionism, Johns added ordinary objects to his works, as in *Target with Plaster Casts* (1955) (Figure 21.14). In this work, he paints a banal image below a row of wooden boxes enclosing molds of body parts. A basic feature of his art is the contrast between the precisely rendered human parts (above) and the painterly target (below). Johns's fascination with such tensions paved the way for the self-contradicting style of Post-Modernism. Similarly, Rauschenberg abandoned pure painting to become an **assemblage** artist, mixing found objects with junk and adding a dash of paint. In *Monogram,* he encircles a stuffed goat with a rubber tire and splashes the goat's head with color, thus turning ready-made objects into an abstract image (Figure 21.15).

Johns and Rauschenberg, with their playful attack on serious art, opened the door to the **Pop Art** movement. Rejecting the Modernist belief that spiritual values may be expressed in nonrealistic works, the Pop artists frankly admitted that they had no spiritual, metaphysical, or philosophic purpose—they simply created two-dimensional images. Even though a kind of Pop Art developed in London in the 1950s, it was not until a new generation of New York artists began to explore commercial images in the early 1960s that the movement took off.

Figure 21.13 HELEN FRANKENTHALER. *Jacob's Ladder*. 1957. Oil on unprimed canvas, 9′5⅜″ × 5′9⅞″ (287.9 × 177.5 cm). The Museum of Modern Art, New York. Gift of Hyman N. Glickstein. Photograph © 1997 Museum of Modern Art, New York. *Frankenthaler's staining method—pouring paint onto a canvas—illustrates the tension between spontaneity and control typical of Abstract Expressionism. On the one hand, this technique leads naturally to surprises because of the unpredictable flow of the paint. On the other hand, the artist exercises control over the process, from choosing the colors and thickness of the paint to manipulating the canvas during the staining. In effect, she becomes both a participant in and the creator of the final work of art.*

way of looking at art in terms of randomness, spontaneity, "alloverness," and stress on the actual physical process of painting. Pollock's tendency to move around the canvas during its execution also introduced the idea of the artist interacting with the artwork.

The first generation of Abstract Expressionists was attracted by the movement's energy, rawness, and seriousness. An outstanding recruit to the new art was Mark Rothko [RAHTH-koh] (1903–1970), a Russian émigré who painted in a style very different from Pollock's. A mystic, Rothko envisioned eliminating pigment and canvas and suspending clouds of shimmering colors in the air. After 1950 he settled for creat-

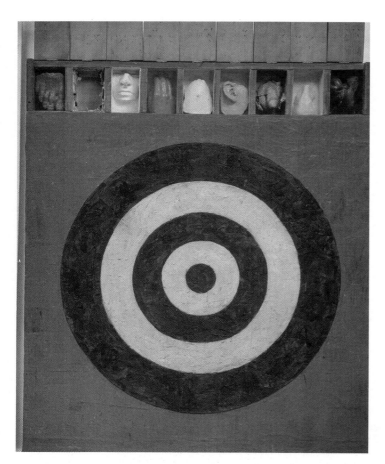

Figure 21.14   JASPER JOHNS. *Target with Plaster Casts.* 1955. Encaustic on canvas with plaster cast objects, 51 × 44 × 3½". Courtesy Leo Castelli Gallery, New York. © Jasper Johns/ Licensed by VAGA, New York, NY. *Johns is a key figure in the transitional generation of painters between the Abstract Expressionists and the Pop artists. He rebelled against the pure abstraction of the older movement, yet he shied away from embracing mass culture images as directly as did the younger school of painters. His Target with Plaster Casts is typical of his playful, witty style. In this work, he makes a visual play on words, juxtaposing a bull's-eye with plaster casts of body parts, each of which has been a "target"—that is, a subject for artists to represent throughout history.*

Figure 21.15   ROBERT RAUSCHENBERG. *Monogram.* 1959. Multimedia construction, 4 × 6 × 6'. Moderna Museet, KSK, Stockholm. Art © Robert Rauschenberg/Licensed by VAGA, New York, NY. *In his glorification of junk, Rauschenberg helped to open the door to Post-Modernism. In works such as Monogram, he showed that anything, no matter how forlorn, even a stuffed goat and a discarded automobile tire, could be used to make art. Such irreverence reflected a democratic vision in which no object is seen as having greater artistic merit than any other.*

Figure 21.16   ANDY WARHOL. *Marilyn Monroe.* 1962. Oil, acrylic, and silkscreen enamel on canvas, 20 × 16". *Warhol's portrait of Marilyn Monroe, America's most famous postwar sex symbol, was typical of his style, which placed little value on originality. Working from a photograph supplied by her Hollywood studio, he merely used his brushes and paint to exaggerate the image that studio hairdressers and cosmetologists had already created. His commercial approach to portraiture made him the most celebrated society artist of his generation.*

Figure 21.17   DAVID SMITH. *Cubi XIX.* 1964. Stainless steel, 9'5⅛" × 21¾" × 20¾". Photo © Tate Gallery / Art Resource, NY. Art © Estate of David Smith / Licensed by VAGA, New York, NY. *Smith's ability as a sculptor of enormous and rather destructive energies shines through in the monumental* Cubi *series, the last artworks he made before his accidental death. A machinist by training, Smith liked to work with industrial metals, welding and bending them into geometric units to meet his expressive needs. His desire to shape mechanical images into expressive forms related him to the Abstract Expressionist movement in painting.*

The most highly visible Pop artist was Andy Warhol (1927–1987), a former commercial artist who was fascinated by the vulgarity and energy of popular culture. Warhol's deadpan treatment of mass culture icons became legendary, whether they were Campbell's Soup cans, Coca Cola bottles, or Marilyn Monroe (Figure 21.16). By treating these icons in series, much in the same way that advertisers blanket the media with multiple images, he conveyed the ideas of repetitiveness, banality, and boredom. An artist who courted fame, Warhol recognized America's obsession with celebrity in his often-quoted line, "In the future everyone will be famous for fifteen minutes."

Sculpture   Styles in sculpture were similar to those in painting. Abstract Expressionist painting had its equivalent in the works of several American sculptors, notably David Smith (1906–1965) and Louise Nevelson (1899–1988), a Russian émigrée. Smith's point of departure, however, differed from that of the

painters in that he drew inspiration from the symbols of primitive cultures, as in *Cubi XIX*, a geometric work that, according to the artist, represents an altar with a sacrificial figure (Figure 21.17). If the viewer is unaware of this intended meaning, however, this stainless steel work has the inaccessible look of a Pollock drip canvas. In contrast, the wooden sculptures of Louise Nevelson are not about representation at all but are simple compositions fashioned from old furniture and wooden odds and ends (Figure 21.18). The use of found objects allowed Nevelson to realize the Abstract Expressionist's goal of spontaneous art devoid of references to the artist's life.

Figure 21.18 LOUISE NEVELSON. *Sky Cathedral*. 1958. Assemblage: wood construction, painted black, 11'1¼" × 10'1¼" × 1'6" (343.9 × 305.4 × 45.7 cm). Museum of Modern Art, New York. Gift of Mr. and Mrs. Ben Mildwoff. Photograph © 1997 Museum of Modern Art, New York. *Though a Modernist, Nevelson anticipated Post-Modernism by combining genres, as in this free-standing wall that integrates architecture, sculpture, and painting. She divided the wall into a grid, stuffed found objects into the wall's compartments, and painted the finished work black.*

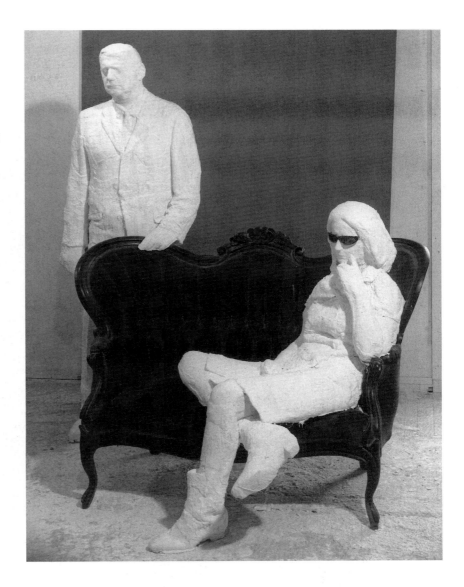

Figure 21.19 GEORGE SEGAL. *Robert and Ethel Scull*. 1965. Plaster, canvas, wood, and cloth, 8 × 6 × 6'. Private collection. Courtesy Sidney Janis Gallery, New York. Photograph © Geoffrey Clements. Art © George and Helen Segal Foundation/Licensed by VAGA, New York, NY. *Unlike his fellow Pop artists, Segal looks at the world through existential eyes. Where Warhol glamorized his celebrity subjects, Segal portrays his wealthy patrons, the Sculls, as beset by anxiety. He conveys their boredom and depression through fixed facial expressions and heavy limbs, while keeping their appearances generalized. His modeling technique, which requires subjects not to move until the plaster dries, reinforces the melancholy image.*

Pop Art was an influence in the works of George Segal (1924–2000). Segal's ghostly sculptures are plaster casts of live subjects, such as his dual portrait of Robert and Ethel Scull, leading patrons of the Pop Art movement (Figure 21.19). Segal himself rejects the Pop Art label—pointing out that his sculptures have expressionistic surfaces, like Rodin's works (see Chapter 19)—but his method reduces the body to a cartoon form and thus relates it to popular culture.

Architecture   In Late Modernist architecture, the most influential architect was the German-born Ludwig Mies van der Rohe [mees van duh ROH] (1886–1969). The last head of the Bauhaus, Germany's premier design school before World War II, Mies closed its doors in 1933 and moved to the United States in 1938. In the 1950s, he captured the world's attention with a glass skyscraper, New York's Seagram Building (Figure 21.20). Based on the artistic creed "less is more," this building's design is simple, a bronze skeletal frame on which are hung tinted windows—the building's only decorative feature. The implementation of his ideals of simplicity and restraint also led him to geometrize the building, planning its structural relationships according to mathematical ratios. So successful was Mies van der Rohe's "glass box" building that skyscrapers built according to similar designs dominate the skylines of cities around the world.

Post-Modernism and the Arts

The arts had begun to change by about 1970, as artists and architects moved beyond Late Modernism, which seemed to have dissolved into weak minimalist

Figure 21.20 LUDWIG MIES VAN DER ROHE AND PHILIP JOHNSON. Seagram Building. 1954–1958. New York City. Ezra Stoller © Esto. *Mies's decision to use bronze-tinted windows as virtually the only decorative feature of the Seagram Building's simple geometrical design had a profound impact on his contemporaries. Following his lead, other architects made the high-rise skeleton-frame building with tinted windows the most recognizable symbol of Late Modernism.*

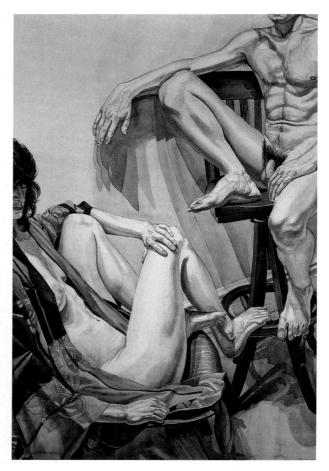

Figure 21.21 PHILIP PEARLSTEIN. *Female on Eames Chair, Male on Swivel Stool.* 1981. Watercolor, 60 × 40″. Collection of Eleanor and Leonard Bellinson. Courtesy Donald Morris Gallery, Birmingham, Mich. *Pearlstein's refusal to glamorize his nude subjects is part of a democratizing tendency in Post-Modernism. Just as some Post-Modernist authors borrow freely from mass-circulation genres such as Sherlock Holmes and science fiction, so Pearlstein focuses attention on bodily features like sagging breasts and bulging veins that had been overlooked by realistic painters.*

schools. In Post-Modernism, the shock of the new gave way to the shock of the old. Seeking a way out of Late Modernism's chaotic pessimism and its focus on abstraction, Post-Modern artists were more optimistic and revived earlier styles, although always with added layers of meaning, nuance, or irony. Realism made a triumphant return to art, flourishing as **Neorealism,** a style based on photographic clarity of detail; as **Neoexpressionism,** a style that offers social criticism and focuses on nontraditional painting methods; and as **Neoclassicism** (not to be confused with the Neoclassicism of the late eighteenth century), which had been dormant since the early twentieth century and pronounced dead by the Late Modernists. Neoclassicism is the most striking style within Post-Modernism, in both painting and architecture, perhaps because it looks so fresh to modern eyes. In addition to these various forms of realism, Modernist abstraction remains a significant facet of Post-Modernism. In their openness to artistic possibilities and their refusal to adopt a uniform style, the Post-Modernists very much resemble the Post-Impressionists of the late nineteenth century.

Figure 21.22 ANSELM KIEFER. *Osiris and Isis.* 1985–1987. Diptych, mixed media on canvas, 12′6″ × 18′4½″ × 6½″. Courtesy Marian Goodman Gallery, New York. *Kiefer drew on an ancient Egyptian myth (see Figure 4.8) to give shape to his fears of modern technology. He represents Isis, the goddess who restored her husband-brother Osiris to life, as an electronic keyboard at the top of a pyramid. He adds actual copper wires to connect the circuit board to broken bits of ceramics, his symbol of Osiris's fragmented body. In Kiefer's Post-Modern imagination, technology has become a deity with the capacity to destroy or create.*

Painting An outstanding Neorealist painter is the American Philip Pearlstein (b. 1924), who specializes in nonidealized nudes. Starting in the 1960s, he made his chief subject human bodies beyond their prime, perhaps as a way of reflecting the melancholy of the age. His nudes are rendered in stark close-up, the bodies at rest like hanging meat, and with cropped heads and limbs as in a photograph (Figure 21.21). His works seem to parody the "centerfold sexuality" that accompanied the sexual revolution brought on in part by the birth control pill.

Whereas Neorealism tends to neutrality or moral subtlety, Neoexpressionism uses realism to create paintings that are overtly socially critical. The outstanding Neoexpressionist and the most highly regarded painter among the Post-Modernists is the German artist Anselm Kiefer [KEE-fuhr] (b. 1945). Kiefer's works have blazed new trails with nontraditional painting materials, including dirt, tar, and copper threads. Existential anguish is alive in his works, which tend to focus on apocalyptic images of a blasted earth—a chilling reference to the threat of nuclear destruction (Figure 21.22). Post-Modern opti-

mism may nevertheless be read in his borrowings from Mesopotamia and Egypt, which affirm the continuity of Western culture from its earliest stages to the present. In his use of personal references and historical allusions, Kiefer is perhaps the contemporary artist closest to the German Expressionists of the early twentieth century.

The British painter Sue Coe (b. 1951), who now lives and works in America, is another important Neoexpressionist whose art serves social and political causes. Daughter of a working-class London family, she is a counterculturalist who came of age in the stormy 1960s. Committed to feminist and overtly political art, she does not espouse any specific ideology but simply confronts injustice wherever she sees it. She once described her creed in these words: "If you remove your armies from other people's countries, I won't paint war." In a broad sense, she wants her art to be a tool for change, to bear witness to the vices of capitalist and urban society, as in *Modern Man Followed by the Ghosts of His Meat* (Figure 21.23), one of the works in her indictment of the meat industry and its shocking treatment of animals. Although the message constantly

Figure 21.23   SUE COE. *Modern Man Followed by the Ghosts of His Meat.* 1990. Copyright © 1990 Sue Coe. Courtesy Galerie St. Etienne, New York. *This is one of the works in the protest booklet* Meat: Animals and Industry *by Sue Coe and her sister Mandy, inspired by visits to slaughter-houses and factory farms. This work is in the vein of an editorial cartoon inspired by a Dickens novel. Coe prefers to work with graphic arts ("handmade, mechanically reproduced images") because they engage the viewer more directly and allow the artist to reach a larger audience than do more traditional means.*

threatens to overpower the art, Coe's paintings are meant to move viewers to share the artist's concerns and thus work for reform.

A painter who uses Neoclassicism to make subtle commentary on art history is Peter Blake (b. 1920). In *The Meeting,* or *"Have a Nice Day, Mr. Hockney,"* he depicts a meeting of three 1960s British Pop artists who in the 1980s joined the ranks of Post-Modernism (Figure 21.24). This new version of Courbet's *The Meeting,* or *"Bonjour Monsieur Courbet"* (see Figure 18.11), is both an ironic comment on contemporary Neoclassicism and a classical composition in itself. The three artists depicted here are, from left to right, Howard Hodgkin (b. 1932), Peter Blake, and David Hockney (b. 1937), the last-named grasping a huge paintbrush. Blake's *Meeting* abounds in ironic juxtapositions: age versus youth, Old World versus the New, the aesthetic life versus consumerism, work versus play, and timeless present versus fleeting moment. Blake's Post-Modernism fuses rival traditions, the eternal values of Classicism and the transience of Pop Art.

Modernist abstraction continues to have a powerful impact on Post-Modernism. The most brilliant current disciple of abstraction is Frank Stella (b. 1936), a painter who has produced an immense and varied body of work. A minimalist in the 1950s, painting black-striped canvases, he became a forerunner of Neoexpressionism in the 1970s, using gaudy color and decorative effects. He has remained true to abstract ideals, as in *Norisring,* one of the *Shard series,* which uses the scraps left over from other works (Figure 21.25). Fully abstract and nonrepresentational, this work is nevertheless Post-Modernist, since it combines the genres of painting and sculpture—an ambition of many Post-Modernists.

Sculpture Like painters, Post-Modernist sculptors began to work with realistic forms. For example, serving as complements to the Neorealist paintings of Philip Pearlstein are the sculptures of the American John De Andrea (b. 1941). Typically, De Andrea uses

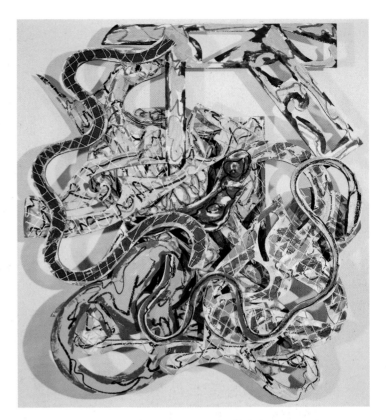

Figure 21.25 FRANK STELLA. *Norisring (XVI, 3X).* 1983. Mixed media on etched aluminum, 6'7" × 5'7" × 1'3". Collection of Ann and Robert Freedman. Courtesy Knoedler & Company, New York. *Largely because of his lively intelligence, Stella has stayed on the cutting edge of Post-Modernism. He has kept abstraction alive almost single-handedly at a time when realist styles are dominant. His 1960s innovation, the shaped canvas, allowed him to replace the rectilinear canvas with an abstract form. By the early 1980s, he had transformed the shaped canvas into a blend of sculpture and painting, as in the* Circuits *series.*

◄ **Figure 21.24** PETER BLAKE. *The Meeting,* or *"Have a Nice Day, Mr. Hockney."* 1981–1983. Oil on canvas, 39 × 49". Tate Gallery. *Blake brings Classicism up-to-date by applying its features and principles to a contemporary California setting. He fills the sun-drenched scene with double-coded references, including the pose of the girl in the right foreground (borrowed partly from a skating magazine and partly from Classical sculpture), the dog (an allusion to American youth culture and Alberti's Renaissance artistic theory), and the winged hat of the person in the Dodgers shirt (a contemporary sports emblem and a symbol of the god Mercury). The result is a hybrid scene, marked by the ironic contrast between the grave and self-contained central figures and the "cool" teenagers in the background.*

traditional poses, as in *Sphinx* (Figure 21.26). But De Andrea's human figures are fully contemporary, suggestive of young upwardly mobile professionals ("yuppies") who have taken off their clothes. Whether or not his works are satirical, he manages to capture in sculptural form the erotic quality considered so desirable by modern advertising, movies, and mass media.

The outstanding school of artists to emerge recently is the "Brit Pak," or, more seriously, the YBA, Young British Artists. Just as Labor prime minister Tony Blair has waged a campaign to nudge Great Britain from her stodgy past into a new era as "Cool Britannia," so has the YBA traded in the low-key style of older British art for an art that is attention-grabbing and often associated with scandal. Not surprising, the YBA's 1997 show—which opened in London and then traveled to the Continent, reaching

Figure 21.26 JOHN DE ANDREA. *Sphinx.* 1987. Polyvinyl, oil paint, life-size. Courtesy ACA Galleries, New York. *Unlike Pearlstein, who uses nudity to register his disgust, De Andrea designs his polyvinyl nudes to celebrate the glossy lives of the upper middle class. The bodies of his nude subjects convey what today's consumer culture urges everyone to be: healthy, sleek, athletic, and sexy.*

Figure 21.27 RACHEL WHITEREAD. *Untitled (Yellow Bath).* 1996. Cast made of rubber and polystyrene. Luhring Augustine Gallery, New York. *Whiteread's wide-ranging eye has led her to sculpt many household objects, including mattresses, chairs and tables, bookshelves, and bathtubs. Her works are more than mere representations; she makes a cast of the spaces around an object, trying to capture traces of a human presence. In its new incarnation, Whiteread's bathtub has been compared to a sarcophagus. Such an interpretation is acceptable to the artist, as she is on record as comparing her casting technique to the making of a death mask. Indeed, there is a faint air of melancholy about Whiteread's sculptures, since they seem to affirm human mortality.*

New York in 1999—was entitled "Sensations." Probably the most praised artist among the YBA is the sculptor Rachel Whiteread (b. 1964). Unlike the works of many of this British school, Whiteread's sculptures are deeply serious and modest in execution. Inspired by American minimalist art of the 1960s and 1970s, her works usually represent simple ideas using familiar, everyday objects (Figure 21.27). She works in various mediums, including plaster, concrete, resin, and rubber.

Installation Art Enjoying a vogue today is **installation art,** a boundary-challenging type of art born in the 1960s that creates architectural tableaux, using objects drawn from and making references to artistic sources (such as music, painting, sculpture, and theater) and the workaday world (such as everyday tasks, media images, and foodstuffs); the work may include a human presence. One of the most gifted installation artists is the American Ann Hamilton (b. 1956), who is known for her sensory works layered with meaning. The piece *mantle,* installed at the Miami Art Museum in 1998 (Figure 21.28), filled up a second-floor gallery and had as its human focus a woman performing a household task before an open window—a homage to Dutch genre art, which often pictured women in similar poses. The task the seated woman is performing—sewing sleeves onto the bodies

of wool coats—gives rise to the piece's name (a "mantle" is, among other things, a sleeveless garment). Multiple wires dangle down the gallery's wall into a mound of 60,000 cut flowers displayed on a 48-foot-long table behind the woman. This mountainous display of slowly decaying flowers is a memento mori, or a reminder of death—a frequent theme of Renaissance art. Hamilton's growing reputation led to her choice as the American representative at the prestigious Venice Art Bienniale in 1999.

Video Art Nam June Paik (b. 1932) is virtually the founder of video art and certainly the most influential artist working in this medium. **Video art** is made with a video monitor, or monitors, and may be produced using computerized programs or with handheld cameras; the work may be ephemeral or permanent. Working with videotapes since 1959,

Figure 21.28   ANN HAMILTON. View of *mantle*. Miami Art Museum. 1998. *Installation art has affinities with other innovative art forms, but it lacks the centrality of the videotaped image, as in video art, or a strong musical component, as in performance art. In* mantle, *there is a minor musical aspect: Radio receivers, placed amid the flowers, transmitted musical and other sounds during the event. Feminist in perspective, this installation may be interpreted as an ironical comment on the male-dominated art world, because, until recently, this world discouraged women from becoming artists and limited their artistic choices mainly to domestic chores, such as making clothes. In the photograph, Ann Hamilton is the woman sewing; volunteers and paid attendants performed this task when the artist was absent.*

Paik has evolved from an artist intent on being entertaining into one devoted to serious issues in his projects and, starting in the 1980s, embracing political ideas. A sophisticated work that represents his political beliefs is *My Faust (Stations): Religion* (1989–1991), which is part of a series of thirteen individual multimonitor installations (see Figure 21.6). Rich in allusions, this work refers to the thirteen channels available at the time for Manhattan television viewers and the word *stations* in the title, reinforced by the neogothic altarpieces, suggests Christianity's Stations of the Cross, the thirteen stages of Jesus' journey to his crucifixion. *Faust* was a symbol of both restlessness and relentless seeking of knowledge, even to the loss of the soul (see Chapter 17). Thus, Paik's *Faust* suggests humanity's pact with the devil for secular power and glory.

Architecture   The chief exponent of Post-Modern architecture is the American Robert Venturi (b. 1925), whose ideas are summarized in his book *Complexity and Contradiction in Architecture* (1966). Rejecting Modernist architecture, which he thinks inhuman because of its starkness, he attempts to create buildings that express the energy and ever-changing quality of contemporary life. Fascinated by mass culture, he is inspired by popular styles of architecture, such as Las Vegas casinos and motels in the form of Indian tepees—a kitsch style sometimes called "vernacular." A work that enshrines his love of the ordinary is his Guild House, a retirement home in a lower-middle-class section of Philadelphia (Figure 21.29). Faceless and seemingly artless, this building is indebted to popular culture for its aesthetic appeal; for instance, the wire sculpture on the roof looks like a television antenna, and the recessed entrance and the sign evoke memories of old-time movie houses. Venturi's playful assault on Modernism opened the door to the diversity of Post-Modernism.

One of the strains in Post-Modernism is **high tech,** a style that uses industrial techniques and whose roots stretch back to the Crystal Palace (see Figure 18.5) and the Eiffel Tower. Richard Rogers (b. 1933) of England and Renzo Piano (b. 1937) of Italy launched this revival with the Pompidou Center in Paris, which boldly displays its factory-made metal parts and transparent walls (Figure 21.30). Commissioned by France to restore Paris's cultural position over New York, the Pompidou Center has spawned many imitations as well as a style of interior decoration.

One of the most controversial buildings in Post-Modern architecture is the thirty-seven-story, pink granite headquarters building of American Telephone and Telegraph, executed in a Neoclassical

Figure 21.29 ROBERT VENTURI. Guild House. 1965. Philadelphia. *Venturi's aesthetic aim is to transform the ordinary into the extraordinary. He followed this democratic ideal in Guild House, where he took a "dumb and ordinary" (his term) concept and tried to give it a monumental look. His ironic intelligence and his perverse delight in mass culture have made him a guiding spirit of Post-Modernism.*

Figure 21.30 RICHARD ROGERS AND RENZO PIANO. The Georges Pompidou Center for Art and Culture. 1971–1977. Paris. *Designed in a gaudy industrial style and erected in the heart of a quiet section of Paris called Beaubourg, the Pompidou Center was controversial from the start, as it was planned to be. Its showy appearance sharply contrasted with the historic styles of neighboring structures—a contrast that has become a guiding ideal of Post-Modernist architects. The furor that greeted the Pompidou Center on its opening has occurred in other places where city governments have placed colorful and brash high-tech temples amid their more traditional buildings.*

PERSONAL PERSPECTIVE

YO-YO MA
A Journey of Discovery

The Juilliard-trained, Harvard-educated cellist Yo-Yo Ma (b. 1955) founded, in 1998, the Silk Road Project, a series of concerts, festivals, and other events to explore the traditions of the Silk Road countries. Perhaps the earliest known example of globalization, the Silk Road, mainly an overland trading route, stretched from China to Korea and Japan in the east and to Italy in the west and flourished off and on between about 200 B.C. and the fourteenth century A.D.

These days, the Silk Road is mostly remembered as a string of fabled places—Samarkand [Uzbekistan], Nishapur [Iran], Bukhara [Uzbekistan], Kashgar [China]. For me, however, the Silk Road has always been fundamentally a story about people, and how their lives were enriched and transformed through meeting other people who were at first strangers. By starting a conversation and building shared trust, strangers could become allies, partners, and friends, learning from one another along the way and working creatively together.

If you accept that the Silk Road is still present in our world as an inspirational symbol of intercultural meetings, then there are many people alive today whose lives exemplify modern-day Silk Road stories. I am one of them. I was born in Paris to Chinese parents. My father was a violinist and composer who devoted his career to building musical bridges between China and the West. When I was seven, my family moved to the United States. I began playing Western classical music as a youngster but have always been curious about other cultures.

As a cellist who loves working in different musical styles, I've had the good fortune to travel and learn about music outside my own tradition. I have visited the Khoisan people of the Kalahari Desert and listened to Buddhist chant in Japan's ancient Todaiji Temple. I have learned Celtic and Appalachian dance tunes and have taken lessons on the *morin huur*, the Mongolian horsehead fiddle. These encounters have led me to think about the way that music reveals the connections among us.

For example, is the horsehead fiddle, held upright and played with a horsehead bow, in fact an ancient ancestor of European viols? How did a Japanese stringed instrument, the *biwa*, originally created in the 8th century and now part of the Imperial Shosoin collection in Nara, come to be decorated with West and Central Asian motifs? Why does music from the Celtic lands, Mongolia, India, and many other disparate places rely so heavily on the concept of melody played against a steady drone? Answers to these questions are not always fully known, but persuasive evidence suggests that peoples now separated by great distances had at some time been connected. Moreover, these connections were not passive but based on a vigorous exchange of ideas, artifacts, technologies, and fashions. Cultural exchange has in turn inspired innovation and creativity.

The message seems clear: We all have much to gain by staying in touch, and much to lose by throwing up walls around ourselves. We live in a world of increasing interdependence where it is ever more important to know what other people are thinking and feeling, particularly in the vast and strategic regions of Asia that were linked by the Silk Road. . . .

As a crucible for cultural intermingling, the lands of the Silk Road, then and now, offer an unparalleled vantage point from which to understand vitally alive and ever-evolving languages of music, art, and craft that may seem by turns familiar and exotic. Our challenge is to embrace the wondrous diversity of artistic expression while remaining mindful of the common humanity that links us all.

Figure 21.31   PHILIP C. JOHNSON AND JOHN BURGEE. American Telephone and Telegraph Headquarters. 1979–1984. New York. © Peter Mauss/Esto. *Although Classical rules were followed in the planning of Johnson and Burgee's AT&T Headquarters, it was built using Modernist methods. Like Modernist structures, the building has a steel frame to which exterior panels are clipped. Despite its Modernist soul, the physical presence of this Post-Modernist building conveys the gravity and harmony customarily associated with Classical architecture.*

style (Figure 21.31). Designed by Philip C. Johnson (b. 1906), an American disciple of Mies van der Rohe, this building was a slap in the face to the Modernist ideal because it used Classical forms. The AT&T Headquarters has a base, middle, and top, corresponding to the foot, shaft, and capital of a Greek column—the basic element of Greco-Roman building style. As a final blow to Modernist purity, Johnson topped his building with a split pediment crown, causing a hostile critic to compare it to an eighteenth-century Chippendale highboy. Notwithstanding the furor surrounding its creation, this building heralded the resurgence of Neoclassicism in the Post-Modern age.

The Guggenheim Museum in the Basque city of Bilbao, Spain, designed by the American Frank Gehry (b. 1929), was recognized immediately as a classic when it opened in 1997. Hired by city officials to build the museum as part of a civic rejuvenation project, Gehry chose a building site on the Nervion River, a stream that has played a major role in the city's history. Gehry's design is in the form of a rose, or "metallic flower," with a rotunda at its center and the petals spiraling in waves of centrifugal force (Figure 21.32). Typical of Gehry's expressionist handling of flexible materials, strips of metal ripple and flare outward into the city. Within the Baroque interior are exhibition spaces, an auditorium, a restaurant, a café, retail space, and an atrium that functions as a town square. The choice of a rose, the symbol of the Virgin Mary, was appropriate for Catholic Spain. Gehry, by shifting this emblem from a church to a museum, transformed it into an ambiguous sign of the Post-Modern period.

Late Modern and Post-Modern Music

The major musical styles that were dominant before World War II persisted in Late Modernism. New York was the world's musical capital, and styles were still polarized into tonal and atonal camps, led by Stravinsky and Schoenberg, respectively. After Schoenberg's death in 1951, however, Stravinsky abandoned tonality and adopted his rival's serial method. Stravinsky's conversion made twelve-tone serialism the most respected type of atonal music, though other approaches to atonality sprang up, notably in the United States. Under Late Modernism, this dissonant style became the musical equivalent of the spontaneous canvases painted by Pollock and the Abstract Expressionist school.

Despite embracing the dissonance and abstraction of serialism, Stravinsky filled his Late Modernist works with energy and feeling, the touchstones of his

Figure 21.32   FRANK O. GEHRY. Guggenheim Museum. 1997. Bilbao, Spain. *Gehry is famed for pushing the boundaries of architecture, which has often been confined by set rules, because he, as a friend of painters and sculptors, sees himself as both an artist and an architect. Thus, the Bilbao Guggenheim has been labeled sculptural architecture, considered a work of art in itself. Gehry relied on a sophisticated computer program to achieve the building's dramatic curvature, and he chose metal titanium to sheath the exterior, thereby giving it a gleaming, wavy-in-a-stong-wind appearance.*

Figure 21.33   WILLIAM STRUHS. Laurie Anderson performing at the Spoleto Festival
U.S.A., June 1999. *Laurie Anderson, second from left, whose works virtually define performance
art, is pictured here in the midst of a performance of* Songs and Stories from "Moby Dick" *at
the Spoleto Festival U.S.A., held in Charleston, South Carolina. Her nineteenth-century costume,
the stovepipe top hat and frock coat, reflects the time period of Melville's famous novel. The setting
of the performance, with its alienating effects created by electronic means, suggests the technological world that is the principal concern of her art. For example, on a background screen are
projected, among other things, constantly shifting lines and words of Melville's text, letters of the
alphabet, blown-up images of the performers, and dictionary definitions; similarly, in addition to
instrumental music, there are songs, chanted passages, and spoken words, some of whose sounds
are deliberately distorted by electronic means.*

musical style. Two of his finest serial works are
Agon (1957), a score for a ballet with no other plot than
a competition among the dancers, and *Requiem Canti-
cles* (1968), a religious service for the dead, marked by
austere solemnity.

Dissonance also characterizes the music of Krzystof
Penderecki [pahn-duhr-ETS-key] (b. 1933), a member
of the "Polish School" who is anything but a doctri-
naire Modernist. Committed to an older musical ideal,
he believes that music, above all things, must speak to
the human heart. Nevertheless, he has been a constant
innovator, seeking especially to create new sounds
through the unconventional use of stringed instruments and the human voice. Marked by Classical
restraint, his compositions are clearly structured works

permeated by fluctuating clouds of sounds, as in
Threnody for the Victims of Hiroshima (1960), scored for
fifty-two stringed instruments. (A "threnody" is a
"song of lamentation.") Reflective of the melancholy
mood of Late Modernism, this work conjures up the
eerie minutes, in 1945 at Hiroshima, between the
dropping of the atomic bomb and its detonation.
Penderecki achieves unearthly effects through the use
of **glissando** (the blending of one tone into the next in
scalelike passages) in an extremely high register and
by the string players' bowing their instruments in
abnormal ways.

The most influential Late Modernist was John Cage
(1912–1992), whose unusual, even playful, approach
to music opened the door to Post-Modernism. Briefly

Schoenberg's student, Cage gained most of his controversial notions—in particular, his goal of integrating noise into music—from the enigmatic teachings of Zen Buddhism. A work that demonstrates this goal is called *4'33" (Four Minutes and Thirty-three Seconds).* The title describes the time period that the performer is to sit immobile before a piano keyboard so that the concert hall sounds, in effect, become the music during the performer's silence. Cage's spirited experiments made him the darling of the avant-garde. Along with assemblage artists, choreographers, and sculptors, he helped to break down the divisions among the art forms—in anticipation of a Post-Modernist development.

In the 1960s, some innovative composers rejected atonality for its overintellectuality and its apparent devotion to harsh sounds. In place of atonality, they founded a Post-Modern style devoted to making music more emotionally appealing, though they remained committed to experimental methods. Among the most notable composers working within this style is the American Philip Glass (b. 1937), who has made it his mission to return exuberance to music. He has pursued this goal while working in a minimalist tradition, although he draws on varied sources, including classical Indian music, African drumming, and rock and roll. Much of Glass's music is written for **synthesizer,** a machine with a simple keyboard that can duplicate the sounds of up to twelve instruments simultaneously. He composes with simple tonal harmonies, pulsating rhythms, unadorned scales, and, above all, lilting arpeggios, the cascading sounds produced by playing the notes of a chord in rapid sequences. A Glass piece is instantly recognizable for its repetitiveness and obsessive quality.

A composer of symphonies, chamber works, film scores, and dance pieces, Glass has gained the widest celebrity for his operas. His first opera, *Einstein on the Beach* (1976), produced in collaboration with the equally controversial American director Robert Wilson (b. 1941), was staged at New York's Metropolitan Opera, a rarity for a living composer in recent times. In their kaleidoscopic work, Glass and Wilson redefined the operatic form, staging a production lasting four and one-half hours without intermission and with Glass's driving music set to Wilson's texts with no recognizable plot, no formal arias, and no massed choruses. So successful was this venture that Glass followed it with operas based on other remarkable figures, *Satyagraha* (1978), dealing with the life of Gandhi, India's liberator, and *Akhnaten* (1984), focusing on the Egyptian pharaoh who is sometimes called the first monotheist (see Chapter 1). Glass's interests took an even more multicultural turn in 1998

with the premiere and world tour of his multimedia opera *Monsters of Grace,* with a libretto based on the thirteenth-century mystical poetry of the Persian poet Jalal ad-Din ar-Rumi (see Chapter 8). In 2000, he returned to Western themes with *In the Penal Colony*—a "pocket opera" he terms it—based on Kafka's short story.

One of the best-known living composers is the American John Adams (b. 1947). Like many other composers of his generation, Adams is a minimalist, but he stands out for his resonant sounds and firm grasp of musical form. He has written for a wide range of media, including orchestra, opera, video, film, and dance, and he has composed both electronic and instrumental music. His operas, *Nixon in China* (1987), *The Death of Klinghoffer* (1991), and *I Was Looking at the Ceiling and Then I Saw the Sky* (1998), based on historical events, have been viewed by more audiences than any other operas in recent history. Two orchestral works, *The Chairman Dances,* adapted from *Nixon in China,* and *Shaker Loops* (1996), have been called "among the best known and most frequently performed of contemporary American music." Adams frequently conducts some of the world's most prestigious orchestras.

Performance Art

Laurie Anderson (b. 1947) is a key artist in **performance art**—a democratic type of mixed media art born in the 1960s that ignores artistic boundaries, happily mixing high art (such as music, painting, and theater) and popular art (such as rock and roll, film, and fads) to create a unique, nonreproducible, artistic experience. Anderson's performance art consists of sing-and-tell story-songs about mundane events of daily life, which somehow take on unearthly significance. These monologues are often tinged with humor and are delivered in a singsong voice backed up by mixed media images, strange props, and varied electronic media, including electronic musical instruments, photo projection, manipulated video, and devices that alter the sound of her voice. Central to the performance is her stage persona, rather like Dorothy in *The Wizard of Oz,* in which she gazes with wide-eyed wonder on the modern technological world. A gifted violinist, she intends her music to play only a supporting role in her art, though her recordings—for example, *The Ugly One with the Jewels* (1995), based on a work called *Readings from the New Bible* (1992–1995)—have found eager listeners. In *Songs and Stories from "Moby Dick"* (1999), based on Herman Melville's nineteenth-century novel, she broke new ground by composing for male voices as well as her own (Figure 21.33).

Figure 21.34   CINDY SHERMAN. *Untitled #298.* Photograph, 73 × 49½". 1994. *In this photograph from the Fairy Tale Series, Sherman impersonates a medieval wizard, standing in profile against a star-filled "sky" and wearing a blonde wig and flowing robe whose inner lining is emblazoned with skulls. The props have been assembled by Sherman, based on some plan of her own, making this photograph a unique image. Works such as this bring into question the creating of art when there is no preexisting prototype. Interpretation of Sherman's art is difficult, as she is dismissive of what critics say, calling their analyses "a kind of side effect."*

Anderson's ongoing popularity is a testament to her ability to stay ahead of the ever-shifting zeitgeist.

The American Cindy Sherman (b. 1954) also has created a body of performance art, but without music. Sherman first attracted notice in the 1970s with photographs of herself in elaborately staged poses, evocative of old movie scenes. Although these photographs focused on women as victims, their ambiguous nature made her controversial, especially to feminists. In the eighties, she made a series of History Portraits, in which she impersonated famous art subjects. In the nineties, she made photographs using pornographic subjects, mock fashion images, and fairy-tale characters (Figure 21.34). Sherman's art, with its staged and rather tacky quality, seeks to dethrone high art and bring it down to earth for today's audiences.

Mass Culture

In the postwar era, American mass culture began to serve as the common denominator of an emerging world civilization. Because of its democratic and energetic qualities, sexual content, and commitment to free expression, this culture has attracted people around the globe. Scenes of American life—conveyed through television, movies, and advertising—have mesmerized millions, who imitate these images as far as they are able. The popularity of the clothing (jeans, T-shirt, and running shoes), the food (hamburgers, fries, and cola), and the music (rock and roll) of the American teenager has influenced behavior even in Eastern Europe, Russia, the Third World, and the Middle East.

The information boom has been the explosive force Americanizing the world and transforming it into a global village, with television providing the initial means of transformation. As the earth has shrunk, more electronic gear—the videocassette recorder, the compact-disc player, the digital recorder, the camcorder, the computer—has reduced the individual's world even more, turning each home into a communications center. Further shrinkage is taking place with the coming of the global information highway, which includes the Internet and the World Wide Web, and developments in international communications technology, such as the cellular telephone.

The rise of a worldwide mass culture has produced an insatiable demand for popular entertainment. It has led to the replacement of old types of amusements with new forms, such as the rock concert and the rock video, along with the creation of innovative means of media coverage, including cable television with MTV and all-sports channels. This demand has given birth to extravagantly popular figures: Elvis Presley (1935–

1977), America's first postwar music idol; Michael Jackson (b. 1958), superstar of the mid-1980s; Madonna (b. 1959), queen of popular songs in the early 1990s, and Eminem (born Marshall Mathers III in 1972), a white rapper and the reigning king of current pop music. Except for the Beatles, the British rock quartet that was the most popular rock group of the 1960s, few superstars are non-American. Only time will tell if Post-Modernist mass culture can produce a civilization that is truly pluralistic and global.

A SUMMING UP

Between 1945 and the present, the world has passed from a cold war "fought" between two superpowers and their allies into a period dominated by a single superpower. With the United States as the reigning superpower, its democratic institutions and free-market economy have become widely imitated by much of the world. However, the revival of militant nationalism and ethnic warfare and, most recently, the spread of terrorism threaten the triumph of liberal democracy and laissez-faire capitalism.

Considering over fifty years of breathtaking changes in the political, social, and economic realms, we offer two contradictory interpretations of the near future. On the one hand, in our Post-Modern era, a new vision of the world can be seen—global and democratic, embracing the contributions, tastes, and ideas of men and women from many races and countries and borrowing freely from high culture and mass culture. In this optimistic view, the world continues to take its lead from Western civilization, largely because of its proven capacity to adapt and survive. On the other hand, in light of the mounting tensions around the world, these trends toward unity seem mere illusions. In our pessimistic view, the future may be filled with renewed disruptions and clashes among societies, which could manifest themselves in various ways, ranging from economic sanctions to armed conflicts to terrorist campaigns.

So much for the immediate future, but what of the millennium? When we consider our past, as we have in this book, one major lesson is clear: The long term in history is unpredictable. For example, five thousand years ago in 3000 B.C., who could have predicted that the fledgling Egyptian and Mesopotamian societies would become cradles of civilization, leaving enduring cultural forms before falling into decay? Or in 2000 B.C., who could have foreseen that a rejuvenated Egypt and Mesopotamia would eventually be undermined by Iron Age invaders? Or would it have been possible to guess in 1000 B.C., a time of disarray and decline in the eastern Mediterranean, that first Greece and later Rome would evolve into the civilizations that became the standard in the West? Or at the dawn of the Christian era, with the Roman Empire at its height, who would have dared forecast that Roman power would spread so widely but then collapse, to be succeeded by three separate and distinct civilizations—Islam, Byzantium, and the West? Or in A.D. 1000, who could have anticipated that the backward West would become the constantly revolutionizing industrial giant whose culture would dominate the world? Drawing a lesson from this quick survey, we readily admit that we cannot know what this millennium will bring. Perhaps all we can say is that, based on past history, civilization as we know it is likely to undergo fundamental change, for good or ill, as a consequence of some currently unforeseen technological, political, religious, economic, or social innovation.

KEY CULTURAL TERMS

Late Modernism	Neoexpressionism
Post-Modernism	Neoclassicism
structuralism	installation art
theater of the absurd	video art
magic realism	high tech
Abstract Expressionism	glissando
assemblage art	synthesizer
Pop Art	performance art
Neorealism	

SUGGESTIONS FOR FURTHER READING

Primary Sources

The Autobiography of Malcolm X. With the assistance of A. Haley. Secaucus, N.J.: Castle Books, 1967. In his own words, Malcolm X describes his rise from obscurity to become a powerful figure posing radical solutions to racial problems.

BALDWIN, J. *Go Tell It on the Mountain.* New York: Grossett and Dunlap, 1953. A novel representative of Baldwin's early optimism about reconciliation of the black and white races.

———. *No Name in the Street.* New York: Dial Press, 1972. A novel representative of Baldwin's bitterness after the murder of Martin Luther King, Jr.

BECKETT, S. *Waiting for Godot.* Edited and with an introduction by H. Bloom. New York: Chelsea House Publishers, 1987. The central image of Beckett's absurdist play—pointless waiting—has become a metaphor for the disappointed hopes of Late Modernism.

CAMUS, A. *The Fall.* Translated by J. O'Brien. New York: Knopf, 1957. Camus's most autobiographical novel, dealing with self-deceit and spiritual yearning.

CHOMSKY, N. *Syntactic Structures.* The Hague: Mouton, 1957. The work that revolutionized linguistics by claiming that there is a structure that lies hidden beneath the surface of language.

DE BEAUVOIR, S. *The Second Sex.* Translated and edited by H. M. Parshley. New York: Vintage, 1974. One of the books that helped launch the feminist revival by arguing that women must abandon "femininity" and create their own immortality just as men do.

FANON, F. *The Wretched of the Earth.* Translated by C. Farrington. New York: Grove Press, 1968. Fanon's groundbreaking study of racism and colonial liberation; a classic of modern revolutionary theory.

FRIEDAN, B. *The Feminine Mystique.* New York: Norton, 1963. The first acknowledgment of housewives' dissatisfaction with their role and desire for a career, this work was a milestone in the rebirth of feminism in the United States.

GARCÍA MÁRQUEZ, G. *One Hundred Years of Solitude.* New York: Cambridge University Press, 1990. A classic of Post-Modernism that mixes magical happenings with realistic events in the mythical Colombian town of Macondo.

GINSBERG, A. *Collected Poems, 1947–1980.* New York: Harper & Row, 1984. A Late Modernist, Ginsberg wrote poetry that reflected his openness to diversity and his passion for freedom.

KING, M. L., JR. *A Testament of Hope: The Essential Writings of Martin Luther King, Jr.* New York: Harper & Row, 1986. A good introduction to the thought of the most influential black American in history.

KINGSTON, M. H. *China Men.* New York: Knopf, 1980. Dealing with Kingston's patriarchal heritage, this autobiographical work complements *The Woman Warrior,* which focuses on matriarchal influences.

———. *The Woman Warrior: Memoirs of a Girlhood Among Ghosts.* New York: Knopf, 1976. A novel dealing with the confusion of growing up Chinese American in California; the "ghosts" of the subtitle refer to both the pale-faced Americans of the author's childhood and the spirits of Chinese ancestors and legendary female avengers brought to life by immigrant tales.

KUNDERA, M. *The Unbearable Lightness of Being.* Translated by M. H. Heim. New York: Harper & Row, 1984. A novel that explores the anguish of life under communism in Eastern Europe.

LESSING, D. *Children of Violence.* (Includes *Martha Quest, A Proper Marriage, A Ripple from the Storm, Landlocked.*) New York: Simon and Schuster, 1964–1966. *The Four-gated City.* New York: Knopf, 1969. Covering the period between the 1930s and 1960s, this series is Lessing's literary meditation on the transformation of her colonial homeland, Rhodesia, into the black state of Zimbabwe. Martha Quest, the focal point of this quintet of novels, is the author's surrogate witness to these turbulent events.

LÉVI-STRAUSS, C. *The Elementary Structures of Kinship.* Translated by J. H. Bell and others. Boston: Beacon Press, 1969. A classic of social anthropology, this work established that there are only a few basic patterns of kinship relationships in all societies.

MAILER, N. *The Naked and the Dead.* New York: Rinehart, 1948. Mailer's novel of World War II, his first and best work.

MORRISON, T. *Beloved*. New York: Plume, 1998. First published in 1987, *Beloved* widened Morrison's audience after it was made into a movie. Morrison transformed a true incident from pre–Civil War America into a haunting and complex story with the dimensions of a Greek tragedy.

SARTRE, J.-P. *The Age of Reason* and *The Reprieve*. Translated by E. Sutton. *Troubled Sleep*. Translated by G. Hopkins. New York: Knopf, 1947, 1947, and 1950. Sartre's trilogy of novels, called *The Roads to Freedom*, demonstrates existentialism in action.

———. *No Exit and Three Other Plays*. Translated by L. Abel and S. Gilbert. New York: Vintage, 1976. *No Exit* is Sartre's most famous drama, illustrating his idea that "hell is other people" because they strive to define us and see us as objects; also includes *Dirty Hands, The Respectful Prostitute,* and *The Flies*.

SOLZHENITSYN, A. *One Day in the Life of Ivan Denisovich*. Translated by R. Parker. New York: Dutton, 1963. Published with permission of the Soviet authorities, this novel revealed the existence of Stalin's slave labor camps.

THOMAS, D. *The Collected Poems of Dylan Thomas*. New York: New Directions, 1953. The finest lyric poet of the Late Modern period, Thomas wrote on such themes as sex, love, and death.

———. *Under Milk Wood, A Play for Voices*. New York: New Directions, 1954. A verse play set in a mythical Welsh village that comes to symbolize a lost world in an urbanized age.

WALKER, A. *The Color Purple*. New York: Harcourt Brace Jovanovich, 1982. An uplifting novel that describes the central black female character's rise from degradation to modest dignity. The heroine's awkward but poignantly moving letters reveal the difficulty and the ultimate heroism of her victory.

WRIGHT, R. *Black Boy: A Record of Childhood and Youth*. New York: Harper, 1945. Wright's description of his rise from sharecropper status to international renown.

———. *Native Son*. New York: Grossett and Dunlap, 1940. Wright's most celebrated novel, the powerful story of the violent consequences of racism in the life of a young black man.

SUGGESTIONS FOR LISTENING

ADAMS, JOHN (b. 1947). Adams, a minimalist, has emerged as one of the freshest composers working today. Noted for resonant sounds and strong mastery of form, his music embraces a wide array of media, including orchestra, as in *Harmonium* (1997), and especially opera, as in *Nixon in China* (1987), *The Death of Klinghoffer* (1991), and *I Was Looking at the Ceiling and Then I Saw the Sky* (1998).

ANDERSON, LAURIE (b. 1947). The premier performance artist of our time, Anderson has come a long way since 1973's *Duets on Ice*, when, dressed in a kilt and skating on ice, she played duets with herself on the violin (it had been altered to play a prerecorded solo) on Manhattan street corners, the duration of the piece dependent on the melting ice. More recent performances are memorialized through records such as *Mister Heartbreak* (1984); *Sharkey's Day* (1984), based on a Bauhaus work by Oskar Schlemmer; *Strange Angels* (1989), taken from the performance piece entitled *Empty Places; The Ugly One with the Jewels* (1995), generated by the performance called *Stories from the New Bible* (1992–1995); and *Life on a String* (2001), inspired by the material in *Songs and Stories from "Moby Dick"* (1999), based on Herman Melville's novel. Her most popular work to date—almost 900,000 copies sold—is *O Superman* (1980), a single record that was later incorporated into the epic-length *United States I–IV* (1983).

CAGE, JOHN (1912–1992). After the late 1950s, Cage's music came to be characterized by wholly random methods that he called *aleatory* (from the Latin *alea* for dice), as represented by *4'33" (Four Minutes and Thirty-three Seconds)* (1952), *Variations IV* (1963), and *Aria with Fonatana Mix* (1958).

GLASS, PHILIP (b. 1937). Glass's pulsating rhythms and cascading sounds have made him a popular and successful figure in Post-Modern music. He is best known for his operas, including *Einstein on the Beach* (1976), *Satyagraha* (1978), *Akhnaten* (1984), and *Monsters of Grace* (1998), and for his film scores, such as *Koyaanisqatsi* (1983), *Mishima* (1985), *Kundun* (1998), the classic silent film *Dracula* (1999), and *The Hours* (2002).

PENDERECKI, KRZYSTOF (b. 1933). Penderecki, an eclectic composer, draws inspiration from diverse sources, including Stravinsky and Classical and church music. Reflective of the turbulence of contemporary Poland, his music centers on themes of martyrdom, injustice, and persecution. The first work that made him an international musical star was *Threnody for the Victims of Hiroshima* (1960), a piece for orchestra that uses stringed instruments and human voices in unusual ways. Perhaps his masterpiece is the more traditional oratorio *Passion and Death of Our Lord Jesus Christ According to St. Luke,* more commonly called "The St. Luke Passion" (1966), which incorporates Gregorian chant, folk music, nonverbal choral sounds, and modified serialism. He also has had success with operas, as in the simultaneously dissonant and lyrical *Paradise Lost* (1978), based on Milton's epic poem (see Chapter 14).

STRAVINSKY, IGOR (1882–1971). After 1951 Stravinsky replaced his Neoclassical style with the technique of serial music, as in the song *In Memoriam Dylan Thomas* (1954), the ballet *Agon* (1954–1957), and the orchestral works *Movements* (1959) and *Orchestral Variations* (1964).

CHAPTER *21* HIGHLIGHTS
The Age of Anxiety and Beyond, 1945—

1945

SARTRE, from *The Humanism of Existentialism* (1945)

WRIGHT, *Black Boy* (1945)

MAILER, *The Naked and the Dead* (1948)

BEAUVOIR, from *The Second Sex* (1949)

LESSING, from *Martha Quest* (1952)

BECKETT, *Waiting for Godot* (1952)

BALDWIN, from "Stranger in the Village" (1953)

THOMAS, *Under Milk Wood* (1954)

GINSBERG, "A Supermarket in California" (1955)

CAMUS, *The Fall* (1956)

CHOMSKY, *Syntactic Structures* (1957)

FANON, *The Wretched of the Earth* (1961)

SOLZHENITSYN, from *One Day in the Life of Ivan Denisovich* (1962)

KING, JR., from "Letter from a Birmingham Jail" (1963)

FRIEDAN, *The Feminine Mystique* (1963)

MALCOLM X AND HALEY, from *The Autobiography of Malcolm X* (1964)

LÉVI-STRAUSS, *The Elementary Structures of Kinship* (1967)

LATE MODERNISM

21.1   United Nations Headquarters (1949–1951)

21.11 POLLOCK, *Blue Poles* (1952)

21.12 ROTHKO, *Ochre and Red on Red* (1954)

21.14 JOHNS, *Target with Plaster Casts* (1955)

21.13 FRANKENTHALER, *Jacob's Ladder* (1957)

21.18 NEVELSON, *Sky Cathedral* (1958)

21.15 RAUSCHENBERG, *Monogram* (1959)

21.16 WARHOL, *Marilyn Monroe* (1962)

21.8   BEARDEN, *The Prevalence of Ritual: Baptism* (1964)

21.17 SMITH, *Cubi XIX* (1964)

21.19 SEGAL, *Robert and Ethel Scull* (1965)

21.20 VAN DER ROHE AND JOHNSON, Seagram Building (1954–1958)

CAGE, *4'33" (Four Minutes and Thirty-three Seconds)* (1952)

STRAVINSKY, *Agon* (1957)

PENDERECKI, *Threnody for the Victims of Hiroshima* (1960)

1970

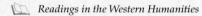

■ *Literature & Philosophy*   ■ *Art & Architecture*   ■ *Music & Dance*

📖 *Readings in the Western Humanities*   💿 *CD, The Western Humanities*

AFRICA

AMERICAS

HISTORY

North Africa   *Morocco, Algeria, Tunisia, Libya, Egypt.* Became independent. *Egypt.* Suez Canal nationalized. Wars with Israel followed by peace negotiations.

Northeast Africa   *Ethiopia.* Flourished under Emperor Haile Selassie (to 1977), followed by military coups, civil war, famine, secession of Eritrea.

West Africa   *Nigeria.* Independent. Unstable rule.

Central Africa   *Democratic Republic of Congo.* Independent (as Zaire).

East Africa   *Tanzania.* Independent (as Tanganyika); union with Zanzibar formed Tanzania.

South Africa: *Zimbabwe.* Independent (as Rhodesia). Black majority to power; renamed Zimbabwe. *Republic of South Africa.* Apartheid segregated nonwhite majority (1948–1990). Black majority rule (1994).

Caribbean   *Cuba.* Shift from right-wing to Marxist dictatorship, under Fidel Castro (1959). U.S.-Cuban missile crisis (1962). Loss of Soviet aid (1991); growing crisis.

Latin America   *Mexico.* One-party governments. Joined Canada and U.S. in free-trade zone (1993). *Argentina.* Ruled by military juntas, starting with Juan Perón. Stability and prosperity under civilian president Carlos Menem. *Colombia.* Decade of political violence; followed by two-party government. Beset by guerrilla and drug wars. *Peru.* Military junta seized power; began to nationalize industries. Return to civilian government; fought Marxist rebels. *Brazil.* "Boom and bust" years, followed by military dictatorship, then civilian rule. Exploitation of Amazon basin.

Native North America   Attempts in Congress to dismantle reservation system and Indian access to federal services (1948–62). Founding of American Indian Movement.

ART

Central Africa   *Democratic Republic of Congo.* Kuba peoples: Textiles in patterns with natural motifs; carved wooden drinking vessels, masks, and royal thrones.

East Africa   *Tanzania.* Carved wooden game boards. *Zimbabwe.* Art school teaching African painting and sculpture founded in Harare (1957).

Northwest Africa   *Senegal.* School of the Beaux Arts founded in Dakar (1960s).

West Africa   *Nigeria.* Nupe artists carved wooden doors, decorated with stylized figures and other designs. Art workshops *(mbari)* founded in Yoruba town of Oshogbo (1960s).

Latin America   *Mexico. Ruptura* movement, inspired by Rufino Tamayo and led by José Luis Cuevas. *Argentina.* Neoexpressionism and Post-Modernism. *Brazil and Chile.* Conceptual, assemblage, and site-specific works. São Paulo Biennial International Art Exhibition founded. *Colombia.* On coast: folk art based on popular images. In interior: exaggerated figural style of painter and sculptor Fernando Botero and ironic style of Ramiro Arango.

FERNANDO BOTERO. Matador. *1986. Oil on canvas, 79⅕ × 47⅗". Galerie Brusberg, Berlin.*

ARCHITECTURE

Sub-Saharan Africa   International and other European styles in African cities; traditional styles in towns and rural areas.

West Africa   *Cameroon.* Rectangular forms used in forest, circular in grasslands. Palaces, regal tombs, and seats of secret societies built at bottom of slopes; less important buildings placed on higher ground.

State Throne Representing Chief Mene. Bamileke art. Musée de la Chefferie, Bansha. Cameroon.

Latin America   *Mexico.* Thin-shell concrete design, in the Baroque spirit, pioneered by Spanish immigrant Félix Candela. University City complex, integrating visual and architectural design (1950s). *Brazil.* Brasilia, the futuristic capital city, built in the International Style of Le Corbusier; designed by Oscar Niemeyer. Use of thin-shelled, reinforced concrete.

OSCAR NIEMEYER. National Congress Building. 1958. Brasilia.

RELIGION, PHILOSOPHY, LITERATURE

North Africa   Egyptian short-story writer and novelist Naguib Mahfouz awarded Nobel Prize for literature (1988). Upsurge in Muslim fundamentalism threatens secular regimes (after 1990).

South Africa   Archbishop Desmond Tutu, a leader of anti-apartheid movement, won Nobel Peace Prize (1984).

West Africa   *Guinea.* Camara Laye, one of first sub-Saharan authors to win international acclaim. *Nigeria.* Igbo novelist Chinua Achebe, author of *Things Fall Apart* (1958); first major African writer to publish in English. Poet, playwright, and novelist Wole Soyinka awarded Nobel Prize for literature (1986). Novelist, poet, and sociologist Buchi Emecheta's *The Rape of Shavi* (1986).

Latin America   Boom, Latin America's first major literary movement. Liberation theology, radical Catholic movement dedicated to helping the poor. *Mexico.* Poet Octavio Paz awarded Nobel Prize for literature (1990). *Argentina.* Julio Cortázar, author of *Hopscotch.* Manuel Puig, author of *Kiss of the Spider Woman. Chile.* Poet Pablo Neruda awarded Nobel Prize for literature (1971). *Colombia.* Gabriel García Márquez, author of *One Hundred Years of Solitude,* awarded Nobel Prize for literature (1982). *Peru.* Mario Vargas Llosa, author of *The War at the End of the World.* Gustavo Gutiérrez's *A Theology of Liberation,* the seminal text for liberation theology.

Native North America   *House Made of Dawn,* by N. Scott Momaday (Kiowa), won Pulitzer Prize (1969). Other noted writers: Louise Erdrich, Vine Deloria, Simon Ortiz, Leslie Marmon Silko, Sherman Alexie.

China

Republic of China Civil war between Kuomintang and Communists before and after WWII.

People's Republic of China (PRC), 1949–present Nationalist forces retreated to Taiwan; Communists under Mao Zedong proclaimed People's Republic of China. Industry and agriculture nationalized. Cultural Revolution tore country apart (1966–76). Relations with U.S. restored, and relations with Soviet Union worsened (1971). Student demonstrations in Tiananmen Square (1989) and the rise of dissident voices. Relations with U.S. under stress (1990s). Moves toward controlled market economy.

India

British Crown. Self-rule (1947); mainly Muslim Pakistan and mainly Hindu India given independence. *Republic of India, 1947–present.* Stayed in British Commonwealth. Politics controlled by Congress Party and prime ministers drawn chiefly from Nehru family (to 1990). Pursued industrialization at home and neutrality in foreign affairs.

Pakistan Lost Bangladesh to Bengali separatists (1971); political instability.

Bangladesh Independent (1971). Political chaos, ethnic unrest, famine.

Japan

Shōwa period, ended 1989. Defeated (1945); occupied by U.S. troops (to 1952). New constitution (1947); monarchy based on English model with Shōwa emperor as figurehead; military dismantled; civil rights guaranteed. *Heisei period, 1989–present.* Economy prospered (to 1991). Ruled by single party (until 1993).

PRC Traditional landscape painting with political overtones. Hundred Flowers movement, a government program designed to open debate (1956–57). Cultural Revolution; artists executed and their works destroyed. Artistic controls loosened (1979); period of experimentation, especially with Western Expressionism.

Republic of India Art scene influenced by Western schools and "isms." Leading painters: Ram Kumar, Jyoti Bhatt, and Maqbool Fida Husain.

Maqbool Fida Husain. The Prancing Horse. *Oil on canvas, 25½ × 29½".*

Zhang Xiaogang. Painter with Mother as a Young Woman. *1993. Oil on canvas, 48 × 52". Collection of the Fukuoka Asian Art Museum, Japan.*

Shōwa period. Free expression returned with peace. Two schools: Nihonga, modified traditional painting, led by Kobayashi Kokei and Maeda Seison; Yoga, Western-style oil painting. Avant-garde artists, active in international circles, lacked audience at home.

PRC Massive building program in the wake of the Great Leap Forward, a drive to expand industry and agriculture (1958–60). Tiananmen Square complex, Beijing Great Hall of the People, surrounded by series of province halls.

Republic of India Indigenous vernacular buildings in villages and towns; hybrid style blending Indian and Western forms in large cities; and traditional styles for temple building. Designs by Western architects: the Swiss-French Le Corbusier in Chandigarh; the American Louis Kahn in Ahmadabad.

Shōwa period. Japanese architects, led by Tange Kenzo, developed a hybrid of Japanese and Western traditions, emphasizing simple lines, diffused lighting, and warm textures of Japanese style.

Tange Kenzo. Aerial view, Olympic Stadium. *1964. Reinforced steel, concrete. Tokyo.*

PRC *Quotations of Chairman Mao* (1966), an instant classic. Writers suppressed or driven to suicide during Cultural Revolution. Founding (1980s) of "Search for Roots," a cultural movement led by Zhang Yimou, director of the film *Raise the Red Lantern* (1991).

Republic of India Anantha Murthy's novel *Samskara* (1965) in the Kannada language. Popularity of English-language novels, led by the Hindu R. K. Narayan and the Muslim Salman Rushdie. Satyajit Ray's films, including *Pather Panchali* (1955).

Shōwa period. Mishima Yukio, author of *Confessions of a Mask* (1949) and director of *The Temple of the Golden Pavilion* (1959). Novelist Kawabata Yasunari won Nobel Prize for literature (1968). Film directors Akira Kurosawa (*Rashomon*, 1950; *Throne of Blood*, 1957); Juzo Itami (*A Taxing Woman*, 1988). *Heisei period.* Kenzaburo Oë, author of *A Personal Matter* (1964), won Nobel Prize for literature (1994).

APPENDIX
Writing for the Humanities: Research Papers and Essay Examinations

The most important part of a man's education is the ability to discuss poetry intelligently.

—PROTAGORAS, FIFTH CENTURY B.C.

I would have the ideal courtier accomplished in those studies that are called the humanities.

—CASTIGLIONE, SIXTEENTH CENTURY A.D.

The idea of "writing for the humanities" has a long history, extending back over twenty-five centuries to ancient Greece. There, in fifth-century B.C. Athens, the Sophists invented what we today call a "liberal education." These philosophers, who could be termed the first humanists, taught literature, the arts, music, and philosophy, along with what we call political science, anthropology, psychology, and history, to young Athenians, particularly those who hoped to play a leading role in politics. Not only did the Sophists demand that their students master a specific body of knowledge, but they also took care to instruct them in putting the humanistic disciplines into practice. They believed that individuals who had honed their analytical skills in the study of the humanities would be able to make wise judgments in private and public matters and to contribute to the community's political affairs.

The Sophists' educational ideal—training for good citizenship—was later adopted by the Romans, who transmitted it to the medieval West, where it became a guiding principle of university education down to the present. Today, college humanities professors give writing assignments because of their belief in the liberal education ideal as well as because of their conviction that writing, despite the spread of the mass media and information technology, remains an essential tool of private and public communication and the hallmark of the truly educated person.

AN INTEGRATIVE APPROACH TO WRITING ABOUT THE HUMANITIES

In your study of the humanities, you will probably be given writing assignments that reflect the integrative approach of *The Western Humanities* (see the Introduction). This means that your papers and examinations will not be limited to a single humanistic discipline. Instead, you will be expected to draw information from all the humanities as well as other disciplines that help illuminate the historical setting, such as political science, economics, and psychology. For example, if you were assigned a term paper on some aspect of nineteenth-century Europe, you would have to consider the civilization as a whole, both its material and its cultural developments, and at the same time bring into clearer focus such specific factors as the impact of the ruling middle class on stylistic changes in the arts and literature or the influence of the rise of nationalism on cultural developments. This integrative approach to writing reinforces the message of the textbook—that the humanities are best understood when studied holistically in their historical setting.

GENERAL RULES FOR WRITING

Typically, writing assignments for a college-level humanities course are out-of-class research or term papers and in-class essay examinations. Regardless of the writing format, keep in mind three general rules. First, think of writing as an exercise in persuasion. Assume the teacher is unfamiliar with the topic, and write to demonstrate your mastery of the material. Second, follow basic principles of good grammar and punctuation. Some teachers will penalize you for mistakes in grammar and punctuation. Even if that is not the case, instructors cannot help but be skeptical of your learning if your writing is riddled with errors. Third, accept criticism and learn from past mistakes. Few individuals are born with a gift for writing; most have to struggle to reach a writing level that is personally satisfying. Even many authors, including famous ones, still find the writing process itself deeply frustrating. Like swimming, writing cannot be learned by talking about it; it is a skill you acquire through experience. Writing well requires patience, practice, and the willingness to learn from mistakes.

RESEARCH AND TERM PAPERS

Learning to write well starts with good work habits. Establish a quiet and comfortable work space, such as a table at a library, a desk in a dormitory room, a computer station, or a desk in an empty classroom. A computer is necessary, as is access to references, such as dictionaries, biographical books, and the Internet. Develop an orderly schedule of study; plan ahead so things are not left until the last minute. Balancing work and play is a prelude to writing well, since you need brief respites from intense study to rest and refresh your mind. If you arm yourself with good work habits, you will be ready to face the challenge of writing a research or term paper.

Steps in Writing a Paper

The first step in writing a research or term paper is to pick a topic. Choose a topic that is interdisciplinary, involving at least two humanistic fields of study, such as the arts and literature of a specific historical period. Make sure your topic is manageable, neither too narrowly nor too broadly focused for your paper's length. Above all, select a topic that sparks some intellectual interest in you. Otherwise, your finished paper, even if it is carefully researched, may turn out to be uninspired and pedestrian. If you cannot find something that appeals to you on a list of suggested topics, consult with your instructor about a new subject satisfactory to both of you. As part of choosing a topic, you should also decide what approach to use in your paper, such as analytical, impressionistic, overview, or other. These approaches are described in detail in the next section.

The next step is to establish a basic bibliography. Scan your school library's holdings, either through the card catalogue system or by computer, to identify books and articles relevant to your topic. Once you have accumulated a bibliography of perhaps twenty to thirty sources, check the library stacks for additional books with appropriate call numbers that you may have overlooked in your search thus far. Then survey all these sources, treating them as background reading. At this preparatory level, take some notes on file cards and draw up a fuller list of secondary and, if needed, primary sources, such as diaries or documents, from the bibliographies in the books you are examining. Information and data from the Internet can also be helpful, but remember that much of it cannot be documented or authenticated. After completing this survey, you are ready to make an outline.

The outline—whether for a five-page paper or a major research project—is mandatory. The outline is a memory device that serves several functions: It forces you to stick to the main topics, keep an accurate perspective, incorporate relevant information, follow the framing narrative, and proceed in an orderly fashion from the opening to the conclusion. Rework your outline until it includes all relevant points and ideas. Think of it as the framework on which you raise your final piece of writing, molded into a coherent shape.

With the outline set, you are ready to make a first draft of your paper. One approach is to expand each section of the outline into a paragraph, incorporating your ideas, the facts, your examples, and your references into a narrative. Be sure to relate each paragraph to both the preceding and the succeeding paragraphs, keeping in mind the overall organization of the paper. Each paragraph should begin with a topic sentence, include examples and references to support the topic, and conclude with a summary sentence or an idea that leads into the next paragraph. Strive to remain invisible in the narrative except where a personal observation might be helpful, and try to write in the active rather than the passive voice. At times you will have to search for the word or phrase that best expresses your thought, perhaps with the help of a dictionary or a thesaurus.

The next step is to edit and re-edit your work until it sounds right. When you reread a first draft, it usually sounds like a first draft, tentative and filled with half-finished thoughts. A good test of your first draft is to read it aloud, either to yourself or to a fellow student. You will be more likely to notice gaps in logic, infelicitous words or phrases, and obvious errors in fact when you hear them out loud. At this point your good work habits will pay off, because you should now have time to polish and improve the text. Don't forget to proof the papers for misspelled words, typographical errors, and misstatements. Attention to literary style and correctness makes the difference between a satisfactory and an excellent paper.

Especially critical in writing a research paper is the citation of sources, or footnotes. Instructors have their varying policies about the use of footnotes, but the following rules apply in most situations. Short quotations (that is, a phrase or one or two sentences) may be cited in the text if the proper recognition is given. Sources for longer quotations (that is, three or more sentences) should be placed in a footnote. A full bibliography listing all books consulted, whether cited directly in the paper or not, should be included at the end of the paper. Regardless of the style you use, make sure the citation forms for footnotes are consistent throughout the paper. You should purchase a writing and style manual; often the instructor will tell you which one to buy. Two of the most frequently used manuals are the following:

Gibaldi, J. *MLA Handbook for Writers of Research Papers*. 5th ed. New York: Modern Language Association of America, 1999.

Turabian, K. Revised by J. Grossman and A. Bennett. *A Manual for Writers of Term Papers, Theses, and Dissertations*. 6th ed. Chicago: University of Chicago Press, 1996.

Types of Term Papers Assigned in the Humanities

In your humanities course you may be assigned any one of various types of research or term papers, reflecting the breadth of the disciplines that are covered under the humanities rubric. The most common types are the impressionistic paper, the analytical paper, the historical overview, the integrative paper, and the comparative culture paper. Each type requires a different approach, even though the basic writing techniques described above are valid for all.

The Impressionistic Paper   In this type of paper you offer a personal, though informed, reaction to some aspect of culture, such as the Gothic style or Post-Modernist art and architecture. Despite its focus on subjective feelings, the impressionistic paper nevertheless has to be documented with specific information, such as key historical events, biographical data, and details about particular works of art, literature, and music.

The Analytical Paper   Here, you compare and contrast two creative works. More strictly scholarly than an impressionistic paper, the analytical research paper usually requires that you study both the original works and the leading secondary sources that provide critical commentaries. Using this approach, you might examine two works within the same historical period, such as Aeschylus's tragedy *Agamemnon* and Sophocles' tragedy *Oedipus Rex;* or works across historical periods, such as Aeschylus's tragedy *Agamemnon* and Shakespeare's tragedy *Hamlet;* or works across genres, such as Aeschylus's tragedy *Agamemnon* and Verdi's opera *Rigoletto.*

The Historical Overview   In this type of paper you survey a specific time period to establish or explain a particular outcome, such as the prevailing worldview, or the leading cultural characteristics, or the impact of a particular social class. For example, if your topic were the role of aristocratic courts in the arts of the Italian Renaissance, you would have to survey fifteenth- and sixteenth-century Italian history and culture as well as the history of specific courts, such as that of the Medici in Florence and the Sforza in Milan.

The Integrative Paper   This type of paper offers a versatile approach, since it allows for a combination of many topics. For example, if you wanted to write on Freudian theory and its application to culture, you would have to research the principles of Freudian theory and discuss Freudian interpretations of specific examples of art and literature. Or, if your topic were the Classical ideal of restraint in the late eighteenth century, you would have to research the period's music, art, literature, economic theory, and political theory.

The Comparative Culture Paper   The comparative culture paper requires you to take a cultural movement, idea, or artistic, literary, or philosophical work in the West, as described in a chapter of *The Western Humanities,* and compare it with a similar development, chronologically, from a non-Western culture mentioned in one of the Windows on the World (WOW). For example, you might compare Christianity, its ideas, and influence (Chapters 6 and 7), with Confucianism in China (WOW, Chapter 5). This would mean, in particular, that you would research the topic of Confucianism, to determine its similarities to and differences from Christianity. Or, as another illustration, you could write about European and Chinese royal residences and parks, using as your cross-cultural examples Versailles, France (Chapter 14), and the rebuilding of the Forbidden City in Beijing (WOW, Chapter 14). For your paper, you could research and compare European and Chinese plans, functions, and construction of these royal palaces and gardens.

ESSAY EXAMINATIONS

Besides research papers, you will also have to write essay tests in most college-level humanities courses. The purpose of such tests is to allow you to demonstrate how well you comprehend the course lectures and readings. To succeed on essay tests, you must learn to take notes efficiently during class and while reading out-of-class assignments and to analyze the assigned material in study sessions.

The following steps will help you write better essays on examinations:

1. Before the exam, master the assigned material through sound and productive work habits. This means keeping up with daily assignments, rereading and studying lecture notes, and reviewing study materials over a four- to five-day period before the test.

2. During the exam, read the entire test carefully before beginning to write. This will ensure that you understand all the questions and allow you to set a time frame for completing each section of the exam. If you are unsure about the meaning of a question, do not hesitate to ask the instructor for a clarification.

3. If there are choices, answer those questions first that seem the easiest. This rule simply reflects common sense; it is always best to lead with your strength.

4. Briefly outline the answer to each question. The outline should include an introduction, a section for each part of the question, and a conclusion. If time permits, it is also helpful to include the major points you want to cover, specific examples or illustrations, and ideas for topic sentences and conclusions of paragraphs. The outline will help you stick to the main topics and finish the exam on time. It can also trigger more ideas while you are writing it.

5. Follow sound writing rules in composing each essay. Begin each paragraph with a topic sentence; then give examples from a wide range of sources in the humanities to support the opening statement; and conclude with a paragraph that pulls the main arguments together. Take nothing for granted. Be concise but specific. Unless they are asked for, keep your own opinions to a bare minimum.

6. Review the exam. Before turning in the exam to the monitor, review your test to correct errors, give added examples, and clarify arguments, where needed. Always allow time to proofread an essay exam.

If you score poorly on the first essay exam in a course, consult with the instructor about how to improve your performance. But remember that improvement is seldom instantaneous and good writing is achieved only after practice. Old habits die hard; the only way to do better on papers and essay exams is to keep on writing.

GLOSSARY

Italicized words within definitions are defined in their own glossary entries.

abstract art   Art that presents a subjective view of the world—the artist's emotions or ideas—or art that presents *line, color,* or shape for its own sake.

Abstract Expressionism   Also known as Action Painting, a nonrepresentational artistic style that flourished after World War II and was typified by randomness, spontaneity, and an attempt by the artist to interact emotionally with the work as it was created.

abstraction   In Modern art, nonrepresentational or nonobjective forms in sculpture and painting that emphasize shapes, *lines,* and *colors* independent of the natural world.

a cappella [ah kuh-PEL-uh]   From the Italian, "in chapel style"; music sung without instrumental accompaniment.

adab [ah-DAHB] An Arabic term. Originally, it meant good manners or good conduct. In the eighth century, it appeared as a literary *genre;* later, it indicated the possession of athletic skills and literary knowledge and applied especially to the elite. Today, *adab* refers to the whole of literature.

aesthete   One who pursues and is devoted to the beautiful in art, music, and literature.

aisles   The side passages in a church on either side of the central nave.

Alexandrianism [al-ig-ZAN-dree-an-ism]   A literary style developed in the *Hellenistic* period, typically formal, artificial, and imitative of earlier Greek writing.

ambulatory [AM-bue-la-tor-e]   A passageway for walking found in many religious structures, such as outdoors in a cloister or indoors around the *apse* or the *choir* of a church.

Anglicanism   The doctrines and practices of the Church of England, which was established in the early sixteenth century under Henry VIII.

anthropomorphism [an-thro-po-MOR-fizm]   The attributing of humanlike characteristics and traits to nonhuman things or powers, such as a deity.

apocalypse [uh-PAHK-uh-lips]   In Jewish and early Christian thought, the expectation and hope of the coming of God and his final judgment; also closely identified with the last book of the New Testament, Revelation, in which many events are foretold, often in highly symbolic and imaginative terms.

apse   In architecture, a large projection, usually rounded or semicircular, found in a *basilica,* usually in the east end; in Christian *basilicas,* the altar stood in this space.

arabesque [air-uh-BESK]   Literally, "Arabian-like"; decorative lines, patterns, and designs, often floral, in Islamic works of art.

arcade   A series of arches supported by *piers* or columns, usually serving as a passageway along a street or between buildings.

Archaic style   The style in Greek sculpture, dating from the seventh century to 480 B.C., that was characterized by heavy Egyptian influence; dominated by the *kouros* and *kore* sculptural forms.

architrave [AHR-kuh-trayv]   The part of the *entablature* that rests on the *capital* or column in Classical *post-beam-triangle construction.*

aria [AH-ree-uh]   In music, an elaborate *melody* sung as a solo or sometimes a duet, usually in an *opera* or an *oratorio,* with an orchestral accompaniment.

ars nova   Latin, "new art"; a style of music in fourteenth century Europe. It used more secular themes than the "old art" music of earlier times, which was closely identified with sacred music.

art song *(lied)*   In music, a *lyric* song with *melody* performed by a singer and instrumental accompaniment usually provided by piano; made popular by Schubert in the nineteenth century.

ashlar [ASH-luhr]   A massive hewn or squared stone used in constructing a fortress, palace, or large building.

assemblage art   An art form in which the artist mixes and/or assembles "found objects," such as scraps of paper, cloth, or junk, into a three-dimensional work and then adds paint or other decorations to it.

ataraxia [at-uh-RAK-see-uh]   Greek, "calmness"; in *Hellenistic* philosophy, the state of desiring nothing.

atonality [ay-toe-NAL-uh-tee]   In music, the absence of a *key* note or tonal center and the use of the *tones* of the chromatic *scale* impartially.

atrium [AY-tree-uhm]   In Roman architecture, an open courtyard at the front of a house; in Christian *Romanesque* churches, an open court, usually colonnaded, in front of the main doors of the structure.

attic   The topmost section or crown of an arch.

audience   The group or person for whom a work of art, architecture, literature, drama, film, or music is intended.

aulos   In music, a reed woodwind instrument similar to the oboe, usually played in pairs by one player as the double aulos; used in Greek music.

autarky [AW-tar-kee]   Greek, "self-sufficient"; in *Hellenistic* thought, the state of being isolated and free from the demands of society.

avant-garde [a-vahn-GARD]   French, "advanced guard"; writers, artists, and intellectuals who push their works and ideas ahead of more traditional groups and movements.

baldacchino [ball-duh-KEE-no]   An ornamental structure in the shape of a canopy, supported by four columns, built over a church altar, and usually decorated with statues and other ornaments.

balustrade   In architecture, a rail and the row of posts that support it, as along the edge of a staircase or around a dome.

baptistery   A small, often octagonal structure, separated from the main church, where baptisms were performed.

bard   A tribal poet-singer who composes and recites works, often of the *epic poetry* genre.

Baroque [buh-ROKE]   The prevailing seventeenth-century artistic and cultural style, characterized by an emphasis on grandeur, opulence, expansiveness, and complexity.

barrel vault   A ceiling or *vault* made of sets of arches placed side by side and joined together.

basilica [buh-SILL-ih-kuh]   A rectangular structure that included an *apse* at one or both ends; originally a Roman building used for public purposes, later taken over by the Christians for worship. The floor plan became the basis of nearly all early Christian churches.

bay   A four-cornered unit of architectural space, often used to identify a section of the *nave* in a *Romanesque* or *Gothic* church.

bel canto [bell KAHN-toe]   Italian, "beautiful singing"; a style of singing characteristic of seventeenth-century Italian *opera* stressing ease, purity, and evenness of tone along with precise vocal technique.

blank verse   Unrhymed iambic pentameter (lines with five feet, or units, each consisting of an unaccented and an accented syllable).

blind arcade   A decorative architectural design that gives the appearance of an open *arcade* or window but is filled in with some type of building material such as stone or brick.

blues   A type of music that emerged around 1900 from the rural African American culture, was originally based on work songs and religious spirituals, and expressed feelings of loneliness and hopelessness.

Byzantine style [BIZ-uhn-teen] In painting, decoration, and architecture, a style blending Greco-Roman and oriental components into a highly stylized art form that glorified Christianity, notably in domed churches adorned with *mosaics* and polished marble; associated with the culture of the Eastern Roman Empire from about 500 until 1453.

Cajun A descendant of French pioneers, chiefly in Louisiana, who in 1755 chose to leave Acadia (modern Nova Scotia) rather than live under the British Crown.

calligraphy Penmanship or handwriting, usually done with flowing lines, used as a decoration or as an enhancement of a written work; found in Islamic and Christian writings.

Calvinism The theological beliefs and rituals set forth in and derived from John Calvin's writings, placing emphasis on the power of God and the weakness of human beings.

campanile From the Latin "campana," bell; a bell tower, especially one near but not attached to a church; an Italian invention.

canon A set of principles or rules that are accepted as true and authoritative for the various arts or fields of study; in architecture, it refers to the standards of proportion; in painting, the prescribed ways of painting certain objects; in sculpture, the ideal proportions of the human body; in literature, the authentic list of an author's works; in religion, the approved and authoritative writings that are accepted as divinely inspired, such as the *Scriptures* for Jews and Christians; and in religious and other contexts, certain prescribed rituals or official rules and laws. In music, a canon is a *composition* in which a *melody* sung by one voice is repeated exactly by successive voices as they enter.

canzone [kan-ZOH-nee] Latin, "chant"; a type of love poem popular in southern France during the twelfth and thirteenth centuries.

capital In architecture, the upper or crowning part of a column, on which the *entablature* rests.

cathedral The church of a bishop that houses a cathedra, or throne symbolizing the seat of power in his administrative district, known as a diocese.

cella [SELL-uh] The inner sanctum or walled room of a *Classical* temple where sacred statues were housed.

chanson [shahn-SAWN] French, "song"; a fourteenth- to sixteenth-century French song for one or more voices, often with instrumental accompaniment. Similar to a *madrigal.*

chanson de geste [shahn-SAWN duh zhest] A poem of brave deeds in the *epic* form developed in France during the eleventh century, usually to be sung.

character A person in a story or play; someone who acts out or is affected by the *plot.*

chiaroscuro [key-ahr-uh-SKOOR-oh] In painting, the use of dark and light contrast to create the effect of modeling of a figure or object.

chivalric code The rules of conduct, probably idealized, that governed the social roles and duties of aristocrats in the Middle Ages.

chivalric novel A late medieval literary form that presented romantic stories of knights and their ladies; the dominant literary form in Spain from the Late Middle Ages into the Renaissance.

choir In architecture, that part of a *Gothic* church in which the service was sung by singers or clergy, located in the east end beyond the *transept;* also, the group of trained singers who sat in the choir area.

chorus In Greek drama, a group of performers who sang and danced in both *tragedies* and *comedies,* often commenting on the action; in later times, a group of singers who performed with or without instrumental accompaniment.

Christian humanism An intellectual movement in sixteenth-century northern Europe that sought to use the ideals of the *Classical* world, the tools of ancient learning, and the morals of the Christian *Scriptures* to rid the church of worldliness and scandal.

chthonian deities [THOE-nee-uhn] In Greek religion, earth gods and goddesses who lived underground and were usually associated with peasants and their religious beliefs.

civilization The way humans live in a complex political, economic, and social structure, usually in an urban environment, with some development in technology, literature, and art.

Classic, or Classical Having the forms, values, or standards embodied in the art and literature of Greek and Roman *civilization;* in music, an eighteenth-century style characterized by simplicity, proportion, and an emphasis on structure.

Classical Baroque style A secular variation of the *Baroque* style that was identified with French kings and artists, was rooted in *Classical* ideals, and was used mainly to emphasize the power and grandeur of the monarchy.

Classicism A set of aesthetic principles found in Greek and Roman art and literature emphasizing the search for perfection or ideal forms.

clavier [French, KLAH-vyay; German, KLAH-veer] Any musical instrument having a keyboard, such as a piano, organ, or harpsichord; the term came into general usage with the popularity of Bach's set of studies entitled *The Well-Tempered Clavier.*

clerestory windows [KLEER-stor-ee] A row of windows set along the upper part of a wall, especially in a church.

collage [koh-LAHZH] From the French "coller," to glue, a type of art, introduced by Picasso, in which bits and pieces of materials such as paper or cloth are glued to a painted surface.

color Use of the hues found in nature to enhance or distort the sense of reality in a visual image.

comedy A literary genre characterized by a story with a complicated and amusing *plot* that ends with a happy and peaceful resolution of all conflicts.

comedy of manners A humorous play that focuses on the way people in a particular social group or class interact with one another, especially regarding fashions and manners.

composition The arrangement of constituent elements in an artistic work; in music, composition also refers to the process of creating the work.

concerto [kuhn-CHER-toe] In music, a composition for one or more soloists and *orchestra,* usually in a symphonic *form* with three contrasting movements.

congregational or Friday mosque A type of *mosque* used for Friday prayers, inspired by Muhammad's original example. Characterized by a central courtyard along with a domed fountain for ablutions; found across the Islamic world.

consort A set of musical instruments in the same family, ranging from bass to soprano; also, a group of musicians who entertain by singing or playing instruments.

Constructivism A movement in nonobjective art, originating in the Soviet Union and flourishing from 1917 to 1922 and concerned with planes and volumes as expressed in modern industrial materials such as glass and plastic.

content The subject matter of an artistic work.

context The setting in which an artistic work arose, its own time and place. Context includes the political, economic, social, and cultural conditions of the time; it can also include the personal circumstances of the artist's life.

contrapposto [kon-truh-POH-stoh]   In sculpture and painting, the placement of the human figure so the weight is more on one leg than the other and the shoulders and chest are turned in the opposite direction from the hips and legs.

convention   An agreed-upon practice, device, technique, or form.

Corinthian   The third Greek architectural order, in which temple columns are slender and *fluted,* sit on a base, and have *capitals* shaped like inverted bells and decorated with carvings representing the leaves of the acanthus bush; this style was popular in *Hellenistic* times and widely adopted by the Romans.

cornice   In architecture, the crowning, projecting part of the *entablature.*

Counter-Reformation   A late-sixteenth-century movement in the Catholic Church aimed at reestablishing its basic beliefs, reforming its organizational structure, and reasserting itself as the authoritative voice of Christianity.

covenant   In Judaism and Christianity, a solemn and binding agreement or contract between God and his followers.

Creole   An ambiguous term, sometimes referring to descendants of French and Spanish settlers of the southern United States, especially Louisiana; used by Kate Chopin in her short stories and novels in this sense. In other contexts, *Creole* can refer either to blacks born in the Western Hemisphere (as distinguished from blacks born in Africa) or to residents of the American Gulf States of mixed black, Spanish, and Portuguese ancestry.

cruciform [KROO-suh-form]   Cross-shaped; used to describe the standard floor plan of a church.

Cubism   A style of painting introduced by Picasso and Braque in which objects are broken up into fragments and patterns of geometric structures and depicted on the flat canvas as if from several points of view.

culture   The sum of human endeavors, including the basic political, economic, and social institutions and the values, beliefs, and arts of those who share them.

cuneiform [kue-NEE-uh-form]   Wedge-shaped characters used in writing on tablets found in Mesopotamia and other ancient *civilizations.*

Cynicism   A *Hellenistic* philosophy that denounced society and its institutions as artificial and called on the individual to strive for *autarky.*

Dada [DAH-dah]   An early-twentieth-century artistic movement, named after a nonsense word that was rooted in a love of play, encouraged deliberately irrational acts, and exhibited contempt for all traditions.

Decadence   A late-nineteenth-century literary style concerned with morbid and artificial subjects and themes.

deductive reasoning   The process of reasoning from the general to the particular—that is, beginning with an accepted premise or first statement and, by steps of logical reasoning or inference, reaching a conclusion that necessarily follows from the premise.

Deism [DEE-iz-uhm]   A religion based on the idea that the universe was created by God and then left to run according to *natural laws,* without divine interference; formulated and practiced in the eighteenth century.

de Stijl [duh STILE]   Dutch, "the style"; an artistic movement associated with a group of early-twentieth-century Dutch painters who used rectangular forms and primary colors in their works and who believed that art should have spiritual values and a social purpose.

devotio moderna [de-VO-tee-oh mo-DER-nuh]   The "new devotion" of late medieval Christianity that emphasized piety and discipline as practiced by lay religious communities located primarily in northern Europe.

Diaspora [dye-AS-puhr-uh]   From the Greek, "to scatter"; the dispersion of the Jews from their homeland in ancient Palestine, a process that began with the Babylonian Captivity in the sixth century B.C. and continued over the centuries.

Dionysia [DYE-uh-NYSH-ee-ah]   Any of the religious festivals held in ancient Athens honoring Dionysus, the god of wine; especially the Great Dionysia, celebrated in late winter and early spring in which *tragedy* is thought to have originated.

Doric   The simplest and oldest of the Greek architectural orders, in which temple columns have undecorated *capitals* and rest directly on the *stylobate.*

drum   In architecture, a circular or polygonal wall used to support a dome.

drypoint   In art, the technique of incising an image, using a sharp, pointed instrument, onto a metal surface or block used for printing. Also, the print made from the technique.

Early Renaissance style   A style inspired by *Classical* rather than *Gothic* models that arose among Florentine architects, sculptors, and painters in the late fourteenth and early fifteenth century.

empiricism   The process of collecting data, making observations, carrying out experiments based on the collected data and observations, and reaching a conclusion.

engraving   In art, the technique of carving, cutting, or etching an image with a sharp, pointed instrument onto a metal surface overlaid with wax, dipping the surface in acid, and then printing it. Also, the print made from the technique.

Enlightenment   The eighteenth-century philosophical and cultural movement marked by the application of reason to human problems and affairs, a questioning of traditional beliefs and ideas, and an optimistic faith in unlimited progress for humanity, particularly through education.

entablature [en-TAB-luh-choor]   In architecture, the part of the temple above the columns and below the roof, which, in *Classical* temples, included the *architrave,* the *frieze,* and the *pediment.*

entasis [EN-ta-sis]   In architecture, convex curving or enlarging of the central part of a column to correct the optical illusion that the column is too thin.

epic   A poem, novel, or film that recounts at length the life of a hero or the history of a people.

epic poetry   Narrative poetry, usually told or written in an elevated style, that recounts the life of a hero.

epic theater   A type of theater, invented by Brecht, in which major social issues are dramatized with outlandish props and jarring dialogue and effects, all designed to alienate middle-class audiences and force them to think seriously about the problems raised in the plays.

Epicureanism [ep-i-kyoo-REE-uh-niz-uhm]   A *Hellenistic* philosophy, founded by Epicurus and later expounded by the Roman Lucretius, that made its highest goals the development of the mind and an existence free from the demands of everyday life.

eschatology [es-kuh-TAHL-uh-jee]   The concern with final events or the end of the world, a belief popular in Jewish and early Christian communities and linked to the concept of the coming of a *Messiah.*

evangelists   From the Greek *evangelion,* a term generally used for those who preach the Christian religion; more specifically, the four evangelists, Matthew, Mark, Luke, and John, who wrote about Jesus Christ soon after his death in the first four books of the New Testament.

evolution   The theory, set forth in the nineteenth century by Charles Darwin, that plants and animals, including humans, evolved over millions of years from simpler forms through a process of natural selection.

existentialism [eg-zi-STEN-shuh-liz-uhm]   A twentieth-century philosophy focusing on the precarious nature of human existence, with its uncertainty, anxiety, and ultimate death, as well as on individual freedom and responsibility and the possibilities for human creativity and authenticity.

Expressionism   A late-nineteenth-century literary and artistic movement characterized by the expression of highly personal feelings rather than of objective reality.

fan vault   A decorative pattern of *vault* ribs that arch out or radiate from a central point on the ceiling; popular in English *Perpendicular* architecture.

Faustian [FAU-stee-uhn]   Resembling the character Faust in Goethe's most famous work, in being spiritually tormented, insatiable for knowledge and experience, or willing to pay any price, including personal and spiritual integrity, to gain a desired end.

Fauvism [FOH-viz-uhm]   From the French "fauve," wild beast; an early-twentieth-century art movement led by Matisse and favoring exotic colors and disjointed shapes.

fête galante [fet gah-LAHNN]   In *Rococo* painting, the *theme* or scene of aristocrats being entertained or simply enjoying their leisure and other worldly pleasures.

First Romanesque   The first stage of *Romanesque* architecture, about 1000–1080. First Romanesque churches had high walls, few windows, and flat wooden roofs, and were built of stone rubble and adorned with *Lombard bands* and *Lombard arcades.* Begun along the Mediterranean, in the area ranging from Dalmatia, across Northern Italy and Provence, to Catalonia.

Flamboyant style [flam-BOY-uhnt]   A Late French *Gothic* architectural style of elaborate decorations and ornamentation that produce a flamelike effect.

Florid Baroque style   A variation of the *Baroque* style specifically identified with the Catholic Church's patronage of the arts and used to glorify its beliefs.

fluting   Decorative vertical grooves carved in a column.

flying buttress   An external masonry support, found primarily in *Gothic* churches, that carries the thrust of the ceiling or *vault* away from the upper walls of the building to an external vertical column.

forms   In music, particular structures or arrangements of elements, such as *symphonies,* songs, concerts, and *operas.*

forum   In Rome and many Roman towns, the public place, located in the center of the town, where people gathered to socialize, transact business, and administer the government.

Fourth Century style   The sculptural style characteristic of the last phase of the *Hellenic* period, when new interpretations of beauty and movement were adopted.

fresco   A painting done on wet or dry plaster that becomes part of the plastered wall.

friars   Members of a thirteenth-century mendicant (begging) monastic order.

frieze [FREEZ]   A band of painted designs or sculptured figures placed on walls; also, the central portion of a temple's *entablature* just above the *architrave.*

fugue [fewg]   In music, a *composition* for several instruments in which a *theme* is introduced by one instrument and then repeated by each successively entering instrument so that a complicated interweaving of themes, variations, imitations, and echoes results; this compositional technique began in the fifteenth century and reached its zenith in the *Baroque* period in works by Bach.

gallery   In architecture, a long, narrow passageway or corridor, usually found in churches and located above the *aisles,* and often with openings that permit viewing from above into the *nave.*

gargoyle [GAHR-goil]   In architecture, a water spout in the form of a grotesque animal or human, carved from stone, placed on the edge of a roof.

genre [ZHON-ruh]   From the French, "a kind, a type, or a class"; a category of artistic, musical, or literary composition, characterized by a particular *style, form,* or *content.*

genre subject   In art, a scene or a person from everyday life, depicted realistically and without religious or symbolic significance.

geocentrism   The belief that the earth is the center of the universe and that the sun, planets, and stars revolve around it.

ghazal [GUZ-l]   A short *lyric,* usually dealing with love, composed in a single rhyme and based on the poet's personal life and loves.

glissando [gle-SAHN-doe] (plural, **glissandi**)   In music, the blending of one *tone* into the next in scalelike passages that may be ascending or descending in character.

goliards [GOAL-yuhrds]   Medieval roaming poets or scholars who traveled about reciting poems on topics ranging from moral lessons to the pains of love.

Gospels   The first four books of the New Testament (Matthew, Mark, Luke, and John) that record the life and sayings of Jesus Christ; the word itself, from Old English, means good news or good tales.

Gothic style   A *style* of architecture, usually associated with churches, that originated in northern France and whose three phases—Early, High, and Late—lasted from the twelfth to the sixteenth century. Emerging from the *Romanesque* style, Gothic is identified by pointed arches, *ribbed vaults, stained-glass* windows, *flying buttresses,* and carvings on the exterior.

Greek cross   A cross in which all the arms are of equal length; the shape used as a floor plan in many Greek or Eastern Orthodox churches.

Gregorian chant   A style of *monophonic* church music sung in unison and without instrumental accompaniment and used in the *liturgy;* named for Pope Gregory I (590–604).

groined vault, or cross vault   A ceiling or *vault* created when two *barrel vaults,* set at right angles, intersect.

harmony   The simultaneous combination of two or more *tones,* producing a chord; generally, the chordal characteristics of a work and the way chords interact.

heliocentrism   The belief that the sun is the center of the universe and that the earth and the other planets revolve around it.

Hellenic [hell-LENN-ik]   Relating to the time period in Greek civilization from 480 to 323 B.C., when the most influential Greek artists, playwrights, and philosophers, such as Praxiteles, Sophocles, and Plato, created their greatest works; associated with the *Classical* style.

Hellenistic [hell-uh-NIS-tik]   Relating to the time period from about 323 to 31 B.C., when Greek and oriental or Middle Eastern cultures and institutions intermingled to create a heterogeneous and cosmopolitan *civilization.*

hieroglyphs [HI-uhr-uh-glifs]   Pictorial characters used in Egyptian writing, which is known as hieroglyphics.

High Classical style   The *style* in Greek sculpture associated with the ideal physical form and perfected during the zenith of the Athenian Empire, about 450–400 B.C.

higher criticism   A rational approach to Bible study, developed in German Protestant circles in the nineteenth century, that treated the biblical *Scriptures* as literature and subjected them to close scrutiny, testing their literary history, authorship, and meaning.

High Renaissance   The period from about 1495 to 1520, often associated with the patronage of the popes in Rome, when the most influential artists and writers of the *Renaissance*, including Michelangelo, Raphael, Leonardo da Vinci, and Machiavelli, were producing their greatest works.

high tech   In architecture, a *style* that uses obvious industrial design elements with exposed parts serving as decorations.

Homeric epithet   A recurring nickname, such as "Ox-eyed Hera," used in Homer's *Iliad* or *Odyssey*.

hubris [HYOO-bris]   In Greek thought, human pride or arrogance that leads an individual to challenge the gods, usually provoking divine retribution.

humanism   An attitude that is concerned with humanity, its achievements, and its potential; the study of the *humanities*; in the *Renaissance*, identified with *studia humanitatis*.

humanities   In the nineteenth century, the study of Greek and Roman languages and literature; later set off from the sciences and expanded to include the works of all Western peoples in the arts, literature, music, philosophy, and sometimes history and religion; in *Post-Modernism* extended to a global dimension.

hymn   From the Greek and Latin, "ode of praise of gods or heroes"; a song of praise or thanksgiving to God or the gods, performed both with and without instrumental accompaniment.

idealism   in Plato's philosophy, the theory that reality and ultimate truth are to be found not in the material world but in the spiritual realm.

idée fixe [ee-DAY FEEX]   French, "fixed idea"; in music, a recurring musical *theme* that is associated with a person or a concept.

ideogram [ID-e-uh-gram]   A picture drawn to represent an idea or a concept.

idyll   A relatively short poem that focuses on events and themes of everyday life, such as family, love, and religion; popular in the *Hellenistic Age* and a standard form that has been periodically revived in Western literature throughout the centuries.

illuminated manuscript   A richly decorated book, painted with brilliant colors and gold leaf, usually of sacred writings; popular in the West in the Middle Ages.

illusionism   The use of painting techniques in *Florid Baroque* art to create the appearance that decorated areas are part of the surrounding architecture, usually employed in ceiling decorations.

impasto [ihm-PAHS-toe]   In painting, the application of thick layers of pigment.

Impressionism   In painting, a *style* introduced in the 1870s, marked by an attempt to catch spontaneous impressions, often involving the play of sunlight on ordinary events and scenes observed outdoors; in music, a style of *composition* designed to create a vague and dreamy mood through gliding melodies and shimmering tone colors.

impressionistic   In art, relating to the representation of a scene using the simplest details to create an illusion of reality by evoking subjective impressions rather than aiming for a totally realistic effect; characterized by images that are insubstantial and barely sketched in.

inductive reasoning   The process of reasoning from particulars to the general or from single parts to the whole and/or final conclusion.

installation art   A boundary-challenging type of art born in the 1960s that creates architectural tableaux, using objects drawn from and making references to artistic sources (such as music, painting, sculpture, and theater) and the workaday world (such as everyday tasks, media images,

and foodstuffs) and that may include a human presence. Associated with the work of Ann Hamilton.

International style   In twentieth-century architecture, a *style* and method of construction that capitalized on modern materials, such as ferro-concrete, glass, and steel, and that produced the popular "glass box" skyscrapers and variously shaped private houses.

Ionic   The Greek architectural order, developed in Ionia, in which columns are slender, sit on a base, and have *capitals* decorated with scrolls.

isorhythm   In music, a unifying method based on rhythmic patterns rather than *melodic* patterns.

Italo-Byzantine style [ih-TAL-o-BIZ-uhn-teen]   The *style* of Italian *Gothic* painting that reflected the influence of *Byzantine* paintings, *mosaics*, and icons.

iwan [eye-van]   In Islamic architecture, a vaulted hall. In the 4-*iwan* mosque, one *iwan* was used for prayers and the other three for study or rest.

jazz   A type of music, instrumental and vocal, originating in the African American community and rooted in African, African American, and Western musical forms and traditions.

Jesuits [JEZH-oo-its]   Members of the Society of Jesus, the best-organized and most effective monastic order founded during the *Counter-Reformation* to combat Protestantism and spread Roman Catholicism around the world.

jihad [JEE-HAD]   Originally, this Arabic term meant "to strive" or "to struggle," and, as such, was identified with any pious Muslim combating sin and trying not to do evil. In modern times, radical Islamic states and groups have given the term new meaning as "Holy War" and then used it to justify military and other violent action against their enemies. A central belief in Islam.

key   In music, a tonal system consisting of seven *tones* in fixed relationship to a tonic, or keynote. Since the Renaissance, *key* has been the structural foundation of the bulk of Western music, down to the *Modernist* period.

keystone   The central stone at the top of an arch that locks the other stones in place.

koine [KOI-nay]   A colloquial Greek language spoken in the *Hellenistic* world that helped tie together that *civilization.*

kore [KOH-ray]   An *Archaic* Greek standing statue of a young draped female.

kouros [KOO-rus]   An *Archaic* Greek standing statue of a young naked male.

Late Gothic style   A *style* characterized in architecture by ornate decoration and tall cathedral windows and spires and in painting and sculpture by increased refinement of details and a trend toward naturalism; popular in the fourteenth and fifteenth centuries in central and western Europe.

Late Mannerism   The last stage of the *Mannerist* movement, characterized by exaggeration and distortion, especially in painting.

Late Modernism   The last stage of *Modernism,* characterized by an increasing sense of existential despair, an attraction to non-Western cultures, and extreme experimentalism.

lay   A short *lyric* or narrative poem meant to be sung to the accompaniment of an instrument such as a harp; based on Celtic legends but usually set in feudal times and focused on courtly love themes, especially adulterous passion. The oldest surviving lays are those of the twelfth-century poet Marie de France.

leitmotif [LITE-mo-teef]   In music, and especially in Wagner's *operas,* the use of recurring *themes* associated with particular characters, objects, or ideas.

liberalism   In political thought, a set of beliefs advocating certain personal, economic, and natural rights based on assumptions about the perfectibility and autonomy of human beings and the notion of progress, as first expressed in the writings of John Locke.

libretto [lih-BRET-oh] In Italian, "little book"; the text or words of an *opera,* an *oratorio,* or a musical work of a similar dramatic nature involving a written text.

line The mark—straight or curved, thick or thin, light or dark—made by the artist in a work of art.

Linear A In Minoan civilization, a type of script still undeciphered that lasted from about 1800 to 1400 B.C.

Linear B In Minoan civilization, an early form of Greek writing that flourished on Crete from about 1400 until about 1300 B.C. and lasted in a few scattered places on the Greek mainland until about 1150 B.C.; used to record commercial transactions.

liturgical drama Religious dramas, popular between the twelfth and sixteenth centuries, based on biblical stories with musical accompaniment that were staged in the area in front of the church, performed at first in Latin but later in the *vernacular languages;* the mystery plays (*mystery* is derived from the Latin for "action") are the most famous type of liturgical drama.

liturgy A rite or ritual, such as prayers or ceremonies, practiced by a religious group in public worship.

local color In literature, the use of detail peculiar to a particular region and environment to add interest and authenticity to a narrative, including description of the locale, customs, speech, and music. Local color was an especially popular development in American literature in the late nineteenth century.

logical positivism A school of modern philosophy that seeks truth by defining terms and clarifying statements and asserts that metaphysical theories are meaningless.

logos [LOWG-os] In *Stoicism,* the name for the supreme being or for reason—the controlling principle of the universe—believed to be present both in nature and in each human being.

Lombard arcades In architecture, a sequence of *arcades* beneath the eaves of a building. First used in churches in Lombardy (North Central Italy). A defining feature of the *First Romanesque.*

Lombard bands In architecture, a web of vertical bands or buttresses along the sides of a building. First used in churches in Lombardy (North Central Italy). A defining feature of the *First Romanesque.*

luminism In nineteenth century American landscape painting, a group of artists, who were inspired by the vastness of the American west and influenced by Transcendentalism, approached their work by consciously removing themselves from their paintings.

lute In music, a wooden instrument, plucked or bowed, consisting of a sound box with an elaborately carved sound hole and a neck across which the (often twelve) strings pass. Introduced during the High Middle Ages, the lute enjoyed a height of popularity in Europe from the seventeenth to eighteenth century.

Lutheranism The doctrine, liturgy, and institutional structure of the church founded in the sixteenth century by Martin Luther, who stressed the authority of the Bible, the faith of the individual, and the worshiper's direct communication with God as the bases of his new religion.

lyre In music, a hand-held stringed instrument, with or without a sound box, used by ancient Egyptians, Assyrians, and Greeks. In Greek culture, the lyre was played to accompany song and recitation.

lyric A short subjective poem that expresses intense personal emotion.

lyric poetry In Greece, verses sung and accompanied by the *lyre;* today, intensely personal poetry.

Machiavellianism [mahk-ih-uh-VEL-ih-uhn-iz-uhm] The view that politics should be separated from morals and dedicated to the achievement of desired ends through any means necessary ("the end justifies the means"); derived from the political writings of Machiavelli.

madrasa [mah-DRASS-ah] An Arabic term meaning a religious school for advanced study; a forerunner of the Islamic university. Today, *madrasas* are schools for Islamic youth, and their curriculum is based on the *Qur'an.*

madrigal [MAD-rih-guhl] A *polyphonic* song performed without accompaniment and based on a secular text, often a love *lyric;* especially popular in the sixteenth century.

maenad [MEE-nad] A woman who worshiped Dionysus, often in a state of frenzy.

magic realism A literary and artistic *style* identified with Latin American *Post-Modernism* that mixes realistic and supernatural elements to create imaginary or fantastic scenes.

Mannerism A cultural movement between 1520 and 1600 that grew out of a rebellion against the *Renaissance* artistic norms of symmetry and balance; characterized in art by distortion and incongruity and in thought and literature by the belief that human nature is depraved.

maqamah [mah-kah-mah] In Arabic, "assembly." A Muslim literary *genre,* intended for educated readers, that recounted stories of rogues and con men; filled with wordplay, humor, and keen usage of Arabic language and grammar. Created by al-Hamadhani in the tenth century.

Mass In religion, the ritual celebrating the Eucharist, or Holy Communion, primarily in the Roman Catholic Church. The Mass has two parts, the Ordinary and the Proper; the former remains the same throughout the church year, whereas the latter changes for each date and service. The Mass Ordinary is composed of the Kyrie, Gloria, Credo, Sanctus, and Agnus Dei; the Mass Proper includes the Introit, Gradual, Alleluia or Tract, Sequence, Offertory, and Communion. In music, a musical setting of certain parts of the Mass, especially the Kyrie, Gloria, Credo, Sanctus, Benedictus, and Agnus Dei. The first complete Mass Ordinary was composed by Guillaume de Machaut [mah-SHOH] (about 1300–1377) in the fourteenth century.

mass culture The tastes, values, and interests of the classes that dominate modern industrialized society, especially the consumer-oriented American middle class.

medallion In Roman architecture, a circular decoration often found on triumphal arches enclosing a scene or portrait; in more general architectural use, a tablet or panel in a wall or window containing a figure or an ornament.

medium The material from which an artwork is made.

melody A succession of musical *tones* having a distinctive shape and rhythm.

Messiah A Hebrew word meaning "the anointed one," or one chosen by God to be his representative on earth; in Judaism, a savior who will come bringing peace and justice; in Christianity, Jesus Christ (*Christ* is derived from a Greek word meaning "the anointed one").

metope [MET-uh-pee] In architecture, a panel, often decorated, between two *triglyphs* on the *entablature* of a *Doric* Greek temple.

microtone In music, an interval, or distance between a sound (pitch) on a *scale,* that is smaller than a semi-*tone*—the smallest interval in mainstream Western music prior to *jazz.* Muslim music uses a microtonal system.

minaret   In Islamic architecture, a tall, slender tower with a pointed top, from which the daily calls to prayer are delivered; located near a *mosque*.

minbar [min-bar]   In Muslim *mosque* architecture, a pulpit with steps, sometimes on wheels for portability; used by a cleric for leading prayers and giving sermons.

miniature   A small painting, usually of a religious nature, found in *illuminated manuscripts*; also, a small portrait.

minstrel   A professional entertainer of the twelfth to the seventeenth century; especially a secular musician; also called "jongleur."

Modernism   A late-nineteenth- and twentieth-century cultural, artistic, and literary movement that rejected much of the past and focused on the current, the secular, and the revolutionary in search of new forms of expression; the dominant style of the twentieth century until 1970.

modes   A series of musical *scales* devised by the Greeks and believed by them to create certain emotional or ethical effects on the listener.

monophony [muh-NOF-uh-nee]   A *style* of music in which there is only a single line of melody; the *Gregorian chants* are the most famous examples of monophonic music.

monotheism   From the Greek *monos,* single, alone, and the Greek *theos,* god; the belief that there is only one God.

mood   In music, the emotional impact of a *composition* on the feelings of a listener.

mosaic   An art form or decoration, usually on a wall or a floor, created by inlaying small pieces of glass, shell, or stone in cement or plaster to create pictures or patterns.

mosque   A Muslim place of worship, often distinguished by a dome-shaped central building placed in an open space surrounded by a wall.

motet   A multivoiced song with words of a sacred or secular text, usually sung without accompanying instruments; developed in the thirteenth century.

mural   A wall painting, usually quite large, used to decorate a private or public structure.

muse   In Greek religion, any one of the nine sister goddesses who preside over the creative arts and sciences.

music drama   An *opera* in which the action and music are continuous, not broken up into separate *arias* and *recitatives,* and the music is determined by its dramatic appropriateness, producing a work in which music, words, and staging are fused; the term was coined by Wagner.

narrator   The speaker whose voice we hear in a story or poem.

narthex   The porch or vestibule of a church, usually enclosed, through which worshipers walk before entering the *nave*.

Naturalism   In literature, a late-nineteenth-century movement inspired by the methods of science and the insights of sociology, concerned with an objective depiction of the ugly side of industrial society.

natural law   In *Stoicism* and later in other philosophies, a body of laws or principles that are believed to be derived from nature and binding on human society and that constitute a higher form of justice than civil or judicial law.

nave   The central longitudinal area of a church, extending from the entrance to the *apse* and flanked by *aisles*.

Neoclassical style   In the late eighteenth century, an artistic and literary movement that emerged as a reaction to the *Rococo* style and that sought inspiration from ancient *Classicism*. In the twentieth century, between 1919 and 1951, *Neoclassicism* in music was a style that rejected the emotionalism favored by Romantic composers as well as the dense orchestral sounds of the Impressionists; instead, it borrowed features from seventeenth- and eighteenth-century music and practiced the ideals of balance, clarity of texture, and nonprogrammatic works.

Neoclassicism   In the late third century B.C., an artistic movement in the disintegrating Hellenistic world that sought inspiration in the Athenian Golden Age of the fifth and fourth centuries B.C.; and, since 1970, *Neoclassicism* has been a highly visible submovement in *Post-Modernism,* particularly prominent in painting and architecture, that restates the principles of *Classical* art—balance, harmony, idealism.

Neoexpressionism   A submovement in *Post-Modernism,* associated primarily with painting, that offers social criticism and is concerned with the expression of the artist's feelings.

Neolithic   Literally, "new stone"; used to define the New Stone Age, when human *cultures* evolved into agrarian systems and settled communities; dating from about 10,000 or 8000 B.C. to about 3000 B.C.

Neo-Platonism   A philosophy based on Plato's ideas that was developed during the Roman period in an attempt to reconcile the dichotomy between Plato's concept of an eternal World of Ideas and the ever-changing physical world; in the fifteenth-century *Renaissance,* it served as a philosophical guide for Italian humanists who sought to reconcile late medieval Christian beliefs with *Classical* thinking.

Neorealism   A submovement in *Post-Modernism* that is based on a photographic sense of detail and harks back to many of the qualities of nineteenth-century *Realism*.

New Comedy   The style of comedy favored by *Hellenistic* playwrights, concentrating on gentle satirical themes—in particular, romantic *plots* with stock *characters* and predictable endings.

Nominalism [NAHM-uh-nuhl-iz-uhm]   In medieval thought, the school that held that objects were separate unto themselves but could, for convenience, be treated in a collective sense because they shared certain characteristics; opposed to *Realism*.

Northern Renaissance   The sixteenth-century cultural movement in northern Europe that was launched by the northward spread of Italian *Renaissance* art, culture, and ideals. The Northern Renaissance differed from the Italian Renaissance largely because of the persistence of the *Late Gothic style* and the unfolding of the *Reformation* after 1520.

octave   In music, usually the eight-tone interval between a note and a second note of the same name, as in C to C.

oculus [AHK-yuh-lus]   The circular opening at the top of a dome; derived from the Latin word for "eye."

Old Comedy   The style of *comedy* established by Aristophanes in the fifth century B.C., distinguished by a strong element of political and social satire.

oligarchy   From the Greek *oligos,* few; a state ruled by the few, especially by a small fraction of persons or families.

Olympian deities   In Greek religion, sky gods and goddesses who lived on mountaintops and were worshiped mainly by the Greek aristocracy.

opera   A drama or play set to music and consisting of vocal pieces with *orchestral* accompaniment; acting, scenery, and sometimes *choruses* and dancing are used to heighten the dramatic values of operas.

oratorio   A choral work based on religious events or *scripture* employing singers, *choruses,* and *orchestra* but without scenery or staging and performed usually in a church or a concert hall.

orchestra   In Greek theaters, the circular area where the *chorus* performed in front of the audience; in music, a group of instrumentalists, including string players, who play together.

organum [OR-guh-nuhm]   In the ninth through the thirteenth centuries, a simple and early form of *polyphonic* music consisting of a main melody sung along with a *Gregorian chant;* by the thirteenth century it had developed into a complex multivoiced song.

Paleolithic   Literally, "old stone"; used to define the Old Stone Age, when crude stones and tools were used; dating from about 2,000,000 B.C. to about 10,000 B.C.

pantheism   The doctrine of or belief in multitudes of deities found in nature.

pantomime   In Roman times, enormous dramatic productions featuring instrumental music and dances, favored by the masses; later, a type of dramatic or dancing performance in which the story is told with expressive or even exaggerated bodily and facial movements.

pastoral   A type of *Hellenistic* poetry that idealized rural customs and farming, especially the simple life of shepherds, and deprecated urban living.

pavane [puh-VAHN]   A sixteenth- and seventeenth-century English court dance of Italian origin; the dance is performed by couples to stately music. Ravel based *Pavane for a Dead Princess* (1899) on this *Baroque* dance form.

pediment   In *Classical*-style architecture, the triangular-shaped area or gable at the end of the building formed by the sloping roof and the *cornice*.

pendentive [pen-DEN-tiv]   In architecture, a triangular, concave-shaped section of *vaulting* between the rim of a dome and the pair of arches that support it; used in Byzantine and Islamic architecture.

performance art   A democratic type of mixed media art born in the 1960s that ignores artistic boundaries, mixing high art (such as music, painting, and theater) and popular art (such as rock and roll, film, and fads), to create a unique, nonreproducible, artistic experience. Associated with the work of Laurie Anderson.

peristyle [PAIR-uh-stile]   A colonnade around an open courtyard or a building.

Perpendicular style   The highly decorative style of *Late Gothic* architecture that developed in England at the same time as the *Late Gothic* on the European continent.

Persian miniature   A style of *miniature* painting that flourished in Persia from the thirteenth to the seventeenth centuries; characterized by rectangular designs, the depiction of the human figure as about one-fifth the height of the painting, and refined detail.

perspective   A technique or formula for creating the illusion or appearance of depth and distance on a two-dimensional surface. **Atmospheric perspective** is achieved in many ways: by diminishing color intensity, by omitting detail, and by blurring the lines of an object. **Linear perspective,** based on mathematical calculations, is achieved by having parallel lines or lines of projection appearing to converge at a single point, known as the *vanishing point*, on the horizon of the flat surface and by diminishing distant objects in size according to scale to make them appear to recede from the viewer.

philosophes [FEEL-uh-sawfs]   A group of European thinkers and writers who popularized the ideas of the *Enlightenment* through essays, novels, plays, and other works, hoping to change the climate of opinion and bring about social and political reform.

phonogram   A symbol used to represent a syllable, a word, or a sound.

Physiocrats [FIZ-ih-uh-kratz]   A group of writers, primarily French, who dealt with economic issues during the *Enlightenment*, in particular calling for improved agricultural productivity and questioning the state's role in economic affairs.

pianoforte [pee-an-o-FOR-tay]   A piano; derived from the Italian for "soft/loud," terms used to describe the two types of sound emitted by a stringed instrument whose wires are struck with felt-covered hammers operated from a keyboard.

picaresque novel   From the Spanish term for "rogue." A type of literature, originating in sixteenth-century Spain, that recounted the comic misadventures of a roguish hero who lived by his wits, often at the expense of the high and mighty; influenced novel writing across Europe, especially in England, France, and Germany, until about 1800; the anonymous "Lazarillo de Tormes" (1554) was the first picaresque novel.

pictogram   A carefully drawn, often stylized, picture that represents a particular object.

pier   In architecture, a vertical masonry structure that may support a *vault*, an arch, or a roof; in *Gothic* churches, piers were often clustered together to form massive supports.

Pietà [pee-ay-TAH]   A painting or sculpture depicting the mourning Virgin and the dead Christ.

pilaster [pih-LAS-tuhr]   In architecture, a vertical, rectangular decorative device projecting from a wall that gives the appearance of a column with a base and a *capital;* sometimes called an applied column.

Platonism   The collective beliefs and arguments presented in Plato's writings stressing especially that actual things are copies of ideas.

plot   The action, or arrangement of incidents, in a story.

podium   In architecture, a low wall serving as a foundation; a platform.

poetry   Language that is concentrated and imaginative, marked by meter, rhythm, rhyme, and imagery.

Pointillism [PWANT-il-iz-uhm]   Also known as Divisionism, a style of painting, perfected by Seurat, in which tiny dots of paint are applied to the canvas in such a way that when they are viewed from a distance they merge and blend to form recognizable objects with natural effects of color, light, and shade.

polyphony [puh-LIF-uh-nee]   A style of musical *composition* in which two or more voices or melodic lines are woven together.

polytheism [PAHL-e-the-iz-uhm]   The doctrine of or belief in more than one deity.

Pop Art   An artistic *style* popular between 1960 and 1970 in which commonplace commercial objects drawn from *mass culture,* such as soup cans, fast foods, and comic strips, became the subjects of art.

portico   In architecture, a covered entrance to a building, usually with a separate roof supported by columns.

post-and-lintel construction   A basic architectural form in which upright posts, or columns, support a horizontal lintel, or beam.

post-beam-triangle construction   The generic name given to Greek architecture that includes the post, or column; the beam, or lintel; and the triangular-shaped area, or *pediment.*

Post-Impressionism   A late-nineteenth-century artistic movement that extended the boundaries of *Impressionism* in new directions to focus on structure, composition, fantasy, and subjective expression.

Post-Modernism   An artistic, cultural, and intellectual movement, originating in about 1970, that is more optimistic than *Modernism*, embraces an open-ended and democratic global civilization, freely adapts elements of high culture and *mass culture,* and manifests itself chiefly through revivals of earlier styles, giving rise to *Neoclassicism, Neoexpressionism*, and *Neorealism.*

Praxitelean curve [prak-sit-i-LEE-an]   The graceful line of the sculptured body in the *contrapposto* stance, perfected by the *Fourth Century style* sculptor Praxiteles.

primitivism   In painting, the "primitives" are those painters of the Netherlandish and Italian schools who flourished before 1500, thus all Netherlandish painters between the van Eycks and Dürer and all Italian painters between Giotto and Raphael; more generally, the term reflects modern artists' fascination with non-Western art forms, as in Gauguin's Tahitian-inspired paintings. In literature, primitivism has complex meanings; on the one hand, it refers to the notion of a golden age, a world of lost innocence, which appeared in both ancient pagan and Christian writings; on the other hand, it is a modern term used to denote two species of cultural relativism, which either finds people isolated from civilization to be superior to those living in civilized and urban settings, as in the cult of the Noble Savage (Rousseau), or respects native peoples and their cultures within their own settings, yet accepts that natives can be as cruel as Europeans (the view expressed by Montaigne).

problem play   A type of drama that focuses on a specific social problem; the Swedish playwright Ibsen was a pioneer of this *genre*, as in *A Doll's House* (1879), concerning women's independence.

program music   Instrumental music that depicts a narrative, portrays a *setting*, or suggests a sequence of events; often based on other sources, such as a poem or a play.

prose   The ordinary language used in speaking and writing.

Puritanism   The beliefs and practices of the Puritans, a small but influential religious group devoted to the teachings of John Calvin; they stressed strict rules of personal and public behavior and practiced their beliefs in England and the New World during the seventeenth century.

putti [POOH-tee]   Italian, plural of *putto;* in painting and sculpture, figures of babies, children, or sometimes angels.

qasida [kah-SEE-dah]   In Arabic, "ode." An ode, composed in varied meters and with a single rhyme, that is, all lines end in the same rhyming sound. The leading poetic *genre* in Muslim literature.

qiblah [kee-blah]   In Islamic *mosque* architecture, a niche, often richly decorated, pointing the direction for prayer, that is, toward the Kaaba in Mecca.

ragtime   A type of instrumental music, popularized by African Americans in the late nineteenth and early twentieth centuries, with a strongly syncopated rhythm and a lively *melody.*

Rayonnant [ray-yo-NAHNN]   A decorative *style* in French architecture associated with the High *Gothic* period, in which walls were replaced by sheets of *stained glass* framed by elegant stone *traceries.*

Realism   In medieval philosophy, the school that asserted that objects contained common or universal qualities that were not always apparent to the human senses but that were more real or true than the objects' physical attributes; opposed to *Nominalism*. In art and literature, a mid- to late-nineteenth-century style that focused on the everyday lives of the middle and lower classes, portraying their world in a serious, accurate, and unsentimental way; opposed to *Romanticism.*

recitative [ress-uh-tuh-TEEV]   In music, a rhythmically free but often stylized declamation, midway between singing and ordinary speech, that serves as a transition between *arias* or as a narrative device in an *opera.*

Reformation   The sixteenth-century religious movement that looked back to the ideals of early Christianity, called for moral and structural changes in the church, and led ultimately to the founding of the various Protestant churches.

refrain   In music, a recurring musical passage or phrase; called *"ritornello"* in Italian.

regalia   Plural in form, often used with a singular verb. The emblems and symbols of royalty, as the crown and scepter.

relief   In sculpture, figures or forms that are carved so they project from the flat surface of a stone or metal background. **High relief** projects sharply from the surface; **low relief,** or **bas relief,** is more shallow.

Renaissance [ren-uh-SAHNS]   From the French for "rebirth"; the artistic, cultural, and intellectual movement marked by a revival of *Classical* and *humanistic* values that began in Italy in the mid–fourteenth century and had spread across Europe by the mid–sixteenth century.

representational art   Art that presents a likeness of the world as it appears to the naked eye.

Restrained Baroque style   A variation of the *Baroque* style identified with Dutch and English architects and painters who wanted to reduce Baroque grandeur and exuberance to a more human scale.

revenge tragedy   A type of play popular in sixteenth-century England, probably rooted in Roman *tragedies* and concerned with the need for a family to seek revenge for the murder of a relative.

ribbed vault   A masonry roof with a framework of arches or ribs that reinforce and decorate the *vault* ceiling.

rocaille [roh-KYE]   In *Rococo* design, the stucco ornaments shaped like leaves, flowers, and ribbons that decorate walls and ceilings.

Rococo style [ruh-KOH-koh]   An artistic and cultural *style* that grew out of the *Baroque* style but that was more intimate and personal and that emphasized the frivolous and superficial side of aristocratic life.

romance   A story derived from legends associated with Troy or Celtic culture but often set in feudal times and centered on themes of licit and illicit love between noble lords and ladies.

Romanesque style [roh-muhn-ESK]   A *style* of architecture, usually associated with churches built in the eleventh and twelfth centuries, that was inspired by Roman architectural features, such as the *basilica,* and was thus Roman-like. Romanesque buildings were massive, with round arches and *barrel* or *groined vaulted* ceilings, and had less exterior decoration than *Gothic* churches.

Romanticism   An intellectual, artistic, and literary movement that began in the late eighteenth century as a reaction to *Neoclassicism* and that stressed the emotional, mysterious, and imaginative side of human behavior and the unruly side of nature.

rose window   A large circular window, made of *stained glass* and held together with lead and carved stones set in patterns, or *tracery,* and located over an entrance in a *Gothic* cathedral.

sacred music   Religious music, such as Gregorian chants, *masses,* and hymns.

sarcophagus [sahr-KAHF-uh-guhs]   From the Greek meaning "flesh-eating stone"; a marble or stone coffin or tomb, usually decorated with carvings, used first by Romans and later by Christians for burial of the dead.

satire   From the Latin, "medley"—a cooking term; a literary *genre* that originated in ancient Rome and that was characterized by two basic forms: (a) tolerant and amused observation of the human scene, modeled on Horace's style, and (b) bitter and sarcastic denunciation of all behavior and thought outside a civilized norm, modeled on Juvenal's style. In modern times, a literary work that holds up human vices and follies to ridicule or scorn.

satyr-play [SAT-uhr]   A comic play, often featuring sexual themes, performed at the Greek drama festivals along with the *tragedies.*

scale   A set pattern of tones (or notes) arranged from low to high.

scenographic [see-nuh-GRAF-ik]   In *Renaissance* architecture, a building style that envisioned buildings as composed of separate units; in the painting of stage scenery, the art of *perspective* representation.

scherzo [SKER-tso]   From the Italian for "joke"; a quick and lively instrumental *composition* or movement found in *sonatas* and *symphonies*.

scholasticism   In medieval times, the body or collection of knowledge that tried to harmonize Aristotle's writings with Christian doctrine; also, a way of thinking and establishing sets of arguments.

Scientific Revolution   The seventeenth-century intellectual movement, based originally on discoveries in astronomy and physics, that challenged and overturned medieval views about the order of the universe and the theories used to explain motion.

scripture   The sacred writings of any religion, as the Bible in Judaism and Christianity.

Second Romanesque   The second and mature stage of *Romanesque* architecture, about 1080–1200. Second Romanesque churches were richly decorated and built on a vast scale, including such features as double *transepts,* double aisles, crossing towers, and towers at the ends of the *transepts;* associated with Cluniac monasticism.

secular music   Nonreligious music, such as *symphonies,* songs, and dances.

serial music   A type of musical composition based on a *twelve-tone scale* arranged any way the composer chooses; the absence of a tonal center in serial music leads to *atonality.*

setting   In literature, the background against which the action takes place; in a representational artwork, the time and place depicted.

Severe style   The first sculptural style of the *Classical* period in Greece, which retained stylistic elements from the *Archaic* style.

sfumato [sfoo-MAH-toh]   In painting, the blending of one tone into another to blur the outline of a form and give the canvas a smokelike appearance; a technique perfected by Leonardo da Vinci.

shaft graves   Deep pit burial sites; the dead are usually placed at the bottom of the shafts.

skene [SKEE-nee]   A small building behind the *orchestra* in a Greek theater, used as a prop and as a storehouse for theatrical materials.

Skepticism   A *Hellenistic* philosophy that questioned whether anything could be known for certain, argued that all beliefs were relative, and concluded that *autarky* could be achieved only by recognizing that inquiry was fruitless.

slave narrative   A literary *genre,* either written by slaves or told by slaves to secretaries, which emerged prior to the American Civil War; the genre was launched by the *Narrative of the Life of Frederick Douglass, an American Slave* (1845); the harsh details of the inhumane and unjust slave system, as reported in these narratives, contributed to *Realist* literature.

social contract   In political thought, an agreement or contract between the people and their rulers defining the rights and duties of each so that a civil society might be created.

socialism   An economic and political system in which goods and property are owned collectively or by the state; the socialist movement began as a reaction to the excesses of the factory system in the nineteenth century and ultimately called for either reforming or abolishing industrial capitalism.

Socialist Realism   A Marxist artistic theory that calls for the use of literature, music, and the arts in the service of the ideals and goals of socialism and/or communism, with an emphasis in painting on the realistic portrayal of objects.

sonata [soh-NAH-tah]   In music, an instrumental *composition,* usually in three or four movements.

sonata form   A musical *form* or structure consisting of three (or sometimes four) sections that vary in *key, tempo,* and mood.

stained glass   An art form characterized by many small pieces of tinted glass bound together by strips of lead, usually to produce a pictorial scene of a religious theme; developed by *Romanesque* artists and a central feature of *Gothic* churches.

stele [STEE-lee]   A carved or inscribed vertical stone pillar or slab, often used for commemorative purposes.

Stoicism [STO-ih-sihz-uhm]   The most popular and influential *Hellenistic* philosophy, advocating a restrained way of life, a toleration for others, a resignation to disappointments, and a resolution to carry out one's responsibilities; Stoicism appealed to many Romans and had an impact on early Christian thought.

stream-of-consciousness   A writing technique used by some modern authors in which the narration consists of a *character's* continuous interior monologue of thoughts and feelings.

structuralism   In *Post-Modernism,* an approach to knowledge based on the belief that human behavior and institutions can be explained by reference to a few underlying structures that themselves are reflections of hidden patterns in the human mind.

studia humanitatis [STOO-dee-ah hu-man-ih-TAH-tis] **(humanistic studies)**   The Latin term given by *Renaissance* scholars to new intellectual pursuits that were based on recently discovered ancient texts, including moral philosophy, history, grammar, rhetoric, and poetry. This new learning stood in sharp contrast to medieval *scholasticism.*

Sturm und Drang [STOORM oont drahng]   German, "Storm and Stress"; a German literary movement of the 1770s that focused on themes of action, emotionalism, and the individual's revolt against the conventions of society.

style   The combination of distinctive elements of creative execution and expression, in terms of both form and *content.*

style galant [STEEL gah-LAHNN]   In *Rococo* music, a *style* of music developed by French composers and characterized by graceful and simple *melodies.*

stylobate [STY-luh-bate]   In Greek temples, the upper step of the base that forms a platform on which the columns stand.

Sublime [suh-BLIME]   In *Romanticism,* the term used to describe nature as a terrifying and awesome force full of violence and power.

Suprematism [suh-PREM-uh-tiz-uhm]   A variation of abstract art, originating in Russia in the early twentieth century, characterized by the use of geometric shapes as the basic elements of the composition.

Surrealism [suh-REE-uhl-iz-uhm]   An early-twentieth-century movement in art, literature, and theater, in which incongruous juxtapositions and fantastic images produce an irrational and dreamlike effect.

symbolic realism   In art, a *style* that is realistic and true to life but uses the portrayed object or person to represent or symbolize something else.

symphony   A long and complex *sonata,* usually written in three or four movements, for large *orchestras;* the first movement is traditionally fast, the second slow, and the third (and optional fourth) movement fast.

syncopation [sin-ko-PAY-shun]   In music, the technique of accenting the weak beat when a strong beat is expected.

syncretism [SIN-kruh-tiz-uhm]   The combining of different forms of religious beliefs or practices.

synthesizer [SIN-thuh-size-uhr]   An electronic apparatus with a keyboard capable of duplicating the sounds of many musical instruments, popular among *Post-Modernist* composers and musicians.

tabula rasa [TAB-yuh-luh RAH-zuh]   "Erased tablet," the Latin term John Locke used to describe the mind at birth, empty of inborn ideas and ready to receive sense impressions, which Locke believed were the sole source of knowledge.

technique   The systematic procedure whereby a particular creative task is performed.

tempo   In music, the relative speed at which a composition is to be played, indicated by a suggestive word or phrase or by a precise number such as a metronome marking. (A metronome is a finely calibrated device used to determine the exact tempo for a musical work.)

terza rima [TER-tsuh REE-muh]   A three-line stanza with an interlocking rhyme scheme (*aba bcb cdc ded,* and so on), used by Dante in his *Divine Comedy.*

texture   In a musical composition, the number and nature of voices or instruments employed and how the parts are combined.

theater of the absurd   A type of theater that has come to reflect the despair, anxieties, and absurdities of modern life and in which the characters seldom make sense, the plot is nearly nonexistent, bizarre and fantastic events occur onstage, and tragedy and comedy are mixed in unconventional ways; associated with *Late Modernism.*

theme   The dominant idea of a work; the message or emotion the artist intends to convey.

theocracy   From the Greek *theos,* god; a state governed by a god regarded as the ruling power or by priests or officials claiming divine sanction.

theology   The application of philosophy to the study of religious truth, focusing especially on the nature of the deity and the origin and teachings of an organized religious community.

tone   A musical sound of definite pitch; also, the quality of a sound.

tracery   Ornamental architectural work with lines that branch out to form designs, often found as stone carvings in *rose windows.*

tragedy   A serious and deeply moral drama, typically involving a noble protagonist brought down by excessive pride (hubris) and describing a conflict between seemingly irreconcilable values or forces; in Greece, tragedies were performed at the festivals associated with the worship of Dionysus.

transept   In church architecture, the crossing arm that bisects the *nave* near the *apse* and gives the characteristic *cruciform* shape to the floor plan.

triglyph [TRY-glif]   In Greek architecture, a three-grooved rectangular panel on the frieze of a *Doric* temple; triglyphs alternated with *metopes.*

triptych [TRIP-tik]   In painting, a set of three hinged or folding panels depicting a religious story, mainly used as an altarpiece.

trope [TROHP]   In *Gregorian chants,* a new phrase or melody inserted into an existing chant to make it more musically appealing; also called a turn; in literature, a figure of speech.

troubador [TROO-buh-door]   A composer and/or singer, usually an aristocrat, who performed secular love songs at the feudal courts in southern France.

twelve-tone scale   In music, a fixed *scale* or series in which there is an arbitrary arrangement of the twelve *tones* (counting every half-tone) of an *octave;* devised by Arnold Schoenberg.

tympanum [TIM-puh-num]   In medieval architecture, the arch over a doorway set above the lintel, usually decorated with carvings depicting biblical themes; in *Classical*-style architecture, the recessed face of a *pediment.*

ukiyo-e [oo-key-yoh-AY]   A type of colorful Japanese print, incised on woodblocks, that is characterized by simple design, plain backgrounds, and flat areas of color. Developed in seventeenth-century Japan; admired by late-nineteenth-century Parisian artists, who assimilated it to a Western style that is most notable in the prints of Mary Cassatt.

Utilitarianism [yoo-til-uh-TARE-e-uh-niz-uhm]   The doctrine set forth in the social theory of Jeremy Bentham in the nineteenth century that the final goal of society and humans is "the greatest good for the greatest number."

vanishing point   In linear *perspective,* the point on the horizon at which the receding parallel lines appear to converge and then vanish.

vault   A ceiling or roof made from a series of arches placed next to one another.

vernacular language [vuhr-NAK-yuh-luhr]   The language or dialect of a region, usually spoken by the general population as opposed to the wealthy or educated elite.

vernacular literature   Literature written in the language of the populace, such as English, French, or Italian, as opposed to the language of the educated elite, usually Latin.

via antiqua [VEE-uh ahn-TEE-kwah]   The "old way," the term used in late medieval thought by the opponents of St. Thomas Aquinas to describe his *via media,* which they considered outdated.

via media [VEE-uh MAY-dee-ah]   The "middle way" that St. Thomas Aquinas sought in reconciling Aristotle's works to Christian beliefs.

via moderna [VEE-uh moh-DEHR-nah]   The "new way," the term used in late medieval thought by those thinkers who opposed the school of Aquinas.

video art   A type of art made with a video monitor, or monitors; produced using either computerized programs or handheld cameras; can be ephemeral or permanent.

virtuoso [vehr-choo-O-so]   An aristocratic person who experimented in science, usually as an amateur, in the seventeenth century, giving science respectability and a wider audience; later, in music, a person with great technical skill.

voussoir [voo-SWAR]   A carved, wedge-shaped stone or block in an arch.

woodcut   In art, the technique of cutting or carving an image onto a wooden block used for printing; originated in the Late Middle Ages. Also, the print made from the technique.

word painting   In music, the illustration of an idea, a meaning, or a feeling associated with a word, as, for example, using a discordant *melody* when the word *pain* is sung. This technique is especially identified with the sixteenth-century *madrigal;* also called word illustration, or madrigalism.

ziggurat [ZIG-oo-rat]   A Mesopotamian stepped pyramid, usually built with external staircases and a shrine at the top; sometimes included a tower.

CREDITS

TEXT CREDITS

Chapter 1 p. 9 Samuel N. Kramer, excerpt from *History Begins at Sumer* (New York: Doubleday/Anchor, 1959). Reprinted with the permission of Mildred Kramer; p. 19, Miriam Lichtheim, excerpt from "The Man Who Was Tired of Life" from *Ancient Egyptian Literature, Volume I.* Copyright © 1973-1980 by the Regents of the University of California. Reprinted with the permission of the University of California Press. Reprinted by permission. **Chapter 2** p. 44, Sappho, "He Seems to Be a God" from *Seven Greeks,* translated by Guy Davenport. Copyright © 1995 by Guy Davenport. Reprinted with the permission of New Directions Publishing Corporation; Alcaeus, "Longing for Home" and "Drinking Song" from *Greek Lyric Poetry,* translated by M.L. West. Copyright © 1993 by M.L. West. Reprinted with the permission of Oxford University Press, 1993, p. 54–55, 61. **Chapter 3** p. 74, Xenophon, excerpt from *Oeconomicus: A Social and Historical Commentary,* translated by S.B. Pomeroy. Copyright © 1994 by Clarendon Press, a division of Oxford University Press. Reprinted with the permission of the translator. **Chapter 4** p. 92, Theocritus, "Getting to the Concert on Time" from *The Idylls of Theocritus: A Verse Translation,* translated by Thelma Sargent. Copyright © 1982 by Thelma Sargent. Reprinted with the permission of W. W. Norton & Company, Inc. **Chapter 6** p. 152, Flavius Josephus, "The Destruction of the Temple at Jerusalem" (excerpt) from *The History of the Jewish War,* translated by G.A. Williamson. Copyright © 1959 by G.A. Williamson. Reprinted with the permission of Penguin Books Ltd.; p. 162, Vibia Perpetua, "Account of Her Last Days Before Martyrdom" (excerpt) from *The Acts of the Christian Martyrs,* edited by Herbert Musurillo. Copyright © 1972. Reprinted with the permission of Oxford University Press. **Chapter 7** p. 174, Paulina, "Epitaph for Agorius Praetextatus" from Peter Dronke, *Women Writers of the Middle Ages.* Copyright © 1984. Reprinted with the permission of Cambridge University Press. **Chapter 8** p. 220, Abu 'l Faraj al-Isfahani, excerpt from *Kitabal-Aghani (The Book of Songs)* (Bulaq, 1285), 20 volumes. Reprinted in *Islam from the Prophet Muhammed to the Capture of Constantinople: II, Religion and Society,* edited and translated by Bernard Lewis. Copyright © 1987 by Bernard Lewis. Reprinted with the permission of Oxford University Press, 1987, pp. 147–48. **Chapter 9** p. 238, Abelard and Heloise, "My Sorrow and My Loss" (excerpt) from *The Letters of Abelard and Heloise,* translated by Betty Radice. Copyright © 1974 by Betty Radice. Reprinted with the permission of Penguin Books Ltd., 1974, p. 113. **Chapter 11** p. 304, Laura Cereta, excerpt from "Defense of the Liberal Instruction of Women" (January 13, 1488). Reprinted with the permission of MRTS, SUNY Binghamton, New York. From *Her Immaculate Hand: Selected Works by and about the Women Humanists of Quattrocento Italy.* Edited by Margaret King & Albert Rabil, 1992. Pegasus Press, #13. Reprinted by permission of MRTS, SUNY Binghamton, NY. **Chapter 12** p. 343, Georgio Vasari, "Michelangelo Has the Last Word" from *Lives of the Artists, Volume I,* translated by George Bull. Copyright © 1965 by George Bull. Reprinted with the permission of Penguin Books Ltd. Reprinted by permission of Penguin Books, Ltd. **Chapter 14** p. 388 Louis XIV, "Réflections sur le métier du Roi" (1679), Bibliothèque national, mss. fr. 1033, fol. 125-130. Reprinted in *The Century of Louis XIV,* edited by Orest and Patricia Ranum. Copyright © 1972. Reprinted with the permission of HarperCollins Publishers, Inc., pp. 71–72; Duke of Saint-Simon, *Mémoirs de Saint-Simon,* ed. by A. Chéruel (Paris 1857), XII, 461–71. Preprinted in *The Century of Louis XIV*, ed. by Orest and Patricia Ranum, New York: Harper & Row, 1972, p. 87. **Chapter 15** p. 423 Suzanne Gaudry, excerpt from *Witchcraft in Europe, 1100-1700: A Documentary History,* edited by Alan C. Kors and Edward Peters. Copyright © 1972. Reprinted with the permission of The University of Pennsylvania Press, 1972, pp. 274–75. **Chapter 20** p. 568, Elie Wiesel, excerpt from *Night,* translated by Stella Rodway. Copyright © 1960 by MacGibbon and Kee. Copyright renewed © 1988 by the Collins Publishing Group. Reprinted with the permission of Hill and Wang, a division of Farrar, Straus & Giroux, LLC. **Chapter 21** p. 627, Yo-Yo Ma, "A Journey of Discovery" from *The Silk Road Connecting Cultures, Creating Trust* (Washington, DC: Smithsonian Institution Center for Folklife and Cultural Heritage and The Silk Road Project, 2002). Copyright © 2002. Reprinted with the permission of the Silk Road Project. Catalogue to the festival, held June 26–30, July 3–7, 2002, p. 7, "A Journey of Discovery," by Yo-Yo Ma.

PHOTO CREDITS

Chapter 1 CO1, © The Boltin Picture Library; 1.1, © The British Museum; 1.2, © Jean-Marie Chauvet/Corbis Sygma; 1.3, © Naturhistorisches Museum, Wien; 1.5a, © The British Museum; 1.5b, © The British Museum; 1.6, © Erich Lessing/Art Resource, NY; 1.7, © The British Museum; 1.8, © Hirmer Fotoarchiv, Munich; 1.9, Erwin Boehm, Mainz; 1.10, © David Sutherland/Getty Images/Stone; 1.12, © Tim Schermerhorn; 1.13, © Inge Morath/Magnum Photos, Inc.; 1.14, © AKG London; 1.15, Museum Expedition. Courtesy Museum of Fine Arts, Boston; 1.16, The Metropolitan Museum of Art, Rogers Fund and contribution from Edward S. Harkness, 1929. (29.3.2) Photograph © 1997 The Metropolitan Museum of Art; 1.17, © Margarete Büsing/Bildarchiv Preußischer Kulturbesitz; 1.18, Staatliche Museen zu Berlin, Ägyptisches Museum/BPK. Photo: Margarete Büsing; 1.19, © The British Museum; 1.20, © The British Museum; 1.21, © The Boltin Picture Library; 1.22, © The British Museum; 1.23, Persepolis, Iran/© Bridgeman Art Library; p. 28T, © David Coulson/Robert Estall Photograph Library; p. 28B, © Robert & Linda Mitchell; p. 29L, British Museum, London, UK/© Bridgeman Art Library; p. 29R, © J.M. Kenoyer/Harappa **Chapter 2** CO2, © George Grigoriou/Getty Images/Stone; 2.1, © C.M. Dixon; 2.2, © Erich Lessing/Art Resource, NY; 2.3, © Erich Lessing/Art Resource, NY; 2.4, © SEF/Art Resource, NY; 2.5, © Hirmer Fotoarchiv, Munich; 2.6, © Ira Block/National Geographic Image Collection; 2.7, © Erich Lessing/Art Resource, NY; 2.8, © George Grigoriou/Getty Images/Stone; 2.9, © The Granger Collection, New York; 2.10, © The British Museum; 2.13, © Vanni/Art Resource, NY; 2.14, © Erich Lessing/Art Resource, NY; 2.15, The Metropolitan Museum of Art, Fletcher Fund, 1932. (32.11.1) Photograph © 1997 The Metropolitan Museum of Art; 2.17, © Hirmer Fotoarchiv, Munich;

2.18, © Craig & Marie Mauzy, Athens Greece; 2.19, 2.20 © Hirmer Fotoarchiv, Munich **Chapter 3** CO3, © Erich Lessing/Art Resource, NY; 3.1, Courtesy of the Arthur M. Sackler Museum, Harvard University Art Museums, Bequest of David M. Robinson. Photo by Michael Nedzweski, © President and Fellows of Harvard College, Harvard University; 3.2, 3.3, © Hirmer Fotoarchiv, Munich; 3.4, © Bildarchiv Preußischer Kulturbesitz; 3.5, © Hirmer Fotoarchiv, Munich; 3.6, © Ara Guler/Magnum Photos, Inc.; 3.7, © Erich Lessing/Art Resource, NY; p. 62, © Staatliche Museen zu Berlin/Preußischer Kulturbesitz Antikensammlung. Photo by Johannes Laurentius; 3.8, © Ronald Sheridan/Ancient Art & Architecture Collection; 3.10, © Kunsthistorisches Museum; 3.11, © The British Museum; 3.12, © The Granger Collection, New York; 3.13, © C.M. Dixon; 3.14, © Ronald Sheridan/Ancient Art & Architecture Collection; 3.15, © Scala/Art Resource, NY; 3.16, © René Burri/Magnum Photos, Inc.; 3.17, 3.18, © Hirmer Fotoarchiv, Munich; 3.19, © Réunion des Musées Nationaux/Art Resource, NY; 3.20, 3.21, © Scala/Art Resource, NY; 3.22, © Hirmer Fotoarchiv, Munich; 3.24, © The British Museum; 3.25, © Erich Lessing/Art Resource, NY; 3.26, © Hirmer Fotoarchiv, Munich; p. 84TL, © R. Sheridan/Ancient Art & Architecture Collection; p. 84TR, © Corbis/Gianni Dagli Orti; p. 84B, © Christie's Images, Ltd.; p. 85L, © Dumbarton Oaks, Pre-Columbian Collection, Washington, DC; p. 85R, © Kyodo News International, Inc. **Chapter 4** CO4, Louvre, Paris, France/© Lauros-Giraudon/Bridgeman Art Library; 4.1, © Bibliothèque Nationale de France, Paris; 4.2, © Bildarchiv Preußischer Kulturbesitz; 4.4, © Réunion des Musées Nationaux/Art Resource, NY; 4.5, Courtesy Yale University Art Gallery, Dura Europos Collection, Neg #258; 4.6, © Alinari/Art Resource, NY; 4.7, The Metropolitan Museum of Art, Rogers Fund, 1911. (11.90); 4.9, © C.M. Dixon; 4.10, © Art Resource, NY; 4.11, © Foto Marburg/Art Resource, NY; 4.12, Pinacoteca Capitolina, Palazzo Conservatori, Rome, Italy/Index/© Bridgeman Art Library; 4.13, The Metropolitan Museum of Art, Rogers Fund, 1909. (09.39) Photograph © 1997 The Metropolitan Museum of Art; 4.14, © Erich Lessing/Art Resource, NY; 4.15, Louvre, Paris, France/© Lauros-Giraudon/Bridgeman Art Library; 4.16, © Réunion des Musées Nationaux/Art Resource, NY; 4.17, © Nimatallah/Art Resource, NY; 4.18, Courtesy Archivio Fotografico dei Musei Capiolini. Photo by Maria Teresa Natale; 4.19, Araldo de Luca **Chapter 5** CO5, © Scala/Art Resource, NY; 5.1, © Alinari/Art Resource, NY; 5.2, © Scala/Art Resource, NY; 5.3, Ministero per i Beni e le Attivita Culturali. Soprintendenza Archeologica delle province di Napoli e Caserta; 5.4, © Hirmer Fotoarchiv, Munich; 5.5, © Fototeca Unione, Rome. American Academy in Rome; 5.6, © Réunion des Musées Nationaux/Art Resource, NY; 5.7, © Ronald Sheridan/Ancient Art & Architecture Collection; 5.8, © AKG London; 5.9, © Scala/Art Resource, NY; 5.11, © Giraudon/Art Resource, NY 5.12, © Scala/Art Resource, NY; 5.13, © Paul Chesley/Getty Images/Stone; 5.14, © Stephen Studd/Getty Images/Stone; p. 128, © Scala/Art Resource, NY; 5.15, Rome, Italy/Index/© Bridgeman Art Library; 5.16, © Scala/Art Resource, NY; 5.17, © Guido Rossi/The Image Bank; 5.18, © Corbis/Bettmann; 5.19, © Williams A. Allard/Getty Images/National Geographic; 5.20, © C.M. Dixon; 5.21, Museum of Art, Rhode Island School of Design, Museum of Appropriation, Photograph by Del Bogart; 5.22, © Scala/Art Resource, NY; 5.23, © Nimatallah/Art Resource, NY; 5.24, © Ronald Sheridan/Ancient Art & Architecture Collection; 5.25, © Alinari/Art Resource, NY; 5.26, 5.27, © Scala/Art Resource, NY; 5.28, © R. Sheridan/Ancient Art & Architecture Collection; 5.29, © Erich Lessing/Art Resource, NY; p. 142T, © Boltin Picture Library; p. 142B, © Staatliche Museen zu Berlin/Bildarchiv Preußischer Kulturbesitz; p. 143T, © Dinodia Picture Agency; p. 143M, © Robert Harding Picture Library, London; p. 143B, © Mary Evans Picture Library **Chapter 6** CO6, National Museum, Damascus, Syria/Topham Picturepoint/© Bridgeman Art Library; 6.1, © Israel Museum, Jerusalem; 6.2, © The Oriental Institute of the University of Chicago; 6.3, © The Jewish Museum, NY/Art Resource, NY; 6.4, © Zev Radovan, Jerusalem; 6.5, © Richard T. Nowitz; 6.6, National Museum, Damascus, Syria/Topham Picturepoint/© Bridgeman Art Library; 6.7, © Israel Museum, Jerusalem; 6.9, Courtesy of Nancy L. Lapp; 6.10, 6.11, © Zev Radovan, Jerusalem; 6.12, © Carl Purcell/Words & Pictures; 6.13, 6.14, © Phototheque André Held; 6.15, © Hirmer Fotoarchiv, Munich; 6.16, © Scala/Art Resource, NY; 6.17, © Erich Lessing/PhotoEdit; 6.18, © Hirmer Fotoarchiv, Munich **Chapter 7** CO7, © C.M. Dixon; 7.1, © Scala/Art Resource, NY; 7.2, © Superstock; 7.3, © Vanni/Art Resource, NY; 7.4, © C.M. Dixon; 7.5, © Scala/Art Resource, NY; 7.6, © Foto Marburg/Art Resource, NY; 7.7, © Scala/Art Resource, NY; 7.9, © AKG London; 7.10, © Erich Lessing/Art Resource, NY; 7.11, Arch. Phot. Paris/© C.N.M.H.S ; 7.12, Courtesy Ministero oer i beni Culturali e Ambientali, Istituto Centrale per il Catalogo e la Documentazione; 7.13, © Deutsches Archäologisches Institut; 7.14, © Biblioteca Apostolica Vaticana, Minature 15 (Fol. 106); 7.15, © Scala/Art Resource, NY; 7.16, © Phototheque André Held; 7.17, © Scala/Art Resource, NY; 7.18, © C.M. Dixon; 7.19, © Scala/Art Resource, NY; 7.20, © Ian Berry/Magnum Photos, Inc.; 7.21, 7.22, © Scala/Art Resource, NY; 7.23, © Colorphoto Hinz Allschwil-Basel; 7.24, © Erich Lessing/Art Resource, NY; 7.26, © Bibliothèque Nationale de France, Paris.; 7.27, © Foto Marburg/Art Resource, NY; 7.28, © Istituto Poligrafico e Zecca dello Stato; 7.29, © Bayerische Staatsbibliothek/ Bildarchiv Preußischer Kulturbesitz; p. 200T, © Tony Morrison/South American Pictures; p. 200M, © D. Donne Bryant/Art Resource, NY; p. 200B, © Frank Willet; p. 201T, © The British Museum; p. 201B, © Adam Woolfitt/Woodfin Camp and Associates **Chapter 8** CO8, © Erich Lessing/Art Resource, NY; 8.1, © AP/Wide World Photos; 8.2, Reproduced by kind permission of the Trustees of the Chester Beatty Library, Dublin; 8.3, © Vanni Archive/Corbis; 8.4, The Nelson-Atkins Museum of Art, Kansas City, Missouri. Purchase: Nelson Trust.; 8.5, Minbar from Kutubiyya Mosque, Marrakesh, Morocco. Islamic. Woodwork. 12th C., 1137-ca.-1145. H. 12 ft. 10 in.; W. 2 ft. 10-1/4 in.; D. 11 ft. 4-1/4 in. Three quarter view from the right. Photography by Bruce White. Photograph © 1998, The Metropolitan Museum of Art; 8.6, © Bibliothèque Nationale de France, Paris. AR 5847. Fol. 21; p. 213, © The Granger Collection, New York; 8.7, Used by permission of the Edinburgh University Library. Or Ms. 161, folio 16r; 8.8, © Victoria & Albert Museum; 8.9, © J. Pate/Robert Harding Picture Library; 8.10, © Werner Foreman Archive/Art Resource, NY; 8.11, © Ronald Sheridan/Ancient Art & Architecture Collection; 8.12, Courtesy of the World of Islam Festival Trust; 8.13, © Adam Lubroth/Art Resource, NY; 8.14, © Bibliothèque Nationale de France, Paris. AR. 5847. Fol. 95; 8.15, Reproduced by the kind permission of the Trustees of the Chester Beatty Library, Dublin; 8.16, © Erich Lessing/Art Resource, NY **Chapter 9** CO9, © AKG London/Stefan Drechsel; 9.1, © Erich Lessing/Art Resource, NY; 9.2, © C.N.M.H.S; 9.3, © Scala/Art Resource, NY; 9.4, © Erich Lessing/Art Resource, NY; 9.5, © Alinari/Art Resource, NY; p. 231, © English Heritage Photograph Library; 9.6, © The Granger Collection, New York; 9.7, © AKG London/Stefan Diller; 9.8, © Catherine Karnow/Woodfin Camp and Associates; 9.9, © Giraudon/Art Resource, NY; 9.10, © Jean Bernard; 9.12, © AKG London/Schütze/Rodemann; 9.13, © AKG London/Stefan Drechsel; 9.14, © Lee Snider Photo Images; 9.15, © Photographie Bulloz; 9.16, © C.N.M.H.S; 9.17, © Giraudon/Art Resource, NY; 9.18, Courtesy the Master and Fellows of Corpus Christi College, Cambridge. © Corpus Christi College, Cambridge;

9.20, © Hirmer Fotoarchiv, Munich; 9.21, From *Gardner's Art Through the Ages*, 6/e by Horst de la Croix and Richard G. Tansey, © 1975 by Harcourt Brace & Company. Reproduced by permission of the publisher, Thomson Learning; 9.22, From *Drawings of Great Buildings* by W. Blaser and O. Hannaford. Birkhauser Verlag, Basel. Drawing by Charlotte Myhrum; 9.23, © Hirmer Fotoarchiv, Munich; 9.24, 9.25, © Ronald Sheridan/Ancient Art & Architecture Collection; 9.26, 9.27, © Hirmer Fotoarchiv, Munich; 9.28, Jean Feuille/© C.N.M.H.S.; 9.29, © Scala/Art Resource, NY; 9.30, From *Drawings of Great Buildings* by W. Blaser and O. Hannaford. Birkhauser Verlag, Basel. Drawing by James McCahon; 9.31, 9.32, © Hirmer Fotoarchiv, Munich; 9.33, © Bibliothèque Nationale de France, Paris.; 9.34, Universitats Bibliothek, Munich; p. 256TL, © Frank Willet; p. 256TR, Courtesy Fundación Miguel Mujica Gallo, Museo Oro del Peru; p. 256B, © Werner Foreman Archive/Art Resource, NY; p. 257T,

INDEX

Page numbers in *italics* indicate pronunciation guides; page numbers in **boldface** indicate illustrations. For readers using the two-volume set of *The Western Humanities*, page numbers 1–351 (Chapters 1–12) refer to material in Volume I: *Beginnings through the Renaissance*, and page numbers 297–637 (Chapters 11–21) refer to material in Volume II: *The Renaissance to the Present*.